Disability Law
Cases, Materials, Problems

Disability Law
Cases, Materials, Problems

Fifth Edition

Laura Rothstein
Professor of Law and
Distinguished University Scholar
University of Louisville
Louis D. Brandeis School of Law

Ann C. McGinley
William S. Boyd Professor of Law
William S. Boyd School of Law
University of Nevada Las Vegas

ISBN: 978-1-4224-7633-8

Library of Congress Cataloging-in-Publication Data
Rothstein, Laura F.
Disability law : cases, materials, problems / Laura Rothstein, Ann C. McGinley. -- 5th ed.
p. cm.
Includes bibliographical references and index.
978-1-4224-7633-8 (hard cover : alk. paper) 1. People with disabilities--Legal status, laws, etc.--United States--Cases.
I. McGinley, Ann C. II. Title.
1. Vendors and purchasers--United States. 2. Commercial leases--United States. 3. Real estate investment--Law and legislation--United States. I. Stark, Debra P. II. White, Thomas R. (Thomas Raeburn) III. Title.
KF3738.R68 2010
346.7301'3--dc22   2010000717

NOTE TO USERS

To ensure that you are using the latest materials available in this area, please be sure to periodically check the LexisNexis Law School web site for downloadable updates and supplements at www.lexisnexis.com/lawschool.

Editorial Offices

121 Chanlon Rd., New Providence, NJ 07974 (908) 464-6800

201 Mission St., San Francisco, CA 94105-1831 (415) 908-3200

www.lexisnexis.com

MATTHEW◆BENDER

Dedication

To my family

Laura Rothstein

To Jeff, Ryan, Shanen, and Reed

Ann McGinley

Preface

This book is intended to provide a comprehensive overview of most of the major laws relating to individuals with disabilities. Before the late 1980s and early 1990s, few law schools had comprehensive courses on disability law, although some of the issues were covered in courses related to employment law and mental health law. The major topics not addressed in depth in this book relate primarily to entitlements and benefits, such as Social Security and workers' compensation. Also not covered are many of the issues relating to individuals with mental disabilities. While discrimination issues for that population are discussed, the topics related to competency, right to treatment, right to refuse treatment, and deinstitutionalization are not addressed to a great extent. These issues merit coverage in separate books and courses.

The book includes selected cases, problems, questions, and statutory and regulatory references. The notes are designed to highlight additional cases of interest, while the questions are intended to provoke thought about unresolved and complex issues. While there may be case citations following some of the problems, it is essential to note that these often represent only one jurisdiction's view of the issue raised by the problem.

This new edition of the casebook includes important updating and new materials designed to focus students on the important issues in disability law. Now that the Americans with Disabilities Act Amendments Act (ADAAA) has gone into effect, it is important for lawyers and law students to understand the changes the amendments made in both the Americans with Disabilities Act and the Rehabilitation Act. This edition includes several sections that analyze the ADAAA and its effect on the interpretation of the ADA and the Rehabilitation Act. While all the chapters deal with the ADAAA, Chapter 2 explains and analyzes the new amendments in depth.

The new edition also offers a number of features that should make the book more user-friendly and should enable students to further their understanding of the law. First, besides the questions and notes following the case materials, each chapter has a number of hypothetical problems that are introduced at the beginning of the material to be studied. Students are encouraged to read the hypothetical problems and to consider the questions in the hypothetical problems as they read the new material in the text. After studying the new materials, students and faculty members should discuss the hypothetical in order to assure that the students have gained a working knowledge of the law and analysis.

Second, the new edition also has information about many up-to-date issues that affect persons with disabilities. It includes discussions of the Genetic Information Nondiscrimination Act (GINA), the Mental Health Parity and Addiction Equity Act, (MHPAEA), the Lily Ledbetter Act, and the recent debate on national health care reform. It also includes a chart designed to explain the basics of the Americans with Disabilities Act, the Family Medical Leave Act and the state Worker's Compensation statutes.

Chapter 3, the chapter on employment and disabilities, is expanded to include further materials on burdens of proof and persuasion in the areas of reasonable accommodation and undue hardship, the different proof models in employment discrimination law, disability-related hostile work environment and retaliation claims.

Chapter 7, covering education, adds the 2009 Supreme Court decision in *Forest Grove*

Preface

School District v. T.A. which clarifies the issue of reimbursement for unilateral placement.

Chapter 9, the chapter on health care and insurance, has an expanded section on health insurance and Title III and includes discussion of the Genetic Information Non-discrimination Act and the Mental Health Parity and Addiction Equity Act. It also discusses the debate on national health insurance that currently exists in the country.

In an overview course on this topic, it is difficult to address in depth all of the legal issues affecting individuals with disabilities. These materials focus on issues of rights and nondiscrimination in the areas of employment, governmental programs and services, public accommodations (by private providers), higher education, education, housing, and health care. As is evident in reading the materials, some areas (such as education and employment) have an enormous body of case law. Others (such as housing and health care) have been more recently developing.

The importance of awareness of these issues has never been greater. With the 1990 passage of the Americans with Disabilities Act (which affects almost all aspects of society), problems with access to health care, and the 2008 amendments to the ADA, it is critical that members of the legal profession, as well as many social service providers and educators, have a working knowledge of this important area of law.

"String" citations and non-quote source citations have been omitted from cases without any note of their omission. Footnotes in the cases generally have been deleted, but where retained, they have been renumbered within the case. Many of the cases are not the full opinion, and material has been omitted in many instances without notation within the case. Some material is not indented and blocked in the same format as the original. The reader should check the full case report when doing research in reliance on the decision.

Because disability law is an evolving area of law, it is essential that reliance on the precedents and materials in this book be followed up by research on the current status in each area.

Laura Rothstein
Ann C. McGinley
October 2009

Acknowledgments

Thanks to James Chen, Dean of the University of Louisville Louis D. Brandeis School of Law and to University of Louisville Provost Shirley Willihnganz for their institutional support in preparing this edition.

Thanks to Elaine Shoben for suggesting Ann McGinley as coauthor for the new edition.

To my research assistant, Guion Johnstone, for her excellent research, to Kurt Metzmeier, Peter Scott Campbell, and Will Hilyerd (library faculty members), to Rebecca Wenning and Marilyn Peters for their administrative assistance in preparing the manuscript, to Julia Rothstein and Lisa Rothstein for their research support.

To Charles B. Craver, Freda H. Alverson Professor of Law at George Washington University, for encouraging and supporting publication of this book.

To Joe Smith, Bonnie Tucker, Lex Frieden, Wendy Wilkinson, Peg Nosek, Laurie Gerken Redd, Kathleen DeSilva, and the late Gretchen George, my thanks for challenging me to think about these issues from their unique perspectives. A similar thanks to all of the students with disabilities who have helped me to consider how to address the challenges they face in new and creative ways.

To Paul Steven Miller, Jan Sheldon Sherman, Ilene Shane, Elaine Roberts, Rud Turnbull, Michael Perlin, Robert Silverstein, Peter Blanck, Chai Feldblum, Larry Gostin, and John Wodatch for their positive influence, in my early work on disability law.

To my former colleagues Mary Anne Bobinski, Ron Turner, Mary Anderlik, and Bill Winslade for their insights.

To my current colleague, Sam Marcosson, thanks for engaging in thought provoking discussions about disability law.

Special acknowledgements to Stanley Herr, a law professor at the University of Maryland, who died in 2001. Stan had been involved in several important disability rights issues, including special education, deinstitutionalization, mental health histories for professional licensing, and prohibition of execution of individuals who are mentally retarded. And to Adam Milani, a law professor at Mercer University, who died in 2005. Adam and I shared an interest in writing about sports and disability law, and a mutual respect for each other's work. Their advocacy and intellect are missed, but their work has enabled others to build on the foundations they have laid.

Additional special acknowledgement to my friend, the late H. Joan Ehrlich, who served in leadership positions within the EEOC until she died in December 2008. Her proactive approach to educating and informing everyone about employment discrimination was extremely valuable and is greatly missed.

In summer 2009, the world lost the great Senator Edward Kennedy. His constant, unfailing and effective leadership is responsible for most of the major legislation providing protection and rights for individuals with disabilities. He inspired many to make sure that the "dream lives on."

And finally, as always, I thank my parents, Dorothy Friesen and the late Eric J. Friesen, for their constant support and example; to my daughters, Julia and Lisa for their patience; and to Mark, my husband and colleague for his valuable contributions and suggestions on issues of employment, genetics, and privacy.

Acknowledgments

Laura Rothstein

Thanks to Dean John White of the William S. Boyd School of Law, University of Nevada, Las Vegas, for supporting this project.

Thanks also to Jeanne Price, Associate Professor of Law and Director of the Wiener-Rogers Law Library at UNLV, who supported this project wholeheartedly. Thanks also to library faculty at the Wiener-Rogers Law Library, Chad Schatzle, Jennifer Gross and David McClure for their excellent and often very quick research.

Thanks to my colleagues at UNLV, Boyd School of Law for supporting this project, especially Steve Johnson, Elaine Shoben, Terry Pollman, Linda Edwards and Jeff Stempel.

Thanks to those students, friends and family members who live with disabilities and have helped me understand the difficulties they face and the important and creative role that law and understanding can play in helping them face those disabilities.

Special thanks go to my mother, Mary McGinley, who turned ninety years old as I was preparing this manuscript, and who never waivered in her support, to my late father, Paul McGinley, a lawyer's lawyer who gave me courage as a child to be what I wanted to be, to my brother and sisters, Paul, Laurie and Ellin, who are always supportive of my projects.

Special thanks to Jeff Stempel, my colleague and husband, for his valuable contributions, especially on issues of insurance and disabilities, and to my children, Ryan, Shanen, and Reed for their understanding and patience.

Thanks also to Keith Moore and Sean Caldwell of LexisNexis for their efforts and support.

Ann McGinley

Summary Table of Contents

Summary Table of Contents

Summary Table of Contents

TABLE OF CONTENTS

TABLE OF CONTENTS

TABLE OF CONTENTS

TABLE OF CONTENTS

TABLE OF CONTENTS

TABLE OF CONTENTS

TABLE OF CONTENTS

TABLE OF CONTENTS

TABLE OF CONTENTS

TABLE OF CONTENTS

TABLE OF CONTENTS

TABLE OF CONTENTS

TABLE OF CONTENTS

Chapter 1

INTRODUCTION

A THE PEOPLE AND THEIR STORIES

Bill Carney was in his twenties when he became a quadriplegic as a result of a jeep accident. Before the accident, he had had custody of his seven- and five-year old sons for four years since separating from his wife, Ellen. She had not visited them once during that time, and her other contact was limited to an occasional phone call or letter. After the accident, however, Ellen Carney sought custody of the boys because she thought that Bill could not be a good father. See *Carney v. Carney*, 24 Cal. 3d 725, 598 P.2d 36, 157 Cal. Rptr. 383 (1979).

Judith Gurmankin became blind at age twelve. After outstanding academic achievement in public high school in Philadelphia and completion of a Bachelor of Science degree at Temple University, she wanted to teach high school in the regular public schools in Philadelphia. Although she was academically qualified to do so, she was rejected because it was thought that a blind teacher would not be competent to teach sighted students. See *Gurmankin v. Costanzo*, 411 F. Supp. 982 (E.D. Pa. 1976), *aff'd*, 556 F.2d 184 (3d Cir. 1977), *cert. denied*, 450 U.S. 923 (1981).

Trina Hairston's disability was spina bifida, which resulted in incontinence and a limp, but she had no mental problems to prevent her attendance at public kindergarten in West Virginia. Her attendance in the regular classroom, however, was made contingent on her mother's presence at school to attend to Trina's needs — primarily diapering. Her mother needed to be home to take phone orders for coal deliveries and to attend to the needs of Trina's terminally-ill grandmother. See *Hairston v. Drosick*, 423 F. Supp. 180 (S.D. W. Va. 1976).

Rick Duran had a history of epilepsy, but had been seizure-free for over fifteen years when he applied to be a policeman in Tampa, Florida. He was successful in passing the oral and written tests, but when his history of epilepsy was noted in the physical exam, he was told he would be excluded automatically from consideration. See *Duran v. City of Tampa*, 430 F. Supp. 75 (M.D. Fla. 1977).

Catherine McDermott wanted to be a computer programmer. Although her technical skills were acceptable, she was denied the job because of her obesity — not because the condition would affect her work, but because she was a risk to the company's insurance benefit programs. See *State Div. of Human Rights ex rel. McDermott v. Xerox Corp.*, 65 N.Y.2d 213, 480 N.E.2d 695 (1985).

A California fifth grader, Andrew Adams was average in intelligence, but his dyslexia prevented him from benefiting from the education being provided at public schools. Because the school was so slow in obtaining an appropriate placement, Mrs.

Adams enrolled her son in a special private school. See *Adams v. Hansen*, 632 F. Supp. 858 (N.D. Cal. 1985).

Ryan White got AIDS from a blood transfusion necessitated by his hemophilia. A pleasant teenager, who just wanted to go to school with other kids, he was repeatedly excluded from attending by court orders based on the fear of contagion — in spite of overwhelming evidence that one cannot get AIDS by casual contact. See DAVID L. KIRP, LEARNING BY HEART 26–64 (1989).

Michael Bunjer could not order his food through the speaker system at a fast food restaurant because of his hearing impairment. When he tried to order using a paper and pencil, he was initially refused, later laughed at, and then given the wrong change and warm water instead of a soda. When he refused to leave the restaurant after complaining, he was arrested. See *Bunjer v. Edwards*, 985 F. Supp. 165 (D.D.C. 1997).

When the tenant of a mobile home installed a ramp with her own funds to accommodate her post polio syndrome and other disabilities, the mobile home park told her that she should consider moving to a "handicapped facility." See *Elliott v. Sherwood Manor Mobile Home Park*, 947 F. Supp. 1574 (M.D. Fla. 1996).

Kathy Adams has always wanted to work for the Foreign Service. After passing all the tests, she found out that she had early stage breast cancer. She was treated with a mastectomy and later had her ovaries and fallopian tubes removed, but the State Department revoked her medical clearance and did not assign her a position because it believed that not all posts to which she could be assigned would have proper follow-up medical care for her. See *Adams v. Rice*, 531 F.3d 936 (D.C. Cir. 2008).

Charles Littleton is a 29 year old man who is mentally retarded. He lives with his mother and receives social security benefits because of his disability. He applied for a job with Wal-Mart as a cart-pusher. He asked to have his job coach accompany him for the interview. Wal-Mart refused, and, because the interview did not go well, did not hire Charles. See *Littleton v. Wal-Mart Stores*, 231 Fed. Appx. 874 (11th Cir. 2007).

There are other people with other stories, and there are other kinds of problems. These individuals are mentally retarded, they are deaf, they have cystic fibrosis, and they have cancer. They have problems climbing the steps to get on the bus. They are deinstitutionalized and given bus fare to the next city because there is no community program available in the city where the institution is located. Often there is no program at the other end of the bus ride. And where there is a community program available, there are often problems of neighbors using zoning laws and private deed restrictions to exclude group homes for mentally retarded individuals.

What all of these people have in common is that because of some physical or mental impairment (or a record of such an impairment or a perception that they have an impairment) — they face unique problems functioning in the everyday world. Sometimes these problems result from thoughtless planning of the environment, with no malice to the person with a disability. Sometimes these problems are the result of clear prejudice about conditions, such as epilepsy. And sometimes the problems result simply from misplaced assumptions about the inabilities and abilities of individuals with disabilities.

What these individuals also generally have in common is that they have similar goals in life — they want to go to school, to work, to play, to travel, to obtain health care, to live, and to participate in the community and other activities, just like everyone else.

For some of them, their disabilities have been with them from birth. For others, like Bill Carney, an accident suddenly has changed their lives. For still others, the impairment has occurred gradually, such as blindness resulting from diabetes. Those who became disabled before age 21 are considered to be developmentally disabled, because the disability has affected them during the time when many important basic skills are normally developed. For some, the disability is not obvious to the casual observer: the individual who has epilepsy, is HIV-positive, or who is an alcoholic. These individuals are said to have "hidden disabilities."

What they also have in common is that they now receive some protection from a variety of laws — protection that was largely unavailable until the early 1970s. Beginning in 1973 with the passage of amendments to the Vocational Rehabilitation Act and continuing to 1990 when the most comprehensive disability rights statute, the Americans with Disabilities Act (ADA) was passed, there has been an increase in the legal rights created for people with disabilities. In examining these statutes and applying them to a particular situation, care must be taken in evaluating whether the condition in question is treated as a handicap or disability under applicable law. In addition, the party whose conduct is in question must be subject to the statute in question. Even if both these criteria exist, there still may be other procedural and substantive obstacles to protection or application.

As is evident from the brief descriptions of the individuals mentioned previously, there are many types of disabilities. Unlike most other groups who are given statutory protection against discrimination, a person can become a member of the class at any moment — merely by being involved in an accident and becoming paralyzed or visually impaired, for example. The members of this class are of all ages, all incomes, all religions, all ethnic groups, both sexes, and from all kinds of backgrounds. The problems they face in many cases are not unlike discrimination problems of other protected classes: they have problems obtaining employment, they have problems obtaining housing, and they are excluded from education. But unlike the other protected classes, the problems are not always the result of prejudicial attitudes or even institutionalized discrimination. The problems arise because much of the world has been designed for the average able-bodied person, with little thought of the person with limited mobility, limited vision, health problems, or other disabilities.

There is much debate over appropriate terminology — whether "impairment," "disability," or "handicap" is the most appropriate word. Federal statutes use both "disability" and "handicap," although most statutes currently use "disability." At present, "disability" is generally accepted as the preferred term, but these materials will use handicap/disability interchangeably. Many of the reported judicial decisions that are included in the materials use terminology that existed before amendments to change the language.

This book provides legal materials covering issues involving people with physical and mental impairments. In most cases, the statutes apply to both groups — employment laws and education laws, for example. Some laws relate primarily to persons with physical impairments, i.e., architectural barrier laws, transportation laws, etc. Other laws relate primarily to individuals whose impairments are mental — who are either mentally retarded or mentally ill — i.e., guardianship, institutionalization, and sterilization.

B   HOW MANY PEOPLE HAVE DISABILITIES?

Precise statistics on the number of Americans with disabilities are very difficult to obtain. There are several reasons for this. First, the definition of handicap or disability varies depending on whether it is a Social Security benefit, employment, or education that is in question. (This is discussed in Chapter 2.) Often the individual is not required to self-identify. In other cases, an individual may not consider himself/herself to be disabled. In some instances, individuals may over-identify, such as people who have correctable conditions (e.g., near-sightedness).

About one in five Americans has some disability — approximately 43 million Americans according to the legislative history of the Americans with Disabilities Act. About 7.5% of the population have a severe disability. There are relationships of disability to age, race, education, income and where one lives, but the causal connections, if there are any, are unclear. The increase in the incidence of HIV also has had a significant impact on the number of individuals with disabilities.

Technology has had an impact on disabilities. Today, low-birthweight infants are surviving as a result of technology, and in many cases these infants have severe disabilities. Individuals with spinal cord injuries are surviving at very high rates today as a result of technology developed during the Viet Nam conflict to save wounded soldiers. In addition, computers and microchips and other technology have improved the functioning ability of many people with disabilities. For example, voice synthesizers, reading machines, and adapted automobiles have made a great deal of difference for many individuals. On the other hand, computers can be a barrier for individuals with visual impairments or mobility impairments who cannot see computer graphics and/or cannot use a mouse. Computer program design can limit who is able to use this technology.

The following are statistics of interest from various sources describing the incidence of disability.

AMERICANS WITH DISABILITIES IN 2005

Have trouble walking	22.5 million
(including 13 million in need of a wheelchair, cane, crutches or walker)	
Visual impairments	7.7 million
(including 1.8 million blind or unable to see printed words)	
Hearing impairments	7.8 million
(including 1 million deaf or unable to hear conversations at all)	
Have trouble speaking	2.5 million
Total	40.5 million

Source: Matthew Brault, *Americans With Disabilities: 2005*, Current Population Reports, 70-117, U.S. Census Bureau, Washington, DC, 2008.

The number is much higher if the following "other" disabilities are counted.

Hypertension	72 million[1]
Coronary Heart Disease	16.8 million[2]
Cancer (all types)	10.7 million[3]
Bi-Polar Disorder	5.7 million[4]
Schizophrenia	2.4 million[5]
Diabetes	24 million[6]
Polycystic Kidney Disease	600,000[7]
Alzheimer's Disease, senility or dementia	2.1 million[8]
Multiple Sclerosis	400,000[9]

---

[1] American Heart Association, "Know the Facts, Get the Stats, 2007."

[2] "Cardiovascular Disease Statistics," American Heart Association, retrieved June 2, 2009 at http://www.americanheart.org/presenter.jhtml?identifier=4478.

[3] Ries LAG, Melbert D, Krapcho M., et al. (eds.). SEER Cancer Statistics Review, 1975-2005, National Cancer Institute. Bethesda, MD, http://seer.cancer.gov/csr/1975_2005/, based on November 2007 SEER data submission, posted to the SEER Web site, 2008.

[4] Kessler RC, Chiu WT, Demler O, Walters EE. Prevalence, severity, and comorbidity of twelve-month DSM-IV disorders in the National Comorbidity Survey Replication (NCS-R). *Archives of General Psychiatry*, 2005 June: 62(6):617–27.

[5] Regier DA, Narrow WE, Rae DS, Manderscheid RW, Locke BZ, Goodwin FK. The de facto mental and addictive disorders service system. Epidemiologic Catchment Area prospective 1-year prevalence rates of disorders and services. *Archives of General Psychiatry*. 1993 Feb: 50(2):85–94.

[6] "Number of People with Diabetes Increases to 24 Million," Centers for Disease Control and Prevention, Press Release, June 24, 2008.

[7] "Polycystic Kidney Disease," National Kidney Foundation (2003).

[8] Matthew Brault, *Americans With Disabilities: 2005*, Current Population Reports, P70-117, U.S. Census Bureau, Washington, DC, 2008.

[9] "Who Gets MS?", National Multiple Sclerosis Society, retrieved June 2, 2009, http://www.nationalmssociety.org/about-multiple-sclerosis/who-gets-ms/index.aspx.

U.S. Census data about individuals with disabilities indicates that in 2000, approximately 19 percent of Americans had some degree of disability. U.S. Census Bureau of Public Information Office, Census 2000. The definition of disability for these purposes, however, does not mean that all of these individuals meet the definition of disability within the ADA.

The impact of disability on personal life is documented by a 1986 ICD Survey of Disabled Americans called *Bringing Disabled Americans into the Mainstream*. A comparison of disabled adults and all others indicates that while 87 percent of all others shop in a grocery store at least once a week, only 62 percent of disabled adults do so. While 78 percent of all others attended a movie last year, only 36 percent of disabled adults did. This demonstrates the importance of the ADA in reaching everyday activities in addition to the workplace, educational settings, housing, and social service providers.

C THE LAWS AND HOW THEY DEVELOPED

Until the late 1960s, the philosophy towards Americans with disabilities was a combination of paternalism and fear — the result was usually segregation. Originally, the child with a disability was completely removed from the classroom to alleviate the stress on the teacher and other children, although in more recent years the child was placed in a special classroom setting where no stress could be placed on the child with the disability — the child was being taught diluted academic skills or manual activities. See Max L. Hutt & Robert Gwyn Gibby, The Mentally Retarded Child (2d ed. 1982).

For the adult, the philosophy was to provide disability benefits — financial support so the individual could exist, but with little attempt to move the individual back into the mainstream of society. Edward D. Berkowitz, in his 1987 book, *Disabled Policy*, describes from the perspective of a historian how disability policy began as financial support for the retirement of individuals with disabilities. Disability policy began in the early part of the 20th century with income-maintenance programs (Workers' Compensation (in 1911) and Social Security Disability Insurance (in 1935)). "Vocational rehabilitation" as policy began in 1920. The philosophy of this program was "corrective." The intent was to rehabilitate the individual for the workplace, the attitude being one of making the individual fit into the world as it was, rather than adapting the world to the needs of the individual with a disability.

Because of these policies most individuals with disabilities remained in their homes, in institutions, or otherwise outside the mainstream of society. There was, therefore, little reason to consider the needs of these individuals in the design of our environment. People in wheelchairs did not go to work — so subways and office buildings were not designed to accommodate them. Children who were mentally retarded were thought to be incapable of functioning in society, so little attempt was made to teach them skills needed to work and manage their lives.

In the 1960s, a change in attitude began to occur. The philosophy became one of recognizing the worth and potential of all persons. The attitude included the idea that this potential could be realized only if persons with disabilities were allowed to participate in the mainstream of everyday life. *Brown v. Board of Ed.*, 347 U.S. 483 (1954), had already established that separation was inherently unequal in the context of race. This change in attitude resulted in a number of important changes in the law. These changes were initially found in judicial opinions. But, as is often the case when significant case law is made, Congress and state lawmakers recognized the need to clarify and codify many of the concepts from these early decisions.

The changes in the area of education occurred beginning in 1971 and 1972 with two separate but related lower court decisions approving consent decrees involving education of children with disabilities. These cases involved Fourteenth Amendment constitutional theories of equal protection and due process. See *Pennsylvania Ass'n for Retarded Children (PARC) v. Pennsylvania*, 334 F. Supp. 1257 (E.D. Pa. 1971); 343 F. Supp. 279 (E.D. Pa. 1972), and *Mills v. Board of Ed.*, 348 F. Supp. 866 (D.D.C. 1972). These decisions established that where a state undertakes to provide education at public expense, it must do so on an equal basis for *all* children and it must provide procedural safeguards before there is exclusion or differing treatment. Because of the potential for similar holdings in other pending cases and in recognition of the cost of providing special education, Congress passed the Education for All Handicapped Children Act (now known as the Individuals with Disabilities Education Act (IDEA)) in 1975, 20 U.S.C. § 1400 et seq. This statute incorporated the basic principles and requirements from the *PARC* and *Mills* cases.

The IDEA is essentially a hybrid statute, funding states to provide education for students with disabilities within a framework of substantive and procedural protection, while also creating enforceable rights and individual remedies. The underlying premise of the IDEA is that *all* children are educable, and that they should receive public education in the *least restrictive appropriate* placement at *no cost*, that their educational program should be *individualized*, and that they should be provided *procedural protections*. There have been several significant amendments to the IDEA — providing for attorneys' fees, implementing preschool programming, eliminating governmental immunity, adding some substantive programming, and expanding on the definition of who is protected — but the basic premise of the IDEA is the same as it was in 1975. There have been hundreds of judicial decisions, including several Supreme Court cases, that have clarified some of the questions arising under this statute.

The Rehabilitation Act was passed in 1973, and until 1990 was the only other major federal statute providing for nondiscrimination on the basis of disability. The 1973 Rehabilitation Act was actually an amendment to a much older law providing for vocational rehabilitation — the focus of the older law being solely on employment. Early vocational rehabilitation legislation was passed after World War I as a response to the number of veterans with disabilities. See 1973 U.S. Code Cong. & Ad. News 2076. The 1973 Act provided that the federal government (under Section 501), federal contractors (under Section 503), and recipients of federal financial assistance (under Section 504) should not discriminate on the basis of handicap against otherwise qualified individuals. See 29 U.S.C. §§ 791, 793, 794. Amendments in 1992 included changing the terminology to use "disability" instead of "handicap" throughout the statute. The most significant substantive section of the Rehabilitation Act is Section 504, which reaches not only employment, but also institutions such as public schools, welfare providers, hospitals, federally supported transportation, and so forth. Most of the private sector, however, was not covered by federal law. Reliance on state laws, which were inconsistent and often provided little enforcement power, was necessary for individuals with disabilities who wanted to bring discrimination claims.

Most early litigation under the Rehabilitation Act focused on procedural issues, such as whether the recipient was covered, whether there was a private right of action, and whether one must exhaust administrative remedies. Subsequent judicial opinion has addressed more substantive issues such as whether the particular person is within the protected class, whether the individual is otherwise qualified, whether discriminatory action actually occurred, whether reasonable accommodations are required, and whether defenses such as undue burden apply. Like the IDEA, there are many cases interpreting the Rehabilitation Act. This judicial interpretation is important not only for understanding the Rehabilitation Act, but also because it was incorporated into the language of the Americans with Disabilities Act (ADA), 42 U.S.C. § 12101 et seq. The Rehabilitation Act has been amended to more clearly define coverage for individuals with contagious and infectious diseases, to define coverage applicable to individuals who are drug and alcohol users, and to provide that states and state agencies are not immune from suit under the statute.

Until the Americans with Disabilities Act was passed in 1990, there were several other federal statutes providing a patchwork of protection for individuals with disabilities. The Architectural Barriers Act of 1968, 42 U.S.C. §§ 4151–4157, requires newly constructed federal government buildings to be accessible. The Federal Aid Highway Act of 1972, 23 U.S.C. § 142, mandates accessibility in federally assisted transportation programs and on federal highways. The Air Carrier Access Act of 1986, 49 U.S.C. § 1374, prohibits discrimination against people with disabilities by providers of air transportation. In 1988 the Fair Housing Act, 42 U.S.C. § 3601 et seq., was amended to provide protection against discrimination on the basis of disability in housing and to require barrier-free design for certain multi-unit dwelling construction. Other federal statutes relate to voter accessibility, telecommunications access, and a variety of other areas.

Comprehensive coverage was not a reality, however, until the passage of the Americans with Disabilities Act. The ADA prohibits discrimination on the basis of disability in both public and private employment (Title I), in public services provided by state and local governmental authorities (Title II), and in programs of public accommodation provided by private parties (Title III). Improvement in access to telecommunications (Title IV) is a significant part of the statute, as well. Miscellaneous provisions (Title V) relate to coverage of Congress and access in wilderness areas. As a result of the ADA, most schools (public and private), most places of business open to the public, most governmental services, most transportation services, and most employers must take steps to ensure reasonable accommodation in addition to the nondiscrimination mandates. As was noted previously, the ADA is intended to be interpreted consistently with the Rehabilitation Act in most situations. For that reason, there was a significant body of case law that applied to the ADA as soon as it was enacted.

Common to most of these statutes are concepts of nondiscrimination, reasonable accommodation, and least restrictive environment (sometimes referred to as mainstreaming). Individualized assessment is also a key principle. Depending on the activity, more than one of these statutes might apply. In the chapters that follow, the application of these various laws to particular life experiences such as employment or education is clarified in greater detail.

To be entitled to protection under any of the federal statutes, one must meet the definition of disability or handicap, must be otherwise qualified to carry out the fundamental requirements of the program with or without reasonable accommodation, must bring an action within the appropriate statute of limitations, must prove discrimination, and must have been discriminated against by an entity that is covered by the statute in question. As the following chapters will illustrate, these issues can be quite complex.

One other major area of legal development applicable to the study of disability rights should be noted. This area relates to issues affecting individuals with mental disabilities. Issues such as commitment, deinstitutionalization, right to treatment, right to refuse treatment, right to treatment in the least restrictive environment, competency, and sterilization are currently the subject of substantial judicial debate and uncertainty. One major case, *Halderman v. Pennhurst State Sch. & Hosp.*, 451 U.S. 1 (1981), involved many of these issues and applied constitutional principles as well as state mental health law, the Rehabilitation Act, and the Developmental Disabilities Assistance and Bill of Rights Act. Unfortunately, the *Pennhurst* case and other similar cases continue to leave many questions unanswered. A comprehensive discussion of these issues is found in MICHAEL J. PERLIN, MENTAL DISABILITY AND LAW: CIVIL AND CRIMINAL, Vol. 2 (LEXIS 2d ed. 1998), Vol. 3 (2000) Vol. 4 (2001).

Advocates are beginning to use traditional discrimination theories as an avenue to obtain more community services and access to independent living. While the discrimination statutes afford some opportunity for redress, the major problem is that the benefits and services needed in the communities, such as supervised housing and access to mental health treatment, are not available because of funding deficiencies. For example, using the Fair Housing Act has been quite successful as a means of challenging exclusionary zoning that is used to keep out group homes for individuals with mental retardation. The major obstacle to independent living is the lack of funding to provide this type housing and related supportive services in the first place.

The Constitution has been the basis of some of the litigation in the area of disability discrimination law. Major constitutionally based judicial decisions will be included in appropriate chapters. For the most part, however, disability rights law has developed in response to statutory requirements and judicial interpretations of those requirements.

One of the earliest Supreme Court decisions to address issues arising under a disability discrimination statute focused on whether intentional discrimination was the only prohibited discrimination on the basis of disability. Although the case arises in the context of the provision of certain health benefits, the reasoning is applicable to most other areas of disability discrimination law.

ALEXANDER v. CHOATE
469 U.S. 287 (1985)

JUSTICE MARSHALL delivered the opinion for a unanimous Court:

In 1980, Tennessee proposed reducing the number of annual days of inpatient hospital care covered by its state Medicaid program. The question presented is whether the effect upon the handicapped that this reduction will have is cognizable under § 504 of the Rehabilitation Act of 1973 or its implementing regulations. We hold that it is not.

I.

Faced in 1980–1981 with projected state Medicaid costs of $42 million more than the State's Medicaid budget of $388 million, the directors of the Tennessee Medicaid program decided to institute a variety of cost-saving measures. Among these changes was a reduction from 20 to 14 in the number of inpatient hospital days per fiscal year that Tennessee Medicaid would pay hospitals on behalf of a Medicaid recipient. Before the new measures took effect, respondents, Tennessee Medicaid recipients, brought a class action for declaratory and injunctive relief in which they alleged, *inter alia*, that the proposed 14-day limitation on inpatient coverage would have a discriminatory effect on the handicapped. Statistical evidence, which petitioners do not dispute, indicated that in the 1979–1980 fiscal year, 27.4% of all handicapped users of hospital services who received Medicaid required more than 14 days of care, while only 7.8% of nonhandicapped users required more than 14 days of inpatient care.

Based on this evidence, respondents asserted that the reduction would violate § 504 of the Rehabilitation Act of 1973, 29 U.S.C. § 794, and its implementing regulations. Section 504 provides:

> "No otherwise qualified handicapped individual . . . shall, solely by reason of his handicap, be excluded from the participation in, be denied the benefits of, or be subjected to discrimination under any program or activity receiving Federal financial assistance. . . . "

Respondents' position was twofold. First, they argued that the change from 20 to 14 days of coverage would have a disproportionate effect on the handicapped and hence was discriminatory.[1] The second, and major, thrust of respondents' attack was directed at the use of any annual limitation on the number of inpatient days covered, for respondents acknowledged that, given the special needs of the handicapped for medical care, any such limitation was likely to disadvantage the handicapped disproportionately. Respondents noted, however, that federal law does not require States to impose any annual durational limitation on inpatient coverage, and that the Medicaid programs of only 10 States impose such restrictions.[2]

---

[1] The evidence indicated that, if 19 days of coverage were provided, 16.9% of the handicapped, as compared to 4.2% of the nonhandicapped, would not have their needs for inpatient care met.

[2] As of 1980 the average ceiling in those States was 37.6 days. Six States also limit the number of

Respondents therefore suggested that Tennessee follow these other States and do away with any limitation on the number of annual inpatient days covered. Instead, argued respondents, the State could limit the number of days of hospital coverage on a per-stay basis, with the number of covered days to vary depending on the recipient's illness (for example, fixing the number of days covered for an appendectomy); the period to be covered for each illness could then be set at a level that would keep Tennessee's Medicaid program as a whole within its budget. The State's refusal to adopt this plan was said to result in the imposition of gratuitous costs on the handicapped and thus to constitute discrimination under § 504.

II.

The first question the parties urge on the Court is whether proof of discriminatory animus is always required to establish a violation of § 504 and its implementing regulations, or whether federal law also reaches action by a recipient of federal funding that discriminates against the handicapped by effect rather than by design. The State of Tennessee argues that § 504 reaches only purposeful discrimination against the handicapped. As support for this position, the State relies heavily on our recent decision in *Guardians Assn. v. Civil Service Commission of New York City*, 463 U.S. 582 (1983).

In *Guardians*, we confronted the question whether Title VI of the Civil Rights Act of 1964, 42 U.S.C. § 2000d et seq., which prohibits discrimination against racial and ethnic minorities in programs receiving federal aid, reaches both intentional and disparate-impact discrimination.[3] No opinion commanded a majority in *Guardians*, and Members of the Court offered widely varying interpretations of Title VI. Nonetheless, a two-pronged holding on the nature of the discrimination proscribed by Title VI emerged in that case. First, the Court held that Title VI itself directly reached only instances of intentional discrimination. Second, the Court held that actions having an unjustifiable disparate impact on minorities could be redressed through agency regulations designed to implement the purposes of Title VI. In essence, then, we held that Title VI had delegated to the agencies in the first instance the complex determination of what sorts of disparate impacts upon minorities constituted sufficiently significant social problems, and were readily enough remediable, to warrant altering the practices of the federal grantees that had produced those impacts. The premise of the State's reliance on *Guardians* is that § 504 was modeled in part on Title VI, and that the evolution of Title VI regulatory and judicial law is therefore relevant to ascertaining the intended scope of § 504. Nonetheless, as we point out *infra*, too facile an assimilation of Title VI law to § 504 must be resisted.

Guardians, therefore, does not support petitioners' blanket proposition that federal law proscribes only intentional discrimination against the handicapped. Indeed, to the extent our holding in *Guardians* is relevant to the interpretation of

---

reimbursable days per admission, per spell of illness, or per benefit period.

[3] Section 601 of the Civil Rights Act of 1964, 42 U.S.C. § 2000d, provides:

"No person in the United States shall, on the ground of race, color, or national origin, be excluded from participation in, be denied the benefits of, or be subjected to discrimination under any program or activity receiving Federal financial assistance."

§ 504, *Guardians* suggests that the regulations implementing § 504, upon which respondents in part rely, could make actionable the disparate impact challenged in this case. Moreover, there are reasons to pause before too quickly extending even the first prong of *Guardians* to § 504.

Discrimination against the handicapped was perceived by Congress to be most often the product, not of invidious animus, but rather of thoughtlessness and indifference — of benign neglect. Thus, Representative Vanik, introducing the predecessor to § 504 in the House, described the treatment of the handicapped as one of the country's "shameful oversights," which caused the handicapped to live among society "shunted aside, hidden, and ignored." Similarly, Senator Humphrey, who introduced a companion measure in the Senate, asserted that "we can no longer tolerate the invisibility of the handicapped in America. . . . " And Senator Cranston, the Acting Chairman of the Subcommittee that drafted § 504, described the Act as a response to "previous societal neglect." Federal agencies and commentators on the plight of the handicapped similarly have found that discrimination against the handicapped is primarily the result of apathetic attitudes rather than affirmative animus.

In addition, much of the conduct that Congress sought to alter in passing the Rehabilitation Act would be difficult if not impossible to reach were the Act construed to proscribe only conduct fueled by a discriminatory intent. For example, elimination of architectural barriers was one of the central aims of the Act, yet such barriers were clearly not erected with the aim or intent of excluding the handicapped. Similarly, Senator Williams, the chairman of the Labor and Public Welfare Committee that reported out § 504, asserted that the handicapped were the victims of "[discrimination] in access to public transportation" and "[discrimination] because they do not have the simplest forms of special educational and rehabilitation services they need. . . . " And Senator Humphrey, again in introducing the proposal that later became § 504, listed, among the instances of discrimination that the section would prohibit, the use of "transportation and architectual [sic] barriers," the "discriminatory effect of job qualification . . . procedures," and the denial of "special educational assistance" for handicapped children. These statements would ring hollow if the resulting legislation could not rectify the harms resulting from action that discriminated by effect as well as by design.

At the same time, the position urged by respondents — that we interpret § 504 to reach all action disparately affecting the handicapped — is also troubling. Because the handicapped typically are not similarly situated to the nonhandicapped, respondents' position would in essence require each recipient of federal funds first to evaluate the effect on the handicapped of every proposed action that might touch the interests of the handicapped, and then to consider alternatives for achieving the same objectives with less severe disadvantage to the handicapped. The formalization and policing of this process could lead to a wholly unwieldy administrative and adjudicative burden. Had Congress intended § 504 to be a National Environmental Policy Act for the handicapped, requiring the preparation of "Handicapped Impact Statements" before any action was taken by a grantee that affected the handicapped, we would expect some indication of that purpose in the statute or its legislative history. Yet there is nothing to suggest that such was Congress' purpose. Thus, just as there is reason to question whether Congress intended § 504 to reach only intentional discrimination, there is similarly reason to question whether Congress intended § 504 to embrace all claims of disparate-impact discrimination.

Any interpretation of § 504 must therefore be responsive to two powerful but countervailing considerations — the need to give effect to the statutory objectives and the desire to keep § 504 within manageable bounds. Given the legitimacy of both of these goals and the tension between them, we decline the parties' invitation to decide today that one of these goals so overshadows the other as to eclipse it. While we reject the boundless notion that all disparate-impact showings constitute prima facie cases under § 504, we assume without deciding that § 504 reaches at least some conduct that has an unjustifiable disparate impact upon the handicapped. On that assumption, we must then determine whether the disparate effect of which respondents complain is the sort of disparate impact that federal law might recognize.

III.

To determine which disparate impacts § 504 might make actionable, the proper starting point is *Southeastern Community College v. Davis*, 442 U.S. 397 (1979), our major previous attempt to define the scope of § 504. *Davis* involved a plaintiff with a major hearing disability who sought admission to a college to be trained as a registered nurse, but who would not be capable of safely performing as a registered nurse even with full-time personal supervision. We stated that, under some circumstances, a "refusal to modify an existing program might become unreasonable and discriminatory. Identification of those instances where a refusal to accommodate the needs of a disabled person amounts to discrimination against the handicapped [is] an important responsibility of HEW." We held that the college was not required to admit Davis because it appeared unlikely that she could benefit from any modifications that the relevant HEW regulations required, and because the further modifications Davis sought — full-time, personal supervision whenever she attended patients and elimination of all clinical courses — would have compromised the essential nature of the college's nursing program. Such a "fundamental alteration in the nature of a program" was far more than the reasonable modifications the statute or regulations required. *Davis* thus struck a balance between the statutory rights of the handicapped to be integrated into society and the legitimate interests of federal grantees in preserving the integrity of their programs: while a grantee need not be required to make "fundamental" or "substantial" modifications to accommodate the handicapped, it may be required to make "reasonable" ones.[5]

---

[5] In *Davis*, we stated that § 504 does not impose an "affirmative-action obligation on all recipients of federal funds." Our use of the term "affirmative action" in this context has been severely criticized for failing to appreciate the difference between affirmative action and reasonable accommodation; the former is said to refer to a remedial policy for the victims of past discrimination, while the latter relates to the elimination of existing obstacles against the handicapped. Regardless of the aptness of our choice of words in *Davis*, it is clear from the context of *Davis* that the term "affirmative action" referred to those "changes," "adjustments," or "modifications" to existing programs that would be "substantial," or that would constitute "fundamental [alterations] in the nature of a program . . . ," rather than to those changes that would be reasonable accommodations.

The balance struck in *Davis* requires that an otherwise qualified handicapped individual must be provided with meaningful access to the benefit that the grantee offers. The benefit itself, of course, cannot be defined in a way that effectively denies otherwise qualified handicapped individuals the meaningful access to which they are entitled; to assure meaningful access, reasonable accommodations in the grantee's program or benefit may have to be made. In this case, respondents argue that the 14-day rule, or any annual durational limitation, denies meaningful access to Medicaid services in Tennessee. We examine each of these arguments in turn.

A.

The 14-day limitation will not deny respondents meaningful access to Tennessee Medicaid services or exclude them from those services. The new limitation does not invoke criteria that have a particular exclusionary effect on the handicapped; the reduction, neutral on its face, does not distinguish between those whose coverage will be reduced and those whose coverage will not on the basis of any test, judgment, or trait that the handicapped as a class are less capable of meeting or less likely of having. Moreover, it cannot be argued that "meaningful access" to state Medicaid services will be denied by the 14-day limitation on inpatient coverage; nothing in the record suggests that the handicapped in Tennessee will be unable to benefit meaningfully from the coverage they will receive under the 14-day rule.[6] The reduction in inpatient coverage will leave both handicapped and nonhandicapped Medicaid users with identical and effective hospital services fully available for their use, with both classes of users subject to the same durational limitation. The 14-day limitation, therefore, does not exclude the handicapped from or deny them the benefits of the 14 days of care the State has chosen to provide. To the extent respondents further suggest that their greater need for prolonged inpatient care means that, to provide meaningful access to Medicaid services, Tennessee must single out the handicapped for more than 14 days of coverage, the suggestion is simply unsound. At base, such a suggestion must rest on the notion that the benefit provided through state Medicaid programs is the amorphous objective of "adequate health care." But Medicaid programs do not guarantee that each recipient will receive that level of health care precisely tailored to his or her particular needs. Instead, the benefit provided through Medicaid is a particular package of health care services, such as 14 days of inpatient coverage. That package of services has the general aim of assuring that individuals will receive necessary medical care, but the benefit provided remains the individual services offered — not "adequate health care."

The federal Medicaid Act makes this point clear. The Act gives the States substantial discretion to choose the proper mix of amount, scope, and duration limitations on coverage, as long as care and services are provided in "the best interests of the recipients." 42 U.S.C. § 1396a(a)(19). The District Court found that the 14-day limitation would fully serve 95% of even handicapped individuals eligible

---

[6] The record does not contain any suggestion that the illnesses uniquely associated with the handicapped or occurring with greater frequency among them cannot be effectively treated, at least in part, with fewer than 14 days' coverage. In addition, the durational limitation does not apply to only particular handicapped conditions and takes effect regardless of the particular cause of hospitalization.

for Tennessee Medicaid, and both lower courts concluded that Tennessee's proposed Medicaid plan would meet the "best interests" standard. That unchallenged conclusion indicates that Tennessee is free, as a matter of the Medicaid Act, to choose to define the benefit it will be providing as 14 days of inpatient coverage.

Section 504 does not require the State to alter this definition of the benefit being offered simply to meet the reality that the handicapped have greater medical needs. To conclude otherwise would be to find that the Rehabilitation Act requires States to view certain illnesses, i.e., those particularly affecting the handicapped, as more important than others and more worthy of cure through government subsidization. Nothing in the legislative history of the Act supports such a conclusion. Section 504 seeks to assure evenhanded treatment and the opportunity for handicapped individuals to participate in and benefit from programs receiving federal assistance. The Act does not, however, guarantee the handicapped equal results from the provision of state Medicaid, even assuming some measure of equality of health could be constructed.

Regulations promulgated by the Department of Health and Human Services (HHS) pursuant to the Act further support this conclusion.[7] These regulations state that recipients of federal funds who provide health services cannot "provide a qualified handicapped person with benefits or services that are not as effective as the benefits or services provided to others." The regulations also prohibit a recipient of federal funding from adopting "criteria or methods of administration that have the purpose or effect of defeating or substantially impairing accomplishment of the objectives of the recipient's program with respect to the handicapped." 45 CFR § 84.4(b)(4)(ii) (1984).

While these regulations, read in isolation, could be taken to suggest that a state Medicaid program must make the handicapped as healthy as the nonhandicapped, other regulations reveal that HHS does not contemplate imposing such a requirement. Title 45 CFR § 84.4(b)(2) (1984), referred to in the regulations quoted above, makes clear that

> "[for] purposes of this part, aids, benefits, and services, to be equally effective, are not required to produce the identical result or level of achievement for handicapped and nonhandicapped persons, but must afford handicapped persons equal opportunity to obtain the same result, to gain the same benefit, or to reach the same level of achievement. . . . "

This regulation, while indicating that adjustments to existing programs are contemplated,[8] also makes clear that Tennessee is not required to assure that its handicapped Medicaid users will be as healthy as its nonhandicapped users. Thus,

---

[7] We have previously recognized these regulations as an important source of guidance on the meaning of § 504.

[8] The interpretive analysis accompanying these regulations states:

"[The] term 'equally effective,' defined in paragraph (b)(2), is intended to encompass the concept of equivalent, as opposed to identical, services and to acknowledge the fact that in order to meet the individual needs of handicapped persons to the same extent that the corresponding needs of nonhandicapped persons are met, adjustments to regular programs or the provision of different programs may sometimes be necessary." 45 CFR, pt. 84, App. A, para. 6 (1984).

to the extent respondents are seeking a distinct durational limitation for the handicapped, Tennessee is entitled to respond by asserting that the relevant benefit is 14 days of coverage. Because the handicapped have meaningful and equal access to that benefit, Tennessee is not obligated to reinstate its 20-day rule or to provide the handicapped with more than 14 days of inpatient coverage.

B.

We turn next to respondents' alternative contention, a contention directed not at the 14-day rule itself but rather at Tennessee's Medicaid plan as a whole. Respondents argue that the inclusion of any annual durational limitation on inpatient coverage in a state Medicaid plan violates § 504. The thrust of this challenge is that all annual durational limitations discriminate against the handicapped because (1) the effect of such limitations falls most heavily on the handicapped and because (2) this harm could be avoided by the choice of other Medicaid plans that would meet the State's budgetary constraints without disproportionately disadvantaging the handicapped. Viewed in this light, Tennessee's current plan is said to inflict a gratuitous harm on the handicapped that denies them meaningful access to Medicaid services.

Whatever the merits of this conception of meaningful access, it is clear that § 504 does not require the changes respondents seek. In enacting the Rehabilitation Act and in subsequent amendments,[9] Congress did focus on several substantive areas — employment, education, and the elimination of physical barriers to access — in which it considered the societal and personal costs of refusals to provide meaningful access to the handicapped to be particularly high. But nothing in the pre- or post-1973 legislative discussion of § 504 suggests that Congress desired to make major inroads on the States' longstanding discretion to choose the proper mix of amount, scope, and duration limitations on services covered by state Medicaid. And, more generally, we have already stated, that § 504 does not impose a general NEPA-like requirement on federal grantees.

The costs of such a requirement would be far from minimal, and thus Tennessee's refusal to pursue this course does not, as respondents suggest, inflict a "gratuitous" harm on the handicapped. On the contrary, to require that the sort of broad-based distributive decision at issue in this case always be made in the way most favorable, or least disadvantageous, to the handicapped, even when the same benefit is meaningfully and equally offered to them, would be to impose a virtually unworkable requirement on state Medicaid administrators. Before taking any across-the-board action affecting Medicaid recipients, an analysis of the effect of the proposed change on the handicapped would have to be prepared. Presumably, that analysis would have to be further broken down by class of handicap — the change at issue here, for example, might be significantly less harmful to the blind,

---

[9] The year after the Rehabilitation Act was passed, Congress returned to it with important amendments that clarified the scope of § 504. While these amendments and their history cannot substitute for a clear expression of legislative intent at the time of enactment, as virtually contemporaneous and more specific elaborations of the general norm that Congress had enacted into law the previous year, the amendments and their history do shed significant light on the intent with which § 504 was enacted. We have previously relied on the post-1973 legislative actions to interpret § 504.

who use inpatient services only minimally, than to other subclasses of handicapped Medicaid recipients; the State would then have to balance the harms and benefits to various groups to determine, on balance, the extent to which the action disparately impacts the handicapped. In addition, respondents offer no reason that similar treatment would not have to be accorded other groups protected by statute or regulation from disparate-impact discrimination.

It should be obvious that administrative costs of implementing such a regime would be well beyond the accommodations that are required under *Davis*. As a result, Tennessee need not redefine its Medicaid program to eliminate durational limitations on inpatient coverage, even if in doing so the State could achieve its immediate fiscal objectives in a way less harmful to the handicapped.

IV.

The 14-day rule challenged in this case is neutral on its face, is not alleged to rest on a discriminatory motive, and does not deny the handicapped access to or exclude them from the particular package of Medicaid services Tennessee has chosen to provide. The State has made the same benefit — 14 days of coverage — equally accessible to both handicapped and nonhandicapped persons, and the State is not required to assure the handicapped "adequate health care" by providing them with more coverage than the nonhandicapped. In addition, the State is not obligated to modify its Medicaid program by abandoning reliance on annual durational limitations on inpatient coverage. Assuming, then, that § 504 or its implementing regulations reach some claims of disparate-impact discrimination, the effect of Tennessee's reduction in annual inpatient coverage is not among them. For that reason, the Court of Appeals erred in holding that respondents had established a prima facie violation of § 504. The judgment below is accordingly reversed.

NOTES

1. *Legislative History of the Rehabilitation Act:* The history of Section 504 of the Rehabilitation Act was summarized briefly in the 1985 Supreme Court decision in *Alexander v. Choate*, 469 U.S. 287 (1985), *supra*. What is not obvious from the opinion, however, is what politically led up to the passage of the Rehabilitation Act and the promulgation of the regulations. See RICHARD K. SCOTCH, FROM GOOD WILL TO CIVIL RIGHTS: TRANSFORMING FEDERAL DISABILITY POLICY (1984), describing the evolution of Section 504 of the Rehabilitation Act. The research the author conducted from the perspective of a sociologist involved contacts and interviews with more than one hundred individuals involved in the development of Section 504 and its subsequent regulations. Signed by President Nixon, in 1973, Section 504 was patterned after other civil rights legislation as a "routine inclusion" in the reauthorization of the Vocational Rehabilitation Act. *Id.* at 5. It is surprising to know that the social reform found in the 1973 amendments was not the result of the activism of disability rights advocates or any other strong political activism by federal legislators. "Rather, the adoption and development of a nondiscrimination policy was carried out by individuals working at the subpolitical, or staff, level." *Id.* at 148. Initially, the reauthorization did not include Section 504. It was "conceived by Senate committee staff members and added to the bill at a relatively late point

in the legislative process." *Id.* at 49. "It appears that most members of Congress either were unaware that Section 504 was included in the act or saw the section as little more than a platitude, a statement of a desired goal with little potential for causing institutional change." *Id.* at 54. There was little discussion or debate of Section 504 in either committees or on the floor of either the House or Senate. The promulgation of the regulations also has an unusual political history, as is further described in Scotch's fascinating book.

2. *Legislative History of the Americans with Disabilities Act:* Unlike Section 504 of the Rehabilitation Act, which did not result from lengthy debate and discussion, the Americans with Disabilities Act (ADA) went through extensive Congressional committee discussion and floor debate. Major efforts to pass a comprehensive antidiscrimination statute began in 1988. The ADA was almost passed in 1989, but concerns from several constituencies, such as small business, resulted in going back to the drawing board for another year of discussion. After considerable discussion by several Congressional Committees, and a potential eleventh-hour derailment on the issue of employees with AIDS in the food industry, the ADA was passed by Congress and signed by President Bush in July of 1990. For a detailed overview of the ADA, its history and its major provisions, see THE AMERICANS WITH DISABILITIES ACT: FROM POLICY TO PRACTICE (Jane West ed. 1991). See also BARNARD D. REAMS, PETER J. MCGOVERN & JON S. SCHULTZ, DISABILITY LAW IN THE UNITED STATES: A LEGISLATIVE HISTORY OF THE AMERICANS WITH DISABILITIES ACT OF 1990 (1992).

Unlike the nondiscrimination mandates in the Rehabilitation Act, which are relatively short in terminology, the ADA is a lengthy statute incorporating directly into the statute many of the issues that are covered by the Rehabilitation Act through its regulations and through case law interpretation. The ADA is truly a descendant of the Rehabilitation Act, and it specifically refers to the Rehabilitation Act judicial interpretation as precedent for the ADA. It is thus incorrect to state, as many ADA opponents did, that the ADA is unclear in its mandates. It is true that in some areas, particularly public accommodations, there was little guidance from the Rehabilitation Act interpretation. In other areas, however, such as employment, higher education, and health services, there was a substantial and growing body of case law to draw upon.

The ADA and Rehabilitation Act were amended by the ADA Amendments Act of 2008, which took effect on January 1, 2009. As subsequent chapters will demonstrate, Congress passed the amendments to overturn a number of United States Supreme Court opinions interpreting the ADA and their application by the lower federal courts that had the effect of significantly narrowing the definition of individuals with disabilities. Some of these opinions concluded that persons with serious impairments such as mental retardation, deafness, diabetes and cancer were not individuals with disabilities and were therefore not protected by the Act from discrimination.

A 1995 circuit court opinion provides a useful summary and outline of the history of the ADA in the context of the Rehabilitation Act history. The following is the portion of that opinion with the historical information.

HELEN L. v. DIDARIO
46 F.3d 325 (3d Cir. 1995)

McKEE, CIRCUIT JUDGE:

In order to appreciate the scope of the ADA and its attendant regulations, it is necessary to examine the circumstances leading to its enactment. Section 504 of the Rehabilitation Act of 1973, 29 U.S.C. § 794, was the first broad federal statute aimed at eradicating discrimination against individuals with disabilities.[10] "Section 504 of the Rehabilitation Act of 1973, [is] commonly known as the civil rights bill of the disabled." Section 504 now reads in relevant part:

> No otherwise qualified individual with a disability . . . shall, solely by reason of her or his disability, be excluded from the participation in, be denied the benefits of, or be subjected to discrimination under any program or activity receiving Federal financial assistance . . . .

29 U.S.C. § 794.[11]

Section 504's sponsors described it as a response to " 'previous societal neglect' " and introduced it to rectify "the country's 'shameful oversights' which caused the handicapped to live among society 'shunted aside, hidden and ignored.' " *Alexander v. Choate*, 469 U.S. 287, 296 (1985).

As originally enacted, section 504 referred to a "handicapped" individual being discriminated against solely by reason of a "handicap." The change in nomenclature from "handicap" to "disability" reflects Congress' awareness that individuals with disabilities find the term "handicapped" objectionable. Burgdorf, *The Americans with Disabilities Act Analysis and Implication of a Second-Generation Civil Rights Statute*, 26 Harv. C.R.-C.L. L.Rev. 413, 522 n. 7 (1991).

On April 26, 1976 then-President Gerald Ford signed Executive Order No. 11914, 3 C.F.R. § 117 (1977), which authorized the Department of Health, Education and Welfare to coordinate enforcement of section 504 and which required the Secretary of HEW to promulgate regulations for enforcement.[12] Subsequently, HEW's section 504 rulemaking and enforcement authority was transferred to the Department of Health and Human Services ("HHS"). See 20 U.S.C. § 3508.

---

[10] The law developed under section 504 of the Rehabilitation Act is applicable to Title II of the ADA. 28 C.F.R. § 35.103 ("This part [applying to the ADA] shall not be construed to apply a lesser standard than the standards applied under title V of the Rehabilitation Act of 1973 (29 U.S.C. § 791)").

[11] The general prohibition against disability-based discrimination contained in § 504 was first proposed in the 92nd Congress as an amendment to Title VI of the Civil Rights Act of 1984, 42 U.S.C. § 2000d et seq. Although it was ultimately enacted by the 93rd Congress as part of a pending Vocational Rehabilitation Act, its language was patterned after other civil rights statutes. *Alexander v. Choate*, 469 U.S. 287, 296 n. 13 (1985). The language of section 504 is virtually identical to that of section 601 of Title VI of the Civil Rights Act of 1964 that bars discrimination based upon race, color or national origin in federally-assisted programs.

[12] The Rehabilitation Act did not mandate that any regulations be promulgated. Accordingly the Department of Health, Education and Welfare (now the Department of Health and Human Services), did not promulgate any regulations to implement that Act. *Southeastern Community College v. Davis*, 442 U.S. 397, 404 n. 4 (1979).

On November 2, 1980, President Carter signed Executive Order No. 12250, 45 Fed. Reg. 72995, entitled "Leadership and Coordination of Nondiscrimination Laws". That Executive Order transferred HHS's coordination and enforcement authority to the Attorney General. Section 1-105 of that Executive Order provided that the HHS guidelines "shall be deemed to have been issued by the Attorney General pursuant to this Order and shall continue in effect until revoked or modified by the Attorney General." Thereafter, the Department of Justice adopt the HHS coordination and enforcement regulations and transferred them from 45 C.F.R. part 84 to 28 C.F.R. part 41, 46 Fed. Reg. 40686 (the "coordination regulations"). The section 504 coordination regulations begin by stating that the purpose of 28 C.F.R. part 41 is to "implement Executive Order 12250, which requires the Department of Justice to coordinate the implementation of section 504 of the Rehabilitation Act 1973." 28 C.F.R. § 41.1. A subsequent section requires all federal agencies to issue regulations "to implement section 504 with respect to programs and activities to which it provides assistance." 28 C.F.R. § 41.4. The coordination regulations contain a separate section which lists a number of general prohibitions against disability-based discrimination. 28 C.F.R. § 41.51. That section mandates that all recipients of federal financial assistance "shall administer programs and activities in the most integrated setting appropriate to the needs of qualified handicapped persons." 28 C.F.R. § 41.51(d). Although Section 504 has been called "the cornerstone of the civil rights movement of the mobility-impaired," its shortcomings and deficiencies quickly became apparent. See, e.g., Cook, *The Americans with Disabilities Act: The Move to Integration*, 64 Temp. L. Rev. 393, 394–408 (1991) (The Rehabilitation Act and its regulations have been practically a dead letter as a remedy for segregated public services). One commentator has written that the weaknesses of section 504 arise from its statutory language, the limited extent of its coverage, inadequate enforcement mechanisms and erratic judicial interpretations. Burgdorf, *The Americans with Disabilities Act: Analysis and Implications of a Second-Generation Civil Rights Statute*, 26 Harv. C.R.-C.L. L. Rev. 413, 431 (1991).

Toward the end of the 1980's the United States Senate and the House of Representatives both recognized that then current laws were "inadequate" to combat "the pervasive problems of discrimination that people with disabilities are facing." S. Rep. No. 116, 101st Cong., 1st Sess. 18 (1989); H.R. Rep. No. 485 (II), 101st Cong., 2d Sess. 47 (1990). The Senate recognized the need for "omnibus civil rights legislation" for the disabled. S. Rep. No. 116, 101st Cong., 1st Sess. 19 (1989). Similarly, the House addressed the need for legislation that "will finally set in place the necessary civil rights protections for people with disabilities." H. R. Rep. No. 485 (II), 101st Cong., 2d Sess. 40 (1990). Both branches of Congress concluded:

> There is a compelling need to provide a clear and comprehensive national mandate for the elimination of discrimination against individuals with disabilities and for the integration of persons with disabilities into the economic and social mainstream of American life. Further, there is a need to provide clear, strong, consistent, enforceable standards addressing discrimination against individuals with disabilities.

S. Rep. No. 116, 20: H. R. Rep. No. 485 (II), 50. It was against this backdrop that the ADA was enacted.[13]

[B]ecause Congress mandated that the ADA regulations be patterned after the section 504 coordination regulations, the former regulations have the force of law. When Congress re-enacts a statute and voices its approval of an administrative interpretation of that statute, that interpretation acquires the force of law and courts are bound by the regulation. The same is true when Congress agrees with an administrative interpretation of a statute which Congress is re-enacting.

In enacting the ADA, Congress found that "historically, society has tended to isolate and segregate individuals with disabilities, and . . . such forms of discrimination . . . continue to be a serious and pervasive social problem." 42 U.S.C. § 12101(a)(2). Congress also concluded that "individuals with disabilities continually encounter various forms of discrimination, including . . . segregation. . . . " 42 U.S.C. § 12101(a)(5).

In furtherance of the objective of eliminating discrimination against the disabled, Congress stated that "the Nation's proper goals regarding individuals with disabilities are to assure equality of opportunity, full participation, independent living, and economic self-sufficiency for such individuals[.]" 42 U.S.C. § 12101(a)(8). Similarly, in response to its mandate, the Department of Justice stated "integration is fundamental to the purposes of the Americans with Disabilities Act." 28 C.F.R. Part 35, App. A. § 35.130.[14] Thus, the ADA and its attendant regulations clearly define unnecessary segregation as a form of illegal discrimination against the disabled.[15]

NOTE

Judicial Decisions as the Basis for New Legislation and Amendments to Existing Federal Legislation: Although neither the Rehabilitation Act nondiscrimination mandates nor the ADA were a direct result of any specific judicial activity, other major legislation has been. The passage of the Education for All Handicapped Children Act (now the Individuals with Disabilities Education Act) was a direct result of the judicial settlements in the *PARC* and *Mills* decisions. Amendments to the IDEA also have been the direct result of judicial activity. In 1986, the EAHCA/IDEA was amended by the Handicapped Children's Protection Act to provide for attorneys' fees in special education cases. This amendment was a direct result of a Supreme Court decision that these fees could

[13] For a concise history of the ADA's "tortuous legislative journey", see Nancy Lee Jones, *Overview and Essential Requirements of the Americans with Disabilities Act*, 64 Temp. L. Rev. 471, 472–475 (1991).

[14] We note that this is consistent with the Fair Housing Act of 1988, 52 U.S.C. § 3604(f), another predecessor of the ADA. In enacting that Act, the House Judiciary Committee stated "the Fair Housing Amendments Act, like Section 504 of the Rehabilitation Act of 1973, as amended, is a clear pronouncement of a national commitment to end the unnecessary exclusion of persons with handicaps from the American mainstream." H. Rep. No. 711, 100th Cong., 2d Sess., 18 (1988).

[15] Even if it could be argued that the Act and its regulations are ambiguous on this point, the heading of the regulation at issue here, and the legislative history of the ADA confirm that Congress intended to define unnecessary segregation of the disabled as a form of illegal discrimination.

not be implied in the EAHCA/IDEA. See *Smith v. Robinson*, 468 U.S. 992 (1984). The EAHCA/IDEA was amended again in 1990 as a response to the decision in *Dellmuth v. Muth*, 491 U.S. 223 (1989), in which the Supreme Court held that states and state agencies are immune from suits under the EAHCA/IDEA.

The Air Carrier Access Act, which is an amendment to the Federal Aviation Act, was the direct result of a Supreme Court decision, *Department of Transp. v. Paralyzed Veterans of Am.*, 477 U.S. 597 (1986), which had held that commercial airlines are not recipients of federal financial assistance and, thus, were not subject to Section 504 of the Rehabilitation Act.

Although the ADA was not a direct result of judicial activity, it is probable that the mass transit portions of the ADA were, at least in part, a response to the confusion surrounding what was required for mass transit by the various federal laws (including Section 504 of the Rehabilitation Act, the Federal Aid Highway Act, and the Urban Mass Transportation Act), that became apparent as a result of several lower court cases interpreting these statutes.

History of the ADA Amendments Act of 2008

Although in passing the ADA Congress had an intent to provide broad protection to individuals with disabilities, Supreme Court and lower court opinions interpreted the definition of disability under the ADA narrowly, finding that many persons with severe impairments were not covered by the Act. Defendants prevailed in an extremely high percentage of cases brought under the ADA (some say as high as 97%), with many of plaintiffs' cases defeated because the courts concluded that the plaintiff was not an individual with a disability. See Chai R. Feldblum, et al., *The ADA Amendments Act of 2008*, 13 TEX. J. ON C.L. & C.R. 187, 202–03 (2008). Disability activists were disappointed that the courts had not interpreted the ADA of 1990 broadly to prohibit discrimination against persons with mental and physical disabilities. They had expected broad coverage, because the ADA definition of disability was the same as that in Section 504 of the Rehabilitation Act, whose definition had been interpreted broadly for years, and because of the more extensive legislative history of the ADA which indicated the Congressional intent to define disability broadly. See *id.* at 187, 203–04. The cases, in which the defendants often prevailed on motions for summary judgment, led to the ADA Amendments Act of 2008 ("ADAAA") which overturned a number of Supreme Court decisions and expressly directed courts to construe the definition of disability in favor of broad coverage of individuals. The changed definition applies to both the ADA and the Rehabilitation Act. This text will incorporate the amendments in light of court interpretation of the definition of disability in subsequent chapters.

D   GOALS AND STRATEGIES FOR STUDYING DISABILITY LAW

This book is designed to provide an introduction to the major substantive legal requirements affecting individuals with disabilities, as well as to provide an understanding of the underlying philosophical reasons for the public policies that are currently in place.

In addition to federal laws, there are a number of state laws that apply to these issues. For the most part, federal law does not preempt existing state law. Local requirements, such as nondiscrimination ordinances and building codes, are applicable as well. It is useful to be aware of these requirements, but because of the differing coverage in each state, state materials are not included in this text except as examples of interesting fact settings or interpretations.

In addition to understanding the major federal substantive requirements, *Notes* and *Questions* raise questions about whether current policies are working and whether change is needed. If change is needed, should it be legislative, regulatory, judicial, or sociological? It may be that a particular policy is currently appropriate, but additional funding is needed to carry out that policy. Practical and tactical aspects of achieving goals should also be considered. *Hypothetical Problems* allow the readers to consider a fact problem and to apply knowledge of the statutes, regulations, and policies of the disability statutes.

Another goal is to sensitize the reader to what life is like for individuals with various types of disabilities. What does it mean to the individual in a wheelchair that she cannot use public transportation to go to work? What does it mean to the regular classroom teacher that students with serious behavior problems may be mainstreamed into the classroom? Why are neighbors afraid of having a group of individuals who are mentally retarded move in next door? What is the impact on health insurance coverage for someone with HIV who is fired from his job? What is the impact on the family when a seriously ill infant is born into that family? What is the impact of these infants on hospital resources or on the nurse in charge of the neonatal intensive care unit? When groups of individuals who are mentally retarded are taken to a baseball game by a well-meaning civic group, are they really being exposed to the mainstream of society? How does someone with a hearing impairment enjoy a television program?

In analyzing the problems in this book, the following considerations should be taken into account where relevant:

1. What additional **information** is needed?

    Where can that information be obtained?

    What documents are needed — medical reports, copies of correspondence, work evaluations, school records?

    What limitations apply to obtaining records — confidentiality, cost?

    When did the discrimination, denial of benefits, or exclusion take place (for statute of limitations purposes)?

2. What **laws** have been violated?

    Is there a constitutional issue? Is there requisite state action?

    If there is state action, what test applies — strict scrutiny, rational basis, or some other test?

    Is the party carrying out the conduct in question covered by applicable law?

Is the party a program receiving federal financial assistance, a federal contractor, or is it covered by state law?

Is the party claiming discrimination disabled or handicapped within the applicable definition?

Is the party claiming discrimination otherwise qualified, within the applicable definition?

Is there a private right of action; is exhaustion of administrative remedies required?

3. What are the best means of pursuing the problem, i.e., what **tactics** — negotiation, litigation (in which court?), administrative action?

4. What **procedures** need to be understood in order to represent your client?

5. What **remedy** is sought — damages, injunction, debarment, etc.?

    What is most appropriate?

    What is provided for by statute?

    If damages, what kind of damages?

    What about attorneys' fees and costs?

6. What kind of **defenses** might bar the action — statute of limitations, mootness, immunity, lack of jurisdiction, undue administrative or financial burden, direct threat to health and safety of others?

Chapter 2

WHO IS PROTECTED UNDER THE LAWS?
HISTORICAL AND CONTEMPORARY PERSPECTIVES

A CONSTITUTIONAL PROTECTIONS

There is some protection for persons with disabilities under the Equal Protection and Due Process Clauses of the Fourteenth Amendment to the United States Constitution. This protection, however, is limited to irrational classification by state law or irrational discrimination engaged in by state actors. It does not apply to private actors. And, there is some debate as to the extent that the federal Constitution protects persons with disabilities. Federal laws such as the Rehabilitation Act and the Americans with Disabilities Act (ADA), therefore, provide most of the protections enjoyed by persons with disabilities. There are, however, problems with liability against the states for damages under the ADA because of immunity created by the Eleventh Amendment to the Constitution. Chapter 3 will deal with those issues. A state or municipality's potential liability for disability-based discrimination under the federal Constitution is addressed in this chapter.

CITY OF CLEBURNE v. CLEBURNE LIVING CENTER, INC.
473 U.S. 432 (1985)

JUSTICE WHITE delivered the opinion of the Court.

A Texas city denied a special use permit for the operation of a group home for the mentally retarded, acting pursuant to a municipal zoning ordinance requiring permits for such homes. The Court of Appeals for the Fifth Circuit held that mental retardation is a "quasi-suspect" classification and that the ordinance violated the Equal Protection Clause because it did not substantially further an important governmental purpose. We hold that a lesser standard of scrutiny is appropriate, but conclude that under that standard the ordinance is invalid as applied in this case.

I

In July 1980, respondent Jan Hannah purchased a building at 201 Featherston Street in the city of Cleburne, Texas, with the intention of leasing it to Cleburne Living Center, Inc. (CLC), for the operation of a group home for the mentally retarded. It was anticipated that the home would house 13 retarded men and women, who would be under the constant supervision of CLC staff members.

The city informed CLC that a special use permit would be required for the operation of a group home at the site, and CLC accordingly submitted a permit application. In response to a subsequent inquiry from CLC, the city explained that under the zoning regulations applicable to the site, a special use permit, renewable annually, was required for the construction of "[hospitals] for the insane or feeble-minded, or alcoholic [*sic*] or drug addicts, or penal or correctional institutions." The city had determined that the proposed group home should be classified as a "hospital for the feebleminded." After holding a public hearing on CLC's application, the City Council voted 3 to 1 to deny a special use permit.

CLC then filed suit in Federal District Court against the city and a number of its officials, alleging, *inter alia*, that the zoning ordinance was invalid on its face and as applied because it discriminated against the mentally retarded in violation of the equal protection rights of CLC and its potential residents. The court deemed the ordinance, as written and applied, to be rationally related to the city's legitimate interests in "the legal responsibility of CLC and its residents, . . . the safety and fears of residents in the adjoining neighborhood," and the number of people to be housed in the home.

The Court of Appeals for the Fifth Circuit reversed, determining that mental retardation was a quasi-suspect classification and that it should assess the validity of the ordinance under intermediate-level scrutiny. The court considered heightened scrutiny to be particularly appropriate in this case, because the city's ordinance withheld a benefit which, although not fundamental, was very important to the mentally retarded. Without group homes, the court stated, the retarded could never hope to integrate themselves into the community.

II

The Equal Protection Clause of the Fourteenth Amendment commands that no State shall "deny to any person within its jurisdiction the equal protection of the laws," which is essentially a direction that all persons similarly situated should be treated alike. Section 5 of the Amendment empowers Congress to enforce this mandate, but absent controlling congressional direction, the courts have themselves devised standards for determining the validity of state legislation or other official action that is challenged as denying equal protection. The general rule is that legislation is presumed to be valid and will be sustained if the classification drawn by the statute is rationally related to a legitimate state interest. When social or economic legislation is at issue, the Equal Protection Clause allows the States wide latitude, and the Constitution presumes that even improvident decisions will eventually be rectified by the democratic processes.

The general rule gives way, however, when a statute classifies by race, alienage, or national origin. These factors are so seldom relevant to the achievement of any legitimate state interest that laws grounded in such considerations are deemed to reflect prejudice and antipathy — a view that those in the burdened class are not as worthy or deserving as others. For these reasons and because such discrimination is unlikely to be soon rectified by legislative means, these laws are subjected to strict scrutiny and will be sustained only if they are suitably tailored to serve a compelling state interest. Similar oversight by the courts is due when state laws impinge on personal rights protected by the Constitution.

[W]here individuals in the group affected by a law have distinguishing characteristics relevant to interests the State has the authority to implement, the courts have been very reluctant, as they should be in our federal system and with our respect for the separation of powers, to closely scrutinize legislative choices as to whether, how, and to what extent those interests should be pursued. In such cases, the Equal Protection Clause requires only a rational means to serve a legitimate end.

III

Against this background, we conclude for several reasons that the Court of Appeals erred in holding mental retardation a quasi-suspect classification calling for a more exacting standard of judicial review than is normally accorded economic and social legislation. First, it is undeniable, and it is not argued otherwise here, that those who are mentally retarded have a reduced ability to cope with and function in the everyday world. Nor are they all cut from the same pattern: as the testimony in this record indicates, they range from those whose disability is not immediately evident to those who must be constantly cared for.[9] They are thus different, immutably so, in relevant respects, and the States' interest in dealing with and providing for them is plainly a legitimate one. How this large and diversified group is to be treated under the law is a difficult and often a technical matter, very much a task for legislators guided by qualified professionals and not by the perhaps ill-informed opinions of the judiciary. Heightened scrutiny inevitably involves substantive judgments about legislative decisions, and we doubt that the predicate for such judicial oversight is present where the classification deals with mental retardation.

Second, the distinctive legislative response, both national and state, to the plight of those who are mentally retarded demonstrates not only that they have unique problems, but also that the lawmakers have been addressing their difficulties in a manner that belies a continuing antipathy or prejudice and a corresponding need for more intrusive oversight by the judiciary.

---

[9] Mentally retarded individuals fall into four distinct categories. The vast majority — approximately 89% — are classified as "mildly" retarded, meaning that their IQ is between 50 and 70. Approximately 6% are "moderately" retarded, with IQs between 35 and 50. The remaining two categories are "severe" (IQs of 20 to 35) and "profound" (IQs below 20). These last two categories together account for about 5% of the mentally retarded population. App. 39 (testimony of Dr. Philip Roos).

Mental retardation is not defined by reference to intelligence or IQ alone, however. The American Association on Mental Deficiency (AAMD) has defined mental retardation as " 'significantly subaverage general intellectual functioning existing concurrently with deficits in adaptive behavior and manifested during the developmental period.' " Brief for AAMD et al. as *Amici Curiae* 3 (quoting AAMD, Classification in Mental Retardation 1 (H. Grossman ed. 1983)). "Deficits in adaptive behavior" are limitations on general ability to meet the standards of maturation, learning, personal independence, and social responsibility expected for an individual's age level and cultural group. Brief for AAMD et al. as *Amici Curiae* 4, n. 1. Mental retardation is caused by a variety of factors, some genetic, some environmental, and some unknown. *Id.*, at 4.

Such legislation thus singling out the retarded for special treatment reflects the real and undeniable differences between the retarded and others. That a civilized and decent society expects and approves such legislation indicates that governmental consideration of those differences in the vast majority of situations is not only legitimate but also desirable. It may be, as CLC contends, that legislation designed to benefit, rather than disadvantage, the retarded would generally withstand examination under a test of heightened scrutiny. The relevant inquiry, however, is whether heightened scrutiny is constitutionally mandated in the first instance. Even assuming that many of these laws could be shown to be substantially related to an important governmental purpose, merely requiring the legislature to justify its efforts in these terms may lead it to refrain from acting at all. Much recent legislation intended to benefit the retarded also assumes the need for measures that might be perceived to disadvantage them. Especially given the wide variation in the abilities and needs of the retarded themselves, governmental bodies must have a certain amount of flexibility and freedom from judicial oversight in shaping and limiting their remedial efforts.

Third, the legislative response, which could hardly have occurred and survived without public support, negates any claim that the mentally retarded are politically powerless in the sense that they have no ability to attract the attention of the lawmakers. Any minority can be said to be powerless to assert direct control over the legislature, but if that were a criterion for higher level scrutiny by the courts, much economic and social legislation would now be suspect.

Fourth, if the large and amorphous class of the mentally retarded were deemed quasi-suspect for the reasons given by the Court of Appeals, it would be difficult to find a principled way to distinguish a variety of other groups who have perhaps immutable disabilities setting them off from others, who cannot themselves mandate the desired legislative responses, and who can claim some degree of prejudice from at least part of the public at large. One need mention in this respect only the aging, the disabled, the mentally ill, and the infirm. We are reluctant to set out on that course, and we decline to do so.

Doubtless, there have been and there will continue to be instances of discrimination against the retarded that are in fact invidious, and that are properly subject to judicial correction under constitutional norms. But the appropriate method of reaching such instances is not to create a new quasi-suspect classification and subject all governmental action based on that classification to more searching evaluation. Rather, we should look to the likelihood that governmental action premised on a particular classification is valid as a general matter, not merely to the specifics of the case before us. Because mental retardation is a characteristic that the government may legitimately take into account in a wide range of decisions, and because both State and Federal Governments have recently committed themselves to assisting the retarded, we will not presume that any given legislative action, even one that disadvantages retarded individuals, is rooted in considerations that the Constitution will not tolerate.

Our refusal to recognize the retarded as a quasi-suspect class does not leave them entirely unprotected from invidious discrimination. To withstand equal protection review, legislation that distinguishes between the mentally retarded and others must be rationally related to a legitimate governmental purpose.

IV

The constitutional issue is clearly posed. The city does not require a special use permit in an R-3 zone for apartment houses, multiple dwellings, boarding and lodging houses, fraternity or sorority houses, dormitories, apartment hotels, hospitals, sanitariums, nursing homes for convalescents or the aged (other than for the insane or feebleminded or alcoholics or drug addicts), private clubs or fraternal orders, and other specified uses. It does, however, insist on a special permit for the Featherston home, and it does so, as the District Court found, because it would be a facility for the mentally retarded. May the city require the permit for this facility when other care and multiple-dwelling facilities are freely permitted?

It is true, as already pointed out, that the mentally retarded as a group are indeed different from others not sharing their misfortune, and in this respect they may be different from those who would occupy other facilities that would be permitted in an R-3 zone without a special permit. But this difference is largely irrelevant unless the Featherston home and those who would occupy it would threaten legitimate interests of the city in a way that other permitted uses such as boarding houses and hospitals would not. Because in our view the record does not reveal any rational basis for believing that the Featherston home would pose any special threat to the city's legitimate interests, we affirm the judgment below insofar as it holds the ordinance invalid as applied in this case.

The District Court found that the City Council's insistence on the permit rested on several factors. First, the Council was concerned with the negative attitude of the majority of property owners located within 200 feet of the Featherston facility, as well as with the fears of elderly residents of the neighborhood. But mere negative attitudes, or fear, unsubstantiated by factors which are properly cognizable in a zoning proceeding, are not permissible bases for treating a home for the mentally retarded differently from apartment houses, multiple dwellings, and the like. It is plain that the electorate as a whole, whether by referendum or otherwise, could not order city action violative of the Equal Protection Clause, and the city may not avoid the strictures of that Clause by deferring to the wishes or objections of some fraction of the body politic.

Second, the Council had two objections to the location of the facility. It was concerned that the facility was across the street from a junior high school, and it feared that the students might harass the occupants of the Featherston home. But the school itself is attended by about 30 mentally retarded students, and denying a permit based on such vague, undifferentiated fears is again permitting some portion of the community to validate what would otherwise be an equal protection violation. The other objection to the home's location was that it was located on "a five hundred year flood plain." This concern with the possibility of a flood, however, can hardly be based on a distinction between the Featherston home and, for example, nursing homes, homes for convalescents or the aged, or sanitariums or hospitals, any of which could be located on the Featherston site without obtaining a special use permit. The same may be said of another concern of the Council —

doubts about the legal responsibility for actions which the mentally retarded might take. If there is no concern about legal responsibility with respect to other uses that would be permitted in the area, such as boarding and fraternity houses, it is difficult to believe that the groups of mildly or moderately mentally retarded individuals who would live at 201 Featherston would present any different or special hazard.

Fourth, the Council was concerned with the size of the home and the number of people that would occupy it. The District Court found, and the Court of Appeals repeated, that "[if] the potential residents of the Featherston Street home were not mentally retarded, but the home was the same in all other respects, its use would be permitted under the city's zoning ordinance." Given this finding, there would be no restrictions on the number of people who could occupy this home as a boarding house, nursing home, family dwelling, fraternity house, or dormitory. The question is whether it is rational to treat the mentally retarded differently. It is true that they suffer disability not shared by others; but why this difference warrants a density regulation that others need not observe is not at all apparent. At least this record does not clarify how, in this connection, the characteristics of the intended occupants of the Featherston home rationally justify denying to those occupants what would be permitted to groups occupying the same site for different purposes. Those who would live in the Featherston home are the type of individuals who, with supporting staff, satisfy federal and state standards for group housing in the community; and there is no dispute that the home would meet the federal square-footage-per-resident requirement for facilities of this type.

The short of it is that requiring the permit in this case appears to us to rest on an irrational prejudice against the mentally retarded, including those who would occupy the Featherston facility and who would live under the closely supervised and highly regulated conditions expressly provided for by state and federal law.

The judgment of the Court of Appeals is affirmed insofar as it invalidates the zoning ordinance as applied to the Featherston home. The judgment is otherwise vacated, and the case is remanded.

JUSTICE MARSHALL, with whom JUSTICE BRENNAN and JUSTICE BLACKMUN join, concurring in the judgment in part and dissenting in part.

I cannot agree . . . with the way in which the Court reaches its result or with the narrow, as-applied remedy it provides for the city of Cleburne's equal protection violation. The Court holds the ordinance invalid on rational-basis grounds and disclaims that anything special, in the form of heightened scrutiny, is taking place. Because I dissent from this novel and truncated remedy, and because I cannot accept the Court's disclaimer that no "more exacting standard" than ordinary rational-basis review is being applied, I write separately.

The refusal to acknowledge that something more than minimum rationality review is at work here is, in my view, unfortunate . . . .

II

I have long believed the level of scrutiny employed in an equal protection case should vary with "the constitutional and societal importance of the interest adversely affected and the recognized invidiousness of the basis upon which the particular classification is drawn." When a zoning ordinance works to exclude the retarded from all residential districts in a community, these two considerations require that the ordinance be convincingly justified as substantially furthering legitimate and important purposes.

First, the interest of the retarded in establishing group homes is substantial. The right to "establish a home" has long been cherished as one of the fundamental liberties embraced by the Due Process Clause. For retarded adults, this right means living together in group homes, for as deinstitutionalization has progressed, group homes have become the primary means by which retarded adults can enter life in the community.

Second, the mentally retarded have been subject to a "lengthy and tragic history," of segregation and discrimination that can only be called grotesque. During much of the 19th century, mental retardation was viewed as neither curable nor dangerous and the retarded were largely left to their own devices. By the latter part of the century and during the first decades of the new one, however, social views of the retarded underwent a radical transformation. Fueled by the rising tide of Social Darwinism, the "science" of eugenics, and the extreme xenophobia of those years, leading medical authorities and others began to portray the "feebleminded" as a "menace to society and civilization . . . responsible in a large degree for many, if not all, of our social problems." A regime of state-mandated segregation and degradation soon emerged that in its virulence and bigotry rivaled, and indeed paralleled, the worst excesses of Jim Crow. Massive custodial institutions were built to warehouse the retarded for life; the aim was to halt reproduction of the retarded and "nearly extinguish their race." Retarded children were categorically excluded from public schools, based on the false stereotype that all were ineducable and on the purported need to protect nonretarded children from them. State laws deemed the retarded "unfit for citizenship."

Segregation was accompanied by eugenic marriage and sterilization laws that extinguished for the retarded one of the "basic civil rights of man" — the right to marry and procreate. Marriages of the retarded were made, and in some States continue to be, not only voidable but also often a criminal offense. The purpose of such limitations, which frequently applied only to women of child-bearing age, was unabashedly eugenic: to prevent the retarded from propagating. To assure this end, 29 States enacted compulsory eugenic sterilization laws between 1907 and 1931.

Prejudice, once let loose, is not easily cabined. As of 1979, most States still categorically disqualified "idiots" from voting, without regard to individual capacity and with discretion to exclude left in the hands of low-level election officials. Not until Congress enacted the Education of the Handicapped Act, 84 Stat. 175, as amended, 20 U. S. C. § 1400 *et seq.*, were "the [doors] of public education" opened wide to handicapped children. But most important, lengthy and continuing isolation of the retarded has perpetuated the ignorance, irrational fears, and stereotyping that long have plagued them.

The searching scrutiny I would give to restrictions on the ability of the retarded to establish community group homes leads me to conclude that Cleburne's vague generalizations for classifying the "feeble-minded" with drug addicts, alcoholics, and the insane, and excluding them where the elderly, the ill, the boarder, and the transient are allowed, are not substantial or important enough to overcome the suspicion that the ordinance rests on impermissible assumptions or outmoded and perhaps invidious stereotypes.

NOTES AND QUESTIONS

1.   The *City of Cleburne* is known by Constitutional scholars for adopting a variation of the rational relationship test under the Equal Protection Clause that imposes more scrutiny than most classifications subject to the test. Justice Marshall's dissent (in part) challenges the Court as being somewhat disingenuous in its application of the test, and argues that the Court should apply heightened scrutiny to the classification in question. He also argues that the Court's scrutiny goes beyond that applied to other laws subject to the rational relationship test.

2.   Justice Marshall refers to the history of segregation of persons with mental retardation and to the eugenics movement. Why is this background important to his argument? Can the argument be made that persons with disabilities, and, in particular, those with mental retardation, possess immutable characteristics that have caused them to suffer a history of unfair and discriminatory treatment and political powerlessness? Explain.

3.   The Court notes that there has been a great deal of legislation to protect the rights of individuals with disabilities as evidence that this group is not politically powerless, and thus does not require special constitutional treatment. Why then are racial minorities, who are treated as a suspect class, considered to be politically powerless when there is a substantial body of civil rights legislation prohibiting race discrimination?

4.   Justice Marshall refers to the case of *Buck v. Bell*, 274 U.S. 200 (1927). In that case, Carrie Buck was institutionalized because she was categorized by the state of Virginia as "feebleminded." According to the opinion, Carrie's mother was also "feebleminded," and Carrie had an illegitimate "feebleminded" child. Under Virginia law, the state ordered the institution to sterilize Carrie. When she challenged the forced sterilization, the Supreme Court, in an opinion by Justice Holmes, held that the procedure would not violate Buck's federal constitutional rights. A famous portion of the opinion states:

> It is better for all the world, if instead of waiting to execute degenerate offspring for crime, or to let them starve for their imbecility, society can prevent those who are manifestly unfit from continuing their kind. . . . Three generations of imbeciles is enough.

Id. at 207.

5. Disagreement about the meaning of *Cleburne* continues. In *Board of Trustees v. Garrett*, 531 U.S. 356 (2001), see Chapter 3, Section [G][2], *infra*, Chief Justice Rehnquist, who authored the majority opinion in *Garrett*, interpreted *Cleburne* as holding merely that minimum rational-basis review is required, and that no special scrutiny applies to classifications of persons with disabilities. He stated that no matter how hardhearted, states do not have to grant reasonable accommodations to persons with disabilities. Justice Breyer, in dissent in *Garrett*, however, interpreted *Cleburne* to hold that state laws that rest either on a desire to harm or on negative attitudes, fear or irrational prejudices would unconstitutionally discriminate against persons with disabilities. Which of these interpretations makes more sense? Does the interpretation of *Cleburne* depend on the composition of the Supreme Court? In what way?

In the next case, the Supreme Court addresses whether differing treatment between two different types of disabilities can withstand constitutional scrutiny. The decision was a result of a challenge by a class of mentally retarded persons who had been involuntarily committed to mental institutions. In Kentucky, the standard for commitment of individuals who are mentally ill is that there must be a showing that the individual is a danger to self, family, or others "beyond a reasonable doubt." The standard for committing individuals who are mentally retarded is there must be a showing of danger to self, family, or others by "clear and convincing evidence."

The following is the Court's justification of the distinction between these two groups.

HELLER v. DOE
507 U.S. 970 (1993)

Mr. Justice Kennedy delivered the opinion of the Court:

[A] classification neither involving fundamental rights nor proceeding along suspect lines is accorded a strong presumption of validity. Such a classification cannot run afoul of the Equal Protection Clause if there is a rational relationship between the disparity of treatment and some legitimate governmental purpose. Further, a legislature that creates these categories need not "actually articulate at any time the purpose or rationale supporting its classification."

A State, moreover, has no obligation to produce evidence to sustain the rationality of a statutory classification. A statute is presumed constitutional and "[t]he burden is on the one attacking the legislative arrangement to negate every conceivable basis which might support it," whether or not the basis has a foundation in the record.

Kentucky argues that a lower standard of proof in commitments for mental retardation follows from the fact that mental retardation is easier to diagnose than is mental illness. That general proposition should cause little surprise, for mental retardation is a developmental disability that becomes apparent before adulthood. By the time the person reaches 18 years of age the documentation and other evidence of the condition have been accumulated for years. Mental illness, on the other hand, may be sudden and may not occur, or at least manifest itself, until adulthood. Furthermore, as we recognized in an earlier case, diagnosis of mental illness is difficult. Kentucky's basic premise that mental retardation is easier to diagnose than is mental illness has a sufficient basis in fact.

The differences between the two conditions justifies Kentucky's decision to assign a lower standard of proof in commitment proceedings involving the mentally retarded. In assigning the burden of proof, Kentucky was determining the "risk of error" faced by the subject of the proceedings. If diagnosis is more difficult in cases of mental illness than in instances of mental retardation, a higher burden of proof for the former tends to equalize the risks of an erroneous determination that the subject of a commitment proceeding has the condition in question.

There is moreover, a "reasonably conceivable state of facts," from which Kentucky could conclude that the second prerequisite to commitment — that "[t]he person presents a danger or a threat of danger to self, family, or others," — is established more easily, as a general rule, in the case of the mentally retarded. Previous instances of violent behavior are an important indicator of future violent tendencies. Mental retardation is a permanent, relatively static condition, so a determination of dangerousness may be made with some accuracy based on previous behavior. We deal here with adults only, so almost by definition in the case of the retarded there is an 18 year record upon which to rely.

This is not so with the mentally ill. Manifestations of mental illness may be sudden, and past behavior may not be an adequate predictor of future actions. Prediction of future behavior is complicated as well by the difficulties inherent in diagnosis of mental illness. It is thus no surprise that psychiatric predictions of future violent behavior by the mentally ill are inaccurate. For these reasons, it would have been plausible for Kentucky to conclude that the dangerousness determination was more accurate as to the mentally retarded than the mentally ill.

[I]t would have been plausible for the Kentucky legislature to believe that most mentally retarded individuals who are committed receive treatment which is different from, and less invasive than, that to which the mentally ill are subjected.

Kentucky's burden of proof scheme, then, can be explained by differences in the ease of diagnosis and the accuracy of the prediction of future dangerousness and by the nature of the treatment received after commitment. Each of these rationales, standing on its own, would suffice to establish a rational basis for the distinction in question.

PROBLEMS

1. Does the *Heller* decision indicate whether the Supreme Court would be likely to view the denial of the special use permit in a case involving a group home for mentally ill persons more or less favorably than their decision in *Cleburne*, *supra*.

2. Would the analysis be any different if a genetic predisposition to certain kinds of mental illness were discovered?

3. Does this analysis provide guidance on whether distinctions in health care insurance between mental and physical conditions are valid?

B DEFINING DISABILITY: STATUTORY DEFINITIONS AND JUDICIAL INTERPRETATIONS

Authors' Note on the ADA Amendments Act of 2008 (ADAAA)

Congress passed the ADA Amendments Act in September 2008. The statute became effective January 1, 2009, and amends both the ADA and the Rehabilitation Act. The ADAAA was passed to reject the courts' narrow interpretation of the definition of "individual with a disability," and to ensure that more persons with serious impairments would be protected by the law. Most courts have held that the ADAAA does not apply retroactively to conduct occurring before the effective date of the ADAAA, unless the relief requested is limited to injunctive relief. Therefore, at the time of this book's publication there were few cases interpreting the new amendments.

This chapter includes historical and contemporary accounts of the statutory provisions, judicial interpretations and the Congressional override of Supreme Court cases that narrowly define those individuals who are protected by the ADA. When Congress first enacted the ADA, drafters of the statute erroneously believed that courts would look to the previous broad interpretations of the Rehabilitation Act to provide for a broad coverage of the ADA. Unfortunately, the Supreme Court significantly narrowed the definition of "individual with a disability" instead.

The ADAAA instructs courts to broadly interpret the definition of individual with a disability and to focus attention more on the question of whether the covered entity discriminated against the individual based on his or her disability. While it is crucial for students to understand the history of the ADA, the Rehabilitation Act, and the ADAAA in order to interpret the definition of disability in the future, it is equally important for students to recognize that the law that is now in effect encourages more focus on causation and on the issue of whether the covered entity illegally discriminated against the individual. Those issues will be studied in subsequent chapters. This portion of this chapter focuses on the evolution of the definition of "individual with a disability" under the ADA and the Rehabilitation Act.

[1] Statutory Definitions

The following is the statutory language of the five major federal disability discrimination statutes that provide substantive protection. In reading the statutes, note the similarity and differences among them. The Architectural Barriers Act of 1968, 42 U.S.C. §§ 4151–4157, is not discussed here because it relates primarily to physical aspects of federal buildings and has been subject to very little judicial interpretation. Some other statutes are not discussed here for similar reasons.

AMERICANS WITH DISABILITIES ACT

42 U.S.C. § 12102(1) **Disability**

[Author's Note: This definition applies to all subchapters of the ADA.]

The term "disability" means, with respect to an individual —

(A) a physical or mental impairment that substantially limits one or more major life activities of such individual;

(B) a record of such an impairment; or

(C) being regarded as having such an impairment.

Major Life Activity

The ADAAA of 2008 amended the 42 U.S.C. § 12102 of the ADA to add a non-exhaustive list to the definition of "major life activity:"

> "caring for oneself, performing manual tasks, seeing, hearing, eating, sleeping, walking, standing, lifting, bending, speaking, breathing, learning, reading, concentrating, thinking, communicating, and working."

It also includes in the definition the operation of a "major bodily function," including but not limited to:

> "functions of the immune system, normal cell growth, digestive, bowel, bladder, neurological, brain, respiratory, circulatory, endocrine, and reproductive functions."

The ADAAA amended Section 7 of the Rehabilitation Act of 1973, 29 U.S.C. § 705, by granting it "the meaning given [major life activities] in . . . the Americans with Disabilities Act of 1990." 122 Stat. 3558.

Title I (Employment)

42 U.S.C. § 12111(8) **Qualified individual with a disability**

> The term "qualified individual with a disability" means an individual who, with or without reasonable accommodation, can perform the essential functions of the employment position that such individual holds or desires. For the purposes of this title, consideration shall be given to the employer's judgment as to what functions of a job are essential, and if an employer has prepared a written description before advertising or interviewing applicants for the job, this description shall be considered evidence of the essential functions of the job.

42 U.S.C. § 12112(b)(4) **Construction**

> As used in subsection (a) of this section, the term "discriminate" . . . includes —

> (4) excluding or otherwise denying equal jobs or benefits to a qualified individual because of the known disability of an individual with whom the qualified individual is known to have a relationship or association;

42 U.S.C. § 12113(b) **Qualification standards**

The term "qualification standards" may include a requirement that an individual shall not pose a direct threat to the health or safety of other individuals in the workplace.

42 U.S.C. § 12114(a) **Illegal use of drugs**

For purposes of this title, the term "individual with a disability" does not include any employee or applicant who is currently engaging in the illegal use of drugs, when the covered entity acts on the basis of such use.

42 U.S.C. § 12114(b) **Rules of construction**

Nothing in subsection (a) shall be construed to exclude as a qualified individual with a disability an individual who —

(1)   has successfully completed a supervised drug rehabilitation program and is no longer engaging in the illegal use of drugs, or has otherwise been rehabilitated successfully and is no longer engaging in such use;

(2)   is participating in a supervised rehabilitation program and is no longer engaging in such use; or

(3)   is erroneously regarded as engaging in such use, but is not engaging in such use;

except that it shall not be a violation of this Act for a covered entity to adopt or administer reasonable policies or procedures, including but not limited to drug testing, designed to ensure that an individual described in paragraph (1) or (2) is no longer engaging in the illegal use of drugs.

Title II (Public Services)

42 U.S.C. § 12131(2) **Qualified individual with a disability**

The term "qualified individual with a disability" means an individual with a disability who, with or without reasonable modifications to rules, policies, or practices, the removal of architectural, communication, or transportation barriers, or the provision of auxiliary aids and services, meets the essential eligibility requirements for the receipt of services or the participation in programs or activities provided by a public entity.

Title III (Public Accommodations)

42 U.S.C. § 12182(b)(1)(E) **Association**

It shall be discriminatory to exclude or otherwise deny equal goods, services, facilities, privileges, advantages, accommodations, or other opportunities to an individual or entity because of the known disability of an individual with whom the individual or entity is known to have a relationship or association.

Title IV (Miscellaneous Provisions)

42 U.S.C. § 12208 Transvestites

For purposes of this Act, the term "disabled" or "disability" shall not apply to an individual solely because that individual is a transvestite.

42 U.S.C. § 12210 Illegal use of drugs

(a) In general

For purposes of this Act, the term "individual with a disability" does not include an individual who is currently engaging in the illegal use of drugs, when the covered entity acts on the basis of such use.

(b) Rules of construction

Nothing in subsection (a) shall be construed as to exclude as an individual with a disability an individual who —

    (1)   has successfully completed a supervised drug rehabilitation program and is no longer engaging in the illegal use of drugs, or has otherwise been rehabilitated successfully and is no longer engaging in such use;

    (2)   is participating in a supervised rehabilitation program and is no longer engaging in such use; or

    (3)   is erroneously regarded as engaging in such use, but is not engaging in such use;

except that it shall not be a violation of this Act for a covered entity to adopt or administer reasonable policies or procedures, including, but not limited to drug testing, designed to ensure that an individual described in paragraph (1) or (2) is no longer engaging in the illegal use of drugs; however, nothing in this section shall be construed to encourage, prohibit, restrict, or authorize the conducting of testing for the illegal use of drugs.

42 U.S.C. § 12211(a) Homosexuality and bisexuality

For purposes of the definition of "disability" in section 12102(2) of this title, homosexuality and bisexuality are not impairments and as such are not disabilities under this Act.

42 U.S.C. § 12211(b) Certain conditions

Under this Act, the term "disability" shall not include —

    (1)   transvestism, transsexualism, pedophilia, exhibitionism, voyeurism, gender identity disorders not resulting from physical impairments, or other sexual behavior disorders;

    (2)   compulsive gambling, kleptomania, or pyromania; or

    (3)   psychoactive substance use disorders resulting from current illegal use of drugs.

REHABILITATION ACT

29 U.S.C. § 705(20)

(A) Except as otherwise provided in subparagraph (B), the term "individual with a disability" means any individual who (i) has a physical or mental impairment which for such individual constitutes or results in a substantial impediment to employment and (ii) can benefit in terms of an employment outcome from vocational rehabilitation services provided pursuant to subchapters I, II, III, VI, and VIII of this chapter.

(B) Subject to subparagraphs (C), (D), (E), and (F), the term "individual with a disability" means, for purposes of [29 U.S.C. §§ 701, 714, 715, 760 et seq., 780 et seq.], any person who has a disability as defined in section 3 of the Americans with Disabilities Act of 1990 (42 U.S.C. § 12102).

(C)(i) For purposes of title V of [29 U.S.C. § 791 et seq.], the term "individual with a disability" does not include an individual who is currently engaging in the illegal use of drugs, when a covered entity acts on the basis of such use.

(ii) Nothing in clause (i) shall be construed to exclude as an individual with a disability an individual who —

(I)   has successfully completed a supervised drug rehabilitation program and is no longer engaging in the illegal use of drugs, or has otherwise been rehabilitated successfully and is no longer engaging in such use;

(II)   is participating in a supervised rehabilitation program and is no longer engaging in such use; or

(III)   is erroneously regarded as engaging in such use, but is not engaging in such use;

except that it shall not be a violation of this Act for a covered entity to adopt or administer reasonable policies or procedures, including but not limited to drug testing, designed to ensure that an individual described in subclause (I) or (II) is no longer engaging in the illegal use of drugs.

(iii) Notwithstanding clause (i), for purposes of programs and activities providing health services and services provided under subchapters I, II and III [29 U.S.C. §§ 720 et seq., 760 et seq., 771 et seq.] of this chapter, an individual shall not be excluded from the benefits of such programs or activities on the basis of his or her current illegal use of drugs if he or she is otherwise entitled to such services.

(iv) For purposes of programs and activities providing educational services, local educational agencies may take disciplinary action pertaining to the use or possession of illegal drugs or alcohol against any student who is an individual with a disability and who currently is engaging in the illegal use of drugs or in the use of alcohol to the same extent that such disciplinary action is taken against students who are not individuals with disabilities. Furthermore, the due process procedures at 34 CFR 104.36 shall not apply to such disciplinary action.

(v) For purposes of sections 793 and 794 of this title as such sections relate to employment, the term "individual with a disability" does not include any individual who is an alcoholic whose current use of alcohol prevents such individual from performing the duties of the job in question or whose employment, by reason of such current alcohol abuse, would constitute a direct threat to property or the safety of others.

(D) For the purpose of sections 793 and 794 of this title, as such sections relate to employment, such term does not include an individual who has a currently contagious disease or infection and who, by reason of such disease or infection, would constitute a direct threat to the health or safety of other individuals or who, by reason of the currently contagious disease or infection is unable to perform the duties of the job.

(E) For the purposes of sections 791, 793, 794 of this title —

(i) for purposes of the application of subparagraph (B) to such sections, the term "impairment" does not include homosexuality or bisexuality; and

(ii) therefore the term "individual with a disability" does not include an individual on the basis of homosexuality or bisexuality.

(F) For the purposes of sections 791, 793, 794 of this title, the term "individual with a disability" does not include an individual on the basis of

(i) transvestism, transsexualism, pedophilia, exhibitionism, voyeurism, gender identity disorders not resulting from physical impairments, or other sexual behavior disorders;

(ii) compulsive gambling, kleptomania, or pyromania; or

(iii) psychoactive substance use disorders resulting from current illegal use of drugs.

FAIR HOUSING ACT

42 U.S.C. § 3602(h)

Handicap means, with respect to a person —

(1) a physical or mental impairment which substantially limits one or more of such person's major life activities,

(2) a record of having such an impairment, or

(3) being regarded as having such an impairment,

but such term does not include current, illegal use of or addiction to a controlled substance (as defined in section 102 of the Controlled Substances Act).

The Note under Section 3602 states: "For the purposes of this Act . . . neither the term 'individual with a handicap' nor the term 'handicap' shall apply to an individual solely because that individual is a transvestite."

AIR CARRIER ACCESS ACT

49 U.S.C. § 41705

(a) In providing air transportation an air carrier including . . . any foreign air carrier may not discriminate against an otherwise qualified individual on the following grounds:

  (1) the individual has a physical or mental impairment that substantially limits one or more major life activities.

  (2) the individual has a record of such an impairment.

  (3) the individual is regarded as having such an impairment.

14 C.F.R. § 382.3

As used in this definition, the phrase:

(a) Physical or mental impairment means:

  (1) any physiological disorder or condition, cosmetic disfigurement, or anatomical loss affecting one or more of the following body systems: neurological, musculoskeletal, special sense organs, respiratory including speech organs, cardio-vascular, reproductive, digestive, genito-urinary, hemic and lymphatic, skin, and endocrine; or

  (2) any mental or psychological disorder, such as mental retardation, organic brain syndrome, emotional or mental illness, and specific learning disabilities.

The term physical or mental impairment includes, but is not limited to, such diseases and conditions as orthopedic, visual, speech, and hearing impairments, cerebral palsy, epilepsy, muscular dystrophy, multiple sclerosis, cancer, heart disease, diabetes, mental retardation, emotional illness, drug addiction, and alcoholism.

14 C.F.R. § 382.21

(a) You must not do any of the following things on the basis that a passenger has a communicable disease or infection, unless you determine that the pasenger's condition poses a direct threat:

  (1) Refuse to provide transportation . . . ;

  (2) Delay the passenger's transportation . . . ;

  (3) Impose on the passenger any condition, restriction, or requirement not imposed on other passengers; or

  (4) Require the passenger to provide a medical certificate.

INDIVIDUALS WITH DISABILITIES EDUCATION ACT

20 U.S.C. § 1401(3) Child with a disability.

(A)   In general. The term "child with a disability" means a child —

(i)   with mental retardation, hearing impairments (including deafness), speech or language impairments, visual impairments (including blindness), serious emotional disturbance (referred to . . . as "emotional disturbance"), orthopedic impairments, autism, traumatic brain injury, other health impairments, or specific learning disabilities; and

(ii)   who, by reason thereof, needs special education and related services.

(B)   Child aged 3 through 9. . . . The term "child with a disability" for a child aged 3 through 9 may, at the discretion of the State and the local educational agency, include a child —

(i)   experiencing developmental delays, as defined by the State and as measured by appropriate diagnostic instruments and procedures, in one or more of the following areas; physical development; cognitive development; communication development; social or emotional development; or adaptive development; and

(ii)   who, by reason thereof, needs special education and related services.

20 U.S.C. § 1401(30) Specific learning disability.

(A)   In general. The term "specific learning disability" means a disorder in one or more of the basic psychological processes involved in understanding or in using language, spoken or written, which disorder may manifest itself in imperfect ability to listen, think, speak, read, write, spell, or do mathematical calculations.

(B)   Disorders included. Such term includes such conditions as perceptual disabilities, brain injury, minimal brain dysfunction, dyslexia, and developmental aphasia.

(C)   Disorders not included. Such term does not include a learning problem that is primarily the result of visual, hearing, or motor disabilities, of mental retardation, of emotional disturbance, or of environmental, cultural, or economic disadvantage.

[2]   Prong One: A Physical or Mental Impairment that Substantially Limits A Major Life Activity

Historically, to be protected under federal disability discrimination law, one must be substantially limited in a major life activity. After the ADA Amendments Act of 2008, a person must still prove a substantial limitation in a major life activity in order to qualify for protection under prongs (A) and (B) of the statute. The individual no longer has to prove the substantial limitation or perceived substantial limitation to qualify for protection under prong (C) (the "regarded as" prong) of the statute so long as the person has an impairment or is perceived as having one.

SCHOOL BOARD OF NASSAU COUNTY v. ARLINE
480 U.S. 273 (1987)

[Authors' Note: In 1987, the Supreme Court decided *School Bd. of Nassau County v. Arline*, 480 U.S. 273 (1987), under Section 504 of the Rehabilitation Act. *Arline* broadly defined "substantially limits" and "major life activity." The Court held that Arline, a school teacher with inactive tuberculosis, had a record of a disability and was regarded as having a disability and was therefore protected by the Rehabilitation Act. It rejected the defendant's argument that firing the plaintiff for her contagiousness was not firing her based on her disability. This portion of the opinion deals only with the question of whether Arline was an individual with a disability. The portion of the opinion dealing with whether she was a "qualified individual" is reproduced *infra* in Section [C].]

JUSTICE BRENNAN delivered the opinion of the Court.

Section 504 of the Rehabilitation Act of 1973 prohibits a federally funded state program from discriminating against a handicapped individual solely by reason of his or her handicap. This case presents the questions whether a person afflicted with tuberculosis, a contagious disease, may be considered a "handicapped individual" within the meaning of § 504 of the Act, and, if so, whether such an individual is "otherwise qualified" to teach elementary school.

I

From 1966 until 1979, respondent Gene Arline taught elementary school in Nassau County, Florida. She was discharged in 1979 after suffering a third relapse of tuberculosis within two years. After she was denied relief in state administrative proceedings, she brought suit in federal court, alleging that the school board's decision to dismiss her because of her tuberculosis violated § 504 of the Act.

A trial was held in the District Court, at which the principal medical evidence was provided by Marianne McEuen, M.D., an assistant director of the Community Tuberculosis Control Service of the Florida Department of Health and Rehabilitative Services. According to the medical records reviewed by Dr. McEuen, Arline was hospitalized for tuberculosis in 1957. For the next 20 years, Arline's disease was in remission. Then, in 1977, a culture revealed that tuberculosis was again active in her system; cultures taken in March 1978 and in November 1978 were also positive.

The superintendent of schools for Nassau County, Craig Marsh, then testified as to the school board's response to Arline's medical reports. After both her second relapse, in the spring of 1978, and her third relapse in November 1978, the school board suspended Arline with pay for the remainder of the school year. At the end of the 1978-1979 school year, the school board held a hearing, after which it discharged Arline, "not because she had done anything wrong," but because of the "continued occurrence [*sic*] of tuberculosis."

In her trial memorandum, Arline argued that it was "not disputed that the [school board dismissed her] solely on the basis of her illness. Since the illness in this case qualifies the Plaintiff as a 'handicapped person' it is clear that she was dismissed solely as a result of her handicap in violation of Section 504." The District Court held, however, that although there was "[no] question that she suffers a handicap," Arline was nevertheless not "a handicapped person under the terms of that statute." The court found it "difficult . . . to conceive that Congress intended contagious diseases to be included within the definition of a handicapped person." The court then went on to state that, "even assuming" that a person with a contagious disease could be deemed a handicapped person, Arline was not "qualified" to teach elementary school.

The Court of Appeals reversed, holding that "persons with contagious diseases are within the coverage of section 504," and that Arline's condition "falls . . . neatly within the statutory and regulatory framework" of the Act. The court remanded the case "for further findings as to whether the risks of infection precluded Mrs. Arline from being 'otherwise qualified' for her job and, if so, whether it was possible to make some reasonable accommodation for her in that teaching position" or in some other position. We granted certiorari and now affirm.

II

In enacting and amending the Act, Congress enlisted all programs receiving federal funds in an effort "to share with handicapped Americans the opportunities for an education, transportation, housing, health care, and jobs that other Americans take for granted." To that end, Congress not only increased federal support for vocational rehabilitation, but also addressed the broader problem of discrimination against the handicapped by including § 504, an antidiscrimination provision patterned after Title VI of the Civil Rights Act of 1964. Section 504 of the Rehabilitation Act reads in pertinent part:

> "No otherwise qualified handicapped individual in the United States, as defined in section 706(7) of this title, shall, solely by reason of his handicap, be excluded from participation in, be denied the benefits of, or be subjected to discrimination under any program or activity receiving Federal financial assistance. . . . "

In 1974 Congress expanded the definition of "handicapped individual" for use in § 504 to read as follows:

> "[Any] person who (i) has a physical or mental impairment which substantially limits one or more of such person's major life activities, (ii) has a record of such an impairment, or (iii) is regarded as having such an impairment."

The amended definition reflected Congress' concern with protecting the handicapped against discrimination stemming not only from simple prejudice, but also from "archaic attitudes and laws" and from "the fact that the American people are simply unfamiliar with and insensitive to the difficulties [confronting] individuals with handicaps." To combat the effects of erroneous but nevertheless prevalent perceptions about the handicapped, Congress expanded the definition of "handicapped individual" so as to preclude discrimination against "[a] person who has a record of, or is regarded as having, an impairment [but who] may at present have no actual incapacity at all."

In determining whether a particular individual is handicapped as defined by the Act, the regulations promulgated by the Department of Health and Human Services are of significant assistance. As we have previously recognized, these regulations were drafted with the oversight and approval of Congress; they provide "an important source of guidance on the meaning of § 504." The regulations are particularly significant here because they define two critical terms used in the statutory definition of handicapped individual. "Physical impairment" is defined as follows:

"[Any] physiological disorder or condition, cosmetic disfigurement, or anatomical loss affecting one or more of the following body systems: neurological; musculoskeletal; special sense organs; respiratory, including speech organs; cardiovascular; reproductive, digestive, genitourinary; hemic and lymphatic; skin; and endocrine." 45 CFR § 84.3(j)(2)(i) (1985).

In addition, the regulations define "major life activities" as

"functions such as caring for one's self, performing manual tasks, walking, seeing, hearing, speaking, breathing, learning, and working." § 84.3(j)(2)(ii).

III

Within this statutory and regulatory framework, then, we must consider whether Arline can be considered a handicapped individual. According to the testimony of Dr. McEuen, Arline suffered tuberculosis "in an acute form in such a degree that it affected her respiratory system," and was hospitalized for this condition. Arline thus had a physical impairment as that term is defined by the regulations, since she had a "physiological disorder or condition . . . affecting [her] respiratory [system]." This impairment was serious enough to require hospitalization, a fact more than sufficient to establish that one or more of her major life activities were substantially limited by her impairment. Thus, Arline's hospitalization for tuberculosis in 1957 suffices to establish that she has a "record of . . . impairment" within the meaning of 29 U. S. C. § 706(7)(B)(ii), and is therefore a handicapped individual.

Petitioners concede that a contagious disease may constitute a handicapping condition to the extent that it leaves a person with "diminished physical or mental capabilities," and concede that Arline's hospitalization for tuberculosis in 1957 demonstrates that she has a record of a physical impairment. Petitioners maintain, however, that Arline's record of impairment is irrelevant in this case, since the school board dismissed Arline not because of her diminished physical capabilities, but because of the threat that her relapses of tuberculosis posed to the health of others.

We do not agree with petitioners that, in defining a handicapped individual under § 504, the contagious effects of a disease can be meaningfully distinguished from the disease's physical effects on a claimant in a case such as this. Arline's contagiousness and her physical impairment each resulted from the same underlying condition, tuberculosis. It would be unfair to allow an employer to seize upon the distinction between the effects of a disease on others and the effects of a disease on a patient and use that distinction to justify discriminatory treatment.[7]

Nothing in the legislative history of § 504 suggests that Congress intended such a result. That history demonstrates that Congress was as concerned about the effect of an impairment on others as it was about its effect on the individual. Congress extended coverage, in 29 U. S. C. § 706(7)(B)(iii), to those individuals who are simply "regarded as having" a physical or mental impairment. The Senate Report provides as an example of a person who would be covered under this subsection "a person with some kind of visible physical impairment which in fact does not substantially limit that person's functioning." Such an impairment might not diminish a person's physical or mental capabilities, but could nevertheless substantially limit that person's ability to work as a result of the negative reactions of others to the impairment.

Allowing discrimination based on the contagious effects of a physical impairment would be inconsistent with the basic purpose of § 504, which is to ensure that handicapped individuals are not denied jobs or other benefits because of the prejudiced attitudes or the ignorance of others. By amending the definition of "handicapped individual" to include not only those who are actually physically impaired, but also those who are regarded as impaired and who, as a result, are substantially limited in a major life activity, Congress acknowledged that society's accumulated myths and fears about disability and disease are as handicapping as are the physical limitations that flow from actual impairment. Few aspects of a handicap give rise to the same level of public fear and misapprehension as contagiousness. Even those who suffer or have recovered from such noninfectious diseases as epilepsy or cancer have faced discrimination based on the irrational fear that they might be contagious. The Act is carefully structured to replace such reflexive reactions to actual or perceived handicaps with actions based on reasoned and medically sound judgments: the definition of "handicapped individual" is broad, but only those individuals who are both handicapped *and* otherwise qualified are eligible for relief. The fact that *some* persons who have contagious diseases may pose a serious health threat to others under certain circumstances does not justify excluding from the coverage of the Act *all* persons with actual or perceived contagious diseases. Such exclusion would mean that those accused of being contagious would never have the opportunity to have their condition evaluated in light of medical evidence and a determination made as to whether they were "otherwise qualified." Rather, they would be vulnerable to discrimination on the basis of mythology — precisely the type of injury Congress sought to prevent. We conclude that the fact that a person with a record of a physical impairment is also

---

[7] This case does not present, and we therefore do not reach, the questions whether a carrier of a contagious disease such as AIDS could be considered to have a physical impairment, or whether such a person could be considered, solely on the basis of contagiousness, a handicapped person as defined by the Act.

contagious does not suffice to remove that person from coverage under § 504.

NOTES AND QUESTIONS

1. Although the Court barely mentions "substantially limits a major life activity," it does come to the conclusion that Arline's tuberculosis, when active, fulfilled this requirement. How can the Court's reasoning be explained?

2. In footnote 7, the Court reserved the question of whether HIV positivity constitutes a disability. Using *Arline*, how would it be argued that HIV positivity is a disability?

After *Arline*, and the enactment of the ADA in 1990, *Bragdon v. Abbott*, 524 U.S. 624 (1998), raised the question of whether a woman who was HIV positive but was asymptomatic had a disability covered by the statute. *Bragdon* was important because it, like *Arline*, defined "person with a disability" broadly. Only a year later, however, the Court decided a number of cases that significantly narrowed the definition of disability. And, in response to these later cases, the lower courts strictly limited the definition of disability. It is these later cases with which the drafters of the ADAAA took issue. In reading the following cases, consider the Supreme Court's reasoning and how it appears to change from *Arline* and *Bragdon* to *Sutton* and *Toyota*. Also pay close attention to how the Congress overturned much of the reasoning of the Supreme Court to restore a broader definition of person with a disability under the ADA and the Rehabilitation Act.

BRAGDON v. ABBOTT
524 U.S. 624 (1998)

JUSTICE KENNEDY delivered the opinion of the Court.

We address in this case the application of the Americans with Disabilities Act of 1990 (ADA), 42 U.S.C. § 12101 et seq., to persons infected with the human immunodeficiency virus (HIV).

[This portion of the opinion addresses only whether the plaintiff is disabled within the statute. The portion addressing whether discrimination occurred is found in Chapter 9.]

I

Respondent Sidney Abbott has been infected with HIV since 1986. When the incidents we recite occurred, her infection had not manifested its most serious symptoms. On September 16, 1994, she went to the office of petitioner Randon Bragdon in Bangor, Maine, for a dental appointment. She disclosed her HIV infection on the patient registration form. Petitioner completed a dental examination, discovered a cavity, and informed respondent of his policy against filling cavities of HIV-infected patients. He offered to perform the work at a hospital with no added fee for his services, though respondent would be responsible for the cost of using the hospital's facilities. Respondent declined.

II

We first review the ruling that respondent's HIV infection constituted a disability under the ADA. The statute defines disability as:

(A)   a physical or mental impairment that substantially limits one or more of the major life activities of such individual;

(B)   a record of such an impairment; or

(C)   being regarded as having such impairment. § 12102(2).

We hold respondent's HIV infection was a disability under subsection (A) of the definitional section of the statute. In light of this conclusion, we need not consider the applicability of subsections (B) or (C).

Our consideration of subsection (A) of the definition proceeds in three steps. First, we consider whether respondent's HIV infection was a physical impairment. Second, we identify the life activity upon which respondent relies (reproduction and child bearing) and determine whether it constitutes a major life activity under the ADA. Third, tying the two statutory phrases together, we ask whether the impairment substantially limited the major life activity. In construing the statute, we are informed by interpretations of parallel definitions in previous statutes and the views of various administrative agencies which have faced this interpretive question.

A

The ADA's definition of disability is drawn almost verbatim from the definition of "handicapped individual" included in the Rehabilitation Act of 1973, and the definition of "handicap" contained in the Fair Housing Amendments Act of 1988. Congress' repetition of a well-established term carries the implication that Congress intended the term to be construed in accordance with pre-existing regulatory interpretations. In this case, Congress did more than suggest this construction; it adopted a specific statutory provision in the ADA directing as follows:

Except as otherwise provided in this chapter, nothing in this chapter shall be construed to apply a lesser standard than the standards applied under title V of the Rehabilitation Act of 1973 or the regulations issued by Federal agencies pursuant to such title.

The directive requires us to construe the ADA to grant at least as much protection as provided by the regulations implementing the Rehabilitation Act.

1

The first step in the inquiry under subsection (A) requires us to determine whether respondent's condition constituted a physical impairment. The Department of Health, Education and Welfare (HEW) issued the first regulations interpreting the Rehabilitation Act in 1977. The regulations are of particular significance because, at the time, HEW was the agency responsible for coordinating the implementation and enforcement of § 504. The HEW regulations, which appear without change in the current regulations issued by the Department of Health and Human Services, define "physical or mental impairment" to mean:

(A)   any physiological disorder or condition, cosmetic disfigurement, or anatomical loss affecting one or more of the following body systems: neurological; musculoskeletal; special sense organs; respiratory, including speech organs; cardiovascular; reproductive, digestive, genito-urinary; hemic and lymphatic; skin; and endocrine; or

(B)   any mental or psychological disorder, such as mental retardation, organic brain syndrome, emotional or mental illness, and specific learning disabilities.

In issuing these regulations, HEW decided against including a list of disorders constituting physical or mental impairments, out of concern that any specific enumeration might not be comprehensive. 42 Fed.Reg. 22685 (1977), reprinted in 45 CFR pt. 84, App. A, p. 334 (1997). The commentary accompanying the regulations, however, contains a representative list of disorders and conditions constituting physical impairments, including "such diseases and conditions as orthopedic, visual, speech, and hearing impairments, cerebral palsy, epilepsy, muscular dystrophy, multiple sclerosis, cancer, heart disease, diabetes, mental retardation, emotional illness, and . . . drug addiction and alcoholism."

In 1980, the President transferred responsibility for the implementation and enforcement of § 504 to the Attorney General. The regulations issued by the Justice Department, which remain in force to this day, adopted verbatim the HEW definition of physical impairment quoted above. In addition, the representative list of diseases and conditions originally relegated to the commentary accompanying the HEW regulations were incorporated into the text of the regulations.

HIV infection is not included in the list of specific disorders constituting physical impairments, in part because HIV was not identified as the cause of AIDS until 1983. HIV infection does fall well within the general definition set forth by the regulations, however.

The disease follows a predictable and, as of today, an unalterable course. Once a person is infected with HIV, the virus invades different cells in the blood and in body tissues. Certain white blood cells, known as helper T-lymphocytes or CD4+ cells, are particularly vulnerable to HIV. The virus attaches to the CD4 receptor site of the target cell and fuses its membrane to the cell's membrane. HIV is a retrovirus, which means it uses an enzyme to convert its own genetic material into a form indistinguishable from the genetic material of the target cell. The virus' genetic material migrates to the cell's nucleus and becomes integrated with the cell's chromosomes. Once integrated, the virus can use the cell's own genetic machinery to replicate itself. Additional copies of the virus are released into the body and infect other cells in turn. Although the body does produce antibodies to combat HIV infection, the antibodies are not effective in eliminating the virus.

The virus eventually kills the infected host cell. CD4+ cells play a critical role in coordinating the body's immune response system, and the decline in their number causes corresponding deterioration of the body's ability to fight infections from many sources. Tracking the infected individual's CD4+ cell count is one of the most accurate measures of the course of the disease.

The initial stage of HIV infection is known as acute or primary HIV infection. In a typical case, this stage lasts three months. The virus concentrates in the blood. The assault on the immune system is immediate. The victim suffers from a sudden and serious decline in the number of white blood cells. There is no latency period. Mononucleosis-like symptoms often emerge between six days and six weeks after infection, at times accompanied by fever, headache, enlargement of the lymph nodes (lymphadenopathy), muscle pain (myalgia), rash, lethargy, gastrointestinal disorders, and neurological disorders. Usually these symptoms abate within 14 to 21 days. HIV antibodies appear in the bloodstream within 3 weeks; circulating HIV can be detected within 10 weeks.

After the symptoms associated with the initial stage subside, the disease enters what is referred to sometimes as its asymptomatic phase. The term is a misnomer, in some respects, for clinical features persist throughout, including lymphadenopathy, dermatological disorders, oral lesions, and bacterial infections. Although it varies with each individual, in most instances this stage lasts from 7 to 11 years. The virus now tends to concentrate in the lymph nodes, though low levels of the virus continue to appear in the blood. It was once thought the virus became inactive during this period, but it is now known that the relative lack of symptoms is attributable to the virus' migration from the circulatory system into the lymph nodes. The migration reduces the viral presence in other parts of the body, with a corresponding diminution in physical manifestations of the disease. The virus, however, thrives in the lymph nodes, which, as a vital point of the body's immune response system, represents an ideal environment for the infection of other CD4+ cells. Studies have shown that viral production continues at a high rate. CD4+ cells continue to decline an average of 5% to 10% (40 to 80 cells/mm3) per year throughout this phase.

A person is regarded as having AIDS when his or her CD4+ count drops below 200 cells/mm3 of blood or when CD4+ cells comprise less than 14% of his or her total lymphocytes. During this stage, the clinical conditions most often associated with HIV, such as pneumocystis carninii pneumonia, Kaposi's sarcoma, and non-Hodgkins lymphoma, tend to appear. In addition, the general systemic disorders present during all stages of the disease, such as fever, weight loss, fatigue, lesions, nausea, and diarrhea, tend to worsen. In most cases, once the patient's CD4+ count drops below 10 cells/mm3, death soon follows.

In light of the immediacy with which the virus begins to damage the infected person's white blood cells and the severity of the disease, we hold it is an impairment from the moment of infection. As noted earlier, infection with HIV causes immediate abnormalities in a person's blood, and the infected person's white cell count continues to drop throughout the course of the disease, even when the attack is concentrated in the lymph nodes. In light of these facts, HIV infection must be regarded as a physiological disorder with a constant and detrimental effect on the infected person's hemic and lymphatic systems from the moment of infection. HIV infection satisfies the statutory and regulatory definition of a physical impairment during every stage of the disease.

2

The statute is not operative, and the definition not satisfied, unless the impairment affects a major life activity. Respondent's claim throughout this case has been that the HIV infection placed a substantial limitation on her ability to reproduce and to bear children. Given the pervasive, and invariably fatal, course of the disease, its effect on major life activities of many sorts might have been relevant to our inquiry. Respondent and a number of amici make arguments about HIV's profound impact on almost every phase of the infected person's life. In light of these submissions, it may seem legalistic to circumscribe our discussion to the activity of reproduction. We have little doubt that had different parties brought the suit they would have maintained that an HIV infection imposes substantial limitations on other major life activities.

From the outset, however, the case has been treated as one in which reproduction was the major life activity limited by the impairment. It is our practice to decide cases on the grounds raised and considered in the Court of Appeals and included in the question on which we granted certiorari. We ask, then, whether reproduction is a major life activity.

We have little difficulty concluding that it is. As the Court of Appeals held, "[t]he plain meaning of the word 'major' denotes comparative importance" and "suggest[s] that the touchstone for determining an activity's inclusion under the statutory rubric is its significance." Reproduction falls well within the phrase "major life activity." Reproduction and the sexual dynamics surrounding it are central to the life process itself.

While petitioner concedes the importance of reproduction, he claims that Congress intended the ADA only to cover those aspects of a person's life which have a public, economic, or daily character. The argument founders on the statutory language. Nothing in the definition suggests that activities without a public, economic, or daily dimension may somehow be regarded as so unimportant or insignificant as to fall outside the meaning of the word "major." The breadth of the term confounds the attempt to limit its construction in this manner.

As we have noted, the ADA must be construed to be consistent with regulations issued to implement the Rehabilitation Act. See 42 U.S.C. § 12201(a). Rather than enunciating a general principle for determining what is and is not a major life activity, the Rehabilitation Act regulations instead provide a representative list, defining term to include "functions such as caring for one's self, performing manual tasks, walking, seeing, hearing, speaking, breathing, learning, and working." As the use of the term "such as" confirms, the list is illustrative, not exhaustive.

These regulations are contrary to petitioner's attempt to limit the meaning of the term "major" to public activities. The inclusion of activities such as caring for one's self and performing manual tasks belies the suggestion that a task must have a public or economic character in order to be a major life activity for purposes of the

ADA. On the contrary, the Rehabilitation Act regulations support the inclusion of reproduction as a major life activity, since reproduction could not be regarded as any less important than working and learning. Petitioner advances no credible basis for confining major life activities to those with a public, economic, or daily aspect. In the absence of any reason to reach a contrary conclusion, we agree with the Court of Appeals' determination that reproduction is a major life activity for the purposes of the ADA.

3

The final element of the disability definition in subsection (A) is whether respondent's physical impairment was a substantial limit on the major life activity she asserts. The Rehabilitation Act regulations provide no additional guidance.

Our evaluation of the medical evidence leads us to conclude that respondent's infection substantially limited her ability to reproduce in two independent ways. First, a woman infected with HIV who tries to conceive a child imposes on the man a significant risk of becoming infected. The cumulative results of 13 studies collected in a 1994 textbook on AIDS indicates that 20% of male partners of women with HIV became HIV-positive themselves, with a majority of the studies finding a statistically significant risk of infection.

Second, an infected woman risks infecting her child during gestation and childbirth, i.e., perinatal transmission. Petitioner concedes that women infected with HIV face about a 25% risk of transmitting the virus to their children. Published reports available in 1994 confirm the accuracy of this statistic.

Petitioner points to evidence in the record suggesting that antiretroviral therapy can lower the risk of perinatal transmission to about 8%. The Solicitor General questions the relevance of the 8% figure, pointing to regulatory language requiring the substantiality of a limitation to be assessed without regard to available mitigating measures. We need not resolve this dispute in order to decide this case, however. It cannot be said as a matter of law that an 8% risk of transmitting a dread and fatal disease to one's child does not represent a substantial limitation on reproduction.

The Act addresses substantial limitations on major life activities, not utter inabilities. Conception and childbirth are not impossible for an HIV victim but, without doubt, are dangerous to the public health. This meets the definition of a substantial limitation. The decision to reproduce carries economic and legal consequences as well. There are added costs for antiretroviral therapy, supplemental insurance, and long-term health care for the child who must be examined and, tragic to think, treated for the infection. The laws of some States, moreover, forbid persons infected with HIV from having sex with others, regardless of consent.

In the end, the disability definition does not turn on personal choice. When significant limitations result from the impairment, the definition is met even if the difficulties are not insurmountable. For the statistical and other reasons we have cited, of course, the limitations on reproduction may be insurmountable here. Testimony from the respondent that her HIV infection controlled her decision not to have a child is unchallenged. In the context of reviewing summary judgment, we must take it to be true. Fed. Rule Civ. Proc. 56(e). We agree with the District Court and the Court of Appeals that no triable issue of fact impedes a ruling on the question of statutory coverage. Respondent's HIV infection is a physical impairment which substantially limits a major life activity, as the ADA defines it. In view of our holding, we need not address the second question presented, i.e., whether HIV infection is a per se disability under the ADA.

B

Our holding is confirmed by a consistent course of agency interpretation before and after enactment of the ADA. Every agency to consider the issue under the Rehabilitation Act found statutory coverage for persons with asymptomatic HIV. Responsibility for administering the Rehabilitation Act was not delegated to a single agency, but we need not pause to inquire whether this causes us to withhold deference to agency interpretations under *Chevron U.S.A. Inc. v. Natural Resources Defense Council Inc.*, 467 U.S. 837, 844 (1984). It is enough to observe that the well-reasoned views of the agencies implementing a statute "constitute a body of experience and informed judgment to which courts and litigants may properly resort for guidance."

One comprehensive and significant administrative precedent is a 1988 opinion issued by the Office of Legal Counsel of the Department of Justice (OLC) concluding that the Rehabilitation Act "protects symptomatic and asymptomatic HIV-infected individuals against discrimination in any covered program." Relying on a letter from Surgeon General C. Everett Koop stating that, "from a purely scientific perspective, persons with HIV are clearly impaired" even during the asymptomatic phase, OLC determined asymptomatic HIV was a physical impairment under the Rehabilitation Act because it constituted a "physiological disorder or condition affecting the hemic and lymphatic systems." OLC determined further that asymptomatic HIV imposed a substantial limit on the major life activity of reproduction. The Opinion said:

> Based on the medical knowledge available to us, we believe that it is reasonable to conclude that the life activity of procreation . . . is substantially limited for an asymptomatic HIV-infected individual. In light of the significant risk that the AIDS virus may be transmitted to a baby during pregnancy, HIV-infected individuals cannot, whether they are male or female, engage in the act of procreation with the normal expectation of bringing forth a healthy child.

In addition, OLC indicated that "[t]he life activity of engaging in sexual relations is threatened and probably substantially limited by the contagiousness of the virus." Either consideration was sufficient to render asymptomatic HIV infection a handicap for purposes of the Rehabilitation Act. In the course of its Opinion, OLC considered, and rejected, the contention that the limitation could be discounted as a voluntary response to the infection. The limitation, it reasoned, was the infection's manifest physical effect. Without exception, the other agencies to address the problem before enactment of the ADA reached the same result. Agencies have adhered to this conclusion since the enactment of the ADA as well.

Every court which addressed the issue before the ADA was enacted in July 1990, moreover, concluded that asymptomatic HIV infection satisfied the Rehabilitation Act's definition of a handicap. We are aware of no instance prior to the enactment of the ADA in which a court or agency ruled that HIV infection was not a handicap under the Rehabilitation Act.

Had Congress done nothing more than copy the Rehabilitation Act definition into the ADA, its action would indicate the new statute should be construed in light of this unwavering line of administrative and judicial interpretation. All indications are that Congress was well aware of the position taken by OLC when enacting the ADA and intended to give that position its active endorsement. As noted earlier, Congress also incorporated the same definition into the Fair Housing Amendments Act of 1988. We find it significant that the implementing regulations issued by the Department of Housing and Urban Development (HUD) construed the definition to include infection with HIV. Again the legislative record indicates that Congress intended to ratify HUD's interpretation when it reiterated the same definition in the ADA.

We find the uniformity of the administrative and judicial precedent construing the definition significant. When administrative and judicial interpretations have settled the meaning of an existing statutory provision, repetition of the same language in a new statute indicates, as a general matter, the intent to incorporate its administrative and judicial interpretations as well. The uniform body of administrative and judicial precedent confirms the conclusion we reach today as the most faithful way to effect the congressional design.

C

Our conclusion is further reinforced by the administrative guidance issued by the Justice Department to implement the public accommodation provisions of Title III of the ADA. As the agency directed by Congress to issue implementing regulations, see 42 U.S.C. § 12186(b), to render technical assistance explaining the responsibilities of covered individuals and institutions, § 12206(c), and to enforce Title III in court, § 12188(b), the Department's views are entitled to deference.

The Justice Department's interpretation of the definition of disability is consistent with our analysis. The regulations acknowledge that Congress intended the ADA's definition of disability to be given the same construction as the definition of handicap in the Rehabilitation Act. The regulatory definition developed by HEW to implement the Rehabilitation Act is incorporated verbatim in the ADA regulations. § 36.104. The Justice Department went further, however. It added "HIV infection (symptomatic and asymptomatic)" to the list of disorders constituting a physical impairment. § 36.104(1)(iii). The technical assistance the Department has issued pursuant to 42 U.S.C. § 12206 similarly concludes that persons with asymptomatic HIV infection fall within the ADA's definition of disability. Any other conclusion, the Department reasoned, would contradict Congress' affirmative ratification of the administrative interpretations given previous versions of the same definition.

We also draw guidance from the views of the agencies authorized to administer other sections of the ADA. These agencies [EEOC, the Attorney General, and the

Secretary of Transportation], too, concluded that HIV infection is a physical impairment under the ADA. Most categorical of all is EEOC's conclusion that "an individual who has HIV infection (including asymptomatic HIV infection) is an individual with a disability." In the EEOC's view, "impairments . . . such as HIV infection, are inherently substantially limiting."

The regulatory authorities we cite are consistent with our holding that HIV infection, even in the so-called asymptomatic phase, is an impairment which substantially limits the major life activity of reproduction.

[Author's Note: The portion of the *Bragdon v. Abbott* opinion addressing whether the dentist could refuse to treat Ms. Abbott because of concerns about whether her condition posed a direct threat to Dr. Bragdon is found in Chapter 9, *infra*.]

NOTES AND QUESTIONS

1. Most readers of this case believe that it is odd that the Court relied on reproduction as the major life activity that is impaired by HIV. Even Justice Kennedy seems to consider this a weaker argument than others that could have been presented in this case. Why did the plaintiff prevail using this argument? Is it because the defendant did not challenge her testimony that she had refrained from having children because of her impairment? What will happen in the next case? If an attorney is representing a gay man who is HIV positive who the dentist refused to treat and the client has never had any interest in having children, how should he be represented? What arguments could be made if the ADAAA is not applicable?

2. The ADAAA changed the definition of major life activity by adding bodily functions. See *supra* for the list of bodily functions. How would this change affect the arguments that could be made on behalf of the gay client?

In 1999, only one year after *Bragdon v. Abbott*, the Supreme Court decided three cases that had the effect of severely narrowing the definition of a person with a disability. The issue raised in these cases was, in determining whether a person's impairment substantially limits a major life activity, whether the court should take into account mitigating measures that may affect the impairment. An excerpt of one of these three cases follows.

SUTTON v. UNITED AIR LINES, INC.
527 U.S. 471 (1999)

JUSTICE O'CONNOR delivered the opinion of the Court.

The Americans with Disabilities Act of 1990 (ADA or Act), 42 U.S.C. § 12101 *et seq.*, prohibits certain employers from discriminating against individuals on the basis of their disabilities. Petitioners challenge the dismissal of their ADA action for failure to state a claim upon which relief can be granted. We conclude that the complaint was properly dismissed. In reaching that result, we hold that the determination of whether an individual is disabled should be made with reference to measures that mitigate the individual's impairment, including, in this instance, eyeglasses and contact lenses. In addition, we hold that petitioners failed to allege properly that respondent "regarded" them as having a disability within the meaning of the ADA.

I

Petitioners are twin sisters, both of whom have severe myopia. Each petitioner's uncorrected visual acuity is 20/200 or worse in her right eye and 20/400 or worse in her left eye, but "[w]ith the use of corrective lenses, each . . . has vision that is 20/20 or better." Consequently, without corrective lenses, each "effectively cannot see to conduct numerous activities such as driving a vehicle, watching television or shopping in public stores," but with corrective measures, such as glasses or contact lenses, both "function identically to individuals without a similar impairment."

In 1992, petitioners applied to respondent for employment as commercial airline pilots. They met respondent's basic age, education, experience, and FAA certification qualifications. After submitting their applications for employment, both petitioners were invited by respondent to an interview and to flight simulator tests. Both were told during their interviews, however, that a mistake had been made in inviting them to interview because petitioners did not meet respondent's minimum vision requirement, which was uncorrected visual acuity of 20/100 or better. Due to their failure to meet this requirement, petitioners' interviews were terminated, and neither was offered a pilot position.

In light of respondent's proffered reason for rejecting them, petitioners filed a charge of disability discrimination under the ADA with the Equal Employment Opportunity Commission (EEOC). After receiving a right to sue letter, petitioners filed suit in the United States District Court for the District of Colorado, alleging that respondent had discriminated against them "on the basis of their disability, or because [respondent] regarded [petitioners] as having a disability" in violation of the ADA. Specifically, petitioners alleged that due to their severe myopia they actually have a substantially limiting impairment or are regarded as having such an impairment, and are thus disabled under the Act.

The District Court dismissed petitioners' complaint for failure to state a claim upon which relief could be granted. . . . [T]he Court of Appeals for the Tenth Circuit affirmed the District Court's judgment.

The Tenth Circuit's decision is in tension with the decisions of other Courts of Appeals.

II

The ADA prohibits discrimination by covered entities, including private employers, against qualified individuals with a disability. Specifically, it provides that no covered employer "shall discriminate against a qualified individual with a disability because of the disability of such individual in regard to job application procedures, the hiring, advancement, or discharge of employees, employee compensation, job training, and other terms, conditions, and privileges of employment." A "qualified individual with a disability" is identified as "an individual with a disability who, with or without reasonable accommodation, can perform the essential functions of the employment position that such individual holds or desires." In turn, a "disability" is defined as:

> "(A) a physical or mental impairment that substantially limits one or more of the major life activities of such individual;

> "(B) a record of such an impairment; or

> "(C) being regarded as having such an impairment."

Accordingly, to fall within this definition one must have an actual disability (subsection (A)), have a record of a disability (subsection (B)), or be regarded as having one (subsection (C)).

The parties agree that the authority to issue regulations to implement the Act is split primarily among three Government agencies. According to the parties, the EEOC has authority to issue regulations to carry out the employment provisions in Title I of the ADA, pursuant to § 12116. The Attorney General is granted authority to issue regulations with respect to Title II, subtitle A, §§ 12131–12134, which relates to public services. Finally, the Secretary of Transportation has authority to issue regulations pertaining to the transportation provisions of Titles II and III. Moreover, each of these agencies is authorized to offer technical assistance regarding the provisions they administer.

No agency, however, has been given authority to issue regulations implementing the generally applicable provisions of the ADA, which fall outside Titles I-V. Most notably, no agency has been delegated authority to interpret the term "disability." Justice Breyer's contrary, imaginative interpretation of the Act's delegation provisions, is belied by the terms and structure of the ADA. The EEOC has, nonetheless, issued regulations to provide additional guidance regarding the proper interpretation of this term. . . .

The agencies have also issued interpretive guidelines to aid in the implementation of their regulations. For instance, at the time that it promulgated the above regulations, the EEOC issued an "Interpretive Guidance," which provides that "[t]he determination of whether an individual is substantially limited in a major life activity must be made on a case by case basis, without regard to mitigating measures such as medicines, or assistive or prosthetic devices." The Department of Justice has issued a similar guideline. Although the parties dispute the persuasive force of these interpretive guidelines, we have no need in this case to decide what deference is due.

III

With this statutory and regulatory framework in mind, we turn first to the question whether petitioners have stated a claim under subsection (A) of the disability definition, that is, whether they have alleged that they possess a physical impairment that substantially limits them in one or more major life activities. Because petitioners allege that with corrective measures their vision "is 20/20 or better," they are not actually disabled within the meaning of the Act if the "disability" determination is made with reference to these measures. Consequently, with respect to subsection (A) of the disability definition, our decision turns on whether disability is to be determined with or without reference to corrective measures.

Petitioners maintain that whether an impairment is substantially limiting should be determined without regard to corrective measures. They argue that, because the ADA does not directly address the question at hand, the Court should defer to the agency interpretations of the statute, which are embodied in the agency guidelines issued by the EEOC and the Department of Justice. These guidelines specifically direct that the determination of whether an individual is substantially limited in a major life activity be made without regard to mitigating measures.

Respondent, in turn, maintains that an impairment does not substantially limit a major life activity if it is corrected. It argues that the Court should not defer to the agency guidelines cited by petitioners because the guidelines conflict with the plain meaning of the ADA. The phrase "substantially limits one or more major life activities," it explains, requires that the substantial limitations actually and presently exist. Moreover, respondent argues, disregarding mitigating measures taken by an individual defies the statutory command to examine the effect of the impairment on the major life activities "of such individual." And even if the statute is ambiguous, respondent claims, the guidelines' directive to ignore mitigating measures is not reasonable, and thus this Court should not defer to it.

We conclude that respondent is correct that the approach adopted by the agency guidelines — that persons are to be evaluated in their hypothetical uncorrected state — is an impermissible interpretation of the ADA. Looking at the Act as a whole, it is apparent that if a person is taking measures to correct for, or mitigate, a physical or mental impairment, the effects of those measures — both positive and negative — must be taken into account when judging whether that person is "substantially limited" in a major life activity and thus "disabled" under the Act. The dissent relies on the legislative history of the ADA for the contrary proposition that individuals should be examined in their uncorrected state. Because we decide that, by its terms, the ADA cannot be read in this manner, we have no reason to consider the ADA's legislative history.

Three separate provisions of the ADA, read in concert, lead us to this conclusion. The Act defines a "disability" as "a physical or mental impairment that substantially limits one or more of the major life activities" of an individual. Because the phrase "substantially limits" appears in the Act in the present indicative verb form, we think the language is properly read as requiring that a person be presently — not potentially or hypothetically — substantially limited in order to demonstrate a disability. A "disability" exists only where an impairment "substantially limits" a major life activity, not where it "might," "could," or "would" be substantially limiting if mitigating measures were not taken. A person whose physical or mental impairment is corrected by medication or other measures does not have an impairment that presently "substantially limits" a major life activity. To be sure, a person whose physical or mental impairment is corrected by mitigating measures still has an impairment, but if the impairment is corrected it does not "substantially limi[t]" a major life activity.

The definition of disability also requires that disabilities be evaluated "with respect to an individual" and be determined based on whether an impairment substantially limits the "major life activities of such individual." Thus, whether a person has a disability under the ADA is an individualized inquiry.

The agency guidelines' directive that persons be judged in their uncorrected or unmitigated state runs directly counter to the individualized inquiry mandated by the ADA. The agency approach would often require courts and employers to speculate about a person's condition and would, in many cases, force them to make a disability determination based on general information about how an uncorrected impairment usually affects individuals, rather than on the individual's actual condition. For instance, under this view, courts would almost certainly find all diabetics to be disabled, because if they failed to monitor their blood sugar levels and administer insulin, they would almost certainly be substantially limited in one or more major life activities. A diabetic whose illness does not impair his or her daily activities would therefore be considered disabled simply because he or she has diabetes. Thus, the guidelines approach would create a system in which persons often must be treated as members of a group of people with similar impairments, rather than as individuals. This is contrary to both the letter and the spirit of the ADA.

The guidelines approach could also lead to the anomalous result that in determining whether an individual is disabled, courts and employers could not consider any negative side effects suffered by an individual resulting from the use of mitigating measures, even when those side effects are very severe. [The Court references the effects of antipsyhotic drugs, potential liver damage for drugs for Parkinson's disease, and potential negative effects of antiepileptic drugs.] This result is also inconsistent with the individualized approach of the ADA.

Finally, and critically, findings enacted as part of the ADA require the conclusion that Congress did not intend to bring under the statute's protection all those whose uncorrected conditions amount to disabilities. Congress found that "some 43,000,000 Americans have one or more physical or mental disabilities, and this number is increasing as the population as a whole is growing older." This figure is inconsistent with the definition of disability pressed by petitioners.

Although the exact source of the 43 million figure is not clear, the corresponding finding in the 1988 precursor to the ADA was drawn directly from a report prepared by the National Council on Disability. That report detailed the difficulty of estimating the number of disabled persons due to varying operational definitions of disability. It explained that the estimates of the number of disabled Americans ranged from an overinclusive 160 million under a "health conditions approach," which looks at all conditions that impair the health or normal functional abilities of an individual, to an underinclusive 22.7 million under a "work disability approach," which focuses on individuals' reported ability to work. It noted that "a figure of 35 or 36 million [was] the most commonly quoted estimate." The 36 million number included in the 1988 bill's findings thus clearly reflects an approach to defining disabilities that is closer to the work disabilities approach than the health conditions approach.

Because it is included in the ADA's text, the finding that 43 million individuals are disabled gives content to the ADA's terms, specifically the term "disability." Had Congress intended to include all persons with corrected physical limitations among those covered by the Act, it undoubtedly would have cited a much higher number of disabled persons in the findings. That it did not is evidence that the ADA's coverage is restricted to only those whose impairments are not mitigated by corrective measures.

The dissents suggest that viewing individuals in their corrected state will exclude from the definition of "disab[led]" those who use prosthetic limbs, or take medicine for epilepsy or high blood pressure. This suggestion is incorrect. The use of a corrective device does not, by itself, relieve one's disability. Rather, one has a disability under subsection A if, notwithstanding the use of a corrective device, that individual is substantially limited in a major life activity. For example, individuals who use prosthetic limbs or wheelchairs may be mobile and capable of functioning in society but still be disabled because of a substantial limitation on their ability to walk or run. The same may be true of individuals who take medicine to lessen the symptoms of an impairment so that they can function but nevertheless remain substantially limited. Alternatively, one whose high blood pressure is "cured" by medication may be regarded as disabled by a covered entity, and thus disabled under subsection C of the definition. The use or nonuse of a corrective device does not determine whether an individual is disabled; that determination depends on whether the limitations an individual with an impairment actually faces are in fact substantially limiting.

Applying this reading of the Act to the case at hand, we conclude that the Court of Appeals correctly resolved the issue of disability in respondent's favor. As noted above, petitioners allege that with corrective measures, their visual acuity is 20/20, and that they "function identically to individuals without a similar impairment." In addition, petitioners concede that they "do not argue that the use of corrective lenses in itself demonstrates a substantially limiting impairment." Accordingly, because we decide that disability under the Act is to be determined with reference to corrective measures, we agree with the courts below that petitioners have not stated a claim that they are substantially limited in any major life activity.

NOTES

1. The Supreme Court used similar reasoning in two other cases decided simultaneously with *Sutton. Albertson's, Inc. v. Kirkingburg*, 119 S. Ct. 2162 (1999), involved an individual whose vision affected his binocular acuity. Mr. Kirkingburg was denied a truck driving position at a grocery chain, based on his vision deficiencies. His ADA claim of discrimination failed because his brain had developed coping mechanisms for dealing with his limitations. These mitigating measures, when taken into account, meant that he was not "disabled" within the statute.

The third case also involved transportation related employment. In *Murphy v. United Parcel Service, Inc.*, 119 S. Ct. 2133 (1999), a United Parcel Service mechanic was dismissed from his job because of high blood pressure. The position description required driving commercial motor vehicles. Because Mr. Murphy's condition was mitigated when he took medication, he was found not to be "substantially limited" in major life activities.

A fourth case, *Bartlett v. New York State Board of Law Examiners*, 527 U.S. 1031 (1999), was remanded on the same day that these cases were decided. *Barlett* involved a learning disability and whether the condition substantially limited a major life activity.

2. After the *Sutton* trilogy, there was a significant change in lower court decisions regarding whether a person had a disability. Whereas before the trilogy, courts had held that persons with conditions such as epilepsy, diabetes and cancer were persons with disabilities, after the trilogy, more restrictive rulings emerged from the lower courts. Courts now held that the following were not disabilities in most cases: epilepsy, muscular dystrophy, mental retardation, hearing impairment, heart disease and HIV infection. *See* Jonathan R. Mook, ADA Amendments Act of 2008 8–9 (2009 LexisNexis). Individuals with these conditions were much more likely to lose a defense motion to dismiss or for summary judgment based on noncoverage. For recent cases demonstrating this trend, see Laura Rothstein & Julia Rothstein, Disabilities and the Law, § 4.8 (2009).

3. In *Sutton*, what is the Court's point about the effect of the regulations drafted by the Justice Department and the EEOC with reference to whether the courts should consider mitigating measures in determining whether an impairment substantially limits a major life activity? What is the difference between how the Supreme Court in *Arline* treated the regulations pursuant to the Rehabilitation Act and how the Court in *Sutton* treated those drafted pursuant to the ADA?

4. Why didn't the Court in *Sutton* consider the legislative history in determining whether mitigating measures should be taken into account in determining whether the plaintiffs had a disability? What did the legislative history say about mitigating measures?

5. Is *Sutton* an example of the saying, "Bad facts make bad law?" Explain.

6. The ADAAA overturned the reasoning of *Sutton* and the other cases in the trilogy, while maintaining an exception for persons wearing eyeglasses or contact lenses. The purposes section of the ADAAA states that one of the purposes of the ADAAA is "to reject the requirement enunciated by the Supreme Court in *Sutton v. United Air Lines, Inc.*, 527 U.S. 471 (1999), and its companion cases that whether an impairment substantially limits a major life activity is to be determined with reference to the ameliorative effects of mitigating measures" 110 P.L. 325(b)(2).

7. Section 3 of the ADA, 42 U.S.C. § 12102, is amended to read:

(4) Rules of construction regarding the definition of disability. The definition of "disability" in paragraph (1) shall be construed in accordance with the following:

(E)(i) The determination of whether an impairment substantially limits a major life activity shall be made without regard to the ameliorative effects of mitigating measures such as —

(I) medication medical supplies, equipment, or appliances, low-vision devices (which do not include ordinary eyeglasses or contact lenses), prosthetics including limbs and devices, hearing aids and cochlear implants or other implantable hearing devices, mobility devices, or oxygen therapy equipment and supplies:

(II) use of assistive technology;

(III) reasonable accommodations or auxiliary aids or services; or

(IV) learned behavioral or adaptive neurological modifications.

(ii) The ameliorative effects of the mitigating measure of ordinary eyeglasses and contact lenses shall be considered in determining whether an impairment substantially limits a major life activity.

Section 103 of the ADA, 42 U.S.C. § 12113, is amended by adding the following:

. . . Notwithstanding section 3(4)(E)(ii), a covered entity shall not use qualification standards, employment tests, or other selection criteria based on an individual's uncorrected vision unless the standard, test, or other selection criteria, as used by the covered entity, is shown to be job-related for the position in question and consistent with business necessity.

8. If the Sutton sisters were to bring a lawsuit now against United Airlines, would the company be permitted legally to refuse to hire them based on their uncorrected vision? Would the Sutton sisters be able to allege that they were "regarded as" having a disability? Explain. If not, would there be another portion of the statute on which they could rely? What would United Airlines have to prove under the amended Section 12113? What if a law firm decided not to hire new associates unless their uncorrected vision is 20/40 or better? Would this be permissible? Explain.

9. What if the mitigation for the disease actually caused other problems? For example, what if a plaintiff who has cancer surgery is treated with radiation and chemotherapy that make her very sick and tired? After the ADAAA, would the court be permitted to take into account the harmful effects of the radiation and chemotherapy in determining whether her impairment substantially limits a major life activity?

10. The Court in *Sutton* relies on the finding of the ADA that states that there are 43 million persons with disabilities to bolster its interpretation that Congress could not have intended to take mitigating factors into account. The ADAAA amends its findings by deleting the reference to 43 million persons.

11. The Court in *Sutton* suggests that no agency has the authority to issue regulations implementing the generally applicable provisions of the ADA — those defining what a disability is. This is because the Act was divided into separate titles. In each Title, the Act gave authority to an agency to write regulations pursuant to the Act. Title I, for example, which is the employment section, authorized the Equal Employment Opportunity Commission to write regulations in Section 12116. The definition of the term "disability," however, applies to all titles and appears in a separate section that precedes Title I of the Act. The ADAAA corrects the problem

that there was no agency designated to write regulations concerning the definition of the term "disability" by adding a new rule of construction that grants such authority:

> The authority to issue regulations granted to the Equal Employment Opportunity Commission, the Attorney General, and the Secretary of Transportation under this Act includes the authority to issue regulations implementing the definitions of disability in section 3 (including rules of construction) and the definitions in section 4, consistent with the ADA Amendments Act of 2008 . . . .

ADAAA § 6(a)(1).

―――――――

As mentioned above, the *Sutton* trilogy led to more limited coverage of persons with impairments, because with great frequency, the courts held that their impairments did not substantially limit a major life activity. In the case that follows, the Supreme Court further narrowed the definition of disability. It dealt with the issue of what demonstration a plaintiff must make to prove that she is substantially limited in the major life activity of performing manual tasks.

TOYOTA MOTOR MANUFACTURING v. WILLIAMS
534 U.S. 184 (2002)

JUSTICE O'CONNOR delivered the opinion of the Court.

Under the Americans with Disabilities Act of 1990 (ADA or Act), a physical impairment that "substantially limits one or more . . . major life activities" is a "disability." Respondent, claiming to be disabled because of her carpal tunnel syndrome and other related impairments, sued petitioner, her former employer, for failing to provide her with a reasonable accommodation as required by the ADA.

I

Respondent began working at petitioner's automobile manufacturing plant in Georgetown, Kentucky, in August 1990. She was soon placed on an engine fabrication assembly line, where her duties included work with pneumatic tools. Use of these tools eventually caused pain in respondent's hands, wrists, and arms. She sought treatment at petitioner's in-house medical service, where she was diagnosed with bilateral carpal tunnel syndrome and bilateral tendinitis. Respondent consulted a personal physician who placed her on permanent work restrictions that precluded her from lifting more than 20 pounds or from "frequently lifting or carrying of objects weighing up to 10 pounds," engaging in "constant repetitive . . . flexion or extension of [her] wrists or elbows," performing "overhead work," or using "vibratory or pneumatic tools."

In light of these restrictions, for the next two years petitioner assigned respondent to various modified duty jobs. Nonetheless, respondent missed some work for medical leave, and eventually filed a claim under the Kentucky Workers' Compensation Act. The parties settled this claim, and respondent returned to work. She was unsatisfied by petitioner's efforts to accommodate her work restrictions, however, and responded by bringing an action in the United States District Court for the Eastern District of Kentucky alleging that petitioner had violated the ADA by refusing to accommodate her disability. That suit was also settled, and as part of the settlement, respondent returned to work in December 1993. Upon her return, petitioner placed respondent on a team in Quality Control Inspection Operations (QCIO). QCIO is responsible for four tasks: (1) "assembly paint"; (2) "paint second inspection"; (3) "shell body audit"; and (4) "ED surface repair." Respondent was initially placed on a team that performed only the first two of these tasks, and for a couple of years, she rotated on a weekly basis between them. In assembly paint, respondent visually inspected painted cars moving slowly down a conveyor. When respondent began working in assembly paint, inspection team members were required to open and shut the doors, trunk, and/or hood of each passing car. Sometime during respondent's tenure, however, the position was modified to include only visual inspection with few or no manual tasks. Paint second inspection required team members to use their hands to wipe each painted car with a glove as it moved along a conveyor. The parties agree that respondent was physically capable of performing both of these jobs and that her performance was satisfactory.

During the fall of 1996, petitioner announced that it wanted QCIO employees to be able to rotate through all four of the QCIO processes. Respondent therefore received training for the shell body audit job, in which team members apply a highlight oil to the hood, fender, doors, rear quarter panel, and trunk of passing cars at a rate of approximately one car per minute. Wiping the cars required respondent to hold her hands and arms up around shoulder height for several hours at a time.

A short while after the shell body audit job was added to respondent's rotations, she began to experience pain in her neck and shoulders. Respondent again sought care at petitioner's in-house medical service, where she was diagnosed with [conditions causing] pain in the nerves that lead to the upper extremities. Respondent requested that petitioner accommodate her medical conditions by allowing her to return to doing only her original two jobs in QCIO, which respondent claimed she could still perform without difficulty.

The parties disagree about what happened next. According to respondent, petitioner refused her request and forced her to continue working in the shell body audit job, which caused her even greater physical injury. According to petitioner, respondent simply began missing work on a regular basis. Regardless, it is clear that on December 6, 1996, the last day respondent worked at petitioner's plant, she was placed under a no-work-of-any-kind restriction by her treating physicians. On January 27, 1997, respondent received a letter from petitioner that terminated her employment, citing her poor attendance record. Respondent filed a charge of disability discrimination with the Equal Employment Opportunity Commission (EEOC). After receiving a right to sue letter, respondent filed suit against petitioner in the United States District Court for the Eastern District of Kentucky.

Respondent based her claim that she was "disabled" under the ADA on the ground that her physical impairments substantially limited her in (1) manual tasks; (2) housework; (3) gardening; (4) playing with her children; (5) lifting; and (6) working, all of which, she argued, constituted major life activities under the Act. Respondent also argued, in the alternative, that she was disabled under the ADA because she had a record of a substantially limiting impairment and because she was regarded as having such an impairment.

III

The question presented by this case is whether the Sixth Circuit properly determined that respondent was disabled under subsection (A) of the ADA's disability definition at the time that she sought an accommodation from petitioner. The parties do not dispute that respondent's medical conditions, which include carpal tunnel syndrome, myotendinitis, and thoracic outlet compression, amount to physical impairments. The relevant question, therefore, is whether the Sixth Circuit correctly analyzed whether these impairments substantially limited respondent in the major life activity of performing manual tasks. Answering this requires us to address an issue about which the EEOC regulations are silent: what a plaintiff must demonstrate to establish a substantial limitation in the specific major life activity of performing manual tasks.

Our consideration of this issue is guided first and foremost by the words of the disability definition itself. "[S]ubstantially" in the phrase "substantially limits" suggests "considerable" or "to a large degree." The word "substantial" thus clearly precludes impairments that interfere in only a minor way with the performance of manual tasks from qualifying as disabilities.

"Major" in the phrase "major life activities" means important. "Major life activities" thus refers to those activities that are of central importance to daily life. In order for performing manual tasks to fit into this category — a category that includes such basic abilities as walking, seeing, and hearing — the manual tasks in question must be central to daily life. If each of the tasks included in the major life activity of performing manual tasks does not independently qualify as a major life activity, then together they must do so.

That these terms need to be interpreted strictly to create a demanding standard for qualifying as disabled is confirmed by the first section of the ADA, which lays out the legislative findings and purposes that motivate the Act. When it enacted the ADA in 1990, Congress found that "some 43,000,000 Americans have one or more physical or mental disabilities." If Congress intended everyone with a physical impairment that precluded the performance of some isolated, unimportant, or particularly difficult manual task to qualify as disabled, the number of disabled Americans would surely have been much higher.

We therefore hold that to be substantially limited in performing manual tasks, an individual must have an impairment that prevents or severely restricts the individual from doing activities that are of central importance to most people's daily lives. The impairment's impact must also be permanent or long-term.

It is insufficient for individuals attempting to prove disability status under this test to merely submit evidence of a medical diagnosis of an impairment. Instead, the ADA requires those "claiming the Act's protection . . . to prove a disability by offering evidence that the extent of the limitation [caused by their impairment] in terms of their own experience . . . is substantial." That the Act defines "disability" "with respect to an individual," makes clear that Congress intended the existence of a disability to be determined in such a case-by-case manner.

An individualized assessment of the effect of an impairment is particularly necessary when the impairment is one whose symptoms vary widely from person to person. Carpal tunnel syndrome, one of respondent's impairments, is just such a condition. While cases of severe carpal tunnel syndrome are characterized by muscle atrophy and extreme sensory deficits, mild cases generally do not have either of these effects and create only intermittent symptoms of numbness and tingling. Studies have further shown that, even without surgical treatment, one quarter of carpal tunnel cases resolve in one month, but that in 22 percent of cases, symptoms last for eight year or longer. When pregnancy is the cause of carpal tunnel syndrome, in contrast, the symptoms normally resolve within two weeks of delivery. Given these large potential differences in the severity and duration of the effects of carpal tunnel syndrome, an individual's carpal tunnel syndrome diagnosis, on its own, does not indicate whether the individual has a disability within the meaning of the ADA.

IV

The Court of Appeals' analysis of respondent's claimed disability suggested that in order to prove a substantial limitation in the major life activity of performing manual tasks, a "plaintiff must show that her manual disability involves a 'class' of manual activities . . . " and that those activities "affec[t] the ability to perform tasks at work." Both of these ideas lack support.

The Court of Appeals relied on our opinion in *Sutton v. United Air Lines, Inc.*, for the idea that a "class" of manual activities must be implicated for an impairment to substantially limit the major life activity of performing manual tasks. But *Sutton* said only that "*[w]hen the major life activity under consideration is that of working*, the statutory phrase 'substantially limits' requires . . . that plaintiffs allege that they are unable to work in a broad class of jobs." Because of the conceptual difficulties inherent in the argument that working could be a major life activity, we have been hesitant to hold as much, and we need not decide this difficult question today. In *Sutton*, we noted that even assuming that working is a major life activity, a claimant would be required to show an inability to work in a "broad range of jobs," rather than a specific job. But *Sutton* did not suggest that a class-based analysis should be applied to any major life activity other than working. Nor do the EEOC regulations. In defining "substantially limits," the EEOC regulations only mention the "class" concept in the context of the major life activity of working. Nothing in the text of the Act, our previous opinions, or the regulations suggests that a class-based framework should apply outside the context of the major life activity of working.

While the Court of Appeals in this case addressed the different major life activity of performing manual tasks, its analysis circumvented *Sutton* by focusing on respondent's inability to perform manual tasks associated only with her job. This was error. When addressing the major life activity of performing manual tasks, the central inquiry must be whether the claimant is unable to perform the variety of tasks central to most people's daily lives, not whether the claimant is unable to perform the tasks associated with her specific job. Otherwise, *Sutton*'s restriction on claims of disability based on a substantial limitation in working will be rendered meaningless because an inability to perform a specific job always can be recast as an inability to perform a "class" of tasks associated with that specific job. There is also no support in the Act, our previous opinions, or the regulations for the Court of Appeals' idea that the question of whether an impairment constitutes a disability is to be answered only by analyzing the effect of the impairment in the workplace. Indeed, the fact that the Act's definition of "disability" applies not only to Title I of the Act, which deals with employment, but also to the other portions of the Act, which deal with subjects such as public transportation, and privately provided public accommodations, demonstrates that the definition is intended to cover individuals with disabling impairments regardless of whether the individuals have any connection to a workplace.

Even more critically, the manual tasks unique to any particular job are not necessarily important parts of most people's lives. As a result, occupation-specific tasks may have only limited relevance to the manual task inquiry. In this case, "repetitive work with hands and arms extended at or above shoulder levels for extended periods of time," the manual task on which the Court of Appeals relied, is not an important part of most people's daily lives. The court, therefore, should not have considered respondent's inability to do such manual work in her specialized assembly line job as sufficient proof that she was substantially limited in performing manual tasks.

At the same time, the Court of Appeals appears to have disregarded the very type of evidence that it should have focused upon. It treated as irrelevant "[t]he fact that [respondent] can . . . ten[d] to her personal hygiene [and] carr[y] out personal or household chores." Yet household chores, bathing, and brushing one's teeth are among the types of manual tasks of central importance to people's daily lives, and should have been part of the assessment of whether respondent was substantially limited in performing manual tasks.

The District Court noted that at the time respondent sought an accommodation from petitioner, she admitted that she was able to do the manual tasks required by her original two jobs in QCIO. In addition, according to respondent's deposition testimony, even after her condition worsened, she could still brush her teeth, wash her face, bathe, tend her flower garden, fix breakfast, do laundry, and pick up around the house. The record also indicates that her medical conditions caused her to avoid sweeping, to quit dancing, to occasionally seek help dressing, and to reduce how often she plays with her children, gardens, and drives long distances. But these changes in her life did not amount to such severe restrictions in the activities that are of central importance to most people's daily lives that they establish a manual-task disability as a matter of law. On this record, it was therefore inappropriate for the Court of Appeals to grant partial summary judgment to respondent on the issue whether she was substantially limited in performing manual tasks, and its decision to do so must be reversed.

Accordingly, we reverse the Court of Appeals' judgment granting partial summary judgment to respondent and remand the case for further proceedings consistent with this opinion.

NOTES AND QUESTIONS

1. In *Toyota*, the Court held that a plaintiff alleging that carpal tunnel or other impairment substantially limits a major life activity would have to prove that the impairment "prevents or severely restricts the individual from doing activities that are of central importance to most people's daily lives." The impairment must also be shown to be permanent or long-term. How much of the decision turns on the plaintiff's reliance on the major life activity of performing manual tasks? Is there something different about this major life activity? How does the ADAAA treat this major life activity? What was wrong with the lower court's analysis according to the Supreme Court? Is this analysis correct under the ADAAA?

2. *Findings and Purposes of the ADAAA.* One finding of the ADAAA is that due to the *Sutton* trilogy and *Toyota*, the lower courts have incorrectly found that persons with substantially limiting impairments are not individuals with disabilities. The ADAAA further finds that, in particular, *Toyota* interpreted the definition of "substantially limits" "to require a greater degree of limitation than was intended by Congress." It also finds that the EEOC regulations interpreting "substantially limits" as "significantly restricted" sets too high a standard. P.L. 110-325(2)(a)(6), (7) & (8). One of the purposes of the ADAAA is to reject *Toyota*'s holding that the terms "substantially limits" and "major" be interpreting strictly in order to ensure a demanding standard for determining whether a person has a disability; another is to reject the holding that a person must demonstrate that in order to prove that an impairment substantially limits a major life activity, the individual "must have an impairment that prevents or severely restricts the individual from doing activities that are of central importance to most people's daily lives." P.L. 110-325(2)(b)(4). Another purpose is to convey congressional intent that the primary issue should be whether a covered entity complied with its obligations under the ADA, and that the question of whether an individual's impairment constitutes a disability should "not demand extensive analysis." P.L. 110-325(2)(b)(5). Finally, the ADAAA states that it expects the EEOC to rewrite the part of its regulations that define "substantially limits" as "significantly restricted" in order to comply with the ADA and the amendments. P.L. 110-325(2)(b)(6).

3. *Definition of Individual with a Disability under the ADAAA.* As mentioned above, the ADAAA clarifies the meaning of "major life activity" in two ways. First, it makes a non-exclusive list of major life activities. See [B][1], *supra.* Second, it also defines bodily functions to be major life activities. See [B][1], *supra.*

4. *Rules of Construction of the ADAAA.* In addition to the rule of construction discussed above, concerning the effect of ameliorative methods on the definition of "substantially limits," the Act lists as rules of construction the following:

- The Act shall be construed in favor of broad coverage to the maximum extent permitted by the terms of the Act;

- The term "substantially limits" shall be construed consistent with the findings and purposes of the ADAAA;

- An impairment that substantially limits one major life activity need not substantially limit another in order for the individual to have a covered disability;

- An impairment that is episodic or in remission is a disability if it would substantially limit a major life activity when active

P.L. 110-325 (4) (a).

5. Assuming that the ADAAA were applicable, how would the Supreme Court decide the issue in the *Toyota* case today? How would the case be argued under the ADAAA for the plaintiff? For the defendant?

6. Does the ADAAA change the ADA's original directive that the courts should make an individual determination as to whether a person has a disability?

[3]   Prong Two: A Record of Such an Impairment

The major federal statutes recognize that it would be inappropriate to deny protection to someone who does not currently have a disability, but who had a disability in the past. The goal of ensuring full participation by individuals who had been historically discriminated against would not be accomplished without including those with a history of disability.

In *Arline, supra* at [B][2], the Court held that the plaintiff had a record of an impairment that substantially limited a major life activity. Thus, even though the plaintiff no longer had an impairment that substantially limited a major life activity, Section 504 of the Rehabilitation Act protected her against discrimination based on her record of her impairment. While the ADA defined disability the same as the Rehabilitation Act, after the *Sutton* trilogy and *Toyota*, plaintiffs had difficulty proving that they had a record of a disability. While the ADAAA did not explicitly change the law concerning a "record of" a disability, the amendments strongly favor a broad definition of disability, so the "record of" should be construed broadly as well.

In a case decided under the ADA before the effective date of the ADAAA, *Adams v. Rice*, 531 F.3d 936 (D.C. Cir. 2008), the plaintiff was a candidate for Foreign Service. After passing all the tests, the plaintiff found out that she had early stage breast cancer. She was treated with a mastectomy and later had her ovaries and fallopian tubes removed, but the State Department revoked her medical clearance because it believed that not all posts to which she could be assigned would have proper follow-up medical care for her. She sued alleging violation of the Rehabilitation Act. She alleged that she had a disability, was regarded as having an impairment, and had a record of an impairment.

The court of appeals held that because Adams' illness had been cured, she no longer had a disability, but it stated that having a record of an impairment does not necessarily require a document demonstrating an impairment. Rather, it requires only that the plaintiff prove that she had a history of an impairment, and that the impairment substantially limited a major life activity. This reasoning seems to be consistent with that in *Arline*. Would this be decided differently after the 2008 amendments?

[4]   Prong Three: Being "Regarded As" Having Such An Impairment

SUTTON v. UNITED AIR LINES, INC.
527 U.S. 471 (1999)

[Author's Note: The remainder of the case appears earlier in this Chapter.]

IV

Our conclusion that petitioners have failed to state a claim that they are actually disabled under subsection (A) of the disability definition does not end our inquiry. Under subsection (C), individuals who are "regarded as" having a disability are disabled within the meaning of the ADA. Subsection (C) provides that having a disability includes "being regarded as having," § 12102(2)(C), "a physical or mental impairment that substantially limits one or more of the major life activities of such individual." There are two apparent ways in which individuals may fall within this statutory definition: (1) a covered entity mistakenly believes that a person has a physical impairment that substantially limits one or more major life activities, or (2) a covered entity mistakenly believes that an actual, nonlimiting impairment substantially limits one or more major life activities. In both cases, it is necessary that a covered entity entertain misperceptions about the individual — it must believe either that one has a substantially limiting impairment that one does not have or that one has a substantially limiting impairment when, in fact, the impairment is not so limiting. These misperceptions often "resul[t] from stereotypic assumptions not truly indicative of . . . individual ability."

There is no dispute that petitioners are physically impaired. Petitioners do not make the obvious argument that they are regarded due to their impairments as substantially limited in the major life activity of seeing. They contend only that respondent mistakenly believes their physical impairments substantially limit them in the major life activity of working. To support this claim, petitioners allege that respondent has a vision requirement, which is allegedly based on myth and stereotype. Further, this requirement substantially limits their ability to engage in the major life activity of working by precluding them from obtaining the job of global airline pilot, which they argue is a "class of employment." In reply, respondent argues that the position of global airline pilot is not a class of jobs and therefore petitioners have not stated a claim that they are regarded as substantially limited in the major life activity of working.

Standing alone, the allegation that respondent has a vision requirement in place does not establish a claim that respondent regards petitioners as substantially limited in the major life activity of working. By its terms, the ADA allows employers to prefer some physical attributes over others and to establish physical criteria. An employer runs afoul of the ADA when it makes an employment decision based on a physical or mental impairment, real or imagined, that is regarded as substantially limiting a major life activity. Accordingly, an employer is free to decide that physical characteristics or medical conditions that do not rise to the level of an impairment — such as one's height, build, or singing voice — are preferable to others, just as it is free to decide that some limiting, but not substantially limiting, impairments make individuals less than ideally suited for a job.

Considering the allegations of the amended complaint in tandem, petitioners have not stated a claim that respondent regards their impairment as substantially limiting their ability to work. The ADA does not define "substantially limits," but "substantially" suggests "considerable" or "specified to a large degree." The EEOC has codified regulations interpreting the term "substantially limits" in this manner, defining the term to mean "[u]nable to perform" or "[s]ignificantly restricted."

When the major life activity under consideration is that of working, the statutory phrase "substantially limits" requires, at a minimum, that plaintiffs allege they are unable to work in a broad class of jobs. Reflecting this requirement, the EEOC uses a specialized definition of the term "substantially limits" when referring to the major life activity of working:

> "significantly restricted in the ability to perform either a class of jobs or a broad range of jobs in various classes as compared to the average person having comparable training, skills and abilities. The inability to perform a single, particular job does not constitute a substantial limitation in the major life activity of working."

The EEOC further identifies several factors that courts should consider when determining whether an individual is substantially limited in the major life activity of working, including the geographical area to which the individual has reasonable access, and "the number and types of jobs utilizing similar training, knowledge, skills or abilities, within the geographical area, from which the individual is also disqualified." To be substantially limited in the major life activity of working, then, one must be precluded from more than one type of job, a specialized job, or a particular job of choice. If jobs utilizing an individual's skills (but perhaps not his or her unique talents) are available, one is not precluded from a substantial class of jobs. Similarly, if a host of different types of jobs are available, one is not precluded from a broad range of jobs.

Because the parties accept that the term "major life activities" includes working, we do not determine the validity of the cited regulations. We note, however, that there may be some conceptual difficulty in defining "major life activities" to include work, for it seems "to argue in a circle to say that if one is excluded, for instance, by reason of [an impairment, from working with others] . . . then that exclusion constitutes an impairment, when the question you're asking is, whether the exclusion itself is by reason of handicap." Indeed, even the EEOC has expressed reluctance to define "major life activities" to include working and has suggested that working be viewed as a residual life activity, considered, as a last resort, only "[i]f an individual is not substantially limited with respect to any other major life activity."

Assuming without deciding that working is a major life activity and that the EEOC regulations interpreting the term "substantially limits" are reasonable, petitioners have failed to allege adequately that their poor eyesight is regarded as an impairment that substantially limits them in the major life activity of working. They allege only that respondent regards their poor vision as precluding them from holding positions as a "global airline pilot." Because the position of global airline pilot is a single job, this allegation does not support the claim that respondent regards petitioners as having a substantially limiting impairment. Indeed, there are a number of other positions utilizing petitioners' skills, such as regional pilot and pilot instructor to name a few, that are available to them. Even under the EEOC's Interpretative Guidance, to which petitioners ask us to defer, "an individual who cannot be a commercial airline pilot because of a minor vision impairment, but who can be a commercial airline co-pilot or a pilot for a courier service, would not be substantially limited in the major life activity of working."

Petitioners also argue that if one were to assume that a substantial number of airline carriers have similar vision requirements, they would be substantially limited in the major life activity of working. Even assuming for the sake of argument that the adoption of similar vision requirements by other carriers would represent a substantial limitation on the major life activity of working, the argument is nevertheless flawed. It is not enough to say that if the physical criteria of a single employer were imputed to all similar employers one would be regarded as substantially limited in the major life activity of working only as a result of this imputation. An otherwise valid job requirement, such as a height requirement, does not become invalid simply because it would limit a person's employment opportunities in a substantial way if it were adopted by a substantial number of employers. Because petitioners have not alleged, and cannot demonstrate, that respondent's vision requirement reflects a belief that petitioners' vision substantially limits them, we agree with the decision of the Court of Appeals affirming the dismissal of petitioners' claim that they are regarded as disabled.

NOTES AND QUESTIONS

1. *ADAAA changes.* The ADAAA reverses this holding of *Sutton.* It states,

> An individual meets the requirement of "being regarded as having such an impairment" if the individual establishes that he or she has been subjected to an action prohibited under this Act because of an actual or perceived physical or mental impairment whether or not the impairment limits or is perceived to limit a major life activity.

P.L. 110-325(4)(a).

This prong does not apply, however, to transitory impairments under the ADAAA. A transitory impairment is defined as one with an actual or expected duration of six months or less. *Id.* For example, a broken leg or the flu would in most instances be a transitory impairment.

2. Why did Congress amend the statute in this way? What is the policy involved in holding an entity liable for discriminating against a person because of a perceived impairment without requiring proof that the entity believed that the perceived impairment substantially limited a major life activity? What are the policies supporting passage of the Act? What are the issues involved in proving the entity's state of mind concerning the perceived impairment and its effects?

3. To eliminate *all* discrimination based on disability, the ADA protects individuals who are *regarded as* or *perceived as* substantially impaired, in addition to those who are actually currently impaired. For example, an employer who believes that an individual has epilepsy and will thus be unable to do the job will probably be in violation of the law if the employer acts discriminatorily on that basis even if it turns out that the employee or job applicant does not in fact have epilepsy. Similarly, if an individual actually has a particular condition that is not substantially limiting, but the covered entity regards it as substantially limiting, that employee may be protected under the definition of disability.

In Chapter 3, the use of drug tests and medical screening will be discussed. Assume that it is permissible to give a drug test to a job applicant, and that the drug test erroneously indicates that the applicant is taking dilantin (a drug used to control epilepsy), and that the employer does not hire the employee based on this condition. Even though this seems to be a clear violation of the ADA, as a practical matter, how does the job applicant prove that this was the basis of employment decision?

4. *Reasonable accommodation or modifications.* One important difference under the ADAAA is that Congress made clear that if the plaintiff's *only* means of qualifying as an individual with a disability is under the "regarded as" prong, the covered entity under Title I, the public entity under Title II, and the owner, lessor or occupier of a place of public accommodation under Title III are not required to provide a reasonable accommodation to the individual or reasonable modifications to policies, practices or procedures for the individual. P.L. 110-325(6).

HYPOTHETICAL PROBLEMS APPLYING THE ADAAA

Before and After. The following fact patterns describe what courts decided about an individual's coverage or lack of coverage by the ADA or the Rehabilitation Act after the *Sutton* trilogy and *Toyota*, but before the ADAAA. Read the descriptions carefully and using specific statutory provisions of the ADAAA predict how courts would decide the cases if they arose under the ADAAA. Explain the arguments that the plaintiffs' lawyers would use under the ADAAA. What arguments would the defendants use to rebut these arguments?

1. *Before*: Allen Epstein was an executive of an insurance brokerage firm. He was hospitalized for heart disease. His employer demoted him. Then he told his employer that he had been diagnosed with diabetes. The employer fired him. He sued, alleging that the company violated the ADA. Holding: Epstein was not an individual with a disability because he was able to manage his heart disease and his diabetes with medication. Therefore, the court granted summary judgment to the employer. See *Epstein v. Kalvin-Miller Int'l*, 100 F. Supp. 2d 222 (S.D.N.Y. 2000). *After?*

2. *Before:* Charles Littleton was a 29 year old man with mental retardation. He lived with his mother and collected disability payments. He applied for a job at Wal-Mart and when the company called to schedule an interview, he requested that they permit a job coach to sit in on the interview. Wal-Mart refused and he went to the interview alone, which did not go well. Wal-Mart did not hire him. He sued alleging a violation of the ADA because Wal-Mart refused to accommodate him in the interview. He claimed that he was substantially limited in the major life activities of learning, thinking, and communicating. The court granted Wal-Mart summary judgment, holding that Littleton was not a person with a disability because he could drive, read and talk. See *Littleton v. Wal-Mart Stores, Inc.*, 231 Fed. Appx. 874 (11th Cir. 2007). *After?*

3. *Before.* Kent Furnish suffered from cirrhosis of the liver caused by Hepatitis B. He notified his employer of his illness and he was soon fired. When he sued under the ADA, the court granted the employer's motion for summary judgment, concluding that Kent had an impairment, but that it did not substantially impair a "major life activity." According to the court, "liver function" was not a major life activity, and therefore the plaintiff did not have a disability. See *Furnish v. SVI Systems, Inc.*, 270 F.3d 445 (7th Cir. 2001). *After?*

4. *Before.* Dawn Holt was diagnosed with a form of cerebral palsy which affected her speech and her ability to chew and swallow, to button her clothes, etc. When her employer fired her, the court granted the defendant summary judgment, concluding that the plaintiff had not proved that she was a person with a disability because she was able to perform many manual tasks. See *Holt v. Grand Lake Mental Health Center, Inc.*, 443 F. 3d 762 (10th Cir. 2006). *After?*

NOTES ON OTHER ISSUES CONCERNING DEFINITION OF DISABILITY

1. *Known Disabilities:* While there is not much case law on this issue, it seems clear from what there is that a covered entity will not be found to have discriminated against someone on the basis of disability unless that entity knows or should know that the individual actually has a disability. If the individual has a disability and wants that to be taken into account in an admissions, hiring, or other initial application process or after the individual is participating in the program, it is the responsibility of the individual to bring the disability to the attention of the covered entity. In certain situations, it will be the obligation of the individual to provide documentation to prove that the disability exists in order to qualify for accommodations or special consideration.

In demonstrating substantial limitation, it will often be required that appropriate documentation from qualified professionals be provided. While the issue of documentation can be disputed in other contexts, it often arises in cases involving learning disabilities and higher education and professional licensing. This is discussed in greater detail in Chapters 5 and 6. The issues include the credentials of the evaluator, what instruments were used to make the assessment, and how current the documentation should be. In addition, courts have grappled with the question of whether the evaluations by the treating professional or defendant's professional have greater weight.

2. *Individualized Assessments:* While certain conditions, such as total blindness and quadriplegia, will be determined to be disabilities within the definitional requirements, other conditions must be evaluated on an individualized basis, taking into account the nature and severity of the condition for that person, its long term effects, and the effects of mitigating measures. As the *Bragdon* decision indicates, HIV seems no longer to automatically be considered to be substantially limiting. The Court determined that circumstances related to Sidney Abbott indicated that she was substantially limited in the major life activity of reproduction. The Court left undecided whether a person with HIV who is asymptomatic is per se disabled under the "regarded as" prong of the definition.

As mentioned above, however, because the ADAAA adds to the definition of "major life activity" to include bodily functions, and because the immune system is listed as one of these bodily functions, it is likely that HIV positivity will be considered a per se disability.

3. *Requiring Special Education Because of Disability:* The definitional coverage under Individuals with Disabilities Education Act (IDEA) differs somewhat from the other major statutes discussed above. This statute is intended to protect individuals not only from discrimination, but to provide the basis for benefits and services that would exceed their entitlements under basic nondiscrimination statutes. The definition provides a specific listing of several disabling conditions. Not only must a child meet the label of one of those conditions, but the child must also require special education and related services because of the condition. For example, a child who uses a wheelchair, but who does not require any special education, probably does not fit within the definitional coverage of the IDEA. That child, however, probably would be protected from discrimination under the Americans with Disabilities Act and the Rehabilitation Act. E.g., *Wolff v. South Colonie Cent. Sch. Dist.*, 534 F. Supp. 758 (N.D.N.Y. 1982) (claim by high school girl with a limb deficiency that § 504 was violated when she was prohibited from taking a school sponsored trip to Spain).

4. *Age Eligibility in Special Education:* While all of the other statutes referred to above include the concept of qualification by virtue of being able to carry out the essential or fundamental requirements of the program, the Individuals with Disabilities Education Act is unique in its age eligibility requirement. While assuming that all children with disabilities are able to benefit from education, the IDEA requires that the child fall within certain age eligibility requirements. This issue is discussed more fully in Chapter 7.

5. *Retroactivity of the ADAAA.* Most courts have held that the ADAAA does not apply to facts occurring before the effective date of the amendments (January 1, 2009), but at least one case in the Sixth Circuit applied the ADAAA retroactively where the plaintiff sought injunctive relief. In *Jenkins v. National Bd. Medical Examiners*, 2009 U.S. App. LEXIS 2660, 2009 Fed. App. 0117N (6th Cir. Feb. 11, 2009) (unpublished opinion), the plaintiff, a third year medical student, sought additional time on the United States Medical Licensing Exam because of a reading

disability. The lower court found that his reading was slow and labored compared to the rest of the population, but it concluded, under *Toyota* that because he was able to perform tasks central to most persons' daily lives like reading a menu and the newspaper, that his impairment did not substantially limit a major life activity. On appeal, the Sixth Circuit concluded that because the plaintiff sought only prospective relief and not damages, the law in effect at the time of the appeal — the ADAAA — would govern. The plaintiff's attorneys' fees request did not defeat the retroactivity of his claim. The court distinguished *Landgraf v. USI Film Products*, 511 U.S. 244 (1994), which held that a right to a jury trial and compensatory and punitive damages created by the 1991 Civil Rights Act would not apply retroactively to cases already pending on appeal. What is the likely outcome with respect to attorneys' fees in this case?

[5]   Exemptions for Stated Conditions

The ADA excludes individuals with specific stated conditions from coverage because Congress was concerned about some cases decided earlier under the Rehabilitation Act in which courts held that conditions such as compulsive gambling and kleptomania could potentially be handicaps. See, e.g., *Fields v. Lyng*, 705 F. Supp. 1134 (D. Md. 1988); *Rezza v. Department of Justice*, 698 F. Supp. 586 (E.D. Pa. 1988). The ADA specifically excludes homosexuality, bisexuality, transvestism, transsexualism, pedophilia, exhibitionism, voyeurism, gender identity disorders not resulting from physical impairments, or other sexual behavior disorders, compulsive gambling, kleptomania, pyromania and psychoactive substance abuse disorders resulting from current illegal drug use. 42 U.S.C. § 12208, 12211. The Rehabilitation Act was amended to incorporate similar language. 29 U.S.C. § 705(20)(E) & (F). The Fair Housing Act does not protect persons based on transvestism. 42 U.S.C. § 3606(b)(3).

In one unusual case under state law, *Doe v. Boeing Co.*, 121 Wash. 2d 8, 846 P.2d 531 (1993), the court addressed the question of whether the state disability discrimination law required an employer to accommodate a transsexual who was transitioning from male to female. In accordance with medical standards that recommend that a male to female transsexual live as a woman for a year before undergoing a sex change operation, the plaintiff requested that (s)he be permitted to wear women's clothing to work. Holding that there was no illegal discrimination under state law, the court found that gender dysphoria is not a handicap unless the employer discriminates against the employee on the basis of the condition. Because the employer did not fire the employee, the employee did not have a handicap. The court states the following:

> Under [state law] the question of whether a person is "handicapped" is a question of fact and not a question of law. [T]he . . . definition requires both the "presence" of a handicapping condition and evidence that this condition was the reason for the discharge. The inquiry as to the "presence" of a handicapping condition . . . is factual in nature because it depends upon expert medical testimony, relevant medical documentation, and state of mind. The question of whether a condition was the reason for a dismissal is also a factual inquiry because it depends upon documentation

of the employer, testimony regarding the dismissal, and other relevant facts.

The [state] definition requires a factual finding of discrimination because of the condition in order to determine whether the condition is a "handicap" in the first place. . . . [T]he trial court should have held that Doe was not "handicapped". The Court of Appeals . . . declared gender dysphoria a "handicap" as a matter of law.

Gender dysphoria is a medically cognizable and diagnosable condition. Those who suffer from the condition surely endure great mental and emotional agony. However, unless a plaintiff can prove he or she was discriminated against because of the abnormal condition, his or her condition is not a "handicap" for purposes of the Act.

Despite the circular nature of the applicable regulation we [hold] that the definition of "handicap" for enforcement purposes . . . requires factual findings of both (1) the presence of an abnormal condition, and (2) employer discrimination against the employee plaintiff because of that condition.

The record substantially supports the . . . findings that Boeing did not discriminate against Doe because of her condition. Boeing discharged Doe because she violated Boeing's directives on acceptable attire [she was told not to wear feminine women's clothing until after the sex change operation, but wore pink pearls specifically to test the limits of this mandate], not because she was gender dysphoric. Doe was treated in a respectful way by both her peers and supervisors at Boeing. Doe's supervisor consistently rated her work as satisfactory on her performance evaluations. While complaints were filed with Boeing management about Doe's use of the women's restroom, the record is void of any evidence that Doe suffered harassment because of her use of the restroom or because of her attire.

Does the reasoning in this case make sense? Or is it unique to the statutory language in the State of Washington, which specifically defines handicap as requiring both the condition and that the individual be discriminated against because of the condition and that the condition be abnormal?

[6]   Special Situations

There are a number of special situations in which the definition of who is protected arises. For some of these situations, there is substantial judicial or regulatory guidance. For others there is not. The following are some of the most important or interesting of these situations.

Substance Use and Abuse: Individuals who use controlled substances and/or alcohol present some of the most complex questions. The statutory language of Title I of the ADA specifically precludes coverage of an individual *currently* engaged in the *illegal use* of drugs, when the entity acts on that basis. The ADA generally exempts as a disability psychoactive substance use disorders resulting from current illegal use of drugs.

The Rehabilitation Act precludes from coverage in employment discrimination those individuals who are alcoholic and whose *current* use of alcohol prevents them from performing the job or cause a threat to property or safety of others. With respect to drug usage, the Rehabilitation Act does not cover individuals currently using illegal drugs when the entity acts on the basis of that use. Individuals with a record of drug use, those regarded as being drug users, and those in rehabilitation who are currently not using are protected under the Rehabilitation Act. Special provisions relating to drug and alcohol use in educational agencies are also included.

The Fair Housing Act statutory language refers to illegal use of or addiction to controlled substances. The statute states that an individual currently illegally using or addicted to controlled substances is not covered. Interestingly, the Air Carrier Access Act specifically defines drug addiction and alcoholism as impairments.

A unique issue was addressed by the Supreme Court in *Traynor v. Turnage*, 485 U.S. 535 (1988). The issue was whether the Veteran's Administration violated the Rehabilitation Act by providing differential treatment benefits for primary and secondary alcoholism. The plaintiffs claimed that treating primary alcoholism and secondary alcoholism differently in this context violated Section 504 of the Rehabilitation Act. The differential treatment was based on a determination that primary alcoholism was based on willful misconduct under Veterans Benefits regulations. Secondary alcoholism was treated as a manifestation of an acquired psychiatric disorder. Although, as the dissent noted, the plaintiffs had begun drinking as minors and their alcoholism should thus not be treated as a result of their own willful misconduct, the majority held that providing a governmental benefit on a differential basis was not impermissible discrimination. It should be noted, however, that discrimination on the basis of disability generally, does not focus on whether the alcoholism is primary or secondary.

PROBLEMS

1. What if new research indicates a greater linkage between alcoholism and genes? Would this be a justification for genetic testing to determine the causation of the alcoholism in deciding whether an individual should receive Veteran's benefits? What are the potential dangers of such testing?

2. An individual is seeking a job at an automobile manufacturing plant. In the course of the preplacement medical assessment, the employer learns that the individual is carrying a gene that if passed on to her child (she has no children at this point), could result in the child having cystic fibrosis, a condition that would probably result in substantial medical costs. The employer is concerned that hiring the woman would result in increased costs to the company insurance plan. The employer decides not to hire the applicant. Assuming the applicant can prove that this is the reason she was not hired, is she protected against disability discrimination based on her unborn (and unconceived) child's potential genetic condition? What if the genetic condition were one where it is less certain that the condition would have substantial medical implications? For a comprehensive discussion of this issue, see Mark A. Rothstein, *Genetic Discrimination in Employment and the Americans with Disabilities Act*, 29 Hous. L. Rev. 23, 47–50 (1992).

For cases on this issue, see LAURA ROTHSTEIN & JULIA ROTHSTEIN, DISABILITIES AND THE LAW § 4.8 (2009). Generally courts have permitted adverse action when based on misconduct, even if the misconduct is related to alcoholism or drug addiction. Some of the issues addressed by the courts include what it means to be in rehabilitation and the use of drug testing as the basis for determining whether someone is using drugs or alcohol.

Communicable Diseases and Infections: The presence of HIV infection in society has resulted in significant attention to how individuals with communicable diseases and infections are to be treated in employment and other settings. In some respects, the treatment is similar to drug and alcohol use and addiction, i.e., the condition is covered, but not if it poses a danger to others. There was a great deal of controversy over this issue during the Congressional debate about the ADA. The compromise was to include statutory language to study the issue. Indirectly, the ADA provision relating qualification standards for employment mentions that for an individual to be protected, there should be no direct threat to the health or safety of other individuals in the workplace. The key issue, then, is whether a particular communicable disease or infection poses such a danger. The ADA also includes language indicating that state and local requirements relating to food handling and infectious or communicable diseases are not to be preempted. 42 U.S.C. § 12113(3).

The Rehabilitation Act, like the ADA, addresses this condition in the context of employment. It does so by exempting individuals whose current contagious disease or infection would constitute a direct threat to the health or safety of others, or whose condition results in the individual being unable to perform the job.

The Fair Housing Act does not address this in the statutory language. The Air Carrier Access Act refers to this condition in the context of when an individual might be refused transportation, required to provide a medical certificate, or have some restriction or condition placed upon the right to transportation.

In *School Bd. v. Arline*, 480 U.S. 273 (1987), the Court held that tuberculosis is a handicap under Section 504, but in footnote 7, the Court specifically noted that it was not deciding whether the carrier of a contagious disease such as AIDS would be covered by the Rehabilitation Act solely on the basis of "contagiousness." Subsequent amendments to the Rehabilitation Act and the initial definition of disability under the ADA seemed to clearly cover individuals with AIDS or who are HIV positive.

Following this decision and the statutory clarifications under the Rehabilitation Act and the ADA, individuals with HIV or AIDS and similar conditions were routinely found by courts to be individuals with disabilities under federal discrimination law. These decisions focused on the issue of whether the individual was otherwise qualified, particularly in cases involving medical care service providers. While many of these individuals ultimately lost their cases, they did not lose based on not being a person with a disability.

In 1998, the Supreme Court provided some guidance on this issue. In *Bragdon v. Abbott, supra*, the Court held that reproduction is a major life activity, and that the plaintiff had demonstrated that her HIV status, even though asymptomatic, had substantially limited her decision to reproduce. The Court left undecided whether a person with HIV who is asymptomatic is per se disabled under the "regarded as" prong of the definition.

After *Sutton*, and the narrowing of the definition, courts began to consider more closely whether an individual who was HIV positive, but asymptomatic was "substantially limited" in any major life activity. The ADAAA, which defines the immune system as a major life activity, should result in coverage of persons with HIV.

Associational Disabilities: The Americans with Disabilities Act and the Fair Housing Act make it illegal to discriminate against individuals because of their association with someone who is disabled. There has been little judicial guidance on situations when this would apply. Case excerpts in Chapters 3 (Employment) and 9 (Health Care) include that issue. In one of the few cases on this issue, *Saladin v. Turner*, 936 F. Supp. 1571 (N.D. Okla. 1996), a waiter was able to establish that his association with his HIV positive partner was a motivating factor in his dismissal from employment as a waiter and was a violation of the ADA. AIDS advocacy was found not to be enough for an associational discrimination claim in *Oliveras-Sifre v. Puerto Rico Dept. of Health*, 214 F.3d 23 (1st Cir. 2000).

The judicial decisions seem also to indicate that there is no obligation to accommodate the disability of the person with whom the claimant is associating. For example, in *Den Hartog v. Wasatch Academy*, 129 F.3d 1076 (10th Cir. 1997), the court allowed the termination of an employee because of the conduct of his son who had a mental disability. The court held that the employer was not required to accommodate the disability of the family member. This would probably mean, for example, that while a reasonable accommodation for a disability might require allowing time off for treatment, that the employer would not be required to allow the employee time off to assist with treatment for a family member with a disability. There may be coverage for such accommodation under the Family and Medical Leave Act, which allows for 12 weeks unpaid leave to care for a loved one, but probably not under the Rehabilitation Act or the ADA.

Behavior Related Conditions: As was noted previously in this chapter, there are a number of behavior related conditions that have been specifically exempted from coverage by the Americans with Disabilities Act statutory language, and now by the Rehabilitation Act, as a result of a 1992 amendment. A number of conditions not exempted, such as bipolar disorder, depression, and other mental illnesses, often raise concerns in various settings because of myths and prejudices about mental conditions.

Learning Disabilities: In the early years of disability discrimination law, the issue of learning disabilities was addressed primarily in the context of special education (which has separate statutory definitional protection), higher education and professional licensing. In the special education setting, the disputes were not primarily about whether the individual met the definition, but rather whether the educational programming was appropriate.

Substantial judicial attention to whether a learning disability (or other conditions such as attention deficit disorder or attention deficit and hyperactivity disorder) are substantially limiting to qualify as disabilities has been given in the higher education and professional licensing contexts. Numerous cases and Office for Civil Rights opinions have addressed questions related to whether the appropriate documentation of the condition has been provided. In the pre-*Sutton* cases, the courts tended to be more likely to find the person to be disabled within the statute, although many of the cases found the individual not to be "otherwise qualified." Simultaneous with deciding the *Sutton* trilogy, the Court remanded a case involving accommodations on the New York bar exam requested by an individual claiming a learning disability. The Court remanded for the lower court to consider the issue in light of the guidance on "mitigating measures."

More recently, attention to this issue has begun to occur in the employment setting. The trend, like the trend in higher education and professional licensing, has been that increasingly these individuals are found not to be substantially limited in major life activities. *See* Laura Rothstein & Julia Rothstein, Disabilities and the Law § 4.9 (2009).

Other: There are a number of other conditions that have given rise to interesting or unusual fact settings.

• *Facial Disfigurement.* One of these conditions is facial disfigurement. A few judicial decisions have considered conditions that fall into the category of facial or other disfigurements. In most of these cases, the individual is not substantially limited in carrying out the requirements of the program. Prejudicial attitudes towards individuals with disfigurements, however, may place these individuals in the category of someone who is "perceived to be" or "regarded as" disabled. Someone with scars from a serious burn might be covered, but perhaps only where the disfigurement is serious, but not where there is a small scar. Two decisions applying state law demonstrate contrary results on this issue. In *Chico Dairy Co. v. West Virginia Human Rights Comm'n*, 181 W. Va. 238, 382 S.E.2d 75 (1989), the court upheld the refusal to promote an employee with a sunken eye socket to be manager of a restaurant. The court found that this was not a protected condition. In contrast, the court in *Hodgdon v. Mt. Mansfield Co.*, 160 Vt. 150, 624 A.2d 1122 (1992), found that a toothless chambermaid was protected under state law because her employer regarded her as having a disabling condition. Should it matter whether the employment involves a position where appearance is of greater concern to others? For example, should severe burn scars on the face of a waitress at an upscale restaurant be treated differently than the same condition on the face of a bus driver, or a clerical employee with his own office? One author has discussed this issue in depth. See Comment, *Facial Discrimination: Extending Handicap Law to Employment Discrimination on the Basis of Physical Appearance*, 100 Harv. L. Rev. 2035 (1987).

In 2009, the EEOC settled a case on facial disfigurement for $95,000 and ADA training of its employees. The EEOC sued employer Extra Space Management, Inc. for violating the ADA when it fired its maintenance employee whose face was disfigured by burns. When the employee met the acting district manager, the manager fired him and said that "he was handicapped, deformed or something" and that "it's clear he can't get the job done." See *Extra Space Management to Pay*

$95,000 for Disability Bias Against Employee with Cosmetic Disfigurement,
http://eeoc.gov/press/5-28-09.html.

• *Size, Obesity*. It is not always clear when size will constitute a disability under
any of the statutes. In *Dexler v. Tisch*, 660 F. Supp. 1418 (D. Conn. 1987), the court
held that dwarfism is a handicap, while in *Tudyman v. United Airlines*, 608 F.
Supp. 739 (C.D. Cal. 1984), the court found that being heavier than the maximum
weight for flight attendants as a result of bodybuilding is not a handicap under
§ 504. It is possible that the difference in these results stems from the obvious
disparity in underlying causes.

When size might be a condition within the control of the individual, there are
complex and unresolved questions about whether the condition is covered. The
courts, the Equal Employment Opportunity Commission (EEOC), and the commentators are at odds about how obesity should be treated, how it should be
defined, and whether it matters that the obesity is a result of a physiological or
psychological condition or just that the person likes to eat. The case of *Cook v. State
of Rhode Island*, 10 F.3d 17 (1st Cir. 1993), involves a woman who was denied a job
as an attendant in a state facility for mentally retarded individuals. She was 5'3" tall
and weighed 329 pounds, a condition that would be considered morbid obesity, i.e.,
weighing at least two times the normal amount for a person of that height. The
federal court in its decision addressing whether the employer violated the Rehabilitation Act, stated the following:

> [T]he prophylaxis of section 504 embraces not only those persons who are
> in fact disabled, but also those persons who bear the brunt of discrimination
> because prospective employers view them as disabled.

> On the one hand, the jury could plausibly have found that plaintiff had a
> physical impairment; after all, she admittedly suffered from morbid
> obesity, and she presented expert testimony that morbid obesity is a
> physiological disorder involving a dysfunction of both the metabolic system
> and the neurological appetite-suppressing signal system, capable of causing
> adverse effects within the musculoskeletal, respiratory and cardiovascular
> systems. On the second hand, the jury could have found that plaintiff,
> although not handicapped, was treated by [the employer] as if she had a
> physical impairment. Indeed [its] stated reasons for its refusal to hire — its
> concern that Cook's limited mobility impeded her ability to evacuate
> patients in case of an emergency, and its fear that her condition augured a
> heightened risk of heart disease, thereby increasing the likelihood of
> workers' compensation claims — show conclusively that [the employer]
> treated plaintiff's obesity as if it actually affected her musculoskeletal and
> cardiovascular systems.

> Detached jurors reasonably could have found that [the employer's] pessi-
> mistic assessment of plaintiff's capabilities demonstrated that appellant
> regarded Cook's condition as substantially limiting a major life activity —
> being able to work.

> Accordingly, the district court appropriately refused to direct a verdict for
> the employer.

In the *Cook v. Rhode Island* case, the Equal Employment Opportunity Commission weighed in on the side of the plaintiff, filing a brief arguing that obesity is a disability. The EEOC specifically rejected the assertion that obesity is not a disability because it is a voluntary condition subject to individual control. Furthermore, its position is that whether obesity is a disability should be decided on a case-by-case basis, and it is not limited to situations where it results from some physiological condition rendering it an immutable condition. The EEOC suggested that factors to determine coverage should include duration of the condition and its long-term impact. With the national attention and concern about obesity in America, this will certainly continue to be an issue facing the courts. As the *Cook* case highlights, there is an unresolved question as to whether it makes a difference when the obesity is a voluntary condition.

In *Coleman v. Georgia Power Co.*, 81 F. Supp. 2d 1365 (N.D. Ga. 2000), the court held that obesity is an impairment under the ADA only where it is shown to affect a bodily system and is related to a physiological disorder.

There have been a number of other interesting cases involving conditions such as cancer, chemical and other environmental sensitivities, health impairments (such as diabetes and epilepsy), and back injuries. Several of the cases in subsequent chapters involve these conditions in the context of issues of reasonable accommodation and qualifications.

C   OTHERWISE QUALIFIED AND REASONABLE ACCOMMODATION

The statutes in the previous section require not only that the individual meet the definition of having a disability, but either explicitly in the statute or implicitly through interpretation, the individual is required to be otherwise qualified in order to be protected against discrimination. Although the Rehabilitation Act did not include the concept of reasonable accommodation in the statutory language, the Americans with Disabilities Act does incorporate the language directly. As the next case illustrates, this is a concept that was incorporated early on in the interpretation of the Rehabilitation Act.

The first Supreme Court decision to address any issue under the major federal disability discrimination statutes is the following case. It involves a nurse with a serious hearing impairment who was seeking admission into the clinical training program. This clinical training was required for her to become a registered nurse. During the admissions interview process, Ms. Davis had difficulty understanding questions, and upon inquiry it was learned that she had a history of hearing problems and needed a hearing aid. After examination it was determined that she would need to lip-read in addition to relying on her hearing aid support in order to have effective communication. The program was concerned with whether her disability would make it unsafe for her to practice as a nurse. The following excerpt examines the Supreme Court's analysis of how to determine whether someone is entitled to protection under the Rehabilitation Act. Section 504 of the Rehabilitation Act originally used the term "handicap." This was amended in 1992, and current statutory language uses "disability."

SOUTHEASTERN COMMUNITY COLLEGE v. DAVIS
442 U.S. 397 (1979)

MR. JUSTICE POWELL:

Section 504 by its terms does not compel educational institutions to disregard the disabilities of handicapped individuals or to make substantial modifications in their programs to allow disabled persons to participate. Instead, it requires only that an "otherwise qualified handicapped individual" not be excluded from participation in a federally funded program "solely by reason of his handicap," indicating only that mere possession of a handicap is not a permissible ground for assuming an inability to function in a particular context.

The court below, however, believed that the "otherwise qualified" persons protected by § 504 include those who would be able to meet the requirements of a particular program in every respect except as to limitations imposed by their handicap. Taken literally, this holding would prevent an institution from taking into account any limitation resulting from the handicap, however disabling. It assumes, in effect, that a person need not meet legitimate physical requirements in order to be "otherwise qualified." . . . An otherwise qualified person is one who is able to meet all of a program's requirements in spite of his handicap.

The regulations . . . reinforce . . . this conclusion. According to these regulations, a "[q]ualified handicapped person" is, "[w]ith respect to postsecondary and vocational education services, a handicapped person who meets the academic and technical standards requisite to admission or participation in the [school's] education program or activity. . . . " An explanatory note states:

> "The term 'technical standards' refers to *all* nonacademic admissions criteria that are essential to participation in the program in question." (emphasis supplied).

A further note emphasizes that legitimate physical qualifications may be essential to participation in particular programs.

The remaining question is whether the physical qualifications Southeastern demanded of respondent might not be necessary for participation in its nursing program. It is not open to dispute that, as Southeastern's Associate Degree Nursing program currently is constituted, the ability to understand speech without reliance on lipreading is necessary for patient safety during the clinical phase of the program. [T]his ability also is indispensable for many of the functions that a registered nurse performs.

Respondent contends nevertheless that § 504, properly interpreted, compels Southeastern to undertake affirmative action that would dispense with the need for effective oral communication. First, it is suggested that respondent can be given individual supervision by faculty members whenever she attends patients directly. Moreover, certain required courses might be dispensed with altogether for respondent. It is not necessary, she argues, that Southeastern train her to undertake all the tasks a registered nurse is licensed to perform. Rather, it is sufficient to make § 504 applicable if respondent might be able to perform satisfactorily some of the duties of a registered nurse or to hold some of the positions available to a registered nurse.

[The Court rejected these arguments.]

NOTES

1. *Fundamental or Essential Requirements:* The nondiscrimination statutes are fairly consistent in requiring that the individual must be able to carry out the fundamental requirements of the program with or without reasonable accommodation. The factual disputes arise as to what constitutes a fundamental requirement. Fundamental requirements differ, depending on the context. For example, what is essential or fundamental in attending a higher education professional program such as law school may be different from what is fundamental in the practice of law.

As the statutory language in the Americans with Disabilities Act notes, employers will be given deference in determining what are essential requirements, particularly where they have prepared in advance a job description and qualifications. See the definition of "qualified individual with a disability" under Title I, *supra*, Section [B][1]. The courts have given particular deference to schools in establishing their educational programming requirements. Similarly, the courts have been reluctant to second guess the essential admission and academic requirements for institutions of higher education.

This aspect of nondiscrimination requirements is discussed in more detail in each context in later chapters. The following are some examples of typical judicial responses. In the context of education, the Supreme Court in *Board of Ed. v. Rowley*, 458 U.S. 176 (1982), noted that:

> The primary responsibility for formulating the education to be accorded a handicapped child, and for choosing the educational method most suitable to the child's needs, was left by the [Individuals with Disabilities Education Act], to state and local educational agencies in cooperation with the parents or guardian of the child. The Act expressly charges States with the responsibility of "acquiring and disseminating to teachers and administrators of programs for handicapped children significant information derived from educational research, demonstration, and similar projects, and [of] adopting, where appropriate, promising educational practices and materials." In the face of such a clear statutory directive, it seems highly unlikely that Congress intended courts to overturn a State's choice of appropriate educational theories in a proceeding conducted pursuant to § 1415(e)(2).

For higher education, the decision in *Southeastern Community College v. Davis*, indicates the deference the courts give to institutions of higher education. Laura Rothstein, *The Story of* Southeastern Community College v. Davis: *The Prequel to the Television Series "ER,"* Chapter 7 of EDUCATION STORIES (2008) (discussing the impact of the *Davis* decision on higher education and students with disabilities).

Professional licensing agencies, many of which are not subject to the Rehabilitation Act because they do not receive federal financial assistance, but which are generally subject to Title II of the Americans with Disabilities Act because such agencies are state governmental entities, have recently been challenged with respect to their requirements. The Virginia Board of Education requirement that a teacher pass a national teacher examination was challenged under the Rehabilitation Act (because the state receives federal financial assistance). In *Pandazides v. Virginia Bd. of Ed.*, 804 F. Supp. 794 (E.D. Va. 1992), the court noted:

> Section 504 [of the Rehabilitation Act] does not prohibit minimum competency tests; nor does it mean that the handicapped are excused from reasonable standards of minimum competence.

> The Rehabilitation Act was not intended to eliminate academic or professional requirements that measure proficiency in analyzing written information by attaining a passing score on a multiple choice test.

> Courts are prohibited from requiring a fundamental alteration in a defendant's program to accommodate a handicapped individual.

> The ability to read intelligently, to comprehend written and spoken communication accurately, effectively and quickly, and to respond to written and spoken communication professionally, effectively and quickly, are "essential functions" of a special education, public school teacher in Virginia. Moreover, the ability to manage a classroom is an "essential function" for a public school teacher . . . .

The court also addressed the fact that reasonable accommodations to take the test should be, and in fact, were provided.

In the area of employment, there is an enormous body of emerging judicial interpretation of what is meant by "essential requirements." These cases involve a variety of types of employment and a wide range of disabilities. The courts have been fairly consistent in requiring employees to meet job attendance requirements, although employers may be obligated to consider scheduling adjustments in certain cases, and unpaid leave for medical or psychological treatment. For example, in *Jackson v. Veterans Admin.*, 22 F.3d 277 (11th Cir. 1994), a housekeeping aide with rheumatoid arthritis was competent in performing his custodial tasks, but the court held that his unpredictable and excessive absences need not be excused. Attendance was an essential aspect of the job.

Many cases involve whether a police officer must be able to perform the entire range of duties in order to meet the fundamental requirements of the program. Often these cases involve police officers who are no longer able to perform all of their previous duties because they were injured on the job. Generally, the courts have required that all duties must be performed. E.g., *Simon v. St. Louis County*, 735 F.2d 1082 (8th Cir. 1984); *Kees v. Wallenstein*, 973 F. Supp. 1191 (W.D. Wash. 1997) (employees unable to be in direct, physical contact with inmates unable to perform essential functions of corrections officer); *Karbusicky v. City of Park Ridge*, 950 F. Supp. 878 (N.D. Ill. 1997) (a police officer with hearing loss in one ear is not qualified).

2. *Safety and Health Concerns:* Consistent with substantial judicial deference about fundamental requirements relating to safety in the area of health related professional programs, the courts have been deferential to the medical institutions in the employment context. Some of these are discussed later in Chapter 3. In *Bradley v. University of Texas M.D. Anderson Cancer Ctr.*, 3 F.3d 922 (5th Cir. 1993), the court addressed the issue of whether a surgical technician, who is HIV-positive, whose job requires him to be close to open wounds and handle surgical instruments, poses an undue risk of transmission of the virus to patients. The court found that Bradley was not otherwise qualified because of this risk.

SCHOOL BOARD OF NASSAU COUNTY v. ARLINE
480 U.S. 273 (1987)

[In the portion of the *Arline* decision reproduced in [B][2], *supra*, the Court considered whether discriminating against a person based on contagiousness of her tuberculosis is discrimination based on disability. After the Court decided that question in the affirmative, it went on to consider whether Arline is otherwise qualified for the job and what test should be used to determine whether Arline's contagiousness posed an unacceptable risk to the health and safety of others.]

IV

The remaining question is whether Arline is otherwise qualified for the job of elementary schoolteacher. To answer this question in most cases, the district court will need to conduct an individualized inquiry and make appropriate findings of fact. Such an inquiry is essential if § 504 is to achieve its goal of protecting handicapped individuals from deprivations based on prejudice, stereotypes, or unfounded fear, while giving appropriate weight to such legitimate concerns of grantees as avoiding exposing others to significant health and safety risks.[16] The basic factors to be considered in conducting this inquiry are well established. In the context of the employment of a person handicapped with a contagious disease, we agree with *amicus* American Medical Association that this inquiry should include:

> "[findings of] facts, based on reasonable medical judgments given the state of medical knowledge, about (a) the nature of the risk (how the disease is transmitted), (b) the duration of the risk (how long is the carrier infectious), (c) the severity of the risk (what is the potential harm to third parties) and (d) the probabilities the disease will be transmitted and will cause varying degrees of harm." Brief for American Medical Association as *Amicus Curiae* 19.

---

[16] A person who poses a significant risk of communicating an infectious disease to others in the workplace will not be otherwise qualified for his or her job if reasonable accommodation will not eliminate that risk. The Act would not require a school board to place a teacher with active, contagious tuberculosis in a classroom with elementary school children. "An otherwise qualified person is one who is able to meet all of a program's requirements in spite of his handicap." In the employment context, an otherwise qualified person is one who can perform "the essential functions" of the job in question. When a handicapped person is not able to perform the essential functions of the job, the court must also consider whether any "reasonable accommodation" by the employer would enable the handicapped person to perform those functions. Accommodation is not reasonable if it either imposes "undue financial and administrative burdens" on a grantee or requires "a fundamental alteration in the nature of [the] program."

In making these findings, courts normally should defer to the reasonable medical judgments of public health officials. The next step in the "otherwise-qualified" inquiry is for the court to evaluate, in light of these medical findings, whether the employer could reasonably accommodate the employee under the established standards for that inquiry.

NOTES AND QUESTIONS

1. Safety and health concerns have been raised in a number of judicial decisions, not only in the context of medical professions. Individuals with disabilities such as diabetes, serious mental conditions, and epilepsy in settings such as driving, operating heavy equipment, law enforcement, working in hazardous environments such as construction or at a high altitude, and employment related to children have been the subject of several decisions. In most, if not all, of these decisions, the courts also consider whether reasonable accommodation could be made to eliminate or adequately reduce the risk. For example, in *Wood v. Omaha Sch. Dist.*, 25 F.3d 667 (8th Cir. 1994), the court found that an insulin dependent school van driver could not be reasonably accommodated and would pose a risk of lost consciousness. Thus, it did not violate Section 504 of the Rehabilitation Act to demote the plaintiffs to non-driving positions. The court in *Chandler v. City of Dallas*, 2 F.3d 1385 (5th Cir. 1993), reached a similar decision with respect to city employees who had driving responsibilities.

2. There have been a number of decisions involving safety issues where the Postal Service has been the employer, many of these involving psychological conditions. E.g., *Marino v. United States Postal Serv.*, 25 F.3d 1037 (1st Cir. 1994) (employee with psychiatric problems had assaulted her supervisor); *Mazzarella v. Postal Serv.*, 849 F. Supp. 89 (D. Mass. 1994) (employee with personality disorder was discharged because of destructive behavior and was not qualified). But in *Kupferschmidt v. Runyon*, 827 F. Supp. 570 (E.D. Wis. 1993), the court held that a Postal Service employee who had threatened to kill her supervisor and fellow employees must be allowed to prove that she is qualified. In *Lussier v. Runyon*, 1994 U.S. Dist. LEXIS 4668, 3 Am. Disabilities Cas. (BNA) 223 (D. Maine 1994), the court found that the Postal Service employee with post-traumatic stress disorder had been improperly discharged out of fear of violent behavior, not because the employee had actually done anything.

3. The courts have held that under Section 504 of the Rehabilitation Act, the definition of "qualified individual" also includes a personal safety requirement. An otherwise qualified individual is one who "can perform the essential functions of the position in question without endangering the health and safety of the individual or others." *Chandler v. City of Dallas*, 2 F.3d at 1393. Title I of the ADA has an explicit defense that states in Section 12113(b): "The term 'qualification standards' may include a requirement that an individual shall not pose a direct threat to the health or safety of other individuals in the workplace." The Supreme Court has interpreted this defense to include when the individual poses a direct threat to the health or safety of the individual him or herself as well. *Chevron U.S.A. v. Echazabal*, 536 U.S. 73 (2002).

In cases involving concerns about health and safety, what should the employer be required to prove before deciding that the individual is not otherwise qualified because of the risk? In the case of mental impairments, should it be enough that the employee has made threats? What if the employee's behavior occurs before the employee is diagnosed and begins treatment? Should the behavior be forgiven? Does it matter whether the behavior was violent towards a person where physical harm resulted or if it was minor property damage for which the employee has paid?

If there is concern about risk of contagion in the case of disease, does it matter what the resulting harm might be? Is the employee more likely to be found not qualified because of health risk concerns where the disease is HIV/AIDS (which is virtually always fatal) as compared to tuberculosis? The mode and likelihood of transmission are also relevant considerations. For example, tuberculosis becomes airborne and is more highly transmissible compared to the HIV virus.

Does it matter whether the risk is to children or adults? Why or why not? Are there other vulnerable populations where there is a greater need to protect against risk because the individuals are not able to do so themselves?

Chapter 3

EMPLOYMENT

A APPLICABILITY OF TITLE I OF THE AMERICANS WITH DISABILITIES ACT AND THE REHABILITATION ACT

Until the 1990 passage of the Americans with Disabilities Act (ADA), 42 U.S.C. § 12101 et seq., individuals with disabilities had little comprehensive protection against employment discrimination on the basis of disability. Most states had statutes, but the definition of who was protected, which employers were covered, and the rights and remedies varied significantly from state to state. The Rehabilitation Act of 1973 only covered federal government employers, federal contractors, and programs receiving federal financial assistance. 29 U.S.C. §§ 791, 793, 794. This left the majority of employees and job applicants without any protection against discrimination, or with state laws that might be ineffective.

[1] Which Employers are Covered?

Title I of the ADA provided that as of July 26, 1992, employers with 25 or more employees are not to discriminate on the basis of disability against otherwise qualified individuals with disabilities. On July 26, 1994, employers with 15 or more employees became subject to the Title I requirements. Title II of the ADA applies to state and local governmental agencies and prohibits those entities from discriminating in their programs, both in the provision of services and in the employment practices of the agency. The advantage of seeking redress for employment discrimination under Title II instead of Title I is that individuals are not required to exhaust administrative (i.e., Equal Employment Opportunity Commission) remedies under Title II. Because of Eleventh Amendment immunity, money damages in employment cases against state entities are not available according to the Supreme Court in *Board of Trustees v. Garret*, excerpted in Section [G][2], *infra*. Under Title I, however, damages up to $300,000 may be awarded against non-state defendants. The amount of damages available depends on the size of the employer. Title III, which prohibits discrimination by private providers of services considered to be public accommodations, does not cover employment discrimination.

Under the Rehabilitation Act, there are three major categories of employers prohibited from discriminating on the basis of disability. Section 501 applies to federal government employers; Section 503 applies to federal contractors with contracts in excess of $10,000 (increased from $2,500 in the original statute); Section 504 applies to recipients of federal financial assistance.

In 1984, the Supreme Court held, in *Grove City College v. Bell*, 465 U.S. 555 (1984), that statutes like Section 504 do not subject an entire institution to their mandates when only one program within an institution receives federal financial assistance. Only the program receiving the federal support would be subject to the nondiscrimination requirements. In 1987, Congress overturned *Grove City* by enacting the Civil Rights Restoration Act, which provides that if any part of an institution receives federal financial assistance, all of its programs are subject to Section 504. 29 U.S.C. § 794(b).

There is some confusion about whether federal employers are subject to both Sections 501 and 504. The weight of authority is that both statutes apply. See LAURA ROTHSTEIN & JULIA ROTHSTEIN, DISABILITIES AND THE LAW § 4.03 (2009).

NOTES

1. *Individual Liability:* Title I makes an employer liable in respondeat superior for the discriminatory acts of its supervisory employees. It defines an employer as a "person engaged in an industry affecting commerce . . . and any agent of such person . . . ." Despite this language, the courts of appeals are fairly settled that there is no individual liability under the anti-discrimination provisions of Title I of the ADA. The Seventh, Ninth, Tenth and Eleventh Circuits have declined to find individual liability. The courts reason that because Title I of the ADA is based on Title VII of the 1964 Civil Rights Act and there is no individual liability under Title VII, there is no individual liability under Title I of the ADA for discrimination. See, e.g., *Walsh v. Nevada Dept. of Human Res.*, 471 F.3d 1033 (9th Cir. 2006). While at least two courts — the Fourth and the Eleventh Circuits — apply this same reasoning to the anti-retaliation provisions of Title I, it has not been clearly settled whether or not there is individual liability where a person retaliates against an individual based on disability, because a number of the other courts of appeals have not yet ruled on this issue. See Jonathan R. Mook, *Jonathan R. Mook on Individual Liability Under Disability Discrimination Laws*, 2008 EMERGING ISSUES 797 (Oct. 26, 2007). Despite the lack of individual liability under federal law, a number of state anti-discrimination laws hold individuals personally liable for discriminating in the workplace based on disability. States finding an individual liable for disability discrimination in employment include New York, Massachusetts, Pennsylvania and West Virginia. *Id.*

2. *Standing: Former Employees — Standing to Sue under Title I of the ADA?* There is a split in the circuits as to whether former employees who collect disability insurance have standing to sue their employers under the ADA for provision of fringe benefits in discriminatory fashion. Those opposing standing argue that the statute requires that a former employee be a "qualified individual," and former employees who are collecting benefits are not qualified to work. In *McKnight v. GM Corp.*, 2008 U.S. App. LEXIS 24373 (6th Cir. Dec. 4, 2008), the plaintiffs were former employees who sued, alleging that the employer discriminated against them based on their disability with respect to payment of post-employment fringe benefits. The lower court granted summary judgment to the defendant. The Sixth Circuit affirmed, concluding that former employees are not qualified individuals and therefore do not have standing to sue. The Second and Third Circuits, however, have ruled that former employees are "qualified individuals" under the statute and have standing to challenge discriminatory benefits. See *Ford v. Schering-Plough Corp.*, 145 F.3d 601 (3d Cir. 1998); *Castellano v. City of New York*, 142 F.3d 58 (2d Cir. 1998). Because the statute covers discriminatorily granted fringe benefits, would it not obviate the purpose of the Act to not permit former employees collecting those benefits to sue? On the other hand, how can those former employees argue that they are "qualified individuals" either with or without reasonable accommodation? Assuming its applicability, could the ADAAA help plaintiffs make their argument?

Zone of Interest: In *Foote v. Folks, Inc.*, 864 F. Supp. 1327 (N.D. Ga. 1994), an employee's former wife, covered by the employee's health plan, was held not to have standing to challenge the plan as discriminatory. The court held that because she was not an employee, former employee, or a job applicant, but rather a beneficiary of her husband's employment benefits, she did not fall within the "zone of interest" envisioned by the ADA. *Id.* at 1329.

3. *State Disability Laws:* Individuals not protected under federal law may, in many states, be covered by state law. The majority of states and the District of Columbia cover employers with fewer than fifteen employees. State laws may also apply to a wider range of conditions than the ADA or the Rehabilitation Act. Conditions such as genetic predisposition, obesity, or substance abuse may be covered. State laws also may be more restrictive with respect to preemployment hiring practices. For a listing of relevant state laws, see Mark A. Rothstein, Charles B. Craver, Elinor P. Schroeder & Elaine W. Shoben, Employment Law § 3.15 (4th ed. 2009).

Chapter 2, *supra*, focused on the issue of who is protected under the various disability discrimination statutes in a variety of contexts. The *Sutton* trilogy and *Toyota* and *Bragdon* were included as major Supreme Court cases analyzing the definition. *Sutton* and *Toyota* arose in the context of employment. Since these decisions, lower courts have applied the analysis and have been much less likely to find a variety of conditions to be substantially limiting in covered major life activities. As a consequence, litigants have begun to bring more actions under the "regarded as" prong of the definition.

The second prong of the definition protects individuals with a "record of an impairment." Congress intended that individuals with a history of major illness should be protected from discrimination after recovery. There has not been a great deal of judicial interpretation of this definition, but what case law exists has generally not favored plaintiffs. The fact that an individual has a record of medical treatment in the personnel or other record, will not usually establish such a "record of impairment." But see *Adams v. Rice*, 531 F.3d 936 (D.C. Cir. 2008) (holding that a woman who had a mastectomy for breast cancer had a record of a disability).

Before the ADAAA, one was "regarded as having an impairment" when the individual was considered to be substantially limited in a major life activity, even though the impairment does not actually limit the individual. After the ADAAA, the individual will meet the requirement of "being regarded as having such an impairment" by establishing that he or she has been subjected to an action prohibited by the ADA or the Rehabilitation Act because of an actual or perceived physical or mental impairment, whether or not the impairment limits or is perceived as limiting a major life activity. See Chapter 2, *supra.*

Some of the cases that follow in this chapter were decided before the *Sutton* trilogy in 1999. Consequently, the courts were not as likely to focus on whether certain conditions (such as epilepsy or HIV) were actual disabilities. Instead, the focus was on the substantive application of the statutory provisions. After *Sutton*, the courts narrowed the definition of disability, often dismissing cases based on the individual's failure to prove that he or she had a disability. Because of the ADAAA, the courts should again begin to decline to focus extensively on whether the plaintiffs' impairments constitute disabilities and will likely begin to pay more attention to the substantive application of the ADA and the Rehabilitation Act. Thus, many of the pre-1999 cases are good law once again. For additional cases, See LAURA ROTHSTEIN & JULIA ROTHSTEIN, DISABILITIES AND THE LAW § 4:8 (2009).

4. *Definition of Employee:* The Supreme Court in *Clackamas Gastroenterology Associates v. Wells*, 538 U.S. 440 (2003), addressed the definition of "employee" for purposes of determining whether a medical clinic was subject to the ADA. The clinic had four physicians who were actively involved in practicing medicine and who were shareholders and directors of the clinic corporation. Whether the clinic employed 15 or more employees depended on whether these individuals were considered to be "employees" under the ADA. The Court in a 7-2 opinion remanded for further proceedings, providing the standard for review. The factors the Court instructed for consideration were that the common-law element of control should be the primary guideline. In this case, the Court was persuaded by the EEOC guidelines on the issue of control in which six factors are considered. These factors included: whether the organization can hire or fire individuals or set rules and regulations for work; supervision of individual work; whether individuals report to someone higher in an organization; the ability of individuals to influence organizations; the intent of the parties as evidenced by written agreements or contracts; and whether individuals share in profits, losses, and liabilities of the organization. The dissent by Justice Ginsburg (with whom Justice Breyer joined) focused more on the fact that the physicians had employment contracts and they worked at the facilities owned or leased by the corporation and that they were required to conform with standards set by the corporation.

[2] Applicability of The Three-Prong Definition of Disability to Employment

For an individual to be protected against employment discrimination on the basis of disability under the ADA, the individual must be one who has an impairment that substantially limits one or more of the individual's major life activities, has a record of such an impairment, or is regarded as having such an impairment. 29 U.S.C. § 121101. These definitions are virtually identical to language under the Rehabilitation Act. Under Title I of the ADA, a qualified individual with a disability is one "who, with or without reasonable accommodation, can perform the essential functions of the employment position that such individual holds or desires." 42 U.S.C. § 12111(8).

The ADA contemplates consistency with the Rehabilitation Act. Most cases addressing substantive issues would be decided similarly under either the ADA or the Rehabilitation Act.

NOTES AND QUESTIONS

1. *Employees with Disabled Family Members:* The Rehabilitation Act does not specifically provide protection based on "associational disability" (i.e., protection for individuals who are associated with someone with a disability), although the ADA does provide this protection. 42 U.S.C. § 12112(b)(4). Although it is generally appropriate to incorporate interpretations of Section 504 of the Rehabilitation Act into the ADA, it is less clear that interpretations of the ADA should be incorporated into Section 504. This question is presented in the case of James Patterson, a federal employee (who is thus not covered by the ADA), who has a family member with a chronic medical condition. The federal agency where he was employed did not want to send him to an appointment outside the United States because of the high cost and risks associated with providing treatment for his daughter's congenital heart problem. Barbara Presley Noble, *Promotions and Family Matters*, N.Y. TIMES p. 23 (Jan. 22, 1995). In *Den Hartog v. Wasatch Academy*, 129 F.3d 1076 (10th Cir. 1997), the plaintiff was discharged as a teacher at a boarding school. The discharge was a result of Den Hartog's son's behavior, which had included attacks and threatening behavior towards individuals in the boarding school community. Den Hartog's son had bipolar disorder. Den Hartog requested that he and his family be allowed to live off campus to minimize the threat. The court held that there is no requirement to reasonably accommodate an individual who is associated with someone with a disability, rather than having a disability himself or herself.

2. *Short Term and Minor Impairments:* A number of judicial decisions have addressed conditions of short duration or where there was not a substantial limitation and have held that individuals are not disabled within the ADA and other disability discrimination statutes. See *Boren v. Wolverine Tube, Inc.*, 966 F. Supp. 457 (N.D. Miss. 1997) (chemical allergy not covered); *Cehrs v. Northeast Ohio Alzheimer Research Ctr.*, 959 F. Supp. 441 (N.D. Ohio 1997) (psoriasis not covered); *Williams v. City of Charlotte*, 899 F. Supp. 1484 (W.D.N.C. 1995) (seasonal affective disorder not covered); *Dutton v. Johnson County Bd. of Comm'rs*, 859 F. Supp. 498 (D. Kan. 1994) (fact question whether migraine headache substantially limits major life activities); *Huffman v. Ace Elec. Co.*, 1994 U.S. Dist. LEXIS 15165, 3 A.D. Cases 1347 (D. Kan. 1994) (temporary cough resulting from hypersensitivity to unknown substances is not a disability); *Schultz v. Spraylat*, 866 F. Supp. 1535 (C.D. Cal. 1994) (sinus condition preventing air travel not a disability under state law); *Shaw v. Citicorp Credit Servs.*, No. C93-3696 (N.D. Cal., Aug. 3, 1994) (offensive body odor is not a disability); *Laurence v. Metro-Dade Police Dep't*, 3 A.D. Cases 1396 (S.D. Fla. 1993) ("hammer toes" not a disability).

The ADAAA states that temporary and minor impairments do not create liability under the "regarded as" prong of the definition of disability. It defines temporary impairments as those lasting 6 months or fewer. P.L. 110-325 § 3(3)(B).

3. *Mental Conditions:* A number of cases have addressed a variety of mental conditions from bipolar disorder to panic attacks and mood swings. While a few of these cases have been resolved by finding that the condition does not constitute a disability, most of the cases focused on other issues, such as whether the individual is otherwise qualified (i.e., because of behavior problems in the workplace, chronic attendance problems, or dangerous or threatening conduct) or whether the accommodation sought by the individual is reasonable. After the 1999 *Sutton* narrowing of who is protected, courts looked at mitigating measures with respect to a number of mental health conditions. Conditions such as bipolar disorder and severe depression were often found not covered when medication alleviates the symptoms. For example, in *Rohan v. Networks Presentations*, 375 F.3d 266 (4th Cir. 2004), an actress/singer with post-traumatic stress disorder and depression was not covered, because her psychological episodes were sporadic and short-lived.

The dilemma in these cases was that the mitigating measures might cause side effects that need to be accommodated, but the individual is not entitled to an accommodation unless there is a disability. For example, some medications taken for mental health conditions cause "dry mouth." An employee might want to have water at the work station. An employer might have a "no exceptions" policy of not allowing food or water at the work station. The reasons might be for appearance, or they might be for safety or similar reasons. At a computer station, spilling water could damage a keyboard. Not allowing an exception, however, could be burdensome for the individual taking the medication. Under *Sutton*, while on the medication, the employee is not currently substantially limited, so the case would not go forward on the issue of reasonable accommodation. If the employee stops taking the medication, however, the individual may not longer be "otherwise qualified." The ADAAA attempted to resolve this problem. Under the ADAAA, may the courts consider the side effects of medications in determining whether the employee's impairment substantially limits a major life activity? If not, will the individual with mental health conditions still be covered by the Act? Will the employer be required to provide a reasonable accommodation to the side effects of the medicine?

4. *Statistics on Employment and Disabilities:* As Chapter 2 indicates, it is extremely difficult to determine with precision just how many individuals meet the definition of disability under the various discrimination statutes. In the area of employment, however, it was estimated by the Centers for Disease Control and Prevention in 2008 that approximately 19 million Americans have a work disability, i.e., a disability lasting six or more months. (U.S. Census Bureau, CPS, March 2008).

5. *Major Life Activity of Working and Back Problems:* Before the ADAAA was enacted, it was settled that for a plaintiff to prove that she was substantially limited in the major life activity of working, she would have to demonstrate that her impairment significantly restricted her "ability to perform either a class of jobs or a broad range of jobs in various classes as compared to the average person having comparable training, skills and abilities." The inability to perform a single, particular job was insufficient to prove a substantial limitation in the major life activity of working. 29 C.F.R. § 1630.2(j)(3). The ADAAA instructed the EEOC to rewrite its regulations that define "substantially limits" as "significantly restricted" because this standard, which is based on *Toyota*, is too high. The ADAAA also includes "working" in the definition of "major life activity." It is unclear, however, whether the ADAAA rejects the former requirement that a plaintiff relying on the major life activity of working demonstrate that the impairment limits the individual's ability to perform either a class of jobs or a broad range of jobs in various classes.

The highest number of complaints to the EEOC based on disability involve back problems. From 1997 to 2008, 12.2% of charges filed with the EEOC were orthopedic and structural impairments of the back. See *ADA Charge Data by Impairments/Bases-Receipts*, FY 1997-FY2008, EEOC. A good example of a case addressing this issue is *Partlow v. Runyon*, 826 F. Supp. 40 (D.N.H. 1993), which involved an auto mechanic with an extensive history of back problems. When Mr. Partlow applied for a position as a mechanic with the United States Postal Service, he was rejected (after passing the pre-employment road-test) when his pre-employment medical exam led to a conclusion that his long history of chronic back problems was incompatible with the demands of the job. In the case, the court addresses the claim that he was covered by the Rehabilitation Act because the Postal Service "regarded him" as disabled. The critical fact in deciding that Partlow did not meet the statutory definition was that there was still a wide range of employment available to him. However, courts have disagreed about whether lifting restrictions substantially limit a major life activity. In *Thompson v. Holy Family Hosp.*, 121 F.3d 537 (9th Cir. 1997), the court found that lifting restrictions did not substantially limit a major life activity. However, in *Frix v. Florida Tile Indus., Inc.*, 970 F. Supp. 1027 (N.D. Ga. 1997), the court found that lifting restrictions prevented an employee from performing an entire class of jobs and therefore substantially limited the major life activity of working. For additional cases, see LAURA ROTHSTEIN & JULIA ROTHSTEIN, DISABILITIES AND THE LAW § 4.9 (2009). See also *Daugherty v. Sajar Plastics, Inc.*, 544 F. 3d 696 (6th Cir. 2008) (back injury case where the plaintiff could not prove that he was incapable of, or his employer perceived him to be incapable of, doing a class of jobs or a broad range of jobs in various classes); *Cook v. Union Pac. R.R. Co.*, 2008 U.S. Dist. LEXIS 80005 (D. Neb. 2008).

6. *HIV/AIDS as Per Se Disability:* After *Bragdon v. Abbott, supra*, it was not as easy as one would have thought to prove that a person with asymptomatic HIV was a person with a disability because *Abbott* relied on proof from the plaintiff that she was substantially limited in the major life activity of reproduction. Many other plaintiffs were not able to provide this proof. Because the ADAAA has amended the ADA to define "major life activity" to include bodily functions and includes the immune system as a "bodily function," it should be much easier to prove that asymptomatic HIV substantially limits a major life activity. Because HIV is a defect of the immune system, it is likely that it will be considered a per se disability in the future.

7. *ADA Employment Cases Often Fail on Definitional Issues:* A 1998 survey by the American Bar Association concluded that employers prevail in 92 percent of the court rulings where a final decision was reached. Of significance in the survey is the conclusion that the judiciary is defining disability in a very restrictive manner, one that was probably not intended by the drafters and supporters of the ADA.

Study Finds Employers Win Most ADA Title I Judicial and Administrative Complaints, 22 MENTAL & PHYSICAL DISABILITY L. REP. 403 (May-June 1998). Later studies found the plaintiffs' win rates range between 2% and 7.9%. This information relating to judicial outcomes may underestimate the success of the ADA. In a study of EEOC resolutions, settlement statistics and survey responses by Human Resources personnel, Professor Sharona Hoffman concluded that employers are "reasonably responsive" to claimants' informal internal requests for accommodation, EEOC conciliations, and settlement requests. See Sharona Hoffman, *Settling the Matter: Does Title I of the ADA Work?* 59 ALA. L. REV. 305 (2008). The ADAAA has amended the ADA and the Rehabilitation Act to encourage courts to define disability broadly. See Ch. 2, *supra*.

QUESTIONS

1. *Traynor v. Turnage*, 485 U.S. 535 (1988), involved eligibility for a government benefit where distinctions are based on whether the disability is self imposed. The Court treated differing types of alcoholism differently. Would the courts be likely to apply similar reasoning to cases involving obesity? What about impairments resulting from cigarette smoking? What about a mobility impairment that resulted from skydiving? Should it matter whether the issue is eligibility for a benefit as compared to discrimination in employment? What are the costs of sorting out the levels of individual fault in these cases?

2. In *Bragdon v. Abbott*, in Chapter 2, the Supreme Court held that the plaintiff who was HIV-positive, but asymptomatic, was protected because she had demonstrated that she was substantially limited in the major life activity of reproduction. In reading the decision, determine whether the *Bragdon* holding applies to employment, or whether it was limited to discrimination in health care services? Also, does it protect all individuals with HIV or only that particular individual?

[3]   Drug and Alcohol Users and Persons with Contagious and Infectious Diseases

HYPOTHETICAL PROBLEM 3.1

Read the following hypothetical problem before reading the materials that follow on alcoholics and illegal drug use and the ADA, as well as the conduct/disability distinction. After reading the materials, analyze this problem.

3.1. Janet Jones and Sam Sneck work for Duosoftcorp, a company that develops software for personal computers. Janet and Sam develop software for university online courses. They are good friends and occasionally go out for beers after work. Janet develops a serious drinking problem. She drinks in bars every evening after work for four or five hours. She then goes home and drinks well into the night. Sam does not drink much when he accompanies Janet to the bars. Sam had suffered from bouts of depression for two years before meeting Janet, and takes medication daily. At times, Sam's medication makes him sleepy, and he finds it difficult to get to work on time. At other times, Sam is irritable at work because of his depression.

On at least two occasions, Sam has snapped at the supervisor, Louisa Lopez, when she asked how his work was coming along. On occasion, Janet finds it difficult to get to work on time. She is also very tired at work, occasionally nodding off at her desk. She never drinks at work or before going to work.

Louisa Lopez speaks to Janet and Sam and tells them that they have to arrive at work on time. She tells Sam that she does not appreciate his irritable moods, and that he will be on probation if he arrives late again or continues to show irritability. She tells Janet that she must come to work better-rested, and that the company does not tolerate employees' falling asleep at work. She says that the company will place Louisa on probation if she arrives late again or if she falls asleep at her desk again. Sam tells Louisa that he suffers from depression, that the medication makes it difficult for him to arrive on time and that his depression makes him irritable. Janet tells Louisa that she thinks she has a drinking problem.

1. Assume that the meetings with Louisa occurred after the effective date of the ADAAA. Analyze whether Sam and Janet are individuals with disabilities under the ADA.

2. Assuming that Janet is an individual with a disability under the ADA, consider the options open to Louisa Lopez and Duosoftcorp. Discuss whether Louisa can place Janet on probation if she arrives late to work or falls asleep again. What information would you like to know before answering this question? Should Louisa explore the possibility of rehabilitation with Janet? If Janet goes to her lawyer after the meeting and Louisa has not explored rehabilitation with Janet, what advice should the lawyer give Janet?

3. Assuming that Sam is an individual with a disability under the ADA, consider the options open to Louisa Lopez and Duosoftcorp. Discuss whether Louisa can place Sam on probation if he arrives late or snaps at her again. What information would a lawyer need to know before answering this question? Should Louisa explore the possibility of a reasonable accommodation with Sam? If Sam went to his lawyer after the meeting above with Louisa, what advice should the lawyer give him?

4. Sam gets upset at Louisa and brings a gun to work. What advice should the in-house counsel at Duosoftcorp give Louisa about her options with Sam?

Use of Illegal Drugs and Alcohol

The ADA, 42 U.S.C. § 12114(a), states that the "term 'qualified individual with a disability' shall not include any employee or applicant who is currently engaging in the illegal use of drugs, when the covered entity acts on the basis of such use." Exceptions to this exclusion include an individual who has successfully completed a supervised drug rehabilitation program and is no longer engaging in the illegal use of drugs or is one who is participating in a drug rehabilitation program and is no longer using illegal drugs.

Section 12114(c) permits a covered entity to prohibit the illegal use of drugs and the use of alcohol at work, to require that employees not be under the influence of alcohol or engage in illegal use of drugs at work, to require that employees behave in conformance with the requirements of the Drug Free Workplace Act of 1988, and to hold "an employee who engages in the illegal use of drugs or who is an alcoholic to the same qualification standards for employment or job performance and behavior that such entity holds other employees, even if any unsatisfactory performance or behavior is related to the drug use or alcoholism of such employee . . . ."

The Rehabilitation Act has a similar exclusion for current illegal drug users. 29 U.S.C. § 705(10). It also excludes from the definition of "individual with a disability" an alcoholic whose current use of alcohol prevents the individual from performing the duties of the job or whose presence would constitute a direct threat to the property or safety of others. 29 U.S.C. § 705(2)(D).

Contagious and Infectious Diseases

Except for food handlers, the ADA does not have a specific provision that exempts employers from employing persons with infectious or communicable disease. 42 U.S.C. § 12113(d)(1), (2) & (3). It does, however create a defense that an individual shall not pose a direct threat to the health or safety of others in the workplace. 42 U.S.C. § 12113(b).

The Rehabilitation Act states that for employment under federal contracts and federal grant programs, an individual is excluded from protection of the Act if he or she has a currently contagious disease or infection and would constitute a direct threat to the health or safety of others or by virtue of the disease or infection would not be able to perform the job duties. 29 U.S.C. § 705(20)(D).

Theoretically, there is no reason for any of the statutes to separately define how users of drugs and alcohol and individuals with communicable and infectious diseases are to be treated for purposes of discrimination. That is because someone who is unable to perform the essential requirements of the job or who is a threat to the health or safety of self or others would be considered not to be otherwise qualified and thus would not be protected against adverse treatment.

Mostly for political reasons, Congress has developed statutory clarifications of how users of drugs and alcohol and individuals with communicable diseases are to be treated. These separate definitions began in 1974 with an amendment to the Rehabilitation Act and evolved to the current definition. The ADA treatment is similar to that of the Rehabilitation Act. Chapter 2 discusses this issue. Some of the cases in this chapter will illustrate how these definitions have been applied.

The decision in *Burch v. Coca-Cola Co.*, 119 F.3d 305 (5th Cir. 1997), demonstrates the difference between alcohol addiction (which is covered) and inebriation (which is not). The Supreme Court has also addressed whether a neutral no-rehire policy has a discriminatory impact on rehiring of rehabilitated drug addicts. See *Raytheon Co. v. Hernandez*, 540 U.S. 44 (2003), *infra*.

The *Maddox* case excerpt is an interesting fact setting that clarifies when an individual who is alcoholic is not protected from adverse employment action. The case should be kept in mind when considering defenses, later in this chapter.

MADDOX v. UNIVERSITY OF TENNESSEE
62 F.3d 843 (6th Cir. 1995)

BAILEY BROWN, CIRCUIT JUDGE.

I. *Facts*

On February 17, 1992, Doug Dickey, acting as UT's athletic director, extended to Maddox an offer of employment as an assistant football coach. The position did not carry tenure and was terminable at will in accordance with the policies of the Personnel Manual. As part of the hiring process, Maddox completed an application. On the line after "Describe any health problems or physical limitations, which . . . would limit your ability to perform the duties of the position for which you are applying," Maddox wrote "None." In response to the question "have you ever been arrested for a criminal offense of any kind?" Maddox replied "No." These responses were not accurate. According to what Maddox alleges in this lawsuit, he suffers from the disability of alcoholism. Also, Maddox was arrested three times before 1992, once for possession of a controlled substance, and twice for driving a motor vehicle under the influence of alcohol. As to the first answer, Maddox claims that it is in fact correct because "it has never affected my coaching ability . . . I never drank on the job." As to the second question, Maddox claims that another university employee, Bill Higdon, advised him not to include the information concerning his prior arrests on the application.

On May 26, 1992, after Maddox began working at UT, a Knoxville police officer arrested Maddox and charged him with driving under the influence of alcohol and public intoxication. According to newspaper reports, the accuracy of which is not contested, Maddox backed his car across a major public road at a high rate of speed, almost striking another vehicle. When stopped by the officer, Maddox was combative, his pants were unzipped, and he refused to take a breathalyzer. He also lied to the arresting officer, stating that he was unemployed. This incident was highly publicized, and UT was obviously embarrassed by the public exposure surrounding the event.

Maddox entered an alcohol rehabilitation program at a UT hospital after his arrest. UT first placed Maddox on paid administrative leave. In June 1992, however, Dickey and then Head Coach Johnny Majors determined that the allegations were accurate and jointly issued a letter notifying Maddox that his employment was being terminated. They testified that termination was necessary because of: 1) the criminal acts and misconduct of Maddox; 2) the bad publicity surrounding the arrest; and 3) the fact that Maddox was no longer qualified, in their minds, for the responsibilities associated with being an assistant coach.[8] Both Dickey and Majors deny that they were aware that Maddox was an alcoholic or

---

[8] In addition to the "coaching" responsibilities on the field, Coach Majors described other essential job functions of an assistant coach as: 1) the recruitment of high school football players, 2) serving as a positive role model for athletes on the university's football team, 3) counseling players on various issues, including the use and abuse of alcohol and drugs, and 4) promoting a positive image as a representative of not only the football program but the university as well.

that Maddox's alcoholism played any part in the decision to discharge him. Nevertheless, Maddox brought this action alleging that the termination was discriminatory on the basis of his alcoholism in violation of his rights under the Rehabilitation Act and the ADA. . . .

II. *Analysis*

. . . [O]ur analysis focuses on whether Maddox is "otherwise qualified" under the Act and whether he was discharged "solely by reason of" his disability. The burden of making these showings rests with Maddox.

In support of its motion for summary judgment, UT contended that both factors weighed in its favor. First, Dickey and Majors contended that they did not even know that Maddox was considered an alcoholic in making both the decision to hire and fire him. Moreover, they contended that Maddox was discharged, not because he was an alcoholic, but because of his criminal conduct and behavior and the significant amount of bad publicity surrounding him and the school. UT alternatively contended that Maddox is nevertheless not "otherwise qualified" to continue in the position of assistant football coach.

The district court granted UT's motion for summary judgment, specifically holding that UT did not discharge Maddox solely by reason of his disability. The court found it beyond dispute that Maddox's discharge resulted from his misconduct rather than his disability of alcoholism. . . . The affidavit testimony of Mr. Dickey and Mr. Majors is clear on the point that it was this specific conduct, not any condition to which it might be related, which provoked the termination of Mr. Maddox's employment. As a result, the court found it unnecessary to decide the alternative ground of whether Maddox was "otherwise qualified."

Maddox contends that the district court erred in distinguishing between discharge for misconduct and discharge solely by reason of his disability of alcoholism. Maddox claims that he has difficulty operating a motor vehicle while under the influence of alcohol and therefore he characterizes drunk driving as a causally connected manifestation of the disability of alcoholism. Thus, Maddox contends that because alcoholism caused the incident upon which UT claims to have based its decision to discharge him, UT in essence discharged him because of his disability of alcoholism. In support, Maddox relies on *Teahan v. Metro-North Commuter R.R., Co.*, 951 F.2d 511, 516–17 (2d Cir. 1991), in which the Second Circuit held that a Rehabilitation Act plaintiff can show that he was fired "solely by reason of" his disability, or at least create a genuine issue of material fact, if he can show that he was fired for conduct that is "causally related" to his disability. In *Teahan*, the defendant company discharged the plaintiff because of his excessive absenteeism. The plaintiff responded by claiming that his absenteeism was caused by his alcoholism and therefore protected under the Rehabilitation Act. The district court disagreed and granted summary judgment for the employer because, the court found, Teahan was fired for his absenteeism and not because of his alcoholism. The Second Circuit reversed the district court's grant of summary judgment on appeal, however, rejecting the court's distinction between misconduct (absenteeism), and the disabling condition of alcoholism. The court presumed that Teahan's absenteeism resulted from his alcoholism and held that one's disability should not be distinguished from its consequences in determining whether he was fired "solely by reason" of his disability. Thus, Maddox argues that, in the instant case, when UT acted on the basis of the conduct allegedly caused by the alcoholism, it was the same as if UT acted on the basis of alcoholism itself.

We disagree and hold that the district court correctly focused on the distinction between discharging someone for unacceptable misconduct and discharging someone because of the disability. As the district court noted, to hold otherwise, an employer would be forced to accommodate all behavior of an alcoholic which could in any way be related to the alcoholic's use of intoxicating beverages; behavior that would be intolerable if engaged in by a sober employee or, for that matter, an intoxicated but non-alcoholic employee.

Despite *Teahan*, a number of cases have considered the issue of misconduct as distinct from the status of the disability. In *Taub v. Frank*, 957 F.2d 8 (1st Cir. 1992), the plaintiff Taub, a heroin addict, brought suit against his former employer, the United States Postal Service, alleging discriminatory discharge under the Rehabilitation Act. The Post Office discharged Taub after he was arrested for possession of heroin for distribution. . . . The First Circuit . . . held that Taub could not prevail on his Rehabilitation Act claim because his discharge resulted from his misconduct, possession of heroin for distribution, rather than his disability of heroin addiction. The court reasoned that addiction-related criminal conduct is simply too attenuated to extend the Act's protection to Taub.

The conduct/disability distinction was also recognized by the Fourth Circuit in *Little v. F.B.I.*, 1 F.3d 255 (4th Cir. 1993). In *Little*, the F.B.I. discharged the plaintiff, known by his supervisors to be an alcoholic, after an incident in which he was intoxicated on duty. . . . The Fourth Circuit affirmed [the district court], noting as an additional basis that the plaintiff's employment was not terminated because of his handicap. The court noted, "based on no less authority than common sense, it is clear that an employer subject to the . . . [Rehabilitation] Act must be permitted to terminate its employees on account of egregious misconduct, irrespective of whether the employee is handicapped."

Moreover, language within the respective statutes makes clear that such a distinction is warranted. Section 706(8)(C) of the Rehabilitation Act states: " '[I]ndividuals with a disability' does not include any individual who is an alcoholic whose current use of alcohol prevents such individual from performing the duties of the job in question or whose employment, by reason of such current alcohol abuse, would constitute a direct threat to property or the safety of others." Likewise, the ADA specifically provides that an employer may hold an alcoholic employee to the same performance and behavior standards to which the employer holds other employees "even if any unsatisfactory performance is related to the alcoholism of such employee." These provisions clearly contemplate distinguishing the issue of misconduct from one's status as an alcoholic.

At bottom, we conclude that the analysis of the district court is more in keeping with the purposes and limitations of the respective Acts, and therefore, we decline to adopt the Second Circuit's reasoning in *Teahan*. Employers subject to the Rehabilitation Act and ADA must be permitted to take appropriate action with respect to an employee on account of egregious or criminal conduct, regardless of whether the employee is disabled. In the instant case, for example, while alcoholism might compel Maddox to drink, it did not compel him to operate a motor vehicle or engage in the other inappropriate conduct reported. Likewise, suppose an alcoholic becomes intoxicated and sexually assaults a coworker? We believe that it strains logic to conclude that such action could be protected under the Rehabilitation Act or the ADA merely because the actor has been diagnosed as an alcoholic and claims that such action was caused by his disability.

Maddox alternatively contends that even if UT has successfully disclaimed reliance on his disability in making the employment decision, the district court nevertheless erred in determining that Maddox had produced no evidence that the reasons articulated by UT were a pretext for discrimination. A Rehabilitation Act plaintiff may demonstrate pretext by showing that the asserted reasons had no basis in fact, the reasons did not in fact motivate the discharge, or, if they were factors in the decision, they were jointly insufficient to motivate the discharge.

Maddox first alleges that Dickey and Majors knew that Maddox was an alcoholic. Setting aside for a moment the legal significance of this statement, it is not supported factually in the record. Dickey and Majors, the district court found, had no knowledge of Maddox's previous criminal history prior to the DUI arrest involved here. In fact, Dickey states that if he had known of the prior arrests, he would not have hired him. More importantly, however, assuming that Dickey and Majors did know of Maddox's alcoholism, as we must do on a summary judgment motion, that knowledge does not translate into evidence that alcoholism was the basis for the termination. To the contrary, the university stated that the criminal conduct and the bad publicity surrounding it formed the basis of the termination, which we conclude is sufficient to motivate the discharge.

Maddox also claims that he knew of other coaches in the football program who drank alcohol in public and who were arrested for DUI but who were not discharged. This point is also irrelevant. Whether Maddox had such knowledge is immaterial. There is no evidence in the record establishing that Majors or Dickey had knowledge of the public intoxication of any other coach, or failed to reprimand or terminate any coach who they knew to have engaged in such behavior.

Maddox finally contends that UT's conclusion that he is no longer qualified to be an assistant coach at UT is without merit. Maddox claims that his misconduct did not affect his "coaching" responsibilities because an assistant coach's duties are limited to the practice and playing fields, and do not comprise of serving as a counselor or mentor to the players or serving as a representative of the school. Maddox relies on the fact that none of these functions were explained to him in his formal job description.

We first note that this allegation seems more appropriate for determining whether he was "otherwise qualified" rather than whether he was discharged because of his disability. Nevertheless, Maddox's position is simply unrealistic. It is obvious that as a member of the football coaching staff, Maddox would be representing not only the team but also the university. As in the instant case, UT received full media coverage because of this "embarrassing" incident. The school falls out of favor with the public, and the reputation of the football program suffers. Likewise, to argue that football coaches today, with all the emphasis on the misuse of drugs and alcohol by athletes, are not "role models" and "mentors" simply ignores reality.

The district court's grant of summary judgment in favor of the defendants is AFFIRMED.

NOTES

1. *History of Falling Off the Wagon:* Courts have been consistent that individuals with records of recently using illegal drugs are not protected under the ADA. In *McDaniel v. Mississippi Baptist Med. Ctr.*, 869 F. Supp. 445 (S.D. Miss. 1994), the court held that an individual who has a relapse of a drug abuse problem within two months of treatment violated the employer's official policy and was not covered under the ADA. See also *Wormley v. Arkla, Inc.*, 871 F. Supp. 1079 (E.D. Ark. 1994). The courts also have been fairly consistent in upholding employer policies that employees can be discharged or otherwise disciplined for violating rules about drinking on the job or working under the influence of alcohol.

The court in *Wormley v. Arkla, Inc.*, 871 F. Supp. 1079 (E.D. Ark. 1994), held that merely entering into a rehabilitation program does not convert a current drug user into a person with a disability who is protected under Section 12210(b)(2) of the ADA. Further, the court in *Wolfe v. Jurczyski*, 241 A.D.2d 88 (3d Dep't 1998), held that an employer did not violate the ADA by discharging an employee who had agreed to obtain treatment for alcoholism but had failed to do so. Also, as in *Peyton v. Otis Elevator Co.*, 72 F. Supp. 2d 915 (N.D. Ill. 1999), an employer was not liable for firing an employee who is an alcoholic, if the same conduct by another employee would result in discharge. Neither was the employer liable for failure to rehire him after he voluntarily completed an alcoholism treatment program.

What is not clearly resolved is to what degree an employer is obligated to reasonably accommodate an employee with a drug or alcohol problem. In *Gallagher v. Catto*, 778 F. Supp. 570 (D.D.C. 1991), the court held that an individual with a substance abuse problem first must be offered counseling, then must be given a "firm choice" between rehabilitation and discipline if the counseling offer was rejected, and may be terminated only if that is the only viable option and other measures fail. It is far from certain that all courts would apply this standard. The obligation to accommodate may depend on what conduct led up to the disciplinary action in the first place. For example, in *Sizemore v. Department of Rehabilitation & Corrections*, 63 Ohio Misc. 2d 319, 629 N.E.2d 1096 (1992), the court held that the employer did not have a duty to accommodate the employee's alcoholism where the discharge was based on driving under the influence of alcohol. Federal employers have higher duties, however.

In *Vandenbroek v. PSEG Power Conn., L.L.C.*, 2009 U.S. Dist. LEXIS 18320 (D. Conn. 2009), the court held that under the ADA, employers are not required to make reasonable accommodation for employees who are illegal drug users or alcoholics if the disability affects job performance. But the right to participate in an alcohol or drug rehabilitation program as a reasonable accommodation may exist under state law. See, e.g., *Lamke v. Sunstate Equip. Co.*, 387 F. Supp. 2d 1044 (N.D. Cal. 2004).

For citations to other cases on this issue, see LAURA ROTHSTEIN & JULIA ROTHSTEIN, DISABILITIES AND THE LAW § 4.09 (2009).

2. *Conduct/Disability Distinction.* The court in *Maddox* states that courts recognize a difference between discrimination based on conduct related to a disability and discrimination based on the disability itself. Not all courts would agree to so general a proposition. In *Humphrey v. Memorial Hospitals Ass'n*, 239 F.3d 1128 (9th Cir. 2001), *infra*, the plaintiff had obsessive compulsive disorder (OCD) and had difficulty arriving at work on time and many absences. With reference to the conduct/disability distinction, the court stated:

> In this case, MHA's stated reason for Humphrey's termination was absenteeism and tardiness. For purposes of the ADA, with a few exceptions, conduct resulting from a disability is considered to be part of the disability, rather than a separate basis for termination. The link between the disability and termination is particularly strong where it is the employer's failure to reasonably accommodate a known disability that leads to discharge for performance inadequacies resulting from that disability. Humphrey has presented sufficient evidence to create a triable issue of fact as to whether her attendance problems were caused by OCD. In sum, a jury could reasonably find the requisite causal link between a disability of OCD and Humphrey's absenteeism and conclude that MHA fired Humphrey because of her disability.

The court wrote, in footnote 18:

> The text of the ADA authorizes discharges for misconduct or inadequate performance that may be caused by a "disability" in only one category of cases — alcoholism and illegal drug use: "[An employer] may hold an employee who engages in the illegal use of drugs or who is an alcoholic to the same qualification standards for employment or job performance and behavior that such entity holds other employees, even if any unsatisfactory performance or behavior is related to the drug use or alcoholism of such employee." 42 U.S.C. § 12114(c)(4). In line with this provision, we have applied a distinction between disability-caused conduct and disability itself as a cause for termination only in cases involving illegal drug use or alcoholism. In *Newland*, however, we suggested that an additional exception might apply in the case of "egregious and criminal conduct" regardless of whether the disability is alcohol- or drug-related. *See Newland v. Dalton*, 81 F.3d 904, at 906 (9th Cir. 1995) ("Attempting to fire a weapon at individuals is the kind of egregious and criminal conduct which employees are responsible for regardless of any disability."). Any such exception would not be applicable to Humphrey's absences or tardiness.

To what extent does the conduct/disability distinction make sense in *Maddox* and the other cases it cites precisely because they deal with misconduct relating to alcohol or illegal drug use and because there is a statutory provision permitting employers to hold employees to the same performance or behavior standards to which the employer holds other employees "even if any unsatisfactory performance is related to the alcoholism of such employee"? Should there be a judge-created exception for egregious criminal conduct that *Humphrey* mentions in its discussion of *Newland*? If there is an egregious criminal conduct exception, does that undercut the argument that the conduct/disability distinction should be limited to the statutory-based exceptions (i.e., the provisions on employees' use of drugs and alcohol)?

3. *HIV/AIDS as a Disability:* The Supreme Court in *School Board v. Arline*, 480 U.S. 273 (1987), expressly declined to decide whether AIDS or AIDS-related conditions constitute disabilities under the Rehabilitation Act. Congress resolved this issue when it passed the Americans with Disabilities Act, which not only addressed the issue with respect to the ADA, but also amended the Rehabilitation Act to clarify coverage on this issue. The legislative history makes it clear that individuals with contagious and infectious diseases were to be protected. The ADA and the Rehabilitation Act provide that individuals who pose a direct threat to the health or safety of others in the workplace are not protected. 42 U.S.C. § 12113(b); 29 U.S.C. § 706(8)(D).

The ADA also provides for the Secretary of Health and Human Services to study infectious and communicable diseases and list those that present a risk in the food handling industry. Individuals with these conditions may be legally excluded from food handling jobs. 42 U.S.C. § 12113(e). HIV has not been found to be a risk in the food handling industry. The ADA specifically states that it will not preempt state, county, or local laws regarding food handling by persons with infectious or communicable diseases. However, such local laws must be made pursuant to the list from the Secretary of Health and Human Services, and must include the requirement of reasonable accommodation. 42 U.S.C. § 12113(e).

In *Bragdon v. Abbott*, 524 U.S. 624 (1998), the Court held that the plaintiff was covered because reproduction is a major life activity, and that this plaintiff had demonstrated that her HIV status substantially limited her in that activity. The Court did not hold that all individuals with asymptomatic HIV are covered, so that issue has yet to be completely decided. The case of *Bragdon v. Abbott* is excerpted in Chapter 2.

Later in this chapter, the issues of direct threat and reasonable accommodation are discussed in the context of cases involving employees with HIV and other contagious and infectious diseases. For citations to other employment cases involving individuals with impairments, see LAURA ROTHSTEIN & JULIA ROTHSTEIN, DISABILITIES AND THE LAW § 4.09 (2009).

B QUALIFICATION STANDARDS UNDER THE ADA AND REHABILITATION ACT: TECHNICAL STANDARDS AND MEDICAL EXAMINATIONS AT THE HIRING STAGE

Section D of this chapter contains a discussion of when an individual with a disability is qualified to perform the essential job functions. This section focuses on evaluative mechanisms for making that determination. The issues are what tests and evaluations may be performed and when. The question of what must be done with the evaluation results in the case of medical information is also addressed.

This section addresses three stages of the employment process. At the *preem-ployment* stage the individual is a mere applicant. At this stage the ADA prohibits all medical inquiries into whether the individual has a disability or the nature and extent of the disability. Medical questionnaires and examinations are not permitted. The *post-offer* or *preplacement* stage occurs after a conditional offer of employment has been made. At this stage medical examinations and inquiries are permitted. The examinations are referred to as *employment entrance examinations* or *preplace-ment* examinations. Once the employee has been hired, this stage is referred to as the *post-hiring stage*. The employer may conduct limited examinations at this point. The specifics of these provisions are discussed below. See 42 U.S.C. § 12112(d).

HYPOTHETICAL PROBLEM 3.2

Read the following hypothetical problem before reading the materials on preemployment and postemployment medical examinations and inquiries. After reading the materials, analyze this problem.

Risa Kim applies for a job as a teacher's aide at the public school district in Fallow, Ohio. Her interviewer explains that there is a job open in the first grade classroom. She tells Risa, a 48-year-old woman, that "you have to be very energetic to do this job" and asks Risa if she has any disabilities that would prevent her from "chasing first graders around." Is this question legal at this stage? If not, explain how the interviewer could have posed a legal question?

1. Assume that the interviewer does not ask the question above, but instead offers Risa a job conditioned upon the principal's approval and her passing the security check and the medical examination. The interviewer sends Risa to get a blood test for the medical exam. Is this legal?

2. Assume that the interviewer offers Risa a job conditioned upon taking a blood and a urine test. When the blood test comes back, it shows that Risa is a hemophiliac. The school district refuses to hire Risa. Is it legal to ask Risa to take a urine test at this stage? Why? Why not? Is it legal to ask Risa to take the blood test at this stage? Why? Why not? Once the school district has the information about Risa's hemophilia, is it legal to refuse to hire her because of her hemophilia? Explain. See 29 C.F.R. § 1630.14(b)(3).

3. Assume that Risa has been employed as a teacher's aide and she is diagnosed with HIV. The school has a mandatory blood test for all employees at the end of each school year. Is the mandatory blood test for all employees legal? Under what conditions might it be legal? Assume that Risa has been employed as a teacher's aide in a private school and her son, who is 15 years old and lives with her, is diagnosed with HIV. The school hears about Risa's son's diagnosis because Risa had told the teacher she worked with who then told her principal. Is it legal for the school to refuse to renew her contract because of the fear that Risa will be absent many days caring for her son? See 42 U.S.C. § 12112(b)(4).

[1]   Preemployment

Issues at the preemployment stage include whether the qualification standards, tests, and other criteria are discriminatory; the administration of tests required for employment; and preemployment inquiries. Before hiring for a specific position, it is useful in many situations for employers to develop and maintain written job descriptions listing essential functions. The ADA does not require employers to do this, however. 29 C.F.R. § 1630.2(n). See also 56 Fed. Reg. 35,743 (July 26, 1991) (Interpretive Guidance on Title I of the ADA).

Essential functions are fundamental job duties considered to be essential for reasons such as the following: 1) the position exists to perform that function; 2) a limited number of employees are available among whom that responsibility can be distributed; 3) the function is so specialized that the person is being hired for the expertise to perform the job. 29 C.F.R. § 1630.2(n)(2).

It is unlawful for employers to use standards, criteria, or methods of administering evaluations that are not job-related and consistent with business necessity, where such practices have the effect of discriminating on the basis of disability or perpetuate such discrimination. 29 C.F.R. § 1630.7. Related to this requirement is the mandate that covered employers may not use qualification standards, tests, and other selection criteria that screen out or tend to screen out an individual with a disability or a class of individuals with disabilities, unless this can be shown to be job-related and consistent with business necessity. 29 C.F.R. § 1630.10. Employment tests are to be administered to reflect abilities that are intended to be measured, and they may not reflect impairments except where such skills are the factors to be measured. 29 C.F.R. § 1630.11.

Related to the issue of qualification standards is the question of what employer inquiries and medical examinations are permitted at the preemployment stage. The following case involves a discussion of the types of qualifications employers can set with respect to a particular position. Following this case, the issue of preemployment inquiries is addressed.

STUTTS v. FREEMAN
694 F.2d 666 (11th Cir. 1983)

FAY, CIRCUIT JUDGE:

Facts

The uncontroverted facts show that in 1971, Mr. Stutts was hired by TVA as a laborer at TVA's Colbert Steam Plant in Colbert County, Alabama where he worked temporarily until 1973 when he was hired on a permanent basis. In 1979, Mr. Stutts applied for an opening with TVA in an apprenticeship training program to become a heavy equipment operator. His application was denied on the basis of a "low" score on the General Aptitude Test Battery (GATB), a test used by TVA to predict the probability of success of an applicant in the training program.

Mr. Stutts has been diagnosed as having the condition of dyslexia, which impairs his ability to read. The record indicates that this disability renders Mr. Stutts incapable of reading beyond the most elementary level, and leads to an inability to perform well on written tests such as the GATB. There is evidence that Mr. Stutts was evaluated by doctors and tested with non-written tests after receiving results of his GATB test and was judged to have above average intelligence, coordination and aptitude for a position as a heavy equipment operator. TVA tried to obtain the results of these non-verbal tests in connection with Mr. Stutts' application for the apprenticeship training program, but was unable to do so. Attempts to persuade the testing service to give Mr. Stutts an oral GATB were unsuccessful because scoring on the written GATB is based on standardized and uniform testing conditions and cannot be accurately translated from an oral test. Despite TVA's knowledge of and unsuccessful efforts to obtain alternate forms of evaluation, Mr. Stutts' nonselection was based solely on his low score on the written GATB test.

Discussion

The policy underlying the Rehabilitation Act of 1973 is clear — "to promote and expand employment opportunities in the public and private sectors for handicapped individuals." 29 U.S.C. § 701(8). Both parties agree that Mr. Stutts is a handicapped individual and that the main hiring criteria — the GATB test — could not accurately reflect Mr. Stutts' abilities. There is considerable evidence supporting Mr. Stutts' contention that he is fully capable of performing well as a heavy equipment operator and we find a genuine issue as to whether or not he could successfully complete the training program, either with the help of a reader or by other means. Congress has clearly directed entities in its sphere of control to make efforts to expand employment opportunities for handicapped persons. TVA has not satisfied its obligation under the statute by merely asking for results of alternate testing methods and accepting a rejection.

We do not hold that Mr. Stutts must be given a position as a heavy equipment operator, nor do we hold that he must be admitted into the training program. We do hold that when TVA uses a test which cannot and does not accurately reflect the abilities of a handicapped person, as a matter of law they must do more to accommodate that individual than TVA has done in regard to Mr. Stutts. TVA argues that their efforts on behalf of Mr. Stutts showed that he received better treatment than a non-handicapped applicant. TVA sought to have a non-written GATB test given to Mr. Stutts. They tried to obtain the results of other examinations and tests given Mr. Stutts after his dyslexic condition was discerned. But the fact remains that these efforts were not successful. In the final analysis TVA made its decision based on the GATB test. TVA's unsuccessful efforts do not amount to "reasonable accommodation" of the handicapped as required by 45 C.F.R. § 84.12 (1981).

When an employer like TVA chooses a test that discriminates against handicapped persons as its sole hiring criterion, and makes no meaningful accommodation for a handicapped applicant, it violates the Rehabilitation Act of 1973.

The summary judgment is set aside and the case *Remanded* for further proceedings consistent with this opinion.

NOTES AND QUESTIONS

1. Are courts more likely to be deferential to the employer when the employment position involved is a professional one, such as teaching or the practice of medicine, than where the employment position is skilled labor? Why or why not?

2. In *Ricci v. DeStefano*, 2009 U.S. LEXIS 4945 (June 29, 2009), the city of New Haven used a written test to count 60% toward selection of firefighters for promotions. Although black firefighters passed the test, they did not perform well enough to earn any of the promotions, according to the formula that was previously agreed upon with the union. The city refused to promote the white and Latino firefighters who were successful in the promotion process because it feared that the test had a disparate impact on black firefighters and that the black firefighters would sue the city. The city had not had the test validated before administering it, but it had hired a consultant to establish the test who spent time studying the responsibilities of the positions to which the successful test takers would be promoted. The white and Latino firefighters then sued the city under Title VII of the 1964 Civil Rights Act for race discrimination because the city failed to promote them because of their race. The United States Supreme Court held that once a city gives a test, it cannot then decide not to promote the successful candidates because of their race merely because it fears that the test had a disparate impact on members of another race. It may, however, refuse to promote based on the test if it can demonstrate that it has a strong basis in evidence that it would lose a disparate impact suit. What behavior on the part of cities and other defendants using employment tests do you believe this opinion will evoke? Should employers discontinue the use of written tests for jobs such as firefighters? Does this opinion affect the decision in *Stutts* where the plaintiff was applying for a job as a heavy equipment operator? How should Stutts' lawyer distinguish *Ricci*? What arguments will the employer make in response?

3. The ADA prohibits an employer from asking an applicant disability-related questions or conducting medical examinations before making a conditional offer of employment. After a conditional offer of employment, the employer may require that the applicant submit to disability-related questions and medical examinations if all applicants for that particular position are treated the same way. Once the information is gleaned, it must be kept confidential. While the employer does not have to prove that the disability-related questions and medical examinations of an applicant are job-related for the job in question and consistent with business necessity, the employer may not use the information to discriminate on the basis of the individual's disability.

4. In response to these provisions, the EEOC promulgated a regulation that states:

> A covered entity may make preemployment inquiries into the ability of an applicant to perform job-related functions, and/or may ask an applicant to

describe or to demonstrate how, with or without reasonable accommodation, the applicant will be able to perform job-related functions.

29 C.F.R. § 1630.14(a).

5. On October 10, 1995, the EEOC provided guidance of this issue in the *EEOC Enforcement Guidance: Preemployment Disability-Related Questions and Medical Examinations*. http://eeoc.gov/policy/docs/preemp.html. One of the most difficult complex issues is what questions may be asked at the pre-employment stage. While some have criticized the guidance as exceeding the scope of the statute, and the guidance does not have the force of law, many courts give EEOC guidances some deference.

6. The guidance defines a disability-related question by stating:

> At the pre-offer stage, an employer cannot ask questions that are likely to elicit information about a disability. This includes directly asking whether an applicant has a particular disability. It also means that an employer can not ask questions that are closely related to disability.

> On the other hand, if there are many possible answers to a question and only some of those answers would contain disability-related information, that question is not disability-related.

7. *Questions the Employer May Ask.* At the pre-offer stage, the Guidance states that the employer may ask:

- Whether the applicant can perform the job functions

- To describe or demonstrate how the applicant would perform a job function (as long as all applicants are asked this question)

- If not all other applicants for the job category are asked to describe or demonstrate how they would perform the job function, the employer may ask a person with a known disability how he or she would perform the job function. The applicant has a "known" disability if it is obvious or if the applicant has told the employer that he of she has a disability.

8. The Guidance covers the permissibility of a number of other types of questions the employer may ask such as whether the individual will need a reasonable accommodation, attendance records, drug use, third party inquiries about medical conditions, etc.

9. The Guidelines also define a "medical examination" as a procedure or test that seeks information about an individual's physical or mental impairments or health. The Guidelines provide factors to be considered in determining whether a procedure falls within the definition of a medical examination. They further clarify that physical agility and physical fitness tests, where the applicant demonstrates a job-related task, are not considered medical examinations. Therefore, such tests may be administered at the preoffer stage.

Psychological examinations that are not medical in nature are permitted. A psychological test is medical if it "provides evidence that would lead to identifying a mental disorder or impairment." Personality and intelligence tests are considered medical exams, and may not be permitted at the preoffer stage. Whether other, more general tests of aptitude, interest, and personality are considered medical examinations depends on a number of factors, such as whether the test is intended to identify underlying psychological conditions and whether trained health professionals are needed to administer and interpret the results of the test. Polygraphs, which purport to measure whether individuals are telling the truth, are not generally considered to be medical examinations. Some inquiries made before polygraphs are given, however, such as asking about prescription medications taken, are impermissible inquiries. In a separate piece of legislation, however, preemployment polygraph testing has been made illegal in all but a few situations. See the Employee Polygraph Protection Act of 1988, 29 U.S.C. §§ 2001-2009. Whether a vision test to diagnose the ability to see is a medical examination depends on the type of test and the circumstances.

In a case involving medical exams, the Seventh Circuit in *Karraker v. Rent-A-Center, Inc.*, 411 F.3d 831 (7th Cir. 2005), held that the MMPI test (which is intended in part to identify mental illness) is a medical exam, subject to the ADA requirement that it be administered to current employees only if it is job-related and consistent with business necessity.

Drug tests are not considered medical examinations under the ADA, and therefore may be given at any time, including the preoffer stage. 42 U.S.C. § 12114(d)(1). The problem with drug tests is that to account for "cross-reactivity" (i.e., the positive test results caused ingestion of substances other than illegal drugs), it is necessary to inquire into the prescription medications taken by the individual. Although inquiry into what prescription medications an individual is taking is generally prohibited at the preoffer stage (because they often indicate a medical disability), EEOC has taken the position that after an initial positive result on a drug test, an employer may ask an applicant about any prescription medications that he or she is taking. Alcohol tests are considered medical examinations if they are invasive, i.e., when such tests would require the drawing of blood, urine, or breath.

In spite of the fact that the Guidelines provide a number of examples for each guideline, these Guidelines have been viewed as complex and confusing by some, and are likely targets for litigation.

10. If a third party is asked to respond to questions about disabilities, what is the potential liability? For example, if a prior employer is asked whether the individual has any impairments that may interfere with the job, how should that third party respond if the party is aware that the employee had undergone treatment or therapy, but is unaware whether there are any current performance problems as a result? Are there confidentiality issues under the ADA? Are there privacy issues protected by tort law? If so, what are they? What possible causes of action might the plaintiffs have?

11. Would the questions asked of Maddox when he was hired be permissible preemployment practices under the ADA?

12. In *Armstrong v. Turner Industries, Inc.*, 141 F.3d 554 (5th Cir. 1999), an applicant for a pipefitter's position was given a written, skill-based qualification exam. In addition, he was required to fill out paperwork, which included a question about whether he had any of approximately seventy ailments. General questions about medical history were also included. Worker's compensation history was also requested. Applicants were then given medical exams while background checks to verify medical information were conducted. During Armstrong's background check, it was determined that he had possible asbestos exposure about three years before the application. Turner Industries rejected Armstrong's application because he had falsified the questionnaire asking about asbestos exposure.

While it was determined in judicial proceedings that the questions were impermissible preemployment inquiries in violation of the ADA, the appellate court declined to award damages or injunctive or declaratory relief. The court found that there was no compensable injury. Under the "make whole" purpose of civil rights statutes, the court found that the violation of preemployment inquiry prohibitions does not give rise to an action for damages. With respect to the injunctive relief, the court found that the plaintiff had not demonstrated a likelihood that he would seek employment with Turner again.

Given this court's reluctance to remedy this violation, are there any incentives for employers to eliminate such impermissible inquiries and activities, if the potential remedies are so limited? What incentives are there for plaintiff attorneys to take cases involving these facts?

[2] Preplacement Examinations

The cases regarding preplacement examinations involve situations where the employer has made an initial determination that an individual is eligible for the job and has made a conditional offer. At this stage, the employer often wishes to conduct medical examinations and drug, psychological, or intelligence testing. The EEOC Guidelines referred to previously address Post-Offer, Preemployment Examinations and Inquiries. The Guidance states:

> [T]he ADA permits employers to make disability-related inquiries and to require medical examinations after a conditional offer of employment has been extended, but before the individual has started work.

The statutory language of the ADA provides:

> [A] covered entity may require a medical examination after an offer of employment has been made to a job applicant and prior to the commencement of the employment duties of such applicant, and may condition an offer of employment on the results of such examination.

42 U.S.C. § 12112(d)(3).

To be permissible, such employment entrance exams must meet the following requirements: 1) all entering employees are subject to such exams regardless of disability; 2) information on the medical condition or history is collected and maintained on separate forms and in separate medical files and is treated confidentially; and 3) the results of such exams are used only for job-related reasons. 42 U.S.C. §§ 12112(d)(3), 12112(b)(6).

Exceptions to the confidentiality requirements are permitted where supervisors and managers need to be informed because of necessary work restrictions or accommodations, where first aid and safety personnel need to be informed because of potential emergency treatment concerns, and where government officials investigating compliance request such relevant information. 42 U.S.C. § 12112(d)(3)(B).

An incongruous result of the language in the ADA seems to permit preplacement exams that are *not* job-related to be given, so long as the results of such exams are not used to discriminate. 29 C.F.R. § 1630.14(b)(3). For example, HIV testing appears to be permitted at the preplacement stage, although the results could not be used to exclude an employee.

Because drug testing is specifically excluded from the definition of "medical examination," it can occur at any stage. 42 U.S.C. § 12114(d)(1) & (2).

NOTE

Non-ADA Preplacement Tests: For a discussion of laws applicable to preplacement medical examinations, see MARK A. ROTHSTEIN ET AL., EMPLOYMENT LAW § 1.22 (4th ed. 2009). This discussion includes constitutional law, the Occupational Safety and Health Act, Title VII of the Civil Rights Act of 1964, state statutes, and common law.

The following case explains the policy behind requiring an offer of employment before conducting a medical exam, and demonstrates the importance of timing of medical examinations at the pre-employment stage.

LEONEL v. AMERICAN AIRLINES
400 F.3d 702 (9th Cir. 2005)

FISHER, CIRCUIT JUDGE:

Appellants Walber Leonel, Richard Branton and Vincent Fusco, who all have the human immunodeficiency virus ("HIV"), applied for flight attendant positions with American Airlines ("American"). American interviewed them at its Dallas, Texas, headquarters and then issued them conditional offers of employment, contingent upon passing both background checks and medical examinations. Rather than wait for the background checks, American immediately sent the appellants to its on-site medical department for medical examinations, where they were required to fill out medical history questionnaires and give blood samples. None of them disclosed his HIV-positive status or related medications. Thereafter, alerted by the appellants' blood test results, American discovered their HIV-positive status and rescinded their job offers, citing their failure to disclose information during their medical examinations.

The appellants now challenge American's medical inquiries and examinations as prohibited by the Americans with Disabilities Act ("ADA"), 42 U.S.C. § 12101 *et seq.* (1999). They argue that American could not require them to disclose their personal medical information so early in the application process — before the company had completed its background checks such that the medical examination would be the only remaining contingency — and thus their nondisclosures could not be used to disqualify them.

I.

Leonel, Branton and Fusco all participated in American's standard application process for flight attendant positions. They first responded to questions in telephone surveys and then provided more extensive information about their language abilities, previous employment and educational backgrounds in written applications. Based on these initial screening forms, American selected the appellants to fly to the company's headquarters in Dallas, Texas, for in-person interviews. Leonel, Branton and Fusco flew to Dallas at American's expense. There, they participated first in group interviews, and then, having been chosen to progress in the application process, in individual interviews. Immediately after these interviews, members of the American Airlines Flight Attendant Recruitment Team extended the appellants conditional offers of employment.

After making the offers, American Airlines representatives directed the appellants to go immediately to the company's medical department for medical examinations.

There, the appellants were instructed to fill out series of forms. One informed them that they would be asked to provide a urine specimen which would be tested for certain specified drugs, and solicited their written consent for the testing. This form also required them to list all medications they were taking at the time. None of the appellants listed the medications he was taking for HIV.

American also required the appellants to complete medical history forms that asked whether they had any of 56 listed medical conditions, including "blood disorder." Here, too, none of the appellants disclosed his HIV-positive status.

At some point during the appellants' medical examinations, nurses drew blood samples. Unlike the urinalysis procedure, American did not provide notice or obtain written consent for its blood tests. Nor did any of the company's representatives disclose that a complete blood count would be run on the blood samples. When Fusco explicitly asked what his blood would be tested for, a nurse replied simply, "anemia."

A few days after the appellants' medical examinations, American's medical department ran CBC tests on their blood samples and discovered that they had elevated "mean corpuscular volumes" ("MCV"s). The appellants' expert, Dr. Shelley Gordon, testified that approximately 99% of individuals with HIV have elevated MCV levels. As nothing in any of the appellants' medical histories indicated cause for an elevated MCV level, American wrote the appellants and requested explanations for the results. All of the appellants, acting through their personal physicians, then disclosed their HIV-positive status and medications.

After learning that the appellants had HIV, American's medical department sent forms to the company's recruiting department stating, as final dispositions, that the appellants "[did] not meet AA medical guidelines." The forms also specified the ground on which the appellants had failed to meet the medical guidelines as "nondisclosure." The recruiting department then wrote the appellants and rescinded their conditional offers of employment.

Upon learning that their offers had been rescinded, the appellants brought individual suits against American. [T]he United States District Court for the Northern District of California . . . consolidated the appellants' cases and, in April 2003, granted summary judgment for American on all claims.

II.

We review de novo the district court's summary judgment order. We must determine "whether, viewing the evidence in the light most favorable to the nonmoving party, there are any genuine issues of material fact and whether the district court correctly applied the relevant substantive law."

III.

The federal Americans with Disabilities Act regulate[s] the *sequence* of employers' hiring processes. [It] prohibit[s] medical examinations and inquiries until *after* the employer has made a "real" job offer to an applicant. *See* 42 U.S.C. § 12112(d) (1999). "A job offer is real if the employer has evaluated all relevant non-medical information which it reasonably could have obtained and analyzed prior to giving the offer." Equal Employment Opportunity Commission, ADA Enforcement Guidance: Preemployment Disability-Related Questions and Medical Examinations, 17 (1995) ("EEOC's ADA Enforcement Guidance"). To issue a "real" offer under the ADA, therefore, an employer must have either completed all non-medical components of its application process or be able to demonstrate that it could not reasonably have done so before issuing the offer.

This two-step requirement serves in part to enable applicants to determine whether they were "rejected because of disability, or because of insufficient skills or experience or a bad report from a reference." When employers rescind offers made conditional on both non-medical and medical contingencies, applicants cannot easily discern or challenge the grounds for rescission. When medical considerations are isolated, however, applicants know when they have been denied employment on medical grounds and can challenge an allegedly unlawful denial.

The two-step structure also protects applicants who wish to keep their personal medical information private. Many hidden medical conditions, like HIV, make individuals vulnerable to discrimination once revealed. The ADA allow[s] applicants to keep these conditions private until the last stage of the hiring process. Applicants may then choose whether or not to disclose their medical information once they have been assured that as long as they can perform the job's essential tasks, they will be hired.

American's offers to the appellants here were by their terms contingent not just on the appellants successfully completing the medical component of the hiring process but also on the completion of a critical *non-medical* component: undergoing background checks, including employment verification and criminal history checks. Other courts have found offers not real, and medical examinations thus unlawfully premature, when an offer remained contingent upon a polygraph test, personal interview and background investigation. Here, it is undisputed that American's offers were subject to both medical and non-medical conditions when they were made to the appellants and the appellants were required to undergo immediate medical examinations. Thus the offers were not real, the medical examination process was premature and American cannot penalize the appellants for failing to disclose their HIV-positive status — unless the company can establish that it could not reasonably have completed the background checks before subjecting the appellants to medical examinations and questioning. It has not done so.

As justification for accelerating the medical examinations, American's Manager of Flight Service Procedures, Julie Bourk-Suchman, explained that the company found it important to minimize the length of time that elapsed during the hiring process in order to compete for applicants. But competition in hiring is not in itself a reason to contravene the ADA's mandates to defer the medical component of the hiring process until the non-medical component is completed. The appellants' expert, Craig Pratt, a management consultant, testified that it is "the accepted practice for employers to complete such [background] checks *prior to* conducting a preemployment medical examination of the job applicant." American has not established that there are no reasonable alternatives that would address its asserted need for expedited hiring of flight attendants that would avoid jumping medical exams ahead of background checks.

American also suggests that it conducted the medical examinations before completing the background checks for the convenience of the applicants. As Bourk-Suchman put it, "it's not a business reason. It just has to do with the applicants and trying to have it be convenient for them." Not only does this testimony undercut American's meeting-competition rationale, applicants' supposed convenience does not justify reordering the hiring process in a manner contrary to that set out by the ADA. Congress [has] determined that job applicants should not be required to undergo medical examinations before they hold real offers of employment. American — even if well-intentioned — cannot avoid that mandate simply because it believes doing so will be more convenient for its applicants.

In short, at the summary judgment stage, American has failed to show that it could not reasonably have completed the background checks and so notified the appellants before initiating the medical examination process. It might, for example, have performed the background checks before the appellants arrived in Dallas, kept them in Dallas longer, flown them to Dallas twice, performed the medical examinations at satellite sites or relied on the appellants' private doctors, as it did for explanation of the CBC results. American may be able to prove that alternatives such as these were not feasible and that it could not reasonably have implemented the sequence prescribed by the ADA, but on this record it has not. Without such proof, American cannot require applicants to disclose personal medical information — and penalize them for not doing so — before it assures them that they have successfully passed through all non-medical stages of the hiring process.

American argues in the alternative that even if the offers were not real, the company did not violate the ADA because it *evaluated* the appellants' non-medical information before it considered their medical information. Bourk-Suchman asserted that American's recruiting department actually performed the background check for each appellant before receiving the medical department's disposition of "does not meet AA guidelines." As we have explained, however, the statutes regulate the sequence in which employers collect information, not the order in which they evaluate it.

The words of the ADA plainly address when employers can make medical inquiries or conduct medical examinations. *See* 42 U.S.C. § 12112(d)(3) (1999) ("A covered entity may require a medical examination after an offer of employment has been made . . . and prior to the commencement of the employment duties."). As the EEOC has stated explicitly, "an employer may not ask disability-related questions or require a medical examination, *even if* the employer intends to shield itself from the answers to the questions or the results of the examination until the post-offer stage." EEOC's ADA Enforcement Guidance, 2.

The focus on the collection rather than the evaluation of medical information is important to the statutes' purposes. [T]he ADA deliberately allow[s] job applicants to shield their private medical information until they know that, absent an inability to meet the medical requirements, they will be hired, and that if they are not hired, the true reason for the employer's decision will be transparent. American's attempt to focus on the evaluation rather than the collection of medical information squares with neither the text nor the purposes of the statutes. Whether or not it looked at the medical information it obtained from the appellants, American was not entitled to get the information at all until it had completed the background checks, unless it can demonstrate it could not reasonably have done so before initiating the medical examination process. As to that question, we hold that there are material issues of fact that require reversal of summary judgment on the appellants' claims that American's hiring process violated the ADA. We therefore reverse summary judgment. . . .

NOTES AND QUESTIONS

1.   Why was the timing of the medical test important?

2.   The Swine Flu, also known as the H1N1 virus, has caused considerable concern around the world and has been named a pandemic. See http://pandemicflu.gov. The EEOC has written advice for employers to explain legal ways to react to the H1N1 virus under the ADA. See http://eeoc.gov/factsh1n1flu.html

3.   *Back Problems and EEOC Complaints.* In *City of Lacrosse Police & Fire Comm'n v. Labor & Industry Rev. Comm'n,* 139 Wis. 2d 740, 407 N.W.2d 510 (1987), the plaintiff sued the police department for failing to hire him after making a conditional offer of employment. After accepting the offer, he underwent a physical examination in which his back strength was tested on a "Cybex" machine. The purpose of the test was to measure his back strength and flexibility of his back muscles. He received a "B" rating based on the Cybex test which recommended an exercise program before beginning heavy labor. The defendant refused to hire him

because of the "B" rating. He subsequently retook the Cybex test and received an "A" rating, but the police department refused to hire him despite notice of the "A" result and notice that the Cybex test had not been validated for certain back movements. In plaintiff's lawsuit, the defendant argued that it had a right to establish tests and to assure that the individual applying for a job would not constitute a direct threat to health of the individual or of others. The Wisconsin Supreme Court, however, rejected these arguments, holding that the issue was whether the defendant perceived the plaintiff as an individual with a disability. The Court held that the plaintiff was a qualified individual for the job. It held that there was no evidence that demonstrated that the plaintiff could not adequately perform his job as a police officer because there was insufficient evidence in the record that the Cybex machine was a reliable indicator of the adequacy of performance.

The decision in this case is significant, because back problems account for the largest percentage of complaints filed with the EEOC. See Note 6 in Section [A][2], *supra*. Employer costs for back injuries also are the highest workers' compensation expense, and therefore, employers have a great incentive to try to screen out individuals with the potential for back problems, even though doing so may be unlawful in most instances. After *Sutton* and *Toyota*, most individuals claiming they were individuals with disabilities who had back injuries have not been successful in proving that they have a disability. Will the ADAAA amendments change the way courts and employers view back injuries?

4. *Job-relatedness. Genetic testing.* In *Norman-Bloodsaw v. Lawrence Berkeley Laboratory*, 135 F.3d 1260 (9th Cir. 1998), the plaintiffs sued the defendant alleging violations of privacy and the ADA based on pre-employment blood and urine testing in which the employer tested for intimate medical conditions such as syphilis, sickle cell trait and pregnancy without the plaintiffs' consent. When alleging an ADA violation, the plaintiffs argued that the employer was permitted to use only tests that were job related and consistent with business necessity. The Ninth Circuit rejected this argument, holding that at the pre-employment stage, the employer may engage in testing after the conditional offer of employment, and such testing does not have to be job related and consistent with business necessity. The job-related and business necessity test is applied, however, when testing of current employees takes place. *Norman-Bloodsaw* is interesting because the testing for sickle cell trait would likely constitute testing for genetic information. Subsequent to this case, Congress passed the Genetic Information Nondiscrimination Act (GINA), which prohibits testing for genetic information. A number of state laws also prohibit testing for genetic information. See *infra* pp. 256–258 for a description of GINA.

[3]   Posthiring

Once an individual has been hired, there are two circumstances under which medical examinations may be given. These are where the exam is job-related, such as OSHA-mandated medical examinations, and where it is voluntary, including employee assistance programs. 42 U.S.C. § 12112(d)(4). The provisions regarding the treatment of medical information that were discussed in the previous section also apply at this stage.

Many employers, especially large ones, have employee assistance programs (EAPs). Employees are encouraged to avail themselves of these voluntary programs. Although the programs may differ in specifics, they often feature health promotion activities (e.g., exercise, weight loss, smoking cessation), counseling (e.g., marital, stress reduction), and substance abuse treatment (e.g., drugs and alcohol). Employers have found that EAPs are cost-effective by contributing to a happier, more stable, and healthier work force. Nevertheless, there are concerns that EAPs may run afoul of the ADA and other discrimination laws. Employees are told that information provided to EAP counselors will be kept "confidential." Nevertheless, when information is learned that could threaten public safety or the employer's business, such as a drug abuse problem in an employee with a safety-sensitive job, the counselor is faced with a dilemma. If confidentiality is breached, then the employee trust on which the EAP is built may be irrevocably lost. If confidentiality is not breached, then a tragedy could result. One possible solution is for the EAP counselors to advise employers about their disclosure policies in advance. As yet, there have been few cases.

The following case discusses when employers may make medical inquiries of their employees, and sets the standard for the employer's proof of business necessity.

CONROY v. NEW YORK STATE DEPT. OF CORRECTIONAL SERVICES
333 F.3d 88 (2d Cir. 2003)

POOLER, CIRCUIT JUDGE:

Defendants the New York State Department of Correctional Services ("DOCS") appeal from the judgment of the District Court denying DOCS's motion for summary judgment and granting Plaintiff-Appellee Belinda Fountain's motion for summary judgment. The DOCS sick leave policy requires employees to submit general diagnoses as part of a medical certification procedure following certain absences. Fountain challenged the policy as violating Americans with Disabilities Act ("ADA") prohibitions against inquiries into the disabilities of a current employee. She sought a declaratory judgment that the relevant parts of DOCS's policy violates (sic) the statute and injunctive relief preventing DOCS from requiring her to comply with the general diagnosis requirement. Although we agree with the district court that the policy falls within the ADA's general prohibition, we find that genuine issues of material fact preclude summary judgment on the issue of the business necessity defense provided for in the statute. We therefore affirm in part and vacate and remand in part.

BACKGROUND

This case involves a DOCS Sick Leave Directive ("the Directive" or "the Policy") which Plaintiff contends violates the ADA's prohibition against inquiry into the disabilities of current employees. DOCS is the New York State agency responsible for the maintenance of correctional facilities throughout the state.

Under some circumstances, the challenged Directive requires that an employee bring medical certification upon returning to work after an absence. The certification must include a brief general diagnosis that is "sufficiently informative as to allow [DOCS] to make a determination concerning the employee's entitlement to leave or to evaluate the need to have an employee examined by [the Employee Health Service] prior to returning to duty." Certification is usually not required for absences of less (sic) than four days. However, the Directive indicates that "in exceptional cases, a supervisor may exercise the right to request certification for any absence charged to sick leave or family sick leave regardless of duration." The Directive then references another DOCS directive, Controlling Unexcused and Unauthorized Absences, which reads "medical certification may be required of any employee who requests to charge an absence to sick leave credits." However, this second directive may limit the reach of the requirement by clarifying that only "employees suspected of attendance abuse may be required to furnish medical certification for all absences which they seek to charge to sick leave." In addition to these directives, a memorandum indicates that when an employee has an attendance problem, and informal discussions have not remedied the problem, the supervisor should have a formal discussion with the employee, and instruct the employee that certification will be required for all future absences regardless of the duration of the illness. The guidelines for identifying attendance abusers explicitly leave a great deal of discretion in the hands of lower management.

Fountain is a Corrections Officer employed by DOCS since 1989. Fountain suffers from asthma and severe pulmonary obstructive disease. She has asked DOCS for accommodation because of these conditions in the past. Fountain filed a complaint about the Policy with the Equal Employment Opportunity Commission ("EEOC") in August of 1998. She sought declaratory relief that the general diagnosis requirement violates the ADA and an injunction prohibiting DOCS from requiring her to submit a general diagnosis.

The District Court denied DOCS's motion for summary judgment, and granted Fountain's cross-motion for summary judgment. Thus, the court concluded that the certification requirement was an "inquiry" under the ADA. The court then interpreted the Policy as "allowing inquiry after only a single day's absence from work." It found that because the Policy was not "based upon a reasonable expectation that the inquiry into the protected information would reveal that the employee was unable to perform work related functions or was a danger to the health and safety of the workplace," the Policy did not fall within the ADA's business necessity exception.

This appeal followed.

DISCUSSION

Fountain brings her challenge under a provision of the ADA which provides:

A covered entity shall not require a medical examination and shall not make inquiries of an employee as to whether such employee is an individual with a disability or as to the nature or severity of the disability, unless such examination or inquiry is shown to be job-related and consistent with business necessity.

42 U.S.C. § 12112(d)(4)(A).

I. Fountain Has Standing To Challenge the Policy under 42 U.S.C. § 12112(d)(4)(A)

Before turning to the merits of the case, we address DOCS's contentions that Fountain is not a proper plaintiff to challenge the Policy. Because of their jurisdictional nature, we may of course address standing arguments, even where, as here, they were not raised in the district court. DOCS's basic contention is that because Fountain has disabilities of which it is already aware, the ADA authorizes it to make certain types of inquiries. Therefore, DOCS maintains, Fountain has suffered no injury from the Policy and she lacks standing to bring this challenge on her own behalf or on behalf of others.

Since Fountain has already revealed her disability to and requested accommodation from DOCS, DOCS argues that it can permissibly make inquiries into her disability that are "necessary to the reasonable accommodation process." 29 C.F.R. Pt. 1630, App. § 1630.14(c). This argument fails because DOCS submitted no evidence in the district court to support the conclusion that either the Policy generally or inquiries of Fountain specifically were intended to aid in the accommodation process. This alleged justification for the medical certification requirement appears nowhere in any of the directives or memorandums submitted as evidence, but only in DOCS's appellate briefs.

Besides contending that its inquiries are a legitimate part of the accommodation process, DOCS also relies more generally on the ADA's approval of inquiries to determine "the ability of an employee to perform job-related functions." 42 U.S.C. § 12112(d)(4)(B). DOCS notes that one purpose of the sick leave Policy is to provide information necessary to ensure that a corrections officer can safely return to work. Therefore, it argues that application of the Policy to Fountain, who testified to her physical limitations, is acceptable because of a legitimate need to verify her ability to perform the sometimes strenuous functions of a corrections officer. But a general diagnosis is not a narrowly tailored inquiry into the employee's ability to carry out her job-related functions. Accordingly, this argument is also unavailing.

Finally, DOCS argues that Fountain suffers no injury because even if DOCS's inquiries into Fountain's health result from the broad sick leave policy rather than an appropriately narrow inquiry, they will still reveal no information that DOCS could not obtain through legitimate inquiries. We disagree. Certainly DOCS's broad policy requiring general diagnoses may sometimes reveal information about Fountain's known disabilities that DOCS could obtain through a focused inquiry. But inquiries made pursuant to the Policy could also reveal disabilities of Fountain previously unknown to DOCS.

There is no evidence in the record that Fountain has any disabilities other than those already known to DOCS. Therefore, this raises the question whether only those employees with unknown disabilities may challenge an impermissible medical inquiry or examination under the ADA. Other circuit courts have found that a plaintiff need not prove a disability in order to challenge a medical examination or inquiry under 42 U.S.C. § 12112(d).

We agree with our sister circuits that a plaintiff need not prove that he or she has a disability unknown to his or her employer in order to challenge a medical inquiry or examination under 42 U.S.C. § 12112(d)(4)(a). In contrast to other parts of the ADA, the statutory language does not refer to qualified individuals with disabilities, but instead merely to "employees." 42 U.S.C. § 12122(d)(4)(A). Moreover, we agree with the Tenth Circuit that "it makes little sense to require an employee to demonstrate that he has a disability to prevent his employer from inquiring as to whether or not he has a disability." We also note that EEOC enforcement guidance supports this interpretation. See Enforcement Guidance on Disability-Related Inquiries and Medical Examinations of Employees Under the Americans with Disabilities Act (ADA), (EEOC, July 27, 2000), available at http://www.eeoc.gov/docs/guidance-inquiries.html ("This statutory language makes clear that the ADA's restrictions on inquiries and examinations apply to all employees, not just those with disabilities."). Even when they are not formally promulgated as regulations, such agency publications are "at least a body of experience and informed judgment to which courts and litigants may properly resort for guidance."

We conclude that Fountain has sufficiently alleged that she has suffered and will continue to suffer the injury prohibited by the ADA's prohibition against inquiries into disability. She is therefore an appropriate plaintiff to bring this challenge to the Policy under 42 U.S.C. § 12112(d)(4)(A).

II.   The Policy Falls within the ADA's General Prohibition

DOCS contends that requiring medical certification is not an "inquiry" prohibited under 42 U.S.C. § 12112(d)(4)(A). The ADA does not forbid all medical inquiries, but only those "as to whether such employee is an individual with a disability or as to the nature or severity of the disability." DOCS argues that because the Policy only requires a "general" diagnosis, its inquiries are insufficient to reveal whether the employee has a disability. Fountain argues that the Policy falls within the statute, because the inquiries would tend to reveal an employee's disability.

A DOCS memorandum described the types of diagnoses that would be acceptable under the Policy:

> Medical documentation need only to be sufficiently informative as to allow [DOCS] to make a determination concerning the employee's entitlement to leave or to evaluate the need to have an employee examined by [the Employee Health Service] prior to returning to duty. If a doctor's note states that an employee is "under my care", this is not sufficient. However, if a doctor's note, for example, states "recuperating from minor surgery" or "treated for a minor foot injury", this is a sufficient diagnosis.

It is clear that even what DOCS refers to as a "general diagnosis" may tend to reveal a disability. We hold that requiring a general diagnosis is sufficient to trigger the protections of the ADA under this provision and that summary judgment in Fountain's favor was appropriate on this element.

Few courts have interpreted this provision, but one court has found that a requirement that employees disclose what prescription drugs they use is a prohibited inquiry, since such a policy would reveal disabilities (or perceived disabilities) to employers. Similarly, we believe that since general diagnoses may expose individuals with disabilities to employer stereotypes, the Policy implicates the concerns expressed in these provisions of the ADA.

Even where a diagnosis alone is not sufficient to establish that an employee is disabled, the diagnosis may give rise to the perception of a disability, and discrimination on the basis of a perceived disability is also prohibited by the ADA.

The EEOC's own definition of a "disability-related inquiry" further undercuts DOCS's argument:

> *What is a "disability-related inquiry"? (Question 1)*
>
> A "disability-related inquiry" is a question that is likely to elicit information about a disability, such as asking employees about: whether they have or ever had a disability; the kinds of prescription medications they are taking; and, the results of any genetic tests they have had.
>
> Disability-related inquiries also include asking an employee's co-worker, family member, or doctor about the employee's disability.
>
> Questions that are not likely to elicit information about a disability are always permitted, and they include asking employees about their general well-being; whether they can perform job functions; and about their current illegal use of drugs.

See Questions and Answers: Enforcement Guidance on Disability-Related Inquiries and Medical Examinations of Employees Under the Americans with Disabilities Act (ADA), (EEOC, July 27, 2000), available at http://www.eeoc.gov/docs/qanda-inquiries.html (emphasis in original). DOCS's requirement of a general diagnosis is much more akin to the examples of prohibited inquiries than to inquiries into general well-being or ability to perform job functions.

III. Genuine Issues of Material Fact Exist as to whether the Policy Is Job-related and Consistent with Business Necessity

The ADA creates an exception to generally prohibited inquiries when "such . . . inquiry is shown to be job-related and consistent with business necessity." 42 U.S.C. § 12112(d)(4)(A). DOCS contends that, based on this exception, summary judgment for Fountain was inappropriate and that we should instead grant summary judgment in its favor. We agree that the facts, when viewed in the light most favorable to DOCS, create genuine issues of material fact with respect to the business necessity defense. On the other hand, we do not think that the facts, viewed in the light most favorable to Fountain, can support a grant of summary judgment for DOCS. Therefore, we remand for further discovery and, if necessary, for trial.

A. The business necessity standard

Relatively little case law concerns the proper interpretation of business necessity in this context. Even fewer cases involve generally applicable policies like DOCS's rather than individualized inquiries. Faced with this limited case law, the district court reasoned:

> In order to fall within the [business necessity] exception . . ., the employer must demonstrate some reasonable basis for concluding that the inquiry was necessary. That is, the employer must show that it had some reason for suspecting that the employee, or class of employees, would be unable to perform essential job functions or would pose a danger to the health and safety of the workplace.

The court concluded that "no reasonable factfinder could conclude that an inquiry triggered by a single day's absence from work is the type of reasonable expectation" that it had described.

We believe that the district court's approach here was generally sound. Nonetheless, because we find that material issues of genuine fact exist, a remand is necessary to allow the district court to reconsider DOCS's business necessity defense.

The Ninth Circuit has held that the "the business necessity standard is quite high, and is not [to be] confused with mere expediency." We endorse the views of the Ninth Circuit and hold that in proving a business necessity, an employer must show more than that its inquiry is consistent with "mere expediency." An employer cannot simply demonstrate that an inquiry is convenient or beneficial to its business. Instead, the employer must first show that the asserted "business necessity" is vital to the business. For example, business necessities may include ensuring that the workplace is safe and secure or cutting down on egregious absenteeism. The employer must also show that the examination or inquiry genuinely serves the asserted business necessity and that the request is no broader or more intrusive than necessary. The employer need not show that the examination or inquiry is the only way of achieving a business necessity, but the examination or inquiry must be a reasonably effective method of achieving the employer's goal.

The case law on inquiries directed towards individual employees thus demonstrates that courts will readily find a business necessity if an employer can demonstrate that a medical examination or inquiry is necessary to determine 1) whether the employee can perform job-related duties when the employer can identify legitimate, non-discriminatory reasons to doubt the employee's capacity to perform his or her duties (such as frequent absences or a known disability that had previously affected the employee's work) or 2) whether an employee's absence or request for an absence is due to legitimate medical reasons, when the employer has reason to suspect abuse of an attendance policy. These two business necessity justifications are merely illustrative, and an employer may be able to demonstrate other business necessities. For example, here, DOCS has suggested that it must guard against the severe disruption that would result from infectious diseases being spread through the staff or inmate population. On remand, DOCS will have the chance to submit evidence that it has a legitimate and vital need to protect against this occurrence, and that its general diagnosis requirement helps to alleviate the concern.

QUESTIONS

1. What are DOCS' legitimate reasons for making medical inquiries?

2. Why would it be more difficult to prove business necessity if the policy affects a broad group of "attendance abuses"?

In the following case, the court addressed whether an employer could inquire into matters other than technical qualifications at the postemployment stage.

ROE v. CHEYENNE MOUNTAIN CONFERENCE RESORT, INC.
124 F.3d 1221 (10th Cir. 1997)

HOLLOWAY, CIRCUIT JUDGE.

I

Plaintiff-appellant Jane Roe . . . is an accounts manager for the defendant-appellee Cheyenne Mountain Conference Resort (hereinafter CMCR or simply defendant). . . . In the summer of 1995, CMCR adopted a new Drug and Alcohol Testing Policy (the Policy). On July 7, 1995, CMCR's employees, including plaintiff, were given copies of the Policy and told that their written consent to the Policy and their adherence to its requirements were mandatory for their continued employment.

Preceding its provisions on drug and alcohol testing, the Policy contained these provisions:

The following rules on alcohol, drugs and illegal substances are the policy of CMCR. Adherence to these rules is a condition of employment:

1. Employees are strictly prohibited from possessing, consuming, or being under the influence of alcohol during work hours or on company property.

2. Employees are strictly prohibited from possessing, consuming, or being under the influence of any illegal drugs, controlled substance, any prescribed or over the counter drug or medication that has been illegally obtained or is being used in an improper manner.

3. Employees must report without qualification, all drugs present within their body system [sic]. Further, they must remain free of drugs while on the job. They must not use, possess, conceal, manufacture, distribute, dispense, transport, or sell drugs while on the job, in CMCR vehicles or on CMCR property or to the property to which they have been assigned in the course

of their employment. Additionally, prescribed drugs may be used only to the extent that they have been reported and approved by an employee supervisor and that they can be taken by the employee without risk of sensory impairment and/or injury to any person or employee.

The Policy provided further for drug and alcohol testing of employees in various situations. . . . As it pertains to this lawsuit, the only significant aspect of the drug and alcohol testing under the Policy is a provision for random testing to which any employee might be subjected. The Policy does not state whether blood or urine testing is contemplated, nor how samples will be taken.

Plaintiff refused to sign the consent form. Alleging that some of the requirements of the Policy were so unreasonable and intrusive as to violate her legal rights, she instead initiated this action to enjoin its implementation . . . . Plaintiff . . . alleged that the prescription drug disclosure provisions violated section 102 of the Americans With Disabilities Act, 42 U.S.C. § 12112(d)(4), which prohibits a medical examination or inquiries as to whether an employee is an individual with a disability, unless shown to be job-related and consistent with business necessity.

B

Defendant also contends that federal jurisdiction is lacking because Roe has no standing to pursue an ADA claim. This is so, defendant argues, because Roe has not shown that she is a person with a "disability" as that term is defined in the Act. This argument has no merit. The argument is miscast because it actually does not go to plaintiff's standing, and the particular challenge plaintiff has brought does not require her to meet the statutory definition of a person with a disability.

First, whether a plaintiff suing under the ADA comes within the definition of a person with a disability is simply not a question of standing but of whether an essential element of the claim can be established. Standing concerns whether the plaintiff "is entitled to have the court decide the merits of the dispute or of particular issues." Thus,

> [a] plaintiff has standing when (1) she has suffered an injury in fact, (2) there is a causal connection between the injury and the conduct complained of, and (3) it is likely that the injury will be redressed by a favorable decision.

Plaintiff has sufficiently alleged each of these elements.

Second, plaintiff's ability to maintain the particular ADA claim she has alleged does not require her to prove that she is an individual with a disability. As the district judge aptly observed, adopting defendant's position would defeat the very purpose of prohibiting disability related inquiries: "It makes little sense to require an employee to demonstrate that he has a disability to prevent his employer from inquiring as to whether or not he has a disability." We also agree with the district court's reasoning that this common sense rejection of defendant's argument is consistent with the statutory language.

The ADA explicitly prohibits employers from making disability-related inquiries of employees, unless the inquiry is job-related or consistent with business necessity. 42 U.S.C. § 12112(d)(4)(A). This provision applies to all employees. Unlike suits based on a failure to provide a reasonable accommodation, this provision is not limited to qualified individuals with disabilities. Cf. 42 U.S.C. § 12112(b)(5)(A).

Defendant further argues that plaintiff lacks standing because she faced no real or immediate threat of injury due to the fact that defendant suspended enforcement of the policy pending the district court's determination of the controversy. This argument does indeed address one of the elements of standing, but we believe that plaintiff has at all times been threatened with injury in fact. We note that this argument is essentially the same as defendant's third purportedly jurisdictional argument, which is that jurisdiction is lacking because the controversy is moot. We reject both of these arguments. It is well settled that voluntary cessation of illegal conduct by itself does not make the case moot. As will be made clear in discussing the issues raised by the plaintiff-appellant in this appeal, we believe that under the particular circumstances presented here, the controversy was not mooted. Defendant's voluntary suspension of its unlawful policy did not completely remove the threat of injury; consequently plaintiff's standing is unaffected by defendant's suspension of the Policy.

In sum, the arguments made by defendant do not show a lack of jurisdiction in the district court.

NOTES AND QUESTIONS

1. *Job Relatedness.* One of the best judicial decisions illustrating how testing must be job-related is *Crane v. Dole*, 617 F. Supp. 156 (D.D.C. 1985). The employee had been an air traffic control specialist for several years, a position that required in-flight communications with pilots and handling air traffic emergencies. Toward the end of this ten year period, it was determined that he had a hearing loss requiring a hearing aid, and that the stringent hearing requirements for air traffic control specialists could no longer be met. In the course of his application for another position with the Federal Aviation Administration (which required no in-flight communications with pilots), the agency decided to develop a "test" which basically consisted of being able to listen to information and write down what was heard. The test therefore purported to measure not only hearing, but also speed writing. The test had not been validated, it had been developed by individuals with no experience in test development, and the FAA did not they seek any professional advice on test development. The court held the test was not job-related.

2. *Standing.* The issue of standing was raised in both *Conroy* and *Roe* in different ways. Explain. Also explain the courts' holdings concerning standing in both cases.

3. *Grenier v. Cyanamic Plastics, Inc.*, 70 F.3d 667 (1st Cir. 1997), is one of the early circuit court opinions interpreting the ADA and EEOC Enforcement Guidance. The employee was a shift electrician who had worked at a plant for nine years, at which time his behavior became unusual. He reacted in a highly emotional and irrational manner to questioning about vandalism, and was reported to have other

behavior concerns. He was placed on medical leave and was informed that he would have to be cleared to return through the company doctor. He refused voluntary termination and remained on indefinite disability until his employment automatically terminated. When he reapplied for the position, he was requested to provide medical certification from a physician that he was prepared to return to work without restrictions or identifying accommodations. He was eventually denied the position.

The court recognized that the position's essential functions were not limited to technical ability and experience as an electrician. Because the employee had himself claimed disability and inability to perform the job because of a mental psychiatric treatment, it was reasonable to raise questions about the ability to do the job. The court noted

> The EEOC regulations . . . [provide] that an employer can ask an applicant with a known disability to describe or demonstrate how "with or without reasonable accommodation" the applicant will be able to do the job. . . . We hold that this employer did not violate the [ADA] [prohibition] by inquiring into Grenier's ability to function effectively in the workplace and to get along with his co-workers and supervisor, rather than just his technical qualifications as an electrician.

The court held that an employer does not violate the ADA

> by requiring a former employee with a recent known disability applying for re-employment to provide medical certification as to ability to return to work with or without reasonable accommodation, and as to the type of any reasonable accommodation necessary, as long as it is relevant to the assessment of ability to perform essential job functions.

C   WHAT CONSTITUTES DISCRIMINATION?

[1]   Prohibited Activities Related To Wages, Hours, And Conditions Of Employment

The ADA defines discrimination in employment as:

(1)   limiting, segregating, or classifying a job applicant or employee in a way that adversely affects the opportunities or status of such applicant or employee because of the disability of such applicant or employee.

(2)   participating in a contractual or other arrangement or relationship that has the effect of subjecting a covered entity's qualified applicant or employee with a disability to the discrimination prohibited by this title . . .

(3)   utilizing standards, criteria, or methods of administration —

    (A)   that have the effect of discrimination on the basis of disability; or

    (B)   that perpetuate the discrimination of others who are subject to common administrative control;

(4)   excluding or otherwise denying equal jobs or benefits to a qualified individual because of the known disability of an individual with whom the qualified individual is known to have a relationship or association;

(5)   (A) not making reasonable accommodations . . . ; [or]

(B)   denying employment opportunities . . .

(6)   using qualification standards, employment tests or other selection criteria that screen out or tend to screen out an individual with a disability . . . unless . . . shown to be job related . . . and consistent with business necessity; and

(7)   failing to select and administer tests concerning employment in the most effective manner to ensure that . . . such test results accurately reflect the skills, aptitude, or whatever other factor . . . that such test purports to measure, rather than reflecting the impaired sensory, manual, or speaking skills of such employee or applicant (except where such skills are the factors that the test purports to measure).

42 U.S.C. § 12112(b).

Employers are prohibited from such conduct in employee selection, upgrading, promotion, transfer, layoff, compensation, job assignment, seniority, and a variety of other aspects. See 29 C.F.R. § 1630.4.

The following case excerpt is an early decision under the ADA. If such a fact setting arose after *Sutton* and *Toyota*, the case would probably be dismissed because cancer was rarely found to be a disability. After the ADAAA, it is more likely that the courts will find cancer to be a disability.

U.S. EQUAL EMPLOYMENT OPPORTUNITY COMMISSION v. AIC SECURITY INVESTIGATIONS, LTD.
820 F. Supp. 1060 (N.D. Ill. 1993)

GUZMAN, UNITED STATES MAGISTRATE JUDGE:

Background Facts

This action is brought pursuant to Title I of the Americans with Disabilities Act of 1990, and Title I of the Civil Rights Act of 1991. The EEOC and the Intervening Plaintiff, Charles Wessel ("Wessel"), allege that AIC discriminated against Wessel on the basis of his disability, terminal cancer, by discharging him from his position as Executive Director at AIC.

AIC is a wholly owned subsidiary of AIC International. AIC has been and is currently engaged in the business of providing commercial security services, hardware, and investigative services to customers in the Chicago area. The security guard business, as compared to other service industries, is highly competitive; it is a dynamic, unpredictable business that requires continual and prompt adaptations to the clients' needs as they arise.

Wessel was hired by Victor Vrdolyak [AIC's owner] in February 1986 and reported to Victor Vrdolyak until his death on June 6, 1992, and to David Pack, President of AIC International, until Pack's termination on July 6, 1992. In his position of Executive Director, Charles Wessel was the Chief Executive of the security guard division. The Executive Director position which Wessel held was at all times during his employment the highest management position in AIC, and accordingly, Wessel was responsible for the overall management and profitability of AIC. The position of Executive Director required, as an essential function, overall management and direction of the 300 plus employees of the company, from all management level personnel to watch commanders and ultimately hundreds of security guards employed by AIC. This position also required, as an essential function, dealing with labor unions, supervising investigations, tracking litigation AIC was involved in, the development of policy, site walk throughs, handling labors matters, establishing price rates and monitoring and disciplining subordinates.

Wessel is a widely recognized leader in the security guard industry, having worked in the industry for approximately thirty years. He is licensed as a private detective and a private security contractor by the State of Illinois and the State of Florida. . . .

When Wessel started with AIC, he had emphysema caused by smoking 2–4 packs of cigarettes a day for approximately 25 years and 8-10 cigars a day for 15 years, and he had a back injury rendering him 20 percent disabled under his V.A. disability. In June, 1987, Wessel was diagnosed with lung cancer. Following surgery and recuperation Wessel returned to work at AIC. In July, 1991, Wessel suffered pneumothorax during a biopsy and went into respiratory arrest. Thereafter, Wessel was again diagnosed with lung cancer, this time affecting his right lung. Surgery was performed, and following a period of treatment and recuperation, Wessel again returned to work as Executive Director of AIC. In April, 1992, Wessel was initially diagnosed . . . with 2 tumors, and subsequently, in June, 1992, with 2 additional tumors, for a total of 4. Wessel's doctors considered his condition to be terminal and he was told sometime in April, 1992 that he had six to twelve months to live. Wessel has received radiation treatments since this diagnosis but these treatments have been palliative, that is, not for the purpose of a cure, but to prolong and assure some quality of Wessel's life.

Wessel continued to work at AIC throughout the course of the treatments, although on the days when the radiation treatments were scheduled in the afternoon, he had to leave work at approximately 2:30 p.m. The amount of time Wessel was absent from work is disputed. The EEOC and Wessel allege that Wessel had two treatments in July of 1992 and he did not miss a full day of work on either of those two days nor did he miss any other work in July of 1992. AIC claims that he missed 15 workdays in April and May of 1992, several days in June, 1992 and 2 days in July, 1992. Further, between July 29th and August 13th, 1991 Wessel missed 16 days of work when he experienced a pneumothorax during his routine one-day biopsy. He missed 2 half days and one full day in August of 1991, and he missed approximately 33 days between October 3rd and November 4th, 1991 for surgery to remove his right lung. Dr. Nomanbhoy, Wessel's primary treating physician, restricted Wessel's driving because of lesions in the occipital lobe of the brain and in December of 1992 Wessel experienced seizures. Dr. Petras, a radiation oncologist treating Wessel, informed Ruth Vrdolyak in a telephone conversation that Wessel had been advised not to drive. Larry Roberts, the Executive Vice President of AIC's Systems Division, offered Wessel a driver which Wessel refused.

On or about June 10, 1992, Mrs. Vrdolyak hired Beverly Kay to work for AIC. On July 28, 1992, Kay had a meeting with Wessel. During that meeting, Kay apprised Wessel that Mrs. Vrdolyak had decided that it was time for Wessel to retire. On July 30, 1992, Kay advised Wessel by telephone that his employment at AIC was terminated effective July 31, 1992. Wessel was paid through July 31, 1992. Prior to his termination from AIC, Wessel was never subject to any warnings relating to his performance, his attendance, or any disciplinary action.

Discussion

AIC first contends that Wessel cannot meet his initial burden of proof that he was a qualified individual with a disability. In particular, AIC argues that regular, predictable, full-time attendance was an essential function of the position of Executive Director which Wessel could not perform regardless of any reasonable accommodations.

To support this contention AIC points to the deposition testimony of Wessel in which Wessel stated as follows:

Q.   . . . When you went to work on a given day, did you typically know everything that, every issue that you were going to confront that day, or did things come up a daily basis?

A.   Absolutely, I did not know what was going to come up. We're in a business that is subject to surprises. Nothing is routine. There is no day-to-day "do this," "do that."

Q.   Hectic pace, your workplace?

A.   Sometimes

Q.   Need for quick decisions?

A.   Often.

Q.   Is the industry highly competitive in your estimation?

A.   Probably one of the most highly competitive service industries.

Likewise, Wessel testified that a "normal" workday had been 8:00 to 8:30 a.m. to 6:00 to 6:30 p.m. at night, but this changed significantly in 1991 and 1992. AIC also points to Wessel's testimony regarding the search for his replacement in which Wessel stated: "No, Ed was one who came in at five to ten after 9 and left at five to ten before 5. And then once I told him that I was terminal and he'd either better get in shape or they were going to look elsewhere, he did make an effort.["] This testimony[,] AIC argues, clearly indicates that AIC, and indeed, Wessel himself, would exclude individuals from any consideration for the Executive Director position unless they could put in the necessary long hours.

AIC claims that during the last 12 months of his employment at AIC, Wessel was absent approximately 25 percent of the time. In consideration of the responsibilities of Executive Director and the heavy day-to-day demands of the Guard Division, attendance was an extremely important essential function which Wessel was unable to perform.

The EEOC's response to these arguments puts forth the counter-argument that while it is undisputed that Wessel was required to miss a certain amount of work for surgery and treatment of his cancer during his employment at AIC, there remains a genuine issue of material fact as to whether Wessel's absence resulted in his not being able to perform the essential functions of the position of Executive Director. The EEOC points to the deposition testimony of David Pack, Wessel's supervisor for all but one month of his employment, who stated the following:

Q.   Did it affect the hours he put in at work?

A.   No. He put in quite a few hours.

Thereafter, Pack stated that although Wessel missed time for surgery and treatment, it was no different than instances when other employees at AIC had to take time off for surgery. In addition Pack elaborated that typically Wessel worked long hours and Saturdays and did "a ton of work at home."

Similarly, Kenneth Bartels, an AIC customer who dealt with Charles Wessel for years[,] testified that his ability to contact Wessel at AIC did not change at all in 1992, from what it had been in prior years. Bartels further stated that whenever he needed to talk to Wessel he was able to do so up to and including 1992.

The EEOC finally argues that perhaps the most telling indication that a genuine issue of fact remains as to whether Wessel's absences, necessitated by surgery and treatment, resulted in his inability to perform the essential functions of the position of Executive Director is the complete absence of any evidence in the record that Wessel was ever advised by anyone at AIC that his lack of attendance was interfering with the performance of his duties.

The disposition of this action is, of course, controlled by Title I of the Americans with Disabilities Act ("ADA"). Although the ADA is relatively new law, Section 504 of the federal Rehabilitation Act of 1973, and many state handicap laws form the basis of parallel decision which will assist with questions of law in this action. In fact, the ADA expressly contemplates that the voluminous precedent arising out of Section 504 of the Rehabilitation Act may serve as guidance for determinations involving the ADA.

Accordingly, only those persons who are qualified — that is, able, with or without reasonable accommodation, to perform the essential functions of a particular job — may state a claim under the ADA.

The record demonstrates that there remains a factual dispute as to whether Wessel's absences rendered him "unqualified" for purposes of the ADA. As the EEOC has argued, Pack's deposition testimony clearly indicates that he, as Wessel's immediate supervisor, was completely satisfied with Wessel's attendance and performance, despite the time that Wessel had to be absent for [from] work for his surgery and treatment. Likewise, there is no evidence that Wessel was given notice that his attendance was unsatisfactory.

In light of these disputed facts a genuine issue remains as to whether as of July 29, 1992, Wessel was a "qualified individual with a disability" as that term is defined. To be sure, attendance is necessary to any job, but the degree of such, especially in an upper management position such as Wessel's, where a number of tasks are effectively delegated to other employees requires close scrutiny. Further, an executive such as Wessel more than likely handled a number of his business matters through customer contact, and this usually is done by phone or in person at the customer's site. Whether a phone call is made from the office, a car phone, or a home is immaterial. Whether a contract is negotiated in the office or out of the office is immaterial. What is material is that the job gets done. Therefore, a genuine issue of fact remains as to whether Wessel was meeting that threshold of both attendance and regularity necessary to perform his job successfully at the time he was discharged. This is necessarily a fact intensive determination.

AIC's next argument raises the allegation that Wessel was unable to perform his job because of alleged short term memory problems. This allegation is supported by Wessel's deposition testimony that in part stated "My short-term memory is somewhat limited, but by the — an hour from now I remember everything."

AIC also contends that the people who worked with Wessel on a daily basis during his course of employment with AIC during 1992 observed Wessel exhibiting severe short-term memory loss directly related to his performance of the functions of this job as Executive Director. AIC also emphasizes that in July of 1992, Wessel was involved in a serious problem with one of AIC's largest accounts. Apparently a contract renewal was mistitled when mailed to a renewal account and in a second instance an incorrect estimate was submitted to an AIC customer. It is undisputed that if this estimate had not been corrected, it would have caused AIC an account loss.

AIC claims that in order to insure the survival of the company, Wessel's job responsibilities were being transferred to other AIC personnel as his condition deteriorated. Further, the pace of these transfers was hastened once Wessel was diagnosed in April, 1992 with inoperable brain tumors and given 6 to 12 months to live. Finally, AIC points out that Wessel upon his termination immediately became qualified for total disability Social Security benefits.

Once again, I agree with the EEOC that Mr. Wessel's alleged short-term memory loss and its effect on Mr. Wessel's qualification to perform his job as Executive Director is a disputed issue of fact. It is important to note that Wessel's own testimony was "[m]y short-term memory is somewhat limited, but the — an hour from now I remember everything." The fact that Wessel admits to some limitation of his short-term memory is not evidence of the severity of such or that the limitation had any impact on Wessel's performance. In fact, deposition testimony reveals that the lobes of Mr. Wessel's brain where the tumors were located were not the lobes where the short-term memory function takes place. Rather, the functions of balance and possibly some visual coordination had the potential to be affected. Further, AIC's contentions that "there is simply no accommodation for memory loss" is contradicted by AIC's own expert witness, Dr. Peter Lewitt who stated in his deposition that if memory is a problem, for example writing things down and keeping logical notes is one strategy to improve a deficient memory. In addition, Dr. Lewitt acknowledged that experience and expertise could also aid in overcoming memory loss. It is undisputed that Mr. Wessel has such substantial experience and expertise.

As to the two errors that AIC has alleged, Wessel acknowledges that he failed to catch both and explained that they were the result of clerical error. Wessel further indicated, and AIC does not dispute that the estimate error was rectified shortly thereafter, and AIC did not suffer any adverse consequences, financial or otherwise. Further, AIC has failed to establish that the above errors have any connection whatsoever to short-term memory loss.

Therefore a factual question exists, as to whether Wessel's errors can lead to a finding that Wessel could not perform the essential functions of this position of Executive Director. As the EEOC has persuasively argued, if perfection is to be the standard for qualification under the ADA, very few individuals would be qualified.

As to AIC's assertion that over time, Wessel's job responsibilities were being transferred to other AIC employees because of Wessel's alleged inability to perform such, this assertion is refuted by the testimony of David Pack and Larry Roberts. Specifically, Pack stated in his affidavit that "Wessel maintained overall responsibility for all of these essential functions throughout his employment." Pack further testified that to the extent that Wessel began to delegate and transfer some of his functions to others, the reasons for the transfer were unrelated to Wessel's illness. Rather, Pack stated that he wanted Wessel to transfer his duties to others, so that Pack could promote Wessel and begin to delegate some of his own duties to Wessel. Roberts confirmed that the discussion to transfer some of Wessel's job responsibilities preceded Wessel's illness. In addition, Pack acknowledged the terminal nature of Wessel's illness, indicating that he wanted to take advantage of Wessel's experience and knowledge for purposes of selecting and training a successor.

Finally, there is substantial evidence in the record to create a genuine issue on the question of whether Wessel could perform the essential functions of his job. AIC's audited financial's show that the profits of AIC's division under Wessel's direction increased from July 31, 1991 to July 31, 1992, while the overall profits of AIC decreased. Likewise, there is disputed evidence to refute the allegation that Wessel was unable to perform the "essential functions" of labor negotiations, supervising investigations, tracking litigation and development of policy. Therefore, there exists disputed material issues of fact and summary judgment must be denied.

AIC's final argument contends that Wessel could not perform his job without risk to himself and others, regardless of any reasonable accommodation. This argument stems from Wessel's treating physician's recommendation that he not drive a car because of his potential to suffer a seizure. Wessel's refusal to discontinue driving, AIC argues[,] poses a direct threat to other AIC employees, the public at large, as well as exposes to AIC to potential liability.

Direct threat is defined as "a significant risk of substantial harm to the health and safety of the individual or others that cannot be eliminated or reduced by reasonable accommodation." A "direct threat" defense is to be evaluated on a individualized assessment of the individual's present ability to safely perform the essential functions of the job.

AIC's direct defense obviously fails for purposes of this motion. AIC cannot establish that driving was an essential function of the position of Executive Director of AIC. Therefore, any inability to drive could not serve as the basis for asserting the defense. In order to rely on a safety requirement to screen out disabled individuals the employer must demonstrate that the requirement, as applied to the individual, satisfies the direct threat standard under the ADA in order to show that the requirement is job related and consistent with business necessity.

In the instant case, AIC does not assert and cannot demonstrate that driving is an essential function of Wessel's job. Even if they had, an accommodation, i.e. alternative mode of transportation could be provided. In fact, one such accommodation was offered voluntarily by AIC prior to this lawsuit. AIC offered Wessel a driver. So the company determined of its own accord that such an accommodation was reasonable. Further, the deposition testimony of Dr. Nomanbhoy, indicates that he has on occasion initiated proceedings to have patients' licenses suspended due to their being a risk to the public at large behind the wheel. Mr. Wessel was not one of those patients.

AIC in their reply brief primarily argue that the record is clear that all four physicians who are to give expert medical testimony at trial have declared Wessel unable to perform his former position of Executive Director for AIC. Allegedly this conclusive medical testimony is not disputed anywhere.

At the outset, I disagree with AIC's statement that this medical testimony is not disputed anywhere. Dr. Nomanbhoy in his deposition clearly stated that he had never observed Mr. Wessel suffering from memory problems and that up until a few weeks ago when Mr. Wessel fell he had no qualms in answering that Mr. Wessel could still perform his job. Further, as to the information that Dr. Nomanbhoy supplied to Social Security, Dr. Nomanbhoy clearly stated that this information was premised on the fact that Mr. Wessel had been fired from his job and that he should be able to get some compensation because no one is going to hire him. Further, I don't agree that Dr. Petras has stated that Mr. Wessel was not capable of performing his job. In fact, Dr. Petras went into great detail explaining that the tumors were located in areas of the brain that did not affect mental functions. As to Dr. Lewitt and Dr. Milner's testimony the weight to be afforded to such is for the trier of fact to determine.

Although the excerpted *AIC* decision is included here for purposes of defining discrimination (in this case discrimination in the form of termination of employment), the case also addresses themes that recur in many of the decisions in this area, i.e., whether the individual is qualified to perform the requirements of the position and whether there are reasonable accommodations that could have been provided that would allow the individual to be able to carry out the job functions.

In *AIC*, the jury ultimately awarded $22,000 in back pay, $50,000 in compensatory damages, and $500,000 in punitive damages (reduced to $150,000 by the court).

United States EEOC v. AIC Security Investigations, Ltd., 823 F. Supp. 571 (N.D. Ill. 1993).

QUESTIONS

If a professional job such as the one in *AIC* is involved, should it be permissible to inquire at the hiring stage whether the individual will be able to perform the job for two or three years? What if the search for such a professional position is an expensive process? Does that justify such a preemployment inquiry? For example, would it make a difference if the position were superintendent for a large urban school district, college president, a fourth grade teacher, or the school custodian?

[2] Disparate Treatment and Disparate Impact

HYPOTHETICAL PROBLEM 3.3

Read the following hypothetical problem before reading the materials on disparate treatment and disparate impact. After reading the materials, analyze this problem.

3.3 Review the following from the perspective of an attorney specializing in plaintiff's employment discrimination cases. Ruben Allen, is considering a possible lawsuit. He tells his attorney that he works as a lawyer in a small law firm. The firm just recently denied him partnership based on a longstanding assumption that all associates in the law firm must bill a minimum of 2,000 hours a year. Ruben has worked for the firm for five years. He billed 2,000 hours the first three years, but in years four and five, Ruben billed 1,900 and 1,875 respectively. At the end of each year, the partners have evaluated Ruben. His evaluations were always very positive. Nothing was said about his failure to meet the 2,000 hour goal in his last two years. Ruben was diagnosed with fibromyalgia two years ago, which made him very tired, and it was impossible to meet the 2,000 hour goal. Nonetheless, Ruben worked diligently during the past two years, and came to work often when he did not feel well. About six months before his partnership vote, a young partner asked Ruben if he was "ok" and told him that he had been looking very tired and sick recently. Ruben told the partner that he had fibromyalgia, but that he was determined to ignore it. There was a woman who was up for partnership in the same year. She had been pregnant during her fourth year, and told Ruben that because she had morning sickness, she was only able to bill 1,800 hours that year. In her fifth year, she took a 12 week maternity leave, which prevented her from meeting the 2,000 hour goal. She was elected to the partnership.

1. Consider the possible theories under which Ruben could bring a lawsuit under the ADA. Explain whether Ruben can make out a prima facie case under the disparate treatment theory. If so, explain how the case would proceed from there.

2. Discuss whether Ruben has a potential disparate impact cause of action against the firm. Analyze that cause of action and the employer's defense.

3.   Consider what evidence would be needed to prove both the disparate treatment and the disparate impact cases. Make a discovery plan for the case.

NOTE

Title VII of the 1964 Civil Rights Act, 42 U.S.C. § 2000e, et seq., prohibits discrimination in employment based on a person's race, color, national origin, sex and religion. The ADA, in many respects, was modeled on Title VII and the courts apply Title VII law to the ADA, where it is relevant. In particular, Title VII permits an employee or applicant to prove two different types of discrimination. First, the employee can prove disparate treatment. Proof of disparate treatment requires proof that the covered entity intended to discriminate against the individual because of his or her protected characteristic. A plaintiff who brings a cause of action for disparate treatment is entitled to a jury and, if the party proves intentional discrimination, backpay, frontpay, injunctive and declaratory relief and compensatory and punitive damages may be awarded. Because backpay, frontpay and injunctive and declaratory relief are equitable in nature, the judge decides what backpay and other equitable relief will be granted. The jury determines what damages will be awarded. Damages are capped, however, depending on the size of the employer. See 42 U.S.C. § 1981a(a) & (b). Under Title VII, an individual may also prove that the employer uses a neutral practice that creates a disparate impact on a protected group. Disparate impact cases do not require proof of intentional discrimination. Rather, they require proof that the employer uses the particular employment practice and that the practice caused the disparate impact. Once the employee proves the disparate impact, the employer can defeat the suit by demonstrating that the practice is job related and consistent with business necessity. Even if the employer makes this proof, the plaintiff can still prevail if she proves that there are less discriminatory alternatives to the employment practice that the employer refused to adopt.

Like Title VII, the ADA also permits employment discrimination actions based on disparate treatment and disparate impact. The disparate treatment cases, as in Title VII, require a showing of discriminatory intent. The caps for compensatory and punitive damages under 42 U.S.C. § 1981a apply expressly to the ADA and the Rehabilitation Act as well as to Title VII. The disparate impact cases, like those brought under Title VII, do not require a showing of discriminatory intent. Recall that *Alexander v. Choate*, excerpted in Chapter 1, established that intentional discrimination is not always required to find a violation of the Rehabilitation Act. It is also clear that a disparate impact cause of action exists under the ADA. While a plaintiff proving disparate impact may receive equitable relief such as backpay, declaratory and injunctive relief, she is not entitled to damages.

Proving Disparate Treatment under Title VII and the ADA

The courts have created different mechanisms to prove intent in Title VII cases. The most commonly known method is that set forth in *McDonnell Douglas Corp. v. Green*, 411 U.S. 792 (1973). That case and its progeny set up a three step process for proving intentional discrimination. First, the plaintiff proves a prima facie case by demonstrating in a failure to hire case that: 1) the plaintiff is a member of a protected class; 2) the plaintiff is qualified for the job; 3) the plaintiff applied for the job; and 4) the plaintiff was rejected and a person who is not a member of the protected class was hired or the job remained open after plaintiff's application was rejected. When neither of these situations exists, if sufficient facts exist to create an inference of discrimination, the courts will ordinarily conclude that the plaintiff has made out a prima facie case. Once the plaintiff produces evidence to support a prima facie case, the burden of production shifts to the defendant to articulate a legitimate, non-discriminatory reason for the adverse employment action. Once the defendant produces this evidence, the burden of production shifts back to the plaintiff and at this point, the burden of production merges with the plaintiff's ultimate burden of persuasion. The plaintiff must now demonstrate that the defendant's articulated reason is a pretext for discrimination. Ordinarily, the plaintiff can meet this burden by demonstrating that the defendant's articulated reason is either untrue or is not the real reason for the adverse employment action. The courts have adjusted this proof to discharge and failure to promote cases as well.

A second method of proving discriminatory intent under Title VII is to demonstrate that the protected characteristic is a "motivating factor" in the employment decision. Once this proof is made under the 1991 Civil Rights Act, the plaintiff prevails. The employer, however, can limit the remedies by proving that there were other legitimate reasons for the discrimination and because of those legitimate reasons, it would have taken the adverse employment action against the employee even without the illegitimate motivating factor. This method of proof is often called the "mixed motives" proof method. See § 703(m) of the 1991 Civil Rights Act.

Courts hold that the *McDonnell Douglas* methodology applies to ADA cases as well as Title VII cases. But this methodology should be used only when the issue is whether the employer intentionally discriminated against a person with a disability because of the disability. While the ADA may also use the mixed motives method of proof, it is unclear whether Section 703(m) applies to the ADA, because the 1991 Civil Rights Act does not expressly apply to the ADA. The ADA, however incorporates the "powers, remedies, and procedures" set forth in Title VII. Consequently, a number of courts have found § 703(m) applicable to the ADA. See MICHAEL J. ZIMMER, ET AL., CASES AND MATERIALS ON EMPLOYMENT DISCRIMINATION 565 (7th ed. 2008). Nonetheless, a recent Supreme Court case, *Gross v. FBL Financial Servs., Inc.*, 129 S. Ct. 2343 (2009), suggests that mixed motives methodology may not be applicable to ADA and Rehabilitation Act cases. *Gross* held that neither the 1991 Act mixed motives method nor the method applied before the 1991 Act applies to age discrimination cases. By analogy, the courts may also decide that ADA plaintiffs may not employ a mixed motives proof method. For a description of methods of proving intentional discrimination with examples, see Ann C. McGinley, *Viva la Evolucion!: Recognizing Unconscious Motive in Title VII*, 9 CORNELL J. L. & PUB. POL'Y 415, 447–66 (2000).

Proving Disparate Impact Under Title VII and the ADA

The 1991 Civil Rights Act also codified the disparate impact cause of action in Title VII cases. Once again, while the 1991 Civil Rights Act does not expressly apply to the ADA, the courts ordinarily conclude that Title VII disparate impact analysis does apply. The ADA itself expressly provides for liability in a disparate impact employment discrimination case. It states that "the term 'discriminate' includes . . . using qualification standards, employment tests or other selection criteria that screen out or tend to screen out an individual with a disability or a class of individuals with disabilities unless the standard, test or other selection criteria, as used by the covered entity, is shown to be job-related for the position in question and is consistent with business necessity." 42 U.S.C. § 12112(b)(6).

The following case demonstrates the importance of knowing the difference between disparate treatment and disparate impact causes of action and pleading the proper cause of action.

RAYTHEON CO. v. HERNANDEZ
540 U.S. 44 (2003)

JUSTICE THOMAS delivered the opinion of the Court.

The Americans with Disabilities Act of 1990 (ADA), 42 U.S.C. § 12101 *et seq.*, makes it unlawful for an employer, with respect to hiring, to "discriminate against a qualified individual with a disability because of the disability of such individual." § 12112(a). We are asked to decide in this case whether the ADA confers preferential rehire rights on disabled employees lawfully terminated for violating workplace conduct rules. The United States Court of Appeals for the Ninth Circuit held that an employer's unwritten policy not to rehire employees who left the company for violating personal conduct rules contravenes the ADA, at least as applied to employees who were lawfully forced to resign for illegal drug use but have since been rehabilitated. Because the Ninth Circuit improperly applied a disparate-impact analysis in a disparate-treatment case in order to reach this holding, we vacate its judgment and remand the case for further proceedings consistent with this opinion.

I

Respondent, Joel Hernandez, worked for Hughes Missile Systems for 25 years. On July 11, 1991, respondent's appearance and behavior at work suggested that he might be under the influence of drugs or alcohol. Pursuant to company policy, respondent took a drug test, which came back positive for cocaine. Respondent subsequently admitted that he had been up late drinking beer and using cocaine the night before the test. Because respondent's behavior violated petitioner's workplace conduct rules, respondent was forced to resign. Respondent's "Employee Separation Summary" indicated as the reason for separation: "discharge for personal conduct (quit in lieu of discharge)."

More than two years later, on January 24, 1994, respondent applied to be rehired by petitioner. Respondent stated on his application that he had previously been employed by petitioner. He also attached two reference letters to the application, one from his pastor, stating that respondent was a "faithful and active member" of the church, and the other from an Alcoholics Anonymous counselor, stating that respondent attends Alcoholics Anonymous meetings regularly and is in recovery.

Joanne Bockmiller, an employee in the company's Labor Relations Department, reviewed respondent's application. Bockmiller testified in her deposition that since respondent's application disclosed his prior employment with the company, she pulled his personnel file and reviewed his employee separation summary. She then rejected respondent's application. Bockmiller insisted that the company had a policy against rehiring employees who were terminated for workplace misconduct. Thus, when she reviewed the employment separation summary and found that respondent had been discharged for violating workplace conduct rules, she rejected respondent's application. She testified, in particular, that she did not know that respondent was a former drug addict when she made the employment decision and did not see anything that would constitute a "record of" addiction.

Respondent subsequently filed a charge with the Equal Employment Opportunity Commission (EEOC). Respondent's charge of discrimination indicated that petitioner did not give him a reason for his nonselection, but that respondent believed he had been discriminated against in violation of the ADA.

Petitioner responded to the charge by submitting a letter to the EEOC, in which George M. Medina, Sr., Manager of Diversity Development, wrote:

> "The ADA specifically exempts from protection individuals currently engaging in the illegal use of drugs when the covered entity acts on the basis of that use. Contrary to Complainant's unfounded allegation, his non-selection for rehire is not based on any legitimate disability. Rather, Complainant's application was rejected based on his demonstrated drug use while previously employed and the complete lack of evidence indicating successful drug rehabilitation."

This response, together with evidence that the letters submitted with respondent's employment application may have alerted Bockmiller to the reason for respondent's prior termination, led the EEOC to conclude that petitioner may have "rejected [respondent's] application based on his record of past alcohol and drug use." The EEOC thus found that there was "reasonable cause to believe that [respondent] was denied hire to the position of Product Test Specialist because of his disability." The EEOC issued a right-to-sue letter, and respondent subsequently filed this action alleging a violation of the ADA.

Respondent proceeded through discovery on the theory that the company rejected his application because of his record of drug addiction and/or because he was regarded as being a drug addict. In response to petitioner's motion for summary judgment, respondent for the first time argued in the alternative that if the company really did apply a neutral no-rehire policy in his case, petitioner still violated the ADA because such a policy has a disparate impact. The District Court granted petitioner's motion for summary judgment with respect to respondent's disparate-treatment claim. However, the District Court refused to consider respondent's disparate-impact claim because respondent had failed to plead or raise the theory in a timely manner.

The Court of Appeals agreed with the District Court that respondent had failed timely to raise his disparate-impact claim. In addressing respondent's disparate-treatment claim, the Court of Appeals proceeded under the familiar burden-shifting approach first adopted by this Court in *McDonnell Douglas Corp. v. Green*, 411 U.S. 792, 93 S. Ct. 1817, 36 L. Ed. 2d 668 (1973).[3] First, the Ninth Circuit found that with respect to respondent's prima facie case of discrimination, there were genuine issues of material fact regarding whether respondent was qualified for the position for which he sought to be rehired, and whether the reason for petitioner's refusal to rehire him was his past record of drug addiction. The Court of Appeals thus held that with respect to respondent's prima facie case of discrimination, respondent had proffered sufficient evidence to preclude a grant of summary judgment.

The Court of Appeals then moved to the next step of *McDonnell Douglas*, where the burden shifts to the defendant to provide a legitimate, nondiscriminatory reason for its employment action. Here, petitioner contends that Bockmiller applied the neutral policy against rehiring employees previously terminated for violating workplace conduct rules and that this neutral company policy constituted a legitimate and nondiscriminatory reason for its decision not to rehire respondent. The Court of Appeals, although admitting that petitioner's no-rehire rule was lawful on its face, held the policy to be unlawful "as applied to former drug addicts whose only work-related offense was testing positive because of their addiction." The Court of Appeals concluded that petitioner's application of a neutral no-rehire policy was not a legitimate, nondiscriminatory reason for rejecting respondent's application:

> "Maintaining a blanket policy against rehire of *all* former employees who violated company policy not only screens out persons with a record of addiction who have been successfully rehabilitated, but may well result, as [petitioner] contends it did here, in the staff member who makes the employment decision remaining unaware of the "disability" and thus of the fact that she is committing an unlawful act. . . . Additionally, we hold that a policy that serves to bar the reemployment of a drug addict despite his successful rehabilitation violates the ADA."

In other words, while ostensibly evaluating whether petitioner had proffered a legitimate, nondiscriminatory reason for failing to rehire respondent sufficient to rebut respondent's prima facie showing of disparate treatment, the Court of

---

[3] The Court in *McDonnell Douglas* set forth a burden-shifting scheme for discriminatory-treatment cases. Under *McDonnell Douglas*, a plaintiff must first establish a prima facie case of discrimination. The burden then shifts to the employer to articulate a legitimate, nondiscriminatory reason for its employment action. If the employer meets this burden, the presumption of intentional discrimination disappears, but the plaintiff can still prove disparate treatment by, for instance, offering evidence demonstrating that the employer's explanation is pretextual. The Courts of Appeals have consistently utilized this burden-shifting approach when reviewing motions for summary judgment in disparate-treatment cases.

Appeals held that a neutral no-rehire policy could never suffice in a case where the employee was terminated for illegal drug use, because such a policy has a disparate impact on recovering drug addicts. In so holding, the Court of Appeals erred by conflating the analytical framework for disparate-impact and disparate-treatment claims. Had the Court of Appeals correctly applied the disparate-treatment framework, it would have been obliged to conclude that a neutral no-rehire policy is, by definition, a legitimate, nondiscriminatory reason under the ADA. And thus the only remaining question would be whether respondent could produce sufficient evidence from which a jury could conclude that "petitioner's stated reason for respondent's rejection was in fact pretext."

II

This Court has consistently recognized a distinction between claims of discrimination based on disparate treatment and claims of discrimination based on disparate impact. The Court has said that " '[d]isparate treatment' . . . is the most easily understood type of discrimination. The employer simply treats some people less favorably than others because of their race, color, religion, sex, or [other protected characteristic]." Liability in a disparate-treatment case "depends on whether the protected trait . . . actually motivated the employer's decision." By contrast, disparate-impact claims "involve employment practices that are facially neutral in their treatment of different groups but that in fact fall more harshly on one group than another and cannot be justified by business necessity." Under a disparate-impact theory of discrimination, "a facially neutral employment practice may be deemed [illegally discriminatory] without evidence of the employer's subjective intent to discriminate that is required in a 'disparate-treatment' case."

Both disparate-treatment and disparate-impact claims are cognizable under the ADA. See 42 U.S.C. § 12112(b) (defining "discriminate" to include "utilizing standards, criteria, or methods of administration . . . that have the effect of discrimination on the basis of disability" and "using qualification standards, employment tests or other selection criteria that screen out or tend to screen out an individual with a disability"). Because "the factual issues, and therefore the character of the evidence presented, differ when the plaintiff claims that a facially neutral employment policy has a discriminatory impact on protected classes," courts must be careful to distinguish between these theories. Here, respondent did not timely pursue a disparate-impact claim.

Petitioner's proffer of its neutral no-rehire policy plainly satisfied its obligation under *McDonnell Douglas* to provide a legitimate, nondiscriminatory reason for refusing to rehire respondent. Thus, the only relevant question before the Court of Appeals, after petitioner presented a neutral explanation for its decision not to rehire respondent, was whether there was sufficient evidence from which a jury could conclude that petitioner did make its employment decision based on respondent's status as disabled despite petitioner's proffered explanation. Instead, the Court of Appeals concluded that, as a matter of law, a neutral no-rehire policy was not a legitimate, nondiscriminatory reason sufficient to defeat a prima facie case of discrimination. The Court of Appeals did not even attempt, in the remainder of its opinion, to treat this claim as one involving only disparate treatment. Instead, the

Court of Appeals observed that petitioner's policy "screens out persons with a record of addiction," and further noted that the company had not raised a business necessity defense, factors that pertain to disparate-impact claims but not disparate-treatment claims. By improperly focusing on these factors, the Court of Appeals ignored the fact that petitioner's no-rehire policy is a quintessential legitimate, nondiscriminatory reason for refusing to rehire an employee who was terminated for violating workplace conduct rules.

The Court of Appeals rejected petitioner's legitimate, nondiscriminatory reason for refusing to rehire respondent because it "serves to bar the re-employment of a drug addict despite his successful rehabilitation." We hold that such an analysis is inapplicable to a disparate-treatment claim. Once respondent had made a prima facie showing of discrimination, the next question for the Court of Appeals was whether petitioner offered a legitimate, nondiscriminatory reason for its actions so as to demonstrate that its actions were not motivated by respondent's disability. To the extent that the Court of Appeals strayed from this task by considering not only discriminatory intent but also discriminatory impact, we vacate its judgment and remand the case for further proceedings consistent with this opinion.

NOTES AND QUESTIONS

1. This case was remanded to the lower court to determine whether there was a genuine issue of material fact concerning whether the employer intentionally refused to rehire the plaintiff because of his disability. On remand, the Ninth Circuit held that there were genuine issues of material fact as to whether the employer had refused to re-hire the plaintiff because of his status as an alcoholic rather than in reliance upon a neutral no-rehire policy. 362 F.3d 564 (9th Cir. 2004).

2. *Raytheon* did not reach the question of whether a no-rehire policy creates a disparate impact on persons with disabilities. How should the plaintiff's lawyer argue that such a policy does create a disparate impact on persons with disabilities? Assuming that it creates a disparate impact, the employer may still escape liability if it can prove that the policy is job related and consistent with business necessity. Plaintiff worked for Hughes Missile Systems, a company that made defense air missiles, as a Calibration Service Technician. 298 F.3d 1030 (9th Cir. 2002). Raytheon Company subsequently acquired Hughes. Given this information, what arguments should the defendant make concerning job-relatedness and business necessity? How should plaintiff's counsel respond to these arguments?

3. *Wellness Programs:* To reduce health benefits costs, many companies have recognized the value of preventive medicine and have implemented a variety of "wellness" programs to encourage good health. These programs take the forms of exercise equipment and incentives for participating in exercise and other "good health" type programming. To what extent could such programs be challenged as violative of the ADA? Suppose employees are given cash bonuses if they lose weight, stop smoking, or lower their cholesterol levels?

What about reduced insurance premiums as an incentive to participate in a wellness program? What if the reduction required the employee to provide and update health related information? What assurance should the employee seek that this information would remain confidential and not be used as the basis for discrimination?

4. *Employment Benefits.* Employer subsidized health insurance is the primary means by which people in the United States receive health care. Individual insurance policies are often quite expensive, and individuals with preexisting conditions are often denied coverage for individual policies. For this reason, access to health insurance benefits is an important issue in employment discrimination cases. Chapter 9 addresses health insurance issues generally. Chapter 4 also includes cases involving insurance benefits. It should be noted here, however, that in 2000, EEOC issued guidance on employer provided health benefits in 2000. EEOC Compliance Manual Section 627 (2000). The guidance covers distinctions in health benefit plans and how actuarial principles are to be used in setting benefits. One of the most controversial issues is the differential benefits provided for physical disabilities and mental disabilities. Most courts have upheld these differentials as being permissible under the ADA. *See* LAURA ROTHSTEIN & JULIA ROTHSTEIN, DISABILITIES AND THE LAW Ch. 10 (2009). The Mental Health Parity and Addiction Act applies to group insurance offered by employers, and mandates that if employer's insurance grants mental health benefits, there must be equality in coverage and costs. See *infra* p. 259.

5. *Differential Coverage.* Under Section 501 of the ADA, insurers or other medical service providers may offer differential coverage for different health conditions based on medical risks. 42 U.S.C. § 12201(c). The EEOC issued enforcement guidance in 2000.

6. Would it violate the ADA to give smaller payouts for accrued, unused sick leave to employees who retired on the basis of disability than for those who retired on some other basis? See *Felde v. City of San Jose*, 839 F. Supp. 708 (N.D. Cal. 1994).

D QUALIFICATIONS

Under the ADA, employers are free to establish "qualification standards" for jobs. As interpreted by the EEOC, "qualification standards" means:

> the personal and professional attributes including the skill, experience, education, physical, medical, safety and other requirements established by a covered entity as requirements which an individual must meet in order to be eligible for the position held or desired.

29 C.F.R. § 1630.2(q).

This issue was previously discussed in the context of hiring. This section focuses primarily on employees already in the work setting who either become unable to do the job or who are found to be unable to do the job after being hired as qualified.

[1]   Fundamental and Essential Aspects

"Essential functions" under the ADA mean "the fundamental job duties of the employment position of the individual with a disability. . . . [It] does not include marginal functions of the position." 29 C.F.R. § 1630.2(n)(1).

Job functions are considered essential for reasons such as the following: the position exists for the performance of that function, there are a limited number of employees available among whom the job function can be distributed, and/or it is highly specialized, and the person has been hired because of the expertise to perform the function. 29 C.F.R. § 1630.2(n)(2).

Evidence of whether something is an essential function includes factors such as employer's judgment, written job descriptions prepared in advance of hiring, amount of time performing the function, consequences of not requiring the employee to perform the function, collective bargaining agreement terms, and work experience of previous employees in that position. 29 C.F.R. § 1630.2(n)(3).

The cases in this section do not all address each of these issues. Some of the cases involve Rehabilitation Act claims, rather than ADA claims, but the standards applied on these issues are generally the same.

[a]   Attendance Requirements

TYNDALL v. NATIONAL EDUCATION CENTERS
31 F.3d 209 (4th Cir. 1994)

WILKINSON, CIRCUIT JUDGE:

Plaintiff Mary Tyndall suffers from lupus erythematosus, an autoimmune system disorder that causes joint pain and inflammation, fatigue, and urinary and intestinal disorders. In 1989, Tyndall enrolled in a career training program in medical assisting at the Kee Business College Campus ("Kee"), a school in Richmond, Virginia owned by defendant National Education Centers ("NEC"). Tyndall successfully completed her coursework in January 1990. At that time, Dale Seay, the head of Kee's Allied Health Department, hired Tyndall as a parttime instructor in the medical assisting program. Seay and the other Kee staff members knew of Tyndall's disability when she was hired.

During Tyndall's tenure at Kee, the school made every effort to accommodate her lupus condition. Kee permitted Tyndall to take sick leave, to come into work late or leave early, and to take breaks from ongoing classes whenever she felt ill. If Tyndall became ill during the work day, Seay and other colleagues would accompany her to the rest room to help her, and would offer her a ride home. Indeed, Tyndall admitted that she never made a request for accommodation of her lupus condition that Kee refused.

In 1992, Tyndall began missing work with increasing frequency. From January until July 15, 1992, she missed nineteen days of work: one day to help a friend with legal work, ten days because of her lupus condition, and eight days to take care of her son, Kevin, who suffered from gastro-esophageal reflux disease. Kee approved each of those absences. However, Seay mentioned in a meeting with Tyndall that she had been missing a lot of work.

In mid-July, Tyndall submitted a request for a leave of absence from July 23 to August 17, 1992, because her son was undergoing surgery in Birmingham, Alabama. Again, Kee approved the leave of absence. On August 10, after returning home from Birmingham, Tyndall called Seay to confirm that she would return to work on August 17 as scheduled. However, she informed Seay that she would need to take off more time in order to take care of her son's post-operative problems. Seay responded by asking Tyndall to meet with her and Zoe Thompson, the Executive Director of Kee, regarding the additional leave of absence. That meeting took place on August 12.

At the meeting, Tyndall stated that she could teach for a week beginning August 17 before taking more time off to accompany her son on a post-operative trip to Birmingham. Tyndall said she was not sure how long she would be gone on that trip. Seay told Tyndall that she could return to work on August 17 as scheduled and continue to work, but that she could not take additional time off. Seay explained that the additional leave of absence would cause Tyndall to miss the beginning of an instructional cycle for the third time in a row. Because students in Tyndall's classes and teachers who had to work overtime to cover her classes had complained about her absences, Seay was concerned that another absence would further disrupt the operations of the school. When Tyndall insisted that she had to take her son to Birmingham, Seay suggested that Tyndall resign because of everything that was going on in her life. Seay prepared a report explaining that the separation was "mutual," and Tyndall signed it. Before Tyndall left the meeting, Thompson encouraged her to apply to Kee for re-employment when she was ready to return to work.

[Lower court proceedings omitted.]

II.

Tyndall first challenges her termination under the Americans with Disabilities Act. In order to establish a violation of this section, three criteria must be met: first, Tyndall must have a "disability"; second, Tyndall must be "qualified" for the job; and third, Kee's termination of Tyndall must constitute an unlawful "discrimination" based on her disability. Because it is undisputed that Tyndall's lupus condition constituted a "disability" under the ADA, we need address only the latter two elements.

A.

Under the ADA, only persons who are "qualified" for the job in question may state a claim for discrimination. The ADA defines "qualified individual with a disability" as an individual with a disability who, with or without reasonable accommodation, can perform the essential functions of the employment position that such individual holds or desires. 42 U.S.C. § 12111(8). The Supreme Court has interpreted this provision to mean that a "qualified" person must be "able to meet all of a program's requirements in spite of his handicap." Accordingly, to determine whether Tyndall was qualified for the teaching position, we must decide (1) whether she could "perform the essential functions of the job, i.e., functions that bear more than a marginal relationship to the job at issue," and (2) if not, whether "any reasonable accommodation by the employer would enable [her] to perform those functions." Plaintiff bears the burden of demonstrating that she could perform the essential functions of her job with reasonable accommodation.

Tyndall contends that she was qualified for her job because she could perform all of her teaching duties and received "excellent" and "good" performance evaluations at Kee. We agree, and NEC does not dispute, that the quality of Tyndall's performance when she was working was more than adequate. However, an evaluation of the quality of Tyndall's performance does not end our inquiry. In addition to possessing the skills necessary to perform the job in question, an employee must be willing and able to demonstrate these skills by coming to work on a regular basis. Except in the unusual case where an employee can effectively perform all work-related duties at home, an employee "who does not come to work cannot perform any of his job functions, essential or otherwise." Therefore, a regular and reliable level of attendance is a necessary element of most jobs. An employee who cannot meet the attendance requirements of the job at issue cannot be considered a "qualified" individual protected by the ADA.

Here, Tyndall held a job that could not be performed away from the Kee campus; her position required that she teach the assigned courses during the scheduled class times and spend time with her students. Despite this obvious need for regular attendance, Tyndall missed almost forty days of work during a seven-month period. Moreover, she missed the beginning of an instructional cycle twice in a row and requested permission to be absent for yet a third time, even though the start of an instructional period is a crucial time for Kee's operations. Accordingly, regardless of the fact that she possessed the necessary teaching skills and performed well when she was at work, Tyndall's frequent absences rendered her unable to function effectively as a teacher.

Furthermore, Kee's extensive accommodations of Tyndall's lupus condition did not improve her attendance level. From the beginning of Tyndall's tenure at Kee, Seay permitted her to take sick leave, come into work late, leave early, and take mid-class breaks when necessary to alleviate her condition. Despite the numerous attempts to assist her, Tyndall continued to miss an excessive number of days from work. Indeed, Kee's accommodations of Tyndall's disability could not have significantly improved Tyndall's attendance level, as a majority of her absences were not related to her own disability. Rather, they were caused by her personal need to tend to her son's disability, which an employer is not obligated to accommodate through scheduling modifications. See 29 C.F.R. § 1630, App. ("[A]n employee would not be entitled to a modified work schedule as an accommodation to enable the employee to care for [a family member] with a disability."). Because Tyndall's attendance problems rendered her unable to fulfill the essential functions of her job, and because these problems occurred even with Kee's more than reasonable accommodations for her own disability, we hold that she was not a "qualified individual with a disability," as required by § 12112(a) of the ADA.

B.

Even if Tyndall were a "qualified" employee covered by the ADA, she nonetheless could not recover under the Act because she has failed to show that Kee in any way discriminated against her. Tyndall alleges that Kee discriminated against her in two different ways, but neither of her claims has merit.

First, Tyndall contends that Kee's termination constituted discrimination based on her association with her disabled son. The ADA prohibits employers from taking adverse employment action "because of the known disability of an individual with whom the qualified individual is known to have a relationship or association." 42 U.S.C. § 12112(b)(4). More specifically, the Interpretive Guidelines to the ADA provide that an employer may not make decisions based on the "belie[f] that the [employee] would have to miss work" in order to take care of a disabled person. Tyndall contends that Seay's decision to terminate her stemmed from the assumption that Tyndall would have to take additional time off in order to take care of her disabled son, Kevin.

We find no merit in this argument. Seay did not make an unfounded assumption that Tyndall would have to miss work to take care of Kevin. Rather, Seay responded to Tyndall's record of extended absences in connection with Kevin's care and her actual statement that she would, in fact, have to miss additional work in order to be with her son. It is undisputed that when Seay informed Tyndall she could not take another leave of absence at the start of an instructional cycle, Tyndall replied that she had to take Kevin back to Birmingham for post-operative treatment. The ADA does not require an employer to restructure an employee's work schedule to enable the employee to care for a relative with a disability. Because Tyndall's termination was not based on any assumption regarding future absences related to Kevin's care, but instead resulted from her record of past absences and her clear indication that she needed additional time off, we hold that Kee's actions did not constitute discrimination based on Tyndall's association with a disabled individual.

Second, Tyndall maintains that even if Kee did not discriminate against her based on her association with her son, Kee's termination violated § 12112(b)(5)(B), which prohibits employers from taking adverse employment action "based on the need of [the employer] to make reasonable accommodation to the physical or mental impairments of the employee or applicant." 42 U.S.C. § 12112(b)(5)(B). In evaluating Tyndall's claim that her disability was a motivating factor for her termination, we must focus on the undisputed fact that Seay, the person responsible for terminating Tyndall, is the same person who hired Tyndall with full knowledge of her disability. At least two other circuits have taken [the view that] employees who were discharged by the same person who had earlier hired or promoted them were not victims of age discrimination.

Here, Seay not only hired Tyndall, but actively encouraged her to apply for the teaching position at Kee, despite having full knowledge of her lupus condition. Seay fully accommodated Tyndall's disability during her employment with Kee, and discharged Tyndall only when informed that she had to take an indefinite amount of time off just a week after returning from a leave of absence nearly a month long. These undisputed facts create a strong inference that Tyndall's termination was not motivated by bias against disabled workers or by a desire to avoid making reasonable accommodations for Tyndall's disability.

Viewed against this strong presumption of nondiscrimination, Tyndall's evidence is plainly inadequate to establish that discrimination motivated her termination. Tyndall relies on three pieces of evidence to argue that considerations of her disability played a role in Kee's decision: (1) after Tyndall returned from a sick leave in July, Seay warned Tyndall that she was missing a lot of time from work; (2) at the August 12 meeting at which Tyndall was terminated, Seay commented that Tyndall "didn't sound too great" and asked if she was doing okay; and (3) at the same meeting, Thompson told Tyndall that her health and the health of her family seemed more important than her job. Far from disclosing discriminatory motive, however, these statements are unexceptional remarks regarding Tyndall's work performance or general welfare. Seay's comment about Tyndall "not sounding great," for example, was prompted by Tyndall's cold symptoms, not by her disability. More basically, an employer must feel free to explore workplace problems with an employee without fear of making actionable statements at every turn. The civil rights laws prohibit discrimination, not discussion. The ADA does not discontinue the dialogue on problems such as substandard job performance or absence from work.

[Discussion of state discrimination claim omitted.]

For the foregoing reasons, the judgment of the district court is Affirmed.

NOTES AND QUESTIONS

1. In *Tyndall*, the employee had lupus and other health conditions. The court stated that "it is undisputed that Tyndall's lupus condition constituted a 'disability.'" See Laura Rothstein & Julia Rothstein, Disabilities and the Law § 4.9 *Orthopedic and Mobility Impairments* (2009). Is lupus likely to be found to be a disability under the ADAAA?

2. *Application of Family and Medical Leave Act:* The court notes that the employer has no obligation to accommodate an employee's needs to care for a family member. This case was decided before the Family and Medical Leave Act (FMLA), 29 U.S.C. §§ 2601–2654, was passed in 1993. The FMLA requires employers with 50 or more employees to provide up to 12 weeks of unpaid leave to care for an immediate family member with a serious health condition and for several other family and medical reasons. Would this statute have had any impact on the decision in the *Tyndall* case?

3. *Job Reassignment and Other Accommodations in Response to Attendance Requirements:* The *Tyndall* decision demonstrates the issue of attendance as a legitimate requirement for employment. In *Carr v. Reno*, 23 F.3d 525 (D.C. Cir. 1994), the employee had an ear disability causing periodic dizziness, nausea, and vomiting. Ms. Carr worked for the Department of Justice as a data transcriber on a flexible schedule. Although she performed her work satisfactorily, she began missing a great deal of work, and because her dizzy spells were unpredictable, she was often unable to call in to advise her employer. She accumulated an extensive number of hours (477 hours in her first seven months of work) of leave. The

Department attempted to accommodate her by providing a sofa in a nearby office, but this did not help. The court noted that:

> If the Office falls behind in [its data transcribing], it must expend considerable resources to catch up. When Ms. Carr, without advance warning or prompt explanation, did not show up for work, the Office was forced to rely on a single clerk because it could not know when a replacement (assuming one could be found) would be needed.

Ms. Carr failed to produce a detailed doctor's report in response to the employer's request for documentation. When at one point she was allowed to work on her own schedule, she received an "outstanding" performance rating, but she still did not put in an eight-hour day. After over four years of poor attendance, she was discharged.

In response to her challenges under Sections 501 and 504 of the Rehabilitation Act, the court noted the following requirements under the Rehabilitation Act:

[T]he "model employer" standard requires that:

> (1) An agency shall make reasonable accommodation to the known physical or mental limitations of an applicant or employee who is a qualified individual with handicaps unless the agency can demonstrate that the accommodation would impose an undue hardship on the operations of its program.

> (2) Reasonable accommodation may include, but shall not be limited to:

>> (i) Making facilities readily accessible to and usable by individuals with handicaps; and (ii) Job restructuring, part-time or modified work schedules, acquisition or modification of equipment or devices, appropriate adjustment or modification of examinations, the provision of readers and interpreters, and other similar actions.

29 C.F.R § 1614.203(c). Currently, the model employer requirement appears at 29 C.F.R. § 1614.203(a), and the standards are those set forth in the EEOC's ADA regulations at 29 C.F.R. part 1630. See 29 C.F.R. § 1614.203.

The court addressed the question of "whether any reasonable accommodation would have allowed Ms. Carr to perform all the essential functions of her job without creating an undue hardship for the agency."

> Ms. Carr asked for the following accommodation: a flexible arrival time (between 8:00 a.m. and noon); release from the requirement of continually providing doctors' reports; and job restructuring to ensure that the time-sensitive portions of her job were taken care of when she was unable to attend. But the district court considered this an unsatisfactory solution. Because of Ms. Carr's erratic (at best) attendance record and her inability to inform the Office when she could not attend, the court found that the U.S. Attorney's Office could not function normally without having others do her work on a daily basis. The U.S. Attorney's Office has demonstrated that its 4:00 p.m. deadline renders a flexible schedule an undue hardship. Its chosen accommodation, to allow Ms. Carr as-needed access to the health unit and to a sofa in a nearby office, did not result in improved attendance.

As for giving Ms. Carr a flexible schedule, the court noted, even for the short period in 1986 when this was tried Ms. Carr could not work a full eight-hour day. With or without reasonable accommodation, then, she could not perform the "essential function" of coming to work regularly.

We are reminded that section 501 demands a great deal from federal employers in the way of accommodation. Indeed, in appropriate cases, that section requires an agency to consider work at home, as well as reassignment in another position, as potential forms of accommodation. But under the facts of this case the U.S. Attorney's Office properly rejected these options. Ms. Carr concedes that she could not work as a Coding Clerk at home, as the job involves tight 4:00 p.m. deadlines. Even if a job could be found for her that allowed her to work at home, there is no reason to think her periodic dizziness and nausea would allow her to work regular hours on a consistent basis.

Although reassignment in another job may be one form of reasonable accommodation, and the regulations specifically provide that "job restructuring" or "part-time or modified work schedules" should be considered, 29 C.F.R. § 1614.203(b)(2), the district court held that Ms. Carr's attendance was so erratic as to make her unqualified for any position. We agree with the proposition that an essential function of any government job is an ability to appear for work (whether in the workplace or, in the unusual case, at home) and to complete assigned tasks within a reasonable period of time. Ms. Carr's record demonstrates that the Office could not count on her to fulfill these minimum expectations. If it is unreasonable to ask the Office to continue to put up with Ms. Carr's poor attendance, it is equally unreasonable to require the Office to refer an unqualified employee to another government agency for employment.

4. *Other Cases Involving Attendance: Jackson v. Veterans Admin.*, 22 F.3d 277 (11th Cir. 1994), involved a housekeeping aide with rheumatoid arthritis whose condition resulted in excessive and unpredictable absences. Although he performed his custodial tasks satisfactorily while he was at work, the employer argued that his "presence on a routine basis is also an essential element of the job that he has failed to satisfy." The court agreed, and found that:

> [u]nlike other jobs that can be performed off site or deferred until a later day, the tasks of a housekeeping aide by their very nature must be performed daily at a specific location . . . .

The heart of the problem was the "unpredictable nature" of the absences which would unduly burden the employer to accommodate.

Guice-Mills v. Derwinski, 967 F.2d 794 (2d Cir. 1992), involved a head nurse at a Veterans Administration hospital. The complainant's position was an administrative one, with job duties such as participating in major administrative activities concerning her unit, meetings near the beginning of her shift, and reviewing and modifying scheduling for patient care. The court noted that "the hospital's standard requirement is that a head nurse be present and fulfill the prescribed tasks during the designated administrative shift" and to work different shifts and cover more than one unit if other head nurses are absent.

When she requested a number of accommodations to her position as head nurse related to scheduling, including being able to arrive late, she was denied this request. The court agreed with the district court's finding that: "[A]n administrative work week tour of duty was a critical requirement for the position of Head Nurse at the Hospital." Testimony at trial had indicated that "an administrative shift commencing at 7:30 or 8:00 a.m. was an essential requirement of the head nurse position."

> The fact that occasional exceptions were made to the shift requirements does not undermine the district court's finding that compelling the hospital to place appellant permanently in a head nurse position with a 10:00 a.m. starting time would affect the services offered by the hospital to patients in the particular unit and thus constitute an undue burden. Because Guice-Mills' ailments prevented her from fulfilling the justified requirements of a head nurse position, she was not "otherwise qualified" for that position.
>
> Moreover, with regard to an offer of reasonable accommodation, the hospital offered Guice-Mills a position as a staff nurse with the hours requested and with no reduction in remuneration. In addition to making changes in job requirements that do not create undue hardship for the employer, an employer may reassign the handicapped employee as a "reasonable accommodation." When an employer offers an employee an alternative position that does not require a significant reduction in pay and benefits, that offer is a "reasonable accommodation" virtually as a matter of law. Accordingly, the offer of a staff nurse position — a position at the requested hours, for which appellant was qualified by training and experience, without loss of grade or salary — constituted a "reasonable accommodation."

In *Mason v. Avaya Communications*, Inc., 357 F.3d 1114 (10th Cir. 2004), the plaintiff, who suffered from post traumatic stress disorder, requested for the right to work at home after a coworker pulled a knife on another coworker and threatened her. The court discussed whether being present was an essential function of the job:

> According to Avaya, Mason's physical attendance at the center is an essential function of the service coordination position because the low-level hourly position is administrative in nature and requires supervision. Furthermore, a service coordinator's duties require teamwork. Consistent with 29 C.F.R. § 1630.2(n)(3), Avaya presented evidence to the district court demonstrating four of the evidentiary factors set forth by the EEOC regulations. Specifically, Avaya presented evidence that (1) it considers attendance at the administration center, supervision, and teamwork as essential functions of the service coordinator position, (2) all of its service coordinators work their entire shift at the administration centers, (3) it has never permitted a service coordinator to work anywhere other than an administration center, and (4) service coordinators cannot be adequately trained or supervised if they are not at the administration center.

Mason responds that her physical attendance at the administration center was not an essential function of the service coordinator position because she can perform all of the essential functions of the job at home using a computer, telephone, and fax machine. In support of her argument, Mason relies on her own firsthand experience[.]

Assuming Avaya had the technology to permit Mason to work from home, Avaya established it still could not adequately supervise Mason if she was at home. Although Avaya could tell if Mason was logged into her computer, Avaya's supervisors would not be able to ascertain what she was doing while logged into the computer. Mason could, for example, engage in any number of non-work related activities while logged into her computer without Avaya's knowledge. The EEOC regulations recognize that "the inquiry into essential functions is not intended to second guess an employer's business judgment with regard to production standards, whether qualitative or quantitative, nor to require employers to lower such standards." See 29 C.F.R. § 1630 App. at 356. At a time when employers are justifiably concerned with productivity at the workplace, we are in no position to second guess Avaya's desire to directly supervise its lower level employees.

Similarly, Avaya presented significant evidence demonstrating teamwork is an essential function of the service coordinator position because the coordinators typically assist and cover for one another in a job even Mason described as "very hectic."

Mason's own testimony that she could perform the essential functions of the service coordinator position from home is insufficient under Fed. R. Civ. P. 56(c) to create a "genuine" issue of material fact concerning the essential functions of the service coordinator position. [T]he only evidence Mason proffered in support of her argument that she could perform the essential functions of her job from home, other than her own self-serving testimony, was the absence of attendance, supervision, and teamwork from the service coordinator job description. We are not persuaded the absence of those functions from the job description demonstrates those functions were non-essential. [W]e find the omission of physical attendance, teamwork, and supervision from the job description entirely unremarkable. In cases arising under the ADA, we do not sit as "as a 'super personnel department' that second guesses employers' business judgments."

Additional cases involving attendance as a job requirement can be found at Laura Rothstein & Julia Rothstein, Disabilities and the Law § 4.11 (2009).

––––––––––––

In the following case, the court takes a different view of whether an employer should be required under the ADA to permit an employee to work at home. Consider the differences between this and the previous case.

HUMPHREY v. MEMORIAL HOSPITALS ASSOCIATION
239 F.3d 1128 (9th Cir. 2001).

REINHARDT, CIRCUIT JUDGE:

Carolyn Humphrey brought suit against her former employer, Memorial Hospitals Association (MHA), under the Americans with Disabilities Act (ADA) for failure to reasonably accommodate her disability and wrongful termination. We reverse the district court's grant of summary judgment in favor of MHA.

I. BACKGROUND

Humphrey worked for MHA as a medical transcriptionist from 1986 until her termination in 1995. Throughout her employment at MHA, Humphrey's transcription performance was excellent and consistently exceeded MHA's standards for speed, accuracy, and productivity.

In 1989, Humphrey began to experience problems getting to work on time, or at all. She engaged in a series of obsessive rituals that hindered her ability to arrive at work on time. She felt compelled to rinse her hair for up to an hour, and if, after brushing her hair, it didn't "feel right," she would return to the shower to wash it again. This process of washing and preparing her hair could take up to three hours. She would also feel compelled to dress very slowly, to repeatedly check and recheck for papers she needed, and to pull out strands of her hair and examine them closely because she felt as though something was crawling on her scalp. She testified that these obsessive thoughts and rituals made it very difficult to get to work on time. Once she realized that she was late, she would panic and become embarrassed, making it even more difficult for her to leave her house and get to work.

Due to Humphrey's difficulties with tardiness and absenteeism, MHA gave her a "Level I" disciplinary warning in June 1994. This warning required her to call her supervisor before the time she was due to be at work if she was going to be late or absent. Humphrey's mental obsessions and peculiar rituals only grew worse after the warning, and her attendance record did not improve; nor did her call-in rate. In December 1994, she received a "Level III" warning, which documented four tardy days and one unreported absence over a two week period.

When MHA gave Humphrey the Level III warning, she was told that she was expected to schedule and keep counseling appointments with the Employee Assistance Program (EAP). This counseling consisted of "tips," helpful hints such as getting up earlier and laying out clothes the night before. Humphrey found this somewhat helpful and attended several sessions, but her efforts to follow the "tips" were not particularly successful. In May, 1995, she asked MHA's EAP nurse, Elizabeth Pierson, if she could see a psychiatrist for an evaluation. Pierson agreed, and set up an appointment for a diagnostic evaluation and psychological testing with Dr. John Jacisin. MHA paid for the consultation through its EAP program.

Humphrey first saw Dr. Jacisin on May 12, 1995. Dr. Jacisin diagnosed her with obsessive compulsive disorder (OCD).[2] He sent a letter explaining that diagnosis to Pierson on May 18, 1995, telling her that Humphrey's OCD "is directly contributing to her problems with lateness." In addition, the letter stated:

> I believe that we can treat this, although, the treatment may take a while. I do believe that she would qualify under the Americans with Disability Act, although, I would like to see her continue to work, but if it is proving to be a major personnel problem, she may have to take some time off until we can get the symptoms better under control.

Humphrey sought treatment from Dr. Jacisin and from a psychologist, Dr. Litynsky. Dr. Litynsky, like Dr. Jacisin, diagnosed Humphrey with OCD and concluded that it was probable that the OCD caused her absenteeism and tardiness.

Humphrey had difficulty paying for the necessary services, however, because her insurance did not cover the treatment. In addition, due to the severe symptoms of her ailment, Humphrey had great difficulty showing up for appointments. Both doctors considered her inconsistency in treatment in 1995 and 1996 to be the result of the disorder as well as her financial problems.

On June 7, 1995, Humphrey met with Pierson and Humphrey's supervisor, Carol Evans-Bowlsby, to review Dr. Jacisin's letter. What happened at this meeting is disputed. MHA contends that Humphrey rejected the leave of absence alluded to in the doctor's letter. Humphrey says that she was never offered a leave of absence and never rejected one. Instead, she testified that "they asked if I would like to keep working. And I said yes." She did not remember anyone using the term "leave of absence." (As it turns out, this factual dispute is not material to our ruling on appeal.)

Humphrey did want to try to keep working, if possible, and Pierson offered a flexible start-time arrangement in which Humphrey could begin work any time within a 24 hour period on days on which she was scheduled to work. A few days later, Humphrey sent Pierson a letter accepting the flexible start time arrangement, and saying that she "would still do my best to be at my work station at the earliest possible hour."

Nevertheless, Humphrey continued to miss work. It is disputed whether Humphrey's supervisor warned her about her conduct during the remainder of that summer. It is undisputed, however, that no one from MHA broached the subject of modifying the accommodation during that period. On September 18, 1995, Humphrey, upset about her continuing problems, sent Pierson an e-mail message asking for a new accommodation because the then-current one seemed to be failing:

---

[2] Individuals with obsessive compulsive disorder experience obsessions or compulsions or both. *See American Psychiatric Ass'n, Diagnostic and Statistical Manual of Mental Disorders 417* (4th ed. 1994). Obsessions are recurring or persistent thoughts, images, or impulses that, rather than being voluntarily produced, seem to invade a person's consciousness despite his attempts to ignore, suppress, or control them. Compulsions are urges or impulses to commit repetitive acts that are apparently meaningless, stereotyped, or ritualistic. The disorder was recently made famous by Jack Nicholson's Oscar-winning portrayal of a man with OCD in the 1998 film *As Good As it Gets.*

Dear Liz:

It has now been a few months since I sent you a memo regarding how my disability would best be accommodated as far as my job performance. I have since come to the conclusion that I would be able to put in considerable more hours [sic] and be much more productive if I were able to work from my home as a lot of other transcriptionists are doing. . . . I think this would be the ideal way to accommodate my diagnosed disability.

MHA allows certain medical transcriptionists to work out of their homes. Dr. Jacisin was not asked by anyone at MHA for his opinion on the work-at-home request. After Humphrey's termination, Jacisin said that working at home "might accommodate some of her work issues" but might be "anti-therapeutic." He testified, in his deposition in this lawsuit, that he felt working at home was an accommodation which would have been worth trying because it was necessary for Humphrey to earn money and increase her self-confidence.

In any event, Humphrey's request was summarily denied. [Pierson wrote:]

It is departmental policy that if you are involved in any disciplinary action you are ineligible to be a home based transcriptionist as per the AT HOME ARRANGEMENT FOR TRANSCRIPTIONISTS. Since you are currently involved in the discipline process, you are ineligible for being based at home. During our 6/7/95 meeting, you requested to be accommodated for your disability by having a flexible start time, stating that you would have no problems staying for a full shift once you arrived. You were given this flexible start time accommodation which continues to remain in effect. As for your productivity, your manager indicated that you consistently meet your hourly productivity requirements when you are at work.

Pierson's comment regarding Humphrey's productivity at work was typical of Humphrey's performance evaluations, which recognized her high level of competence but were tarnished by the problems caused by her disability.

Humphrey's evaluation indicates that were it not for her ailment, she would have been a model employee. The only negative ratings she received were in relation to the problems caused by the interference of her symptoms and the accommodation of flexible start time. Her evaluation stated that her recent unscheduled absences were "unacceptable," and advised that correcting her attendance problem was "a major goal for the upcoming year." During a meeting with her supervisor, Julie Vieira, to discuss her evaluation, Humphrey again raised the issue of working at home, but was told that she would have to be free of attendance problems for a year before she could be considered for an at-home transcriptionist position. Neither Humphrey nor her supervisor suggested a medical leave of absence at this meeting.

Humphrey was absent two more times, and on October 10, 1995, Vieira fired her. MHA's stated reason for the termination was Humphrey's history of tardiness and absenteeism. Humphrey testified that after learning of her termination, she went across the hall to Pierson's office and asked if she might take a leave of absence instead of lose her job, but that Pierson refused and told her that she had had her chance at accommodation. Pierson denies that Humphrey requested a leave of absence on the day of her discharge. MHA concedes that it would have granted the request if Humphrey had asked for a leave of absence prior to her termination, as MHA had a policy of permitting medical leaves of absence to employees with disabilities.

On September 6, 1996, Humphrey brought suit against MHA for violation of the ADA. The district court granted MHA's motion for summary judgment on the theory that MHA had satisfied its duty to reasonably accommodate Humphrey's disability.

II. DISCUSSION

Humphrey contends that MHA violated the ADA by failing to reasonably accommodate her disability and by terminating her because of that disability. The ADA provides that "no covered entity shall discriminate against a qualified individual with a disability because of the disability . . . ." 42 U.S.C. § 12112(a). Title I of the ADA insures full opportunities for people with disabilities in the workplace by requiring reasonable accommodation of employees' disabilities by their employers. Under the ADA, the term "discriminate" is defined as including "not making reasonable accommodations to the known physical or mental limitations of an otherwise qualified individual with a disability who is an applicant or employee, unless such covered entity can demonstrate that the accommodation would impose an undue hardship on the operation of the business of such covered entity." 42 U.S.C. § 12112(b)(5)(A). To prevail on a claim of unlawful discharge under the ADA, the plaintiff must establish that he is a qualified individual with a disability and that the employer terminated him because of his disability. The ADA defines a "qualified individual with a disability" as "an individual with a disability who, with or without reasonable accommodation, can perform the essential functions of the employment position that such individual holds or desires." 42 U.S.C. § 12111(8). A "disability" is "a physical or mental impairment that substantially limits one or more of the major life activities of such individual." 42 U.S.C. § 12102(2)(a).

A. QUALIFIED INDIVIDUAL WITH A DISABILITY

Because the district court granted summary judgment to MHA on the ground that it reasonably accommodated Humphrey, the court did not address whether Humphrey is a qualified individual with a disability.

MHA . . . argues that Humphrey was not "qualified" for the medical transcriptionist position within the meaning of the ADA. A qualified individual is "an individual with a disability who, with or without reasonable accommodation, can perform the essential functions of the employment position that such individual holds or desires." 42 U.S.C. § 12111(8). It is undisputed that Humphrey had the skills, training, and experience to transcribe medical records. MHA contends that Humphrey's inability to show up for work and to notify her employer when she would be absent renders her not otherwise qualified under the ADA because regular and predictable attendance is an essential function of the position. However,

Humphrey is a "qualified individual" under the ADA so long as she is able to perform the essential functions of her job "with or without reasonable accommodation." 42 U.S.C. § 12111(8). Either of two potential reasonable accommodations might have made it possible for Humphrey to perform the essential functions of her job: granting her a leave of absence or allowing her to become a "home-based transcriptionist."

A leave of absence for medical treatment may be a reasonable accommodation under the ADA. See 29 C.F.R. 1630 app. § 1630.2(o). We have held that where a leave of absence would reasonably accommodate an employee's disability and permit him, upon his return, to perform the essential functions of the job, that employee is otherwise qualified under the ADA. MHA contends that Humphrey is not otherwise qualified because the results of the leave of absence were speculative. However, the ADA does not require an employee to show that a leave of absence is certain or even likely to be successful to prove that it is a reasonable accommodation.

The statements in Dr. Jacisin's letter that Humphrey's condition was treatable and that "she may have to take some time off until we can get the symptoms better under control" are sufficient to satisfy the minimal requirement that a leave of absence could plausibly have enabled Humphrey adequately to perform her job. We discuss in Section C below MHA's contention that it was not required to offer Humphrey a leave of absence or other accommodation unless she specifically requested it.

There is another reasonable accommodation that could also serve to render Humphrey a "qualified individual." There is at least a triable issue of fact as to whether Humphrey would have been able to perform the essential duties of her job with the accommodation of a work-at-home position. Working at home is a reasonable accommodation when the essential functions of the position can be performed at home and a work-at-home arrangement would not cause undue hardship for the employer. EEOC Enforcement Guidance: Reasonable Accommodation and Undue Hardship Under the Americans with Disabilities Act, FEP (BNA) 405:7601, at 7626 (March 1, 1999) [hereinafter EEOC Enforcement Guidance on Reasonable Accommodation]. Humphrey does not dispute that regular and predictable performance of the job is an essential part of the transcriptionist position because many of the medical records must be transcribed within twenty-four hours, and frequent and unscheduled absences would prevent the department from meeting its deadlines. However, physical attendance at the MHA offices is not an essential job duty; in fact, the record makes it clear that MHA permits some of its medical transcriptionists to work at home.

MHA denied Humphrey's application for a work-at-home position because of her disciplinary record, which consisted of Level I and Level III warnings for tardiness and absenteeism prior to her diagnosis of OCD. It would be inconsistent with the purposes of the ADA to permit an employer to deny an otherwise reasonable accommodation because of past disciplinary action taken due to the disability sought to be accommodated. Thus, Humphrey's disciplinary record does not constitute an appropriate basis for denying her a work-at-home accommodation.

Although Dr. Jacisin was less optimistic about Humphrey's working at home than he was about a leave of absence, Humphrey has submitted sufficient evidence to raise an issue of fact as to whether she could perform the job with the accommodation of a work-at-home position. She testified that her ailment interfered primarily with her ability to leave her house in the morning. Dr. Jacisin stated that working at home "might accommodate some of her work issues," and later testified that he felt working at home would have been worth trying because "her OCD really didn't interfere necessarily with her ability to do the work, that is to actually do the typing and transcription." A reasonable jury could conclude that if Humphrey was relieved of the stress of having to leave the house, she could perform her transcriptionist duties and thus was "qualified" under the ADA.

Accordingly, we hold that MHA is not entitled to summary judgment on the issue of whether Humphrey is a "qualified individual with a disability" for purposes of the ADA.

NOTES AND QUESTIONS

1. *Humphrey* is one of the only cases that holds that it may not be an essential function of the job to work at the office. Is this case inconsistent with the previous cases or can the cases be reconciled? How are the facts in *Humphrey* different? Do these different facts justify a different result, at least in response to a motion for summary judgment? Why? Why not?

2. The EEOC has concluded that working at home can be a reasonable accommodation under Title I of the ADA. See http://www.eeoc.gov/facts/telework.html for a discussion of the EEOC's position on the matter. Many of the courts seem to have disregarded the EEOC's position. Which position is correct? Defend the argument by citing to the statute and the policies supporting it. Does the ADAAA add to either of the arguments? Explain.

3. What is the difference with respect to attendance requirements between a custodian, a college teacher, a head nurse, a data analyst, and a computer programmer?

[b] Working Overtime

In *Rohr v. Salt River Project Agric. Improvement and Power Dist.*, 2009 U.S. App. LEXIS 2856 (9th Cir. Feb.13, 2009), the plaintiff was an insulin-dependent type 2 diabetic who appealed the lower court's grant of summary judgment for the employer whom he sued alleging discrimination under the ADA. He tires easily especially when he has to drive long ways, has chronic high blood pressure and deteriorating vision. He works as a metallurgy specialist in the tech support group. The plaintiff was occasionally called upon to travel to another power plant and work long days. This occurred only on 12 occasions throughout his 23 years at the company As his diabetes began to take more time to control, his doctor recommended that he not work more than nine hour days and that he not travel. After accommodating him for a while, the company told him that he would have to travel and be ready to work overtime. When he sued, one issue was whether the plaintiff could perform the essential functions of the job. The court overturned the lower court's summary judgment for the defendant, and held that there was a genuine issue of material fact as to whether the travel and long hours were essential functions of the job. The court noted that although consideration should be given to the employer's judgment as to what an essential function is, such evidence is not conclusive even if the function is included in a job description.

[c]   Coping with Stress

A number of cases have addressed whether coping with stress is a fundamental requirement of the job. In other words, is stress so inherent in the position, that removal of stress is not a reasonable accommodation that can be made?

JOHNSTON v. MORRISON, INC.
849 F. Supp. 777 (M.D. Ala. 1994)

EDWIN L. NELSON, DISTRICT JUDGE:

Ms. Johnston was hired as a food server in Morrison's L & N Seafood restaurant in Birmingham, Alabama, on September 18, 1992, and was employed there until December 31, 1992, as a food server. She contends that she suffers from mitral valve prolapse, dysautonomia, panic attack disorder, and hypoglycemia, rendering her unable to perform the duties of a food server. Morrison learned of the plaintiff's conditions after she began working as a food server and, thereafter, assigned her to the least busy work station in the restaurant where she was responsible for the fewest number of customers. On December 31, 1992, the restaurant became very crowded and Ms. Johnston stated that she suffered what she described as a "meltdown" because she was unable to handle the pressure of the work. Ms. Johnston alleges that on December 31, 1992, while in the midst of her "meltdown," Mr. Mitchell "grabbed and twisted [her] arm and dug his fingernails into her skin, breaking the skin."

Under the ADA, "[n]o covered entity shall discriminate against a qualified individual with a disability." 42 U.S.C. § 12112(a). A "qualified individual with a disability" is one "who, with or without reasonable accommodation, can perform the essential functions of the employment position that such individual holds or desires." 42 U.S.C. § 12111(8). . . .

"The term essential functions means the fundamental job duties of the employment position the individual with a disability holds or desires." 29 C.F.R. § 1630.2(n)(1). . . . Morrison has the right to determine that an essential function of being a food server at its L & N Seafood restaurant includes knowing and being able to communicate the ingredients, portion sizes, and prices of items on the menu. See 42 U.S.C. § 12111(8) ("consideration shall be given to the employer's judgment as to what functions of a job are essential") and 29 C.F.R. § 1630.2(n)(3)(i) (an employer can determine which functions are essential). Plaintiff testified that Morrison constantly made changes in what she was required to know and be able to communicate to the customers. Morrison also has the right to determine whether changes in matters such as food ingredients, portion sizes, and pricing are necessary in order to stay competitive. See 29 C.F.R.

§ 1630.2(n)(3)(i) and 29 C.F.R. § 1630.2(n)(3)(iv) (the consequences of not requiring the incumbent to perform the function can be used to determine whether a function is essential).

However, Ms. Johnston testified that, because of her disability, she could not handle such changes. She testified that changes of the kind described caused "a panic attack all the time," and these attacks resulted in "constant headache, constant fear," and "confusion inside." She stated that "[t]he constant changes just screwed up [her] whole body." If Ms. Johnston were not required to perform the essential function of learning and communicating information concerning ingredients, portion sizes, and prices, then she would be something other than a food server as defined by the day-to-day operation at Morrison's L & N Seafood restaurant. "The essential functions are by definition those that the individual who holds the job would have to perform, with or without reasonable accommodation, in order to be considered qualified for the position." Interpretive Guidance on Title I of the Americans with Disabilities Act, 29 C.F.R.App. § 1630.2(o).

Ms. Johnston also testified that her disability prevented her from performing her food server duties when Morrison's L & N Seafood restaurant became crowded. She stated that in order to accommodate her disability Morrison assigned her to the restaurant's least busy area where she was responsible for the fewest number of tables. Even with this accommodation, however, Ms. Johnston stated that she was unable to handle the work when the restaurant became crowded. She testified that on December 31, 1992, the restaurant was "packed" and that due to the pace of the work she suffered a "meltdown." Under the ADA, a reasonable accommodation may include "job restructuring, part-time or modified work schedules," 42 U.S.C. § 12111(9)(B); however, "[a]n employer or other covered entity is not required to reallocate essential functions." Interpretive Guidance on Title I of the Americans with Disabilities Act, 29 C.F.R.App. § 1630.2(o). Ms. Johnston's food server position required her to serve the customers in her work station. Morrison was not required to provide another employee to handle the plaintiff's food server duties. Morrison also was not required to simply remove plaintiff from her work station when her work station became crowded. In cases interpreting the Rehabilitation Act of 1973, courts have found that an employee's inability to work necessary hours justified an employee's termination.

Ms. Johnston contends that until December 31, 1992, she was able to perform her duties as a food server with the accommodation Morrison provided. Plaintiff would segregate her employment experience at Morrison's restaurant on December 31, 1992, from the remainder of her employment there, apparently conceding that she was unable on that evening to perform the essential functions of the job of food server. However, Ms. Johnston's position as a food server required her to perform her duties during all times she was at her work station, whether the situation presented slow or busy periods. Ms. Johnston's employment at L & N Seafood during December 31, 1992, may not be viewed as a discrete incident in determining whether she is a qualified individual for purposes of the ADA. Her employment during December 31, 1992, is relevant, because it shows that her disabilities caused her to suffer a "meltdown" when her work station became busy, and thus, she was unable to perform the essential functions of the job.

In conclusion, Ms. Johnston's disability prevented her from performing the essential functions required of a food server at Morrison's L & N Seafood restaurant. Since she cannot perform the essential functions of the position, she is not a qualified individual for purposes of the ADA. Since the 42 U.S.C. § 12112(a) requirement that plaintiff be a "qualified individual with a disability" has not been met, the Court need not address whether Morrison's pre-employment inquiries would otherwise have been in violation of 42 U.S.C. § 12112(d)(2)(A).

NOTES

In *Doe v. Region 13 Mental Health-Mental Retardation Commission*, 704 F.2d 1402 (5th Cir. 1983), a psychologist working for a state operated mental health center suffered from a variety of mental health problems that had become more serious over time. She was ordered not to see any more patients and was advised that she should consider employment elsewhere or long term leave for hospitalization, after which she might be considered for rehiring. Although she had an exemplary work record and her attendance, paper work, and interpersonal relationships with other staff members were all positive, she had exhibited serious suicidal tendencies over a long period of time. The court looked at the totality of the circumstances, including the potential adverse effect of a suicide or attempted suicide on patients, and determined that she was not otherwise qualified.

Relationship of Difficulty with Stress and Direct Threat Cases. A later section in this chapter includes cases and discussion of situations where mental health problems present a direct threat to the health or safety of others. Difficulty dealing with stress does not always result in violent or dangerous behavior. It can result in the person's not being able to carry out the job requirements. In *Carrozza v. Howard County*, 847 F. Supp. 365 (D. Md. 1994), the court held it was not discriminatory to discharge a clerk-typist with bipolar disorder who was rude and insubordinate and who had outbursts directed toward supervisors. Another court found that a customer service representative who was unable to answer customer telephone calls due to panic attacks and mood swings was not a qualified individual. *Larkins v. CIBA Vision Corp.*, 858 F. Supp. 1572 (N.D. Ga. 1994).

Assigning to Different Supervisor as a Reasonable Accommodation. In *Gaul v. Lucent Techs*, 134 F.3d 576 (3d Cir. 1998), the court held that the ADA did not oblige the employer to accommodate a worker with depression and anxiety by assigning him to work with different supervisors. The court concluded that the request for different supervisors was unreasonable. See also *Weiler v. Household Finance Corp.*, 101 F. 3d 519 (7th Cir. 1996) (holding that the plaintiff, who suffered from anxiety and depression, was not entitled to the accommodation of changing her supervisor, because the ADA does not give the employee the right to make the employer's decision about terms and conditions of employment); *Poff v. Rockford Pub. Sch. Dist.*, 2009 U.S. Dist. LEXIS 16217 (N.D. Ill. Feb. 25, 2009) (same).

The discussion of reasonable accommodation later in this chapter, however, provides guidance on the fact that while major changes might not be required to reduce stress in certain situations involving individuals with mental impairments, there are nonetheless, a number of steps that can easily be taken in many employment settings. The issue of job reassignment as an accommodation is also important on this issue.

[d]   Professional and Technical Competence

In the section on standards at the hiring stage, the issue of professional and technical competence to perform work requirements was discussed. This issue also is discussed in Chapter 6 (Higher Education). If the job is to drive a bus, the employee must be able to drive. If the position is that of a teacher, skills such as those discussed in the following case are necessary.

The *Pandazides* case addresses both qualification standards and reasonable accommodation in the context of Section 504. It is also one of the few decisions in the employment discrimination area involving a learning disability. Most such cases arise in the context of education or higher education.

PANDAZIDES v. VIRGINIA BOARD OF EDUCATION
804 F. Supp. 794 (E.D. Va. 1992)

HILTON, DISTRICT JUDGE:

Findings of Fact

1.   This action has been brought under section 504 of the Rehabilitation Act of 1973.

2.   Plaintiff, Sofia P. Pandazides is 26 years old. Following Plaintiff's graduation from Longwood College, she was employed as a special education teacher at Woodbridge Middle School in the Prince William County School System for a one-year appointment for the 1988–89 school year.

3.   The State Board of Education granted Plaintiff a one-year nonrenewable probationary certificate to teach in Prince William County from September 1988 to September 1989 in 1988. Plaintiff's probationary teaching certificate was subject to the condition that she meet the Board of Education's requirement that she pass the National Teacher Examination ("NTE") during the one-year period for which she was granted leave to teach.

8.   The NTE is composed of two categories of tests: (1) Core Battery, and (2) Specialty Area Tests.

9.   The NTE Core Battery provides a comprehensive assessment of the basic knowledge and skills required for the beginning teacher and consists of three separate tests: Communication Skills, General Knowledge, and Professional Knowledge.

10.   The Communication Skills test covers listening, reading, and writing.

[Descriptions of General Knowledge and Professional Knowledge portions omitted.]

17. Dr. Cross's validation study concluded that the skills tested by the NTE Communication Skills Test were strongly endorsed by classroom teachers and by teacher educators as essential functions which were actually needed on a constant basis in the professional teacher's job.

18. The conclusion reached by Dr. Cross in his Virginia validation study that the NTE measured skills necessary for minimally competent performance for certified professional teachers was the same result found in a study of teacher educators and classroom teachers who examined the contents of the Communications Skills Test for ETS in over 15 states.

19. On June 21, 1984, the Virginia Board of Education approved the cut scores for the Core Battery which were recommended by Dr. Cross's validation study.

21. Although Plaintiff passed the NTE's general knowledge test on her first attempt and passed the NTE's professional knowledge test on her second attempt, Plaintiff has failed the NTE's communication skills test eight times.

22. The NTE's communications skills test measures the ability of prospective teachers to understand and use elements of written and spoken language.

[Description of listening and writing skills sections omitted.]

28. The NTE's communication skills test is an objective standardized examination designed to have no interaction between an examinee and an exam administrator. The communication skills test was designed to be non-interactive in order to avoid the possibility that the examinee's answers could be cued or shaped by a person administering or interpreting the examination and to present the same challenges to all examinees independent of the qualifications of the administrator.

29. After having failed the NTE communications skills test [on six occasions], Plaintiff wrote to the Virginia Department of Education asking that she be exempted from the licensure requirement of passing the NTE communications skills section on January 25, 1989. This letter made no mention of any learning disabilities.

30. In a letter dated February 10, 1989, Plaintiff again wrote the Virginia Department of Education in which she stated her belief that "a subtle learning disability prevents me from passing this one part of the NTE." Plaintiff enclosed two letters to support this assertion.

[Details of letters omitted.]

34. The Virginia Department of Education denied Plaintiff's request. . . .

35. Plaintiff wrote to ETS in a letter dated March 17, 1989 seeking two special arrangements for taking the Communication Skills Test: "A reader and unlimited response time.

38. The NTE Program ETS considered this request for special arrangements in accordance with the policies and procedures in the NTE Programs Policy for Testing Examinees with Disabilities.

39. The NTE Program's Policy for Testing individuals with Disabilities was developed in collaboration with the ETS Committee on People with Disabilities to

develop sensitive and appropriate testing alternatives for individuals with disabilities who are taking NTE tests to be licensed to practice as classroom teachers and other educational positions.

40. Other than a literal reading for blind test takers, neither the NTE nor any other ETS test are administered on terms which would allow a third person to mediate between the examinee and the test itself. Hearing-impaired test takers are provided a sign-language interpreter for spoken instruction, but must handle the test content alone.

41. Following the ETS policy of granting special testing accommodations for disabilities when an applicant provides sufficient documentation to justify test accommodations, ETS granted Plaintiff four accommodations, relying solely on the letters Plaintiff had submitted. These accommodations were granted without making any finding or assessment on its own regarding Plaintiff's alleged disabilities. [Accommodations that were allowed were extended time, a script of the tape used in the listening session, a tape recorder that would permit listening to the tape more slowly, and a separate testing room.]

46. Plaintiff took the NTE communications skills test twice during June 1989. She took the test on June 17 under standard testing conditions and on June 30, 1989 with accommodations.

47. Although Plaintiff failed the exam on both occasions, she achieved the same score under standard testing conditions as she had under multiple accommodations. In both test sittings, Plaintiff had her lowest percentages of correct answers in the reading and writing test categories, not the listening section. Even without special accommodations, Plaintiff had her highest percentage of correct answers on the listening portion of the test.

56. In evaluation by Prince William County Public Schools in February 1989 Plaintiff was rated "needs improvement" in 3 of 5 job categories. Those were: (1) delivery of instruction, (2) classroom management, and (3) planning and knowledge of content. She was rated as an "effective teacher" only in "providing favorable psychological environment" and "professional responsibilities."

57. To help Miss Pandazides with her teaching shortcomings, Plaintiff's supervisors gave her the assistance of an experienced classroom teacher and guidance in planning lessons.

58. Because of Plaintiff's poor evaluations and her failure to pass the NTE following her first year probationary period, Plaintiff was not rehired on a full-time basis for the next school year, but on a temporary substitute basis until a competent and certified special education teacher was hired to replace her.

59. Mid-way through the school year, her supervisors requested that she be removed from the classroom immediately because of her weaknesses as a teacher. Because school administrators viewed her classroom management skills as "lacking," school administrators sought to avert "a potentially explosive situation."

60. The Superintendent of Schools for Prince William County testified at trial that even if Plaintiff had passed the NTE communications skills test, she would not have been rehired because of her inability to manage her classroom.

61. In evaluation by Prince William County Public Schools in June 1990, Plaintiff received an overall rating as "effective," but still was rated as "needs improvement" in classroom management. The overall rating of "effective" was given when her evaluators knew she would not be returning to that school and in an attempt to be helpful to Miss Pandazides.

Conclusions of Law

"The state has the right to adopt academic requirements and to use written achievement tests designed and validated to disclose the minimum amount of knowledge necessary to effective teaching."

Section 504 does not prohibit minimum competency tests; nor does it mean that the handicapped are excused from reasonable standards of minimum competence.

The Rehabilitation Act was not intended to eliminate academic or professional requirements that measure proficiency in analyzing written information by attaining a passing score on a multiple choice test.

The Rehabilitation Act never requires that basic academic standards be altered, or that substantial modifications in professional requirements be made to allow entry to a handicapped candidate.

"That defendant could have provided a different set of reasonable accommodations or more accommodations does not establish that the accommodations provided were unreasonable or that additional accommodations were necessary." Courts are prohibited from requiring a fundamental alteration in a defendant's program to accommodate a handicapped individual.

[The court raises the question of whether the plaintiff is even handicapped within the statute.]

Plaintiff has failed to establish that the accommodations made by ETS, with the concurrence of defendants, were not reasonable accommodations which were directly responsive to those difficulties which the Plaintiff claimed as disabilities. Unlimited time would not be a reasonable accommodation because similar modifications could not be expected in the job of teaching. The listening, reading and writing skills being measured in the Test of Communication Skills are those judged necessary to competent performance as a beginning classroom teacher. There is some variability in how quickly or slowly a teacher needs to read or write as required on the job, but the real world requirements do not permit totally unlimited time to accomplish work in the classroom such as reading and correcting students' work, working directly with students in groups or as a whole unit, or writing comments and directions for them about their work. The limitations of time are even more demanding when one considers the listening skills required of a classroom teacher. Similarly, interaction with the examiner would have been a fundamental change to the test design which would compromise the integrity of the test as a measure of minimum skills.

The Virginia Board of Education requirement that those seeking a professional license to teach in Virginia public schools pass the Communication Skills Test of the NTE is a reasonable and legitimate professional licensing requirement.

The Communications Skills Test of the NTE accurately measures "essential functions" of the job of teaching in grades 1 through 12 in the public schools of Virginia. The NTE Communications Skills Test measures a prospective teacher's ability to understand and use the elements of written or spoken language.

Because of Plaintiff's poor teaching evaluations and the extraordinary measures taken by her supervisors in pursuit of her removal from the classroom, Plaintiff has failed to establish that she is an excellent or effective teacher despite her inability to demonstrate minimum professional communication skills as measured by the NTE.

Plaintiff is not "otherwise qualified" under § 504 because she cannot perform "essential functions" of public school teacher in Virginia. The ability to read intelligently, to comprehend written and spoken communication accurately, effectively and quickly, and to respond to written and spoken communication professionally, effectively and quickly, are "essential functions" of a special education, public school teacher in Virginia. Moreover, the ability to manage a classroom is an "essential function" for a public school teacher in grades 1 through 12 in Virginia. Plaintiff has failed to prove competence in this essential function.

There is no evidence on which the Court can conclude that the Virginia Board of Education has discriminated against the plaintiff based on a handicap. Thus, the Court cannot conclude that plaintiff must be excused from meeting the legitimate and valid requirements for a teachers license in Virginia.

NOTES

1. On appeal, the Fourth Circuit reversed and remanded the previous decision, holding that there is a right to a jury trial under the Rehabilitation Act where the relief sought is damages. The court did not decide the merits of the case. *Pandazides v. Virginia Bd. of Ed.*, 13 F.3d 823 (4th Cir. 1994).

2. *Police Officers.* There have been a number of cases involving police officers who have become disabled (often in the line of duty), who are then no longer able to carry out the requirements of a police officer. These decisions usually involve a discussion of whether certain duties, such as effecting a forcible arrest, are essential, and whether transfer to light duty or a desk job is a reasonable accommodation that should be required. The majority of these decisions have resulted in substantial deference to the law enforcement agency regarding its job descriptions, but some recent cases have examined more closely whether a job reassignment should be considered. In August 1994, the Department of Justice issued a letter of finding in the case of *Davoll v. Webb*, 943 F. Supp. 1289 (D. Colo. 1995). It is the Department's position that job reassignment should be considered in cases involving police officers who can no longer carry out all the requirements of the position.

In *Simon v. St. Louis County*, 563 F. Supp. 76 (E.D. Mo. 1983), the court was required to decide on remand whether a police officer who had become a paraplegic after a gunshot wound was qualified to perform all of the "reasonable, legitimate, and necessary" requirements of a commissioned police officer. The ability to perform a forceful arrest and to work in all positions of the department were deemed to be essential technical requirements of the position. See also *Mathes v. Harris County, Tex.*, 96 F. Supp. 2d 650 (S.D. Tex. 2000) (requiring that person with hand deformity, applying for communication position in sheriff's department, be certified as a peace officer did not rationally relate to the job functions under the ADA); *Kees v. Wallenstein*, 973 F. Supp. 1191 (W.D. Wash. 1997) (employees unable to be in direct, physical contact with inmates unable to perform essential functions of corrections officer); *Karbusicky v. City of Park Ridge*, 950 F. Supp. 878 (N.D. Ill. 1997) (a police officer with hearing loss in one ear is not qualified); *Siefken v. Arlington Heights*, 3 A.D. Cases (BNA) 1281 (N.D. Ill. 1994) (police officer with diabetes who was fired after driving erratically and then collapsing into a coma was not qualified). For additional case citations, see LAURA ROTHSTEIN & JULIA ROTHSTEIN, DISABILITIES AND THE LAW § 4.11 (2009).

3. Other cases involving physical qualifications for certain positions include *Cook v. Rhode Island*, 10 F.3d 17 (1st Cir. 1993) (whether mobility and lifting ability related to job of nursing); *Lowe v. Angelo's Italian Foods, Inc.*, 1994 LEXIS 17150, 3 A.D. Cases (BNA) 1654 (D. Kan. 1994) (restaurant employee with multiple sclerosis was not qualified because she was unable to perform lifting and carrying heavy objects, which were essential functions of the job).

4. *Health Care Professions.* The unique concerns of health care professionals make these positions subject to close scrutiny by the courts. See Laura F. Rothstein, *Health Care Professionals with Mental and Physical Impairments: Developments in Disability Discrimination Law*, 41 ST. LOUIS U. L.J. 973 (1997). See also LAURA ROTHSTEIN & JULIA ROTHSTEIN, DISABILITIES AND THE LAW Ch. 10 (2009).

The Interpretive Guidance to the ADA regulations notes the following with respect to qualifications:

> It is important to note that the inquiry into essential functions is not intended to second guess an employer's business judgment with regard to production standards . . . nor to require employers to lower such standards. If an employer requires its typists to be able to accurately type 75 words per minute, it will not be called upon to explain why an inaccurate work product, or a typing speed of 65 words per minute, would not be adequate. Similarly, if a hotel requires its service workers to thoroughly clean 16 rooms per day, it will not have to explain why it requires thorough cleaning, or why it chose a 16 room rather than a 10 room requirement. However, if any employer does [have such requirements] it will have to show that it actually imposes such requirements on its employees in fact, and not simply on paper. It should also be noted that, if it is alleged that the employer intentionally selected the particular level of production to exclude individuals with disabilities, the employer may have to offer a legitimate, nondiscriminatory reason for its selection.

56 Fed. Reg. 35,743–35,744 (July 26, 1991).

Many of the cases on qualifications also address the issue of reasonable accommodation, because in some instances, the person would have the technical or professional competence with reasonable accommodation. Examples of these cases are found later in this chapter.

[e]   Marginal Functions

In the *AIC* decision, *supra*, the court addressed Mr. Wessell's ability to drive a car as a job requirement. The employer was unable to establish that this was an essential function of the position of Executive Director of AIC. The ADA regulations specifically note that "The term 'essential functions' does not include the marginal functions of the position." 26 C.F.R. § 1630.2(n)(1). In the *AIC* case, it is questionable whether driving was a function of any kind; at most, it was only a marginal function.

Just because an activity is performed only occasionally does not make it marginal. "For example, although a firefighter may not regularly have to carry an unconscious adult out of a burning building, the consequences of failing to perform this function would be serious." 56 Fed. Reg. 35,743 (July 26, 1991). Therefore, being able to carry 180 pounds would not be a marginal function, although the firefighter may do this rarely. In contrast, if a person is hired as a receptionist, where the job functions are to answer the phone, make appointments, and greet clients, it might be found that typing is a marginal function, where the receptionist is called upon only rarely to perform this function, and where there are others in the workforce who can readily carry out this function.

The employer usually has the burden of demonstration that functions are not marginal. In *Kuehl v. Wal-Mart Stores, Inc.*, 909 F. Supp. 794 (D. Colo. 1995), the employer had demonstrated that the ability to stand for a full shift was an essential function of the job of a door greeter. For additional cases and discussion, see LAURA ROTHSTEIN & JULIA ROTHSTEIN, DISABILITIES AND THE LAW § 4.11 (2009).

[2]   Direct Threat

HYPOTHETICAL PROBLEM 3.4

Read the following hypothetical problem before reading the materials on direct threat to the health and safety of the individual and of others. After reading the materials, analyze this problem.

3.4   Tala Rashad is a truck driver for a delivery service. She is diagnosed with diabetes. She is dependent on insulin to control her diabetic seizures. The insulin does a fairly good job but once over the past two years, Tala went into a diabetic coma while she was at home. Her husband gave her the proper medication to bring her back to consciousness. The employer requires that all truck drivers take and pass a medical examination every five years. Its stated purpose is to protect the safety of the driver and of others. When Tala had her most recent medical examination, the test demonstrated that her diabetes had worsened. The company doctor asked her questions about whether she had control over her diabetes. She told the doctor about the one incident two years ago. The employer fired Tala because of her diabetes. Consider whether Tala is a qualified individual with a disability. Assuming that she is, explain whether Tala has a cause of action under the ADA against her employer for 1) the medical testing; and 2) the discharge.

1. Look at Hypothetical Problem 3.2, *supra*. Can the school district refuse to renew Risa's contract because it fears she may pass the HIV on to the children in the playground if the children have injuries that cause bleeding? What if an assistant hockey coach has HIV and one of the duties of the assistant hockey coach is to play hockey during the practices with the children?

2. Look at the Genetic Information Nondiscrimination Act, *infra*, pp. 256–258. Would it be legal under GINA for the principal to call Risa in to ask about her son's condition?

It is clear that neither the ADA nor the Rehabilitation Act requires employment of individuals where such action would result in a direct threat to the health or safety of the individual or others in the workplace. Both statutes, however, intend that unfounded fears may not be the basis for denying employment.

Questions about direct threat arise in situations involving employees with contagious and infectious diseases, those who have mental disabilities where violent or dangerous behavior may occur, individuals with health impairments such as epilepsy or diabetes where sudden loss of consciousness or functioning may result in a safety problem to others, workers with limitations in jobs requiring physical strength or dexterity, and in a number of other settings.

The following cases illustrate some of these issues.

MAURO v. BORGESS MEDICAL CENTER
137 F.3d 398 (6th Cir. 1998)

JOHN R. GIBSON, CIRCUIT JUDGE.

Borgess [Medical Center] employed [William C.] Mauro from May 1990 through August 24, 1992 as an operating room technician. In June of 1992, an undisclosed source telephoned Robert Lambert, Vice President of Human Resources for Borgess Medical Center and Borgess Health Alliance, and informed Lambert that Mauro had "full blown" AIDS. Because of Borgess's concern that Mauro might expose a patient to HIV, Georgiann Ellis, Vice President of Surgical, Orthopedic and Clinical Services at Borgess, and Sharon Hickman, Mauro's supervisor and Operating Room Department Director, created a new full-time position of case cart/instrument coordinator, a position that eliminated all risks of transmission of the HIV virus. In July of 1992, Borgess officials offered Mauro this position, which he refused.

After Mauro's refusal of the case cart/instrument coordinator position, Borgess created a task force to determine whether an HIV-positive employee could safely perform the job responsibilities of a surgical technician. Lambert and Ellis informed Mauro by a letter dated August 10, 1992, that the task force had determined that a job requiring an HIV-infected worker to place his or her hands into a patient's body cavity in the presence of sharp instrumentation represented a direct threat to patient care and safety. Because the task force had concluded that an essential function of a surgical technician was to enter a patient's wound during surgery, the task force concluded that Mauro could no longer serve as a surgical technician. Lambert and Ellis concluded by offering Mauro two choices: to accept the case cart/instrument coordinator position, or be laid off. Mauro did not respond by the deadline stated in the letter, and Borgess laid him off effective August 24, 1992. Mauro filed this suit in January 1994.

[Lower court proceedings omitted.]

II.

Mauro argues that the district court erred in concluding that there was no genuine issue of material fact about whether the likelihood of him transmitting HIV in the course of his job posed a significant risk or direct threat to the health and safety of others, thus rendering him unqualified.

Mauro's first claim alleges that Borgess discriminated against him in violation of section 504 of the Rehabilitation Act. . . .

Through the passage of the Rehabilitation Act, Congress intended to protect disabled individuals "from deprivations based on prejudice, stereotypes, or unfounded fear, while giving appropriate weight to such legitimate concerns . . . as avoiding exposing others to significant health and safety risks."

In order to recover under the Rehabilitation Act, a plaintiff must establish that he or she is "otherwise qualified" to do the job within the meaning of the Act. An "otherwise qualified" person is one who can perform the "essential functions" of the job at issue. In a situation regarding the employment of a person with a contagious disease, the inquiry should also include a determination of whether the individual poses "a significant risk of communicating the disease to others in the workplace."

Mauro's second claim alleges that Borgess discriminated against him in violation of the Americans with Disabilities Act. . . .

To prevail under his Americans with Disabilities Act claim, Mauro must show that he is "otherwise qualified" for the job at issue. A person is "otherwise qualified" if he or she can perform the essential functions of the job in question. A disabled individual, however, is not "qualified" for a specific employment position if he or she poses a "direct threat" to the health or safety of others which cannot be eliminated by a reasonable accommodation.

The "direct threat" standard applied in the Americans With Disabilities Act is based on the same standard as "significant risk" applied by the Rehabilitation Act. Our analysis under both Acts thus merges into one question: Did Mauro's activities as a surgical technician at Borgess pose a direct threat or significant risk to the health or safety of others?

[*School Board v.*] *Arline* laid down four factors to consider in this analysis:

(a) the nature of the risk (how the disease is transmitted), (b) the duration of the risk (how long is the carrier infectious), (c) the severity of the risk (what is the potential harm to third parties) and (d) the probabilities the disease will be transmitted and will cause varying degrees of harm.

To show that one is "otherwise qualified," neither Act requires the elimination of all risk posed by a person with a contagious disease. In *Arline* the Supreme Court determined that a person with an infectious disease "who poses a significant risk of communicating an infectious disease to others in the workplace," is not otherwise qualified to perform his or her job. If the risk is not significant, however, the person is qualified to perform the job. The EEOC guidelines provide further insight:

> An employer, however, is not permitted to deny an employment opportunity to an individual with a disability merely because of a slightly increased risk. The risk can only be considered when it poses a significant risk, i.e. high probability, of substantial harm; a speculative or remote risk is insufficient.

29 C.F.R. § 1630.2(r) (1996) (citations omitted). The legislative history further supports the premise that the risk does not have to be eliminated. "The plaintiff is not required to prove that he or she poses no risk." Thus, our analysis in the instant case must not consider the possibility of HIV transmission, but rather focus on the probability of transmission weighed with the other three factors of the *Arline* test.

III.

The parties agree that the first three factors of the *Arline* test: the nature, duration, and severity of the risk, all indicate that Mauro posed a significant risk to others. Mauro argues, however, that because the probability of transmission, the fourth factor of *Arline*, was so slight, it overwhelmed the first three factors and created a genuine issue of material fact.

In determining whether Mauro posed a significant risk or a direct threat in the performance of the essential functions of his job as a surgical technician, *Arline* instructs that courts should defer to the "reasonable medical judgments of public health officials." The Centers for Disease Control is such a body of public health officials. The Centers for Disease Control has released a report discussing its recommendations regarding HIV-positive health care workers.

The Report states that the risk of transmission of HIV from an infected health care worker to a patient is very small, and therefore recommends allowing most HIV-positive health care workers to continue performing most surgical procedures, provided that the workers follow safety precautions outlined in the Report. The Report, however, differentiates a limited category of invasive procedures, which it labels exposure-prone procedures, from general invasive procedures. General invasive procedures cover a wide range of procedures from insertion of an intravenous line to most types of surgery. Exposure-prone procedures, however, involve those that pose a greater risk of percutaneous (skin-piercing) injury. Though the Centers for Disease Control did not specifically identify which types of procedures were to be labeled exposure-prone, it supplies a general definition: "Characteristics of exposure-prone procedures include digital palpation of a needle tip in a body cavity or the simultaneous presence of the [health care worker's] fingers and a needle or other sharp instrument or object in a poorly visualized or highly confined anatomic site." The Report advises that individual health care institutions take measures to identify which procedures performed in their hospital should be labeled exposure-prone and recommends that HIV-infected health care workers should not perform exposure-prone procedures unless they have sought counsel from an expert review panel and have been advised under what circumstances they may continue to perform these procedures. The Report further recommends that those health care workers who engage in exposure-prone procedures notify prospective patients of their condition.

We must defer to the medical judgment expressed in the Report of the Centers for Disease Control in evaluating the district court's ruling on whether Mauro posed a direct threat in the essential functions of his job.

Mauro stated in his deposition that during surgery his work did not include assisting in surgery, but instead handing instruments to the surgeon and helping the surgeon with whatever else he or she needed. During surgery, Mauro would at times hold a retractor with one hand in the wound area, and pass instruments as needed with his other hand. When asked if he would be actually inside a wound holding a retractor, Mauro answered "Me personally, no." But when questioned further about his hands in the wound area, he stated: "Usually if I have my hands near the wound, it would be to like, on an abdominal incision, to kind of put your finger in and hold — kind of pull down on the muscle tissue and that — where the two met in like a V shape at the bottom and the top, and pull that back. But it happened very, very rarely because they had retractors to do that." The purpose of this action was to give the surgeon more room and more visibility.

The continued questioning led to a distinction between the wound and the body cavity. Mauro was asked if he ever had his hands in a body cavity, described as being past the wound area, and Mauro stated that he personally never had his hand in a body cavity because the small size of the surgical incision prevented too many hands from being placed inside the body cavity.

Mauro was also questioned about the work of other surgical technicians at Borgess. When asked if other surgical technicians would have their hands in a wound, he could not give a definite answer because he did not work with other surgical technicians. Mauro further testified that he was told that some hospitals have their technicians assist, and that therefore no distinctions existed between the duties of surgical technicians and surgical assistants. Mauro believed, however, that Borgess did not allow technicians to assist because of union requirements, but he was not sure if this was correct.

Mauro explained that during his training, discussion had occurred indicating that nicks and cuts were always a possibility for a surgical technician. In fact, the record included two incident reports involving Mauro. One report indicated that Mauro had sliced his right index finger while removing a knife blade from a handle on June 25, 1991, and another report indicated that he had scratched his hand with the sharp end of a dirty needle while threading it on June 8, 1990.

Mauro further stated in his deposition that when Dr. Mark DeYoung, his family physician, first expressed concern that Mauro might have the HIV virus, he was of the impression that Mauro should refrain from working in surgery because of the possibility of a needle stick. Dr. DeYoung referred Mauro to Dr. David Davenport, an infectious disease specialist.

After examining Mauro, Dr. Davenport wrote a letter to Dr. DeYoung. The letter quoted Mauro as telling Dr. Davenport that he double gloved and wore orthopedic gloves when he worked, but that he still suffered cuts and needle sticks frequently with his job. Dr. Davenport's letter expressed concerns about Mauro's current job, but stated that he had told Mauro that the current consensus was that infected health care workers could continue to work in the surgical field provided that they had no underlying illnesses and used extraordinary care in their work. Dr. Davenport concluded by stating that he had suggested to Mauro that he may want to seek another type of job at Borgess that did not involve continuous direct exposure to blood and eventual needle sticks.

Dr. Davenport testified in his deposition that even if HIV-infected health care workers followed universal precautions, methods designed to ensure that health care workers do not come into contact with blood, some risk of exposure existed when HIV-infected health care workers come into contact with patients. Dr. Davenport stated that this can happen because of human error, as health care workers would not completely follow the precautions; through needle injuries; and because there was always potential for blood exposure in situations that could not be controlled, such as when surgical gloves tore.

Dr. Davenport identified the Centers for Disease Control Report as one of the best resources available on preventing transmission of the HIV virus. He stated that he was familiar with the theoretical model estimating that the risk of a patient being infected by an HIV-positive surgeon during a single operation as being somewhere between one in 42,000, and one in 420,000. He further stated that any patient who comes in contact with the HIV-infected blood of a health care worker has some risk of the virus being transferred to that patient. Though a few people infected with HIV suffer no consequences, Dr. Davenport stated that in general most people consider HIV a uniformly lethal disease. Dr. Davenport agreed that if a job required an HIV-infected worker to place his or her hands into a patient's body cavity in the presence of sharp instrumentation, it represented a real risk to patient care and safety because it could result in blood to blood contact which could lead to the transmission of the AIDS virus.

Sharon Hickman, a registered nurse, was the interim director of operating rooms at Borgess in June and July of 1992. While serving as interim director Hickman supervised the surgical technicians at Borgess, including Mauro. In her affidavit Hickman described a meeting of the Ad Hoc HIV Task Force for the hospital on July 23, 1992 and the statements she made at that meeting. Hickman stated that she told the task force that the duties of a surgical technician include preparing and maintaining the equipment used during surgery, but that:

>   on an infrequent basis, the Surgical Technician is required to assist in the performance of surgery by holding back body tissue, with the use of either retractors or the Technician's hands, to assist the surgeon in visualizing the

operative site. The Surgical Technician also may assist the surgeon with suturing and other duties related to the performance of the operation.

She also advised the task force that, although the need for a surgical technician's assistance in the performance of a surgical procedure arises infrequently, it is not possible to restructure the job to eliminate the surgical technician from performing such functions because this need arises on an emergency basis and cannot be planned in advance. In some cases, particularly on off-shifts, Hickman stated that the surgical technician is required to assist at the surgery because a registered nurse or surgical assistant is not available. In other surgical proceedings a nurse or surgical assistant may be present, but due to the complexity or other unexpected requirements of the procedure, another pair of hands may be needed in the operative site, and the surgical technician is then required to assist. Most often, the surgical technician is required to assist in the operative site because more hands are needed to visualize the surgical area. Finally, Hickman stated that Mauro had been involved in two incidents during the course of his employment, one of which might have resulted in patient exposure. [Two other Task Force members also confirmed the risk in this case.]

The written offer of an alternative employment position to Mauro provides further support for the task force's conclusion concerning a surgical technician's job responsibilities. This offer stated that an essential function of the O.R. surgical technician position is the ability to enter a patient's wound during surgery as directed by the attending surgeon. The offer concluded that because instruments such as needles and scalpels are used while the technician's hands are inside a patient's body cavity, potential exists for direct patient exposure to the surgical technician's blood.

The material issue as to whether Mauro was a direct threat or significant risk to the health and safety of others turns on whether his job duties require him, even on rare occasions, to have his hands in or near an operative site in the presence of sharp instrumentation where visibility is poor. Mauro's statement above, that at times he would place his finger in an incision in order to pull down on and pull back the muscle tissue, is consistent with Hickman's uncontradicted statement that the duties of a surgical technician require a surgical technician, on an infrequent basis, to hold back body tissue with a retractor or his or her hands to assist the surgeon in visualizing the operative site. Mauro's statements that he never had his hands in the operative cavity are not material, in light of the fact that on infrequent occasions he might be required to engage in invasive, exposure-prone activities. Further, his technical reliance on the written job description is not persuasive, as it does not purport to enumerate all activities Mauro might be required to perform, and Hickman provided a more detailed description of his job duties, that was the basis of the hospital Ad Hoc HIV Task Force decision. This Task Force was an expert review panel such as recommended in the Centers for Disease Control Report to consider Mauro's continued placement in the operating room as a surgical technician.

We also reject Mauro's argument that Dr. Davenport and Dr. DeYoung both gave favorable testimony on the risk issue, because Dr. Davenport's testimony acknowledged a risk of transmission, and Dr. DeYoung, when asked if his opinion would change if he knew a surgical technician had to have his or her hands in the body cavity, said he would consider this information.

We conclude that the district court did not err in determining that Mauro's continued employment as a surgical technician posed a direct threat to the health and safety of others. The district court based this conclusion on both the description of a Borgess surgical technician's duties indicating the necessity for a surgical technician to place his or her hands upon and into the surgical incision to provide room and visibility for the surgeon, and the risk of sustaining a needle stick or minor laceration which Mauro had in the past sustained. All the evidence, together with the uncontradicted fact that a wound causing an HIV-infected surgical technician to bleed while in the body cavity could have catastrophic results and near certainty of death, indicates that Mauro was a direct threat.

Accordingly, we affirm the judgment of the district court.

NOTES AND QUESTIONS

1. What other medical jobs are likely to be affected by the holding in the previous case? What about optometry? Obstetrics and gynecology? See *Doe v. Attorney Gen.*, 34 F.3d 781 (9th Cir. 1994). Or the general practice of medicine? For cases involving health care workers with contagious and infectious diseases, see LAURA ROTHSTEIN & JULIA ROTHSTEIN, DISABILITIES AND THE LAW Ch. 10 (2009).

2. What if health care professionals were willing to disclose their HIV condition to patients and allow the patients to decide whether the health care profession should be permitted to participate in invasive procedures?

3. Should physicians or nurses be required to inform patients if they are HIV-positive? Is there a greater risk to patients from HIV than from drug or alcohol usage, stress and emotional problems, or general incompetence? For a discussion of this issue, see Mary Anne Bobinski, *Autonomy and Privacy: Protecting Patients from Their Physicians*, 55 U. PITT. L. REV. 291 (1994).

4. It is unclear who has the burden of persuasion on the issue of direct threat to the health and safety of others. Some courts conclude that it is an affirmative defense and that the employer has the burden of proving direct threat. See *Bates v. UPS*, 2007 U.S. App. LEXIS 29870, 20 Am. Disabilities Cases (BNA) 1 (9th Cir. 2007). At least one other case says that it may depend on the type of threat involved. If the job is to protect the health or safety of others, the plaintiff must prove that she does not pose a direct threat when demonstrating that she is qualified to occupy the position, but when the job is one that does not deal with the safety of others, the employer may have the burden of proving that the plaintiff poses a direct threat. See *EEOC v. Amego, Inc.*, 110 F.3d 135 (1st Cir. 1997).

5. *Infectious Diseases as Direct Threats:* Several other courts have addressed issues of contagious and infectious diseases as being a danger to others. For example, in *Roe v. District of Columbia*, 842 F. Supp. 563 (D.D.C. 1993), the court held that the District of Columbia Fire Department violated Section 504 by refusing to allow a firefighter infected with Hepatitis B to perform mouth-to-mouth resuscitation. Other cases involving firefighters have reached similar results.

In *Arline v. School Bd.*, 480 U.S. 273 (1987), the Supreme Court decision that first addressed the issue of contagious diseases, the Court remanded for a determination about the risk that a school teacher with inactive tuberculosis presented to her students. The district court found that she did not present a risk and ordered reinstatement with back pay. 692 F. Supp. 1286 (M.D. Fla. 1988).

For citations to cases on the issue of direct threat, see LAURA ROTHSTEIN & JULIA ROTHSTEIN, DISABILITIES AND THE LAW § 4.12 (2009).

The following case focuses on the issue of qualifications in the context of direct threat. In reading the excerpt, think about whether under the ADAAA the plaintiffs are individuals with disabilities.

CHANDLER v. CITY OF DALLAS
2 F.3d 1385 (5th Cir. 1993)

WIENER, CIRCUIT JUDGE:

In 1978, the City of Dallas, Texas (Dallas or the City) adopted a Driver Safety Program (the Program) to reduce the risk of vehicular collisions. The Program established certain physical standards for city employees who drive on public roads as an intrinsic part of their job duties. Employees of this type are referred to as Primary Drivers. The physical standards required by the Program were patterned on safety regulations promulgated by the United States Department of Transportation. If an employee did not meet these standards, he could not be certified as a primary driver and thus was ineligible for Primary Driver jobs.

Two of the medical standards for Primary Drivers are of particular importance to the instant appeal. A Primary Driver: (1) cannot have an established medical history of diabetes mellitus severe enough to require insulin for control; and (2) must have 20/40 vision (corrected) and a field of vision of at least 70 degrees in the horizontal meridian in each eye. Plaintiff Lyle Chandler has diabetes mellitus that requires insulin for control. Plaintiff Adolphus Maddox has impaired vision in his left eye that cannot be corrected to meet minimum standards. Both of these plaintiffs held positions with the City that were classified as Primary Driver jobs. Only 138 of the City's job classifications were considered Primary Driver jobs.

[Chandler required insulin to control his diabetes and had failed a driver's physical at one point because of his diabetes. He also had major and minor episodes at work related to hypoglycemia. Maddox failed an initial driver's physical because of uncorrectable vision. They filed suit against the City under a number of theories when they were denied certain Primary Driver positions.]

A. *The Rehabilitation Act*

Under the Program, the City established three distinct categories of drivers. Primary Drivers are those City employees who are certified to operate a motor vehicle on public thoroughfares for the City as an intrinsic part of their job duties. Secondary Drivers are those City employees who are certified to operate a motor vehicle on public thoroughfares for the City as an adjunct duty to their job.

Tertiary Drivers are those City drivers who operate motor vehicles and automotive equipment on City property where public access is limited. Only Primary Drivers are subject to the strict physical standards of the Program.

The plaintiffs do not seriously contest the City's assertion that driving is an essential function of every Primary Driver position. Instead, they argue that they can safely perform all of the functions of their respective jobs, including driving, without accommodation. In taking that approach, the plaintiffs failed to adduce sufficient evidence that would support a finding that they were otherwise qualified for Primary Driver positions.

The Program is based on regulations promulgated by the Federal Highway Administration, Department of Transportation, to promote, *inter alia*, safe operation of motor vehicles. These regulations provide in pertinent part that:

"A person is physically qualified to drive a motor vehicle if that person — . . . (3) Has no established medical history or clinical diagnosis of diabetes mellitus currently requiring insulin for control; [and] . . . (10) Has distant visual acuity of at least 20/40 (Snellen) in each eye without corrective lenses or visual acuity separately corrected to 20/40 (Snellen) or better with corrective lenses, distant binocular acuity of at least 20/40 (Snellen) in both eyes with or without corrective lenses, field of vision of at least 70 degrees in the horizontal meridian in each eye, and the ability to recognize the colors of traffic signals and devices showing standard red, green and amber; . . . . "

These regulations, including the provisions relating to insulin dependent diabetes and impaired vision, have been in effect since 1970. Since that time, the Federal Highway Administration has had numerous opportunities to revisit these regulations, and to update and amend them if need be. Yet, the physical requirements regarding insulin dependent diabetes and impaired vision have remained unchanged. The statement of the Administrator of the Federal Highway Administration in the preamble to the proposed regulations remains valid to this day: "Accident experience in recent years has demonstrated that reduction of the effects of organic and physical disorders, emotional impairments, and other limitations of the good health of drivers are increasingly important factors in accident prevention."

After implementing these regulations, the Federal Highway Administration received several petitions for reconsideration. The Director of the Bureau of Motor Carrier Safety (acting under authority delegated to him by the Administrator) responded to objections that the medical qualifications of § 391.41 were unduly stringent by stating: "In this area, however, the Director believes that the risks are so well known and so serious as to dictate the utmost caution. Hence, except as noted below, the physical qualifications are unchanged." The standards for diabetes and vision are not among those that were altered in response to these petitions for reconsideration.

The issue whether an insulin dependent diabetic is otherwise qualified for positions involving driving or other high risk activities has been addressed by several federal courts. Those courts have uniformly held that insulin dependent diabetics present an unacceptable risk, and are thus not otherwise qualified, to be employed as, *inter alia*, sanitation truck drivers or special agents with the Federal Bureau of Investigation. We are aware of no cases holding that insulin dependent diabetes does not present a significant risk in connection with the operation of motor vehicles on public highways.

We hold that, as a matter of law, a driver with insulin dependent diabetes or with vision that is impaired to the extent discussed in 49 C.F.R. § 391.41 presents a genuine substantial risk that he could injure himself or others. We echo the sentiment expressed [previously] by this court: "Woe unto the employer who put such an employee behind the wheel of a vehicle owned by the employer which was involved in a vehicular accident."

As neither Chandler nor Maddox was otherwise qualified for Primary Driver positions in the absence of any employer accommodation, we must answer the second question of the analysis — whether any reasonable accommodation by the City would have enabled them to perform the essential functions of those positions. For if reasonable accommodation will not eliminate a significant safety risk, a handicapped person is not otherwise qualified.

The record is conspicuously devoid of any evidence from Chandler or Maddox that reasonable accommodation was possible, much less that it would eliminate any safety risk inherent in their driving. This evidentiary void is fatal to Plaintiffs' claims, given their burden of establishing that reasonable accommodation is possible so that they would be otherwise qualified for their respective positions if they were so accommodated. As we find that neither plaintiff was otherwise qualified, in the absence of accommodation, because they posed a substantial risk of injury, the absence of evidence that reasonable accommodation could be made precludes the possibility that either plaintiff was "otherwise qualified." . . .

NOTES AND QUESTIONS

1. *Risks Related to Diabetes and Similar Conditions:* Several courts have addressed employment discrimination involving diabetes and other health related conditions. The courts are particularly deferential to the employer's determination relating to risk when the position involves potential danger to a large number of people, such as truck drivers and bus drivers. See *Wood v. Omaha Sch. Dist.*, 25 F.3d 667 (8th Cir. 1994) (insulin-dependent school van driver constituted safety risk). But see *Lawson v. CSX Transp. Inc.*, 245 F.3d 916 (7th Cir. 2001) (holding that the plaintiff, an insulin-dependent diabetic who sought a job as a train conductor, had created a prima facie case that he had a disability and was qualified).

After the *Sutton* trilogy in 1999, courts have rarely found individuals with diabetes and similar conditions to be individuals with disabilities. This analysis may change under the ADAAA. See LAURA ROTHSTEIN & JULIA ROTHSTEIN, DISABILITIES AND THE LAW § 4.9 *Diabetes* (2009). See also *Rohr v. Salt River Project Agricultural Improvement & Power Dist.*, 555 F.3d 850 (9th Cir. 2009) (stating that if the case were brought under the ADAAA, the plaintiff employee, who was an insulin-dependent type 2 diabetic, would have an even stronger case that he was a qualified individual with a disability, and deciding that even without the ADAAA there was a question of fact as to whether he had a disability); *Parker v. Midwest Air Traffic*

Control, 2009 U.S. Dist. LEXIS 40054 (W.D. Pa. May 12, 2009) (assuming that if it applied the ADAAA, the plaintiff, a Type I diabetic, would be covered).

2. *Seizure Disorders and Direct Threat.* The courts have been unlikely to find seizure disorders to be disabilities since 1999. See LAURA ROTHSTEIN & JULIA ROTHSTEIN, DISABILITIES AND THE LAW, § 4.9 *Epilepsy and Seizure Disorders*. Several pre-1999 cases, however, provide insight into how courts are likely to analyze issues of direct threat under the ADAAA in the context of cases involving employees with these conditions.

In *Jansen v. Food Circus Supermarket's Inc.*, 110 N.J. 363, 541 A.2d 682 (1988), the court placed the issue in context by noting the following.

> An estimated 2,135,000 Americans suffer from epilepsy. Nearly half that number eliminate or "control" epileptic seizures through medication; for another 30% medication significantly reduces the number of seizures-. . . . The term "epilepsy" itself evokes stereotypical fears that perpetuate discrimination against its victims in all aspects of life, including employment. Epileptics are not all alike. Some may suffer one or two seizures in a lifetime; others suffer them more frequently. Accordingly, epileptics must be viewed not as fungible members of a class, but as individuals.

The court then addressed the discrimination claim of Mr. Jansen, whose condition was mild and generally controlled and who was hired as a meat cutter by a supermarket, with their knowledge of his condition. When he later had a seizure while cutting meat, followed by comments that were not clear in their meaning, his employment was terminated because of concerns about the risk of injury to himself and others. This was based on medical evaluations and reports. In deciding whether the termination was justifiable, the court noted:

> The appropriate test is not whether the employee suffers from epilepsy or whether he or she may experience a seizure on the job, but whether the continued employment of the employee in his or her present position poses a reasonable probability of substantial harm.

The court further noted that the safety defense should be based on a "probability" rather than a "possibility" of injury. The opinion "that an employee might suffer a seizure at work does not necessarily support the conclusion that such a seizure would present a risk of injury." An individualized assessment of the safety risk is required.

The court further noted that

> An employer may not rely on a deficient report to support its decision to fire a handicapped worker. If, however, the employer relies on an adequate report, courts should not second-guess its decision. [T]he employer should review not only the reports of its medical experts, but also relevant records such as the employee's work and medical histories. . . . In an appropriate case, an employer might reasonably be expected to communicate with its expert about the meaning of the report.

Here, the court found the medical report to be deficient to support the decision that Jansen could not safely work as a meat cutter.

Employment as a shoe salesman would not generally be viewed as one involving direct threat situations. In *Martinson v. Kinney Shoe Corp.*, 104 F.3d 683 (4th Cir. 1997), however, the position required that maintaining store security was an essential function for a salesperson. This was because the salesperson could often be the only individual in the sales area and the store did not employ security guards. Mr. Martinson was a good salesman, but his epilepsy had resulted in a number of episodes where he was not conscious. Because of his inability to control the timing of seizures, his employment was terminated. The court noted that there was no dispute that providing security was an essential function and that Martinson could not perform the function. "Safeguarding the store and its goods is a task that cannot reasonably be abandoned for even 'a brief period.' " The court noted that no reasonable accommodation was possible. "The ADA simply does not require an employer to hire an additional person to perform an essential function of a disabled employee's position."

Ross v. Beaumont Hosp., 687 F. Supp. 1115 (E.D. Mich. 1988), involved a surgeon with narcolepsy whose relationship with a hospital was terminated. The opinion discusses the plaintiff's abusive behavior and other conduct as the basis for the dismissal and finds no discrimination. The court does, however, quote from an article on this issue about the burden of proof in such cases.

An excellent and detailed commentary on the burden of proof on this subject states:

> Where the lives of critically ill patients are at stake, public policy may dictate exclusion if there is any doubt concerning an individual's ability to serve such patients. To use the allocation of the burden of proof as a means of addressing this concern, however, would be a mistake. There are more suitable methods of analysis to protect valid exclusions. As previously discussed, program operators may establish eligibility criteria that reflect their legitimate needs to ensure the public safety. A nursing or medical school is entitled to ensure that persons who serve as hospital staff present no significant safety risk to patients. A medical school might legitimately contend that no individual who may foreseeably cause significant injury to patients should be permitted on its staff. If it can then demonstrate, for example, that an individual with a history of mental disability may foreseeably cause significant injury, it will have carried the requisite burden of persuasion.

Judith Wegner, *The Antidiscrimination Model Reconsidered: Ensuring Equal Opportunity Without Respect to Handicap Under Section 504 of the Rehabilitation Act of 1973*, 59 CORNELL L. REV. 401, 490 (1984).

3. *Mental Illness as Presenting a Direct Threat:* There is much concern by employers about potential dangers presented by individuals with mental health problems, which may manifest in violent behavior. As with other conditions raising concern about a direct threat, it is essential that employers address these concerns on a case-by-case basis and make individualized determinations about the dangers in each situation. Employers should not base their actions on myths and beliefs about mental illness. The justification for the adverse employer action should be based on conduct, behavior, or some other reasonable basis for these concerns.

Several cases involving mental health problems are discussed in Chapter 6 on Higher Education and in Chapter 8 on Housing. See also *Hindman v. GTE Data Serv.*, 1994 LEXIS 9522 (M.D. Fla. 1994) (whether employee with a mental condition who carried a gun to work constituted a direct threat); *Mazzarella v. Postal Serv.*, 849 F. Supp. 89 (D. Mass. 1994) (postal worker with personality disorder was legally discharged because of destructive behavior); *Kupferschmidt v. Runyon*, 827 F. Supp. 570 (E.D. Wis. 1994) (Postal Service employee with mental disability who threatened to kill her supervisor and fellow employees must be allowed to prove that she is qualified).

Are courts more likely to allow adverse treatment by employers where the employee with mental problems is in a position such as a school teacher or medical professional? It should be noted that in some cases involving employees with mental illness, the direct threat could be eliminated with reasonable accommodation. The unresolved issues are whether the employer can take adverse action unless there is evidence that the employee presents a threat of violence or harm. What evidence is enough? The factors for determining direct threat (i.e., duration, nature, and severity, likelihood that harm will occur, and imminence of harm) are found in the ADA regulations. 29 C.F.R. § 1630.2(4). The Interpretive Guidance states that:

> Such consideration must rely on objective, factual evidence — not on subjective perceptions, irrational fears, patronizing attitudes, or stereotypes — about the nature or effect of a particular disability or of disability generally.

56 Fed. Reg. 35,745 (July 26, 1991). For a discussion of this issue, see Laura Rothstein, *The Employer's Duty to Accommodate Performance and Conduct Deficiencies of Individuals with Mental Impairments Under Disability Discrimination Laws*, 47 SYRACUSE L. REV. 931 (1997).

4. *Threat to Self or Others:* The statutory language of the ADA states that individuals are not qualified if they are a direct threat, i.e., present a significant risk to the health or safety "of *others* that cannot be eliminated by reasonable accommodation." 42 U.S.C. § 12111(3) (emphasis added). The regulations, however, state that: "direct threat means a significant risk of substantial harm to the health or safety of *the individual or others* that cannot be eliminated or *reduced* by reasonable accommodation." 29 C.F.R. § 1630.2(r). Although the interpretation by EEOC probably represents a more reasonable definition of this term, it is without textual support in the statute.

In 2002, the Supreme Court decided *Chevron U.S.A., Inc. v. Echazabal*, 536 U.S. 73 (2002), and adopted the EEOC's interpretations. Where an individual poses a direct threat to his or her own safety or health, that individual is not otherwise qualified. The Court emphasized that employers must make this determination not on "untested and pretextual stereotypes," but on "reasonable medical judgement that relies on the most current medical knowledge and/or the best available evidence." Furthermore, the evaluation must be one that is individualized.

In this case, the Court deferred to the EEOC interpretation, while it had rejected the EEOC interpretation in the *Sutton* trilogy decisions on defining who is disabled. The contrast between the two cases regarding deference to legislative history is noteworthy. In *Echazabal*, the Court adopts legislative history. In *Sutton*, the Court chooses to reject the legislative history supporting a broad interpretation of "disability."

5. *Future Risk and Predisposition.* Although the EEOC guidelines recognize the one of the factors in a direct threat case is the imminence of the harm, the courts have not focused on this issue extensively. One way in which the issue could arise is where a currently symptom-free individual is at a genetically increased risk of a condition that might manifest itself suddenly and constitute a direct threat to self or others. For example, the individual who had a genetic predisposition to hereditary cardiomyopathy is at risk of a sudden and severe heart attack. To what extent should such an individual be permitted to engage in a range of activities, such as driving a bus, working in a retail store, or being a professional athlete?

6. *Genetic Conditions:* The research done as part of the Human Genome Project continues to provide information about genetic markers and other genetic indicators of predisposition to a variety of conditions and diseases, such as cancer and Huntington's disease. This raises a variety of questions in the context of disability law. Is a genetic predisposition a "disability"? Is someone predisposed to certain genetically related conditions "regarded as" having a disability? How do we analyze the potential future risk that such a disease might have? For example, if an individual is working in a nuclear power plant in a sensitive position and it is learned that the individual has the gene for Huntington's disease (the first symptom of which is often dementia), is it permissible to terminate the employment? Huntington's disease usually has onset at about age 40 and results in significantly deteriorating mental capacity and ultimately death. Would it be permissible to not hire an applicant with the Huntington's gene who is age 25? Age 35? See the discussion of the new Genetic Information Nondiscrimination Act, *infra* p. at 256–258.

7. *Other Conditions:* In addition to potential impairments relating to orthopedic or mobility problems and those related to genetic predispositions, another area of concern is the predictability of the future onset of mental illness. For a discussion of other cases addressing this issue and an analysis of future risk as a disability, see MARK A. ROTHSTEIN, MEDICAL SCREENING AND THE EMPLOYEE HEALTH COST CRISIS 128–131 (1989); Bryan P. Neal, *The Proper Standard for Risk of Future Injury under the Americans with Disabilities Act: Risk to Self or Risk to Others*, 46 S.M.U. L. REV. 483 (1992).

E   REASONABLE ACCOMMODATION AND UNDUE HARDSHIP

There is no question that reasonable accommodation is required under both the Rehabilitation Act and the ADA. The Rehabilitation Act standard was established by the courts. The ADA, incorporating these interpretations, does not define reasonable accommodation in the statute, but gives a list of possible accommodations, including:

(A)   making existing facilities used by employees readily accessible to and usable by individuals with disabilities; and

(B)   job restructuring, part-time or modified work schedules, reassignment to a vacant position, acquisition or modification of equipment or devices, appropriate adjustment or modifications of examination, training materials or policies, the provision of qualified readers or interpreters, and other similar accommodations for individuals with disabilities.

42 U.S.C. § 12111(9). See also 29 C.F.R. § 1630.2(o). The statute and the regulations also provide that reasonable accommodation is not required if it would result in undue hardship, defined as "an action requiring significant difficulty or expense." 42 U.S.C. § 12111(10). See also 29 C.F.R. § 1630.2(p). This is to be determined in light of factors such as the following:

1.   The nature and cost of the accommodation.

2.   The overall financial resources of the facility involved in providing the accommodation; the number of employees at that facility; the effect or impact on the facility operation.

3.   The overall financial resources of the covered entity; the overall size of the business (number of employees); the number, type, and location of facilities.

4.   The type of operation of the entity, including the composition, structure, and function of the workforce; the geographic separateness, administrative, or fiscal relationship of the facility or facilities in question to the covered entity.

42 U.S.C. § 12111(10); 29 C.F.R. § 1630.2(p)(2).

The cases in this section illustrate the variety of accommodations that may be considered. Individuals new to the issues of disability rights and accommodations often want a checklist of exactly what type of accommodation should be provided to individuals with specific disabilities. What such requests fail to recognize is that the types and severity of disabilities vary dramatically, the manifestations and needs resulting even from the same disability also vary, and the type of job and the circumstances of the employer are different. Often, a common sense and interactive approach is most useful. The factors listed above are only a general guideline. For additional cases, see LAURA ROTHSTEIN & JULIA ROTHSTEIN, DISABILITIES AND THE LAW § 4.20 (2009).

A 1990 census report estimates that the cost in medical expenses and lost wages due to work disabilities is $111.6 billion a year. 43 MORBIDITY AND MORTALITY WEEKLY REPORT 757 (Oct. 8, 1993). The societal costs can be compared with costs of accommodation. A 1994 study assessing ADA compliance by Sears, Roebuck & Company indicates the average cost of accommodation was $121.42. More than two-thirds of the accommodations cost nothing; 28 percent cost less than $1,000; and only three percent cost more than $1,000. Sears 1994 Work Force Data, U.S. Bureau of the Census.

HYPOTHETICAL PROBLEM 3.5

Read the following hypothetical problem before reading the materials on qualified individuals, reasonable accommodations and undue hardship. After reading the materials, analyze this problem.

3.5 Leon Katz has a heart condition entitled "bicuspid aortic valve." The aortic valve ordinarily has three flaps, but because of a genetic anomaly, some people are born with aortic valves with two flaps. Ordinarily people with bicuspid valves can live a long time without the condition's affecting their quality of life. Leon is 50 years old and has always been healthy, but within the past 8 months, he has begun noticing shortness of breath when he climbs stairs. He also gets dizzy easily. His cardiologist tells him that he will need aortic valve replacement surgery in about eight months because his valve is beginning to deteriorate, but that for now he should take it easy and get plenty of rest. He recommends that he not climb steps or engage in strenuous exercise. Leon is a tennis pro at a hotel. He ordinarily teaches children to play tennis, but he also plays with hotel guests who want a good game. While he can teach children without exercising strenuously, Leon tells the hotel management that he is not able to play tennis with hotel guests because that exercise would be too strenuous on his heart. Leon asks the hotel to give him more children's classes and teams to make up for his failure to play with hotel guests. He says that he knows that some of the other tennis pros at the facility who currently teach children and play with guests prefer playing with guests to teaching children's classes. Hotel management is concerned because it has fewer children whose parents want instruction for their children and fewer hotel guests asking for pros to hit balls with them. It would like to eliminate one of the positions of tennis pro at the hotel.

1. Hotel management tells its corporate attorney that it has less business all around calling for a tennis pro and asks whether it can fire Leon because of his inability to play with guests. How should the attorney explain to the hotel the legal issues involved with the decision? Is Mr. Katz a qualified individual with a disability and does he have a viable cause of action under the ADA if the hotel fires him? What is the possibility of a reasonable accommodation?

2. What are the burdens of persuasion and production on the issues of "reasonableness" of the proposed accommodation and whether the proposed accommodation poses an undue hardship on the hotel. How would this analysis differ depending on which circuit the hotel is in?

[1] Proving Reasonable Accommodation and Undue Hardship

All seem to agree that when it comes to proving that a plaintiff is a qualified individual with a disability, the burden of persuasion falls on the plaintiff. It is more complicated than this, however. Proving that an individual is qualified requires proof that the plaintiff can perform the essential functions of the job with or without reasonable accommodation. This requires a decision about what the essential functions of the job are, an analysis of the plaintiff's objective qualifications and of whether she is qualified to perform the essential functions of the particular job in question. It often also requires a discussion of whether a proposed accommodation is reasonable and, if so, whether the accommodation, even if reasonable, imposes an undue hardship on the defendant employer. Some cases demonstrate that the dividing line between essential function and reasonable accommodation is often unclear. For example, in the attendance cases above, many of the courts discussed attendance at work as an essential function of the job. If that is the case, working at home can not be a reasonable accommodation to that essential function. If, on the other hand, as in *Humphrey*, the court sees the attendance issue not as an essential function of the job, but rather as whether working at home is a reasonable accommodation, the case may come out differently. In this section, the courts struggle with the burdens of production and persuasion in reasonable accommodation and undue hardship. All courts seem to agree that the employer has the burden of persuasion on the issue of undue hardship. In other words, it is an affirmative defense. On the other hand, the courts of appeals disagree about who bears the burden of production and persuasion on the issue of reasonableness of accommodation. Consider the different viewpoints expressed by the courts below.

BARTH v. GELB
2 F.3d 1180 (D.C. Cir. 1993)

BUCKLEY, *CIRCUIT JUDGE*

Donald Barth, a severe diabetic, appeals a judgment in favor of his employer, the Voice of America, on his claim that the VOA illegally discriminated on the basis of handicap by failing to clear him for service at the VOA's overseas radio relay stations. The district court found that the agency was justified in denying Mr. Barth an overseas assignment because the special arrangements required to accommodate his medical condition would have imposed an undue burden on its operations. Mr. Barth's principal challenge is directed to the court's allocation to him of the ultimate burden of proof on that issue. Because a claim of undue burden is an affirmative defense in actions under the Rehabilitation Act of 1973, we find that the burden of proving it should have been placed on the VOA. But because we also find that this error was harmless, we affirm the district court's judgment.

I. Background

Donald Barth is a Washington-based computer specialist and employee of the VOA who applied for admittance into the permanent Foreign Service. Mr. Barth passed all requirements for admittance into the Service, except that he failed a State Department medical clearance examination designed to assess his availability for worldwide service. Mr. Barth suffers from an advanced and degenerative form of diabetes requiring the care of a skilled endocrinologist to control the diabetes, plus an array of other specialists (in ophthalmology, for example) to control its complications. The State Department found that Mr. Barth could not serve worldwide, but only in locations with advanced medical facilities.

After the denial of the medical clearance, Mr. Barth requested a medical waiver from the VOA. His particular suggestion was that the VOA grant a limited waiver restricting his assignments to posts with suitable medical facilities. After protracted deliberations, the VOA denied Mr. Barth's waiver request without a written statement of reasons. Upon exhausting his administrative remedies, Mr. Barth brought suit under the Rehabilitation Act of 1973, as amended, 29 U.S.C. § 701-96i (1988), asking the court to order his assignment to a suitable overseas relay station position and to award him backpay.

After a four-day bench trial, the district court found that Mr. Barth's diabetic condition was the sole reason for his exclusion from the VOA's Overseas Radio Relay Station Program and that, although the waiver panel had not recorded its findings, it had focused on whether a reasonable accommodation could be made to his handicap. The court noted that the entire corps of American overseas relay station engineers consists of only seventy persons divided among the twelve stations, most of which were located in remote, sparsely populated areas. It found that Mr. Barth "could function at only three or four posts" and that

> the thin staffing at each post required flexibility of assignment, put a premium on workers not subject to serious health risks, and offered few options for initial assignment of Mr. Barth. Accepting applicants who could basically only work at a few non-hardship posts would be considered unfair to other Specialists and detrimental to morale and success of the program.

The court concluded "as a matter of law" that accommodating Mr. Barth by limiting his assignments would "place an undue burden on the VOA program," and it granted judgment in favor of the agency. This appeal followed.

II. Analysis

A. The Burden of Proof

Mr. Barth's principal claim is that he was improperly assigned the burden of proving that the requested accommodation would not constitute an undue hardship. Specifically, he objects to the court's holding that "Mr. Barth has the ultimate burden of proof." The court explained its allocation of the burden in the following footnote:

The Court of Appeals has stated that in a Rehabilitation Act case claiming wrongful denial of a federal job, the plaintiff has the initial burden to make a prima facie showing that reasonable accommodation of his handicap was possible. The burden then shifts to the defendant to show inability to accommodate. Credible evidence in that regard shifts the burden back to the plaintiff.

2. Burden of Proof Standards

A court's allocation of the burdens of proof in a federal agency handicap discrimination case will be determined in part by whether the court looks to Title VII case law or to the EEOC regulations for guidance. The EEOC regulations direct that "an agency shall make reasonable accommodation [for qualified handicapped persons] unless the agency can demonstrate that the accommodation would impose an undue hardship on the operation of its program." 29 C.F.R. § 1613.704(a). This rule apparently calls for a two-part approach in which plaintiffs bear their usual burden of showing a breach of duty — namely, that they are qualified handicapped persons who have been denied reasonable accommodations for their handicaps — but in which agencies may "demonstrate," as an affirmative defense, that fulfilling this duty would impose "undue hardships" on their programs.

Section 505(a)(1), on the other hand, states, in relevant part:

> The remedies, procedures, and rights set forth in section 717 of the Civil Rights Act of 1964 (42 U.S.C. § 2000e-16) . . . shall be available, with respect to any complaint under section 791 of this title, to any employee or applicant for employment aggrieved by the final disposition of such complaint . . . .

29 U.S.C. § 794a(a)(1). Section 717 prohibits discrimination on the basis of race, color, religion, sex, or national origin. [C]ourts focusing on this language have tended to look to the allocations of the burdens of proof developed for Title VII race and sex discrimination complaints in shaping rules under the Rehabilitation Act. Thus, courts allocating burdens of proof under the Rehabilitation Act have been prone to adapt and employ the familiar principles of *McDonnell Douglas* [as interpreted by *Burdine*].

Burdine places on the plaintiff an initial burden of producing sufficient evidence to support a prima facie case of discrimination. If the plaintiff establishes a prima facie case, the burden shifts to the defendant, which must then produce evidence of an articulable non-discriminatory reason for the challenged action. If the defendant produces such a reason, the plaintiff then bears the ultimate burden of persuading the trier of fact that the reason was pretextual and that intentional discrimination had in fact occurred.

The allocation of the burdens of production in the first two steps is designed to "sharpen the inquiry" into an "elusive" fact — an employer's discriminatory motivation. Because of the difficulties inherent in establishing such motivation, the Supreme Court placed only a modest initial burden on a Title VII plaintiff; namely, that he establish that although qualified for an available position, he was "rejected under circumstances which give rise to an inference of unlawful discrimination." Once this burden is met, it becomes necessary for the employer to produce admissible evidence of legitimate reasons for the plaintiff's rejection, thus "framing the factual issue with sufficient clarity so that the plaintiff will have a full and fair opportunity to demonstrate pretext." Such a demonstration having been made, it remains the plaintiff's ultimate burden to show that he was in fact the victim of intentional discrimination. In short, the requirement of only a minimal prima facie showing strips the defendant of the ability to remain silent as to its motive while recognizing the plaintiff's ultimate obligation to prove that motive's illegality.

An individual bringing an action under section 501 of the Rehabilitation Act, however, may face a quite different situation from that faced by plaintiffs charging racial discrimination under Title VII. Unlike a person's race, an employer may legitimately take a handicap into consideration in determining whether an applicant or employee is qualified for a particular position. Thus, while an agency would never admit to basing an employment decision on race, agencies frequently acknowledge that they have taken a person's handicap into consideration. Under such circumstances, the ultimate purpose of *Burdine*'s requirements is typically achieved from the outset.

It is apparent, then, that the *Burdine* test is not equally applicable to all cases brought under section 501. To illustrate this point, we describe three of the various categories of handicap discrimination cases that may be brought under that section. The first is one in which the employing agency asserts that it refused a job application, or denied an employee a promotion or discharged him, for reasons unrelated to the person's handicap. A second category involves suits in which the employer challenges a plaintiff's claim that he is a "qualified handicapped person" who, with "reasonable accommodation, can perform the essential functions of the position in question." In these cases, the agency will usually contend that no reasonable accommodation is available. In a third category we have those cases, such as the one before us, in which the employing agency offers the affirmative defense of "undue hardship on the operation of its program." 29 C.F.R. § 1613.704(a). This last may at times merge with the second, however, as indicated by the regulation's reference to "the nature and the cost" of a proposed accommodation as an example of "undue hardship."

The first of these categories involves the sort of inquiry into subjective facts — the employing agency's true motivation — that the *Burdine* three-step approach was designed to address. But in the last two categories, the fact that the plaintiff's handicap was taken into explicit account in the agency's employment or personnel decision is acknowledged. These cases deal with objective claims that may be tested through the application of traditional burdens of proof. In the second category, for example, a plaintiff must establish that (a) he is handicapped but, (b) with reasonable accommodation (which he must describe), he is (c) able to perform "the essential functions" of the position he holds or seeks. *See* 29 C.F.R. § 1613.702(f); *see also id.* § 1613.704(a), (b). As in the usual case, it would then be up to the employing agency to refute that evidence. The burden, however, remains with the plaintiff to prove his case by a preponderance of the evidence.

In the third category, the agency invokes the affirmative defense of "undue hardship," an inquiry for which the regulations provide three factors for consideration:

(1)   The overall size of the agency's program with respect to the number of employees, number and type of facilities and size of budget;

(2)   the type of agency operation, including the composition and structure of the agency's work force; and

(3)   the nature and the cost of the accommodation.

29 C.F.R. § 1613.704(c). In such a case the agency has the burden of proving the undue hardship.

As a general matter, a reasonable accommodation is one employing a *method of accommodation* that is reasonable in the run of cases, whereas the undue hardship inquiry focuses on the hardships imposed by the plaintiff's preferred accommodation in the context of the particular agency's operations. As noted earlier, a grey area will arise where a proposed accommodation is so costly or of such a nature that it would impose an undue burden on the employer's operations. Thus, an accommodation would be both unreasonable and impose an undue burden "if it either imposes undue financial and administrative burdens on [an agency] or requires a fundamental alteration in the nature of [its] program."

3. The Burden of Proof in this Case

In this case, the issue has been joined in a manner that places us squarely within the third category described above. Therefore, the district court erred in two respects on the question of burdens of proof: Because the VOA acknowledged that it had refused Mr. Barth's application on account of his handicap, the court should not have invoked the *Burdine* three-step scheme; and, more to the point, it wrongly assigned the burden of persuasion on the undue hardship issue to Mr. Barth instead of the agency.

The VOA does not claim that limiting Mr. Barth's overseas assignments to posts at which adequate medical facilities are available would be unreasonable in the abstract. Rather, it asserts that the requested accommodation would result in undue hardship as a result of considerations peculiar to its operation; essentially, its need for flexibility in the difficult task of rotating a small number of radio engineering specialists among twelve far-flung relay stations, most of them "hardship posts," while trying to maintain the efficiency of its operation. The VOA notes that its non-hardship posts, the only ones at which Mr. Barth would be eligible to serve, function as short-term havens for its specialists. Yet, given the "thin staffing" of VOA posts, every transfer from, say, Liberia to Munich, Germany, implies the need for another transfer in the opposite direction. Mr. Barth, however, would be medically disqualified for such transfers, thereby imposing additional burdens on the remaining engineers. For these and other operational reasons, the VOA maintains that its staffing problems would be greatly compounded by admitting someone into the Service who from the outset had Mr. Barth's serious limitations on assignability.

The accommodation Mr. Barth seeks is assignment to one of three or four "non-hardship" posts in the VOA radio relay system. As the VOA admits that it restricts the assignments of certain of its current radio specialists for medical and family reasons, there can be no claim that such an accommodation would mark a "fundamental alteration" in the nature of the VOA's program. The agency argues instead that permanently assigning Mr. Barth to non-hardship postings would impose, in these particular circumstances, undue hardship on the VOA. This is an affirmative defense that the VOA had the burden of proving. The issue to be resolved, then, is whether it has met that burden. But because the district court erred in assigning the ultimate burden of proof to Mr. Barth, we must also decide whether that error was harmless.

Mr. Barth does not claim that the Government failed to produce evidence of undue hardship. Therefore, the only conceivable prejudice from the district court's error is the possibility that its misallocation of the ultimate burden of proof affected the outcome of the case. For this to occur, the evidence presented would have to be in sufficient balance so that the outcome would depend on who had the burden. Here, the district court examined the administrative record and concluded that the VOA's decision that Mr. Barth's handicap could not be reasonably accommodated "was proper and consistent with the requirements of the Rehabilitation Act." The court observed that "the thin staffing at each post required flexibility of assignment, put a premium on workers not subject to serious health risks, and offered few options for initial assignment of Mr. Barth." It found that "at the time he sought waiver Mr. Barth could function only at three or four posts." Mr. Barth does not challenge the court's findings.

Our examination of the records satisfies us that the VOA introduced sufficient evidence to support a claim of undue hardship by virtue of the loss of essential operational flexibility that would have resulted from an attempt to accommodate Mr. Barth's medical needs. And because Mr. Barth does not challenge the district court's findings of fact, we must accept those findings as true. Viewing the evidence through the lens of those findings, we conclude that it was not so closely balanced that the court's error in assigning the burden of persuasion to Mr. Barth would have affected the outcome.

B. Mr. Barth's Other Claims

Mr. Barth maintains that the court erred in allowing the VOA to refuse to offer an accommodation to an applicant for employment that it has extended to current employees. Mr. Barth notes that the VOA has made special accommodations for employees who have incurred medical problems while on duty overseas or whose children have particular educational needs. From this, he argues that (1) if such limitations on the assignment of an existing employee do not create an undue hardship, similar restrictions on the assignment of an applicant will not do so; and (2) if the VOA restricts the assignments of a current employee for medical or family reasons, it must be equally willing to restrict the assignment of a handicapped applicant.

These arguments overlook the benefits that agencies derive from accommodating the special needs of existing employees, which they do not gain from serving those of applicants. A willingness to accommodate incumbent employees increases the likelihood that they — and their knowhow — will be retained by the employing agency. It will also contribute to employee morale and, presumably, to productivity. Thus there is economic logic as well as moral truth behind the intuition that distinguishes between "family" and "stranger" and the level of obligation owed to each. Robert Frost captured that intuition in his poem, "The Death of the Hired Man":

> Home is the place where, when you have to go there,
> They have to take you in.

The Poetry of Robert Frost at 38 (Edward C. Lathem ed., 1967). Mr. Barth may knock at the door, but he is not family, and his handicap does not give him the right to be treated as such. An agency is entitled both to take the measure of the burden imposed by an accommodation net of its benefits and to take account of the duty of care, whether legal or not, that is owed employees who develop problems while on the job. Accordingly, we decline to find that the disparate treatment Mr. Barth complains of constitutes handicap discrimination within the meaning of the Act.

Mr. Barth also contends that even if the VOA had offered admissible evidence of an adverse effect on employee morale, it was inappropriate to take that factor into account. For support, he relies on cases holding, for example, that racial animus may not be used to defend race-based policies or practices.

This argument, however, confuses animus against the handicapped with the morale effects of a particular means of accommodating them. Consider an extreme example: An agency is asked to accommodate an employee with extra-sensitive eyes by moving operations underground. It seems clear that in considering this request, the agency could not properly take into account the other workers' animus against the handicapped or their resentment over the handicapped's protected legal status. But this does not mean the agency must ignore the probable effects of subterranean working conditions on the morale of other employees, however pure of heart.

An element of the undue hardship calculus cited in the EEOC regulation is the relationship between the number of employees and the size of the agency's program. 29 C.F.R. § 1613.704(c). This factor is relevant, we presume, precisely because the degree of the imposition of a particular accommodation on non-handicapped employees as a group, and the effects of such impositions on a small work force, are legitimate concerns under the Rehabilitation Act.

NOTES AND QUESTIONS

1. In *Barth*, the court talks about the three different types of cases, and explains that the *McDonnell Douglas* proof mechanism is used for only one of these three different types. Explain these different types of cases and why *McDonnell Douglas* applies only to the one that it does apply.

2. Employers sometimes attempt to justify discriminatory conduct on the basis of customer or coworker preference. For example, employers in the restaurant industry may be concerned that customers will not come to a restaurant where they know that employees are HIV positive. Using customer preference as a defense has been routinely struck down by the courts in the context of race and sex discrimination cases, and this defense is similarly likely to be struck down in disability discrimination cases.

3. *The ADA and Stigmatizing Appearance:* The Interpretive Guidance to ADA regulation 29 C.F.R. § 1630.2(l) (relating to the definition of disability as including individuals who are "regarded as" substantially limited in a major life activity) states the following:

> An individual satisfies the second part of the "regarded as" definition if the individual has an impairment that is only substantially limiting because of the attitudes of others toward the condition. For example, an individual may have a prominent facial scar or disfigurement, or may have a condition that periodically causes an involuntary jerk of the head but does not limit the individual's major life activities. If an employer discriminates against

such an individual because of the negative reaction of customers, the employer would be regarding the individual as disabled and acting on the basis of that perceived disability.

56 Fed. Reg. 35,742 (July 26, 1991).

There are few reported cases involving stigmatizing appearance as disability discrimination. In a case decided under West Virginia state law, *Chico Dairy Co. v. West Virginia Human Rights Commission*, 181 W. Va. 238, 382 S.E.2d 75 (1989), the assistant manager of a dairy mart store was blind in her left eye, which had been removed because of cancer when she was an infant. She wore an artificial eye, and the socket around it was somewhat sunken. She was denied promotion to manager, because her supervisor considered her appearance to be unacceptable for dealing with customers and vendors. The dissent found this decision to be "insensitive, outrageous and wrong as a matter of law." The majority, however, found that the state Human Rights Commission's definition that a "handicapped" person was one who was "regarded as" handicapped was invalid because it conflicted with legislative intent. For that reason, she lost. The case was decided before the ADA took effect. Would the Interpretive Guidance noted above be the basis for protection should this same situation occur after the ADAAA's passage? What if the position is as a waiter in an expensive restaurant and the condition is a serious burn scar on the applicant's face? Were these conditions covered after *Sutton*? Will they now be covered under the ADAAA? The new amendments state that a person qualified as "regarded as" having a disability if the person has an impairment that caused the employer's discriminatory act.

In *Baldetta v. Harborview Med. Ctr.*, 116 F.3d 482 (9th Cir. 1997), a nurse's aide refused to cover a 1-inch red tattoo on his forearm reading "HIV POSITIVE". The court held that this refusal could be the basis for discipline because the interest in facilitating patient recovery outweighed First Amendment protections. For citations to other customer and coworker preference cases, see Laura Rothstein & Julia Rothstein, Disabilities and the Law § 4.14 (2009).

KATHLEEN BORKOWSKI v. VALLEY CENTRAL SCHOOL DISTRICT
63 F.3d 131 (2d Cir. 1995)

Calabresi, *Circuit Judge:*

Can a teacher with disabilities, whose disabilities directly affect her capacity to perform her job, insist that her employer provide a teacher's aide as a form of reasonable accommodation under Section 504 of the Rehabilitation Act, 29 U.S.C. § 794? That question is at the heart of this appeal from the entry of summary judgment for the defendant Valley Central School District ("the School District"). We acknowledge that, on a proper factual showing, the answer may prove to be "no." But because we believe that issues of material fact have not been resolved, we vacate the entry of judgment in favor of the School District and remand the matter for further proceedings consistent with this opinion.

I.

In 1972, as a result of a motor vehicle accident, Kathleen Borkowski suffered a major head trauma and sustained serious neurological damage. During long years of difficult rehabilitative therapy, Ms. Borkowski's condition improved significantly. She was unable to make a complete recovery, however. According to her treating physician and to a psychologist who evaluated her in connection with this litigation, Ms. Borkowski has continuing difficulties with memory and concentration, and as a result has trouble dealing with multiple simultaneous stimuli. In addition, Ms. Borkowski's balance, coordination, and mobility continue to show the effects of her accident.

In the fall of 1987, Ms. Borkowski applied for the position of library teacher with the School District. During interviews with School District officials, Ms. Borkowski discussed her accident and its lingering consequences. Following these interviews, Ms. Borkowski was appointed to serve as a library teacher at two elementary schools within the school district. Ms. Borkowski's duties as a library teacher went beyond those of a librarian; she also was responsible for teaching library skills to classes of elementary school students.

Ms. Borkowski's appointment was for a probationary term. Under New York law, such a term may last up to three years. At the end of the third year, unless the teacher and the school district agree to extend the probationary term for a fourth year, a decision is made whether or not to grant the teacher tenure. If tenure is not granted, the teacher's employment is ended.

During her three years of probationary employment, Ms. Borkowski received regular performance evaluations. These were based on observations of Ms. Borkowski's work by the Superintendent of the School District, James Coonan, the district's Director of Elementary Education, Robert Schoonmaker, and the principals of the two schools at which Ms. Borkowski taught, Harvey Gregory and John Schmoll. While Mr. Gregory's evaluations generally were positive, those of Messrs. Schoonmaker and Schmoll were not. Of particular significance was an unannounced observation of Ms. Borkowski's class by Mr. Schmoll during Ms. Borkowski's third and final year of probationary employment. Based on his observation, Mr. Schmoll found that Ms. Borkowski had difficulty controlling the class and noted that students had talked, yelled, and whistled without being corrected. Mr. Schmoll also criticized Ms. Borkowski for remaining seated during the lesson. He concluded that little learning had occurred during the observed class.

In the spring of 1990, Mr. Coonan, as Superintendent of the School District, determined that Ms. Borkowski should not be granted tenure. Mr. Coonan informed Ms. Borkowski of this decision on May 1, 1990. Two weeks later, replying to Ms. Borkowski's inquiry, Mr. Coonan set forth in writing the reasons for the denial of tenure. Mr. Coonan focused primarily on what he termed Ms. Borkowski's poor classroom management; he also noted that it was inappropriate for Ms. Borkowski to remain seated during class. In response, Ms. Borkowski, citing her disability, requested reconsideration of the tenure decision, but stated that if reconsideration was denied she would resign. Having received no answer from the School District, Ms. Borkowski submitted her resignation on June 1, 1990.

Ms. Borkowski subsequently offered to provide the School District with a letter from her neurologist detailing her disability. The School District responded that Ms. Borkowski's disability "had absolutely nothing to do with" the decision to deny her tenure. The present action ensued.

II.

The basic framework of a claim of employment discrimination under Section 504 of the Rehabilitation Act is well settled. To prevail on her claim, Ms. Borkowski must establish that (1) she is an individual with a disability within the meaning of the Act, (2) she is otherwise qualified to perform the job in question, (3) she was excluded from the job solely because of her disability, and (4) her employer received federal funding.

For the purposes of its motion for summary judgment, the School District concedes that Ms. Borkowski is an individual with a disability within the meaning of the Act. It is also undisputed that the School District receives federal funds. The matter therefore turns on the second and third elements of the claim, namely, whether Ms. Borkowski was otherwise qualified for the position of tenured library teacher, and whether she was denied that position solely on the basis of her disability.

The School District and the district court misapprehend the nature of the inquiry into whether Ms. Borkowski was otherwise qualified and whether her termination was due to her disability. Ms. Borkowski claims, and the School District concedes, that she was otherwise qualified in a formal sense, in that she had the necessary educational background and certifications to be hired. By determining that Ms. Borkowski's performance was inadequate without considering whether her known disabilities could be accommodated reasonably, and by relying on that determination to justify denying her tenure, the School District in effect concluded that Ms. Borkowski was not otherwise qualified and that she could be dismissed. It is this decision that brings her claim within the bounds of Section 504, and requires us to examine whether, under the terms of that section, Ms. Borkowski (1) was, in fact, otherwise qualified for tenure, and (2) was denied tenure solely because of her disability.

1. Was Ms. Borkowski otherwise qualified for the position of tenured library teacher?

Although the phrase "otherwise qualified" is hardly unambiguous on its face, its meaning in the context of an employment discrimination claim is fairly clear: an individual is otherwise qualified for a job if she is able to perform the essential functions of that job, either with or without a reasonable accommodation. This definition plays off the regulatory language that requires an employer to "make reasonable accommodation to the known physical or mental limitations of an otherwise qualified handicapped applicant or employee unless the [employer] can demonstrate that the accommodation would impose an undue hardship on the operation of its program." 34 C.F.R. § 104.12(a); 45 C.F.R. § 84.12(a).

a. The allocation of the burdens of production and persuasion

Given the rather obscure regulatory language, it is perhaps not surprising that courts have struggled to give content to the terms reasonable accommodation and undue hardship. It is also not surprising, in view of the lack of any direct statutory guidance, that they have found the assignment of the burdens of production and persuasion particularly difficult as to reasonable accommodation.

The D.C. Circuit, for example, places the burden of both production and persuasion on the plaintiff. *See Barth v. Gelb*, 2 F.3d 1180, 1186 (D.C. Cir. 1993), *cert. denied*, 114 S. Ct. 1538 (1994). The D.C. Circuit divides the issue of reasonable accommodation into two elements. First, the accommodation must be effective — that is, the plaintiff must show that the accommodation allows her to perform the essential functions of the job in question. *See Carr v. Reno*, 23 F.3d 525, 529 (D.C. Cir. 1994). Second, the plaintiff must show that the accommodation is reasonable in terms of the burdens that it places on employers. *Barth*, 2 F.3d at 1187. It appears that the *Barth* court requires plaintiffs to demonstrate that a proposed accommodation does not put an unreasonable burden on typical employers in a given industry. If, on the other hand, the employer were to argue that a proposed accommodation was unreasonable in light of factors particular to its own operation, the court would treat the argument as a defense based on undue hardship. And then the burden of proof would fall on the employer, in accordance with the regulations. *Id.* at 1186–87.[2]

We are barred by our precedents from adopting the D.C. Circuit's approach. In addition, the D.C. Circuit's analysis raises at least two difficulties. First, it may be contrary to the intent of Congress. In passing the Americans With Disabilities Act, 42 U.S.C. §§ 12101 *et seq.*, which imposes obligations equivalent to those under Section 504, *see* 29 U.S.C. § 794(d), Congress apparently contemplated that an accommodation that imposed burdens that would be unreasonable for most members of an industry might nevertheless be required of an individual defendant in light of that employer's particular circumstances. Under the D.C. Circuit's approach, however, an accommodation that imposed a burden so significant as to be unreasonable "in the run of cases" would never be required, because the plaintiff would be unable to carry her burden of persuasion on the question of reasonable accommodation, and the issue of whether the accommodation would unduly burden the particular employer would never be reached.

---

[2] In *Vande Zande v. Wisconsin Department of Administration*, 44 F.3d 538 (7th Cir. 1995), Judge Posner, writing for the Seventh Circuit, attributes to the District of Columbia Circuit the view that undue hardship "permits an employer to escape liability if he can carry the burden of proving that a disability accommodation reasonable for a normal employer would break him." This suggests that an employer could escape liability even if the only reason the accommodation "would break him" is his own inefficiency relative to others in the industry. We do not read the D.C. Circuit as going quite that far in *Barth*. Such a holding would require the Rehabilitation Act to be read, in effect, to subsidize inefficient employers by relieving them of burdens that are imposed on their more efficient competitors. The listing of regulatory factors pertinent to the individual employer does not on its face require such an interpretation. But the issue is not before us, and so we need not resolve it at this time.

Second, the employer has far greater access to information than the typical plaintiff, both about its own organization and, equally importantly, about the practices and structure of the industry as a whole. Requiring a plaintiff not merely to proffer evidence that a proposed accommodation is reasonable, but to bear the risk of nonpersuasion on that issue as well, means that the plaintiff's burden, viewed in the context of all of the other elements that she must also establish to prevail is a heavy one indeed.

In contrast to the D.C. Circuit, the Fifth and Ninth Circuits have essentially placed the burden on the issue of reasonable accommodation, as well as on undue hardship, on the employer.

Our precedents have rejected the approach taken by the Fifth and Ninth Circuits. The approach of these two circuits does not run into direct difficulties with the regulatory language. It does have a consequence, however, that the courts do not discuss and appear not to recognize. In effect, it puts on the employer the burden of demonstrating that the plaintiff is not otherwise qualified for employment. A plaintiff is otherwise qualified only if she can perform the essential functions of her job with or without reasonable accommodation. And the Fifth and Ninth Circuits' approach essentially places on the employer both the initial burden of production and the ultimate burden of persuading the factfinder that no reasonable, effective accommodation exists.

This court charts a middle course. Under our approach, the plaintiff bears the burden of production and persuasion on the issue of whether she is otherwise qualified for the job in question. A plaintiff cannot be considered "otherwise qualified" unless she is able, with or without assistance, to perform the essential functions of the job in question. It follows that the plaintiff bears the burden of proving either that she can meet the requirements of the job without assistance, or that an accommodation exists that permits her to perform the job's essential functions.

Whether a proposed accommodation is *reasonable*, however, is another question. "Reasonable" is a relational term: it evaluates the desirability of a particular accommodation according to the consequences that the accommodation will produce. This requires an inquiry not only into the benefits of the accommodation but into its costs as well. We would not, for example, require an employer to make a multi-million dollar modification for the benefit of a single individual with a disability, even if the proposed modification would allow that individual to perform the essential functions of a job that she sought. In spite of its effectiveness, the proposed modification would be unreasonable because of its excessive costs. In short, an accommodation is reasonable only if its costs are not clearly disproportionate to the benefits that it will produce.[3]

---

[3] In evaluating the costs and benefits of a proposed accommodation, it must be noted that Section 504 does not require that the *employer* receive a benefit commensurate with the cost of the accommodation. The concept of reasonable accommodation, developed by regulation under Section 504, received the imprimatur of congressional approval with the passage of the Americans With Disabilities Act, 42 U.S.C.A. §§ 12101 *et seq.* (stating, in a 1992 amendment, that Section 504 is to be interpreted consistently with the employment-related provisions of the Americans With Disabilities Act). As set forth by statute and regulation, the concept of reasonable accommodation permits the employer to expect the same level

As to the requirement that an accommodation be reasonable, we have held that the plaintiff bears only a burden of production. This burden, we have said, is not a heavy one. It is enough for the plaintiff to suggest the existence of a plausible accommodation, the costs of which, facially, do not clearly exceed its benefits. Once the plaintiff has done this, she has made out a *prima facie* showing that a reasonable accommodation is available, and the risk of nonpersuasion falls on the defendant.

At this point the defendant's burden of persuading the factfinder that the plaintiff's proposed accommodation is unreasonable merges, in effect, with its burden of showing, as an affirmative defense, that the proposed accommodation would cause it to suffer an undue hardship. For in practice meeting the burden of non-persuasion on the reasonableness of the accommodation and demonstrating that the accommodation imposes an undue hardship amount to the same thing.

Does Section 504 require, for example, that employers be driven to the brink of insolvency before a hardship becomes too great? We think not. Similarly, where the employer is a government entity, Congress could not have intended the only limit on the employer's duty to make reasonable accommodation to be the full extent of the tax base on which the government entity could draw.

What, then, does undue hardship mean? We note that "undue" hardship, like "reasonable" accommodation, is a relational term; as such, it looks not merely to the costs that the employer is asked to assume, but also to the benefits to others that will result. The burden on the employer, then, is to perform a cost/benefit analysis. In a sense, of course, that is what the plaintiff also had to do to meet her burden of making out a *prima facie* case that a reasonable accommodation existed. But while the plaintiff could meet her burden of production by identifying an accommodation that facially achieves a rough proportionality between costs and benefits, an employer seeking to meet its burden of persuasion on reasonable accommodation and undue hardship must undertake a more refined analysis. And it must analyze the hardship sought to be imposed through the lens of the factors listed in the regulations, which include consideration of the industry to which the employer belongs as well as the individual characteristics of the particular defendant-employer. If the employer can carry this burden, it will have shown both that the hardship caused by the proposed accommodation would be undue in light of the enumerated factors, and that the proposed accommodation is unreasonable and need not be made.[4]

---

of performance from individuals with disabilities as it expects from the rest of its workforce. But the requirement of reasonable accommodation anticipates that it may cost more to obtain that level of performance from an employee with a disability than it would to obtain the same level of performance from a non-disabled employee. And Congress fully expected that the duty of reasonable accommodation would require employers to assume more than a *de minimis* cost. It follows that an accommodation is not unreasonable simply because it would be more efficient, in the narrow sense of less costly for a given level of performance, to hire a non-disabled employee than a disabled one.

[4] With our approach and those of the D.C., Fifth, and Ninth Circuits, contrast that which the Seventh Circuit appears to adopt in *Vande Zande*. Under that case, the plaintiff is required to do a rough cost/benefit analysis to demonstrate that a reasonable accommodation exists, but the employer may defend by showing that "upon more careful consideration" the accommodation imposes an undue hardship. *Vande Zande* does not deal expressly with questions of burdens of production and persuasion.

Despite the ambiguities of the statutory and regulatory language, we believe that the resulting standards should not prove difficult to apply. First, the plaintiff bears the burden of proving that she is otherwise qualified; if an accommodation is needed, the plaintiff must show, as part of her burden of persuasion, that an effective accommodation exists that would render her otherwise qualified. On the issue of reasonable accommodation, the plaintiff bears only the burden of identifying an accommodation, the costs of which, facially, do not clearly exceed its benefits. These two requirements placed on the plaintiff will permit district courts to grant summary judgments for defendants in cases in which the plaintiff's proposal is either clearly ineffective or outlandishly costly. Second, we do not at all intend to suggest that employers, in attempting to meet their burden of persuasion on the reasonableness of the proposed accommodation and in making out an affirmative defense of undue hardship, must analyze the costs and benefits of proposed accommodations with mathematical precision. District courts will not be required to instruct juries on how to apply complex economic formulae; a common-sense balancing of the costs and benefits in light of the factors listed in the regulations is all that is expected.

b. Ms. Borkowski's claim

With these standards in mind, we proceed to analyze Ms. Borkowksi's claim. Ms. Borkowski concedes that her performance was inadequate, and that she was unable to meet the School District's legitimate expectations without help. She maintains, however, that with the provision of a teacher's aide to assist her in maintaining classroom control, she would be able to perform all of the functions of a library teacher, and therefore was otherwise qualified. She further contends that the provision of a teacher's aide is not unreasonable.

i. Ms. Borkowski's ability to perform the essential functions of her job

In evaluating Ms. Borkowski's claim that she could perform all of the essential functions of a tenured library teacher, we encounter a difficulty: it is not immediately apparent what the essential functions of Ms. Borkowski's job were. In denying Ms. Borkowski tenure, the School District focused primarily on Ms. Borkowksi's poor classroom management. But is classroom management — the ability to maintain appropriate behavior among the students — an essential function of a tenured library teacher's job? We might intuitively think so. But Section 504 does not permit us to rely on intuition — indeed, unthinking reliance on intuition about the methods by which jobs are to be performed and how an individual's disabilities relate to those methods is among the barriers that the Rehabilitation Act was designed to overcome. To avoid unfounded reliance on uninformed assumptions, the identification of the essential functions of a job requires a fact-specific inquiry into both the employer's description of a job and how the job is actually performed in practice.

Determining what is an essential part of Ms. Borkowski's job and examining in detail the manner in which a teaching aide might assist Ms. Borkowski in

It is possible, therefore, that in the Seventh Circuit the burdens of production and of persuasion on the issue of reasonableness — although subject only to a rough cost/benefit analysis — nevertheless rest with the plaintiff.

maintaining classroom control are of critical importance to this case because those inquiries establish the framework for determining whether Ms. Borkowski has met her burden of showing that she is otherwise qualified. As we noted earlier, an individual who cannot perform the essential functions of a job, either with or without assistance, is not otherwise qualified within the meaning of Section 504. It follows that an employer is not required to accommodate an individual with a disability by eliminating essential functions from the job. And so we have held, for instance, that individuals whose physical condition precludes them from engaging in heavy lifting, and who seek jobs for which such lifting is shown to be an essential function, need not be accommodated by shifting responsibility for the lifting to other individuals.

Admittedly, then, having someone else do part of a job may sometimes mean eliminating the essential functions of the job. But at other times providing an assistant to help with a job may be an accommodation that does not remove an essential function of the job from the disabled employee. Thus, for example, a visually impaired administrator or clerk may be provided with a reader. What matters to that individual's job is not the ability to read *per se*, but rather the ability to take in, process, and act on information. The provision of a reader in these circumstances does not eliminate an essential function, but rather permits the individual with a disability to perform that essential function.

The accommodation suggested by Ms. Borkowski appears, at first blush, to resemble more closely one that would eliminate an essential function of a library teacher in a classroom setting than one that would permit Ms. Borkowski to perform that function. Yet, viewing the record at this stage of the proceedings in the light most favorable to Ms. Borkowski, we cannot say that no reasonable jury could conclude otherwise. This is especially so since the regulations implementing Section 504 explicitly contemplate that teachers with disabilities may require the assistance of teachers' aides. *See* 45 C.F.R. Part 84 Appendix A at 376.

A number of factors might be relevant in the present case. One might be the age of the students that Ms. Borkowski taught. We know that they were elementary school students, but, within that category, children of different ages may require different degrees of supervision. Another would be the availability of teacher's aides within the School District. We know from the record that Ms. Borkowski was provided with an aide to assist her in the performance of her library duties, although not of her teaching duties. But were other teachers within the school system provided with teacher's aides to assist in maintaining appropriate student behavior? If so, then classroom management might not be considered an essential function.

Under the circumstances of this case, three conclusions are possible: either (a) classroom management was an essential function of Ms. Borkowski's job, and Ms. Borkowski's proposed accommodation would eliminate that function; or (b) classroom management was an essential function of Ms. Borkowski's job, but providing Ms. Borkowski with an assistant would permit *her* to perform that function, though with assistance; or (c) classroom management was not an essential function of Ms. Borkowski's job, and it does not matter whether Ms. Borkowski's proposed accommodation would result in her performing the function, albeit with assistance, or in the reassignment of that function to the teacher's aide. Only the first of these conclusions would support a grant of summary judgment in favor of the School District. And we cannot say that such a conclusion is required on the record as it currently exists.

Ms. Borkowski has introduced evidence that an accommodation — provision of an aide — is available and would allow her to perform the essential functions of a tenured library teacher. Ms. Borkowski therefore has established, as a *prima facie* matter, that an effective accommodation exists. The School District to date has not brought in any evidence that would permit a court to rule as a matter of law that Ms. Borkowski's performance would be inadequate even with the proposed accommodation or that the accommodation would eliminate the essential functions of the job. Accordingly, an issue of fact remains as to whether Ms. Borkowski's proposed accommodation would render her otherwise qualified.

ii. *Ms. Borkowski's prima facie showing of reasonableness*

Turning, then, to the reasonableness of Ms. Borkowski's proposed accommodation, we conclude that Ms. Borkowski has met her burden of production. The proposed accommodation plainly falls within the range of accommodations that may, in a general sense, be considered reasonable in light of their costs and benefits. Both the regulations implementing Section 504 and the cases applying the Rehabilitation Act contemplate the possibility that the use of assistants may be reasonable accommodations. Accordingly, we conclude that Ms. Borkowski has made a showing adequate to carry her burden of production on the reasonableness of her proposed accommodation.

c. The School District's claim of undue hardship

Since Ms. Borkowski has introduced enough evidence to raise a factual issue as to whether, with an accommodation, she is otherwise qualified, and also has made out a *prima facie* case that the proposed accommodation is reasonable, a summary judgment can be entered on this issue only if the School District has demonstrated, as a matter of law, that the accommodation is unreasonable or that it imposes an undue hardship. The School District, however, has thus far presented no evidence concerning the cost of providing a teacher's aide, its budget and organization, or any of the other factors made relevant by the regulations. Instead, the School District argues that the provision of an assistant is unreasonable and creates an undue hardship as a matter of law, regardless of the particular facts of the case. This argument need not long detain us. As was noted above, there is nothing inherently unreasonable or undue in the burden that an employer would assume by providing an assistant to an employee with disabilities; the regulations clearly contemplate, and courts have held, that employers may be required to assume the cost of providing assistants for otherwise qualified individuals with disabilities absent a showing by the employer that the cost is excessive in light of the factors enumerated in the regulations. It may be that the School District can show that the benefits that an aide would give are too small in relation to the cost of an aide. It may also be that the District can demonstrate that in this and other districts provision of an aide would impact school budgets sufficiently as to be an unreasonable or undue burden. It may even be that the School District can show these so powerfully that a judgment as a matter of law would be appropriate. But in the absence of evidence regarding school district budgets, the cost of providing an aide of this sort, or any like kind of information, we are unable to conclude that unreasonableness or undue hardship has been established, and we certainly cannot say that either has been established as a matter of law.

. . . .

Because Ms. Borkowski has raised a fact question on whether with the provision of an aide she would be able to perform the essential functions of a library teacher, and because she has met her burden of production on the issue of whether the provision of such an aide would be a reasonable accommodation, and finally because the School District has not established as an affirmative defense that the provision of such an aide would, as a matter of law, either be unreasonable or impose an undue hardship, a summary judgment on the question of whether Ms. Borkowski is "otherwise qualified" cannot issue on the present record.

NOTES AND QUESTIONS

1. The court discusses the different circuits and their approaches to the proof of the reasonableness of a proposed accommodation. Does the court correctly characterize the rule adopted in *Barth v. Gelb*? Explain what that rule is. How is the Second Circuit rule different from the rule in the District of Columbia and the Ninth Circuits?

2. Note that the court used a cost benefit analysis in determining reasonableness. What are the limits on that analysis?

VANDE ZANDE v. WISCONSIN DEPARTMENT OF ADMINISTRATION
44 F.3d 538 (7th Cir. 1995)

POSNER, *CHIEF JUDGE.*

The concept of reasonable accommodation is at the heart of this case. The plaintiff sought a number of accommodations to her paraplegia that were turned down. The principal defendant as we have said is a state, which does not argue that the plaintiff's proposals were rejected because accepting them would have imposed undue hardship on the state or because they would not have done her any good. The district judge nevertheless granted summary judgment for the defendants on the ground that the evidence obtained in discovery, construed as favorably to the plaintiff as the record permitted, showed that they had gone as far to accommodate the plaintiff's demands as reasonableness, in a sense distinct from either aptness or hardship — a sense based, rather, on considerations of cost and proportionality — required. On this analysis, the function of the "undue hardship" safe harbor, like the "failing company" defense to antitrust liability is to excuse compliance by a firm that is financially distressed, even though the cost of the accommodation to the firm might be less than the benefit to disabled employees.

This interpretation of "undue hardship" is not inevitable — in fact probably is incorrect. It is a defined term in the Americans with Disabilities Act, and the definition is "an action requiring significant difficulty or expense," 42 U.S.C. § 12111(10)(A). The financial condition of the employer is only one consideration in determining whether an accommodation otherwise reasonable would impose an undue hardship. See 42 U.S.C. §§ 12111(1)(B)(ii), (iii). The legislative history equates "undue hardship" to "unduly costly." These are terms of relation. We must ask, "undue" in relation to what? Presumably (given the statutory definition and the legislative history) in relation to the benefits of the accommodation to the disabled worker as well as to the employer's resources.

So it seems that costs enter at two points in the analysis of claims to an accommodation to a disability. The employee must show that the accommodation is reasonable in the sense both of efficacious and of proportional to costs. Even if this prima facie showing is made, the employer has an opportunity to prove that upon more careful consideration the costs are excessive in relation either to the benefits of the accommodation or to the employer's financial survival or health. In a classic negligence case, the idiosyncrasies of the particular employer are irrelevant. Having above-average costs, or being in a precarious financial situation, is not a defense to negligence. One interpretation of "undue hardship" is that it permits an employer to escape liability if he can carry the burden of proving that a disability accommodation reasonable for a normal employer would break him.

Lori Vande Zande, aged 35, is paralyzed from the waist down as a result of a tumor of the spinal cord. Her paralysis makes her prone to develop pressure ulcers, treatment of which often requires that she stay at home for several weeks. The defendants and the amici curiae argue that there is no duty of reasonable accommodation of pressure ulcers because they do not fit the statutory definition of a disability. Intermittent, episodic impairments are not disabilities, the standard example being a broken leg. But an intermittent impairment that is a characteristic manifestation of an admitted disability is, we believe, a part of the underlying disability and hence a condition that the employer must reasonably accommodate. Often the disabling aspect of a disability is, precisely, an intermittent manifestation of the disability, rather than the underlying impairment. The AIDS virus progressively destroys the infected person's immune system. The consequence is a series of opportunistic diseases which (so far as relevant to the disabilities law) often prevent the individual from working. If they are not part of the disability, then people with AIDS do not have a disability, which seems to us a very odd interpretation of the law, and one expressly rejected in the regulations. We hold that Vande Zande's pressure ulcers are a part of her disability, and therefore a part of what the State of Wisconsin had a duty to accommodate — reasonably.

Vande Zande worked for the housing division of the state's department of administration for three years, beginning in January 1990. The housing division supervises the state's public housing programs. Her job was that of a program assistant, and involved preparing public information materials, planning meetings, interpreting regulations, typing, mailing, filing, and copying. In short, her tasks were of a clerical, secretarial, and administrative assistant character. In order to enable her to do this work, the defendants, as she acknowledges, "made numerous accommodations relating to the plaintiff's disability." As examples, in her words, "they paid the landlord to have bathrooms modified and to have a step ramped;

they bought special adjustable furniture for the plaintiff; they ordered and paid for one-half of the cost of a cot that the plaintiff needed for daily personal care at work; they sometimes adjusted the plaintiff's schedule to perform backup telephone duties to accommodate the plaintiff's medical appointments; they made changes to the plans for a locker room in the new state office building; and they agreed to provide some of the specific accommodations the plaintiff requested in her October 5, 1992 Reasonable Accommodation Request."

But she complains that the defendants did not go far enough in two principal respects. One concerns a period of eight weeks when a bout of pressure ulcers forced her to stay home. She wanted to work full time at home and believed that she would be able to do so if the division would provide her with a desktop computer at home (though she already had a laptop). Her supervisor refused, and told her that he probably would have only 15 to 20 hours of work for her to do at home per week and that she would have to make up the difference between that and a full work week out of her sick leave or vacation leave. In the event, she was able to work all but 16.5 hours in the eight-week period. She took 16.5 hours of sick leave to make up the difference. As a result, she incurred no loss of income, but did lose sick leave that she could have carried forward indefinitely. She now works for another agency of the State of Wisconsin, but any unused sick leave in her employment by the housing division would have accompanied her to her new job. Restoration of the 16.5 hours of lost sick leave is one form of relief that she seeks in this suit.

She argues that a jury might have found that a reasonable accommodation required the housing division either to give her the desktop computer or to excuse her from having to dig into her sick leave to get paid for the hours in which, in the absence of the computer, she was unable to do her work at home. No jury, however, could in our view be permitted to stretch the concept of "reasonable accommodation" so far. Most jobs in organizations public or private involve team work under supervision rather than solitary unsupervised work, and team work under supervision generally cannot be performed at home without a substantial reduction in the quality of the employee's performance. This will no doubt change as communications technology advances, but is the situation today. Generally, therefore, an employer is not required to accommodate a disability by allowing the disabled worker to work, by himself, without supervision, at home. [W]e think the majority view is correct. An employer is not required to allow disabled workers to work at home, where their productivity inevitably would be greatly reduced. No doubt to this as to any generalization about so complex and varied an activity as employment there are exceptions, but it would take a very extraordinary case for the employee to be able to create a triable issue of the employer's failure to allow the employee to work at home.

And if the employer, because it is a government agency and therefore is not under intense competitive pressure to minimize its labor costs or maximize the value of its output, or for some other reason, bends over backwards to accommodate a disabled worker — goes further than the law requires — by allowing the worker to work at home, it must not be punished for its generosity by being deemed to have conceded the reasonableness of so far-reaching an accommodation. That would hurt rather than help disabled workers. Wisconsin's housing division was not required by the Americans with Disabilities Act to allow Vande Zande to work at home; even more clearly it was not required to install a computer in her home so that she could avoid using up 16.5 hours of sick leave. It is conjectural that she will ever need those 16.5 hours; the expected cost of the loss must, therefore, surely be slight. An accommodation that allows a disabled worker to work at home, at full pay, subject only to a slight loss of sick leave that may never be needed, hence never missed, is, we hold, reasonable as a matter of law.

Vande Zande complains that she was reclassified as a part-time worker while she was at home, and that this was gratuitous. She was not reclassified. She received her full pay (albeit with a little help from her entitlement to sick leave), and full benefits, throughout the period. It is true that at first her supervisor did not think he would have fulltime work for her to do at home. Had that turned out to be true, we do not see on what basis she could complain about being reclassified; she would be working on a part-time basis. It did not turn out to be true, so she was not reclassified, and we therefore do not understand what she is complaining about.

Her second complaint has to do with the kitchenettes in the housing division's building, which are for the use of employees during lunch and coffee breaks. Both the sink and the counter in each of the kitchenettes were 36 inches high, which is too high for a person in a wheelchair. The building was under construction, and the kitchenettes not yet built, when the plaintiff complained about this feature of the design. But the defendants refused to alter the design to lower the sink and counter to 34 inches, the height convenient for a person in a wheelchair. Construction of the building had begun before the effective date of the Americans with Disabilities Act, and Vande Zande does not argue that the failure to include 34-inch sinks and counters in the design of the building violated the Act. She could not argue that; the Act is not retroactive. But she argues that once she brought the problem to the attention of her supervisors, they were obliged to lower the sink and counter, at least on the floor on which her office was located but possibly on the other floors in the building as well, since she might be moved to another floor. All that the defendants were willing to do was to install a shelf 34 inches high in the kitchenette area on Vande Zande's floor. That took care of the counter problem. As for the sink, the defendants took the position that since the plumbing was already in place it would be too costly to lower the sink and that the plaintiff could use the bathroom sink, which is 34 inches high.

Apparently it would have cost only about $ 150 to lower the sink on Vande Zande's floor; to lower it on all the floors might have cost as much as $ 2,000, though possibly less. Given the proximity of the bathroom sink, Vande Zande can hardly complain that the inaccessibility of the kitchenette sink interfered with her ability to work or with her physical comfort. Her argument rather is that forcing her to use the bathroom sink for activities (such as washing out her coffee cup) for which the other employees could use the kitchenette sink stigmatized her as different and inferior; she seeks an award of compensatory damages for the resulting emotional distress. We may assume without having to decide that emotional as well as physical barriers to the integration of disabled persons into the workforce are relevant in determining the reasonableness of an accommodation. But we do not think an employer has a duty to expend even modest amounts of money to bring about an absolute identity in working conditions between disabled and nondisabled workers. The creation of such a duty would be the inevitable consequence of deeming a failure to achieve identical conditions "stigmatizing." That is merely an epithet. We conclude that access to a particular sink, when access to an equivalent sink, conveniently located, is provided, is not a legal duty of an employer. The duty of reasonable accommodation is satisfied when the employer does what is necessary to enable the disabled worker to work in reasonable comfort.

In addition to making these specific complaints of failure of reasonable accommodation, Vande Zande argues that the defendants displayed a "pattern of insensitivity or discrimination." She relies on a number of minor incidents, such as her supervisor's response, "Cut me some slack," to her complaint on the first day on which the housing division moved into the new building that the bathrooms lacked adequate supplies. He meant that it would take a few days to iron out the bugs inevitable in any major move. It was clearly a reasonable request in the circumstances; and given all the accommodations that Vande Zande acknowledges the defendants made to her disability, a "pattern of insensitivity or discrimination" is hard to discern. But the more fundamental point is that there is no separate offense under the Americans with Disabilities Act called engaging in a pattern of insensitivity or discrimination. The word "pattern" does not appear in the employment subchapter, and the Act is not modeled on RICO. As in other cases of discrimination, a plaintiff can ask the trier of fact to draw an inference of discrimination from a pattern of behavior when each individual act making up that pattern might have an innocent explanation. The whole can be greater than the sum of the parts. But in this case all we have in the way of a pattern is that the employer made a number of reasonable and some more than reasonable — unnecessary — accommodations, and turned down only requests for unreasonable accommodations. From such a pattern no inference of unlawful discrimination can be drawn.

NOTES AND QUESTIONS

1.   How does the Seventh Circuit rule concerning proof of reasonableness differ from that of the Second Circuit?

2.   Would this case have come out differently if the focus were on the issue of undue hardship rather than unreasonableness?

3.   Like the court in *Borkowski*, Judge Posner assumes that it is proper to engage in a cost benefit analysis in determining the reasonableness of a requested accommodation and in determining whether the request is an undue hardship for the defendant. In a portion of the opinion that is not reproduced here, the court concludes that the fact that the defendant is wealthy or large, or as in this case, the state, and can therefore raise the money to make the accommodation through taxes, does not mean that it has a greater responsibility to provide all accommodations requested. Here, the cost of the accommodation is very low, but the court nonetheless rejected the request as unreasonable. Thus, although a defendant may defend on the reasonableness question by arguing that it would not be economically sound to spend the money on the accommodation, even if the accommodation

requested is for a modest amount of money, the defendant is not necessarily required to make the accommodation. Why is this the case?

4. Note the tone of this opinion. What is the author's attitude toward the plaintiff? What is the basis for this conclusion? Does this attitude affect the result?

[2]   Health Impairments and Reasonable Accomodations

The following case demonstrates the importance of considering not only the cost of the requested accommodation but also the feasibility of the accommodation given the job requirements.

HUBER v. HOWARD COUNTY, MARYLAND
849 F. Supp. 407 (D. Md. 1994)

FRANK A. KAUFMAN, SENIOR DISTRICT JUDGE:

Facts

In Howard County, Maryland, firefighting services are provided by both volunteer fire corporations and career employees of the County's Department of Fire and Rescue. Volunteer firefighters are not required to meet all the requirements established for career firefighters or to participate in County sponsored training or testing. Rather, they may choose to limit the functions which they perform during a fire emergency.

Huber applied and was accepted for membership in the Ellicott City Volunteer Fireman's Association, Inc. in March of 1986, and in the West Friendship Volunteer Fireman's Association, Inc. in February 1987. . . . As a volunteer firefighter, Huber successfully completed several training courses and also became certified as a cardiac rescue technician.

[Huber's condition and record of employment is omitted. He had asthma, which necessitated the use of an inhaler on occasion. This condition affected his ability to pass agility tests (running exercises) that were part of the recruit training. He was evaluated by his physician, who indicated that his performance of the duties of firefighter would require using his inhaler. His employment was terminated on grounds that without the inhaler he could not complete the agility requirements, and he would be a risk to himself and others. He brought suit under Section 504 of the Rehabilitation Act.]

The Rehabilitation Act

The County asserts that Huber cannot fulfill the essential functions of a firefighter because, as Dr. Hayes concluded, Huber's asthma poses the risk that he may be incapacitated at the scene of a fire when confronted in an outdoor environment with a variety of allergens, variable weather conditions, including cold weather, and hazardous and toxic fumes and substances. Huber does not contest Dr. Hayes' assessment of the risks involved in firefighting, but responds that he is otherwise qualified because he can and has performed the functions of a volunteer firefighter for eight years.

However, the position of a volunteer firefighter differs in several important ways from that of a career firefighter. To begin with, the volunteer corporations are funded separately from the County department and have their own membership standards. Most importantly, unlike County firefighters, volunteer firefighters have the discretion of not responding to a fire and Huber has stated in depositions that he has, on numerous occasions, declined from going on calls because he was not feeling well. Career firefighters simply do not have that discretion. Finally, Huber's performance as a volunteer is not necessarily indicative of his future performance given the unpredictable nature of asthma, which in Huber's case, according to his own expert, is cold and exercise induced, conditions which are faced by firefighters. Huber simply may not impose the standards of a volunteer firefighter upon the County in the light of the differences between the two jobs. Rather, he must demonstrate that he is qualified to serve in the specific job at issue.

As to the second level of the "otherwise qualified" inquiry, whether the employer's requirements are representative of the essential functions of the job, this Court concludes that the County's requirement that firefighters not have a chronic medical condition such as Huber's is directly linked to the duties which inhere in the position of a County firefighter. In the case now before us, the uncontradicted evidence in this record, . . . serves only to confirm a fact that is self-evident — firefighting is strenuous, hazardous, demanding work. [Firefighters] must wear heavy protective gear in fighting fires, and are often required to lift heavy loads. Dependable firefighting services are crucial to the public, and the danger involved in the work requires that each firefighter be confident in the abilities and stamina of his fellow workers. Firefighting is simply a job for which physical fitness is a most basic qualification. Some conditions simply are not compatible with certain lines of work. Huber has not provided or even proffered evidence that he can perform a most essential function of a career firefighter, namely to be available, in a healthy physical condition at any, random moment during a shift — "in spite of his handicap." Thus, in terms of the Act, Huber is not "otherwise qualified" unless his would-be employer can reasonably accommodate him in the performance of the job.

Reasonable Accommodation

A disabled individual may be qualified under the Act if provided by his employer with reasonable accommodation in the handling of his disability. Thus, the question arises as to whether Huber can perform the essential functions of a firefighter with such accommodation and if so, whether the County has failed reasonably to accommodate him. "[P]laintiff bears the burden of demonstrating that she could perform the essential functions of her job with reasonable accommodation." While plaintiff has produced evidence that he could perform most of the essential functions of the job with accommodation by the County, he has not shown that the type of accommodation which would be necessary would also be reasonable.

Huber states that the County failed to accommodate him when it denied him use of his inhaler during exercises at the academy. However, an exhibit provided by Huber, apparently from a Physician's Desk Reference, states that his brand of inhaler should not be used or stored near open flame and that exposure to high temperatures could cause bursting of the device. In the light of these facts, the County has not acted unreasonably in determining that such device would be improper if used at the scene of a fire. Further, Huber does not contest the fact that, in denying Huber use of his inhaler during exercises, the County was concerned with how a firefighter, at the scene of a fire, would use an inhaler, given the breathing apparatus, helmet, facepiece and gloves a firefighter wears, and that the County was also concerned with how long it would take for such medication to have effect. Thus, Huber has provided no evidence that the County's direction regarding the inhaler was not job related or supported by legitimate safety concerns; rather, the opposite appears true.

Beyond the medication controversy, Huber has provided the opinion of Dr. James L. Gamble, a specialist in occupational medicine, who states that Huber could perform the duties of a firefighter with several accommodations, above and beyond permitting use of the inhaler. According to Dr. Gamble, the County could have other firefighters, who are trained to use a stethoscope, evaluate Huber on a daily basis to determine whether he is having a wheezing problem, and if he is having a problem he could be referred to the fire department's medical department for further determination of his work status. At the scene of a fire when the firefighters report for rehabilitation, the paramedics on sight could listen to Huber's lungs to see if there is a wheezing problem. Again, if he is found to have a problem he could report to the firefighter's medical department. Dr. Gamble states that with those accommodations, the risk of any sort of problem would be less than ten percent.

However, an employer need not make accommodations which "would result in an undue hardship," to the employer. The accommodation urged by Huber would appear to add up to just that. To begin with, contrary to Dr. Gamble's assumption, the County fire department has no on-site medical department or rehabilitation center, and common sense suggests that establishing and maintaining such departments to accommodate plaintiff would entail substantial cost. Moreover, the fact that plaintiff's lungs are clear at the start of the day would not guarantee that Huber's lungs would remain clear at the scene of a fire or at any other time during a work shift. Even if Huber were further examined at the site of a fire, his potential incapacitation could require that he be removed from service. That contingency would mean that the County would have to increase its staffing requirements at stations to which Huber is assigned in order to have enough active firefighters at the scene. An accommodation which permits an employee to work only when his or her impairment permits is not reasonable in a job, such as firefighting, where active attendance and immediate, undelayed participation is crucial.

Huber's requested accommodation would also pose an undue burden upon the County in the light of the fact that the County provides only one day of disability leave a month, which experience has shown will not be enough to accommodate Huber. During training as a recruit, Huber was often incapacitated for several days within a single month. Providing Huber with extra disability days would affect staffing and hours of the other firefighters.

It bears repeating that the applicable regulation defines an otherwise qualified person as one who, with or without reasonable accommodation, does not pose a safety or health risk to others. Numerous cases have held that an individual who is at risk of danger to himself or others is not otherwise qualified.

Huber's enthusiasm, sincerity, and commendable desire to serve his community, as well as the competent work he has done as a volunteer firefighter, all deserve to be noted and taken into account. But the Rehabilitation Act and its ensuing caselaw provide that the County need not accommodate Huber's disability where so to do would result in an undue burden for the County and a risk of harm to Huber himself, to his fellow firefighters, and to the general public. Accordingly, the County is entitled to the summary judgment which it seeks.

Courts have frequently addressed disability cases involving respiratory conditions, and have generally found the conditions not to be covered under the ADA. *See* LAURA ROTHSTEIN & JULIA ROTHSTEIN, DISABILITIES AND THE LAW § 4.9 *Respiratory Conditions* (2009).

NOTES

1. *Accommodating Smoke Sensitivities.* One of the earliest decisions addressing this issue arose under Section 504 of the Rehabilitation Act. In *Vickers v. Veterans Admin.*, 549 F. Supp. 85 (W.D. Wash. 1982), a government employee requested a work environment free of tobacco smoke. The court noted that it is not clear whether someone who is unusually sensitive to tobacco smoke is even covered under Section 504, but the court discussed the problem of balancing the rights of smokers and nonsmokers. The court observed that the following accommodations were provided to the plaintiff.

> In an effort to accommodate the plaintiff's handicap the following has been done by the Veterans Administration: (a) After plaintiff's initial complaint, the desks of smokers were physically separated in the office from the desks of the nonsmokers. (b) Thereafter, Mr. Radke sought and was able to secure a voluntary agreement by those who work in the same office as plaintiff (Room 105-C) not to smoke at any time in that room. (c) Later, Mr. Radke sought and was able to secure a voluntary agreement by those who work in Room 105-D, the office adjacent to Room 105-C, that they would not smoke at any time in that room. (d) Mr. Radke submitted a requisition for an exhaust system to be installed in Room 105-C in the hope that this system would remove whatever tobacco smoke might drift into Room 105-C from rooms where smoking was still permitted. This request was, however, turned down by the Engineering Department because its cost was considered to be excessive in light of the fact that Building 15 was only a temporary building and the employees in Supply Service were to be transferred from that building to a new building. (e) Mr. Radke was able to have two vents installed in the ceiling of Room 105-C in an effort to withdraw from that room any tobacco smoke that might drift into it from

other areas. (f) Mr. Radke purchased at his own expense an air purifier in an effort to alleviate the effects of his smoking in his own private office, Room 105-B. (g) Mr. Radke offered to have a partition constructed around plaintiff's desk. This partition would have extended from floor to ceiling and have a door. (h) Plaintiff was given the opportunity to move his desk farther away from the door leading from Room 105-C to 105-D and closer to a window. (i) Plaintiff has been offered an outside maintenance job by defendant Veterans Administration.

The voluntary action by the smokers in Rooms 105-C and 105-D has significantly reduced the presence of tobacco smoke in plaintiff's work space in Room 105-C.

The only tobacco smoke to which plaintiff is now exposed is that which may at times drift into Room 105-C from Room 105-A or 105-B. This drifting in of smoke is not a constant phenomenon and, when it does occur, the smoke is normally not heavy in concentration. At the time of the voluntary commitments by the smokers in Rooms 105-C or 105-D, and as an accommodation to them in exchange for their agreeing not to smoke at their desks, Mr. Radke gave them permission to smoke in Room 105-A, the office of the Assistant Chief of Supply Service, or, when on business, to smoke in his own office, Room 105-B.

In light of all of the foregoing, the Court finds that the Veterans Administration did make a reasonable effort to accommodate to plaintiff's handicap while at the same time attempting to accommodate to those who felt the need to smoke during working hours.

Plaintiff would like to have everyone in Supply Service be forbidden to smoke in order that he would not be exposed at any time to tobacco smoke. The Director of the Medical Center has not, however, banned smoking in any of the office spaces of the Center. The Veterans Administration has not adopted a policy against smoking in any of its offices. Congress has not enacted any legislation which forbids smoking in office working spaces in any of the office buildings owned by the United States.

In order to minimize the effect of tobacco smoke upon himself, plaintiff must himself take action to avoid his exposure to tobacco smoke. It appears that plaintiff can at any time close the door which separates Room 105-C from 105-D and that this would have the effect of preventing the entrance into Room 105-C of any smoke which might drift out of Rooms 105-A or 105-B. Although it is somewhat of an inconvenience and perhaps a nuisance to close that door, it appears to the Court that plaintiff would choose to do that rather than to have himself exposed to the tobacco smoke to which he is sensitive. There is no prohibition against the closing of that door, and the Chief of the Purchasing and Contracts Section testified that it was immaterial to him whether that door was kept in a closed or an open position.

In addition the desk of plaintiff is located but one desk away from the door which separates Rooms 105-C and 105-D. Plaintiff was advised that he could move his desk farther away from that door and closer to a window if he desired to do so, but he has chosen to have his desk remain in its present position. The Court is of the opinion that moving his desk would undoubtedly reduce his exposure to smoke.

By reason of the foregoing the Court finds that plaintiff is not entitled to injunctive relief nor to damages as against defendant Veterans Administration.

See also *Gupton v. Virginia*, 14 F.3d 203 (4th Cir. 1994) (no right to smoke-free environment).

The plaintiff in *Harmer v. Virginia Electric & Power Co.*, 831 F. Supp. 1300 (E.D. Va. 1993), also sought a smoke-free workplace to accommodate his bronchial asthma. Mr. Harmer was a buyer in the purchasing department of the corporate headquarters, and he and other sought to make the twelfth floor smoke-free. The court denied Harmer's request of a complete smoking ban because of evidence that "he can perform the essential functions of his position with the reasonable accommodations made by Virginia Power . . . ." Because his job performance indicated that he could meet his job requirements without an absolute smoking ban, the accommodations provided were sufficient.

In light of the increasing social and political pressures to limit smoking, would it be permissible for employers to refuse to hire smokers? Could they ask this at the preemployment stage? Could they do drug tests to determine whether someone had violated this? Is it a good social policy to regulate what people do off the job? See Mark A. Rothstein, *Refusing to Employ Smokers: Good Public Health or Bad Public Policy?*, 62 NOTRE DAME L. REV. 940 (1987). See also Mark W. Pugsley, *Nonsmoking Hiring Policies: Examining the Status of Smokers under Title I of the Americans with Disabilities Act of 1990*, 43 DUKE L.J. 1089 (1994).

2. *Chemical and Environmental Sensitivities:* There has been an increase in the number of complaints in the workplace and in other settings about environmental factors affecting the health of individuals. This type of complaint raises not only the issue of whether hypersensitivities of this type are disabilities under the applicable statutes, but also what types of accommodations would be viewed as reasonable in a given case. Chapter 8 (Housing) illustrates an example of such a case.

[3] Physical Impairments and Reasonable Accomodations

The following case illustrates an unusual fact setting where the employee is requesting that the employer "provide" parking, not simply designate a specific parking space in a parking area already provided to employees.

LYONS v. LEGAL AID SOCIETY
68 F.3d 1512 (2d Cir. 1995)

KEARSE, CIRCUIT JUDGE:

[Betty Lyons was an attorney with the Legal Aid office in lower Manhattan. Two years into her employment, she was injured in a car accident, which left her with a number of serious physical impairments that substantially affected her working. Upon returning to work, she requested that Legal Aid pay for a parking space near the office and courts, because she could not take public transportation which would require walking substantial distances. This request was denied, and Ms. Lyons has been paying $300–$520 a month (which was 15-26 percent of her monthly net salary) for a parking space since that time.]

Lyons commenced the present action in April 1994. Citing an Equal Employment Opportunity Commission ("EEOC") guideline which stated that "reasonable accommodation of a disability 'could include . . . providing reserved parking spaces'" the complaint alleged that Legal Aid had refused to provide reasonable accommodations for Lyons's disability, thereby violating her rights under the ADA, the Rehabilitation Act, state law, and municipal law.

II. *Discussion*

The only question is whether Lyons's request that Legal Aid provide her with a parking space near work is, as a matter of law, not a request for a "reasonable" accommodation.

Neither the ADA nor the Rehabilitation Act provides a closed-end definition of "reasonable accommodation." The ADA sets out a nonexclusive list of different methods of accommodation encompassed by that term, stating that

> [t]he term "reasonable accommodation" may include —
>
> (A) making existing facilities used by employees readily accessible to and usable by individuals with disabilities; and
>
> (B) job restructuring, part-time or modified work schedules, reassignment to a vacant position, acquisition or modification of equipment or devices, appropriate adjustment or modifications of examinations, training materials or policies, the provision of qualified readers or interpreters, and other similar accommodations for individuals with disabilities.

42 U.S.C. § 12111(9). The Rehabilitation Act does not include a definition of reasonable accommodation, but the regulations promulgated under that Act use virtually the same language as § 12111(9) of the ADA. See 45 C.F.R. § 84.12. The term is to be interpreted in the same way with respect to both the ADA and the Rehabilitation Act.

Additional regulations promulgated by the EEOC under the ADA give further guidance as to what may or may not be within the employer's obligation to provide "reasonable accommodation." The employer is required to provide [m]odifications or adjustments to the work environment, or to the manner or circumstances under which the position held or desired is customarily performed, that enable a qualified individual with a disability to perform the essential functions of that position; or . . . that enable a covered entity's employee with a disability to enjoy equal benefits and privileges of employment as are enjoyed by its other similarly situated employees without disabilities. This description too is nonexclusive. The EEOC notes that "[t]here are any number of other specific accommodations that may be appropriate for particular situations but are not specifically mentioned" in § 1630.2(o). On the other hand, the accommodation obligation does not require the employer to make accommodations that are "primarily for the [individual's] personal benefit," such as an "adjustment or modification [that] assists the individual throughout his or her daily activities, on and off the job," or to provide "any amenity or convenience that is not job-related."

In support of the order of dismissal in the present case, Legal Aid argues that Lyons's claim for financial assistance in parking her car amounts to a demand for unwarranted preferential treatment because the requested accommodation is merely "a matter of personal convenience that she uses regularly in daily life." Legal Aid asserts that it does not provide parking facilities or any other commuting assistance to its nondisabled employees and that Lyons's special needs in getting to work must therefore lie outside the scope of its obligations under the federal disability statutes. We find Legal Aid's contentions to be an inappropriate foundation for the Rule 12(b)(6) dismissal.

First, Legal Aid's assertion that it does not provide parking assistance to any other employee goes beyond the face of the complaint. This assertion cannot be the basis for a dismissal for failure to state a claim.

Further, even if that assertion were established as a matter of fact, it would not dispose of the issue of whether provision of a parking space would be a reasonable accommodation. It is clear that an essential aspect of many jobs is the ability to appear at work regularly and on time, and that Congress envisioned that employer assistance with transportation to get the employee to and from the job might be covered. Thus, the report of the House of Representatives Committee on Education and Labor noted that a qualified person with a disability seeking employment at a store that is "located in an inaccessible mall" would be entitled to reasonable accommodation in helping him "get to the job site." Similarly, the EEOC has stated that possible required accommodations other than those specifically listed in the statute include "making employer provided transportation accessible, and providing reserved parking spaces." So far as we are aware, there has been no judicial interpretation of this EEOC guideline, which may have been intended to mean that the provision of parking spaces can be required, or that the reservation of employer-provided parking spaces can be required, or both.

Whatever the guideline intended, we think that the question of whether it is reasonable to require an employer to provide parking spaces may well be susceptible to differing answers depending on, e.g., the employer's geographic location and financial resources, and that the determination of the reasonableness of such a requirement will normally require some development of a factual record.

Further, we have noted that while reasonableness depends upon "a common-sense balancing of the costs and benefits" to both the employer and the employee, an accommodation may not be considered unreasonable merely because it requires the employer "to assume more than a de minimis cost," or because it will cost the employer more overall to obtain the same level of performance from the disabled employee.

Finally, we reject Legal Aid's contention that Lyons's request for a parking space amounts to no more than a demand for an additional fringe benefit in the nature of a "personal amenity" unrelated to the "essential functions" of her job. According to the complaint, whose factual allegations must be taken as true, Lyons cannot fulfill her responsibilities as a staff attorney at Legal Aid without being able to park her car adjacent to her office. Lyons's ability to reach her office and the courts is an essential prerequisite to her work in that position. There is no suggestion in the complaint that the requested parking space near the Legal Aid office and the courts was sought for any purpose other than to allow Lyons to reach and perform her job.

Plainly there is nothing inherently unreasonable, given the stated views of Congress and the agencies responsible for overseeing the federal disability statutes, in requiring an employer to furnish an otherwise qualified disabled employee with assistance related to her ability to get to work. We conclude that Lyons's complaint stated a claim on which relief can be granted under the ADA and the Rehabilitation Act. We express no view as to whether Legal Aid may be able to develop an evidentiary record prior to trial that is sufficient to demonstrate the unreasonableness of the requested accommodation as a matter of law. At this juncture, we note only that, in light of the need to develop a factual record, it was inappropriate to dismiss the complaint summarily by granting defendant's motion pursuant to Rule 12(b)(6).

NOTES AND QUESTIONS

1.   What should the outcome be on remand? What facts would need to be established to demonstrate undue burden?

2.   Does it make a difference whether Lyons is an existing employee or an applicant for employment?

3.   What if she needed a driver or a special vehicle? Where should the line be drawn?

4.   The court remanded the issue for further review. Does the EEOC guidance that a reasonable accommodation might include "providing reserved parking spaces" mean that an employer would have to pay for a parking space when parking is not provided for any employees?

5.   *Other Parking Issues:* In *Dumas v. Keebler Co.*, 98 F.3d 1354 (11th Cir. 1996), the court found no discrimination when an employer required an employee with a state-issued accessibility parking sticker to prove that she needed to park in a space for people with disabilities. This case raises the difficulty in addressing the abuse in using such stickers, which is becoming an increasing problem.

6. *Barrier Removal Issues:* Reasonable accommodation related to physical access to facilities in employment under the Rehabilitation Act is addressed in 45 C.F.R. §§ 84.21–.23. Some of the Rehabilitation Act cases addressing these issues include *Stolmeier v. Yellow Freight Sys.*, 64 Empl. Prac. Dec. (CCH) ¶ 42,597 (D. Or. 1994) (seating modifications and steering on tractor need not be provided until issue of whether they are required is resolved); *Perez v. Philadelphia Hous. Auth.*, 677 F. Supp. 357 (E.D. Pa. 1987) (employer required to provide straight back chair, use of elevator, and regular breaks for a receptionist with back problems); *AFGE, Local 51 v. Baker*, 677 F. Supp. 636 (N.D. Cal. 1987) (United States Mint required to at least attempt to accommodate disabled coin checkers even though it would entail more than minimal cost).

7. More recent ADA cases have also addressed these issues. Many cases involve clerical employees who have developed problems because of the repetitive nature of this work. A few courts have addressed the issue of accommodating such conditions. They include *Beck v. University of Wisconsin Bd. of Regents*, 75 F.3d 1130 (7th Cir. 1996) (wrist rest rather than adjustable keyboard was reasonable accommodation for employee with osteoarthritis); *Garza v. Abbott Labs.*, 940 F. Supp. 1227 (N.D. Ill. 1996) (employee who experienced pain when typing failed to show that split keyboard and voice activated computer were reasonable accommodations in light of their expense).

For additional cases on equipment and other physical environment accommodations, see Laura Rothstein & Julia Rothstein, Disabilities and the Law § 4.20 (2009).

[4]   Mental Impairments and Reasonable Accomodation

There is a high incidence of mental illness in American society. It includes depression, bipolar disorder, substance addiction, and a number of other conditions. The highly publicized media stories about violent episodes in the workplace unfortunately serve to perpetuate myths that mentally ill individuals are violent and dangerous. There is great fear and stigma surrounding mental illness. For this and other reasons, individuals with mental illness have a number of challenges in gaining and retaining employment.

Discrimination claims by individuals with mental illness are met with several obstacles. In many cases, the mental problems relate to conduct and behavior that is then found to be the legitimate basis for the adverse employment action. In many instances, if accommodations had been provided before the deficient performance, the misconduct would not have occurred. Employers are required to accommodate known disabilities only.

There are a number of reasons why the individual with a mental illness might not make known the disability. The individual may not be aware that he or she has a mental illness. Or the employee may be in denial about the condition or the need to have accommodations. The individual may be justifiably concerned about stigma and negative treatment in the workplace if the disability is made known. Although adverse employment action might violate the ADA, individuals are aware that it can be difficult to prove that the employer's actions are based on the knowledge of the employee's mental illness. For these reasons, perhaps there should be an exception to accommodate the "after-discovered" mental illness disability. Perhaps in these cases, it should be required that employers give a second chance where the misconduct has not been a danger or threat or where the consequences of the adverse employment treatment are unduly severe. The vast majority of courts, however, do not require "second chances" where the adverse treatment is based on behavior and conduct, even if related to the condition.

NOTES

1. An unusual example of a case in which an employee requested accommodations for his manic depression is *Gardner v. Morris*, 752 F.2d 1271 (8th Cir. 1985). The employee was a civilian employee with the Army Corps of Engineers in St. Louis, Missouri. His condition was fairly controlled with careful monitoring of medication and related toxic effects. When chosen for assignment in Saudi Arabia, the medical examining physician advised Gardner that medical facilities were so limited that there was no capability of addressing complicated medical situations.

The court addressed Gardner's Rehabilitation Act claim and noted that the extreme climate, poor communication and transportation facilities and inadequate medical facilities meant that there was a threat that could not be reasonably addressed. Getting him to a place where he could be treated in the event of an episode was infeasible. The court notes that "We emphasize the narrowness of this decision. We do not condone paternalism toward handicapped individuals." Thus it was the potential danger to coworkers, not danger to self, that was the basis for the decision that he could not be accommodated.

2. *Other Accommodations for Individuals with Mental Illness:* Accommodations for individuals with mental illness that should at least be considered in appropriate situations would include education of coworkers and others in the workplace, changing the physical environment, flexible scheduling, job restructuring, job training, improved communication and support, feedback (both critical and positive), and on-the-job support (such as allowing the employee to call friends or counselors). See American Bar Association & National Mental Health Association, The ADA and People with Mental Illness: A Resource Manual for Employers (1993). See also Mickey & Pardo, *Dealing with Mental Disabilities under the ADA*, 9 THE LABOR LAWYER 531 (1993). A 1994 report indicates that job opportunities and income levels have increased substantially for many people with mental disabilities since the passage of the ADA. Peter Blanck, *Employment Integration, Economic Opportunity, and the Americans with Disabilities Act: An Empirical Study from 1990-1993*, 79 IOWA L. REV. 853 (1994). For a discussion proposing giving second chances as an accommodation in the case of some individuals with mental illness, see Laura F. Rothstein, *The Employer's Duty to Accommodate Performance and Conduct Deficiencies of Individuals with Mental Impairments Under Disability Discrimination Laws*, 47 SYRACUSE L. REV. 931 (1997).

3. *Technical Assistance:* Another resource dealing with accommodations for employees with mental and physical disabilities in the workplace is the Job Accommodation Network. See *Mental Illness Cases Handled by the Job Accommodation Network*, Report of the Job Accommodation Network, A Service of the

President's Committee on Employment of People with Disabilities (December 1, 1993).

[5]   Job Restructuring and Job Reassignment

HYPOTHETICAL PROBLEM 3.6

Read the following hypothetical problem before reading the materials on job restructuring and reassignment. After reading the materials, analyze this problem.

3.6   Ken Ko is a police officer who has worked for the municipality of Springfield for 10 years. He has recently been diagnosed with macular degeneration, a condition that leads to blindness, in both eyes. At the time of diagnosis, Ken's eyesight with his glasses was 20/100 in one eye and 20/60 in the other eye. The city's rules require that an officer who works in the field have vision correctable to 20/40 in both eyes. Ken wants the city to transfer him to an open desk job in the police station, answering the phones, filling in as a 911 operator, giving officers orders in the field, and doing some clerical work. While he is qualified for the position, another officer, Sam Clark has asked the police department to transfer him to the desk job because he is getting older and the job on the street is difficult for him. Ordinarily, the municipality grants jobs based on seniority. Sam is a few months ahead of Ken in seniority.

1.   Is Ken a qualified individual with a disability?

2.   Is the city's vision requirement legal under the new amendments to the ADA and the Rehabilitation Act?

3.   If so, is the city obligated to give Ken the job in order to avoid liability under the Rehabilitation Act?

4.   Assume that there is no union and no use of seniority in the workplace. If Ken asks for the desk job as an accommodation to his eye condition, but Sam is better qualified for the clerical part of the job because he can see better, can the city deny the job to Ken? What if Sam is better qualified because he can type better? What if Sam can type better, but the city has never had the policy of hiring the best-qualified person for the job?

The ADA contemplates job restructuring and job reassignment as accommodations that should be considered in appropriate cases. The regulations state that "reasonable accommodation" may include "Job restructuring; part-time or modified work schedules; reassignment to a vacant position. . . . " 29 C.F.R. § 1630.2(o)(2)(ii).

In the EEOC Title I Technical Assistance Manual, guidance on reassignment is provided. This guidance indicates that reassignment should be considered only when it is not possible to accommodate the present job or when such an accommodation would be an undue hardship. Only employees, not applicants, need be accommodated through consideration of reassignment. Reassignment to equivalent positions with equivalent pay should be considered first if such positions are vacant or will be vacant within a reasonable time. The question of reasonable amount of time is to be decided on a case-by-case basis. If there is no equivalent position available, reassignment to a lower graded position may be offered, and the lower salary may be paid. Employers are not required to create new jobs or give jobs that are currently held by other employees. What is unclear from this guidance is whether the employer is required to give preference to an employee with a disability seeking reassignment as a reasonable accommodation over another employee seeking to apply to transfer to the vacant position.

U.S. AIRWAYS, INC. v. BARNETT
535 U.S. 391 (2002)

JUSTICE BREYER delivered the opinion of the Court.

The Americans with Disabilities Act of 1990 (ADA or Act) prohibits an employer from discriminating against an "individual with a disability" who, with "reasonable accommodation," can perform the essential functions of the job. This case, arising in the context of summary judgment, asks us how the Act resolves a potential conflict between: (1) the interests of a disabled worker who seeks assignment to a particular position as a "reasonable accommodation," and (2) the interests of other workers with superior rights to bid for the job under an employer's seniority system. In such a case, does the accommodation demand trump the seniority system?

In our view, the seniority system will prevail in the run of cases. As we interpret the statute, to show that a requested accommodation conflicts with the rules of a seniority system is ordinarily to show that the accommodation is not "reasonable." Hence such a showing will entitle an employer/defendant to summary judgment on the question — unless there is more. The plaintiff remains free to present evidence of special circumstances that make "reasonable" a seniority rule exception in the particular case. And such a showing will defeat the employer's demand for summary judgment.

I

In 1990, Robert Barnett, the plaintiff and respondent here, injured his back while working in a cargo-handling position at petitioner U.S. Airways, Inc. He invoked seniority rights and transferred to a less physically demanding mailroom position. Under U.S. Airways' seniority system, that position, like others, periodically became open to seniority-based employee bidding. In 1992, Barnett learned that at least two employees senior to him intended to bid for the mailroom job. He asked U.S. Airways to accommodate his disability-imposed limitations by making an exception that would allow him to remain in the mailroom. After permitting Barnett to continue his mailroom work for five months while it considered the matter, U.S. Airways eventually decided not to make an exception. And Barnett lost his job.

II
A

US Airways' claim that a seniority system virtually always trumps a conflicting accommodation demand rests primarily upon its view of how the Act treats workplace "preferences." Insofar as a requested accommodation violates a disability-neutral workplace rule, such as a seniority rule, it grants the employee with a disability treatment that other workers could not receive. Yet the Act, U.S. Airways says, seeks only "equal" treatment for those with disabilities. It does not, it contends, require an employer to grant preferential treatment. Hence it does not require the employer to grant a request that, in violating a disability-neutral rule, would provide a preference.

While linguistically logical, this argument fails to recognize what the Act specifies, namely, that preferences will sometimes prove necessary to achieve the Act's basic equal opportunity goal. The Act requires preferences in the form of "reasonable accommodations" that are needed for those with disabilities to obtain the *same* workplace opportunities that those without disabilities automatically enjoy. By definition any special "accommodation" requires the employer to treat an employee with a disability differently, *i.e.*, preferentially. And the fact that the difference in treatment violates an employer's disability-neutral rule cannot by itself place the accommodation beyond the Act's potential reach.

Were that not so, the "reasonable accommodation" provision could not accomplish its intended objective. Neutral office assignment rules would automatically prevent the accommodation of an employee whose disability-imposed limitations require him to work on the ground floor. Neutral "break-from-work" rules would automatically prevent the accommodation of an individual who needs additional breaks from work, perhaps to permit medical visits. Neutral furniture budget rules would automatically prevent the accommodation of an individual who needs a different kind of chair or desk. Many employers will have neutral rules governing the kinds of actions most needed to reasonably accommodate a worker with a disability. Congress, while providing such examples, said nothing suggesting that the presence of such neutral rules would create an automatic exemption. Nor have the lower courts made any such suggestion.

In sum, the nature of the "reasonable accommodation" requirement, the statutory examples, and the Act's silence about the exempting effect of neutral rules together convince us that the Act does not create any such automatic exemption. The simple fact that an accommodation would provide a "preference" — in the sense that it would permit the worker with a disability to violate a rule that others must obey — cannot, *in and of itself*, automatically show that the accommodation is not "reasonable." . . .

US Airways also points to the ADA provisions stating that a " 'reasonable accommodation' may include . . . reassignment to a *vacant* position." And it claims that the fact that an established seniority system would assign that position to another worker automatically and always means that the position is not a "vacant" one. Nothing in the Act, however, suggests that Congress intended the word "vacant" to have a specialized meaning. And in ordinary English, a seniority system can give employees seniority rights allowing them to bid for a "vacant" position. The position in this case was held, at the time of suit, by Barnett, not by some other worker; and that position, under the U.S. Airways seniority system, became an "open" one. Moreover, U.S. Airways has said that it "reserves the right to change any and all" portions of the seniority system at will. Consequently, we cannot agree with U.S. Airways about the position's vacancy; nor do we agree that the Act would automatically deny Barnett's accommodation request for that reason.

B

[The discussion of the interpretation whether reasonable accommodation means only effective accommodation is omitted.]

III

The question in the present case focuses on the relationship between seniority systems and the plaintiff's need to show that an "accommodation" seems reasonable on its face, *i.e.*, ordinarily or in the run of cases. We must assume that the plaintiff, an employee, is an "individual with a disability." He has requested assignment to a mailroom position as a "reasonable accommodation." We also assume that normally such a request would be reasonable within the meaning of the statute, were it not for one circumstance, namely, that the assignment would violate the rules of a seniority system. Does that circumstance mean that the proposed accommodation is not a "reasonable" one?

In our view, the answer to this question ordinarily is "yes." The statute does not require proof on a case-by-case basis that a seniority system should prevail. That is because it would not be reasonable in the run of cases that the assignment in question trump the rules of a seniority system. To the contrary, it will ordinarily be unreasonable for the assignment to prevail.

A

Several factors support our conclusion that a proposed accommodation will not be reasonable in the run of cases. Analogous case law supports this conclusion, for it has recognized the importance of seniority to employee-management relations. This Court has held that, in the context of a Title VII religious discrimination case, an employer need not adapt to an employee's special worship schedule as a "reasonable accommodation" where doing so would conflict with the seniority rights of other employees. The lower courts have unanimously found that collectively bargained seniority trumps the need for reasonable accommodation in the context of the linguistically similar Rehabilitation Act. And several Circuits, though differing in their reasoning, have reached a similar conclusion in the context of seniority and the ADA. All these cases discuss *collectively bargained* seniority systems, not systems (like the present system) which are unilaterally imposed by management. But the relevant seniority system advantages, and related difficulties that result from violations of seniority rules, are not limited to collectively bargained systems.

For one thing, the typical seniority system provides important employee benefits by creating, and fulfilling, employee expectations of fair, uniform treatment. These benefits include "job security and an opportunity for steady and predictable advancement based on objective standards." They include "an element of due process," limiting "unfairness in personnel decisions." And they consequently encourage employees to invest in the employing company, accepting "less than their value to the firm early in their careers" in return for greater benefits in later years.

Most important for present purposes, to require the typical employer to show more than the existence of a seniority system might well undermine the employees' expectations of consistent, uniform treatment — expectations upon which the seniority system's benefits depend. That is because such a rule would substitute a complex case-specific "accommodation" decision made by management for the more uniform, impersonal operation of seniority rules. Such management decisionmaking, with its inevitable discretionary elements, would involve a matter of the greatest importance to employees, namely, layoffs; it would take place outside, as well as inside, the confines of a court case; and it might well take place fairly often. We can find nothing in the statute that suggests Congress intended to undermine seniority systems in this way. And we consequently conclude that the employer's showing of violation of the rules of a seniority system is by itself ordinarily sufficient.

B

The plaintiff (here the employee) nonetheless remains free to show that special circumstances warrant a finding that, despite the presence of a seniority system (which the ADA may not trump in the run of cases), the requested "accommodation" is "reasonable" on the particular facts. That is because special circumstances might alter the important expectations described above. The plaintiff might show, for example, that the employer, having retained the right to change the seniority system unilaterally, exercises that right fairly frequently, reducing employee expectations that the system will be followed — to the point where one more departure, needed to accommodate an individual with a disability, will not likely make a difference. The plaintiff might show that the system already contains exceptions such that, in the circumstances, one further exception is unlikely to matter. We do not mean these examples to exhaust the kinds of showings that a plaintiff might make. But we do mean to say that the plaintiff must bear the burden of showing special circumstances that make an exception from the seniority system reasonable in the particular case. And to do so, the plaintiff must explain why, in the particular case, an exception to the employer's seniority policy can constitute a "reasonable accommodation" even though in the ordinary case it cannot.

IV

In its question presented, U.S. Airways asked us whether the ADA requires an employer to assign a disabled employee to a particular position even though another employee is entitled to that position under the employer's "established seniority system." We answer that *ordinarily* the ADA does not require that assignment. Hence, a showing that the assignment would violate the rules of a seniority system warrants summary judgment for the employer — unless there is more. The plaintiff must present evidence of that "more," namely, special circumstances surrounding the particular case that demonstrate the assignment is nonetheless reasonable.

Because the lower courts took a different view of the matter, and because neither party has had an opportunity to seek summary judgment in accordance with the principles we set forth here, we vacate the Court of Appeals' judgment and remand the case for further proceedings consistent with this opinion.

[Concurring opinions by Justices Stevens and O'Connor omitted.]

[Dissenting opinions by Justices Thomas, Scalia, Ginsburg, and Souter omitted.]

NOTES AND QUESTIONS

1. *Unanswered Questions.* While this decision answers some questions, it raises new questions. The types of accommodations that might be requested that will be affected by seniority include location of workspace (to allow for natural light or better ventilation), parking spaces, and other perks of seniority. Employers will need to prove in challenges to denials of exceptions to seniority based award of such benefits that these are truly part of a package of legitimate employee expectations. In addition, employers will need to take care in granting exceptions. Does this decision mean that exceptions can never be granted?

2. The Court places the burden of proving the accommodation is reasonable on the plaintiff in cases where seniority systems exist. Does this indicate that the Court would place the burden of proving reasonableness always on the plaintiff?

3. *Vacant Positions:* A number of cases have addressed this issue. In *Fedro v. Reno*, 21 F.3d 1391 (7th Cir. 1994), the court held that there is no duty to reassign an individual when there is no vacant position. But, both the Ninth and the Tenth Circuits conclude that reassignment includes those positions that an employer reasonably anticipates will become vacant in the near future or within a reasonable time period. See *Smith v. Midland Brake, Inc.*, 180 F.3d 1154 (10th Cir. 1999); *Dark v. Curry County*, 451 F.3d 1078 (9th Cir. 2006). The court in *Howell v. Michelin Tire Corp.*, 860 F. Supp. 1488 (M.D. Ala. 1994), addressed the issue of whether there is an obligation to offer reassignment to a permanent light-duty position to an employee who becomes injured. The court held that this was an issue for jury determination. See also *Bates v. Long Island R.R. Co.*, 997 F.2d 1028 (2d Cir. 1993) (employer not required to reassign pipefitter with ankle injury); *DiPompo v. West Point Military Academy*, 770 F. Supp. 887 (S.D.N.Y. 1991), *aff'd*, 960 F.2d 326 (2d Cir. 1992) (major restructuring of job requirements which would lead to obvious safety risks is not a reasonable accommodation for a firefighter with dyslexia); *Taylor v. Secretary of Navy*, 852 F. Supp. 343 (E.D. Pa. 1994) (Navy failed to show undue hardship in reassignment of shipyard employee); *Carrozza v. Howard County*, 847 F. Supp. 365 (D. Md. 1994) (job restructuring for clerical employee with bipolar disorder not required because the stresses sought to be removed were inherent); *Lillback v. Metropolitan Life Ins. Co.*, 640 N.E.2d 250 (Ohio Ct. App.

1994) (salesman with back problems not entitled to promotion to managerial position as reasonable accommodation).

4. *Otherwise Qualified to Perform Original Job:* One of the most questionable opinions regarding job reassignments is the Tenth Circuit's opinion in *Smith v. Midland Brake Inc.*, 138 F.3d 1304 (10th Cir. 1998), in which the court held that there is no obligation to reassign to another job where the individual is not qualified for the job from which reassignment is being sought. The ruling was a 2-1 decision and is viewed as a very conservative position on the duty to reassign. The decision essentially negates any duty to reassign because if the employee were qualified to perform the current job, a reassignment would not be needed as an accommodation.

5. *Permanent Light Duty:* The courts have been quite consistent in holding that employees are not entitled to permanent light duty positions as an accommodation, although courts seem to recognize temporary light duty as an accommodation where such positions exist. Courts do not seem to require employers to create light duty positions as an accommodation where they did not exist before.

For cases on the issue of reassignment and change in duty as an accommodation, see LAURA ROTHSTEIN & JULIA ROTHSTEIN, DISABILITIES AND THE LAW § 4.20 (2009). E.g., *Malabarba v. Chicago Tribune Co.*, 149 F.3d 690 (7th Cir. 1998) (although ADA provides that reassignment to vacant position may constitute reasonable accommodation, it does not require employers to convert temporary light-duty jobs into permanent ones); *Dalton v. Subaru-Isuzu Automotive, Inc.*, 141 F.3d 667 (7th Cir. 1998) (no ADA violation by limiting access to light-duty program to employees with only temporary disabilities to fulfill employer's obligation under worker's compensation statute); *Mengine v. Runyon*, 114 F.3d 415 (3d Cir. 1997) (employer not required to make light duty position permanent); *Soone v. Kyo-Ya Co., Lts.*, 353 F. Supp. 2d 1107 (D. Hawaii 2005) (not reasonable to fire nondisabled employee to create vacancy for disabled employee).

6. *Requirement to Assign Less Qualified Employee.* Neither the statutes nor the regulations clarify whether an employer must assign a less qualified employee to a vacant position when there is another applicant with better qualifications. There is now a split on this issue.

The next case deals with the issue of whether an employer is required to transfer a qualified employee with a disability to a position for which the employer has a better qualified applicant.

HUBER v. WAL-MART STORES, INC.
486 F.3d 480 (8th Cir. 2007)

RILEY, CIRCUIT JUDGE.

We are faced with an unanswered question: whether an employer who has an established policy to fill vacant job positions with the most qualified applicant is required to reassign a qualified disabled employee to a vacant position, although the disabled employee is not the most qualified applicant for the position. Pam

Huber (Huber) brought an action against Wal-Mart Stores, Inc. (Wal-Mart), claiming discrimination under the Americans with Disabilities Act of 1990 (ADA), 42 U.S.C. §§ 12101 to 12213. The parties filed cross-motions for summary judgment. The district court granted summary judgment in favor of Huber. Wal-Mart appeals. For the reasons stated below, we reverse.

I. BACKGROUND

Huber worked for Wal-Mart as a dry grocery order filler earning $13.00 per hour, including a $0.50 shift differential. While working for Wal-Mart, Huber sustained a permanent injury to her right arm and hand. As a result, she could no longer perform the essential functions of the order filler job. The parties stipulated Huber's injury is a disability under the ADA.

Because of her disability, Huber sought, as a reasonable accommodation, reassignment to a router position, which the parties stipulated was a vacant and equivalent position under the ADA. Wal-Mart, however, did not agree to reassign Huber automatically to the router position. Instead, pursuant to its policy of hiring the most qualified applicant for the position, Wal-Mart required Huber to apply and compete for the router position with other applicants. Ultimately, Wal-Mart filled the job with a non-disabled applicant and denied Huber the router position. Wal-Mart indicated, although Huber was qualified with or without an accommodation to perform the duties of the router position, she was not the most qualified candidate. The parties stipulated the individual hired for the router position was the most qualified candidate.

Wal-Mart later placed Huber at another facility in a maintenance associate position (janitorial position), which paid $6.20 per hour. Huber continues to work in that position and now earns $7.97 per hour.

Huber filed suit under the ADA, arguing she should have been reassigned to the router position as a reasonable accommodation for her disability. Wal-Mart filed a motion for summary judgment, contending it had a legitimate non-discriminatory policy of hiring the most qualified applicant for all job vacancies and was not required to reassign Huber to the router position. Huber filed a cross-motion for summary judgment, and the district court granted Huber's motion. Wal-Mart appeals.

II. DISCUSSION

We review de novo the district court's grant of summary judgment.

[T]he parties do not dispute Huber (1) has a disability under the ADA, (2) suffered an adverse employment action, or (3) possessed the requisite skills for the router position. The parties' only dispute is whether the ADA requires an employer, as a reasonable accommodation, to give a current disabled employee preference in filling a vacant position when the employee is able to perform the job duties, but is not the most qualified candidate.

The ADA states the scope of reasonable accommodation may include:

[J]ob restructuring, part-time or modified work schedules, *reassignment to a vacant position*, acquisition or modification of equipment or devices, appropriate adjustment or modifications of examinations, training materials or policies, the provision of qualified readers or interpreters, and other similar accommodations for individuals with disabilities.

42 U.S.C. § 12111(9)(B) (emphasis added).

Huber contends Wal-Mart, as a reasonable accommodation, should have automatically reassigned her to the vacant router position without requiring her to compete with other applicants for that position. Wal-Mart disagrees, citing its non-discriminatory policy to hire the most qualified applicant. Wal-Mart argues that, under the ADA, Huber was not entitled to be reassigned automatically to the router position without first competing with other applicants. This is a question of first impression in our circuit. As the district court noted, other circuits differ with respect to the meaning of the reassignment language under the ADA.

In the Tenth Circuit, reassignment under the ADA results in automatically awarding a position to a qualified disabled employee regardless whether other better qualified applicants are available, and despite an employer's policy to hire the best applicant.

On the other hand, [i]n the Seventh Circuit, ADA reassignment does not require an employer to reassign a qualified disabled employee to a job for which there is a more qualified applicant, if the employer has a policy to hire the most qualified applicant.

Wal-Mart urges this court to adopt the Seventh Circuit's approach and to conclude (1) Huber was not entitled, as a reasonable accommodation, to be reassigned automatically to the router position, and (2) the ADA only requires Wal-Mart to allow Huber to compete for the job, but does not require Wal-Mart to turn away a superior applicant. We find this approach persuasive and in accordance with the purposes of the ADA. As the Seventh Circuit noted in *Humiston-Keeling*:

> The contrary rule would convert a nondiscrimination statute into a mandatory preference statute, a result which would be both inconsistent with the nondiscriminatory aims of the ADA and an unreasonable imposition on the employers and coworkers of disabled employees. A policy of giving the job to the best applicant is legitimate and nondiscriminatory. Decisions on the merits are not discriminatory.

We agree and conclude the ADA is not an affirmative action statute and does not require an employer to reassign a qualified disabled employee to a vacant position when such a reassignment would violate a legitimate nondiscriminatory policy of the employer to hire the most qualified candidate. This conclusion is bolstered by the Supreme Court's decision in *U.S. Airways, Inc. v. Barnett*, holding that an employer ordinarily is not required to give a disabled employee a higher seniority status to enable the disabled employee to retain his or her job when another qualified employee invokes an entitlement to that position conferred by the employer's seniority system. We previously have stated in dicta that "an employer is not required to make accommodations that would subvert other, more qualified applicants for the job."

Thus, the ADA does not require Wal-Mart to turn away a superior applicant for the router position in order to give the position to Huber. To conclude otherwise is "affirmative action with a vengeance. That is giving a job to someone solely on the basis of his status as a member of a statutorily protected group."

Here, Wal-Mart did not violate its duty, under the ADA, to provide a reasonable accommodation to Huber. Wal-Mart reasonably accommodated Huber's disability by placing Huber in a maintenance associate position. The maintenance position may not have been a perfect substitute job, or the employee's most preferred alternative job, but an employer is not required to provide a disabled employee with an accommodation that is ideal from the employee's perspective, only an accommodation that is reasonable. In assigning the vacant router position to the most qualified applicant, Wal-Mart did not discriminate against Huber. On the contrary, Huber was treated exactly as all other candidates were treated for the Wal-Mart job opening, no worse and no better.

III. CONCLUSION

We reverse the judgment of the district court, and we remand for entry of judgment in favor of Wal-Mart consistent with this opinion.

NOTES AND QUESTIONS

1.   The Supreme Court granted certiorari in this case, but the case was dismissed before the case was decided due to the parties' settlement. See Jonathan R. Mook, *Mook on Reassignment as an ADA Reasonable Accommodation*, 2008 EMERGING ISSUES 1851 (Jan. 31, 2008). As noted in the Eighth Circuit opinion, there is a split in the circuits on the issue of whether the employer must reassign a qualified individual with a disability to an open position if there is another applicant who is better qualified.

2.   The Eighth Circuit notes that Wal-Mart had a policy of hiring the most qualified individual for the position and states that it is this policy that permits Wal-Mart to hire the more qualified candidate for the position in question. What would an employer have to prove in order to establish that it has such a policy and that it acts pursuant to the policy regularly? What type of discovery should a plaintiff's lawyer do on the issue of whether an employer has such a policy and follows the policy?

3.   What is the danger of the Eighth Circuit opinion? Does this mean that there will never be reassignment as a reasonable accommodation? On the other hand, what would be the burden on the employer of automatically granting the open position to the person with a disability?

4.   Is the Eighth Circuit's point that the ADA is not an affirmative action statute convincing?

5.   Consider the following fact pattern: Employee A works as a photocopier in a large university copy center. The employee develops a sensitivity to photocopy chemicals that cannot be accommodated. She asks to be reassigned to another job within the university. A large university typically has a number of low skill jobs

available, but there are also often a number of current employees seeking to transfer to those positions through the regular transfer process. Should Employee A be given priority over other transfer applicants for the same position? What if Employee A is qualified for the position, but the University finds other transfer applicants to be preferable? How would the *Barth* court, *supra*, p. 188, analyze the issue from the perspective of employee morale?

6. It is not unusual for law firms to assign corner offices to senior partners based on seniority. What if a new associate has seasonal affective disorder which is exacerbated by his interior office with no natural light? Is the firm required to give him a corner office? How might this assignment affect morale at the law firm?

[6] Duty to Engage in Interactive Process

HYPOTHETICAL PROBLEM 3.7

Read the following hypothetical problem before reading the materials on the duty to engage in the interactive process. After reading the materials, analyze this problem.

3.7 Edward Elkins, a university professor who teaches Philosophy, becomes deaf in one ear and finds it difficult to hear his students while engaging in classroom discussion. He believes he would be able to do a better job if he were assigned to teach courses online only. The university has a very small online program that is used primarily for students who live outside of the area and cannot travel to the university town. Never before has the Philosophy Department taught a course online, and a large percentage of the freshmen take Philosophy in their first year. The Chair of the Philosophy Department and the Dean of Arts and Sciences fear that if they permit Elkins to teach exclusively online, other professors will want to do the same in order to avoid the commute to campus. Moreover, they fear that they might not be able to accommodate all of the freshmen Philosophy courses if Elkins teaches online. How should the General Counsel for the university explain to the Chair of the Philosophy Department and the Dean of Arts and Sciences what obligations they have in deciding whether to grant Elkins this or any other accommodation?

An employer and a qualified individual with a disability should engage in an interactive process to determine whether there is a reasonable accommodation to the individual's disability. Courts have found an employer liable for failing to engage in the interactive process. The requirement to engage in the interactive process is ongoing.

HUMPHREY v. MEMORIAL HOSPITALS ASSOCIATION
239 F.3d 1128 (9th Cir. 2001)

[An earlier portion of this opinion is reproduced at p. 156, *supra*.] Reread that section and then read the following which deals with the employer's duty to engage in an interactive process to determine whether there is a reasonable accommodation to the plaintiff's disability.]

B. BREAKDOWN OF THE INTERACTIVE PROCESS

The remaining question with respect to the duty to accommodate is purely a legal one: was MHA obligated to suggest a leave of absence or to explore other alternatives in response to Humphrey's request for a work-at-home position, or was it Humphrey's burden to make an express request for a leave of absence before she was terminated? We conclude, as a matter of law, that (assuming Humphrey was a qualified individual with a disability) MHA had an affirmative duty under the ADA to explore further methods of accommodation before terminating Humphrey.

Once an employer becomes aware of the need for accommodation, that employer has a mandatory obligation under the ADA to engage in an interactive process with the employee to identify and implement appropriate reasonable accommodations. "An appropriate reasonable accommodation must be effective, in enabling the employee to perform the duties of the position." The interactive process requires communication and good-faith exploration of possible accommodations between employers and individual employees, and neither side can delay or obstruct the process. Employers, who fail to engage in the interactive process in good faith, face liability for the remedies imposed by the statute if a reasonable accommodation would have been possible.

Moreover, we have held that the duty to accommodate "is a 'continuing' duty that is 'not exhausted by one effort.'" The EEOC Enforcement Guidance notes that "an employer must consider each request for reasonable accommodation," and that "if a reasonable accommodation turns out to be ineffective and the employee with a disability remains unable to perform an essential function, the employer must consider whether there would be an alternative reasonable accommodation that would not pose an undue hardship." EEOC Enforcement Guidance on Reasonable Accommodation, at 7625. Thus, the employer's obligation to engage in the interactive process extends beyond the first attempt at accommodation and continues when the employee asks for a different accommodation or where the employer is aware that the initial accommodation is failing and further accommodation is needed. This rule fosters the framework of cooperative problem-solving contemplated by the ADA, by encouraging employers to seek to find accommodations that really work, and by avoiding the creation of a perverse incentive for employees to request the most drastic and burdensome accommodation possible out of fear that a lesser accommodation might be ineffective.

When MHA received Dr. Jacisin's letter diagnosing Humphrey with OCD, MHA properly initiated the interactive process by arranging a meeting to discuss possible accommodations. Dr. Jacisin's statement "I would like to see her continue to work, but if it is proving to be a major personnel problem, she may have to take some time off until we can get the symptoms better under control" alerted MHA to the possibility that any initial arrangement that kept Humphrey on the job might not be effective and that a leave of absence might ultimately be necessary to accommodate her disability.

In fact, it is MHA's position, disputed by Humphrey, that MHA explicitly offered her a leave at the June 7 meeting, and that it was Humphrey who decided that flexible scheduling was the better choice. Even if we assume that Humphrey turned down the leave of absence in June in favor of a flexible start-time arrangement, her attempt to perform her job functions by means of a less drastic accommodation does not forfeit her right to a more substantial one upon the failure of the initial effort.

By the time of her annual performance review in September, it was abundantly clear to MHA that the flexible start time accommodation was not succeeding; Humphrey had accumulated six unreported absences in each of the months of August and September, and her evaluation stated that her attendance record was "unacceptable." At this point, MHA had a duty to explore further arrangements to reasonably accommodate Humphrey's disability.

Humphrey also realized that the accommodation was not working, and requested a work at home position. When it received that request, MHA could have either granted it or initiated discussions with Humphrey regarding other alternatives.[16] Instead, MHA denied her request without suggesting any alternative solutions, or exploring with her the possibility of other accommodations. Rather than fulfill its obligation to engage in a cooperative dialogue with Humphrey, Pierson's e-mail suggested that the matter was closed: "During our 6/7/95 meeting, you requested to be accommodated for your disability by having a flexible start time, stating that you would have no problems staying for a full shift once you arrived. You were given this flexible start time accommodation which continues to remain in effect." We held in *Barnett* that an employer fails to engage in the interactive process as a matter of law where it rejects the employee's proposed accommodations by letter and offers no practical alternatives. Similarly, MHA's rejection of Humphrey's work-at-home request and its failure to explore with Humphrey the possibility of other accommodations, once it was aware that the initial arrangement was not effective, constitutes a violation of its duty regarding the mandatory interactive process.

Given MHA's failure to engage in the interactive process, liability is appropriate if a reasonable accommodation without undue hardship to the employer would otherwise have been possible. As we have already discussed, a leave of absence was a reasonable accommodation for Humphrey's disability. Ordinarily, whether an accommodation would pose an undue hardship on the employer is a factual question. Here, however, MHA has conceded that granting a leave of absence would not have posed an undue hardship. MHA had a policy of granting leaves to disabled employees, and admits that it would have given Humphrey a leave had she asked for one at any time before her termination. MHA's ultimate position, therefore, is simply that Humphrey is not entitled to a leave of absence because she failed to ask for one before she was fired. As we have explained, however, MHA was under a continuing duty to offer a reasonable accommodation.

---

[16] As we have discussed, working at home is a reasonable accommodation when the essential functions of the position can be performed at home and a work-at-home arrangement would not cause an undue hardship for the employer. EEOC Enforcement Guidance on Reasonable Accommodation, at 7626.

Accordingly, we hold as a matter of law (again, assuming that Humphrey is a qualified individual with a disability) that MHA violated the ADA's reasonable accommodation requirement.

NOTE

The importance of good faith efforts to reasonably accommodate under 42 U.S.C. § 1981a (a)(3). In cases where the employer has engaged in good faith efforts in consultation with the individual with a disability to identify and make a reasonable accommodation and the alleged discrimination is based on an alleged failure to make a reasonable accommodation, the employer is not liable for damages to the individual. The section reads:

> In cases where a discriminatory practice involves the provision of a reasonable accommodation pursuant to section 102(b)(5) of the Americans with Disabilities Act of 1990 [42 U.S.C.A. § 12112(b)(5)] or regulations implementing section 791 of Title 29, damages may not be awarded under this section where the covered entity demonstrates good faith efforts, in consultation with the person with the disability who has informed the covered entity that accommodation is needed, to identify and make a reasonable accommodation that would provide such individual with an equally effective opportunity and would not cause an undue hardship on the operation of the business.

42 U.S.C. § 1981a(a)(3).

[7]   Adverse Employment Actions, Constructive Discharge and Reasonable Accommodation

NOTES AND QUESTIONS

1. *Adverse Employment Actions and Constructive Discharge.* In order to prove a violation of Title I of the ADA or of the Rehabilitation Act, the plaintiff must demonstrate that he or she suffered an adverse employment action. Ordinarily, adverse employment actions include failures to hire or to promote, discharges, demotions, decreases in salary, or transfers to jobs that do not afford the individual the opportunities for advancement that the employee had in the former job. The ADA, however, makes it illegal to fail to make a reasonable accommodation "to the known physical or mental limitations of an otherwise qualified individual with a disability" unless doing so would impose an undue hardship on the employer. 42 U.S.C. § 12112(5). It is clear from the statutory language, then, that failing to make a reasonable accommodation where there is no proof of undue hardship constitutes a violation of the statute, and it appears that no additional adverse employment action is necessary. A question arises, however, as to whether an employee has the right to resign once the employer refuses to grant an accommodation. Does the employee who resigns forfeit his right to bring suit under the ADA? The courts have considered this issue in light of the law of constructive discharge. In *Talley v. Family Dollar Stores of Ohio, Inc.*, 2008 U.S. App. LEXIS 19342 (6th Cir. Sept. 11,

2008), the plaintiff was a cashier at the defendant store who had used a stool because of back pain. She took medical leave several times because of her degenerative osteoarthritis in her back. She alleged that she could not stand or sit for long periods. After her last medical leave, the plaintiff provided a note saying she had no restrictions. Before she returned to work, her boss asked her to sign a statement saying she understood she would not be allowed to use a stool at work and would be limited to three five-minute breaks during a six hour shift. She wrote a letter in response stating that she could not sign the letter because it would prohibit her use of a stool, and returned to work. She eventually provided a doctor's note saying she needed a stool. Her boss allegedly refused to open the note, but told her that he would schedule a meeting with the plaintiff, himself, and the district manager. The plaintiff attempted to call about the meeting a number of times but her boss did not return her calls. She never returned to work. The lower court granted the defendant's motion for summary judgment because it concluded that there was no adverse employment action.

The Sixth Circuit concluded that the key issue was whether the defendant's alleged refusal to accommodate her converted her resignation into a constructive discharge. The court concluded that there was a genuine issue of material fact as to whether the plaintiff proposed a reasonable accommodation that would have allowed her to be "otherwise qualified." Before her medical leave, the plaintiff had used a stool and her supervisors were evidently pleased with her work. Now, she proposed using the stool again and taking all the evidence in the light most favorable to the plaintiff, her boss would not look at the doctor's note and would not return her phone calls concerning the meeting with him and the district manager. The court held that a reasonable jury could conclude based on these facts that she proposed a reasonable accommodation and that defendant failed to engage in an interactive process with her, leaving her with no choice but to resign.

2. In *Ekstrand v. School Dist. of Somerset*, 603 F. Supp. 2d 1196 (W.D. Wisc. 2009), the plaintiff was an elementary school teacher who suffered from fibromyalgia, anxiety disorder and panic attacks, depression and seasonal affective disorder (SAD). She was assigned an interior classroom that had many distractions because it was near a common room, had poor ventilation and was dark. She asked the employer repeatedly to move her to a different room. The plaintiff believed that her depression and SAD worsened as a result of the classroom and the parents' complaints about it. The employer made a number of accommodations to the plaintiff such as installing improved ventilation and better lights, but refused to grant her a room change, even though another teacher offered to change rooms with the plaintiff. The plaintiff became very anxious and depressed which required her to go out on medical leave. She hoped to return to teach in a different room. During her leave, the employer asked the plaintiff to return her keys to her room and she asked to keep the keys to work in her room at times. The employer ordered the plaintiff to stay away unless she submitted written permission from a physician. The plaintiff also asked the employer to permit her to draw from a voluntary leave bank, to which other employees donate their unused sick days. After delaying for a number of months, the employer finally permitted the plaintiff access to the leave bank. Finally, during her leave, the plaintiff requested a room change from the Superintendent of schools. He refused to grant her the room change, stating that he did not micromanage his principals. The plaintiff made no more requests for a new classroom. The plaintiff finally resigned and sued under the ADA and the Rehabilitation Act. The court held that because the employer had made numerous reasonable accommodations to the plaintiff's disability and continued to make them after she was so disabled that she had to go on leave, the plaintiff never tested whether those accommodations would be sufficient by returning to work. The plaintiff's constructive discharge claim, therefore, failed. The court stated:

> A claim for constructive discharge requires that the working environment become "so intolerable that [the plaintiff's] resignation qualified as a fitting response." *Rooney v. Koch Air, LLC*, 410 F.3d 376, 382–83 (7th Cir. 2005) (internal quotations omitted).The treatment must be "so severe or pervasive as to alter the conditions of employment and create an abusive working environment." *Mannie v. Potter*, 394 F.3d 977, 982 (7th Cir. 2005) (internal quotations omitted). Even assuming, as plaintiff asserts, that defendant's treatment showed that it did not want her to return to work, the incidents she identifies were not severe enough to create the type of abusive environment that has been found to amount to constructive discharge. *Taylor v. Western & Southern Life Insurance Co.*, 966 F.2d 1188, 1191 (7th Cir. 1992) (boss consistently made racial comments and once held a gun to employee's head, took photo, and showed it at staff meeting while making racial jokes); *Brooms v. Regal Tube Co.*, 881 F.2d 412, 417 (7th Cir. 1989) (human resource manager repeatedly showed employee racist pornographic photos and made threatening comments to her including threat to kill her). Therefore, defendant's motion for summary judgment will be granted as to plaintiff's constructive discharge claim as well.

3.   How should *Talley* and *Ekstrand* be reconciled? Do the different results in these cases depend on the plaintiffs' behavior? Or, are the courts using different standards in determining whether there is a constructive discharge? Explain. Under *Talley*, does an employee have the right to resign and preserve her lawsuit if the employer refuses to engage in the interactive process? Or, does this right depend on the severity of the pain/disability to which the plaintiff is seeking an accommodation combined with the employer's failure to engage in the interactive process? In *Ekstrand*, could it be argued that the employer failed to engage in the interactive process when the Superintendent refused to meddle with the principal's decision? Compare this case to *Humphrey, supra.*

F   DISABILITY-BASED HARASSMENT AND RETALIATION

HYPOTHETICAL PROBLEM 3.8

Read the following hypothetical problem before reading the materials on disability-based harassment and retaliation. After reading the materials, analyze this problem.

3.7   Agnes Coppola has severe facial disfigurement as a result of an accident. At the time of her accident, Agnes worked as a receptionist in a health club. Because the bosses fear that Agnes will "turn people off" with her looks, after the accident, they move Agnes to the laundry facility of the health club, where her job is to wash and dry all of the towels used at the club. This job is a demotion. Agnes makes only $8 per hour, as opposed to her previous $13 per hour. Agnes' supervisor checks up on her daily in the laundry and on at least seven or eight occasions, he looked at her face and asked her when she was going to get reconstructive surgery. Unfortunately, Agnes has already had reconstructive surgery and no more can be done. One day Agnes left the laundry to take the towels to the locker room and two women customers told her that she was "disgusting" and that she should "quit her job" because they "hated to look at her." Agnes complained to her supervisor, who said nothing to the customers. The same customers returned a number of times that month and made similar comments, some within the earshot of the supervisor, who did nothing. Agnes complained again to her supervisor, who forbade Agnes from leaving the laundry, even over her lunch hour. He also told her to enter the building through the back door. Finally, Agnes filed a charge of disability discrimination and harassment against the health club. Four days after the charge was filed, her supervisor told her that he thought her face looked worse. Agnes was so upset that she left the building and never went back. She subsequently filed a charge of retaliation. The health club had a policy that encouraged employees to report any harassment, based on any reason, to the management.

1. Is Agnes a qualified individual with a disability for the job of receptionist? Explain. If so, does she have a viable claim against the health club based on her demotion? Explain. Analyze the defendant's possible defenses.

2. Analyze whether the comments by the customers and those by Agnes' supervisor constituted disability-based harassment. Consider whether the health club would be liable for the comments of the customers and the supervisor. Do not forget the differing standards applicable to supervisors and customers in this analysis.

3. Does Agnes have a viable retaliation claim against the health club? Explain.

[1] Disability-Based Harassment

Although the Supreme Court has not ruled on whether there is a cause of action for disability-based harassment, most courts assume that the ADA and the Rehabilitation Act would support a cause of action for hostile work environment based on an individual's disability. A hostile work environment cause of action based on disability would require the plaintiff to prove that the harassing behavior alleged to constitute a hostile work environment is: 1) unwelcome; 2) sufficiently severe or pervasive to alter the terms or conditions of employment; and 3) based on the individual's disability. As in Title VII, employers would likely be liable for harassment caused by supervisors, coworkers and third parties such as customers and clients depending on the behavior. Under Title VII, employers are strictly liable for hostile work environments created by supervisors if the supervisors create a tangible employment action. That is, the plaintiff is harassed and is subject to an adverse employment action as part of the harassment such as a firing, demotion, transfer, etc. If there is no tangible employment action, but the environment is hostile because of the individual's disability, the employer will be strictly liable unless it can prove an affirmative defense that it "exercised reasonable care to prevent and correct promptly any sexually harassing behavior," and that the "plaintiff unreasonably failed to take advantage of any preventive or corrective opportunities provided by the employer or to avoid the harm otherwise." *Faragher v. Boca Raton*, 524 U.S. 775, 807 (1998). Finally, if customers or clients harass the individual with a disability, the employer will be liable based on negligence principles, if it knew or had reason to know of the harassment and did not correct the behavior.

[2]   Retaliation

42 U.S.C. § 12203 states:

> No person shall discriminate against any individual because such individual has opposed any act or practice made unlawful by this chapter or because such individual made a charge, testified, assisted, or participated in any manner in an investigation, proceeding, or hearing under this chapter.

The following case demonstrates how allegations of harassment and retaliation interact.

QUILES-QUILES v. HENDERSON
439 F.3d 1 (1st Cir. 2006)

HOWARD, CIRCUIT JUDGE.

This appeal arises from a civil action under the Rehabilitation Act brought against the Postmaster General of the United States by Genaro Quiles-Quiles, a former postal employee. See 29 U.S.C. § 791 et seq. Quiles alleges that his Postal Service supervisors harassed him because of his disability and retaliated against him when he complained about the harassment. A jury found for Quiles on both claims and awarded him $950,000 in compensatory damages, which the district court reduced to the statutory cap of $300,000. See 42 U.S.C. § 1981a (a)(2). The Postmaster General filed a post-trial motion for judgment as a matter of law, which the district court allowed. We reverse and reinstate the verdict in the statutorily-capped amount.

I.

The jury could have found the following facts. Quiles began his employment for the Postal Service in 1986 as a mail carrier. In 1995, he was assigned to the Bayamon Gardens station where he worked as a window cashier. Among his duties, he sold stamps and other postal products. His immediate supervisor was Doris Vazquez, who served under Virgilio Lopez. Luther Alston was the station manager.

Soon after Quiles moved to Bayamon Gardens station, Vazquez began to bother him. Vazquez frequently interfered with Quiles' running his window, dealing with customers, and handling the cash drawer money. This conduct made Quiles "anxious and nervous" because he was afraid that he would be held responsible for any accounting errors. Quiles complained to Lopez, who did nothing to stop the interference.

On October 4, 1997, Vazquez screamed at Quiles because he had gone to lunch "without authorization." The incident took place in front of several employees and customers. Immediately thereafter, Quiles suffered a panic attack and sought psychiatric help for anxiety and depression. Quiles missed three days of work because of his distress. When Quiles returned, he presented to Lopez a certificate from his psychiatrist stating that the absence was medically necessary.

After Quiles returned to work, Vazquez interrupted his work more frequently. Quiles complained on several occasions, but neither Lopez nor Alston intervened. On March 5, 1998, Quiles was crossing the street outside the post office when (so the jury could have found) Vazquez drove at him in her truck. Quiles reported the incident to his supervisors and the police. Afterwards, Quiles entered a state of "acute anxiety."

As a result of Quiles' worsening mental condition, his psychiatrist prescribed a week-long leave of absence and recommended that he be reassigned from his cashier duties after returning to work. Quiles brought Lopez a sealed envelope containing the medical certificate referencing this information. Lopez opened the envelope, read the medical certificate, and brought it to Vazquez. Vazquez read the certificate and laughingly exclaimed, "He is crazy!" Lopez laughed as well. When Quiles informed Alston of the incident, Alston told Quiles to "stop acting."

From this point forward, Vazquez and Lopez called Quiles "crazy" on a daily basis. They also constantly "joked" in front of coworkers and customers about the fact that Quiles saw a psychiatrist and took medication for his condition. This commentary included remarks about the effect that the medication had on Quiles' ability to have sexual relations with his wife. In addition, Lopez often remarked that Quiles posed a "great risk" to the other employees because he was under on-going psychiatric treatment. Alston frequently stated that Quiles was a "risk to the floor" because he was undergoing psychiatric treatment. And Vazquez remarked several times a day that Quiles should "not be working" in the post office because he was "crazy."

On April 14, 1998, Quiles filed a complaint with the Equal Employment Office of the Postal Service, claiming that Vazquez, Lopez, and Alston had harassed him because of his mental disability. Through the remainder of 1998 and 1999, the harassment and derogatory comments continued. Two weeks after Quiles filed his EEO complaint, Alston threw Quiles out of his office, screamed at him, and slammed the door as Quiles was leaving. Several weeks later, Lopez stopped a union grievance meeting between Quiles and a shop steward and shouted at Quiles in front of coworkers. Alston approached Quiles in the bathroom and told him that he would "soon be without a job," called Quiles a "punk," challenged Quiles to a fight, and grabbed his (own) crotch while calling Quiles a "coward."

Quiles' mental condition deteriorated. On March 31, 2000, Quiles' psychiatrist found him totally disabled because of severe depression, and Quiles began a leave of absence. Quiles was hospitalized for several days during this period to treat his depression. A year later, Quiles returned to his position because of financial need. He worked until August 14, 2003, when Vazquez again called him "crazy." This triggered a relapse of Quiles' depression and required another hospitalization. He has since been totally disabled.

Following the close of evidence, the Postmaster General moved for judgment as a matter of law. The district court denied the motion and submitted the case to the jury. After the jury returned a verdict for Quiles, the district court allowed the Postmaster General's renewed motion for judgment as a matter of law, and entered judgment against Quiles. The court rejected the jury's disability-harassment finding because Quiles had not demonstrated that he was disabled. The court also rejected the jury's retaliation finding because Quiles had failed to prove either that he was subjected to a hostile work environment, or that any harassment he suffered was causally related to his filing of an EEO complaint.

II.

We review the ruling on a motion for judgment as a matter of law de novo. Our review is "weighted toward preservation of the jury verdict" because a verdict should be set aside only if the jury failed to reach the only result permitted by the evidence.

As a Postal Service employee, Quiles' claim arises under the Rehabilitation Act, not the Americans with Disabilities Act (ADA). Nevertheless, the liability standards are the same under each statute. See 29 U.S.C. § 791(g). Therefore, "the caselaw construing the ADA generally pertains equally to claims under the Rehabilitation Act."

A. Disability Harassment

[The discussion of whether the plaintiff is an individual with a disability is omitted.]

We turn next to the Postmaster General's first alternative argument for affirmance: Quiles failed to adduce sufficient evidence that he was forced to endure a hostile work environment. The Postmaster General acknowledges that Quiles was subject to daily ridicule about his mental impairment. He contends, however, that this sort of conduct is common in blue- collar workplaces such as a post office, and that conduct of this sort, while inappropriate, does not constitute a hostile work environment.

To establish a hostile work environment, Quiles had to show that his "workplace [was] permeated with discriminatory intimidation, ridicule, and insult that [was] sufficiently severe or pervasive to alter the conditions of . . . [his] employment and create an abusive working environment." Among the factors relevant to this inquiry are the severity of the conduct, its frequency, and whether it unreasonably interfered with the victim's work performance.

There was testimony that Quiles was subject to such constant ridicule about his mental impairment that it required him to be hospitalized and eventually to withdraw from the workforce. This evidence was, in our view, sufficient for a reasonable jury to find a hostile work environment.

Finally, we consider the Postmaster General's other alternate ground for affirmance: the hostile conduct at issue was not directed at Quiles because of his disability. In presenting this argument, the Postmaster General highlights the fact that Vazquez harassed Quiles before she knew of his impairment.

The Supreme Court has emphasized that the federal employment discrimination laws do not establish "a general civility code" for the workplace. Rather, an employee claiming harassment must demonstrate that the hostile conduct was directed at him because of a characteristic protected by a federal anti-discrimination statute.

The Postmaster General correctly posits that some of Vazquez's conduct does not constitute actionable harassment because it occurred before Vazquez knew that Quiles was suffering from depression. But, even discounting this conduct, there was ample proof that Quiles was harassed because of his disability. On March 5, 1998, Quiles brought a medical certificate to Lopez identifying his mental impairment. And, for the next two years, Quiles' superiors harassed and ridiculed him relentlessly, frequently mentioning the disability in the course of their actions. This evidence was sufficient to ground the jury's finding that Quiles was discriminated against because of his perceived disability.

B. Retaliation

As explained above, the jury also found that Quiles' supervisors retaliated against him after he complained about the harassment. The Rehabilitation Act prohibits retaliation against employees for complaining about violations of the Act. To prove retaliation, Quiles had to establish that (1) he engaged in protected conduct; (2) he experienced an adverse employment action; and (3) there was a causal connection between the protected conduct and the adverse employment action. The adverse employment action requirement may be satisfied by showing the creation of a hostile work environment or the intensification of a pre-existing hostile environment. And, in proper circumstances, the causation element may be established by evidence that there was a temporal proximity between the behavior in question and the employee's complaint.

The district court rejected the retaliation claim on two grounds. It concluded that Quiles did not satisfy the adverse-action requirement because the evidence of a hostile environment was insufficient. The court also ruled that, even if Quiles had introduced sufficient proof of a hostile environment, he had failed to show that the hostility was caused by his complaint.

We have already addressed the hostile-environment issue in the disability-harassment discussion, but now consider it as it relates to the retaliation claim. The relevant conduct is that which occurred after Quiles complained about his superiors' disability-related harassment.

There was proof that, within a few weeks of Quiles filing a harassment complaint with the Postal Service's Equal Employment Office, the harassment intensified. Prior to the EEO complaint, the harassment related primarily to comments concerning Quiles' mental impairment. But, after Quiles filed his complaint, the harassment expanded to include, inter alia, threats by Alston, screaming tirades directed at Quiles by both Alston and Lopez, and efforts by Lopez to interrupt Quiles' pursuit of a union grievance.

"Subject to some policing at the outer bounds, [the hostile environment question] is . . . to be resolved by the trier of fact on the basis of inferences drawn from a broad array of circumstantial and often conflicting evidence." We cannot say on this record that the jury's conclusion that Quiles endured a hostile work environment after he made his EEO complaint was irrational.

We also think that there was sufficient evidence for the jury to have found that the hostile environment was motivated by a desire to retaliate against Quiles. The district court found no evidence of such causation because Quiles did not "even present one stray hearsay remark as to the motivation for these particular supervisors' actions." But there is no requirement for the plaintiff to present such "smoking gun" evidence; circumstantial evidence can suffice. The proof that the intensified harassment commenced shortly after Quiles filed his EEO complaint is sufficient evidence from which the jury could infer causation.

III.

Quiles presented sufficient evidence that he was the victim of harassment by his supervisors because of his perceived disability. He also presented sufficient evidence that his supervisors retaliated against him after he complained about their harassment. Accordingly, the district court erred in granting the Postmaster General's motion for judgment as a matter of law.

Reversed and remanded.

NOTES

1.   Although some courts make the mistake of stating that a plaintiff alleging a hostile work environment must show that the harassing behavior was severe *and* pervasive, the actual standard established by the Supreme Court was that the conduct be severe *or* pervasive. This means that the behavior need not be severe, but that repeated pervasive behavior may be sufficient to create a hostile work environment that alters the terms or conditions of employment. In *Casas v. El Paso*, 502 F. Supp. 2d 542 (W.D. Tex. 2007), a case brought under Title II of the ADA, the plaintiff alleged that the defendant subjected the plaintiff to a hostile environment based on rudeness of city bus drivers who argued with the plaintiff and treated him rudely when the plaintiff attempted to board city buses with a personal care assistant without the assistant's paying a fare. The court held that the behavior was not severe or pervasive enough to constitute a hostile environment even though the plaintiff alleged 17 different instances of rude behavior based on his disability over a two year period.

2.   The retaliation in this case is retaliatory harassment. In many traditional retaliation cases, the employer or its agents subject the plaintiff to an adverse employment action, such as firing, demotion or unfavorable reassignment, in retaliation for the employee's opposition to illegal discriminatory behavior or because the employee testifies or participates in a lawsuit or proceeding brought against the employer. Here, the retaliation alleged is not a particular adverse action such as a firing but the worsening of a hostile work environment. Many courts today recognize a cause of action for retaliatory harassment.

3. In *Crawford v. Metropolitan Gov't of Nashville & Davidson County*, 129 S. Ct. 846 (2009), the Supreme Court held that an employee who responds to questions asked during an employer's internal investigation of a sexual harassment complaint is protected by the anti-retaliation provision of Title VII. Similar protection likely exists under the ADA.

G DEFENSES

[1] Employee Misconduct

Defenses to an ADA claim discussed previously include the following: the employer is not covered by the statute under which a claim is brought; the individual bringing the claim is not disabled within the statutory definition; the employer does not know of the disability; the individual is not otherwise qualified; or the requested accommodation is not reasonable or is an undue hardship.

Other defenses include downsizing and selection or promotion of a more qualified individual. One frequent defense is misconduct, which can include an array of employee behavior ranging from insubordination, attendance (discussed previously), providing false information, dishonesty, and sexual harassment. Courts disagree as to whether an employer must accommodate a person whose misconduct is caused by the disability.

There are cases in which the employee is able to carry out the technical, physical, or professional requirements of the job competently, and the employee has no problems with attendance or dealing with stress, but engages in some type of misconduct. Depending on the seriousness of the misconduct, courts have been inclined to find that certain levels of conduct are qualifications for the job.

For example, truthfulness and honesty often are deemed to be legitimate job requirements. In *Hartman v. City of Petaluma*, 841 F. Supp. 946 (N.D. Cal. 1994), the court held that the deliberate failure to disclose past drug use supported a discharge. Insubordination or failure to comply with employer instructions also have been found to be misconduct meriting termination of employment. See *Schartle v. Motorola, Inc.*, 1994 LEXIS 6241 (N.D. Ill. 1994); *Fehr v. McLean Packaging Corp.*, 860 F. Supp. 198 (E.D. Pa. 1994).

Using drugs and alcohol at work or working under the influence of these substances also are often deemed misconduct disqualifying the individual from employment. See *McDaniel v. Mississippi Baptist Med. Ctr.*, 869 F. Supp. 445 (S.D. Miss. 1994); *Flynn v. Raytheon Co.*, 868 F. Supp. 383 (D. Mass. 1994).

The excerpt from *Maddox v. University of Tennessee*, 62 F.3d 843 (6th Cir. 1995), in Section 3[A][3], *supra*, highlights that defense in the context of a case in which the employee claimed that because the disability related to the misconduct, the adverse employment action violated the Rehabilitation Act.

[2]   Immunity

One of the areas receiving substantial attention from the Supreme Court is the defense of Eleventh Amendment immunity from damage claims. The following case addresses this issue in the context of employment and Title I of the ADA.

BOARD OF TRUSTEES v. GARRETT
531 U.S. 356 (2001)

CHIEF JUSTICE REHNQUIST delivered the opinion of the Court.

We decide here whether employees of the State of Alabama may recover money damages by reason of the State's failure to comply with the provisions of Title I of the Americans with Disabilities Act of 1990 (ADA or Act). We hold that such suits are barred by the Eleventh Amendment.

[The claimants were a registered nurse who had been treated for breast cancer and who was employed by the University of Alabama, a state university, and a security officer with chronic asthma employed by the state Department of Youth Services. Both were denied requested relief under the ADA, and they filed claims for money damages.]

The Eleventh Amendment provides:

> "The Judicial power of the United States shall not be construed to extend to any suit in law or equity, commenced or prosecuted against one of the United States by Citizens of another State, or by Citizens or Subjects of any Foreign State."

Although by its terms the Amendment applies only to suits against a State by citizens of another State, our cases have extended the Amendment's applicability to suits by citizens against their own States. The ultimate guarantee of the Eleventh Amendment is that nonconsenting States may not be sued by private individuals in federal court.

We have recognized, however, that Congress may abrogate the States' Eleventh Amendment immunity when it both unequivocally intends to do so and "acts pursuant to a valid grant of constitutional authority." The first of these requirements is not in dispute here. The question, then, is whether Congress acted within its constitutional authority by subjecting the States to suits in federal court for money damages under the ADA.

Congress may not, of course, base its abrogation of the States' Eleventh Amendment immunity upon the powers enumerated in Article I. [We have held] that "the Eleventh Amendment, and the principle of state sovereignty which it embodies, are necessarily limited by the enforcement provisions of § 5 of the Fourteenth Amendment." Congress may subject nonconsenting States to suit in federal court when it does so pursuant to a valid exercise of its § 5 power. Our cases have adhered to this proposition. Accordingly, the ADA can apply to the States only to the extent that the statute is appropriate § 5 legislation.

Section 1 of the Fourteenth Amendment provides, in relevant part:

"No State shall make or enforce any law which shall abridge the privileges or immunities of citizens of the United States; nor shall any State deprive any person of life, liberty, or property, without due process of law; nor deny to any person within its jurisdiction the equal protection of the laws."

Section 5 of the Fourteenth Amendment grants Congress the power to enforce the substantive guarantees contained in § 1 by enacting "appropriate legislation." Congress is not limited to mere legislative repetition of this Court's constitutional jurisprudence. "Rather, Congress' power 'to enforce' the Amendment includes the authority both to remedy and to deter violation of rights guaranteed thereunder by prohibiting a somewhat broader swath of conduct, including that which is not itself forbidden by the Amendment's text."

[I]t is the responsibility of this Court, not Congress, to define the substance of constitutional guarantees. Accordingly, § 5 legislation reaching beyond the scope of § 1's actual guarantees must exhibit "congruence and proportionality between the injury to be prevented or remedied and the means adopted to that end."

The first step in applying these now familiar principles is to identify with some precision the scope of the constitutional right at issue. Here, that inquiry requires us to examine the limitations § 1 of the Fourteenth Amendment places upon States' treatment of the disabled.

In *Cleburne v. Cleburne Living Center, Inc.*, 473 U.S. 432 (1985) we considered an equal protection challenge to a city ordinance requiring a special use permit for the operation of a group home for the mentally retarded. The specific question before us was whether the Court of Appeals had erred by holding that mental retardation qualified as a "quasi-suspect" classification under our equal protection jurisprudence. We answered that question in the affirmative, concluding instead that such legislation incurs only the minimum "rational-basis" review applicable to general social and economic legislation. In a statement that today seems quite prescient, we explained that

> "if the large and amorphous class of the mentally retarded were deemed quasi-suspect for the reasons given by the Court of Appeals, it would be difficult to find a principled way to distinguish a variety of other groups who have perhaps immutable disabilities setting them off from others, who cannot themselves mandate the desired legislative responses, and who can claim some degree of prejudice from at least part of the public at large. One need mention in this respect only the aging, the disabled, the mentally ill, and the infirm. We are reluctant to set out on that course, and we decline to do so."

Under rational-basis review, where a group possesses "distinguishing characteristics relevant to interests the State has the authority to implement," a State's decision to act on the basis of those differences does not give rise to a constitutional violation. "Such a classification cannot run afoul of the Equal Protection Clause if there is a rational relationship between the disparity of treatment and some legitimate governmental purpose." Moreover, the State need not articulate its reasoning at the moment a particular decision is made. Rather, the burden is upon the challenging party to negative " 'any reasonably conceivable state of facts that could provide a rational basis for the classification.' "

Justice Breyer suggests that *Cleburne* stands for the broad proposition that state decisionmaking reflecting "negative attitudes" or "fear" necessarily runs afoul of the Fourteenth Amendment. Although such biases may often accompany irrational (and therefore unconstitutional) discrimination, their presence alone does not a constitutional violation make. [S]tate action subject to rational-basis scrutiny does not violate the Fourteenth Amendment when it "rationally furthers the purpose identified by the State."

Thus, the result of *Cleburne* is that States are not required by the Fourteenth Amendment to make special accommodations for the disabled, so long as their actions towards such individuals are rational. They could quite hard headedly — and perhaps hardheartedly — hold to job-qualification requirements which do not make allowance for the disabled.

Once we have determined the metes and bounds of the constitutional right in question, we examine whether Congress identified a history and pattern of unconstitutional employment discrimination by the States against the disabled. Just as § 1 of the Fourteenth Amendment applies only to actions committed "under color of state law," Congress' § 5 authority is appropriately exercised only in response to state transgressions. The legislative record of the ADA, however, simply fails to show that Congress did in fact identify a pattern of irrational state discrimination in employment against the disabled.

Congress made a general finding in the ADA that "historically, society has tended to isolate and segregate individuals with disabilities, and, despite some improvements, such forms of discrimination against individuals with disabilities continue to be a serious and pervasive social problem." The record assembled by Congress includes many instances to support such a finding. But the great majority of these incidents do not deal with the activities of States.

Respondents in their brief cite half a dozen examples from the record that did involve States. A department head at the University of North Carolina refused to hire an applicant for the position of health administrator because he was blind; similarly, a student at a state university in South Dakota was denied an opportunity to practice teach because the dean at that time was convinced that blind people could not teach in public schools. A microfilmer at the Kansas Department of Transportation was fired because he had epilepsy; deaf workers at the University of Oklahoma were paid a lower salary than those who could hear. The Indiana State Personnel Office informed a woman with a concealed disability that she should not disclose it if she wished to obtain employment.

Several of these incidents undoubtedly evidence an unwillingness on the part of state officials to make the sort of accommodations for the disabled required by the ADA. Whether they were irrational under our decision in *Cleburne* is more debatable, particularly when the incident is described out of context. But even if it were to be determined that each incident upon fuller examination showed unconstitutional action on the part of the State, these incidents taken together fall far short of even suggesting the pattern of unconstitutional discrimination on which § 5 legislation must be based. Congress, in enacting the ADA, found that "some

43,000,000 Americans have one or more physical or mental disabilities." 42 U.S.C. § 12101(a)(1). In 1990, the States alone employed more than 4.5 million people. It is telling, we think, that given these large numbers, Congress assembled only such minimal evidence of unconstitutional state discrimination in employment against the disabled.

Justice Breyer maintains that Congress applied Title I of the ADA to the States in response to a host of incidents representing unconstitutional state discrimination in employment against persons with disabilities. A close review of the relevant materials, however, undercuts that conclusion. Justice Breyer's Appendix C consists not of legislative findings, but of unexamined, anecdotal accounts of "adverse, disparate treatment by state officials." Of course, as we have already explained, "adverse, disparate treatment" often does not amount to a constitutional violation where rational-basis scrutiny applies. These accounts, moreover, were submitted not directly to Congress but to the Task Force on the Rights and Empowerment of Americans with Disabilities, which made no findings on the subject of state discrimination in employment. And, had Congress truly understood this information as reflecting a pattern of unconstitutional behavior by the States, one would expect some mention of that conclusion in the Act's legislative findings. There is none. Although Justice Breyer would infer from Congress' general conclusions regarding societal discrimination against the disabled that the States had likewise participated in such action, the House and Senate committee reports on the ADA flatly contradict this assertion. After describing the evidence presented to the Senate Committee on Labor and Human Resources and its subcommittee (including the Task Force Report upon which the dissent relies), the Committee's report reached, among others, the following conclusion: "Discrimination still persists in such critical areas as *employment in the private sector*, public accommodations, public services, transportation, and telecommunications." The House Committee on Education and Labor, addressing the ADA's employment provisions, reached the same conclusion: "After extensive review and analysis over a number of Congressional sessions, . . . there exists a compelling need to establish a clear and comprehensive Federal prohibition of discrimination on the basis of disability in the areas of *employment in the private sector*, public accommodations, public services, transportation, and telecommunications." Thus, not only is the inference Justice Breyer draws unwarranted, but there is also strong evidence that Congress' failure to mention States in its legislative findings addressing discrimination in employment reflects that body's judgment that no pattern of unconstitutional state action had been documented.

Even were it possible to squeeze out of these examples a pattern of unconstitutional discrimination by the States, the rights and remedies created by the ADA against the States would raise the same sort of concerns as to congruence and proportionality as were found in *City of Boerne*. For example, whereas it would be entirely rational (and therefore constitutional) for a state employer to conserve scarce financial resources by hiring employees who are able to use existing facilities, the ADA requires employers to "make existing facilities used by employees readily accessible to and usable by individuals with disabilities." The ADA does except employers from the "reasonable accommodation" requirement where the employer "can demonstrate that the accommodation would impose an undue hardship on the operation of the business of such covered entity." However, even with this exception, the accommodation duty far exceeds what is constitutionally required in that it makes unlawful a range of alternate responses that would be reasonable but would fall short of imposing an "undue burden" upon the employer. The Act also makes it the employer's duty to prove that it would suffer such a burden, instead of requiring (as the Constitution does) that the complaining party negate reasonable bases for the employer's decision.

The ADA also forbids "utilizing standards, criteria, or methods of administration" that disparately impact the disabled, without regard to whether such conduct has a rational basis. § 12112(b)(3)(A). Although disparate impact may be relevant evidence of racial discrimination, such evidence alone is insufficient even where the Fourteenth Amendment subjects state action to strict scrutiny.

JUSTICE BREYER, with whom JUSTICE STEVENS, JUSTICE SOUTER and JUSTICE GINSBURG join, dissenting.

The Court says that its primary problem with this statutory provision is one of legislative evidence. It says that "Congress assembled only . . . minimal evidence of unconstitutional state discrimination in employment." In fact, Congress compiled a vast legislative record documenting " 'massive, society-wide discrimination' " against persons with disabilities. In addition to the information presented at 13 congressional hearings, and its own prior experience gathered over 40 years during which it contemplated and enacted considerable similar legislation, Congress created a special task force to assess the need for comprehensive legislation. That task force held hearings in every State, attended by more than 30,000 people, including thousands who had experienced discrimination first hand. The task force hearings, Congress' own hearings, and an analysis of "census data, national polls, and other studies" led Congress to conclude that "people with disabilities, as a group, occupy an inferior status in our society, and are severely disadvantaged socially, vocationally, economically, and educationally." As to employment, Congress found that "two-thirds of all disabled Americans between the age of 16 and 64 [were] not working at all," even though a large majority wanted to, and were able to, work productively. And Congress found that this discrimination flowed in significant part from "stereotypic assumptions" as well as "purposeful unequal treatment."

The powerful evidence of discriminatory treatment throughout society in general, including discrimination by private persons and local governments, implicates state governments as well, for state agencies form part of that same larger society. There is no particular reason to believe that they are immune from the "stereotypic assumptions" and pattern of "purposeful unequal treatment" that Congress found prevalent. The Court claims that it "makes no sense" to take into consideration constitutional violations committed by local governments. But the substantive obligation that the Equal Protection Clause creates applies to state and local governmental entities alike.

There are roughly 300 examples of discrimination by state governments themselves in the legislative record. I fail to see how this evidence "falls far short of even suggesting the pattern of unconstitutional discrimination on which § 5 legislation must be based."

The congressionally appointed task force collected numerous specific examples, provided by persons with disabilities themselves, of adverse, disparate treatment by state officials. They reveal, not what the Court describes as "half a dozen" instances of discrimination, but hundreds of instances of adverse treatment at the hands of state officials — instances in which a person with a disability found it impossible to obtain a state job, to retain state employment, to use the public transportation that was readily available to others in order to get to work, or to obtain a public education, which is often a prerequisite to obtaining employment. State-imposed barriers also frequently made it difficult or impossible for people to vote, to enter a public building, to access important government services, such as calling for emergency assistance, and to find a place to live due to a pattern of irrational zoning decisions similar to the discrimination that we held unconstitutional in *Cleburne*, 473 U.S. at 448.

The Court's failure to find sufficient evidentiary support may well rest upon its decision to hold Congress to a strict, judicially created evidentiary standard, particularly in respect to lack of justification. Justice Kennedy's empirical conclusion — which rejects that of Congress — rests heavily upon his failure to find "extensive litigation and discussion of constitutional violations," in *"the courts* of the United States." Or as Justice Brandeis, writing for the Court, put the matter many years ago, " 'if any state of facts reasonably can be conceived that would sustain' " challenged legislation, then " 'there is a presumption of the existence of that state of facts, and one who assails the classification must carry the burden of showing . . . that the action is arbitrary.' "

There is simply no reason to require Congress, seeking to determine facts relevant to the exercise of its § 5 authority, to adopt rules or presumptions that reflect a court's institutional limitations. Unlike courts, Congress can readily gather facts from across the Nation, assess the magnitude of a problem, and more easily find an appropriate remedy.

The Court argues in the alternative that the statute's damage remedy is not "congruent" with and "proportional" to the equal protection problem that Congress found. The Court suggests that the Act's "reasonable accommodation" requirement, 42 U.S.C. § 12112(b)(5)(A), and disparate impact standard, § 12112(b)(3)(A), "far exceed what is constitutionally required." But we have upheld disparate impact standards in contexts where they were not "constitutionally required."

And what is wrong with a remedy that, in response to unreasonable employer behavior, requires an employer to make accommodations that are reasonable? Of course, what is "reasonable" in the statutory sense and what is "unreasonable" in the constitutional sense might differ. In other words, the requirement may exceed what is necessary to avoid a constitutional violation. But it is just that power — the power to require more than the minimum- that § 5 grants to Congress, as this Court has repeatedly confirmed. As long ago as 1880, the Court wrote that § 5 "brought within the domain of congressional power" whatever "tends to enforce submission" to its "prohibitions" and "to secure to all persons . . . the equal protection of the laws."

In keeping with these principles, the Court has said that "it is not for us to review the congressional resolution of" the various conflicting considerations — the risk or pervasiveness of the discrimination in governmental services . . . , "the adequacy or availability of alternative remedies, and the nature and significance of the state interests that would be affected." "It is enough that we be able to perceive a basis upon which the Congress might resolve the conflict as it did." Nothing in the words "reasonable accommodation" suggests that the requirement has no "tendency to enforce" the Equal Protection Clause, that it is an irrational way to achieve the objective, that it would fall outside the scope of the Necessary and Proper Clause, or that it somehow otherwise exceeds the bounds of the "appropriate."

The Court had left open the issue of immunity under Title II of the ADA in the 2001 *Board of Trustees v. Garrett* opinion. In 2004, the Court addressed this issue again, although not in the context of employment discrimination. In *Tennessee v. Lane*, 124 S. Ct. 1978 (2004) (excerpted in Chapter 5, *infra*), the Court held that Title II does not exceed Congressional power under the Fourteenth Amendment in allowing actions for damages against state agencies in the context of access to the judicial system. What remains unresolved in that opinion is the applicability of Eleventh Amendment immunity in the context of employment discrimination cases under Title II. Given the analysis in *Garrett*, it seems probable that the Supreme Court would disallow damages against state agencies under Title II. The Supreme Court has not addressed whether state agencies are immune from damages in employment settings under Section 504 of the Rehabilitation Act. For more recent cases on immunity, see LAURA ROTHSTEIN & JULIA ROTHSTEIN, DISABILITIES AND THE LAW § 4.26 (2009).

H   RELATIONSHIP OF ADA TO OTHER FEDERAL AND STATE LAWS

There are a number of other federal and state laws that are not disability discrimination laws, but nonetheless interact with the ADA and/or the Rehabilitation Act.

[1]   Benefits Statutes

Statutes providing benefits for disability are particularly problematic because the definition for one statute does not necessarily equate to the definition in the other statute. For example, to be eligible for workers' compensation or Social Security disability benefits, one must meet the definition of being either totally or partially disabled. Does meeting this definition preclude the individual claiming the benefits from seeking reinstatement to the job with accommodations? Is the individual precluded from claiming that he or she is otherwise qualified to perform the job when the individual had indicated an inability to do the work as a basis for receiving the benefits? An employee who is injured on the job is less likely to be eligible for workers' compensation if the employer reasonably accommodates the injured employee and makes reasonable efforts to return the worker to the job.

Section 510 of the Employee Retirement Income Security Act (ERISA) of 1974, 29 U.S.C. § 1140, makes it unlawful for an employer to discriminate against an employee for the purpose of interfering with the right to become a participant in an employee welfare plan, such as health insurance.

There has been a great deal of debate about tension between benefits statutes and discrimination statutes and how the definition of whether one is qualified and able to work under one statute affects the individual's ability to bring suit under another statute.

NOTE

The Supreme Court has clarified whether individuals are judicially estopped from claiming that they are otherwise qualified to carry out employment requirements when they have sought or obtained benefits in situations where one must indicate the inability to work.

In *Cleveland v. Policy Management Systems Corp.*, 526 U.S. 795 (1999), the plaintiff was employed by the defendant and suffered a stroke, which damaged her concentration, memory and language skills. She filed for disability benefits with the Social Security Disability Insurance Program (SSDI), stating that she was "disabled" and "unable to work." Her condition improved, and three months later she returned to work and reported her return to the Social Security Administration. The SSDI noted that she had returned to work and denied her SSDI benefits. Four days later, the plaintiff was fired. She appealed her denial of her benefits from the SSDI, stating that she had attempted to work but that her employer had fired her because she could no longer do the job. She alleged that she was unable to work because of her disability. She then filed a lawsuit against her former employer, alleging that it violated the ADA because it failed to grant her a reasonable accommodation. Her complaint alleged that she could perform the essential functions of the job with an accommodation.

The federal district court granted summary judgment to the defendant of the ADA suit because of the plaintiff's claims that she was unable to work in her appeal to the SSDI, and the court of appeals affirmed. The case went to the United States Supreme Court. The issue was whether there is a presumption that a person who receives SSDI benefits because she is unable to work may not bring an ADA claim because she would not be a qualified individual. The Court held that there is no special presumption against a recipient of SSDI that she is not a qualified individual for purposes of the ADA. The two laws have different definitions of disability, and collecting SSDI benefits is not necessarily inconsistent with proving a violation of the ADA. The definition of a qualified individual with a disability under the ADA provides that she is a person who can perform the essential functions of the job either with or without reasonable accommodation. In contrast, the SSDI does not take into account the possibility of a reasonable accommodation in defining whether an individual is unable to work. Moreover, SSDI benefits are processed with reference to a list of questions, one of which asks the former employee whether he or she has an impairment that meets or equals those on a list of impairments. Because of the differences in the definitions of disability of the two statutes, a person who collects SSDI benefits will not have a presumption against her in an ADA case. But, the ADA plaintiff cannot ignore the apparent contradiction. Her sworn assertion in an SSDI application that she is unable to work will likely negate an essential element of the ADA unless the plaintiff can offer a sufficient explanation.

For cases since this decision, see LAURA ROTHSTEIN & JULIA ROTHSTEIN, DISABILITIES AND THE LAW § 4.25 (2009).

[2]   Family and Medical Leave Act

The Family and Medical Leave Act (FMLA) of 1993, 29 U.S.C. §§ 2601–2654, provides that employers with 50 or more employees must provide up to 12 weeks of unpaid leave for the birth or adoption of a child; to care for the spouse, child or parent of an employee; or the serious health condition of the employee. The FMLA and ADA are not mutually exclusive. For example, an individual with a disability requiring physical therapy might be entitled to have reasonable leave (unpaid) from the job under the ADA, which might in some cases be more extensive than the maximums provided for in the FMLA.

Where the employee has a disability or a serious medical condition or injury, there is often an intersection of issues concerning the FMLA, the ADA and the state worker compensation laws. Much of the FMLA and ADA litigation arises from work-related illnesses or injuries. An employee who is absent from work because of a work-related condition or illness often has rights under the FMLA or the ADA. The following chart, using Nevada's worker's compensation act as a model, examines in a broad fashion the rights and obligations under the different statutes, but does not contain the specific details of the FMLA and WC statutes:

	ADA	FMLA	WORKER'S COM-PENSATION
Purpose	To prevent discrimination against qualified persons with disabilities. To get persons with disabilities working.	To grant leaves to persons who have serious medical conditions, birth or adoption, or family members with serious medical conditions.	To compensate workers injured at work or caused by work related industrial disease.
Covered Employers	Those with 15 employees.	Those with 50 employees within 75 miles.	Every person, firm, voluntary association and private corporation that has any person under contract for hire.

	ADA	FMLA	WORKER'S COMPENSATION
Eligible Individuals	Qualified applicants or employees with disabilities. Mental or physical impairment that substantially limits a major life activity; a record of such an impairment; or regarded as having an impairment.	Employees who have worked at least 1 year, with at least 1,250 hours within the past 12 months. Employee has "serious health condition."	Every person in service of an employer whose injuries arise out of work and in scope of employment or whose occupational disease is incidental to the business.
Medical Information (inquiries and medical examinations)	Pre-offer (no) Post-offer but pre-employment (yes if all in same job category, must reveal); Employees — only if job related and consistent with business necessity	Evidence from Employee's doctor of "serious health condition." Need not defer to WC's authorized treating physician. Employee may seek second opinion from another doctor. Employer then must pay for a third opinion by a mutually agreed upon doctor.	Employer's doctor certifies. ("authorized treating physician). Before ADA, could ask questions in interviews about prior WC claims to assess risks — no longer permissible. Post-conditional offer of employment, may require medical exams and information if required for all employees in unit, but must keep confidential and separate under ADA. If applicant has a disability under ADA, may not refuse to hire based on the disability unless person would pose a direct threat to his or others' health or safety.

	ADA	FMLA	WORKER'S COMPENSATION
Medical Records	Separate confidential file	May keep FMLA medical info in same ADA file. WC information may be kept in same file, but ADA information can only be revealed in limited circumstances.	May submit under the ADA information obtained through medical exams or inquiries to state WC offices or SIF (Second Injury Fund) — to promote employment of individuals with disabilities.
Requests for Leaves	Only as reasonable accommodation	To care for oneself or loved ones	Because of injury.
Terms of Leave	Won't necessarily need leave unless leave is a reasonable accommodation; unpaid. If leave taken under ADA, may run concurrently with FMLA leave. Must permit Employee able to perform essential functions of the job with or without accommodation to return to work, unless undue hardship based on cost to Employer, # of jobs and persons at facility, other business issues.	12 weeks unpaid over one year period; may be intermittent. Qualifying exigency leave of up to 12 weeks for persons with family members on active duty or where active duty is impending. Employee caregiver has up to 26 weeks leave to care for family service member.	Paid medical and disability benefits until maximum medical improvement; if injury persists, may be eligible for permanent, partial or total disability payments, vocational rehabilitation. May consider any leave taken under WC as FMLA leave. 100% healed policy before returning to work violates ADA.

	ADA	**FMLA**	**WORKER'S COMPENSATION**
Return to Work	If Employee can perform essential functions of the same job; or as accommodation, place in another vacant position for which she is qualified. If Employee cannot perform essential functions of same job, and there is no vacant position, Employer not required to create a position for Employee, but must consider what jobs may become vacant in reasonable future.9th Circuit case required Employer to permit Employee to work from home as reasonable accommodation where some other Employees worked from home; Employer not ordinarily required to create part time positions if there are none.	Employee entitled to same job or equivalent job with equal pay and benefits; may return on intermittent schedule if provides certification that medically necessary. Must attempt to schedule intermittent leaves during mutually convenient times. Employer may move Employee to different equal position during intermittent leave.	Employer should provide light duty assignment or permanent reassignment in accordance with state law. Under ADA, if Employer has light duty jobs for Worker's Comp Employees, must give one to non WC disabled Employee as accommodation. But if light duty jobs are temporary, Employer not required to give it to a disabled Employee permanently. Employer may still have to give reasonable accommodation to disabled Employee.

NOTES

1. Definitions of persons covered under the ADA, FMLA, and WC differ. Under the ADA, a qualified individual is one who can perform the essential functions of the job with or without reasonable accommodation. Under the ADA, a person with a disability has a mental or physical impairment that substantially limits a major life activity. Until recently, it has been difficult to establish that an individual has a disability, but after the ADAAA, it should be easier to prove that a person has a disability. Under the FMLA, the person must have a "serious health condition." This is not a difficult standard to meet and a person can have a serious health condition without having a disability under the ADA. The definition under the FMLA is very broad: it requires 1) inpatient care; 2) any period of incapacity requiring absence of more than three days involving treatment by health care provider; or 3) continuing treatment by a health-care provider.

2. A person with a "serious health condition" may qualify for up to 12 weeks of unpaid leave under the FMLA, and may take the leave intermittently. The employer may require an employee who takes intermittent leave to transfer to another equal job if doing so better accommodates the employer's need during the intermittent leave. If the "serious health condition" or a disability is a work injury or illness, the employee may also be covered by WC, and the 12 week FMLA leave may run concurrently with the WC absence.

3. Where it is "medically necessary" to care for a serious health condition, an employee may take FMLA leave intermittently, e.g., weekly physical therapy. The employer must track the hours taken. An employee need not call it FMLA leave, but must ask for time off. The employer must notify the employee that it is FMLA leave that s/he is taking.

4. FMLA leave is unpaid, but the employer may require the employee to substitute any paid leave the employee has accrued for any part of the 12 weeks.

5. While on FMLA leave, the employee may continue coverage under the employer's health plan.

6. When the employee returns from FMLA leave, he or she must be returned to the position held before the leave or an equivalent position in benefits, pay, other terms or conditions of employment.

7. When rights under the FMLA and ADA apply simultaneously, the statute with the greater protection controls. For example, FMLA grants 12 weeks unpaid leave. ADA grants a reasonable accommodation. The reasonable accommodation may include an unpaid leave of less than or greater than 12 weeks if no undue hardship. But undue hardship is not a defense under the FMLA. So, there is a minimum of 12 weeks unpaid leave, but an employee may have the right to more unpaid leave under the ADA if it is a reasonable accommodation that does not impose an undue hardship.

8. Under the ADA, as a reasonable accommodation, the employer may reassign a person to a position that is a demotion, if the employer first considers a lateral move and there is no available position. The employer need not bump an employee with more seniority, if the seniority system has been uniformly applied.

9. The FMLA was amended and the regulations updated for FMLA. The new U.S. Department of Labor update of the FMLA regulations went into effect on January 16, 2009. The amended statute includes increased leave for members of military families. The rules are very specific and detailed and must be consulted before employers/employees act.

See John H. Geaney, *The Relationship of Workers' Compensation to the Americans with Disabilities Act and Family and Medical Leave Act*, 4 CLIN. OCCUP. ENVIRON. MED. 273 (2004). Other sources of useful information are the following:

a.   EEOC website: www.eeoc.gov (for ADA information)

b.   Dept. of Labor website: www.dol.gov (for FMLA information)

c.   For cases on the Family and Medical Leave Act and its relationship to disability discrimination law, see LAURA ROTHSTEIN & JULIA ROTHSTEIN, DISABILITIES AND THE LAW § 1.33 (2009).

[3]   National Labor Relations Act

Another law that may intersect with the ADA is the National Labor Relations Act (NLRA), 29 U.S.C. §§ 151–169, the law that regulates unionization and collective bargaining. For example, under the ADA, one type of reasonable accommodation is to reassign an individual to a vacant position. In companies with collective bargaining agreements, however, job transfer rights are usually set out in the collective bargaining agreement and often are determined on the basis of seniority.

The Supreme Court's decision in *Barnett* is included earlier in this chapter in the section on job reassignment. It should be noted that the Court held that seniority system expectations generally take precedence over requests for reasonable accommodation, regardless of whether such systems are based on a collective bargaining agreement or if they are based on an employer established system.

[4]   Genetic Information Nondiscrimination Act (GINA)

Congress passed GINA, 42 U.S.C. § 2000ff, et seq., overwhelmingly, but only after thirteen years of attempts to pass a bill on genetic discrimination. While proponents of the Act presented testimony of persons who had suffered genetic discrimination by employers and insurance companies, it was acknowledged that there were few documented instances of genetic discrimination. *See* Jessica L. Roberts, *Preempting Discrimination: Lessons from the Genetic Information Nondiscrimination Act,* ___ VAND. L. REV. ___ (2010). Nonetheless, with the Human Genome Project and medicine's ability to track the genes in humans and an expected movement toward personalized medicine based on an individual's genetic makeup, genetics have moved into the treating physician's office. There is a belief that individuals will resist genetic testing or participation in genetic studies, however, because of their fear that they and their family members will suffer discrimination in employment and insurance coverage if their genetic information is dispersed.

GINA passed Congress and was signed by then President Bush on May 21, 2008. The law became effective on November 21, 2009. GINA protects against discrimination based on genetic information in the insurance and employment contexts. Title II deals with employment and prohibits employers, labor organizations, employment agencies and employment training programs from discriminating against an employee or applicant on the basis of genetic information. The term "employee" includes those employees and applicants covered by various acts protecting government and private employees including Title VII of the Civil Rights Act, the Government Employees Rights Act of 1991, the Congressional Accountability Act of 1995, Chapter 5 of Title 3 of the United States Code, and Section 717 of the Civil Rights Act of 1964. "Genetic information" includes genetic tests of the individual or family members and manifestation of disease or disorder of family members. Discrimination is defined as it is in Title VII of the 1964 Civil Rights Act and the ADA:

(1)   to fail or refuse to hire, or to discharge, any employee, or otherwise to discriminate against any employee with respect to the compensation, terms, conditions, or privileges of employment of the employee, because of genetic information with respect to the employee; or

(2)   to limit, segregate, or classify the employees of the employer in any way that would deprive or tend to deprive any employee of employment opportunities or otherwise adversely affect the status of the employee as an employee, because of genetic information with respect to the employee.

P.L. 110-233

The Act also prohibits employers, with certain exceptions, from acquiring genetic information of an employee, applicant, or family member of the employee or applicant. The exceptions include:

(1)   an employer's inadvertent acquisition of information (known as the "water cooler exception");

(2)   where the employer offers health or genetic services including a wellness program and the employee participates knowingly and voluntarily;

(3)   where the employer needs information to comply with certification provisions under the Family Medical Leave Act or state family medical leave laws;

(4)   where the employer purchases documents that are publicly available (such as newspapers) that contain such information;

(5)   where the information is used for genetic monitoring of biological effects of toxic substances in the workplace and the employee knowingly and voluntarily participates;

(6)   where the employer conducts DNA analysis for law enforcement purposes and requests employees' DNA to assure no contamination of samples.

The Act also requires that if an employer, labor organization, employment agency or joint labor-management committee possesses genetic information about an employee or member, the information be maintained on separate forms in separate medical files and be treated as the confidential medical record of the employee. Complying with confidentiality of medical records under the ADA, 42 U.S.C. § 12112 (d)(3)(B), is deemed compliance with this provision. Disclosure is limited to exceptions listed and required by law. P.L. 110-233 § 205 & 206.

Finally, the Act grants remedies in accordance with the remedies provided by the Acts listed above which cover the employee. For example, employees covered by Title VII of the 1964 Civil Rights Act have the same procedural pre-requisites (filing a charge with the EEOC) and remedies available to them as those available to persons proving discrimination under that Act. These include the same remedies as those found under the ADA and the same caps on compensatory and punitive damages as apply to plaintiffs under Title VII and the ADA. See Section [I], *infra,* for a discussion of the caps. One major difference, however, is that GINA does not grant a cause of action for violations that cause a disparate impact. Thus, unintentional discrimination having a disparate impact does not violate GINA. The Act does, however, establish a Commission to study disparate impact six years after the Act goes into effect.

EEOC Regulations

GINA gives the EEOC the authority to write regulations implementing the statute. The EEOC issued proposed regulations and expects to have final regulations implemented in late 2009. To find the regulations, questions and answers on GINA, see http://www.eeoc.gov.

This is an important and useful source for employment lawyers to get up-to-date information on the EEOC regulations, rules and guidances.

GINA, the ADA, and the ADAAA

Before GINA, the EEOC took the position that discrimination based on genetic information was discrimination under the "regarded as" prong of the ADA and the Rehabilitation Act. While the EEOC filed a lawsuit under this theory, the case settled, and the EEOC did not have the opportunity to make its arguments before the courts. Given the narrow interpretation of "individual with a disability" after the *Sutton* trilogy, particularly the requirement that the employee must prove that the employer believed that the impairment substantially limited a particular major life activity of the employee in order to prove his case under the "regarded as" prong of the statute, and the Supreme Court's willingness to ignore the agencies' regulations interpreting the definition of disability, there is a serious question as to whether the courts would have given much deference to the EEOC's regulation.

Given the passage of GINA, the landscape is significantly improved for persons with genetic predisposition to specific diseases, but there are significant problems with the confidentiality and the coverage provisions. GINA does not amend the ADA, which permits employers to condition employment after an offer on passing medical tests. Thus, when an employer asks for medical information, it is likely that it will be impossible to separate the genetic information protected by GINA from the other information in an employee's medical records. *See* Mark A. Rothstein, *GINA, the ADA, and Genetic Discrimination in Employment*, HEALTH CARE 837, 838 (Winter 2008). Furthermore, as Professor Mark Rothstein demonstrates, there is a problem with coverage. Under GINA, individuals are protected from discrimination based on their genes, but not from discrimination based on the disease once it is manifested. The gap between persons who fit the definition of having a disability and those who are asymptomatic but have a genetic anomaly may prove to be problematic. *Id.* at 839.

[5]   Mental Health Parity and Addiction Equity Act

The Mental Health Parity and Addiction Equity Act (MHPAEA), 29 U.S.C. § 1185a and 42 U.S.C. § 300gg-5, applies to group insurance offered by employers. Although insurance plans are not required to offer mental health or addiction benefits, if they do offer these benefits, the financial requirements such as deductibles, copayments and out-of-pocket expenses may not be more burdensome than those for physical health or surgical coverage. The treatment limitation, such as caps on number of visits and days of coverage, may not be more restrictive than limitations applying to physical health or surgical coverage, and there must be equality in the coverage of out-of-network providers. The Act provides for government enforcement as well as a private cause of action. There is, however, an escape clause that states that if the mental health and addiction coverage results in more than a 2% increase in the first year or than 1% in the second year, the plan obtains a one year exemption from statutory compliance.

I   ENFORCEMENT

Enforcement of employment discrimination rights under the Rehabilitation Act and the Americans with Disabilities Act includes both administrative and private procedures and remedies.

[1]   Section 501 of The Rehabilitation Act

Section 501 of the Rehabilitation Act prohibits discrimination on the basis of disability by federal agencies. 29 U.S.C. § 791(a). It also requires federal agencies to have affirmative action plans for the hiring, placement, and advancement of individuals with disabilities. 29 U.S.C. § 791(b). The 1978 amendments to the Rehabilitation Act clarified that there is a private right of action under Section 501 of the Rehabilitation Act. 42 U.S.C. §§ 2003-16, 20003-5(f)-(k). Individuals pursuing actions under Section 501 are required to exhaust administrative remedies by complaint mechanisms through the agency which is the employer.

The remedies available to complainants under Section 501 are the remedies found in the Civil Rights Act of 1964, which is incorporated by reference. These remedies include equitable and legal relief and are discussed later in this section.

Although the majority of courts addressing the issue have held that Sections 501 and 504 may both be applied to cases involving federal agencies, this has not been finally resolved by either the Supreme Court or Congress. For citations to cases on this issue, see LAURA ROTHSTEIN & JULIA ROTHSTEIN, DISABILITIES AND THE LAW § 4.03 (2009).

[2]   Section 503 of The Rehabilitation Act

Section 503 of the Rehabilitation Act prohibits discrimination on the basis of disability by federal contractors with over $10,000 in annual federal contracts. 29 U.S.C. § 793. Like federal agencies, federal contractors must have affirmative action plans.

Complainants under Section 503 must pursue relief by filing a complaint with the Department of Labor, Office of Federal Contract Compliance Programs (OFCCP). This office has a detailed procedure for resolving these complaints. The majority of jurisdictions have ruled that relief through OFCCP procedures is the exclusive avenue of redress and that individuals may not bring private actions in court. For citations to cases on this issue, see LAURA ROTHSTEIN & JULIA ROTHSTEIN, DISABILITIES AND THE LAW § 4.03 (2009).

The remedies available for Section 503 violations include injunctive relief, withholding progress payments, terminating the contract, and debarring the violator from receiving future government contracts. 41 C.F.R. § 60-741.28. The availability of damages is an unresolved issue.

[3]   Section 504 of The Rehabilitation Act

Section 504 of the Rehabilitation Act prohibits discrimination on the basis of disability by recipients of federal financial assistance. 29 U.S.C. § 794. Like Section 501, the remedies and procedures of the Civil Rights Act of 1964 are incorporated by reference. 34 C.F.R. §§ 100.6–.10, 101.1–.131. Section 501 requires covered entities to have affirmative action policies, but Section 504 does not. 29 U.S.C. § 791(b).

Section 504 requires employers with 15 or more employees to adopt grievance procedures with procedural safeguards to ensure prompt and equitable complaint resolution. These procedures are to be available to employees, but they need not be provided to applicants for employment. 45 C.F.R. § 84.7(b).

Complainants are not required to resort to internal grievance procedures before filing an administrative complaint with the granting agency. Nor are they required to exhaust administrative remedies before bringing action in court.

For a discussion of enforcement under Section 504, see LAURA ROTHSTEIN & JULIA ROTHSTEIN, DISABILITIES AND THE LAW § 4.04 (2009).

In 1996, the Supreme Court held that Congress had not waived the federal government's sovereign immunity against awards of monetary damages for violations of section 504 of the Rehabilitation Act. The following is part of the Court's reasoning. Justices Stevens and Breyer dissented. The case involved a Merchant Marine Academy cadet, who was terminated from the Academy because of his diabetes mellitus. The termination was found by the District Court to violate the Rehabilitation Act, and the court ordered reinstatement, but denied compensatory damages on the basis of sovereign immunity.

LANE v. PENA

518 U.S. 187 (1996)

JUSTICE O'CONNOR delivered the opinion of the Court.

I

The clarity of expression necessary to establish a waiver of the Government's sovereign immunity against monetary damages for violations of § 504 is lacking in the text of the relevant provisions. The language of § 505(a)(2), the remedies provision, is telling. In that section, Congress decreed that the remedies available for violations of Title VI would be similarly available for violations of § 504(a) "by any recipient of Federal assistance or Federal provider of such assistance." This provision makes no mention whatsoever of "program[s] or activit[ies] conducted by any Executive agency," the plainly more far-reaching language Congress employed in § 504(a) itself. Whatever might be said about the somewhat curious structure of the liability and remedy provisions, it cannot be disputed that a reference to "federal provider[s]" of financial assistance in § 505(a)(2) does not, without more, establish that Congress has waived the Federal Government's immunity against monetary damages awards beyond the narrow category of § 504(a) violations committed by federal funding agencies acting as such — that is, by "federal provider[s]."

The lack of clarity in § 505(a)(2)'s "federal provider" provision is underscored by the precision with which Congress has waived the Federal Government's sovereign immunity from compensatory damages claims for violations of § 501 of the Rehabilitation Act, which prohibits discrimination on the basis of disability in employment decisions by the Federal Government. In § 505(a)(1), Congress expressly waived the Federal Government's sovereign immunity against certain remedies for violations of § 501.

But our analysis need not end there. In the Civil Rights Act of 1991, Congress made perfectly plain that compensatory damages would be available for certain violations of § 501 by the Federal Government (as well as other § 501 defendants), subject to express limitations: "In an action brought by a complaining party under the powers, remedies, and procedures set forth in . . . section 794a(a)(1) of title 29 [which applies to violations of § 501 by the Federal Government] . . . against a respondent who engaged in unlawful intentional discrimination (not an employment practice that is unlawful because of its disparate impact) under section 791 of title 29 and the regulations implementing section 791 of title 29, or who violated the requirements of section 791 of title 29 or the regulations implementing section 791 of title 29 concerning the provision of a reasonable accommodation . . . the complaining party may recover compensatory and punitive damages as allowed in subsection (b) of this section . . . from the respondent." The Act's attorney's fee provision makes a similar point. Section 505(b) provides that, "[i]n any action or proceeding to enforce or charge a violation of a provision of this title, the court, in its discretion, may allow the prevailing party, other than the United States, a reasonable attorney's fee as part of the costs." This provision likewise illustrates Congress' ability to craft a clear waiver of the Federal Government's sovereign immunity against particular remedies for violations of the Act. The clarity of these provisions is in sharp contrast to the waiver Lane seeks to tease out of §§ 504 and 505(a)(2) of the Act.

Given the care with which Congress responded to our decision in *Atascadero* by crafting an unambiguous waiver of the States' Eleventh Amendment immunity in § 1003, it would be ironic indeed to conclude that that same provision "unequivocally" establishes a waiver of the Federal Government's sovereign immunity against monetary damages awards by means of an admittedly ambiguous reference to "public . . . entit[ies]" in the remedies provision attached to the unambiguous waiver of the States' sovereign immunity.

For the reasons stated, the judgment of the Court of Appeals for the District of Columbia Circuit is affirmed.

[4] Title I of The Americans with Disabilities Act

Title I of the Americans with Disabilities Act prohibits employers with 15 or more employees from discriminating in employment on the basis of disability. 42 U.S.C. § 12112. Like Sections 501 and 504 of the Rehabilitation Act, Title I of the ADA incorporates the powers, remedies, and procedures of the Civil Rights Act of 1964. 42 U.S.C. § 12117(a). The ADA also specifies that agencies with enforcement authority under Title I and under the Rehabilitation Act are to coordinate enforcement. 42 U.S.C. § 12117(b).

Individuals seeking redress under Title I of the ADA are required to bring actions through the Equal Employment Opportunity Commission administrative complaint resolution procedures. The EEOC will first attempt conciliation after a complaint has been investigated. Only after conciliation has failed will the EEOC pursue a civil action through the courts. The EEOC may also provide the complainant with a "Letter of Right to Sue." Only after administrative remedies through the EEOC have been exhausted may the complainant seek redress in the courts. 42 U.S.C. § 2000e-5.

For a discussion of Title I enforcement, see LAURA ROTHSTEIN & JULIA ROTHSTEIN, DISABILITIES AND THE LAW § 4.26 (2009).

Arbitration Clauses and the ADA

The Supreme Court has twice addressed remedies available to individual complainants in ADA employment claims where they have entered into arbitration agreements to resolve controversies. In *Circuit City Stores, Inc. v. Adams*, 532 U.S. 105 (2001), the Court upheld the validity of arbitration agreements by individuals waiving the right to bring ADA claims in court or to obtain relief in a judicial forum are bound by those agreements. Individual plaintiffs are bound by agreements to arbitrate their ADA claims so long as their waiver of rights is knowing and voluntary. The Court further clarified the role of such arbitration agreements in *EEOC v. Waffle House, Inc.* 534 U.S. 279 (2002). The Court held that while these arbitration agreements are binding against individuals seeking recourse through the courts, they do not bar the Equal Employment Opportunity

Commission from bringing victim-specific cases. The EEOC may seek back pay, reinstatement, and damages in ADA enforcement actions on behalf of individuals. The Court notes, however, that the individual's recovery through the arbitration process may limit the relief in an EEOC case.

In *14 Penn Plaza LLC v. Pyett*, 129 S. Ct. 1456 (2009), the Supreme Court held that a union may waive the rights of its members to a judicial forum in an age discrimination case if the waiver is clear and unmistakable in the collective bargaining agreement and the agreement provides for arbitration of the statutory claim. This analysis will likely be applied to ADA cases as well as Age Discrimination in Employment Act cases.

[5]   Title II of The Americans with Disabilities Act

Title II of the Americans with Disabilities Act prohibits discrimination on the basis of disability by state and local governmental agencies. 42 U.S.C. § 12132. Unlike Title III of the ADA (prohibiting discrimination by private providers of public accommodations), which does not apply to employment discrimination, Title II prohibits not only discrimination in the provision of services, but also employment discrimination. See 28 C.F.R. § 35.140 for applicable regulations.

Unlike Title I of the ADA, which requires individuals complaining about employment discrimination to exhaust administrative remedies by pursuing redress through the EEOC, employees of state or local governmental agencies may go directly to court to seek redress. Individuals covered by Title II would also be covered by Title I, unless the governmental agency has fewer than 15 employees.

Title II applies the remedies, procedures, and rights of Section 504 of the Rehabilitation Act, which in turn incorporates the remedies, procedures, and rights of the Civil Rights Act of 1964.

[6]   Civil Rights Act of 1964

The Civil Rights Act of 1964, as amended by the Civil Rights Act of 1991, 42 U.S.C. § 2000e, provides for a number of remedies for discrimination. These remedies include injunctive relief, appropriate affirmative action, equitable relief, back pay, front pay, and declaratory relief.

The 1991 amendments clarify that damages are available as a remedy, but limit compensatory and punitive damages to certain circumstances. The damages provisions can be found at 42 U.S.C. § 1981a and are applicable to the ADA and the Rehabilitation Act. Damages are not available where the employer has made good faith efforts at reasonable accommodation. Punitive damages are recoverable only where there has been malice or reckless indifference to federally protected rights. Compensatory damages include future pecuniary losses, emotional pain, suffering, inconvenience, mental anguish, loss of enjoyment of life, and other nonpecuniary losses. Punitive damages are not available against state and local governmental agencies. Caps on total damage awards (the sum of compensatory and punitive damages) range from $50,000 per violation (for employers with 15–100 employees) up to $300,000 per violation (for employers with more than 500 employees).

Lilly Ledbetter Fair Pay Act of 2009

The Lilly Ledbetter Fair Pay Act is an amendment to the ADA and the Rehabilitation Act. It overturns the decision in *Ledbetter v. Goodyear Tire & Rubber Co.*, 550 U.S. 618 (2007). It applies to Title I of the ADA and to Sections 501 and 504 of the Rehabilitation Act as well as Title VII of the Civil Rights Act. It states that an unlawful employment practice occurs, with respect to discrimination in compensation, when a discriminatory compensation decision is adopted, when an individual becomes subject to a discriminatory compensation decision, including each time wages, benefits, or other compensation is paid, resulting in whole or part from a discriminatory decision.

[7] Other Remedies Issues

The availability of attorneys' fees is a significant factor in whether an individual can find representation in disability discrimination cases. This is increasingly the case because of the complexity and difficulty in succeeding in such cases. Settlement of these claims may be less likely because of a 2001 Supreme Court ruling. In *Buckhannon Board & Care Home, Inc. v. West Virginia Department of Health and Human Resources*, 532 U.S. 598 (2001), the Supreme Court held that attorneys' fees under the ADA or the Fair Housing Act are only available where a favorable judgment on the merits or a consent decree approved by the court favors the plaintiff. As a result of this decision, it would seem that settlement agreements should specify recovery of attorneys' fees. Otherwise settlements would be discouraged. It may be problematic, however, for counsel to bargain for attorneys' fees at the same time they are negotiating settlements. Consider the conflicts of interest that might arise.

The issue of damages as a remedy is also one that is receiving greater attention in the courts, including the Supreme Court. In a case that was not an employment case, but which has implications for all disability discrimination claims, the Court held that while compensatory damages would be available in claims against state agencies, punitive damages are not available under Section 202 of the ADA or Section 504 of the Rehabilitation Act. *Barnes v. Gorman*, 536 U.S. 181 (2002). This decision does not necessarily govern employment cases, however, because they specifically are covered by 42 U.S.C. § 1981a, which provides for capped compensatory and punitive damages and does not limit punitive damages to private entities.

Chapter 4

PUBLIC ACCOMMODATIONS

A OVERVIEW

"Public accommodations" in the context of disability discrimination law refers to privately operated facilities that are used by the public. The most comprehensive coverage of these facilities is found under the Americans with Disabilities Act (ADA), 42 U.S.C. § 12101 et seq. Title III of the Americans with Disabilities Act (ADA), 42 U.S.C. § 12181, lists twelve specific categories. These are

> Lodging (other than apartments), eating establishments, entertainment facilities, public gathering places, stores and sales establishments, service establishments (including law offices and health care provider facilities), transportation stations, public display facilities (such as museums), places of recreation (such as parks), places of education, social service centers, and exercise facilities (such as golf courses).

The ADA is the primary disability discrimination law affecting such privately operated programs. Most of these programs do not receive federal financial assistance and, therefore, are not subject to Section 504 of the Rehabilitation Act, 29 U.S.C. § 794. The major exceptions are probably some private health care programs receiving federal research grants, education programs such as private colleges receiving federal financial assistance through government loan programs or federal grants, and private schools receiving funding for school lunches and similar federal funding, and some social service centers that receive federal support.

In addition to the twelve categories specified within Title III of the ADA, there are a number of other types of privately provided services or accommodations that are the subject of nondiscrimination mandates. The two major categories of private providers of public accommodations that are not included within the scope of the ADA are airline transportation and housing. Both of these types of public accommodations were exempted for the most part from the ADA because of earlier Congressional enactments. For airline travel, Congress amended the Federal Aviation Act by passing the Air Carrier Access Act in 1986. This issue is discussed later in this chapter. Housing, which is subject to the 1988 amendments to the Fair Housing Act, is covered in Chapter 8.

Mass transit and driver's licensing are primarily governmental operated or controlled programs. For that reason, these issues are treated in Chapter 5, on Governmental Services and Programs. Transportation provided by private taxi services and interstate bus services provided by private entities are also addressed in Chapter 5 because of the pervasive governmental regulation of these services, and to avoid duplication of coverage in both chapters.

Chapters 6 (Higher Education) and 7 (Education) address the concepts of privately operated public accommodations (i.e., private schools) and state and local governmentally operated public services (i.e., public schools). This chapter will address other categories of programs.

Health care providers, which are both private and public programs, present unique issues. For that reason, Chapter 9 treats health care separately.

The three major issues applicable to public accommodations are nondiscrimination, reasonable accommodation (requiring modification of policies, practices, and procedures), and barrier-free design. While the ADA is the major and most comprehensive federal statutory coverage for privately operated public accommodations, many states and local governments also have mandates in one or more of these areas. The ADA contemplates that services and programs will be provided in the least restrictive setting possible. The principle of mainstreaming is consistent with the application of all federal statutes related to disability discrimination.

There are some programs that may be affected by more than one part of the ADA or by other federal laws. For example, a private store leasing space in an airport terminal may be subject to Section 504 of the Rehabilitation Act because of federal funding in subsidizing the terminal; Title II because the terminal is operated by a local municipal governmental authority; and Title III because it is one of the categories of public accommodations. If the private store had 15 or more employees, it would also be subject to Title I of the ADA.

The cases in this section focus primarily on whether the entity is subject to Title III of the ADA. The cases have been selected to highlight unusual situations or emerging issues as well as two Supreme Court decisions on specific types of programs — professional golf tournaments and cruise ships. The decisions along with the statutory and regulatory language provide guidance for other settings.

HYPOTHETICAL PROBLEM 4.1

Shane is a 35-year-old who is the Deputy Director of Finance for Springfield College, located in the Midwest. In 2005, he was called from National Guard Reserves to active duty in the military. He served in Iraq and Afghanistan until early 2007, when the vehicle in which he was riding hit a land mine and he sustained serious injuries resulting in some paralysis to his lower extremities. In Spring 2009, after extensive rehabilitation, he returned to his previous employment (from which he had been granted a leave of absence). Although he does not have total paralysis in his legs, he uses a wheelchair for mobility. He was always athletic and had played basketball and golf before his injury. He has begun to play wheelchair basketball on campus and has even gone to the driving range to hit some balls. He can stand for long enough to hit the ball, although his accuracy and distance are not good. He still enjoys playing.

He has learned about a three day conference for university finance directors in Clayton, a city some distance from Springfield. The conference brochure notes that the hotel (which is part of a chain hotel) is located in an historic renovated railroad station, which now includes conference meeting rooms and ballrooms. Connected to the hotel is an arcade with shops, restaurants, a casino, and a movie theater. Extra events that conference attendees can sign up for are a trolley tour of the historic area of Clayton and a conference attendee golf tournament.

Shane was eager to get back to his previous life and to network again with colleagues he had known before. It is essential to him that he have an accessible hotel room, particularly for access in the bathroom. He could not tell from the hotel website how many hotel rooms are accessible and when he tried to register on-line through the web, there was no way to know if his request for an accessible room would be honored. The website does provide some general information about access, but there is no specific contact information link for more details. Shane tried to call the hotel directly, but the person to whom he spoke assured him that there were plenty of accessible rooms and that he should not worry. Shane's conference registration also included his selection of the golf outing and the trolley tour.

When Shane arrived at the conference, he had difficulty registering at the hotel because the reception desk clerk could not see him over the counter. He learned that all the accessible rooms had been taken. The clerk was apologetic and said this was unusual. The clerk called a nearby hotel (two blocks away) and found an accessible room for Shane, although the room rate was a bit higher. Shane also encountered the following challenges during his conference attendance.

- Meeting Rooms — One of the breakout meeting rooms was located in a room that had three steps. Other attendees offered to carry him in and out of the room. He declined and attended a different session.

- Cocktail Lounges — There were three different cocktail lounge/bar facilities in the hotel and two of them were divided so there were steps to reach some of the areas. In one of the lounges, in order to be allowed to sit at a table (rather than at the bar), the customer had to order food, not just a drink. Smoking was allowed in all of the lounges, which caused a serious reaction because of lung damage during the explosion when he was injured.

- Casino — In the casino, he could not play blackjack because the table was too high.

- Golf tournament — His request to drive the golf cart onto the putting green was denied, so he quit after the first hole.

- Trolley ride — The trolley cars had no hydraulic lifts, and he was told that they were historic and could not be made accessible without destroying the appearance.

- Movie attendance — When he tried to attend the movie which had only stadium seating, he was only able to sit in the front of the first row, requiring him to view the screen at a very painful angle.

During the conference he met another veteran, Jeffrey, who told him that he had post traumatic stress disorder, and his psychologist had recommended that he bring a companion dog to relieve stress to public places. His dog, Trusty, was a large German Shepherd. Jeffrey told Shane that the hotel and the adjacent arcade would not allow Trusty in the public areas because Jeffrey did not have any "official" documentation about Trusty's training and it was not apparent that Jeffrey required assistance of any kind.

The conference was not the positive experience Shane had hoped it would be. Although he had not had a problem flying to Clayton, on the flight back, the airline would not allow him to exit first in order to make a tight connection at the airport where he had to change planes. He missed the flight and had to wait four hours for the next flight. Upon his return, Shane has become so angry that he has contacted a local attorney and given her this information. He wants advice about whether to bring a legal action, what his rights might be, who might be liable, what strategies to take, and whether it might be a good idea to contact Jeffrey about a possible class action to address some of the concerns.

The ADA is not entirely clear in its language about the extent to which providers of insurance of various types are considered to be public accommodations subject to Title III of the ADA. See LAURA ROTHSTEIN & JULIA ROTHSTEIN, DISABILITIES AND THE LAW § 5.02 (2009). The following case is one of the major cases holding that long term disability insurance is not covered by the ADA.

PARKER v. METROPOLITAN LIFE INSURANCE CO.
121 F.3d 1006 (6th Cir. 1997)

[The employee claimed that the long term disability plan which contained longer benefits for physical disabilities than mental disabilities violates Title I and Title III of the ADA. The portion of the case addressing the Title I and the ERISA claims is omitted. The decision affirms the lower court decision. The *Parker* decision highlights one judicial viewpoint about what is sometimes referred to as the "four walls" requirement of Title III, that the entity be a physical place. As noted in the dissent, other courts have taken a different view. The case does not address the substantive issue of potential discrimination in health insurance. This is addressed in Chapter 9.]

KENNEDY, CIRCUIT JUDGE. [Joined by seven other judges.]

I.

Plaintiff, Ouida Sue Parker, was employed by Schering-Plough Health Care Products, Inc. ("Schering-Plough") from April 20, 1981 through October 29, 1990. During her employment, Parker participated in a long-term disability plan offered by Schering-Plough to its employees; the plan was issued by Metropolitan Life Insurance Co. ("MetLife"). Under the plan, an individual who is deemed to be totally disabled due to a mental or nervous disorder may receive benefits for up to twenty-four months, unless at the termination of the twenty-four month period, the individual was hospitalized or receiving inpatient care for the disorder. For physical disorders, however, the plan provides for benefits until the individual reaches sixty-five years of age.

The District Court . . . dismissed Parker's claim against the defendants under Title III of the ADA, 42 U.S.C. §§ 12165–12189. Met Life was not a proper defendant under Title III, the court concluded, because Title III only covers discrimination in the physical access to goods and services, not discrimination in the terms of insurance policies.

III.

A. *Title III: Places of Public Accommodation*

To determine whether a benefit plan provided by an employer falls within the prohibitions of Title III, we must begin by examining the statutory text. Title III of the ADA specifically addresses discrimination by owners, lessors, and operators of public accommodations. It provides as follows:

> No individual shall be discriminated against on the basis of disability in the full and equal enjoyment of the goods, services, facilities, privileges, advantages, or accommodations of any place of public accommodation by any person who owns, leases (or leases to), or operates a place of public accommodation. 42 U.S.C. § 12182(a).

Section 12181 sets forth [a] list of private entities that are considered public accommodations for purposes of Title III.

. . . .

> (F) a laundromat, dry-cleaner, bank, barber shop, beauty shop, travel service, shoe repair service, funeral parlor, gas station, office of an accountant or lawyer, pharmacy, insurance office, professional office of a health care provider, hospital, or other service establishment.

Title III specifically prohibits, inter alia, the provision of unequal or separate benefits by a place of public accommodation. See 42 U.S.C. §§ 12182(b)(1)(A)(i)-(iii). For example, 42 U.S.C. § 12182(b)(1)(A)(ii) provides that it is "discriminatory to afford an individual or class of individuals, on the basis of a disability . . . with the opportunity to participate in or benefit from a good, service, facility, privilege, advantage, or accommodation that is not equal to that afforded to other individuals . . ." 42 U.S.C. § 12182(b)(1)(a)(ii). To the extent that subsections (i), (ii), and (iii) do not explicitly state that they apply only to public accommodations, subsection (iv) expressly provides that ". . . the term 'individual or class of individuals' refers to the clients or customers of the covered public accommodation . . . " 42 U.S.C. § 12182(b)(1)(a)(iv).

While we agree that an insurance office is a public accommodation as expressly set forth in § 12181(7), plaintiff did not seek the goods and services of an insurance office. Rather, Parker accessed a benefit plan provided by her private employer and issued by MetLife. A benefit plan offered by an employer is not a good offered by a place of public accommodation. As is evident by § 12187(7), a public accommodation is a physical place and this Court has previously so held. . . . This Court [in

---

other cases has] rejected the plaintiffs' contention holding that the defendants did not fall within any of the twelve categories enumerated in § 12181(7). Furthermore, we held that "the prohibitions of Title III are restricted to 'places' of public accommodation . . . " A "place," as defined by the applicable regulations, is " 'a facility, operated by a private entity, whose operations affect commerce and fall within at least one of the' twelve 'public accommodation' categories." " 'Facility,' in turn, is defined as 'all or any portion of buildings, structures, sites, complexes, equipment, rolling stock or other conveyances, roads, walks, passageways, parking lots, or other real or personal property, including the site where the building, property, structure, or equipment is located.' " [In the case of *Stoutenborough v. National Football League, Inc.*, 59 F.3d 580 (6th Cir.), *cert. denied*, 516 U.S. 1028 (1995),] the court acknowledged that the football games were played in a place of accommodation and that the television broadcasts were a service provided by the defendants, the court concluded that the broadcasts "do not involve a 'place of public accommodation.' " Accordingly, we held that the service offered by the defendants did not involve a place of public accommodation. Quoting the district court's opinion, we explained that " '[i]t is all of the services which the public accommodation offers, not all services which the lessor of the public accommodation offers' which fall within the scope of Title III.' " Finally, the court noted that "plaintiffs' argument that the prohibitions of Title III are not solely limited to 'places' of public accommodation contravenes the plain language of the statute."

Similarly, the good that plaintiff seeks is not offered by a place of public accommodation. The public cannot enter the office of MetLife or Schering-Plough and obtain the long-term disability policy that plaintiff obtained. Parker did not access her policy from MetLife's insurance office. Rather, she obtained her benefits through her employer. There is, thus, no nexus between the disparity in benefits and the services which MetLife offers to the public from its insurance office.

The Department of Justice's explanation of whether wholesale establishments are places of public accommodation supports our conclusion that MetLife's offering of a disability plan to Schering-Plough is not a service offered by a place of public accommodation. As the Department explains:

> . . . The Department intends for wholesale establishments to be covered . . . as places of public accommodation except in cases where they sell exclusively to other businesses and not to individuals . . . [However], [i]f th[e wholesale company] operates a road side stand where its crops are sold to the public, the road side stand would be a sales establishment covered by the ADA . . .

> Of course, a company that operates a place of public accommodation is subject to this part only in the operation of that place of public accommodation. In the example given above, the wholesale produce company that operates a road side stand would be a public accommodation only for the purposes of the operation of that stand. The company would be prohibited from discriminating on the basis of disability in the operation of the road side stand, and it would be required to remove barriers to physical access

> . . .

28 C.F.R. pt. 36, app. B at 604 (1996). Thus, the offering of disability policies on a discounted rate solely to a business is not a service or good offered by a place of public accommodation.

Furthermore, Title III does not govern the content of a long-term disability policy offered by an employer. The applicable regulations clearly set forth that Title III regulates the availability of the goods and services the place of public accommodation offers as opposed to the contents of goods and services offered by the public accommodation. According to the Department of Justice:

> The purpose of the ADA's public accommodations requirements is to ensure accessibility to the goods offered by a public accommodation, not to alter the nature or mix of goods that the public accommodation has typically provided. In other words, a bookstore, for example, must make its facilities and sales operations accessible to individuals with disabilities, but is not required to stock Brailled or large print books. Similarly, a video store must make its facilities and rental operations accessible, but is not required to stock closed-captioned video tapes.

While Title IV of the ADA, 42 U.S.C. § 12201(c), may address the contents of insurance policies provided by a public accommodation, Title IV does not address the contents of a long-term disability plan offered by an employer because it is not a place of public accommodation. We, therefore, disagree with the First Circuit's decision in *Carparts Distribution Center, Inc. v. Automotive Wholesaler's Association of New England Inc.*, 37 F.3d 12 (1st Cir. 1994). In *Carparts*, the health benefit plan offered by the employer contained a $25,000 cap on benefits for AIDS related illnesses while the plan provided $1,000,000 in coverage for any other illness. The executors of the estate of an employee, who suffered from AIDS, brought suit against the provider of the self-funded medical reimbursement plan under the ADA alleging that the lifetime cap on health benefits for individuals with AIDS was discriminatory. The court rejected the district court's conclusion that defendants were not liable under Title III because they were not places of public accommodation. In rejecting the district court's construction, the court cited to the list of private entities considered public accommodations in § 12181(7) of Title III. The court particularly noted that the list includes a " 'travel service,' a 'shoe repair service,' an 'office of an accountant, or lawyer,' an 'insurance office,' a 'professional office of a healthcare provider,' and 'other service establishment[s].' " The plain meaning of those terms, the court concluded, "does not require 'public accommodations' to have physical structures for persons to enter." The court further noted that "[b]y including 'travel service' among the list of services considered 'public accommodations,' Congress clearly contemplated that 'service establishments' include providers of services which do not require a person to physically enter an actual physical structure." The court, therefore, concluded that a defendant who provides medical benefit plans could be considered a public accommodation under Title III.

In arriving at this conclusion, the First Circuit disregarded the statutory canon of construction, noscitur a sociis. The doctrine of noscitur a sociis instructs that "a . . . term is interpreted within the context of the accompanying words 'to avoid the giving of unintended breadth to the Acts of Congress.' "

The clear connotation of the words in § 12181(7) is that a public accommodation is a physical place. Every term listed in § 12181(7) and subsection (F) is a physical place open to public access. The terms travel service, shoe repair service, office of an accountant or lawyer, insurance office, and professional office of a healthcare provider do not suggest otherwise. Rather than suggesting that Title III includes within its purview entities other than physical places, it is likely that Congress simply had no better term than "service" to describe an office where travel agents provide travel services and a place where shoes are repaired. Office of an accountant or lawyer, insurance office, and professional office of a healthcare provider, in the context of the other terms listed, suggest a physical place where services may be obtained and nothing more. To interpret these terms as permitting a place of accommodation to constitute something other than a physical place is to ignore the text of the statute and the principle of noscitur a sociis.

Accordingly, we conclude that the provision of a long-term disability plan by an employer and administered by an insurance company does not fall within the purview of Title III.

[Title I portion omitted.]

For the foregoing reasons, the judgment of the District Court is AFFIRMED.

BOYCE F. MARTIN, JR., CHIEF JUDGE, dissenting.

I join Judge Merritt and others in dissenting from the opinion of the Court in this case. I write separately to highlight my agreement with Judge Merritt regarding congressional intent and to emphasize my disagreement with the majority's interpretation of *Stoutenborough v. National Football League, Inc.*, 59 F.3d 580 (6th Cir. 1995).

In *Stoutenborough*, a hearing impaired individual and an association of hearing impaired individuals sought to prohibit the National Football League, its member clubs, and several broadcast companies from using the so-called "blackout rule" to avoid broadcasting live local football games when tickets to the live game had not been completely sold seventy-two hours before the game. With regard to Stoutenborough's Title III claim, we stated that "plaintiff's argument that the prohibitions of Title III are not solely limited to 'places' of public accommodation contravenes the plain language of the statute."

The majority takes this language to mean that Title III's mandates are limited to physical structures. However, *Stoutenborough* recognized that, in the context of a Title III claim, the term "place" is a defined term; we recognized that "a 'place' is '[1] a facility, [2] operated by a private entity, [3] whose operations affect commerce and [4] fall within at least one of the twelve "public accommodation" categories.'" Because the defendants in *Stoutenborough*, did not fall within one of the twelve public accommodation categories, they were not "places" of public accommodation as required for Title III protection. Thus, although *Stoutenborough* limited Title III's applicability to "places," it did so in the context of the defined meaning of the term "place." Unlike the defendants in *Stoutenborough*, Title III specifically identifies an "insurance office" as a public accommodation.

Not only does the majority view incorrectly apply *Stoutenborough*, it also directly conflicts with the conclusion reached by the First Circuit. In *Carparts Distribution Ctr. v. Automotive Wholesalers Ass'n of New England*, 37 F.3d 12 (1st Cir. 1994), the First Circuit held that, by including travel services in the list of public accommodations, Congress chose not to limit Title III protections to physical structures. The *Carparts* court wrote: "It would be irrational to conclude that persons who enter an office to purchase services are protected by the ADA, but persons who purchase the same services over the telephone or by mail are not. Congress could not have intended such an absurd result." Similarly, Judge Merritt notes that, under the majority view, individuals who purchase insurance through an insurance office are entitled to Title III protections while those who purchase insurance through their employers receive no Title III protections.

In my view, Judge Merritt and the First Circuit present a more compelling argument. As the First Circuit noted, "[t]he purpose of Title III is 'to bring individuals with disabilities into the economic and social mainstream of American life . . . in a clear, balanced, and reasonable manner.'"

By limiting Title III's applicability to physical structures, the majority interprets Title III in a manner completely at odds with clear congressional intent. In recent years, the economic and social mainstream of American life has experienced significant change due to technological advances. An increasing array of products and services are becoming available for purchase by telephone order, through the mail, via the Internet, and other communications media. Unfortunately, under the majority view, the same technological advances that have offered disabled individuals unprecedented freedom may now operate to deprive them of rights that Title III would otherwise guarantee. As the modern economy increases the percentage of goods and services available through a marketplace that does not consist of physical structures, the protections of Title III will become increasingly diluted.

In my view, the majority view incorrectly applies a prior opinion of this Court and reaches a conclusion clearly at odds with congressional intent. Accordingly, I join Judge Merritt and respectfully dissent.

[The dissent by Judge Merritt addresses the merits of whether the policy itself was discriminatory and whether the "safe harbor" provision applies and whether actuarial principles would allow the practice.]

NOTE

Although this court determines that this insurance program is not covered by Title III of the ADA, most other courts have disagreed.

The cases instead focus on issues of differential treatment for mental and physical conditions and caps on certain conditions, such as cancer and HIV. The courts have upheld the mandate that disability based distinctions must be based on legitimate actuarial data or reasonable experience. For cases on this issue, see LAURA ROTHSTEIN & JULIA ROTHSTEIN, DISABILITIES AND THE LAW § 10.2 (2009).

In the following case, the court addressed whether the Professional Golf Association is an entity covered by Title III of the ADA. In addition to addressing that issue, the court also addresses some of the substantive issues of Title III of the ADA.

PGA TOUR, INC. v. CASEY MARTIN
121 S. Ct. 1879 (2001)

JUSTICE STEVENS delivered the opinion of the Court:

Petitioner PGA TOUR, Inc., a nonprofit entity formed in 1968, sponsors and cosponsors professional golf tournaments conducted on three annual tours. About 200 golfers participate in the PGA TOUR; about 170 in the NIKE TOUR; and about 100 in the SENIOR PGA TOUR. PGA TOUR and NIKE TOUR tournaments typically are 4-day events, played on courses leased and operated by petitioner. The entire field usually competes in two 18-hole rounds played on Thursday and Friday; those who survive the "cut" play on Saturday and Sunday and receive prize money in amounts determined by their aggregate scores for all four rounds. The revenues generated by television, admissions, concessions, and contributions from cosponsors amount to about $300 million a year, much of which is distributed in prize money.

There are various ways of gaining entry into particular tours. For example, a player who wins three NIKE TOUR events in the same year, or is among the top-15 money winners on that tour, earns the right to play in the PGA TOUR. Additionally, a golfer may obtain a spot in an official tournament through successfully competing in "open" qualifying rounds, which are conducted the week before each tournament. Most participants, however, earn playing privileges in the PGA TOUR or NIKE TOUR by way of a three-stage qualifying tournament known as the "Q-School."

Any member of the public may enter the Q-School by paying a $3,000 entry fee and submitting two letters of reference from, among others, PGA TOUR or NIKE TOUR members. The $3,000 entry fee covers the players' greens fees and the cost of golf carts, which are permitted during the first two stages, but which have been prohibited during the third stage since 1997. Each year, over a thousand contestants compete in the first stage, which consists of four 18-hole rounds at different locations. Approximately half of them make it to the second stage, which also includes 72 holes. Around 168 players survive the second stage and advance to the final one, where they compete over 108 holes. Of those finalists, about a fourth qualify for membership in the PGA TOUR, and the rest gain membership in the NIKE TOUR. The significance of making it into either tour is illuminated by the fact that there are about 25 million golfers in the country.

Three sets of rules govern competition in tour events. First, the "Rules of Golf," jointly written by the United States Golf Association (USGA) and the Royal and Ancient Golf Club of Scotland, apply to the game as it is played, not only by millions of amateurs on public courses and in private country clubs throughout the United States and worldwide, but also by the professionals in the tournaments conducted by petitioner, the USGA, the Ladies' Professional Golf Association, and the Senior Women's Golf Association. Those rules do not prohibit the use of golf carts at any time.

Second, the "Conditions of Competition and Local Rules," often described as the "hard card," apply specifically to petitioner's professional tours. The hard cards for the PGA TOUR and NIKE TOUR require players to walk the golf course during tournaments, but not during open qualifying rounds. On the SENIOR PGA TOUR, which is limited to golfers age 50 and older, the contestants may use golf carts. Most seniors, however, prefer to walk.

Third, "Notices to Competitors" are issued for particular tournaments and cover conditions for that specific event. Such a notice may, for example, explain how the Rules of Golf should be applied to a particular water hazard or man-made obstruction. It might also authorize the use of carts to speed up play when there is an unusual distance between one green and the next tee.

The basic Rules of Golf, the hard cards, and the weekly notices apply equally to all players in tour competitions. As one of petitioner's witnesses explained with reference to "the Masters Tournament, which is golf at its very highest level . . . the key is to have everyone tee off on the first hole under exactly the same conditions and all of them be tested over that 72-hole event under the conditions that exist during those four days of the event."

Casey Martin is a talented golfer. Martin is also an individual with a disability as defined in the Americans with Disabilities Act of 1990 (ADA or Act). Since birth he has been afflicted with Klippel-Trenaunay-Weber Syndrome, a degenerative circulatory disorder that obstructs the flow of blood from his right leg back to his heart. The disease is progressive; it causes severe pain and has atrophied his right leg. During the latter part of his college career, because of the progress of the disease, Martin could no longer walk an 18-hole golf course. Walking not only caused him pain, fatigue, and anxiety, but also created a significant risk of hemorrhaging, developing blood clots, and fracturing his tibia so badly that an amputation might be required. For these reasons, Stanford made written requests to the Pacific 10 Conference and the NCAA to waive for Martin their rules requiring players to walk and carry their own clubs. The requests were granted.

When Martin turned pro and entered petitioner's Q-School, the hard card permitted him to use a cart during his successful progress through the first two stages. He made a request, supported by detailed medical records, for permission to use a golf cart during the third stage. Petitioner refused to review those records or to waive its walking rule for the third stage. Martin therefore filed this action.

Congress enacted the ADA in 1990 to remedy widespread discrimination against disabled individuals. At issue now, as a threshold matter, is the applicability of Title III to petitioner's golf tours and qualifying rounds, in particular to petitioner's treatment of a qualified disabled golfer wishing to compete in those events.

The phrase "public accommodation" is defined in terms of 12 extensive categories, which the legislative history indicates "should be construed liberally" to afford people with disabilities "equal access" to the wide variety of establishments available to the nondisabled.

It seems apparent, from both the general rule and the comprehensive definition of "public accommodation," that petitioner's golf tours and their qualifying rounds fit comfortably within the coverage of Title III, and Martin within its protection. The events occur on "golf courses," a type of place specifically identified by the Act as a public accommodation. § 12181(7)(L). In addition, at all relevant times, petitioner "leases" and "operates" golf courses to conduct its Q-School and tours. § 12182(a). As a lessor and operator of golf courses, then, petitioner must not discriminate against any "individual" in the "full and equal enjoyment of the goods, services, facilities, privileges, advantages, or accommodations" of those courses. Certainly, among the "privileges" offered by petitioner on the courses are those of competing in the Q-School and playing in the tours; indeed, the former is a privilege for which thousands of individuals from the general public pay, and the latter is one for which they vie. Martin, of course, is one of those individuals. It would therefore appear that Title III of the ADA, by its plain terms, prohibits petitioner from denying Martin equal access to its tours on the basis of his disability.

Petitioner argues otherwise. To be clear about its position, it does not assert (as it did in the District Court) that it is a private club altogether exempt from Title III's coverage. In fact, petitioner admits that its tournaments are conducted at places of public accommodation. Nor does petitioner contend (as it did in both the District Court and the Court of Appeals) that the competitors' area "behind the ropes" is not a public accommodation, notwithstanding the status of the rest of the golf course. Rather, petitioner reframes the coverage issue by arguing that the competing golfers are not members of the class protected by Title III of the ADA.

According to petitioner, Title III is concerned with discrimination against "clients and customers" seeking to obtain "goods and services" at places of public accommodation, whereas it is Title I that protects persons who work at such places. As the argument goes, petitioner operates not a "golf course" during its tournaments but a "place of exhibition or entertainment," and a professional golfer such as Martin, like an actor in a theater production, is a provider rather than a consumer of the entertainment that petitioner sells to the public. Martin therefore cannot bring a claim under Title III because he is not one of the "clients or customers of the covered public accommodation." Rather, Martin's claim of discrimination is "job-related" and could only be brought under Title I-but that Title does not apply because he is an independent contractor (as the District Court found) rather than an employee.

The reference to "clients or customers" that petitioner quotes appears in 42 U.S.C. § 12182(b)(1)(A)(iv), which states: "For purposes of clauses (i) through (iii) of this subparagraph, the term 'individual or class of individuals' refers to the clients or customers of the covered public accommodation that enters into the contractual, licensing or other arrangement." Clauses (i) through (iii) of the subparagraph prohibit public accommodations from discriminating against a disabled "individual or class of individuals" in certain ways either directly or indirectly through contractual arrangements with other entities. Those clauses make clear on the one hand that their prohibitions cannot be avoided by means of contract, while clause (iv) makes clear on the other hand that contractual relationships will not expand a public accommodation's obligations under the subparagraph beyond its own clients or customers.

As petitioner recognizes, clause (iv) is not literally applicable to Title III's general rule prohibiting discrimination against disabled individuals. Title III's broad general rule contains no express "clients or customers" limitation, § 12182(a), and § 12182(b)(1)(A)(iv) provides that its limitation is only "for purposes of" the clauses in that separate subparagraph. Nevertheless, petitioner contends that clause (iv)'s restriction of the subparagraph's coverage to the clients or customers of public accommodations fairly describes the scope of Title III's protection as a whole.

We need not decide whether petitioner's construction of the statute is correct, because petitioner's argument falters even on its own terms. If Title III's protected class were limited to "clients or customers," it would be entirely appropriate to classify the golfers who pay petitioner $3,000 for the chance to compete in the Q-School and, if successful, in the subsequent tour events, as petitioner's clients or customers. In our view, petitioner's tournaments (whether situated at a "golf course" or at a "place of exhibition or entertainment") simultaneously offer at least two "privileges" to the public — that of watching the golf competition and that of competing in it. Although the latter is more difficult and more expensive to obtain than the former, it is nonetheless a privilege that petitioner makes available to members of the general public. In consideration of the entry fee, any golfer with the requisite letters of recommendation acquires the opportunity to qualify for and compete in petitioner's tours. Additionally, any golfer who succeeds in the open qualifying rounds for a tournament may play in the event. That petitioner identifies one set of clients or customers that it serves (spectators at tournaments) does not preclude it from having another set (players in tournaments) against whom it may not discriminate. It would be inconsistent with the literal text of the statute as well as its expansive purpose to read Title III's coverage, even given petitioner's suggested limitation, any less broadly.

Our conclusion is consistent with case law in the analogous context of Title II of the Civil Rights Act of 1964. Title II of that Act prohibits public accommodations from discriminating on the basis of race, color, religion, or national origin. In *Evans v. Laurel Links, Inc.*, 261 F. Supp. 474, 477 (E.D. Va. 1966), a class action brought to require a commercial golf establishment to permit black golfers to play on its course, the District Court held that Title II "is not limited to spectators if the place of exhibition or entertainment provides facilities for the public to participate in the entertainment."

As we have noted, 42 U.S.C. § 12182(a) sets forth Title III's general rule prohibiting public accommodations from discriminating against individuals because of their disabilities. The question whether petitioner has violated that rule depends on a proper construction of the term "discrimination," which is defined by Title III to include:

"a failure to make reasonable modifications in policies, practices, or procedures, when such modifications are necessary to afford such goods, services, facilities, privileges, advantages, or accommodations to individuals with disabilities, unless the entity can demonstrate that making such modifications would fundamentally alter the nature of such goods, services, facilities, privileges, advantages, or accommodations."

Petitioner does not contest that a golf cart is a reasonable modification that is necessary if Martin is to play in its tournaments. Martin's claim thus differs from one that might be asserted by players with less serious afflictions that make walking the course uncomfortable or difficult, but not beyond their capacity. In such cases, an accommodation might be reasonable but not necessary. In this case, however, the narrow dispute is whether allowing Martin to use a golf cart, despite the walking requirement that applies to the PGA TOUR, the NIKE TOUR, and the third stage of the Q-School, is a modification that would "fundamentally alter the nature" of those events.

In theory, a modification of petitioner's golf tournaments might constitute a fundamental alteration in two different ways. It might alter such an essential aspect of the game of golf that it would be unacceptable even if it affected all competitors equally; changing the diameter of the hole from three to six inches might be such a modification. Alternatively, a less significant change that has only a peripheral impact on the game itself might nevertheless give a disabled player, in addition to access to the competition as required by Title III, an advantage over others and, for that reason, fundamentally alter the character of the competition. We are not persuaded that a waiver of the walking rule for Martin would work a fundamental alteration in either sense.

As an initial matter, we observe that the use of carts is not itself inconsistent with the fundamental character of the game of golf. From early on, the essence of the game has been shot-making — using clubs to cause a ball to progress from the teeing ground to a hole some distance away with as few strokes as possible. That essential aspect of the game is still reflected in the very first of the Rules of Golf, which declares: "The Game of Golf consists in playing a ball from the teeing ground into the hole by a stroke or successive strokes in accordance with the rules." Over the years, there have been many changes in the players' equipment, in golf course design, in the Rules of Golf, and in the method of transporting clubs from hole to hole. Originally, so few clubs were used that each player could carry them without a bag. Then came golf bags, caddies, carts that were pulled by hand, and eventually motorized carts that carried players as well as clubs. "Golf carts started appearing with increasing regularity on American golf courses in the 1950's. Today they are everywhere. And they are encouraged. For one thing, they often speed up play, and for another, they are great revenue producers." There is nothing in the Rules of Golf that either forbids the use of carts, or penalizes a player for using a cart. That set of rules, as we have observed, is widely accepted in both the amateur and professional golf world as the rules of the game. The walking rule that is contained in petitioner's hard cards, based on an optional condition buried in an appendix to the Rules of Golf, is not an essential attribute of the game itself.

Indeed, the walking rule is not an indispensable feature of tournament golf either. As already mentioned, petitioner permits golf carts to be used in the SENIOR PGA TOUR, the open qualifying events for petitioner's tournaments, the first two stages of the Q-School, and, until 1997, the third stage of the Q-School as well. Moreover, petitioner allows the use of carts during certain tournament rounds in both the PGA TOUR and the NIKE TOUR. In addition, although the USGA enforces a walking rule in most of the tournaments that it sponsors, it permits carts in the Senior Amateur and the Senior Women's Amateur championships.

Petitioner, however, distinguishes the game of golf as it is generally played from the game that it sponsors in the PGA TOUR, NIKE TOUR, and (at least recently) the last stage of the Q-School — golf at the "highest level." According to petitioner, "the goal of the highest-level competitive athletics is to assess and compare the performance of different competitors, a task that is meaningful only if the competitors are subject to identical substantive rules." The waiver of any possibly "outcome-affecting" rule for a contestant would violate this principle and therefore, in petitioner's view, fundamentally alter the nature of the highest level athletic event. The walking rule is one such rule, petitioner submits, because its purpose is "to inject the element of fatigue into the skill of shot-making," and thus its effect may be the critical loss of a stroke. As a consequence, the reasonable modification Martin seeks would fundamentally alter the nature of petitioner's highest level tournaments even if he were the only person in the world who has both the talent to compete in those elite events and a disability sufficiently serious that he cannot do so without using a cart.

The force of petitioner's argument is, first of all, mitigated by the fact that golf is a game in which it is impossible to guarantee that all competitors will play under exactly the same conditions or that an individual's ability will be the sole determinant of the outcome. For example, changes in the weather may produce harder greens and more head winds for the tournament leader than for his closest pursuers. A lucky bounce may save a shot or two. Whether such happenstance events are more or less probable than the likelihood that a golfer afflicted with Klippel-Trenaunay-Weber Syndrome would one day qualify for the NIKE TOUR and PGA TOUR, they at least demonstrate that pure chance may have a greater impact on the outcome of elite golf tournaments than the fatigue resulting from the enforcement of the walking rule.

Further, the factual basis of petitioner's argument is undermined by the District Court's finding that the fatigue from walking during one of petitioner's 4-day tournaments cannot be deemed significant. The District Court credited the testimony of a professor in physiology and expert on fatigue, who calculated the calories expended in walking a golf course (about five miles) to be approximately 500 calories — "nutritionally . . . less than a Big Mac." What is more, that energy is expended over a 5-hour period, during which golfers have numerous intervals for rest and refreshment. In fact, the expert concluded, because golf is a low intensity activity, fatigue from the game is primarily a psychological phenomenon in which stress and motivation are the key ingredients. And even under conditions of severe heat and humidity, the critical factor in fatigue is fluid loss rather than exercise from walking.

Moreover, when given the option of using a cart, the majority of golfers in petitioner's tournaments have chosen to walk, often to relieve stress or for other strategic reasons.

Even if we accept the factual predicate for petitioner's argument — that the walking rule is "outcome affecting" because fatigue may adversely affect performance — its legal position is fatally flawed. Petitioner's refusal to consider Martin's personal circumstances in deciding whether to accommodate his disability runs counter to the clear language and purpose of the ADA. As previously stated, the ADA was enacted to eliminate discrimination against "individuals" with disabilities, 42 U.S.C. § 12101(b)(1), and to that end Title III of the Act requires without exception that any "policies, practices, or procedures" of a public accommodation be reasonably modified for disabled "individuals" as necessary to afford access unless doing so would fundamentally alter what is offered," § 12182(b)(2)(A)(ii). To comply with this command, an individualized inquiry must be made to determine whether a specific modification for a particular person's disability would be reasonable under the circumstances as well as necessary for that person, and yet at the same time not work a fundamental alteration.

To be sure, the waiver of an essential rule of competition for anyone would fundamentally alter the nature of petitioner's tournaments. As we have demonstrated, however, the walking rule is at best peripheral to the nature of petitioner's athletic events, and thus it might be waived in individual cases without working a fundamental alteration. Therefore, petitioner's claim that all the substantive rules for its "highest-level" competitions are sacrosanct and cannot be modified under any circumstances is effectively a contention that it is exempt from Title III's reasonable modification requirement. But that provision carves out no exemption for elite athletics, and given Title III's coverage not only of places of "exhibition or entertainment" but also of "golf courses," its application to petitioner's tournaments cannot be said to be unintended or unexpected. Even if it were, "the fact that a statute can be applied in situations not expressly anticipated by Congress does not demonstrate ambiguity. It demonstrates breadth."

Under the ADA's basic requirement that the need of a disabled person be evaluated on an individual basis, we have no doubt that allowing Martin to use a golf cart would not fundamentally alter the nature of petitioner's tournaments. As we have discussed, the purpose of the walking rule is to subject players to fatigue, which in turn may influence the outcome of tournaments. Even if the rule does serve that purpose, it is an uncontested finding of the District Court that Martin "easily endures greater fatigue even with a cart than his able-bodied competitors do by walking." The purpose of the walking rule is therefore not compromised in the slightest by allowing Martin to use a cart. A modification that provides an exception to a peripheral tournament rule without impairing its purpose cannot be said to "fundamentally alter" the tournament. What it can be said to do, on the other hand, is to allow Martin the chance to qualify for and compete in the athletic events petitioner offers to those members of the public who have the skill and desire to enter. That is exactly what the ADA requires. As a result, Martin's request for a waiver of the walking rule should have been granted.

The ADA admittedly imposes some administrative burdens on the operators of places of public accommodation that could be avoided by strictly adhering to general rules and policies that are entirely fair with respect to the able-bodied but that may indiscriminately preclude access by qualified persons with disabilities. But surely, in a case of this kind, Congress intended that an entity like the PGA not only give individualized attention to the handful of requests that it might receive from talented but disabled athletes for a modification or waiver of a rule to allow them access to the competition, but also carefully weigh the purpose, as well as the letter, of the rule before determining that no accommodation would be tolerable.

The judgment of the Court of Appeals is affirmed.

It is so ordered.

[Dissent by Justice Scalia, with whom Justice Thomas joined is omitted.]

NOTES

1. In the case of *Brown v. 1995 Tenet ParaAmerica Bicycle Challenge*, 959 F. Supp. 496 (N.D. Ill. 1997), the court held that a cross country bike tour organizer was not a public accommodation.

2. In the Spring of 1998, the National Collegiate Athletic Association, reached a settlement with the Department of Justice regarding the NCAA initial-eligibility requirements. Individuals had complained that these requirements discriminate against students with learning disabilities. The NCAA agreed to adopt a policy of evaluating applications for waivers of eligibility filed by students with learning disabilities. One of the issues that was not resolved as a result of the settlement was whether the NCAA is a public accommodation within the meaning of Title III of the ADA. The NCAA has taken the position that it is not such an entity, but that it is willing to provide accommodations to student athletes with disabilities in determining eligibility on an individualized basis. There had been a number of challenges by students with learning disabilities that the NCAA core course and other requirements for scholarship eligibility have a disparate impact on students with disabilities. *Bowers v. NCAA*, 118 F. Supp. 2d 494 (D.N.J. 2000). In *Cureton v. NCAA*, 198 F.3d 107 (3d Cir. 1999), the court held that the NCAA does not have sufficient control of member schools to be a recipient of federal financial assistance, and in *Matthews v. NCAA*, 79 F. Supp. 2d 1199 (E.D. Wash. 1999), the court held that the NCAA is not a Title III entity. The Supreme Court ruling in *PGA v. Casey Martin*, *supra*, however broadly interpreted Title III coverage, and those cases in which the NCAA was found not to be covered by Title III may be called into question as a result. The issue has not yet been definitively resolved by the Supreme Court, and because the NCAA voluntarily changed its policies, there has been less litigation.

The following decision was quite complex with respect to the Justices joining in various parts of the opinion and the decision. The final decision including four dissents by Justices Scalia, Rehnquist, O'Connor and Thomas. The reader should review the full opinion by all Justices to determine which parts of the decision were joined by which Justices. The following is only the opinion by Justice Kennedy, which reflects the basic general determination of a majority of the Court that cruise lines operating foreign-flag ships departing from, and returning to, United States ports, are subject to Title III of the Americans with Disabilities Act. Statutory references and case citations are deleted from the edited excerpt in most instances.

SPECTOR v. NORWEGIAN CRUISE LINE LTD.
125 S. Ct. 2169 (2005)

JUSTICE KENNEDY

Our cases hold that a clear statement of congressional intent is necessary before a general statutory requirement can interfere with matters that concern a foreign-flag vessel's internal affairs and operations, as contrasted with statutory requirements that concern the security and well-being of United States citizens or territory. While the clear statement rule could limit Title III's application to foreign-flag cruise ships in some instances, when it requires removal of physical barriers, it would appear the rule is inapplicable to many other duties Title III might impose. We therefore reverse the decision of the Court of Appeals for the Fifth Circuit that the ADA is altogether inapplicable to foreign vessels; and we remand for further proceedings.

I

The respondent Norwegian Cruise Line Ltd (NCL), a Bermuda Corporation with a principal place of business in Miami, Florida, operates cruise ships that depart from, and return to, ports in the United States. The ships are essentially floating resorts. They provide passengers with staterooms or cabins, food, and entertainment. The cruise ships stop at different ports of call where passengers may disembark. Most of the passengers on these cruises are United States residents; under the terms and conditions of the tickets, disputes between passengers and NCL are to be governed by United States law; and NCL relies upon extensive advertising in the United States to promote its cruises and increase its revenues. Despite the fact that the cruises are operated by a company based in the United States, serve predominately United States residents, and are in most other respects United States-centered ventures, almost all of NCL's cruise ships are registered in other countries, flying so-called flags of convenience. The two NCL cruise ships that are the subject of the present litigation, the Norwegian Sea and the Norwegian Star, are both registered in the Bahamas.

The petitioners are disabled individuals and their companions who purchased tickets in 1998 or 1999 for round-trip cruises on the Norwegian Sea or the Norwegian Star, with departures from Houston, Texas. Naming NCL as the defendant, the petitioners filed a class action in the United States District Court for the Southern District of Texas on behalf of all persons similarly situated. They sought declaratory and injunctive relief under Title III of the ADA, which prohibits discrimination on the basis of disability.

II
A
1

Title III of the ADA prohibits discrimination against the disabled in the full and equal enjoyment of public accommodations, and public transportation services.

2

This Court has long held that general statutes are presumed to apply to conduct that takes place aboard a foreign-flag vessel in United States territory if the interests of the United States or its citizens, rather than interests internal to the ship, are at stake. The general rule that United States statutes apply to foreign-flag ships in United States territory is subject only to a narrow exception. Absent a clear statement of congressional intent, general statutes may not apply to foreign-flag vessels insofar as they regulate matters that involve only the internal order and discipline of the vessel, rather than the peace of the port. This qualification derives from the understanding that, as a matter of international comity, "all matters of discipline and all things done on board which affect only the vessel or those belonging to her, and [do] not involve the peace or dignity of the country, or the tranquility of the port, should be left by the local government to be dealt with by the authorities of the nation to which the vessel belonged." This exception to the usual presumption, however, does not extend beyond matters of internal order and discipline. "If crimes are committed on board [a foreign-flag vessel] of a character to disturb the peace and tranquility of the country to which the vessel has been brought, the offenders have never by comity or usage been entitled to any exemption from the operation of the local laws."

The two cases in recent times in which the presumption against applying general statutes to foreign vessels' internal affairs has been invoked concern labor relations. The Court held that the general terms of the National Labor Relations Act (NLRA) did not govern the respective rights and duties of a foreign ship and its crew because the NLRA standards would interfere with the foreign vessel's internal affairs in those circumstances. These cases recognized a narrow rule, applicable only to statutory duties that implicate the internal order of the foreign vessel rather than the welfare of American citizens. The Court held the NLRA inapplicable to labor relations between a foreign vessel and its foreign crew not because foreign ships are generally exempt from the NLRA, but because the particular application of the NLRA would interfere with matters that concern only the internal operations of the ship. In contrast, the Court held that the NLRA is fully applicable to labor relations between a foreign vessel and American longshoremen because this relationship, unlike the one between a vessel and its own crew, does not implicate a foreign ship's internal order and discipline.

This narrow clear statement rule is supported by sound principles of statutory construction. It is reasonable to presume Congress intends no interference with matters that are primarily of concern only to the ship and the foreign state in which it is registered. It is also reasonable, however, to presume Congress does intend its statutes to apply to entities in United States territory that serve, employ, or otherwise affect American citizens, or that affect the peace and tranquility of the United States, even if those entities happen to be foreign-flag ships.

Cruise ships flying foreign flags of convenience offer public accommodations and transportation services to over 7 million United States residents annually, departing from and returning to ports located in the United States. Large numbers of disabled individuals, many of whom have mobility impairments that make other kinds of vacation travel difficult, take advantage of these cruises or would like to do so. To hold there is no Title III protection for disabled persons who seek to use the amenities of foreign cruise ships would be a harsh and unexpected interpretation of a statute designed to provide broad protection for the disabled. The clear statement rule adopted by the Court of Appeals for the Fifth Circuit, moreover, would imply that other general federal statutes — including, for example, Title II of the Civil Rights Act of 1964 — would not apply aboard foreign cruise ships in United States waters. A clear statement rule with this sweeping application is unlikely to reflect congressional intent.

The relevant category for which the Court demands a clear congressional statement, then, consists not of all applications of a statute to foreign-flag vessels but only those applications that would interfere with the foreign vessel's internal affairs. This proposition does not mean the clear statement rule is irrelevant to the ADA, however. If Title III by its terms does impose duties that interfere with a foreign-flag cruise ship's internal affairs, the lack of a clear congressional statement can mean that those specific applications of Title III are precluded. On remand, the Court of Appeals may need to consider which, if any, Title III requirements interfere with the internal affairs of foreign-flag vessels. As we will discuss further, however, Title III's own limitations and qualifications may make this inquiry unnecessary.

B
1

It is plain that Title III might impose any number of duties on cruise ships that have nothing to do with a ship's internal affairs. The pleadings and briefs in this case illustrate, but do not exhaust, the ways a cruise ship might offend such a duty. The petitioners allege the respondent charged disabled passengers higher fares and required disabled passengers to pay special surcharges; maintained evacuation programs and equipment in locations not accessible to disabled individuals; required disabled individuals, but not other passengers, to waive any potential medical liability and to travel with a companion; and reserved the right to remove from the ship any disabled individual whose presence endangers the "comfort" of other passengers. The petitioners also allege more generally that respondent "failed to make reasonable modifications in policies, practices, and procedures" necessary to ensure the petitioners' full enjoyment of the services respondent offered. These are bare allegations, and their truth is not conceded. We express no opinion on the factual support for those claims. We can say, however, that none of these alleged Title III violations implicate any requirement that would interfere with the internal affairs and management of a vessel as our cases have employed that term.

At least one subset of the petitioners' allegations, however, would appear to involve requirements that might be construed as relating to the internal affairs of foreign-flag cruise ships. These allegations concern physical barriers to access on board. For example, according to the petitioners, most of the cabins on the respondent's cruise ships, including the most attractive cabins in the most desirable locations, are not accessible to disabled passengers. The petitioners also allege that the ships' coamings — the raised edges around their doors — make many areas of the ships inaccessible to mobility-impaired passengers who use wheelchairs or scooters. Removal of these and other access barriers, the petitioners suggest, may be required by Title III's structural barrier removal requirement. Although these physical barriers affect the passengers as well as the ship and its crew, the statutory requirement could mandate a permanent and significant alteration of a physical feature of the ship — that is, an element of basic ship design and construction. If so, these applications of the barrier removal requirement likely would interfere with the internal affairs of foreign ships. A permanent and significant modification to a ship's physical structure goes to fundamental issues of ship design and construction, and it might be impossible for a ship to comply with all the requirements different jurisdictions might impose. The clear statement rule would most likely come into play if Title III were read to require permanent and significant structural modifications to foreign vessels. It is quite a different question, however, whether Title III would require this. The Title III requirements that might impose permanent and substantial changes to a ship's architecture and design, are, like all of Title III's requirements, subject to the statute's own specific limitations and qualifications. These limitations may make resort to the clear statement rule unnecessary.

2

Title III requires barrier removal if it is "readily achievable." The statute defines that term as "easily accomplishable and able to be carried out without much difficulty or expense." Title III does not define "difficulty" . . . , but use of the disjunctive — "easily accomplishable and able to be carried out without much difficulty or expense" — indicates that it extends to considerations in addition to cost. Furthermore, Title III directs that the "readily achievable" determination take into account "the impact . . . upon the operation of the facility."

Surely a barrier removal requirement under Title III that would bring a vessel into noncompliance with the International Convention for the Safety of Life at Sea (SOLAS), or any other international legal obligation, would create serious difficulties for the vessel and would have a substantial impact on its operation, and thus would not be "readily achievable." This understanding of the statute, urged by the United States, is eminently reasonable. If, moreover, Title III's "readily achievable" exemption were not to take conflicts with international law into account, it would lead to the anomalous result that American cruise ships are obligated to comply with Title III even if doing so brings them into noncompliance with SOLAS, whereas foreign ships — which unlike American ships have the benefit of the internal affairs clear statement rule — would not be so obligated. Congress could not have intended this result.

It is logical and proper to conclude, moreover, that whether a barrier modification is "readily achievable" under Title III must take into consideration the modification's effect on shipboard safety. A separate provision of Title III mandates that the statute's nondiscrimination and accommodation requirements do not apply if disabled individuals would pose "a significant risk to the health or safety of others that cannot be eliminated by a modification of policies, practices, or procedures or by the provision of auxiliary aids or services." This reference is to a safety threat posed by a disabled individual, whereas here the question would be whether the structural modification itself may pose the safety threat. It would be incongruous, nevertheless, to attribute to Congress an intent to require modifications that threaten safety to others simply because the threat comes not from the disabled person but from the accommodation itself. The anomaly is avoided by concluding that a structural modification is not readily achievable . . . if it would pose a direct threat to the health or safety of others.

III

The Court of Appeals for the Fifth Circuit held that general statutes do not apply to foreign-flag ships in United States waters. This Court's cases, however, stand only for the proposition that general statutes are presumed not to impose requirements that would interfere with the internal affairs of foreign-flag vessels. Except insofar as Title III regulates a vessel's internal affairs — a category that is not always well defined and that may require further judicial elaboration — the statute is applicable to foreign ships in United States waters to the same extent that it is applicable to American ships in those waters.

Title III's own limitations and qualifications prevent the statute from imposing requirements that would conflict with international obligations or threaten shipboard safety. These limitations and qualifications, though framed in general terms, employ a conventional vocabulary for instructing courts in the interpretation and application of the statute. If, on remand, it becomes clear that even after these limitations are taken into account Title III nonetheless imposes certain requirements that would interfere with the internal affairs of foreign ships — perhaps, for example, by requiring permanent and substantial structural modifications — the clear statement rule would come into play. It is also open to the court on remand to consider application of the clear statement rule at the outset if, as a prudential matter, that appears to be the more appropriate course.

We reverse the judgment of the Court of Appeals and remand the case for further proceedings.

It is so ordered.

NOTES

1. The *Spector* decision leaves unresolved a number of issues, including the specifics of what accommodations must be provided and what barrier issues must be addressed. What is the best means of resolving those questions — federal design standards, case by case litigation, or other means? What is likely to be the difference in addressing standards related to the location of activities? For example, should a cruise ship be required to consider locating certain events, such as bingo games, in more accessible locations, where there is a choice of where to locate the activity? What about shore access? What would be required to make tender accessible or should cruise ships not be permitted to dock where accessible landings are not possible?

Should cruise lines be able to charge more for larger rooms that are designed to allow wheelchair access? Should they be required to ensure a choice of cabin prices for accessible cabins?

2. In an unusual case, a court held that Title III does not apply to the process of selecting contestants to participate on a network television quiz show through an automated phone system. The plaintiff alleges that a disability prevented being able to participate on an equivalent basis. *Rendon v. Valleycrest Productions, Ltd.*, 119 F. Supp. 2d 1344 (S.D. Fla. 2000). Would this mean that the quiz show could exclude, for example, a deaf individual on the show as a contestant?

B   NONDISCRIMINATION

The previous section focused on whether an activity is considered to be one of the twelve categories within Title III of the ADA. In reviewing the cases on whether the program had discriminated or not, it is useful to review cases in earlier sections to assess whether the program had engaged in impermissible discrimination. Often that determination involves an interrelated analysis of whether the individual was otherwise qualified and whether reasonable accommodations could have been provided to ensure qualification and/or to ensure access. Hypothetical Problem 4.1 raises all of these issues.

The following is one of the first cases decided under the ADA involved a Title III claim. The case involved an individual who used a wheelchair due to a spinal cord injury, who had coached Little League Baseball for three years as an on-field base coach. Because of safety concerns, a policy was adopted allowing him to coach only from the dugout, but not from the coacher's box. The plaintiff challenged this policy as violating the ADA.

ANDERSON v. LITTLE LEAGUE BASEBALL, INC.
794 F. Supp. 342 (D. Ariz. 1992)

EARL H. CARROLL, DISTRICT JUDGE:

Discussion

Despite its prohibition against discrimination in public accommodations, Subchapter III provides:

> Nothing in this subchapter shall require an entity to permit an individual to participate in or benefit from the goods, services, facilities, privileges, advantages and accommodations of such entity where such individual poses a direct threat to the health or safety of others. The term "direct threat" means a significant risk to the health or safety of others that cannot be eliminated by a modification of policies, practices, or procedures or by the provision of auxiliary aids or services.

In determining whether an individual, such as plaintiff, poses a direct threat to the health or safety of others, a public accommodation must make an individualized assessment, based on reasonable judgment that relies on current medical knowledge or on the best available objective evidence, to ascertain: (1) the nature, duration, and severity of the risk; (2) the probability that the potential injury will actually occur; and (3) whether reasonable modifications of policies, practices, or procedures will mitigate the risk. 28 C.F.R. § 36.208(c).

The Act's definition of "direct threat" codifies the standard first articulated by the United States Supreme Court in *School Board of Nassau County, Fla. v. Arline*, 480 U.S. 273 (1987), in which the Court held that a person suffering from the contagious disease of tuberculosis can be a handicapped person with the meaning of Section 504 of the Rehabilitation Act of 1973. The Court recognized that there is a need to balance the interests of people with disabilities against legitimate concerns for public safety. "The determination that a person poses a direct threat to the health or safety of others may not be based on generalizations or stereotypes about the effects of a particular disability; it must be based on an individual assessment that conforms to the requirements of [28 C.F.R. § 36.208(c)]." An individualized inquiry is essential if the law is to achieve its goal of protecting disabled individuals from discrimination based on prejudice, stereotypes, or unfounded fear.

There is no indication in the pleadings, affidavits, or oral arguments presented by the parties that defendants conducted an individualized assessment and determined that plaintiff poses a direct threat to the health and safety of others. In fact, there is no indication that defendants undertook any type of inquiry to ascertain "the nature, duration, and severity of the risk" posed by plaintiff; "the probability that the potential injury will actually occur;" or "whether reasonable modifications of policies, practices, or procedures will mitigate the risk" allegedly posed by plaintiff. Defendants' policy amounts to an absolute ban on coaches in wheelchairs in the coachers box, regardless of the coach's disability or the field or game conditions involved. Regrettably, such a policy — implemented without public discourse — falls markedly short of the requirements enunciated in the Americans with Disabilities Act and its implementing regulations.

The Court gives great weight to the fact that plaintiff has served as a Little League coach at either first base or third base for three years without incident. Moreover, plaintiff's significant contributions of time, energy, enthusiasm, and personal example benefit the numerous children who participate in Little League activities as well as the community at large. Plaintiff's work with young people teaches them the importance of focusing on the strengths of others and helping them rise to overcome their personal challenges.

The Court has no doubt that both plaintiff and the children with whom he works will suffer irreparable harm if defendants are permitted to arguably discriminate against plaintiff based upon his disability. Such discrimination is clearly contrary to public policy and the interests of society as a whole. In particular, such discrimination is contrary to the interests of plaintiff and everyone who is interested or participates in Little League activities, including the defendant organization and its officers.

The Court anticipates that the parties will respect these interests and cooperate so that the tournament will begin on schedule and the games will be played as they were during the regular season.

It Is Ordered that plaintiff's Application for Temporary Restraining Order is granted. Defendants are enjoined from preventing or attempting to prevent plaintiff from participating fully, coaching on the field, or otherwise being involved to the full extent of his responsibilities as coach, under the auspices of Little League Baseball, Inc. Furthermore, defendants are enjoined from intimidating or threatening players, parents of players, coaches, officials, umpires, or other persons involved in Little League Baseball and from attempting to induce them to boycott games because of plaintiff's participation.

PROBLEMS

1. Is the Little League in violation of the ADA by providing official uniforms, caps, and insignias to players in the regular league, but not to those in a special league created for individuals with disabilities? *Suhansky v. Little League Baseball Inc.*, No. C.A. 393CV01255 (D. Conn. filed June 25, 1993). Must the Little League provide a separate program in the first place?

2. In any of the Little League cases, is there a Title II claim against the city if it allows the Little League program known to be discriminating to use city operated recreational facilities?

3. In a September 22, 1986, Ann Landers column, several letters responded to a previous column in which Ann had "told off a 'Chicago Reader' who complained about having her appetite spoiled by the sight of a woman with a disability whose husband was feeding her in the restaurant." One response states that "I am a picky eater with a queasy stomach. . . . The sight of a woman in a wheelchair with food running down her chin would make me throw up." Another suggested that "restaurants should have a special section for handicapped people — partially hidden by palms or other greenery so they are not seen by other guests." *Ask Ann Landers*, HOUSTON CHRONICLE, Sept. 22, 1986, at D2.

While Ann Landers had a lot of influence, she was not a judge. Would exclusion of the woman in this case by a restaurant be permissible under the ADA? What about the suggestion to have a special section, would that be permitted under Title III?

4. In 1985, environmentalists tried to stop air tour operators from flying groups below the rim of the Grand Canyon. The environmentalists argued that the activity spoiled the quiet of the canyon as well as adversely affecting wildlife. The air tour operators countered by claiming that a ban on such flights would mean that senior citizens and individuals with disabilities would not have the same access to the canyon as those who could hike the trails or take mule rides into the canyon.

If such flights were banned, what is the likely outcome of an individual suit based on discrimination? Would this be a Title III case or would some other avenue for redress be required?

See *Plane Flights in Grand Canyon Spur Debate*, N.Y. TIMES, Nov. 3, 1985, at I30. The proposed regulations for wilderness areas are found at 61 Fed. Reg. 66968 (Dec. 19, 1996).

5. Would it violate the ADA for an amusement park to demand medical documentation that a child was fit to be on the rides where the request was made because the child appeared to be retarded? What if the child appeared to have severe mobility problems? Would it matter whether it was the roller coaster or the merry-go-round?

6. *Newspapers as Public Accommodations:* In *Treanor v. Washington Post Co.*, 826 F. Supp. 568 (D.D.C. 1993), the court held that a newspaper column is not a public accommodation under Title III of the ADA. Because a newspaper column is not covered, an editorial decision not to publish a review of a book written by an author who is disabled could not be challenged under the ADA. The court also raised concerns about the First Amendment. Does that mean that a newspaper that refuses to include obituaries of individuals who die of HIV complications would not be subject to a Title III challenge? What about a practice that a newspaper would not publish an obituary of anyone under the age of 40 without being advised of the cause of death?

NOTES

1. *A Day at the Movies?* A group trip of individuals with mental retardation to the movies resulted in a negative experience at a Kansas City theater in 1992. Five individuals from a neurological center were turned away from a movie theater because they had made noise in the ticket line. An employee thought they would be disruptive and refused to sell them a ticket. Is this a violation of Title III? Donald Bradley, *Theater Turns Away Disabled*, KANSAS CITY STAR, March 25, 1992, at C1.

23. *Mother's Day Discrimination:* The New York City Commission on Human Rights found a florist in violation of state law by refusing to allow a patron in a wheelchair to enter the store, claiming it was too crowded. This occurred on Mother's Day in 1991. The patron claimed that when he tried to enter, the florist yelled, "No wheelchairs allowed in here — you will break everything." The florist was ordered to pay $5,000 to the customer, but a $3,000 settlement was reached. *No Bouquets for Florist*, NEWSDAY, Feb. 4, 1994, at A22.

C MODIFICATION OF POLICIES, PRACTICES, AND PROCEDURES

Title III of the ADA prohibits as discriminatory the refusal to make reasonable modifications in policies, practices, or procedures necessary to afford access to individuals with disabilities. 42 U.S.C. § 12182(b)(2)(A)(ii). For example, the refusal to accept a state identification card by a business that usually requires a driver's license to write checks would almost always be viewed as discriminatory. *United States v. Venture Stores*, 1994 U.S. Dist. LEXIS 3053, 3 Am. Disabilities Cas. (BNA) 768 (N.D. Ill. 1994).

In a separate section of Title III, it is required that providers of examinations or courses relating to applications, licensing, certification, or credentialing for secondary, postsecondary education, professional, or trade purposes must make these services available in a place and manner accessible to individuals with disabilities.

42 U.S.C. § 12189. In 1994, two settlement agreements were reached in response to cases involving a bar exam test prep program and a CPA test prep program and requests for auxiliary services such as interpreters. *United States v. Harcourt Brace Legal & Prof. Publications, Inc.*, No. CA-94-C-3295 (N.D. Ill. settled May 27, 1994); *United States v. Becker C.P.A. Review*, No. CV-92-2879 (D.D.C. settled May 16, 1994). Cases addressing professional exam modifications have addressed issues such as testing time and format modifications, provision of auxiliary services such as interpreters, and other accommodations. See LAURA ROTHSTEIN & JULIA ROTH-STEIN, DISABILITIES AND THE LAW § 5:7 (2009) (citing cases on these and other issues).

The following decision illustrates that issues of undue hardship are not the only consideration. Considerations of public safety also are relevant.

BREECE v. ALLIANCE TRACTOR-TRAILER TRAINING II, INC.
824 F. Supp. 576 (E.D. Va. 1993)

HILTON, DISTRICT JUDGE:

Findings of Fact

1.   This action has been brought under the Americans with Disabilities Act of 1990.

2.   Plaintiff Michael K. Breece suffers from a severe hearing impairment. Mr. Breece's hearing impairment constitutes a physical impairment that substantially limits one or more of his major life activities. In addition, Mr. Breece has a record of having such impairment and is regarded as having such an impairment. As such, Mr. Breece has a disability within the meaning of 42 U.S.C. § 12102(2).

3.   Defendant Alliance Tractor-Trailer Training II, Inc. is a North Carolina corporation which operates a school for training individuals to operate tractor-trailer vehicles in Wytheville, Virginia. As a place of education, Alliance is a public accommodation under the Americans with Disabilities Act. 42 U.S.C. § 12181(7).

4.   Alliance's training program is known within the trucking industry for its special emphasis on having students drive tractor-trailers on public roads with individualized instruction from teachers sitting with the student drivers in the truck cab. Sixty percent of the seven week course — over 200 hours — is spent driving first on single lane roads, then on larger thruways and finally on the interstate system itself. Students begin the public road driving segment with empty trailers, progress to driving semi-full trailers, and finally drive fully-loaded tractor-trailers.

5.   On January 23, 1992, Mr. Breece applied for admission in Alliance's tractor-trailer training school and attended an interview at the school where he met with Mr. Jerry Patrick, an Alliance recruiter, and Mr. Mark Pressley, Alliance's President.

6.   During the interview, Mr. Patrick questioned Breece's qualifications for admission because of the impairment. Mr. Breece proposed that his hearing impairment could be accommodated by having a sign language interpreter in the cab of the tractor-trailer during the public road training segment of the course. He suggested that the truck cab could be modified so that the instructor could stand behind him and plaintiff could continually "glance around" at the interpreter in order to understand the instructor's instructions, questions, comments, and warnings.

7.   Mr. Patrick and Mr. Pressley gave Mr. Breece a tour of Alliance's facilities and pointed to Mr. Hoback, Alliance's training director and chief instructor, while he was teaching a class, and said that Mr. Breece should return to meet with Mr. Hoback to discuss his application and suggested modification to accommodate his hearing impairment.

8.   Mr. Breece never contacted Mr. Hoback or returned to Alliance. Finally, after Mr. Patrick and Mr. Pressley consulted with Mr. Hoback, Alliance concluded that it could not safely accommodate Mr. Breece's hearing impairment during the integral public road training segment of the course and thereafter rejected Mr. Breece's application.

11.   Mr. Breece demonstrated at trial the extent of his hearing impairment. Despite having his attorney stand next to him at the witness stand in the stillness of the courtroom, Mr. Breece could not understand and repeat some of the words his attorney called out in a loud voice. Even with a sign-language interpreter, Mr. Breece had difficulty understanding the questions he was asked in court.

12.   Dr. Allen R. Robinson teaches education courses in automobile, motorcycle, and truck driving at Indiana University of Pennsylvania. Since beginning his career in traffic safety education in 1964, he has trained individuals to drive cars, motorcycles, medium trucks and developed instructor training programs. Dr. Robinson's only experience training tractor-trailer drivers was a summer course for 28 individuals at the National Institutes of Health.

13.   Dr. Robinson testified at trial that Mr. Breece could be safely accommodated with an earphone amplification device on Alliance's trucks, a truck driving simulator, and expanded in-class training. Mr. Robinson thought that these accommodations could even substitute for the road driving segment of the course.

14.   Alliance's officers testified at trial that truck simulators have little pedagogical value because they lack the requisite fear element of truck driving on the interstate highway system.

15.   Alliance's Mr. Jack Hoback testified that the modifications sought by Mr. Breece would not only be unsafe, but would fundamentally alter the nature of Alliance's road driving oriented tractor-trailer training program.

16.   Mr. Jack Hoback has been an instructor at Alliance for a decade and has trained over 4,000 students how to drive a tractor-trailer. Prior to becoming a driving instructor, Mr. Hoback was a tractor-trailer truck driver for 11 years and trained other truck drivers for his employers. Before becoming a truck driver, Mr. Hoback attended a truck driving school. Mr. Hoback has experience driving over

2,000,000 miles of public roads on a tractor-trailer.

17.   Mr. Hoback described the importance of the public road driving segment of the course and how it cannot be replaced by expanded in-class training. He said that regardless of the amount of in-class training prior to driving trucks on the road, every one of his thousands of students has gotten into a morass when driving on the road that has required personal interaction and instruction with the in-cab trainer making quick commands to get out of it. These intense situations constitute the major pedagogical benefit of Alliance's road training segment.

18.   Mr. Hoback further testified that based upon the evidence available to him he determined that the modifications requested by Mr. Breece and Mr. Breece's inability to understand an instructor in a truck cab with the engine running balanced against the severity of risking a major accident on a public highway in a tractor-trailer led to his conclusion that Mr. Breece's admission to the school would constitute a direct threat to public safety.

19.   Mr. Hoback testified that Mr. Breece's inability to repeat words his lawyers said at trial provided him with further evidence that Mr. Breece would be unable to understand his instructors in a tractor-trailer and that it would be impossible to communicate with him during the public road driving segment of the course, even with a sign language interpreter.

20.   Mr. Hoback thought that an earphone voice amplification system would be unsafe and possibly illegal.

Conclusions of Law

The Americans with Disabilities Act prohibits discrimination by public accommodations on the basis of a disability. The Act specifies that discrimination includes "a failure to make reasonable modifications in policies, practices, or procedures" when the modifications are necessary to afford the services to individuals with disabilities "unless the entity can demonstrate that making such modifications would fundamentally alter the nature of such goods, services, facilities, privileges, advantages, or accommodations." 42 U.S.C. § 12182(b)(2)(A)(ii). This section extends the Rehabilitation Act of 1973's prohibition against discrimination on the basis of disabilities to public accommodations and services operated by private entities.

Both the text of the Americans with Disabilities Act and precedent interpreting the Rehabilitation Act forbid courts from requiring a fundamental alteration in a defendant's program to accommodate a handicapped individual. In *Southeastern Community College v. Davis*, 442 U.S. 397 (1979), the Supreme Court found that a nursing school did not illegally discriminate against a rejected hearing impaired nursing applicant who could communicate only by reading lips and sign language by refusing to modify its program in such a way as to "dispense with the need for effective oral communication" with a nursing instructor. Even though the nursing applicant could read lips, the nature of the clinical phase of the training program required that students be able to "instantly follow" instructions. Justice Powell said that the Rehabilitation Act "imposes no requirement upon an educational institution to lower or to effect substantial modifications of standards to accommodate a handicapped person."

Mr. Breece contends that his hearing impairment can be accommodated by: 1) a driving simulator; 2) more direction or instruction before taking the wheel; 3) a sign language interpreter standing with him in the truck cab; or 4) a speaker on his shoulder near his less hearing impaired ear amplifying his instructor's voice.

Although Dr. Robinson, Mr. Breece's expert witness, testified that Mr. Breece's hearing impairment can be accommodated, Dr. Robinson's has had both significantly less tractor-trailer driving and teaching experience than Mr. Hoback. The testimony of Mr. Hoback is thus entitled to greater weight than Dr. Robinson's testimony.

Mr. Breece's hearing impairment cannot be accommodated without fundamentally altering the nature of Alliance's intensive training program of driving tractor-trailers on the road accompanied by an instructor. Expanded theoretical classroom training could not substitute for the actual road driving experience that is the integral part of Alliance's training program. A simulator based training program substituting for the road segment would also fundamentally alter the school's program because such a simulator lacks the fear element of driving a tractor trailer which is essential to graduating competent drivers from the training course.

In addition, nothing in the Americans with Disabilities Act requires "an entity to permit an individual to participate in or benefit from the goods, services, facilities, privileges, advantages and accommodations of such entity where such individual poses a direct threat to the health or safety of others." 42 U.S.C. § 12182(b)(3). A "direct threat" is a "significant risk to the health or safety of others that cannot be eliminated by a modification of policies, practices, or procedures or by the provision of auxiliary aids or services."

These provisions dealing with direct threats to public safety codify the standards requiring an "individualized inquiry" about the handicapped plaintiff expressed by the Supreme Court in *School Board of Nassau County v. Arline*, 480 U.S. 273 (1987). The finding of a direct threat is to be based on a reasonable judgment relying either upon current medical evidence or "on the best available objective evidence, to determine: the nature, duration and severity of the risk; the probability that the potential injury will actually occur; and whether reasonable modifications of policies, practices, or procedures will mitigate the risk."

Alliance made a reasonable judgment based on the best available objective evidence upon Mr. Breece's application and interview that any accommodation for his disability during the road driving segment would pose a direct threat to the safety of himself, his instructor, and the public at large on the public highway system. Mr. Breece could not possibly keep his eyes on the road, gauges, and mirrors and simultaneously watch a sign-language interpreter translating his teacher's instructions. The severity of Mr. Breece's hearing impairment would also make voice amplification devices useless in a noisy truck cab. Because Mr. Breece would be unable to communicate with his instructor in the cab, his presence on the road would constitute a direct threat to public safety.

Because accommodations could not be made to Alliance's tractor-trailer training program without fundamentally altering that program or posing a direct threat to public safety, the court concludes that the defendant has not violated the Americans with Disabilities Act by rejecting the plaintiff's application.

———

The unique challenges of daycare programs as a public accommodation have been at issue in several cases, although most of these cases seem to have reached settlement, so there is little judicial guidance on this issue. One of the few cases to address daycare settings is *Roberts v. Kindercare Learning Centers, Inc.*, 896 F. Supp. 921 (D. Minn. 1995). The parents of a four year old child with developmental delays, seizures, attention deficit hyperactivity disorder, and other behavior problems, and who was not toilet trained sought to enroll Brandon and requested the availability of a one-on-one Personal Care Attendant (PCA) to accompany him on a continuous basis. The following is the court's response. The PCA was paid for by the school system and was part of the Individualized Educational Program (IEP). The issue for this court was whether the day care program was required to accommodate the child by providing one-on-one staffing when the school-provided PCA was unable to be present.

ROBERTS v. KINDERCARE LEARNING CENTERS, INC.
896 F. Supp. 921 (D. Minn. 1995)

Magnuson, Chief Judge.

Findings of Fact

On May 11, 1994, Ms. Rodenberg-Roberts contacted KinderCare Learning Centers, Inc. ("KinderCare"), in Apple Valley, Minnesota, and spoke with Center Director Ann Marie Donahue to enroll Brandon. KinderCare is a for-profit corporation operating day care centers throughout the United States, including the State of Minnesota. KinderCare provides a "public accommodation" within the meaning of the ADA and the MHRA. KinderCare generally provides group child care, as opposed individualized, or one-on-one child care. Ms. Rodenberg-Roberts was acquainted with the Apple Valley KinderCare; the Roberts had enrolled Becky, Brandon's sister, there, and were satisfied with the care KinderCare had been providing her. Becky, too, was a special-needs child, having Spina Bifida and a tendency to run away. However, Becky did not require the one-on-one care that Brandon required.

Ms. Donahue informed Ms. Rodenberg-Roberts that the center had room for another child. Ms. Rodenberg-Roberts advised Ms. Donahue of Brandon's special needs, including his continuous need for one-on-one personal care while participating in day care as directed by his IEP. Among other things, she also informed Ms. Donahue that Brandon had a traumatic brain injury, a seizure disorder, a tendency to bolt, but that he was "not terribly disruptive." Ms. Rodenberg-Roberts also advised Ms. Donahue that they had been dissatisfied with the decision of Children's World's to provide Brandon's one-on-one care in the office with a staff member when his PCA was absent.

Ms. Rodenberg-Roberts requested that Ms. Donahue enroll Brandon at the Apple Valley KinderCare on a "full-time" basis. However, Ms. Rodenberg-Roberts did not suggest that "full-time" had anything but its common meaning, and Ms. Donahue believed Ms. Rodenberg-Roberts was seeking day care for Brandon for 40 to 50 hours per week. Ms. Rodenberg-Roberts' request for "full-time" child care without any attempt to clarify her meaning, despite further discussions and correspondence with KinderCare regarding its responsibility to provide one-on-one care for Brandon at all times his PCA would be absent, caused KinderCare decision-makers reasonably to conclude Ms. Rodenberg-Roberts was requesting Brandon be enrolled for 40 hours per week. Ms. Rodenberg-Roberts also advised Ms. Donahue that while a PCA ordinarily would accompany Brandon, the Roberts currently did not have a PCA for Brandon, and that they were seeking to acquire one who would accompany Brandon to KinderCare for 30 hours per week. Ms. Roberts requested KinderCare provide the one-on-one care Brandon required for all times a PCA did not accompany him. Thus, based on Ms. Rodenberg-Roberts' representations to KinderCare about the need for "full-time" day care service and the understanding that PCA service is occasionally disrupted due to illness, turnover, or as anticipated from past PCA unreliability to the Roberts, and the additional fact that the Roberts sought PCA service for only about 30 hours per week, KinderCare would likely have to provide substantial one-on-one care for Brandon.

KinderCare does not provide one-on-one care on a regular basis for any child, but does provide one-on-one care for brief periods due to injuries or immediate disciplinary problems. The wages of a KinderCare full-time aid employed for Brandon's one-on-one care would have been about $200 per week, or nearly double the revenue KinderCare would earn in tuition for Brandon's care. Never having faced the issue of substantial one-on-one care, Ms. Donahue contacted Dee Ann Besch, a KinderCare regional director. Several telephone discussions took place between Ms. Besch, Ms. Donahue and Ms. Rodenberg-Roberts. On May 20, 1994, Ms. Donahue informed Ms. Rodenberg-Roberts that KinderCare would enroll Brandon, but that Brandon could attend KinderCare only when accompanied by a PCA; KinderCare would not provide an employee to care for Brandon on a one-on-one basis in the absence of a PCA. Ms. Rodenberg-Roberts testified that both she and her husband needed to work, and therefore it would be unacceptable to them to come to assist with Brandon at KinderCare or pick up Brandon in the event his PCA would become ill or would otherwise be unable to accompany Brandon at KinderCare.

One year before KinderCare's decision here, it had distributed to its center directors a list of "helpful guidelines" for enrolling children with disabilities. Those guidelines included the center director's meeting with the child and family in the center before enrollment, observing the child in the classroom, assessing the staff person's ability to cope with the disability and the child's ability to adapt to the group, discussing the potential enrollment with a supervisor and with the staff, and enrolling the child for a "trial period." There was no evidence that KinderCare intended these to be anything more than what they purport to be: "helpful guidelines." Ms. Donahue did not invite Brandon for a meeting with KinderCare staff at the center, did not observe him in the classroom, and did not follow any of the other guidelines before making the decision concerning Brandon's enrollment.

KinderCare also has produced a reference booklet, KinderCare and the ADA, The Americans With Disabilities Act and the Enrollment Process. This booklet contains KinderCare's policy statement regarding care for children with disabilities. That statement indicates that KinderCare "reviews each child's situation on a case-by-case basis to determine if the child's needs can be met in the KinderCare setting." The booklet directs KinderCare employees to "[a]scertain if you have sufficient resources for the child and her unique needs . . . while still having the caring responsibility for the other children in the group." The booklet indicates that enrollment for a trial period is "usually" a good idea, but that a KinderCare director should "not put off telling the family once [the director] know[s] the situation is not going to work."

Discussion

The Roberts brought this action on behalf of Brandon, alleging that KinderCare's acceptance of Brandon only when accompanied by a PCA violates the ADA and the MHRA. They argue that KinderCare did not make reasonable efforts to accommodate Brandon's needs, and that KinderCare's policies "dictate" that KinderCare must not make an admission decision regarding a disabled child "until the child has had at least two visits to the center." Essentially, they argue that because KinderCare did not follow its own policy regarding enrollment of disabled children, KinderCare failed to reasonably accommodate Brandon or otherwise discriminated against Brandon. The Roberts seek injunctive relief, as well as compensatory and punitive damages.

I. *Duty to Provide One-on-One Care*

KinderCare argues that it had no duty under the ADA or the MHRA to provide one-on-one care to Brandon because providing such care would alter the nature of KinderCare's business, and would place an undue financial burden on KinderCare. The Roberts argue that KinderCare is in the business of providing child care generally, and that providing one-on-one child care therefore would not affect its business function. The Roberts also argue that KinderCare would have no financial burden to provide additional staffing "on most days," because the absence of Brandon's PCA would have been "rare." Additionally, they argue that KinderCare has "numerous mechanisms in place to provide replacement staffing on a[n] emergency basis;" that KinderCare could have directed a substitute teacher or the center director to provide one-on-one care in the absence of Brandon's PCA.

A. *Fundamentally Altering the Service Provided*

The ADA prohibits an entity that provides a public accommodation from failing to take steps to ensure disabled persons are not denied service "unless the entity can demonstrate that taking such steps would fundamentally alter the nature of the . . . service . . . or accommodation being offered."

This Court has no difficulty concluding that requiring KinderCare to provide one-on-one child care would fundamentally alter the nature of its service. The undisputed evidence at trial establishes that there are at least two distinct types of child care service: group child care and individual child care. KinderCare is in the group child care business and does not seek to provide individual child care. It does not provide one-on-one child care on a regular basis to any child except as necessary to deal with temporary, urgent needs. Requiring KinderCare to provide one-on-one service essentially places it into a child care market it did not intend to enter.

The Court is unpersuaded by the Roberts' argument that because KinderCare is in the business of providing child care, requiring one-on-one child care would not fundamentally alter its service. The Roberts construe "service" too broadly.

B. *Undue Burden*

The ADA and MHRA also do not require an entity offering a public accommodation to endure an undue burden in order to provide its service to a disabled person. The Roberts point to KinderCare's $2.4 million 1994 first quarter net income for the proposition that provision of one-on-one service would not impose an undue financial burden on KinderCare.

To determine whether an action would result in an undue burden, the Court considers several factors: the nature and cost of the action; the financial resources of the site involved; the number of persons employed at the site; the effect on expenses and resources; the administrative and financial relationship of the site to the corporation; and, if applicable, the overall financial resources of the parent corporation and the number of its facilities. 28 C.F.R. § 36.104. KinderCare argues it would have to hire a full-time care-giver to ensure one-on-one care for Brandon on those dates and times his PCA does not accompany him. The Roberts argue that a part-time employee would be sufficient.

The evidence revealed that PCA care is unpredictable, at best. Certainly, KinderCare would not be able to predict those dates Brandon's PCA would be ill or through some other circumstance unable to accompany Brandon. The Court agrees that to ensure the one-on-one care Brandon needed likely would have required KinderCare to employ a full-time care-giver. The evidence revealed that KinderCare would pay this employee approximately $200 per week, plus provide benefits. The evidence also revealed that KinderCare would have received $105 per week in tuition for Brandon's care.

The Roberts do not dispute that the Apple Valley KinderCare operates "on a shoestring budget," and offered no evidence contrary to trial testimony indicating that the $95 per week loss for Brandon's care would constitute a substantial financial detriment to the site. Additionally, the evidence established that KinderCare has recently emerged from bankruptcy.

The Roberts argument that KinderCare could simply transfer the center's director or some other staff member to provide Brandon's one-on-one care without any cost is unpersuasive. Ms. Donahue testified that in those rare events that she, as center director, must serve as a replacement for an absent teacher for whom no substitute is available, her work as director simply piles up and she must work into the night to compensate. Because of the frequent one-on-one service KinderCare would be required to provide in lieu of Brandon's absent PCA, simply juggling staff is not a quick, cost-free fix to the problem. The facts produced at trial relevant to issues listed above, point to a finding that requiring KinderCare to provide one-on-one care to Brandon in the absence of his PCA would impose an undue financial or administrative burden on KinderCare; thus, the accommodation the Roberts sought was not a reasonable accommodation within the meaning of the ADA or the MHRA.

II. *Duty to Provide Day Care Services Without One-on-One Care*

The Plaintiff presented evidence at trial challenging Brandon's actual need for one-on-one care due to Brandon's improvement. However, it is undisputed that KinderCare was required at least to incorporate Brandon's existing IEP into the care it provided him, if not to follow the IEP directly. The evidence established that Brandon's mother, his treating psychologist and his existing IEP, all indicated that Brandon required one-on-one care for his own safety. KinderCare certainly had no duty to ignore Brandon's safety needs, or to seek ways to circumvent those needs in order to gain his enrollment.

NOTES

1. *It's a Dog's World:* In a case decided under New York State Law, the court may have reached the right decision, but for the wrong reasons. In *Perino v. St. Vincent's Medical Center*, 132 Misc. 2d 20, 502 N.Y.S.2d 921 (Sup. Ct. 1986), a blind man wanted to have his guide dog accompany him to the delivery room of a hospital where his wife was to give birth. The court held that the delivery room of a hospital was not a public facility subject to the state's nondiscrimination in public accommodations law. Therefore, it was not a violation of the statute to deny the requested accommodation. Surely if the hospital had denied a blind woman access to the delivery room, she would have succeeded in a discrimination claim under the same statute. What seems more appropriate would be a decision that denied access based on reasonable concerns about safety and health in a crowded delivery room. Although the *Perino* case allowed the dog to be excluded, the special circumstances of the case should be taken into account. A hospital delivery room is quite different from many other places of accommodation. Generally speaking, service animals will be allowed in such places as a modification of usual business practice. While most operators of public accommodations are familiar with seeing eye dogs and readily permit them to enter, problems can occur with other service animals, especially where the need for the animal is not as obvious. A restaurant owner who refused to allow Lucky, the dog, to enter found himself on the receiving end of a fine. He had refused to even look at the owner's ID card explaining a state law requiring access for animals assisting people with hearing impairments. In court, the dog demonstrated his assistance abilities and showed that he could behave in a public place. Deborah Quinn Hensel, *Dog Proves He's Man's Best Friend — in Court*, Houston Post, Nov. 11, 1993, at A29. The ADA probably would result in a consistent ruling. It should be noted that while modification of "no animals" policies is probably going to be required in most instances, the operators of public accommodations will not be responsible for caring for the animals.

In *Thompson v. Dover Downs, Inc.*, 31 Nat'l Disability L. Rep. ¶ 135 (Del. 2005), a casino denied entry to an individual accompanied by a four-month-old dog. The puppy arrived wearing a vest indicating that it was a support animal. The security guard asked what the dog was trained to do, and when the individual refused to answer, the dog was not allowed entry. The court held that while it was not permissible to ask about one's disability, it is permitted to ask about training.

In *Lentini v. California Center for the Arts*, 370 F.3d 837 (9th Cir. 2004), the court allowed service animals to be in a concert hall where disruptive noises would have been acceptable if engaged in by humans.

In *Johnson v. Gambrinus Co.*, 116 F.3d 1052 (5th Cir. 1997), Judge Carolyn King held that a brewery's policy of denying access to individuals with guide dogs violated Title III of the ADA. The court held that modifying its "no animals" policy did not jeopardize safety. The court noted that the marginal increase in the risk of contamination resulting from such an accommodation did not justify the refusal to modify the policy.

There is increasing attention and awareness about the need to have clearer policies on service and other animals in places of public accommodation. While there is some guidance from court decisions and the Department of Justice, clarity is necessary on what level of training is required, what documentation the individual should be required to present about the animal, health and safety concerns, and disruption concerns. See LAURA ROTHSTEIN & JULIA ROTHSTEIN, DISABILITIES AND THE LAW § 5:5 (2009) (citing cases on these and other issues).

2. *Fast Food Drive Through Accommodation:* In March of 1994, Burger King entered into a settlement, agreeing to develop, test, and implement an electronic ordering system to assist individuals with hearing and speech impairments. *Sacchetti v. King*, No. CV-93-7667-SVM (C.D. Cal. settled March 22, 1994).

The case of *Bunjer v. Edwards*, 985 F. Supp. 165 (D.D.C. 1997), involved a deaf customer at a Washington, D.C. McDonald's restaurant, who was arrested after a dispute involving the restaurant's treatment of him when he attempted to order food through the drive-through facility. When he tried to order by driving directly to the drive-through window and giving a written order, he was initially refused, eventually served, snickered at by employees, allegedly given the wrong change and warm water with a white substance instead of the Sprite he had ordered. When he went inside to complain, his dissatisfaction with the restaurant's handling of his complaint eventually resulted in his refusal to leave and an arrest. The court in finding that he had been discriminated against, noted the following:

> Under the current system, deaf and hearing impaired patrons have no way to make use of the drive-through facility. There is an easy way to make provision for these patrons. All that needs to be done is for the restaurant to put up a sign at the initial speaker/menu point instructing deaf patrons to proceed directly to the window to have their orders filled.

Additionally, the employees of Defendant's McDonald's franchise were inadequately trained to deal with the special needs of deaf and hearing impaired patrons. Defendants' McDonald's restaurant is located in close proximity to Gallaudet University, the foremost national university devoted entirely to the deaf and the hearing impaired. Despite the numerous deaf patrons at the restaurant, Defendant has in place no policies or training to instruct employees about the special needs of such customers. The circumstances in this case illustrate that the employees of Defendants' restaurant were far from capable of dealing effectively with deaf patrons. Had Defendants provided adequate training to their employees, the offensive treatment of the Plaintiff that occurred in this case might have been avoided. Accordingly, the Court will order Defendants to implement policies and provide training for their employees to accommodate the deaf and hearing impaired. Although the injunction will be limited to Defendants' McDonald's franchise, [because] ("[A] nationwide or companywide injunction is appropriate only when the facts indicate a company policy or practice in violation of the statute."), the Court hopes that it will serve as a "wake-up call" for the national McDonald's Corporation to put in place training and other appropriate procedures for dealing with the deaf and the hearing impaired. It was conceded at trial that the parent McDonald's Corporation provides no training to its own employees or its franchise proprietors with respect to dealing with the deaf and hearing impaired.

Should the duty to provide training be any different because the restaurant is located where there will likely be a number of deaf customers?

3. *Not Everyone Loves Peanut Butter:* Most people think of peanut butter as a staple food for children. Unfortunately, some children are severely allergic to peanut products and the reaction could be so severe as to result in death. In the 1997 settlement in *United States v. La Petite Academy, Inc.*, the child care program with 750 locations nationwide, agreed to implement procedures to ensure that children with such allergies could be accommodated. The program also agreed to implement procedures relating to glucose testing of children with insulin-dependent diabetes. A related issue involves allowing children to carry and use Epi-Pens at camp or school as an accommodation to a policy that prohibits children from having or administering medication.

4. *Golf Carts and Fundamental Alterations:* The Court's opinion in *PGA Tour, Inc. v. Martin* earlier in the chapter addresses whether the PGA is a public accommodation within Title III. The case should be reviewed at this point. Note that the Court makes a careful individualized assessment not only on whether carrying clubs is fundamental to to the game of golf, but also on whether Casey Martin was unfairly advantaged by riding a golf cart instead of walking. The individualized assessment was that Martin still suffered substantial fatigue in spite of riding a golf cart, and thereby was not unfairly advantaged.

5. The use of Segways and similar devices in public places is becoming more of an issue. The court in *McElroy v. Simon Property Group, Inc.*, 37 Nat'l Disability L. Rep. ¶ 235 (D. Kan. 2008), denied a motion to dismiss a case brought by an individual who was required to sign an indemnification form when using a Segway at the mall. Other issues include complete prohibition of Segways. These have yet to be resolved.

PROBLEM

Don't Roll in My Parade: Sponsors of parades often have restrictions against wheeled vehicles. If an individual with a disability requested to be in the parade using a wheelchair, would it violate the ADA to deny this accommodation? What if the parade sponsor claimed that this would slow down the parade and thus adversely affect television coverage? See *Handicapped Group Left Out of Parade — Too Slow for TV*, L.A. TIMES, Nov. 20, 1985 at I2.

See also Laura Rothstein, *Don't Roll in My Parade: The Impact of Sports and Entertainment Cases on Public Awareness and Understanding of the Americans with Disabilities Act*, 19 REVIEW OF LITIGATION (University of Texas) 400 (2000). The article examines litigation and advocacy involving sports and entertainment cases under the ADA and how the print media have covered these cases. The article discusses cases involving impaired athletes and issues related to sports venues and movie theatres. The conclusion of the review is that while there has been some adverse media coverage about the ADA, the media coverage of issues relating to sports and entertainment has given a more positive light to the ADA and has increased awareness and support by the public.

D   ARCHITECTURAL BARRIERS

[1]   Covered Facilities

When most people think about individuals with disabilities, they think about those who use wheelchairs. The international symbol for handicap/disability access is a graphic design wheelchair. When considering physical access to the environment, many of the barriers do affect individuals who use wheelchairs or who have other mobility impairments. Lack of access, however, affects individuals with other kinds of disabilities, such as those related to hearing and visual impairments.

For example, a coat rack in a hallway that protrudes from the wall may be a barrier for a person who is blind. Audible fire warnings will be of no use to an individual who is deaf. And some access features may detrimentally affect individuals with one type of disability while benefitting others. For example, lowering elevator buttons for individuals with wheelchairs may adversely affect individuals who are not in wheelchairs, but who have limited range of motion.

In recognition of the various types of disabilities and the barriers that affect individuals with these disabilities, a number of federal, state, and local laws have been enacted to ensure that the environment is more accessible. This chapter focuses primarily on federal laws, but it is important to recognize that state and local laws may be more comprehensive in some cases. For example, religious entities and private clubs have certain exemptions under the major federal laws, but state and local requirements often apply to these facilities. The differences in enforcement are also important in comparing state and local requirements with federal law. For example, local law may work primarily by requiring accessibility as a requirement to obtain a building permit. This law may not include a mechanism for an individual to challenge noncompliance.

The three major federal laws requiring architectural access are the Architectural Barriers Act of 1968 (ABA), 42 U.S.C. §§ 4151–4157; Section 504 of the Rehabilitation Act of 1973, 29 U.S.C. § 794; and the Americans with Disabilities Act of 1990, 42 U.S.C. § 12101 et seq. (ADA). For the most part, accessibility in housing is not covered in this chapter because it is separately treated in Chapter 8, which addresses housing. There has been little litigation under the ABA or the Rehabilitation Act, so most of the judicial interpretation of architectural barrier requirements arises under the ADA. There are some requirements that may arise under Sections 501 and 503 of the Rehabilitation Act, 29 U.S.C. §§ 791, 793, but generally the Rehabilitation Act requirements arise as a result of Section 504.

Which law applies depends primarily on whether the facility is public or private, whether it meets certain definitional requirements within the statute, and who is challenging the lack of access. For example, Title I of the ADA does not apply to employers with fewer than 15 employees, so a small employer, such as a "mom and pop" grocery store, would not be subject to the mandates to remove architectural barriers as a reasonable accommodation to an individual working there. That same employer, however, may be a public accommodation under Title III of the ADA, so that the public portions of the store would be subject to accessibility requirements for customers.

The Architectural Barriers Act (ABA) was the first major federal statute to affect building design. Passed in 1968, it applies to buildings and facilities built with federal funds or leased by the federal government. The four major federal agencies that have facilities subject to the ABA are the General Services Administration, the Department of Housing and Urban Development, the Department of Defense, and the United States Postal Service. Minimum accessibility guidelines were developed pursuant to the ABA. The enforcing agency for the ABA is the Architectural and Transportation Barriers Compliance Board, which was not created until 1973. The ABA mandates only apply to new construction or renovations and alterations. They do not require retrofitting. The ABA has no major impact on private entities that are considered to be public accommodations.

It is obvious that only a small percentage of all buildings and facilities are subject to the ABA. Section 504 of the Rehabilitation Act, passed in 1973, expands the zone of coverage to facilities receiving federal financial assistance. Like the ABA, Section 504 does not require retrofitting, except to the extent that barrier removal or other accessibility changes might be required to make the facility accessible when viewed in its entirety. The Fair Housing Act Amendments of 1988, 42 U.S.C. § 3601 et seq., expanded accessibility requirements to housing.

Even with these federal mandates, there are a great number of buildings and facilities subject to none of the major federal mandates. The passage of the Americans with Disabilities Act in 1990 is particularly significant because of its expanded coverage to most workplaces, most places of public accommodation, and most facilities and buildings operated by state and local governmental agencies. Title I of the ADA has accessibility requirements for the workplace, Title II for state and local governmental bodies, and Title III for private operators of public accommodation. The ADA mandates specific design standards for new construction under Titles II and III, requires some access when there are renovations or alterations, and requires barrier removal. The specific barrier removal requirements depend on whether the entity is an employer (where removal would be subject to reasonable accommodation standards), a state or local government agency (requiring barriers to be removed to the extent that the program is accessible when viewed in its entirety), or a place of public accommodation (requiring barrier removal to the extent it is readily achievable). There are also a number of barrier removal tax incentives and grant programs from agencies that are designed to provide carrots as well as sticks in making the environment accessible.

As some of the cases in this chapter illustrate, it is possible for more than one statute to apply. It is also possible that more than one of the titles of the ADA may apply. Furthermore, more than one entity may be liable for noncompliance with the architectural access requirements.

FIEDLER v. AMERICAN MULTI-CINEMA, INC.
871 F. Supp. 35 (D.D.C. 1994)

JACKSON, DISTRICT JUDGE.

Plaintiff Marc Fiedler is a quadriplegic movie-goer in Washington, D.C., who uses a wheelchair to ambulate.[1] Defendant American Multi-Cinema, Inc. ("AMC") is a nationwide operator of movie theaters, one of which is the Avenue Grand, located on the basement concourse of Union Station, the principal passenger railway terminal in Washington, D.C.[2] The only wheelchair seating available to Mr. Fiedler when he attends the Avenue Grand Theater is one of two wheelchair sites situated at the very back of the theater, in the last row of conventional seats farthest from the screen.

Union Station is owned by the United States and managed by the Department of Transportation, ("DOT"), an agency in the executive branch of the federal government. The Avenue Grand premises (and its sister theaters) are leased to AMC by DOT. Both the construction of the Avenue Grand Theater and the lease thereof to AMC antedate the enactment and the effective date of the Americans with Disabilities Act of 1990 ("ADA").

Plaintiff Fiedler brings this three-count complaint against AMC alleging, in the first count, that AMC's placement of wheelchair seating in the Avenue Grand Theater violates the ADA. By relegating him to inferior seating in the back of the theater when he goes to see a movie at the Avenue Grand, Fiedler alleges that AMC deprives him of full and equal enjoyment of the facilities to which he, as a

---

[1] Although a quadriplegic, Fiedler has some use of his upper body, arms, and hands. His wheelchair is manually powered.

[2] The Avenue Grand is the largest of nine movie theaters that AMC operates as a single complex at Union Station.

disabled person, is entitled under the ADA. As the ADA authorizes a private victim of discrimination to do, he prays for an injunction directing AMC to so reconfigure the seating in the Avenue Grand as to enable him to occupy a wheelchair seat situated in the fourth or fifth rows of the theater.

In the second count of his complaint, Fiedler asks for similar injunctive relief under the District of Columbia Human Rights Act, D.C. Code § 1-2501 et seq., with respect to the Avenue Grand's eight smaller sister theaters, each of which has a seating capacity below the ADA's threshold of 300 seats. In the third and final count of his complaint, Fiedler asks for an award of compensatory damages from AMC for the common law tort of failing to furnish facilities to a member of the public without discrimination.

AMC has moved for summary judgment on the entire complaint, on several grounds. AMC contends that the ADA is inapplicable to its Union Station premises by virtue of its status as a lessee of an entity itself not subject to the provisions of the ADA, namely, the executive branch of the federal government. Second, AMC argues that even if it must comply with the ADA generally, dispersed seating for wheelchair-bound patrons[3] is not required at the Avenue Grand because the theater actually conforms to a technical exception the United States Department of Justice has written into its implementing literature for the ADA, allowing the "clustering" of seating for the disabled in certain circumstances.[4] Lastly, AMC asserts that the ADA does not require equivalent treatment of the disabled and the able-bodied when to do so would present a "direct threat" to the health or safety of others.

I.

AMC contends that Title III of the ADA is inapplicable to it because it leases the space for its theaters from an agency in the executive branch of the federal government. The parties agree that the executive branch is exempt from the requirements of Title III of the ADA, and that insofar as government buildings are concerned, executive branch real estate is subject to another federal anti-discrimination regime, namely, the Architectural Barriers Act ("ABA") of 1968.[5] AMC argues that since Union Station is a federal building, it is covered only by the ABA, and AMC, as lessee of a federal landlord, can therefore claim the benefit of Union Station's ADA-exempt status for the purpose of avoiding the requirements of the ADA.

---

[3] [Authors' Note: This term is generally not considered to be appropriate. The preferred term would be wheelchair user].

[4] The United States Department of Justice is charged by statute with the implementation of Title III of the ADA, and to that end it has promulgated conventional regulations and published literature interpreting the regulations, including a "technical assistance" manual. Although the parties do not agree as to the force and effect each is to be given, the Court will deem them as regulations and interpretations of regulations, the latter to be given controlling weight as to the meaning of the former.

[5] The ABA generally applies to buildings and facilities that are constructed or altered on behalf of the government; leased by the government; financed by certain government grants or loans; or constructed under authority vested by certain statutes. See 42 U.S.C. §§ 4151–52.

By its terms, however, Title III of the ADA applies to a "place of public accommodation," which in turn is defined as "a facility, operated by a private entity, whose operations affect commerce and fall within at least one of the following categories . . . (3) A motion picture house, theater, concert hall, stadium, or other place of exhibition or entertainment." The Avenue Grand Theater is indisputably a "motion picture house." It is "operated by a private entity," the defendant AMC. And by regulation it has been declared to "affect commerce."[6] Thus, the Court concludes that the Avenue Grand Theater is a "place of public accommodation" and, as such, is subject to Title III of the ADA.

Moreover, the ADA itself expressly contemplates that entities to which it applies might be subject to two or more separate sets of obligations with respect to their treatment of handicapped patrons. See 42 U.S.C. § 12201(b) ("Nothing in this chapter shall be construed to invalidate or limit the remedies, rights and procedures of any Federal law . . . that provides greater or equal protection for the rights of individuals with disabilities than are afforded by this chapter."). AMC maintains that the provisions of the ABA and the ADA may potentially conflict with one another, but it has made no showing here that its compliance with the ADA in this case would be inconsistent with any obligation it may also have inherited under the ABA as the lessee of a federal landlord. Accordingly, the Court finds that the ADA is applicable to AMC notwithstanding the federal government's fee simple ownership of the leased property.

II.

Having determined that the ADA is applicable, the Court must next consider whether AMC has complied with its requirements for retrofitting existing structures to accommodate the disabled. The requirements are found in the regulations promulgated by the Department of Justice, which, as they pertain to this case, provide as follows:

To the extent that it is readily achievable, a public accommodation in assembly areas shall —

(i)   Provide a reasonable number of wheelchair seating spaces and seats with removable aisle-side arm rests; and

---

[6] See Title III Manual § III-1.2000.A (Supp.1994) (a facility that is "open to out-of-state visitors," as Union Station and all of its amenities, including the Avenue Grand Theater, are, "affects commerce"). The Department of Justice also directly addresses the status of private lessees of government property in its Title III Manual:

> If the owner of a building is not covered by the ADA, is it possible for a private tenant to still have title III responsibility?
>
> Yes. The fact that a landlord in a particular case is not covered by the ADA does not necessarily negate title III's coverage of private entities that lease or operate places of public accommodation within the facility.
>
> ILLUSTRATION: A Federal Executive agency owns a building in which several spaces are rented to retail stores. Although Federal executive agencies are not covered by the ADA, the private entities that rent and operate the retail stores, which are places of public accommodation, are covered by title III.

Title III Manual § III-1.2000.B (Supp.1994).

(ii)   Locate the wheelchair seating spaces so that they —

(A)   Are dispersed throughout the seating area;

(B)   Provide lines of sight and choice of admission prices comparable to those for members of the general public;

(C)   Adjoin an accessible route that also serves as a means of egress in case of emergency; and

(D)   Permit individuals who use wheelchairs to sit with family members or other companions.

AMC acknowledges that dispersion of wheelchair seating throughout the Avenue Grand is "readily achievable." It is exempted from any obligation to do so, however, it says, by an "exception" found in an explanatory portion of the technical regulations allowing it to "cluster" wheelchair seating at a single location (presumably of its choice) in "bleachers, balconies, and other areas having sight lines that require slopes of greater than 5 percent." The defendant argues that the underlined portion of Section 4.33.3 should be interpreted to mean that if the "slope," or grade, of the aisle in a theater or other place of public exhibition exceeds five percent, then it is not required to disperse wheelchair seating throughout the theater. Specifically, when the grade of the floor exceeds a one-inch rise in twenty inches of horizontal travel — an arguably more difficult ascent for a person in a wheelchair — as is the grade on all of the aisle areas of the Avenue Grand except at the rear, then the theater operator is entitled to "cluster" its wheelchair seating, ostensibly where it concludes it is safest for its wheelchair patrons, but in practical effect wherever it chooses.

Fiedler and the government maintain that the "exception" has nothing to do with the slope of floors or aisles; the exception speaks to the angle of vision between spectator and spectacle, or, more precisely, the angular distance a spectator must drop or raise his line of sight below or above the horizontal to observe what he came to see.

The mandatory portion of the regulation to which the "exception" relates, provides: Wheelchair areas shall be an integral part of any fixed seating plan and shall be provided so as to provide people with physical disabilities a choice of admission prices and lines of sight comparable to those for members of the general public. In context, therefore, both the mandate and the exception appear to concern, as Fiedler contends, a criterion of visual vantage, not physical safety. In other words, disabled people are to have equal access to the less desirable (and presumably cheaper) seats at theatrical events, as well as the most coveted.

The government, agreeing with Fiedler's interpretation of Section 4.33.3, asserts that the clustering exception is intended to have very limited application to discrete parts of assembly areas, such as balconies, bleachers, and the like. These seating areas are unique, it says, in that they are almost always situated high above the spectacle to be observed (i.e., where the sight lines almost always exceed five percent). To the extent safety is implicated at all in the reason for the exception, it is because access to these seats is almost always afforded by steps, not ramps. Thus, wheelchair seating can only be provided at the top or bottom of those areas. This narrow exception is inapplicable, according to the government, to a typical single-level movie theater, where steep lines of sight are not generally found.

As the author of the regulation, the Department of Justice is also the principal arbiter as to its meaning. The Court concludes that the exception to ADAAG Section 4.33.3 affords AMC no warrant to consign its wheelchair patrons to the back of the Avenue Grand Theater.

III.

AMC's most persuasive argument in support of a right to retain its wheelchair seating in the back of the Avenue Grand despite the ADA is that the presence of a wheelchair and its occupant in the midst of able-bodied patrons in fear for their own safety could impede a mass exodus of the theater in the case of an emergency. It would thus constitute a "direct threat to the health or safety of others," in which case compliance with the ADA is no longer obligatory. A "direct threat" is defined as "a significant risk to the health or safety of others that cannot be eliminated by a modification of policies, practices, or procedures, or by the provision of auxiliary aids or services." "In determining whether an individual poses a direct threat to the health or safety of others," thus justifying disparate treatment of the disabled in the interest of public health or safety, "a public accommodation must make an individualized assessment, based on reasonable judgment that relies on current medical knowledge or on the best available objective evidence, to ascertain: the nature, duration, and severity of the risk; the probability that the potential injury will actually occur; and whether reasonable modifications of policies, practices, or procedures will mitigate the risk."

Fiedler cites to several cases recently decided under the ADA that have held that the right to treat a disabled person disparately, and less favorably, on the ground that to do otherwise would endanger others must be preceded by an individualized assessment of the nature and extent of danger in relation to the specific disability of the person to be disfavored.

Making his own individualized assessment in his case, Fiedler dismisses the threat to safety he poses as de minimis. He has, he says, ample upper body strength to move his own wheelchair rapidly up the aisles at the Avenue Grand. He also never attends a performance in a theater with a steeply sloped aisle unless he is accompanied by a companion who is willing and able to assist him in the event of an emergency. Moreover, he states, he customarily waits for the other patrons to exit before he leaves a movie theater. He observes that the likelihood of a theater fire is so remote — none having occurred in the United States, he says, in more than fifty years — and of a magnitude sufficient to force a general evacuation of the audience, given modern fire safety precautions, is such as to render the risk to others virtually non-existent.

AMC is not so sanguine. By scattering wheelchair seating throughout the audience, unless all of a theater's emergency exits are equipped with ramps (as those at the Avenue Grand are not), a wheelchair-bound patron can exit only at the rear, which he can reach only by negotiating his way up the aisle from a seat toward the screen. In event of an emergency evacuation, he would be proceeding against substantial crowd traffic heading for nearer exits in the opposite direction. Even those patrons moving in the same direction but behind the wheelchair will be able to proceed only at a pace determined by the ability of the occupant of the wheelchair to propel his or her chair upgrade.

A theater fire, moreover, while representing the classic crisis situation, is not the only event that could precipitate the flight of the audience: a bomb threat, a deranged patron with a gun, or a riot could have a similar effect.

Finally, the cases cited by plaintiff are only marginally apposite. Fiedler's prayer for relief is not concerned with AMC's policies, practices, or procedures, but with its structural amenities. Thus, unlike policies, practices, and procedures — which are more readily adaptable and can be discretely applied in individual cases — structural changes, such as wheelchair seating dispersed throughout a movie theater, once built, would be available not only to Fiedler, but also to other handicapped individuals who may pose a far greater "direct threat" to other patrons than Fiedler.

Therefore, the "individualized assessment" called for in this case will require the taking of evidence to determine not only whether Mr. Fiedler's presence in the fourth or fifth row of the Avenue Grand Theater in his wheelchair poses a significant risk to his fellow theater-goers, but also whether others similarly limited by disability, but less agile or prudent than he, might also do so, and whether AMC can readily achieve an accommodation that might ameliorate the dangers so posed.

NOTES

1. There have been a number of cases involving movie theaters and sports venues since this decision. Some of the issues raised in these cases are discussed in later sections of this chapter. See also LAURA ROTHSTEIN & JULIA ROTHSTEIN, DISABILITIES AND THE LAW § 6:13 (2009) (citing cases on these and other issues).

2. Hotels and casinos are also covered entities. In *Long v. Coast Resorts, Inc.*, 49 F. Supp. 2d 1177 (D. Nev. 1999), a hotel/casino was ordered to provide additional counter space in all bar areas in order to provide wheelchair users with bar access in each bar in the casino. The court found that wheelchair users should be able to use every bar in the casino, as each had its own theme and ambiance. Does that mean that every patron should be able to reach every section of the room?

[2] Accessibility Requirements

Programs subject to Section 504 of the Rehabilitation Act must meet its requirements. 34 C.F.R. §§ 104.21–.23. These requirements apply to both private and public entities receiving federal financial assistance. Private entities such as colleges and hospitals are covered by these requirements.

All programs subject to Section 504 are to be readily accessible when viewed in their entirety. 34 C.F.R. § 104.22(a). Programs were to have conducted a self evaluation and developed a transition plan for removing barriers necessary to carry out this requirement. 34 C.F.R. § 104.22(e). Thus, Section 504 does not require retrofitting of existing facilities to meet the same degree of accessibility that would be required for new construction and substantial alterations. Construction and alterations made after June 3, 1977, were to have met specified accessibility standards.

The ADA has very detailed and specific guidelines for new construction contained in the Americans with Disabilities Act Accessibility Guidelines (ADAAG). Existing facilities in programs subject to Title III of the ADA are subject to the requirement that barriers should be removed to the extent it is readily achievable to do so. This was to have been done by January 26, 1992. 28 C.F.R. § 36.304. "Readily achievable" means easily accomplishable without much difficulty or expense. 28 C.F.R. § 36.304.

For Title III covered programs, new construction and alterations made after January 26, 1993, are to meet ADA Accessibility Guidelines for Buildings and Facilities. 28 C.F.R. pt. 36, app. A. One of the major issues that can arise under the ADA is whether a change rises to the level of an alteration subject to these requirements. Minor changes such as a new coat of paint would not trigger the requirements. Major alterations must affect a primary function area for the requirements to apply. Therefore, repairing a roof would probably not require accessibility compliance. Even where an alteration is significant enough to trigger access requirements, programs are not required to make changes that would be unduly expensive.

[a]   Alterations

Sidewalks are an architectural feature that for most locations were in place before the effective date of the ADA. The ADA requires retrofitting only where removal is needed to make the program accessible when viewed in its entirety (Title II) or if it is readily achievable (Title III). For many municipalities, retrofitting all of the sidewalks and making curbcuts at every corner is not financially feasible. Self evaluations done in many places have prioritized such removals. The ADA, however, does expect corrections when there are alterations. The following decision involves a local governmental facility that would be covered by Title II instead of Title III, but it raises the same issue, which is when a change is considered an alteration.

KINNEY v. YERUSALIM
9 F.3d 1067 (3d Cir. 1993)

Roth, Circuit Judge:

This appeal requires us to determine whether 28 C.F.R. § 35.151(e)(1) (1992), issued by the Attorney General pursuant to Section 204 of the Americans with Disabilities Act (the "ADA"), 42 U.S.C. § 12134 requires the City of Philadelphia (the "City") to install curb ramps[7] at intersections when it resurfaces city streets.

---

[7] The terms "curb ramps" and "curb cuts" are used interchangeably.

At issue is whether resurfacing constitutes an "alteration" within the scope of the regulation.

I.

Plaintiffs are Disabled in Action, a non-profit organization, and twelve individuals with ambulatory disabilities who live and work in Philadelphia. In their complaint, plaintiffs sought injunctive relief for alleged violations of the ADA. These allegations were based on the City's practice of installing curb cuts only when work on the city streets otherwise affected the curb or sidewalk or when a complete reconstruction of the street was required.

The lack of curb cuts is a primary obstacle to the smooth integration of those with disabilities into the commerce of daily life. Without curb cuts, people with ambulatory disabilities simply cannot navigate the city; activities that are commonplace to those who are fully ambulatory become frustrating and dangerous endeavors. At present, people using wheelchairs must often make the Hobson's choice between travelling in the streets — with cars and buses and trucks and bicycles — and travelling over uncut curbs which, even when possible, may result in the wheelchair becoming stuck or overturning, with injury to both passenger and chair.

The City of Philadelphia has some 2,400 miles of streets, roads and highways. These streets typically consist of three components: a sub-base of stone, covered by a concrete base, finished with a layer of asphalt. For routine maintenance — patching, pothole repairs, and limited resurfacing — the City maintains a crew of roughly 300 people. For more extensive work, including most resurfacing, bids are solicited from outside contractors.

Resurfacing of the streets is done in a variety of ways, affecting different parts of the street structure. Resurfacing at its simplest is "paving," which consists of placing a new layer of asphalt over the old. In other instances, a more complicated process of "milling" is used to ensure proper drainage or contouring of the road. Milling requires the use of heavy machinery to remove the upper 2 to 3 1/2 inches of asphalt. During an ordinary milling and resurfacing job, cracks in the concrete base may be discovered, and, if so, repaired. The most extensive form of resurfacing is "reconstruction," which involves removal and replacement of both the asphalt and the concrete or stone layers.

Whatever the extent of work performed under a contract, the City has certain minimum requirements for resurfacing. Thus, by the City's own specifications, resurfacing requires laying at least 1 1/2 inches of new asphalt, sealing open joints and cracks, and patching depressions of more than one inch. At issue in this appeal are those resurfacings which cover, at a minimum, an entire street from intersection to intersection. Thus, we are not called upon to decide whether minor repairs or maintenance trigger the obligations of accessibility for alterations under the ADA.

At present the City does not include the installation of curb cuts in its milling and resurfacing contracts unless the curb is independently intended to be altered by the scope of the contract. Thus, only those contracts calling for alterations to curbs include curb cuts; contracts for alterations limited to the street surface itself do not.

Plaintiffs brought this class action against Alexander Hoskins, the Commissioner of the Philadelphia Streets Department, and Howard Yerusalim, the Secretary of the Pennsylvania Department of Transportation ("PennDOT"), to compel the installation of curb cuts on all streets resurfaced since the effective date of the ADA.

III.

Title II of the ADA prohibits discrimination in the provision of public services. Section 202 of the Act, 42 U.S.C. § 12132 provides: "[N]o qualified individual with a disability shall, by reason of such disability, be excluded from participation in or be denied the benefits of the services, programs, or activities of a public entity, or be subjected to discrimination by any such entity." Congress' concern with physical barriers is apparent in both the history and the text of the legislation. For example, the findings section of the Act recounts:

. . . .

(2) historically, society has tended to isolate and segregate individuals with disabilities . . . ;

(3) discrimination against individuals with disabilities persists in such critical areas as . . . transportation . . . and access to public services;

. . . .

(5) individuals with disabilities continually encounter various forms of discrimination, including . . . the discriminatory effects of architectural, transportation and communication barriers . . . .

42 U.S.C. § 12101. These general concerns led to a particular emphasis on the installation of curb cuts. The House Report for the legislation noted that "[t]he employment, transportation, and public accommodation sections of this Act would be meaningless if people who use wheelchairs were not afforded the opportunity to travel on and between the streets." As such, "under this title, local and state governments are required to provide curb cuts on public streets."

The Act itself does not set forth implementing standards, but rather directs the Attorney General to do so. 42 U.S.C. § 12134(a). As guidance, Congress directed that the regulations be consistent both with the ADA and with the coordination regulations issued by the Department of Health, Education, and Welfare under Section 504 of the Rehabilitation Act of 1973, concerning nondiscrimination by recipients of federal financial assistance. With regard to program accessibility in existing facilities and communications, Congress directed that the regulations be consistent with the Department of Justice's Section 504 regulations for federally conducted activities.

Following this mandate, the Department of Justice issued regulations maintaining the previously established distinction between existing facilities, which are covered by 28 C.F.R. § 35.150, and new construction and alterations, which are covered by 28 C.F.R. § 35.151. With limited exceptions, the regulations do not require public entities to retrofit existing facilities immediately and completely. Rather, a flexible concept of accessibility is employed, and entities are generally excused from making fundamental alterations to existing programs and bearing undue financial burdens. In contrast, the regulations concerning new construction and alterations are substantially more stringent. When a public entity independently decides to alter a facility, it "shall, to the maximum extent feasible, be altered in such a manner that the altered portion of the facility is readily accessible to and usable by individuals with disabilities." This obligation of accessibility for alterations does not allow for non-compliance based upon undue burden.

Consistent with the emphasis on architectural barriers, the installation of curb cuts is specifically given priority in both the "existing facilities" and the "new constructions and alterations" sections of the regulations. Streets are considered existing facilities under the regulations,[8] and, as such, they are subject to the more lenient provisions of § 35.150. However, because of the importance attributed to curb cuts, the regulations direct public entities to fashion a transition plan for existing facilities, containing a "schedule for providing curb ramps or other sloped areas where pedestrian walks cross curbs, giving priority to walkways serving entities covered by the Act."

The existence of a transition plan for the installation of curb cuts on existing streets does not, however, negate the City's obligations under § 35.151, governing alterations. In addition to the general provision in subpart (b), § 35.151 has a second subpart addressed solely to the installation of curb ramps. This subpart provides that when a public entity undertakes to construct new streets or to alter existing ones, it shall take that opportunity to install curb ramps.

Newly constructed or altered streets, roads, and highways must contain curb ramps or other sloped areas at any intersection having curbs or other barriers to entry from a street level pedestrian walkway. The City does not dispute the literal requirement that the regulation mandates the installation of curb cuts when the City "alters" a street. The City does, however, protest the notion that the resurfacing of a street constitutes an "alteration."

Subpart (e) does not explicitly define "alteration," either in general or as applied in particular instances. Our focus here is the specific application of the general provision in subpart (b) (alterations to existing facilities) to one subject in subpart (e) (streets). We will look first to subpart (b) for guidance:

> Alteration. Each facility or part of a facility altered by, on behalf of, or for the use of a public entity in a manner that affects or could affect the usability of the facility or part of the facility shall, to the maximum extent feasible, be altered in such a manner that the altered portion of the facility is readily accessible to and usable by individuals with disabilities, if the alteration was commenced after January 26, 1992.

---

[8] The regulations define "facility" to include "all or any portions of . . . roads, walks, [or] passageways."

In addition, subpart (c) provides that alterations made in conformity with the Americans with Disabilities Act Accessibility Guidelines for Buildings and Facilities (the "ADAAG") or with the Uniform Federal Accessibility Standards (the "UFAS") shall be deemed to comply with the requirements of this section. Both guidelines provide technical and engineering specifications. The ADAAG definition of "alteration" is substantially the same as that in the regulation: "a change to a building or facility . . . that affects or could affect the usability of the building or facility or part thereof." It continues: "[n]ormal maintenance . . . [is] not [an] alteration unless [it] affect[s] the usability of the building or facility."

These provisions lead one to the conclusion that an "alteration" within the meaning of the regulations is a change that affects the usability of the facility involved. If we then read the "affects usability" definition into subpart (e), the regulation serves the substantive purpose of requiring equal treatment: if an alteration renders a street more "usable" to those presently using it, such increased utility must also be made fully accessible to the disabled through the installation of curb ramps.

Subpart (e) effectively unifies a street and its curbs for treatment as interdependent facilities. If a street is to be altered to make it more usable for the general public, it must also be made more usable for those with ambulatory disabilities. At the time that the City determines that funds will be expended to alter the street, the City is also required to modify the curbs so that they are no longer a barrier to the usability of the streets by the disabled. This interpretation helps to implement the legislative vision, for Congress felt that it was discriminatory to the disabled to enhance or improve an existing facility without making it fully accessible to those previously excluded.

Although there is limited analysis of the "alterations" sections of Title II, the discussion of the parallel provision in Title III (addressing public accommodations) is helpful in our analysis here.[9] In the context of Title III, Congress' discussion of "affecting usability" focused on the "primary function" of a facility. "Areas containing primary functions refer to those portions of a place of public accommodations where significant goods, services, facilities, privileges, advantages or accommodations are provided."

Thus, while Congress chose not to mandate full accessibility to existing facilities, it required that subsequent changes to a facility be undertaken in a non-discriminatory manner. The use of such changes must be made available to all. The emphasis on equal treatment is furthered, as well, by an expansive, remedial construction of the term "usability." "Usability should be broadly defined to include renovations which affect the use of a facility, and not simply changes which relate directly to access."

With this directive, we must now determine whether resurfacing a street affects its usability. Both physically and functionally, a street consists of its surface; from a utilitarian perspective, a street is a two-dimensional, one-plane facility. As intended, a street facilitates smooth, safe, and efficient travel of vehicles and

---

[9] Like Title II, Title III bears the distinction between existing and new or altered facilities. Congress intended that the provisions of both titles be read consistently.

pedestrians — in the language above, this is its "primary function."

As such, we can only agree with the district court that resurfacing a street affects it in ways integral to its purpose. As discussed above, "resurfacing" involves more than minor repairs or maintenance. At a minimum, it requires the laying of a new asphalt bed spanning the length and width of a city block. The work is substantial, with substantial effect. As the district court described in its opinion . . . :

> Resurfacing makes driving on and crossing streets easier and safer. It also helps to prevent damage to vehicles and injury to people, and generally promotes commerce and travel. The surface of a street is the part of the street that is "used" by both pedestrians and vehicular traffic. When that surface is improved, the street becomes more usable in a fundamental way.

Finally, we must consider the City's suggestion that interpretation of the ADA is always subject to a requirement of reasonableness. It is true that reasonableness language appears in the text of § 35.151(b): "Each facility or part of a facility altered . . . shall, *to the maximum extent feasible*, be altered in such a manner that the altered portion of the facility is readily accessible to and usable by individuals with disabilities" (emphasis added). The City relies on a prior decision of this court, [citation omitted], interpreting a Department of Transportation regulation that is similar to 28 C.F.R. § 35.151(b).[10] There we stated that the relevant questions were "to what extent any alterations to a facility provide an opportunity to make the facility more accessible to handicapped persons" and "what degree of accessibility . . . becomes 'feasible' within the scope of alterations." Because the . . . regulation referred to "accessibility" rather than "usability," with resulting limits on scope and effect, the district court found the case to be inapposite. We need not decide that issue. Were we considering alterations only covered by § 35.151(b), the relevance of [that decision] would be at issue. However, in this case the Attorney General has already determined, in promulgating § 35.151(e), that the installation of curb cuts is feasible during the course of alterations to a street. Subpart (e) is a specific application of the general principle contained in subpart (b).

IV.

As a final argument, the City contends that, even if resurfacing is an "alteration" requiring the installation of curb cuts, it is entitled to assert an "undue burden" defense excusing compliance. There is no general undue burden defense in the ADA. Rather, following the Section 504 regulations for program access in existing facilities, as Congress intended, the ADA regulations provide for the defense only in limited circumstances. For example, § 35.150(a)(3), governing "existing facilities," excuses a public entity from taking "any action that it can demonstrate would result in a fundamental alteration in the nature of a service, program, or activity or

---

[10] The regulation was promulgated to comply with Section 504 of the Rehabilitation Act of 1973, also the predecessor to section 202 of the ADA. The regulation is as follows:

> Each facility or part of a facility which is altered by, on behalf of, or for the use of a recipient [of Federal financial assistance] . . . in a manner that affects or could affect the accessibility of the facility shall, to the maximum extent feasible, be altered in such a manner that the altered portion of the facility is readily accessible to and usable by handicapped persons.

in undue financial and administrative burdens."

As discussed above, there are logical reasons for the distinction between existing and new or altered facilities. Allowance of an undue burden defense for existing facilities serves as recognition that modification of such facilities may impose extraordinary costs. New construction and alterations, however, present an immediate opportunity to provide full accessibility. Congress recognized the competing social interests at stake: "While the integration of people with disabilities will sometimes involve substantial short-term burdens, both financial and administrative, the long-range effects of integration will benefit society as a whole." Balancing these interests, Congress acknowledged the existence of an undue burden defense for existing facilities but clearly warned, "[n]o other limitation should be implied in other areas."

The City acknowledges that the defense is not available for alterations. Nonetheless, it makes a last-ditch attempt at characterizing a street and its curbs as separate facilities. As such, a curb would remain an existing facility susceptible to the "undue burden" defense even while the street that it abuts is being altered. As with our discussion . . . above, the express language of § 35.151(e) refutes this reasoning. That section requires the installation of curb ramps if a street is altered. When the City decides that funds are available for the alteration of the street, the City must now understand that such a determination is to be made with the awareness that subpart (e) also requires alteration of the curbs. Thus, once the City undertakes to resurface a street, the accompanying curbs are no longer to be considered as existing facilities, subject to the "undue burden" defense of § 35.150(a)(3). They are now, pursuant to the language of subpart (e), incorporated with a facility under alteration, pursuant to § 35.151, so that the "undue burden" defense is no longer available.

V.

For the foregoing reasons, we find that resurfacing of the city streets is an alteration within the meaning of 28 C.F.R. § 35.151(b) which must be accompanied by the installation of curb cuts under 28 C.F.R. § 35.151(e). We will affirm the decision of the district court.

NOTE

The chapter on governmental services (Chapter 5) includes an excerpt from the Supreme Court decision in *Pennsylvania Department of Corrections v. Yeskey*, 524 U.S. 206 (1998). The excerpt focuses on whether prisons are covered under Title II of the ADA. A later section includes an excerpt in the Supreme Court's decision in *Tennessee v. Lane*, 541 U.S. 509 (2004), focusing on whether state and local governmental agencies are immune from damage actions under Title II in cases involving access to the judicial system. These decisions together mean that such programs are covered, and that they are subject to damages as a remedy. What they do not decide is what is specifically required in terms of architectural access for jails, prisons, courthouses, police stations, and other criminal justice facilities. These are challenging issues, because most of them are existing facilities and their use for criminal justice includes challenging issues of safety and security. In the case of courthouses, many are historical structures built decades ago, and exist in areas where economic challenges make it difficult to engage in expensive retrofitting. For cases on these issues, see LAURA ROTHSTEIN & JULIA ROTHSTEIN, DISABILITIES AND THE LAW § 9:11 (2009) (citing cases on these and other issues).

[b]   Existing Facilities

The next decision involves a facility that is subject to Title III of the ADA and demonstrates the concerns about what is required of existing facilities. It provides a broad overview of the various defenses that might be raised.

PINNOCK v. INTERNATIONAL HOUSE OF PANCAKES
844 F. Supp. 574 (S.D. Cal. 1993)

RHOADES, DISTRICT JUDGE:

I. *Background*

Plaintiff, Theodore A. Pinnock ("Pinnock") filed the complaint in this action against Defendant, Majid Zahedi, owner of an International House of Pancakes franchise ("Zahedi"). Pinnock, an attorney representing himself, is unable to walk and uses a wheelchair. Pinnock dined at the defendant's restaurant on June 21, 1992, and then attempted to use the restroom. The entrance to the restroom, however, was not wide enough to admit his wheelchair. Pinnock therefore removed himself from his wheelchair and crawled into the restroom. As a result of this encounter, Pinnock alleges nine causes of action against Zahedi. Five of the causes of action arise under state law, alleging violations of the state health and safety code, the Unruh Civil Rights Act, and infliction of emotional distress. The remaining four causes of action are alleged under the Americans with Disabilities Act of 1990 ("ADA"), arising from Zahedi's alleged failure to comply with the statute's provisions governing access for disabled individuals in public accommodations ("title III").

Zahedi argues that Congress does not have constitutional authority to regulate his facility, asserting that title III of the ADA exceeds the powers granted Congress by the U.S. Constitution. Congress enacted title III pursuant to Article I, Section 8, of the United States Constitution, which grants Congress the power to "regulate Commerce . . . among the several States" and to enact all laws necessary and proper to this end. The Supreme Court has consistently held that Congress is empowered under the Commerce Clause to regulate not only interstate activities, but also intrastate activities that substantially affect interstate commerce. The Commerce Clause allows Congress to regulate any entity, regardless of its individual impact on interstate commerce, so long as the entity engages in a class of activities that affects interstate commerce.

Courts must defer to congressional findings that an activity affects commerce, so long as there is a rational basis for such a finding. As the Supreme Court recognized in the context of racial discrimination, the restaurant industry unquestionably affects interstate commerce in a substantial way.

Even aside from its membership in an interstate industry, Zahedi's restaurant demonstrates characteristics which place it squarely in the category of interstate commerce. It is a franchise of a large, international, publicly traded corporation ("IHOP Corp."), organized under Delaware law. IHOP Corp. had total retail sales of $479 million in 1992, operates 547 franchises in thirty-five states, Canada, and Japan, and employs 16,000 persons. Furthermore, Zahedi's restaurant is located directly across the street from State Highway 163, and within two miles of two interstate highways. There are three hotels within walking distance, and three motels within one and one-half miles of the restaurant. The courts have found these facts to be indicia of a business operating in interstate commerce.

Congressional enactment of title III of the ADA was well within Congress' power to regulate interstate commerce under the Commerce Clause. As part of the restaurant industry, Zahedi is subject to the provisions of title III, which by its own terms, reaches as broadly as the Commerce Clause permits. As a member of the restaurant industry and as an individual enterprise which caters to travelers, Zahedi's restaurant is properly regulated by title III of the ADA.

III. *Title III of the ADA is Not Unconstitutionally Vague*

Zahedi argues that many of the terms used in section 12182(b)(2) of title III are unconstitutionally vague and are therefore in violation of the Due Process Clause of the Fifth Amendment. Statutes which fail to adequately specify the actions or conduct necessary to conform with the law pose problems for which the Supreme Court has expressed serious concern. However, the terms with which Zahedi takes issue do not deprive private businesses of the ability to steer between lawful and unlawful conduct. To the contrary, the statute, its preamble, the legislative history, and the accompanying guidelines provide more than ample explanation of the statute's application.

A. *Statutes Regulating Commercial Activity are Subject to Lower Standards of Specificity*

Vagueness challenges are considered under varying standards, depending upon the nature of the statute. Statutes which threaten to inhibit freedom of speech or other constitutionally protected rights face a more stringent vagueness test. Criminal statutes, in general, face a higher vagueness standard than do civil statutes: "The Court has . . . expressed greater tolerance of enactments with civil rather than criminal penalties because the consequences of imprecision are qualitatively less severe." *Village of Hoffman Estates v. Flipside*, 455 U.S. 489 (1982).

By contrast, purely economic regulations are subject to lower standards of specificity. . . . Title III of the ADA is a civil statute regulating commercial conduct. As such, Zahedi can successfully sustain its challenge only if he can prove that the enactment specifies "no standard of conduct . . . at all."

B. *Limiting Constructions Offered by the Department of Justice are Properly Considered*

In evaluating a vagueness challenge, a court should consider the words of the ordinance, interpretations given to analogous statutes, and "the interpretation of the statute given by those charged with enforcing it."

Zahedi argues that the limiting constructions offered by the Department of Justice should not be considered when examining the statute for vagueness because none of the cases cited by the Government involve federal statutes. [W]hen federal and state statutes are challenged on the same constitutional grounds, they should be held to the same standard. The reasons for applying limiting constructions to state statutes apply with equal force to federal statutes. Therefore, the limiting constructions offered by the Department of Justice and the title III Technical Assistance Manual, which are available to the public, are properly considered.

C. *Each of the Challenged Terms, When Considered in Conjunction With Limiting Constructions, is Sufficiently Precise*

[T]he terms of title III are marked by well-reasoned flexibility and breadth. When considered in conjunction with the Department of Justice guidelines, these terms are not unconstitutionally vague.

1. *Readily Achievable Barrier Removal*

Title III requires existing places of public accommodation to remove architectural barriers to access, where such removal is "readily achievable." 42 U.S.C. § 12182(b)(2)(A)(iv). The term is defined in the statute as "easily accomplishable and able to be carried out without much difficulty or expense." 42 U.S.C. § 12181(9). The statute enumerates four factors to consider when determining whether a modification is readily achievable, and the legislative history lists examples of the types of changes Congress believes are readily achievable. These include specific examples for small stores and restaurants such as rearranging tables and chairs and installing small ramps and grab bars in restrooms.

In addition, the federal regulation further elucidates the term "readily achievable" by adding other factors. These include the overall financial resources of the parent corporation and safety requirements. 28 C.F.R. § 36.104, at 460–61. The regulation lists 21 examples of barrier removal likely to be "readily achievable" in many circumstances, such as installing ramps and repositioning shelves and telephones.

Finally, the preamble to the regulation provides further explanation and notes that use of a more specific standard would contravene the goals of the ADA:

> the Department has declined to establish in the final rule any kind of numerical formula for determining whether an action is readily achievable. It would be difficult to devise a specific ceiling on compliance costs that would take into account the vast diversity of enterprises covered by the

ADA's public accommodation requirements and the economic situation that any particular entity would find itself in at any moment.

The specifications easily met the requirements for economic regulation announced in *Hoffman Estates*.

2. *Alternatives to Barrier Removal*

Title III provides that where barrier removal is not readily achievable, a covered entity must make its goods or services available through "alternative methods if such methods are readily achievable." 42 U.S.C. § 12182(b)(2)(A)(v). The legislative history, the regulation itself, and the preamble all provide specific examples of appropriate alternatives to barrier removal. These include providing curb service or home delivery, coming to the door of the facility to handle transactions, serving beverages at a table for persons with disabilities where a bar is inaccessible, providing assistance to retrieve items from inaccessible shelves, and relocating services and activities to accessible locations. These provisions also meet the specificity requirements for economic regulations.

3. *Reasonable Modifications of Policies and Procedures*

The statute requires public accommodations to: make reasonable modifications in policies, practices or procedures, when such modifications are necessary to afford such goods, services . . . to individuals with disabilities, unless the entity can demonstrate that making such modifications would fundamentally alter the nature of such goods, services, facilities, privileges, advantages, or accommodations; 42 U.S.C. § 12182(b)(2)(A)(ii). Zahedi argues that the phrases "reasonable modifications" and "fundamentally alter" are unconstitutionally vague.

Illustrations of the term "reasonable modifications" are provided in the title III regulation and its preamble. For example, stores in which all of the checkout aisles are not accessible are required to ensure that an adequate number of accessible checkout aisles are left open at all times. Likewise, facilities that do not permit entry to animals would be required to modify such policies as they apply to service animals accompanying disabled individuals.

The preamble to the title III regulation contains a lengthy explanation of the concept of fundamental alteration, and explains that the "rule does not require modifications to the legitimate areas of specialization of service providers." The preamble also provides an example of an acceptable referral to another provider who specializes in a requested service.

Furthermore, as the Government points out, the term "fundamentally alter" has been previously used in *Southeastern Community College v. Davis*, 442 U.S. 397 (1979). That decision construed section 504 of the Rehabilitation Act of 1973, which prohibits discrimination on the basis of disability in federally assisted or operated programs or activities. In *Davis*, the Court concluded that programs did not discriminate if they failed to make accommodations that would "fundamentally alter" the nature of the program. The terms "reasonable modifications" and "fundamental alteration" are therefore not unconstitutionally vague.

4. *Most Integrated Setting Appropriate*

Title III requires covered entities to afford their goods and services to an individual with a disability "in the most integrated setting appropriate to the needs of the individual." 42 U.S.C. § 12182(b)(1)(B). The preamble to the title III regulation provides two pages of examples and explanations illustrating the meaning of this provision. One example provides that it would be a violation of this provision to require persons with mental disabilities to eat in the back room of a restaurant or to refuse to allow a person with a disability to full use of a health spa because of stereotypes about the person's ability to participate. The legislative history provides further illustration, noting that the "integrated settings" provision is intended to prevent segregation based on fears and stereotypes about persons with disabilities. The term "most integrated setting appropriate," as used in title III, is not unconstitutionally vague.

5. *Undue Burden*

Under title III, public accommodations are required to provide auxiliary aids in order to extend their services to persons with disabilities, unless to do so would pose an "undue burden" to the covered entity or would "fundamentally alter" the nature of its goods or services. 42 U.S.C. § 12182(b)(2)(A)(iii). The term "undue burden" is defined in the regulation as a "significant difficulty or expense." The regulation lists factors for determining whether a particular action will create an undue burden. These are the same factors as those provided for assessing whether an action is "readily achievable." The preamble, however, clarifies that: "[R]eadily achievable" is a lower standard than "undue burden" in that it requires a lower level of effort on the part of the public accommodation. . . . [A] public accommodation is not required to provide any particular aid or service that would result in either a fundamental alteration in the nature of the goods, services, facilities, privileges, advantages, or accommodations offered or in an undue burden. Both of these statutory limitations are derived from case law under section 504 [of the Rehabilitation Act of 1973] and are to be applied on a case-by-case basis . . . . Furthermore, the regulation is supplemented by discussion in the Technical Assistance Manual, which provides explanations of both "undue burden" and "fundamental alteration."

6. *Full and Equal Enjoyment and Opportunity to Participate*

Title III's general prohibition against discrimination provides as follows: "No individual shall be discriminated against on the basis of disability in the full and equal enjoyment of the goods, services, facilities, privileges, advantages, or accommodations of any place of public accommodation. . . . " 42 U.S.C. § 12182(a). Zahedi claims that the phrase "full and equal enjoyment" is impermissibly vague. However, the next subsection of the statute, entitled "Construction" enumerates categories of actions that constitute such discrimination. These categories include denying a person with a disability public accommodations, or providing accommodations not equal to that afforded to other individuals.

Furthermore, the legislative history explains that [f]ull and equal enjoyment does not encompass the notion that persons with disabilities must achieve the identical result or level of achievement of nondisabled persons, but does mean that persons with disabilities must be afforded equal opportunity to obtain the same result. Thus, the terms "full and equal enjoyment" are given ample operational definition, as are the specific subsections of this provision that Zahedi challenges. As the government argues, the prohibition denying individuals with disabilities an "opportunity to participate in or benefit from" the goods or services of a covered entity clearly means that persons with disabilities may not be excluded from receiving the services of a place of public accommodation.

IV. *Title III is Not Retroactive Legislation*

Zahedi challenges the ADA on the grounds that it is retroactive legislation and therefore violates the Due Process Clause of the Fifth Amendment.

The fact that title III applies to existing places of public accommodation does not render the statute retroactive. Congress routinely acts to regulate existing businesses, programs, and structures, imposing new guidelines which reflect the changing social and environmental standards of our democratic system. The fact that such legislation affects existing entities does not insulate responsible parties from compliance with the law.

The relevant inquiry is whether the legislation imposes liability or penalty for conduct occurring prior to the effective date of the statute. "The determination of whether a statute's application in a particular situation is prospective or retroactive depends upon whether the conduct that allegedly triggers the statute's application occurs before or after the law's effective date." The ADA provided an 18 month notice period in which businesses could comply with the Act's requirements, and no liability was imposed prior to the end of that period. Small businesses were given an even lengthier notice period. Pinnock's complaint was not filed until September 9, 1992, nearly two years after the ADA was passed on July 26, 1990. The requirements of the title III do not subject Zahedi to retroactive legislation.

V. *Promulgation by the Attorney General's Office of Regulations Implementing the Provisions of Title III of the ADA is not an Unconstitutional Delegation of Authority by Congress*

[Omitted.]

VI. *Requiring Alterations to Property in Compliance with Title III of the ADA Is Not an Unconstitutional Taking Without Just Compensation*

Zahedi contends that the expenditure of funds necessary to make the restrooms in his facility accessible to individuals in wheelchairs, if required under the ADA, would constitute a taking of private property "for public use, without just compensation" in violation of the Fifth Amendment's Due Process Clause. In *Lucas v. South Carolina Coastal Council*, 112 S. Ct. 2886 (1992), the Supreme Court delineated three situations in which a governmental restraint is considered a taking, therefore requiring compensation. These three situations are: 1) When the regulation compels a permanent physical invasion of the property; 2) When the regulation denies an owner all economically beneficial or productive use of its land; 3) When the regulation in question does not substantially advance a legitimate governmental objective. If either of the first two situations occur, the regulation will be considered a taking regardless of whether the action achieves an important public benefit or has only minimal impact on the owner. The expenditure of funds required by title III does not constitute a taking under the Fifth Amendment as defined in *Lucas*.

[Authors' Note: The remainder of this discussion is omitted, but holds that compliance with the ADA is not a physical taking, a denial of all economically beneficial or productive use of the owner's land, and Title III substantially advances a legitimate governmental interest.]

VII. *Title III does not Intrude Upon State Sovereignty in Violation of the Tenth Amendment*

[Omitted.]

VIII. *Conclusion*

A district court . . . is limited to considering the constitutionality of the challenged regulations, rather than their political or economic desirability. Although members of the judiciary have occasionally taken forays into the political arena, I agree with Justice Frankfurter, who once noted: "The Framers carefully and with deliberate forethought refused to so enthrone the judiciary."

Having carefully considered each of Zahedi's constitutional challenges, it is clear that none of these challenges can prevail. The United States' cross-motion for summary judgment is granted. Zahedi's motion for summary judgment is denied, and Zahedi's counterclaim is dismissed.

NOTE

Wilderness Areas: Must the Grand Canyon be accessible? The answer is "sort of." Congress recognized that many wilderness areas would be infeasible to make accessible, and provided for study of this issue. 42 U.S.C. § 12207. Hiking trails maintained by the United States Government would fall under this part of the ADA. What about private vendors licensed to operate in national wilderness areas? Are they subject to Title III or this federal wilderness area requirement? What would be the theories under which an individual might seek redress against a lodge that had not removed architectural barriers? Who would be the defendant(s)?

PROBLEMS

1. If a professional football team contracts to use a domed stadium owned by the county, who is liable for failure to meet accessibility guidelines? Which guidelines apply, those for Title II or Title III? Alexandra Hardy, *Disabled Hope Dome Pact Means More Than Seats*, Houston Post, June 26, 1993, at A29.

2. Must a state-operated lottery program ensure that all vendors of lottery tickets meet accessibility requirements? The State of Texas has implemented a policy of inspecting stores with lottery licenses and revoking those licenses where the merchants do not meet Title II accessibility standards. According to a 1994 survey by the Texas Lottery Commission, 65 percent of Lottery Retailers have obstacles to people with disabilities from the door to the checkout counter. Retailers are entitled to a one percent bonus of lottery winnings, but the money can be withheld if the store does not meet disability requirements.

Lottery programs are an interesting avenue for encouraging access because of the method of distribution. The state agency granting the license to sell lottery tickets does not necessarily have to demonstrate accessibility to receive the license, although there should be an expectation of accessibility. When lottery programs sell winning tickets, the states have an opportunity to check for access before giving the vendor the share for selling the winning ticket. This has the potential for being an area for advocates to monitor and enforce. For additional cases on lotteries, see LAURA ROTHSTEIN & JULIA ROTHSTEIN, DISABILITIES AND THE LAW § 6:13 (2009). Should states be required to monitor access before granting the license? See *Paxton v. State Dept. of Tax & Revenue*, 192 W. Va. 213, 451 S.E.2d 779 (1994) (holding that the state lottery commission is required by the ADA to ensure that vendors selling lottery tickets be accessible).

3. Is an adult nightclub with a stage for nude dancing in violation of Title I of the ADA because a nude dancer in a wheelchair would be unable to access the dance area? No one in a wheelchair had applied to work as a nude dancer at the nightclub, and the area for customers was accessible. Mike Comeaux, *L.A. Pulls the Plug on Club Shower*, HOUSTON CHRONICLE, April 21, 1994, at A19.

4. An associate minister at a church becomes mobility impaired as a result of the progressive symptoms of multiple sclerosis. The church refuses to build ramps or make other structural changes to provide her access to carry out her job. Does this violate the ADA? Steven A. Holmes, *When the Disabled Face Rejection From Churches That Nurtured Them*, N.Y. TIMES, Sept. 30, 1991, at A8.

[c]   New Construction

There are certainly challenges to ensuring access for existing facilities. There is less understanding where a new facility subject to the ADA or other discrimination statute is built without meeting access design standards. There are some standards that are not as clear, and there are occasionally conflicts between federal, state, and local requirements. One of the questions that arises when there is new construction that is not in compliance is whether the party who contracted to have the facility built is the only party liable, or whether the architects and/or engineers might also be directly liable under the ADA or other statute. The following case highlights one perspective. It also demonstrates how substantive protection is only the first step to compliance. Without adequate enforcement or remedies, the promise of these requirements may not be met.

PARALYZED VETERANS OF AMERICA v. ELLERBE BECKET ARCHITECTS & ENGINEERS
945 F. Supp. 1 (D.D.C. 1996)

THOMAS F. HOGAN, DISTRICT JUDGE.

The plaintiffs brought this action seeking declaratory and injunctive relief in connection with the building of the MCI Center, a sports and multi-purpose arena now being erected in Washington, D.C. In Count I of the complaint, the plaintiffs allege that the design and construction of the arena violate the ADA. Among the named defendants are Ellerbe Becket Architects & Engineers, P.C. and Ellerbe Becket, Inc. The former is the architectural and engineering firm that designed the arena, and the latter is its parent company. These two defendants argue that the ADA does not hold architects liable for the design and construction of facilities in violation of the statute's provisions.

Two provisions of the ADA are relevant to architects' potential liability. First, § 302(a) states that "[n]o individual shall be discriminated against on the basis of disability in the full and equal enjoyment of . . . any place of public accommodation by any person who owns, leases . . . or operates a place of public accommodation." It is conceded in this case that the Ellerbe defendants do not own, lease, or operate the MCI Center. This is typical of construction work: architects generally provide their design services by contract to other parties involved in the project. Therefore, standing alone, § 302(a) does not provide grounds for a suit against the Ellerbe defendants.

The next provision of the ADA, § 303, is entitled "New construction and alteration in public accommodations and commercial facilities," and states that as applied to public accommodations and commercial facilities, discrimination for purposes of section 302(a) includes . . . a failure to design and construct facilities . . . that are readily accessible to and usable by individuals with disabilities.

The plaintiffs argue that since § 303 mentions the design function, the provision encompasses architects. However, the plain language of the statute reveals at least two reasons why this argument is untenable. First, the phrase "design and construct" is distinctly conjunctive. It refers only to parties responsible for both functions, such as general contractors or facilities owners who hire the necessary design and construction experts for each project. Since architects in general, and the Ellerbe defendants in particular, are not responsible for both the design and the construction of the MCI Center, § 303 does not refer to them. Second, § 303 defines "discrimination for purposes of § 302(a)." Therefore, the limitation in § 302 to owners, operators, and lessors also applies to § 303 and thereby excludes architects from liability under the section.

The United States Department of Justice filed an amicus brief arguing that its interpretation of § 303, which includes architects as liable parties, should be awarded the deference described in *Chevron v. Natural Resources Defense Council*, 467 U.S. 837 (1984). However, the issue of such deference only arises when the statute is ambiguous. "If the intent of Congress is clear, that is the end of the matter." Because the plain language of the statute makes clear that architects are not covered by §§ 302 and 303 of the ADA, there is no need for the Court to apply the second part of the *Chevron* analysis and consider the interpretation pressed by the Department of Justice.

The Court's interpretation does not frustrate the intent of the statutory scheme. If entities who are responsible for both design and construction can be held liable for violations of the ADA, those entities will ensure that the firms or individuals with whom they contract — experts in design or construction — will hew to the dictates of the statute and regulations. If a violation is nonetheless alleged, interested parties with standing may seek effective relief by naming as defendants the high-level entities responsible for both design and construction, as the remaining defendants in this case are aware.

NOTES

1. On April 24, 1998, Ellerbe Becket architectural firm entered into a consent decree with the Department of Justice in which they agreed that future designs would ensure appropriate line of sight seating for wheelchair users. In addition to the MCI Center, the firm had designed four other sports arenas that were the subject of the original Department of Justice Act. The Department itself agreed not to bring enforcement actions with respect to any of those facilities. The settlement leaves undecided whether architects or architectural firms may be held liable under Title III of the ADA, nor does it resolve suits brought by private plaintiffs, such as Paralyzed Veterans. *United States v. Ellerbe Becket, Inc.*, C.A. No. 4-96-995 (D. Minn. Consent Decree 1998). For additional cases on this issue, see LAURA ROTHSTEIN & JULIA ROTHSTEIN, DISABILITIES AND THE LAW § 6:13 (2009).

2. There has been a substantial amount of litigation involving stadium seating in movie theaters. The issue is whether the front row seats, which are accessible to wheelchair users, provide reasonable access. The angle of view can be quite uncomfortable for anyone, but particularly an individual with a spinal cord injury or other mobility impairment. The stadium seating areas have generally been designed so that they are reached only by use of steps. The current trend by most, although not all, courts is that such design violates the ADA because it does not allow for a comparable line of sight for viewing angles. See LAURA ROTHSTEIN & JULIA ROTHSTEIN, DISABILITIES AND THE LAW Ch. 5 (2009), for cases on this issue.

E EXEMPTIONS FROM THE ADA AND SPECIAL SITUATIONS

[1] Religious Entities

Title III of the ADA does not apply to "religious organizations or entities controlled by religious organizations, including places of worship." 42 U.S.C. § 12187; 28 C.F.R. § 36.102(e). The analysis accompanying the regulations clarifies the application. For example:

> [I]f a church itself operates a day care center, a nursing home, a private school, or a diocesan school system, the operations of the center, home,

school or schools would not be subject to the requirements of the ADA . . . merely because the services provided were open to the general public. The test is whether the church or other religious organization operates the public accommodation, not which individuals receive the public accommodation's services . . . .

The test [is] whether the church or other religious organization controls the operations of the school or of the service or whether the school or service is itself a religious organization . . . .

[A] public accommodation . . . that operates a place of public accommodation in leased space on the property of a religious entity, which is not a place of worship, is subject to the rule's requirements if it is not under control of a religious organization.

46 Fed. Reg. 35554 (July 26, 1991).

PROBLEM

Would a private Jewish day school that receives federal financial assistance through meal subsidies be subject to any mandates relating to nondiscrimination on the basis of disability? What information would be necessary to decide this question?

[2]   Private Clubs

Just as private clubs are exempt from other federal civil rights statutes, Title III of the ADA specifically exempts private clubs or establishments, except to the extent that the facilities are made available to customers or patrons of a place of public accommodation. 42 U.S.C. § 12187; 28 C.F.R. § 36.102(e). The definition of what constitutes a private club is found in Title II of the Civil Rights Act of 1964, 42 U.S.C. § 2000-a(e). Courts deciding whether the exemption applies have considered factors such as

the degree of member control of club operations, the selectivity of the membership selection process, whether substantial membership fees are charged, whether the entity is operated on a nonprofit basis, the extent to which the facilities are open to the public, the degree of public funding, and whether the club was created specifically to avoid compliance with the Civil Rights Act.

56 Fed. Reg. 35552 (July 26, 1991).

For example, a wedding held at a country club where membership is truly private would not be subject to Title III of the ADA. If, however, a continuing education program were held at the club, sponsored by a private entity with enrollment open to the public, the exemption would probably not apply for purposes of the event.

The case of *Martin v. PGA Tour, Inc.* excerpted *supra* in section A should be reviewed at this point.

PROBLEMS

1. If an individual using a wheelchair wishing to attend the education program found that barriers had not been removed to make attendance possible, would there be liability against the club, the sponsor of the education program, or both entities? Assume that barriers could be removed without undue burden.

2. Is a Boy Scout troop that uses donated space in a private club subject to Title III requirements? Is the club? See 56 Fed. Reg. 35556 (July 26, 1991).

3. Would a private club operating a day care center open only to its own members be subject to Title III? What about a church that offers day care only to members? See *id.*

[3]   Mixed Use Residential Facilities

One of the specified categories of public accommodations relates to places of lodging. The statute lists the following:

> an inn, hotel, motel, or other place of lodging, except for an establishment located within a building that contains not more than five rooms for rent or hire and that is actually occupied by the proprietor of such establishment as the residence of such proprietor.

42 U.S.C. § 12181(7)(A). The regulations clarify that facilities covered by the Fair Housing Act of 1968, as amended in 1988, 42 U.S.C. § 3601 et seq., are not subject to Title III mandates. 28 C.F.R. § 36.104. Thus, an apartment building would be subject to the Fair Housing Act, but probably not Title III of the ADA.

It has been recognized, however, that facilities may have mixed use.

> For example, in a large hotel that has a separate residential apartment wing, the residential wing would not be covered by the ADA because of the nature of the occupancy of that part of the facility. This residential wing would, however, be covered by the Fair Housing Act. The separate nonresidential accommodations in the rest of the hotel would be a place of lodging, and thus a public accommodation subject to the requirements of this final rule. If a hotel allows both residential and short-term stays, but does not allocate space for these different uses in separate, discrete units, both the ADA and the Fair Housing Act may apply to the facility.
>
> . . . Although [residential] hotels or portions of such hotels may fall under the Fair Housing Act when operated or used as long-term residences, they are also considered "places of lodging" under the ADA when guests of such hotels are free to use them on a short-term basis. In addition, "single room occupancy hotels" may provide social services to their guests. . . . In such a situation, the facility would be considered a "social service center establishment" and thus covered by the ADA as a place of public accommodation, regardless of the length of stay of the occupants.

56 Fed. Reg. 35552 (July 26, 1991) (Regulatory Analysis).

PROBLEM

Would homeless shelters or battered women's shelters be subject to the Fair Housing Act, Title III of the ADA, or any other statutes? What information would be needed to decide this issue?

[4]   Leased Space

The regulations under Title III of the ADA provide that

> Both the landlord who owns the building that houses a place of public accommodation and the tenant who owns or operates the place of public accommodation are public accommodations subject to the requirements of this part. As between the parties, allocation of responsibility for complying with the obligations of this part may be determined by lease or other contract.

28 C.F.R. § 36.201(b).

The analysis of this regulation is interesting in its recognition of allocating responsibility when the lease is either silent on the tenant's right to make alterations or where the lease prohibits the landlord from entering the premises to make alterations. The analysis further notes the issue that is raised when a lease contains a "compliance clause," allocating responsibility for complying with various legal requirements. The analysis also recognizes a number of practical problems with this kind of shared responsibility. Other questions relating to short term leases were raised. The interpretation of the regulation, however, specifies that the time remaining in a lease is not a factor in allocating responsibility for accessibility, but is relevant to the factual issue of what is readily achievable in a particular instance. 56 Fed. Reg. 35555–35556 (July 26, 1991). The analysis somewhat naively notes that

> As between the landlord and tenant, the extent of responsibility for particular obligations may be, and in many cases probably will be, determined by contract.

Id. at 35556. First, many long term leases, such as a lease by a major department store in a shopping center, may have been negotiated long before 1990. These leases may include general compliance clauses, but were not written in contemplation of the major affirmative responsibilities that would accrue as a result of the ADA. Second, many leases are silent on these types of responsibilities. Questions arising from the landlord/tenant relationship are likely to be the subject of much debate, either through negotiation of new leases or renegotiation of existing leases or through litigation after an individual with a disability seeks relief against the landlord and/or tenant. See Wade Lambert, *Disabilities Act May Spur Lease Changes*, WALL ST. J., April 5, 1994, at B7.

PROBLEMS

1.   If a restaurant leasing space in a building refuses to seat a patron because he or she is blind, who is likely to be liable as between the restaurant owner and the building owner in a Title III action? What if the restaurant has inaccessible restrooms? See 56 Fed. Reg. 35556 (July 26, 1991). See James R. Carrsel, *Veterans*

Take Aim at Hilton, COURIER JOURNAL, May 8, 2006, at A1 (regarding termination of a restaurant lease with a hotel and disputes over access).

2. What if the lease in the previous problem specified a "no pets" rule, and the tenant refused to allow a blind patron's guide dog onto the premises as a result, who is likely to be liable as between the restaurant owner and the building owner in a Title III action? See 56 Fed. Reg. 35556 (July 26, 1991).

[5]   Parent/Subsidiary Responsibility

Like the landlord/tenant issue, the parent/subsidiary relationship promises to be a topic of debate. The responsibility for nondiscrimination, for removing barriers and for making other accommodations will have to be resolved on a case-by-case basis. The Department of Justice responded to numerous commenters seeking guidance about this issue in its analysis of the Title III regulations by stating just that. The Department recognized that the wide variety of relationships between parent corporations and other entities made it "unwise" to establish specific guidance. The factors to be considered, however, in order of priority are

> the overall financial resources of any parent corporation or entity; the overall size of the parent corporation or entity with respect to the number of its employees; the number, type, and location of its facilities; and . . . [i]f applicable, the type of operation or operations of any parent corporation or entity, including the composition, structure, and functions of the workforce of the parent corporation or entity.

28 C.F.R. § 36.104 (definition of *undue burden*); 56 Fed. Reg. 35553–35554 (July 26, 1991).

Cases have begun to address liability of parent companies. In *United States v. Days Inns*, 997 F. Supp. 1080 (C.D. Ill. 1998), the court held that the parent company may be liable for ADA design violations because of its careful licensing and planning involvement in the design and construction of hotels. Decisions on this issue are likely to be individualized and should focus on the specific involvement of the parent or franchisor in architectural design. For additional cases on this issue, see LAURA ROTHSTEIN & JULIA ROTHSTEIN, DISABILITIES AND THE LAW § 6:13 (2009).

PROBLEM

Most drive-through service lines for fast food restaurants do not have a communication mechanism permitting individuals with hearing impairments to communicate over the microphone. As between the parent corporation of a major national chain and the local franchisee, who should bear the responsibility for providing accommodations for individuals with hearing impairments?

[6]   Private Homes

A physician working out of his or her home is an example of when Title III of the ADA would apply to a private home. Other common examples are day care centers, real estate businesses, and law practices operated out of one's home.

The regulations under Title III specify that

When a place of public accommodation is located in a private residence, the portion of the residence used exclusively as a residence is not covered by this part, but that portion used exclusively in the operation of the place of public accommodation or that portion used both for the place of public accommodation and for residential purposes is covered by this part.

28 C.F.R. § 36.207(a).

PROBLEM

Would a physician be required to make the bathroom in his or her home accessible? What about the entry to the house? 56 Fed. Reg. 35559–35560 (July 26, 1991).

[7]   Smoking

Pressure from a variety of interest groups has made smoking in public places (as well as in the workplace) less and less popular. Most states and local governments, however, have not prohibited smoking altogether. More likely is the decision of a place of public accommodation or an employer to prohibit smoking or to restrict smoking to specific areas. Perhaps recognizing the potential for smokers to claim that their addictions should be accommodated (leaving aside whether addiction to tobacco is a protected disability), the ADA specifies that nothing in the ADA should "be construed to preclude the prohibition of, or the imposition of restrictions on, smoking. . . . " 42 U.S.C. § 12210(b); 28 C.F.R. § 36.210. See also Gottlieb, Daynard & Lew, *Second-Hand Smoke and the ADA: Ensuring Access for Persons with Breathing and Heart Disorders*, 13 St. Louis U. Pub. L. Rev. 635 (1994). Nonetheless, the regulators specifically declined to prohibit or restrict smoking in places of public accommodation. Already attempts have been made by litigants to extend the interpretation of Title III of the ADA to do so.

EMERY v. CARAVAN OF DREAMS
879 F. Supp. 640 (N.D. Tex. 1995)

Sanders, District Judge.

Findings of Fact

2.   Plaintiff Emery has cystic fibrosis, a progressive genetic disease of the respiratory and digestive systems. As a result of her disability, she is substantially impaired in the major life function of breathing.

3.   Plaintiff Young is allergic to tobacco, ragweed, pollen, and dust mites. She has also been diagnosed as having asthma.

4.   Plaintiff Young leads a normal life, according to Dr. Michael. She has worked continuously as a flight attendant for American Airlines for twenty-nine years. She is learning how to roller blade. Her allergies and asthma do not substantially impair any major life function.

5. Cigarette smoke is an irritant to mucous membranes in general, and to respiratory tissue in particular. It increases mucus production in the lungs, and patients with cystic fibrosis have a difficult time moving mucus out of their lungs. The presence of mucus in the lungs increases the chance that opportunistic bacterial infections will develop. Most cystic fibrosis patients die from opportunistic bacterial infections.

6. Plaintiff Emery's physician has advised her to avoid cigarette smoke whenever possible. After two or three breaths of cigarette smoke, Plaintiff Emery begins to wheeze and cough; this lasts from twenty to twenty-five minutes.

7. For non-smoking patrons, Defendant provides a non-smoking section in the first two rows of seats in the theater.

8. Defendant's policy of allowing smoking in all areas of the theater except for the seats reserved for non-smoking patrons has the effect of denying Plaintiff Emery access to Defendant's musical venue.

9. The only accommodation that would allow Plaintiff Emery to have access to Caravan of Dreams is a complete ban on smoking when Plaintiff attends a performance.

10. Banning smoking in the Caravan of Dreams would have a major adverse economic effect on the Defendant, and would endanger the Defendant theater's viability. Nationally known performers would not play at the club if smoking were not permitted.

11. Defendant's only requirement for admission to a show is possession of a ticket.

Conclusions of Law

A. *Background Conclusions*

1. Defendant Caravan of Dreams is a public accommodation under the ADA.

2. Plaintiff Young is not a person with a disability as that term is defined in the ADA. Although Young has a physical impairment, that impairment does not substantially limit any major life activity as required by the ADA.

3. The regulations promulgated under the ADA define major life activities as "functions such as caring for one's self, performing manual tasks, walking, seeing, hearing, speaking, breathing, learning, and working." As the Justice Department's explanation of the regulations notes, whether or not an allergy to cigarette smoke can be termed a disability within the meaning of the ADA requires a case-by-case analysis of whether the respiratory or neurological functioning is so severely affected that it impairs a major life function.

4. Testimony showed that Plaintiff Young is not substantially impaired in her ability to work, recreate, breathe or to have a normal life. Accordingly, she is not disabled within the meaning of the ADA.

5. Plaintiff Emery is a person with a disability as that term is defined under the ADA. She is substantially impaired in the major life activity of breathing.

B. *Discrimination Conclusions*

1. The findings and conclusions previously made do not end the Court's inquiry. The Court must still determine whether Emery has been discriminated against on account of her disability.

2. Section 302(a) of Title III of the ADA establishes a general rule that "no individual shall be discriminated against on the basis of disability in the full and equal enjoyment of the goods, services, facilities, privileges, advantages, or accommodations of any place of public accommodation. . . . "

5. Plaintiffs here have insisted that their claim is based on § 302(b)(2)(A)(i). That section states that discrimination includes "the imposition or application of eligibility criteria that screen out or tend to screen out an individual with a disability or any class of individuals with disabilities from fully and equally enjoying any goods, services, facilities, privileges, advantages, or accommodations, unless such criteria can be shown to be necessary for the provision of the goods, services, facilities, privileges, advantages, or accommodations being offered."

6. Plaintiffs argue that because Defendant allowed smoking, Defendant has imposed eligibility criteria which screen out persons with severe respiratory ailments. The Court concludes that Plaintiffs' argument amounts to a torturous misreading of the statutory language just quoted, and that it is without merit.

Plaintiffs' argument fails with respect to the term "criteria." No case authority being available, the Court turns first to Webster's New Universal Unabridged Dictionary, which defines criterion as "a standard of judging; any established law, rule, principle or fact by which a correct judgment may be formed." "Criteria" thus implies the necessity of making a judgment, and because judging is necessarily an active rather than a passive endeavor, the Court views the quoted section as applying only to those rules or policies that are or could be used to make a specific or conscious decision as to whether or not to permit an individual or individuals to have access to goods, services, facilities, privileges, advantages, or accommodations which are being offered in this case by Defendant.

The Department of Justice commentary on the regulations supports the reading and analysis which I have just given. The Justice Department stated that it would violate the regulation implementing this section to "bar, for example, all persons who are deaf from playing on a golf course or all individuals with cerebral palsy from attending a movie theater, or limit the seating of individuals with Down's syndrome to only particular areas of a restaurant." Each of these decisions would involve a conscious decision directed at who will have access to the services offered by the public accommodation.

The smoking policy in question in this case clearly does not fall within the Court's construction or a fair analysis of § 302(b)(2)(A)(i). The only criterion for eligibility or access to Defendant's theater is the possession of a ticket. Plaintiffs are therefore not entitled to recover under § 302(b)(2)(A)(i).

7. Plaintiffs' suit appears to come within the provisions of § 302(b)(2)(A)(ii), which provides that discrimination includes "a failure to make reasonable modifications in policies, practices, or procedures, when such modifications are necessary to afford such goods, services, facilities, privileges, advantages, or accommodations to individuals with disabilities, unless the entity can demonstrate that making such modifications would fundamentally alter the nature of such goods, services, facilities, privileges, advantages, or accommodations."

As I understood Plaintiffs' testimony and evidence, a modification of Defendant's smoking policy would be necessary in order for Plaintiffs to take advantage of Defendant's facilities. Plaintiffs requested that Defendant modify its policy, and Defendant refused to do so. Plaintiffs do not base their case on a violation of § 302(b)(2)(A)(ii). I cover it, however, because it's another possibility here.

In the Court's view, even if Plaintiffs had relied on Section 302(b)(2)(A)(ii), their claim would fail because the section provides that a failure to make necessary modifications to policies is not discrimination under the ADA, when such modifications would fundamentally alter the services offered. It should be noted that there is some similarity between this provision and a similar phrase in the section under which Plaintiffs brought their case.

The "fundamental alteration" test is rooted in the Supreme Court's opinion in *Southeastern Community College v. Davis*, 442 U.S. 397 (1979), a Rehabilitation Act case. There the Court held that a college was not required to modify its clinical nursing program by converting it to a program of purely academic classes to accommodate a woman with a hearing impairment. The Court held that such a modification would amount to a "fundamental alteration" in the nature of the program, which was more than the Rehabilitation Act required. I understand that preceded the ADA, but it's a reference to the same phrase which makes it important to the Court.

8. Defendant's President testified that banning smoking would have a major economic impact and would result in major national bands not coming to play at Caravan of Dreams. This testimony was not contradicted. The uncontroverted evidence is that the requested modification would endanger Defendant's viability as a business, and such modifications are not required.

PROBLEMS

1. What would the likely result be if a less healthy plaintiff had brought this suit?

2. Does the fact that major bands would not play there matter? Isn't this somewhat like the customer/coworker preference argument, which is generally not allowed as an exemption from compliance?

NOTES AND QUESTIONS

1. In the previous case, the court found that Ms. Young did not have a disability. Would a court today be as likely to reach that decision under the ADA Amendments Act of 2008, which broadens the definition and makes it more likely that individuals with asthma and allergies will be covered? Or will she still have to make a stronger case that these conditions substantially limit her major life activity of breathing in more than a bar-type setting?

2. The fact that the *Emery* case was decided in 1995 is also significant. For a variety of reasons, the political climate for making more public places smoke free has changed substantially. The following case involves a fast food restaurant. These places are more likely to be smoke free in most states today. Would that be the same for the *Caravan of Dreams* type settings?

The following case involves a different type of facility — a fast food restaurant rather than a nightclub — and children rather than adults.

STARON v. McDONALD'S CORP.
51 F.3d 353 (2d Cir. 1995)

WALKER, CIRCUIT JUDGE:

These actions are brought by three children with asthma and a woman with lupus against two popular fast-food restaurant chains, McDonald's Corporation ("McDonald's") and Burger King Corporation ("Burger King"). Plaintiffs claim that defendants' policies of permitting smoking in their restaurants violate § 302 of the Americans with Disabilities Act (the "ADA" or "Act").

Background

The facts alleged in plaintiffs' complaints are rather straightforward. During one week in February, 1993, each plaintiff entered both a McDonald's and a Burger King restaurant in Connecticut. Each plaintiff found the air in each restaurant to be full of tobacco smoke, and, because of his or her condition, was unable to enter the restaurant without experiencing breathing problems. Each plaintiff has also encountered similar difficulties at other times in other restaurants owned by McDonald's and Burger King.

After registering complaints with the defendants and the State of Connecticut Human Rights Commission without satisfactory results, plaintiffs filed separate suits against McDonald's and Burger King on March 30, 1993. Their complaints alleged that the defendants' policies of permitting smoking in their restaurants constituted discrimination under the Act. Each complaint requested a declaratory judgment that such policies are discriminatory under the ADA, as well as an injunction to prohibit defendants from maintaining any policy which interfered with plaintiffs' rights under the Act, "and more specifically to require [defendants and their franchisees] to establish a policy of prohibiting smoking in all of the facilities they own, lease, or operate."

[The lower court granted the defendants' motion to dismiss.]

The ADA and cases interpreting it do not articulate a precise test for determining whether a particular modification is "reasonable." However, because the Rehabilitation Act, which applies to recipients of federal funding, uses the same "reasonableness" analysis, cases interpreting that act provide some guidance.

The Supreme Court, addressing the issue of the reasonableness of accommodations under the Rehabilitation Act in the employment context, stated that "[a]ccommodation is not reasonable if it either imposes 'undue financial and administrative burdens' . . . or requires 'a fundamental alteration in the nature of [the] program.'" Other courts have articulated factors that they consider relevant to the determination, including the nature and extent of plaintiff's disability.

Although neither the ADA nor the courts have defined the precise contours of the test for reasonableness, it is clear that the determination of whether a particular modification is "reasonable" involves a fact-specific, case-by-case inquiry that considers, among other factors, the effectiveness of the modification in light of the nature of the disability in question and the cost to the organization that would implement it.

While there may be claims requesting modification under the ADA that warrant dismissal as unreasonable as a matter of law, in the cases before us a fact-specific inquiry was required. None has occurred at this early stage of the suits. The magistrate judge instead concluded — and the district court agreed — that plaintiffs' request for a ban on smoking in all of defendants' restaurants was unreasonable as a matter of law. The magistrate judge offered two grounds for this conclusion: first, that "the ADA, by itself, does not mandate a 'blanket ban' on smoke in 'fast food' restaurants," and second, that "[i]t is not reasonable, under the ADA, to impose a blanket ban on every McDonald's [and Burger King] restaurant where there are certain restaurants which reasonably can accommodate a 'no-smoking' area." We believe that neither ground justifies dismissal of the complaints.

I. *The Permissibility of Smoking Bans Under the ADA*

The magistrate judge correctly noted that the ADA on its face does not ban smoking in all public accommodations or all fast-food restaurants. Defendants carry this point a significant step further, however, and argue that the ADA precludes a total smoking ban as a reasonable modification. They assert that Congress did not intend to restrict the range of legislative policy options open to state and local governments to deal with the issue of smoking. Their argument rests on § 501(b) of the ADA: Nothing in this chapter shall be construed to invalidate or limit the remedies, rights, and procedures of any Federal law or law of any State or political subdivision . . . that provides greater or equal protection for the rights of individuals with disabilities than are afforded by this chapter. Nothing in this chapter shall be construed to preclude the prohibition of, or the imposition of restrictions on, smoking . . . in places of public accommodation covered by subchapter III of this chapter. The magistrate judge echoed a sentiment similar to defendants', stating that "[t]he significant public policy issues regarding smoking in 'fast food' restaurants are better addressed by Congress or by the Connecticut General Assembly. . . . "

It is plain to us that Congress did not intend to isolate the effects of smoking from the protections of the ADA. The first sentence of § 501(b) simply indicates that Congress, states, and municipalities remain free to offer greater protection for disabled individuals than the ADA provides. The passage does not state, and it does not follow, that violations of the ADA should go unredressed merely because a state has chosen to provide some degree of protection to those with disabilities.

As to the second sentence of § 501(b), the Department of Justice regulations state that it "merely clarifies that the Act does not require public accommodations to accommodate smokers by permitting them to smoke." Nothing in the second sentence precludes public accommodations from accommodating those with smoke-sensitive disabilities. In fact, this language expressly permits a total ban on smoking if a court finds it appropriate under the ADA. We therefore reject any argument by defendants to the contrary.

Cases in which individuals claim under the ADA that allergies to smoke constitute a disability and require smoking restrictions are simply subject to the same general reasonableness analysis as are other cases under the Act.

II. *The Scope of Plaintiffs' Proposed Accommodation*

The magistrate judge's principal objection to plaintiffs' proposed modification was that plaintiffs were seeking a total ban on smoking in all of defendants' restaurants even though "there are certain restaurants which reasonably can accommodate a 'no-smoking' area." We do not think that it is possible to conclude on the pleadings that plaintiffs' suggested modification in this case is necessarily unreasonable.

To be sure, the few courts that have addressed the question of reasonable modification for a smoke-sensitive disability have found a total ban unnecessary. See *Harmer v. Virginia Elec. & Power Co.*, 831 F. Supp. at 1303-04, 1307; *Vickers v. Veterans Admin.*, 549 F. Supp. at 87–89. Yet these courts only reached this conclusion after making a factual determination that existing accommodations were sufficient. In granting summary judgment to the defendant, the *Harmer* court concluded that the plaintiff could perform the essential functions of his job with the modifications already made by the defendant, which included moving smokers further from the plaintiff's desk, mandatory use of smokeless ashtrays, and installation of air filtration and oxygen infusion devices. In *Vickers*, the court found after a bench trial that the nine steps defendants had taken to alleviate plaintiff's suffering constituted sufficient accommodation, and that a total ban was therefore not necessary. *Vickers*, 549 F. Supp. at 87–88. Neither case held that a ban on smoking would be unreasonable if less drastic measures were ineffective, much less that a ban on smoking is unreasonable as a matter of law.

Plaintiffs in this case are entitled to the same opportunity afforded to the plaintiffs in *Harmer* and *Vickers* to prove that a ban on smoking is a reasonable modification to permit them access to defendants' restaurants. Given that

McDonald's has voluntarily banned smoking in all corporate-owned restaurants, the factfinder may conclude that such a ban would fully accommodate plaintiffs' disabilities but impose little or no cost on the defendants. The magistrate judge's unsupported assumption that certain restaurants "reasonably can accommodate a 'no-smoking' area" does not obviate the need for a factual inquiry. Plaintiffs have alleged that, regardless of the different structural arrangements in various restaurants, the environment in each establishment visited by the plaintiffs contained too much smoke to allow them use of the facilities on an equal basis as other non-disabled patrons. These allegations belie the magistrate judge's assumption that no-smoking areas offer a sufficient accommodation to plaintiffs. In such a case, it is not possible to conclude that "plaintiff can prove no set of facts in support of his claim which would entitle him to relief." Accordingly, defendants' motions to dismiss should have been denied.

In addition, we note that plaintiffs do not solely request a ban on smoking. Their complaints ask that defendants be enjoined "from continuing or maintaining any policy" that denies plaintiffs access to their restaurants, as well as "such other and further relief as it may deem just and proper." We do not think that it is necessary at this point in the lawsuit to bind plaintiffs to the one specific modification they prefer. If plaintiffs should fail in their quest for an outright ban on smoking, they may still be able to demonstrate after discovery that modifications short of an outright ban, such as partitions or ventilation systems, are both "reasonable" and "necessary," and plaintiffs should be allowed the opportunity to do so.

Defendants raise another objection to the scope of plaintiffs' request for an injunction. They contend that plaintiffs' request for a smoking ban is unreasonable because it applies to all of defendants' restaurants "regardless of whether these four Plaintiffs have ever visited, will visit, might visit or never will visit" the many McDonald's and Burger King restaurants across the country. This objection pertains to the permissible scope of injunctive relief in this case, an issue which neither the magistrate judge nor the district court has reached. But whatever may be the appropriate scope of an injunction, doubts about that scope do not justify dismissal of the complaints where plaintiffs have alleged cognizable claims at least with respect to the restaurants they expect to visit.

We therefore reverse the judgments of the district court and remand for proceedings consistent with this opinion.

NOTE

One of the procedural barriers to cases such as the *McDonald's* case and many of the architectural barrier cases against places of accommodation is whether the plaintiff has standing. Several cases have now addressed whether the plaintiff must demonstrate an intent to return or a likelihood of returning. Some of this litigation has occurred because of what are sometimes referred to as "vexatious litigants." For additional discussion of that issue, see Section 4[H][1] Enforcement under the ADA, *infra*.

F   AIR TRANSPORTATION

It has been argued that limitations on transportation are a violation of the constitutional right to travel. This generally will be a successful argument only if there is a direct limitation of some sort by the state or federal government. Usually the limitations on individuals with disabilities are not direct, but indirect limitations — created primarily by design barriers.

The importance of transportation to an active involvement in everyday life — work, education, recreation — is obvious. Imagine that all of the buildings in the United States had been designed to be barrier free, and that employers provided all the necessary reasonable accommodation for disabled employees to carry out their jobs, but that the transportation policies do not provide for access. The individual with epilepsy might be unable to obtain a driver's license and might be unable to get to work as a result. The individual with a mobility impairment might be able to obtain a driver's license and buy a specially-designed vehicle, but unless adequate parking were provided, there would still be difficulties in gaining access. If that individual wanted to use mass transit, in most cities there would be problems with doing so, although the mass transit requirements of the Americans with Disabilities Act have made improvements. In the past, the airlines provided little assistance for the disabled traveler.

There is not much judicial analysis of transportation issues relating to individuals with disabilities. This is because most of the legal requirements only recently have become more clearly established. In assessing transportation access, it is necessary to examine policies relating to the vehicle, the fixed facilities, and practices and policies relating to transportation.

Until 1986, there was little comprehensive application of nondiscrimination policy to airline transportation. This was because airlines are not generally recipients of federal financial assistance and are not subject to § 504 of the Rehabilitation Act. Airport terminals were recipients of federal financial assistance and were required to be accessible, but this was of little comfort to the disabled passenger who could not get on the plane.

In 1986, the Supreme Court addressed a case in which it was claimed that airlines were subject to Section 504 by virtue of receiving grants from a federal trust fund for airport operators and by receiving benefits from the operation of the air traffic control system. The following is an excerpt from the analysis of that claim.

UNITED STATES DEPARTMENT OF TRANSPORTATION v. PARALYZED VETERANS OF AMERICA
477 U.S. 597 (1986)

JUSTICE POWELL:

The grant statutes are the Airport and Airway Improvement Act of 1982. . . . The 1970 Act established the Airport and Airway Trust Fund, appropriations from which are used to fund airport development. The purpose of disbursements . . . is to establish a "nationwide system of public airports adequate to meet the present and future needs of civil aeronautics." Congress directed the Secretary of Transportation to prepare a national airport system plan, and required airport project applications to be consistent with that plan. Funds are disbursed for a variety of airport construction projects: e.g., land acquisition, runway paving, and buildings, sidewalks, and parking. The use of the Trust Funds is strictly limited to projects that concern airports.

It is not difficult to identify the recipient of federal financial assistance under these Acts: Congress has made it explicitly clear that these funds are to go to airport operators. Not a single penny of the money is given to the airlines. Thus, the recipient for purposes of § 504 is the operator of the airports and not its users.

Congress limited the scope of § 504 to those who actually "receive" federal financial assistance because it sought to impose § 504 coverage as a form of contractual cost of the recipient's agreement to accept the federal funds. By limiting coverage to recipients, Congress imposes the obligations of § 504 upon those who are in a position to accept or reject those obligations as a part of the decision whether or not to "receive" federal funds. In this case, the only parties in that position are the airport operators.

Respondents attempt to avoid the straightforward conclusion that airlines are not recipients within the meaning of § 504 by arguing that airlines are "indirect recipients" of the aid to airports. They contend that the money given to airports to comply is converted by the airports into nonmoney grants to airlines. Under this reasoning, federal assistance is disbursed to airport operators in the form of cash. The airport operators convert the cash into runways and give the federal assistance — now in the form of a runway — to the airlines.

Congress tied the regulatory authority to those programs or activities that *receive* federal financial assistance; the key is to identify the recipient of that assistance. In this case, it is clear that the recipients of the financial assistance extended by Congress under the Trust Fund are the airport operators.

Even if the reach of § 504 were limited to those whom Congress specifically intended to benefit, the scope of the statute would be broad indeed, covering whole classes of persons and businesses with only an indirect relation to aviation. The statutory "limitation" on § 504's coverage would virtually disappear, a result Congress surely did not intend.

Respondents . . . assert that the ultimate beneficiaries under the Act are the passengers, while the economic benefit derived by the airlines is intended to aid the airlines in benefiting the passengers. Section 504 provides no basis for this distinction. Nor can we find a basis in the Trust Fund Acts for preferring passengers over other beneficiaries. Rather, Congress recognized a need to improve airports in order to benefit a wide variety of persons and entities, all of them classified together as beneficiaries.

The Court of Appeals also held that the federally-provided air traffic control system is a form of federal financial assistance to airlines. The Federal Government spends some two billion dollars annually to run this system 24 hours a day nationwide and in various spots around the world. The air traffic controllers are federal employees and the Federal Government finances operation of the terminal control facilities. In short, the air traffic control system is "owned and operated" by the United States. For that reason, the air traffic control system is not "federal financial assistance" at all. Rather, it is a federally conducted program that has many beneficiaries but no recipients. The legislative history of Title VI makes clear that such programs do not constitute federal financial assistance to anyone.

JUSTICE MARSHALL, dissenting:

The Court . . . infers that commercial airlines . . . do not "receive" federal financial assistance. The appropriate question is thus not whether commercial airlines "receive" federal financial assistance. Rather, it is whether commercial airlines are in a position to "exclude [disabled persons] from the participation in . . . or deny [them] the benefits of or . . . subject [them] to discrimination under" a program or activity receiving federal financial assistance or conducted by an Executive agency.

[T]he nature of airline transportation demands that DOT have [authority to regulate commercial airlines to ensure that disabled individuals are not discriminated against]. If commercial airline companies barred the handicapped from traveling on their airlines at all, then that conduct would deny the handicapped the benefits of federally funded and conducted programs and activities relating to the airport and airway system.

[C]ommercial airlines are in a unique position to deny public access to federally funded airport and airway services. The vast majority of members of the general public can enjoy that benefit [flying] only to the extent allowed, and under conditions set, by commercial airlines. Commercial airlines thus necessarily act as gatekeepers controlling who shall enjoy, and under what conditions, important benefits under federally funded and conducted programs.

DOT has the power, through regulation of *airport operators*, to ensure that commercial airlines do not discriminatorily deprive handicapped persons of the benefits of federal programs supporting the airport and airway systems. In order to serve an airport, an air carrier must enter into a lease with the airport operator for the use of airport facilities. DOT has power to direct each federally-assisted airport, as part of that lease, to secure from all air carriers serving the airport an assurance of compliance with regulatory standards for service to handicapped person.

NOTE

Air Carrier Access Act. After the decision in this case, Congress passed the Air Carrier Access Act of 1986, 49 U.S.C. app. § 1374(c), which prohibits airlines from discriminating against individuals with disabilities. The statute does not state whether there is a private right of action to enforce this provision. The regulations implementing the Air Carrier Access Act, 14 C.F.R. pt. 382, provide clarification of the reasonable accommodation requirements under the statute. The statute contemplates the same principles that are found under other disability nondiscrimination statutes — i.e., the definitional coverage of who is a person with a disability is similar; reasonable accommodation is contemplated; least restrictive environment is contemplated; and airlines are not expected to make fundamental alterations to their program. There are still a number of issues left open even with the statute and promulgation of regulations. The following case illustrates some of the issues left unresolved. Other issues include exclusion from emergency row seating and other areas. For cases under the ACAA, see Laura Rothstein & Julia Rothstein, Disabilities and the Law Ch. 8 (2009).

The following case is one of the first decisions under the Air Carrier Access Act, and raises several of the issues that still have not been resolved in a compelling fact setting. In reading the case, one should question whether the lack of awareness of federal changes in the law would make a difference today, more than two decades after the ACAA. In a jurisdiction that recognized damages, would it be more likely that higher punitive damages would be awarded today than in 1989?

TALLARICO v. TRANS WORLD AIRLINES, INC.
881 F.2d 566 (8th Cir. 1989)

Beam, Circuit Judge:

I. *Background*

Polly Tallarico, who is fourteen years old, has cerebral palsy which impedes her ability to walk and talk. She generally uses a wheelchair, but is able to move about on her own by crawling. Although Polly is able to speak only short words, she is able to hear and understand the spoken word. She communicates by use of a variety of communication devices such as a communication board, a memo writer and a "Minispeak."

On November 25, 1986, the day before the Thanksgiving holiday, Polly arrived at Houston's Hobby Airport intending to fly to St. Louis, Missouri, unaccompanied. When the TWA ticket agent, Richard Wattleton, learned that Polly intended to fly alone he contacted Lynn Prothero, acting TWA station manager, and asked for directions as to how he should handle the situation. Wattleton had learned from the limousine driver assisting Polly that she could not speak or walk. Wattleton relayed this information to Prothero and also informed her that Polly could communicate by use of a communication board. From this information, Prothero determined that Polly would not be allowed to fly unaccompanied and informed Wattleton of her decision. This decision was apparently made on the basis of Prothero's conclusion that Polly could not take care of herself in an emergency and could not exit the plane expeditiously. As a result of this decision, Polly's father had to fly to Houston to accompany Polly to St. Louis.

The Tallaricos brought suit alleging that TWA violated the ACAA by denying Polly the right to board the plane because of her physical handicaps. The jury found for the Tallaricos awarding damages in the amount of $80,000. The district court entered judgment notwithstanding the verdict on the issue of damages reducing the award to $1,350 which is equivalent to the Tallaricos' actual out-of-pocket expenses.

II. *Discussion*

A. *Private cause of action*

Logic dictates that we begin with TWA's cross-appeal in which TWA contends that the ACAA does not provide for a private cause of action. The Act states that "[n]o air carrier may discriminate against any otherwise qualified handicapped individual, by reason of such handicap, in the provision of air transportation." 49 U.S.C.App. § 1374(c)(1) The ACAA does not expressly provide for a cause of action to enable private citizens to seek a remedy for a violation of the Act. Consequently, we must determine if a private cause of action is implied under the ACAA.

TWA claims that Polly is not an intended beneficiary of the ACAA because the Act is intended to benefit only "otherwise qualified handicapped individuals." Because we find that Polly is an otherwise qualified handicapped individual, we do not need to decide whether the ACAA was intended to benefit handicapped persons who are not otherwise qualified.

No definition of otherwise qualified handicapped individual is given in the Act. Although the ACAA requires the Secretary of Transportation "to promulgate regulations to ensure nondiscriminatory treatment of qualified handicapped individuals," no regulations were in effect at the time of the incident. However, the legislative history of the Act states that the definition of otherwise qualified handicapped individual is intended to be consistent with the Department of Transportation's definition in 14 C.F.R. § 382.3(c) (1988). Section 382.3(c) defines a "qualified handicapped person" as a handicapped individual (1) who tenders payment for air transportation, (2) whose carriage will not violate Federal Aviation Administration (FAA) regulations, and (3) who is willing and able to comply with reasonable safety requests of the airline personnel or, if unable to comply, who is accompanied by a responsible adult passenger who can ensure compliance with such a request. 14 C.F.R. § 382.3(c) (1988). An instruction based upon section 382.3(c) was given to the jury which instruction required the jury to find that Polly was an otherwise qualified handicapped individual before it could allow her to recover. Although the jury obviously determined that Polly was an otherwise qualified handicapped individual, the district court stated in its memorandum that had it been the trier of fact, it would have concluded differently.

We agree with the jury's conclusion and hold that Polly is an otherwise qualified handicapped individual within the meaning of the ACAA. The evidence at trial showed that Polly had tendered payment for air transportation, that her carriage would not violate any FAA regulations (in fact she had flown alone before), and that she was capable of complying with the reasonable safety requests of airline personnel. The evidence demonstrated that Polly is able to crawl on her knees or her hands and knees, that she has normal intelligence, and that she is capable of communicating her needs. Polly has a variety of ways of communicating including the use of communication boards which contain the letters of the alphabet and some short phrases; a memo writer, an electronic typewriter-like device; and a "Minispeak," a portable computer with an electronic voice attached. Polly is able to fasten her own seatbelt as well as put on an oxygen mask. In addition, Polly's mother testified that she was confident that Polly could crawl to the bathroom (and, presumably, an exit) on the plane if necessary. From this evidence we conclude, as did the jury, that Polly is an otherwise qualified handicapped individual and, consequently, one of the class for whose especial benefit the ACAA was enacted.

The second factor is whether there is any indication of legislative intent to create such a remedy or to deny one. As the district court noted, the ACAA was enacted in response to the Supreme Court ruling in *United States Dep't of Transp. v. Paralyzed Veterans of America*, 477 U.S. 597 (1986), which case held that section 504 of the Rehabilitation Act of 1973 applies only to those commercial airlines receiving direct federal subsidies. Congress felt that "the practical effect of [PVA was] to leave handicapped air travelers subject to the possibility of discriminatory, inconsistent and unpredictable treatment on the part of air carriers." Consequently, Congress amended the Federal Aviation Act of 1958 to specifically prohibit discrimination against otherwise qualified handicapped individuals. Relying on this portion of the legislative history and the fact that the ACAA is patterned after the Rehabilitation Act of 1973, which Act has been held to imply a private cause of action, the district court concluded that "Congress implicitly intended that handicapped persons would have an implied private cause of action to remedy perceived violations of the [ACAA]." We agree.

We believe that to allow a private cause of action is consistent with the underlying purposes of the ACAA. In addition, we conclude that the area of discrimination against handicapped persons by air carriers is not an area which is basically the concern of the states. Accordingly, we affirm the district court's decision that the ACAA impliedly provides a private cause of action.

B. *Damages for emotional injuries*

The jury awarded the Tallaricos $80,000. The district court then granted judgment n.o.v. in favor of TWA as to $78,650 of the damages award. The court concluded that there was insufficient evidence to support the total award and that as a matter of law, the award was not sustainable. The court determined that $1,350 of the award was compensation for out-of-pocket damages as a result of TWA's refusal to allow Polly to board and the remainder was damages for emotional distress. The court held that because the ACAA is an anti-discrimination statute, "as a matter of law, emotional distress damages are not recoverable for violations of the Act." In reaching this conclusion, the court relied upon cases under Title VII of the Civil Rights Act of 1964, the Age Discrimination in Employment Act of 1967, and the Rehabilitation Act of 1973, which did not allow emotional distress damages for violations of the acts.

The Tallaricos argue that these cases should not have been relied upon by the court in making its determination as to whether emotional distress damages are allowable under the ACAA because each of the acts, Title VII, the ADEA, and the Rehabilitation Act, specifically provide a complete remedial scheme for violations. As the Tallaricos note, where a statute provides a specific remedial scheme, it is evidence that any other remedies are excluded. Because the ACAA does not provide a remedial scheme, evidence of a Congressional intent to exclude emotional distress damages does not exist.

Further, the district court's conclusion that all antidiscrimination statutes disallow emotional distress damages is incorrect. The Supreme Court has held that damages for mental and emotional distress are compensable under 42 U.S.C. § 1983. In addition, damages for mental distress are allowed under 42 U.S.C. § 1982 and the Fair Housing Act, 42 U.S.C. § 3601 et seq. (1982). We believe that the purpose and operation of the ACAA are more closely analogous to section 1983 than to Title VII, the ADEA and the Rehabilitation Act. Consequently, we conclude that emotional distress damages are allowable under the ACAA.

The district court also held that there was no evidentiary basis for that portion of the award which exceeded the Tallaricos' out-of-pocket expenses. We disagree. "Because of the difficulty of evaluating . . . emotional injuries . . . , courts do not demand precise proof to support a reasonable award of damages for such injuries." The Supreme Court in *Carey v. Piphus* stated that although the award "must be supported by competent evidence," injury in the form of mental suffering or emotional anguish "may be evidenced by one's conduct and observed by others." 435 U.S. at 264 n. 20. In addition, the Seventh Circuit held that "[h]umiliation can be inferred from the circumstances as well as established by the testimony."

In this case the proof of the emotional distress which Polly suffered after TWA denied her boarding came from the testimony of her mother, her father, the assistant director for Polly's school and the driver who was with Polly when the incident occurred. Theodore Sherwood, the driver who took Polly to the airport, testified that Polly was with him when he was told she would not be allowed to board the aircraft. He stated he noticed that Polly was getting disturbed as she listened to his conversations with TWA employees. Sherwood also testified that he felt it necessary to call Polly's school to see if someone there could talk to Polly and calm her down because after the incident she was crying and upset about what had happened. Polly's father testified that Polly was very angry and upset about the incident. In addition, he stated that since the incident Polly has seemed more withdrawn, quiet and reserved. Polly's mother also testified that Polly was upset about what happened and that Polly was anxious about the situation and concerned about having to fly back to Houston after the Thanksgiving holiday. Susan Oldham, the assistant director of Polly's school, testified that prior to the incident Polly was very outgoing and socialized well with the other students. After the incident, Ms. Oldham testified, Polly seemed more withdrawn and would spend large amounts of time by herself in her room after school was over. Ms. Oldham stated that when she asked Polly if something about her trip home had upset her, Polly replied that what had happened had made her feel badly and had hurt her feelings.

We find that sufficient evidence was presented to support the jury's award of $80,000. Consequently, we reverse the district court's judgment n.o.v.

C. *Punitive damages*

At the close of the Tallaricos' evidence, the district court granted TWA's motion for a directed verdict on the issue of punitive damages. The Tallaricos assert that the court erred in granting TWA's motion because the evidence adduced by the Tallaricos was sufficient to make a prima facie case that TWA acted in such a manner as to warrant granting punitive damages. Punitive damages are awarded where the "defendant exhibits oppression, malice, gross negligence, willful or wanton misconduct, or reckless disregard" for the rights of the plaintiff. A trial court should grant a motion for a directed verdict only if all the evidence points one way and is susceptible of no reasonable inference sustaining a finding of such behavior on the part of TWA. We apply the same standard as the trial court in considering such a motion.

The district court did not question whether punitive damages are allowed under the ACAA but instead merely concluded that there was insufficient evidence to submit the question to the jury. We agree with the district court that the Tallaricos failed to present sufficient evidence to support an award of punitive damages and similarly do not reach the question of whether punitive damages would be allowed under the ACAA.

The Air Carrier Access Act applies to nondiscrimination related to the airline's activities. That leaves open the issue of access to the fixed facilities, i.e., the airport terminal and related services, such as car rental agencies, shuttle bus service, etc. While Section 504 of the Rehabilitation Act applied to the airport terminal itself even before the Air Carrier Access Act, there were many unanswered questions. For example, what requirements applied to food vendors and gift shops leasing space in the airport? Most, if not all, of these questions have been resolved as a result of the passage of the Americans with Disabilities Act in 1990. Title II would apply to any aspects that were operated by a state or local governmental entities, such as a municipally operated parking garage or airport. Title III applies to private entities providing public accommodations. Thus, the food service vendors, the car rental agencies, and other private parties with services in the airport or adjoining areas would be subject to these requirements. These issues would be covered by the ADA, as discussed earlier in this chapter.

HYPOTHETICAL PROBLEM 4.2

Review the facts in Problem 4.1 regarding Shane's unhappy experience at the conference. What should counsel do with respect to his complaints about how he was treated during his air travel experience?

For more information on cases relating to air transportation, see LAURA ROTHSTEIN & JULIA ROTHSTEIN, DISABILITIES AND THE LAW §§ 8:1–8:3 (2009).

NOTES

1. *Treatment of Passengers During Layovers and in the Airport:* A complaint against United Airlines and O'Hare International Airport by a passenger who uses a wheelchair claimed that the ADA and the Air Carrier Access Act were violated when the passenger was not permitted to move around the terminal in an airport wheelchair during a layover. The passenger was given the option of waiting in a special room for travelers with disabilities or waiting at the gate in a standard chair. What claims are the defendants likely to make in such a case? *Michael Auberger v. City of Chicago*, No. C.A. 93C-6060 (N.D. Ill. filed Oct. 4, 1993.)

Passenger's Duty to Request Accommodations: In the case of *Adiutori v. Sky Harbor International Airport*, 880 F. Supp. 696 (D. Ariz. 1995), a passenger suffered a heart attack after difficulties and overexertion in moving from one terminal to another via a shuttle bus. A sky cap had taken him by wheelchair to the the shuttle bus stop. Although he was elderly and used canes to walk, he did not request that the skycap remain with the wheelchair, nor did he request assistance in boarding the shuttle bus. Help was offered by another man, but it was refused. He also refused an offer of a seat on the shuttle bus and remained standing. The court found the evidence did not demonstrate any request for additional assistance or that any responsible party should have known that he needed assistance, Therefore no violation of either the Americans with Disabilities Act or the Air Carrier Access Act was found.

2. *Application to Cargo Flights:* An interesting decision involved whether the Air Carrier Access Act applies to cargo carriers that allow employees to fly in available space on cargo flights. An employee of Federal Express Corporation who was disabled was denied this benefit, and successfully challenged this denial as a violation of the ACAA. *Bower v. Federal Express Corp.*, 96 F.3d 200 (6th Cir. 1996).

3. *Obligation to Provide Wheelchairs:* In *Rivera v. Delta Air Lines, Inc.*, 1997 U.S. Dist. LEXIS 14989 (E.D. Pa. 1997), the court held that Title II of the ADA does not require a city airport to provide wheelchairs for passengers with disabilities, but that the ACAA may apply to the airline and create such a requirement.

G TELECOMMUNICATIONS

[1] Telephones

Before the passage of the Americans with Disabilities Act, the only major federal statute addressing accessibility to telephone communication by individuals with disabilities was the Telecommunications for the Disabled Act, 47 U.S.C. § 610(b), which was passed in 1982. This Act amended the Communications Act of 1934, and requires reasonable accessibility to essential telephones for individuals with hearing impairments. Essential telephones are defined as "coin-operated telephones, telephones provided for emergency use, and other telephones frequently needed for use by persons using . . . hearing aids [specially designed for telephone use]." 47 U.S.C. § 610(b).

The requirements of the Telecommunications for the Disabled Act were enhanced with the passage of the ADA. Title IV of the ADA applies to common carriers that provide interstate wire or radio communications. By 1993, common carriers, as defined by the Federal Communications Commission, are to provide telecommunications relay services on an equivalent basis to voice communications service. 47 U.S.C. §§ 152(b), 225; 47 C.F.R. parts 0 and 64. This provision is intended to enable individuals who use telecommunications devices for the deaf (TDDs) to communicate with those who do not have such devices.

The ADA incorporates into its Accessibility Guidelines for Buildings and Facilities regulations related to construction and alterations of public telephones. 36 C.F.R. Part 36, Appendix A, Standard 4.31., 46 Fed. Reg. 35660–35662 (July 26, 1991). Whether a particular facility is required to have a telephone communication device for the deaf (TDD) depends whether a public accommodation offers users of its services the opportunity to make outgoing phone calls on more than an incidental basis. 36 C.F.R. § 36.303(d). Hotels are required to have TDDs or similar devices available to allow guests who use TDDs in their rooms to communicate with the front desk and for ordering room service. 56 Fed. Reg. 35567 (July 26, 1991).

Issues of particular concern to advocates with respect to telephone service are telephone access in medical facilities and access for law enforcement purposes.

PROBLEM

What kind of liability is likely against a hotel that did not have an emergency warning system or communications devices as required by the ADA, such as no TDD for the telephone, no visual or tactical alarm or warning devices, when deaf individuals are not warned of a fire that had burned for two hours before they were rescued? *Gardner v. SeaVenture Restaurant*, No. 2:94-CV-07767 (C.D. Cal. filed Nov. 17, 1994). Are damages recoverable?

[2]   Television and Other Audiovisual Communication

Most television stations do not receive federal financial assistance. The major exception is public television. Because of that, Section 504 of the Rehabilitation Act does not apply to require that accommodations be made to people with disabilities. Such accommodations might include closed captioning for individuals with hearing impairments or descriptive narration for individuals with visual impairments. A 1983 Supreme Court decision, *Community Television of Southern Cal. v. Gottfried*, 459 U.S. 498 (1983), clarified that licensing renewal was an insufficient nexus to mandate Section 504 application.

The only federal mandates related to accessibility in broadcasting television programming relate to emergency broadcasting, 47 C.F.R. § 73.1250, and public service announcements, 47 U.S.C. §§ 152(b), 221(b), 611. In addition, the Television Decoder Circuitry Act, 47 U.S.C. § 303(u), provides that television sets manufactured in the United States or sold in the United States after 1993 (with picture size of 13 inches or more) must be equipped for closed captioning. Regulations under Title III of the ADA specify the availability of closed caption decoding devices for places of lodging and hospitals. 37 C.F.R. § 36.303(f).

Movie theaters are not required to ensure that the movies are captioned for individuals with hearing impairments. Where other public accommodations deliver verbal information by film, videotape or slide shows, this information must be made accessible to individuals with disabilities. Analysis of Title III Regulations, 56 Fed.

Reg. 35567 (July 26, 1991). For example, a natural history museum that shows the history of mummies on a repeating videotape would apparently be required to ensure that this information is accessible. It would be a factual issue whether closed captioning, a transcript of the audio portion, a sign language interpreter, or other accommodation would be reasonable in a particular context. This portion of the analysis does not discuss whether similar accommodations, such as oral description, might be required to enable individuals with visual impairment to better appreciate the programming.

Producers of training films and other educational materials on film or videotape are not directly required to prepare such materials with captioning or to make them otherwise accessible. The employer or educational program contracting for the audiovisual materials, however, might be required to do so.

Recent requirements specify what must be provided for closed captioning of video programming. The requirements apply to television stations and video programming distributors. These FCC requirements do not allow for a private right of action. See 47 C.F.R. Section 79.1.

[3]   Internet and Other Web-Based Communication

For individuals with mobility or vision impairments, the use of computer technology can be difficult or impossible unless adaptations are made. Web pages may be designed so as not to be usable by someone who cannot see or who has difficulty using a mouse instead of a keyboard. Technical assistance is becoming available to ensure accessibility. Technical assistance is becoming available to ensure   accessibility.   Information   can   be   found   at www.itpolicy.gsa.gov/coca/nii.htm;   www.w3.org/Press/19948/WAI-Guide); www.w3org/TR/WD-WAI-PAGEAUTH.

Although the Workforce Investment Act of 1998 (which includes § 508 of the Rehabilitation Act, 29 U.S.C. § 794d) requires federal departments and agencies to provide a level of information accessibility, it is less clear what is required of the private sector. There has been some initial litigation about whether websites are even entities covered under Title III of the ADA. Even where they are covered, this is an area where it is not clear what must be done. If the website meets federal accessibility standards, is that sufficient? The federal agency design regulations are found at 36 C.F.R. § 1194.4. For more information on these issues, see LAURA ROTHSTEIN & JULIA ROTHSTEIN, DISABILITIES AND THE LAW § 9:5 (2009).

NOTES

Assistive Listening System Requirements? Although movie theaters are not mandated by the ADA to provide movies with captioning, it is possible that assistive listening systems might be a reasonable accommodation required of theaters with the financial means to install them. Such devices are readily available and easily installed, costing about $2,000 per theater screen. *Isbell & The Disability Rights Council of Greater Washington v. Cineplex Odeon Corp.*, C.A. No. 94-0679 (D.D.C. filed March 30, 1994).

H ENFORCEMENT

[1] Americans with Disabilities Act

Where the discriminating party is in violation of Title III of the ADA, Congress contemplated dual enforcement by private parties and governmental agencies. Private parties may obtain equitable relief by direct civil action in court. 42 U.S.C. § 12188; 36 C.F.R. § 36.501. The Attorney General of the United States also may seek to intervene. Such intervention is at the discretion of the court. 42 U.S.C. § 12188(b); 36 C.F.R. §§ 36.501–.503. The benefit of Attorney General intervention is the potential for monetary damages, which can be awarded only if the Attorney General requests. Damages in this context include compensatory damages, such as out-of-pocket expenses, and damages for pain and suffering. 46 Fed. Reg. 35590 (July 26, 1991). Civil penalties also are available in certain instances where the Attorney General has intervened. 42 U.S.C. § 12188(b)(2); 36 C.F.R. § 36.504. Punitive damages are not available under Title III. 42 U.S.C. § 12188(b)(4); 36 C.F.R. § 36.504(c). In determining whether civil penalties should be assessed, the courts are to consider good faith efforts to comply. 42 U.S.C. § 12188(b)(5); 36 C.F.R. § 36.504(d). Attorneys' fees, litigation expenses, and costs in judicial or administrative proceedings may be awarded at the discretion of the court or agency to prevailing parties, except where that party is the United States. 42 U.S.C. § 12205; 36 C.F.R. § 36.505.

Individual complainants are not entitled to monetary damages under Title III. Monetary relief is possible in instances where the Attorney General intervenes, but ordinarily an individual would be limited to injunctive relief and attorneys' fees and costs. This may be an inadequate incentive for individual complainants to challenge the failure to comply with ADA accessibility requirements.

While a private litigant whose claim does not merit Attorney General intervention seemingly may be limited to equitable relief, Title III of the ADA may, in appropriate cases, indirectly be the basis for damage awards in common-law tort actions. If such a theory is to be allowed, it will become necessary to prove the elements of the applicable tort, such as negligence. Particularly with respect to physical facilities existing before the effective date of the ADA, it may be difficult to prove exactly what barriers were to have been removed or what physical modifications made in order to demonstrate a duty and a breach thereof. Unlike the kind of situation occurring in the *Morgan* case, *infra*, it is likely that many situations may prove too vague for courts to identify a clear standard.

Plaintiffs have begun to use tort theories in claims involving ADA issues. The cases use ADA standards for architectural accessibility to establish a duty of care as an element of a common law negligence action. One of the most interesting of these cases is *Morgan v. Idaho Department of Public Works*, 124 Idaho 568, 862 P.2d 1080 (1993). A totally blind individual who was trying to unload goods onto a hand truck on a loading dock was severely injured when he fell backwards from an area that did not have tactile warning devices, in violation of the state building code. The court upheld the lower court's determination that the state law applied to such areas. In *Swartz v. Huffmaster Alarms Sys., Inc.*, 145 Mich. App. 431, 377 N.W.2d 393 (1985), the plaintiff who had eaten at a restaurant and who had consumed several alcoholic beverages was hit by a car in crossing the road to his own car. He brought an action against the restaurant for violating state disability discrimination laws. His claim was that he had become intoxicated and anxious as a result of drinking and that he was also legally blind. As a result, he claimed that there was a duty to take special steps for his safety. The court found that the plaintiff was not absolutely blind, and the anxiety was not sufficient to impose a special duty. This case raises the issue as to whether application of ADA standards would have achieved a different result.

[2]   Air Carrier Access Act

Courts have addressed a number of cases involving plaintiffs with disabilities under the ACAA. These cases have involved issues of boarding assistance and seat selection among others. Whether there is a private right of action and the remedies under the ACAA are also addressed. There is not yet clear guidance on all of these issues resulting from these decisions. See Laura Rothstein & Julia Rothstein, Disabilities and the Law § 8.2 (2009).

As the *Tallarico* decision indicates, at least some courts have permitted private actions to enforce the ACA as well as recognizing the availability of monetary damages. The regulations under the ACAA provide for compliance procedures, including a complaint resolution mechanism, but they do not really address the issues of private right of action and remedies. 14 C.F.R. § 382.65. It is not surprising, therefore, that the courts have reached inconsistent results in deciding these issues. See Laura Rothstein & Julia Rothstein, Disabilities and the Law § 8.02, note 24 (2009).

[3]   Telecommunications Enforcement

The Telecommunications for the Disabled Act of 1982, 47 U.S.C. § 396 and Television Decoder Communications Circuitry Act of 1990, 47 U.S.C. §§ 154, 302, 303, 304, 307 both contemplate administrative agency enforcement. An individual believing that either of these statutes had been violated would complain to the Federal Communications Commission or the Department of Justice. The statutes are silent about private rights of action and individual remedies.

Chapter 5

GOVERNMENTAL SERVICES AND PROGRAMS

A OVERVIEW

Title II of the Americans with Disabilities Act (ADA) defines public services as programs of state or local governments and their departments, agencies, and other instrumentalities. 42 U.S.C. § 12131(1). Programs operated or funded by the federal government are not subject to this section of the ADA. They are, however, subject to Sections 501 and 504 of the Rehabilitation Act. 29 U.S.C. §§ 791, 794.

Publicly operated programs include a wide range of activities. Unlike Title III, relating to public accommodations, which defines twelve categories of programs, Title II is more general. It applies to programs such as public transportation, social services and health care, public schools and universities, criminal and civil justice programs, voting, and public recreational areas. As was noted in previous chapters, there may be overlapping authority for certain activities, subjecting them to more than one title of the ADA, more than one federal law, and additional state and local requirements. For example, a "fun run" open to the public and sponsored by a private corporation that refused to allow individuals in wheelchairs to participate might implicate both Title III of the ADA and Title II if the city arranged for routing and other use of city facilities and protection.

Title II also subjects those programs covered under this portion of the ADA to nondiscrimination in employment. This issue is not covered in this chapter, but is treated in Chapter 3. Federal government employment is also covered in Chapter 3.

This chapter also references state and local governmental activities that are not services in the common sense of that term. Activities such as licensing and oversight fall within this category. In addition, state and local laws that are discriminatory in fact or in practice are also briefly discussed. Legal requirements related to family rights, such as child custody, are an example.

B NONDISCRIMINATION

[1] Federal Government Programs

Sections 501, 503, and 504 of the Rehabilitation Act prohibit federal agencies, federal contractors, and recipients of federal financial assistance from discriminating on the basis of disability. Chapter 3 (Employment) discusses the nondiscrimination in employment mandates under those statutory provisions.

The model regulations under Section 504 have separate sections applying to the major types of recipients of federal financial assistance. The three major categories of recipients for which model regulations were developed are preschool, elementary and secondary education; postsecondary education; and health, welfare and social services. 34 C.F.R. part 104. The application of nondiscrimination requirements of the Rehabilitation Act to these settings is addressed in Chapters 6, 7, and 9, and to a lesser extent in Chapter 8. Application to settings such as the judicial system and mass transit is discussed later in this chapter.

[2] State and Local Government Programs

For state and local government programs receiving federal financial assistance, Section 504 of the Rehabilitation Act applies. The more significant statute, however, is the Americans with Disabilities Act (ADA), because it reaches virtually every state and local public service regardless of whether the program receives federal financial assistance.

HYPOTHETICAL PROBLEM 5.1

Springfield is a city with a population of 750,000. The city's economic base includes two colleges, several museums, some manufacturing of household goods and appliances, a health care center with several hospitals, including a veterans' rehabilitation hospital, and a technology park. It is located on a lake, and there is also substantial regional tourism connected with waterfront activities.

During times when there was full employment and a strong economy, the city government planned improvements in several recreational areas, including biking trails, new boat docks on the city-owned lakefront area, and four new swimming pools to be built in underserved areas. In addition, the budget includes retrofitting all ten existing pools to be accessible for individuals with mobility impairments (at a cost of $1 million over five years). One of the existing pools is located near the veterans' hospital. The four new pools would all be accessible. The boat dock improvements, the bike trail additions, new pool construction, and retrofitting had a phase-in schedule of five years. The total budget for the five year period was $5 million. The bike trail additions were begun in the first year (with an expenditure of $250,000), and the contracts for the new pools ($2 million) and the renovations ($1 million) were put out for bid during that first year. Before the contracts had been finalized, there was a significant economic downturn in the area, due to some unpredicted events, including a major tornado and loss of substantial manufacturing. The regional economy was also affected, and the downturn adversely affected tourism.

The city board of supervisors, which makes decisions on the city budget, has revisited the budget and decided to go forward with the boat dock improvements as an investment in revitalization (cost of $1 million over the next three years). The city has decided to shift some of the $5 million budgeted for recreational improvements to city building repair costs resulting from the tornado, but to go forward with the bike trail and boat dock expenditures. The Board has decided at the present not to go forward with the new swimming pool construction or the accessibility retrofitting and to use the $3 million budgeted for that for storm cleanup. The city is considering closing down all existing swimming pools for the summer because of the costs of maintenance and staffing.

Tina is a veteran who was injured in Afghanistan and who is being rehabilitated in the veterans' hospital. She plans to remain in the community to continue rehabilitation and had been looking forward to using an accessible swimming pool. Only one of the city's existing pools is accessible, and that one is in a remote suburb that would require transportation time of over an hour each way.

In addition, Tina uses the paratransit system that is currently funded through a combination of a city subsidy, federal grant funding, and passenger fares. The metro system (Springfield Transit Authority for Riders (STAR)), which provides both scheduled bus service and paratransit service is a nonprofit private agency, but it is regulated by the city board of supervisors and must have all changes in service and rates approved by the city. Because of the economic downturn, STAR has requested to eliminate all bus service (including paratransit service) to suburban areas of the city. There is very low ridership in these areas. This would mean that Tina could not use paratransit service to reach the one existing accessible swimming pool and a worksite where she is seeking employment.

Tina has become a member of an injured veterans' advocacy group, and was advised by the director of the group that an examination of the city's ADA/504 self-evaluation plan did not address recreational facilities at all, and only addressed city office buildings. She is considering whether to seek redress regarding the swimming pool planning and the changes in the paratransit service. She is also considering whether to ask the advocacy group to seek redress in court.

What are the considerations that the advocacy group should give to the substantive, procedural, and strategic issues? What remedies are available? Are there other avenues of redress other than litigation that might be more effective?

One of the first cases to address the nondiscrimination aspects of Title II of the ADA, which prohibits discrimination by public services, is the following.

CONCERNED PARENTS TO SAVE DREHER PARK CENTER v. CITY OF WEST PALM BEACH
846 F. Supp. 986 (S.D. Fla. 1994)

RYSKAMP, DISTRICT JUDGE:

I. *Background*

Concerned Parents to Save Dreher Park Center is an unincorporated association of over fifty parents and volunteers organized in response to the elimination of certain recreational programs for persons with disabilities, which had previously been provided by the Defendant City of West Palm Beach (the "City"). The other named plaintiffs are individuals with disabilities who had been participating in these programs prior to their elimination, or parents or guardians of such participants.

In 1986 the City conducted a needs assessment to determine the need for leisure services for persons with physical and/or mental disabilities of West Palm Beach. The City determined that West Palm Beach had a significant disabled population in need of such services. As a result, and since that time, the City has made available a variety of recreational and social programs and activities for individuals with disabilities and their families at the Dreher Park Center.

As of the 1992–1993 fiscal year, the City was offering at its Dreher Park Center such programs as Jammin' in the Sun Day Camp (summer day camp services for a variety of children with varying disabilities), Awesome Adventurer Club (club-type program for children with varying disabilities), T.G.I.F. (monthly social program for mentally handicapped adults to develop leisure skills), Good Times Club (monthly social program for visually-impaired and blind adults), Sib Shop (designed as an outlet for children with siblings with disabilities), a lip reading instruction program, the Out and About Club (a quarterly activity program for visually-impaired teens), Leisure Alternatives (leisure activities for mentally handicapped adults), little league baseball for disabled youth, swimming for physically disabled persons, and other regular and occasional programs or activities. During fiscal year 1992–1993 approximately 300 disabled persons participated in the Dreher Park Center programs.

The 1992–1993 budget for the entire Department of Leisure Services was $6,573,550. Of this amount, the Special Populations section was allotted $384,560 for their budget. Of the $384,560, the Dreher Park Center's share of the budget was $170,694.

In the fall of 1993, as a result of budget constraints the City made various cuts to the 1993–1994 budget, including those for programs in the Department of Leisure Services. The entire budget of the Department of Leisure Services was reduced from $6,573,550 in Fiscal Year 1992–1993 to $5,919,731 in Fiscal Year 1993–1994. The budget for the Special Population Section was reduced from $384,560 to $82,827. The remaining $82,827 is apparently specifically designated for the salary and benefits for one staff member (a Special Population Supervisor) and for utilities and maintenance of the Howard Park Senior Citizens Center building and liability insurance. Three other positions in the Special Populations section (those for personnel at the Dreher Park Center) were eliminated, as was maintenance for the Dreher Park Center facility. The effective result was that all previously existing programs for the persons with disabilities were completely eliminated.

Plaintiffs instituted this action for injunctive relief in the Court of Fifteenth Judicial Circuit alleging violation of the Americans with Disabilities Act, 42 U.S.C. § 12101, et seq. (the "ADA") and Article I, Section 2 of the Florida Constitution.

II. *Preliminary Injunction*

A. *Substantial Likelihood of Prevailing on the Merits*

The ADA became effective on July 26, 1992, and there is relatively little case law interpreting the reach of the statute. Neither party has directed the Court to any case that applies Title II (relating to public services) of the ADA to city-sponsored recreational programs, nor has this Court been able to locate any cases directly applicable. However, the statute and regulations promulgated thereunder are clear enough to decide this particular case of first impression.

Title II of the ADA provides that ". . . no qualified individual with a disability shall, by reason of such disability, be excluded from participation in or be denied the benefits of the services, programs, or activities of a public entity, or be subjected to discrimination by any such entity." 42 U.S.C. § 12132. Thus, to show a violation of Title II, a plaintiff must show: (1) that he is, or he represents, the interests of a "qualified individual with a disability"; (2) that such individual was either excluded from participation in or denied the benefits of some public entity's services, programs, or activities or was otherwise discriminated against; and (3) that such exclusion, denial of benefits, or discrimination was by reason of the plaintiff's disability.

First, there is no dispute that Plaintiffs or those whose interests Plaintiffs represent are "qualified individuals with disabilities." The definition of the term is: an individual with a disability who, with or without reasonable modifications to rules, policies, or practices . . . meets the essential eligibility requirements for the receipt of services or the participation in programs or activities provided by a public entity. 28 C.F.R. § 35.104. There is no dispute as to the fact that Plaintiffs are individuals with disabilities. However, although Defendant has not raised it, the Court considered the issue of whether Plaintiffs were qualified individuals with disabilities. It could be argued that in many recreational/athletic activities a threshold level of physical and mental abilities constitute "essential eligibility requirements" that disabled persons may not meet. As a paradigmatic scenario, it may be the case that there are wheelchair-bound children who cannot meet the "essential requirements" for a soccer team because they cannot run or cannot kick a ball. However, such an analysis would be persuasive only if the full and entire extent of the City's recreational program was one soccer team. An "essential eligibility requirement" of a soccer team may be the ability to run and kick, but the only "essential eligibility requirement" of the City's recreational program (which is the sum of a variety of individual recreational, social, and educational activities and programs) is the request for the benefits of such a program. Therefore, the only "essential eligibility requirement" that Plaintiffs must meet is to request the benefits of a recreational program.

Further, even if certain physical or mental abilities were considered to be essential eligibility requirements, the same "non-qualifying" disabled individuals may be able to meet such requirements when "reasonable modifications" to the program are made. Thus, if the City's recreational program is not merely one athletic or other activity but rather an entire network of individual activities and services, a creation of a wheelchair soccer team or something of comparable recreational value may be a "reasonable modification" of the City's recreational program. The physical ability requirements for wheelchair soccer, obviously, are different than for non-disabled soccer and may be met by the same disabled persons disqualified for "regular" soccer.[1]

Second, the elimination of the Dreher Park Center programs has the effect of denying persons with disabilities the benefits of the City's recreational programs. The City emphasizes that none of the City's recreational programs are closed to individuals with disabilities, and in this round-about way the City seems to be arguing that because no discriminatory animus exists, there is no Title II violation. Certainly intentional discrimination is banned by Title II. But further, actions that have the effect of discriminating against individuals with disabilities likewise violate the ADA. The most directly applicable part of the regulations under Title II provides:

> A public entity may not, directly or through contractual or other arrangements, utilize criteria or methods of administration: (i) That have the effect of subjecting qualified individuals with disabilities to discrimination on the basis of disability; (ii) That have the purpose or effect of defeating or substantially impairing accomplishment of the objectives of the public entity's program with respect to individuals with disabilities . . . . 28 C.F.R. § 35.130(b)(3).

Thus, although the City is not required to offer to the public (disabled or non-disabled) any type of recreational or leisure programs in the first place, when it does provide and administer such programs, it must use methods or criteria that do not have the purpose or effect of impairing its objectives with respect to individuals with disabilities.

The complete elimination of the Dreher Park Center programs clearly has the effect of impairing the Leisure Services Department's self-professed "Mission Statement" to "[provide] comprehensive and quality recreation services/ entertainment" with respect to Plaintiffs and other disabled persons. There are no equivalent programs provided by the County of Palm Beach or any other neighboring municipal or private entities (which are also facing shrinking budgets) that can fill the void left by the elimination of these programs. While it is true that there is no evidence of deliberate exclusion of disabled persons from the general recreational programs offered by the City, it is clear that many of the general programs are unable to offer the benefits of recreation to individuals with

---

[1] The Court recognizes that such an analysis opens a Pandora's Box of questions as to what are "reasonable modifications" to the City's recreational program. If for some reason a child is unable to play wheelchair soccer, must the City create another "soccer-like" team for those children? Such a question, a thorny one to answer is not at issue before the Court and will not be decided here, but the Court does note a couple of important guideposts. First, the ADA does not require that persons with disabilities be given "adequate recreational programs" or, for that matter, any recreational programs. However, the ADA does require that persons with disabilities be given equal access to whatever benefits the City offers to persons without disabilities. Further, although the City is permitted to provide recreational benefits that are better than those provided to non-disabled persons, the City is not required to do so. Secondly, the City is not required to make any modifications that would "fundamentally alter the nature of the service, program or activity," or that would be futile in eliminating a "direct threat to the health or safety of others."

disabilities because of the nature of the recreational activities and the physical and other limitations of persons with disabilities. Although the ADA contemplates that public entities will provide "integrated settings" for services and programs, the requirement is for "the most integrated setting appropriate to the needs of qualified individuals with disabilities." 28 C.F.R. § 35.130(d). Therefore, the ADA contemplates that different or separate benefits or services be provided if they are "necessary to provide qualified individuals with disabilities with aids, benefits, or services that are as effective as those provided to others." 28 C.F.R. § 35.130(b)(1)(iv). It appears from the evidence that City had offered the Dreher Park Center programs precisely because they were needed to give equal benefits of recreation to persons with disabilities. When these programs were eliminated, Plaintiffs were denied the benefits of the City's leisure services in contravention of Title II.

Lastly, there is strong evidence that the denial of the benefits of recreation was by reason of Plaintiffs' disabilities. The City argues that there is no discriminatory intent against the disabled population, but rather that fiscal concerns dictated the elimination of the Dreher Park Center programs. However, at oral argument the City was unable to account for the extreme disparity between the extent of the budget cuts for the disabled population and the non-disabled, nor has any evidence of any other legitimate reason been presented. This is a significant failure of proof because while Title II does not require any particular level of services for persons with disabilities in an absolute sense, it does require that any benefits provided to non-disabled persons must be equally made available for disabled persons. Therefore, had the City cut their entire budget for the Department of Leisure Services, effectively eliminating recreational programs for disabled and non-disabled alike, the ADA would not be implicated because both groups would be equally affected. However, if the City chooses to provide leisure services to non-disabled persons, the ADA requires that the City provide equal opportunity for persons with disabilities to receive comparable benefits.

The Court accordingly holds that Plaintiffs have shown a substantial likelihood of prevailing on the merits of the ADA claim because there is persuasive evidence for and a lack of any evidence against the finding that the complete elimination of the Dreher Park Center programs denies the Plaintiffs of an equal access to recreational services provided by the City on account of Plaintiffs' disabilities.

B. *Irreparable Injury*

The Court finds that Plaintiffs are suffering irreparable injury in the absence of the kinds of programs previously offered by the City, which cannot be remedied by monetary damages. These City sponsored programs are of great importance in the lives of individuals with disabilities. Indeed, they are even more essential to disabled than to non-disabled persons because various factors (i.e., the limited access to leisure activities, the need for greater supervision, need for trained personnel, physical and other impairments) make it much more difficult for individuals with disabilities to create their own recreational opportunities. The elimination of the Dreher Park Center programs creates irreparable harm because these social, athletic, and other leisure programs present opportunities for recreation that are not being otherwise offered. These programs, prior to their elimination, were contributing to a sense of emotional and psychological well-being, the injury for which injunctive relief is appropriately granted.

C. *Greater Injury to Plaintiffs than Potential Harm to Defendant*

The Court also finds that irreparable harm suffered by Plaintiffs outweighs the potential harm to the City. The City argues that the public purpose of fiscal integrity and maintaining a balanced budget outweighs the injury to Plaintiffs. First, the expenditure of funds cannot be considered a harm if the law requires it. Further, some $170,000 in the context of a $6.5 million budget does not create any real issues of "fiscal integrity" nor present a threat to an otherwise balanced budget.[2]

D. *Public Interest*

Although there is a substantial public interest in balancing the City's budget, as discussed above this interest is not disserved to any significant extent by the continued funding of the Dreher Park Center programs. Further, beyond the interests of the 300 plus disabled individuals that participate in the programs offered by the City, the public also has an interest in meeting the recreational needs of people with disabilities, as well as in upholding the principle of equal rights for individuals with disabilities. The equality of all persons is the underlying principle of the ADA, and one which the public has a strong interest in promoting.

PROBLEMS

1.   The court implies that special recreational programming is probably not required in the first place. Is that a correct interpretation of the ADA?

2.   Might this decision result in a deterrent to Title II agencies to offer specialized programming initially? What about the court's statement that the special programs were offered in order to give equal benefits to people with disabilities?

C   MODIFICATION OF RULES, POLICIES, AND PRACTICES

Title II regulations under the ADA define a qualified individual with a disability as one who can meet the eligibility requirements of the program "with or without reasonable modifications to rules, policies, or practices." 28 C.F.R. § 35.130(b)(7).

---

[2] The City also casts the $9.8 million dollar budget deficit as constituting "undue financial and administrative hardship," which is a defense against the requirements of the ADA. Again, the issue at hand is the Dreher Park Center and its programs, the funding of which plays a very minor part in the overall budget of the City. The Court is not without sympathy for the difficult budgetary decisions the City must make in attempting to balance the budget. However, under the facts as presented, the Court cannot conclude that the requirements of Title II would create an undue financial hardship in this case.

The *Dreher Park* decision in the previous section, gave some insight as to some of the accommodations that were provided by a city operated recreational program. The court does not address whether any or all of these accommodations would be required in the first place, but rather focuses on the complete elimination of the programs as part of a budget cut.

There are a number of government programs where modifications or accommodations could be at issue. Several of these areas are discussed separately in later sections of this chapter. These are treated separately because they are areas in which the stakes are high and/or litigation has begun to address the issues in a number of cases. These include licenses to do business, professional licensing, mass transit, driving and parking, access to justice, and voting.

The following case excerpt is a unique set of facts that raises interesting issues requiring the court to balance public safety concerns with nondiscrimination policies. It provides a useful insight into the test to be applied and the deference to be given to regulatory and legislative bodies that have considered modifications.

CROWDER v. KITAGAWA
81 F.3d 1480 (9th Cir. 1996)

DAVID R. THOMPSON, CIRCUIT JUDGE

[Author's Summary: The plaintiffs were a class of visually-impaired persons who use guide dogs. Hawaii's quarantine law is designed to prevent rabies. It requires a 120-day quarantine for dogs, cats and other animals that adversely affects individuals who use assistance animals. While there is a process for the individual with a disability entering Hawaii to have some access to a guide dog during that time, the limitations effectively denies meaningful use of the service of the dog for the 120 days. Plaintiffs sought reasonable modifications such as vaccinations, a program that had already been debated by veterinarians, scientists and academicians during a legislative debate that resulted in no change to the policy.]

Discussion

The plaintiffs allege Hawaii's quarantine system violates section 12132 of the ADA, which provides that "no qualified individual with a disability shall by reason of such disability be excluded from participation in or be denied the benefits of the services, programs or activities of a public entity, or be subjected to discrimination by any such entity."

The linchpin of the district court's summary judgment on the ADA claim, and the state's argument, is that "[t]he quarantine requirement is a public health measure, and not a 'service' or benefit furnished by the state to eligible participants." Because, according to the district court, the quarantine requirement is not a service or benefit provided by the state, the quarantine does not deny the plaintiffs any benefits, and as a result they have no claim under the ADA.

The flaw in this analysis is the assumption that no violation of the ADA occurs unless a service or benefit of the state is provided in a manner that discriminates against disabled individuals. This simply is not so.

Section 12132 of the ADA precludes (1) exclusion from/denial of benefits of public services, as well as (2) discrimination by a public entity. Due to the insertion of "or" between exclusion from/denial of benefits on the one hand and discrimination by a public entity on the other, we conclude Congress intended to prohibit two different phenomena. Congress intended to prohibit outright discrimination, as well as those forms of discrimination which deny disabled persons public services disproportionately due to their disability.

In section 12101(a)(5), Congress declared its intent to address "outright intentional exclusion" as well as "the discriminatory effects of architectural, transportation, and communication barriers, overprotective rules and policies, [and] failure to make modifications to existing facilities and practices." It is thus clear that Congress intended the ADA to cover at least some so-called disparate impact cases of discrimination, for the barriers to full participation listed above are almost all facially neutral but may work to effectuate discrimination against disabled persons.

Few would argue that architectural barriers to disabled persons such as stairs, or communication barriers such as the preference for the spoken word, are intentionally discriminatory. Yet, stairs can deny the wheelchair-bound access to services provided on the second floor of a government building; and communicating only by the spoken word can deny deaf persons the ability to find out that it is the second floor where they must go to obtain the services they seek.

These and other types of barriers to participation by the disabled in public life do not provide any benefits themselves. Neither stairs nor the spoken word is a "service, program, or activit[y]" of a public entity, yet each can effectively deny disabled persons the benefits of state services, programs or activities.

A further indication of Congress' intent to cover both intentional discrimination and discrimination as a result of facially neutral laws is the explicit mandate in the ADA that federal regulations adopted to enforce the statute be consistent with the Rehabilitation Act. Section 12133 of the ADA provides that "[t]he remedies, procedures, and rights set forth in [the Rehabilitation Act] shall be the remedies, procedures, and rights" applicable to section 12132 discrimination claims.

The Supreme Court interpreted the Rehabilitation Act in *Alexander v. Choate*, 469 U.S. 287 (1985). In *Choate*, the Court concluded that Congress intended to protect disabled persons from discrimination arising out of both discriminatory animus and "thoughtlessness," "indifference," or "benign neglect." The Court held, however, that judicial review over each and every instance of disparate impact discrimination would be overly burdensome. Rather than attempt to classify a type of discrimination as either "deliberate" or "disparate impact," the Court determined it more useful to assess whether disabled persons were denied "meaningful access" to state-provided services.

Although Hawaii's quarantine requirement applies equally to all persons entering the state with a dog, its enforcement burdens visually-impaired persons in a manner different and greater than it burdens others. Because of the unique dependence upon guide dogs among many of the visually-impaired, Hawaii's quarantine effectively denies these persons — the plaintiffs in this case — meaningful access to state services, programs, and activities while such services, programs, and activities remain open and easily accessible by others. The quarantine, therefore, discriminates against the plaintiffs by reason of their disability.[3]

During the four days of each week of the quarantine period when guide dogs must remain in the quarantine station this denial is especially acute. On the other three days when the dogs are allowed out of the quarantine station grounds, the negative impact of the regulation is only slightly alleviated, because during these days the regulations require that the guide dogs avoid all physical contact with other humans or animals. This effectively precludes visually-impaired persons from using a variety of public services, such as public transportation, public parks, government buildings and facilities, and tourist attractions, where humans or animals are inevitably present.

It is no response to assert that the visually-impaired, like anyone else, can leave their dogs in quarantine and enjoy the public services they desire. As the Department of Justice has noted in related regulations, "the general intent of Congress" was "to ensure that individuals with disabilities are not separated from their service animals," such as guide dogs.

We conclude that Hawaii's quarantine requirement is a policy, practice or procedure which discriminates against visually-impaired individuals by denying them meaningful access to state services, programs and activities by reason of their disability in violation of the ADA.

When a state's policies, practices or procedures discriminate against the disabled in violation of the ADA, Department of Justice regulations require reasonable modifications in such policies, practices or procedures "when the modifications are necessary to avoid discrimination on the basis of disability, unless the public entity can demonstrate that making the modifications would fundamentally alter the nature of the service, program, or activity."

There is a genuine dispute of material fact as to whether the plaintiffs' proposed modifications to Hawaii's quarantine amount to "reasonable modifications" which should be implemented, or "fundamental alter[ations]," which the state may reject. The district court refused to consider this question because [t]he legislature has already thoroughly considered [the plaintiffs'] proposed alternatives and has rejected them. As noted earlier, it is the province of the legislature, and not this

---

[3] In his dissent, Judge O'Scannlain argues that if the quarantine discriminates or denies state services "by reason of blindness, then all people who are blind could" assert this ADA claim. Judge O'Scannlain explains that "the quarantine does nothing by reason of blindness; it affects the plaintiffs only because of their use of guide dogs." We respectfully disagree. Many barriers to full participation of the disabled work their discriminatory effects due to the auxiliary aids upon which the disabled rely, and not due solely to the disabling impairment. For example, stairs do not affect victims of multiple sclerosis solely by reason of their disease; some victims of multiple sclerosis, particularly in its early stages, may still be able to walk. The architectural barrier of stairs works its discriminatory effect because other victims of the disease rely on wheelchairs to move around. In this instance, it is not the disease which renders the disabled incapable of accessing services, it is the reliance on a particular type of auxiliary aid which does so.

court, to assess the efficacy of public health measures against the risks they are designed to reduce, particularly when the questions are debatable and experts disagree as to the best solution to the problem.

The district court concluded it could not assess the reasonableness of the plaintiffs' proposed modifications in light of the legislature's own consideration of the issue. Yet in virtually all controversies involving the ADA and state policies that discriminate against disabled persons, courts will be faced with legislative (or executive agency) deliberation over relevant statutes, rules and regulations.

The court's obligation under the ADA and accompanying regulations is to ensure that the decision reached by the state authority is appropriate under the law and in light of proposed alternatives. Otherwise, any state could adopt requirements imposing unreasonable obstacles to the disabled, and when haled into court could evade the antidiscrimination mandate of the ADA merely by explaining that the state authority considered possible modifications and rejected them.

We are mindful of the general principle that courts will not second-guess the public health and safety decisions of state legislatures acting within their traditional police powers.

Whether the plaintiffs' proposed alternatives to Hawaii's quarantine for guide dogs constitute reasonable modifications or fundamental alterations cannot be determined as a matter of law on the record before us. Once again turning to the Rehabilitation Act, we have held that the determination of what constitutes reasonable modification is highly fact-specific, requiring case-by-case inquiry. Moreover, inquiry into reasonable modification would necessitate findings of fact regarding the nature of the rabies disease, the extent of the risk posed by the disease, and the probability that the infected animals would spread it.[4]

Conclusion

We reverse the district court's grant of summary judgment in favor of Hawaii. We remand this case to the district court for determination of the factual dispute whether the plaintiffs' proposed modifications to Hawaii's quarantine are reasonable under the ADA.

NOTE

Following this decision, the parties settled the case (the Justice Department had intervened), agreeing that the state of Hawaii would establish regulations permitting guide dogs, with proper documentation (including certification of training from a recognized guide dog school) and testing, to enter the state without

---

[4] This analysis is particularly important when, as here, there is evidence that the risk of rabies being imported by guide dogs is low, vaccine-based alternatives may be equally or more effective in preventing the importation of rabies, and the quarantine has not once in over 75 years detected a single case of rabies among imported dogs.

the usual waiting period of four months. *Crowder v. Nakatani*, CA No. 93-00213DAE (Jan. 15, 1998).

PROBLEMS

1. Does a state law requiring motorcyclists to wear helmets discriminate against hearing impaired individuals because they cannot hear as well with a helmet? *Buhl v. Hannigan*, 16 Cal. App. 4th 1612, 20 Cal. Rptr. 2d 740 (1993).

2. Electronic bingo devices, with touch sensitive video screens allowing individuals to play several bingo cards at a time, are illegal in some states. A disabled person with limited manual dexterity might need such a device to play bingo. Would a state law prohibiting their use violate the ADA? See *Video Bingo Device OK'd for Disabled*, HOUSTON CHRONICLE, Dec. 21, 1994, at A26.

3. Does a statute that prohibits issuing marriage licenses to people with HIV violate the ADA? *T.E.P. v. Leavitt*, 840 F. Supp. 110 (D. Utah 1993). See also LAURA ROTHSTEIN & JULIA ROTHSTEIN, DISABILITIES AND THE LAW § 9.01 (2009).

D ARCHITECTURAL BARRIERS

[1]   Application of the Architectural Barriers Act, the Rehabilitation Act, and the Americans with Disabilities Act

Programs operated by state and local governmental agencies are potentially subject to several sets of requirements with respect to barrier-free access. In addition to state and local building code and requirements, which are beyond the scope of this book to address, most state and local governmental programs are subject to the architectural barrier requirements found under Title II of the Americans with Disabilities Act. In addition, those programs receiving federal financial assistance would be subject to Section 504 of the Rehabilitation Act. Buildings and facilities constructed or altered by or on behalf of the federal government are subject to the Architectural Barriers Act, 42 U.S.C. § 4151; 36 C.F.R. Part 1191. This would apply to buildings such as post offices, military bases, and federal housing projects.

Like the requirements related to public accommodations, discussed in Chapter 4 (Public Accommodations), the mandates related to physical access in state and local programs depend on whether the facility is already in existence at the time of the applicable date or whether the construction is new or whether there is renovation after the applicable date.

Under Section 504 of the Rehabilitation Act, programs are not required to make facilities accessible to the same degree that would be required for new construction. Barriers were to have been removed so that the program would be readily accessible when viewed in its entirety. 34 C.F.R. § 104.22(a). This is the standard that would still apply for federal programs.

Title II of the ADA applies essentially the same mandate as Section 504 with respect to existing facilities. State and local governmental programs are required to make existing programs accessible when viewed in their entirety. 28 C.F.R. § 35.150. Private entities considered to be public accommodations, however, must remove barriers to the extent it is readily achievable to do so. 28 C.F.R. § 36.305. This issue is addressed in Chapter 4.

For construction subject to the Architectural Barriers Act, Minimum Guidelines and Requirements for Accessible Design, 36 C.F.R. Part 1191 app. C, apply. These standards apply to the General Services Administration, the Department of Housing and Urban Development, the Department of Defense, and the United States Postal Service. New construction by programs subject to Section 504 of the Rehabilitation Act must comply with the Uniform Federal Accessibility Standards, 34 C.F.R. § 104.23(c). Programs subject to Title II of the ADA must meet the standards of either the ADA Accessibility Guidelines for Buildings and Facilities (ADAAG), 28 C.F.R. part 36, app. A, 36 C.F.R. Part 1191 app. B. New construction was to be accessible by January 26, 1992, for programs subject to Title II. For programs subject to Title III, the applicable deadline for new construction is January 26, 1993.

Which design standards are required for new construction and renovations depends on which statute applies and when the new construction occurred because of the varying dates that the requirements have gone into effect. As a result of the confusion in applying these various standards, particularly when there is overlapping legislative application, some of the standards have been consolidated. The revised and consolidated standards for new construction under the Rehabilitation Act, the Americans with Disabilities Act, and the Architectural Barriers Act were published in 2004. For commentary and analysis, see 69 Fed. Reg. 44085 (July 23, 2004).

Later in this chapter the issue of immunity from damage actions is discussed in the context of two Supreme Court decisions that addressed the issue in the context of architectural barriers. In *Tennessee v. Lane* (reproduced later in this chapter), two claimants with mobility impairments claimed that they were adversely affected in accessing the judicial system because county courthouses lacked elevators and had other barriers. The case of *United States v. Georgia*, 126 S. Ct. 877, 163 L. Ed. 2d 650 (2006), involved architectural barriers in the prison setting. Again, the Court focused on the issue of immunity, and left to other courts the analysis of what was required to remove barriers. The plaintiff, who is paraplegic, challenged prison conditions in Georgia. Included in his assertions was a claim that "he was confined for 23-to-24 hours per day in a 12-by-3 foot cell in which he could not turn his wheelchair around. He alleged that the lack of accessible facilities rendered him unable to use the toilet and shower without assistance . . . ." The Court did not reach the substantive issue of what would be required in either case, because the decisions focused on issues of Eleventh Amendment immunity.

[2]   Self Evaluation and Transition Plans

Under the ADA, state and local governmental programs have additional mandates with respect to accessibility. These programs are required to conduct a self-evaluation, to the extent it had not already been completed pursuant to Section 504 of the Rehabilitation Act. 28 C.F.R. § 35.105. The ADA self-evaluation was to have been completed by January 26, 1993. Programs subject to Section 504 were to have conducted a self-evaluation by 1978. Considering the amount of time between these dates — fifteen years — a considerable update probably would be required in most cases. In addition to the self-evaluation requirements of the ADA, programs were to develop transition plans for removing barriers, which were to be implemented by January 26, 1995. The following case is one of the first, and still one of the few, cases to address this issue under the ADA.

TYLER v. CITY OF MANHATTAN
849 F. Supp. 1429 (D. Kan. 1994)

SAFFELS, SENIOR DISTRICT JUDGE:

Plaintiff Lewis "Toby" Tyler ("Tyler") seeks declaratory, injunctive, and monetary relief against the City of Manhattan ("City") under the Americans with Disabilities Act. Count I of his complaint claims that the City has violated the ADA by failing to complete an acceptable self-evaluation as required by 28 C.F.R. § 35.105 and by failing to adopt an acceptable transition plan as required by 28 C.F.R. § 35.150(d). Count II alleges that the City has subjected plaintiff to discrimination by failing to carry out its obligations to permit him to participate equally in its services, activities, and programs, in particular its recreational programs, city council meetings, and advisory board activities.

Plaintiff is partially paralyzed as a result of a gunshot wound to the head, and he is confined to a wheelchair. The City does not dispute that he is a "qualified individual with a disability" as defined by Title II of the ADA.

The City is a political subdivision of the state of Kansas. There is no dispute that the defendant is a "public entity" for purposes of Title II of the ADA. The City employs more than 50 persons.

The City appointed a committee ("ADA Committee") to facilitate compliance with the ADA and to identify priorities. The ADA Committee's membership included City employees and persons with disabilities. The ADA Committee met monthly. Plaintiff attended and participated in virtually all its meetings, except during a three to four-week period when he was recovering from a broken hip and arm. Plaintiff contends that the City did not maintain a list of interested parties consulted by the ADA Committee. Although the City concedes that no such formal list was compiled, it contends that the Committee's records include references to all interested parties, so that such a list could be produced.

Plaintiff regularly attends meetings of the City Commission, held at City Hall. On one occasion in November 1992, plaintiff was unable to attend a City Commission meeting held on the second floor of City Hall, because the elevator was not working. City Commission members were aware that the elevator was not functioning and nevertheless went ahead with the meeting. However, some of the agenda items were deferred to the Commission's next meeting, which the plaintiff attended. City Commission meetings include a time for public comments, when any individual is allowed three minutes to address the Commission. City Commission meetings are televised on the City's cable access channel.

The City timely prepared a self-evaluation for the purpose of complying with ADA's implementing regulations. In preparing the ADA self-evaluation, the City and its ADA Committee reviewed and relied upon the 1984 self-evaluation prepared by the City for the purpose of complying with Section 504 of the Rehabilitation Act of 1973. Plaintiff was not prevented from talking with City personnel regarding the self-evaluation, and in fact submitted comments both verbally and in writing.

Plaintiff asserts that the self-evaluation was inadequate in scope because it did not address all programs, activities, policies, and procedures; and because it did not include streets, sidewalks, parking spaces, and buildings leased by the City. In response, the City contends that all city programs, activities, policies, and practices were evaluated; that the self-evaluation included sidewalks and parking areas adjoining each of the facilities evaluated; and that the ADA does not require evaluation of buildings leased by the City. The City's ADA self-evaluation is available for public review.

The ADA Committee prioritized each of the evaluated facilities with regard to the need for modifications. Within the time permitted by the ADA and its implementing regulations, the City made a list of some planned structural modifications to existing City buildings and facilities that were deemed necessary in order to comply with the ADA. This list was prepared for the purpose of complying with the regulatory requirement that the City prepare a "transition plan."

Plaintiff contends that the City has not adequately complied with the transition plan requirement. Plaintiff contends that the transition plan completed by the City is not broad enough in scope nor complete enough in detail. Further, plaintiff contends that a list of completed facility modifications does not exist, and that no place has been designated for public inspection of such a list. The ADA transition plan itself, however, is available for public review.

Plaintiff contends that his visual impairments prevent him from reading notices in the normal written format, and that the City did not offer public notices in any alternative media as required by the ADA. The City does not produce all its documents in alternative media, but will do so upon request. Some city documents, such as City Commission agendas, are available on audiotape at the city library. The plaintiff has not submitted any requests to the City for notices or other documents in alternative formats.

The City administers a licensing program for purveyors of cereal malt beverages, including liquor stores.

Discussion

The City first argues that its self-evaluation and its transition plan meet the minimum requirements of the regulations implementing the ADA.

The ADA itself does not require local governments to initiate self-evaluations or to adopt transition plans. The ADA, however, does direct the Attorney General to promulgate regulations to implement Part A of Title II of the ADA, which generally prohibits discrimination by public entities against qualified individuals with disabilities. See 42 U.S.C. § 12134(a).

The regulations promulgated by the Department of Justice to implement Part A of Title II generally require each public entity to conduct a "self-evaluation" as follows:

§ 35.105 Self-evaluation.

(a) A public entity shall, within one year of the effective date of this part, evaluate its current services, policies, and practices, and the effects thereof, that do not or may not meet the requirements of this part and, to the extent modification of any such services, policies, and practices is required, the public entity shall proceed to make the necessary modifications.

(b) A public entity shall provide an opportunity to interested persons, including individuals with disabilities or organizations representing individuals with disabilities, to participate in the self-evaluation process by submitting comments.

(c) A public entity that employs 50 or more persons shall, for at least three years following completion of the self-evaluation, maintain on file and make available for public inspection:

(1) A list of the interested persons consulted;

(2) A description of areas examined and any problems identified;

(3) A description of any modifications made.

(d) If a public entity has already complied with the self-evaluation requirement of a regulation implementing section 504 of the Rehabilitation Act of 1973, then the requirements of this section shall apply only to those policies and practices that were not included in the previous self-evaluation.

Among other things, the implementing regulations also prohibit a public entity from excluding a qualified individual with a disability from participation in its services, programs, or activities or denying such an individual the benefits of its services, programs, or activities, because the entity's facilities are inaccessible. See 28 C.F.R. § 35.149. The transition plan requirement addresses the accessibility of existing facilities, as opposed to new construction. Under 28 C.F.R. § 35.150(a)(1), a public entity need not necessarily make each of its existing facilities accessible. However, the entity's services, programs, and activities must be operated so as to be readily accessible to and usable by individuals with disabilities. 28 C.F.R. § 35.150(a). This mandate may be met by a variety of means, which may not necessarily include structural changes in existing facilities. 28 C.F.R.

§ 35.150(b)(1).[5] If a public entity elects to make such structural changes in existing facilities in order to achieve compliance, however, and if it employs 50 or more persons, it must develop a "transition plan" setting forth the steps necessary to complete such changes. 28 C.F.R. § 35.150(d).

The regulation sets forth the requirements for the transition plan as follows:

(d) Transition Plan.

(1) In the event that structural changes to facilities will be undertaken to achieve program accessibility, a public entity that employs 50 or more persons shall develop, within six months of January 26, 1992, a transition plan setting forth the steps necessary to complete such changes. A public entity shall provide an opportunity to interested persons, including individuals with disabilities or organizations representing individuals with disabilities, to participate in the development of the transition plan by submitting comments. A copy of the transition plan shall be made available for public inspection.

(2) If a public entity has responsibility or authority over streets, roads, or walkways, its transition plan shall include a schedule for providing curb ramps or other sloped areas where pedestrian walks cross curbs, giving priority to walkways serving entities covered by the Act, including State and local government offices and facilities, transportation, places of public accommodation, and employers, followed by walkways serving other areas.

(3) The plan shall, at a minimum —

(i)   Identify physical obstacles in the public entity's facilities that limit the accessibility of its programs or activities to individuals with disabilities;

(ii)   Describe in detail the methods that will be used to make the facilities accessible;

(iii)   Specify the schedule for taking the steps necessary to achieve compliance with this section and, if the time period of the transition plan is longer than one year, identify steps that will be taken during each year of the transition period; and

(iv)   Indicate the official responsible for implementation of the plan.

(4) If a public entity has already complied with the transition plan requirement of a Federal agency regulation implementing section 504 of the Rehabilitation Act of 1973, then the requirements of this paragraph (d) shall apply only to those policies and practices that were not included in the previous transition plan. If the public entity undertakes structural changes in existing facilities, such changes must be made "as expeditiously as

---

[5] For example, a public entity may comply with the accessibility requirement by relocating services to accessible buildings, by constructing new facilities, or by delivering services by assigning aides to program beneficiaries. The regulations expressly provide that an entity need not make structural changes in existing facilities "where other methods are effective in achieving compliance with this section." 28 C.F.R. § 35.150(b)(1).

possible," but no later than January 26, 1995.

28 C.F.R. § 35.150(c).

In Count I of his complaint, the plaintiff essentially challenges the adequacy of the City's efforts to comply with the regulation requiring a self-evaluation, and the regulation requiring the City to prepare a transition plan in the event that it elects to make structural changes in existing facilities in order to meet the accessibility mandate of the ADA. Whether or not the City's self-evaluation and transition plan comply with the regulations are essentially questions of law, although the determination of those legal issues depends upon certain underlying facts.

The court has carefully reviewed the City's self-evaluation documents submitted as an exhibit to its motion for summary judgment. The self-evaluation prepared for the purpose of complying with the ADA and its implementing regulations consists of the following:

1. A one-page document listing the programs and services originally evaluated in 1984 as part of the transition plan required by § 504 of the Rehabilitation Act of 1973. The document also states that programs, activities, or services that could be made accessible to the handicapped by non-structural means were deemed to be accessible.

2. A one-page document captioned "ADA Services and Programs Policy," which essentially states the City's policy prohibiting discrimination on the basis of disability, and provides that the policy applies to all City-funded services, programs, and activities. The policy document designates the Department of Human Resources as being responsible for compliance with the ADA.

3. An undated one-page list of city buildings and facilities identified for purposes of the self-evaluation, indicating whether the facility is used by the general public, for programs, or as an employee work center.

4. An undated one-page list of buildings surveyed for purposes of evaluating their physical accessibility. The buildings listed duplicate those in Item 3.

5. Several multi-page self-evaluation checklists prepared in 1984 by recipients of federal housing funds and federal revenue sharing funds.

Plaintiff essentially claims in Count I that the City's self-evaluation does not comply with 28 C.F.R. § 35.105. In its motion for summary judgment, the defendant argues that its self-evaluation appropriately relied upon and adopted the self-evaluation it conducted in 1984 for purposes of complying with § 504 of the Rehabilitation Act of 1973. The City argues that the regulation does not require public entities that have completed Section 504 self-evaluations to complete duplicative evaluations of facilities for purposes of the ADA. Essentially, the City argues that it has met the "minimum" requirements of Title II in performing the required self-evaluation.

From the present record, the court is unable to conclude as a matter of law that the City's self-evaluation complies with 28 C.F.R. § 35.105. The City is correct that the regulation does not require duplication of the self-evaluation conducted by the

City for purposes of complying with § 504 of the Rehabilitation Act. On the other hand, the regulation does not permit a public entity to rely solely on its § 504 evaluation to meet the ADA's requirement for a self-evaluation. Indeed, § 35.105(d) explicitly provides that the self-evaluation requirement applies only to those policies and practices that were not included in the previous self-evaluation. The language of the regulation clearly recognizes that the scope of the ADA self-evaluation is broader than that required by § 504. Yet, the City's ADA self-evaluation appears to be nothing more than the previous self-evaluation conducted in 1984 for purposes of complying with § 504, with the addition of two new pages which essentially do nothing more than assert that the City will comply with the ADA.

Indeed, the great bulk of the documents included within the City's exhibit labelled "self-evaluation plan" are in fact exact duplicates of documents prepared in 1984. The regulation upon which the City relies, however, explicitly provides that the ADA self-evaluation requirement applies only to policies and practices not included in the previous self-evaluation. Only the first two pages of the exhibit appear to have been newly generated for purposes of meeting the ADA self-evaluation requirement. The court would be hard pressed to conclude that these two pages alone reflect a good faith intent on the part of the City to carry out the type of self-evaluation envisioned by the ADA regulations. One of the two pages is a statement of the City's policy against discriminating on the basis of disability. While the court finds this policy completely consistent with the ADA, a statement of anti-discrimination policy is not the same as an evaluation of the extent to which current services, policies, and practices do not or may not meet the requirements of Title II and its implementing regulations.

The City's reply brief states that its ADA policy allows for a "day-to-day evaluation of programs and activities and the flexibility to modify or move programs that are or may become inaccessible under individual circumstances." However, the Title II implementing regulations clearly call for the City to conduct a comprehensive self-evaluation within one year of the effective date of the regulations. Further, to the extent the City elects to comply with the ADA's accessibility mandate by making structural modifications to existing facilities, the regulations require the City to adopt a specific transition plan by July 26, 1992, showing specifically how the City plans to achieve such compliance. In short, the regulations promulgated by the Department of Justice to enforce Title II do not permit the City to exercise a "day-to-day evaluation;" nor do they afford the City the "flexibility" to make modifications of programs that "are or may become inaccessible" on a case-by-case basis. Rather, the regulations impose an affirmative duty on the City to ensure its services, programs, and activities are accessible to those with disabilities. The City is required by the regulations to conduct a self-evaluation to identify compliance deficiencies, and proceed to correct those deficiencies whether or not a particular qualified individual with disabilities is presently excluded from access by such deficiencies.

The City's 1984 self-evaluation appears to have comprehensively reviewed the accessibility of city buildings and facilities as of 1984, and at least some programs and activities that were recipients of federal funds in 1984. However, it is a disputed issue of fact whether the ADA self-evaluation addressed all of the City's current services, policies, and practices, and the effects thereof, to determine the degree of their compliance with the ADA. This is the explicit requirement of 28 C.F.R. § 35.105(a).

. . . Paragraph (d) provides that the self-evaluation required by this section shall apply only to programs not subject to section 504 or those policies and practices, such as those involving communications access, that have not already been included in a self-evaluation required under an existing regulation implementing section 504. Because most self-evaluations were done from five to twelve years ago, however, the Department expects that a great many public entities will be reexamining all of their policies and programs. Programs and functions may have changed, and actions that were supposed to have been taken to comply with section 504 may not have been fully implemented or may no longer be effective. In addition, there have been statutory amendments to section 504 which have changed the coverage of section 504, particularly the Civil Rights Restoration Act of 1987, which broadened the definition of a covered "program or activity."

Because the City's ADA self-evaluation appears to rely almost exclusively on the self-evaluation conducted in 1984 for purposes of compliance with § 504, the court cannot conclude that the City is entitled to judgment as a matter of law on plaintiff's claim that the self-evaluation falls short of compliance with 28 C.F.R. § 35.105.

Count I of the complaint also challenges the adequacy of the transition plan adopted by the City for the purpose of complying with 28 C.F.R. § 35.150(d), with regard to the accessibility of existing facilities. The court has carefully reviewed the City's transition plan, which has been submitted as an exhibit to the City's motion for summary judgment. The plan includes a preprinted one-page form for each of several city buildings and facilities, such as City Hall and the public library, which includes a listing of the structural changes to the facility deemed necessary in order to achieve accessibility. An additional preprinted form in the plan designates a need for "[c]urb ramps as required throughout the community with priority given to those sidewalks serving public facilities and public accommodations." On each form, the City has indicated that the proposed modifications have been "[i]ncluded in CDBG [Community Development Block] Grant for possible funding after August 1992." The only other item included in the transition plan is a city map showing the locations of each facility designated for improvements.

The City contends in its motion for summary judgment that the transition plan meets the minimum requirements of 28 C.F.R. § 35.150(d). The court disagrees. The plan does not include a schedule for providing curb ramps in accordance with the priorities forth in § 35.150(d)(2), but merely echoes the language of the regulation that "priority" will be given to curb ramps on walkways serving public facilities and accommodations. Nor does the plan comply with the minimum requirements explicitly set forth in § 35.150(d)(3). The plan does not identify existing physical barriers but simply indicates generally the parts of the listed facilities that need to be modified or added. The plan does not describe "in detail" the methods to be used to make the facilities accessible. Nor does it specify a schedule for taking the necessary steps to make the facilities accessible.[6] Finally,

---

[6] 28 C.F.R. § 35.150(d)(3)(iii) specifically provides that if the period of the transition plan exceeds one

the transition plan itself does not designate the official responsible for implementation of the transition plan. Consequently, the court must deny the City's motion for summary judgment on the plaintiff's claim that the transition plan fails to comply with the requirements of the ADA regulations, in particular 28 C.F.R. § 35.150(d).

NOTE

The High Cost of Litigation: In a subsequent decision in the *Tyler* case, the court awarded attorneys' fees because "the plaintiff has prevailed on the merits as evidenced by the remedial action taken by the defendant." *Tyler v. City of Manhattan*, 866 F. Supp. 500, 501 (D. Kan. 1994). The court recognized that the claimed fees and costs amounting to close to $62,000 were substantial. "Because the litigation has led to the development of a new field of law, both parties have expended sizable amounts of time, energy, and resources." *Id.* at 502.

E   LICENSING PRACTICES

The Americans with Disabilities Act prohibits discrimination on the basis of disability by state and local governmental entities. As the following opinions illustrate, this raises interesting questions about whether a governmental agency acting in a regulatory capacity, rather than in the direct provision of services, is subject to Title II of the ADA.

HYPOTHETICAL PROBLEM 5.2

Springfield is being proactive in addressing economic downturn challenges and in 2008 built a new sports arena (SPARENA) that can be used as a venue for concerts, conventions, and other large audience events. To pay for the costs of building and maintaining the arena, the city will lease space within the arena's common areas to vendors of food, gifts, sportswear, and alcohol. Some of these leases will be long term (three to five years, with renewable options) to vendors such as major national fast food chains. Some will be short term licenses (for the duration of the event) to vendors associated with a particular event. Other long term leases will be granted to corporations for viewing spaces with 20 to 50 seats and social space with a bar for food and beverage service and other amenities. For the ten year leases, the tenant is given flexibility about how to arrange the space. The shorter term arrangements provide that the city is to specify the design, and also allows the city to license the space to other parties when there is not a major scheduled sports event or concert in the facility. There is also a closed room press box. All private boxes and the press box are accessible to enter, but within the ten year corporate boxes, some have been fitted out in a way that is not accessible in some areas for wheelchair users. Some of the private boxes are fully accessible and are in close proximity to the parking lot.

---

year, the plan must identify which steps will be taken during each year of the multi-year transition period. The City's transition plan makes no attempt to do so, although the City argues that it has three years, until January 26, 1995, to implement the modifications listed in the transition plan.

The number of accessible seats in areas other than the private boxes meet the numerical expectation for an arena of this size, but they are all located in one area. The accessible area is also the most distance from the entrance to the public parking lots, requiring a wheelchair user to travel long distances to reach. These are also often not desirable seats when certain concerts and other events are held at the arena. There is one small more desirable accessible area, but these seats are almost always sold at the most expensive price range.

Tina (from Hypothetical Problem 5.1) purchased a ticket along with a friend to attend a concert at SPARENA. Because of her financial situation, she could only afford the $25 ticket in the area far from parking. The close area accessible seating tickets were $150. When she attended, she discovered the challenge of parking. She also discovered that to purchase food from vendors was very hard because of the high counters making it difficult for them to see her. One of the sportswear shops has clothing racks so close together that she cannot enter the store. In discussing this with friends, she also became aware that the TV sets in the common areas that broadcast what is happening in the venue did not have closed captioning, although within the arena, there was closed captioning on the display boards. Through an open records request, she has learned that the city contracted with a developer/contractor to build the arena, and the developer/contractor entered into contracts with architects and engineers for various aspects of the construction. She has also found correspondence that one of the architects had advised the contractor that the plans the contractor requested for accessible seating seemed problematic under federal requirements, but that the developer had told the architect to build it that way anyway.

A private college and a public university in Springfield have both entered into several year contracts to hold sports events and graduation events at SPARENA. Tina is enrolled at the public university and plans to attend sports events and her graduation at SPARENA and would like to be sure these events are accessible.

The attorney that she consults about her options is considering possible liability and remedies against the city, the contractor/developer, the architect, the engineer, the event sponsors, and the vendors. What are the various substantive, procedural, and strategic considerations? What remedies would be available? Are there avenues other than litigation that might be more effective in achieving the goal?

[1]   Licenses to Do Business

TYLER v. CITY OF MANHATTAN
849 F. Supp. 1429 (D. Kan. 1994)

[The first part of this decision is reported in the preceding section.]

The City next argues that plaintiff cannot prevail on Count III of his complaint, as a matter of law. Count III alleges that the City has entered into licensing and contractual arrangements with local businesses in violation of 28 C.F.R. § 35.130(b)(1). Specifically, the plaintiff argues that the City knowingly issues liquor licenses and building permits for facilities that are not accessible to persons with disabilities. As a result, plaintiff alleges that he has been denied access to services, activities, and programs offered either by the City or by facilities licensed by the City, in particular eating and drinking establishments and liquor stores. Further, plaintiff contends that the City fails to evaluate its licensees for compliance with the ADA, and has failed to require ADA compliance as a condition for licensure.

In seeking summary judgment on Count III, the City correctly argues that the regulations implementing Title II of the ADA do not cover the programs and activities of entities that are licensed or certified by a public entity. See 28 C.F.R. § 35.130(b)(6). Although City programs operated under contractual or licensing arrangements may not discriminate against qualified individuals with disabilities, see 28 C.F.R. § 35.130(b)(1), "[t]he programs or activities of licensees or certified entities are not themselves programs or activities of the public entity merely by virtue of the license or certificate."[7] Therefore, except to the extent that plaintiff asserts in Count III that he has been denied access to services, aids, and programs provided by the City under licensing or contractual arrangements, the defendant is entitled to judgment as a matter of law on Count III.

In response to the City's motion for summary judgment, the plaintiff contends that the City provides a service to the nondisabled public by physically inspecting licensed facilities. If those facilities are not accessible to persons with disabilities, he argues, the City's inspection service and the accompanying safety benefits are not available equally to persons with disabilities. While that may be true, individuals with disabilities are not denied access to such licensed facilities, or to the claimed benefits flowing from the City's inspection of them, by virtue of any act of the City in the manner it conducts those activities. Rather, they are excluded from the benefits of the City's inspection and licensing services solely because the licensed structure itself happens to be inaccessible. Title II of the ADA and its implementing regulations prohibit discrimination against qualified individuals only by public entities. It simply does not go so far as to require public entities to impose on private establishments, as a condition of licensure, a requirement that they make their facilities physically accessible to persons with disabilities.

The plaintiff has not asserted any facts in his response showing that a genuine issue of material fact exists with regard to Count III of his complaint. He relies solely on the argument that the City licenses inaccessible restaurants, vendors of cereal malt beverages, and liquor stores. As previously discussed, such facilities are not "services, programs, or activities of a public entity" under the ADA and hence are not covered by Title II or by the implementing regulations. The City is therefore entitled to summary judgment on Count III.

---

[7] For example, a concessionaire operating in a city park under a contractual arrangement with the city might be considered a city service. However, a licensed food service establishment operating on private property would not be considered a city service, activity, or program just because the city granted it a license to conduct its food service business. In this case, the City has not contracted with any establishment licensed to sell or serve liquor for the purpose of providing any kind of government service or benefit to those who frequent such establishments.

PROBLEMS

1. In Texas, it is a policy that the businesses licensed to sell lottery tickets must meet ADA accessibility requirements. This is a more proactive way to ensure accessibility than after-the-fact challenges against a state or local governmental agency, such as in the *Tyler* case. The program was begun in January 1994. See also *Paxton v. State of West Virginia Dep't of Tax & Revenue*, 5 N.D.L.R. ¶ 473 (W. Va. 1994), in which the lottery commission was directed to require lottery vendors to be accessible.

2. Would it violate Title II for a governmental agency to issue building permits to parties where the proposed construction is in violation of ADA building guidelines? *Schnall v. Levin*, C.A. No. CA-93-5707 (E.D. Pa. filed Oct. 28, 1993).

[2] Professional Licensing

Courts have given substantial attention to the governmental participation in professional licensing, particularly for the legal and medical professions. There are two primary areas in which disability discrimination arises — accommodations to the professional licensing exams and character and fitness questions.

There have been a number of cases addressing accommodations on professional licensing exams, including a Supreme Court case remanded for further proceedings. These cases have addressed both whether the individual met the definition of disabled within the statute, and whether the accommodations being requested were reasonable in light of concerns about security of the exam and whether there was a fundamental alteration to the program by providing certain accommodations.

In *Bartlett v. New York State Board of Law Examiners*, 119 S. Ct. 2388 (1999) (vacating judgment and remanding), the Court was to have addressed whether Marilyn Barlett's learning disability was a "disability" within the ADA. The Supreme Court had simultaneously decided the *Sutton* trilogy, discussed in early chapters of the text, in which mitigating measures were to be considered in deciding that issue. On remand, the lower court determination was that she met the definition. The ADA Amendments Act of 2008 broadened the definition, as discussed earlier in the text. As a result, it is probably less likely that status as a person with a disability will be the focus of professional licensing board denial of requested accommodations, although it is probable that documentation issues will still arise. These will include whether the documentation has been prepared by someone with appropriate expertise and whether it is appropriately recent.

Decisions today are more likely to focus on the accommodations themselves. Judicial decisions have addressed accommodation issues involving additional time on a particular day of the exam, taking an exam over multiple dates, using Braille and large print, use of readers and transcribers. For case references, see LAURA ROTHSTEIN & JULIA ROTHSTEIN, DISABILITIES AND THE LAW § 5:7 (2009).

The 2008 Amendments included language applicable to institutions of higher education that are applicable to the professional licensing setting. This language provides that

Nothing in this Act alters the provision specifying that reasonable modifications in policies, practices, or procedures shall be required unless an entity can demonstrate that making such modifications in policies, practices, or procedures, including academic requirements in postsecondary education, would fundamentally alter the nature of the goods, services, facilities, privileges, advantages, or accommodations involved.

42 U.S.C. § 12201(f).

NOTES

Professional Licensing Exam Accommodations: There have been a number of other cases in which courts have addressed accommodations on the bar exam. In *D'Amico v. New York State Bd. Of Law Exmrs.*, 813 F. Supp. 217 (W.D.N.Y. 1993), the plaintiff had a severe visual disability. The New York State Board of Law Examiners was willing to offer her unlimited time on two exam days, but was unwilling to allow her to take the bar exam over four days. The accommodation suggested by the Board was found to exacerbate her condition, deferring to the treating physician because the Board had provided no medical opinion to support its conclusion. The court, while recognizing legitimate concerns about maintaining the integrity of the exam process, also recognized the plaintiff's willingness to comply with reasonable security requirements. The court found that

> the Board's opinion as to what is "reasonable" for a particular applicant can be given very little weight when the Board has no knowledge of the disability or disease, no expertise in its treatment, and no ability to make determinations about the physical capabilities of one afflicted with the disability or disease.

The denial of the accommodation was found to violate the ADA.

In *Florida Bd. of Bar Exmrs.* 707 So. 2d 323 (Fla. 1998), the court held that it was not a reasonable accommodation to have the score of separate sections of the bar taken at separate sittings calculated as though they were taken at the same administration. This can be contrasted with *In re Rubenstein*, 637 A.2d 1131 (Del. 1994), in which a different result was reached. In an unusual decision, the Delaware Supreme Court ordered the state board of bar admissions to issue a certificate to practice to an applicant with a learning disability who had not passed the bar exam. The court held that she had been unfairly denied extra time to complete the exam in violation of Title II of the ADA. While this may initially seem to be an extraordinary remedy, inappropriate because professional competence should be demonstrated before licensure, additional facts explain the decision. The applicant had previously passed the multistate and the professional conduct portion of the exam, but not at the same time passing the essay section. On her fourth attempt to pass all portions simultaneously, she passed the essay portion of the exam, but fell just short of the multistate section. The examiners had denied her accommodations recommended by an appropriate professional. The court found that there was sufficient evidence of competence to justify the equitable remedy of admission to the bar, rather than requiring that she be given the exam again with appropriate accommodations.

PROBLEMS

1. *Fundamental Aspects of the Program*: Parties are not required to make fundamental alterations to the program or to lower standards in order to comply with the ADA. Parties may also demonstrate that a requested accomodation would be unduly burdensome either administratively or financially as the basis for showing that the accommodation is not reasonable. How would courts be likely to respond to concerns raised about exam security if an applicant requested to take an exam over several days? If a blind applicant requested to take the bar exam in his or her home city rather than at the designated locations elsewhere, would that be a reasonable accommodation? Would there be any situations where speed would be an appropriate measured skill for the practice of the law? What about a policy limiting the number of times an individual could take a professional licensing exam? There have been a number of other challenges involving accommodations on the bar exam with a variety of results. See LAURA ROTHSTEIN & JULIA ROTHSTEIN, DISABILI-TIES AND THE LAW § 5:7 (2009).

2. *Prep Courses for Professional Licensing*: It is clear that the ADA applies not only to professional exams, but to courses offered to prepare individuals for these exams. Such programs probably would be subject to Title III of the ADA rather than Title II. Should such courses be required to provide sign language interpreters and Brailled study aids if they already are providing transcripts of the lectures? See *United States v. Harcourt Brace Legal & Prof. Publications, Inc.*, No. CA 94-C-3295 (N.D. Ill., settled May 27, 1994); *United States v. Becker* C.P.A. Review, No. CV-92-2879 (D.D.C. settled May 16, 1994).

3. A blind individual who uses a seeing eye dog wants to bring the dog to the three day bar exam and has requested assistance in taking the dog to be walked to relieve itself at intervals during the exam because the individual is not familiar with the venue for the exam. The individual also wants to stop the clock whenever he takes a break with the dog. The exam is given in four hour blocks of time. What if the individual requests that a friend be available to walk the dog as needed? What considerations are relevant in that situation?

In the professional licensing process, professional education programs and the individuals themselves, often must provide information about the qualifications and character and fitness for the profession. This information includes academic performance information, details about accommodations received during the educational process, and information about the character and fitness of the individual. Character and fitness questions can relate to truthfulness and trustworthiness. A common practice is to ask about mental health or substance abuse history. Early litigation challenged these questions in both the medical and legal professions as being discriminatory under the Americans with Disabilities Act. In addition to the claim of discrimination, there is substantial concern that these inquiries actually deter students from seeking treatment. There is also concern about ensuring the confidentiality of the treatment records provided to the state licensing boards as part of this process.

In one of the earliest decisions, the court in *Medical Society of New Jersey v. Jacobs*, 1993 U.S. Dist. LEXIS 14294; 2 Am. Disabilities Cas. (BNA) 1318 (D.N.J. 1993), struck down broad questions, not limited in time, about substance abuse and mental health treatment, as imposing extra burdens on qualified individuals with disabilities when those burdens are not necessary. The court noted that the licensing board could "formulate a set of effective questions that screen out applicants based only on their behavior and capabilities. For example, the Board is not foreclosed by Title II from screening out applicants based on their employment histories; based on whether applicants can perform certain tasks or deal with certain emotionally or physically demanding situations; or based on whether applicants have been unreliable, neglected work, or failed to live up to responsibilities. . . . [T]he Board may discriminate against individuals based on their current illegal use of drugs."

The court provided the following additional guidance.

The parties do not dispute that all of the challenged questions inquire into the existence of "disabilities," as that term is employed in the ADA. Thus each of the challenged questions inquire into disabilities, because each question asks for information regarding physical or mental impairments, or alcohol or drug abuse.

It is also unquestionable that many qualified individuals with disabilities will be singled out through their affirmative answers to the challenged questions. Title II defines "qualified individual with a disability" as "an individual with a disability who, with or without reasonable modification to rules, policies, or practices . . . meets the essential eligibility requirements for the receipt of services or the participation in programs or activities provided by a public entity."

Furthermore, these additional burdens are unnecessary. The Court is confident that the Board can formulate a set of effective questions that screen out applicants based only on their behavior and capabilities. For example, the Board is not foreclosed by Title II from screening out applicants based on their employment histories; based on whether applicants can perform certain tasks or deal with certain emotionally or physically demanding situations; or based on whether applicants have been unreliable, neglected work, or failed to live up to responsibilities. In these areas, the applicants' references remain a valuable source of information. Also noteworthy is that the Board may discriminate against individuals based on their current illegal use of drugs.

The Court further notes that there remain to the Board other sources of information, besides license applications, to determine the fitness of applicants and physicians. For instance, information about malpractice payments, along with information about sanctions taken by boards of medical examiners and health care entities, is available to the Board through the Health Care Quality Improvement Act of 1986, 42 U.S.C. § 11101 et seq. Furthermore, New Jersey doctors are required to report to the Board "information which reasonably indicates that another practitioner has demonstrated an impairment, gross incompetence or unprofessional conduct which would present an imminent danger to an individual patient or to the public health, safety or welfare." And, of course, the Board will always have available that most important source of information of all, patient complaints.

The essential problem with the present questions is that they substitute an impermissible inquiry into the status of disabled applicants for the proper, indeed necessary, inquiry into the applicants' behavior. In the context of other anti-discrimination statutes, it has been held to be fundamental that an individual's status cannot be used to make generalizations about that individual's behavior.

The Court stresses, however, that it is not actually the questions themselves that are discriminatory under the Title II regulations. Theoretically, the Board could ask questions concerning the status of applicants, yet neither have the time nor the manpower to act upon the answers. Rather, it is the extra investigations of qualified applicants who answer "yes" to one of the challenged questions that constitutes invidious discrimination under the Title II regulations.

NOTE

The High Cost of Litigation: Following the *Jacobs* decision on the substantive issues, a settlement was reached. As part of the settlement, the court ordered the New Jersey Board of Medical Examiners to pay $233,293 for attorneys' fees incurred following attempts to resolve the matter at an early stage, which would have avoided excessive costs. *Medical Soc'y of New Jersey v. Jacobs*, 1994 U.S. Dist. LEXIS 15261, 62 U.S.L.W. 2238 (D.N.J. Sept. 26, 1994).

A number of challenges have been brought similar to the claim in the *Jacobs* case. The most notable decision reaching a different result than the *Jacobs* decision is the following case. The question at issue is more narrow than the question in the New Jersey case and the questions used by many state licensing agencies.

APPLICANTS v. THE TEXAS STATE BOARD OF LAW EXAMINERS
C.A. No. A-93-CA-740 (Oct. 11, 1994)

SPARKS, JUDGE:

Pursuant to Texas Government Code Section 82.022(b), the Texas Supreme Court adopted the Texas Rules of Court that "govern the administration of the [Board's] functions relating to the licensing of lawyers." The Texas Government Code further requires each person intending to apply for admission to the Texas Bar to file with the Board a declaration of intention to study law and, before taking the bar examination, an application for examination.

The Board is charged with assessing each applicant's moral character and fitness to practice law based on its investigation of the character and fitness of applicants. The Board, in fulfilling its statutory duties, must recommend denial of a license if the Board finds "a clear and rational connection between the applicant's present mental or emotional condition and the likelihood that the applicant will not discharge properly the applicant's responsibilities to a client, a court, or the legal profession if the applicant is licensed to practice law."

The Board's investigation is limited to areas "clearly related to the applicant's moral character and present fitness to practice law." The rules promulgated by the Texas Supreme Court that govern admission to the Texas Bar define fitness as "the assessment of mental and emotional health as it affects the competence of a prospective lawyer." The fitness requirement is designed to exclude from the practice of law in Texas those persons having a mental or emotional condition that "would present the person from carrying out duties to clients, courts, or the profession." The fitness requirement is limited to present fitness; "prior mental or emotional illness or conditions are relevant only so far as they indicate the existence of a present lack of fitness."

Persons intending to seek admission to the Texas Bar usually file their declarations during the first year of law school. The rules require each applicant filing a declaration to provide extensive information about his or her background, including a history of mental illness. The Rules also provide that the Board may require the applicant to execute a consent form authorizing the release of records to the Board.

The questions formulated by the Board to seek information about an applicant's mental health history have been substantially revised since 1992 in efforts to comply with the [Americans with Disabilities Act.] [Author's Note: Language of various versions is omitted.] The current version of question 11 asks:

> 11. a) Within the last ten years, have you been diagnosed with or have you been treated [for] bipolar disorder, schizophrenia, paranoia, or other psychotic disorder?
>
> b) Have you, since attaining the age of eighteen or within the last ten years, whichever period is shorter, been admitted to a hospital or other facility for the treatment of bi-polar disorder, schizophrenia, paranoia, or any other psychotic disorder?
>
> If you answered "YES" to any part of this question, please provide details on a *Supplemental Form*, including date(s) of diagnosis or treatment, a description of the course of treatment, and a description of your present condition. Include the name, current mailing address, and telephone number of each person who treated you, as well as each facility where you received treatment, and the reason for the treatment.

Dr. Richard Coons, one of the experts who testified on the Board's behalf and who is educated as a lawyer, medical doctor, and psychiatrist, was a consultant to the Board in the Board's formulation of the current version of question 11.

An affirmative answer to any part of question 11 triggers a requirement that the applicant provide a detailed description of the diagnosis or treatment and identify and provide the address of each individual that has treated the applicant. The current declaration also includes a general authorization and release for records that each applicant must sign. The current authorization limits the release of mental health records to only those pertaining to diagnosis of the conditions specified in question 11.

As part of the investigation process, each applicant must identify employers or clients and provide character references. The Board then sends forms to the identified references requesting information about the applicant. The current form sent to individuals listed in the declaration by the applicant as character references, employers, or former clients includes a question regarding the reference's knowledge about whether the applicant has been diagnosed or treated in the past ten years for bipolar disorder, schizophrenia, paranoia, or any psychotic disorder.

In addition to the declaration, each person . . . must file an application . . . [including] a verified affidavit that requires, among other statements, an assertion that the applicant is not mentally ill. . . . [E]ach applicant [must] sign a verified affidavit . . . that the applicant has not been diagnosed, treated, or hospitalized since the filing of the declaration for bipolar disorder, schizophrenia, or any psychotic disorder.

Bipolar disorder, schizophrenia, paranoia, and psychotic disorders are serious mental illnesses that may affect a person's ability to practice law. People suffering from these illnesses may suffer debilitating symptoms that inhibit their ability to function normally. The fact that a person may have experienced an episode of one of these mental illnesses in the past but is not currently experiencing symptoms does not mean that the person will not experience another episode in the future or that the person is currently fit to practice law. Indeed, a person suffering from one of these illnesses may have extended periods between episodes, possibly as much as ten years for bipolar disorder or schizophrenia. Although a past diagnosis of the mental illness will not necessarily predict the applicant's future behavior, the mental health history is important to provide the Board with information regarding the applicant's insight into his or her illness and degree of cooperation in controlling it through counseling and medication. In summary, inquiry into past diagnosis and treatment of the severe mental illnesses is necessary to provide the Board with the best information available with which to assess the functional capacity of the individual.

[Factual information about the plaintiffs omitted.]

The prohibition against discrimination [under Title II of the ADA] extends to "qualified individual[s] with a disability." A person is a "qualified individual with a disability" in the context of licensing or certification if the person can meet the essential eligibility requirements for receiving a license or certification. The regulations prohibit the imposition of eligibility criteria that "screen out or tend to screen out" a disabled individual from "fully and equally enjoying any service, program, or activity, *unless such criteria can be shown to be necessary for the provision of the service, program, or activity being offered.*" 28 C.F.R. § 28.130(b) (emphasis added). When, as in this case, questions of public safety are involved, the determination of whether an applicant meets "essential eligibility requirements" involves consideration of whether the individual with a disability poses a direct threat to the health and safety of others. However, a determination that a person poses such a threat may not be based on generalizations or stereotypes about the effects of a particular disability but must be based on

> an individualized assessment, based on reasonable judgment that relies on current medical evidence or on the best available objective evidence, to determine: the nature, duration, and severity of the risk; the probability that the potential injury will actually occur; and whether reasonable modifications of policies, practices, or procedures will mitigate the risk.

The plaintiffs argue that all the mental health questions the Board has used, including the present narrow inquiry, inquire into an individual's status as mentally ill rather than focusing on behaviors that would affect the individual's ability to practice law. They contend that such inquiry is not necessary, the standard required by the ADA to justify the application of criteria that "screen out or tend to screen out," because the same information can be ascertained through other sources and means.

The plaintiffs suggest that applicants to the Board have already been extensively screened by virtue of successfully completing college and achieving admission to law school. Further, any aberrant behavior that might bear on their present mental fitness would be apparent from a criminal, educational, or employment history. The plaintiffs presented evidence that, in fact, the current question was imperfect in that some who suffer from the specified mental illnesses may be missed by the current question because they have not sought diagnosis or treatment. The plaintiffs suggest reliance on other facets of the investigatory process applied to all applicants or a series of questions aimed at behavior would comply with the ADA and would be just as effective as the process the Board currently employs. Alternatively, the plaintiffs suggest asking applicants to voluntarily disclose if they suffer from any mental illness that could affect their ability to perform the functions essential to being a lawyer.

The defendant's expert testified that a direct mental health inquiry . . . is necessary in the licensing process to get a full understanding of the functional capacity of the applicant's mental fitness. The defendant's expert further testified that the inquiry should go back a minimum of five years and optimally ten years because of the chronic nature of the severe mental illnesses specified in the current question 11, which often have an onset during adolescence. Although relying on past behavior in other areas may reveal behavior relevant to mental fitness, the evidence reflected that in the majority of cases already reviewed by the Board, this was not the case.

The inquiries courts in other states have held prohibited by the ADA were virtually identical to the previous broad-based forms of question 11 used by the Board that intruded into an applicant's mental health history without focusing on only those mental illnesses that pose a potential threat to the applicant's present fitness to practice law. The Court concurs that such a broad-based inquiry violates the ADA.

As stated above, the ADA does not preclude a licensing body from any inquiry and investigation related to mental illness, instead allowing for such inquiry and investigation when they are necessary to protect the integrity of the service provided and the public. [R]eliance on "behavior" occurring in other facets of an individual's life as triggers to indicate a mental illness affecting present fitness may be present is a much more inexact and potentially unreliable method of ascertaining mental fitness.

The Board has a duty not to just the applicants, but also to the Bar and the citizens of Texas to make every effort to ensure that those individuals licensed to practice in Texas have the good moral character and present fitness to practice law and will not present a potential danger to the individuals they will represent. The Board has a limited opportunity to accomplish this task — the time of the filing of the declaration and application.

In each of these [varied] proceedings, the lawyer must be prepared to offer competent legal advice and representation despite the stress of understanding the responsibility the lawyer has assumed while balancing other clients' interests and time demands.

[T]he Court finds, by a preponderance of the evidence that the Board's use of the current question 11, a narrowly focused question, and the subsequent investigation based on an affirmative response to the question are necessary to ensure the integrity of the Board's licensing procedure, as well as to provide a practical means of striking an appropriate balance between important societal goals.

PROBLEMS

1. Are *Jacobs* and *Applicants* distinguishable?

2. The argument for inquiring into the mental health status of prospective job applicants as a protection of clients can be made by employers, such as law firms. Would such questions by firms be likely to withstand an ADA challenge? If not, then how could the Texas decision be justified? Are Title I and Title II simply to be read differently? What if answering in the affirmative to any of the mental health history cases resulted in not being able to obtain malpractice insurance? Would a Title I analysis then be more appropriate?

3. There are legitimate concerns about safety of clients and the public and competency to practice law or medicine. What types of questions could state licensing agencies ask to more directly determine character and fitness to practice law or medicine without risking violation of the ADA or without asking about mental health history? The Medical Society of New Jersey has changed its questions to ask about current medical conditions that impair the ability to practice and other questions about *current* conditions that are limiting.

4. What is the likelihood that questions about current illegal use of controlled substances would withstand ADA scrutiny in the professional licensing context? Questions about a history of drug addiction? A history of alcohol addiction? Current alcohol addiction?

5. Would the kinds of questions permitted depend on the profession involved? Would there be a different analysis with respect to teacher certificates, pharmacy licensing, nursing license, or other professions compared with law and medicine?

NOTE

1. *Mental Health Questions:* The issue of mental health history questions in the professional licensing context has been evaluated in several states. The majority have either removed the questions voluntarily or the courts have determined that the questions violate the ADA. *See* LAURA ROTHSTEIN & JULIA ROTHSTEIN, DISABILITIES AND THE LAW § 5.08 (2009). For an excellent discussion of the issues raised in professional licensing mental health questions, see Stanley Herr, *Questioning the Questionnaires: Bar Admissions and Candidates with Disabilities*, 42 VILLANOVA L. REV. 635 (1997). There is evidence that asking such questions is a deterrent to getting treatment for individuals in professional programs who fear that they will not be admitted to the profession if they answer affirmatively to questions about treatment and diagnosis. See also Laura Rothstein, *Law Students and Lawyers with Mental Health and Substance Abuse Problems: Protecting the Public and the Individual*, 69 U. PITT. L. REV. 531 (2008).

2. *Myths and Stereotypes:* The following is an edited excerpt from Laura Rothstein, *Millennials and Disability Law: Revisiting* Southeastern Community College v. Davis, 34 J. COLL. & UNIV. L. 169, 182–184 (2007) (citations to footnotes are omitted).

> The April 2007 shootings at Virginia Tech University raised extensive concern and reaction across the country. Everyone wanted to know how to keep dangerous and "crazy" people off campus. One frequent reaction was that the students should be required to disclose mental health status and that this should be reported to a wide variety of university and law enforcement offices to ensure the safety of these students. This is not only inappropriate in most cases under current legal doctrine, but such a practice would have a deterrent effect on students who might want treatment. In addition it might violate the treating professional's confidentiality obligation of a therapist.

> It should be emphatically noted that most individuals with mental illness are not violent or dangerous and do not present a direct threat. Some, however, are disruptive and may seem threatening in some instances because of their behavior. This behavior may or may not be a result of the mental illness. For that reason, it is critical to focus on behavior and conduct and not diagnosis or history of treatment.

> Some would suggest that asking about mental health problems during the admissions process might reduce problems on campus. While the courts have upheld narrow questions about mental health status and substance abuse in the context of professional licensing certification, they are unlikely to do so in the context of higher education admission. The public protection issues that arise in professional licensing are not the same as those in higher education. The appropriate and permissible questions in higher

education are those relating to behavior and conduct, not to diagnosis and status. While institutions need not admit or continue enrollment of students who present a direct threat to self, others, or property, they should not treat adversely those who are diagnosed with a mental illness or a substance abuse problem, unless that individual's condition has raised direct threat concerns in the past or there is a justifiable basis for the likelihood of concerns in the future. It is also important that the institution keep this information confidential.

Misconduct and misbehavior need not be excused even if caused by a mental impairment or a substance abuse problem. . . . A difficult situation is presented to a university where a student exhibits self destructive behaviors, including threats of suicide, eating disorders, engaging in substance or alcohol abuse, and engaging in antisocial behaviors. While there may not be a threat to others, there can be a disruption or interference with the educational process in the classroom or in a campus living situation. Roommates, other students, instructors, and even patients in health care settings may be challenged by such conduct. For example, a roommate who feels the need to keep a constant eye on a student who is suicidal will be disrupted in the educational process. The focus should be on documenting the destructive behavior, and determining the best course of action based on that. One of the challenges is to identify what code of conduct or disciplinary code is being violated by such behaviors and to ensure that university policies are in place that address that.

3. In response to concerns about overly broad mental health history questions, the court in *Clark v. Virginia Board of Bar Examiners*, 880 F. Supp. 430 (E.D. Va. 1995), addressed a case involving an applicant for admission to the Virginia bar. The applicant alleged that the question on the license application violated the ADA. It asked whether the applicant had within the past five years been treated or counseled for mental, emotional or nervous disorders. An affirmative response required the applicant to provide additional information about the dates of treatment, the treating physician or institution, a description of the diagnosis and treatment and prognosis.

The court held that the question was too broad and should be rewritten to achieve the objective of protecting the public. The broadly worded question was found to discriminate by imposing additional eligibility criteria. The court found that the Board had not obtained evidence that mental health counseling or treatment is effective in guarding against direct threat. The court recognized the deterrent effect of asking a question about mental health counseling, and recognized that past behavior would probably be the best predictor of present and future mental fitness. The decision provides in a footnote a useful listing of approaches that all states had taken to asking mental health questions. The listing was updated in a recent article by Theresa Esquerra, *Mental Illness Disclosure Requirements on State Bar Moral Character and Fitness Applications: A Qualitative Survey*, at www.activeminds.org/storage/activeminds/documents/ theresa_esquerra_part_a.pdf.

F MASS TRANSIT

Mass transit refers to a broad array of transportation services. This includes service offered to the public by both public and private entities on either a demand responsive or fixed route basis. Because of the cost, this is one of the most controversial areas of public policy relating to individuals with disabilities. For example, making subway systems accessible in older cities can be extraordinarily costly. There has been some debate about whether individuals with disabilities would use mass transit even if the systems were made accessible.

A Third Circuit opinion from 1989, *Americans Disabled for Accessible Public Transportation (ADAPT) v. Burnley*, 867 F.2d 1471 (3d Cir. 1989), was withdrawn and the judgement vacated, so it has no value as precedent. The opinion, however, provides a useful history of the attempt to regulate accessible mass transit under the myriad of federal statutes. These included the Urban Mass Transportation Act, the Federal Aid Highway Act, the Architectural Barriers Act of 1968, the Surface Transportation Assistance Act, and Section 504 of the Rehabilitation Act. The guidance and regulations from the various federal agencies involved (Department of Transportation, the Department of Health, Education and Welfare (now Health and Human Services)) created confusion as to whether all public transportation vehicles were to be retrofitted to be accessible or only whether new vehicles must be accessible. There was additional confusion as to whether there was a "safe harbor" limiting the amount of spending for special services. Requirements relating to paratransit systems were also unclear.

In 1990, with the passage of the Americans with Disabilities Act (ADA), 42 U.S.C. § 12101 et seq., Congress specified nondiscrimination and access policy related to demand responsive systems, designated public transportation (not including public school transportation) provided to the general public on a regular and continuing basis, fixed route system transportation, paratransit systems, intercity and commuter rail systems, and rail transportation. 42 U.S.C. §§ 12141–12165; 49 C.F.R. pts 27, 37 and 38. The Section-by-Section Analysis clarifying the regulations is found at 56 Fed. Reg. 45584-45621 (Sept. 6, 1991). The regulations apply to both public and private entities providing mass transit, and implement Titles II and III of the ADA, as well as Section 504 of the Rehabilitation Act, the Urban Mass Transportation Act, and the Federal Aid Highway Act.

Paratransit services present a complex set of issues. These issues include whether it is required, the level of service that should be provided, and what eligibility requirements must be met. Basically, public transit programs providing a fixed-route transportation system must provide a complementary paratransit system. In recognition that it might be unduly burdensome to provide such service, there is a waiver provision. Eligibility requirements are also addressed in the statute and regulations. 42 U.S.C. § 12143(a); 49 C.F.R. §§ 37.121 to 37.156.

The ADA includes reference to how over-the-road bus systems (such as Greyhound) are affected, as well as specifying some requirements relating to taxicabs. The ADA, primarily through its regulations, mandates access for both the vehicles and the fixed facilities as well as providing for nondiscrimination and accommodation to policies and practices of mass transit providers.

In recognition of the high cost in some cases of implementing some of the requirements, there is a phase-in schedule for compliance. For example, mass transit providers need not immediately make all vehicles accessible. They must, however, purchase only accessible vehicles in the future, and there must be some assurance that the overall program is accessible. This may mean the provision of a paratransit system. New stations must be accessible immediately, but not all existing stations require immediate barrier removal. By July of 1993, however, those stations identified as key stations must be accessible. There are provision for extensions of some deadlines in the case of undue hardship. Challenges by individuals with disabilities to the new requirements have not yet reached the courts in any great number.

The difficulty of making over-the-road buses (buses with elevated passenger decks located over the baggage compartment) accessible was recognized. The issue was referred for further study. 42 U.S.C. § 12185.

In *Wray v. National R.R. Passenger Corp.*, 10 F. Supp. 2d 1036 (E.D. Wisc. 1998), disabled passengers sued Amtrak for violations of the ADA. The plaintiffs were passengers who were taking a trip from Milwaukee to Memphis. The plaintiffs, who are elderly and suffer from a variety of medical conditions sat in the car reserved by Amtrak for persons with disabilities, although they had not previously made reservations to do so. When the conductor realized that the plaintiffs were sitting in the disability-accessible seats without reservations, he firmly requested that they move or he would call the police. The plaintiffs moved to the upper level. However, the restroom was on the lower level, and one of the plaintiffs, who took medication causing her to urinate frequently, was on several occasions unable to get down the steep steps before urinating. The question the court analyzed in this case was "does the ADA grant plaintiffs a right to sit in the disabled seating section, notwithstanding that they did not have reservations and that there were more disabled passengers than there were available seats?" The court found that the ADA does not grant such a right. Amtrak has disability-accessible seats, and their reservation system is a reasonable response to excess demand. Therefore, the plaintiffs had no right to stay in the disability-access seats, and the defendants did not violate the ADA by requiring them to move.

PROBLEM

1. The ADA regulations relating to mass transit vehicles include a number of design specifications relating to elements such as grab bars and other safety features. Would a failure to comply with such an ADA requirement be the basis for establishing a breach of duty in a common-law tort action? See *Greater Houston Transp. Co. v. Zrubeck*, 850 S.W.2d 579 (Ct. App. Tex. 1993).

2. Hypothetical Problem 5.1 includes issues regarding elimination of some paratransit service by the City of Springfield. What is the likely outcome of a legal challenge to this decision? What parties might be subject to challenge? The City, the STAR program? What about Eleventh Amendment immunity? Would that affect the remedies that Tina or other plaintiffs could recover?

NOTE

The Right To Travel: Before the passage of any of the major statutes relating to accessible transportation, advocates attempted to raise constitutional arguments to force governmental authorities to make buses accessible. The claim was that the failure to make public transportation accessible was a denial of the Equal Protection Clause of the Fourteenth Amendment to the Constitution. The response to such claims was that public transportation is not a fundamental right. Applying the rational basis test to such claims thus resulted in a finding that there was no denial of equal protection. See *Snowden v. Birmingham-Jefferson County Transit Auth.*, 407 F. Supp. 394 (N.D. Ala. 1975), *aff'd*, 551 F.2d 862 (5th Cir. 1977). One of the earliest discussions of this issue, is found in Note, *Abroad in the Land: Legal Strategies to Effectuate the Rights of the Physically Disabled*, 61 Geo. L.J. 1501 (1973). A pre-ADA discussion of public transportation policy is found in Robert A. Katzmann, Institutional Disability: The Saga of Transportation Policy for the Disabled (1986).

G DRIVING AND PARKING

For the individual with a disability who does not want to use mass transit or some public transportation system, but would rather drive, there are three major obstacles. These are obtaining a driver's license, access to a vehicle, and access to parking and highways. Disability discrimination law addresses these issues in varying ways.

[1] The Driver's License

Obtaining a driver's license is an essential requirement to being able to drive legally. Most licensing requirements fall under state law, although federal licensing requirements relate to operators of vehicles in interstate commerce, such as truck drivers, and operators of railroad vehicles, etc. These laws vary substantially in who may not be licensed, when a license may be revoked, and whose license may be restricted. They also vary as to how impairments are evaluated and how an individual may challenge an adverse decision. The condition probably most affected by such restrictions is epilepsy. In many states, individuals with epilepsy have great difficulty in obtaining driver's licenses. It remains to be seen whether the ADA will have any impact on this issue.

PROBLEMS

1.   Marvin is a medical student who has epilepsy, but he has been seizure-free for ten years. One evening he forgot to take his medication, and had a seizure on the freeway causing a minor accident. After the police report was filed, indicating the facts surrounding Marvin's epileptic seizure, he was notified that his license was being revoked pursuant to a state law revoking driver's licenses for medical reasons (including drug or alcohol addiction). What action should Marvin take? Is Marvin tactically helped or hurt by the fact that he is a medical student? See *Labenski v. Goldberg*, 4 N.D.L.R. ¶ 447 (Conn. App. Ct. 1994).

2.   If a state acted negligently in renewing an unrestricted driver's license to an individual known to be prone to epileptic seizures, and another individual was killed as a result of an auto accident resulting from a seizure by the licensee, would the state be liable for negligence? See *Johnson v. Department of Pub. Safety & Corrections*, 636 So. 2d 644 (La. Ct. App. 1993).

NOTES

1. *Interstate Truck and Common Carrier Drivers:* The federal government is involved in the licensing of drivers in interstate trucking and interstate common carriers, such as bus drivers. The Interstate Commerce Commission (ICC) regulates drivers subject to its jurisdiction. In one of the major cases on this issue, a truck driver requested the Department of Transportation to waive its rule disqualifying drivers with a history of epilepsy. In deciding that the denial of the waiver did not violate Section 504 of the Rehabilitation Act, the court noted that there was not an absolute "anti-epilepsy" rule. The court found that a Task Force, which had been appointed to study medical qualifications of drivers, had recommended against permitting individuals with epilepsy to drive unless they had had no seizures and had not taken anticonvulsant drugs for ten years. The plaintiff had been seizure-free for six years, but he took anticonvulsant drugs.

In holding that the Department of Transportation was not required to make an individualized inquiry as to plaintiff's fitness, the court deferred to the Task Force's recommendation. It concluded that the Task Force's rule was a reasonable one based on sound statistics and that it was sufficiently individualized in its application. See *Ward v. Skinner*, 943 F.2d 157 (1st Cir. 1991). Is there a justification for having a more stringent rule with respect to licensing individuals with epilepsy for interstate trucking and common carrier driving than for a regular automobile driver's license? The Supreme Court's decision in *Albertson's, Inc. v. Kirkingburg*, 119 S. Ct. 2162 (1999), involved termination of employment in a commercial truck driver position because the individual did not meet Department of Transportation vision requirements. The plaintiff alleged that the requirements could be waived, and that denial of waiver violated the ADA. In deciding that the employer was not required to waive the requirement the Court noted the following:

> Is it reasonable . . . to read the ADA as requiring an employer . . . to shoulder the general statutory burden to justify a job qualification that would tend to exclude the disabled, whenever the employer chooses to abide by the otherwise clearly applicable, unamended substantive regulatory standards despite the Government's willingness to waive it experimentally and without any finding of its being inappropriate? If the answer were yes, an employer would in fact have an obligation of which we can think of no comparable example in our law. The employer would be required in effect to justify de novo an existing and otherwise applicable safety regulation issued by the Government itself. The employer would be required on a case-by-case basis to reinvent the Government's own wheel when the Government had merely begun an experiment to provide data to consider changing the underlying specifications. . . . It is simply not credible that Congress enacted the ADA (before there was any waiver program) with the understanding that employers choosing to respect the

Government's sole substantive visual acuity regulation in the face of an experimental waiver might be burdened with an obligation to defend the regulation's application according to its own terms.

As noted in previous chapters, the ADA Amendments Act of 2008 returns the definition of a person with a disability to a broad reading. While generally the amendments prohibit considering ameliorative effects of mitigating measures in determining disability, they allow for considering the ameliorative effect of mitigating measures of "ordinary eyeglasses or contact lenses in determining whether there is a substantial limitation." 42 U.S.C. § 12102(4)(E)(iii). The amendments prohibit covered entities, however, from using qualification standards or selection criteria that are based on uncorrected vision unless these are job-related and consistent with business necessity. 42 U.S.C. § 12113(c). In sum, the 2008 amendments do not really change the *Albertsons* decision with respect to whether the individual was otherwise qualified.

2. *Recipients of Federal Financial Assistance:* Programs, such as public schools, city metro bus systems, etc., also are subject to federal regulation with respect to driver's licensing. 49 C.F.R. part 391. In *Strathie v. Pennsylvania Dep't of Transp.*, 716 F.2d 227 (3d Cir. 1983), the court vacated a lower court decision which had upheld the denial of a school bus driver's license to an individual with a hearing impairment. The case was remanded for a determination as to whether the plaintiff was otherwise qualified.

Should standards for school bus drivers be more stringent than for interstate truck drivers? See also *Chandler v. City of Dallas*, 2 F.3d 1385 (5th Cir. 1993), in which the court held that city employees who were insulin dependent driving on public roads were not disabled under Section 504 and were not otherwise qualified.

3. *Associational Discrimination.* Many states provide for special driver permits for minors who drive under the supervision of a parent or legal guardian. In *Barber v. Colorado*, 31 Nat'l Disability Law Rep. ¶ 147 (D. Colo. 2005), the court dismissed a Title II claim based on associational disability. A mother's visual impairment prevented her from having a license that would have allowed her daughter to participate in the permit program. The court held that associational discrimination claims were not allowed under Title II of the ADA, only Title I. This seems to be a narrow reading of the statute, which was probably intended to extend associational discrimination to all aspects of the ADA.

[2]   The Automobile

A 1982 article entitled *Dealing with Handicapped Consumers* asks what obligations apply in selling goods to individuals with disabilities. These questions are still timely. Is there any potential consumer law liability in selling a car to someone "who cannot possibly drive it because of bad eyesight, or a bad heart, or a history of epileptic seizures"? Or tort liability by the car dealer after such a sale where someone else is injured by the consumer with a disability driving a car? Is a dealer obligated to allow someone using a wheelchair to transfer in and out of an automobile although injury to the car's upholstery might result? The article notes that "case law precedents are few and widely scattered throughout the 50 states."

It will be interesting to monitor whether the passage of the ADA has any impact on additional litigation raising these complex issues of the relationship between obligations not to discriminate on the basis of disability and consumer protection and tort law requirements. See *Dealing with Handicapped Consumers: Added Risks and Obligations*, 18 TRIAL 64 (December 1982).

NOTES

1. *Market Forces:* In recognition that consumers with disabilities represent a significant market to target, General Motors at one time offered Saturn buyers $1,000 as reimbursement to cover costs incurred in installing adaptive equipment to their vehicles. *Saturn Offers Reimbursement to Disabled Buyers*, L.A. TIMES, March 3, 1994, at D2.

2. *Rental Cars:* In a settlement with the Department of Justice, Avis agreed to make rental cars with hand controls available and to train its mechanics to install the equipment, so that the adaptations can be made available on short notice. Other settlement terms included allowing an individual with a disability, but without a driver's license, to be financially responsible on the rental agreement when the car was to be driven by an individual accompanying the person with a disability. Accommodations for individuals who do not have credit cards were also part of the settlement. *Avis Inc., Garden City, New York*, Enforcing the ADA: A Status Report Update (U.S. Dept. of Justice, Civil Rights Division, Public Access Section, Washington, D.C.), July-Sept. 1994, at 5.

[3]   Parking and Highways

Access to federal highway facilities is subject to requirements of the Federal Aid Highway Act. 23 U.S.C. § 142. The ADA applies to state and local streets and roads. Parking areas also will be subject to ADA requirements for the most part. The applicable requirements will depend on whether the parking area is part of a public program (Title II) or a private program (Title III). In addition, in many states there are additional requirements relating to provision of spaces for vehicles appropriately designated.

[4]   Taxicab Service

Taxicab service is technically subject to Title III of the ADA, but because it is heavily regulated, the requirements relating to such service are discussed in this chapter. Providers of taxicab service are not required to purchase or lease accessible automobiles. If a provider purchases vehicles other than automobiles, such vehicles must be accessible unless the provider can demonstrate equivalency in service (including scheduling, response time, fares, area and time of service). 27 C.F.R. §§ 37.29, 37.105.

H   ACCESS TO JUSTICE

[1]   Participation on Juries

Individuals with visual or hearing impairments face difficulties as parties to judicial proceedings and as jurors. The categorical exclusion of individuals with sensory impairments from jury lists has been successfully challenged by a number of claimants applying the ADA and Section 504 of the Rehabilitation Act. The following case is an example of such a challenge.

GALLOWAY v. SUPERIOR COURT
816 F. Supp. 12 (D.D.C. 1993)

JOYCE HENS GREEN, DISTRICT JUDGE:

[P]laintiff Donald Galloway ("plaintiff" or "Galloway") initiated this action, alleging that defendants' policy and practice of refusing to permit persons who are blind to serve on juries of the Superior Court of the District of Columbia ("Superior Court") violates the Rehabilitation Act of 1973 ("Rehabilitation Act"). Plaintiff subsequently filed a second amended complaint, which added a cause of action alleging a violation of Title II of the Americans with Disabilities Act ("ADA").

Background

Plaintiff Galloway is a United States citizen, who lives in and is registered to vote in the District of Columbia. He is also blind and has been blind since the age of sixteen. Presently, he is employed as a Special Assistant and Manager by the District of Columbia Department of Housing and Community Development. Prior to attaining his current position, Galloway received both a Bachelors of Arts degree in sociology and a Masters of Arts in social work. After completing his education, he held a variety of research and supervisory positions in both the private and public sectors. For instance, early in his career, Galloway worked for the University of California, assisting the establishment of a prepaid health care program and health care centers. Later, Galloway served for three years as the Director of the Peace Corps for Jamaica, and then became assistant to the Deputy Director of the Peace Corps. In his current position with the District of Columbia government, as well as in his past positions, Galloway has had "to evaluate facts and people and to weigh evidence and make judgments based on this information."

Like many registered voters in the District of Columbia, Galloway received a notice from the Superior Court indicating that he had been selected for jury duty. Accordingly, accompanied by his guide dog, he duly reported to Superior Court at 8:00 a.m. on the specified date, March 1, 1991. Although he attempted to register for the jury pool, Galloway was informed by Superior Court personnel that he was barred from serving as a juror because he is blind — the official policy of the Superior Court excludes all blind persons from jury service.

Discussion

After careful consideration of the statutes invoked and the pleadings submitted, it is clear that defendants have violated the Rehabilitation Act, the ADA, and the Civil Rights Act of 1871 by implementing a policy that categorically excludes blind individuals from jury service. [The Court did not directly address the availability of compensatory damages.]

A. *The Rehabilitation Act*

It is readily apparent that the Superior Court jury system falls within the purview of Section 504 of the Rehabilitation Act. First, the Act defines "program" as "all of the operations of . . . a department, agency, special purpose district, or other instrumentality of a State or of a local government." 29 U.S.C. § 794(b)(1)(A). In addition, the Superior Court receives "Federal financial assistance" in the form of grants from the United States Department of Justice. Nor is there any question that a blind person is a "handicapped individual" within the meaning of the Act.

Accordingly, the sole remaining issue is whether Galloway or any blind person is "otherwise qualified" to sit on a jury. Defendant bases its policy of excluding blind persons from jury service on the assertion that no blind person is ever "qualified" to serve as a juror because he or she is not able to assess adequately the veracity or credibility of witnesses or to view physical evidence and thus cannot participate in the fair administration of justice. Defendants' position is not only profoundly troubling, but clearly violates the Rehabilitation Act.

Without doubt, there exists "the tendency on the part of officialdom to overgeneralize about the handicapped." *Shirey v. Devine*, 670 F.2d 1188, 1204, n. 45 (D.C. Cir. 1985). The policy at issue here is an excellent example of this penchant for overgeneralization. It is furthermore the reason why a court "must look behind the qualifications [invoked by defendants]. To do otherwise reduces the term 'otherwise qualified' and any arbitrary set of requirements to a tautology." Thus, two questions exist: What are the essential attributes of performing jury duty, and can Galloway or other blind persons meet these requirements?

Defendants' policy is based on the assumption that visual observation is an essential function or attribute of a juror's duties. In reaching this conclusion, however, defendants failed to examine any studies or review any literature on the ability of blind individuals to serve on juries or the ability of these individuals to assess credibility.[13] Even now, defendants only conclusorily contend that plaintiff "is not capable of performing all of the essential aspects of jury service." However,

---

[13] Defendants assert that the Court can draw conclusions regarding jury service without recourse to scientific studies or post-verdict polls. Defendants buttress this proposition by noting that the Court analyzes essential juror functions every time it conducts voir dire. The Court agrees and sees no reason why blind jurors cannot serve competently. That is to say, blind jurors can perform the essential juror functions in most instances. This conclusion is based in part on the fact that juries in this United States District Court for the District of Columbia routinely permit blind jurors to serve if they elect to do so, and if, after voir dire, the Court concludes that the juror is qualified for that particular trial. As illustration, there are trials that involve no documentary or physical evidence or the evidence is such that it can be readily described with a "word picture."

plaintiff has offered uncontradicted testimony that blind individuals, like sighted jurors, weigh the content of the testimony given and examine speech patterns, intonation, and syntax in assessing credibility. Thus, "[t]he nervous tic or darting glance, the uneasy shifting or revealing gesture is almost always accompanied by auditory correlates[, including inter alia,] clearing the throat, pausing to swallow, voice quavering or inaudibility due to stress or looking downward," Kaiser, *Juries, Blindness and the Juror Function*, 60 Chicago Kent Law Review 191, 200 (1984), and permits a blind juror to make credibility assessments just as the juror's sighted counterparts do.

. . . In many . . . jurisdictions, visual impairment is not a per se disqualification, but may result in the exclusion of a blind individual from the jury pool if the case involves a significant amount of physical evidence or if the right to a fair trial is otherwise threatened by that juror's service.

Similarly, in the United States, there are several active judges who are blind. Indeed, it is highly persuasive that Judge David Norman, a blind person, served as a judge on the Superior Court of the District of Columbia and presided over numerous trials where he was the sole trier of fact and had to assess the credibility of the witnesses before him and evaluate the documentation and physical evidence. Defendants have never claimed that "those trials were invalid because [Judge Norman] was blind." It is thus illogical to suggest that all blind persons are unqualified to sit on a jury when a blind judge in the same Superior Court successfully fulfilled those very duties a blind juror would have to discharge. No distinction can be drawn between a blind judge's ability to make factual findings and the abilities of a blind juror.[14]

In addition, the Superior Court admits persons who are deaf to jury panels and has never suggested that simply because they cannot hear, they cannot serve. In fact, the Superior Court accommodates those individuals by providing sign language interpreters. Yet, a deaf juror cannot hear a witness' words and cannot make credibility determinations based on inflection and intonation of voice, but still is able to make the requisite credibility determinations. Defendants obviously recognize deaf individuals' qualifications to serve on a Superior Court jury since no policy excluding deaf jurors exists. Applying the same logic to a blind individual demonstrates that although a blind juror cannot rely on sight, the individual can certainly hear the witness testify, hear the quaver in a voice, listen to the witness clear his or her throat, or analyze the pause between question and answer, then add these sensory impressions to the words spoken and assess the witness' credibility. Defendants' policy toward deaf jurors evidences a lack of prejudice towards those with hearing impairments and demonstrates their ability to look behind archaic stereotypes thrust upon disabled persons; it is thus difficult to fathom why the policy differs toward blind jurors.

Moreover, even if the individual does not initially appear to be "otherwise qualified," it must still be determined whether reasonable accommodation would

---

[14] The well-proven capabilities of blind lawyers, although not precisely parallel to those of every blind juror, are nonetheless persuasive. Blind lawyers have tried both civil and criminal cases before this Court and in doing so, they have utilized the same skills that a blind juror would need — they evaluate the credibility of witnesses and the content of physical and documentary evidence.

make the individual otherwise qualified. In the instant case, no accommodation was offered to Galloway or to any other blind person. According to Galloway he was turned away after being expressly informed that blind jurors could not be accommodated. Plaintiff has established that, in many instances, accommodation could indeed result in an "otherwise qualified" individual. As noted above, sign language interpreters are provided to deaf individuals serving on Superior Court juries. A similar service could be employed for blind jurors.[15] With this type of "reasonable accommodation," a blind juror such as plaintiff should be able to serve satisfactorily in most cases.

In addition to the evidence presented showing that visual observation is not necessarily an essential function of a juror, Galloway introduced substantial evidence to support his individual qualifications to serve competently on a jury. Plaintiff's educational and employment history underscores the fact that he can, and does, make credibility determinations daily. Galloway has served in a number of executive positions in the private sector, the federal government, and the state government and is presently responsibly employed by the District of Columbia, one of the defendants herein. In these capacities, Galloway has been called upon to evaluate facts, weigh evidence, and make judgments. He assesses credibility by listening carefully to the content and consistency of a person's speech and pays particular attention to auditory clues: the rhythm of a person's breathing and the sounds of a person moving, for example.

Yet, just as no per se rule of exclusion should be employed against blind persons who wish to serve as jurors, no per se rule of inclusion should apply either. Plaintiff has never argued that he should be permitted to participate in every trial. Rather, he has consistently conceded that there may be cases in which it would be inappropriate for a blind person to serve as a juror — cases in which there is a substantial amount of documentary evidence, for example — and that the decision as to whether he should be empaneled in any particular case should be left to the Judge, the attorneys, and the voir dire process. In many cases, a blind juror can certainly provide competent jury service.[16]

---

[15] An organization called "Metropolitan Washington Ear, Inc." employs "audio describers" — individuals, trained to describe physical movements, dress, and physical settings for the blind. This or a similar service could be utilized in the Superior Court or the attorneys could be reminded to take special care in questioning witnesses to ensure accurate and complete descriptions of exhibits or diagrams. Moreover, if necessary, documentary evidence could be read to a blind juror by a sighted person and physical evidence could be described. In fact, the Library of Congress utilizes a device called a Kurzweil Reading Machine, which translates printed material into audio. Nevertheless, these suggestions are just that, suggestions — because no accommodation was offered to Galloway, the Court takes no position on the reasonableness of any particular accommodation other than to note that solutions are as limitless as a willing imagination can conceive.

[16] Whether a blind juror can serve competently can be addressed on a case-by-case basis. During voir dire, jurors routinely inform the court of physical ailments or disabilities, temporary or otherwise, which could impede their ability to serve during that trial. In these instances, the judge determines, on an individual basis after inquiry, whether that juror can serve on that particular case. This routine process occurs every day in every court. Members of the venire often advance a variety of reasons which may impact upon their ability to serve, including: requiring both smoking and non-smoking areas, needing to take medication at regular hours, taking medication which induces drowsiness, requiring frequent and regular recesses, having dietary requirements which cannot be satisfied by food available in the court cafeteria, and the inability to sit beyond certain hours due to child care, transportation and carpool

[Authors' Note: The court also addressed claims under the ADA and § 1983. The court determined that the ADA requires that an individualized inquiry should be made and that a practice of categorical exclusion of all blind persons from the jury pool violates the ADA. A cognizable claim was also stated under § 1983 for the same reasons.]

NOTE

The previous case addressed discrimination against a blind individual in jury selection. In *DeLong v. Brumbaugh*, 703 F. Supp. 399 (W.D. Pa. 1989), the court addressed this issue in the context of an individual who was deaf and a similar automatic exclusion policy. At one point in the decision which declared this policy invalid, the court addressed several concerns including the following:

> The concern . . . that the presence of an interpreter would violated the sanctity of the jury system and the secrecy of the jury's deliberations was misplaced. The record is clear that qualified interpreters are bound by oath to interpret accurately and perform only the assigned functions during the deliberative process.

PROBLEMS

1. The previous materials address the discriminatory impact of excluding individuals who are blind or deaf from jury pools. If a trial took substantially longer to conduct because of the time necessary for accommodations discussed in the decisions, is it fair to require parties to such litigation to bear the additional costs of their attorneys' hourly rates for trial? Would this be a factor in the case-by-case analysis of jury qualification in a particular case?

2. To what extent are attorneys who are deaf entitled to have interpreters paid for during court proceedings? See *Mosier v. Commonwealth of Kentucky*, 37 Nat'l Disability L. Rep. ¶ 244 (E.D. Ky. 2008).

Even if reasonable accommodations, such as interpreters, are provided to parties to lawsuits, the lack of availability of legal services to individuals with disabilities is a major obstacle. The availability of attorneys' fees under the ADA, the Rehabilitation Act, the Individuals with Disabilities Education Act, and the Fair Housing Act, has provided some incentive for private attorneys to provide representation of individuals in claims involving disability discrimination. These statutes do not, however, provide attorneys' fees for representing clients with disabilities in legal actions unrelated to disability discrimination.

Title III of the ADA prohibits private attorneys from discriminating on the basis of disability in representing clients and requires that private attorneys make

---

constraints. These needs and constraints are addressed in the regular course of choosing a jury and may in some instances result in a determination that a juror cannot be accepted because either the flow of trial would be irreparably injured or a fair trial might not result. It is no different if there is a blind person in the venire. That person can be individually questioned to ascertain his or her abilities vis-a-vis that particular trial.

reasonable accommodations. This means that private attorneys might be required to provide interpreters or remove architectural barriers, if it is not an undue burden to do so.

Another barrier to judicial access is inaccessible design of courthouses and other facilities such as prisons. In a later section on enforcement, two Supreme Court decisions arise in the context of access barriers. The Court focused on the issue of Eleventh Amendment immunity in both cases, and did not decide the substantive issues regarding architectural barriers. In reviewing those cases, consider what the lower courts are likely to do on remand.

[2]   Criminal Justice System

HYPOTHETICAL PROBLEM 5.3

In 2000, Charles was sentenced to state prison for twenty five years for robbery with a deadly weapon, a crime in which the victim had been seriously injured from Charles shooting a gun. After the fifth year of prison, Charles was injured in a prison fight and is now a paraplegic. He is also obese and has developed diabetes, which is beginning to cause vision impairments. After his injury, Charles has found it difficult to access the prison law library to work on his pro se petitions for parole. He has requested, but been denied a single cell to accommodate his wheelchair. He has claimed that insulin treatment has been delayed on many occasions, and that he should be allowed to administer his insulin with a syringe on his own schedule. There is a work program picking up trash on the highway, to allow prisoners credit towards their sentence, but prisoners with mobility impairments are not eligible. Charles would like to have a trained seeing eye dog while in prison. What are Charles' likely rights and remedies under the ADA?

While some might argue that individuals who are jailed or imprisoned give up some of their rights, the courts have interpreted disability discrimination laws to apply in these settings. The first case addressing this issue clarifies the intent of Congress in this respect.

PENNSYLVANIA DEPARTMENT OF CORRECTIONS v. YESKEY
118 S. Ct. 1952 (1998)

SCALIA, J., delivered the opinion for a unanimous Court.

The question before us is whether Title II of the Americans with Disabilities Act of 1990 (ADA), which prohibits a "public entity" from discriminating against a "qualified individual with a disability" on account of that individual's disability, see [42 U.S.C.] § 12132, covers inmates in state prisons. Respondent Ronald Yeskey was such an inmate, sentenced in May 1994 to serve 18 to 36 months in a Pennsylvania correctional facility. The sentencing court recommended that he be placed in Pennsylvania's Motivational Boot Camp for first-time offenders, the successful completion of which would have led to his release on parole in just six months. Because of his medical history of hypertension, however, he was refused admission. He filed this suit against petitioners, the Commonwealth of Pennsylvania's Department of Corrections and several department officials, alleging that his exclusion from the Boot Camp violated the ADA.

Petitioners argue that state prisoners are not covered by the ADA for the same reason we held in *Gregory v. Ashcroft*, 501 U.S. 452 (1991), that state judges were not covered by the Age Discrimination in Employment Act of 1967 (ADEA)/ Gregory relied on the canon of construction that absent an "unmistakably clear" expression of intent to "alter the usual constitutional balance between the States and the Federal Government," we will interpret a statute to preserve rather than destroy the States' "substantial sovereign powers." It may well be that exercising ultimate control over the management of state prisons, like establishing the qualifications of state government officials, is a traditional and essential State function subject to the plain-statement rule of *Gregory*. "One of the primary functions of government," we have said, "is the preservation of societal order through enforcement of the criminal law, and the maintenance of penal institutions is an essential part of that task." "It is difficult to imagine an activity in which a State has a stronger interest."

Assuming, without deciding, that the plain-statement rule does govern application of the ADA to the administration of state prisons, we think the requirement of the rule is amply met: the statute's language unmistakeably includes State prisons and prisoners within its coverage. The situation here is not comparable to that in *Gregory*. There, although the ADEA plainly covered state employees, it contained an exception for " 'appointee[s] on the policymaking level' " which made it impossible for us to "conclude that the statute plainly cover[ed] appointed state judges." Here, the ADA plainly covers state institutions without any exception that could cast the coverage of prisons into doubt. Title II of the ADA provides that:

> Subject to the provisions of this subchapter, no qualified individual with a disability shall, by reason of such disability, be excluded from participation in or be denied the benefits of the services, programs, or activities of a public entity, or be subjected to discrimination by any such entity.

42 U.S.C. § 12132.

State prisons fall squarely within the statutory definition of "public entity," which includes "any department, agency, special purpose district, or other instrumentality of a State or States or local government." § 12131(1)(B).

Petitioners contend that the phrase "benefits of the services, programs, or activities of a public entity," § 12132, creates an ambiguity, because state prisons do not provide prisoners with "benefits" of "programs, services, or activities" as those terms are ordinarily understood. We disagree. Modern prisons provide inmates with many recreational "activities," medical "services," and educational and vocational "programs," all of which at least theoretically "benefit" the prisoners (and any of which disabled prisoners could be "excluded from participation in"). See *Block v. Rutherford*, 468 U.S. 576, 580 (1984) (referring to "contact visitation program");

Hudson v. Palmer, 468 U.S. 517, 552, (1984) (discussing "rehabilitative programs and services"); *Olim v. Wakinekona*, 461 U.S. 238, 246 (1983) (referring to "appropriate correctional programs for all offenders"). Indeed, the statute establishing the Motivational Boot Camp at issue in this very case refers to it as a "program." The text of the ADA provides no basis for distinguishing these programs, services, and activities from those provided by public entities that are not prisons.

We also disagree with petitioners' contention that the term "qualified individual with a disability" is ambiguous insofar as concerns its application to state prisoners. The statute defines the term to include anyone with a disability

> who, with or without reasonable modifications to rules, policies, or practices, the removal of architectural, communication, or transportation barriers, or the provision of auxiliary aids and services, meets the essential eligibility requirements for the receipt of services or the participation in programs or activities provided by a public entity.

42 U.S.C. § 12131(2).

Petitioners argue that the words "eligibility" and "participation" imply voluntariness on the part of an applicant who seeks a benefit from the State, and thus do not connote prisoners who are being held against their will. This is wrong on two counts: First, because the words do not connote voluntariness. See, e.g., Webster's New International Dictionary 831 (2d ed. 1949) ("eligible": "Fitted or qualified to be chosen or elected; legally or morally suitable; as, an eligible candidate"); *id.*, at 1782 ("participate": "To have a share in common with others; to partake; share, as in a debate"). While "eligible" individuals "participate" voluntarily in many programs, services, and activities, there are others for which they are "eligible" in which "participation" is mandatory. A drug addict convicted of drug possession, for example, might, as part of his sentence, be required to "participate" in a drug treatment program for which only addicts are "eligible." And secondly, even if the words did connote voluntariness, it would still not be true that all prison "services," "programs," and "activities" are excluded from the Act because participation in them is not voluntary. The prison law library, for example, is a service (and the use of it an activity), which prisoners are free to take or leave. In the very case at hand, the governing law makes it clear that participation in the Boot Camp program is voluntary.

Finally, petitioners point out that the statute's statement of findings and purpose, 42 U.S.C. § 12101, does not mention prisons and prisoners. That is perhaps questionable, since the provision's reference to discrimination "in such critical areas as . . . institutionalization," § 12101(a)(3), can be thought to include penal institutions. But assuming it to be true, and assuming further that it proves, as petitioners contend, that Congress did not "envisio[n] that the ADA would be applied to state prisoners," in the context of an unambiguous statutory text that is irrelevant. As we have said before, the fact that a statute can be " 'applied in situations not expressly anticipated by Congress does not demonstrate ambiguity. It demonstrates breadth.' "

Our conclusion that the text of the ADA is not ambiguous causes us also to reject petitioners' appeal to the doctrine of constitutional doubt, which requires that we interpret statutes to avoid "grave and doubtful constitutional questions." That doctrine enters in only "where a statute is susceptible of two constructions." And for the same reason we disregard petitioners' invocation of the statute's title, "Public Services." "[T]he title of a statute . . . cannot limit the plain meaning of the text. For interpretive purposes, [it is] of use only when [it] shed[s] light on some ambiguous word or phrase."

Because the plain text of Title II of the ADA unambiguously extends to state prison inmates, the judgment of the Court of Appeals is affirmed.

Individuals with disabilities face a variety of special problems in obtaining access to the judicial system. For individuals with mobility impairments, inaccessible courthouses and other facilities, such as offices of attorneys and facilities for incarceration, can present significant obstacles to participation. Title II of the ADA requires that state and local governmental judicial facilities be accessible when viewed in their entirety. State and local programs that receive federal financial assistance are subject to Section 504 of the Rehabilitation Act, which requires substantially the same degree of access. Federal facilities are subject to Sections 501 and 504 of the Rehabilitation Act.

PROBLEMS

1. Should an individual who is morbidly obese, and whose obesity makes living in an un-airconditioned environment extremely uncomfortable, be provided any reasonable accommodations if the individual has been incarcerated in an un-airconditioned facility?

2. A news story from Wichita, Kansas, reports that a judge had ordered a 500 pound man to a halfway house. The man, who had been convicted of forging checks, had previously been ordered to pay $11,000 in restitution and to diet at a halfway house as a condition of probation. After losing 50 pounds, he left the halfway house. The judge ordered him to return to the halfway house to lose weight because he gained weight after leaving, and the judge believed that the weight affected his ability to get a job, resulting in little repayment of the restitution. Is the ADA implicated in any way in this decision? See *The Scales of Justice: Man Must Diet or Be Jailed*, Houston Chronicle, Jan. 12, 1995, at A6.

NOTES

1. *Competency of Individuals with Disabilities in the Criminal Justice System:* There is increasing awareness that some individuals who are mentally retarded may become incarcerated in error. This may be a result of a number of reasons, such as the lack of understanding of plea bargain procedures. This is perhaps particularly true in cases involving moderately retarded individuals, who can "pass" for not being retarded. See Joseph P. Shapiro, *Innocent, But Behind Bars*, U.S. News & World Report 36 (September 19, 1994).

2. *Training for Law Enforcement Officers:* The ADA regulations do not provide specifically for training of law enforcement officers, but the analysis of the regulations under Title II note that "it would be appropriate for public entities to evaluate training efforts because, in many cases, lack of training leads to discriminatory practices, even when the policies in place are nondiscriminatory." 46 Fed. Reg. 35702 (July 26, 1991). See also *Jackson v. Inhabitants of Sanford*, No. 94-12-P-H, 1994 U.S. Dist. LEXIS 15367, 63 U.S.L.W. 2351, 3 A.D. Cas. 1366 (D. Me. Sept. 23, 1994), in which the court held that unjustified arrests of individuals with disabilities wrongly thought to be under drug or alcohol influence are subject to Title II sanction. The case involved a man who had suffered a stroke which affected his speech and who was wrongfully arrested for drunk driving. This decision emphasizes the importance of adequate law enforcement training.

3. *911 Access:* A settlement agreement between the City of Los Angeles and the Department of Justice involved 911 emergency service access for individuals who are deaf or who have speech impairments. The basis of the suit was that Title II of the ADA was violated when the city did not respond to a 911 call by an individual who was deaf. BNA ADA Manual, Vol. 3, No. 8, p. 47 (August 1994).

4. *Prisoners with HIV.* Individuals in the criminal justice system who are HIV positive have raised some unique issues. Exclusion of HIV-positive prison inmates from working in food service jobs in prison was at issue in a case arising in California. The court upheld the policy, noting that prison riots have resulted from food service, and inmates receiving food from HIV-positive servers would perceive a threat, even thought it might be irrational to do so. *See Gates v. Rowland*, 39 F.3d 1439 (9th Cir. 1994).

I VOTING

In 1984, the Voting Accessibility for the Elderly and Handicapped Act (VAEH), 42 U.S.C. § 1973ee, went into effect. This statute allows either private action or Attorney General suit and provides for accessibility in polling places for federal elections. This does not directly affect state and local elections, except to the extent that many of these elections occur concurrently with federal elections. Title II of the ADA, however, applies to state and local governmental elections. In addition to being subject to the ADA and the VAEH, parties conducting federal elections are also programs subject to both Section 501 and Section 504 of the Rehabilitation Act. For more detailed information on voting for individuals with disabilities, see LAURA ROTHSTEIN & JULIA ROTHSTEIN, DISABILITIES AND THE LAW § 9:8 (2009).

The following decision is one of the few court cases to address disability discrimination in the context of voting. It highlights to complexity of identifying the party responsible for implementing various legal requirements with respect to voting in order to bring about change.

LIGHTBOURN v. COUNTY OF EL PASO, TEXAS
118 F.3d 421 (5th Cir. 1997)

EMILIO M. GARZA, CIRCUIT JUDGE:

I

The plaintiffs are five blind residents of El Paso, Texas, one mobility-impaired El Paso resident, and a private nonprofit group that aids disabled persons. They sued El Paso County ("El Paso") and the local Republican and Democratic parties under § 504 of the Rehabilitation Act of 1973, and Title II of the Americans with Disabilities Act ("ADA"). Subsequently, El Paso impleaded the Secretary, and the plaintiffs also added him as a defendant.

The plaintiffs alleged that the defendants discriminated against them by failing to ensure that persons with visual and mobility impairments have access to "polling sites and voting procedures." Specifically, the blind plaintiffs asserted that the voting equipment available at their polling places only permitted them to vote with the assistance of an election worker or other person, and the defendants had not taken steps to ensure that they could vote with complete secrecy.[17] Thus, they contended, the defendants violated § 504 and the ADA. In addition, the wheelchair-bound plaintiff maintained that she had trouble locating a parking space next to and using the restroom facilities at her polling place. She asserted that the defendants breached their obligation to ensure that polling places are accessible to handicapped voters and hence violated § 504 and the ADA.

[Procedural history omitted.]

II
A

[Class action issue discussion omitted.]

B

The Secretary next argues that the plaintiffs cannot state a claim against him under § 504 of the Rehabilitation Act of 1973 because he does not receive financial assistance from the federal government. . . .

We have held that to state a § 504 claim a plaintiff must allege that the specific program or activity with which he or she was involved receives or directly benefits from federal financial assistance. Certainly, a plaintiff may not predicate a § 504 claim against a state actor on the mere fact that the state itself obtains federal money. Here, the plaintiffs have not even argued that the Secretary receives federal financial assistance — let alone presented any evidence on this point.

---

[17] Texas Election Code § 64.031 provides that a "voter is eligible to receive assistance in marking the ballot . . . if the voter cannot prepare the ballot because of a physical disability that renders the voter unable to write or see. . . . "

Therefore, the plaintiffs have failed to state a claim under § 504 against the Secretary.

C

Last, the Secretary argues that the district court erred in holding that he violated the ADA by breaching a duty to ensure that local election authorities comply with the ADA. . . .

Based on scattered provisions of the Texas Election Code, the district court found that the Secretary had a duty to warrant that local election authorities followed the ADA. Relying on Texas Election Code §§ 31.003 and 31.005 . . . .

Title II of the ADA provides that "[n]o qualified individual with a disability shall, by reason of such disability, be excluded from participation in or be denied the benefits of the services, programs, or activities of a public entity, or be subjected to discrimination by any such entity." 42 U.S.C. § 12132. Thus, to establish a violation of Title II, the plaintiffs here must demonstrate: (1) that they are qualified individuals within the meaning of the Act; (2) that they are being excluded from participation in, or being denied benefits of, services, programs, or activities for which the Secretary is responsible, or are otherwise being discriminated against by the Secretary; and (3) that such exclusion, denial of benefits, or discrimination is by reason of their disability. The Secretary does not dispute that the plaintiffs are qualified individuals within the meaning of the ADA or that he is a public entity for purposes of the statute. The Secretary, however, asserts that he has not denied the plaintiffs the benefit of a program for which he is responsible.

In *Bush v. Viterna*, 795 F.2d 1203 (5th Cir.1986), a class of prisoners sued the Texas Commission on Jail Standards under 42 U.S.C. § 1983, based upon county jail conditions that allegedly violated the Constitution. The plaintiffs claimed, under a theory of "supervisory liability," that the Commission's failure to discharge its state law-imposed duties caused the constitutional violations. The plaintiffs argued that if the Commission had followed its state law obligations to promulgate regulatory standards and enforce those standards, local officials would have ensured that conditions and activities in county jails did not violate the Constitution.

We analyzed the Commission's state law duties, and found that the Commission's purpose was to remedy inadequacies in county jail conditions. We also concluded that the Commission was required to promulgate standards, but was merely authorized to enforce those standards by order or by filing suit against noncomplying counties. We observed that when a federal right is deprived through state action, the court must turn to state law to determine which state actor is legally responsible for the violation. "States have virtually complete freedom to decide who will be responsible for such tasks, and therewith to determine who will be held liable for civil rights violations that occur in the course of carrying them out." We found that the Commission "simply does not appear to have any state-imposed legal duty to correct jail violations or noncompliance that it becomes aware of." Thus, we found that the prisoners did not state a claim against the Commission under § 1983.

The plaintiffs' claim in *Bush* is analogous to the plaintiffs' claim here that the Secretary has a duty to ensure compliance with the ADA with regard to Texas elections. Following *Bush*, we look to Texas law to determine whether responsibility for the violations the plaintiffs allege can properly be attributed to the Secretary.

Review of the provisions of the Texas Election Code that refer to the Secretary's role in elections reveals that most give discretion to the Secretary to take some action. In the absence of such a duty, the Secretary cannot be held responsible for a failure to exercise his discretion.

The Texas Election Code does contain some provisions requiring the Secretary to take action with respect to elections. Specifically, § 31.003 states that the Secretary

> shall obtain and maintain uniformity in the application, operation, and interpretation of [the Texas Election Code] and of the election laws outside this code. In performing this duty, the secretary shall prepare detailed and comprehensive written directives and instructions relating to and based on [the Texas Election Code] and the election laws outside this code. The secretary shall distribute these materials to the appropriate state and local authorities having duties in the administration of these laws.

Moreover, § 31.004 provides that the Secretary

> (a) . . . shall assist and advise all election authorities with regard to the application, operation, and interpretation of this code and of the election laws outside this code.

> (b) The secretary shall maintain an informational service for answering inquiries of election authorities relating to the administration of the election laws or the performance of their duties.

Whether these sections impose a duty on the Secretary to ensure compliance with the ADA throughout Texas turns on whether the phrase "election laws outside this code" includes the ADA.

[T]he ADA does not include even a single provision specifically governing elections. On the contrary, the statute never refers to elections. Indeed, the statute only mentions voting once, and that is in the "findings and purpose" section. This section, 42 U.S.C. § 12101(a)(3), notes that "discrimination against individuals with disabilities persists in such critical areas as employment, housing, public accommodations, education, transportation, communication, recreation, institutionalization, health services, voting, and access to public services. . . ." The mere mention of the word "voting" here does not transform the ADA into an "election law." Such a tangential allusion is insufficient to impose on the Secretary the rather extraordinary duty of ensuring that local election officials interpret and apply the ADA uniformly.

Second, as a general civil rights statute, the ADA involves every area of law. If the ADA is construed as an "election law," then it presumably could also be called an employment law, housing law, transportation law, and so on. However, we do not think that the common, ordinary meaning of "election laws" includes a law that can be characterized in so many different ways. Rather, "election laws" only covers laws that specifically relate to elections, such as the Voting Rights Act of 1965, 42 U.S.C. §§ 1972-1973, or the Voting Accessibility for the Elderly and Handicapped Act, 42 U.S.C. § 1973ee-1.

Third, if the Secretary is responsible for guaranteeing that local election officials comply with the ADA, then presumably he would also have a duty to warrant that these officials follow every other general civil rights statute that could touch on elections. These statutes would include, among others, the Civil Rights Act of 1870; the Civil Rights Act of 1871; the Ku Klux Klan Act of 1871; the Civil Rights Act of 1964; the Education Amendments of 1972; the Age Discrimination Act; the Indian Civil Rights Act of 1968; and various amending statutes such as the Civil Rights Restoration Act of 1987. In addition, the Secretary would need to ensure that local election officials follow other generally applicable laws which could pertain to elections, such as statutes dealing with littering, zoning, fire safety, and so on. We do not believe that the Texas legislature intended § 31.003 to require the Secretary to provide "detailed and comprehensive written directives and instructions relating to and based on" these statutes, at least to the extent that they do not specifically pertain to elections.

In sum, we conclude that the phrase "election laws outside this code" only encompasses laws that specifically govern elections, not generally applicable laws that might cover some aspect of elections. Thus, neither § 31.003 nor § 31.004 imposes a duty on the Secretary to ensure statewide compliance with the ADA by the political subdivisions that administer elections in Texas.

Two other provisions in the Texas Election Code place responsibility on the Secretary for approval of voting systems and equipment used in Texas elections. Section 122.031 states that "[b]efore a voting system or voting system equipment may be used in an election, the system and a unit of the equipment must be approved by the secretary of state. . . . " Section 122.038 provides that the Secretary "shall approve the system or equipment" after reviewing reports on the system or equipment prepared by designated examiners and determining that it "satisfies the applicable requirements for approval."

The plaintiffs maintain that the Secretary has violated the ADA because he has not approved equipment accessible to blind voters. The plaintiffs construe [Texas law] as obliging the Secretary to take affirmative steps to solicit and approve equipment that ensures a completely secret ballot for blind voters. The plaintiffs do not, however, specify where . . . they find this expansive duty, particularly in the absence of any evidence that the Secretary has refused approval of voting equipment that satisfies the plaintiffs' desires. The plaintiffs' assertion that a voting machine for blind voters exists does not prove that the Secretary violated the ADA because the plaintiffs do not allege — let alone prove — that they presented any voting machine to the Secretary or that he failed to approve such a machine. Perhaps the plaintiffs could state a claim under the ADA if they demonstrated that the Secretary wrongly refused to approve such equipment after it was presented to him for approval. However, the record does not reveal that the Secretary has considered any voting equipment that "satisfies the applicable requirements" and then failed to permit it. As a result, the plaintiffs have not demonstrated the

Secretary's responsibility for the alleged ADA violations.

With regard to mobility-impaired voters, we note that § 43.034 of the Texas Election Code places responsibility for accessibility of polling places to the elderly and physically handicapped on the "commissioners court[s]" and the "governing body of each political subdivision that holds elections." The district court stated that § 43.034 imposes a statutory duty on local political subdivisions, but that the statute is unclear about how it is enforced. Without explanation, the district court concluded that it "is of the opinion that the final enforcer of this section is the Secretary of State." Thus, the district court found that the Secretary violated the ADA because some buildings used as polling places are not accessible to mobility-impaired voters.

We disagree with the district court's conclusion. Section 43.034 directs local election officials, not the Secretary, to ensure accessibility of polling places to elderly and physically handicapped voters. However, since § 43.034 is clearly an "election law," we note that § 31.003 commands the Secretary to obtain and maintain uniformity in the application, operation, and interpretation of § 43.034. This means that the Secretary has a duty to maintain uniformity in the operation of a statute that requires local election officials to ensure the accessibility of polling places.

In this regard, the plaintiffs assert that local election officials implement § 43.034 differently and that the Secretary has not issued "detailed and comprehensive written directives and instructions" suggesting that the officials administer that section in a particular way. To allege an ADA violation, though, the plaintiffs must also maintain, among other things, that they are being denied the benefit of a service for which the Secretary is responsible. Here, the service the Secretary has to perform is obtaining the uniform operation of § 43.034. While the plaintiffs may receive a benefit from the accessibility mandate of § 43.034, they do not receive any benefit from the uniformity of this mandate. For instance, assume that local election officials interpret the accessibility mandate differently. Some officials believe that § 43.034 requires them to provide special scooters to ferry handicapped voters from the parking lot to the polling place; others disagree. The Secretary could carry out his duty under § 31.003 either by informing local election officials that § 43.034 does not compel the provision of special scooters or by directing local officials to offer such scooters. In other words, the Secretary can ensure uniformity by acting either to increase or decrease accessibility on the margin; uniformity in and of itself confers no benefit on the disabled. Thus, we determine that while the Secretary has a state-imposed legal duty to ensure the uniformity of the application, operation, and interpretation § 43.034, this uniformity — without more — cannot be a "benefit" to the plaintiffs for purposes of the ADA and the alleged denial of uniformity cannot be an example of discrimination under the ADA. Accordingly, the Secretary cannot be held liable for violation of the ADA because some polling places are inaccessible to mobility-impaired voters.

Finally, § 35.105 of the ADA implementing regulations requires a public entity to "[e]valuate its current services, policies, and practices, and the effects thereof . . . [and] proceed to make the necessary modifications." 28 C.F.R. § 35.105(a). The plaintiffs argue that the Secretary violated the ADA by failing to perform this "self-evaluation." The plaintiffs maintain that "[t]he Secretary's abject failure . . .

most notably by failing to prepare a self-evaluation plan, played a pivotal role in ensuring that, as of the trial in this case, no efforts had been made in Texas to adapt or invent voting systems that would provide secrecy of the ballot for voters who are blind. . . . " The plaintiffs describe § 35.105 as creating a "duty" on the part of the Secretary "to take the initiative and explore, through all means reasonably available, solutions to the discrimination faced by voters who are blind."

Central to the plaintiffs' argument here is the premise that § 35.105 requires the Secretary to evaluate the practices of every electoral subdivision in Texas. We find such an interpretation of the regulation unreasonable. To the contrary, we read § 35.105 as merely requiring the Secretary to evaluate his department, an evalua- tion the Secretary performed. In fact, even the plaintiffs' counsel admitted before the district court that the Secretary performed an internal self-evaluation.

In sum, the Secretary has no duty under either Texas law or the ADA to take steps to ensure that local election officials comply with the ADA. While the Secretary has a duty to approve certain voting equipment, the plaintiffs have failed to allege facts suggesting a breach of that duty. In addition, while the Secretary has a duty to maintain uniformity in the administration of § 43.034 and arguably breached that duty, he could not have denied any benefit to the plaintiffs. Therefore, we determine that the plaintiffs have failed to state a claim under the ADA against the Secretary.

PROBLEM

How likely is it that the reasoning in *Lightbourn* will be adopted by other courts? What are the consequences of this decision?

In *National Coalition for Students with Disabilities Educ. and Legal Defense v. Allen*, 152 F.3d 283 (4th Cir. 1998), action was brought under the National Voter Registration Act (NVRA), 42 U.S.C. § 1973gg-5(a)(2)(B), to require state officials to designate public university offices providing services to students with disabilities as voter registration agencies. The NVRA requires states to designate all offices providing State-funded programs that primarily provide services to persons with disabilities as voter registration agencies. The court found that offices providing services to students with disabilities at public colleges were offices for the purposes of the NVRA, and such university offices must provide voter registration services.

J   ENFORCEMENT

In addition to the enforcement procedures and remedies discussed in the previous sections, the following is an overview of the enforcement mechanisms relating to governmentally provided services that discriminate unlawfully on the basis of disability.

[1]   Americans with Disabilities Act

Unlike Title III of the ADA, which is more restrictive in terms of remedies, Title II of the ADA permits the recovery of damages. Title II incorporates the remedies, procedures, and rights of Section 504 of the Rehabilitation Act. 29 U.S.C.

§ 794; 42 U.S.C. § 12133. The ADA regulations provide for procedures for filing complaints with administrative agencies. 35 C.F.R. §§ 35.170–.178. Several federal agencies are designated to coordinate compliance activities with respect to Title II. 35 C.F.R. § 35.190. The ADA is specific in its statutory language that states are not immune under the eleventh amendment to the Constitution from actions under the ADA. 42 U.S.C. § 12202.

[2]   Section 504 of The Rehabilitation Act

Violations of Section 504 of the Rehabilitation Act can be remedied either by complaint to the agency granting the federal funding or by private complaint in court. The majority of courts recognize a private right of action without exhaustion of administrative remedies. The model regulations under Section 504 specify the administrative review procedure. 28 C.F.R. pt. 41. For a discussion of cases and other information related to enforcement under Section 504, see LAURA ROTHSTEIN & JULIA ROTHSTEIN, DISABILITIES AND THE LAW § 1.13 (2009).

The remedies available under Section 504, and under the ADA as it incorporates Section 504 remedies and procedures, include termination of federal financial assistance, injunctive relief, and attorneys' fees. The statute is not specific as to the availability of damages under Section 504, although the majority of courts have recognized damages as a remedy. See LAURA ROTHSTEIN & JULIA ROTHSTEIN, DISABILITIES AND THE LAW § 1.14 (2009).

Section 504 was amended in 1986 to clarify that states are not immune from damage actions under Section 504 of the Rehabilitation Act. This is consistent with the ADA. 29 U.S.C. § 701.

[3]   The Architectural Barriers Act

The Architectural Barriers Act is enforced by the Architectural Transportation Barriers Compliance Board (ATBCB). 29 U.S.C. § 792. This agency was created in 1973. It is probable that the primary avenue of redress is through the agency review process, and although judicial review of agency activity is permitted, it is not clear whether one may initially seek redress in the courts. See LAURA ROTHSTEIN & JULIA ROTHSTEIN, DISABILITIES AND THE LAW § 1.17 (2009).

PROBLEM

As a tactical matter, when is it best to seek redress through administrative complaint procedures and when is it best to go directly to court? Should one do both?

[4]   Immunity Issues

In *Board of Trustees v. Garrett*, 531 U.S. 356 (2001), reprinted in Section 3[G][2], *supra*, the Court addressed the issue of immunity in the context of ADA employment claims under Title I against state employers. The Court held that states are immune from money damages in private suits under Title I. The Court left undecided whether the same immunity from money damages suits applies in

Title II cases, whether remedies of reasonable accommodation can be ordered against states, and whether there is also state immunity in Section 504 cases. Also undecided was the issue of immunity in Title II cases involving issues other than employment.

The Supreme Court expanded its views on Eleventh Amendment immunity in ADA cases in two decisions involving the justice system. In the case of *Tennessee v. Lane*, 124 S. Ct. 1978 (2004), the Supreme Court addressed the issue of Eleventh Amendment immunity in Title II cases against state agencies in the context of access to the justice system. Justice Stevens, writing for the majority in a 5-4 opinion, held that "the Eleventh Amendment permits suits for money damages under Title II." The following is a portion of the opinion in that case.

TENNESSEE v. LANE
124 S. Ct. 1978 (2004)

Justice Stevens, delivered the opinion of the Court

In August 1998, respondents George Lane and Beverly Jones filed this action against the State of Tennessee and a number of Tennessee counties, alleging past and ongoing violations of Title II. Respondents, both of whom are paraplegics who use wheelchairs for mobility, claimed that they were denied access to, and the services of, the state court system by reason of their disabilities. Lane alleged that he was compelled to appear to answer a set of criminal charges on the second floor of a county courthouse that had no elevator. At his first appearance, Lane crawled up two flights of stairs to get to the courtroom. When Lane returned to the courthouse for a hearing, he refused to crawl again or to be carried by officers to the courtroom; he consequently was arrested and jailed for failure to appear. Jones, a certified court reporter, alleged that she has not been able to gain access to a number of county courthouses, and, as a result, has lost both work and an opportunity to participate in the judicial process. Respondents sought damages and equitable relief.

The State moved to dismiss the suit on the ground that it was barred by the Eleventh Amendment.

The ADA was passed by large majorities in both Houses of Congress after decades of deliberation and investigation into the need for comprehensive legislation to address discrimination against persons with disabilities. In the years immediately preceding the ADA's enactment, Congress held 13 hearings and created a special task force that gathered evidence from every State in the Union.

Invoking "the sweep of congressional authority, including the power to enforce the fourteenth amendment and to regulate commerce," the ADA is designed "to provide a clear and comprehensive national mandate for the elimination of discrimination against individuals with disabilities."

It is not difficult to perceive the harm that Title II is designed to address. Congress enacted Title II against a backdrop of pervasive unequal treatment in the administration of state services and programs, including systematic deprivations of fundamental rights. . . .

This pattern of disability discrimination persisted despite several federal and state legislative efforts to address it.

With respect to the particular services at issue in this case, Congress learned that many individuals, in many States across the country, were being excluded from courthouses and court proceedings by reason of their disabilities. A report before Congress showed that some 76% of public services and programs housed in state-owned buildings were inaccessible to and unusable by persons with disabilities, even taking into account the possibility that the services and programs might be restructured or relocated to other parts of the buildings.

Given the sheer volume of evidence demonstrating the nature and extent of unconstitutional discrimination against persons with disabilities in the provision of public services, the dissent's contention that the record is insufficient to justify Congress' exercises of its prophylactic power is puzzling, to say the least.

The only question that remains is whether Title II is an appropriate response to this history and pattern of unequal treatment. . . .

Congress' chosen remedy for the pattern of exclusion and discrimination described above, Title II's requirement of program accessibility, is congruent and proportional to its object of enforcing the right of access to the courts. The unequal treatment of disabled persons in the administration of judicial services has a long history, and has persisted despite several legislative efforts to remedy the problem of disability discrimination. Faced with considerable evidence of the shortcomings of previous legislative responses, Congress was justified in concluding that this "difficult and intractable proble[m]" warranted "added prophylactic measures in response."

The remedy Congress chose is nevertheless a limited one. Recognizing that failure to accommodate persons with disabilities will often have the same practical effect as outright exclusion, Congress required the States to take reasonable measures to remove architectural and other barriers to accessibility. But Title II does not require States to employ any and all means to make judicial services accessible to persons with disabilities, and it does not require States to compromise their essential eligibility criteria for public programs. It requires only "reasonable modifications" that would not fundamentally alter the nature of the service provided, and only when the individual seeking modification is otherwise eligible for the service. As Title II's implementing regulations make clear, the reasonable modification requirement can be satisfied in a number of ways. In the case of facilities built or altered after 1992, the regulations require compliance with specific architectural accessibility standards. But in the case of older facilities, for which structural change is likely to be more difficult, a public entity may comply with Title II by adopting a variety of less costly measures, including relocating services to alternative, accessible sites and assigned aides to assist persons with disabilities in accessing services. Only if these measures are ineffective in achieving accessibility is the public entity required to make reasonable structural changes. And in no event is the entity required to undertake measures that would impose an undue financial or administrative burden, threaten historic preservation interests, or effect a fundamental alteration in the nature of the service.

This duty to accommodate is perfectly consistent with the well-established due process principle that, "within the limits of practicability, a State must afford to all individuals a meaningful opportunity to be heard" in its courts. Our cases have recognized a number of affirmative obligations that flow from this principle: the duty to waive filing fees in certain family-law and criminal cases, the duty to provide transcripts to criminal defendants seeking review of their convictions, and the duty to provide counsel to certain criminal defendants. Each of these cases makes clear that ordinary considerations of cost and convenience alone cannot justify a State's failure to provide individuals with a meaningful right of access to the courts. Judged against this backdrop, Title II's affirmative obligation to accommodate persons with disabilities in the administration of justice cannot be said to be "so out of proportion to a supposed remedial or preventive object that it cannot be understood as responsive to, or designed to prevent, unconstitutional behavior." It is rather, a reasonable prophylactic measure, reasonably targeted to a legitimate end.

For these reasons, we conclude that Title II, as it applies to the class of cases implicating the fundamental right of access to the courts, constitutions a valid exercise of Congress' Section 5 authority to enforce the guarantees of the Fourteenth Amendment.

Only a year later, the Court, in a unanimous decision, expanded on this issue in the context of access within a state prison system. In *United States v. Georgia*, 126 S. Ct. 877, 163 L. Ed. 2d 650 (2006), Justice Scalia, writing for the Court, determined that in appropriate contexts disabled inmates in state prisons could recover money damages under Title II of the ADA. The claimant, who was paraplegic, alleged lack of accessible facilities within his cell and that he had been denied assistance or access to use the toilet and shower and that he was denied access to physical therapy and medical treatment, and virtually all prison programs, because of his disability. The Court stated as follows:

> [I]nsofar as Title II creates a private cause of action for damages against the States for conduct that actually violates the Fourteenth Amendment, Title II validly abrogates state sovereign immunity.

> From the many allegations . . . it is not clear precisely what conduct [Goodman] intended to allege in support of his Title II claims. . . . Once Goodman's complaint is amended, the lower courts will be best situated to determine in the first instance, on a claim-by-claim basis, (1) which aspects of the State's alleged conduct violated Title II; (2) to what extent such misconduct also violated the Fourteenth Amendment; and (3) insofar as such misconduct violated Title II but did not violate the Fourteenth Amendment, whether Congress's purported abrogation of sovereign immunity as to that class of conduct is nevertheless valid.

PROBLEMS

What do these decisions mean for the plaintiffs in these cases? Are they likely to recover damages? If the court had offered George Lane the reasonable accommodation of relocating the proceedings, would that be likely to be sufficient? What if they offered to have court employees carry him up the stairs? Are Goodman's claims regarding access in his cell more likely not to be immune from damage claims than a claim from his demand for a steam table for his housing unit?

What is likely to happen with employment situations such as Beverly Jones' case? Is that really an employment case or is it an access to justice case? Has the Court left this issue unresolved?

What does the *Tennessee v. Lane* decision mean for old courthouses? What if they are historic?

What issues of security and undue burden are the operators of jails and prisons likely to raise with respect to physical access issues and barrier removal?

Would damages be available in the following kinds of cases (assuming that the conduct was found to violate the ADA), following the Court's reasoning? Charging for parking placards; denial of parental rights; public swimming pool discrimination; police handling of cases involving DUI; prison setting situations; access in state operated museums and sports and entertainment facilities.

Why is it important to be awarded damages and not just injunctive or declaratory relief?

Chapter 6

HIGHER EDUCATION

A NONDISCRIMINATION IN HIGHER EDUCATION

[1] The Rehabilitation Act of 1973

As noted in earlier chapters, Section 504 of the Rehabilitation Act, 29 U.S.C. § 794, prohibits discrimination on the basis of disability against otherwise qualified individuals with disabilities by entities receiving federal financial assistance. Section 504 also has been interpreted to require reasonable accommodation and is intended to incorporate the concept of "least restrictive environment."

Although Section 504 of the Rehabilitation Act has applied to most institutions of higher education since 1973, only in the late 1980s did disability discrimination issues began to receive much attention on college campuses. One factor that probably led to this focus was the passage of special education laws in 1975 (now the Individuals with Disabilities Education Act, as discussed in Chapter 7). As a result, many students with disabilities had reached college age better prepared for college, having been identified as having a disability, expecting procedural safeguards to be in place. Another factor may be the media attention on disability rights surrounding the passage of the Americans with Disabilities Act in 1990.

It is clear that Section 504 of the Rehabilitation Act of 1973 applies to most institutions of higher education because they are recipients of federal financial assistance. The regulations under Section 504, 34 C.F.R. § 104.41 et seq., include a subpart relating specifically to postsecondary educational issues. This subpart includes regulations relating to admissions and recruitment, general treatment of students, academic adjustments, housing, financial and employment assistance to students, and nonacademic services (including athletics, counseling, and social organizations).

While it was always clear that Section 504 applied to institutions of higher education receiving federal financial assistance, it was not always as clear that all programs within a higher education institution were covered if only one program received the federal financial assistance. For example, if the college of education received a federal grant from the Department of Education, did that mean that the athletics programs were subject to the nondiscrimination mandates of Section 504?

In 1984, the Supreme Court addressed this question in the context of a claim of sex discrimination. Grove City College in Pennsylvania, is a small private liberal arts college, whose only nexus to federal financial assistance was that it provided forms to apply for federal guaranteed student loans and that some students who received these loans attended the college. The issue was whether Grove City

College was subject to the nondiscrimination mandate of Title IX of the Civil Rights Act, which prohibits discrimination on the basis of sex by higher education institutions receiving federal financial assistance. The Court in *Grove City College v. Bell*, 465 U.S. 555 (1984), held that the entire institution was not subject to Title IX (nor would it be subject to several other similar nondiscrimination mandates including Section 504) by virtue of receiving federal financial assistance. Congress responded to this ruling by passing the Civil Rights Restoration Act of 1987, Pub. L. No. 100–259, 102 Stat. 28. This Act amends Section 504 to provide that all operations of an institution are subject to its nondiscrimination mandates if any part of a program or activity receives federal financial assistance. The other civil rights statutes were similarly affected. It has since been clarified by the Supreme Court in *Landgraf v. USI Film Products*, 511 U.S. 244 (1993), that the Civil Rights Restoration Act is not retroactive.

The application of Section 504 to various areas affecting student life, including admissions, academic programming, and architectural barriers, is addressed in the remaining sections of this chapter. As the following section indicates, there is now even more comprehensive protection against discrimination for students with disabilities as a result of the Americans with Disabilities Act.

[2] The Americans with Disabilities Act

The Americans with Disabilities Act (ADA), 42 U.S.C. §§ 12101 et seq., applies to public colleges and universities (Title II) and private educational institutions (Title III). Because of the detailed postsecondary education regulations under Section 504, which is to be read consistently with the ADA, regulations under the ADA do not focus directly on postsecondary education, but in essence incorporate the Rehabilitation Act requirements on these issues. There are some areas where regulations under the ADA provide additional clarification for certain aspects of higher education programming beyond what is available in the model regulations under Section 504. Architectural barrier issues and licensing and credentialing issues are two examples. Some issues that would benefit from additional higher education regulations have not yet been addressed. These include issues such as confidentiality, student records, and housing on campus.

It is important to understand the difference between Title II and Title III, why it may make a difference which statute applies, and when there may be overlapping application. It should also be noted that Section 504 will apply to most institutions of higher education because most receive federal financial assistance. Thus, the question will be whether Title II or Title III applies in addition to Section 504. Often it will not matter which statute applies because all three may have similar mandates in certain instances. Occasionally, however, it will be necessary to determine which statute is applicable. This is particularly true for procedural issues and remedies.

Title II, 42 U.S.C. §§ 12131 et seq., prohibits discrimination on the basis of disability by state and local governmental agencies. Thus state universities, community colleges, and other state or local governmentally operated institutions of higher education would fall under the mandates of Title II. Those entities subject to Title II were to have conducted a self-evaluation of their services, policies, and practices by January 26, 1993. They were to identify needed structural changes and develop a plan for making the needed changes. To the extent that a self-evaluation had already been done pursuant to the Section 504 mandate (requiring a self-evaluation by 1978), Title II institutions were not required to repeat this. Given the fact that 15 years intervened between these two deadlines, as a practical matter, it is difficult to imagine that most campuses did not need to do a substantial update of the self-evaluation. In addition to the self-evaluation, Title II higher education institutions were required to make the program accessible when viewed in its entirety by January 26, 1992.

Title III prohibits discrimination on the basis of disability by twelve categories of private entities that provide public accommodations. One of these twelve categories is places of education. Thus, private colleges and universities are subject to Title III mandates. Although private entities are not subject to an additional self-evaluation mandate (beyond what they may have already done pursuant to Section 504), they are required to remove barriers to the extent it is readily achievable to do so. The term readily achievable is defined as "without much difficulty or expense."

There are several examples of when both Title II and Title III (as well as Section 504) probably apply. A private bookstore or fast food vendor that is given a contract to operate out of a student union building on a public university campus is one such instance. The pizza vendor is obligated under Title III to ensure nondiscrimination and accessibility, but the university is obligated under Title II to ensure that private vendors operating on its campus meet Title II mandates. Another example would involve activities held off campus. Where a public university holds an alumni function at a private club or hotel or holds athletic events at private facilities, both Title II and Title III come into play. The specifics of what will be required in various cases will be addressed in some of the decisions discussed and included in the remaining portion of this chapter.

Chapter 2 provided a detailed overview of who is covered under the statutes, including the 2008 amendments that ensure broader coverage. Many of these cases in this chapter on higher education were decided before the 1999 Supreme Court decisions that narrowed the definition, so coverage is not an issue. Rather, the courts focused on the substantive requirements of qualifications and accommodations. In reading these cases, however, it is worth noting whether the individual would be covered applying current definitional standards. "Major life activities include, but are not limited to, caring for oneself, performing manual tasks, seeing, hearing, eating, sleeping, walking, standing, lifting, bending, speaking, breathing, learning, reading, concentrating, thinking, communicating and working." Major bodily functions also include but are not limited to "functions of the immune system, normal cell growth, digestive, bowel, bladder, neurological, brain, respiratory, circulatory, endocrine, and reproductive functions." 42 U.S.C. § 12102(2). Transitory and minor conditions are not covered. Mitigating measures are not to be considered in deciding whether a person is substantially limited in a major life activity.

B   ADMISSIONS

The first step in entering an institution of higher education is the admissions process. At this stage, there are several issues that arise with respect to ensuring that an applicant is not discriminated against on the basis of disability under Section 504 of the Rehabilitation Act or the Americans with Disabilities Act. These issues include how and whether an institution may identify an applicant as having a disability and whether certain criteria may have the effect of being discriminatory at this stage of the process.

HYPOTHETICAL PROBLEM 6.1

Samantha has applied to a relatively competitive public law school, Springfield Law School. She has taken the LSAT without accommodations and scored in the 70th percentile. The law school's median LSAT is in the 75th percentile. During her first two years at College A, an elite private college, she did not do well. Her boyfriend broke up with her, she stopped attending classes, and she was dismissed from college because of her grades.

She has a supportive family, and they had her evaluated by the family physician, who referred her to a psychiatrist. After she was diagnosed with depression, she began medication and was able to re-enroll at a different college (College B) (with a two year interim during which she did volunteer work at a food bank and worked part time at the library). Her physician had prescribed an effective medication regimen, which caused side effects of drowsiness in the morning. Samantha was careful to schedule afternoon only classes, to be sure she was alert. She became involved in extracurricular activities, served in leadership positions in some service organizations, and received excellent grades. Her GPA from College A was a 1.50 and her GPA from College B was a 3.95. Her cumulative GPA was 2.7. The median GPA for the students admitted to Springfield Law School is 3.25.

Springfield Law School's application form includes the following request for information in the section requesting a resume and a personal statement. "You are encouraged to identify hardships that you may have overcome. If these hardships relate to a disability or illness (that affected your academic or other performance), you are encouraged to provide the documentation relating to these conditions." Samantha does not want to share the information about her depression and treatment, although she believes that it not only affected her grades at College A, but the side effects of the medication made it difficult for her to take the LSAT, which was given in the morning. She has heard that Springfield Law School considers all factors in the application and believes that her strong performance and activities record at College B will compensate for the deficiencies. She decides not to discuss any of this in her application.

In May, Samantha receives a rejection letter from Springfield Law School. At this point, she decides to submit a request for reconsideration, in which she includes the background information about her depression, the medication, and her performance. The law school admissions dean and admissions committee is now considering this request. What must/should the admissions office do in response? What are Samantha's options if they deny a reconsideration or upon reconsidering, still deny the admission.

In reviewing this hypothetical while reading the cases and materials in this section, consider whether it matters that she is applying to law school instead of undergraduate school or medical school.

[1]   Determining Qualifications

The admissions process for most institutions of higher education usually involves submitting an application which includes information about previous academic work, extracurricular activities, work experience, and other background information to assist decisionmakers in deciding why to select one applicant over another. Such applications almost always require a submission of letters of recommendation, official transcripts of prior academic work, and submission of scores received on the appropriate standardized test.

There are various aspects of this process that raise potential concerns under Section 504 of the Rehabilitation and/or the Americans with Disabilities Act. These include whether and when preadmissions inquiries can be made and the criteria that may be used to determine whether a student is otherwise qualified for the academic program. The criteria issue includes whether it is permissible to use standardized test scores, whether entities administering these tests must provide reasonable accommodations, and how such test scores must be evaluated. See also *Bowers v. NCAA*, 974 F. Supp. 459 (D.N.J. 1997), for a discussion of the NCAA bylaws and reasonable accommodations to standardized test scores and other factors affecting the eligibility of athletes with learning disabilities.

The first case addresses several of these issues. In addition, it provides an historical perspective on the development of the "otherwise qualified" requirement under Section 504 of the Rehabilitation Act. The *Southeastern Community College v. Davis* decision in Chapter 2, *supra*, should be reviewed at this point. That decision established that for purposes of Section 504, a determination of whether an individual is "otherwise qualified" requires that the person be one who is able to meet all of the program's requirements in spite of the disability. Reference to this decision is included in many of the case excerpts that follow. See also Laura Rothstein & Julia Rothstein, Disabilities and the Law §§ 3:4–3:6 (2009); Laura Rothstein, *The Story of* Southeastern Community College v. Davis: *The Prequel to the Television Series "ER,"* Chapter 7 of Education Stories (2008) (discussing the impact of the *Davis* decision on higher education and students with disabilities).

The following cases involve admissions decisions for different types of programs by students with different types of impairments — college (*Halasz*/learning disability), a medical residency program (*Pushkin*/multiple sclerosis), and medical school (*Case Western*/blindness). The *Case Western* decision applies state rather than federal law. These differences should be kept in mind in comparing the cases and in deciding how they might resolve Samantha's situation.

HALASZ v. UNIVERSITY OF NEW ENGLAND
816 F. Supp. 37 (D. Me. 1993)

GENE CARTER, CHIEF JUDGE:

I.

The undisputed facts as set forth in Defendant's statement of material facts and supported by the record are as follow. The University of New England is a private college in Biddeford. Its catalog for 1990–91 stated its policy that "no discrimination on the grounds of . . . handicap, . . . will exist in any area." Admission to the college is competitive, based upon, inter alia, the applicant's course of study in high school, grades and class standing, written recommendations and scores obtained on standardized college aptitude tests. At the time Plaintiff applied, the university had separate admissions criteria for transfer students. Students with a grade point average of at least 2.5 were considered for, but not guaranteed, admission. Those with averages below 2.5 might be considered, but it would have been a rare exception for a transfer applicant with an average below 2.0 to be admitted.

At the time Plaintiff applied, U.N.E. also ran programs for students with learning disabilities. For example, students who qualified for admission to the university could also participate in the Individual Learning Program (ILP), which offers specific support services appropriate for the learning disabled in a university setting. These services include access to taped textbooks/readers, proctors/readers for untimed exams, diagnostic testing, and supervision and counseling by a learning specialist.

A second program, called First Year Option (FYO), was for learning disabled students who did not have the academic credentials necessary for admission to the degree programs. The FYO program was designed to provide those students with an integration/transition period during which they could, in an unmatriculated status, take one or two degree courses per semester while receiving the same support services for their learning disabilities that are available to students in the ILP.

Students who completed the FYO program could apply for regular admission to U.N.E. Their admission was based on their academic and social adjustment during the FYO program. Only FYO students with a cumulative grade point average of at least 2.0 for "two consecutive regular semesters, i.e. fall and spring or spring and fall," were recommended for regular admission.

Plaintiff applied to U.N.E. seeking admission in January 1991 as a transfer student. His high school record contained many failures and D grades. His cumulative grade point average from three previously attended colleges in New York was 1.98 (out of 4.0). Moreover, he had been required to withdraw from the State University of New York at Fredonia for academic reasons. The admissions officers at U.N.E. had doubts about his ability to adjust to college pressures given his inability to complete any program at the three previous academic institutions.

In both timed and untimed reading tests, Plaintiff got the lowest possible score. On the Scholastic Aptitude Test, which Plaintiff had taken in a timed setting, his scores were also very low. An experienced UNE admissions officer avers that during her tenure the University has never accepted an applicant with academic credentials as poor as those of Plaintiff.

Plaintiff suffers from a learning disability and Tourette's Syndrome. He initially called U.N.E. because he was interested in its program for the learning disabled. In the call he stated he was learning disabled. With his application, he also wrote a letter to the Director of the ILP, stating that his transcripts and test scores did not reflect his abilities because of lack of understanding and accommodation for his disabilities by his former teachers and testers. Based on his academic record, Plaintiff was considered unqualified for admission to U.N.E. as a regular transfer student. He was, however, admitted to the FYO.

Plaintiff enrolled in two college level courses, Psychology I and Human Development I, in his first semester, as well as in several non-college-level remedial courses. He was assigned tutors in both courses, but dropped Psychology very early in the semester. He requested that he be provided with a notetaker as well as a tutor for Human Development, but his ILP learning specialist refused, believing it better to evaluate Plaintiff's own capabilities in that regard before concluding such services were necessary. Plaintiff's grade in Human Development was a C-, giving him a GPA of 1.75 after the first semester.

In his second FYO semester, Plaintiff again enrolled in two college level courses. Although advised to drop one of the courses because of his struggles the previous semester, he declined to do so during the add/drop period. Ultimately, however, he withdrew from one of the courses. He earned a D in the course he finished, giving him a cumulative G.P.A. at the end of his second semester of 1.375.

Plaintiff was offered the same services which had successfully helped other FYO students qualify for regular admission at U.N.E. He received advising from an ILP specialist at least weekly. He had peer tutors, some taped texts, proctored, untimed testing, oral testing, and readers for some of his classes. He also had remedial courses, as well as access to a writing specialist at times during both semesters and to a reading specialist in the fall semester.

ILP and FYO participants are assessed a fee for services provided exclusively to them. The fee varies depending on use of the services. The highest use fee in 1990-91 was $1450. The next year it was $1550. Regularly admitted U.N.E. students taking twelve credit hours per semester were charged $362.50 per credit hour. An FYO student taking a similar load, but including only one or two college level classes and some remedial courses, was charged $145 per credit hour plus the applicable ILP fees.

II.

A. *Count I*

Plaintiff alleges in Count I that Defendant twice discriminated against him on the basis of his handicap: first when it denied him regular admission to its undergraduate program, and again when it denied him admission to the regular program after completion of the FYO program. Plaintiff alleges that he should not have been placed in the FYO program because he met the requirements for admission of transfer students despite his disability.

The undisputed facts submitted by Defendant show that Plaintiff was not academically qualified for admission to U.N.E. as a transfer student. The admissions officer at U.N.E. avers that it would have been a rare exception for a transfer student with a cumulative GPA of less than 2.0 to be admitted. Plaintiff had a cumulative GPA of 1.98 at the other institutions at which he had studied. The other indicia of Plaintiff's academic potential which were available to the admissions office at the time he applied did not mark him as the "rare exception" who would be academically qualified for the U.N.E. program despite a low grade point average.

Plaintiff's SAT scores were "very low," as described both by him and Defendant's admissions officer. Although in his application materials Plaintiff sought to explain these low scores by the fact that he had not taken the test untimed,[1] on both timed and untimed diagnostic reading comprehension tests,

---

[1] Plaintiff now asserts that UNE acted illegally in considering his SAT scores because the giving of the SAT in a timed setting discriminates against students with learning disabilities. The regulations interpreting § 504 prohibit the use by educational institutions of any tests which have a disproportionate, adverse effect on handicapped persons unless the test has been validated as a predictor of success in the education program and alternate tests that have less disproportionate, adverse effects are not shown by the Secretary to be available. 34 C.F.R. § 104.42(b)(2).

The Court rejects Plaintiff's premise. UNE requires students to submit either SAT or ACT standardized aptitude test scores. The SAT, submitted by Plaintiff, is not one that has a disproportionate, adverse effect on handicapped persons because, as noted by Plaintiff himself, it is available in special formats for the handicapped, including an untimed format that does not discriminate against people like him with learning disabilities.

Plaintiff further argues that UNE violated 34 C.F.R. § 104.42(b)(3), which provides that a school must assure itself that admissions tests are selected and administered so as to ensure that the test accurately reflects a handicapped applicant's aptitude or achievement level. The regulation, unlike the previous regulation, speaks only of admissions tests, rather than of "any test or criterion for admission," 34 C.F.R. § 104.42(b)(2). The Court is satisfied that § 104.42(b)(3) applies to admissions tests administered by a school and not to other criteria of admission, and that it does not impose an obligation on UNE and other colleges and universities to oversee the administration of national standardized tests to all of its applicants who, as is evident by Plaintiff's application, come from far-flung states. The SAT is not an admissions test covered by the cited regulation. It is one of many criteria for admission used by UNE.

It was incumbent upon Plaintiff to take the test in the desired form and submit those scores. Plaintiff, knowing full well that another test format suitable to his condition was available, decided to submit his timed SAT scores and then tell Defendant not to consider them. This is tantamount to not submitting the SAT results, and Plaintiff cannot fault UNE for considering what he submitted when the choice was his. Moreover, it is plain that Defendant used the SAT only in addition to a number of other criteria, including specifically an untimed reading test. None of those other criteria suggested that Plaintiff was

Plaintiff scored in the first percentile, the lowest possible score. Moreover, Plaintiff had never completed any of the programs at the schools in which he had been previously been enrolled, even though, as shown in his essay in support of his application, one of them was a special program for learning disabled students. His better grades in those programs were generally in non-academic subjects while he failed or withdrew from many of his academic college courses. Plaintiff does not dispute Ms. Cribby's statement that during her tenure at U.N.E., no student with academic credentials as poor as Plaintiff's was ever accepted as a transfer student.

The record shows that UNE does not discriminate in its admissions process against students with learning disabilities. It regularly evaluates and admits learning disabled students to its baccalaureate program. Some of these students, who demonstrate in the admissions process that they are academically qualified for UNE, are admitted without condition and some on the condition that they participate in the ILP, which is designed "to promote and enhance learning disabled students' independent and successful academic functioning as quickly as possible." Some of the learning disabled students admitted without condition also choose to participate in the ILP. UNE's admissions policy, therefore, accommodates for learning disabled students who are not already functioning independently and successfully in an academic setting. In considering Plaintiff for admission, UNE used not only its regular criteria, but also untimed tests and performance in previous special programs for the learning disabled. The record shows that UNE made reasonable accommodations in its admissions process for learning disabled students like Plaintiff.

Along with the materials required for his application, Plaintiff submitted a letter telling the UNE admission officers not to consider his grades at previous institutions or his bad standardized test scores because they were not representative of his abilities. Rather he sought to be allowed to enroll at UNE "and prove that I can do the work." Plaintiff, therefore, sought to have UNE abandon all criteria for admissions. Section 504 clearly does not require that an educational institution lower its admissions standards to accommodate the handicapped.

In *Alexander v. Choate*, 469 U.S. 287, 301, 105 S. Ct. 712, 720, 83 L. Ed. 2d 661 (1985), the Supreme Court articulated the reasonable accommodation requirement under section 504:

> The balance struck in *Davis* requires that an otherwise qualified handicapped individual must be provided with meaningful access to the benefit that the grantee offers. The benefit itself, of course, cannot be defined in a way that effectively denies otherwise qualified handicapped individuals the meaningful access to which they are entitled; to assure meaningful access, reasonable accommodations in the grantee's program or benefit may have to be made.

Here the benefit sought by Plaintiff is admission to Defendant's regular baccalaureate program. Defendant has provided meaningful access to the benefit

---

a qualified applicant, and the untimed test, on which Plaintiff received the lowest possible score, showed him to be patently unqualified.

for learning disabled students like Plaintiff. Plaintiff is not "otherwise qualified" for admission to UNE and is not, therefore, entitled to relief under section 504.

U.N.E. has submitted undisputed facts that its officials provided even further accommodation to learning disabled students who have not shown themselves to be qualified for regular admission to the baccalaureate program. The FYO program, which provides services, support, and remedial attention to students like Plaintiff, allows them the opportunity to be regularly matriculated upon successful completion of two semesters of the FYO program. Earning a GPA of 2.0 or better in a reduced load of college-level courses and obtaining the recommendation of the faculty demonstrates a disabled student's capabilities after accommodation has been made for his or her disabilities.

In Count I Plaintiff also alleges that after his participation in the FYO program, Defendant did not allow him to matriculate in the baccalaureate program and dismissed him on the basis of higher academic standards than those imposed on nonhandicapped students. The undisputed facts submitted by Defendant show that matriculation into the regular program from the FYO program required a GPA of 2.0 over two consecutive regular semesters, while regularly matriculated students were required to maintain only a GPA of 1.7 to remain in good academic standing. For regularly matriculated students, grades from the short winter term were considered in determining the GPA, while they were not considered for purposes of determining if FYO students could matriculate.

The undisputed facts also show a rationally justifiable academic reason for these distinctions. In her affidavit, U.N.E. admissions officer Patricia Cribby stated:

> The purpose of the FYO program was to provide an opportunity for non-qualified learning disabled applicants to become qualified for matriculated status at U.N.E. By contrast, matriculated students have already demonstrated through the initial admission process that they are qualified for admission and that they possess the academic abilities and other relevant qualifications for successful participation in U.N.E.'s baccalaureate program. Whereas FYO students generally take only three college-level credit hours per semester, matriculated students generally take twelve to eighteen college-level credit hours per semester.

Thus, Defendant requires a higher grade point average for the FYO students who are taking fewer courses to make sure that they are qualified for the regular program which will require them to take many more college level courses and course hours per semester. Were the GPA requirement not higher for the FYO students, Defendant would have run the risk of lowering academic standards in the regular program by admitting students who would not be able to cope when faced with the necessity of taking a full load of college-level courses. The record discloses, however, that even if Plaintiff had only been required to maintain a 1.7 GPA, he would have failed to meet it with his GPA of 1.375.

Ms. Cribby's affidavit also discloses a rationally justifiable pedagogical basis for the decision to exclude winter term courses from the calculation of FYO students' GPAs while including them to determine the academic standing of regularly matriculated students. First, the winter term courses vary greatly in the level of difficulty and the intensity of the required study. Defendant looks to the success of the FYO students in their college level courses, while they are receiving special assistance for their disabilities, to predict whether they will be successful students in the baccalaureate program if provided with adequate support. Courses that are not necessarily comparable to the majority of courses in the curriculum cannot have that predictive value. The winter term is part of the regular curriculum, however, and its courses are used to evaluate regularly matriculated students who, in contrast to FYO students, have previously demonstrated academic qualification for U.N.E. admission.

Plaintiff complains that the accommodations made for him in the FYO program were not adequate and that he would have been more successful in the program with better accommodations. For example, he argues that he requested the assistance of notetakers, but that his request was resisted by UNE. He also complains that the academic counseling he received from his learning specialist was inadequate, that he was provided with inadequate readers in lieu of taped texts and that his tutors were of poor quality.

The undisputed facts show that Plaintiff was offered the same wide array of accommodations which had been offered previously to other learning disabled students in the FYO program and which had enabled them to matriculate successfully in the baccalaureate program at the end of the year. Although the regulations promulgated under section 504 require academic institutions to provide auxiliary aids to handicapped students, Plaintiff was not entitled to "devices or services of a personal nature." The Court finds, therefore, that even after reasonable accommodation was made for Plaintiff's handicaps, he was not "otherwise qualified" for admission to UNE's baccalaureate program, and the university did not discriminate against him by dismissing him after his FYO year. Summary judgment is, therefore, appropriate for Defendant on Count I.

Plaintiff also complains that UNE violated 34 C.F.R. § 104.42(b)(4) which provides that in administering its admissions policies, a recipient of federal financial aid "may not make preadmission inquiry as to whether an applicant for admission is a handicapped person, but after admission, may make inquiries on a confidential basis as to handicaps that may require accommodation." In this case, the record discloses that Plaintiff called UNE precisely because it had a program for the learning disabled and that in his initial contact with the university, he inquired about the ILP program and volunteered information about his handicap. Plaintiff argues that these facts in no way affect Defendant's obligation not to inquire about his handicap. That position is untenable.

UNE's application form does not require a handicapped applicant to disclose his or her handicap. If the applicant wishes to be considered for UNE's ILP program, which is available only to the learning disabled, he or she may indicate that on the form. As discussed above, not all learning disabled students at UNE participate in the ILP.

When a university operates a program specifically for the handicapped, it clearly needs to know about an applicant's handicaps before it can make a decision about admission to the program, for the program may be appropriate for some handicapped individuals and not for others. Section 504 is designed in part to assure that handicapped applicants and students are not, because of their handicaps, denied the benefits of programs offered by federally subsidized universities to nonhandicapped students. None of the purposes of the statute would be served by enforcing the inquiry prohibition when a university offers a program available only to handicapped students and a handicapped person seeks to participate in that program.

Here, Plaintiff did not check the ILP box on the application form. His telephone inquiry, voluntary provision of information about his handicap, and letter seeking recognition of his handicapped status, however, made it clear that he was interested in UNE's special program for the learning disabled. Certainly, UNE could only tell if Plaintiff could benefit from the ILP or FYO programs for the learning disabled by seeking information about his handicaps. The Court finds, therefore, that under the circumstances presented here UNE did not violate the above-cited regulation by requiring Plaintiff to provide information about his handicaps before being admitted to the FYO program.

The *Halasz* decision discusses the preadmissions inquiry prohibition. As the court notes, generally preadmission inquiries are prohibited except in unusual circumstances where the presence of the disability as eligibility for a program or an accommodation is at issue. The following case raises an issue that may arise in higher education admissions programs where an interview is a required aspect for the admissions process. This seems to be particularly true in admission to medical school and other health professional programs. It should be recalled that in the *Southeastern* case the hearing impairment of Ms. Davis was identified by Southeastern Community College in her admissions interview.

The following decision is a rare example of a situation where the stated reasons for the denial of admission are clearly related directly to the disability. It is also unusual for its result. In most cases, institutions of higher education (especially health care professional programs) are given substantial deference and their decisions are upheld by the courts. This is one of the earlier appellate decisions applying the Rehabilitation Act. The decision would probably be the same if this were an ADA claim.

PUSHKIN v. REGENTS OF THE UNIVERSITY OF COLORADO
658 F.2d 1372 (10th Cir. 1981)

WILLIAM E. DOYLE, CIRCUIT JUDGE:

Dr. Pushkin is a medical doctor who alleges that the University of Colorado wrongfully denied him admittance to the Psychiatric Residency Program because he suffers from multiple sclerosis. As a result of this disease Dr. Pushkin is confined to a wheelchair, and is disabled in his abilities to walk and to write.

What is the Proper Standard of Review?

The standards for determining the merits of a case under § 504 are contained in the statute. First, the statute provides that the individual in question must be an "otherwise qualified handicapped individual;" second, the statute provides that a qualified handicapped individual may not be denied admission to any program or activity or denied the benefits of any program or activity receiving federal financial assistance "solely" on the basis of handicap. To ask the court to defer to admissions decisions of a recipient of federal financial assistance whenever such a decision is rationally related to legitimate government needs is to ask the court to ignore the plain statutory language of § 504. To approach § 504 in such a manner, that is by applying the rational basis test, would be to reduce that statute to nothingness, which should always be avoided.

[T]he Supreme Court [has] rejected the argument that admissions decisions of universities should not be subjected to judicial scrutiny. To limit judicial scrutiny of university admissions decisions solely to the rational basis test where § 504 is involved would be to ignore the standards set forth in § 504 and would eliminate judicial scrutiny altogether under the statute. It is, of course, understandable why the University seeks such a soft test. We conclude that the University is not entitled to ignore the statute and focus on equal protection principles, and to have us adopt, in addition, the least demanding of the equal protection tests; one which is at odds with § 504.

The University's argument that discrimination may not be found under § 504 in the absence of recognized discriminatory intent also fails. . . . [T]he statute itself does not contemplate either a disparate treatment or a disparate impact analysis.

We repeat what we said before and that is that § 504 sets forth its own criteria for scrutinizing claims under that statute. First, the individual is required to show that he is otherwise qualified for the position sought; second, the individual must show that even though he is otherwise qualified, he was rejected for the position solely on the basis of his handicap. The two factors are interrelated, since if the individual is not otherwise qualified he cannot be said to have been rejected solely because of his handicap.

In *Southeastern Community College v. Davis*, . . . the Supreme Court considered the express statutory language of § 504 to solve the problem. Under *Davis* the first test applied was whether the individual in question was qualified for the position sought in spite of his handicap. If the plaintiff's handicap would preclude him from doing the job in question, the plaintiff cannot be found to be otherwise qualified. If the handicap would not preclude the individual from performing the job in question, however, and the plaintiff has met all other qualifications for the position in question, the plaintiff cannot be rejected from the program solely on the basis of his handicap. The record is clear that Dr. Pushkin established that he had the necessary ability despite his handicap. The examining committee, however, focused on the handicap continuously in connection with determining whether to admit him to the residency program. It emphasized factors such as the effect of the handicap on patients and the resulting effect on Dr. Pushkin. Thus, the issue is not merely whether the handicap played a prominent part in his rejection, as in cases dealing with alleged discrimination on the basis of race, for example (where race is never expressly mentioned as a consideration), the issue is whether rejecting Dr. Pushkin after expressly weighing the implication of his handicap was justified. The question is whether Dr. Pushkin was qualified for admission to the residency program in spite of his handicap, so that he was wrongfully rejected from the program on the basis of that handicap, or whether Dr. Pushkin's handicap would preclude him from carrying out the responsibilities involved in the residency program and future patient care, so that the University rightfully excluded him from the program after weighing the implications of his disability.

The trial judge quotes in his findings that an interrogatory was submitted by counsel for Dr. Pushkin requesting the defendants to state every reason why the application of plaintiff for the position of psychiatric resident in any defendant institution was rejected and every reason why he was not appointed to said position. The response to that interrogatory was "the plaintiff was not admitted into the 'psychiatric resident, R II program,' because plaintiff's interview mean ratings, based upon plaintiff's four interviews with faculty members of the University of Colorado Psychiatric Hospital, was far below the level of any other person accepted into the program."

The trial court's findings go on to say that the mean interview ratings as a general practice are not necessarily controlling in the selection process. Moreover, in a specific reference to Dr. Pushkin, Dr. Carter stated that "the numbers," i.e. the mean interview ratings, did not dispose of his application. Dr. Pushkin was never told that his mean interview rating was the reason for his rejection. However, even if the mean interview ratings were the reason for his rejection, that is like saying that he was rejected because he was rejected. In other words the interrogatories should have detailed his insufficiencies in specific terms at the very least. The court also found that the narrative contained on each interviewer's report explains the reasons for the rating on the prediction scale. Each instance shows that the interviewer's rating was inextricably involved with Dr. Pushkin's handicap and by the interviewer's perception of the problems the handicap would create. It is not possible to extricate ratings from the reactions to the handicap itself. The court finally noted that neither Pushkin nor his wife were ever given a reason for his rejection from the program other than that specified by Dr. Carter that Pushkin was rejected because of his handicap. They were left to draw inferences in their conversations with Dr. Carter and the only inference to be drawn by each from the statements made and the absence of other statements being made was that the handicap itself was the reason for the rejection.

The record is replete with testimony dealing with the inability of Dr. Pushkin to serve in the residency program based upon his handicap. These observations of the members of the panel are not predicated on any known deficiency of Dr. Pushkin himself, but rather these are reasons that are based upon the examiners' general knowledge of multiple sclerosis and their concern for psychologic reactions of the patient and in turn the doctor, as a result of his being in a wheelchair. The trial court concluded that the evidence in the case clearly established that these general reasons did not apply with regard to Dr. Pushkin, but that Dr. Pushkin was an otherwise qualified handicapped individual who was wrongfully, by sole reason of his handicap, excluded from participation in or denied the benefits of or subjected to discrimination under a program or activity receiving federal financial assistance.

It would be neither correct nor right, under the circumstances presented, to analyze this case in accord with a strict disparate treatment test. . . . Instead, our approach to the case is fully in harmony with the statute, § 504, as the same has been construed by the Supreme Court in *Southeastern Community College v. Davis* . . . . We believe that the appropriate standards to be gleaned from the court's opinion are the following:

1) The plaintiff must establish a prima facie case by showing that he was an otherwise qualified handicapped person apart from his handicap, and was rejected under circumstances which gave rise to the inference that his rejection was based solely on his handicap;

2) Once plaintiff establishes his prima facie case, defendants have the burden of going forward and proving that plaintiff was not an otherwise qualified handicapped person, that is one who is able to meet all of the program's requirements in spite of his handicap, or that his rejection from the program was for reasons other than his handicap;

3) The plaintiff then has the burden of going forward with rebuttal evidence showing that the defendants' reasons for rejecting the plaintiff are based on misconceptions or unfounded factual conclusions, and that reasons articulated for the rejection other than the handicap encompass unjustified consideration of the handicap itself.

The Final Analysis

Unquestionably plaintiff has established a prima facie case by showing that he is a handicapped person who is qualified for the residency program apart from his handicap and that he was rejected from the program under circumstances which support a finding that his rejection was based solely on his handicap. As to his qualifications, plaintiff met the requisite academic standards of the program in that he held an M.D. degree and had obtained a satisfactory "dean's letter." Plaintiff also presented a letter from Dr. Wong, his supervisor during one year of residency in psychiatry at the Menninger Foundation in Topeka, Kansas. [Substance of letter omitted.]

The position of the University is that Dr. Pushkin was denied admittance to the residency program on the basis of the interview reports of four members of the program faculty. Dr. Pushkin's mean interview ratings, when computed by scores granted by the four interviewers, were held to be too low. In addition to the grades given by the interviewers each made comments expressing their views about Pushkin's capabilities. [Observations of four faculty members omitted.]

We next consider the reasons articulated by the University at trial for the plaintiff's rejection.

Dr. Barchilon testified that he viewed Pushkin as an ill person, rather than a handicapped one, since a handicapped person is "stabilized" in that his defect is predictable and can be accounted for, while a sick person is not stabilized. [Substance of this testimony omitted.]

The Pushkins, husband and wife, testified as to what Dr. Carter had told them, which was that Dr. Pushkin had been rejected from the program because of his handicap. According to Dr. and Mrs. Pushkin, Dr. Carter had told them that Pushkin's multiple sclerosis would prevent him from relating well with his patients, and would prevent the patients from relating well to Dr. Pushkin. Mrs. Pushkin also stated that Dr. Carter had told her that Dr. Pushkin might miss work due to hospitalization for his illness, and that would leave his patients without a doctor. Regarding this, both Doctor and Mrs. Pushkin testified that Dr. Pushkin's multiple sclerosis allowed his episodes of hospitalization to be planned in advance, similar to the way vacations were planned in advance by other doctors, and that Dr. Pushkin had always arranged for other doctors to care for his patients when he was hospitalized, just as most doctors arrange for others to care for their patients when they are on vacation. Dr. and Mrs. Pushkin further noted that Dr. Pushkin did not tell his patients he would be hospitalized, any more than other doctors told their patients where they were going on vacation, so that the patients would not be unduly burdened by such information.

There was testimony also from Dr. Gordon Farley, Dr. Pushkin's psychiatrist and a psychiatrist at the University of Colorado Health Center. [The substance of this testimony omitted. It was favorable to Dr. Pushkin.] According to Dr. Farley, Dr. Pushkin would make an "exceptional" psychiatrist.

The reports of the interviewers and the testimony of the other witnesses indicates that on the basis of 45 minute interviews and discussions by some of the interviewers with Dr. Bernstein, the admissions committee made certain assumptions regarding his handicap, such as:

1)   That Dr. Pushkin was angry and so emotionally upset due to his MS that he would be unable to do an effective job as a psychiatrist; and

2)   That Dr. Pushkin's MS and use of steroids had led to difficulties with mentation, delirium and disturbed sensorium; and

3)   That Dr. Pushkin would be unable to handle the work involved in the residency because of his MS; and

4)   That Dr. Pushkin would miss too much time away from his patients whereby they would suffer.

The testimony of the Pushkins and Dr. Farley and the letter from Dr. Wong rebut all these assumptions. Dr. Farley, who actually counseled Dr. Pushkin, and has done so for over a long period of time and was not merely reaching conclusions on the basis of his observations in the interview, stated that after four years of observing Pushkin closely he could not agree that any of the assumptions made by the admissions committee regarding MS applied to Dr. Pushkin.

It is within the power of the trier of the facts, here the trial court, to weigh the evidence and to determine the credibility of the witnesses. The trial judge found that the assumptions made by the admissions committee were rebutted by other evidence, and thus Dr. Pushkin could not be held to be unqualified due to his handicap. When the trial court's decision is supported by substantial evidence in the record, we are not free to reverse that decision. It boils down to that factor. We fully understand also why the trial court would find that the evidence on behalf of Pushkin was the more persuasive. In short, in the absence of a clearly erroneous decision by the trial court, this court is not going to substitute its judgment for that of the trial court.

It is argued that the judgment of Dr. Farley may not be used as a substitute for the judgment of the admissions committee, who are solely responsible for admissions decisions. We do not disagree with this but feel that the defendants' argument misses the point. The trial court did not substitute Dr. Farley's judgment for that of the admissions committee. That witness was offered to rebut the University's articulated reasons for maintaining that Dr. Pushkin was not qualified for the program despite his handicap. The witnesses on behalf of the University, and the reports of the interviewers, alleged that Dr. Pushkin's handicap would preclude him from doing a good job as a psychiatrist. Thus Dr. Farley was offered as a witness to show that, after four years of observing Dr. Pushkin, he believed the University's assumptions to be based on incorrect factual premises. We see no more effective way for Dr. Pushkin to rebut the University's assumptions or unduly restrictive beliefs as to Dr. Pushkin's capabilities when considered in relation to multiple sclerosis. To preclude this kind of evidence would be to preclude individual plaintiffs from ever rebutting the reasons articulated by a defendant for the actions which it has taken. Indeed it would preclude relief under § 504.

An attempt was made by some of the interviewers to say that Dr. Pushkin was not rejected solely because of his handicap, but that he would have been rejected anyway even if he had not been handicapped. The trial court found that this evidence was overshadowed by the contrary evidence, including the interviewers reports, showing that Pushkin was rejected from the residency program solely on the basis of his handicap. The record fully supports the trial court's decision that their conclusions at the interview were centered on the multiple sclerosis. It was only when the interviews reached the trial stage that they sought to expand their reasoning.

Dr. Barchilon testified that Dr. Pushkin was not of the caliber of people usually interviewed for the residency program and that Dr. Pushkin overidentified with his patients. However, Dr. Barchilon testified that he had not communicated any of those thoughts to any of the committee members prior to the time the decision to reject Dr. Pushkin was made. That doctor further testified that on the basis of such a brief interview of Dr. Pushkin, his assessment was merely an "educated guess."

. . .

Dr. Scully also stated at trial that Dr. Pushkin was not of the caliber of residents usually admitted to the program. This is in conflict with the testimony of Dr. Bernstein, who indicated that Dr. Scully was primarily concerned with the fact that Dr. Pushkin had MS. Moreover, Dr. Scully's testimony indicated uncertainty as to factors other than MS causing Dr. Pushkin's rejection, since he stated further that he thought Dr. Pushkin "had more issues going on than his MS or whatever; I wasn't quite sure."

In addition, Dr. Weissberg stated that Dr. Pushkin was not up to the usual quality of applicants to the program. He also stated, however, that he had not made that observation in his interview report.

As noted before, however, the trial court weighed the credibility of the conflicting evidence and rejected the after the fact testimony that Dr. Pushkin was not qualified for the program apart from his handicap. We are disinclined to substitute our judgment for that of the trial court, since that court's conclusion is supported by the record. We have evaluated the evidence and considered the findings and have approved the trial court's action. The conclusions of the examining board rest on psychologic theory. Our reaction is that these are weak and inadequate threads where, as here, the entire future of the plaintiff is at stake. We also hold that he applied the proper tests in determining whether defendants' articulated reasons for finding Dr. Pushkin unqualified on the basis of his handicap were legitimate or whether those reasons were based upon incorrect assumptions or inadequate factual grounds. Based upon the weighing of all the evidence the trial court held that the latter applied and since the decision is supported by the record, this court cannot reach its own factual conclusion and determine otherwise.

Viewing the record as a whole we conclude that the judgment of the district court is affirmed.

The previous decision might also have involved whether Dr. Pushkin was "regarded as" having a disability. The 2008 ADA Amendments provide the following: "An individual meets the requirement of 'being regarded as having such an impairment' if the individual . . . has been subjected to an action prohibited under this Act because of an actual or perceived physical or mental impairment whether or not the impairment limits or is perceived to limit a major life activity." 42 U.S.C. § 12102(3). The Amendments further clarify, however, that programs are not required to provide reasonable accommodations where the individual is covered only under this definition. 42 U.S.C. § 12201(h). Dr. Pushkin might have required reasonable scheduling accommodations for hospitalizations. Would he have been entitled to request these if his condition only met the "regarded as" prong? It is also noteworthy that the symptoms of the MS might be episodic, but the 2008 ADA amendments clarify that impairments that are episodic or in remission are disabilities if they would substantially limit a major life activity when active. 42 U.S.C. § 12102(4)(D).

The following decision, like the previous one, addresses issues of burden of proof and including the issue of reasonable accommodation in the determination of whether the applicant was qualified. It is decided under Ohio, rather than federal law. Would the result have been different under the ADA or the Rehabilitation Act?

OHIO CIVIL RIGHTS COMMISSION v. CASE WESTERN RESERVE UNIVERSITY

76 Ohio St. 3d 168, 666 N.E.2d 1376 (1996)

JUSTICE COOK:

Plaintiff-appellant, Cheryl A. Fischer ("Fischer"), completely lost her vision during her junior year of undergraduate study at CWRU. To accommodate Fischer's handicap while she pursued a chemistry degree, CWRU provided Fischer with lab assistants and readers, modified the written exams to oral ones, and extended the time periods in which to take exams. Fischer also used a closed circuit television to magnify images before she totally lost her sight, and books on tape to assist her. Thus, in spite of her handicap, Fischer successfully completed all of CWRU's academic requirements and received her baccalaureate degree, cum laude, in 1987.

Following graduation, Fischer sought admission to medical school. All medical colleges in the United States belong to the Association of American Medical Colleges ("AAMC"). In January 1979, the AAMC adopted the "Report of the Special Advisory Panel on Technical Standards for Medical School Admission." The AAMC Technical Standards Report requires candidates for a medical school degree to have the ability to observe. Specifically, the report states, "[t]he candidate must be able to observe demonstrations and experiments in the basic sciences. . . . A candidate must be able to observe a patient accurately at a distance and close at hand. Observation necessitates the functional use of the sense of vision and somatic sensation." The Technical Report further states, "a candidate should be able to perform in a reasonably independent manner. The use of a trained intermediary means that a candidate's judgment must be mediated by someone else's power of selection and observation." Although medical colleges are not required to follow the Technical Standards Report, the AAMC encouraged medical schools to use it as a guideline in developing their own standards.

In 1987, Cheryl applied to the medical school at CWRU. CWRU used the AAMC Technical Standards Report as a guideline in evaluating the four thousand to five thousand preliminary applications received annually for a class total of one hundred thirty-eight. Due to Fischer's sufficient academic credentials and extraordinary letters of recommendation, Dr. Albert C. Kirby, Associate Dean for Admissions and Student Affairs at CWRU's medical school, granted Fischer an interview. Subsequently, Dr. Kirby placed Fischer on an alternate list but ultimately denied her application. The following year, Fischer reapplied to CWRU.

In this second application process, Fischer was one of seven hundred applicants granted an interview and the only applicant to be interviewed by three Admission Committee members: Dr. Kirby, Dr. Richard B. Fratianne and Dr. Mildred Lam. Dr. Kirby believed that CWRU should accept Fischer into the class. Drs. Fratianne and Lam concluded that a blind student would be unable to complete the requirements of the medical school program.

CWRU's four-year curriculum consists of three basic components: the core academic program, the flexible program, and the patient-based program. The core academic program occupies the medical student's first two years, and is taught using traditional methods such as lectures, lab experiments and textbooks. The core academic program consists of study in the basic sciences, such as anatomy, histology, pathology, and physiology. The flexible program consists of electives, allowing students to engage in independent research and study in a specific area. The patient-based program includes clerkships in internal medicine, pediatrics, surgery, obstetrics and gynecology, psychiatry and primary care. In these different clerkships, students provide direct patient care. For example, students must perform a complete physical exam, review laboratory test results, review patient charts and perform basic medical procedures, such as starting an I.V., administering medications through veins, drawing blood, and responding in emergency situations. The surgery clerkship includes rotations in the emergency room and intensive care unit.

After interviewing Fischer, Dr. Fratianne, Associate Professor of Surgery at CWRU, concluded that Fischer would be unable to complete the medical school program. He believed that due to her lack of vision, Fischer would be unable to exercise independent judgment when reading an X-ray, unable to start an I.V., and unable to effectively participate in the surgery clerkship.

Following an interview with Fischer, Dr. Lam, Associate Professor of Medicine at CWRU, concluded that a blind student would be unable to complete the first and second year courses in the basic sciences which required the student to observe and identify various tissues and organ structures. For example, histology requires a student to identify tissue and organ structures through a microscope and pathology requires a student to observe how such structures are affected by disease. She believed that no accommodation would enable a blind student to complete these course requirements.

Dr. Lam further opined that a blind medical student could not complete the third and fourth year clerkships. A blind student would be unable to start an I.V., draw blood, take night call, react in emergency situations, or pass the objective clinical exam which required a student to perform a physical exam and to read an EKG and an X-ray. Dr. Lam prepared a list of forty-three medical conditions, such as jaundice or a patient's state of consciousness, which require good vision to diagnose. Dr. Lam also listed twenty-one medical procedures, such as arterial line placement, which require good vision. Dr. Lam concluded that an intermediary could not assist a blind medical student because use of an intermediary would require extra time that is not available in an emergency situation, and the observations during and the accuracy of the physical exam would be "only as good as the intermediary." Fischer recalled that during the interview, Dr. Lam commented that the "whole concept" of a blind medical student was "ridiculous."

After the three interviews and after consulting other CWRU medical school professors and students, CWRU's Admissions Committee, by a unanimous vote, denied Fischer's application.[2] Although the committee was aware of Dr. David W. Hartman, a psychiatrist who graduated from Temple University School of

---

[2] CWRU had previously offered admission to students with handicaps such as paraplegia, visual and hearing impairments, and dyslexia.

Medicine while totally blind in 1976, the committee did not contact Dr. Hartman or Temple University.

Dr. Hartman's experience affected the decision-making in this case. Temple University, in 1972, voluntarily increased the size of the incoming class by one to accept Dr. Hartman. To facilitate his first two years of study in the basic sciences, Dr. Hartman used a raised line drawing board to diagram and illustrate various structures. Postdoctoral or graduate students privately tutored Dr. Hartman by describing to him the slides of structures under microscope and using the raised line drawing board. Other medical students also assisted Dr. Hartman by describing experiments they conducted and otherwise sharing information. Dr. Hartman also listened to books on tapes, used readers, and relied on his sense of touch for classes such as anatomy.

In virtually all of his first and second year courses, Dr. Hartman required one-on-one assistance from his professors. Dr. Hartman estimated that the professors in the anatomy department, which included courses in gross anatomy, neuroanatomy, embryology and histology, spent double or triple the time tutoring him than they spent tutoring the average student. John R. Troyer, Ph.D., a professor who was on the faculty at Temple when Dr. Hartman attended, believed that the extra time he spent with Dr. Hartman took away from time he had to tutor other students. For this reason, Dr. Troyer had reservations about accepting another blind student.

Professors at Temple also modified their lectures to accommodate Dr. Hartman. For example, professors diagrammed structures on the raised line drawing board that the other students viewed under a microscope and verbally described processes instead of visually demonstrating them. One professor even sat next to Dr. Hartman during class and described procedures being conducted in a class demonstration.

To facilitate his clerkships, Dr. Hartman would have a nurse, another student, the resident or intern perform parts of a physical examination which required visual observations and describe their observations to him. Another student or a nurse would read patient charts and laboratory test results to him. Dr. Hartman could not start an I.V. without the supervision and assistance of a nurse and could not read an X-ray without relying on a radiologist.

During the surgical clerkship, Dr. Hartman spent only one or two days a week for three to four hours a day in surgery, where other students spent six or seven hours a day every day in surgery. Instead of being placed on night call alone, Dr. Hartman was paired with another student because the hospital relied on medical students to start I.V.s and draw blood.

Dr. Hartman's testimony revealed that his successful completion of the school's requirements depended on the willingness of the faculty and other students to spend the extra time describing and sharing information with him.

Following the second denial of Fischer's application to medical school, Fischer filed a complaint with the OCRC [Ohio Civil Rights Commission], alleging that CWRU had discriminated against her by denying her admission to the medical school on the basis of her handicap. After an investigation, OCRC found it probable that CWRU engaged in discriminatory practices in violation of R.C. 4112.022 and filed a complaint and notice of hearing.

Following the hearing, the examiner concluded that CWRU had not discriminated against Fischer and recommended dismissal of her complaint. The hearing examiner found that (1) Fischer could not complete the first two years of CWRU's requirements unless CWRU was willing to accommodate Fischer's handicap beyond what is legally required and was willing to place an undue burden on its teaching faculty, and (2) Fischer could not successfully complete the core clerkships without substantial modification to the essential nature of the program.

Upon its review of the hearing examiner's report, OCRC came to a different conclusion. Relying heavily upon Dr. Hartman's experience, OCRC concluded that Fischer could complete the medical school program with reasonable accommodations that would not modify the essential nature of its program. OCRC further found that CWRU violated an affirmative duty to gather substantial information to ascertain whether Fischer could benefit from the medical school's program. Finding CWRU had discriminated against Fischer, OCRC issued a cease and desist order and ordered CWRU to admit Fischer into its next class.

CWRU appealed to the Cuyahoga County Common Pleas Court, which found that reliable, probative and substantial evidence supported OCRC's findings of fact and conclusions of law and affirmed the OCRC order. The Court of Appeals for Cuyahoga County reversed, holding that the record did not support the trial court's finding that admitting Fischer would not necessitate a modification of the essential nature of the program and would not place an undue burden on CWRU. The court of appeals determined that the trial court had abused its discretion by relying upon Dr. Hartman's experience at Temple University and in finding that Temple made only reasonable accommodations.

This cause is now before the court upon the allowance of a discretionary appeal.

A. *Otherwise Qualified Handicapped Person*

Applying principles [of state and federal law] to R.C. 4112.022(A), we define an "otherwise qualified" handicapped person as one who is able to safely and substantially perform an educational program's essential requirements with reasonable accommodation. An accommodation is not reasonable where it requires fundamental alterations in the essential nature of the program or imposes an undue financial or administrative burden.

Because inquiry into reasonable accommodation is not separate from but rather is an aspect of "otherwise qualified," we further hold that as part of its prima facie case, OCRC carries the initial burden of showing that Fischer could safely and substantially perform the essential requirements of the program with reasonable accommodation. Thereafter, the burden shifts to CWRU to demonstrate that Fischer is not "otherwise qualified," i.e., the accommodations are not reasonable because they require fundamental alterations to the essential nature of the program or because they impose undue financial or administrative burdens. CWRU may also rebut a prima facie case of discrimination by "establishing bona fide requirements or standards for admission or assignment to academic programs, courses, internships, or classes . . . which requirements or standards may include reasonable qualifications for demonstrating necessary skill, aptitude, physical capability, intelligence, and previous education." Finally, the burden returns to OCRC and Fischer to rebut the evidence presented by CWRU.

II. *Standard of Review*

A. *Reliable, Probative and Substantial Evidence*

OCRC relied upon Dr. Hartman's experience at Temple University and Fischer's experience at CWRU while she was an undergraduate to demonstrate that she could complete the essential requirements of CWRU's medical program with reasonable accommodations. The trial court agreed that Dr. Hartman's testimony regarding Temple University's accommodations fulfilled the requisite reliable, probative and substantial evidence to support OCRC's order. We disagree.

"Reliable" evidence is dependable or trustworthy; "probative" evidence tends to prove the issue in question and is relevant to the issue presented; and "substantial" evidence carries some weight or value. We find that Dr. Hartman's experience at Temple University is neither probative nor substantial evidence to demonstrate that Fischer is currently able to safely and substantially perform the essential requirements of CWRU's program with reasonable accommodation.

Dr. Hartman is not an expert in medical education. He attended Temple University twenty years ago, under entirely different circumstances than proposed today. Temple voluntarily accepted Dr. Hartman by increasing the class size by one. The faculty at Temple acted upon a commitment to do whatever necessary to assist Dr. Hartman, and not upon a concept of reasonable accommodation. Additionally, Dr. Hartman was accepted prior to the AAMC's adoption of its technical standards for admission requiring each medical school student to have the ability to observe. Fischer, who provided the only testimony that she could complete the requirements of medical school with accommodations, admitted that she had no familiarity with what a medical student is required to do.

With Hartman and Fischer as its witnesses, OCRC failed to present any probative or substantial testimony that Fischer would be able to complete CWRU's course requirements with reasonable accommodation. CWRU, however, presented testimony from several medical educators that a blind student could not perform the requirements of medical school. Consequently, the trial court abused its discretion in finding that OCRC's cease and desist order was supported by probative or substantial evidence that Fischer could complete the medical program at CWRU with reasonable accommodation.

B. *Accommodations Were Not Reasonable*

The court of appeals also found that the trial court abused its discretion by finding that Fischer was otherwise qualified for admission with reasonable accommodations. Whether an accommodation is reasonable is a mixed question of law and fact.

OCRC suggests that certain accommodations such as raised line drawing boards, tutors and faculty assistance, occasional use of sighted students, and laboratory assistance would permit Fischer to realize the benefits of the first two years of the medical school program. OCRC also suggests modifications which would help her complete the required clerkships, such as the use of intermediaries to read X-rays and patient charts and to perform parts of a physical examination as well as the waiver of course requirements she could not perform such as starting an I.V. or drawing blood. OCRC argues that these accommodations are reasonable because those skills are not necessary for Fischer to pursue a practice in psychiatry, are not necessary for CWRU to maintain its accreditation as a medical school, and would not require a fundamental alteration in the nature of the program, since they are not essential to it. For the following reasons, we hold that the trial court's finding that these accommodations were reasonable is clearly erroneous and an abuse of discretion.

First, a similar argument regarding intermediaries, supervision and course waiver was rejected by the United States Supreme Court in *Davis*. The Court held that because the deaf nursing student would not receive "even a rough equivalent of the training a nursing program normally gives," the school was not required to make such a "fundamental alteration" in its program. In the present case, all of the medical educators who testified at the hearing agreed that it would be impossible to modify the traditional methods of teaching in a manner that would impart the necessary skills and information for a blind student to complete the essential course requirements.

Second, CWRU's decision not to modify its program by waiving course requirements or permitting intermediaries to read X-rays or perform physical examinations is an academic decision. Courts are particularly ill-equipped to evaluate academic requirements of educational institutions. As a result, considerable judicial deference must be paid to academic decisions made by the institution itself unless it is shown that the standards serve no purpose other than to deny an education to the handicapped. Furthermore, an educational institution is not required to accommodate a handicapped person by eliminating a course requirement which is reasonably necessary to the proper use of the degree conferred at the end of study.

The goal of medical schools is not to produce specialized degrees but rather general degrees in medicine which signify that the holder is a physician prepared for further training in any area of medicine. As such, graduates must have the knowledge and skills to function in a broad variety of clinical situations and to render a wide spectrum of patient care. All students, regardless of whether they intend to practice in psychiatry or radiology, are required to complete a variety of course requirements, including rotations in pediatrics, gynecology, and surgery.

Both the AAMC technical standards and the medical educators who testified at the hearing rejected the use of an intermediary by a medical student. In these medical educators' opinions, the use of an intermediary would interfere with the student's exercise of independent judgment — a crucial part of developing diagnostic skills. Accordingly, a waiver of the medical school's requirements such as starting an I.V. or reading an X-ray, or the use of an intermediary to perform these functions would fundamentally alter the nature of the program.

Finally, an administrative agency should accord due deference to the findings and recommendations of its referee, especially where there exist evidentiary conflicts. In this case, the referee concluded that Fischer could not complete courses in the basic sciences without placing an undue burden on the faculty, and could not complete the clerkships without substantial modification to the essential nature of the program. OCRC adopted the hearing officer's findings of fact, but did not accept his recommendation. Rather, OCRC placed great weight upon Dr. Hartman's testimony in arriving at a conclusion contrary to the hearing officer's. As discussed *supra*, however, Dr. Hartman's testimony was not probative of the issue and was insufficient to form the basis of a finding that the accommodations were reasonable.

III. *Duty to Investigate*

Finally, OCRC contends that CWRU's failure to inquire into technological advances to assist the blind, its failure to contact Dr. Hartman or Temple University, and its failure to consult experts in educating the blind during its decision-making process violated an affirmative duty to investigate whether accommodations would enable Fischer to complete the medical school program.

> "[I]mpos[ing] demanding information-gathering requirements upon federal employers" is justified by the express "affirmative action" language of Section 501 — language that does not appear in Section 504.

The United States Supreme Court recognized that in order to protect handicapped individuals from "deprivations based on prejudice, stereotypes, or unfounded fear," a determination as to whether an individual is otherwise qualified should in "most cases" be made in the context of an "individualized inquiry into the relation between the requirements of the program and the abilities of the individual."

Similarly, Ohio law does not support the imposition of a duty to investigate in all cases. Rather, [it] contemplates that there will be situations in which a school could justifiably exclude all persons with a particular handicap from admission to a program. [State law] does not consider an act discriminatory where it is based upon a bona fide requirement or standard for admission. OCRC argues that vision is not a bona fide physical requirement for admission to medical school because CWRU failed to adopt the vision requirement prior to the rejection of Fischer's application.

Again, we must disagree. Regardless of when CWRU adopted its own set of admissions standards and whether the AAMC standards are mandatory, the AAMC technical standards represent a comprehensive study supporting denial of admission to blind medical school applicants. Once CWRU confirmed the complete absence of an ability to observe, CWRU could deny Fischer's application based upon a bona fide standard for admission to the medical school.

PROBLEMS

1. Are the *Pushkin* and *Case Western* decisions consistent?

2. In reading the *Case Western* decision, keep in mind the 2008 ADA amendments relating to eyeglasses and vision. While the amendments generally prohibit considering ameliorative effects of mitigating measures in determining disability, they allow for considering the ameliorative effect of mitigating measures of "ordinary eyeglasses or contact lenses in determining whether there is a substantial limitation." 42 U.S.C. § 12102(4)(E)(iii). The amendments prohibit covered entities, however, from using qualification standards or selection criteria that are based on uncorrected vision unless these are job-related and consistent with business necessity. 42 U.S.C. § 12113(c). It is not clear if this clarification applies only to employment, although it probably does. If not, a medical school or other program could have qualification standards related to vision that might screen out individuals with visual impairments, but the program would have to demonstrate that the requirement was necessary. Has Case Western met that burden based on the facts in the case?

The *Halasz, Pushkin, Case Western*, and *Southeastern Community College* decisions have all raised issues of whether the applicant meets the qualifications essential to the program. Higher education institutions are not required to waive fundamental requirements for admission, and they are given substantial deference in setting those criteria. Fundamental requirements relate not only to academic ability, but also to physical qualifications in some cases. Concerns about safety and health of the applicant and others are raised in some cases. Character and conduct can also be relevant for professional programs such as law school.

NOTES

1. *Conditional Admission:* The case of *Crancer v. Board of Regents*, 156 Mich. App. 790, 402 N.W.2d 90 (1986), involved an unusual request for accommodation under state law in the admission process. The claimant sought admission into the University of Michigan Doctoral Program of English Language and Literature. Because of her condition of Post Traumatic Stress Disorder, she requested that she be admitted conditioned on receiving certain level of performance in her master's program. She argued that the conditional admission would relieve the stress so that she would perform at a better level in the master's program. The court rejected this claim giving judicial deference to the university's evaluation standards.

2. *Changing the Requirements:* What happens when an institution admits a student under one set of criteria, and then changes the requirements for completion of the program while the student is enrolled? This was the situation in *Doherty v. Southern College of Optometry*, 862 F.2d 570 (6th Cir. 1988), a case brought under Section 504. A student with retinitis pigmentosa and an associated neurological condition affecting his vision was admitted into a program of optometry. While he was in his first year of the program, the college established a new requirement requiring visual ability to perform certain techniques that had become part of the

professional expectation for practice. Because the student could not perform these techniques due to his visual impairment, he was unable to complete the program. His request for accommodation of waiving this requirement was denied by the college, and subsequently by the court. It was determined that "An educational institution is not required to accommodate . . . by eliminating a course requirement which is reasonably necessary to proper use of the degree conferred at the end of a course of study." Perhaps key to the court's decision was that this profession involves the health and safety of others. In cases such as this, courts generally give substantial deference to the health care professional organization. Problem 2, following the *Case Western* case highlights the 2008 ADA amendments as they relate to vision criteria. Does this make the result in *Doherty* even more valid?

3.   *Discriminatory Intent:* In *Wood v. President & Trustees of Spring Hill College*, 978 F.2d 1214 (11th Cir. 1992), the college requested that a student who was already enrolled defer her admission when it learned that a mistake had been made in her admission. She did not have the requisite grades for admission as a freshman or as a transfer student. The discovery only occurred after the father of her roommate "called the school demanding that his daughter not be assigned to live with a schizophrenic." The plaintiff claimed that after the college learned of her condition, she was treated in such a hostile manner that she withdrew, and that this was a "constructive dismissal." The court disagreed and held that the actions of the college did not amount to intentional discrimination under Section 504. The case is instructive on the importance of developing good practices and procedures in dealing with students with mental health problems.

4.   *Tort and Contract Theories in Disability Discrimination Cases:* Before the passage of the ADA, a private college not receiving federal financial assistance would not have been subject to the mandates of Section 504 of the Rehabilitation Act. Thus, an individual with a disability who believed there had been unfair treatment might have to resort to other theories to redress this treatment. One such case is *Russell v. Salve Regina College*, 890 F.2d 484 (1st Cir. 1989). The student was an extremely overweight woman in a nursing program at a private college. Although she successfully completed her freshman year, she was eventually pressured to lose weight by trying to get her to sign a contract. After a series of events when she did not lose weight, the program dismissed her. She brought claims under several tort and contract theories, including intentional infliction of emotional distress (which was dismissed), invasion of privacy (which was dismissed), and breach of contract (on which she was successful). It is significant that none of the catalogs, manuals, handbooks referred to weight, and her performance in the program was not at issue. It is important that nursing program and other health care professional programs take care in establishing physical requirements and ensure that these requirements relate to the ability to perform or some other essential attribute of participation in the program. Thus a nursing program might want to establish that standing for long periods of time, moving about beds quickly, stamina, and other physical requirements are essential, but it should not make the assumption that being overweight necessarily means that an individual cannot carry out these requirements.

5.   *Deference to Health and Safety Concerns:* Courts have shown substantial deference to health care professional programs in their establishment of health and

safety concerns of patients. In *Doe v. Washington University*, 780 F. Supp. 628 (E.D. Mo. 1991), a dental student with HIV was removed from the program because the dental school and subsequently the court believed that his condition posed a risk to health of patients because of the invasive procedures inherent to dental student training. Because the decision was based on reasonable medical judgments given the state of medical knowledge, the exclusion was allowed. For additional cases on health care professional programs and students with HIV, see LAURA ROTHSTEIN & JULIA ROTHSTEIN, DISABILITIES AND THE LAW §§ 3:5 & 10:2 (2009).

PROBLEMS

1. The *Salve Regina* case is decided on tort and contract theories. The facts in the case occurred before the passage of the ADA. How would this case be decided under the ADA? Could an action under Section 504 of the Rehabilitation Act have been successful?

2. Many law schools have as a requirement that students do an oral argument in moot court as part of the first year. Could a deaf student who does not speak be legally denied admission on the basis that he/she is not otherwise qualified because of the inability to complete the oral argument?

3. Is there any difference when serious psychiatric problems are involved whether the student is attending undergraduate school, law school, medical school, or some other program? What if the problem is alcohol addiction rather than other psychiatric problems? In other words, is emotional stability a more justifiable criteria in some academic programs than in others?

[2]   Standardized Testing and Other Evaluation

For entry into most academic disciplines, it is generally required that the applicant take a standardized test, such as the Law School Admissions Test. Before the passage of the Americans with Disabilities Act, most standardized testing programs were themselves not required to provide accommodations for taking the test because these entities were not recipients of federal financial assistance. The ADA is very clear that such entities are considered covered under Title III as public accommodations. Before the ADA, the issue was whether the institutions of higher education, which were recipients of federal financial assistance, could legally use scores when accommodations were not provided. This question never reached the courts because most, if not all, of the standardized testing by the professional test administrators began voluntarily providing accommodations in response to market forces. Colleges and universities had been raising these questions directly with the testing agencies.

The issues that arise with respect to standardized testing are 1) whether applicants can be required to undergo such testing or if there are circumstances where there should be a waiver; 2) what accommodations should be provided and when; 3) how these scores should be reported to the institution wanting to take them into account; 4) how these scores should be used by the institution.

Section 504 regulations require institutions of higher education to demonstrate that such tests have been validated as a predictor of success when a test has a disproportionate adverse impact on an applicant with a disability. 34 C.F.R. § 104.42. As the following cases demonstrate, courts have generally upheld the use of standardized tests. These cases also illustrate the issue of accommodations that should be provided. The question about whether a testing service can require documentation of a disability before providing an accommodation is discussed in the next section, and is not addressed to any great extent in the following cases in this section. That is addressed in the following sections.

WYNNE v. TUFTS UNIVERSITY SCHOOL OF MEDICINE
932 F.2d 19 (1st Cir. 1991)

COFFIN, SENIOR CIRCUIT JUDGE:

Appellant Wynne, although possessing lower MCAT (Medical College Aptitude Test) scores and undergraduate grades than most Tufts students, was admitted under the school's affirmative action program for minority applicants in 1983. In December of that year he became aware of his difficulty in dealing with written multiple choice examinations; the following spring he had conversations with school officials about his difficulty. At the end of his first year he had failed eight of fifteen courses. Although the school's guidelines provide for dismissal after five course failures, and the Student Evaluations and Promotions Committee and the Student Appeals Committee had both voted to dismiss Wynne, the dean decided to permit him to repeat the first-year program.

During the summer between his first and second years, Wynne underwent a neuropsychological evaluation at the request of the medical school, which arranged and paid for the test. The psychologist began by noting that Wynne had described having difficulties with multiple choice examination questions and experiencing more success on practicum, laboratory, or applied sections of his courses. She summarized his neuropsychological profile as follows:

> [E]valuation reveals average general cognitive abilities with marked variability among individual skills. Significant strengths were noted in conceptual thinking and reasoning abilities. In contrast, Mr. Wynne encountered serious difficulties processing discrete units of information in a variety of domains, both verbal and non-verbal. Formal language testing revealed insecurities in linguistic processing including inefficient retrieval and retention of information. This type of neuropsychological profile has been identified in the learning disabled population.[3]

The difficulties identified by the psychologist impaired Wynne's ability to answer multiple-choice questions, even though he did manage to pass several such examinations. A reading specialist who worked with him after he was dismissed from medical school observed that he had difficulty interpreting "Type K"

---

[3] Subsequent to Wynne's dismissal from Tufts, he underwent testing at the Massachusetts General Hospital Language Disorders Unit. In a report dated January 9, 1986, the reading therapist who evaluated Wynne observed that the 1984 neuropsychological testing, "which showed weaknesses in sequencing, memory, visual memory and part-whole relationships, taken in conjunction with his academic history, strongly suggests dyslexia."

multiple-choice questions because of their structure, which often includes passive constructions and double and triple negatives.

Wynne began his second exposure to the first-year program with the assistance of counselling, tutors, note-takers, and taped lectures, the nature, quantity, and regularity of which are presently subjects of considerable dispute. In addition to retaking the seven courses he had failed, Wynne also was required to attend classes and take exams in three courses he had passed with low-pass scores. At the end of the year he passed all but two courses, Pharmacology and Biochemistry. The Student Evaluations and Promotions Committee permitted him to take make-up exams in these two courses. He subsequently passed Pharmacology but failed Biochemistry for the third time. The two committees, Student Evaluations and Student Appeals, recommended dismissal and the dean agreed. Wynne was dismissed from the medical school in September 1985.

In 1986 Wynne filed a complaint with the United States Department of Education Office for Civil Rights alleging discrimination. On January 12, 1987 that office issued its report, finding no discrimination. A year later Wynne filed suit, alleging that Tufts' treatment of him constituted discrimination on the basis of his handicap. Although the record contains references to various supposed faults in Tufts' response to his disability, Wynne's brief on appeal ties his claim of discrimination solely to the school's failure to offer an alternative to written multiple choice examinations. We therefore treat the appeal as limited to this issue.

Section 504 of the Rehabilitation Act provides that "[n]o otherwise qualified individual with handicaps in the United States . . . shall, solely by reason of her or his handicap, be excluded from the participation in, be denied the benefits of, or be subjected to discrimination under any program or activity receiving Federal financial assistance. . . . "

Our inquiry into the meaning of "otherwise qualified" begins, but does not end, with *Southeastern Community College v. Davis*. That case involved a nursing school applicant who was afflicted with a serious hearing disability and whose dependence on lip reading would prevent her from clinical training and limit her in other ways. The court of appeals had set aside a district court finding that plaintiff was not an "otherwise qualified" handicapped individual, reasoning that the Act required the College to consider the application without regard to hearing ability and that it required " 'affirmative conduct' on the part of Southeastern to modify its program to accommodate the disabilities of applicants, 'even when such modifications become expensive.' "

The Court, in reversing the judgment, addressed both propositions embraced by the court of appeals. It first rejected the idea that an institution had to disregard any limitation resulting from a handicap, saying, "[a]n otherwise qualified person is one who is able to meet all of a program's requirements in spite of his handicap." Second, observing that no action short of a "substantial change" in Southeastern's program would accommodate plaintiff, and that the Act did not impose an affirmative action obligation on all recipients of federal funds, it held that no such "fundamental alteration" in Southeastern's program was required. It also noted that the program, aimed at training persons for "all normal roles of a registered nurse, represents a legitimate academic policy." The Court did, however, leave open the possibility that an insistence on continuing past requirements notwithstanding technological advances might be "unreasonable and discriminatory."

The arguably absolutist principles of *Davis* — a handicapped person must be able to meet all requirements of an institution; and there is no affirmative action obligation on an institution — were meaningfully qualified by the Court in *Alexander v. Choate*, 469 U.S. 287 (1985). The Court signalled its awareness of criticism that the *Davis* pronouncement on "affirmative action" obscured the difference between "a remedial policy for the victims of past discrimination" and "the elimination of existing obstacles against the handicapped." It then distinguished "substantial" and "fundamental" changes (affirmative action) from "changes that would be reasonable accommodations." *Id.* It added this gloss to *Davis*:

> The balance struck in *Davis* requires that an otherwise qualified handicapped individual must be provided with meaningful access to the benefit that the grantee offers. The benefit itself, of course, cannot be defined in a way that effectively denies otherwise qualified handicapped individuals the meaningful access to which they are entitled; to assure meaningful access, reasonable accommodations in the grantee's program or benefit may have to be made.

Thus, in determining whether an individual meets the "otherwise qualified" requirement of section 504, it is necessary to look at more than the individual's ability to meet a program's present requirements. As the court in *Brennan v. Stewart* recognized:

> The question after *Alexander* is the rather mushy one of whether some "reasonable accommodation" is available to satisfy the legitimate interests of both the grantee and the handicapped person. And since it is part of the "otherwise qualified" inquiry, our precedent requires that the "reasonable accommodation" question be decided as an issue of fact . . . .

What we have distilled from [other case precedents] is consistent with the well established principle enunciated in *Regents of University of Michigan v. Ewing*, "When judges are asked to review the substance of a genuinely academic decision, . . . they should show great respect for the faculty's professional judgment." The question in *Ewing* was whether a university had violated substantive due process (i.e., had engaged in wholly arbitrary action) in dropping plaintiff from an academic program after plaintiff had failed several subjects and received the lowest score so far recorded in the program. This was a context where no federal statutory obligation impinged on the academic administrators; their freedom to make genuine academic decisions was untrammeled. This is why the Court added to the above quoted passage the sentence: "Plainly, [judges] may not override [the faculty's professional judgment] unless it is such a substantial departure from accepted academic norms as to demonstrate that the person or committee responsible did not actually exercise professional judgment."

In the context of an "otherwise qualified-reasonable accommodations" inquiry under the Rehabilitation Act, the same principle of respect for academic decision-making applies but with two qualifications. First, as we have noted, there is a real obligation on the academic institution to seek suitable means of reasonably accommodating a handicapped person and to submit a factual record indicating that it conscientiously carried out this statutory obligation. Second, the *Ewing* formulation, hinging judicial override on "a substantial departure from accepted academic norms," is not necessarily a helpful test in assessing whether professional judgment has been exercised in exploring reasonable alternatives for accommodating a handicapped person. We say this because such alternatives may involve new approaches or devices quite beyond "accepted academic norms." As the Court acknowledged in *Davis*, "[t]echnological advances can be expected to enhance opportunities to rehabilitate the handicapped or otherwise to qualify them for some useful employment."

It seems to us that the case before us, where the adversaries are an individual and an academic institution, involves a set of conflicting concerns. . . .

We believe [the approach that is appropriate is] to assess whether an academic institution adequately has explored the availability of reasonable accommodations for a handicapped individual. If the institution submits undisputed facts demonstrating that the relevant officials within the institution considered alternative means, their feasibility, cost and effect on the academic program, and came to a rationally justifiable conclusion that the available alternatives would result either in lowering academic standards or requiring substantial program alteration, the court could rule as a matter of law that the institution had met its duty of seeking reasonable accommodation. In most cases . . . the issue of whether the facts alleged by a university support its claim that it has met its duty of reasonable accommodation will be a "purely legal one." Only if essential facts were genuinely disputed or if there were significantly probative evidence of bad faith or pretext would further fact finding be necessary.

The district court, in granting Tufts' motion for summary judgment, explicitly relied on the fact that Wynne had failed eight of his first year courses, two of the eight a second time, and one a third time. Following the literal language of *Davis* that an "otherwise qualified person" must meet "all of a program's requirements," the court felt compelled to grant the motion. As we have indicated in our review of the caselaw, *Alexander* in effect modified the "all" language of *Davis* and articulated the obligation to make reasonable accommodation part of the "otherwise qualified" inquiry.

If the record were crystal clear that even if reasonable alternatives to written multiple-choice examinations were available, Wynne would have no chance of meeting Tufts' standards, we might be able to affirm on a different ground from that relied on by the district court. But although Wynne has an uphill road to travel, with much to indicate that he has cognitive and other problems that are independent of his difficulties with multiple-choice examinations, we do not think the record permits this course. The results of his neuropsychological evaluation after his first year indicated average general cognitive abilities and well-developed skills in conceptual reasoning and abstract problem solving; he did pass most of his exams; he scored substantially higher in time-measured "practicum," a form of examination requiring him to apply his knowledge to a problem; he assertedly read and digested information from medical journals for his master's thesis; he read and assimilated computer-generated data in his Hematology course, which was successfully completed; experts asserted that he had the ability and motivation to improve his language skills. Whatever may be the ultimate outcome, we think that on the record as made thus far Tufts had the obligation of demonstrating that its determination that no reasonable way existed to accommodate Wynne's inability to perform adequately on written multiple-choice examinations was a reasoned, professional academic judgment, not a mere ipse dixit.

Tufts' submission on this issue consisted of an affidavit from the Dean of its School of Medicine, Dr. Henry Banks. Three paragraphs concern written multiple-choice (Type K) examinations. The first stated the test's purpose: "to measure a student's ability not only to memorize complicated material, but also to understand and assimilate it." The second, and major, paragraph stated:

> In the judgment of the professional medical educators who are responsible for determining testing procedures at Tufts, written multiple choice (Type K) examinations are important as a matter of substance, not merely of form. In our view, the ability to assimilate, interpret and analyze complex written material is necessary for the safe and responsible practice of modern medicine. It is essential for practicing physicians to keep abreast of the latest developments in written medical journals. Modern diagnostic and treatment procedures often call for the reading and assimilation of computer-generated data and other complex written materials. Frequently, and often under stressful conditions fraught with the most serious consequences, physicians are called upon to make choices and decisions based on a quick reading, understanding and interpretation of hospital charts, medical reference materials and other written resources. A degree from the Tufts University School of Medicine certifies, in part, that its holder is able to read and interpret such complicated written medical data quickly and accurately.

The third paragraph asserted that it was the judgment of "the medical educators who set Tufts' academic standards" that the above described demands "are best tested . . . by written, multiple choice examinations."

[A] court's duty is first to find the basic facts, giving due deference to the school, and then to evaluate whether those facts add up to a professional, academic judgment that reasonable accommodation is simply not available. The above quoted affidavit, however, does not allow even the first step to be taken. There is no mention of any consideration of possible alternatives, nor reference to any discussion of the unique qualities of multiple choice examinations. There is no indication of who took part in the decision or when it was made. Were the simple conclusory averment of the head of an institution to suffice, there would be no way of ascertaining whether the institution had made a professional effort to evaluate possible ways of accommodating a handicapped student or had simply embraced what was most convenient for faculty and administration. We say this, of course, without any intent to impugn the present affiant, but only to attempt to underscore the need for a procedure that can permit the necessary minimum judicial review.

We therefore set aside the summary judgment and remand this issue for further proceedings. As is evident from our discussion, the court will be free to consider other submissions, to enter summary judgment thereon if they meet the standard we have set forth, or to proceed with further fact-finding if such should prove necessary.

NOTES

1. On rehearing in the *Wynne* case, the court determined that the standard set out by the previous opinion subsequently had been applied by the medical school, and that there was no violation of the Rehabilitation Act. The medical school had demonstrated that the alternatives proposed would be a substantial program alteration. *Wynne v. Tufts Univ. Sch. of Med.*, 976 F.2d 791 (1st Cir. 1992).

2. In *Price v. National Bd. of Med. Exmrs.*, 966 F. Supp. 419 (S.D. W. Va. 1997), the court held that medical students claiming learning disabilities had not even demonstrated that they were substantially limited in major life activities.

A number of decisions have focused more on whether the individual with a learning disability is even "disabled" within the definition. Often in these cases, courts found that the individual was not "substantially limited" in a major life activity if he or she has succeeded in the previous academic program. Previous to the *Sutton* trilogy, see Chapter 2[B][4], *supra*, the defendant colleges and universities had focused less on dismissing the cases because the claimant was not protected and more on the merits of the case. Higher education and professional licensing cases since *Sutton* have been substantially more focused on whether the individual is covered. See, e.g., *Wong v. Regents of University of California*, 410 F.3d 1052 (9th Cir. 2005) (medical student with a learning disability was not substantially limited for purposes of daily living as compared to most people); *Swanson v. University of Cincinnati*, 268 F.3d 307 (6th Cir. 2001) (surgical resident with major depression not substantially limited in the ability to perform major life activities). The 2008 ADA amendments were an attempt to return courts to the pre-*Sutton* definition of disability. Learning disabilities and related disabilities such as ADD and ADHD are likely to continue to be addressed by the courts. While compensating measures may no longer be considered, the individual must still demonstrate that the condition creates a "substantial" limitation. Just having a diagnosis of an impairment does not mean that requirement has been met.

3. The *Wynne* decision comments on the term "affirmative conduct" and how the Court in *Southeastern Community College* used the term. In light of recent attention to affirmative action programs relating to considering race and ethnicity in higher education admissions, this comment should be reviewed. Neither Section 504 nor the Americans with Disabilities Act were ever intended to mandate preferential admission or discounting of qualifications. The inartful use of the term in *Southeastern Community College* was intended to reference the expectation that individuals with disabilities should be given "reasonable accommodations" and that these do not require lowering standards or fundamentally altering the program.

4. *"Flagged" Test Scores:* An issue that arises in the context of standardized test scores used for entry into higher education programs is whether a testing service may "flag" or indicate that a standardized test was not taken under standard conditions. This issue is not well addressed by the courts. A Department of

Education interim policy from the 1970s allowing flagging has never been retracted. The practice of flagging varies from test to test. The Office for Civil Rights issued a ruling in 1993 that devaluing MCAT scores of individuals who took the test under nonstandard conditions violates Section 504. *SUNY Health Science Ctr. at Brooklyn — College of Med. (NY)*, 5 N.D.L.R. ¶ 77 (OCR 1993). That ruling noted that using flagged test scores is not noncompliance with the Rehabilitation Act, so long as such test scores are not the only basis for admissions decisions and so long as the applicant is not denied admission because an accommodated test was taken.

The permissibility of flagging has not been definitively decided. In *Doe v. National Board of Medical Examiners*, 199 F.3d 146 (3d Cir. 1999), a lower court ruling that had stopped flagging of the MCAT exam was suspended.

PROBLEMS

1.   Is it permissible under the Americans with Disabilities Act to require an earlier deadline for registration for a standardized admission test if the individual is requesting an accommodation? 42 U.S.C. § 12189; 36 C.F.R. § 36.309.

2.   Would it be permissible to set absolute minimum standardized test scores for admission into an academic program? How is that different from requiring a certain grade point for graduation from the program?

[3]   Identifying and Documenting the Disability

Higher education institutions generally may not inquire about a disability in the admissions process. However, where the applicant wishes to put the disability at issue, it is the obligation of the applicant to raise the existence of the disability, and in some cases, to provide documentation to justify accommodation or consideration in the admissions process. The type of documentation required will depend on the circumstances.

For example, an applicant who uses a wheelchair and who wants to meet with the admissions interview committee in an accessible location should not have to provide medical documentation of the disability. An applicant who claims to have a learning disability, and who wants to be given additional time on the SAT test or wants the college to consider the learning disability as justification for poor performance in certain undergraduate classes, will be held to a different standard. The institution will be justified in requiring appropriate documentation. This will mean that the evaluation of the disability must have been done recently enough to be valid, it must be done by a professional qualified to evaluate the disability, and, ideally, the professional should not only identify the disability, but should indicate what accommodations are needed in response to the limitations resulting from the disability. In most cases, the institution will be on solid legal ground to require the applicant to pay for the cost of the documentation.

The following decisions illustrate some of these points.

NATHANSON v. MEDICAL COLLEGE OF PENNSYLVANIA
926 F.2d 1368 (3d Cir. 1991)

SCIRICA, CIRCUIT JUDGE:

I. *Facts and Background*

With noted exceptions, the following facts are undisputed. In 1981, Nathanson was involved in an automobile accident that resulted in continuing back and neck injuries. During the next several years she engaged in physical therapy to recover from her injuries. In 1982, she decided that she wanted to go to medical school and began taking medical-related courses at Temple University and the University of Pennsylvania. In November, 1984, she applied for admission to MCP's 1985 entering class for the M.D. degree. On August 26, 1985, she was accepted for admission to MCP.

During her interviews with two MCP faculty members in July, 1985, and in the narrative section of her application, Nathanson informed MCP about her accident and injuries. She also told the MCP interviewers that she had not been able to sit in the seats provided for examinees for the Medical College Admissions Test (MCAT) because of her disability. Instead, she had been allowed to take the examination at an ordinary table. She stated, however, that she believed at that time that she would not require special accommodations at MCP because she had "never had a problem" with her seating arrangements during her prior course work at Temple and Penn.

At issue in this case is what took place between Nathanson and MCP administrators from the time that Nathanson first attended MCP to the point of her final departure approximately one year later. Nathanson's transactions with MCP are important because they clarify when and whether MCP was ever aware that Nathanson had a handicap and had requested accommodations, and whether her requests were sufficiently specific for MCP to respond.

[The factual background, including the various transactions leading up to this complaint are omitted in this excerpt, but they are referred to throughout the remainder of the opinion.]

At issue here, then, is the district court's conclusion about the fourth requirement [of § 504 of the Rehabilitation Act] relating to discrimination and denial of the program's benefits. As the district court said, "[a]lthough [Nathanson] discussed her physical discomfort in prior correspondence with defendant, no reason existed for defendant to consider plaintiff's condition to be a handicap as contemplated by the statute . . . [or] that plaintiff did not have meaningful access to defendant's program."

For the reasons provided below, we cannot agree with this assessment.

A. *Did MCP Have Reason to Know That Nathanson's Condition Was a Handicap?*

In order to be liable under the Rehabilitation Act, MCP must know or be reasonably expected to know of Nathanson's handicap. Neither the Rehabilitation Act nor the regulations specifies what notification is necessary to adequately inform a recipient of a person's handicap or what constitutes awareness of a handicap.

In this case, Nathanson's handicap was not visibly obvious. The district court found that Nathanson never sufficiently demonstrated to MCP that one of her "major life activities" was impaired. Therefore, MCP had no reason to know that she was handicapped. The district court also found that Nathanson never made a sufficiently direct and specific request for special accommodations that would have put MCP on notice of her handicap. Of course, this would be relevant only if MCP neither knew nor had reason to know that Nathanson was handicapped.

We believe there is sufficient evidence to create a material issue of fact whether MCP knew or had reason to know that Nathanson met the standards of a "handicapped individual" under § 706(8)(B)(i) and (ii). With regard to § 706(8)(B)(i), Nathanson's meeting with Beasley on September 12, 1985, their depictions of this meeting, and her letter to him the next day, raised a factual issue whether Nathanson's "physical impairment," her neck and back injuries, "substantially limited" one of her "major life activities," which was "learning." Beasley's affidavit stated that Nathanson's physical difficulties precluded her from attending classes at MCP for the next academic year. Moreover, Nathanson's letter of September 13, 1985, requesting permission to defer classes for one year "because of the increased pain and spasm" that she had been experiencing, documented that she believed that her handicap was interfering with her learning.

With regard to § 706(8)(B)(ii), there was sufficient evidence to create a material issue of fact whether Nathanson had a "record of impairment." Nathanson wrote Beasley that:

> I had been in a car accident several years ago, injuring my neck, back, and shoulders and have made major strides in terms of recovery each year. Based upon my performance under a full-time load last spring [at Penn], I truly believed that I was physically prepared to handle the burden of a medical curriculum. Sadly this has not been so, each day the situation has worsened in terms of my pain and fatigue and I do not believe my physical condition is good enough to proceed [in attending classes at MCP] successfully.

A person with a record of impairment can still qualify as a handicapped individual even if that individual's impairment does not presently limit one or more of that person's major life activities. Nathanson described to MCP that she had expanded her course load at Penn and at Temple over the years since her injury in part to test and prepare for the endurance needed to handle a fulltime course load in medical school. Thus, her statements created an issue of fact concerning whether she notified MCP that she had a record of impairment that "substantially limited" one of her "major life activities," learning.

MCP contends that it could not have reasonably known about Nathanson's record of impairment because she indicated at her preadmission interviews that she would not require special accommodations at MCP because she had "never had a problem" with her seating arrangements during her prior course work at Temple and Penn. Moreover, the regulations specifically prohibit schools that receive federal funds from asking if an applicant is handicapped although they may do so confidentially after an individual has been admitted for purposes of accommodation. However, as we have noted, there is sufficient evidence to create an issue of fact about whether Nathanson gave notice of her record of impairment after she was admitted to MCP.

Furthermore, it appears that there was a disputed fact whether Nathanson made a specific request for accommodations before August 21, 1986. There is some evidence that Nathanson did ask for direct help with her accommodations at least three times during the course of the year: [Testimony omitted.]

In general, then, we find some evidence that Nathanson made known that she had difficulty in "learning," that her handicap prevented her from attending classes, and that she made direct requests for accommodations. Therefore, we believe that there is a disputed issue of material fact whether MCP knew or reasonably should have known that Nathanson met the standards for a handicapped individual under the Act.

B. *Did MCP Provide Reasonable Accommodations for Nathanson's Handicap?*

For individuals in Nathanson's position, the regulations implement the reasonable accommodation standard under § 504 as follows:

> A recipient [of federal funds] shall make reasonable accommodation to the known physical or mental limitations of an otherwise qualified handicapped applicant or employee unless the recipient can demonstrate that the accommodation would impose an undue hardship on the operation of its program.

[Discussion of *Southeastern Community College v. Davis* and *Alexander v. Choate* omitted.]

Much of the case law interpreting § 504 relates to circumstances like those in *Southeastern* where a plaintiff claims denial of admission into a program because of a handicap. Southeastern's holding was particularly stringent because the admission standards were designed to protect public health and safety, a concern that has been given considerable deference by the courts.

Nathanson does not typify those handicapped individuals to which the "reasonable accommodation" standard in *Southeastern* was directed because that standard was designed to clarify whether an individual was "otherwise qualified" for a program. This distinction is important because Nathanson's case involves alleged discrimination or denial to a handicapped individual who has already been admitted to a program and deemed to be "otherwise qualified" but who requests individual accommodation in order to have access to or to continue benefitting from the program. Moreover, Nathanson's request does not relate to concerns of public safety involving others and does not require the kind of alteration found in *Southeastern* or *Alexander*.

As we have noted, the regulations require that a recipient make reasonable accommodation to the "known physical or mental limitations" of otherwise qualified individuals like Nathanson unless the recipient can show that the accommodation "would impose undue hardship on the operation of its program." We find nothing inconsistent between the regulations and the Supreme Court holdings that we have reviewed. Therefore, if MCP's failure to provide a suitable seating arrangement makes its program effectively unavailable to a student with a back injury, then that failure could constitute the type of "benign neglect" referred to in *Alexander* and a violation of the Rehabilitation Act. MCP would have to show that the required modification entails a substantial alteration in order to avoid a violation of the Act.

Despite Nathanson's conflicting messages over the course of the year and despite her change of expectations from MCP, we believe the following to be disputed issues of fact:

> 1) whether Nathanson left school before MCP had an opportunity to reasonably accommodate her; 2) whether Nathanson assumed the responsibility for finding her own accommodations after her meeting with Beasley on September 12, 1985; and 3) whether MCP made a reasonable effort to accommodate Nathanson even after August 21, 1986, the date that MCP claimed that it first became aware that Nathanson was handicapped.

The district court construed the statute to require that MCP "need only make it possible for [Nathanson] to have 'access' to the building, her classes and other facilities." The court believed that MCP need not make Nathanson "comfortable," and commented that Nathanson "had access to the facilities and building." As is evident from the regulations, a defendant's obligation goes further than making the building and physical facilities accessible.

We note that MCP would not have been in legal jeopardy for seeking more information from Nathanson because the regulations provide that a recipient "may make inquiries [from handicapped individuals] on a confidential basis as to handicaps that may require accommodation." Furthermore, the regulations state that recipients of federal funds are obligated to provide the types of auxiliary aids that Nathanson requested, therefore enabling reasonable accommodation inside a building as well as access outside.

> (d) *Auxiliary aids.* (1) A recipient to which this subpart applies *shall take such steps as are necessary* to ensure that no handicapped student is denied the benefits of, excluded from participation in, or otherwise subjected to discrimination under the education program or activity operated by the recipient because of the absence of educational auxiliary aids for students with impaired sensory, manual, or speaking skills. (2) Auxiliary aids may include taped texts, interpreters or other effective methods of making orally delivered materials available to students with hearing impairments, readers in libraries for visual impairments, *classroom equipment adapted for use by students with manual impairments*, and other similar services and actions. Recipients need not provide

attendants, individually prescribed devices, readers for personal use or study, or other devices or services of a personal nature.

45 C.F.R. § 84.44(d) (emphasis added).

Nathanson requested closer parking and a straight back chair which, she emphasized, did not need to be specifically designed for her. It is therefore a disputed issue of fact whether Nathanson needed "reasonable" accommodations that would not cause "undue financial or administrative burdens" or "impose an undue hardship" upon the functioning of the recipient's program. A district court's estimate of what is reasonable "rests in large part upon factual determinations." In turn, the regulations suggest the following "factors to be considered" in determining whether an accommodation would create an undue hardship:

> 1) The overall size of the recipient's program with respect to the number of employees, number and type of facilities, and size of budget; 2) The type of the recipient's operation, including the composition and structure of the recipient's workforce; and 3) The nature and cost of the accommodation needed.

Accommodations that are "reasonable" must not unduly strain financial resources. Furthermore, a recipient must be allotted sufficient time and opportunity to investigate and acquire accommodations if appropriate. However, we believe there are disputed issues of fact whether MCP provided Nathanson with reasonable accommodations and whether MCP evidenced the type of "benign neglect" referred to in *Alexander*. These matters must be resolved by the factfinder.

In summary, we find that the following disputed issues of fact remain: 1) whether MCP knew or had reason to know that Nathanson's condition was a handicap either because her condition "substantially limited" her ability to learn or because she had a "record of impairment"; 2) whether Nathanson made a sufficiently direct and specific request for special accommodations in either of her three meetings with Beasley (on September 12, 1985, August 21, 1986, or September 3, 1986) that would have put MCP on notice of Nathanson's handicap if MCP neither knew nor had reason to know that Nathanson was handicapped; 3) whether MCP's failure to provide Nathanson with "reasonable accommodations" in the form of a suitable seating arrangement constituted "benign neglect" and effectively made its program unavailable to her; 4) whether Nathanson gave MCP a fair opportunity to provide the necessary reasonable accommodations; and 5) whether MCP demonstrated that the modifications that Nathanson had requested imposed an "undue hardship," a "financial or administrative burden," or a sufficiently "substantial alteration" to the functioning of MCP's program.

[The court remanded on this issue.]

NOTES

1. In the case of *Guckenberger v. Boston Univ.*, 974 F. Supp. 106 (D. Mass. 1997), the court addressed a number of issues involving students with learning disabilities, including the documentation that was appropriate. The court held that Boston University's policy of requiring that documentation be within the past three years was a significant burden on students with learning disabilities, and that this requirement should be waived where a qualified professional deemed that retesting was not necessary. The court also discussed the credentials of those qualified to make evaluations of students with learning and related disabilities. The court held that those reevaluating individuals for learning disabilities need not have doctorate degrees, so long as they had appropriate training and professional experience. Evaluations of individuals for Attention Deficit Disorder and Attention Hyperactivity Deficit Disorder, however, must be made by evaluators with a Ph.D. or an M.D.

2.   The court in *Price v. National Bd. of Med. Exmrs.*, 966 F. Supp. 419 (S.D. W. Va. 1997), also discussed the credentials of evaluators in finding that the individuals seeking accommodations to medical board examinations had not demonstrated that they were substantially impaired by their "learning disabilities."

PROBLEMS

1.   In *Wynne*, see Section [B][2] of this Chapter, *supra*, the medical school paid for the cost of the evaluation of the student. Is this required under Section 504 or the ADA? Or because the burden is on the individual with a disability to make known the disability when requesting accommodation, could the medical school have required the student to pay for the assessment.

2.   What is the obligation of the program if the student does not succeed academically, but he/she seeks evaluation that identifies the student as having a learning or other disability that might have affected academic performance? Is the program required to give the student a second chance?

3.   If the evaluation paid for by the student is different than an evaluation paid for by the institution, whose documentation is to be given deference? For a brief discussion of this issue, see Laura Rothstein, *Disability Law and Higher Education: A Road Map for Where We've Been and Where We May Be Heading*, 63 MD. L. REV. 101, 115 (2004).

C   THE ENROLLED STUDENT

Once the applicant has been admitted to the higher education program, new questions arise. Some of the issues are similar to those in the admission process. These questions include whether, when, and what auxiliary services and programs must be provided; when modifications of policies and practices must occur; architectural barrier issues; questions that arise in response to behavior and conduct matters; and confidentiality issues. There is also the initial question, of course, when a student challenges the institution in one of these circumstances whether the student is considered to be an individual with a disability under Section 504 of the Rehabilitation Act and/or the Americans with Disabilities Act. This issue was discussed in Chapter 2.

[1]   Auxiliary Aids and Services

Both the Rehabilitation Act and the ADA contemplate reasonable accommodation. Reasonable accommodation does not mean waiver of fundamental requirements. Nor does it require that the institution make accommodations if it would be unduly burdensome to do so, either administratively or financially. What constitutes an undue burden will depend on the nature and cost of the accommodation, financial resources, and the type of operation involved.

Accommodations that would be required under the ADA and the Rehabilitation Act would include auxiliary aids and services, modifications of policies and practices, and barrier removal. The 2008 ADA amendments codify this requirement into the statute itself, which applies to both the ADA and the Rehabilitation Act. 42 U.S.C. § 12103(1). Previously, the auxiliary aids requirement was drawn from the Section 504 regulations. Accommodations might be required in the admissions process or after the student has been accepted. Accommodations for the enrolled student might be required for the academic program itself including test modifications, for extracurricular opportunities, and for housing.

The Supreme Court has addressed the issue of cost in the higher education context only once. It provided little guidance in doing so, but subsequent judicial analysis has helped to shed some light on these issues. See *University of Texas v. Camenisch*, 451 U.S. 390 (1981). One of the few cases to address cost issues after *Camenisch* is the case that follows. The problems following the case suggest why that might be.

HYPOTHETICAL PROBLEM 6.2

Henry is deaf and has been admitted to an undergraduate program at a small private college. He received sign language interpreter services during his K-12 education. Nothing in his college application indicated a need for any services. On the first day of class, he asked his Poli Sci 101 professor to make sure there is an interpreter for him at the next class, which is two days later. Henry sent an email to the college dean of students indicating that he expect to have an interpreter provided for all classes and for all on-campus events (speakers, sports events, student organization meetings) that he plans to attend. He also expects to have all of his classes transcribed and to receive the transcriptions on the day after the class. The college is in a rural area of New England, not close to any major city. In winter, travel to the college town can be difficult because of snow. The college has recently had to terminate a number of clerical, custodial, and non-tenure track faculty employees because of budget challenges. What is the obligation of the college to provide the requested services?

UNITED STATES v. BOARD OF TRUSTEES FOR THE UNIVERSITY OF ALABAMA
908 F.2d 740 (11th Cir. 1990)

CLARK, CIRCUIT JUDGE:

This case requires us to determine the validity of certain portions of the regulations implementing section 504 of the Rehabilitation Act of 1973 promulgated by the Department of Health, Education and Welfare ("HEW"). The University of Alabama at Birmingham ("UAB") appeals the district court's order permanently enjoining UAB from denying auxiliary aids to handicapped students based on consideration of their financial ability, and from failing to grant auxiliary aids to handicapped "special" students and those handicapped students enrolled in the UAB Division of Special Studies. The United States cross-appeals the district court's holding that UAB has made a reasonable accommodation for the transportation of its handicapped students.

Background

This case was tried before the district court mostly on a stipulation of agreed facts. That stipulation, and the factual findings outlined in the district court opinion, reveal the following. At the time of trial there were approximately 175 handicapped students enrolled at UAB, of whom approximately 8 suffered a significant hearing impairment. HEW initiated an investigation in 1979 of UAB's compliance with section 504 of the Rehabilitation Act upon receipt of a complaint by a deaf student whose request for services of a sign language interpreter at UAB's expense was initially denied.

During the pendency of that investigation, UAB adopted an auxiliary aids policy. This policy states that while UAB will provide some aids, such as note-takers or transcriptions of tape recordings of classes to deaf students, UAB generally will not provide interpreters or other "costly" aids. Most of the requests for "costly" auxiliary aids at UAB have been for sign-language interpreters. Students requiring an aid such as an interpreter must notify UAB several months in advance of the academic quarter. Once notified, UAB will direct the student to seek free interpreter services provided by the state Vocational Rehabilitation Service. If the student is not eligible for assistance from the state Vocational Rehabilitation Service and cannot afford to pay for interpreter services, the policy is to direct the student to apply for financial aid (grants, loans, or work-study) and to include the cost of the interpreter services as an educational expense. Only in the case that a student demonstrates to UAB the need for financial aid to pay for an interpreter and an inability to receive the necessary aid or free interpreter services will UAB provide an interpreter for the student.

In addition to its regular educational degree programs, UAB has a Division of Special Studies that offers some courses for credit and some non-degree community education and continuing education courses. The Auxiliary Aids Policy excludes students taking non-credit or non-degree courses from receiving auxiliary aids from UAB. The University of Alabama's Chancellor, Thomas A. Bartlett, describes the Special Studies programs as "a public service that is educational." He also admits that in an ideal world, auxiliary aids should be offered to Special Studies students, but that "it's a lower priority than making those services available in [the] credit programs." The Special Studies budget is part of the overall budget for UAB. Special Studies has received several federal grants for its Cooperative Education Program, and uses UAB buildings on an "as available" basis for its classes.

UAB's Department of Transportation Services runs an on-campus bus transportation system between 6 a.m. and 6 p.m. daily. The bus route covers approximately one-half of the 65 block campus area and connects outlying employee parking lots to UAB buildings and the UAB medical center. Anyone on campus may use the buses. Approximately 73% of the riders are faculty and staff members, while 16% of the riders are students. During the middle of the day only one bus runs at a time, but during the heaviest use times, 7–9 a.m. and 3–6 p.m., two buses are run. For mechanical reasons, UAB uses each of its five buses for no more than one four-hour period per day. The Department of Transportation Services also has seven vans that it uses to provide off-campus transportation for academic and other campus groups. None of the vans is accessible to wheelchair-bound persons.

In 1986, UAB installed a wheelchair lift on one of its five buses at a total cost of $5,000. UAB surveyed 25 handicapped students to determine when peak use for the lift-equipped bus would be each day. Employees and regular visitors to the campus who are also handicapped were not included in the survey. The survey asked the students when they attended classes, and showed the following attendance pattern:

8:00–10:05 a.m.	16%
10:25 a.m.-12:30 p.m.	36%
1:00–3:05 p.m.	19%
3:25–5:30 p.m.	16%
6:00–10:00 p.m.	13%

Based on these results, and its policy of running each bus only four hours per day, UAB decided to run the lift-equipped bus from 10:00 a.m. to 2:00 p.m. each day. If a handicapped individual needs the bus for a different time period, he or she may call the UAB transportation department 48 hours in advance, and the bus will be re-scheduled to run at a different time so as to accommodate that person. The lift-equipped bus service began in June 1987, and had only one rider in June and none in July. No information about handicapped ridership between July, 1987 and present appears on the record. One handicapped employee stated that she would tend to use the bus more on rainy or cold days, and that she needed the bus to make deliveries around campus that are a part of her job. Of course, she cannot use the bus system to make deliveries before 10 a.m. or after 2 p.m.

The district court held that UAB violated section 504 of the Rehabilitation Act of 1973, when it failed to:

1) provide interpreter services to deaf students who were unable to procure such services elsewhere free of charge and who were not eligible for financial aid for such services; 2) provide any auxiliary aids to students in non-degree programs; 3) accommodate mobility impaired students in the business education laboratory; and 4) make the UAB swimming pool accessible to mobility-impaired students.

UAB is not appealing the district court's third and fourth holdings regarding access to the business education lab and the swimming pool. The district court also found that UAB had made a reasonable accommodation for transportation of mobility-impaired students. The court enjoined UAB from denying students auxiliary aids based on financial ability, and from refusing to grant auxiliary aids to non-credit or non-degree students. The court also ordered UAB to reimburse one family for money they spent on interpreter services.

In reaching its decision, the district court found that the Department of Education regulation that precludes the use of a financial needs test in considering whether to provide auxiliary aids to handicapped students is entitled to conclusive weight, because it is neither "unreasonable, 'clearly erroneous,' nor 'demonstrably irrational.' "

[Subpart E of the Section 504 regulations relating to postsecondary education provides:]

> (d) Auxiliary aids. (1) A recipient to which this subpart applies shall take such steps as are necessary to ensure that no handicapped student is denied the benefits of, excluded from participation in, or otherwise subjected to discrimination under the education program or activity operated by the recipient because of the absence of educational auxiliary aids for students with impaired sensory, manual, or speaking skills. (2) Auxiliary aids may include taped texts, interpreters or other effective methods of making orally delivered materials available to students with hearing impairments. . . . Recipients need not provide attendants, individually prescribed devices, readers for personal use or study, or other devices or services of a personal nature.

34 C.F.R. § 104.44. [When HEW proposed these regulations, there were hundreds of comments expressing concerns about cost.]

In response to these comments, HEW modified the auxiliary aids regulation such that universities could meet the requirements of section 504 by referring students to state vocational rehabilitation agencies and private charities as a first step in obtaining auxiliary aids. The regulations nevertheless maintained the requirement that "[w]here no such existing resources supply auxiliary aids, the proposed regulation obligates the recipient to provide the needed auxiliary aid." HEW noted that it anticipated that the bulk of the costs of auxiliary aids would be paid by state and private agencies, and that the proposed regulation allowed universities considerable flexibility in providing auxiliary aids, including using students who are earning degrees in fields related to handicapped persons to provide the necessary services.

After receiving and considering additional comments on the modified proposed regulations, HEW published the final regulations on May 4, 1977. In the accompanying analysis of the final regulations, HEW acknowledged the concern of colleges and universities about the costs of compliance with the auxiliary aids regulation, but emphasized that recipients "can usually meet this obligation by assisting students in using existing resources for auxiliary aids such as state vocational rehabilitation agencies and private charitable organizations." HEW repeated its prediction that the bulk of the costs of auxiliary aids would be paid by these state and private agencies, and that the regulation allowed universities significant flexibility in choosing the methods by which they would provide aids when students were unable to obtain them elsewhere.

UAB argues that its policy is consistent with the HEW auxiliary aids regulation. UAB contends that the regulation only requires it to provide auxiliary aids to handicapped students who are "otherwise qualified" to receive financial aid. The government argues that the history of the formulation of the regulations summarized above clearly indicates that HEW intended for the burden of providing auxiliary aids to be shouldered by the university, whether the university obtained such services for the student through a state vocational rehabilitation service, private charities, or the university's own funds. In response to the concerns voiced by colleges and universities about the costs associated with providing auxiliary aids, HEW noted that the regulation anticipated that recipients would use state vocational rehabilitation services and private charities as a means of meeting this obligation. HEW nevertheless made clear that if these sources were unavailable, the university was responsible for providing the auxiliary aid. In all explanations of the regulation, the government contends that HEW consistently spoke of the obligation of ensuring that an auxiliary aid was available to any handicapped student who needed one as being an obligation of the university. Nothing in these statements indicated that HEW intended for the handicapped student to be responsible for providing an auxiliary aid.

Under the UAB policy, instead of being the primary source for the provision of auxiliary aids, the university merely disseminates information as to possible sources of free services or loans to pay for the services, and becomes a source of last resort for students who have been otherwise unable to procure auxiliary aid services. Thus, the university's policy shifts the burden of providing auxiliary services onto the shoulders of the student. Most handicapped students are forced to either procure the services through state or private agencies, or pay for them themselves from personal resources or by incurring increased financial aid debt. The Department of Education's position in this litigation on the meaning of the auxiliary aids regulation is consistent with the language of the regulation itself and with the original explanation of the regulation during the notice and comment period. Under these circumstances, the Department of Education's assertion that UAB's incorporation of a financial need test into its auxiliary aids policy violates the regulation is entitled to substantial deference.

Having accepted the Department's interpretation of its regulation as prohibiting a university from denying an auxiliary aid to a handicapped student on the basis that the student has failed to demonstrate a need for financial assistance, we must determine whether such a regulation conflicts with Congress' intent in passing section 504. Section 504's general language and sparse legislative history do not reveal that Congress directly addressed the issue of whether universities should be required to provide funding for auxiliary aids only for those students who demonstrate financial need. Our scope of review of the regulations promulgated by HEW is limited, therefore, to a determination of whether the agency's interpretation of section 504 is based on a permissible construction of the statute.

In support of the reasonableness of HEW's auxiliary aids regulation, the government argues that the Supreme Court has repeatedly held that the HEW regulations are due significant deference. We must, therefore, attempt to make an independent determination of Congress' intent in passing section 504 as it relates to the provision of auxiliary aids to university students. Two Supreme Court decisions have established important guidelines for interpreting section 504. In *Southeastern Community College v. Davis*, the Court held that neither the language, purpose nor legislative history of section 504 revealed an intent to impose affirmative action obligations on recipients of federal funds. [In that case t]he Court reasoned that section 504 did not require recipients to make substantial changes in their programs nor to make changes that would cause "undue financial or administrative burdens."

In *Alexander v. Choate*, the Court was presented with an opportunity to clarify its ruling in *Davis*. In *Alexander*, handicapped Medicaid recipients challenged a state's proposal to reduce its Medicaid program's in-patient hospital coverage from 21 days to 14 days for all patients. The plaintiffs argued that because the average hospital stay for handicapped Medicaid recipients was greater than 14 days, this reduction in coverage would violate section 504 by denying them "meaningful access" to Medicaid in-patient hospital coverage. The Court agreed with the plaintiff's assertion that section 504 requires recipients of federal financial assistance to provide the handicapped meaningful access to the benefit conferred, but found that the state's proposed reduction in coverage did not deny handicapped persons such meaningful access.

The Court reasoned that the state's Medicaid program was not intended to guarantee "adequate health care" to all recipients, and that Medicaid programs do not guarantee that each beneficiary will receive a level of health care precisely tailored to his or her needs. Therefore, the Court held, section 504 does not require the state to alter its program to meet the reality that the handicapped have greater medical needs. While section 504 requires that the handicapped have equal access to Medicaid, it does not guarantee them equal results. Because the proposed reduction did not deny handicapped recipients the same access to in-patient coverage that would be offered to non-handicapped recipients, it did not violate section 504. In reaching this conclusion, the Court further explained its holding in *Davis*, stating that "*Davis* struck a balance between the statutory rights of the handicapped to be integrated into society and the legitimate interests of federal grantees in preserving the integrity of their programs." While section 504 does not mandate affirmative action, and thus grantees "may not be required to make 'fundamental' or 'substantial' modifications to accommodate the handicapped, [they] may be required to make 'reasonable' ones."

UAB argues that its auxiliary aids policy, like the state's Medicaid program in *Alexander*, offers the same benefit to all qualified students. That benefit is the opportunity to be educated and earn a college degree. UAB does not, however, guarantee each student equal results. UAB does not offer each student an educational program specifically tailored to his education needs. Some students are smarter than others, some work harder than others. Some students incur more expenses than others. UAB simply opens its doors to those who meet certain academic requirements and who can muster up the funds to pay, and offers them the chance to learn. Therefore, under *Alexander*, UAB is not required to change its program simply to meet the reality that the deaf must spend more money to receive the same results as hearing students.

This argument ignores the fact that in some instances the lack of an auxiliary aid effectively denies a handicapped student equal access to his or her opportunity to learn. In *Alexander*, the 14 days of in-patient coverage offered by the state provided the same benefit to handicapped Medicaid recipients, as non-handicapped, i.e., the benefit of 14 days of hospital care. Depending on the severity of their illness, some people would benefit proportionately more than others, but the handicapped were not excluded from this benefit. A university, by offering lecture, laboratory and discussion courses, also offers a benefit to its students. Some students, by virtue of their innate intelligence or their willingness to study, will benefit more from this opportunity than others. In the case of a deaf student, however, all access to the benefit of some courses is eliminated when no sign-language interpreter is present. In the context of a discussion class held on the third floor of a building without elevators, a deaf student with no interpreter is as effectively denied meaningful access to the class as is a wheelchair bound student. Just as providing 14 days of in-patient coverage was, on the average not as beneficial for handicapped persons as nonhandicapped, the provision of an auxiliary aid still may not eliminate the disadvantages suffered by handicapped students in the classroom. For example, having an interpreter would not be as effective as being able to hear a lecture or the comments and questions of fellow classmates oneself, as some things will probably get lost in the translation. Nevertheless, under *Davis*, if the provision of interpreters when necessary would not impose an undue financial burden on UAB, then it would be a reasonable accommodation which would allow deaf students to get some benefit from attending UAB, just as having 14 days of in-patient coverage provided some benefit to handicapped Medicaid recipients.

UAB acknowledges that the lack of an interpreter may in some instances deny a deaf student meaningful access to education. It contends, however, that by requiring the university to provide auxiliary aids for students who are not eligible for financial aid, the regulation exceeds the scope of section 504 by effectively mandating "affirmative action." The Department of Education argues that the auxiliary aids regulation does not impose an affirmative action requirement, but instead requires universities to make reasonable accommodations to allow handicapped students equal access to a university education.

The Supreme Court noted in *Davis* that the "line between a lawful refusal to extend affirmative action and illegal discrimination against handicapped persons will not always be clear. Identification of those instances where refusal to accommodate the needs of a disabled person amounts to discrimination against the handicapped continues to be an important responsibility of HEW." HEW's decision that the provision of interpreters is necessary to comply with the non-discrimination mandate of section 504, and does not amount to an affirmative action requirement, is a policy choice that HEW is empowered to make. The Supreme Court has repeatedly noted that these types of policy choices made by HEW in promulgating the implementing regulations for section 504 are due substantial deference because the regulations were enacted with the oversight and approval of Congress.

Soon after the final HEW regulations became effective, HEW reported on the rulemaking process and the final regulation to a Congressional oversight committee. In 1978, Congress amended the Rehabilitation Act of 1973 to require state vocational rehabilitation centers to provide technical assistance, including interpreters, to universities to assist them in complying with the Rehabilitation Act, and "particularly the requirements of" section 504. In light of Congress' awareness of HEW's decision that universities should be required to provide interpreters and other auxiliary aids for students, the 1978 amendment requiring state vocational rehabilitation centers to assist universities in meeting this requirement signals Congressional approval of the policy choice made by HEW. We find, therefore, that the legislative history of section 504, along with the Supreme Court interpretations of section 504 in *Davis* and *Alexander*, indicate that HEW's auxiliary aids regulation is based on a permissible construction of the statute.[4]

C. *Non-credit and Non-degree Programs*

The district court held that UAB's auxiliary aids policy violated section 504 insofar as it excludes "special" students from eligibility for assistance in the form of auxiliary aids. "Special" students are those enrolled in non-credit or non-degree programs, which are operated through UAB's Division of Special Studies. Subpart E of the HEW regulations apply to "postsecondary education programs and activities . . . that receive or benefit from Federal financial assistance. . . . " The Department of Education argues that non-credit and non-degree programs, which include both continuing education programs and courses such as canoeing and chess, are nevertheless educational programs, and that nothing in subpart E is intended to limit its coverage to only programs that lead to a college degree. This interpretation of subpart E by the Department is reasonable and consistent with the language of the regulation, and therefore is due substantial deference.

---

[4] In reaching this conclusion, we have considered the possibility that as applied to UAB, the auxiliary aids regulation might impose an "undue financial burden." UAB has not explicitly argued that the regulation would impose such a burden, but does note that sign-language interpreters charge between $5 and $10 per hour, which it considers "costly." Nevertheless, the stipulated facts indicate that the Alabama Vocational Rehabilitation Service ("VRS") will provide interpreters regardless of economic need to full-time students in programs VRS considers reasonably likely to lead to employment. Furthermore, not all hearing-impaired students need sign language interpreters for all classes. Some students can tape-record lectures, and have volunteers at the UAB Handicapped Services office transcribe the tapes, while others have fellow students take notes for them. Our ruling, therefore, will result in UAB being required to furnish interpreters only to those students who are not eligible for VRS assistance, cannot obtain interpreter services from private charitable organizations, and for whom the provision of an interpreter is the only method by which they will have meaningful access to the class.

Moreover, any doubt that section 504 was intended to cover non-degree and non-credit programs was resolved by the Civil Rights Restoration Act of 1987, which provides that section 504 applies to "*all of the operations* of . . . a college, university, or other postsecondary institution. . . . " (emphasis added). The Department of Education's application of its auxiliary aids regulation to the Division of Special Studies and all non-degree and non-credit programs of UAB is therefore based on a permissible construction of section 504.

D. *UAB's Bus System*

The district court held that section 504 applies to UAB's Department of Transportation Services and that UAB has made a reasonable accommodation for the transportation of its handicapped students by providing lift-equipped bus service between 10 a.m. and 2 p.m. every day. Although a district court's determination of what is "reasonable" rests in large part upon factual determinations, our review of the record leaves us with the definite impression that the district court erred in holding that, as a matter of law, UAB has made a reasonable accommodation in the transportation services it offers to students. The Department of Education's regulations provide that a recipient of Federal financial assistance may not "afford a handicapped person an opportunity to participate in or benefit from" any service provided by the recipient that "is not equal to that afforded to others" or that "is not as effective as that provided to others." The stipulated facts in the record indicate that UAB's Department of Transportation offers transportation services beyond the daily on-campus bus service, and that its services are not intended to benefit only students. As the district court noted, the bus system is open to faculty, staff, students and visitors. Approximately 73% of the riders are UAB faculty and staff members, while approximately 16% are students. Although the bus system does not cover the entire campus, it does connect the medical center complex with remote parking areas and the University College. Aside from operating the daily on-campus bus service, the Department of Transportation also maintains 7 vans that are used for academic field trips and other off-campus activities.

The stipulated facts also reveal that UAB is not offering transportation services to handicapped persons on an equivalent basis with those offered to non-handicapped persons. Only one of UAB's five buses and none of its vans are accessible to mobility impaired people. The existence of only one lift-equipped bus, combined with the necessity of running each bus only four hours per day, results in handicapped persons being unable to benefit from the daily on-campus transportation service for 8 out of its 12 hours of operation. The policy of shifting the hours in which the lift-equipped bus runs upon 48 hours notice does not serve to make the daily bus service equally accessible to handicapped persons. Non-handicapped persons benefit from bus service that they can rely on being available all day, every day. Although shifting the hours of operation of the lift-equipped bus may help the person who requested the shift, it prevents any handicapped person from relying on the availability of the bus at any given time during the day. The absence of any lifts on the university's seven vans also means that campus groups with mobility impaired members who wish to make an off-campus trip must reserve the only lift-equipped bus, or have the Department of Transportation arrange for them to rent an accessible vehicle from a commercial agency. Both of these alternatives are more costly to the campus group than the use of one of UAB's vans. Furthermore, on any day that the only lift-equipped bus were used for an off-campus trip, no daily bus service would be available to handicapped persons.

Thus, the transportation services provided to handicapped persons are clearly "not equal to" nor "as effective as" the transportation services offered to non-handicapped persons. Under the Supreme Court's interpretation of section 504, recipients of Federal financial assistance are required to make "reasonable" accommodations, but only to the extent that such accommodations would not cause "undue financial or administrative burdens." The record shows that the cost of installing a lift on UAB's buses is $5,000. By installing lifts on two more buses, UAB could provide handicapped persons full 12 hour on-campus bus service equivalent to that provided to non-handicapped persons. Even if none of the seven vans were equipped with a lift, UAB could reasonably accommodate campus groups with mobility-impaired members by arranging to rent accessible vehicles from commercial agencies, and charging the group the same amount that they would have paid for using a UAB van. In light of UAB's annual transportation budget of $1.2 million, an expenditure of $15,000, plus occasional amounts representing the difference in commercial rental fees versus the UAB rental fee for vans, is not likely to cause an undue financial burden on UAB.

Conclusion

Having determined that the Department of Education's auxiliary aids regulation prohibits universities from denying auxiliary aids to students on the basis that they do not qualify for financial aid, and that this regulation is based on a permissible construction of section 504 of the Rehabilitation Act of 1973, as amended, we *Affirm* the district court's order enjoining UAB from denying auxiliary aids to handicapped students based on consideration of their financial status. We also *Affirm* the district court's order enjoining UAB from denying auxiliary aids to special students or those enrolled in the Special Studies program, based on our conclusion that the auxiliary aids regulation applies to such students and that its application to them is based on a permissible construction of section 504. Because we find that UAB has not made a reasonable accommodation for the handicapped in the provision of its transportation services, we *Reverse* the district court's holding as to this issue, and *Remand* this case to the district court for consideration of an appropriate remedy.

Affirmed in part, *Reversed* in part, and *Remanded*.

PROBLEMS

1. Would mandating auxiliary services for non-degree and non-credit courses be likely to result in colleges deciding not to offer such programming? In evaluating whether accommodations in those programs are reasonable, are only the budgets for the program or department relevant or will undue burden be decided by looking at the entire university budget?

2. The schedule for the lift equipped buses was based on ridership experience of students with disabilities. What is the flaw in using that to set the schedule?

3. The *Halasz* facts, see Section [B][1] of this Chapter, *supra*, noted that ILP and FYO participants were required to pay a fee for services provided only to them. In light of the language in the preceding case, would such a fee be likely to be upheld as permissible in the Eleventh Circuit? Are these services provided exclusively to ILP and FYO students "reasonable accommodations" or are they supplementary services for which a fee might be permissible?

NOTE

In *Witters v. Washington Dep't of Servs. for the Blind*, 474 U.S. 481 (1986), the Supreme Court held that it does not violate the Establishment Clause when a state vocational rehabilitation agency provides funding to a student attending a religious institution. When reading the note on the *Zobrest* opinion following the *Garrett F.* decision in Chapter 7[B][2], keep the *Witters* holding in mind.

[2] Modifications of Requirements

As was noted above, reasonable accommodations may include modifications of requirements. This may mean reduced course loads, waiver of courses, or exam accommodations.

HYPOTHETICAL PROBLEM 6.3

Samantha (from Problem 6.1) decided to attend a less prestigious law school (Oakdale Law Center) when she was not accepted to Springfield Law School. On the first day of class, she realized that the Socratic method of calling on students might mean that she would be called on without any advance notice. She has begun to have panic attacks and wants to have class participation waived. She has asked one of the sympathetic law professors if that would be possible. The professor has consulted with the law school dean of students. Samantha has asked the dean of students about whether class attendance requirements could be waived to allow for more absences, whether the first year moot court competition could be waived, whether all of her classes could be scheduled in the afternoon, and if she could be assigned only to professors who have a reputation for being "nice" in class. She has also been told by her treating psychiatrist that having her small dog, Tootsie, live with her would help. The law school housing does not allow pets. She has requested a waiver of that rule.

In considering this problem, note the following clarification (or perhaps confirmation) from the 2008 ADA amendments, which codifies well settled language from case law:

> Nothing in this Act alters the provision specifying that reasonable modifications in policies, practices, or procedures shall be required unless an entity can demonstrate that making such modifications in policies, practices, or procedures, including academic requirements in postsecondary education, would fundamentally alter the nature of the goods, services, facilities, privileges, advantages, or accommodations involved.

42 U.S.C. § 12201(f). The rules of construction amendments also note that accommodations are not required for an individual who is only "regarded as" having a substantial impairment. 42 U.S.C. § 12210(h).

McGREGOR v. LOUISIANA STATE UNIVERSITY BOARD OF SUPERVISORS
3 F.3d 850 (5th Cir. 1993)

ZAGEL, DISTRICT JUDGE:

Robert T. McGregor suffered permanently disabling head and spinal injuries from a series of unfortunate accidents that occurred in 1968, 1972, and 1979. His injuries have required and continue to require extensive treatment and a number of surgical procedures. Despite these setbacks, McGregor was determined to pursue a legal career. He took the LSAT in October 1987; his score was a 26. Upon recommendation of Professor Joseph from the Louisiana State University Paul M. Hebert Law Center ("Law Center"), McGregor took the LSAT a second time. He scored a 33. This score, combined with his undergraduate grade point average ("GPA") of 2.6, gave him an index of 93. The index cutoff for admission at the Law Center was 90. The Law Center admitted McGregor as a law student in 1988.

This action began after McGregor repeatedly failed to achieve a passing cumulative GPA and after the Law Center refused to allow McGregor to advance to the junior year. Eventually, the district judge granted the defendants' motions for summary judgment and dismissed the case in its entirety. McGregor filed a timely notice of appeal.

I. *Rehabilitation Act*

A. *Accommodations Made*

Prior to freshman registration in the fall [of] 1988, McGregor asked that the Law Center accommodate his disability by permitting him to be a part-time student. The Law Center said no and told him that it had made an academic decision that a full-time freshman schedule is required. Instead, the Law Center made two accommodations for the upcoming freshman year: a handicapped parking permit and, upon McGregor's request toward the end of the first semester, additional time to complete his Criminal Law Examination.

McGregor's overall GPA for the first semester was 61, below the required 65. McGregor, therefore, was supposed to sit out the second semester, reapply for admission, and wait an additional year to return. Instead, during the spring 1989 semester, the Law Center permitted McGregor to audit Professor Devlin's Constitutional Law I, along with a Legal Writing and Research class. The Law Center also assigned Professor Devlin with the specific task of providing McGregor with concentrated and individualized tutorial instruction. Devlin attested that he spent one hour each week working with McGregor outside class, which is considerably more time than he has ever spent with any other student. McGregor received a grade of 70 in Constitutional Law I and passed Legal Writing and Research. However, according to McGregor, these passing grades were at the expense of losing full use of his legs. Toward the end of the spring semester, McGregor's treating physician, Dr. Charles Kennon, authorized a wheelchair, apparently only for endurance purposes. Regardless of the reason, McGregor needed a wheelchair by May 1989.

The Law Center eventually readmitted McGregor as a freshman on scholastic probation for the fall 1989 semester, without waiting an additional year after reapplying to return. In a letter dated June 27, 1989, Professor Howard W. L'Enfant, then also the Chairman of the Admissions Committee, informed McGregor of his readmittance under the following conditions:

> 1. You shall forfeit all credits and quality credits previously earned and shall begin anew as a first year student in the curriculum in effect for 1989-90. 2. You shall be on scholastic probation, and required to earn an average of 68 or better during each of the next two semesters. 3. You shall carry a full load of work during each of the next two semesters. 4. You will not be permitted to engage in any outside work during the fall semester 1989 and spring semester 1990.

In addition to early readmittance, the Law Center made other adjustments for McGregor during this next semester. Prior to the 1989-90 academic year, the Law Center sent McGregor a proposed schedule of first year classes. It is undisputed that classes were switched so that he would attend them in the new instead of the old building, for easier access with a wheelchair. To accommodate further his wheelchair, the Law Center acquired special handicapped tables for the classrooms and removed the inner door in the first floor bathroom. Throughout the year, many of McGregor's professors assisted him with his academic work outside of class.

In the fall 1989, McGregor was allowed to take three of his examinations at home. In the fourth course (Criminal Law), he was allowed eight hours, instead of the usual four, to complete the examination. When examinations came around in the spring 1990 semester, McGregor requested the same arrangements for at-home examinations. Katherine Spaht, as Vice-Chancellor, responded to McGregor's requests by providing alternative accommodations that the Law Center determined were "reasonable while still maintaining the integrity of the examination process." The Law Center gave McGregor:

> (1) extra examination time; (2) a choice of taking the exams on the first or third floor; (3) a room equipped with a handicapped table, a special bench from the library, a typewriter and/or dictaphone; (4) a student proctor to take care of his personal needs as well as assisting him with the men's rest room door; (5) permission to eat and drink in the room to maintain his sugar level.

McGregor did not meet the Law Center's probationary requirements. Although McGregor received a 70.2 in the fall semester, he received an average of 65.53 in the spring semester. The acceptable minimum GPA on probation for each semester is a 68. McGregor again faced flunking out of law school. And again, McGregor petitioned the Law Center for more accommodations.

In response to the spring 1990 petition, the Law Center agreed to readmit McGregor for the 1990–91 academic year as a first year student subject to two conditions. These conditions were first spelled out in the August 20 letter sent by Katherine Spaht, Vice-Chancellor, to McGregor:

1.   permission and encouragement to audit the course in Criminal Law during the fall semester 1990, if, your physical condition permits; and

2.   during the second semester, a course load for credit of the four courses in which you made a grade of less than 68 in spring, 1990 (Obligations, Property, Constitutional Law I, Torts II), unless a committee to be appointed by the Chancellor alter[s] the conditions of readmission for the second semester. You will be timely notified of any such change.

McGregor was unsatisfied and sent a letter renewing his demands for advancement to the junior level in addition to a reduced schedule. For the first time, he threatened litigation. The Law Center responded to each of the items listed by McGregor as a "good faith offer to settle this controversy." The Law Center stood by their August 17, 1990 decision that McGregor be readmitted as a freshman. The faculty committee, however, did perhaps the next best thing and reduced his schedule to make room for junior level courses. Under the new modified schedule, McGregor needed to take only Constitutional Law and Obligations in the spring 1991, scheduled so that he had a day between classes for rest or treatment. Torts and Civil Law Property could be taken in the spring 1992. Moreover, McGregor could take one junior preference course in the summer 1991 and one or two junior preference courses in the fall 1991. If McGregor attained an average of at least 68 in the four first year courses, he could proceed to the junior year; grades in the junior preference courses would not be considered in determining his eligibility to enroll in any semester up to and including the spring 1992 semester. The faculty committee also determined that McGregor could take his examinations at home in the presence of a proctor from the Law Center. After they wrote, McGregor sued them.

B. *Accommodations Required*

McGregor attacks the accommodations because they did not directly address his disability, i.e., fatigue and pain that impaired his ability to learn, and argues that the Law Center discriminated against him by insisting on a full-time schedule, in-class examinations, and advancement only upon achievement of a 68 average in each freshman semester. He says this was equal treatment which resulted in unequal opportunity to participate in the law program. The Law Center says that they "bent over backward" to help McGregor; that what McGregor seeks is to blame the Law Center for his mental ineptitude; and that his additional requests for accommodations amount to demands for preferential treatment or a substantial modification of its program, which is not required by law.

Here, the Law Center has not and does not assume that McGregor cannot function in its legal educational environment. Unlike the plaintiff in *Davis*, McGregor gained admission to the law school program. Some accommodations were made to allow McGregor to participate and to remain a participant in the program.

Despite the Law Center's joint efforts and McGregor's repeated attempts, McGregor did not achieve the necessary GPA to advance to the junior year. McGregor's repeated attempts demonstrate that he cannot function successfully in the Law Center's program.

McGregor argues that he could succeed in law school if the Law Center accommodated him with (1) a part-time schedule and (2) at-home examinations. As proof of his abilities, he points to the spring 1989 semester (during which he earned a 70 in Constitutional I and passed Legal Writing and Research) and the fall 1989 (during which he received a 70.2 cumulative GPA with three at-home examinations and extra time on the fourth in-class examination). First, we are unpersuaded that this is competent evidence that McGregor can meet the academic demands set by the Law Center on a part-time schedule. McGregor received these passing scores after having a second crack at the courses. Second, his ability to pass given a part-time schedule is not dispositive of the issue here. We agree with the Law Center that many more students could succeed in law school on a part-time schedule. While other law schools in Louisiana and in other states have part-time students, the Law Center has made an academic decision to require that all freshman students carry a full-time course load. Any deviation from this constitutes an accommodation for McGregor's disability. We must decide whether § 504 requires the Law Center to accommodate McGregor either by giving him a part-time freshman schedule or at-home examinations or by advancing him to the junior year despite his failure to satisfy the minimum standard GPA, and later the minimum probationary GPA.

The Supreme Court in *Davis* made clear that § 504 does not mandate that an educational institution "lower or effect substantial modifications of standards to accommodate a handicapped person," assuming such standards are reasonable. This rule was crafted in an effort to balance the institution's right to decide the basic requirements pertinent to its program and the handicapped student's right to participate. The extent of an institution's affirmative duties to accommodate handicapped individuals is far from clear. The best that opinions have been able to state definitively is that an educational institution must make "reasonable," but not "fundamental" or "substantial" modifications to accommodate the handicapped. McGregor, therefore, is entitled to the requested accommodations only if he can demonstrate that the accommodations constitute reasonable deviations from the Law Center's usual requirements "which meet his special needs without sacrificing the integrity of the [Law Center's] program." However, absent evidence of discriminatory intent or disparate impact, we must accord reasonable deference to the Law Center's academic decisions. Ultimately, to recover under the Rehabilitation Act, McGregor must demonstrate that his requests are reasonable and do not sacrifice the integrity of the Law Center's program. The imposition of this burden on McGregor is not only consistent with precedent but broadens some plaintiffs' chances of prevailing. Simply placing the burden on the Law Center to explain why McGregor's requests effect a substantial modification only diminishes McGregor's chances of prevailing, since arguably all the regulations require is that the institution articulate a legitimate nondiscriminatory reason for not altering the program.

The record on summary judgment is devoid of evidence of malice, ill-will, or efforts on the part of the Law Center to impede McGregor's progress. Therefore, we must accord deference to the Law Center's decisions not to modify its program if the proposed modifications entail academic decisions. McGregor characterizes the proposed changes as reasonable schedule modifications since the ABA accredits programs with part-time or evening students and the Law Center's bulletin allows such deviation in exceptional circumstances. This does not persuade.

First, whether the ABA accredits part-time programs is not determinative of reasonableness under the Rehabilitation Act, and we refrain from giving ABA accreditation such adjudicatory effect. Second, the fact that the Law Center has recognized in its Bulletin that exceptional circumstances may prompt the institution to alter its full-time attendance does not mean that such an alteration is not substantial. Given the Law Center's history and admittance practices, the full-time attendance requirement is critical to their program and the requested deviation would be a substantial modification under any circumstance. Whether the Law Center yields to such a request and whether § 504 requires the Law Center to yield to such a request are two different questions.

We conclude that the Law Center's decisions to require full-time attendance and in-class examinations for first year students are academic decisions, ones which we find reasonable in light of the Law Center's admittance practices. The first year courses are specifically chosen to simulate the same challenges found in the practice of law, i.e., to assess and assimilate various legal theories in an intelligible manner. The Law Center has structured an intensive program with high academic standards, which it believes is best equipped to produce high quality lawyers. Essential to its program is a level playing field for all students: First year students cannot engage in outside work during the semester; they must take the same required courses in the same semesters; the examinations are given in class at the same time for each class section; and the final grades are generally based entirely on the final examinations.

The Law Center's program, though strict, is effective by some accepted measures. The Law Center has had and continues to have the highest bar passage rate in Louisiana. McGregor proposes that the Law Center create for him a law school program, either with a part-time schedule and at-home examinations or with lowered passing GPA requirements. These additional accommodations clearly force the Law Center either to lower its academic standard and pass McGregor to the next level or to compromise the reasonable policy of its academic program and allow McGregor to attend part-time and take his examinations at home. Section 504 does not require this much.

The Law Center proved, by way of L'Enfant's affidavit, that no other student has ever been allowed to audit a course in the second semester after failing the first semester, and that "no other student, under any circumstances, has ever had a professor assigned to him for the specific purpose of concentrated tutorial instruction on a one on one basis." Also, no student other than McGregor has ever been permitted to take examinations at home, except in the junior or senior level courses in which all students took the examinations at home. Furthermore, no student has ever received the additional accommodations requested. Although the

Bulletin allows for schedule changes under exceptional circumstances, the Law Center has not, in fact, permitted it and says that even under exceptional circumstances, a student must have proven his analytical abilities to succeed in the law program before receiving such an accommodation.

Viewing the undisputed facts, we can conclude only that the Law Center reasonably accommodated McGregor's disability and that the additional accommodations, if granted, would constitute preferential treatment and go beyond the elimination of disadvantageous treatment mandated by § 504. We agree with Judge Duplantier that despite the reasonable accommodations provided, McGregor did not achieve the minimum cumulative GPA as required under the academic standards set by the Law Center. McGregor, therefore, is not an otherwise qualified individual who has been denied the benefits of the Law Center's program solely because of his handicap. We affirm the summary judgment in favor of the defendants on the Rehabilitation Act claims.

PROBLEMS

1. Might the decision in *McGregor* have been different if McGregor had come in with a high GPA and LSAT, was subsequently injured, and then required a part-time schedule as a result?

2. Student A has mild cerebral palsy and was admitted to law school in spite of her low LSAT (which was taken with additional time), because of good undergraduate grades and recommendations. Because it takes her longer to read material, she has been given a lighter course load each semester, and she is allowed extra time to take exams and to complete some assignments. The law school dean for academic affairs wants to know if a notation about these special allowances should be made on her transcript. How should the dean be advised?

The following case deals with an issue that has frequently been raised in complaints to the Office for Civil Rights, whether course requirements must be waived. The court does a careful analysis, following the *Wynne* analysis of how a program should demonstrate that something is a fundamental alteration.

GUCKENBERGER v. BOSTON UNIVERSITY
8 F. Supp. 2d 82 (D.Mass 1998)

SARIS, D.J.

Introduction

A class of students with learning disabilities brought this action against defendant Boston University ("BU") alleging that BU's policies toward them violated the Americans With Disabilities Act ("ADA"), the Rehabilitation Act, and state law. The Court issued its findings of fact, conclusions of law, and order of judgment on August 15, 1997, after a ten-day bench trial. See *Guckenberger v. Boston Univ.*, 974 F. Supp. 106 (D. Mass. 1997) ("*Guckenberger II*"). In paragraph two of its order, the Court required BU to propose and to implement a "deliberative procedure" for considering whether course substitutions for the foreign language requirement of BU's College of Arts and Sciences (the "College") would "fundamentally alter the nature" of BU's undergraduate liberal arts degree. BU, using the College's existing Dean's Advisory Committee to consider the issue, decided that course substitutions would constitute such a fundamental alteration. Plaintiffs challenge that determination. After hearing, the Court holds that BU has complied with the order.

Background

A. *Procedural History*

As part of a wholesale attack on BU's policies toward the learning disabled, plaintiffs alleged that BU's refusal to allow learning disabled students at the College to satisfy its foreign language requirement by completing selected non-language courses constituted a violation of federal and state discrimination law. Unlike some other portions of the case, the dispute over foreign language course substitutions involves only the College of Arts and Sciences and not other BU faculties. The Court rejected plaintiffs' sweeping argument that "any across-the-board policy precluding course substitutions" violates discrimination law. Rather, the Court concluded that "neither the ADA nor the Rehabilitation Act requires a university to provide course substitutions that the university rationally concludes would alter an essential part of its academic program." Plaintiffs did not appeal this or any other aspect of the Court's order of judgment.

Plaintiffs were successful, however, in pressing an inquiry into reasonable accommodation. Based on an administrative regulation that course substitutions "might" be a reasonable means of accommodating the disabled, 34 C.F.R. Pt. 104, App. A ¶ 31 (1997), and evidence introduced at trial, the Court held that plaintiffs had "demonstrated that requesting a course substitution in foreign language for students with demonstrated language disabilities is a reasonable modification." *Guckenberger II*, 974 F. Supp. at 147. Therefore, the burden of demonstrating "that the requested course substitution would fundamentally alter the nature of [BU's] liberal arts degree program" shifted to the University.

The Court determined, for two reasons, that BU had failed to meet its burden at trial of demonstrating why it should not have to accommodate plaintiffs' request. First, BU's president, defendant Jon Westling, had been substantially motivated by uninformed stereotypes (as reflected in the "Somnolent Samantha" metaphor) when he made the decision to deny the request. Second, President Westling did not engage in any form of "reasoned deliberation as to whether modifications would change the essential academic standards of [the College's] liberal arts curriculum." 974 F. Supp. at 149. The Court's conclusion was directly guided by two opinions of the First Circuit in *Wynne v. Tufts University School of Medicine*, which concerned a request for reasonable accommodations by a learning disabled medical student with dyslexia who challenged the multiple choice format of medical school examinations. See 932 F.2d 19 (1st Cir. 1991) (en banc) ("*Wynne I*"); 976 F.2d 791 (1st Cir. 1992) ("*Wynne II*").

Because of BU's failure to "undertake a diligent assessment of the available options," *Guckenberger II*, 974 F. Supp. at 149 (quoting *Wynne II*, 976 F.2d at 795), the Court ordered BU:

> to propose, within 30 days of the receipt of this order, a deliberative procedure for considering whether modification of its degree requirement in foreign language would fundamentally alter the nature of its liberal arts program. Such a procedure shall include a faculty committee set up by the College of Arts and Sciences to examine its degree requirements and to determine whether a course substitution in foreign languages would fundamentally alter the nature of the liberal arts program. The faculty's determination will be subject to the approval of the president, as university by-laws provide. As provided in *Wynne*, BU shall report back to the Court by the end of the semester concerning its decision and the reasons.

Id. at 154–55.

B. *BU's Deliberative Procedure*

The Court considers the following facts to be undisputed.

On October 6, 1997, the Court approved the use of the existing Dean's Advisory Committee (the "Committee") of the College as the mechanism for deliberating the issue of course substitutions for the foreign language requirement in accordance with the Court's order. In the course of normal business, the Committee "is charged by the by-laws of the College with advising the Dean on issues involving academic standards." During the relevant time period, the Committee was composed of eleven faculty members of the College, including professors of mathematics, English, philosophy, natural sciences, engineering and foreign languages.

The Committee convened to consider the issue of course substitutions on seven occasions. In keeping with its practice for general business, the Committee meetings were closed to interested parties and the public, with two exceptions. The first meeting on this issue was attended by Attorneys Lawrence Elswit and Erika Geetter, counsel for BU, who "set out the Committee's responsibilities as outlined in the Court's decision." Also, several College students addressed the Committee at the November 14, 1997 meeting. Their involvement was directed by the Court at a[n] October 6, 1997 hearing and was solicited through notice posted on an internet bulletin board and an advertisement published in BU's student newspaper. On December 2, 1997, the Committee completed its eight-page report (plus attachments) and submitted it to President Westling in accordance with the BU by-laws. Its final recommendation was:

> After extensive review and deliberation, the [Committee's] professional and academic judgment is that the conjunction of the foregoing considerations (which we have merely summarized here) entails but one conclusion: the foreign language requirement is fundamental to the nature of the liberal arts degree at Boston University. The [Committee] therefore recommends against approving course substitutions for any student as an alternative to fulfilling the foreign language requirement.

Two days later, President Westling, in a letter to Dean Berkey, accepted the recommendation of the Committee.

Discussion

A. *The Test*

The First Circuit crafted the following test for evaluating the decision of an academic institution with respect to the availability of reasonable accommodations for the learning disabled:

> If the institution submits undisputed facts demonstrating that the relevant officials within the institution considered alternative means, their feasibility, cost and effect on the academic program, and came to a rationally justifiable conclusion that the available alternatives would result either in lowering academic standards or requiring substantial program alteration, the court could rule as a matter of law that the institution had met its duty of seeking reasonable accommodation.

Wynne I, 932 F.2d at 26, quoted in *Guckenberger II*, 974 F. Supp. at 148. "[T]he point is not whether a [university] is 'right' or 'wrong' in making program-related decisions. Such absolutes rarely apply in the context of subjective decisionmaking, particularly in a scholastic setting." *Wynne II*, 976 F.2d at 795.

B. *Basic Facts Showing Reasoned Deliberation*

The Court's first task under this test is "to find the basic facts, giving due deference to the school . . . ." *Wynne I*, 932 F.2d at 27. Those "basic facts" must include showings of the following: (1) an "indication of who took part in the decision [and] when it was made"; (2) a "discussion of the unique qualities" of the foreign language requirement as it now stands; and (3) "a consideration of possible alternatives" to the requirement. As these elements suggest, the required showing of undisputed facts refers to the "consideration" of the request by BU and not, as plaintiffs suggest, to a broad-ranging consensus of expert or university opinion on the value of foreign languages to a liberal arts curriculum.

The Court concludes that BU has presented sufficient undisputed essential facts, satisfying each of the three aspects of *Wynne*'s requirements. First, the Committee, made up of eminent members of the College faculty, deliberated this issue over the course of two months. The eleven Committee members include four department chairmen and represent diverse disciplines beyond the foreign languages. Though it would have been better to have kept minutes of all seven meetings, the four meetings provide the Court with sufficient insight to allow the Court to review the procedure that BU followed and to "demythologize the institutional thought processes . . . ." *Wynne II*, 976 F.2d at 795. BU took pains to insulate President Westling from the process to remove any concerns about his earlier comments which, in substantial part, necessitated this remedy. The Committee gave adequate notice to College students, both with and without learning disabilities, of the opportunity to provide input into the Committee's decision. The Committee's reliance on only its own academic judgment and the input of College students was reasonable and in keeping with the nature of the decision.

Second, the Committee had vigorous discussions of the "unique qualities" of the foreign language requirement and its importance to the liberal arts curriculum. Its members rallied around an articulated defense, highlighted throughout the Report, of the rigorous foreign language requirement of the College. In both the Minutes and the Report, the Committee mentioned technical educational gains from the learning of foreign languages, such as enhancing an ability to read foreign literature in its original form and laying a "foundation" for other areas of academic concentration. For example, some members at the October 8 meeting believed it was important to be immersed in ancient Greek and Latin to understand Greek and Roman cultures. Another Committee member waxed "that someone who can read in French would realize that Madame Bovary dies in the imperfect tense, something we don't have in the English language, and it makes for a very different understanding of the novel."

Additionally, the Committee repeatedly emphasized its view that foreign language study uniquely contributed to the College's emphasis on multiculturalism: "A mind cooped up within a single culture is not liberally educated, and knowledge of a foreign language is essential to countering parochialism of outlook and knowledge." The Committee also portrayed foreign language study as part of a broader liberal arts education which, in its view, contemplates "some competence in thinking in diverse areas of knowledge." Commenting on the specific contribution of foreign language learning to liberal arts, the Committee reported that "[e]ncountering a foreign culture in and through the complexities of its verbal structures and representations poses a unique challenge to familiar idioms, settled habits of mind, and securities of knowledge."

Third, the Committee "explained what thought it had given to different methods" of meeting the requirement and "why it eschewed alternatives" to meeting the requirement. *Wynne II*, 976 F.2d at 794. The minutes indicate that alternatives were discussed in at least four of the Committee's meetings. The Report discusses objections to the Committee's conclusion. One dissenting member suggested an alternative proposal whereby a "student would select courses from a faculty approved list that focus on the language, culture, history, literature, and art of countries where the language is spoken." However, "[n]o other member shared this belief that the goals of foreign language study could be met by 'alternative paths' outside the foreign languages." Additionally, the objections of several students were noted at length.

As a whole, the Committee concluded that "[n]o content course taught in English can substitute fully for the insider access to other cultures — with its attendant invitation to thoroughgoing critical self-awareness — that is the hallmark of foreign language study." The Committee acknowledged that some students, both learning disabled and not, will "struggle" with the rigorous requirement, but nonetheless concluded "that no other goal could serve the same purpose within the [College] curriculum."

Furthermore, the Committee discussed the College's existing accommodations of learning disabled students attempting to fulfill the foreign language requirement, a consideration that weighs in BU's favor in this analysis. See *Wynne II*, 976 F.2d at 795 (noting with favor Tufts' accommodations of tutoring, taped lectures and untimed examinations). The College allows all its students to satisfy the foreign language requirement in a variety of ways, including a free "Foreign Language Enhancement Program" that provides one-on-one instruction to learning disabled students navigating the required sequences of language classes. Learning disabled students are allowed spelling accommodations in language classes, and student tutoring is provided by the foreign language department at no cost to students. BU provides for additional time on tests, a reading track for French and Spanish, distraction-free testing, distribution of lecture notes in advance, and replacement of written with oral exams.

C. *Professional, Academic Judgment*

Having found undisputed facts of a reasoned deliberation, the Court must "evaluate whether those facts add up to a professional, academic judgment that reasonable accommodation is simply not available." *Wynne I*, 932 F.2d at 27–28. In the unique context of academic curricular decision-making, the courts may not override a faculty's professional judgment "unless it is such a substantial departure from accepted academic norms as to demonstrate that the person or committee responsible did not actually exercise professional judgment."

This standard is in keeping with the policy of judicial deference to academic decision making. The Court previously indicated that BU's decision would be given "great deference" so long as it occurred "after reasoned deliberations as to whether modifications would change the essential academic standards of its liberal arts curriculum." *Guckenberger II*, 974 F. Supp. at 149. Such deference is appropriate in this arena, because "[w]hen judges are asked to review the substance of a genuinely academic decision, . . . they should show great respect for the faculty's professional judgment." *Wynne I*, 932 F.2d at 25. While, of course, "academic freedom does not embrace the freedom to discriminate," the First Circuit has observed that "[w]e are a society that cherishes academic freedom and recognizes that universities deserve great leeway in their operations."

Plaintiffs attack the academic judgment of the Committee in three ways. First, they argue that BU's decision does mark "a substantial departure from accepted academic norms" because a majority of other colleges and universities — including Princeton, Harvard, Yale, Columbia, Dartmouth, Cornell and Brown — either do not have a general foreign language requirement or permit course substitutions for foreign languages. They also point out that the academic program would not be substantially affected because at BU only 15 students (out of 26,000) a semester would require such course modifications and suggest that similar low numbers of students requesting accommodations in other universities inform their willingness to allow substitutions. The evidence that BU is only among a handful of schools of higher education in its decision to deny course substitutions in language requirements is relevant to an evaluation of its decision to deny a reasonable accommodation. However, a court should not determine that an academic decision is a "substantial departure from accepted academic norms" simply by conducting a head-count of other universities. This approach is particularly inappropriate in the protean area of a liberal arts education. The liberal arts curriculum cannot be fit into a cookie cutter mold, unlike the medical school curriculum in *Wynne*, where no one disputed that mastery of biochemistry was necessary.

The *Wynne* decisions indicate that the appropriate question is whether BU's decision is "rationally justifiable" rather than the only possible conclusion it could have reached or other universities have reached. See *Wynne I*, 932 F.2d at 26. In *Wynne II*, the First Circuit endorsed the professional, academic judgment of Tufts Medical School officials, who had concluded after deliberation that allowing a requested accommodation "would require substantial program alterations, result in lowering academic standards, and devalue Tufts' end product. . . . " *Wynne II*, 976 F.2d at 795. The Court of Appeals there rejected a similar argument that at least one other medical school and a national testing service had permitted oral renderings of multiple-choice examinations. 976 F.3d at 795. Instead, because "Tufts decided, rationally if not inevitably, that no further accommodation could be made without imposing an undue (and injurious) hardship on the academic program," *Wynne II*, 976 F.2d at 795, the First Circuit ruled as a matter of law that the medical school had met its burden under the ADA.

This Court concludes that so long as an academic institution rationally, without pretext, exercises its deliberate professional judgment not to permit course substitutions for an academic requirement in a liberal arts curriculum, the ADA does not authorize the courts to intervene even if a majority of other comparable academic institutions disagree.

Second, plaintiffs challenge the substance of the Committee's conclusions and analysis. Specifically, they argue that there are sixteen "material facts" in dispute, such as the following: (1) the two year (four semester) foreign language requirement is not "sufficient to permit the vast majority of students to read major works of literature in a foreign language," thus debunking the Madame Bovary line of argument as involving an imperfect logic, not an imperfect tense; (2) a "foreign language requirement does not provide students with educational benefits regarding a foreign culture"; (3) there is "no particular thinking process involved in learning a foreign language that is distinct from any other type of learning"; and (4) BU's "foreign language requirement does not address ethnocentrism among students."

In particular, Naomi S. Baron, a chair of the Department of Language and Foreign Studies at American University, criticized the foreign language "mystique" on plaintiffs' behalf. Nevertheless, even Professor Baron acknowledges that many academic and governmental institutions in recent years have espoused foreign language requirements, indicating the existence of a genuine academic dispute on this issue. Many colleges and universities (like Harvard and Haverford) have required proficiency in foreign languages based on the rationale that they deepen the students' appreciation of their own language, promote mental discipline, improve understanding between languages and thought, and make students less ethnocentric. While plaintiffs have submitted affidavits of Professor Baron and other academics who strongly disagree with BU's conclusions and label them as "trite," "idealistic" or "cliches," these issues raise the kinds of academic decisions that universities — not courts — are entrusted with making.

Plaintiffs' final mode of attack is to argue that BU's report does not meet the minimum accepted standards of academic study and inquiry, especially in the Committee's not having referred to outside experts. Prior to the initiation of this litigation, President Westling did not substantially consult experts in learning disabilities or engage in any deliberative process in reaching his decision to preclude course substitutions. In *Guckenberger II*, I held that a decision involving reasonable accommodations must involve more than an ipse dixit or blind adherence to the status quo. However, the Committee's deliberative process occurred after a lengthy trial in which experts in the field of learning disabilities testified about the difficulty which students with learning disabilities experience in their efforts to gain proficiency in a foreign language. This testimony summarized in *Guckenberger II* was available to the members of the Committee. In light of the tight timetable which the litigation imposed on the Committee, and the expert evidence in prior proceedings, I am unpersuaded that further academic study (like a "longitudinal" study) would have refined or altered the decision-making process, which ultimately involved a qualitative evaluation: What is essential to a liberal arts education?

Plaintiffs' vigorous attacks on BU's submission generally overstate the Court's level of scrutiny at this stage of litigation. My opinion as to the value of foreign languages in a liberal arts curriculum is not material so long as the requirements of *Wynne* have been met. Despite plaintiffs' attempts to pull truly academic policy debates into the courtroom, the facts "essential" to this order are actually undisputed: BU implemented a deliberative procedure by which it considered in a timely manner both the importance of the foreign language requirement to this College and the feasibility of alternatives. Plaintiffs' argument that the procedure should have been more extensive and inclusive — effectively, more like a legal proceeding — does not have any support in the *Wynne* opinions.

BU's deliberations and conclusions pass muster under *Wynne*. The Court has no cause to doubt the academic qualifications and professionalism of the eleven members of the Committee. There is no evidence that the Committee's decision was mere lip service to the Court's order or was tainted by pretext, insincerity, or bad faith, beyond plaintiffs' unsubstantiated speculation that President Westling's bias infected the Committee. The Report is rationally premised on the Committee's conclusion that the liberal arts degree is "[i]n no sense a technical or vocational degree" like other degrees and that, in its view, the foreign language requirement "has a primarily intellectual, non-utilitarian purpose." With the justifiable belief in mind that this decision could not be made empirically, the Committee concluded that "[k]nowledge of a foreign language is one of the keys to opening the door to the classics and so to liberal learning. It is not the only key, but we do judge it as indispensable."

The Court concludes that the Committee's judgment that "a person holding a liberal arts degree from Boston University ought to have some experience studying a foreign language," is "rationally justifiable" and represents a professional judgment with which the Court should not interfere. Therefore, the Court concludes as a matter of law that BU has not violated its duty to provide reasonable accommodations to learning disabled students under the ADA by refusing to provide course substitutions.

NOTE

It has previously been noted that historically courts have been extremely deferential to institutions of higher education regarding their standards and programming. The *McGregor* and *Guckenberger* decisions demonstrate that deference. The deference is even greater when health care programs are involved. Why might that be the case?

PROBLEMS

1. Student A is blind and has a guide dog. She enrolls in a seminar with ten students that is scheduled in a small room. The professor for the course is allergic to dogs. What should be done? Is the professor protected under § 504 or the ADA? If so, whose disability must be accommodated? Can both needs be met?

2. Student B is enrolled in first year law school. Just before his first exam, he approaches the professor saying that he has "exam anxiety" and asks to take the exam later. Must the professor grant the request?

3. Student C has epilepsy that is not completely controlled with medication. She has advised her professors for the semester that she is likely to have a seizure occasionally in class, and that if that occurs, the emergency medical squad should be called. The professor is concerned about both the disruption and liability should something happen to Student D. What should the university counsel advise if the professor refuses to allow the student into the class?

[3] Architectural Barrier Issues

Chapter 4 discusses architectural barriers issues generally. There are some different issues that arise in the higher education context by virtue of its unique setting. Probably more than any other phase of life, college requires the ability to get from place to place several times a day for full participation. In public school, the student is usually in the same room or at least the same building for most of the day. On the job, the individual generally will be in one place for a substantial part of the day. But the life of the college student involves waking up in one location (a residence hall, apartment, or home), perhaps going somewhere else to eat breakfast, attending classes in three or four different buildings each day, going to the student center for social and extracurricular activities, and on weekends probably attending athletic events or cultural performances in stadiums, arenas, or auditoriums.

Students who attend classes on large campuses and who must rush from one end of campus to another to get to class on time, or students who commute and cannot find a parking space near the classroom building may complain about getting around campus. And students who are in a hurry when the elevator is slow may think they have problems. For most people, however, getting around campus is taken for granted. For the student in a wheelchair or on crutches, the campus experience can be a nightmare. Many buildings were built before the Rehabilitation Act and other architectural barrier requirements were enacted. The result, while not due to intentional discrimination, is that college campuses are often inaccessible.

Under Section 504, not every aspect of every building on campus must be accessible. Rather, the standard is that the program when viewed in its entirety must be readily accessible. 34 C.F.R. § 104.22(a). The Americans with Disabilities Act applies this same standard to public universities. Private institutions, however, are to be made accessible to the extent it is readily achievable to do so. In addition to this general requirement, the regulations under Section 504 make specific reference to housing. 34 C.F.R. § 104.45.

HYPOTHETICAL PROBLEMS 6.4

(1) California Law School's downtown Los Angeles building has little open space such as parks near the building. The administration is considering adding a patio type area for use by students for lunch, etc., on the roof. There is presently no access to the roof. Installation of an elevator would cost approximately $50,000. Stairs could be installed at a cost of $10,000, but it would not be feasible to include a lift system on the stairway. There are presently three students who have mobility impairments. Must the law school install the elevator if it adds the patio? Does it matter if there are no students with mobility impairments? If there is only one? If there are ten?

(2) Midwestern University School of Education has admitted Student A to its graduate education program. At the beginning of the year, she finds that she is suffering from a severe allergic reaction to the chemicals in the newly constructed building (carpet, etc.). She wants to have all her classes moved to a different building, approximately six blocks from the education school. Should the education school be required to make the accommodation she requests? Would it make a difference if she were an undergraduate student enrolled in a basic freshman curriculum and she only had problems in the building in which she was to take English?

(3) The dean of a professional graduate program is a member of a private club (which for purposes of this question would be considered to be exempt from the Title III requirements). The dean entertains candidates for faculty positions, prospective donors, and others at the club. Occasionally the dean hosts a larger event for alumni. If there are no accessible restrooms at the private club, must the dean stop using the club for all college related events? Only for those when the dean knows that a person with a mobility impairment will be attending?

(4) May a professor host a social event for students in his/her home if the house is not accessible? Does it matter what the nature of the event is and whether the professor knows who is coming?

(5) A college of education makes placements for student teachers in local schools. If one of the schools is inaccessible to individuals with mobility impairments, is the college of education precluded from making any placements of student teachers there regardless of whether they require accessibility or not?

(6) College and universities frequently provide summer and semester abroad programs in countries that do not have the same access requirements as the United States. What requirements should there be with respect to accessibility for housing, classrooms, and other activities?

The following cases provide some guidance on barrier issues.

COLEMAN v. ZATECHKA
824 F. Supp. 1360 (D. Neb. 1993)

Piester, United States Magistrate Judge:

Plaintiff, a twenty-one year old student attending the University of Nebraska, Lincoln (UNL), has cerebral palsy. Due to the resulting paresis in her legs plaintiff requires the use of a wheelchair and the services of a personal attendant to assist her with dressing, showering and toileting.

In the summer of 1991 plaintiff applied to and was accepted by UNL as an undergraduate student for the 1991-92 academic year. Prior to beginning classes she completed and submitted a residence housing contract application to secure dormitory housing. On her application plaintiff indicated she wanted a double room in Selleck Hall, and preferred a nonsmoking roommate. Because plaintiff requested a double room but did not specify a particular individual with whom she wished to be housed, she expected that her name would be placed in the pool of roommate candidates and she would be randomly assigned a roommate by the UNL Housing Department, as is UNL's usual procedure. The Residence Hall Handbook, which is provided to all UNL students who request student housing, states that "[b]ecause of Federal and State law, roommate assignments will not be made on the basis of . . . handicap. . . . " There is no dispute that plaintiff, having been admitted to the university and having completed and submitted a residence housing contract application requesting a double room, met all the requirements necessary to be randomly assigned a roommate.

Upon arriving at UNL in August of 1991, plaintiff discovered she had been assigned a dormitory room in Selleck hall but was disappointed to discover she had not been assigned a roommate. She later was informed that university policy prohibits the assignment of roommates to students with disabilities who require personal attendant care. The policy in question reads as follows:

> Although the University will attempt to assign residence hall living accommodations to all students based upon the choices made in a student's residence hall contract application, the University cannot always do so. In the case of students with disabilities or special medical considerations, double rooms will not be assigned if personal attendant service, nursing care, or trained animal assistance is required unless there is a mutual room request. . . . The University will provide a special grant to cover the difference between the double and single room rate for any student assigned to a single room as a result of this policy if the differential cannot be covered by a third party payer.

Thus, although it is UNL's practice to assign roommates to all students who request double rooms but do not specify particular roommates, UNL policy prohibits the assignment of roommates to students with disabilities requiring personal attendant care. This is a blanket policy, and defendants testified that no individualized inquiry is made when a student with a disability requests a roommate to determine the extent of a student's disability, the dimensions of any equipment necessitated by the disability, or the number, duration and nature of any necessary personal attendant visits.

Defendant Zatechka testified that the policy in question was first implemented roughly thirteen years ago, at a time when UNL had a relatively small number of students with disabilities. Responding to complaints from disabled students who expressed embarrassment at having an assigned roommate present during attendant care visits, and hoping to eliminate the room change requests from assigned roommates who found themselves in what Zatechka described as a "less than desirable" situation, the university decided to permanently set aside a block of double rooms to be used as single rooms by students with disabilities requiring attendant care. The policy was intended to accommodate the privacy concerns of students with disabilities requiring attendant care and avoid the hurt feelings and administrative worries that followed the room change requests. It appears plaintiff is the first student at UNL to openly challenge the policy and request the assignment of a roommate.

After plaintiff unsuccessfully renewed her request for an assigned roommate, she filed a formal complaint against UNL with the United States Department of Education's Office for Civil Rights charging that UNL did not provide students with disabilities with housing comparable to that provided other students. Shortly after the complaint was filed a meeting was scheduled between plaintiff, UNL, and the Office for Civil Rights (OCR) in an attempt to resolve the dispute. Following formal discussions, plaintiff agreed to withdraw her OCR charge in exchange for UNL's promise to make a prompt and vigorous effort to find her a "mutually acceptable" roommate for the fall 1992 term.

After withdrawing her OCR complaint, plaintiff heard nothing for two months regarding UNL's attempts to find her a roommate. Believing UNL was not living up to the terms of the agreement, plaintiff filed a second OCR complaint against the university. Although UNL had not been communicating with plaintiff regarding its efforts to locate a roommate for her, the evidence showed the university had in fact been pursuing the matter during the months following the agreement.

Shortly after the agreement was signed UNL housing staff was directed by defendant Zatechka to contact certain female students and ask whether they would voluntarily agree to be plaintiff's roommate. Six women were contacted; none was interested in rooming with plaintiff. Housing staff then contacted eight additional students, none of whom wanted to room with plaintiff. Plaintiff finished out the 1991-92 school year without a roommate.

Prior to beginning classes for the 1992-93 academic year plaintiff again completed and submitted a residence housing application to secure dormitory housing. On her application she once again indicated she wanted a double room in Selleck Hall and preferred a nonsmoking roommate. Due to plaintiff's disability and need for minimal attendant care, her name was not placed in the pool of roommate candidates and she was not assigned a roommate for the 1992-93 academic year.

Despite their persistent refusal to assign plaintiff a roommate, defendants continued their efforts to locate a "voluntary" roommate for her. A form letter was sent to approximately 680 female students who had signed residence hall contracts for the 1992-93 academic year, informing them that a junior studying human development and the family who uses a wheelchair and requires minimal attendant care wanted to share a room in Selleck Hall with a nonsmoking female. Interested parties were instructed to contact housing staff. The letter generated only one response, from a student who mistakenly believed her room and board would be paid by the university if she agreed to room with plaintiff. After being informed she would be required to pay the standard rate for a double room, the student lost interest.

In a final effort to locate a voluntary roommate for plaintiff, six female students were contacted by the university and offered $550.00 off the charge for a double room if they would agree to be plaintiff's roommate. Defendant Zatechka testified that this figure was chosen because students are charged $550.00 more for single rooms than double rooms, and it was determined that a further reduction in privacy was worth an additional $550.00. No student was interested.

At no time during their extensive efforts to locate a voluntary roommate for plaintiff did the university communicate to plaintiff their plans for approaching students, sending letters to students or offering financial incentives to students to persuade them to be her roommate. Plaintiff acknowledges that defendants have expended a great deal of time and energy attempting to locate someone who will agree to be her roommate, but nevertheless is dissatisfied with, and offended by, the approach the university has taken in its efforts. Plaintiff does not wish to be singled out and treated differently merely because she has a disability, and she is not asking that special accommodations be made for her; rather, she wants only to be treated like all other students who request a double room but do not specify a particular roommate — that is, she wants her name placed in the pool of students to be assigned a roommate. The university remains adamant in its position that it "will not require another student to be [plaintiff's] roommate."

Plaintiff testified the university's refusal to assign her a roommate because of her disability, combined with the approach taken in attempting to persuade students to agree to be her roommate, has made her feel isolated and stigmatized.

When asked why she wants a roommate, plaintiff testified that when she transferred to UNL from Peru State College in 1991 she didn't know anyone in Lincoln and believed a roommate would facilitate and enhance her social involvement. Although she has since made some friends and become active in residence-hall government, she continues to believe a roommate would enable her to meet, and perhaps become friends with, people who have different interests, lifestyles and possibly even different cultures from her own. In summary, she wants the growth experience of rooming with another college student while attending UNL. Contrary to defendants' suggestion that plaintiff is seeking the assignment of a roommate hoping to obtain free personal attendant care, plaintiff made it very clear that she does not expect, nor would she want, an assigned roommate to provide her with personal attendant care; that service is, and will continue to be, provided by trained professionals.

Defendants admit plaintiff's name has never been placed in the pool of students to be assigned a roommate, and further admit that due to her disability and need for minimal attendant care, UNL policy excludes her from participating in the assigned roommate program.

II. *Conclusions of Law*

Plaintiff has brought this action pursuant to section 504 of the Rehabilitation Act, and the Americans with Disabilities Act.

In the postsecondary education context, a "qualified" handicapped person is defined as one who:

> meets the academic and technical standards requisite to admission or participation in the recipient's education program or activity.

There is no dispute that plaintiff met these eligibility requirements. Thus, she is "qualified" under the ADA to participate in the roommate assignment program.

Defendants argue, however, that plaintiff is not qualified under either the Rehabilitation Act or the ADA to participate in the roommate assignment program because:

> her disability requires her to use more space than allotted to a double room occupant and to have attendant care visits at least three times a day, thereby impinging on the physical space and solitude her roommate might otherwise be able to enjoy were it not for the plaintiff's medical needs.

Defendants' argument essentially implies that, in addition to being admitted to the university and submitting a proper residence hall contract application, there are two additional, implied eligibility requirements which must be met before a student can be considered "qualified" to be assigned a roommate:

> (1) the student must not use more space than allotted to a double room occupant (presumably half the room), and (2) the student must not routinely have three or more visitors per day.

Defendants suggest that to be "qualified" to participate in the roommate assignment program a student must not utilize more than half the space in the room. For the reasons discussed below I conclude this is not an "essential" eligibility requirement under either the ADA or the Rehabilitation Act.

First, although defendants suggest that students using wheelchairs utilize more physical space in a double room than nondisabled students, I cannot conclude from the evidence presented that plaintiff actually utilizes more than half of the space in the double room she has been assigned, or that the amount of space she does use would unnecessarily impinge upon an assigned roommate's physical space. Moreover, even if the evidence had shown that plaintiff utilized more than half the space in the room, this is not something defendants knew prior to refusing her request to assign her a roommate, as no individualized inquiry was conducted to determine the amount, size or location of the equipment used by plaintiff. Defendants simply made an assumption that because she uses a wheelchair she will utilize more than half the space in the dormitory room. The ADA prohibits using assumptions of this sort rather than facts and conclusions gleaned from individualized inquiry:

> [The provisions of the ADA] are intended to prohibit exclusion and segregation of individuals with disabilities . . . based on, among other things, presumptions, patronizing attitudes, fears, and stereotypes about individuals with disabilities.

Consistent with these standards, public entities are required to ensure their actions are based on facts applicable to individuals and not on presumptions as to what a class of individuals with disabilities can or cannot do. Defendants' assumption that plaintiff's use of a wheelchair causes her to utilize more than half the space in a dormitory room falls far short of the individualized assessment that is required by the ADA.

Second, although the university purports to be concerned about the amount of dormitory room space utilized by students in wheelchairs, the challenged policy does not prohibit students using wheelchairs from being assigned roommates so long as the students do not also require attendant care. Defendants explain they do not apply the challenged policy to these students because they "expect the roommate to yield some to the needs of the other roommate for slightly more physical space. The roommates must, after all, share the room with each other." The university allows students who use wheelchairs but do not require attendant care to participate in the roommate assignment program; this fact effectively undermines the contention that plaintiff cannot be assigned a roommate because her wheelchair utilizes too much physical space.

Third, it is important to note that defendants' concern over equity in the amount of physical space utilized by each roommate is not a concern generally applied to nondisabled students. There is no requirement, for instance, that roommates use only half the space in a double room; rather, students are allowed — indeed encouraged — to arrange and decorate their room how ever they choose. There are no limitations placed on the amount of additional furniture, permissible appliances or personal property a student can bring from home to use in his or her dormitory room. Defendant Zatechka testified that the university does not police how much personal property a roommate brings in, and would become aware that a particular student was dominating room space only if the other roommate complained to housing staff. Absent evidence that defendants actually require dormitory room space to be evenly divided between roommates and actively enforce such a requirement, I cannot conclude that it is an "essential" eligibility requirement that a student not utilize more than half the floor space in the room.

In light of the foregoing, I conclude this particular eligibility requirement — that students use no more than half the space in a room — is not "necessary" to the roommate assignment program and cannot properly be considered an "essential" eligibility requirement which a student must meet in order to be qualified to participate in the program.

Defendants next suggest that plaintiff is not "qualified" to participate in the roommate assignment program because she must be visited three times daily by a personal attendant and it would be unfair, defendants argue, to ask an assigned roommate to endure these daily intrusions. Defendants imply by this argument that to be "qualified" to participate in the roommate assignment program plaintiff cannot receive frequent daily visitors which might disrupt her roommate's solitude. As discussed below, given the nature of dormitory living and the fact that students without disabilities are allowed to participate in the roommate assignment program regardless of the number or frequency of daily visitors, I conclude this is not "necessary" to the roommate assignment program and not an "essential" eligibility requirement under either the ADA or the Rehabilitation Act.

First, I note that the evidence in this case did not indicate that plaintiff's personal attendant visits are unusually disruptive. Two of the three daily visits are relatively brief, and during a good portion of each visit plaintiff and her personal attendant are not even in the room. The daily visits are scheduled, predictable, and amount to nothing more than assisting plaintiff in the daily routine of dressing, showering and toileting — things that all roommates do. No medical care is provided during the visits, and there is no evidence of any reason why the roommate could not remain in the room during the entire visit if she wished.

Second, to the extent the personal attendant visits are disruptive, the disruptions are not of the sort unique to roommates with disabilities, but rather are common disruptions present in all roommate situations. For example, at trial defendants suggested the personal attendant's morning visit (which occurs at either 8:00 or 9:00 a.m. depending on the day of the week) might disturb a roommate who wished to sleep later. While I do not doubt that this could happen, the same problem arises regardless of whether the roommate has a disability. Likewise, interruptions caused by frequent visitors are not unique to students who have disabilities. The argument that it is unfair to require an assigned roommate to tolerate frequent attendant care visits would carry more weight if students were not generally required to tolerate frequent visitors; however, the evidence shows that Selleck hall has 24-hour unlimited visitation, and interruptions caused by frequent visitors are quite common.

Nevertheless, defendants attempt to distinguish the type of intrusion occasioned by attendant care visits from what they term "typical" intrusions encountered by roommates. Defendants suggest that while problems stemming from typical intrusions can be resolved through mutual compromise, plaintiff is not in a position to compromise when it comes to her personal attendant needs and an assigned roommate would be forced to constantly subordinate her interests to accommodate plaintiff's disability. The evidence does not support this argument.

Although plaintiff cannot agree to forgo attendant care altogether (an option which could hardly be termed a compromise), she testified there is some degree of flexibility as to when and where the visits take place.

In light of the foregoing, I conclude this particular implied eligibility requirement — that students not receive frequent daily visitors which might disrupt their roommate's solitude — is not necessary to the roommate assignment program and cannot properly be considered an "essential" eligibility requirement which a student must meet in order to be qualified to participate in the program.

Thus, neither of the additional implied "requirements" advanced by defendants can be considered necessary or essential requirements within the meaning of the

ADA and the Rehabilitation Act. If these additional requirements were actually intended to screen out undesirable roommate candidates who use too much space or who have frequent daily visitors, then one would expect to see the requirements applied to all students requesting an assigned roommate; they are not. The fact that these additional eligibility requirements are not applied to all students indicates the additional requirements are not "essential" to the roommate assignment program, but rather were advanced by defendants in an attempt to legitimize the policy of excluding students who have disabilities from the roommate assignment program.

The only "essential" eligibility requirements for participation in the roommate assignment program are admission to the university and submission of a completed residence hall contract application requesting a double room but not specifying a particular roommate. Because plaintiff met both these eligibility requirements, she is a "qualified individual with handicaps" within the meaning of the Rehabilitation Act and a "qualified individual with a disability" within the meaning of the ADA.

I recognize that the policy of requiring students with disabilities to live in single rooms may have been adopted as an accommodation to students with disabilities who were uncomfortable having an assigned roommate present during attendant care visits. However, nothing in the Rehabilitation Act or the ADA requires that plaintiff accept such accommodations. Even where special accommodations have been made, qualified individuals with disabilities must be given the option to participate in regular programs if they choose. Because the challenged policy forecloses this option to plaintiff, it runs afoul of both the Rehabilitation Act and the ADA.

The defendants argued that the policy exists because the university does not want to "require" students without disabilities to room with students who have disabilities and require attendant care, perceiving such a room assignment to be somehow "unfair" to the students without disabilities. Yet such a policy fosters the very attitudes and stereotypes about individuals with disabilities that the ADA was designed to eliminate.

The ADA's Findings and Purposes illustrate that Congress, in enacting the statute, aimed to bring people with disabilities into society's mainstream, to cause the kinds of interaction which might facilitate recognition of the true equality of human worth as between individuals — regardless of disabilities. In contrast, the university's policy at issue here of excluding plaintiff from the roommate assignment program, however well intentioned it may have been, sanctions the attitude that students with disabilities are less desirable and suggests that others should not be required to live with them. Such standoffishness places less value on the human worth of individuals with disabilities — because of their disabilities. As implemented, the policy unnecessarily separates students with disabilities from those without disabilities and thus strikes at the essence of the ADA and specifically violates the statute's stated purpose "to provide a clear and comprehensive national mandate for the elimination of discrimination against individuals with disabilities."

NOTE

Reduced Cost for Single Occupancy of a Double Room: The case of *Fleming v. New York Univ.*, 865 F.2d 478 (2d Cir. 1989), addressed the reverse side of the issue raised in *Coleman v. Zatechka.* In *Fleming*, the student was a graduate student and a wheelchair user. Unlike the plaintiff in *Coleman*, Mr. Fleming wanted to live alone in a double room, but be charged only the single room rate. He was allowed to live in an undergraduate dormitory as the sole occupant of a room (an accommodation to the usual policy), but was still charged the higher rate, i.e., twice the single occupancy charge. His claim was that he was forced to seek housing in an undergraduate dormitory because of inaccessible graduate housing. The facts are problematic because it was unclear whether graduate housing had been made available to the complainant or whether he had applied for such housing. Unfortunately, because adequate proof of the unavailability of graduate housing was not provided in a timely manner, the court does not really reach the issue of whether the reduced rate must be provided as a reasonable accommodation, but grants the summary judgment because the plaintiff's basis for suit was discrimination by not providing accessible graduate housing. What facts would be important to addressing the reasonableness of such an accommodation, i.e., reduced rate for single room occupancy? Should students with Attention Deficit Disorder, who require solitude in order not to be distracted while studying be able to obtain such an accommodation, i.e., sole occupancy of a room (at either the single or double room rate)? The Department of Justice has recognized the need for clarification about accessibility issues in postsecondary housing. See 73 Fed. Reg. 34466, 34545 (June 17, 2008).

[4]   Behavior and Conduct Issues

HYPOTHETICAL PROBLEM 6.5

Samantha (from Problem 6.1) has dropped out of Oakdale Law Center and decided to go to nursing school instead. She did not indicate anything about her depression and its treatment in her application. The dean of the nursing school learned of this when Samantha asked to have a mid-term exam rescheduled due to stress related to her condition. The dean has also learned that fellow students have complained that Samantha's grooming is not good, she smells, and her hair is often uncombed and her clothes are not clean. This has become more of an issue since Samantha started in the clinical classes where she works with patients under the supervision of a faculty or staff member. It has been reported that Samantha has been rude and abrupt with patients and on one occasion slammed a tray of medication down on a hospital cart.

The dean consults the university counsel's office about whether Samantha should be removed from the program. If she is not to be removed, what other steps can or should be taken? Who should be advised of her condition and how should this be handled in her student records?

An increasing number of cases in a variety of contexts, including employment and housing, raise questions about the degree to which behavior and conduct must be excused or accommodated when it results from mental illness or psychological conditions. Mental problems also raise concerns about when it is permissible to decide that a student is not qualified to participate in a program because of concerns about future behavior and conduct problems. The following cases illustrate some of these points.

The next case involves a lengthy history of serious psychiatric and mental disorders, which had evidenced themselves in a series of very serious self-destructive acts and attacks on self and others. The problems dated back at least as far as when Ms. Doe was age 14. Ms. Doe falsely represented her mental health history in her application to medical school. The court does not address whether the medical school violated the Rehabilitation Act in asking mental health history questions. She was admitted to NYU Medical School in 1975.

The NYU Medical School learned of Ms. Doe's psychiatric history after a post-matriculation mandatory medical examination when it was learned that scars noticed on her arm were self-imposed, and she disclosed some of her psychiatric history. She agreed to begin psychiatric therapy, but did not follow through. It was ultimately agreed that she would take a leave of absence, with the understanding that she could request reinstatement, which was not guaranteed. After various treatments, she worked at an advertising agency in New York.

Eventually she applied for readmission to medical school. Her treating psychiatrists provided letters of support to meet the standards that NYU required for readmission, that a student "must demonstrate that the problems that precipitated the leave are resolved, that the applicant must be able to handle all of the academic and emotional stress of attending medical school, and that the school must be satisfied that the applicant will be able to function properly after graduation as a physician." She was also required to show that she does not pose a significant risk of reexhibiting her prior disorder. She was required also to prove that "in addition to being fully cured, she possesses the additional qualifications of good judgment, personal integrity and truthfulness, and a genuine commitment to the medical profession."

Her request for readmission was denied. She was, however, admitted as a graduate student to the Harvard School of Public Health. She made false statements about her emotional state in her application to Harvard.

Because of the denial of readmission, Doe sought legal assistance, and ultimately brought suit in December of 1977, claiming a violation of § 504 of the Rehabilitation Act. In June of 1978, she completed her Harvard graduate program and began work as a summer intern at the Department of Health, Education and Welfare (HEW) in Washington, D.C., where she continued to work until October 1981, when the lower court ordered her to be readmitted to NYU. Her work at HEW and other government agencies was of high quality under pressure. There was no evidence that she had any mental health related problems since fall 1977.

DOE v. NEW YORK UNIVERSITY
666 F.2d 761 (2d Cir. 1981)

MANSFIELD, CIRCUIT JUDGE:

NYU contended that its decision not to readmit Doe should be upheld against a § 504 challenge as long as it could show that there was a "substantial basis" for its decision. It argued that such a basis had been shown, and thus that its motion for summary judgment should be granted. It pointed to Doe's history of psychiatric difficulties and to the diagnoses of several psychiatrists who had examined her that she had suffered and continued to suffer from a "Borderline Personality disorder," a serious psychiatric problem that is extremely difficult to cure and that can lead to the type of self-destructive behavior that Doe had engaged in the past. NYU relied not only on the opinions of in-house psychiatrists, such as Drs. Fisher, Stern, and Zimmerman, but also on Dr. Lawrence C. Kolb, a former President of the American Psychiatric Association and an eminent clinical psychiatrist. When Doe refused to submit to an examination by Dr. Kolb he executed an affidavit setting forth his opinion on the basis of his study of the pertinent records in the case, including extensive depositions of Doe and the numerous medical reports and interviews. Dr. Kolb stated: "It is my opinion, which I can state with a reasonable degree of medical certainty, that Jane Doe suffers from a Personality Disorder known as Borderline Personality, and that her condition is serious. . . . None of her therapeutic efforts . . . would be considered of sufficient duration or intensity by me or by most experienced therapists to bring about major personality change of such a nature that Jane Doe would not relapse in the face of future emotional stress such as that encountered in medical school." As the result of an order by the district court, Doe finally submitted to an examination by Dr. Kolb on August 27, 1981. He reported, "In my opinion Mrs. Jane Doe remains at high risk of recurrence of personality disorganization if exposed to situations of stress such as would occur on return to medical school."

NYU also produced an affidavit of Dr. Zimmerman, who had re-examined Doe in September of 1978 and had again concluded at that time that she was not qualified for readmission. Dr. Zimmerman reaffirmed this conclusion, stating: "The character of [the] stress [of medical school], Jane Doe's prior history of failing to be able to deal with it, her diagnosis of personality disorder, and her failure to have received any appropriate degree of psychiatric treatment for it leads me to conclude that she has not made any reasonable showing that she is now qualified to re-enter medical school." NYU also relied on the Payne-Whitney diagnosis of Borderline Personality, which confirmed several other medical diagnoses. It pointed out that even one of Jane Doe's own doctors, Dr. Samuel Bojar, although disagreeing with the diagnosis in Doe's case, admitted that "a borderline person is not very treatable. It's a fixed situation." On the basis of these medical diagnoses, which it claimed were well supported by Doe's history, NYU argued that Doe poses a danger to herself, her teachers, her fellow students, and her patients.

In a decision issued on September 25, 1981, Judge Goettel found that Doe was a "handicapped person" under § 504 and implementing regulations. He stated that whether she was "otherwise qualified" for admission to NYU Medical School depended on whether her psychiatric symptoms would recur, preventing her from performing as a medical student and causing her to pose a danger to herself and others. In deciding this issue the judge discounted the testimony of the psychiatrists on both sides and relied upon Doe's "actual behavior and condition over the past five years." He concluded that Doe "will more likely than not be able to complete her course of medical studies and serve creditably as a physician," that she was therefore "otherwise qualified" under the Act, and that she had been denied readmission "solely because of the handicap." [H]e further concluded that NYU had failed to sustain its burden of going forward and proving that Doe was not an otherwise qualified handicapped person or that her application for readmission was rejected for reasons other than her handicap. No deference was given to NYU's evaluation of Doe's qualifications as compared with those of other qualified first-year students. Judge Goettel denied NYU's motion for summary judgment and found that Doe was likely to prevail on the merits.

In claiming to be a handicapped person under the Act, Doe is faced with her representations on applications that she did not suffer from any emotional problems and her testimony that her ability to function in major life activities has never been impaired and that she has never been unable to work or learn, as is attested to by her successful graduation from college, her receipt of a Masters Degree from Harvard and her outstanding record of employment as a member of HEW. Notwithstanding this evidence we believe that for present purposes she should be classified as a handicapped person under the Act, in view of the independent evidence of her extensive history of mental impairments requiring hospitalizations and her departure from NYU in 1976 because of her psychiatric problems, all of which indicate that she has suffered from a substantial limitation on a major life activity, the ability to handle stressful situations of the type faced in a medical training milieu. NYU's refusal to readmit her on the ground that she poses an unacceptable risk to faculty, students, and patients makes clear that she is "regarded as having such an impairment." § 7(7)(B)(iii). Our conclusion is reinforced by the wide scope of the definition in § 7(7)(B), which includes in subdivision (ii) a "record of such impairment," and by its legislative history.

Turning to the Act's term, "otherwise qualified handicapped individual," it is now clear that this refers to a person who is qualified in spite of her handicap and that an institution is not required to disregard the disabilities of a handicapped applicant, provided the handicap is relevant to reasonable qualifications for acceptance, or to make substantial modifications in its reasonable standards or program to accommodate handicapped individuals but may take an applicant's handicap into consideration, along with all other relevant factors, in determining whether she is qualified for admission. The institution need not dispense with reasonable precautions or requirements which it would normally impose for safe participation by students, doctors and patients in its activities. Section 504 simply insures the institution's even-handed treatment of a handicapped applicant who meets reasonable standards so that he or she will not be discriminated against solely because of the handicap. But if the handicap could reasonably be viewed as posing a substantial risk that the applicant would be unable to meet its reasonable standards, the institution is not obligated by the Act to alter, dilute or bend them to admit the handicapped applicant.

In determining whether a handicapped person is "otherwise qualified" for admission to an institution of higher education, a court must also consider other factors not normally encountered in evaluating ability to satisfy employment standards or to qualify for a job. The first of these is a court's limited ability, as contrasted to that of experienced educational administrators and professionals, to determine an applicant's qualifications and whether he or she would meet reasonable standards for academic and professional achievement established by a university or a non-legal profession.

Another factor which must be taken into account is that the qualification of a handicapped person for admission to an institution turns not only on whether he or she meets its reasonable standards but whether the individual, where a few (in this case 170) must be chosen out of thousands of applicants, is as well qualified despite the handicap as others accepted for one of the limited number of openings. In performing the difficult task, where there are more qualified applicants than places available, of making comparative judgments to determine which are the most promising candidates, the institution is not required to accept a qualified handicapped person if the handicap renders that individual less qualified than other qualified applicants.

Since an institution or employer is permitted to take into consideration an applicant's handicap in deciding whether he or she is qualified, a § 504 action frequently does not lend itself easily to the analysis used for allocation of burdens and order of presentation of proof used in suits alleging discrimination based on impermissible factors (race, color, religion, sex or national origin) in violation of Title VII of the Civil Rights Act of 1964. In such suits, although the plaintiff has the ultimate burden of proving by a fair preponderance of the evidence that the defendant discriminated against him on the basis of an impermissible factor, he may establish a prima facie case by proving that he applied for a position for which he was qualified and was rejected under circumstances indicating discrimination on the basis of an impermissible factor. The burden then shifts to the defendant to rebut the presumption of discrimination by coming forward with evidence that the plaintiff was rejected for a legitimate reason, whereupon the plaintiff must prove that the reason was not true but a pretext for impermissible discrimination. That procedure may be appropriate for § 504 suits in which the defendant disclaims any reliance on the plaintiff's handicap.

On the other hand, in the more typical suit under § 504, the defendant acknowledges reliance on the plaintiff's handicap and since the plaintiff's handicap may be a permissible factor to be taken into account in determining whether he is qualified, the order of presentation of proof in such cases cannot be framed in terms of permissible versus impermissible factors. The pivotal issue is not whether the handicap was considered but whether under all of the circumstances it provides a reasonable basis for finding the plaintiff not to be qualified or not as well qualified as other applicants. Accordingly we hold that in a suit under § 504 the plaintiff may make out a prima facie case by showing that he is a handicapped person under the Act and that, although he is qualified apart from his handicap, he was denied admission or employment because of his handicap. The burden then shifts to the institution or employer to rebut the inference that the handicap was improperly taken into account by going forward with evidence that the handicap is relevant to qualifications for the position sought. The plaintiff must then bear the ultimate burden of showing by a preponderance of the evidence that in spite of the handicap he is qualified and, where the defendant claims and comes forward with some evidence that the plaintiff's handicap renders him less qualified than other successful applicants, that he is at least as well qualified as other applicants who were accepted.

Applying these principles, it is clear in the present case that Doe, a handicapped person, was denied readmission because of her handicap. NYU has come forward with evidence that the handicap was relevant to her qualifications for readmission according to its standards which appear reasonable enough and are not challenged. She therefore bears the burden of showing that despite her handicap she is qualified. Since her admission in 1975 was obtained on her false representation that she did not suffer from any recurrent illnesses or emotional problems, that initial admission does not serve to establish that she is "otherwise qualified" under the Act except to indicate that except for her personality disorder, which involved self-destructive and antisocial behavior, she was academically acceptable. NYU, however, was entitled, in determining whether she was qualified, to be advised of and to take into account her mental impairment, since it is directly relevant to her qualifications and bears upon her ability to function as a student and doctor, to get along with other persons, and to withstand stress of the type encountered in medical training and practice. NYU is of necessity concerned with the safety of other students, faculty and patients to whom Doe would be exposed, since this could adversely affect them as well as the success and reputation of its Medical School activities. Any harm done by her as a medical student to others, moreover, might expose it to legal liability for knowingly permitting such exposure.

The crucial question to be resolved in determining whether Doe is "otherwise qualified" under the Act is the substantiality of the risk that her mental disturbances will recur, resulting in behavior harmful to herself and others. The district court adopted as its test that she must be deemed qualified if it appeared "more likely than not" that she could complete her medical training and serve as a physician without recurrence of her self-destructive and antisocial conduct. We disagree with this standard. In our view she would not be qualified for readmission if there is a significant risk of such recurrence. It would be unreasonable to infer that Congress intended to force institutions to accept or readmit persons who pose a significant risk of harm to themselves or others, even if the chances of harm were less than 50%. Indeed, even if she presents any appreciable risk of such harm, this factor could properly be taken into account in deciding whether, among qualified applicants, it rendered her less qualified than others for the limited number of places available. In view of the seriousness of the harm inflicted in prior episodes, NYU is not required to give preference to her over other qualified applicants who do not pose any such appreciable risk at all.

The evidence in the record before us indicates that there is a significant risk that Doe will have a recurrence of her mental disorder, with resulting danger to herself and to others with whom she would be associated as a medical student. The non-recurrence of Doe's self-destructive and antisocial activity for the past four years, during which she has peacefully coexisted with others, is attributed to the fact that the types of stress to which she has been subjected at the Harvard School of Public

Health and as an HEW employee do not approximate the seriousness of those which she would experience as a medical student and doctor. Moreover, her history indicates that although there were no manifestations of disorder for seven years after the earlier episodes in 1963-64, they recurred during the period 1972-1977, indicating that despite a period of dormancy they may recur again.

In support of her claim Doe, on the other hand, has offered the opinions of various psychiatrists to the effect that she is fit to pursue a medical career. However, none of these psychiatrists rules out the risk that she may suffer a recurrence. Moreover, in their depositions Dr. Casella described Doe as having a "Passive-Aggressive personality" (DSM-II, 301.81) which is a type of personality disorder and Dr. Richards, while preferring to describe her as suffering from a "Depressive Neurosis" (DSM-II, 300.4), agreed that she might fall in the category of "Passive-Aggressive personality." Dr. Bojar, while not agreeing that Doe had a Borderline Personality disorder, described his diagnosis as follows:

Q: Did you make a diagnosis of Jane Doe at that time?

A.   Yes. My diagnosis was that of a chronic neurotic depression with anxiety precipitated when her particular needs could not be met. If I may elaborate on my formulation — I prefer "formulations" rather than diagnostic labels. I see her as a perfectionist who is an overachiever, who imposes very high demands on herself and on others; and when these can't be met, she undergoes a great deal of frustration.

                Her security is based on her doing well, and when she cannot utilize this defense of really achieving at a high level she becomes anxious and, well, quite depressed. When she was making demands on others, when she needed others and people could not come through, she felt the same kind of frustration that she would feel from herself if she could not do well; and it was in these settings that the hostility would arise and some of these cutting episodes occurred, which I saw as really expression of anger and hostility against the others.

Dr. Calkins' summary affidavit could hardly be given much weight, since he is not a specialist in psychiatry or behavioral sciences and his training in this area was limited to a one month clerkship at medical school, from which he graduated in 1975, and occasional experience in psychiatry as a resident, principally among outpatients.

For the reasons stated by the district court, it acted properly in refusing to give any weight to the findings of the OCR and, if the action is tried, they should not be accepted as evidence. On the other hand, the court erred in ruling that it would disregard for the most part Doe's prior psychiatric history and treat the expert testimony as being of lesser reliability than her recent behavior. In light of the type of behavioral disorder presented, which could result in a recurrence after a dormant period, expert opinion was entitled to greater weight in reaching a decision as to whether Doe was qualified. The court is required to perform the disagreeable task of considering Doe's entire psychiatric history and weighing the expert testimony on each side.

In our view, Doe, in addition to her failure to show threatened irreparable injury, has not on this record established any likelihood of success in proving that despite her handicap she is qualified for acceptance as a medical student or to engage in the practice of medicine. Moreover, while there may possibly be questions going to the merits that are sufficiently serious to make them a fair ground for litigation, the evidence indicates that there is a significant risk of recurrence of her self-destructive and harmful conduct, which NYU should not be required to bear pending trial and that a substantial basis exists for upholding NYU's decision to deny her readmission.[5] Against this, pending a full decision on the merits, plaintiff can show only the hardship of delay of another year in admission to medical school, which as indicated above, she has voluntarily chosen to do in the past. Thus the balance of hardships tips in NYU's favor, not in Doe's. Accordingly, the grant of a mandatory preliminary injunction must be reversed.

Accordingly, the district court's denial of NYU's motion for summary judgment is affirmed and its grant of mandatory preliminary injunctive relief is reversed.

NOTES

1. The previous case discusses burdens of proof. In employment requirements under the ADA, an interactive process for addressing accommodation needs is expected. Requirements for higher education are not as specific. In light of the burden of proof expectations, what might be the best way to ensure that these issues are negotiated, rather than litigated?

2. Institutions of higher education are concerned about the presence of students and others on campus with difficult behavior problems. The concerns are for the safety of others on campus and related potential liability as well as concern about the disruption to the learning of other students. Finding the appropriate means of ensuring that behavior problems cause neither danger nor disruption is a challenge. In *Aronson v. North Park College*, 94 Ill. App. 3d 211, 49 Ill. Dec. 756, 418 N.E.2d 776 (1981), a private college dismissed a student based on results of a psychological examination, the Minnesota Multiphasic Personality Inventory Test (MMPI), a test required of all incoming students. She was dismissed because the college's psychologist believed that she lacked sufficiently strong mental health to continue college or an educational career. The legal action was not based on disability discrimination theories but rather on whether the dismissal was impermissible under contract theories. There was a dispute about whether students had adequate notice of the process of psychological evaluation and whether the dismissal was arbitrary and capricious. The court held that the college acted reasonably based on the information it received from the counseling center about the student's mental state.

Several things make *Aronson* an interesting contrast with the *Doe v. NYU*

---

[5] Care must be exercised by schools and employers (and courts assessing their decisions under § 504) not to permit prior mental illness to be routinely regarded as a disqualification. This case, however, involves not simply a prior mental illness; Doe has been diagnosed as having a recognized disorder for which long-term treatment has been prescribed by competent psychiatrists and Doe has declined to accept such recommended treatment.

decision. First, there was no indication of any past record of behavior or conduct to raise concerns, only a psychological evaluation. Second, the case was based on common law theories rather than discrimination theories. In 1981, the ADA would not have been applicable, and many private colleges may not have been recipients of federal financial assistance to subject them to Section 504. If this same case occurred today, although Title III of the ADA would apply, it is far from clear that this student would be considered to be "disabled" within the statute after the limitations set out in the *Sutton* Supreme Court opinion.

PROBLEM

1. What ADA or § 504 issues would arise if the facts in *Aronson* occurred today?

2. What are the responsibilities of the institution of higher education in reporting past problems to licensing boards? If a student knows that mental health treatment will be reported to a licensing board, will this be a deterrent from getting the treatment?

3. Would it be a reasonable accommodation to a student with a panic disorder to attend classes by telephone hook-up to the classroom? See *Maczaczyj v. State of New York*, 956 F. Supp. 403 (W.D.N.Y. 1997). What would be the basis for the institution demonstrating fundamental alteration or undue burden? What if the student had HIV and was concerned about being exposed to contagious diseases by class attendance?

[5] Obligations after Disqualification

Higher education enrollment may be terminated for students because of the failure to meet academic standards or for disciplinary reasons resulting from conduct that is disruptive or violent. This raises questions not directly answered in the statutes regarding the degree to which reasonable accommodation requires excusing past behavior. The following cases indicate how some courts have responded to these situations.

HYPOTHETICAL PROBLEM 6.6

Jacob has enrolled in Oakdale Law Center. He had done well in undergraduate school and had an extraordinary record of service in the Peace Corps. Although his LSAT score was fairly low, he was admitted based on the overall record, including his service. In college, Jacob had managed to do well because he took a lot of classes where he had substantial time to write papers, but had taken very few classes requiring essay or multiple choice exams in a timed format. In high school, one of his counselors had mentioned to Jacob that he might have a mild form of ADHD, but Jacob had not received special education.

After his first semester of law school, Jacob received very low grades, and his second semester grades were even lower. He was surprised and upset, and before petitioning for readmission, he had an evaluation by an adult learning disability expert, who diagnosed Jacob with a learning disability. The evaluation recommended that Jacob receive additional time on exams and that he take exams in a distraction-free environment. If Jacob petitions for readmission presenting this documentation, must the law school readmit him? Must his records be expunged? Must it allow him to start over? Must it refund his first year tuition? Does it matter whether Jacob's dismissal was for academic reasons instead of a dismissal for violent and threatening conduct, that is later diagnosed as relating to a mental illness for which the student is now being treated (as was the case for Samantha)?

ANDERSON v. UNIVERSITY OF WISCONSIN
841 F.2d 737 (7th Cir. 1988)

EASTERBROOK, CIRCUIT JUDGE:

The University of Wisconsin Law School at Madison admitted Fradus Lee Anderson to the class entering in August 1979. He completed the semester with an average of 75, below the 77 required by the Law School. He was not permitted to complete the second semester of the 1979-80 year because he had not furnished the Law School with the necessary certification of his undergraduate degree. The Law School allowed him to return for the spring semester in 1981, despite his poor average and the knowledge that he is an alcoholic. Sensing that he was doing poorly Anderson asked to withdraw. The request was granted, but not before he received a D in legal writing and, while drunk, harassed and threatened his legal writing partner. The Law School admitted Anderson for a third time in the spring semester of 1982. He completed this semester with a cumulative average of 76.92. The Law School informed Anderson that he would not be allowed to continue.

The district court recounts Anderson's saga in trying to be readmitted for a fourth try. The Law School generally readmits students whose failure stems from a problem that has been overcome. Anderson attributed his failure to drink and contended that he was recovering. The Retentions Committee thrice concluded that Anderson had not conquered his drinking problem, the third time after receiving live testimony from four of Anderson's supporters, including a counselor at his clinic. The Retentions Committee learned that Anderson generally abstained but still drank on occasions. It concluded both that Anderson was not prepared for a pressure-filled curriculum and that he could not complete the program within the five years ordinarily allowed.

The Petitions Committee of the Law School then reexamined the subject, holding a de novo inquiry in response to Anderson's grievance against the Retentions Committee. The Petitions Committee considered not only Anderson's grades and drinking but also his performance at the Business School. Anderson had received an "A/B" grade in "Legal Aspects of Business Administration," an undergraduate-level course duplicating materials Anderson covered in law school; the other grades were B/C, C, and D (which Anderson had reported as a C). The Business School said that it would not consider this performance sufficient for admission to its graduate program. The Petitions Committee concluded that the record did not augur satisfactory completion of the Law School program and declined to readmit Anderson. The Vice Chancellor for Academic Affairs of the University, after still another inquiry, affirmed this decision. Anderson then filed this suit against the University, its Chancellor and Vice Chancellor, the Law School, and the members of the two committees (collectively the University). He argued that the University violated § 504 of the Rehabilitation Act by discriminating against him on account of alcoholism.

On the Rehabilitation Act aspect of the case, the University does not dispute Anderson's contention that an alcoholic is a "handicapped individual" within the meaning of the Rehabilitation Act; we therefore assume that he is. Anderson does not contend that the Act requires the University to alter its standards or procedures to accommodate his alcoholism; we therefore assume that it need not.

Section 504 provides that an institution receiving federal funds may not discriminate against an "otherwise qualified handicapped individual." The district court ruled in favor of the University because, it believed, Anderson is not "otherwise qualified" to continue as a law student. His average was below 77; the Law School requires an average of 77; that is that. Anderson replies that but for his drinking he could achieve an average of 77, but this misses the point.

Although inability to perform at the required standard as a result of a handicap makes a person not "otherwise qualified," a court still must decide what that standard is. The meaning of a standard lies in the method of its application. A student who cannot maintain an average of 77 at the Law School is not qualified to remain as a student, unless the student shows that the source of the academic problem has been abated, making future work of satisfactory quality likely. The bright line at 77 is diffracted by the Retentions Committee. Its decisions are part of the whole standard the Law School uses. The University wants us to disregard the "unless" clause — to treat the standard of qualification as if there were no Retentions Committee. The exceptions are part of the rule, however, and a university could not say to handicapped persons "None may apply to the Retentions Committee" or "We apply only the basic rules, and not the exceptions, to you." We therefore disagree with the district court's approach to the case.

This does not affect the outcome, however, because no rational jury could return a verdict for Anderson on this record, and the grant of summary judgment therefore was proper. Nothing in the record suggests that the University's decision was based on stereotypes about alcoholism as opposed to honest judgments about how Anderson had performed in fact and could be expected to perform. The Law School allowed Anderson to reenter the program twice, knowing that he is an alcoholic; the Business School also allowed Anderson to take courses. In none of his four stints at the University did Anderson perform up to standard. During spring 1981 he harassed and threatened another student. He did not abstain from alcohol during any substantial portion of the period covered by the record. Although there is a dispute about how serious his drinking remains — the University characterizes Anderson as a person with "fits of sobriety," while Anderson prefers the characterization of a person generally successful at abstaining with periods of inconsequential backsliding — it is undisputed that Anderson sometimes still drinks. His performance at the Business School during a period when he insists he was free from drink does not give confidence that he could succeed at the Law School.

Anderson believes that a jury should evaluate the evidence and determine whether, as his counselor told the Retentions Committee, he had recovered enough to take the stress. There is a dispute about how Anderson would fare if placed back in the classroom, but this is not a "material" issue. The Act does not designate a jury, rather than the faculty of the Law School, as the body to decide whether a would-be student is up to snuff. The Law School may set standards for itself, and jurors unacquainted with the academic program of a law school could not make the readmissions decision more accurately than the faculty of the Law School; the process of litigation would change the substantive standard in addition to raising the costs of its application. The Supreme Court has repeatedly admonished courts to respect the academic judgment of university faculties.

The question is not whether a court believes that Anderson could handle the work. It is whether the University discriminated against him because of his handicap — that is, excluded him even though it would have readmitted a student whose academic performance and prospects were as poor but whose difficulties did not stem from a "handicap." Just as Title VII of the Civil Rights Act of 1964 ensures only equal treatment and not "correct" decisions, so the Rehabilitation Act requires only a stereotype-free assessment of the person's abilities and prospects rather than a correct decision. Not a shred of evidence in the record suggests that the University held a stereotypical view of alcoholism. The committees and the Vice Chancellor looked, hard, at what Anderson had done and could do. If they erred in their appreciation of these things, the error does not violate the Rehabilitation Act.

NOTES

1. *Second Chances*: A decision that raises a difficult issue is *Betts v. Rector & Visitors of Univ. of Va.*, 967 F. Supp. 882 (W.D. Va. 1997), in which a medical student was not identified as having a learning disability until after academic problems occurred. Although the student was given appropriate accommodations after that time, the student could not achieve the requisite cumulative grade point average required to continue in the program because of the earlier low grades. This raises the question of what the obligation of the institution is in such a case. While the courts have been consistent in not requiring the institution to discount or eliminate the grades achieved before the disability was identified, there is a bigger policy question about whether they should do so and if so, in what circumstances. At least two decisions have indicated that institutions should consider a later diagnosed disability in considering dismissal and readmission. See *Singh v. George Washington University*, 368 F. Supp. 2d 58 (D.D.C. 2005), and *Steere v. George Washington University*, 368 F. Supp. 2d 52 (D.D.C. 2005).

2. *Limitations on Exam Attempts:* In *Riedel v. Board of Regents for the State of Kansas*, 1993 U.S. Dist. LEXIS 17262 (D. Kan. 1993), the plaintiff sought relief under § 504 and Title II of the ADA because he was academically dismissed from medical school after unsatisfactory attempts at the National Board Examinations. The National Board policy was that after three unsuccessful attempts, the student must petition to try a fourth time. He was dismissed in 1990, after his petition to take the test a fourth time was denied. Two years after his dismissal he sought to retake the test based on a claimed learning disability that had been identified.

The court concluded that he no longer had standing to petition to retake the test because he was no longer a student. The court thus leaves open the question of whether the four-attempt policy violates § 504 and/or the ADA. The case raises the difficult problem of the later identified disability. In this case, it was not apparent that the claimant had documentation justifying accommodations, but in a case where such documentation did exist, and the disability was not identified until after the failure, it raises the question this court left undecided. Should an institution be required to allow second (or third or fourth) chances where the disability is not known even to the claimant at the time of the failure? Such situations are not unlikely to occur in cases involving learning disabilities and some mental illnesses.

[6]   Athletics

To some, the American college campus could not be imagined without the presence of athletics. Competition in intramural sports or intercollegiate athletics is a big part of campus life. On many college campuses, whether one is interested in athletics or not, completion of the physical education requirement is a part of the required curriculum.

Students with vision in one eye, or with only one kidney or with other impairments are often excluded from participation in college athletics, usually out of paternalistic concerns for the student's safety and welfare.

The Rehabilitation Act regulations, 34 C.F.R. § 104.47(a), provide some guidance, and there have been a few cases on these issues.

NOTES

1. *Deferring to Institutions on Safety Issues:* The two major cases that have addressed this issue have reached consistent results and reflect the general rule that courts will defer to the decisions of academic institutions so long as their decisions are rationally based. In *Knapp v. Northwestern University*, 101 F.3d 473 (7th Cir. 1996), a student who had been awarded an NCAA basketball scholarship at Northwestern University suffered a sudden cardiac death during a pick-up basketball game. He recovered and an internal cardioverter-defibrillator was implanted. Northwestern University later decided, based on recommendations of conference guidance that he was ineligible to play. Although his scholarship continued, the student's ineligibility to play college basketball would certainly have affected his potential to play professional basketball. The court, however, held that Knapp was not substantially limited in obtaining an education. The court further recognized that where the severity of the potential injury is high as in Knapp's case, and where the potential for a further episode was unclear, the university acted reasonably in its decision. The court noted that medical determinations such as these should be left to team doctors and universities so longs as they act reasonably and rationally and "with full regard to possible and reasonable accommodations."

The *Knapp* court cited a similar case of *Pahulu v. University of Kansas*, 897 F. Supp. 1387 (D. Kan. 1995), in which a high risk for permanent and severe neurological injury rendered a college student unqualified for intercollegiate football participation.

2. *Waiver of Liability:* In *Wright v. Columbia Univ.*, 520 F. Supp. 789 (E.D. Pa. 1981), the claimant sought to play college football although he had lost sight in one eye. The college sought to deny his participation although he and his parents were willing to release Columbia from potential liability. The court in granting the plaintiff's request for a preliminary injunction noted that a highly qualified ophthalmologist had indicated that there is no substantial risk of serious eye injury related to football. Other factors of importance were the fact that he was mature enough to make this decision, in contrast to students who might not be old enough to weigh the risks involved. In what ways can this decision be distinguished from *Knapp*?

PROBLEMS

1. Does it violate Section 504 or the ADA if a student with one kidney is prohibited from participating in the football program assuming the student is athletically qualified? How can the college protect itself from liability if participation is permitted?

2. Does it violate Section 504 or the ADA if a student who is HIV-positive is precluded from the basketball team?

3. Is it legal for a deaf student to be prohibited from participating in the football program?

4. What are the implications of a university practice of waiving the physical educational requirement for students who are orthopedically impaired? What if a student does not want waiver, but prefers adaptive physical education? Must that be provided?

5. Must colleges provide equivalent intermural and intramural athletics programs similar to those required under Title IX? For example, must colleges provide opportunities for intermural wheelchair basketball or tennis?

NOTE

Standardized Tests and Athlete Eligibility: A number of cases have been brought since the passage of the ADA challenging NCAA scholarship eligibility based on standardized test scores and curricular requirements. The NCAA was not subject to Section 504 of the Rehabilitation Act because it was not a recipient of federal financial assistance. Title III of the ADA, however, applies to private providers of public accommodations. Although it is unsettled whether the NCAA fits the definition of a Title III entity, the Supreme Court's broad ruling in the case of *PGA v. Casey Martin*, in Chapter 4[A], *supra*, signals that it probably does fall within Title III. The substantive application of the nondiscrimination requirements, however, is also unsettled. Several cases have involved athletes with learning disabilities challenging the absolute requirements of minimum SAT scores and certain core courses. The courts have generally recognized that such requirements have a disparate impact on students with learning and other disabilities, but have recognized that it is legitimate for requirements to be set that ensure that college athletes have the requisite ability to do college academic work. Since these cases began, the NCAA has changed its eligibility requirements and provides for accommodation to allow for individualized assessment of athletes with disabilities. Because of the high stakes in these cases, it is probable that they will continue to be brought.

For a general discussion of college athletes with disabilities, see Laura Rothstein, *Don't Roll in My Parade: The Impact of Sports and Entertainment Cases on Public Awareness and Understanding of the Americans with Disabilities Act*, 19 U. TEX. REV. LITIG. 400 (2000).

[7] Other Programming

Most college campuses offer counseling and placement programs, financial aid programs, and health and insurance services. There are also numerous social activities including fraternities and sororities, and there are a variety of social service and other clubs and organizations on campus. The Section 504 regulations, 34 C.F.R. § 104.46–.47, provide some guidance about discriminatory practices, but they do not answer all of the questions.

PROBLEMS

1. The placement director for the undergraduate program at State College believes that deaf students will have significant difficulty in law school and as lawyers. Student A, a deaf political science major, comes to the placement office seeking advice about attending law school. What kind of counseling is appropriate for the placement director to offer?

2. As part of law school placement programs, law firms interview students on campus. The placement director facilitates these interviews by providing resumes of students to the firms, providing space for the interviews, and by posting notices of firms interested in interviewing. If the director hears that a law firm has refused to interview a student who is in a wheelchair because they do a lot of trial practice and need someone who will be aggressive in the courtroom, what is the obligation of the placement director? Does he/she have any obligation to actively find out whether law firms discriminate?

3. Do athletics scholarships have a disparate discriminatory impact on students with disabilities? Is it illegal to have such scholarships?

4. What obligations do sorority and fraternity houses have to be accessible to individuals with mobility impairments?

D CONFIDENTIALITY ISSUES

The student in a wheelchair is unlikely to be able to have the disability status be treated as a confidential matter. But for the student with a learning disability, with HIV, with epilepsy, or with a history of alcohol problems or mental problems, there may well be a desire to keep that information confidential. The student may be concerned about stigma and discrimination. The institution may need to have documentation of the disability in the student's record in order to justify an accommodation, but it is essential that this information be disclosed only to those at the institution with a need to know. Disclosure to third parties must be made only when there is consent by the student. The Family Education Rights and Privacy Act (FERPA), 20 U.S.C. § 1232g(a)9-(i); 34 C.F.R. pt 5b, not only requires that institutions subject to FERPA comply with this disclosure requirement, but also provides for other protections with respect to student access to their own records and an opportunity to challenge the inclusion of certain information.

There are several problems with FERPA as an avenue for protecting confidentiality. First, FERPA is very vague about who in an institution may have access. Second, there is no private right of action to obtain a remedy under FERPA. The only remedy is to complain to the Department of Education. A student who believes that there have been privacy violations may have to resort to common-law tort theories for protection. Third, it is not entirely clear whether certain types of information would be considered to be academic records or whether they are medical records, subject to protection under other laws.

While it might be argued that student disability documentation should be placed in a separate file, similar to requirements under Title I of the ADA relating to employment, there are logistical reasons in higher education institutions why this may not be feasible. A more appropriate response might be to establish and implement policies and procedures to ensure protection of this information in the student's record.

The following cases illustrate some of the issues that arise with respect to confidentiality. In particular, they raise questions about when there is a privilege to inform another institution or agency about a disability.

DOE v. SOUTHEASTERN UNIVERSITY
732 F. Supp. 7 (D.D.C. 1990)

STANLEY S. HARRIS, DISTRICT JUDGE:

This matter is before the Court on defendant's motion to dismiss and plaintiff's opposition. Upon consideration of the pleadings and the entire record, the Court grants defendant's motion.

Plaintiff is a former student at Southeastern University. Allegedly plaintiff tested positive for Human Immunodeficiency Virus (HIV). Because of a complication which plaintiff associated with having HIV, plaintiff had to be hospitalized and missed a significant portion of a semester of classes. In order to get excused from his fall 1986 classes, he had his physician transmit medical statements to the University confirming plaintiff's inability to have attended classes. According to the plaintiff, this information was improperly leaked to unauthorized faculty and staff. As a result, plaintiff alleges that he was harassed, embarrassed, and finally felt forced to withdraw from Southeastern and transfer to the University of Maryland. Plaintiff also alleges that after his transfer, defendant improperly notified the University of Maryland of his condition. Plaintiff's complaint appears to make several claims: (1) intentional infliction of emotional distress; (2) negligent infliction of emotional distress; (3) invasion of privacy; and (4) violation of § 504 of the Rehabilitation Act of 1973.

Defendant specifically argues that plaintiff's Rehabilitation Act claim . . . should be barred by the one-year statute of limitations. The Court disagrees. The Rehabilitation Act does not contain its own statute of limitations, and therefore the period to be applied must be drawn from the appropriate state statute. Courts have applied a wide variety of state statutes of limitations to the Rehabilitation Act. Some, primarily in cases involving discrimination in employment, have applied the state's statute of limitations involving contracts. Some have found that the applicable standard is found in the state's statute of limitations specially enacted to be used in actions created by statute. Still others have applied the state's applicable personal injury statute.

However, in growing numbers courts have looked to analogous discrimination actions such as those brought under 42 U.S.C. § 1981 and § 1983, and have applied the state's personal injury statute of limitations to Rehabilitation Act claims. Title VI, like § 504, does not have a specific statute of limitations. In determining which state statute of limitations applies to Title VI actions, courts have looked to the statute of limitations used in § 1981 and § 1983 actions. Thus, this Court holds that the District of Columbia's three-year personal injury statute of limitations applies.

Remedies Available under the Rehabilitation Act

Even reading the complaint liberally and assuming that testing positive for AIDS antibodies is a handicap, and assuming he could prove damages, the Court determines that plaintiff would be limited to equitable relief. Plaintiff requests compensatory and punitive damages. Courts are divided as to whether monetary damages are available to a plaintiff in a § 504 case. The Supreme Court has expressly declined to decide "the extent to which money damages are available under § 504." The Supreme Court has allowed back pay and similar types of relief. The remedies allowed in § 504 are set forth in 29 U.S.C. § 794a. Section 794a(a)(2) states that:

> The remedies, procedures, and rights set forth in title VI of the Civil Rights Act of 1964 shall be available to any person aggrieved by any act or failure to act by any recipient of Federal assistance or Federal provider of such assistance under section 794 of this title.

The Supreme Court also is undecided as to whether non-equitable damages apply to Title VI claims. To hold that compensatory and punitive damages are available would be to engage in judicial activism. If Congress feels that additional remedies are necessary to protect the rights of handicapped individuals, Congress must make that law, not this Court. Accordingly, the Court grants defendant's motion to dismiss on this issue.

NOTE

The previous case did not directly address the privilege to transmit certain student information in student records when a student transfers. The problem, however, is when communication beyond privileged parties occurs. In the case of *Rothman v. Emory University*, 123 F.3d 446 (7th Cir. 1997), the court did not directly address the issue of privilege, although it might have. The case involved a law student with epilepsy who claimed that the law school's reporting to the state bar authorities information about his behavior and conduct (which he claimed related to his epilepsy) was discriminatory. The court held that the bar certification letter was not discriminatory, but rather a candid and forthright evaluation of the student. For additional discussion of this issue, see Chapter 5, Governmental Services, E. Licensing and Other Regulatory Practices, 2. Professional Licensing.

Chapter 7

EDUCATION

A HISTORICAL PERSPECTIVE

Before the 1970s, most children with disabilities had minimal access to education, particularly education in regular schools. While some special programming was available in separate settings, such as schools for children who were blind or deaf, children who were mentally retarded or who had serious behavior disorders were more likely to be institutionalized and given minimal, if any, educational programming.

In the early 1970s, an advocacy movement applied the principles established by the Supreme Court in *Brown v. Board of Ed.*, 347 U.S. 483 (1954), relating to schools that were segregated on the basis of race. A number of cases were brought by advocacy groups throughout the United States in several states challenging the exclusion and the different treatment of children with disabilities. The plaintiffs claimed that these practices by schools violated the Fifth and Fourteenth Amendment Due Process and Equal Protection Clauses. Two of these cases resulted in landmark settlement agreements, in which the parties agreed to provide education to children with disabilities. See *Pennsylvania Ass'n for Retarded Children v. Pennsylvania*, 334 F. Supp. 1257 (E.D. Pa. 1971), 343 F. Supp. 279 (E.D. Pa. 1972); and *Mills v. Board of Ed.*, 348 F. Supp. 866 (D.D.C. 1972). In *Mills*, the court approved detailed procedural safeguards to ensure that these substantive rights were carried out.

In recognition of the additional burdens to the state and local educational agencies that educating children with disabilities and the value of consistent policy for all the states, Congress enacted major federal legislation, the Education for All Handicapped Children Act (EAHCA), in 1975 to provide additional funding to states. 42 U.S.C. § 1400 et seq. An earlier version of the statute enacted in 1970 was known as the Education of the Handicapped Act (EHA), 84 Stat. 175, and amended in 1974, 88 Stat. 579. The EHA did not include the elaborate procedural safeguards that are viewed as essential to carrying out the purposes of the EHA. S. Rep. No. 94-168, at 11–12. The condition of funding granted through the Department of Education (formerly the Department of Health, Education and Welfare), was that the state educational agency was required to submit a state plan demonstrating that the state would provide free, appropriate, public education to all children with disabilities in the state. Education was to be individualized and was to be provided in the least restrictive appropriate environment. The state plan was required to include detailed procedural safeguards and a plan for personnel development. The EAHCA became effective in 1977. In 1991 the EAHCA was amended, and the title was changed to the Individuals with Disabilities Education Act (IDEA). The changed title reflected the new preferred language that had been adopted in the Americans with Disabilities Act. The statute was amended in 1997, adding some new requirements, but also renumbering many of the existing sections. Congress again amended and renumbered some sections of the statute in 2004. The statutory and regulatory citations in the case excerpts in this chapter refer to the provisions in effect on the date of the case. Major changes are noted in the text that accompanies relevant sections that follow.

While the EAHCA was being developed, Section 504 of the Rehabilitation Act, 29 U.S.C. § 794, had already been enacted in 1973. Section 504 prohibits discrimination on the basis of handicap (now amended to use "disability") by programs receiving federal financial assistance. Because virtually all public schools receive federal financial assistance through a variety of programs, such as school lunch programs, these schools are subject to the nondiscrimination mandates of the Rehabilitation Act.

In 1990, Congress passed the Americans with Disabilities Act (ADA), 42 U.S.C. § 12101 et seq., which also prohibits discrimination on the basis of disability by both public schools (under Title II) and private schools (under Title III). While the ADA theoretically does not require substantively much more than was already required under Section 504, its application to private schools is a major addition. In addition, it might be interpreted as mandating more than was required under the Rehabilitation Act with respect to architectural barrier removal.

The differences in coverage under the IDEA and Section 504 and the ADA are important in the context of children with disabilities in the school setting. Section 504 and the ADA are nondiscrimination statutes. While they mandate reasonable accommodation as part of nondiscrimination, they do not require schools to carry out activities that would be unduly burdensome or that would fundamentally alter the program. The IDEA mandates more than basic nondiscrimination and reasonable accommodation. The IDEA contemplates special education and related services that may be much more expensive than a reasonable accommodation would require.

The other significant difference between IDEA and Section 504/ADA application relates to who is protected by the statutes. The IDEA categorically defines who is protected as children

> with mental retardation, hearing impairments (including deafness), speech or language impairments, visual impairments (including blindness), serious emotional disturbance, orthopedic impairments, autism, traumatic brain injury, other health impairments, or specific learning disabilities . . . who, by reason thereof, need special education and related services.

20 U.S.C. § 1401(3)(A)(i)(ii) (2004).

In contrast, Section 504 and the ADA protect individuals who have substantial impairments to one or more major life activities (which includes learning), individuals who have a record of such an impairment, or those who are regarded as having such an impairment. 29 U.S.C. § 706(8)(B); 42 U.S.C. § 12102. The ADA also provides protection for individuals who are associated with someone who has a disability. 29 C.F.R. § 1630.8(1). Both statutes have separate definitional clarification related to application for individuals with contagious or infectious diseases, 29 U.S.C. § 706(8)(D), 42 U.S.C. § 12113; and those who illegally use or who are addicted to drugs or alcohol, 29 U.S.C. § 706(8)(C), 42 U.S.C. §§ 12111(6) & 12114.

In 2008, Congress enacted the ADA Amendments Act of 2008, P.L. 110–325 (2008), which took effect on January 1, 2009. The definition of coverage clarifies that the intent of the ADA was to provide for broad coverage. The definition's amendment applies to both the ADA and to the Rehabilitation Act.

The definition of disability basically remains the same and provides as follows:

(A)   a physical or mental impairment that substantially limits one or more major life activities of such individual;

(B)   a record of such an impairment; or

(C)   being regarded as having such an impairment . . .

42 U.S.C. § 12102(1). The definition does not apply to impairments that are transitory and minor. 42 U.S.C. § 12102(4)(D).

Major life activities include, but are not limited to, caring for oneself, performing manual tasks, seeing, hearing, eating, sleeping, walking, standing, lifting, bending, speaking, breathing, learning, reading, concentrating, thinking, communicating and working. A major life activity also includes the operation of a major bodily function, including but not limited to, functions of the immune system, normal cell growth, digestive, bowel, bladder, neurological, brain, respiratory, circulatory, endocrine, and reproductive functions. 42 U.S.C. § 12102(2). This broader definition will result in greater eligibility for services and accommodations under Section 504 for students with impairments such as learning disabilities, ADD, ADHD, diabetes, asthma, peanut allergies, and other conditions that might not require special education.

One of the earliest Supreme Court decisions related to children with disabilities in schools addressed the issue of overlapping application of the IDEA and Section 504. The Court's analysis, which follows in the next case excerpt, would almost certainly be applied to a similar challenge involving the ADA, which had not been enacted in 1984, when the Court decided this case.

SMITH v. ROBINSON
468 U.S. 992 (1984)

JUSTICE BLACKMUN delivered the opinion of the Court:

This case presents questions regarding the award of attorney's fees in a proceeding to secure a "free appropriate public education" for a handicapped child. At various stages in the proceeding, petitioners asserted claims for relief based on state law, on the Education of the Handicapped Act (EHA), 84 Stat. 175, as amended, 20 U.S.C. § 1400 et seq., on § 504 of the Rehabilitation Act of 1973, as amended, 29 U.S.C. § 794, and on the Due Process and Equal Protection Clauses of the Fourteenth Amendment to the United States Constitution. The United States Court of Appeals for the First Circuit concluded that because the proceeding, in essence, was one to enforce the provisions of the EHA, a statute that does not provide for the payment of attorney's fees, petitioners were not entitled to such fees.

I.

The procedural history of the case is complicated, but it is significant to the resolution of the issues. Petitioner Thomas F. Smith, III (Tommy), suffers from cerebral palsy and a variety of physical and emotional handicaps. When this proceeding began in November 1976, Tommy was 8 years old. In the preceding December, the Cumberland School Committee had agreed to place Tommy in a day program at Emma Pendleton Bradley Hospital in East Providence, R.I., and Tommy began attending that program. In November 1976, however, the Superintendent of Schools informed Tommy's parents, who are the other petitioners here, that the School Committee no longer would fund Tommy's placement because, as it construed Rhode Island law, the responsibility for educating an emotionally disturbed child lay with the State's Division of Mental Health, Retardation and Hospitals [MHRH].

Petitioners took an appeal from the decision of the Superintendent to the School Committee. In addition, petitioners filed a complaint under 42 U.S.C. § 1983 in the United States District Court for the District of Rhode Island against the members of the School Committee, asserting that due process required that the Committee comply with "Article IX — Procedural Safeguards" of the Regulations adopted by the State Board of Regents regarding Education of Handicapped Children [Regulations] . . . and that Tommy's placement in his program be continued pending appeal of the Superintendent's decision. [Procedural developments omitted.]

[Petitioners later amended their complaint to seek relief under the Equal Protection Clause of the Fourteenth Amendment and under § 504 of the Rehabilitation Act of 1973, as amended, 29 U.S.C. § 794. They also requested attorney's fees under 42 U.S.C. § 1988 and what was then 31 U.S.C. § 1244(e) (1976 ed.). Attorney's fees had become available directly under the Rehabilitation Act by this time.]

[Lower court proceedings omitted.]

III.

As the legislative history illustrates and as this Court has recognized, § 1988 is a broad grant of authority to courts to award attorney's fees to plaintiffs seeking to vindicate federal constitutional and statutory rights. Congress did not intend to have that authority extinguished by the fact that the case was settled or resolved on a nonconstitutional ground. As the Court also has recognized, however, the authority to award fees in a case where the plaintiff prevails on substantial constitutional claims is not without qualification. Due regard must be paid, not only to the fact that a plaintiff "prevailed," but also to the relationship between the claims on which effort was expended and the ultimate relief obtained.

A similar analysis is appropriate in a case like this, where the prevailing plaintiffs rely on substantial, unaddressed constitutional claims as the basis for an award of attorney's fees. The fact that constitutional claims are made does not render automatic an award of fees for the entire proceeding. Congress' purpose in authorizing a fee award for an unaddressed constitutional claim was to avoid penalizing a litigant for the fact that courts are properly reluctant to resolve constitutional questions if a nonconstitutional claim is dispositive. That purpose does not alter the requirement that a claim for which fees are awarded be reasonably related to the plaintiff's ultimate success. It simply authorizes a district court to assume that the plaintiff has prevailed on his fee-generating claim and to award fees appropriate to that success.

In light of the requirement that a claim for which fees are awarded be reasonably related to the plaintiff's ultimate success, it is clear that plaintiffs may not rely simply on the fact that substantial fee-generating claims were made during the course of the litigation. Closer examination of the nature of the claims and the relationship between those claims and petitioners' ultimate success is required.

Besides making a claim under the EHA, petitioners asserted at two different points in the proceedings that procedures employed by state officials denied them due process. They also claimed that Tommy was being discriminated against on the basis of his handicapping condition, in violation of the Equal Protection Clause of the Fourteenth Amendment.

A.

The first due process claim may be disposed of briefly. Petitioners challenged the refusal of the School Board to grant them a full hearing before terminating Tommy's funding. Petitioners were awarded fees against the School Board for their efforts in obtaining an injunction to prevent that due process deprivation. The award was not challenged on appeal and we therefore assume that it was proper.

The fact that petitioners prevailed on their initial due process claim, however, by itself does not entitle them to fees for the subsequent administrative and judicial proceedings. The due process claim that entitled petitioners to an order maintaining Tommy's placement throughout the course of the subsequent proceedings is entirely separate from the claims petitioners made in those proceedings. Nor were those proceedings necessitated by the School Board's failings. Even if the School Board had complied with state regulations and had guaranteed Tommy's continued placement pending administrative review of its decision, petitioners still would have had to avail themselves of the administrative process in order to obtain the permanent relief they wanted — an interpretation of state law that placed on the School Board the obligation to pay for Tommy's education. Petitioners' initial due process claim is not sufficiently related to their ultimate success to support an award of fees for the entire proceeding. We turn, therefore, to petitioners' other § 1983 claims.

As petitioners emphasize, their § 1983 claims were not based on alleged violations of the EHA, but on independent claims of constitutional deprivations. As the Court of Appeals recognized, however, petitioners' constitutional claims, a denial of due process and a denial of a free appropriate public education as guaranteed by the Equal Protection Clause, are virtually identical to their EHA claims. The question to be asked, therefore, is whether Congress intended that the EHA be the exclusive avenue through which a plaintiff may assert those claims.

B.

We have little difficulty concluding that Congress intended the EHA to be the exclusive avenue through which a plaintiff may assert an equal protection claim to a publicly financed special education. The EHA is a comprehensive scheme set up by Congress to aid the States in complying with their constitutional obligations to provide public education for handicapped children. Both the provisions of the statute and its legislative history indicate that Congress intended handicapped children with constitutional claims to a free appropriate public education to pursue those claims through the carefully tailored administrative and judicial mechanism set out in the statute.

In the statement of findings with which the EHA begins, Congress noted that there were more than 8,000,000 handicapped children in the country, the special education needs of most of whom were not being fully met. Congress also recognized that in a series of "landmark court cases," the right to an equal education opportunity for handicapped children had been established. The EHA was an attempt to relieve the fiscal burden placed on States and localities by their responsibility to provide education for all handicapped children. At the same time, however, Congress made clear that the EHA is not simply a funding statute. The responsibility for providing the required education remains on the States. And the Act establishes an enforceable substantive right to a free appropriate public education.

In light of the comprehensive nature of the procedures and guarantees set out in the EHA and Congress' express efforts to place on local and state educational agencies the primary responsibility for developing a plan to accommodate the needs of each individual handicapped child, we find it difficult to believe that Congress also meant to leave undisturbed the ability of a handicapped child to go directly to court with an equal protection claim to a free appropriate public education. Not only would such a result render superfluous most of the detailed procedural protections outlined in the statute, but, more important, it would run counter to Congress' view that the needs of handicapped children are best accommodated by having the parents and the local education agency work together to formulate an individualized plan for each handicapped child's education. No federal district court presented with a constitutional claim to a public education can duplicate that process.

We do not lightly conclude that Congress intended to preclude reliance on § 1983 as a remedy for a substantial equal protection claim. Since 1871, when it was passed by Congress, § 1983 has stood as an independent safeguard against deprivations of federal constitutional and statutory rights. Nevertheless, § 1983 is a statutory remedy and Congress retains the authority to repeal it or replace it with an alternative remedy. The crucial consideration is what Congress intended.

In this case, we think Congress' intent is clear. Allowing a plaintiff to circumvent the EHA administrative remedies would be inconsistent with Congress' carefully tailored scheme. The legislative history gives no indication that Congress intended such a result. Rather, it indicates that Congress perceived the EHA as the most effective vehicle for protecting the constitutional right of a handicapped child to a public education. We conclude, therefore, that where the EHA is available to a handicapped child asserting a right to a free appropriate public education, based either on the EHA or on the Equal Protection Clause of the Fourteenth Amendment, the EHA is the exclusive avenue through which the child and his parents or guardian can pursue their claim.

[Discussion of due process claim omitted.]

IV.

We turn, finally, to petitioners' claim that they were entitled to fees under § 505 of the Rehabilitation Act, because they asserted a substantial claim for relief under § 504 of that Act.

Much of our analysis of petitioners' equal protection claim is applicable here. The EHA is a comprehensive scheme designed by Congress as the most effective way to protect the right of a handicapped child to a free appropriate public education. We concluded above that in enacting the EHA, Congress was aware of, and intended to accommodate, the claims of handicapped children that the Equal Protection Clause required that they be ensured access to public education. We also concluded that Congress did not intend to have the EHA scheme circumvented by resort to the more general provisions of § 1983. We reach the same conclusion regarding petitioners' § 504 claim. The relationship between the EHA and § 504, however, requires a slightly different analysis from that required by petitioners' equal protection claim.

Section 504 and the EHA are different substantive statutes. While the EHA guarantees a right to a free appropriate public education, § 504 simply prevents discrimination on the basis of handicap. But while the EHA is limited to handicapped children seeking access to public education, § 504 protects handicapped persons of all ages from discrimination in a variety of programs and activities receiving federal financial assistance.

Because both statutes are built around fundamental notions of equal access to state programs and facilities, their substantive requirements, as applied to the right of a handicapped child to a public education, have been interpreted to be strikingly similar. In regulations promulgated pursuant to § 504, the Secretary of Education has interpreted § 504 as requiring a recipient of federal funds that operates a public elementary or secondary education program to provide a free appropriate public education to each qualified handicapped person in the recipient's jurisdiction. 34 CFR § 104.33(a) (1983). The requirement extends to the provision of a public or private residential placement if necessary to provide a free appropriate public education. § 104.33(c)(3). The regulations also require that the recipient implement procedural safeguards, including notice, an opportunity for the parents or guardian to examine relevant records, an impartial hearing with opportunity for participation by the parents or guardian and representation by counsel, and a review procedure. § 104.36. The Secretary declined to require the exact EHA procedures, because those procedures might be inappropriate for some recipients not subject to the EHA, see 34 CFR, subtitle B, ch. 1, App. A, p. 371, but indicated that compliance with EHA procedures would satisfy § 104.36.

On the other hand, although both statutes begin with an equal protection premise that handicapped children must be given access to public education, it does not follow that the affirmative requirements imposed by the two statutes are the same. The significant difference between the two, as applied to special education claims, is that the substantive and procedural rights assumed to be guaranteed by both statutes are specifically required only by the EHA.

Section 504, 29 U.S.C. § 794, provides, in pertinent part, that:

> No otherwise qualified handicapped individual in the United States, . . . shall, solely by reason of his handicap, be excluded from the participation in, be denied the benefits of, or be subjected to discrimination under any program or activity receiving Federal financial assistance . . . .

In *Southeastern Community College v. Davis*, the Court emphasized that § 504 does not require affirmative action on behalf of handicapped persons, but only the absence of discrimination against those persons. In light of *Davis*, courts construing § 504 as applied to the educational needs of handicapped children have expressed confusion about the extent to which § 504 requires special services necessary to make public education accessible to handicapped children.

In the EHA, on the other hand, Congress specified the affirmative obligations imposed on States to ensure that equal access to a public education is not an empty guarantee, but offers some benefit to a handicapped child. Thus, the statute specifically requires "such . . . supportive services . . . as may be required to assist a handicapped child to benefit from special education," . . . including, if the public facilities are inadequate for the needs of the child, "instruction in hospitals and institutions." 20 U.S.C. §§ 1401(16) and (17).

We need not decide the extent of the guarantee of a free appropriate public education Congress intended to impose under § 504. We note the uncertainty regarding the reach of § 504 to emphasize that it is only in the EHA that Congress specified the rights and remedies available to a handicapped child seeking access to public education. Even assuming that the reach of § 504 is coextensive with that of the EHA, there is no doubt that the remedies, rights, and procedures Congress set out in the EHA are the ones it intended to apply to a handicapped child's claim to a free appropriate public education. We are satisfied that Congress did not intend a handicapped child to be able to circumvent the requirements or supplement the remedies of the EHA by resort to the general antidiscrimination provision of § 504.

The [EHA] appears to represent Congress' judgment that the best way to ensure a free appropriate public education for handicapped children is to clarify and make enforceable the rights of those children while at the same time endeavoring to relieve the financial burden imposed on the agencies responsible to guarantee those rights. Where § 504 adds nothing to the substantive rights of a handicapped child, we cannot believe that Congress intended to have the careful balance struck in the EHA upset by reliance on § 504 for otherwise unavailable damages or for an award of attorney's fees.

We emphasize the narrowness of our holding. We do not address a situation where the EHA is not available or where § 504 guarantees substantive rights greater than those available under the EHA. We hold only that where, as here, whatever remedy might be provided under § 504 is provided with more clarity and precision under the EHA, a plaintiff may not circumvent or enlarge on the remedies available under the EHA by resort to § 504.

[Dissenting opinions of Justices Brennan, Marshall, and Stevens are omitted.]

NOTE

Attorneys' Fees Amendment: As the *Smith v. Robinson* opinion indicates, one of the major reasons that Section 504 and Section 1983 were being used as vehicles for relief was to obtain attorneys' fees and possibly damages, which were not specifically provided for in the EAHCA. After this decision was rendered, Congress amended the EAHCA in 1986 by passing the Handicapped Children's Protection Act (HCPA). The HCPA provides that courts may award reasonable attorneys' fees to parents or guardians of disabled children who prevail in EAHCA claims. 20 U.S.C. § 4(e)(4). The statutory amendments did not address the issue of damages as a remedy.

The HCPA has given rise to a substantial amount of litigation addressing issues such as what it means to be a prevailing party, whether such fees are available for administrative proceedings (the majority of courts hold that they are), and what is meant by "reasonable" within a particular set of circumstances. See LAURA ROTHSTEIN & JULIA ROTHSTEIN, DISABILITIES AND THE LAW § 2.51 (2009). The 1997 amendments clarified that attorneys' fees may not generally be recovered for IEP meetings. 20 U.S.C. § 1415(i)(3)(D)(iii) (1997).

B   SUBSTANTIVE PROTECTIONS UNDER THE INDIVIDUALS WITH DISABILITIES EDUCATION ACT

The Individuals with Disabilities Education Act (formerly the Education for All Handicapped Children Act) is more than a nondiscrimination statute. The key substantive principles of the IDEA are that special education and related services are to be provided to *all* children with disabilities; the education is to be *appropriate* and *individualized*; it is to be *free*; and it is to be provided in the *least restrictive appropriate setting.* In addition to the principle substantive provisions, the IDEA provides for an elaborate set of *procedural safeguards.*

The cases in this section illustrate some of the major substantive provisions of the IDEA. The focus is on those provisions that have been the subject of major judicial attention. There have been hundreds of reported decisions addressing a variety of issues under the IDEA. Citations to most of these decisions can be found in LAURA ROTHSTEIN & JULIA ROTHSTEIN, DISABILITIES AND THE LAW ch. 2 (2009).

[1]   Appropriate Education

The term "appropriate" as used in the IDEA is a difficult term to define. Part of the reason it is so difficult to define is that the type of educational programming needed for each child varies significantly depending on the type of disability, the degree of severity, and even the time the child became disabled. For example, a child who is deaf from birth may have very different needs than a child whose hearing impairment occurred as a result of an illness when the child was a teenager.

HYPOTHETICAL PROBLEM 7.1

Helen K. is five years old and became deaf at age three after having meningitis. Her parents placed Helen (at age three) in a private intensive program for children with hearing impairments and paid for the costs of the program themselves. Helen is very bright and has progressed well and, although she has learned American Sign Language, she has become an excellent lip reader, and her parents would prefer that she not rely on sign language but only use lip reading. Helen has a hearing aid that facilitates a small degree of residual hearing. In May, while Helen is still attending the private school, her parents contact the local school district asking for special education for Helen for the following year in first grade. Helen's sixth birthday is in July.

This is a large school district and there are four other children Helen's age with hearing impairments. The closest public school (McKinley School) to Helen's home is two blocks away and would be the school assigned to many of Helen's friends in the neighborhood. After the educational agency evaluates Helen's existing records, it proposes at the IEP meeting in June to place Helen in a mainstream first grade class in Lincoln Elementary School that is fifteen miles away. This would require a one hour bus ride each way. Helen's family lives on the 10th floor of a condominium building, and Helen would need to be at the school bus stop by 6:30 am and would not return home until approximately 4:30 pm each day, and would be dropped at a stop a block from the entrance to the building in which Helen's family lives. Lincoln Elementary has several students with hearing impairments enrolled in various grades and there is a full time deaf education specialist on staff at the school. The four other children Helen's age, who live varying distances from Lincoln Elementary, have all learned sign language and received services from a state agency, facilitated by the local school district for one to five years. A full time sign language interpreter would be placed in the classroom. Helen would also attend separate speech therapy sessions at the school three times a week for an hour. The school has installed microphone systems in all classrooms at Lincoln to benefit those students with residual hearing.

At the IEP meeting, Helen's parents strongly object to the school's proposed placement for several reasons. They are concerned about the time spent in travel and that she would lose the social interaction of after school activities with the other children in her building and neighborhood. They are concerned that Helen will have to wait at a bus stop in the early morning hours and someone would have to wait for her at a busy intersection to take her back to her apartment on the 10th floor. Both of Helen's parents are employed in positions that require them to be at their offices until 5 pm, arriving home between 5:30 and 6:00. McKinley Elementary School has an after school program for enrolled students allowing them to stay there until 5:00 pm at no cost, and a nominal cost after 5:00 until 6:30. The parents strongly object to having a sign language interpreter in the classroom because they think Helen will begin to rely on signing rather than lip reading. They refuse to agree to the proposed IEP, and the dispute remains unresolved by the first day of school. The parents decide to keep Helen enrolled at the private placement until the dispute can be resolved.

The cost of the private school placement is $40,000 a year. The cost to the school district of providing Helen's education at Lincoln Elementary would be $20,000 (including transportation costs and the related service costs divided by the five children in the classroom and the speech therapy). If the school district provided speech therapy at McKinley and installed a microphone, the costs would be $30,000 (because an itinerant speech therapist would have to travel to McKinley), the school would provide a sign language interpreter (although this is a dispute about whether this is needed), and the installation of a microphone system in the classroom would be required and this would be a recurring cost in each classroom to which Helen would move as she moves from grade to grade.

How would this dispute proceed in a best case scenario? What factors would determine whether Helen is receiving an "appropriate" education at Lincoln?

The first Supreme Court decision to address any issue under the IDEA (then EAHCA) is the following case. In this decision, the Court attempts to clarify the meaning of the term "appropriate."

BOARD OF EDUCATION v. ROWLEY
458 U.S. 176 (1982)

JUSTICE REHNQUIST delivered the opinion of the Court:

I.

The Education of the Handicapped Act (Act) provides federal money to assist state and local agencies in educating handicapped children, and conditions such funding upon a State's compliance with extensive goals and procedures. The Act represents an ambitious federal effort to promote the education of handicapped children, and was passed in response to Congress' perception that a majority of handicapped children in the United States "were either totally excluded from schools or [were] sitting idly in regular classrooms awaiting the time when they were old enough to 'drop out.' " The Act's evolution and major provisions shed light on the question of statutory interpretation which is at the heart of this case.

Congress first addressed the problem of educating the handicapped in 1966 when it amended the Elementary and Secondary Education Act of 1965 to establish a grant program "for the purpose of assisting the States in the initiation, expansion, and improvement of programs and projects . . . for the education of handicapped children." That program was repealed in 1970 by the Education of the Handicapped Act, Part B of which established a grant program similar in purpose to the repealed legislation. Neither the 1966 nor the 1970 legislation contained specific guidelines for state use of the grant money; both were aimed primarily at stimulating the States to develop educational resources and to train personnel for educating the handicapped.

Dissatisfied with the progress being made under these earlier enactments, and spurred by two District Court decisions holding that handicapped children should be given access to a public education, . . . Congress in 1974 greatly increased federal funding for education of the handicapped and for the first time required recipient States to adopt "a goal of providing full educational opportunities to all handicapped children." The 1974 statute was recognized as an interim measure only, adopted "in order to give the Congress an additional year in which to study what if any additional Federal assistance [was] required to enable the States to meet the needs of handicapped children." The ensuing year of study produced the Education for All Handicapped Children Act of 1975.

In order to qualify for federal financial assistance under the Act, a State must demonstrate that it "has in effect a policy that assures all handicapped children the right to a free appropriate public education." 20 U.S.C. § 1412(1). That policy must be reflected in a state plan submitted to and approved by the Secretary of Education which describes in detail the goals, programs, and timetables under which the State intends to educate handicapped children within its borders. §§ 1412, 1413. States receiving money under the Act must provide education to the handicapped by priority, first "to handicapped children who are not receiving an education" and second "to handicapped children . . . with the most severe handicaps who are receiving an inadequate education," § 1412(3), and "to the maximum extent appropriate" must educate handicapped children "with children who are not handicapped." § 1412(5). The Act broadly defines "handicapped children" to include "mentally retarded, hard of hearing, deaf, speech impaired, visually handicapped, seriously emotionally disturbed, orthopedically impaired, [and] other health impaired children, [and] children with specific learning disabilities." § 1401(1).

The "free appropriate public education" required by the Act is tailored to the unique needs of the handicapped child by means of an "individualized educational program" (IEP). § 1401(18). The IEP, which is prepared at a meeting between a qualified representative of the local educational agency, the child's teacher, the child's parents or guardian, and, where appropriate, the child, consists of a written document containing "(A) a statement of the present levels of educational performance of such child, (B) a statement of annual goals, including short-term instructional objectives, (C) a statement of the specific educational services to be provided to such child, and the extent to which such child will be able to participate in regular educational programs, (D) the projected date for initiation and anticipated duration of such services, and (E) appropriate objective criteria and evaluation procedures and schedules for determining, on at least an annual basis, whether instructional objectives are being achieved." § 1401(19). Local or regional educational agencies must review, and where appropriate revise, each child's IEP at least annually. § 1414(a)(5). See also § 1413(a)(11).

In addition to the state plan and the IEP already described, the Act imposes extensive procedural requirements upon States receiving federal funds under its provisions. Parents or guardians of handicapped children must be notified of any proposed change in "the identification, evaluation, or educational placement of the child or the provision of a free appropriate public education to such child," and must be permitted to bring a complaint about "any matter relating to" such evaluation and education. §§ 1415(b)(1)(D) and (E). . . . Complaints brought by parents or guardians must be resolved at "an impartial due process hearing," and appeal to the state educational agency must be provided if the initial hearing is held at the local or regional level. §§ 1415(b)(2) and (c). Thereafter, "[a]ny party aggrieved by the findings and decision" of the state administrative hearing has "the right to bring a civil action with respect to the complaint . . . in any State court of competent jurisdiction or in a district court of the United States without regard to the amount in controversy." § 1415(e)(2).

Thus, although the Act leaves to the States the primary responsibility for developing and executing educational programs for handicapped children, it imposes significant requirements to be followed in the discharge of that responsibility. Compliance is assured by provisions permitting the withholding of federal funds upon determination that a participating state or local agency has failed to satisfy the requirements of the Act, §§ 1414(b)(2)(A), 1416, and by the provision for judicial review. At present, all States except New Mexico receive federal funds under the portions of the Act at issue today. [Authors' note: New Mexico has subsequently adopted the requirements of the IDEA.]

II.

This case arose in connection with the education of Amy Rowley, a deaf student at the Furnace Woods School in the Hendrick Hudson Central School District, Peekskill, N.Y. Amy has minimal residual hearing and is an excellent lipreader. During the year before she began attending Furnace Woods, a meeting between her parents and school administrators resulted in a decision to place her in a regular kindergarten class in order to determine what supplemental services would be necessary to her education. Several members of the school administration prepared for Amy's arrival by attending a course in sign-language interpretation, and a teletype machine was installed in the principal's office to facilitate communication with her parents who are also deaf. At the end of the trial period it was determined that Amy should remain in the kindergarten class, but that she should be provided with an FM hearing aid which would amplify words spoken into a wireless receiver by the teacher or fellow students during certain classroom activities. Amy successfully completed her kindergarten year.

As required by the Act, an IEP [individualized educational program] was prepared for Amy during the fall of her first-grade year. The IEP provided that Amy should be educated in a regular classroom at Furnace Woods, should continue to use the FM hearing aid, and should receive instruction from a tutor for the deaf for one hour each day and from a speech therapist for three hours each week. The Rowleys agreed with parts of the IEP, but insisted that Amy also be provided a qualified sign-language interpreter in all her academic classes in lieu of the assistance proposed in other parts of the IEP. Such an interpreter had been placed in Amy's kindergarten class for a 2-week experimental period, but the interpreter had reported that Amy did not need his services at that time. The school administrators likewise concluded that Amy did not need such an interpreter in her first-grade classroom. They reached this conclusion after consulting the school district's Committee on the Handicapped, which had received expert evidence from Amy's parents on the importance of a sign-language interpreter, received testimony from Amy's teacher and other persons familiar with her academic and social progress, and visited a class for the deaf.

[Administrative hearing and lower court proceedings omitted.]

We granted certiorari to review the lower courts' interpretation of the Act. Such review requires us to consider two questions: What is meant by the Act's requirement of a "free appropriate public education"? And what is the role of state and federal courts in exercising the review granted by 20 U.S.C. § 1415? We consider these questions separately. [Authors' Note: The second issue is omitted.]

III.
A.

This is the first case in which this Court has been called upon to interpret any provision of the Act.

We are loath to conclude that Congress failed to offer any assistance in defining the meaning of the principal substantive phrase used in the Act. It is beyond dispute that, contrary to the conclusions of the courts below, the Act does expressly define "free appropriate public education": "The term 'free appropriate public education' means *special education* and *related services* which (A) have been provided at public expense, under public supervision and direction, and without charge, (B) meet the standards of the State educational agency, (C) include an appropriate preschool, elementary, or secondary school education in the State involved, and (D) are provided in conformity with the individualized education program required under section 1414(a)(5) of this title." § 1401(18) (emphasis added). "Special education," as referred to in this definition, means "specially designed instruction, at no cost to parents or guardians, to meet the unique needs of a handicapped child, including classroom instruction, instruction in physical education, home instruction, and instruction in hospitals and institutions." § 1401(16). "Related services" are defined as "transportation, and such developmental, corrective, and other supportive services . . . as may be required to assist a handicapped child to benefit from special education." § 1401(17).

Like many statutory definitions, this one tends toward the cryptic rather than the comprehensive, but that is scarcely a reason for abandoning the quest for legislative intent. Whether or not the definition is a "functional" one, as respondents contend it is not, it is the principal tool which Congress has given us for parsing the critical phrase of the Act. We think more must be made of it than either respondents or the United States seems willing to admit.

According to the definitions contained in the Act, a "free appropriate public education" consists of educational instruction specially designed to meet the unique needs of the handicapped child, supported by such services as are necessary to permit the child "to benefit" from the instruction. Almost as a checklist for adequacy under the Act, the definition also requires that such instruction and services be provided at public expense and under public supervision, meet the State's educational standards, approximate the grade levels used in the State's regular education, and comport with the child's IEP. Thus, if personalized instruction is being provided with sufficient supportive services to permit the child to benefit from the instruction, and the other items on the definitional checklist are satisfied, the child is receiving a "free appropriate public education" as defined by the Act.

Other portions of the statute also shed light upon congressional intent. Congress found that of the roughly eight million handicapped children in the United States at the time of enactment, one million were "excluded entirely from the public school system" and more than half were receiving an inappropriate education. . . .

Noticeably absent from the language of the statute is any substantive standard prescribing the level of education to be accorded handicapped children. Certainly the language of the statute contains no requirement like the one imposed by the lower courts — that States maximize the potential of handicapped children "commensurate with the opportunity provided to other children." That standard was expounded by the District Court without reference to the statutory definitions or even to the legislative history of the Act. . . .

B.
(i)

As suggested in Part I, federal support for education of the handicapped is a fairly recent development. Before passage of the Act some States had passed laws to improve the educational services afforded handicapped children, but many of these children were excluded completely from any form of public education or were left to fend for themselves in classrooms designed for education of their nonhandicapped peers. As previously noted, the House Report begins by emphasizing this exclusion and misplacement, noting that millions of handicapped children "were either totally excluded from schools or [were] sitting idly in regular classrooms awaiting the time when they were old enough to 'drop out.' "

This concern, stressed repeatedly throughout the legislative history, . . . confirms the impression conveyed by the language of the statute. By passing the Act, Congress sought primarily to make public education available to handicapped children. But in seeking to provide such access to public education, Congress did not impose upon the States any greater substantive educational standard than would be necessary to make such access meaningful. Indeed, Congress expressly "recognize[d] that in many instances the process of providing special education and related services to handicapped children is not guaranteed to produce any particular outcome." Thus, the intent of the Act was more to open the door of public education to handicapped children on appropriate terms than to guarantee any particular level of education once inside.

Both the House and the Senate Reports attribute the impetus for the Act and its predecessors to two federal-court judgments rendered in 1971 and 1972. As the Senate Report states, passage of the Act "followed a series of landmark court cases establishing in law the right to education for all handicapped children."

Mills and *PARC* [citations omitted] both held that handicapped children must be given access to an adequate, publicly supported education. Neither case purports to require any particular substantive level of education. Rather, like the language of the Act, the cases set forth extensive procedures to be followed in formulating personalized educational programs for handicapped children. The fact that both *PARC* and *Mills* are discussed at length in the legislative Reports suggests that the principles which they established are the principles which, to a significant extent, guided the drafters of the Act. Indeed, immediately after discussing these cases the Senate Report describes the 1974 statute as having "incorporated the major principles of the right to education cases." Those principles in turn became the basis of the Act, which itself was designed to effectuate the purposes of the 1974 statute.

That the Act imposes no clear obligation upon recipient States beyond the requirement that handicapped children receive some form of specialized education is perhaps best demonstrated by the fact that Congress, in explaining the need for the Act, equated an "appropriate education" to the receipt of some specialized educational services. The Senate Report states: "[T]he most recent statistics provided by the Bureau of Education for the Handicapped estimate that of the more than 8 million children . . . with handicapping conditions requiring special education and related services, only 3.9 million such children are receiving an appropriate education." This statement, which reveals Congress' view that 3.9 million handicapped children were "receiving an appropriate education" in 1975, is followed immediately in the Senate Report by a table showing that 3.9 million handicapped children were "served" in 1975 and a slightly larger number were "unserved." A similar statement and table appear in the House Report.

(ii)

Respondents contend that "the goal of the Act is to provide each handicapped child with an equal educational opportunity." We think, however, that the requirement that a State provide specialized educational services to handicapped children generates no additional requirement that the services so provided be sufficient to maximize each child's potential "commensurate with the opportunity provided other children." Respondents and the United States correctly note that Congress sought "to provide assistance to the States in carrying out their responsibilities under . . . the Constitution of the United States to provide equal protection of the laws." But we do not think that such statements imply a congressional intent to achieve strict equality of opportunity or services.

The educational opportunities provided by our public school systems undoubtedly differ from student to student, depending upon a myriad of factors that might affect a particular student's ability to assimilate information presented in the classroom. The requirement that States provide "equal" educational opportunities would thus seem to present an entirely unworkable standard requiring impossible measurements and comparisons. Similarly, furnishing handicapped children with only such services as are available to nonhandicapped children would in all probability fall short of the statutory requirement of "free appropriate public education"; to require, on the other hand, the furnishing of every special service necessary to maximize each handicapped child's potential is, we think, further than Congress intended to go. Thus to speak in terms of "equal" services in one instance gives less than what is required by the Act and in another instance more. The theme of the Act is "free appropriate public education," a phrase which is too complex to be captured by the word "equal" whether one is speaking of opportunities or services.

The legislative conception of the requirements of equal protection was undoubtedly informed by the two District Court decisions referred to above. But cases such as *Mills* and *PARC* held simply that handicapped children may not be excluded entirely from public education. In *Mills*, the District Court said:

> If sufficient funds are not available to finance all of the services and programs that are needed and desirable in the system then the available funds must be expended equitably in such a manner that no child is entirely excluded from a publicly supported education consistent with his needs and ability to benefit therefrom.

The *PARC* court used similar language, saying "[i]t is the commonwealth's obligation to place each mentally retarded child in a free, public program of education and training appropriate to the child's capacity. . . . " The right of access to free public education enunciated by these cases is significantly different from any notion of absolute equality of opportunity regardless of capacity. To the extent that Congress might have looked further than these cases which are mentioned in the legislative history, at the time of enactment of the Act this Court had held at least twice that the Equal Protection Clause of the Fourteenth Amendment does not require States to expend equal financial resources on the education of each child.

In explaining the need for federal legislation, the House Report noted that "no congressional legislation has required a precise guarantee for handicapped children, i.e. a basic floor of opportunity that would bring into compliance all school districts with the constitutional right of equal protection with respect to handicapped children." Assuming that the Act was designed to fill the need identified in the House Report — that is, to provide a "basic floor of opportunity" consistent with equal protection — neither the Act nor its history persuasively demonstrates that Congress thought that equal protection required anything more than equal access. Therefore, Congress' desire to provide specialized educational services, even in furtherance of "equality," cannot be read as imposing any particular substantive educational standard upon the States.

The District Court and the Court of Appeals thus erred when they held that the Act requires New York to maximize the potential of each handicapped child commensurate with the opportunity provided nonhandicapped children. Desirable though that goal might be, it is not the standard that Congress imposed upon States which receive funding under the Act. Rather, Congress sought primarily to identify and evaluate handicapped children, and to provide them with access to a free public education.

(iii)

Implicit in the congressional purpose of providing access to a "free appropriate public education" is the requirement that the education to which access is provided be sufficient to confer some educational benefit upon the handicapped child. It would do little good for Congress to spend millions of dollars in providing access to a public education only to have the handicapped child receive no benefit from that education. The statutory definition of "free appropriate public education," in addition to requiring that States provide each child with "specially designed instruction," expressly requires the provision of "such . . . supportive services . . . as may be required to assist a handicapped child *to benefit* from special education." § 1401(17) (emphasis added). We therefore conclude that the "basic floor of opportunity" provided by the Act consists of access to specialized instruction and related services which are individually designed to provide educational benefit to the handicapped child.

The determination of when handicapped children are receiving sufficient educational benefits to satisfy the requirements of the Act presents a more difficult problem. The Act requires participating States to educate a wide spectrum of handicapped children, from the marginally hearing-impaired to the profoundly retarded and palsied. It is clear that the benefits obtainable by children at one end of the spectrum will differ dramatically from those obtainable by children at the other end, with infinite variations in between. One child may have little difficulty competing successfully in an academic setting with nonhandicapped children while another child may encounter great difficulty in acquiring even the most basic of self-maintenance skills. We do not attempt today to establish any one test for determining the adequacy of educational benefits conferred upon all children covered by the Act. Because in this case we are presented with a handicapped child who is receiving substantial specialized instruction and related services, and who is performing above average in the regular classrooms of a public school system, we confine our analysis to that situation.

The Act requires participating States to educate handicapped children with nonhandicapped children whenever possible. When that "mainstreaming" preference of the Act has been met and a child is being educated in the regular classrooms of a public school system, the system itself monitors the educational progress of the child. Regular examinations are administered, grades are awarded, and yearly advancement to higher grade levels is permitted for those children who attain an adequate knowledge of the course material. The grading and advancement system thus constitutes an important factor in determining educational benefit. Children who graduate from our public school systems are considered by our society to have been "educated" at least to the grade level they have completed, and access to an "education" for handicapped children is precisely what Congress sought to provide in the Act.

C.

When the language of the Act and its legislative history are considered together, the requirements imposed by Congress become tolerably clear. Insofar as a State is required to provide a handicapped child with a "free appropriate public education," we hold that it satisfies this requirement by providing personalized instruction with sufficient support services to permit the child to benefit educationally from that instruction. Such instruction and services must be provided at public expense, must meet the State's educational standards, must approximate the grade levels used in the State's regular education, and must comport with the child's IEP. In addition, the IEP, and therefore the personalized instruction, should be formulated in accordance with the requirements of the Act and, if the child is being educated in the regular classrooms of the public education system, should be reasonably calculated to enable the child to achieve passing marks and advance from grade to grade.

IV.
A.

As mentioned in Part I, the Act permits "[a]ny party aggrieved by the findings and decision" of the state administrative hearings "to bring a civil action" in "any State court of competent jurisdiction or in a district court of the United States without regard to the amount in controversy." § 1415(e)(2). The complaint, and therefore the civil action, may concern "any matter relating to the identification, evaluation, or educational placement of the child, or the provision of a free appropriate public education to such child." § 1415(b)(1)(E). In reviewing the complaint, the Act provides that a court "shall receive the record of the [state] administrative proceedings, shall hear additional evidence at the request of a party, and, basing its decision on the preponderance of the evidence, shall grant such relief as the court determines is appropriate." § 1415(e)(2).

The parties disagree sharply over the meaning of these provisions, petitioners contending that courts are given only limited authority to review for state compliance with the Act's procedural requirements and no power to review the substance of the state program, and respondents contending that the Act requires courts to exercise de novo review over state educational decisions and policies. We find petitioners' contention unpersuasive, for Congress expressly rejected provisions that would have so severely restricted the role of reviewing courts. In substituting the current language of the statute for language that would have made state administrative findings conclusive if supported by substantial evidence, the Conference Committee explained that courts were to make "independent decision[s] based on a preponderance of the evidence."

But although we find that this grant of authority is broader than claimed by petitioners, we think the fact that it is found in § 1415, which is entitled "Procedural safeguards," is not without significance. When the elaborate and highly specific procedural safeguards embodied in § 1415 are contrasted with the general and somewhat imprecise substantive admonitions contained in the Act, we think that the importance Congress attached to these procedural safeguards cannot be gainsaid. It seems to us no exaggeration to say that Congress placed every bit as much emphasis upon compliance with procedures giving parents and guardians a large measure of participation at every stage of the administrative process, see e.g., §§ 1415(a)-(d), as it did upon the measurement of the resulting IEP against a substantive standard. We think that the congressional emphasis upon full participation of concerned parties throughout the development of the IEP, as well as the requirements that state and local plans be submitted to the Secretary for approval, demonstrates the legislative conviction that adequate compliance with the procedures prescribed would in most cases assure much if not all of what Congress wished in the way of substantive content in an IEP.

Thus the provision that a reviewing court base its decision on the "preponderance of the evidence" is by no means an invitation to the courts to substitute their own notions of sound educational policy for those of the school authorities which they review. The very importance which Congress has attached to compliance with certain procedures in the preparation of an IEP would be frustrated if a court were permitted simply to set state decisions at nought. The fact that § 1415(e) requires that the reviewing court "receive the records of the [state] administrative proceedings" carries with it the implied requirement that due weight shall be given to these proceedings. And we find nothing in the Act to suggest that merely because Congress was rather sketchy in establishing substantive requirements, as opposed to procedural requirements for the preparation of an IEP, it intended that reviewing courts should have a free hand to impose substantive standards of review which cannot be derived from the Act itself. In short, the statutory authorization to grant "such relief as the court determines is appropriate" cannot be read without reference to the obligations, largely procedural in nature, which are imposed upon recipient States by Congress.

Therefore, a court's inquiry in suits brought under § 1415(e)(2) is twofold. First, has the State complied with the procedures set forth in the Act? And second, is the individualized educational program developed through the Act's procedures reasonably calculated to enable the child to receive educational benefits? If these requirements are met, the State has complied with the obligations imposed by Congress and the courts can require no more.

B.

In assuring that the requirements of the Act have been met, courts must be careful to avoid imposing their view of preferable educational methods upon the States. The primary responsibility for formulating the education to be accorded a handicapped child, and for choosing the educational method most suitable to the child's needs, was left by the Act to state and local educational agencies in cooperation with the parents or guardian of the child. The Act expressly charges States with the responsibility of "acquiring and disseminating to teachers and administrators of programs for handicapped children significant information derived from educational research, demonstration, and similar projects, and [of] adopting, where appropriate, promising educational practices and materials." § 1413(a)(3). In the face of such a clear statutory directive, it seems highly unlikely that Congress intended courts to overturn a State's choice of appropriate educational theories in a proceeding conducted pursuant to § 1415(e)(2).

We previously have cautioned that courts lack the "specialized knowledge and experience" necessary to resolve "persistent and difficult questions of educational policy." We think that Congress shared that view when it passed the Act. As already demonstrated, Congress' intention was not that the Act displace the primacy of States in the field of education, but that States receive funds to assist them in extending their educational systems to the handicapped. Therefore, once a court determines that the requirements of the Act have been met, questions of methodology are for resolution by the States.

V.

Entrusting a child's education to state and local agencies does not leave the child without protection. Congress sought to protect individual children by providing for parental involvement in the development of state plans and policies, and in the formulation of the child's individual educational program. As the Senate Report states: "The Committee recognizes that in many instances the process of providing special education and related services to handicapped children is not guaranteed to produce any particular outcome. By changing the language [of the provision relating to individualized educational programs] to emphasize the process of parent and child involvement and to provide a written record of reasonable expectations, the Committee intends to clarify that such individualized planning conferences are a way to provide parent involvement and protection to assure that appropriate services are provided to a handicapped child." 34 CFR § 300.345 (1981). As this very case demonstrates, parents and guardians will not lack ardor in seeking to ensure that handicapped children receive all of the benefits to which they are entitled by the Act.

VI.

Applying these principles to the facts of this case, we conclude that the Court of Appeals erred in affirming the decision of the District Court. Neither the District Court nor the Court of Appeals found that petitioners had failed to comply with the procedures of the Act, and the findings of neither court would support a conclusion that Amy's educational program failed to comply with the substantive requirements of the Act. On the contrary, the District Court found that the "evidence firmly establishes that Amy is receiving an 'adequate' education, since she performs better than the average child in her class and is advancing easily from grade to grade." In light of this finding, and of the fact that Amy was receiving personalized instruction and related services calculated by the Furnace Woods school administrators to meet her educational needs, the lower courts should not have concluded that the Act requires the provision of a sign-language interpreter. Accordingly, the decision of the Court of Appeals is reversed, and the case is remanded for further proceedings consistent with this opinion.

So ordered.

[Concurring and dissenting opinions omitted.]

NOTES

1. *Education for Deaf Students:* There is substantial controversy about the best or most appropriate method of education for children who are deaf. In light of the compelling arguments that are made on behalf of various methodologies, the Supreme Court and other courts have wisely deferred to the educational agencies to make these decisions. Schools are not required to provide the *best* education, but they are required to provide education that is *individualized* to the needs of the particular child. For that reason, it would seem that an educational agency should evaluate each child's needs and abilities and not assume that a particular methodology is necessarily appropriate for all children who are deaf. See Andrew Solomon, *Deaf Is Beautiful*, N.Y. TIMES MAG. 40 (August 28, 1994); Edward Dolnick, *Deafness as Culture*, ATLANTIC MONTHLY 37 (September 1993).

2. *Higher State Standards Than "Appropriate":* Although federal special education law has been interpreted in *Rowley* to mean that schools are not required to provide the best special education or to provide education that will maximize the potential of the child, some states have set higher standards. Courts have consistently held that federal procedural safeguards under the IDEA may be applied to substantive protections that are greater than the IDEA. For example, in *Amann v. Stow Sch. Sys.*, 982 F.2d 644 (1st Cir. 1992), the court upheld the potential maximization standard. In *D.R. v. East Brunswick Bd. of Ed.*, 838 F. Supp. 184 (D.N.J. 1993), the court recognized a standard requiring that students receive services that allow them to best achieve success in learning. Recognizing the limits of even state laws assuring maximum possible development, the court in *Frank S. v. School Committee of Dennis-Yarmouth Regional School Dist.*, 26 F. Supp. 2d 219 (D. Mass. 1998), held that a school is not required to mold a child in to a "responsible and independent individual capable of interacting with the material world around him."

3. *State Minimum Standards Not Dispositive of "Appropriateness":* In the early years after passage of EAHCA, there are some educational policies set by state agencies that were used by the educational agencies as the basis for denying certain programming to children with disabilities. In *Battle v. Commonwealth*, 629 F.2d 269 (3d Cir. 1980), the court addressed a state policy of providing 180 school days per year to all children. The state's position in the class action by special education students claiming a need for year-round programming to avoid significant regression was that the state was required to provide only the same number of school days for special education children as were provided for everyone else. The court found that this policy violated the EAHCA because it did not meet the mandate that education be individualized and appropriate to each child's needs. All other decisions on this and similar issues have reached consistent results. LAURA ROTHSTEIN & JULIA ROTHSTEIN, DISABILITIES AND THE LAW § 2.20, note 17 (2009).

4. *Deference to Educational Agencies:* The *Rowley* decision has been closely adhered to by courts in terms of not second guessing educational agencies and recognizing that schools are in a much better position to evaluate and decide about educational methodology. That does not mean that the courts have never required the schools to provide something different than was initially recommended by the schools. This is particularly true in a number of cases relating to least restrictive environment, which is discussed later in this chapter.

The burden of proof issue was addressed by the Supreme Court in 2005 in its decision in *Schaffer v. Weast*, 126 S. Ct. 528 (2005). The Court recognized that the IDEA is silent on the issue, but decided that the burden of proof falls on the party seeking relief. This recognizes Congressional deference to the expertise of educational agencies, which is balanced through extensive procedural safeguards.

5.   In footnote 23 of the *Rowley* decision, which is omitted from the excerpt in this chapter, the Court quotes from the legislative history and notes that:

> The long range implications of these statistics are that public agencies and taxpayers will spend billions of dollars over the lifetimes of these individuals to maintain such persons as dependents and in a minimally acceptable lifestyle. With proper education services, many would increase their independence, thus reducing their dependence on society.

Although the IDEA is important and necessary primarily to society from an equal protection and due process perspective, the economic benefits should not be forgotten.

[2]   Related Services

One issue that has given educational agencies and, as a result, the courts difficulty is the issue of related services. Such services are to be provided when they are necessary for the child to benefit from special education. When services relate to health care, questions arise about whether such services are required under the special education mandates. The next case illustrates the Supreme Court's response to this question.

HYPOTHETICAL PROBLEM 7.2

Matt is a mature 11-year-old student in 7th grade at a public school. He was recently diagnosed with diabetes and needs to check his insulin levels on a regular basis and inject insulin or have juice or other food, depending on his blood sugar levels. Matt's parents contact the school principal to inquire about the following: whether Matt can carry and self administer the glucose checking apparatus and/or his insulin; whether a school nurse or other school personnel would be available to assist with this if necessary and what arrangements would be made if that person were absent or out of the building. The school has a policy that prohibits students from carrying medication and self administering. Matt's sugar levels are generally stable, but if he has a problem, it is critical that his sugar levels be corrected fairly quickly. Matt also wants to participate on the middle school football team, and the school is concerned about liability and medication issues.

What is legally required under any of the applicable federal statutes? What is the best way to resolve this? What if Matt had asthma instead and needed to be able to use his inhaler and carry it with him? What if Matt had a peanut allergy and wanted to carry an Epi-pen to deal with possible anaphylaxis, a severe allergic reaction from exposure to peanuts or peanut products? What if Matt's parents requested that peanuts and peanut products not be allowed at his school? What if

Matt were 8 instead of 11, or if he were 17? Consider these questions in reading the following materials.

IRVING INDEPENDENT SCHOOL DISTRICT v. TATRO
468 U.S. 883 (1984)

CHIEF JUSTICE BURGER delivered the opinion of the Court:

We granted certiorari to determine whether the Education of the Handicapped Act or the Rehabilitation Act of 1973 requires a school district to provide a handicapped child with clean intermittent catheterization during school hours.

I.

Amber Tatro is an 8-year-old girl born with a defect known as spina bifida. As a result, she suffers from orthopedic and speech impairments and a neurogenic bladder, which prevents her from emptying her bladder voluntarily. Consequently, she must be catheterized every three or four hours to avoid injury to her kidneys. In accordance with accepted medical practice, clean intermittent catheterization (CIC), a procedure involving the insertion of a catheter into the urethra to drain the bladder, has been prescribed. The procedure is a simple one that may be performed in a few minutes by a layperson with less than an hour's training. Amber's parents, babysitter, and teenage brother are all qualified to administer CIC, and Amber soon will be able to perform this procedure herself.

In 1979 petitioner Irving Independent School District agreed to provide special education for Amber, who was then three and one-half years old. In consultation with her parents, who are respondents here, petitioner developed an individualized education program for Amber under the requirements of the Education of the Handicapped Act as amended significantly by the Education for All Handicapped Children Act of 1975, 20 U.S.C. §§ 1401(19), 1414(a)(5). The individualized education program provided that Amber would attend early childhood development classes and receive special services such as physical and occupational therapy. That program, however, made no provision for school personnel to administer CIC.

Respondents unsuccessfully pursued administrative remedies to secure CIC services for Amber during school hours. In October 1979 respondents brought the present action in District Court against petitioner, the State Board of Education, and others. They sought an injunction ordering petitioner to provide Amber with CIC and sought damages and attorney's fees. First, respondents invoked the Education of the Handicapped Act. Because Texas received funding under that statute, petitioner was required to provide Amber with a "free appropriate public education," which is defined to include "related services." Respondents argued that CIC is one such "related service." Second, respondents invoked § 504 of the Rehabilitation Act of 1973, which forbids an individual, by reason of a handicap, to be "excluded from the participation in, be denied the benefits of, or be subjected to discrimination under" any program receiving federal aid.

[Lower court proceedings omitted.]

II.

This case poses two separate issues. The first is whether the Education of the Handicapped Act requires petitioner to provide CIC services to Amber. The second is whether § 504 of the Rehabilitation Act creates such an obligation. We first turn to the claim presented under the Education of the Handicapped Act.

States receiving funds under the Act are obliged to satisfy certain conditions. A primary condition is that the state implement a policy "that assures all handicapped children the right to a free appropriate public education." Each educational agency applying to a state for funding must provide assurances in turn that its program aims to provide "a free appropriate public education to all handicapped children."

A "free appropriate public education" is explicitly defined as "special education and related services." The term "special education" means

> specially designed instruction, at no cost to parents or guardians, to meet the unique needs of a handicapped child, including classroom instruction, instruction in physical education, home instruction, and instruction in hospitals and institutions.

§ 1401(16).

"Related services" are defined as

> transportation, and such developmental, corrective, and other *supportive services (including* speech pathology and audiology, psychological services, physical and occupational therapy, recreation, and *medical* and counseling *services, except that such medical services shall be for diagnostic and evaluation purposes only) as may be required to assist a handicapped child to benefit from special education,* and includes the early identification and assessment of handicapping conditions in children.

§ 1401(17) (emphasis added).

The issue in this case is whether CIC is a "related service" that petitioner is obliged to provide to Amber. We must answer two questions: first, whether CIC is a "supportive servic[e] required to assist a handicapped child to benefit from special education"; and second, whether CIC is excluded from this definition as a "medical servic[e]" serving purposes other than diagnosis or evaluation.

A.

The Court of Appeals was clearly correct in holding that CIC is a "supportive servic[e] required to assist a handicapped child to benefit from special education." It is clear on this record that, without having CIC services available during the school day, Amber cannot attend school and thereby "benefit from special education." CIC services therefore fall squarely within the definition of a "supportive service."

As we have stated before, "Congress sought primarily to make public education available to handicapped children" and "to make such access meaningful." [Citing to *Rowley*.] A service that enables a handicapped child to remain at school during the day is an important means of providing the child with the meaningful access to education that Congress envisioned. The Act makes specific provision for services, like transportation, for example, that do no more than enable a child to be physically present in class; and the Act specifically authorizes grants for schools to alter buildings and equipment to make them accessible to the handicapped. Services like CIC that permit a child to remain at school during the day are no less related to the effort to educate than are services that enable the child to reach, enter, or exit the school.

We hold that CIC services in this case qualify as a "supportive servic[e] required to assist a handicapped child to benefit from special education."

B.

We also agree with the Court of Appeals that provision of CIC is not a "medical servic[e]," which a school is required to provide only for purposes of diagnosis or evaluation. See 20 U.S.C. § 1401(17). We begin with the regulations of the Department of Education, which are entitled to deference. The regulations define "related services" for handicapped children to include "school health services," which are defined in turn as "services provided by a qualified school nurse or other qualified person." "Medical services" are defined as "services provided by a licensed physician." Thus, the Secretary has determined that the services of a school nurse otherwise qualifying as a "related service" are not subject to exclusion as a "medical service," but that the services of a physician are excludable as such.

This definition of "medical services" is a reasonable interpretation of congressional intent. Although Congress devoted little discussion to the "medical services" exclusion, the Secretary could reasonably have concluded that it was designed to spare schools from an obligation to provide a service that might well prove unduly expensive and beyond the range of their competence. . . . From this understanding of congressional purpose, the Secretary could reasonably have concluded that Congress intended to impose the obligation to provide school nursing services.

Congress plainly required schools to hire various specially trained personnel to help handicapped children, such as "trained occupational therapists, speech therapists, psychologists, social workers and other appropriately trained personnel." School nurses have long been a part of the educational system, and the Secretary could therefore reasonably conclude that school nursing services are not the sort of burden that Congress intended to exclude as a "medical service." By limiting the "medical services" exclusion to the services of a physician or hospital, both far more expensive, the Secretary has given a permissible construction to the provision.

Petitioner's contrary interpretation of the "medical services" exclusion is unconvincing. In petitioner's view, CIC is a "medical service," even though it may be provided by a nurse or trained layperson; that conclusion rests on its reading of Texas law that confines CIC to uses in accordance with a physician's prescription and under a physician's ultimate supervision. Aside from conflicting with the

Secretary's reasonable interpretation of congressional intent, however, such a rule would be anomalous. Nurses in petitioner's school district are authorized to dispense oral medications and administer emergency injections in accordance with a physician's prescription. This kind of service for nonhandicapped children is difficult to distinguish from the provision of CIC to the handicapped. It would be strange indeed if Congress, in attempting to extend special services to handicapped children, were unwilling to guarantee them services of a kind that are routinely provided to the nonhandicapped.

To keep in perspective the obligation to provide services that relate to both the health and educational needs of handicapped students, we note several limitations that should minimize the burden petitioner fears. First, to be entitled to related services, a child must be handicapped so as to require special education. In the absence of a handicap that requires special education, the need for what otherwise might qualify as a related service does not create an obligation under the Act.

Second, only those services necessary to aid a handicapped child to benefit from special education must be provided, regardless how easily a school nurse or layperson could furnish them. For example, if a particular medication or treatment may appropriately be administered to a handicapped child other than during the school day, a school is not required to provide nursing services to administer it.

Third, the regulations state that school nursing services must be provided only if they can be performed by a nurse or other qualified person, not if they must be performed by a physician. It bears mentioning that here not even the services of a nurse are required; as is conceded, a layperson with minimal training is qualified to provide CIC.

Finally, we note that respondents are not asking petitioner to provide equipment that Amber needs for CIC. They seek only the services of a qualified person at the school.

We conclude that provision of CIC to Amber is not subject to exclusion as a "medical service," and we affirm the Court of Appeals' holding that CIC is a "related service" under the Education of the Handicapped Act.

III.

Respondents sought relief not only under the Education of the Handicapped Act but under § 504 of the Rehabilitation Act as well. After finding petitioner liable to provide CIC under the former, the District Court proceeded to hold that petitioner was similarly liable under § 504 and that respondents were therefore entitled to attorney's fees under § 505 of the Rehabilitation Act, 29 U.S.C. § 794a. We hold today, in *Smith v. Robinson* . . . that § 504 is inapplicable when relief is available under the Education of the Handicapped Act to remedy a denial of educational services. Respondents are therefore not entitled to relief under § 504, and we reverse the Court of Appeals' holding that respondents are entitled to recover attorney's fees. In all other respects, the judgment of the Court of Appeals is affirmed.

It is so ordered.

[Concurring and dissenting opinions omitted.]

_____

The following opinion addresses some of the issues left unresolved by the *Tatro* decision.

CEDAR RAPIDS COMMUNITY SCHOOL DISTRICT v. GARRET F.
526 U.S. 66 (1999)

JUSTICE STEVENS delivered the opinion of the Court.

The Individuals with Disabilities Education Act (IDEA), was enacted, in part, "to assure that all children with disabilities have available to them . . . a free appropriate public education which emphasizes special education and related services designed to meet their unique needs." Consistent with this purpose, the IDEA authorizes federal financial assistance to States that agree to provide disabled children with special education and "related services." The question presented in this case is whether the definition of "related services" in § 1401(a)(17) requires a public school district in a participating State to provide a ventilator-dependent student with certain nursing services during school hours.

I

Respondent Garret F. is a friendly, creative, and intelligent young man. When Garret was four years old, his spinal column was severed in a motorcycle accident. Though paralyzed from the neck down, his mental capacities were unaffected. He is able to speak, to control his motorized wheelchair through use of a puff and suck straw, and to operate a computer with a device that responds to head movements. Garret is currently a student in the Cedar Rapids Community School District (District), he attends regular classes in a typical school program, and his academic performance has been a success. Garret is, however, ventilator dependent, and therefore requires a responsible individual nearby to attend to certain physical needs while he is in school.[1]

During Garret's early years at school his family provided for his physical care during the school day. When he was in kindergarten, his 18-year-old aunt attended him; in the next four years, his family used settlement proceeds they received after the accident, their insurance, and other resources to employ a licensed practical nurse. In 1993, Garret's mother requested the District to accept financial responsibility for the health care services that Garret requires during the school

_____

[1] He needs assistance with urinary bladder catheterization once a day, the suctioning of his tracheotomy tube as needed, but at least once every six hours, with food and drink at lunchtime, in getting into a reclining position for five minutes of each hour, and ambu bagging occasionally as needed when the ventilator is checked for proper functioning. He also needs assistance from someone familiar with his ventilator in the event there is a malfunction or electrical problem, and someone who can perform emergency procedures in the event he experiences autonomic hyperreflexia. [Explanation of this condition omitted.]

day. The District denied the request, believing that it was not legally obligated to provide continuous one-on-one nursing services.

The administrative judge concluded that the IDEA required the District to bear financial responsibility for all of the services in dispute, including continuous nursing services. The district and appellate court agreed with the administrative decision. [These proceedings are omitted.]

II

The District contends that § 1401(a)(17) does not require it to provide Garret with "continuous one-on-one nursing services" during the school day, even though Garret cannot remain in school without such care. However, the IDEA's definition of "related services," our decision in *Irving Independent School District v. Tatro*, 468 U.S. 883 (1984), and the overall statutory scheme all support the decision of the Court of Appeals.

The text of the "related services" definition, broadly encompasses those supportive services that "may be required to assist a child with a disability to benefit from special education." As we have already noted, the District does not challenge the Court of Appeals' conclusion that the in-school services at issue are within the covered category of "supportive services." As a general matter, services that enable a disabled child to remain in school during the day provide the student with "the meaningful access to education that Congress envisioned." This general definition of "related services" is illuminated by a parenthetical phrase listing examples of particular services that are included within the statute's coverage. § 1401(a)(17). "Medical services" are enumerated in this list, but such services are limited to those that are "for diagnostic and evaluation purposes." The statute does not contain a more specific definition of the "medical services" that are excepted from the coverage of § 1401(a)(17).

The scope of the "medical services" exclusion is not a matter of first impression in this Court. In *Tatro*, we concluded that the Secretary of Education had reasonably determined that the term "medical services" referred only to services that must be performed by a physician, and not to school health services. Accordingly, we held that a specific form of health care (clean intermittent catherization) that is often, though not always, performed by a nurse is not an excluded medical service. We referenced the likely cost of the services and the competence of school staff as justifications for drawing a line between physician and other services, but our endorsement of that line was unmistakable. It is thus settled that the phrase "medical services" in § 1401(a)(17) does not embrace all forms of care that might loosely be described as "medical" in other contexts, such as a claim for an income tax deduction.

Based on certain policy letters issued by the Department of Education, it seems that the Secretary's post-*Tatro* view of the statute has not been entirely clear. We may assume that the Secretary has authority under the IDEA to adopt regulations that define the "medical services" exclusion by more explicitly taking into account the nature and extent of the requested services; and the Secretary surely has the authority to enumerate the services that are, and are not, fairly included within the scope of § 1407(a)(17). But the Secretary has done neither; and, in this Court, she advocates affirming the judgment of the Court of Appeals. We obviously have no authority to rewrite the regulations, and we see no sufficient reason to revise *Tatro* either.

The District does not ask us to define the term so broadly. Indeed, the District does not argue that any of the items of care that Garret needs, considered individually, could be excluded from the scope of § 1401(a)(17). It could not make such an argument, considering that one of the services Garret needs (catheterization) was at issue in *Tatro*, and the others may be provided competently by a school nurse or other trained personnel. As the [Administrative Law Judge] concluded, most of the requested services are already provided by the District to other students, and the in-school care necessitated by Garret's ventilator dependency does not demand the training, knowledge, and judgment of a licensed physician. While more extensive, the in-school services Garret needs are no more "medical" than was the care sought in *Tatro*.

Instead, the District points to the combined and continuous character of the required care, and proposes a test under which the outcome in any particular case would "depend upon a series of factors, such as [1] whether the care is continuous or intermittent, [2] whether existing school health personnel can provide the service, [3] the cost of the service, and [4] the potential consequences if the service is not properly performed."

The District's multi-factor test is not supported by any recognized source of legal authority. The proposed factors can be found in neither the text of the statute nor the regulations that we upheld in *Tatro*. Moreover, the District offers no explanation why these characteristics make one service any more "medical" than another. The continuous character of certain services associated with Garret's ventilator dependency has no apparent relationship to "medical" services, much less a relationship of equivalence. Continuous services may be more costly and may require additional school personnel, but they are not thereby more "medical." Whatever its imperfections, a rule that limits the medical services exemption to physician services is unquestionably a reasonable and generally workable interpretation of the statute. Absent an elaboration of the statutory terms plainly more convincing than that which we reviewed in *Tatro*, there is no good reason to depart from settled law.

Finally, the District raises broader concerns about the financial burden that it must bear to provide the services that Garret needs to stay in school. The problem for the District in providing these services is not that its staff cannot be trained to deliver them; the problem, the District contends, is that the existing school health staff cannot meet all of their responsibilities and provide for Garret at the same time. Through its multi-factor test, the District seeks to establish a kind of undue-burden exemption primarily based on the cost of the requested services. The first two factors can be seen as examples of cost-based distinctions: intermittent care is often less expensive than continuous care, and the use of existing personnel is cheaper than hiring additional employees. The third factor-the cost of the service-would then encompass the first two. The relevance of the fourth factor is likewise related to cost because extra care may be necessary if potential consequences are especially serious.

The District may have legitimate financial concerns, but our role in this dispute is to interpret existing law. Defining "related services" in a manner that accommodates the cost concerns Congress may have had, is altogether different from using cost itself as the definition. Given that § 1401(a)(17) does not employ cost in its definition of "related services" or excluded "medical services," accepting the District's cost-based standard as the sole test for determining the scope of the provision would require us to engage in judicial lawmaking without any guidance from Congress. It would also create some tension with the purposes of the IDEA. The statute may not require public schools to maximize the potential of disabled students commensurate with the opportunities provided to other children; and the potential financial burdens imposed on participating States may be relevant to arriving at a sensible construction of the IDEA. But Congress intended "to open the door of public education" to all qualified children and "require[d] participating States to educate handicapped children with nonhandicapped children whenever possible."[2]

This case is about whether meaningful access to the public schools will be assured, not the level of education that a school must finance once access is attained. It is undisputed that the services at issue must be provided if Garret is to remain in school. Under the statute, our precedent, and the purposes of the IDEA, the District must fund such "related services" in order to help guarantee that students like Garret are integrated into the public schools.

The judgment of the Court of Appeals is accordingly Affirmed.

NOTES

1. *Psychological Services:* Psychological counseling is intended to be a related service that the school is to provide if it is essential to the child's ability to benefit from special education. 34 C.F.R. § 300.13(a). The major difficulty occurs in sorting out the interrelationship between educational and noneducational needs. This same difficulty occurs in deciding when a student is eligible for residential programming to be provided through the educational agency. For example, an adolescent who

---

[2] The dissent's approach, which seems to be even broader than the District's, is unconvincing. The dissent's rejection of our unanimous decision in *Tatro*; comes 15 years too late. Moreover, the dissent's approach apparently would exclude most ordinary school nursing services of the kind routinely provided to nondisabled children; that anomalous result is not easily attributable to congressional intent.

In a later discussion the dissent does offer a specific proposal: that we now interpret (or rewrite) the Secretary's regulations so that school districts need only provide disabled children with "health-related services that school nurses can perform as part of their normal duties." The District does not dispute that its nurses "can perform" the requested services, so the dissent's objection is that District nurses would not be performing their "normal duties" if they met Garret's needs. That is, the District would need an "additional employee." This proposal is functionally similar to a proposed regulation-ultimately withdraw-that would have replaced the "school health services" provision. The dissent's suggestion is unacceptable for several reasons. Most important, such revisions of the regulations are better left to the Secretary, and an additional staffing need is generally not a sufficient objection to the requirements of § 1401(a)(17).

becomes depressed or troubled as part of the growing up process may benefit from psychological counseling, but unless the need for services becomes so great as to interfere with the educational experience, the student is ineligible for the service to be provided through federal special education mandates. This approach has been criticized as a policy because it fails to provide for intervention until the problem is severe. Earlier intervention might prevent severe problems later. This issue is discussed in depth in Theresa Glennon, *Disabled Ambiguities: Confronting Barriers to the Education of Students with Emotional Disabilities*, 60 TENN. L. REV. 295 (1993).

2. *Transportation:* Transportation is perhaps the most expensive service provided for special education because of the capital expenditures involved in purchasing and maintaining school buses and special vehicles with hydraulic lift devices. The Americans with Disabilities Act portions related to mass transit specify that public school transportation is not covered within the ADA. 42 U.S.C. § 12141(2). The IDEA contemplates that transportation is a part of special education programming. 34 C.F.R. § 300.13(b)(13). Requirements relating to time in transit, type of equipment required, bus routes, and transportation personnel, however, are usually found in state and local policies. Cases related to transportation and students with disabilities have addressed what is meant by door-to-door service, whether students can be disciplined by denying them the right to ride the school bus, and whether a school must purchase a special vehicle to reach a child living in a remote area with poor roads. In *Donald v. Board of Sch. Comm'rs*, 117 F.3d 1371 (11th Cir. 1997), the court held that the educational agency is not responsible for transporting a student from a private school to a public school to receive therapy. See LAURA ROTHSTEIN & JULIA ROTHSTEIN, DISABILITIES AND THE LAW § 2.26 (2009).

3. *Providing Related Services to Parochial Schools:* Two Supreme Court decisions have addressed the issue of providing related services to parochial schools. The issue arises because governmental agencies are prohibited from providing direct aid to religious schools because of First Amendment separation of church and state doctrinal interpretations. See *Aguilar v. Felton*, 473 U.S. 402 (1985). In 1993, the Supreme Court permitted public schools to pay for interpreter services for a deaf student in a parochial school. The Court basically held that such services are neutral and benefit the child rather than the parochial school. *Zobrest v. Catalina Foothills Sch. Dist.*, 509 U.S. 1 (1993).

A year later the Court addressed the constitutionality of a state statute creating a new school district within the Hasidic sect community in New York City. The purpose of creating the special public school district was to allow the public school system to provide special education and related services to children in this community. Part of the Hasidic sect's religious practice is to avoid interaction between boys and girls in certain activities and between nonmembers of the community and those who are members of the community. The Court struck down the statute as being unconstitutional. *Board of Ed. v. Grumet*, 512 U.S. 687 (1994).

In *Russman v. Sobol*, 85 F.3d 1050 (2d Cir. 1996), the court held that it did not violate the establishment clause of the Constitution for the public school system to provide a consultant teacher and teacher's aide to a mentally retarded student in a parochial school. The court further held that the IDEA required the provision of such services at the parochial school site.

In 1997, the Supreme Court again looked at the issue of public aid to parochial schools. In *Agostini v. Felton*, 521 U.S. 203 (1997), the Court allowed public school teachers to provide special education and related services to children in parochial schools in the same way that the services are provided in other private school settings. The 2004 IDEA amendments clarified to some degree whether public schools can provide special education services at a parochial school site. The amendments allow, but do not require, services at the parochial site, to the extent it is consistent with law. 20 U.S.C. § 1412(a)(10)(A)(1)(iii). This leaves it to be resolved what is "consistent with law."

For a more detailed discussion of this issue, see LAURA ROTHSTEIN & JULIA ROTHSTEIN, DISABILITIES AND THE LAW § 2.29 (2009).

4. *Providing Services in Private School Settings*: There has been much controversy about the degree of obligation that a public school has to provide special education and related services when parents have voluntarily placed their children in private school settings.

The 1997 amendments to IDEA provided some clarification on this issue. The amendments provide that the educational agency is not obligated to provide certain related services and programming at the private school site, where the student has been offered a free appropriate individualized education program at the public school site, when the parents voluntarily transfer the student to a private school. 20 U.S.C. § 1412(10)(C) (1997). See also LAURA ROTHSTEIN & JULIA ROTHSTEIN, DISABILITIES AND THE LAW § 2.28 (2009).

[3]   Least Restrictive Environment — Mainstreaming

The Individuals with Disabilities Education Act does not use the term "mainstreaming" in the statutory language or in the regulations. The term is commonly used, however, to indicate the philosophy of providing education in the least restrictive environment. The goal is to provide education in the mainstream of the regular class if possible.

In the early 1990s, a strong advocacy movement calling for "full inclusion" as its primary goal has pressed for mainstreaming in the regular classroom to be used much more than it is today. This is a controversial topic. Many teachers feel that they are not adequately prepared or staffed for children with needs that will put significant demands on their time. They also are concerned about children with behavior problems in the regular classroom. Some parents of children without disabilities are concerned about the needs of their children being neglected if children with disabilities are included in the regular classroom. Some parents of children with disabilities also are concerned about the specialized services their children need and may not receive if they are in the regular classroom.

The advocates who press for full inclusion, however, note that mainstreaming is one of the major principles in not only the IDEA, but in other laws enacted to protect individuals with disabilities. The benefits of mainstreaming include stigma avoidance and peer modeling. The other key principle to keep in mind, however, is individualization. Each child's needs are to be met by an individualized placement plan. The needs and development of the child are to be reevaluated periodically. While it may be appropriate to place a child in a separate special education resource room during first and second grades, the goal should be to consider less restrictive placements on an ongoing basis.

HYPOTHETICAL PROBLEM 7.3

Lisa is seven years old with moderate mental retardation. She has been successfully mainstreamed in first and second grade. She is making very good progress, and her classroom teacher believes that she would be able to continue in third grade so long as a summer program were provided to prevent or reduce regression. The school district in which Lisa attends public school has such a summer program, but it is only for students with special education needs. Do the mainstreaming requirements mandate that they enroll other students in the summer program? What if a private school had a summer program for students with disabilities, which also included students who did not have disabilities? If the evaluation determines that Lisa would benefit from having summer programming to retain not only academic skills, but also social skills, would that make a difference?

The following case demonstrates one standard that is applied in determining whether a student should be placed in the regular classroom. It should be noted that the courts have applied a variety of tests in making these determinations. In reading this case, note the weight the court gives to different evidence and the reason for doing so. Review the previous hypothetical problems and consider the evidence that either party might provide and the weight that could be given to that evidence.

SACRAMENTO CITY UNIFIED SCHOOL DISTRICT v. RACHEL H.
14 F.3d 1398 (9th Cir. 1994)

SNEED, CIRCUIT JUDGE:

Facts and Prior Proceedings

Rachel Holland is now 11 years old and is mentally retarded. She was tested with an I.Q. of 44. She attended a variety of special education programs in the District from 1985–89. Her parents sought to increase the time Rachel spent in a regular classroom, and in the fall of 1989, they requested that Rachel be placed full-time in a regular classroom for the 1989–90 school year. The District rejected their request and proposed a placement that would have divided Rachel's time between a special education class for academic subjects and a regular class for non-academic activities such as art, music, lunch, and recess. The district court found that this plan would have required moving Rachel at least six times each day between the two classrooms. The Hollands instead enrolled Rachel in a regular kindergarten class at the Shalom School, a private school. Rachel remained at the Shalom School in regular classes and at the time the district court rendered its opinion was in the second grade.

In considering whether the District proposed an appropriate placement for Rachel, the district court examined the following factors: (1) the educational benefits available to Rachel in a regular classroom, supplemented with appropriate aids and services, as compared with the educational benefits of a special education classroom; (2) the non-academic benefits of interaction with children who were not disabled; (3) the effect of Rachel's presence on the teacher and other children in the classroom; and (4) the cost of mainstreaming Rachel in a regular classroom.

1. *Educational Benefits*

The district court found the first factor, educational benefits to Rachel, weighed in favor of placing her in a regular classroom. Each side presented expert testimony. The court noted that the District's evidence focused on Rachel's limitations but did not establish that the educational opportunities available through special education were better or equal to those available in a regular classroom. Moreover, the court found that the testimony of the Hollands' experts was more credible because they had more background in evaluating children with disabilities placed in regular classrooms and that they had a greater opportunity to observe Rachel over an extended period of time in normal circumstances. The district court also gave great weight to the testimony of Rachel's current teacher, Nina Crone, whom the court found to be an experienced, skillful teacher. Ms. Crone stated that Rachel was a full member of the class and participated in all activities. Ms. Crone testified that Rachel was making progress on her IEP goals: She was learning one-to-one correspondence in counting, was able to recite the English and Hebrew alphabets, and was improving her communication abilities and sentence lengths.

The district court found that Rachel received substantial benefits in regular education and that all of her IEP goals could be implemented in a regular classroom with some modification to the curriculum and with the assistance of a part-time aide.

2. *Non-academic Benefits*

The district court next found that the second factor, non-academic benefits to Rachel, also weighed in favor of placing her in a regular classroom. The court noted that the Hollands' evidence indicated that Rachel had developed her social and communications skills as well as her self-confidence from placement in a regular class, while the District's evidence tended to show that Rachel was not learning from exposure to other children and that she was isolated from her classmates. The court concluded that the differing evaluations in large part reflected the predisposition of the evaluators. The court found the testimony of Rachel's mother and her current teacher to be the most credible. These witnesses testified regarding Rachel's excitement about school, learning, and her new friendships and Rachel's improved self-confidence.

3. *Effect on the Teacher and Children in the Regular Class*

The district court next addressed the issue of whether Rachel had a detrimental effect on others in her regular classroom. The court looked at two aspects: (1) whether there was detriment because the child was disruptive, distracting or unruly, and (2) whether the child would take up so much of the teacher's time that the other students would suffer from lack of attention. The witnesses of both parties agreed that Rachel followed directions and was well-behaved and not a distraction in class. The court found the most germane evidence on the second aspect came from Rachel's second grade teacher, Nina Crone, who testified that Rachel did not interfere with her ability to teach the other children and in the future would require only a part-time aide. Accordingly, the district court determined that the third factor, the effect of Rachel's presence on the teacher and other children in the classroom weighed in favor of placing her in a regular classroom.

4. *Cost*

Finally, the district court found that the District had not offered any persuasive or credible evidence to support its claim that educating Rachel in a regular classroom with appropriate services would be significantly more expensive than educating her in the District's proposed setting.

The District contended that it would cost $109,000 to educate Rachel full-time in a regular classroom. This figure was based on the cost of providing a full-time aide for Rachel plus an estimated $80,000 for school-wide sensitivity training. The court found that the District did not establish that such training was necessary. Further, the court noted that even if such training were necessary, there was evidence from the California Department of Education that the training could be had at no cost. Moreover, the court found it would be inappropriate to assign the total cost of the training to Rachel when other children with disabilities would benefit. In addition, the court concluded that the evidence did not suggest that Rachel required a full-time aide. In addition, the court found that the District should have compared the cost of placing Rachel in a special class of approximately 12 students with a full-time special education teacher and two full-time aides and the cost of placing her in a regular class with a part-time aide. The District provided no evidence of this cost comparison.

The court also was not persuaded by the District's argument that it would lose significant funding if Rachel did not spend at least 51% of her time in a special education class. The court noted that a witness from the California Department of Education testified that waivers were available if a school district sought to adopt a program that did not fit neatly within the funding guidelines. The District had not applied for a waiver.

By inflating the cost estimates and failing to address the true comparison, the District did not meet its burden of proving that regular placement would burden the District's funds or adversely affect services available to other children. Therefore, the court found that the cost factor did not weigh against mainstreaming Rachel.

The district court concluded that the appropriate placement for Rachel was full-time in a regular second grade classroom with some supplemental services and affirmed the decision of the hearing officer.

Discussion

B. *Mainstreaming Requirements of the IDEA*

1. *The Statute*

The IDEA provides that each state must establish:

> [P]rocedures to assure that, to the maximum extent appropriate, children with disabilities are educated with children who are not disabled, and that special classes, separate schooling, or other removal of children with disabilities from the regular educational environment occurs only when the nature or severity of the disability is such that education in regular classes with the use of supplementary aids and services cannot be achieved satisfactorily.

20 U.S.C. § 1412(5)(B).

This provision sets forth Congress's preference for educating children with disabilities in regular classrooms with their peers.

3. *Test for Determining Compliance with the IDEA's Mainstreaming Requirement*

We have not adopted or devised a standard for determining the presence of compliance with 20 U.S.C. § 1412(5)(B). The Third, Fifth and Eleventh Circuits use what is known as the *Daniel R.R.* test. The Fourth, Sixth and Eighth Circuits apply the *Roncker* test.

Although the district court relied principally on *Daniel R.R.* and *Greer*, it did not specifically adopt the *Daniel R.R.* test over the *Roncker* test. Rather, it employed factors found in both lines of cases in its analysis. The result was a four-factor balancing test in which the court considered (1) the educational benefits of placement full-time in a regular class; (2) the non-academic benefits of such placement; (3) the effect Rachel had on the teacher and children in the regular class; and (4) the costs of mainstreaming Rachel. This analysis directly addresses the issue of the appropriate placement for a child with disabilities under the requirements of 20 U.S.C. § 1412(5)(B). Accordingly, we approve and adopt the test employed by the district court.

4. *The District's Contentions on Appeal*

The District strenuously disagrees with the district court's findings that Rachel was receiving academic and non-academic benefits in a regular class and did not have a detrimental effect on the teacher or other students. It argues that the court's findings were contrary to the evidence of the state Diagnostic Center and that the court should not have been persuaded by the testimony of Rachel's teacher, particularly her testimony that Rachel would need only a part-time aide in the future. The district court, however, conducted a full evidentiary hearing and made a thorough analysis. The court found the Hollands' evidence to be more persuasive. Moreover, the court asked Rachel's teacher extensive questions regarding Rachel's need for a part-time aide. We will not disturb the findings of the district court.

The District is also not persuasive on the issue of cost. The District now claims that it will lose up to $190,764 in state special education funding if Rachel is not enrolled in a special education class at least 51% of the day. However, the District has not sought a waiver pursuant to California Education Code § 56101. This section provides that (1) any school district may request a waiver of any provision of the Education Code if the waiver is necessary or beneficial to the student's IEP, and (2) the Board may grant the waiver when failure to do so would hinder compliance with federal mandates for a free appropriate education for children with disabilities.

Finally, the District argues that Rachel must receive her academic and functional curriculum in special education from a specially credentialed teacher. We hold only, under our standard of review, that the school district's decision was a reasonable one under the circumstances of this case. More importantly, the District's proposition that Rachel must be taught by a special education teacher runs directly counter to the congressional preference that children with disabilities be educated in regular classes with children who are not disabled.

We affirm the judgment of the district court. While we cannot determine what the appropriate placement is for Rachel at the present time, we hold that the determination of the present and future appropriate placement for Rachel should be based on the principles set forth in this opinion and the opinion of the district court.

Affirmed.

NOTES

1. The factors cited in *Rachel H.* as being applied in the *Daniel R.R. v. State Bd. of Ed.*, 874 F.2d 1036 (5th Cir. 1989), decision are as follows:

> First, the court must determine "whether education in the regular classroom, with the use of supplemental aids and services, can be achieved satisfactorily. . . . " *Daniel R.R.*, 874 F.2d at 1048. If the court finds that education cannot be achieved satisfactorily in the regular classroom, then it must decide "whether the school has mainstreamed the child to the maximum extent appropriate." *Id.* Factors the courts consider in applying the first prong of this test are (1) the steps the school district has taken to accommodate the child in a regular classroom; (2) whether the child will

receive an educational benefit from regular education; (3) the child's overall educational experience in regular education; and (4) the effect the disabled child's presence has on the regular classroom. *Daniel R.R.*, 874 F.2d at 1048-49; see also *Oberti v. Board of Educ.*, 995 F.2d at 1215–1217; *Greer v. Rome City School Dist.*, 950 F.2d at 696–97. In *Greer* the court added the factor of cost, stating that "if the cost of educating a handicapped child in a regular classroom is so great that it would significantly impact upon the education of other children in the district, then education in a regular classroom is not appropriate." 950 F.2d at 697. Regarding the second factor, the *Oberti* and *Greer* courts compared the educational benefits received in a regular classroom with the benefits received in a special education class. *Oberti*, 995 F.2d at 1216; *Greer*, 950 F.2d at 697.

14 F.3d at 1404, note 5, referring to *Daniel R.R. v. State Bd. of Ed.*, 874 F.2d 1036 (5th Cir. 1989).

2. The *Rachel H.* case stated:

According to the court in *Roncker v. Walter*: "[W]here the segregated facility is considered superior, the court should determine whether the services which make that placement superior could be feasibly provided in a non-segregated setting. If they can, the placement in the segregated school would be inappropriate under the Act." 700 F.2d at 1063. Courts are to (1) compare the benefits the child would receive in special education with those she would receive in regular education; (2) consider whether the child would be disruptive in the non-segregated setting; and (3) consider the cost of mainstreaming. *Id.*

14 F.3d at 1404, note 6, referring to *Roncker v. Walter*, 700 F.2d 1058 (6th Cir. 1983).

PROBLEMS

1. Most of the cases addressing education in the regular classroom involve children in elementary grades. How would these tests work in a high school setting? Can a tenth grade history course be appropriately provided to a severely retarded student? If not, in what classes would that student be appropriately mainstreamed? How could the high school ensure at least the social interaction aspect of the high school experience?

2. For special education students receiving specialized programming during the summer to avoid undue regression, how is mainstreaming accomplished?

The following case raises an issue that is not clearly resolved in the statutory language itself. The case addresses the right to receive education in the neighborhood school. The holding represents how the majority of courts have responded to this issue.

MURRAY v. MONTROSE COUNTY SCHOOL DISTRICT
51 F.3d 921 (10th Cir. 1995)

STEPHEN H. ANDERSON, CIRCUIT JUDGE.

Background

Tyler Murray ("Tyler") is a twelve-year-old boy with multiple disabilities due to cerebral palsy. His disabilities include significant mental and physical impairments, as well as speech difficulties. Tyler lives in Olathe, Colorado, approximately five blocks from Olathe Elementary School.

In late 1987 and in early 1988, Tyler was tested in anticipation of his commencing kindergarten in the fall of 1988. Olathe Elementary offers basic services to disabled children with "mild to moderate" ("M/M") needs. It offers these services through its two resource teachers, as well as through paraprofessionals and itinerant specialists.[3] When Tyler began kindergarten at Olathe, and until early 1991, the school was not fully accessible to children with disabilities like Tyler's. It is now fully accessible. Another school, Northside Elementary School, located in Montrose, some ten miles from Olathe, has a specific program, implementing the Colorado Effective Education Model ("CEEM"), for children with "severe/profound" needs ("S/P"). It is fully accessible to disabled children. It is one of six elementary schools in Colorado implementing CEEM. Northside also contains regular education classrooms which serve nondisabled children.

In April and October of 1988, a multi-disciplinary staffing team at Olathe met to develop an individualized education program ("IEP") for Tyler, as the IDEA requires for each child with disabilities. The staffing team determined that Tyler's IEP could be implemented at Olathe. Tyler was in the regular kindergarten class at Olathe for the full two and one-half hour school day, with two to four hours per week of speech and occupational/physical therapy. As of February 1989 he began spending one and one-quarter to three and three-quarters hours per week in the resource room instead of the regular classroom.

The required annual review of Tyler's IEP occurred in May 1989, at which needs and goals were established for first grade. Tyler remained at Olathe in the regular first grade classroom with five hours served in the resource room, one to two hours of speech and language therapy, and one and one-half hours of occupational therapy per week.

In January 1990 Tyler's IEP was reviewed because the staff at Olathe were concerned that he was not progressing as well as expected, and that his current educational placement might be inappropriate. His time in special education services was increased, and his curriculum was modified.

---

[3] Itinerant specialists travel to different schools, offering specialized services to students at those schools for a part of each day.

Tyler had surgery in July 1990, and spent six weeks in a cast, which caused him to regress in certain areas and made it difficult for him to meet his IEP goals during that time period.

At a meeting in August 1990, between the Murrays, Donald Binder, the Director of Student Services for the District, and others, District personnel suggested that the CEEM program at Northside might be a more appropriate placement for Tyler. The Murrays expressed their strong preference that Tyler remain at Olathe, where his sibling and neighborhood friends attended school.

At a triennial review held on November 27, 1990, Tyler's IEP was carefully reviewed and modified, and the staffing team discussed alternative placements, comparing the benefits of Olathe and Northside. At that time, Tyler was in second grade, but his academic level was determined to be kindergarten in some areas, and beginning first grade in others. His greatest area of strength was in social skills and interaction.

The staffing team was polled, and the Olathe psychologist, one of the resource teachers, the Olathe school principal, Tyler's regular classroom teacher at Olathe, and Mr. Binder all voted to place Tyler at Northside. Mr. Binder testified that the reasons for recommending placement at Northside were that the severe needs program was more appropriate for Tyler and that Olathe was not physically as accessible as Northside. Tyler's parents, his occupational therapist, his physical therapist, and his speech therapist all voted to have Tyler remain at Olathe. It is apparently undisputed that all members of the staffing team, and Tyler's parents, agreed on the needs, goals, and objectives contained in the IEP and that Tyler should spend most of his time outside the regular classroom setting.

On December 13, 1990, Mr. Binder sent the Murrays a letter indicating the District's intent to move Tyler to Northside, effective January 7, 1991, and informing the Murrays of their right to challenge that decision in a due process hearing. The Murrays requested such a due process hearing before an independent hearing officer ("IHO"), as permitted by the IDEA, as well as an independent educational and psychological evaluation of Tyler.

Following Tyler's evaluation by Dr. Sally Rogers, the staffing team reconvened in March 1991, along with Dr. Rogers, and prepared an addendum to Tyler's IEP, which made some clarifications and added some goals and objectives, primarily academic. Nonetheless, the same majority of the team voted for placement at Northside, with the addition that the Olathe social worker also recommended placement at Northside. The Murrays continued to express their strong preference that Tyler remain at Olathe.

Because the matter remained unresolved, the due process hearing took place on March 25–27, 1991. The IHO determined that Olathe was providing an appropriate education for Tyler. The District appealed that decision to an administrative law judge ("ALJ"), who reversed the IHO's decision, holding that Tyler had not achieved any meaningful educational progress at Olathe and that Northside was the appropriate placement for him.

The Murrays thereafter filed a complaint in district court challenging the ALJ's decision. On October 21, 1993, the district court granted the District's motion, affirmed the ALJ's decision, and dismissed the Murrays' claim.

Discussion

A. *Is There a Presumption of Neighborhood Schooling in LRE?*

The Murrays argue that the LRE mandate includes a presumption that the LRE is in the neighborhood school, with supplementary aids and services. They rely upon the "plain meaning" of the statute; the 1973-1975 legislative history of the IDEA; the wording of two regulations implementing the IDEA; and the 1982-1983 legislative history of the IDEA. We reject these arguments.

The statute requires that to the maximum extent appropriate, children with disabilities . . . are educated with children who are not disabled, and that special classes, separate schooling or other removal of children with disabilities from the regular educational environment occurs only when the nature or severity of the disability is such that education in regular classes with the use of supplementary aids and services cannot be achieved satisfactorily. . . . 20 U.S.C. § 1412(5)(B). The Murrays argue that "regular educational environment" implicitly includes neighborhood schools, that "special classes" means non-regular classes; and that "separate schooling" means non-neighborhood schools. They further argue that because Congress has declared that "the neighborhood is the appropriate basis for determining public school assignments," 20 U.S.C. § 1701(a)(2), then the reference to "removal" in section 1412(5)(B) must mean removal from the neighborhood school. Thus, they argue that "supplementary aids and services" must be fully explored before a child is removed from both the neighborhood school and the regular classroom with nondisabled children.

This interpretation strains the plain meaning of the statute. The statute clearly addresses the removal of disabled children from classes or schools with nondisabled children. It simply says nothing, expressly or by implication, about removal of disabled children from neighborhood schools. In other words, while it clearly commands schools to include or mainstream disabled children as much as possible, it says nothing about where, within a school district, that inclusion shall take place.

The Murrays next argue that two implementing regulations make express what the statute merely implies. 34 C.F.R. § 300.552(a)(3) provides that "[t]he educational placement of each child with a disability [shall be] as close as possible to the child's home." 34 C.F.R. § 300.552(c) provides that state agencies must ensure that "[u]nless the IEP of a child with a disability requires some other arrangement, the child is educated in the school that he or she would attend if nondisabled." The Murrays assert that these two regulations create a presumption that the LRE is in the neighborhood school.

We disagree. A natural and logical reading of these two regulations is that a disabled child should be educated in the school he or she would attend if not disabled (i.e., the neighborhood school), unless the child's IEP requires placement elsewhere. If the IEP requires placement elsewhere, then, in deciding where the appropriate placement is, geographical proximity to home is relevant, and the child should be placed as close to home as possible. There is at most a preference for education in the neighborhood school. To the extent the Third Circuit has expressly held in *Oberti* that the IDEA encompasses a presumption of neighborhood schooling, we disagree.

The Murrays next argue that the voluminous legislative history surrounding the enactment of the statute, as well as the legislative history surrounding a subsequent proposal to amend certain implementing regulations and a resulting amendment to the IDEA, support their interpretation of the statute. We disagree.

With respect to legislative statements surrounding the enactment of the IDEA, they all present the same problem for the Murrays as the statute: they simply do not clearly indicate that Congress, in discussing mainstreaming or inclusion and the concept of the LRE for each disabled child, meant anything more than avoiding as much as possible the segregation of disabled children from nondisabled children. They in no way express a presumption that the LRE is always or even usually in the neighborhood school.

The Murrays fare little better with the legislative history surrounding the proposed amendment to certain implementing regulations in 1982 and 1983. In 1982 the Secretary of Education proposed amending some regulations, including 34 C.F.R. § 300.552(a)(3) requiring education as close as possible to a child's home. The regulations were ultimately not amended, but the IDEA was itself amended to include a prohibition against "any regulation . . . which would procedurally or substantively lessen the protections provided to children . . . as embodied in regulations in effect on July 20, 1983 (particularly as such protections relate to . . . least restrictive environment)." 20 U.S.C. § 1407(b). The Murrays cite various statements made in connection with the proposed amendments, as well as the fact of section 1407(b)'s enactment, to support their argument that the LRE concept includes a strong presumption in favor of neighborhood schools. We again reject this argument as simply insufficiently persuasive to overcome the plain meaning of the statute, and the absence therein of any reference to neighborhood schools. Accordingly, we hold that there is no presumption of neighborhood schooling, either in the IDEA or its implementing regulations.

The Murrays ask us to select an LRE standard from those proposed thus far by other circuit courts. We need not adopt an LRE compliance standard in order to decide this case, and we therefore choose not to do so. This is so because we have held that the LRE mandate does not include a presumption of neighborhood schooling, and a school district accordingly is not obligated to fully explore supplementary aids and services before removing a child from a neighborhood school. It is only so obligated before removing a child from a regular classroom with nondisabled children. The Murrays have never objected to the degree to which Tyler was educated outside the regular classroom; they only challenge his removal from his neighborhood school. We therefore need not decide which standard this circuit would apply to determinations of whether the LRE requirement of section 1412(5)(B) has been met.

PROBLEMS

1. *Time in Transit Concerns:* Hypothetical Problem 7.1 noted concerns by the parents about the amount of time Helen would spend on the bus. *Murray* and the majority of other courts seem to have found that there is not a right to be in the neighborhood school under the IDEA mainstreaming mandate. Might there still be issues, however, about the "appropriateness" of a placement at a distant site aside from mainstreaming concerns?

2. *School Choice Issues:* What is the effect of the movement towards school choice on this issue? As an increasing number of school districts adopt a variety of choice programs (including vouchers, magnet school programs, and open enrollment), are students with disabilities entitled to the same choices as those who do not require special education and related services? For a discussion of this issue, see STEPHEN D. SUGARMAN & FRANK KEMERER, SCHOOL CHOICE AND SOCIAL CONTROVERSY: POLITICS, POLICY AND LAW (Brookings Institute 2000) chapter 11, by Laura Rothstein. The 2004 amendments to IDEA clarified the obligation to provide services to students placed in private schools by parents rather than the educational agency. In particular, the amendments specify that the school district where the school is located is responsible for the costs, and the funding formula allows for that. 20 U.S.C. § 1412(a)(10).

[4]   Disciplinary Removal — Denial of Services

As drugs and gangs become increasingly difficult problems, schools are faced with the task of providing discipline that meets constitutional due process and equal protection requirements as well as state and local educational agency policy requirements. Discipline of special education students creates additional complexities, as the following decision illustrates.

HYPOTHETICAL PROBLEM 7.4

Bryan is 16 and a junior at a public high school in Springfield. He is very outgoing and popular and has a C+ grade point average. He has never received special education services. His father is a computer company executive, and the family has moved a lot, although Bryan has lived in Springfield throughout high school. Although some of his teachers in elementary and middle school have raised questions to Bryan's parents in conversation about whether Bryan might have ADD or ADHD, he was never referred for testing. Bryan learned in February that his father is going to be transferred to another state and that Bryan will have to attend his senior year of high school in a new place. This is very troubling to Bryan, and he has begun to act out, yelling at teachers and other students. He was on the high school gymnastics team, and after winning the school competition in the still rings and the pommel horse, which would make him eligible for the state competition, he tells the coach for the first time about the upcoming move. The coach has told the school vice principal that he is worried about Bryan and thinks he should be referred to the school counselor. A week later, the school learns that while at school Bryan purchased "uppers" from a classmate to cope with his depression about the move. Both the classmate and Bryan have been suspended for ten days. Bryan has been removed from the gymnastics team and will not be able to compete in the state competition. Law enforcement authorities have not yet become involved, but the school principal plans to notify them. What are the implications under applicable federal laws and what are the options for Bryan? What if just before the school competition, Bryan's parents requested the school to evaluate him for special education services? Bryan's coach wants him to compete at the state meet. If Bryan wins all of his events, the school will probably win the overall state championship.

HONIG v. DOE
484 U.S. 305 (1988)

JUSTICE BRENNAN delivered the opinion of the Court:

As a condition of federal financial assistance, the Education of the Handicapped Act requires States to ensure a "free appropriate public education" for all disabled children within their jurisdictions. In aid of this goal, the Act establishes a comprehensive system of procedural safeguards designed to ensure parental participation in decisions concerning the education of their disabled children and to provide administrative and judicial review of any decisions with which those parents disagree. Among these safeguards is the so-called "stay-put" provision, which directs that a disabled child "shall remain in [his or her] then current educational placement" pending completion of any review proceedings, unless the parents and state or local educational agencies otherwise agree. 20 U.S.C. § 1415(e)(3). Today we must decide whether, in the face of this statutory proscription, state or local school authorities may nevertheless unilaterally exclude disabled children from the classroom for dangerous or disruptive conduct growing out of their disabilities. In addition, we are called upon to decide whether a district court may, in the exercise of its equitable powers, order a State to provide educational services directly to a disabled child when the local agency fails to do so.

I.

[Legislative history of the EHA omitted.]

In responding to these problems [funding constraints and exclusionary practices], Congress did not content itself with passage of a simple funding statute. Rather, the EHA confers upon disabled students an enforceable substantive right to public education in participating States and conditions federal financial assistance upon a State's compliance with the substantive and procedural goals of the Act. Accordingly, States seeking to qualify for federal funds must develop policies assuring all disabled children the "right to a free appropriate public education," and must file with the Secretary of Education formal plans mapping out in detail the programs, procedures, and timetables under which they will effectuate these policies. 20 U.S.C. §§ 1412(1), 1413(a). Such plans must assure that, "to the maximum extent appropriate," States will "mainstream" disabled children, i.e., that they will educate them with children who are not disabled, and that they will segregate or otherwise remove such children from the regular classroom setting "only when the nature or severity of the handicap is such that education in regular classes cannot be achieved satisfactorily." § 1412(5).

The primary vehicle for implementing these congressional goals is the "individualized educational program" (IEP), which the EHA mandates for each disabled child. Prepared at meetings between a representative of the local school district, the child's teacher, the parents or guardians, and, whenever appropriate, the disabled child, the IEP sets out the child's present educational performance, establishes annual and short-term objectives for improvements in that performance, and describes the specially designed instruction and services that will enable the child to meet those objectives. § 1401(19). The IEP must be reviewed and, where necessary, revised at least once a year in order to ensure that local agencies tailor the statutorily required "free appropriate public education" to each child's unique needs. § 1414(a)(5).

Envisioning the IEP as the centerpiece of the statute's education delivery system for disabled children, and aware that schools had all too often denied such children appropriate educations without in any way consulting their parents, Congress repeatedly emphasized throughout the Act the importance and indeed the necessity of parental participation in both the development of the IEP and any subsequent assessments of its effectiveness. See §§ 1400(c), 1401(19), 1412(7), 1415(b)(1)(A), (C), (D), (E), and 1415(b)(2). Accordingly, the Act establishes various procedural safeguards that guarantee parents both an opportunity for meaningful input into all decisions affecting their child's education and the right to seek review of any decisions they think inappropriate. These safeguards include the right to examine all relevant records pertaining to the identification, evaluation, and educational placement of their child; prior written notice whenever the responsible educational agency proposes (or refuses) to change the child's placement or program; an opportunity to present complaints concerning any aspect of the local agency's provision of a free appropriate public education; and an opportunity for "an impartial due process hearing" with respect to any such complaints. §§ 1415(b)(1), (2).

At the conclusion of any such hearing, both the parents and the local educational agency may seek further administrative review and, where that proves unsatisfactory, may file a civil action in any state or federal court. §§ 1415(c), (e)(2). In addition to reviewing the administrative record, courts are empowered to take additional evidence at the request of either party and to "grant such relief as [they] determine is appropriate." § 1415(e)(2). The "stay-put" provision at issue in this case governs the placement of a child while these often lengthy review procedures run their course. It directs that:

> During the pendency of any proceedings conducted pursuant to [§ 1415], unless the State or local educational agency and the parents or guardian otherwise agree, the child shall remain in the then current educational placement of such child . . . .

§ 1415(e)(3).

The present dispute grows out of the efforts of certain officials of the San Francisco Unified School District (SFUSD) to expel two emotionally disturbed children from school indefinitely for violent and disruptive conduct related to their disabilities. In November 1980, respondent John Doe assaulted another student at the Louise Lombard School, a developmental center for disabled children. Doe's April 1980 IEP identified him as a socially and physically awkward 17-year-old who experienced considerable difficulty controlling his impulses and anger. Among the goals set out in his IEP was "[i]mprovement in [his] ability to relate to [his] peers [and to] cope with frustrating situations without resorting to aggressive acts." Frustrating situations, however, were an unfortunately prominent feature of Doe's school career: physical abnormalities, speech difficulties, and poor grooming habits had made him the target of teasing and ridicule as early as the first grade; his 1980 IEP reflected his continuing difficulties with peers, noting that his social skills had deteriorated and that he could tolerate only minor frustration before exploding.

On November 6, 1980, Doe responded to the taunts of a fellow student in precisely the explosive manner anticipated by his IEP: he choked the student with sufficient force to leave abrasions on the child's neck, and kicked out a school window while being escorted to the principal's office afterwards. Doe admitted his misconduct and the school subsequently suspended him for five days. Thereafter, his principal referred the matter to the SFUSD Student Placement Committee (SPC or Committee) with the recommendation that Doe be expelled. On the day the suspension was to end, the SPC notified Doe's mother that it was proposing to exclude her child permanently from SFUSD and was therefore extending his suspension until such time as the expulsion proceedings were completed. The Committee further advised her that she was entitled to attend the November 25 hearing at which it planned to discuss the proposed expulsion.

After unsuccessfully protesting these actions by letter, Doe brought this suit against a host of local school officials and the State Superintendent of Public Instructions. Alleging that the suspension and proposed expulsion violated the EHA, he sought a temporary restraining order canceling the SPC hearing and requiring school officials to convene an IEP meeting. The District Judge granted the requested injunctive relief and further ordered defendants to provide home tutoring for Doe on an interim basis; shortly thereafter, she issued a preliminary injunction directing defendants to return Doe to his then current educational placement at Louise Lombard School pending completion of the IEP review process. Doe reentered school on December 15, 5 1/2 weeks, and 24 school-days, after his initial suspension.

Respondent Jack Smith was identified as an emotionally disturbed child by the time he entered the second grade in 1976. School records prepared that year indicated that he was unable "to control verbal or physical outburst[s]" and exhibited a "[s]evere disturbance in relationships with peers and adults." Further evaluations subsequently revealed that he had been physically and emotionally abused as an infant and young child and that, despite above average intelligence, he experienced academic and social difficulties as a result of extreme hyperactivity and low self-esteem. Of particular concern was Smith's propensity for verbal hostility; one evaluator noted that the child reacted to stress by "attempt[ing] to cover his feelings of low self worth through aggressive behavior[,] primarily verbal provocations."

Based on these evaluations, SFUSD placed Smith in a learning center for emotionally disturbed children. His grandparents, however, believed that his needs would be better served in the public school setting and, in September 1979, the school district acceded to their requests and enrolled him at A.P. Giannini Middle School. His February 1980 IEP recommended placement in a Learning Disability Group, stressing the need for close supervision and a highly structured environment. Like earlier evaluations, the February 1980 IEP noted that Smith was easily distracted, impulsive, and anxious; it therefore proposed a half-day schedule and suggested that the placement be undertaken on a trial basis.

At the beginning of the next school year, Smith was assigned to a full-day program; almost immediately thereafter he began misbehaving. School officials met twice with his grandparents in October 1980 to discuss returning him to a half-day program; although the grandparents agreed to the reduction, they apparently were never apprised of their right to challenge the decision through EHA procedures. The school officials also warned them that if the child continued his disruptive behavior — which included stealing, extorting money from fellow students, and making sexual comments to female classmates — they would seek to expel him. On November 14, they made good on this threat, suspending Smith for five days after he made further lewd comments. His principal referred the matter to the SPC, which recommended exclusion from SFUSD. As it did in John Doe's case, the Committee scheduled a hearing and extended the suspension indefinitely pending a final disposition in the matter. On November 28, Smith's counsel protested these actions on grounds essentially identical to those raised by Doe, and the SPC agreed to cancel the hearing and to return Smith to a half-day program at A.P. Giannini or to provide home tutoring. Smith's grandparents chose the latter option and the school began home instruction on December 10; on January 6, 1981, an IEP team convened to discuss alternative placements.

[District and appellate court proceedings omitted.]

II.

At the outset, we address the suggestion, raised for the first time during oral argument, that this case is moot. Under Article III of the Constitution this Court may only adjudicate actual, ongoing controversies. That the dispute between the parties was very much alive when suit was filed, or at the time the Court of Appeals rendered its judgment, cannot substitute for the actual case or controversy that an exercise of this Court's jurisdiction requires. In the present case, we have jurisdiction if there is a reasonable likelihood that respondents will again suffer the deprivation of EHA-mandated rights that gave rise to this suit. We believe that, at least with respect to respondent Smith, such a possibility does in fact exist and that the case therefore remains justiciable.

Respondent John Doe is now 24 years old and, accordingly, is no longer entitled to the protections and benefits of the EHA, which limits eligibility to disabled children between the ages of 3 and 21. It is clear, therefore, that whatever rights to state educational services he may yet have as a ward of the State, . . . the Act would not govern the State's provision of those services, and thus the case is moot as to him. Respondent Jack Smith, however, is currently 20 and has not yet completed high school. Although at present he is not faced with any proposed expulsion or suspension proceedings, and indeed no longer even resides within the SFUSD, he remains a resident of California and is entitled to a "free appropriate public education" within that State. His claims under the EHA, therefore, are not moot if the conduct he originally complained of is " 'capable of repetition, yet evading review.' " Given Smith's continued eligibility for educational services under the EHA, the nature of his disability, and petitioner's insistence that all local school districts retain residual authority to exclude disabled children for dangerous conduct, we have little difficulty concluding that there is a "reasonable expectation," that Smith would once again be subjected to a unilateral "change in placement" for conduct growing out of his disabilities were it not for the statewide injunctive relief issued.

We have previously noted that administrative and judicial review under the EHA is often "ponderous," and this case, which has taken seven years to reach us, amply confirms that observation. For obvious reasons, the misconduct of an emotionally disturbed or otherwise disabled child who has not yet reached adolescence typically will not pose such a serious threat to the well-being of other students that school officials can only ensure classroom safety by excluding the child. Yet, the adolescent student improperly disciplined for misconduct that does pose such a threat will often be finished with school or otherwise ineligible for EHA protections by the time review can be had in this Court. Because we believe that respondent Smith has demonstrated both "a sufficient likelihood that he will again be wronged in a similar way," and that any resulting claim he may have for relief will surely evade our review, we turn to the merits of his case.

III.

The language of § 1415(e)(3) is unequivocal. It states plainly that during the pendency of any proceedings initiated under the Act, unless the state or local educational agency and the parents or guardian of a disabled child otherwise agree, "the child *shall* remain in the then current educational placement." § 1415(e)(3) (emphasis added). Faced with this clear directive, petitioner asks us to read a "dangerousness" exception into the stay-put provision on the basis of either of two essentially inconsistent assumptions: first, that Congress thought the residual authority of school officials to exclude dangerous students from the classroom too obvious for comment; or second, that Congress inadvertently failed to provide such authority and this Court must therefore remedy the oversight. Because we cannot accept either premise, we decline petitioner's invitation to rewrite the statute.

Petitioner's arguments proceed, he suggests, from a simple, commonsense proposition: Congress could not have intended the stay-put provision to be read literally, for such a construction leads to the clearly unintended, and untenable, result that school districts must return violent or dangerous students to school while the often lengthy EHA proceedings run their course. We think it clear, however, that Congress very much meant to strip schools of the unilateral authority they had traditionally employed to exclude disabled students, particularly emotionally disturbed students, from school. In so doing, Congress did not leave school administrators powerless to deal with dangerous students; it did, however, deny school officials their former right to "self-help," and directed that in the future the removal of disabled students could be accomplished only with the permission of the parents or, as a last resort, the courts.

As noted above, Congress passed the EHA after finding that school systems across the country had excluded one out of every eight disabled children from classes. In drafting the law, Congress was largely guided by the recent decisions in *Mills v. Board of Education of District of Columbia*, 348 F. Supp. 866 (1972), and *PARC*, 343 F. Supp. 279 (1972), both of which involved the exclusion of hard-to-handle disabled students. *Mills* in particular demonstrated the extent to which schools used disciplinary measures to bar children from the classroom. There, school officials had labeled four of the seven minor plaintiffs "behavioral problems," and had excluded them from classes without providing any alternative education to them or any notice to their parents. After finding that this practice was not limited to the named plaintiffs but affected in one way or another an estimated class of 12,000 to 18,000 disabled students, the District Court enjoined future exclusions, suspensions, or expulsions "on grounds of discipline."

Congress attacked such exclusionary practices in a variety of ways. It required participating States to educate all disabled children, regardless of the severity of their disabilities, and included within the definition of "handicapped" those children with serious emotional disturbances. It further provided for meaningful parental participation in all aspects of a child's educational placement, and barred schools, through the stay-put provision, from changing that placement over the parent's objection until all review proceedings were completed. Recognizing that those proceedings might prove long and tedious, the Act's drafters did not intend § 1415(e)(3) to operate inflexibly, and they therefore allowed for interim placements where parents and school officials are able to agree on one. Conspicuously absent from § 1415(e)(3), however, is any emergency exception for dangerous students. This absence is all the more telling in light of the injunctive decree issued in *PARC*, which permitted school officials unilaterally to remove students in " 'extraordinary circumstances.' " Given the lack of any similar exception in *Mills*, and the close attention Congress devoted to these "landmark" decisions, we can only conclude that the omission was intentional; we are therefore not at liberty to engraft onto the statute an exception Congress chose not to create.

Our conclusion that § 1415(e)(3) means what it says does not leave educators hamstrung. The Department of Education has observed that, "[w]hile the [child's] placement may not be changed [during any complaint proceeding], this does not preclude the agency from using its normal procedures for dealing with children who are endangering themselves or others." Comment following 34 CFR § 300.513 (1987). Such procedures may include the use of study carrels, timeouts, detention, or the restriction of privileges. More drastically, where a student poses an immediate threat to the safety of others, officials may temporarily suspend him or her for up to 10 schooldays. This authority, which respondent in no way disputes, not only ensures that school administrators can protect the safety of others by promptly removing the most dangerous of students, it also provides a "cooling down" period during which officials can initiate IEP review and seek to persuade the child's parents to agree to an interim placement. And in those cases in which the parents of a truly dangerous child adamantly refuse to permit any change in placement, the 10-day respite gives school officials an opportunity to invoke the aid of the courts under § 1415(e)(2), which empowers courts to grant any appropriate relief.

Petitioner contends, however, that the availability of judicial relief is more illusory than real, because a party seeking review under § 1415(e)(2) must exhaust time-consuming administrative remedies, and because under the Court of Appeals' construction of § 1415(e)(3), courts are as bound by the stay-put provision's "automatic injunction," as are schools. It is true that judicial review is normally not available under § 1415(e)(2) until all administrative proceedings are completed, but as we have previously noted, parents may bypass the administrative process where exhaustion would be futile or inadequate. While many of the EHA's procedural safeguards protect the rights of parents and children, schools can and do seek redress through the administrative review process, and we have no reason to believe that Congress meant to require schools alone to exhaust in all cases, no matter how exigent the circumstances. The burden in such cases, of course, rests with the school to demonstrate the futility or inadequacy of administrative review, but nothing in § 1415(e)(2) suggests that schools are completely barred from attempting to make such a showing. Nor do we think that § 1415(e)(3) operates to limit the equitable powers of district courts such that they cannot, in appropriate cases, temporarily enjoin a dangerous disabled child from attending school. As the EHA's legislative history makes clear, one of the evils Congress sought to remedy was the unilateral exclusion of disabled children by schools, not courts, and one of the purposes of § 1415(e)(3), therefore, was "to prevent school officials from removing a child from the regular public school classroom over the parents' objection pending completion of the review proceedings." The stay-put provision in no way purports to limit or pre-empt the authority conferred on courts by § 1415(e)(2); indeed, it says nothing whatever about judicial power.

In short, then, we believe that school officials are entitled to seek injunctive relief under § 1415(e)(2) in appropriate cases. In any such action, § 1415(e)(3) effectively creates a presumption in favor of the child's current educational placement which school officials can overcome only by showing that maintaining the child in his or her current placement is substantially likely to result in injury either to himself or herself, or to others. In the present case, we are satisfied that the District Court, in enjoining the state and local defendants from indefinitely suspending respondent or otherwise unilaterally altering his then current placement, properly balanced respondent's interest in receiving a free appropriate public education in accordance with the procedures and requirements of the EHA against the interests of the state and local school officials in maintaining a safe learning environment for all their students.

IV.

We believe the courts below properly construed and applied § 1415(e)(3), except insofar as the Court of Appeals held that a suspension in excess of 10 schooldays does not constitute a "change in placement." . . .

Affirmed.

[Concurring and dissenting opinions omitted.]

PROBLEM

The Court noted that the case was moot as to John Doe because he was twenty-four years old at the time of the decision. Should John Doe be able to receive compensatory education or damages to compensate for the denial of education? The IDEA is silent on the availability of these remedies. The courts have reached inconsistent results, and commentators have addressed this issue at some length. See LAURA ROTHSTEIN & JULIA ROTHSTEIN, DISABILITIES AND THE LAW §§ 2.46, 2.48, 2.50, 2.57 (2009).

NOTES

The case of *Clyde K. v. Puyallup*, 35 F.3d 1396 (9th Cir. 1994), raises the troubling issue of how to handle extremely disruptive students whose behavior results from the disability. The court noted the importance of having parents and school officials resolve their differences through cooperation and compromise. After an escalating set of behavioral problems by a fifteen year old student with ADHD and Tourette's Syndrome, which resulted in an emergency expulsion after an assault on a staff member of the school, the school recommended a placement in a more structured environment on an interim basis. The parents rejected the placement, claiming it to be too restrictive. Ultimately the court found the school's placement to be appropriate because of his behavior difficulties and the danger and disruption that resulted from them.

The issue of discipline was also the subject of the decision in *Commonwealth v. Riley*, 106 F.3d 559 (4th Cir. 1997), in which the appellate court held that IDEA does not require providing special education to students with disabilities who have been expelled or suspended for criminal or other serious misconduct that is wholly unrelated to their disabilities.

The controversy over this issue was resolved to some degree in 1997, when Congress reauthorized IDEA and amended it to provide for disciplinary removal of students beyond the 10 day limit imposed by *Honig v. Doe*. The amendment allows schools to suspend students with disabilities for up to 45 days if they bring weapons or drugs to school or where they pose a serious threat to other students. 42 U.S.C. § 1415(k)(1)(B).

The 2004 amendments update the 1997 amendments that had addressed issues of disciplinary removal. A child identified as disabled may not be denied educational services, but removal from the current placement to an alternative educational setting is permissible in circumstances involving weapons, drug sale and use, or infliction of bodily harm on another. There are procedures for expedited hearings in these instances. 20 U.S.C. § 1415(k). See also LAURA ROTHSTEIN & JULIA ROTHSTEIN, DISABILITIES AND THE LAW § 2.44 (2009).

The 2004 amendments also incorporate a procedure called a "manifestation determination review." 20 U.S.C. § 1415(k)(1)(E). This process provides for a determination about whether behavior that is subject to disciplinary treatment is related to a disability. If the student currently has an IEP, the procedure is to assess whether any intervention strategies in the IEP are appropriate. This becomes more difficult where a student has not yet been identified as eligible for special education, but where the educational agency knew of the disability before the misconduct. If parents have expressed concern in writing to appropriate personnel or if school personnel have expressed concern, this may trigger the manifestation process.

[5]   Education During Dispute Resolution

It is not unusual for parents to disagree with the educational agency about whether the education of a child is appropriate. The difficult question is where the child should be placed pending resolution of this disagreement. This is an important issue because, as the *Burlington* case illustrates, these matters can sometimes take years to resolve. Unlike employment disputes, where back wages, reinstatement, and similar remedies can go a long way towards putting the employee back in the position he or she would have been in had there been no discrimination, lost educational experience cannot easily be compensated for.

HYPOTHETICAL PROBLEM 7.5

Review the facts from Hypothetical Problem 7.1 involving Helen and her parents' decision to place her in the private school pending resolution of where she should be placed for first grade, Lincoln or McKinley. How would the following cases resolve their rights to reimbursement?

BURLINGTON SCHOOL COMMITTEE v. DEPARTMENT OF EDUCATION
471 U.S. 359 (1985)

JUSTICE REHNQUIST delivered the opinion of the Court:

The Education of the Handicapped Act (Act), 20 U.S.C. § 1401 et seq., requires participating state and local educational agencies "to assure that handicapped children and their parents or guardians are guaranteed procedural safeguards with respect to the provision of free appropriate public education" to such handicapped children. These procedures include the right of the parents to participate in the development of an "individualized education program" (IEP) for the child and to challenge in administrative and court proceedings a proposed IEP with which they disagree. Where as in the present case review of a contested IEP takes years to run its course — years critical to the child's development — important practical questions arise concerning interim placement of the child and financial responsibility for that placement. This case requires us to address some of those questions.

Michael Panico, the son of respondent Robert Panico, was a first grader in the public school system of petitioner Town of Burlington, Mass., when he began experiencing serious difficulties in school. It later became evident that he had "specific learning disabilities" and thus was "handicapped" within the meaning of the Act. This entitled him to receive at public expense specially designed instruction to meet his unique needs, as well as related transportation. The negotiations and other proceedings between the Town and the Panicos, thus far spanning more than eight years, are too involved to relate in full detail; the following are the parts relevant to the issues on which we granted certiorari.

In the spring of 1979, Michael attended the third grade of the Memorial School, a public school in Burlington, Mass., under an IEP calling for individual tutoring by a reading specialist for one hour a day and individual and group counselling. Michael's continued poor performance and the fact that Memorial School was not equipped to handle his needs led to much discussion between his parents and Town school officials about his difficulties and his future schooling. Apparently the course of these discussions did not run smoothly; the upshot was that the Panicos and the Town agreed that Michael was generally of above average to superior intelligence, but had special educational needs calling for a placement in a school other than Memorial. They disagreed over the source and exact nature of Michael's learning difficulties, the Town believing the source to be emotional and the parents believing it to be neurological.

In late June, the Town presented the Panicos with a proposed IEP for Michael for the 1979-1980 academic year. It called for placing Michael in a highly structured class of six children with special academic and social needs, located at another Town public school, the Pine Glen School. On July 3, Michael's father rejected the proposed IEP and sought review under § 1415(b)(2) by respondent Massachusetts Department of Education's Bureau of Special Education Appeals (BSEA). A hearing was initially scheduled for August 8, but was apparently postponed in favor of a mediation session on August 17. The mediation efforts proved unsuccessful.

Meanwhile the Panicos received the results of the latest expert evaluation of Michael by specialists at Massachusetts General Hospital, who opined that Michael's "emotional difficulties are secondary to a rather severe learning disorder characterized by perceptual difficulties" and recommended "a highly specialized setting for children with learning handicaps . . . such as the Carroll School," a state-approved private school for special education located in Lincoln, Mass. Believing that the Town's proposed placement of Michael at the Pine Glen School was inappropriate in light of Michael's needs, Mr. Panico enrolled Michael in the Carroll School in mid-August at his own expense, and Michael started there in September.

The BSEA held several hearings during the fall of 1979, and in January 1980 the hearing officer decided that the Town's proposed placement at the Pine Glen School was inappropriate and that the Carroll School was "the least restrictive adequate program within the record" for Michael's educational needs. The hearing officer ordered the Town to pay for Michael's tuition and transportation to the Carroll School for the 1979-1980 school year, including reimbursing the Panicos for their expenditures on these items for the school year to date.

[Lower court proceedings omitted.]

The Town filed a petition for a writ of certiorari in this Court challenging the decision of the Court of Appeals on numerous issues . . . . We granted certiorari only to consider the following two issues: whether the potential relief available under § 1415(e)(2) includes reimbursement to parents for private school tuition and related expenses, and whether § 1415(e)(3) bars such reimbursement to parents who reject a proposed IEP and place a child in a private school without the consent of local school authorities. We express no opinion on any of the many other views stated by the Court of Appeals.

The modus operandi of the [Education of the Handicapped Act] is the already mentioned "individualized educational program." The IEP is in brief a comprehensive statement of the educational needs of a handicapped child and the specially designed instruction and related services to be employed to meet those needs. § 1401(19) [now § 1402(11)]. The IEP is to be developed jointly by a school official qualified in special education, the child's teacher, the parents or guardian, and, where appropriate, the child. In several places, the Act emphasizes the participation of the parents in developing the child's educational program and assessing its effectiveness. See §§ 1400(c), 1401(19), 1412(7), 1415(b)(1)(A), (C), (D), (E), and 1415(b)(2); 34 CFR § 300.345 (1984).

Apparently recognizing that this cooperative approach would not always produce a consensus between the school officials and the parents, and that in any disputes the school officials would have a natural advantage, Congress incorporated an elaborate set of what it labeled "procedural safeguards" to insure the full participation of the parents and proper resolution of substantive disagreements. Section 1415(b) entitles the parents "to examine all relevant records with respect to the identification, evaluation, and educational placement of the child," to obtain an independent educational evaluation of the child, to notice of any decision to initiate or change the identification, evaluation, or educational placement of the child, and to present complaints with respect to any of the above. The parents are further entitled to "an impartial due process hearing," which in the instant case was the BSEA hearing, to resolve their complaints.

The Act also provides for judicial review in state or federal court to "[a]ny party aggrieved by the findings and decision" made after the due process hearing. The Act confers on the reviewing court the following authority:

> [T]he court shall receive the records of the administrative proceedings, shall hear additional evidence at the request of a party, and, basing its decision on the preponderance of the evidence, shall grant such relief as the court determines is appropriate. § 1415(e)(2).

The first question on which we granted certiorari requires us to decide whether this grant of authority includes the power to order school authorities to reimburse parents for their expenditures on private special education for a child if the court ultimately determines that such placement, rather than a proposed IEP, is proper under the Act.

We conclude that the Act authorizes such reimbursement. The statute directs the court to "grant such relief as [it] determines is appropriate." The ordinary meaning of these words confers broad discretion on the court. The type of relief is not further specified, except that it must be "appropriate." Absent other reference, the only possible interpretation is that the relief is to be "appropriate" in light of the purpose of the Act. As already noted, this is principally to provide handicapped children with "a free appropriate public education which emphasizes special education and related services designed to meet their unique needs." The Act contemplates that such education will be provided where possible in regular public schools, with the child participating as much as possible in the same activities as nonhandicapped children, but the Act also provides for placement in private schools at public expense where this is not possible. See § 1412(5); 34 CFR §§ 300.132, 300.227, 300.307(b), 300.347 (1984). In a case where a court determines that a private placement desired by the parents was proper under the Act and that an IEP calling for placement in a public school was inappropriate, it seems clear beyond cavil that "appropriate" relief would include a prospective injunction directing the school officials to develop and implement at public expense an IEP placing the child in a private school.

If the administrative and judicial review under the Act could be completed in a matter of weeks, rather than years, it would be difficult to imagine a case in which such prospective injunctive relief would not be sufficient. As this case so vividly demonstrates, however, the review process is ponderous. A final judicial decision on the merits of an IEP will in most instances come a year or more after the school term covered by that IEP has passed. In the meantime, the parents who disagree with the proposed IEP are faced with a choice: go along with the IEP to the detriment of their child if it turns out to be inappropriate or pay for what they consider to be the appropriate placement. If they choose the latter course, which conscientious parents who have adequate means and who are reasonably confident of their assessment normally would, it would be an empty victory to have a court tell them several years later that they were right but that these expenditures could not in a proper case be reimbursed by the school officials. If that were the case, the child's right to a free appropriate public education, the parents' right to participate fully in developing a proper IEP, and all of the procedural safeguards would be less than complete. Because Congress undoubtedly did not intend this result, we are confident that by empowering the court to grant "appropriate" relief Congress meant to include retroactive reimbursement to parents as an available remedy in a proper case.

In this Court, the Town repeatedly characterizes reimbursement as "damages," but that simply is not the case. Reimbursement merely requires the Town to belatedly pay expenses that it should have paid all along and would have borne in the first instance had it developed a proper IEP. Such a post hoc determination of financial responsibility was contemplated in the legislative history:

> If a parent contends that he or she has been forced, at that parent's own expense, to seek private schooling for the child because an appropriate program does not exist within the local educational agency responsible for the child's education and the local educational agency disagrees, that disagreement and *the question of who remains financially responsible* is a matter to which the due process procedures established under [the predecessor to § 1415] appl[y]. (emphasis added)

Regardless of the availability of reimbursement as a form of relief in a proper case, the Town maintains that the Panicos have waived any right they otherwise might have to reimbursement because they violated § 1415(e)(3), which provides:

> During the pendency of any proceedings conducted pursuant to [§ 1415], unless the State or local educational agency and the parents or guardian otherwise agree, the child shall remain in the then current educational placement of such child . . . .

We need not resolve the academic question of what Michael's "then current educational placement" was in the summer of 1979, when both the Town and the parents had agreed that a new school was in order. For the purposes of our decision, we assume that the Pine Glen School, proposed in the IEP, was Michael's current placement and, therefore, that the Panicos did "change" his placement after they had rejected the IEP and had set the administrative review in motion. In so doing, the Panicos contravened the conditional command of § 1415(e)(3) that "the child shall remain in the then current educational placement."

As an initial matter, we note that the section calls for agreement by either the State or the local educational agency. The BSEA's decision in favor of the Panicos and the Carroll School placement would seem to constitute agreement by the State to the change of placement. The decision was issued in January 1980, so from then on the Panicos were no longer in violation of § 1415(e)(3). This conclusion, however, does not entirely resolve the instant dispute because the Panicos are also seeking reimbursement for Michael's expenses during the fall of 1979, prior to the State's concurrence in the Carroll School placement.

We do not agree with the Town that a parental violation of § 1415(e)(3) constitutes a waiver of reimbursement. The provision says nothing about financial responsibility, waiver, or parental right to reimbursement at the conclusion of judicial proceedings. Moreover, if the provision is interpreted to cut off parental rights to reimbursement, the principal purpose of the Act will in many cases be defeated in the same way as if reimbursement were never available. As in this case, parents will often notice a child's learning difficulties while the child is in a regular public school program. If the school officials disagree with the need for special education or the adequacy of the public school's program to meet the child's needs, it is unlikely they will agree to an interim private school placement while the review process runs its course. Thus, under the Town's reading of § 1415(e)(3), the parents are forced to leave the child in what may turn out to be an inappropriate educational placement or to obtain the appropriate placement only by sacrificing any claim for reimbursement. The Act was intended to give handicapped children both an appropriate education and a free one; it should not be interpreted to defeat one or the other of those objectives.

The legislative history supports this interpretation, favoring a proper interim placement pending the resolution of disagreements over the IEP . . . . We think at least one purpose of § 1415(e)(3) was to prevent school officials from removing a child from the regular public school classroom over the parents' objection pending completion of the review proceedings.

This is not to say that § 1415(e)(3) has no effect on parents. While we doubt that this provision would authorize a court to order parents to leave their child in a particular placement, we think it operates in such a way that parents who unilaterally change their child's placement during the pendency of review proceedings, without the consent of state or local school officials, do so at their own financial risk. If the courts ultimately determine that the IEP proposed by the school officials was appropriate, the parents would be barred from obtaining reimbursement for any interim period in which their child's placement violated § 1415(e)(3). This conclusion is supported by the agency's interpretation of the Act's application to private placements by the parents . . . .

The judgment of the Court of Appeals is Affirmed.

PROBLEMS

1. If the Court had ultimately determined that the placement chosen by the parents was not appropriate, would the parents be obligated to reimburse the school? See LAURA ROTHSTEIN & JULIA ROTHSTEIN, DISABILITIES AND THE LAW § 2.49 (2009).

2. What remedy is available to parents who do not have the means to place their child in a private school pending dispute resolution? If the placement is ultimately determined to be substantially inappropriate, and the child has been found to have been substantially harmed educationally by such a placement, should the parents be able to recover damages for lost potential earnings or the costs of remedial or compensatory education?

The *Burlington* decision did not decide what happens when the unilateral placement by the parents is in a program that has not been approved by the state or that does not comply with all the IDEA requirements. The following decision addresses those issues.

FLORENCE COUNTY SCHOOL DISTRICT FOUR v. CARTER
510 U.S. 7 (1993)

JUSTICE O'CONNOR delivered the opinion of the Court:

I.

Respondent Shannon Carter was classified as learning disabled in 1985, while a ninth grade student in a school operated by petitioner Florence County School District Four. School officials met with Shannon's parents to formulate an individualized education program (IEP) for Shannon, as required under IDEA. The IEP provided that Shannon would stay in regular classes except for three periods of individualized instruction per week, and established specific goals in reading and mathematics of four months' progress for the entire school year. Shannon's parents were dissatisfied, and requested a hearing to challenge the appropriateness of the IEP. Both the local educational officer and the state educational agency hearing officer rejected Shannon's parents' claim and concluded that the IEP was adequate. In the meantime, Shannon's parents had placed her in Trident Academy, a private school specializing in educating children with disabilities. Shannon began at Trident in September 1985 and graduated in the spring of 1988.

Shannon's parents filed this suit in July 1986, claiming that the school district had breached its duty under IDEA to provide Shannon with a "free appropriate public education," and seeking reimbursement for tuition and other costs incurred at Trident. After a bench trial, the District Court ruled in the parents' favor. The court held that the school district's proposed educational program and the achievement goals of the IEP "were wholly inadequate" and failed to satisfy the requirements of the Act. The court further held that "[a]lthough [Trident Academy] did not comply with all of the procedures outlined in [IDEA]," the school "provided Shannon an excellent education in substantial compliance with all the substantive requirements" of the statute. The court found that Trident "evaluated Shannon quarterly, not yearly as mandated in [IDEA], it provided Shannon with low teacher-student ratios, and it developed a plan which allowed Shannon to receive passing marks and progress from grade to grade." The court also credited the findings of its own expert, who determined that Shannon had made "significant progress" at Trident and that her reading comprehension had risen three grade levels in her three years at the school. The District Court concluded that Shannon's education was "appropriate" under IDEA, and that Shannon's parents were entitled to reimbursement of tuition and other costs.

The Court of Appeals for the Fourth Circuit affirmed. . . .

II.

Reimbursement is [not] necessarily barred by a private school's failure to meet state education standards. Trident's deficiencies, according to the school district, were that it employed at least two faculty members who were not state-certified and that it did not develop IEPs. As we have noted, however, the § 1401(a)(18) requirements — including the requirement that the school meet the standards of the state educational agency, § 1401(a)(18)(B) — do not apply to private parental placements. Indeed, the school district's emphasis on state standards is somewhat ironic. As the Court of Appeals noted, "it hardly seems consistent with the Act's goals to forbid parents from educating their child at a school that provides an appropriate education simply because that school lacks the stamp of approval of the same public school system that failed to meet the child's needs in the first place."

Furthermore, although the absence of an approved list of private schools is not essential to our holding, we note that parents in the position of Shannon's have no way of knowing at the time they select a private school whether the school meets state standards. South Carolina keeps no publicly available list of approved private schools, but instead approves private school placements on a case-by-case basis. In fact, although public school officials had previously placed three children with disabilities at Trident, Trident had not received blanket approval from the State. South Carolina's case-by-case approval system meant that Shannon's parents needed the cooperation of state officials before they could know whether Trident was state-approved. As we recognized in *Burlington*, such cooperation is unlikely in cases where the school officials disagree with the need for the private placement.

III.

The school district also claims that allowing reimbursement for parents such as Shannon's puts an unreasonable burden on financially strapped local educational authorities. The school district argues that requiring parents to choose a state-approved private school if they want reimbursement is the only meaningful way to allow States to control costs; otherwise States will have to reimburse dissatisfied parents for any private school that provides an education that is proper under the Act, no matter how expensive it may be.

There is no doubt that Congress has imposed a significant financial burden on States and school districts that participate in IDEA. Yet public educational authorities who want to avoid reimbursing parents for the private education of a disabled child can do one of two things: give the child a free appropriate public education in a public setting, or place the child in an appropriate private setting of the State's choice. This is IDEA's mandate, and school officials who conform to it need not worry about reimbursement claims.

Moreover, parents who, like Shannon's, "unilaterally change their child's placement during the pendency of review proceedings, without the consent of the state or local school officials, do so at their own financial risk." They are entitled to reimbursement only if a federal court concludes both that the public placement violated IDEA, and that the private school placement was proper under the Act.

Finally, we note that once a court holds that the public placement violated IDEA, it is authorized to "grant such relief as the court determines is appropriate." 20 U.S.C. § 1415(e)(2). Under this provision, "equitable considerations are relevant in fashioning relief," and the court enjoys "broad discretion" in so doing. Courts fashioning discretionary equitable relief under IDEA must consider all relevant factors, including the appropriate and reasonable level of reimbursement that should be required. Total reimbursement will not be appropriate if the court determines that the cost of the private education was unreasonable.

Accordingly, we affirm the judgment of the Court of Appeals.

So ordered.

PROBLEMS

1. Do parents have an obligation to "mitigate damages" by trying to find the least expensive appropriate placement in cases where the school's proposed placement does not seem appropriate? See *Tucker v. Bay Shore Union Free Sch. Dist.*, 873 F.2d 563 (2d Cir. 1989).

2. Under the IDEA can a school district limit rates it will pay for private facilities? See *Fisher v. District of Columbia*, 828 F. Supp. 87 (D.D.C. 1993); *McClain v. Smith*, 793 F. Supp. 756 (E.D. Tenn. 1989).

3. Does a school violate IDEA if it requires parents to use private insurance policies as a source of payment for some services in private school placements? For example, a placement for intense psychiatric treatment may be necessary for the child to benefit from education, and the parents may have private insurance available to cover at least some of the expenses of such a placement. See *Seals v. Loftis*, 614 F. Supp. 302 (E.D. Tenn. 1985). The IDEA has clarified that the school may request, but not require, that private insurance benefits be used to pay for services or programming. 34 C.F.R. § 300.154(e).

The following Supreme Court decision excerpt addresses a reimbursement issue not raised in either *Burlington* or *Florence County* because in both previous cases, the student was already receiving special education services from the public educational agency.

FOREST GROVE SCHOOL DISTRICT v. T.A.
2009 U.S. LEXIS 4645 (2009)

JUSTICE STEVENS delivered the opinion of the Court.

I

T.A. attended public schools in the Forest Grove School District (School District or District) from the time he was in kindergarten through the winter of his junior year of high school. From kindergarten through eighth grade, [his] teachers observed that he had trouble paying attention in class and completing his assignments. When [he] entered high school, his difficulties increased.

In December 2000, during [T.A.]'s freshman year, his mother contacted the school counselor to discuss respondent's problems with his schoolwork. At the end of the school year, [he] was evaluated by a school psychologist. After interviewing him, examining his school records, and administering cognitive ability tests, the psychologist concluded that [T.A.] did not need further testing for any learning disabilities or other health impairments, including attention deficit hyperactivity disorder (ADHD). The psychologist and two other school officials discussed the evaluation results with [T.A.]'s mother in June 2001, and all agreed that respondent did not qualify for special-education services. [T.A.]'s parents did not seek review of that decision, although the hearing examiner later found that the School District's evaluation was legally inadequate because it failed to address all areas of suspected disability, including ADHD.

With extensive help from his family, [T.A.] completed his sophomore year at Forest Grove High School, but his problems worsened during his junior year. In February 2003, [his] parents discussed with the School District the possibility of [T.A.] completing high school through a partnership program with the local community college. They also sought private professional advice, and in March 2003 [T.A.] was diagnosed with ADHD and a number of disabilities related to learning and memory. Advised by the private specialist that [he] would do best in a structured, residential learning environment, [his] parents enrolled him at a private academy that focuses on educating children with special needs.

Four days after enrolling him in private school, [T.A.]'s parents hired a lawyer to ascertain their rights and to give the School District written notice of [his] private placement. A few weeks later, in April 2003, [his] parents requested an administrative due process hearing regarding [his] eligibility for special-education services. In June 2003, the District engaged a school psychologist to assist in determining whether [T.A.] had a disability that significantly interfered with his educational performance. [His] parents cooperated with the District during the evaluation process. In July 2003, a multidisciplinary team met to discuss whether [T.A.] satisfied IDEA's disability criteria and concluded that he did not because his ADHD did not have a sufficiently significant adverse impact on his educational performance. Because the School District maintained that [T.A.] was not eligible for special-education services and therefore declined to provide an individualized education program (IEP), [T.A.]'s parents left him enrolled at the private academy for his senior year.

The administrative review process resumed in September 2003. After considering the parties' evidence, including the testimony of numerous experts, the hearing officer issued a decision in January 2004 finding that [T.A.]'s ADHD adversely affected his educational performance and that the School District failed to meet its obligations under IDEA in not identifying respondent as a student eligible for special-education services. Because the District did not offer respondent a FAPE and his private-school placement was appropriate under IDEA, the hearing officer ordered the District to reimburse [T.A.]'s parents for the cost of the private-school tuition.

[The School District sought judicial review of the reimbursement order. The District Court upheld the hearing decision. The Court of Appeals for the Ninth Circuit reversed and remanded. The Supreme Court granted certiorari in the case because of inconsistent results among the federal circuits.]

II

Justice Rehnquist's opinion for a unanimous Court in *Burlington* provides the pertinent background for our analysis of the question presented. [Discussion of the *Burlington* decision omitted.]

Our decision [in *Burlington*] rested in part on the fact that administrative and judicial review of a parent's complaint often takes years. We concluded that, having mandated that participating States provide a FAPE for every student, Congress could not have intended to require parents to either accept an inadequate public-school education pending adjudication of their claim or bear the cost of a private education if the court ultimately determined that the private placement was proper under the Act. Eight years later, we unanimously reaffirmed the availability of reimbursement in *Florence County School Dist. Four v. Carter*, 114 S. Ct. 361 (1993) (holding that reimbursement may be appropriate even when a child is placed in a private school that has not been approved by the State).

The dispute giving rise to the present litigation differs from those in *Burlington* and *Carter* in that it concerns not the adequacy of a proposed IEP but the School District's failure to provide an IEP at all. And, unlike respondent, the children in those cases had previously received public special-education services. These differences are insignificant, however, because our analysis in the earlier cases depended on the language and purpose of the Act and not the particular facts involved. Moreover, when a child requires special-education services, a school district's failure to propose an IEP of any kind is at least as serious a violation of its responsibilities under IDEA as a failure to provide an adequate IEP. It is thus clear that the reasoning of *Burlington* and *Carter* applies equally to this case. The only question is whether the 1997 Amendments require a different result.

III

Congress enacted IDEA in 1970 to ensure that all children with disabilities are provided " 'a free appropriate public education which emphasizes special education and related services designed to meet their unique needs [and] to assure that the rights of [such] children and their parents or guardians are protected.' " *Burlington*, now codified as amended at §§ 1400(d)(1)(A), (B). After examining the States' progress under IDEA, Congress found in 1997 that substantial gains had been made in the area of special education but that more needed to be done to guarantee children with disabilities adequate access to appropriate services. The 1997 Amendments were intended "to place greater emphasis on improving student performance and ensuring that children with disabilities receive a quality public education."

Consistent with that goal, the Amendments preserved the Act's purpose of providing a FAPE to all children with disabilities. And they did not change the text of the provision we considered in *Burlington*, § 1415(i)(2)(C)(iii), which gives courts broad authority to grant "appropriate" relief, including reimbursement for the cost of private special education when a school district fails to provide a FAPE. "Congress is presumed to be aware of an administrative or judicial interpretation of a statute and to adopt that interpretation when it re-enacts a statute without change." Accordingly, absent a clear expression elsewhere in the Amendments of Congress' intent to repeal some portion of that provision or to abrogate our decisions in *Burlington* and *Carter*, we will continue to read § 1415(i)(2)(C)(iii) to authorize the relief respondent seeks.

[Discussion of School District and dissent arguments and Court's response to those arguments omitted.]

V

The IDEA Amendments of 1997 did not modify the text of § 1415(i)(2)(C)(iii), and we do not read § 1412(a)(10)(C) to alter that provision's meaning. Consistent with our decisions in *Burlington* and *Carter*, we conclude that IDEA authorizes reimbursement for the cost of private special-education services when a school district fails to provide a FAPE and the private-school placement is appropriate, regardless of whether the child previously received special education or related services through the public school.

When a court or hearing officer concludes that a school district failed to provide a FAPE and the private placement was suitable, it must consider all relevant factors, including the notice provided by the parents and the school district's opportunities for evaluating the child, in determining whether reimbursement for some or all of the cost of the child's private education is warranted. As the Court of Appeals noted, the District Court did not properly consider the equities in this case and will need to undertake that analysis on remand. Accordingly, the judgment of the Court of Appeals is affirmed.

It is so ordered.

NOTES

1. *Compensatory Education:* Like reimbursement, compensatory education is a remedy that should be allowed in appropriate circumstances because it is intended to compensate for the denial of appropriate educational services that should have been provided all along. Although the Supreme Court has not directly addressed the availability of compensatory education as a remedy, most lower courts have recognized it as available in appropriate circumstances. A few courts indicate that it may only be provided as long as the child remains age eligible. See LAURA ROTHSTEIN & JULIA ROTHSTEIN, DISABILITIES AND THE LAW § 2.50 (2009).

2. *Damages:* Courts are less likely to award monetary damages for a variety of reasons. There seems to be greater judicial reluctance to read this into the IDEA as a remedy that was intended by Congress. In addition, policy concerns about the financial burden such awards might place on educational agencies seems to be an underlying concern in some of the decisions. The question of immunity has been addressed by a number of courts, with inconsistent outcomes, and the issue remains unresolved by the Supreme Court. See LAURA ROTHSTEIN & JULIA ROTHSTEIN, DISABILITIES AND THE LAW § 2.48 (2009).

3. *Attorneys' Fees:* Arguably, one disincentive to educational agencies dragging their feet in resolving controversies about appropriate placements is the fact that as of 1986, with the enactment of the Handicapped Children's Protection Act, an amendment to the IDEA, attorneys' fees are now available to parents who prevail in special education disputes. 20 U.S.C. § 4(e)(4). The 1997 IDEA amendments clarified that attorneys' fees may not generally be recovered for work done as part of the IEP meeting. 20 U.S.C. § 1415 (i)(3)(D)(ii) (2004). See LAURA ROTHSTEIN & JULIA ROTHSTEIN, DISABILITIES AND THE LAW § 2.51 (2009).

4. *Special Education Malpractice:* The use of constitutional tort type theories for remediating misconduct by educational agencies in the provision of special education has been a much discussed topic. *Smith v. Robinson* seems to clarify that if the IDEA provides a resolution to the dispute, it is the sole avenue through which to proceed. What if the injury is physical (as a result of failure to adequately supervise a mainstreamed special education student) or if it is lost potential earnings (as a result of inappropriately identifying a child as retarded when the child is actually deaf)? Should the school be obligated to pay for medical expenses or lost potential earnings? It remains unsettled whether such theories can be used. Some of the obstacles to using constitutional tort or other malpractice theories are policy objections to having schools pay for such injuries, difficulty in proving the tort elements of negligence (duty, breach of duty, causation, and injury), and state immunity statutes. See LAURA ROTHSTEIN & JULIA ROTHSTEIN, DISABILITIES AND THE LAW § 2.57 (2009).

5. *Reimbursement for Private Schools:* The 1997 IDEA amendments resolved some of the unanswered questions about reimbursement. Where the parents do not inform the educational agency at an IEP meeting of their intent to place the child in a private school or do not given 10 days notice, reimbursement may be reduced or even denied. 20 U.S.C. § 1412(a)(10(C)(iii) (2004).

C   NONDISCRIMINATION AND REASONABLE ACCOMMODATION UNDER SECTION 504 OF THE REHABILITATION ACT AND THE AMERICANS WITH DISABILITIES ACT

HYPOTHETICAL PROBLEM 7.6

Refer back to Hypotheticals 7.2 and 7.4 involving peanut allergies, diabetes, and learning disabilities and consider in reading the following materials whether there might be rights and remedies under the ADA and/or the Rehabilitation Act in addition to the IDEA. How would that affect those situations? What if in hypothetical 7.4, Bryan's grades fell below the average required for eligibility for sports and extracurricular activities?

Consider also the following two situations in reviewing the next section:

Lisa, from hypothetical problem 7.3, has reached the high school level and is receiving a special education program that will lead to a certificate, instead of a diploma. Although she has academic delays, she is quite athletic and tries out for the cross country team. She is allowed to participate in the meets, but her time and place is not counted for the team because she is not in a diploma program.

Bryan, from hypothetical problem 7.4, is identified in first grade as having a learning disability and is provided special education services, including accommodations on exams including additional time. He works very hard and has the grades that would qualify other students for the honor roll. Can the school deny equal recognition by claiming that special education supported classes should not count for eligibility?

[1]   Students Not Covered by the IDEA

In *Smith v. Robinson*, 468 U.S. 992 (1984), reproduced in Section [A] of this Chapter, *supra*, the Court left open the possibility that there might still be some situations in which students with disabilities would not be protected by the IDEA. The following case illustrates one such example.

DOE v. BELLEVILLE PUBLIC SCHOOL DISTRICT
672 F. Supp. 342 (S.D. Ill. 1987)

Foreman, Chief Judge:

Background

Plaintiff Johnny Doe is a six-year-old male child who was diagnosed as having Hemophilia B as an infant. Subsequent to that diagnosis, made in August of 1986, he was diagnosed as having Acquired Immune Deficiency Syndrome (AIDS). During the 1986–87 school year, Johnny attended kindergarten at a public school in Harmony School District No. 175. Sometime before the end of that school year, Johnny and his mother moved to a new school district where, by virtue of the timing of the move, he was required to enroll in the first grade in Belleville District No. 118.

School officials were notified that Johnny was a hemophiliac and that he had been diagnosed as having AIDS. Subsequent to that notification it appears the Board of Education decided that it needed to formulate a "policy" to serve as their basis in placing him. The final version of this policy, titled "Policy Regarding Children With Chronic Communicable Diseases," was adopted by the Board on July 21, 1987. Following the guidelines set forth in the policy, the Board appointed an interdisciplinary Placement Evaluation Committee which supplied a factual analysis of plaintiff's case to the Board for its use in determining appropriate placement for him. On August 25, 1987, the Board met in executive session with plaintiff's mother and her attorney and thereafter unanimously decided to exclude Johnny from the normal classroom and, instead, to provide him with a tutor in his home. It is this exclusion that plaintiff alleges gives rise to his claim of discrimination in violation of Section 504 of the Rehabilitation Act of 1973, 29 U.S.C. § 794.

Discussion

The defendants urge this Court that it lacks subject matter jurisdiction over the case by virtue of plaintiff's alleged failure to exhaust his state law administrative remedies as required by 20 U.S.C. § 1415(e)(2) and the law of this Circuit. The plaintiff, on the other hand, contends that he is not "handicapped," as that term is statutorily defined in EAHCA, and thus is not afforded a remedy by that Act. Consequently, plaintiff argues that he is not required to exhaust his administrative remedies because his claim does not arise under EAHCA, but rather under the Rehabilitation Act. Exhaustion of remedies is not required under the Rehabilitation Act.

Because defendants' argument relies on the applicability of EAHCA to the plaintiff, the Court must determine if plaintiff's diagnosis of AIDS brings him within the statutory definition of a handicapped individual and is, therefore, subject to the exhaustion requirement. EAHCA defines "handicapped children" as children who are:

mentally retarded, hard of hearing, deaf, speech or language impaired, visually handicapped, seriously emotionally disturbed, orthopedically impaired, *or other health impaired children*, or children with specific learning disabilities, *who by reason thereof require special education and related services.*

20 U.S.C. § 1401(a)(1). [Emphasis added.]

In this case the parties agree that the only category into which Johnny fits is that of "other health impaired children." That phrase is defined as children who have:

[l]imited strength, vitality or alertness due to chronic or acute health problems such as a heart condition, tuberculosis, rheumatic fever, nephritis, asthma, sickle-cell anemia, *hemophilia*, epilepsy, lead poisoning, leukemia, or diabetes, *which adversely affects a child's educational performance.*

34 C.F.R. § 300.5(b)(7). [Emphasis added.]

In applying these definitions to the plaintiff, the Court concludes that three tests must be met before the provisions of EAHCA can be made to apply in this case: 1) there must be limited strength, vitality, or alertness due to chronic or acute health problems, 2) which adversely affects a child's educational performance, and 3) which requires special education and related services. Here, the record reveals virtually no evidence that plaintiff suffers from limited strength, vitality, or alertness. Furthermore, given such evidence as is in the record of Johnny's limited strength, there is virtually no evidence that this limitation has adversely affected his educational performance.

The Court also finds it noteworthy that, while the defendants assert that Johnny's hemophilia brings him within the statutory definition of "other health impaired children," the health impairment they are apparently concerned with is Johnny's AIDS virus. AIDS is not listed as an example of an acute or chronic health problem in the statute. Furthermore, the United States Department of Education, directly addressing the applicability of EAHCA to AIDS victims, has opined that a child with AIDS might be considered "handicapped" under EAHCA, depending upon his or her condition. More significantly, the Department's opinion concludes that a child with AIDS is not considered to be "handicapped," as the term is defined in the EAHCA, unless he or she needs special education. With respect to the availability of special education programs for children with AIDS, the opinion states:

Children with AIDS could be eligible for special education programs under the category of "other health impaired," if they have chronic or acute health problems which adversely affect their educational performance.

Based on the Department of Education's opinions and the tenor of the statutory language, the Court concludes that EAHCA would apply to AIDS victims only if their physical condition is such that it adversely affects their educational performance; i.e., their ability to learn and to do the required classroom work. There is no such showing at the present time, and it seems clear that the only reason for the Board's determination that Johnny needs "special education" is the fact that he has a contagious disease — AIDS. In the Court's opinion, given the facts of this case as they now exist, the provisions of EAHCA would not apply to the plaintiff at this time.

This conclusion is further buttressed by the Board's own actions. For example, at no time did the Board or its counsel advise the plaintiff that Johnny's placement was being treated as an individual education program (IEP) under EAHCA. More significantly the "policy" promulgated by the Board did not provide the rather detailed procedural safeguards mandated by EAHCA. In fact, the policy itself states that any appeal procedures otherwise available to an individual (such as those provided in EAHCA), which are contrary to those expressly set forth in the policy, are not applicable. Also, there appears to have been no policy at all regarding placement of children with contagious diseases until the plaintiff attempted to enroll in the district. Thus, the policy appears to be more an ad hoc reaction to plaintiff's case than a well-established plan promulgated by the district under the auspices of EAHCA.

For these reasons, the Court is of the opinion that the Board itself did not consider Johnny's situation one to which EAHCA would apply. That being the case, the Court finds that the plaintiff is not required to exhaust his administrative remedies, and that it has subject matter jurisdiction over this case by virtue of 28 U.S.C. § 1331.

Finally, even assuming arguendo that EAHCA does apply and exhaustion is required, it is well established that a plaintiff need not exhaust administrative remedies where the exercise of those remedies would be futile. Furthermore, exhaustion is not required if the only available administrative remedy is plainly inadequate.

Here, it is abundantly clear from the record that exhaustion would be futile. This conclusion is reached for a variety of reasons, not the least of which is the Board's failure to follow the Illinois Department of Public Health's guidelines for placing children with contagious diseases. The Board's failure to follow the guidelines apparently resulted in the director of that agency writing a letter to the editor of a local newspaper critical of the Board's decision. Additionally, and more importantly, there is the fact that the Board and its counsel apparently advised the plaintiff that his only mechanism for appeal of their decision was the monthly review provision set forth in the policy.

An even cursory review of the language of that provision reveals it to be plainly inadequate. It provides no mechanism for an independent review of an individual's case by any entity other than the Board, which of course made the original decision. Furthermore, it vests the medical decision-making in the school district nurse as opposed to a doctor and, in any event, does not seem to require expertise in infectious or contagious diseases on the nurse's part. These defects, when coupled with the language exempting the policy from other appellate mechanisms inconsistent with its terms, convince the Court that as a practical matter no meaningful administrative remedies exist for this plaintiff. Thus, the Court finds that even if EAHCA does apply, exhaustion in this case would not be required because it would indeed be futile.

For the above-stated reasons, the Court is of the opinion that defendants' Motion to Dismiss should be, and hereby is, *Denied*.

NOTE

Students with Contagious and Infectious Diseases: This decision only reaches the issue of whether Section 504 of the Rehabilitation Act can be used as a theory to challenge the exclusionary practices of the school. While it is legitimate for a school to consider health risks to others in deciding about the appropriateness of a placement, schools will not be permitted to use unsubstantiated fears as a basis for exclusion. The Center for Disease Control has developed policies on this issue. See also LAURA ROTHSTEIN & JULIA ROTHSTEIN, DISABILITIES AND THE LAW § 2.09 (2009).

[2]   Substantive Application

The previous section demonstrated the kinds of situations in which Section 504, the ADA, or Section 1983 might apply in spite of the *Smith v. Robinson* limitations. The following material demonstrates some examples of the substantive application of the nondiscrimination statutes in cases where the IDEA does not provide a remedy.

The following two case excerpts involve athletics and sports participation. In reading these opinions, consider the high value that many students and their parents place on participation in athletics in American culture.

CROCKER v. TENNESSEE SECONDARY SCHOOL ATHLETIC ASS'N
980 F.2d 382 (6th Cir. 1992)

MERRITT, CHIEF JUDGE.

I. *Facts and Procedural History*

The events leading to this appeal were precipitated by Michael Crocker's transfer from Ezell-Harding Christian School, a private secondary school in Nashville, to McGavock High School, Michael's local public secondary school. The Crockers have maintained that Michael transferred to gain access to remedial educational programs that were unavailable to him at Ezell-Harding.

Following the transfer, Carter ruled Michael Crocker ineligible to participate in specified interscholastic sports, including football, for a period of twelve months. Carter based his ruling on the TSSAA transfer rule under which students who transfer from one TSSAA member school to another are ineligible to participate in specified sports for one year unless the transfer was made because of a change of residence.

McGavock High School appealed to Carter on Michael's behalf, requesting a waiver under the TSSAA's hardship rule. The hardship rule permits the Executive Director to waive the transfer rule if its application would unduly burden the student affected. Representatives from McGavock explained to Carter that Michael transferred in order to gain access to an English class less advanced than the college preparatory classes available to him at Ezell-Harding and argued that a transfer to gain access to appropriate educational services should constitute a hardship. Carter denied the appeal because he concluded that Crocker did not suffer a hardship under the TSSAA rules.

Following Carter's denial Metro Schools classified Michael as having a learning disability that qualified as a handicapping condition under the EHA. On August 22, 1988 McGavock submitted a second hardship appeal to the TSSAA urging that Michael's official status as a handicapped child under the EHA justified and required a waiver of the transfer rule. The TSSAA denied the second appeal.

On August 23, 1988, the Crockers filed a civil action in federal district court seeking to enjoin the TSSAA from applying the transfer rule to their son so as to make him ineligible. The Crockers claimed that application of the transfer rule to Michael violated his rights as a handicapped student. Following a trial, the District Court held that to deny Crocker the opportunity to participate in interscholastic athletics if he in fact transferred schools in order to receive educational benefits suitable to his handicapping condition would amount to discrimination on the basis of a handicap. Furthermore, the district court held that the local educational agency and not the TSSAA should determine whether Crocker had genuine educational motivations for his transfer. The court enjoined the TSSAA from applying the transfer rule pending a determination by the municipal government of Metropolitan Nashville-Davidson County as to the reason for Michael's transfer from Ezell-Harding to McGavock.

On appeal, this Court ruled that the federal suit was premature because the Crockers did not first exhaust their administrative remedies under the EHA. Accordingly, we dissolved the District Court's injunction and dismissed the litigation. Prior to our dissolution of the injunction, Crocker had played on the McGavock football team. Subsequent to the dissolution of the injunction, the TSSAA and Carter notified McGavock that the school had to forfeit all football games in which Michael had participated while the District Court's injunction was in effect. The TSSAA and Carter also declared that Michael would be ineligible to participate in interscholastic football and basketball from and after September 23, 1989 because of his court-ordered participation the previous year.

In accordance with the EHA's required procedures, a team of teachers and psychologists met on September 5, 1988 to establish an Individualized Educational Plan ("IEP") for Michael to follow at McGavock. The IEP provided for continued participation in a mainstream educational program with provisions for monitoring Michael's progress and having teachers available for support. Michael's parents agreed with the educational program, but refused to approve the IEP because Metro would not include football on the basis that it would not help Michael's written language handicap.

Because Metro refused to write participation in interscholastic sports into Michael's IEP, the Crockers sought and obtained a due process hearing from the Tennessee Department of Education. The TSSAA was not made a party to the administrative action, nor was it permitted to attend. The hearing was held on

September 29, 1989. Administrative Judge James Mulroy issued his order and opinion on October 13, 1989. He found that Crocker's handicap had motivated his transfer from Ezell-Harding to McGavock and that the TSSAA's refusal to grant a hardship waiver amounted to discrimination. Judge Mulroy ruled that Metro and the TSSAA must allow Crocker to participate in all interscholastic athletics without threat of retaliation. Judge Mulroy did not rule on the question of whether participation in interscholastic athletics was a "related service," as defined by the EHA, that should have been incorporated into Michael's IEP.

After the ruling was announced, legal counsel for Carter and the TSSAA made public statements that the decision did not appear to be binding on the TSSAA and that the TSSAA's position with respect to Michael's participation remained unchanged. Following this announcement, the TSSAA refused to discuss its position on the matter with representatives from McGavock High School or with the Crockers' legal counsel.

On the same day that Judge Mulroy issued his decision, the coach of McGavock High School's football team, unsure of TSSAA's position with respect to Michael's participation, refused to permit him to participate in a game with another member school of the TSSAA. Prior to the next week's game, the coach attempted to ascertain whether the TSSAA would comply with Judge Mulroy's order. He found the TSSAA unresponsive to his inquiries. Unwilling to risk reprisal or retaliation, the coach sidelined Crocker for the next game as well.

On October 18, 1989, Michael Crocker filed this § 1983 action in federal district court claiming that the TSSAA and Carter had deprived him of rights secured by the EHA, and § 504 of the Rehabilitation Act of 1973. Crocker sought an injunction to prohibit the TSSAA from any further interference with his participation in interscholastic sports at McGavock. Crocker also sought compensatory and punitive damages in the amount of $1.5 million dollars.

On October 19, 1989, the District Court issued a temporary restraining order that enjoined Carter and the TSSAA from "all acts which might prevent, prohibit or discourage McGavock High School, its coaches or administrative personnel from allowing Michael Ray Crocker full participation in interscholastic athletics, pending further order of this Court." The District Court held a hearing on October 23, 1989, to determine whether a preliminary injunction should issue. On November 2, 1989, the Court issued a preliminary injunction against Carter and the TSSAA, holding that the defendants had interfered with rights guaranteed to Michael by the EHA and prescribed by the due process hearing held by Judge Mulroy.

The defendants appealed the preliminary injunction. Because Crocker had graduated from McGavock in May 1990, prior to the issuance of this Court's opinion, we held that as it pertained to Michael's eligibility for interscholastic sports, the injunction was moot. We upheld the injunction to the extent that it enjoined the TSSAA from imposing sanctions against Metro in relation to Michael's participation in interscholastic athletics at McGavock during the 1988-89 school year. We found that even though we ultimately vacated the District Court's initial injunction, it was valid and enforceable until it was dissolved by this Court. We concluded that Crocker, Metro, and McGavock should not later be penalized for actions taken in reliance on a valid injunction.

On April 22, 1991, the District Court granted summary judgment in favor of the defendants with respect to the plaintiff's claim for damages. The District Court held that Michael Crocker failed to show that Carter or the TSSAA deprived him of a federal right under the Rehabilitation Act or the EHA. Judge Nixon determined that Crocker did not acquire such a right at the administrative hearing because "Judge Mulroy never reached the gravamen of Michael's complaint: was participation in interscholastic football a related service that should have been incorporated in his [Michael's] IEP for the academic year 1989-1990." Finding no deprivation of a right secured by federal law, the District Court found it unnecessary to determine whether the defendants acted under color of state law within the meaning of § 1983. Plaintiff now appeals the summary judgment against him.

II. *Analysis*

We agree with Chief Judge John Nixon below that the facts alleged in this case do not state a valid claim for damages under the EHA. Section 615(e)(2) of the Act, 20 U.S.C. § 1415(e)(2), confers upon courts reviewing handicapped claims the authority to "grant such relief as the court determines is appropriate." In this case, general damages for emotional anguish, including the pain of missing two high school games, do not constitute "appropriate" judicial relief. Other cases under the Act have limited monetary damages to restitutionary types of relief. They have allowed restitution to parents for the expense of providing educational services for the handicapped child, but we do not find case authority interpreting the Act to allow an award of general damages for emotional injury or injury to a dignitary interest.

In *Burlington School Committee v. Massachusetts Department of Education*, 471 U.S. 359, 370–71 (1985), the Court appears to interpret § 1415(e)(2) as not allowing "damages" in general but as allowing "reimbursement [of] . . . expenses that it [the municipal government] should have paid all along and would have borne in the first instance had it developed a proper IEP."

As a result of the findings of the state administrative process and the federal injunctive relief granted in this case, young Crocker was allowed to play high school interscholastic sports except for two games. TSSAA sought rigidly to enforce its one-year rule against transferring athletes. In doing so it caused young Crocker and his family considerable difficulty and emotional anguish. But TSSAA was not made a party to the state administrative proceeding and was, therefore, not judicially bound by the administrative judgment.

Although under the circumstances the organization may appear stubborn and inflexible in its conduct, it is ordinarily entitled to enforce its athletic rules in order to deter students, parents and school officials from trying to turn high school athletics into an activity that overshadows or unduly interferes with academic life. The main purpose of high school is to learn science, the liberal arts and vocational studies, not to play football and basketball. Young Crocker and his family seem to have taken sports more seriously than academic studies, and the TSSAA seems to have overreacted to this situation. The EHA does not contemplate such actions for damages in these circumstances. There is no case authority for it, and we believe such damage relief would be inequitable and inappropriate.

Because Crocker cannot recover general damages under the EHA, he cannot recover damages under § 1983 for any violation of his rights secured by the EHA. Section 1983 merely secures the federally protected rights a plaintiff already holds. It does not expand those rights. Through § 1983 Crocker was able to bring an action that might otherwise have been foreclosed. Section 1983 did not provide a right to damages where none existed before.

Accordingly, the judgment of the District Court is AFFIRMED.

PROBLEM

Texas has adopted a "no pass-no play" policy requiring that students maintain certain grades to participate in extracurricular activities including interscholastic athletics. Must such a policy incorporate exceptions for special education students? How would such a policy work?

POTTGEN v. MISSOURI STATE HIGH SCHOOL ACTIVITIES ASS'N
40 F.3d 926 (8th Cir. 1994)

BEAM, CIRCUIT JUDGE.

I. *Background*

After Pottgen repeated two grades in elementary school, the school tested him to see whether he needed special classroom assistance. When the school discovered that Pottgen had several learning disabilities, it placed him on an individualized program and provided him with access to special services. With these additional resources, Pottgen progressed through school at a normal rate. It is not clear from the evidence whether he attempted to make up the lost time through summer school or other remedial activities.

Pottgen was active in sports throughout junior high and high school. He played interscholastic baseball for three years in high school and planned to play baseball his senior year as well. However, because he had repeated two grades, Pottgen turned nineteen shortly before July 1 of his senior year. Consequently, MSHSAA By-Laws rendered Pottgen ineligible to play. The MSHSAA By-Law states, in relevant part, "A student shall not have reached the age of nineteen prior to July 1 preceding the opening of school. If a student reaches the age of nineteen on or following July 1, the student may be considered eligible for [interscholastic sports during] the ensuing school year."

Pottgen petitioned MSHSAA for a hardship exception to the age limit since he was held back due to his learning disabilities. Pottgen struck out. MSHSAA determined that waiving the requirement violated the intent of the age eligibility rule.

Pottgen then brought this suit, alleging MSHSAA's age limit violated the Rehabilitation Act of 1973 (the "Rehabilitation Act"), the Americans With Disabilities Act (the "ADA"), and section 1983.

II. *Discussion*

B. *Injunctive Relief*

1. *Section 504 of the Rehabilitation Act*

The district court found Pottgen to be an "otherwise qualified" individual because, except for the age limit, Pottgen meets all MSHSAA's eligibility requirements. The court framed the issue as not whether Pottgen meets all of the eligibility requirements, but rather whether reasonable accommodations existed. We disagree. A Rehabilitation Act analysis requires the court to determine both whether an individual meets all of the essential eligibility requirements and whether reasonable modifications exist.

Here, Pottgen cannot meet all the baseball program's requirements in spite of his disability. He is too old to meet the MSHSAA age limit. This failure to meet the age limit does not keep Pottgen from being "otherwise qualified" unless the age limit is an essential or necessary eligibility requirement.

We find that MSHSAA has demonstrated that the age limit is an essential eligibility requirement in a high school interscholastic program. An age limit helps reduce the competitive advantage flowing to teams using older athletes; protects younger athletes from harm; discourages student athletes from delaying their education to gain athletic maturity; and prevents over-zealous coaches from engaging in repeated red-shirting to gain a competitive advantage. These purposes are of immense importance in any interscholastic sports program.

Even though Pottgen cannot meet this essential eligibility requirement, he is "otherwise qualified" if reasonable accommodations would enable him to meet the age limit. Reasonable accommodations do not require an institution "to lower or to effect substantial modifications of standards to accommodate a handicapped person." Accommodations are not reasonable if they impose "undue financial and administrative burdens" or if they require a "fundamental alteration in the nature of [the] program."

Since Pottgen is already older than the MSHSAA age limit, the only possible accommodation is to waive the essential requirement itself.[4] Although Pottgen contends an age limit waiver is a reasonable accommodation based on his disability, we disagree. Waiving an essential eligibility standard would constitute a fundamental alteration in the nature of the baseball program. Other than waiving

---

[4] Other accommodations may exist when a younger student realizes that he will not be able to meet the age requirement when he is a senior. For example, MSHSAA allows eighth grade students to participate on a high school team if they will be ineligible as a high school senior. This accommodation permits students to play for four years at the high school level.

the age limit, no manner, method, or means is available which would permit Pottgen to satisfy the age limit. Consequently, no reasonable accommodations exist.

Since Pottgen can never meet the essential eligibility requirement, he is not an "otherwise qualified" individual. Section 504 was designed only to extend protection to those potentially able to meet the essential eligibility requirements of a program or activity.

2. *Title II of the ADA*

MSHSAA also appeals the district court's ruling that Pottgen would likely prevail on his ADA claim. MSHSAA contends Pottgen is not a "qualified individual with a disability" under Title II of the ADA.

Consistent with our Rehabilitation Act analysis, we find MSHSAA has demonstrated that the age limit is an essential eligibility requirement of the interscholastic baseball program. . . .

HYPOTHETICAL PROBLEM 7.7

Julia is 13 years old and has fibromyalgia that has worsened over the years. Julia now has extreme difficulty walking up and down stairs, especially during winter months when it is cold or when it is damp. She moves slowly and cannot carry heavy objects for any length of time. Before high school, Julia's classes were generally in the same room, and her condition was not as severe. She is about to begin her freshman year of high school. Her parents have asked that she be provided a school locker on each floor of the three story high school and/or that all of her classes be scheduled for the first floor. They have also asked what the evacuation plan is for Julia if there is a fire or other need for evacuation. They have also asked that a second set of books be provided to Julia so that she does not need to carry her books to and from school to do homework. The high school is an urban school with 1500 students, and a shortage of lockers. Students who are freshmen and sophomores generally are assigned to share lockers. There is an elevator in the building which requires a key and is used only by faculty and staff.

Consider what federal law might require in this situation.

––––––––––

School facilities constructed before the major disability laws were enacted often have substantial barriers. The following two cases demonstrate how the new laws can be applied to these situations. The *Wolff* case highlights not only the barriers within the school building, but also the challenges for off site programming. While the case involves activities in a foreign country, field trips to museums, parks, and other facilities in the United States can present some of the same barriers. The *Bechtel* case focuses more on what *Wolff* did not address, the access in the school facilities themselves.

WOLFF v. SOUTH COLONIE CENTRAL SCHOOL DISTRICT
534 F. Supp. 758 (N.D.N.Y. 1982)

MINER, DISTRICT JUDGE:

Findings of Fact

1. Plaintiff, Jean Wolff, a 15 1/2 year old student attending the 10th grade at South Colonie High School, has a congenital limb deficiency. Her legs are approximately 1 foot in length; her right arm has been amputated above the elbow and fitted with a prosthetic device. At the end of her left arm, which is shorter than normal, are two partially functional digits. Jean is approximately 3 1/2 feet in height.

2. Defendant South Colonie Central School District (hereinafter "School District"), a municipal corporation organized pursuant to the laws of the State of New York, operates the high school Jean attends and is an entity receiving Federal financial assistance.

3. In September, 1979, plaintiff Phyllis Wolff contacted School District officials concerning Jean's attendance in the South Colonie school system and requested that a van or automobile be supplied to transport Jean to and from school. She also requested that an "aide" be supplied to help Jean in school to perform her daily school activities.

4. At a meeting of the South Colonie Board of Education on September 18, 1979, a resolution was passed approving the creation of a 6 1/2 hour school monitor position (hereinafter "aide") at the Sand Creek Jr. High School to provide for Jean's individual safety and welfare. In addition, arrangements were made for a special van to transport Jean to and from school. The School District has continued to supply the special van and aide during Jean's attendance at the High School and plaintiff Phyllis Wolff has not applied to discontinue these services.

5. The special van, which has no riders other than Jean, transports Jean daily from the door of her house to the school entrance. The van is specially equipped with lower than usual access steps.

6. The aide, Mrs. Dorothy Kulzer, meets Jean at the entrance of the school. During the school day she takes Jean's books out of a locker and carries them from class to class. She also protects Jean from inadvertent harm from her fellow classmates by walking behind Jean and to her left, thereby blocking any onrushing students. In addition, the aide guards against slipping or falling when Jean ascends or descends stairways.

7. However, there are occasions when students have bumped into Jean in the hallways during the passing of classes as well as occasions when she has stumbled and fallen. Jean is allowed to use a "short cut" to class through normally restricted hallways. She usually is late for the class to which she has the longest walk with a stairway en route.

8. In order to climb stairs, Jean must place one foot on the next level step and then, using the bannister for leverage, haul the rest of her body up to that level. This procedure is repeated until she reaches the top. Jean descends stairs in the same manner, hopping from stair to stair if no bannister is available.

9. Jean is capable of walking at a speed of approximately one half that of a normal adult for at least three miles, and is capable of "running" for between 5 and 10 minutes. On a short field trip through the Pine Bush, Jean was unable to keep up with the class.

10. This Court has had the opportunity to observe Jean during the course of these proceedings and notes the difficulties she encountered with such tasks as seating herself on the witness chair. Otherwise, Jean appears to be above average in intelligence, friendly and highly motivated for a child of her years.

11. In October, 1981, an announcement was made in Jean's Spanish class concerning a forthcoming trip to Spain. Wishing to participate, Jean fulfilled all the preliminary requirements, including demonstration of a serious interest in languages, completion of Level I Spanish studies, stipulating to certain school and trip policies, obtaining a medical release, attendance at certain planning meetings, paying a deposit of $100, and obtaining her mother's consent and signature. At some point, the balance of the cost of the trip was paid in full.

12. A meeting attended by Jean, her mother, and various school officials and teachers was held thereafter to discuss the itinerary, city by city, in light of problems which might develop for Jean. In January 1982, plaintiffs were informed that Jean would not be allowed to participate in the program without being accompanied by an aide. When plaintiffs made no attempt to obtain such an aide, all payments were returned to plaintiffs and Jean was dropped from the program.

13. The itinerary of the trip includes various Spanish cities, and the tour is to last for approximately twenty days. Much of the trip will include extensive walking tours of the cities, including the crossing of congested highways, ascending and descending stairs, and exploring various sites and monuments of historic significance. Many of the tours would be conducted by a "guide" at a brisk pace. During most of their stay in Madrid, the students will be residing with Spanish families who will accompany the children on additional excursions. Madrid, during the tour, will be particularly crowded due to the Easter holidays.

14. On the day of arrival in Madrid, the Colonie School group is scheduled to take a five mile walking tour of the City. Later that day, there will be a two mile walking tour to dinner. On another day, the students will travel to the outskirts of Madrid, where they will tour El Escorial, involving the descent of a steep and narrow stairway to the tombs of the Spanish Kings, and the Valley of the Fallen, involving the ascent of numerous flights of stairs to the monument dedicated to those who died in the Spanish Civil War.

15. The trip will also include a walking tour of Toledo, lasting almost an entire day. Toledo's streets are uneven and cobblestoned. In addition, the group will spend two days in Seville, including an extensive walking tour of much of the city. It is anticipated that Seville will be particularly crowded due to the upcoming annual spring fair. Generally, past school tours have included a day at the

bullfights. The bullfight is particularly crowded and frenzied, and is apparently on the upcoming tour's agenda for Seville. Attending the bullfight will entail the climbing of numerous stone stairways.

16.   In Granada, the group will visit the Alhambra Palace. The tour bus will stop at some distance from the Palace, which contains numerous steps. The group will also take extensive walking tours of other Spanish cities.

17.   Given her present physical limitations, Jean would be unable to maintain the brisk and physically demanding pace of the group's walking tours and would be unable to ascend and descend the myriad stairways, many of which, as part of historically preserved sites, do not contain bannisters or guardrails necessary for her locomotion and safety.

18.   In addition, the throngs of people encountered in many cities, the heavy urban traffic and the crowds gathered at events such as the bullfight, constitute significant hazards to the well-being and safety of the infant plaintiff.

Conclusions of Law

1.   This action arises under section 504 of the Rehabilitation Act of 1973, 29 U.S.C. § 794, which provides that no otherwise qualified handicapped individual, shall, solely by reason of his handicap, be excluded from participation in any program or activity receiving Federal financial assistance.

4.   Plaintiff Jean Wolff is a handicapped individual within the meaning of this Act.

5.   The trip to Spain can be considered an activity or program receiving Federal financial assistance within the meaning of the Act since, although the students pay for a substantial portion of the expenses of the trip, regular salaried teachers will be attending as chaperones while school is in session, the School District has sponsored and planned the program, and students will be under the supervision of teacher and School District personnel during this trip.

6.   For a determination of whether plaintiff Jean Wolff is "otherwise qualified" within the meaning of the Act, the Court may consider whether the program requires applicants to possess certain physical qualifications necessary for participation, and the Court may also consider a state's parens patriae interest in protecting the disabled against physical harm when the state has shown a risk to safety in a particular activity.

7.   Since Jean is unable to fulfill the physical requirements of the trip, and since a substantial degree of physical risk to her safety has been demonstrated were she to participate in the program, plaintiff Jean Wolff is not otherwise qualified within the meaning of § 504 of the Act.

8.   Accordingly, the relief sought by plaintiffs is denied in all respects and the complaint is dismissed.

The following case raises another issue likely to arise more frequently.

BECHTEL v. EAST PENNSYLVANIA SCHOOL DISTRICT
1994 U.S. Dist. LEXIS 1327, 3 A.D. Cases (BNA) 200 (E.D. Pa. 1994)

EDWARD N. CAHN, CHIEF JUDGE:

Bechtel is a minor who suffers from spina bifida. As a result of his medical condition, Bechtel is confined to a wheelchair. Although not currently a student at Emmaus High School ("Emmaus High"), Bechtel is a resident of the defendant school district and expects to attend Emmaus High next fall. Emmaus High is a public school located within the East Penn School District, and the defendant[s] are responsible for ensuring the school's compliance with all applicable laws and regulations.

Bechtel has long desired to use certain facilities at Emmaus High, specifically the stadium, which are not equipped for usage by those in wheelchairs. As a result, Bechtel has been unable to attend events at the school stadium, such as his sister's band performance. Bechtel's sister is currently enrolled at Emmaus High. On several occasions, the plaintiffs expressed to members of the defendant school board their dissatisfaction with the lack of accommodations for disabled students at Emmaus High.

Sometime in 1991, the defendant school board decided to renovate Emmaus High. In the spring of 1993, the defendants met with an architect to discuss the renovations. At that time, the architect advised the defendants that existing law required access for disabled individuals and that providing such access would not be financially burdensome. Nevertheless, the renovations which defendants undertook did not include providing access for the disabled.

A. *Americans with Disabilities Act Claim*

Plaintiffs have stated a claim of discrimination under Title II of the ADA. Title II of the ADA prohibits discrimination in public services and provides in relevant part that:

> [N]o qualified individual with a disability shall, by reason of such disability, be excluded from participation in or be denied the benefits of the services, programs, or activities of a public entity, or be subjected to discrimination by such entity.

42 U.S.C. at § 12132. A "public entity" includes "any department, agency, special purpose district, or other instrumentality of a State or States or local government." *Id.* at § 12131(1)(B). Defendants do not suggest that they fall outside the definition of "public entity."

Defendants' sole basis for dismissal is the plaintiffs' failure to exhaust their administrative remedies. However, defendants cite no caselaw to support the proposition that such exhaustion is required prior to filing a suit in federal court under Title II of the ADA. Rather, defendants rely exclusively on the enforcement mechanism in place for actions brought pursuant to Title III of the ADA. Defendants are correct that § 12188 makes the enforcement procedures of the Civil

Rights Act of 1964, which provide for exhaustion of administrative remedies, applicable to actions brought under Title III of the ADA. However, the plaintiffs in the instant case do not allege a cause of action under Title III of the ADA and therefore § 12188 is inapplicable. The relevant enforcement provision of Title II, pursuant to which plaintiffs brought their claim, is § 12133 and is distinguishable from § 12188. See 42 U.S.C. at § 12133. In fact, the cases that have addressed this issue uniformly have held that Title II of the ADA, unlike the other titles, does not require the exhaustion of administrative remedies.

In reaching this result, the courts that have addressed the issue have looked to the regulations promulgated by the Department of Justice ("DOJ") interpreting Title II of the ADA, 28 C.F.R. § 35.101 et seq., to help clarify whether exhaustion of remedies is required under Title II in light of the statutory ambiguity. The DOJ regulations specifically provide that although federal agencies are available to hear claims under Title II of the ADA, plaintiffs are not required to file with the agencies prior to filing in federal court. The relevant language reads:

> The Act requires the Department of Justice to establish administrative procedures for resolution of complaints, but does not require complainants to exhaust these administrative remedies. . . . Because the Act does not require exhaustion of administrative remedies, the complainant may elect to proceed with a private suit at any time.

28 C.F.R. at § 35.172. Additionally, a technical assistance manual designed by the DOJ to educate individuals about their rights under Title II of the ADA clearly states that there is no exhaustion of remedies requirement.

Accordingly, defendants' motion to dismiss the plaintiffs claim under the ADA is denied.

B. *Act 166 of the Commonwealth of Pennsylvania*

The plaintiffs have also asserted a claim pursuant to a Pennsylvania statute, 71 P.S. § 1455.1 et seq. The statute at issue requires that certain buildings and facilities meet set standards to make them accessible by persons with physical handicaps.

Where a statute is unambiguous, there is no need for the court to engage in speculative interpretations. The statute at issue makes clear that an individual may not bring a civil action until an initial determination is made by the government agency responsible for processing complaints under the statute. The plaintiffs have not yet filed a complaint with the Department of Labor and Industry as required by the statute. Therefore, the defendants' motion to dismiss this claim is granted.

PROBLEMS

1. Had the *Bechtel* case not involved renovations, what would the school probably have been required to do with respect to making the stadium (and existing structure) accessible?

2. Is this decision consistent with the *Smith v. Robinson, supra* Section [A], analysis?

3. Should the school be required to eliminate programs in which mobility-impaired students cannot participate?

4. If the student in *Wolff* were deaf, rather than mobility-impaired, would the school be required to find a sign language interpreter who understood Spanish to assist in any translation by guides who speak Spanish, assuming that there is an English translator for the other students?

5. Under the ADA, would the school have an obligation to do more than it is currently doing to ensure a student's movement around the school building without such difficulty as occurred in *Wolff*? For example, if it is too expensive to install an elevator, should the classes be rescheduled so as to avoid having to climb stairs? Could the student be required to attend a school that had been built to be barrier free?

NOTES

1. *Doe v. Belleville*, in the previous section, focuses on whether a child with HIV might be protected under statutes other than the IDEA. The excerpt does not really focus on what accommodations might be reasonable as applied to the facts in the case. In addition to students with diseases such as HIV, students with health impairments such as asthma or diabetes also present questions as to the accommodations that might be required. These might include allowing students to carry medication as an exception to school-wide policies prohibiting this. There is not substantial guidance from the courts on this, and each case will be individualized. The *Pottgen* decision includes factors to be addressed in determining whether something is a reasonable accommodation. These factors will be applied by the courts in cases involving accommodations for health impairments.

2. *Use of IQ Tests for Placement Decisions:* Two major judicial decisions have addressed the use of IQ tests for placing children in special education classes. In *Parents in Action on Special Ed. (PASE) v. Hannon*, 506 F. Supp. 831 (N.D. Ill. 1980), the court allowed IQ tests to be used in Illinois, while a court in California struck them down in *Larry P. v. Riles*, 495 F. Supp. 926 (N.D. Cal. 1979), *aff'd*, 793 F.2d 969 (9th Cir. 1984), as being discriminatory. What is significant about these two cases is that in the *PASE* case, the use of IQ tests was only one of many factors used in placement decisions, while in *Larry P.*, it was the primary (and in some cases the only) basis for the placement decision. See Laura Rothstein & Julia Rothstein, Disabilities and the Law § 2.32 (2009).

In *Georgia State Conference of Branches of NAACP v. Georgia*, 775 F.2d 1403 (11th Cir. 1985), the court addresses the procedures for placing children into special education in a number of school districts in Georgia. The plaintiffs had alleged that the use of achievement grouping in Georgia public schools was intended to achieve or resulted in racial segregation. The claim also alleged that black children in Georgia were being assigned to classes for children who are educably mentally retarded in a discriminatory manner in violation of § 504. The lower court found that the local school districts did not act intentionally or in bad faith in their classification, and this finding was upheld. The appellate court held, however, there was evidence of misclassification, although there was insufficient evidence to demonstrate a violation of § 504. The court found a number of procedural violations of § 504 and that some of the school districts had misinterpreted the state I.Q. score regulation. This case illustrates the importance of taking care in relying on standardized tests and the need to use many factors in classifying and placing children into special education.

3. The 2000 amendments to IDEA provided that students with learning disabilities could be tested for such disabilities using tests other than IQ type discrepancy tests. 20 U.S.C. § 1414(b)(6)(A).

D SECTION 1983 ACTIONS AND STUDENTS WITH DISABILITIES IN SCHOOLS

HYPOTHETICAL PROBLEM 7.8

Consider the facts about Helen, the deaf student from Hypothetical Problem 7.1. Helen has lost her dispute about placement at McKinley School. The parents have not been reimbursed for her private placement, and because of the cost, they have decided to send her for second grade to Lincoln School. She now must take the bus or have her parents drive her to school, which is challenging because of their work schedules. On the bus, other students tease her about her hearing impairment. The bus driver is aware of this, but does nothing. The parents learn about this from Helen and ask the school district special education director to stop it. The harassment continues, and after several days, Helen jumps off of the bus and into oncoming traffic and is hit by a car, and suffers broken bones and an extensive hospitalization, although she ultimately recovers. What are the remedies available to the parents in this situation?

What if they are concerned that Helen is dropped at the bus stop a block from her apartment entrance and no one knows whether she gets to the apartment building or to her own apartment? What obligations does the school have in this case?

MANECKE v. SCHOOL BOARD
762 F.2d 912 (11th Cir. 1985)

FAY, CIRCUIT JUDGE:

I. *Factual Background*

Lauren Manecke had suffered brain damage at birth. As a result, she was epileptic and also exhibited other mental and emotional handicaps. Despite these problems, Lauren had been enrolled in "regular" school programs supplemented with special education classes until February, 1979, when her then current high school placement came to a halt.

Lauren left the high school with a thirty-two year old man with whom she was having a sexual relationship. She stayed with him away from her home for six days. Both before and after this episode, Lauren acted in a sexually provocative manner.

It seems she employed sex as a means of asserting her independence and maturity.

When Lauren returned from her stay with the older man, her parents withdrew her from the high school she was attending and enrolled her in a small private school. Mrs. Manecke thereafter requested that the Board enroll Lauren in a county special education school. The Board agreed, and Lauren commenced attending classes at the Nina Harris School for exceptional children ("Nina Harris") in September, 1979. Lauren was evaluated and classified as emotionally handicapped and physically impaired. Before she began at Nina Harris, an individual education program ("IEP") for Lauren was developed by the Board in conjunction with her parents. Lauren seemed to be adjusting well to Nina Harris: she was making adequate academic progress, appeared well-behaved, and participated in some extracurricular social activities. The quality of Lauren's homelife, however, was rapidly deteriorating. She fought incessantly with family members, especially her mother and younger brother.

On December 19, 1979, Mrs. Manecke wrote Dr. Howard J. Hinesley, the Board's Assistant Superintendent for Exceptional Student Education. In a two page typewritten letter, Mrs. Manecke expressed her concern over Lauren's emotionally charged behavior, and the Maneckes' desire to place Lauren in an out-of-state residential facility. Mrs. Manecke attached to the typewritten letter a handwritten note requesting a due process hearing on the issue of Lauren's appropriate educational placement.

Dr. Hinesley forwarded copies of the letter and request for due process hearing to the school district's attorney. Dr. Hinesley assumed that the attorney's office would take any necessary action relative to the due process hearing.

Mrs. Manecke sent a copy of her December 19, 1979, correspondence to the Florida Commission of Education. In response, Diane Wells, an administrator with that agency, instructed Dr. Hinesley to mediate the dispute between the Board and the Maneckes; he was specifically advised to avoid resort to more formal procedures. The Maneckes, Dr. Hinesley and Mr. Delp met on February 13, 1980. The Maneckes stated that because of Lauren's intractability, they believed residential placement was necessary. Dr. Hinesley and Mr. Delp, however, expressed their belief that the Board was providing Lauren with an appropriate education at Nina Harris. Consequently, it was their position that the expense of residential placement need not be borne by the school board.

The Maneckes suggested that Dr. Hinesley and Mr. Delp meet with Dr. Andriola, Lauren's treating neurologist, and Dr. John Mann, an adolescent psychologist. Dr. Hinesley acceded to this request, and, on March 12, 1980, the meeting was held. The Maneckes asked if this meeting was their due process hearing and if their attorney should be present. Dr. Hinesley responded that the meeting was merely an informal effort to resolve the dispute over Lauren's placement. Although Dr. Hinesley did not waiver in his belief that the Board was not required to pay for Lauren's placement in a residential facility, he did end the meeting by promising to furnish the Maneckes with information concerning sundry residential facilities.

Immediately after this meeting, the Maneckes were contacted by the Devereux School for exceptional children. They were told that Devereux, which is located in Texas, had a rare residential placement vacancy which Lauren could fill if she were promptly enrolled. The Maneckes agreed to Devereux's terms and withdrew Lauren from Nina Harris on March 21, 1980. The Board was not informed why Lauren was removed from school. The Maneckes then enrolled Lauren in Devereux.

Mrs. Manecke later complained to the United States Office of Civil Rights (OCR) that the Board unlawfully refused to place Lauren in a residential facility because of her age. As a result of that agency's mediation efforts, the Board, in July of 1980, sent Lauren's parents a standard request for due process hearing form. Although the Maneckes received it, it was never returned to the Board. The OCR dropped the age discrimination charge in December, 1980. The OCR did, however, order the Board to hold a due process hearing. The hearing, scheduled for January 26, 1981, was cancelled by the Maneckes.

II. *Procedural History*

The gravamen of plaintiffs' two-count amended complaint, brought under § 504 of the Rehabilitation Act, 29 U.S.C. § 794, and the Civil Rights Act of 1871, 42 U.S.C. § 1983, was that the board's failure to provide them with a due process hearing on the issue of Lauren's educational placement within 45 days of Mrs. Manecke's December 19, 1979 request, see 34 C.F.R. § 300.512, necessitated their unilateral transfer of Lauren to a residential facility. The relief they sought was an order requiring the Board to reimburse them for Lauren's tuition at Devereux and other expenses.

[Lower court proceedings omitted.]

III. *The EHA*

The EHA provides public school districts with federal funding for the education of handicapped children so long as the "[s]tate has in effect a policy that assures all handicapped children the right to a free appropriate public education." . . . The EHA also contains a detailed procedural component. Any state or local agency receiving federal assistance under the Act must, in accordance with the requirements of 20 U.S.C. § 1415, establish and maintain procedural safeguards. Among these is the requirement that parents be given the opportunity to contest virtually any matter concerning the educational placement of the handicapped child, or the provision of a "free appropriate public education" to such child. Additionally, if the parents of a handicapped child decide to bring a complaint, they must be given an "impartial due process hearing." Federal regulations mandate that a hearing must be held and a final decision must be reached not later than 45 days after the public agency receives a request for a hearing. Upon completion of the administrative process, any party dissatisfied with the administrative final decision may "bring a civil action with respect to the complaint" in either state or federal court.

The Maneckes, relying on *Smith v. Robinson*, 104 S. Ct. 3457 (1984), argue that the district court erroneously dismissed both counts of their amended complaint. They essentially contend that in the unique circumstances of this case, the EHA is not the exclusive avenue through which to seek relief. The Board, of course, disagrees. First, the Board insists that *Smith* requires us to affirm the district court's dismissal of the § 1983 count, albeit for reasons not articulated by the trial court. Second, the Board contends that the § 504 count failed to state a claim because (1) the amended complaint alleges no discrimination; (2) money damages are not available under that statute; and (3) *Smith* holds that the EHA is the sole remedy for handicapped children seeking a free appropriate public education. After carefully considering the arguments of both sides, we conclude that the district court erred in dismissing the § 1983 claim but correctly dismissed the § 504 claim.

IV. (a) *§ 1983 and the EHA*

The plaintiffs and the Board read *Smith* as supporting their respective positions on § 1983. A review of that case is therefore appropriate.

In *Smith* the plaintiffs brought suit under the EHA, § 504 of the Rehabilitation Act, and § 1983. [Discussion of lower court proceedings omitted.]

The Supreme Court affirmed the court of appeals, holding that the plaintiffs were not entitled to attorney's fees under either § 1988 or § 505 of the Rehabilitation Act. The Court arrived at this conclusion after examining the law on awarding attorney's fees on the basis of substantial, though unaddressed, constitutional claims, and the substantive aspects and detailed procedural requirements of the EHA, a statutory scheme which does not mention attorney's fees.

The Court, after noting that the plaintiffs' unaddressed due process and equal protection claims, [brought] under § 1983, were virtually identical to the EHA claims, undertook a separate analysis of these independent constitutional claims. The Court recognized "the comprehensive nature of the procedures and guarantees set out in the EHA" as well as the intent of Congress "to place on local and state educational agencies the primary responsibility for developing a plan to accommodate the needs of each individual handicapped child." The court also noted that in enacting the EHA, Congress attempted to accommodate the equal protection claims of handicapped children. With these factors in mind, the Court concluded that where a handicapped child asserts a right to a free appropriate public education, and the EHA is available, a claim based either on the EHA or on the Equal Protection Clause may be brought only under the EHA. Hence, the plaintiffs were not entitled to fees on the basis of their § 1983 equal protection claims.

The Court was more circumspect in the way it handled the unaddressed due process claim. The Court raised but did not decide the issue of "whether the procedural safeguards set out in the EHA manifest Congress' intent to preclude resort to § 1983 on a due process challenge." It was not necessary to resolve this threshold issue because the due process claim simply had no bearing on the substantive issue of the lawsuit — which agency was required to pay for the education of the minor handicapped plaintiff — and therefore could not support the award of fees.

The Board urges that *Smith* supports the district court's dismissal of the § 1983 claim. The Board, however, reads that decision more broadly than we do, and totally ignores the fact that the Court in *Smith*, admittedly in dicta, took pains to distinguish a due process claim from an equal protection claim.

Smith suggests that not all § 1983 claims are to be treated alike. Indeed, the Court expressly noted that the issue raised by an independent due process challenge "is not the same as that presented by a substantive equal protection claim to a free appropriate public education." Further, "unlike an independent equal protection claim, maintenance of an independent due process challenge to state procedures would not be inconsistent with the EHA's comprehensive scheme." Finally, speaking specifically to the issue of attorney's fees, the Court noted that Congress has not indicated "that agencies should be exempt from a fee award where plaintiffs have had to resort to judicial relief to force the agencies to provide them the process they were constitutionally due."

In our view, the approach the Supreme Court employed in *Smith* counsels holding that where, as here, a party is denied due process by effectively being denied access to "the carefully tailored administrative and judicial mechanism" found in the EHA, that party may seek relief under § 1983. The thrust of the Court's equal protection claim holding is unmistakable: Congress enacted the EHA, with its panoply of procedures, to clarify and make enforceable the handicapped child's right to a free appropriate public education. This right is grounded on the Equal Protection Clause. Accordingly, a plaintiff asserting that equal protection right as a basis for relief understandably should do so via the EHA, with all that that implies. This rationale, however, breaks down in the facts of this case.

The EHA "establishes an enforceable substantive right to a free appropriate public education." Moreover, Congress intended "the carefully tailored administrative and judicial mechanism" set forth in the EHA to be the vehicle to enforce that right. The plain language of the statute itself, however, suggests that Congress must not have intended the EHA to be the exclusive method to redress denial of access to that very mechanism.

The EHA provides that "[a]ny party aggrieved by the findings and decision" resulting from the administrative proceeding may bring an action with respect to the complaint presented initially to educational authorities. Additionally, the court, when reviewing the administrative proceedings, "shall receive the records of the administrative proceedings, shall hear additional evidence [upon request], and, basing its decision on the preponderance of the evidence, shall grant . . . relief." We believe that this language presupposes the existence of an administrative hearing or record. Moreover, the Supreme Court has instructed that this statutory language "is by no means an invitation to the [reviewing] courts to substitute their own notions of sound educational policy for those of school authorities." Rather, the state administrative proceedings are to be given "due weight," mainly because "[t]he primary responsibility for formulating the education to be accorded a handicapped child . . . was left by the Act to state and local educational agencies in cooperation with the parents . . . of the child." The Court therefore also has made it clear that the principal office of a court proceeding under the EHA is to review the administrative determinations contemplated by the Act. With these principles in mind, we conclude that where, as here, the local educational agency deprives a handicapped child of due process by effectively denying that child access to the heart of the EHA administrative machinery, the impartial due process hearing, an action may be brought under § 1983.

Post-*Smith* case law supports our conclusion. [Discussion of caselaw omitted.]

We initially noted that in *Smith* the Supreme Court did not resolve the § 1983 — EHA/exclusivity issue when a due process claim is involved. Rather than simply holding that a due process challenge could not be maintained apart from the EHA, we assumed that the conclusory allegations in the complaint that the defendants violated the Fourteenth Amendment by failing to comply with the procedural provisions of the EHA were sufficient to state a constitutional claim. We held that summary judgment for the defendants was proper, however, because a review of the record revealed that the defendants in no way contravened the procedural requirements of the EHA. That review would have been unnecessary had we not recognized that a due process challenge, at least in certain circumstances, could be maintained outside of the EHA.

In short, based on the language of the EHA itself, the *Smith* decision, and post-*Smith* case-law, we hold that the district court erroneously dismissed plaintiffs' § 1983 due process claim. We accordingly remand on that issue.

[The court's holding that the § 504 claim should be dismissed is omitted. The reason for the holding is that unlike EHA, § 504 does not require affirmative action.]

V. *Remaining Issues*

[The court's discussion of whether the court is bound by the administrative record in reaching its decision or whether it can consider new information is omitted. The court held that usually decisions should be confined to reviewing administrative proceedings.]

VI. *Damages*

Given its rulings, the district court never reached the issue of reimbursement. Since a remand of the § 1983 claim is indicated, we make the following observations which the district court should find useful in determining the amount of reimbursement to be ordered, if any is to be ordered at all. We hasten to add that in making these comments, we do not intend to limit the trial court's inquiry on the damages issue.

We are not remanding this case for an entry of judgment for a sum certain. Rather, on remand the district court's task is to determine the damages that flow from the due process violation. Although the record before us has not been developed to any great extent on the damages issue, there are suggestions in it that cause us some concern.

Lauren was enrolled in Devereux from March 21, 1980, until December 31, 1981, when she graduated. The Maneckes seek reimbursement in the amount of $40,000 for tuition paid and related expenses. It seems, however, that Lauren did not begin her academic classes until September, 1980. The Board, in its Proposed Findings of Fact and Conclusions of Law, indicates that Lauren contracted mononucleosis shortly after she began at Devereux and was unable to attend any academic classes for March and April of 1980. Additionally, during the summer months of that year, Lauren apparently was not enrolled in any academic classes at all. Although the parties have not briefed the issue, it seems to us that if these indeed are the facts, the Board may not be obliged under the EHA or any other statute to pay for boarding unaccompanied by academic classes. The district court should address itself to this question.

Perhaps more important is the Maneckes' refusal to agree to a due process hearing after Lauren was removed from Nina Harris and enrolled in Devereux. The Maneckes received a form in July, 1980, which if completed, would serve as a formal request for a due process hearing. The form was not returned to the Board, and a hearing accordingly was not scheduled. Additionally, the Board, in consultation with counsel for the Maneckes, scheduled a due process hearing for January 26, 1981. The hearing was cancelled at the Maneckes' request. As we view the case, there is a serious question that damages, if there were any, ceased accruing when the Board ceased violating the Maneckes' due process rights. If the facts conform to the Board's version, the Board may not be liable for any reimbursement.

VII. *Conclusion*

We hold that the district court erred when it dismissed plaintiffs' § 1983 claim alleging a deprivation of due process by virtue of the Board's failure to provide them with a timely impartial due process hearing. Lest our holding be broadly construed, we now emphasize its narrowness. We do not hold that § 1983 may be employed whenever a procedural deprivation occurs in the EHA context. We simply conclude that, under the facts of the instant case, the plaintiffs properly invoked § 1983. We affirm the district court's dismissal of the § 504 claim, though for reasons not cited by the district court. We further hold that because of the district court's § 1983 ruling, it improvidently addressed the EHA claim. On remand, the district court shall determine what damages, if any, the plaintiffs sustained as a result of the Board's deprivation of their right to due process.

Affirmed in part, *Reversed* in part, and *Remanded* for proceedings consistent with this opinion.

PROBLEMS

1. What § 1983 liability would be likely if a substitute teacher were not advised about the need to supervise a special education student, and the student was injured as a result? *Collins v. School Bd.*, 471 So. 2d 560 (Fla. Dist. Ct. App. 1985). See also

Greider v. Shawnee Mission Unified Sch. Dist., 710 F. Supp. 296 (D. Kan. 1989).

2. What should the obligation be where the school refuses to administer prescription medicine in excess of PDR recommendations? In *DeBord v. Board of Ed.*, 126 F.3d 1102 (8th Cir. 1997), the school refused to administer the medication, but offered to alter the student's schedule to permit home administration or to allow administration by the parent. The court held that this was a reasonable accommodation. What is the likely concern of the school in a case where such a medication regime is requested?

NOTES

1. *Failure to Supervise:* There have been a number of cases involving failures to supervise students with disabilities. The facts in these cases have included special education students who were sexually assaulted or physically injured by other students, special education students who were injured by equipment because they did not appreciate the dangers, and other circumstances. The injuries include not only physical injuries but also emotional damage in some cases. See LAURA ROTHSTEIN & JULIA ROTHSTEIN, DISABILITIES AND THE LAW § 2.57 (2009).

2. *Special Education Malpractice:* In addition to denial of access to due process procedures and failure to supervise, § 1983 has been used in a number of other situations as a theory of liability. The results have varied, and as *Lopez v. Houston Indep. Sch. Dist.*, 817 F.2d 351 (5th Cir. 1987), illustrates, this is a difficult area of law because of the conflicting standards relating to immunity, the degree of negligence necessary to give rise to a constitutional tort action under § 1983, and other reasons. See LAURA ROTHSTEIN & JULIA ROTHSTEIN, DISABILITIES AND THE LAW §§ 2.56, 2.57 (2009). It is quite unusual for courts to award damages in any case involving special education.

E ENFORCEMENT

One of the key aspects of the IDEA is the procedural safeguards that are required in order for states to receive funding under the Act. The safeguards apply whenever a child is identified, evaluated, or placed initially; when a change is proposed; or where the educational agency refuses to identify, evaluate, or place the child.

The key elements of the procedures include notice and right to a hearing if there is a disagreement about the child's identification, evaluation, or placement. The hearing is to be an impartial hearing, and the parents have a right to have representation at the hearing. The educational agency is not required to pay for the representation unless the parents are ultimately successful in the proceeding. This right to attorneys' fees and costs is a result of a 1986 amendment to the IDEA following the *Smith v. Robinson* decision excerpted at the beginning of the chapter, *supra* Section [A].

The 2004 IDEA amendments provided that attorneys' fees could be obtained against parents in cases involving litigation that is frivolous, unreasonable or without foundation or for an improper purpose. 20 U.S.C. § 1415(8)(3)(B).

The rights related to the hearing include a right to a record of the hearing and written findings of fact and decisions. The parents have a right to have the child present at the hearing, and it is the decision of the parents whether the hearing should be open or closed. The formality of the hearing, such as whether rules of evidence apply, depends on the state.

If either party disagrees with the decision of the hearing officer, a review may be requested of a state administrative agency. If there is still disagreement with the agency's decision, either party may bring an action in a state court with competent jurisdiction or in federal court.

The courts have been consistent and clear that parties must exhaust administrative remedies unless it would be futile to do so. Only on rare occasions have factual circumstances justified a finding of futility.

The procedural safeguards also include specifications about deadlines for bringing actions at various levels, rights related to access to a student's records, and the status of the child during the resolution. A number of procedural issues have been subject to judicial attention. These include whether a hearing officer is impartial in certain cases, whether attorneys' fees are available for prevailing at the administrative level, and whether exhaustion is required in a particular case.

The remedies available are generally equitable in nature. The parents would be likely to obtain injunctive relief ordering a placement or a provision of services, for example. Reimbursement is clearly an available remedy in appropriate cases, but the courts are not clear about compensatory education as a remedy in all jurisdictions. In a few cases, courts have recognized the availability of damages, but the Supreme Court has yet to rule on whether damages are available under the IDEA.

Where the claim is a pure discrimination claim, rather than a claim relating to special education, enforcement occurs through other avenues. Claims involving matters such as a child with HIV who is excluded from school may be brought directly to court alleging violation of Section 504 of the Rehabilitation Act and/or a violation of Title II or Title III of the ADA (depending on whether the school is public or private). In these cases, courts have been much clearer about the availability of damages for Section 504 and Title II cases, although punitive damages are not recoverable against state and local governmental agencies.

Complaints about discrimination under Section 504 or the ADA may also be made to the Department of Education. There is an administrative investigation procedure which follows in appropriate cases, but the complainant is not a party to any action taken, although the party may benefit from the Department of Education's investigation. In addition to injunctive relief, an administrative investigation might result in the termination of funds.

States and local educational agencies are not immune from actions under the IDEA, Section 504, or the ADA.

As noted in the previous material, courts are quite deferential to educational agencies regarding educational programming. In 2005, the Supreme Court gave guidance as to which party bears the burden or proof in administrative proceedings regarding the appropriate placement under IDEA. The Court held that "Absent some reason to believe that Congress intended otherwise . . . we will conclude that the burden of persuasion lies where it usually falls, upon the party seeking relief. . . . The burden of proof in an administrative hearing challenging an IEP is properly placed upon the party seeking relief." *Schaffer v. Weast*, 126 S. Ct. 528 (2005). This rule is to apply with equal effect to school districts and to parents. Whichever party seeks relief bears the burden of persuasion.

NOTE

For a detailed discussion and case citation on issues related to enforcement, see LAURA ROTHSTEIN & JULIA ROTHSTEIN, DISABILITIES AND THE LAW §§ 2.31-2.52, 2.55-2.57 (2009). See also 34 C.F.R. § 300.530-.543.

Chapter 8

HOUSING AND INDEPENDENT LIVING

A   INTRODUCTION

Until 1988, there was no comprehensive protection against housing discrimination on the basis of disability status. There were many state laws, but these varied a great deal in application and effectiveness. Federally funded housing is covered under Section 504 of the Rehabilitation Act, 29 U.S.C. § 794, but this applies to only a small segment of housing.

Section 202 of the federal Housing Act of 1959, 12 U.S.C. § 1701q(a)(2), also provides some protection. Section 202 is a loan program to enable nonprofit, limited-profit, or public agencies to build low cost housing. Recipients are required to provide services to facilitate independent living for their tenants. Only elderly tenants or those with disabilities are eligible for Section 202 housing. The types of disabilities include physical disabilities, mental impairments, and developmental disabilities. The definition under Section 202 refers to individuals whose disability is expected to be long-term and of indefinite duration, who are substantially impeded in the ability to live independently, and whose situation could be improved by more suitable housing conditions. 12 U.S.C. § 1701q(d)(4). A person also is covered if he/she fits within the definition of the Developmentally Disabled Assistance and Bill of Rights Act, 42 U.S.C. § 6001. This covers individuals with severe, chronic disabilities manifested before the age of twenty-two. 42 U.S.C. § 6001(7). Section 8 is another federal housing subsidy program. Under this program, landlords receive rent subsidies for housing that supports individuals with disabilities. 42 U.S.C. § 1437f(t); 24 C.F.R. § 5.403. This makes Section 8 subject to Section 504 nondiscrimination mandates.

In 1988, Congress amended the Fair Housing Act, which up until that time had prohibited housing discrimination only on the basis of race, color, sex, religion, and national origin. The 1988 amendments added familial status and handicap[1] as protected classifications. The definition of handicap under the amendment is virtually identical to the Rehabilitation Act definition. 42 U.S.C. §§ 3601 et seq.

The Fair Housing Act covers most issues related to housing discrimination against individuals with disabilities, with the Rehabilitation Act providing additional coverage for federally supported housing. Title II of the Americans with Disabilities Act, 42 U.S.C. §§ 12131 et seq., may also play a role because of the application to the

---

[1] The Fair Housing Act is the only major disability discrimination law that continues to use the term "handicap" instead of disability in its language, although the terms have virtually identical definitions. Throughout this chapter, except for judicial decision excerpts or direct reference to the statutory language, the authors use the term disability instead of handicap.

oversight of state and local agencies in land use regulation, including zoning. Under the amendments, discrimination on the basis of handicap refers not only to acts and practices such as refusal to rent and charging higher rent, but also requires new multiunit construction to meet specific accessibility guidelines for barrier-free design. Modifications to practices and policies also are required.

Elimination of discrimination, including barrier removal and reasonable accommodations, is an important beginning for individuals with disabilities to ensure mainstream participation in society. For many individuals with disabilities, there is a need for supportive services, such as home health care for individuals with certain health impairments, supervision for individuals with some mental disabilities, and attendant care for individuals with mobility impairments. Without funding support for these services, discrimination laws alone will not ensure the right to live in the community.

B   DISCRIMINATION

Most disability discrimination in housing probably results from unintentional practices, such as barriers in architectural design or policies that have a disparate adverse impact on individuals with disabilities. The most common type of discrimination that results from negative attitudes occurs in cases involving group homes for individuals with disabilities such as HIV, drug and alcohol histories, and mental retardation or mental illness. The manifestation of this discriminatory attitude results in denials of special use permits required for zoning variances for group homes or from enforcement of restrictive covenants in a discriminatory manner. The Supreme Court decision in *City of Cleburne v. Cleburne Living Ctr.*, 473 U.S. 432 (1985), challenged such discriminatory conduct by applying constitutional equal protection and due process principles. The Court applied the rational basis test in striking down the denial of a special use permit by a municipal zoning board as being based on unfounded prejudices against individuals who are mentally retarded.

Challenges to discriminatory conduct under the Constitution are only viable where there is state action. Thus, much private housing discrimination would not be prohibited. For this reason, the Fair Housing Act Amendments of 1988 provide a much more viable alternative for attacking discrimination in housing on the basis of disability.

HYPOTHETICAL PROBLEM 8.1

The Transitional Rehabilitation Access Veterans Equal Living (TRAVEL) Organization is a nonprofit social service provider whose mission is to provide transitional services for veterans of the military who have served in the Middle East and who have been injured during that service. TRAVEL is funded through a combination of federal and state grants, private contributions, and the veterans themselves. One of TRAVEL's major programs is to provide transitional group housing in cities where veterans' rehabilitation hospitals are located to allow individuals who have ongoing medical and rehabilitation needs to live near the hospitals until they can return to their own homes.

TRAVEL accomplishes this goal by purchasing or renting homes in residential neighborhoods that can accommodate eight to ten residents (plus a staff member) with a range of conditions. The average period of residence is generally twelve to eighteen months. The soldiers that seek this housing generally have some type of mobility impairments resulting from lost limbs or paralysis. Many have additional mental health needs such as post traumatic stress disorder. Some have become addicted to drugs or use alcohol, which began as a result of their combat experiences and injuries. One of the goals of TRAVEL is also drug and alcohol rehabilitation.

TRAVEL is seeking to rent two adjacent homes (one for men, one for women) in a residence near Springfield VA hospital and has begun discussing this with the owner of two similar large single-family dwelling with five bedrooms. The owner had originally lived in one home and had allowed adult children to live in the adjacent home. All have relocated to another area of the country. The neighborhood is middle income and has both private deed restrictions and zoning requirements regarding architectural and other issues. The home in question is ideally suited not only for proximity to the VA hospital but its proximity to the metro bus stop, which would allow residents to travel easily to the hospital and to other areas of Springfield for shopping and recreation. Having the male and female housing adjacent to each other will allow for economies of scale for transportation, home health care services, and other services. There is very little suitable rental housing available in this neighborhood.

The private deed restrictions prohibit carports and front entrance ramps because of their appearance and the goal of uniform aesthetic architecture. Zoning restrictions related to occupancy require that housing in the neighborhood should be single-family housing and any variances must be approved by the zoning commission. Zoning restrictions also provide that occupancy levels must ensure that for each resident there is at least 600 square feet of living space. The home at issue has 4500 square feet, which would only accommodate seven total occupants within the zoning requirements. Basement areas are not counted in the zoning regulations, although the houses in question have finished basements with an additional 1,000 square feet (including a finished full bathroom). For reasons of economic viability, TRAVEL seeks to have at least eight veterans plus one staff member live at each residence. There is a zoning and private deed restriction limiting the number of pets to three per residence and requiring that all animals be domesticated. Additional zoning restrictions prohibit "group homes" from being located within three blocks of each other.

TRAVEL has met the following problems in its efforts to locate the home at the desired location. The owner, who was eager to rent, initially has learned of TRAVEL's request to make some renovations in the house (lowering some light switches and adding reinforcements and grab bars in all bathrooms and some bedrooms, adding a temporary carport adjacent to the back entrance so that wheelchairs will not be damaged during inclement weather, and adding a ramp to the front entrance). TRAVEL is requesting a three year renewable lease and has promised to return the homes to their original condition after the lease ends. The goal is to continue to operate the homes so long as there is need and funding. The owner is reluctant to allow these changes and has advised TRAVEL that even if he would allow them, the homeowners' association would have to approve the front ramp and the carport and these variances would be unlikely because other residents would be concerned about the impact on their home value.

Initial discussions with the zoning board have raised concerns about the occupancy levels, the fact that two such residences would be located next to each other, and potential parking problems. Both the homeowner's association and the zoning officials have indicated serious concerns with TRAVEL's indication that occasionally there might be monkeys trained to assist with manual tasks and that there might be more than three animals on site. Both have raised concerns that at the very least, they would expect notification of any residents with drug abuse problems or mental health problems and a right to veto their occupancy.

The legal counsel for TRAVEL has been consulted about the best course of action, both in terms of legal rights in this situation and the feasibility and difficulty and strategic decisions of proceeding further.

The following case sets out the Fair Housing Act Amendment requirements in the context of a case involving a group home permit request. In this case, the group home was intended to be a hospice for HIV-positive, homeless individuals, in the later stages of the disease.

BAXTER v. CITY OF BELLEVILLE
720 F. Supp. 720 (N.D. Ill. 1989)

STIEHL, DISTRICT JUDGE:

On March 27, 1989, Baxter filed an application with the Belleville Zoning Board for a special use permit for a residence he desires to establish in the City of Belleville to provide housing for AIDS infected persons. On April 27, 1989, the Zoning Board voted to recommend that Baxter's request be denied. That recommendation was then presented to the Belleville City Council at its May 15, 1989 meeting. Baxter's request for a special use permit was denied by a 9 to 7 vote of the Council.

[The residence in question was for a one-year lease for a hospice for terminally ill patients.]

The Zoning Board hearing was held on April 27, 1989. Baxter's counsel made a lengthy presentation to the Board including traffic and parking impact, availability of local medical facilities, current zoning of the property and a description of the location. She told the Board that no one in the area opposed the special use request. Copies of an exchange of letters between Hospice of Southern Illinois and Baxter were presented to the Board with respect to the use of the term "hospice." However, not until the end of the presentation to the Zoning Board was it revealed that the residents of Our Place would be AIDS patients.

The Board members asked Baxter a number of questions, including whom he intended to house in the facility. Baxter told the Board that he would be housing

AIDS patients. The majority of the questions asked of Baxter concerned the members' fear of AIDS. The questions included: how potential residents would be screened; supervision of the residents; effect on the junior high school across the street; how Baxter would handle sanitation, including disposal of body fluids; why he chose Belleville for the residence; needs in Belleville for such a residence; and, whether Baxter, himself, was homosexual or had tested positive for the Human Immunodeficiency Virus (HIV).

Baxter informed the Board of his extensive history of providing in-home care for critically ill patients, including AIDS patients in the final stages of their disease. He spoke of three persons in Belleville who were HIV-infected and homeless and of Red Cross statistics to the effect that there are 3000 HIV-positive cases in Madison and St. Clair Counties. He also told the Board that he personally had spoken with the Superintendent of Schools about his plans for Our Place, and that the Superintendent had said that he had no problem with the residence plans. Baxter told the Board that AIDS persons deserved to live with dignity so that they could die with dignity.

Our Place is located in the 6th Ward, and both 6th Ward aldermen were present at the hearing. No opposition was raised by any member of the audience. The Board voted unanimously to recommend to the Board of Aldermen that Baxter's request for special use permit be denied.

The City designated Frank Heafner, one of the members of the Zoning Board, to testify on behalf of the Zoning Board. He testified that one of the important reasons the Board recommended denial of the permit was that Our Place would be close to a junior high school. The Board was also concerned with the potential change in property values in the area, and that people might stay away from that part of Belleville. He also stated that the Board was concerned with Baxter's lack of qualifications and they were uncertain how he was going to accomplish his plans. Heafner testified that it was the belief of the Board that Baxter would need more training, although he was not able to say exactly what training would be necessary to satisfy the Board's concerns. The Board members also expressed concern about the potential spread of AIDS through residents who might be intravenous drug users and homosexuals.

The Belleville City Council considered Baxter's request for a special use permit at its regular meeting held May 15, 1989. Alderman Koeneman of the 6th ward, where 301 South Illinois is located, made a motion to overturn the recommendation of the Zoning Board. The motion was seconded by Alderman Seibert, of the same ward.

Because there were a number of questions from the aldermen, Mayor Brauer requested and received permission from the Council for Baxter to respond to the questions. (No member of the public is permitted to speak at a Council meeting without formal approval by the Council.) Thomas Mabry, a Belleville alderman, was designated by the City to testify on behalf of the City Council. He stated that the majority of the questions from the aldermen were addressed to how the facility would be run and concerns of the aldermen about AIDS. He also testified that the City Council was concerned with the fact that Our Place would affect property values; that many of the residents would be intravenous drug users; and that the facility is located across the street from a junior high school.

Mabry stated that the main factors in his voting to refuse the special use permit were: (1) Baxter did not convince him that Baxter had the ability to run or fund the facility; (2) Baxter did not have sufficient medical or counseling background to run the facility; (3) Baxter did not have a plan for proper sanitation, specifically, disposal of items that would come into contact with the AIDS virus; and, (4) his major concern was the location of the residence — in a commercial area, in close proximity to both a junior high school and a grade school.

He also testified that he understood Baxter's intent to be to establish a residence for seven HIV-infected persons, but that during the meeting Baxter changed the number of prospective residents to four, of whom only two could be in the critical stages of the disease. Mabry admitted that he did not know of Baxter's medical background.

Mabry has served on both the City Council and the Zoning Board. He stated that the Council generally votes unanimously, and if the two aldermen for the ward in which the applicant property is located vote in favor of a variance, special use permit, or other zoning change, the other aldermen will vote with them. Mabry further testified that he could not recall an instance in which a request that was supported by the two aldermen of the ward in which the property was located had been denied by the Council.

Arthur Baum, Belleville City Clerk, testified that he was present at the City Council meeting, and confirmed Mabry's testimony as to the nature of the questions asked by the aldermen, and their concerns. Baum understood Baxter's intended use of the facility to be for the housing of terminally ill AIDS patients in the last stages of their disease. He stated that no one on the Council referred to any medical authorities or experts, and that to his knowledge none were consulted by the Council. He further testified that there was no specific determination by the Council as to the health and safety issues, although the vote indicated the Council's position. Baum testified that the aldermen made it clear that they were concerned about and feared the spread of HIV into the community if Our Place were allowed to open.

Baum testified that he has been City Clerk for ten years, and that he does not know of any other instance during that time when the Council voted against a request supported by the two aldermen of the ward in which the property was located.

[Baxter's background and experience as a home healthcare provider and in caring for individuals with AIDS is long and extensive.]

Plaintiff's expert, Robert L. Murphy, M.D., testified at length and in great detail as to the genesis, transmission and physiological development of the Human Immunodeficiency Virus, commonly referred to as "HIV." The Court finds that Dr. Murphy is qualified as an expert in the field of sexually transmitted diseases.

The City did not attempt to refute or rebut Dr. Murphy's testimony by offering its own expert.

[Medical findings omitted.]

Based on the conclusive medical evidence presented, the Court finds that persons who are HIV-positive pose no risk of its transmission to the community at large.

It is evident from Baxter's testimony that his intention for Our Place, has, from its inception, been to offer housing to persons who are HIV-positive, homeless, and in the later stages of the disease, but still able to care for themselves. However, throughout the evidentiary hearing the parties used the terms "AIDS" and "HIV-positive" interchangeably, although it is clear from the medical evidence before the Court that not all persons who are HIV-positive have progressed to the AIDS stage of the disease. In an effort to minimize confusion with respect to the Court's discussion of this deadly disease, it will be referred to as HIV, understanding AIDS to be included in that term.

(a) *Fair Housing Act*

Sections 3601, et seq. of the FHA are amendments to the Act which became effective March 12, 1989. Among the stated purposes for the amendments were the Congressional interest in expanding the Act to allow private litigants the right to challenge alleged discriminatory housing practices, and including handicapped persons among those protected by the Act.

Plaintiff asserts that his rights under § 3604(f)(1) and § 3617 have been violated by the City's refusal to grant him a special use permit and thereby allow him to open the residence to house up to seven persons with AIDS.

Section 3604(f)(1) makes it unlawful:

> To discriminate in the sale or rental, or to otherwise make unavailable or deny, a dwelling to any buyer or renter because of a handicap of — (A) that buyer or renter; (B) a person residing in or intending to reside in that dwelling after it is so sold, rented, or made available; or (C) any person associated with that buyer or renter.

Section 3617 provides:

> It shall be unlawful to coerce, intimidate, threaten, or interfere with any person in the exercise or enjoyment of, or on account of his having exercised or enjoyed, or on account of his having aided or encouraged any other person in the exercise or enjoyment of, any right granted or protected by section 3603, 3604, 3605, or 3606 of this title. This section may be enforced by appropriate civil action.

Because Baxter's claims under both § 3604 and § 3617 are founded on the same conduct or acts of the City, under the holding in Arlington Heights, for Baxter to have standing under § 3617, the Court must first be persuaded that he has standing under § 3604. Accordingly, the Court will first look to Baxter's standing to sue under § 3604(f)(1). The main thrust of section (f)(1) is to prohibit discrimination in housing based upon handicap. Therefore, the Court must determine whether persons infected with HIV are handicapped within the meaning of the statute.

(i) Determination of Handicap Under the Act

Section 3602(h) defines handicap as follows:

> (h) "Handicap" means, with respect to a person — (1) a physical or mental impairment which substantially limits one or more of such person's major life activities, (2) a record of having such an impairment, or (3) being regarded as having such an impairment, but such term does not include current, illegal use of or addiction to a controlled substance as defined in section 802 of Title 21.

The 1988 amendments to the FHA were modeled on the Rehabilitation Act of 1973.

It is clear from its legislative history that Congress intended to include among handicapped persons those who are HIV-positive. The Fair Housing Amendments [sic] Act, like Section 504 of the Rehabilitation Act of 1973, as amended, is a clear pronouncement of a national commitment to end the unnecessary exclusion of persons with handicaps from the American mainstream. It repudiates the use of stereotypes and ignorance, and mandates that persons with handicaps be considered as individuals. Generalized perceptions about disabilities and unfounded speculations about threats to safety are specifically rejected as grounds to justify exclusion. . . . People with Acquired Immune Deficiency Syndrome (AIDS) and people who test positive for the AIDS virus have been evicted because of an erroneous belief that they pose a health risk to others. All of these groups have experienced discrimination because of prejudice and aversion — because they make non-handicapped people uncomfortable. H.R. 1158 clearly prohibits the use of stereotypes and prejudice to deny critically needed housing to handicapped persons. The right to be free from housing discrimination is essential to the goal of independent living. Although Congress spoke in terms of persons with AIDS and "people who test positive for the AIDS virus," notwithstanding the problems with nomenclature, the legislative history supports a finding that Congress intended to include persons with HIV within the definition of handicapped.

In *School Board of Nassau County v. Arline*, 480 U.S. 273 (1987), the Supreme Court declined to determine whether a carrier of AIDS, that is an HIV-positive person, would fall within the definition of handicap under the Rehabilitation Act. The plaintiff in *Arline* was a tuberculosis victim, and not HIV-positive. Subsequent courts, however, have addressed the application of the Rehabilitation Act to persons with HIV, and have found that those with ARC and AIDS are handicapped under the Act.

[T]he inability to reside in a group residence due to the public misapprehension that HIV-positive persons cannot interact with non-HIV-infected persons adversely affects a major life activity. The Court therefore finds that persons who are HIV-positive are handicapped within the meaning of the FHA.

(b) *Application of § 3604(f)(1)*

In light of the evidence adduced at the hearing, it cannot be said that Baxter is, himself, infected with HIV. Therefore, § 3604(f)(1)(A) is not applicable in this action.

A more difficult question is whether Baxter has standing under (f)(1)(B). The precise language of subsection B prohibits discrimination due to the handicap of "a person residing in or intending to reside in that dwelling after it is so sold, rented or made available." Baxter proceeds alone in this action, and has not been joined as a party plaintiff by a HIV-positive individual who seeks to reside at Our Place.

A number of FHA cases offer some guidance to the Court on the issue of plaintiff's standing to sue. The Supreme Court, in ruling on prior FHA cases, has held that the prudential limitations on standing are not applicable in actions that are brought pursuant to the FHA.

In the case at bar, Baxter has testified that he has suffered economic injury from the loss of income from tenants due to his inability to go forward with his plans for Our Place. In addition, Baxter testified that he has invested his own money to remodel and repair the building, and for the deposit and rental costs of $1,500 per month. Among the renovations were the installation of a kitchen and window repairs. He further testified that he knows of three persons who are HIV-positive, homeless, and would move into Our Place if it were allowed to be opened. The economic injury Baxter has suffered is sufficient to support a finding that he has met the required Article III injury in fact to raise a case or controversy.

The Court further finds that, as a prudential matter, Baxter is the proper proponent of the rights under § 3604(f)(1) on which he bases his suit. As Baxter has standing under § 3604(f)(1), the Court may now address his standing under § 3617. Section 3617 makes it unlawful to interfere with the exercise or enjoyment of a right protected under § 3604. As the Court has determined that the actions of the City violated Baxter's rights under § 3604(f)(1), he may also proceed under § 3617.

Having determined that Baxter has standing to sue under § 3604(f)(1)(B) and 3617 of the FHA, the Court now addresses the issue of his likelihood of success on the merits of his claims. As stated earlier, Baxter's required showing is minimal. He need only establish that his chances of succeeding are more than negligible.

It has long been recognized that to give full measure to the Congressional purpose behind the FHA, courts have given broad interpretation to the statute.

There are two methods of showing a violation of § 3604. The first method is commonly referred to as an "intent" case. That is, plaintiff need only show that the handicap of the potential residents at Our Place, a protected group under the FHA, was in some part the basis for the City's action.

The evidence adduced at the hearing supports plaintiff's claim that irrational fear of AIDS was at least a motivating factor in the City's refusal to grant Baxter's special use permit. Furthermore, due to that fear, the City's actions were both intentional and specifically designed to prevent persons with HIV from residing at Our Place. Therefore, plaintiff has established a sufficient likelihood of success on the merits with respect to his "intent" case to entitle him to injunctive relief.

In addition, Baxter is likely to succeed on the alternative showing of a § 3604 violation. In *Arlington Heights*, the Seventh Circuit set out a four-pronged test for review of § 3604 causes of action in which the conduct produced a discriminatory effect, but was taken without discriminatory intent. This is known as an "impact" analysis. Although the *Arlington Heights* court was faced with racial discrimination under the FHA, the analysis therein is equally applicable to the 1988 handicap amendments to the FHA, and will be applied by this Court in its review of Baxter's claims. The court held:

> Four critical factors are discernible from previous cases. They are: (1) how strong is the plaintiff's showing of discriminatory effect; (2) is there some evidence of discriminatory intent, though not enough to satisfy the constitutional standard of *Washington v. Davis*, 426 U.S. 229 (1976); (3) what is the defendant's interest in taking the action complained of; and (4) does the plaintiff seek to compel the defendant to affirmatively provide housing for members of minority groups or merely to restrain the defendant from interfering with individual property owners who wish to provide such housing.

The court divided the first prong into two kinds of discriminatory effects which can be produced in a facially neutral housing decision. "The first occurs when that decision has a greater adverse impact on one [FHA protected] group than on another. The second is the effect which the decision has on the community involved. . . . " In this action only the first kind of discriminatory effect is applicable. It is evident that the actions of the City adversely impacted handicapped individuals, persons who are HIV-positive, more than non-handicapped individuals. The intent of Baxter was to open a residence for homeless HIV-positive persons. This group of persons has been adversely impacted each day the residence remains unopened. This form of discrimination is strong because all of the persons adversely affected, with the exception of Baxter, himself, are members of an FHA protected group of handicapped individuals.

The second prong is the discriminatory intent present in the conduct. The court noted, however, that this factor is the least important of the four in an impact determination. As previously discussed, it is evident from the testimony of the City's own witnesses that fear of AIDS and a desire to keep persons with HIV out of the Belleville community were, at least, compelling factors in the City's actions.

The third prong is the interest of the defendant in taking the action which produced the alleged discriminatory impact. The City has asserted that it acted pursuant to its legitimate interest in zoning, particularly land use and public health and safety. In support thereof, the City asserts that Baxter failed to demonstrate that he had the background to operate this facility or that he had a firm plan or program for operating the facility.

The Court acknowledges the City's stated concerns, but finds them to have been a pretext. If the City's true concerns were with Baxter's qualifications or his lack of a firm program or plan, it could have continued the Zoning Board or Council hearings, or both, and given Baxter an opportunity to respond to these concerns. The evidence, however, was substantial that both the Zoning Board and the City Council focused on the perceived threat of HIV and voted accordingly. That the City's actions were based on fear of HIV, and not a legitimate zoning interest, is further supported by the fact that although the two 6th ward aldermen were in favor of the special use permit and moved for its passage, they were out-voted by the Council. The City's witnesses, Baum and Mabry, both testified that they could not recall that ever happening before. Furthermore, no zoning ordinance was cited by the City as a basis for its action.

The final prong of the *Arlington Heights* analysis is the nature of the relief which the plaintiff seeks. Baxter is not seeking to compel the City to build public housing for HIV-positive persons, he seeks to be allowed to use available housing provided by him exclusively for a residence for this handicapped group.

Under the *Arlington Heights* analysis, the Court finds that plaintiff is likely to succeed on the merits of his impact claim.

4. *Exclusion Pursuant to § 3604(f)(9)*

The City asserts that its actions did not violate the FHA because they were made in accordance with the provisions of § 3604(f)(9). That section provides: "(9) Nothing in this subsection requires that a dwelling be made available to an individual whose tenancy would constitute a direct threat to the health or safety of other individuals or whose tenancy would result in substantial physical damage to the property of others." The City contends that Our Place constitutes a direct threat to the health or safety of others. In support thereof the City cites the fact that 301 South Illinois is across the street from a junior high school and near a grade school. In addition, the City focuses on the fact that HIV can be transmitted by illegal drug users, a group specifically excluded from the definition of handicap under § 3602(h).

The Court has found that the scientific and medical authority is that HIV-positive persons pose no risk of transmission to the community at large. The City has asserted that the risk of secondary infections, to which the HIV-infected individual is subject, pose a substantial health risk. However, of the secondary infections, only MAI [microbacterium avian intracellular, which is related to tuberculosis] is transmissible to the community at large. Standing alone, this is an insufficient health concern to warrant the City's refusal to allow Baxter's special use under the exclusion of § 3604(f)(9). Furthermore, the fear that intravenous drug users would pose a threat to the community, under the facts of this case, is unfounded. Baxter testified that he would, through a screening process, not accept current illegal drug users as residents at Our Place. Therefore, the Court finds that the exclusions of § 3604(f)(9) do not support the City's actions.

The Court has previously found that Baxter has standing under § 3617. Under the provisions of that section of the Act, the Court finds that the evidence supports Baxter's assertion that the City's refusal to allow his requested special use permit constituted an interference with the exercise of his rights under § 3604, as well as the potential interference with the rights of HIV-positive persons to a dwelling of their choice. Therefore, the Court finds that Baxter is likely to succeed on the merits of his § 3617 claim.

Conclusions

1. The defendant, City of Belleville, is hereby preliminarily RESTRAINED and ENJOINED from refusing to issue to plaintiff, Charles Baxter, a special use

permit for the residence at 301 South Illinois Street as a residence for HIV-infected persons.

2. The City of Belleville may establish reasonable restrictions as related to the issues of sanitation and non-admission of current illegal drug users as residents as conditions of said special use permit.

PROBLEMS

1. *Associational Disabilities:* In Chapter 2 which sets out the major requirements for protection under the major substantive statutes, it is noted that individuals who are associated with someone with a handicap are protected against discrimination under the Fair Housing Act. In fact, the *Baxter* decision involved associational disability protection. Would it violate the FHA to discriminate against gay men because it is believed that they are likely to be HIV positive? *Poff v. Caro*, 228 N.J. Super. 380, 549 A.2d 900 (1987).

2. *Danger to Others:* The *Baxter* case illustrates that the Fair Housing Act does not provide protection for individuals who pose a direct threat to the health or safety of others or whose tenancy would result in substantial physical damage to the property of others. 42 U.S.C. § 3604(f)(9). This case illustrates the general judicial consensus that discrimination in housing based on HIV status is impermissible because generally there is no risk. Would it be permissible for an apartment complex owner to prohibit individuals with HIV from using the apartment complex swimming pool? James Robinson, *Houstonian with AIDS Files Federal Fair Housing Complaint*, HOUSTON CHRONICLE, Aug. 3, 1994, at A23.

3. *Alcohol and Drug Use:* Individuals who are currently illegally using or addicted to controlled substances are not considered "handicapped" within the FHA. Housing specifically designed for recovering drug addicts and alcoholics, however, would be treated differently. Would it be legal for a private apartment complex to require prospective tenants to submit to drug tests? What about a governmental agency? M.R. Kropko, *Tenants Must Submit to Drug Tests*, HOUSTON CHRONICLE, Aug. 3, 1994, at A5.

4. *Disclosure Requirements.* Would a state law requiring realtors and sellers or lessors of housing to disclose any material fact that they know or should know about housing mean that the prior realtor, seller, or lessor must disclose that the prior occupant had HIV? Would such a law violate the Fair Housing Act? See Ralph Bivins, *Realtors Seeking Relief From Thorny AIDS Issue*, HOUSTON CHRONICLE, March 11, 1988, at A32.

5. *HIV and AIDS and the Definition of "Handicap/Disability."* The *Baxter* case does not dwell on whether the residents meet the definition of "handicap" under the Fair Housing Act, noting that "it is clear from its legislative history that Congress intended to include . . . those who are HIV-positive." The *Sutton* Court analysis, narrowing the definition under the ADA, could have been applied in housing cases, although it was more often applied in employment cases after 1999. The ADA Amendments Act of 2008, which returned the broader definition, would probably mean that HIV would today still be considered a "handicap" under the Fair Housing Act and under the ADA and Section 504 as they apply to housing.

Would the conditions (such as PTSD and drug and alcohol addiction) in the Hypothetical Problem be covered, even under the 2008 amendments?

6. *Greater Awareness About HIV.* The *Baxter* case was decided in 1989 at an early point in the public awareness of AIDS and HIV and their transmissibility. Is it more likely today that there would be less stereotype and prejudice in a case like this?

C REASONABLE ACCOMMODATION

Like the Rehabilitation Act and the Americans with Disabilities Act, the Fair Housing Act contemplates within its nondiscrimination prohibition that those entities subject to the Fair Housing Act provisions shall make reasonable accommodations. 42 U.S.C. § 3604(f)(3)(A) & (B). This may mean waiver of certain rules or adjustment of requirements. The following cases illustrate some of the types of accommodations the courts have considered in the context of housing.

[1]   Parking

SHAPIRO v. CADMAN TOWERS, INC.
844 F. Supp. 116 (E.D.N.Y. 1994)

SIFTON, DISTRICT JUDGE:

Background

Plaintiff, Phyllis Shapiro, is a guidance counselor at Middle School 88 in Brooklyn and a resident of Cadman Towers, a residential complex located on the edge of the Brooklyn Heights neighborhood of Brooklyn, New York. In 1975, plaintiff was diagnosed as suffering from multiple sclerosis. Multiple sclerosis is a chronic, progressive disease of the central nervous system, which primarily affects young women. The cause of multiple sclerosis and its cure remain unknown. Its symptoms include physical weakness, difficulty in walking, loss of balance and coordination, visual disturbance, fatigue, loss of stamina and severe headaches. Through the years and at different times, plaintiff has displayed a number of these symptoms, particularly those relating to her motor skills. The onset of these symptoms, their frequency, and severity are unpredictable, although there are some warnings of their onset. In plaintiff's case, the illness has followed a "relapsing progressive" course, meaning a pattern of progressive deterioration which in the course of time will likely totally disable her.

Like many multiple sclerosis sufferers, plaintiff is afflicted not only with problems of stamina and balance but also with a related neurogenic bladder disorder. Due to interference with the nervous system's mechanism for triggering a felt need to urinate, plaintiff's bladder is stretched and progressively collapsing onto itself, with the result that plaintiff has difficulty emptying her bladder. Since she is, as a result of the underlying illness, afflicted with painful bladder spasms of an incompletely voided bladder, she is from time to time rendered incontinent. To minimize the number and extent of these stressful episodes, plaintiff has in the past used a self-catheter. She has, however, frequently found herself involuntarily urinating between catheterizations, when unable to find a nearby restroom. In an attempt to shrink her bladder, plaintiff is currently using an indwelling catheter and an attached leg bag for a three month period. The procedure has its own negative side effects, including increased risk of infection. In fact, plaintiff has developed serious infections since the implant. Medications she takes for her related problems increase her liquid intake, thereby increasing her need to urinate. In the event plaintiff's abnormally large bladder cannot be shrunk, she faces a choice of surgery on her bladder or living with incontinence.

Although plaintiff's condition is slowly deteriorating, the regularity and intensity of her symptoms fluctuate. During good periods, plaintiff is able to walk by herself for short distances on level ground. At other times, however, she can only walk with the assistance of a cane or a wheelchair. In her workplace, plaintiff utilizes a motorized scooter, particularly as she tires in the afternoon. Like other multiple sclerosis patients, plaintiff's condition is aggravated by emotional stress and by extreme temperatures occurring during winter or summer. Also like other patients, plaintiff is periodically subject to episodes in which she experiences near or total paralysis, which so far do not last long.

Plaintiff employs her own car, a present from her mother, to get to work. Her attempts to use public transportation have been unsuccessful. She relies exclusively on her car for transportation beyond the immediate proximity of her apartment, except during such episodes when she cannot drive, when she uses a car service. In July of 1992, plaintiff received a special handicapped parking identification from the New York City Department of Transportation, which allows her to park at parking meters without paying and exempts her from the City's alternate side of the street parking rules.

Plaintiff currently parks her car on the street in Brooklyn Heights. Because plaintiff's apartment building is on the edge of residential Brooklyn Heights, next to the downtown commercial area, plaintiff must, at least until late evening, compete with both residential and nonresidential car owners to find a space. She must then walk from the parking place on the street to her apartment building with greater or lesser difficulty depending on the weather, time of day, whether the walk is uphill or downhill and the distance. At the moment, in New York's most severe recent winter, the dangers of the walk are aggravated due to icy conditions. Until recently, plaintiff's best hope of a spot was on a one block street named Monroe Place just south of her apartment building where she can take advantage of her exemption from alternate side of the street parking rules. However, other drivers, including officials employed at or visiting the courthouse on Monroe Place of the Appellate Division, Second Department, who also enjoy exemption from the City's parking rules, compete with her for this space until they leave in the evening. Moreover, the parking is adjacent to one- and two-family brownstones, one resident of which, plaintiff credibly testified, has threatened her with reprisals if she continues to interfere with the street cleaning schedule of his neighborhood. As a result of these problems, it has, on occasion, taken plaintiff as much as forty-five minutes to find a parking space, and her incontinence has forced her to relieve herself on the street or in the car. On other occasions, as both plaintiff and an employee of her building's security service called by the defendants testified, she has arrived at the building lobby in such distress as to have to use a lavatory in the lobby to relieve herself. Once plaintiff reaches her apartment she describes herself as feeling on occasion "like a prisoner," since the problems of losing her spot and having to find another at a late hour are too daunting to face.

Cadman Towers consists of two buildings located around the corner from each other — one at 101 Clark Street ("101 Clark") and the other at 10 Clinton Street ("10 Clinton"). There are approximately half as many parking spaces in the complex as there are apartments. 101 Clark has 302 apartments and 64 indoor parking spaces, and 10 Clinton has 121 apartments and 136 indoor parking spaces. The parking rate at either location at Cadman Towers is approximately $90 a month plus tax, whereas the nearest commercial parking in the neighborhood is $275 a month.

Due to the disparity in numbers between apartments and parking spaces, the cooperative has in the past generally allocated spaces on a first come/first served basis and required users of parking spaces to live in one of the two buildings and residents to enjoy no more than one parking space per apartment. There are, however, exceptions to this general policy. Six shareholders have two spaces. The explanation for this given by the Board's president is that the six got these spaces during a period when there was low demand. At least one elderly resident is allowed to let her son, who does not live with her, use her space, apparently because she does not drive and her son, on occasion, does errands for her. In the past, a resident with severe emphysema was given a parking space without regard for the waiting list and then accommodated to the extent of being allowed to offer a $1,000 reward for a space closer to his apartment in contravention of the usual policy prohibiting the sale of parking spaces. Also excepted from the first come/first served, residents-only policy are three spaces given without charge to building employees as part of the employees' compensation.

When the first come/first served policy is followed, the resident's name is placed on a waiting list, and when a parking space is awarded, the resident may use the space until he or she vacates the apartment. To obtain a spot on the waiting list, residents are required to communicate their desire to be placed on such list in writing and are placed on the list as of the date their letter is received. . . . The restrictions and the procedure to be followed in requesting a space are spelled out in a building guide, the Cadman Towers Handbook, which is supposed to be provided free to all residents upon taking up residency.

In September of 1989, plaintiff applied to buy an apartment in the complex. At the time, she informed the building management and Board that she suffered from multiple sclerosis and further checked a box on the application form indicating that she would be seeking a parking space. Plaintiff claims not to have been informed that there was a waiting list for these spaces and does not recall receiving the building guide containing the parking space application procedures. Defendants do not consider the application to buy an apartment, even when completed as plaintiff completed it, to be an application to be placed on the waiting list for a parking space.

In June of 1990, plaintiff purchased her apartment at 101 Clark and has resided there since that time. On two occasions in February and March of 1992, plaintiff called the property manager for the complex and requested a parking space in 101 Clark due to her handicap. Plaintiff was informed that she would not be given a space and that her name would have to go on the waiting list. On March 25, 1992, plaintiff renewed her request for an immediate parking space by letter. The letter was written by plaintiff's brother, a lawyer, and contained information regarding plaintiff's handicap. Defendants again denied plaintiff's request. On April 14, plaintiff submitted another letter, this time written by her present counsel. The Board denied this request as well.

At the hearing before the undersigned, defendant Levy testified that the principal reason for denying plaintiff's application was the Board's concern with maintaining the integrity of the waiting lists which the Board felt would be threatened by any type of exception. In addition, it appears clear that the Board was suspicious of plaintiff's handicap. This suspicion remained unexamined, that is, no request for additional medical information or physical examination was made by the Board or any of its members, and Board members, like a number of building residents who testified at trial, confined themselves to remarking that they had not noticed that plaintiff had difficulty walking. (A witness at trial testified that "she seemed normal to me." Plaintiff, in an unrelated response to cross-examination by defendants' counsel at the hearing, gave the appropriate answer to these comments: that discrimination against the handicapped often begins with the thought that she looks just like me — that she's normal — when in fact the handicapped person is in some significant respect different. Prejudice, it bears recalling, includes not just mistreating another because of the difference of her outward appearance but also assuming others are the same because of their appearance, when they are not.) Another ground for the Board's suspicions and for issues raised about plaintiff's credibility at the hearing were questions about her candor in asking for a two-bedroom apartment in her initial application because of a need for a 24-hour-a-day attendant as a result of her progressive disease. So far plaintiff has had an attendant with her only when suffering from near or total paralysis. Given the dire prognosis plaintiff has been given by her doctors, it is not at all incredible that she has and will face the need for a round-the-clock companion, and in fact a companion will undoubtedly in the future be called upon more and more regularly to share plaintiff's living space.

After receiving the letter from plaintiff's brother and after consulting with their own counsel, the Board took the position that any duty to accommodate plaintiff's disability would only come into being at the time she was awarded a parking space, and not before. As expressed by defendant Levy, the Board's position was and remains that no reasonable accommodation is due plaintiff at the waiting list stage and that she must wait the same number of years as a nonhandicapped tenant before she obtains a space. When she is awarded a space, the Board then appears to have in mind considering whether existing spaces should be rearranged so as to place plaintiff's space in 101 Clark rather than in 10 Clinton.

Discussion

42 U.S.C. § 3613(c) provides that, in a civil action under the provisions of the FHAA, the court may grant as relief any permanent or temporary injunction "or other such order (including an order enjoining the defendants from engaging in such practice or ordering such affirmative action as may be appropriate)."

In order for a preliminary injunction to issue, plaintiff must demonstrate (1) irreparable harm and (2) either (a) a likelihood of success on the merits or (b) sufficiently serious questions going to the merits to make them fair ground for litigation and a balance of hardships tipping decidedly toward the party requesting the preliminary relief. Irreparable harm must be shown to be imminent, not remote or speculative, and the injury must be such that it cannot be fully remedied by monetary damages.

Plaintiff easily meets the first requirement for a preliminary injunction, namely, the likelihood of irreparable harm should the injunction not issue. As a patient suffering from multiple sclerosis, plaintiff is subject to an incurable disease that gradually and progressively saps her strength and interferes with her balance and bodily functions. Without a parking space in her building, plaintiff is subjected to risks of injury, infection, and humiliation substantially different in kind and magnitude from the inconveniences the nonhandicapped driver faces in finding parking on the City's streets. Plaintiff's disease makes her a candidate for accidental loss of balance, particularly during the winter season when her condition is aggravated. In addition, her urinary dysfunction results in episodes of embarrassing humiliation and discomfort which could be significantly reduced were she allowed to park indoors. The inconvenience suffered by a typical city resident forced to deice the car after a winter snowstorm is mild when compared to the discomfort, stress, and ensuing fatigue experienced by plaintiff when faced with the same task. Under these situations, it is clear that plaintiff has met her task of demonstrating a likelihood of irreparable harm were her exclusion from parking in the building allowed to continue during the pendency of this litigation.

An analysis of plaintiff's likelihood of success on the merits requires a preliminary discussion of the statutory framework within which plaintiff brings her action. The FHAA was passed by Congress in 1988 with the stated purpose of (1) creating an administrative system to enforce the nation's housing discrimination laws, (2) extending the principle of equal opportunity to handicapped individuals, and (3) extending these civil rights protections to families with children. . . . Section 3604(f)(2) forbids discriminat[ion] against any person in the terms, conditions, or privileges of sale or rental of a dwelling, or in the provision of services or facilities in connection with such dwelling, because of a handicap of . . . that person. . . . Section 3604(f)(3) further defines discrimination as including

> a refusal to make reasonable accommodations in rules, policies, practices, or services, when such accommodations may be necessary to afford such person equal opportunity to use and enjoy a dwelling . . . .

Under the 1988 amendments, a person believing herself to be the target of a discriminatory practice under the Fair Housing Act is entitled to file a complaint with the Secretary of HUD. Upon receiving the complaint, the Secretary is to conduct an investigation, and to attempt conciliation. If a conciliation cannot be attained, the Secretary is to make a determination as to whether reasonable cause exists to believe that a discriminatory housing practice has occurred. If the Secretary believes that discrimination has occurred, he is instructed to issue a charge on behalf of the aggrieved party. Such a finding and charge have been issued in this case. The parties then have the option to elect to bring the proceeding before an administrative judge or commence an action in a federal district court. In this case, plaintiff elected to have her case heard in this Court. [T]he Secretary then authorizes the Attorney General to commence a proceeding on the aggrieved individual's behalf.

42 U.S.C. § 3613(a)(1) also allows an aggrieved person to commence a civil action in an appropriate United States district court or state court no later than two years after the occurrence of the discriminatory housing practice. Because of plaintiff's need for immediate relief, she has filed this action without waiting for the Attorney General to commence hers. The Justice Department filed its action shortly thereafter.

[There is not] much question that defendants' first come/first served policy is a rule, policy, or practice within the meaning of the FHAA and that indoor parking is part of the services and facilities provided at plaintiff's building.

In a case such as this, plaintiff's need to show a likelihood of success on the merits would usually translate into demonstrating that defendants had a duty to reasonably accommodate her request for a parking space and that no such reasonable accommodation was made. In the present case, however, defendants have conceded that they made no attempt at an accommodation, and the central issue for resolution remains only the existence of defendants' duty.

Defendants appear to make the argument that, because plaintiff has not yet made it to the top of the list, when she would be entitled to a parking space under the building's existing regulations, indoor parking is not yet part of the services and facilities provided "in connection with plaintiff's dwelling." Such an argument, however, ignores the fact that parking space at Cadman Towers is something all shareholders, including Ms. Shapiro, own and control in common as members of the cooperative corporation. The first come/first served policy is not, in other words, a creature of the lease to Ms. Shapiro's apartment or her contract of sale but of the building's rules and regulations which may be changed by the appropriate vote of all the members of the cooperative under the building's by-laws.

The fact that the rules and regulations are longstanding does not exempt them from the FHAA. . . .

Defendants also appear to argue that the fact that there are fewer parking spaces than apartments or "dwellings" also somehow severs the connection between the dwellings and the parking spaces. Although the House Report was correct in noting that the phrase "reasonable accommodation" has been much written about in connection with other types of discrimination and discrimination against the handicapped in other areas, there is remarkably little authority on its meaning and requirements in a housing situation such as the one faced here, involving the allocation of a scarce good among handicapped and nonhandicapped individuals.

Nevertheless, it seems common sense that in a situation of scarcity each individual has a connection with the scarce good.

Case law interpreting the "reasonable accommodation" language in the provisions of the FHAA has analogized the language to similar provisions in the Federal Rehabilitation Act.

As with other agencies under the Rehabilitation Act, HUD was given the power to promulgate regulations instituting the provisions of the Fair Housing Act. 24 C.F.R. § 100.204(b) was the regulation specifically promulgated by HUD to implement the "reasonable accommodation" requirements of section 3604. After restating the language of the statute, the regulation proceeds to give two examples of a reasonable accommodation. The first involves a blind applicant for rental housing who wished to keep her seeing eye dog in a building with a "no pets" policy. The example states that allowing the handicapped individual to keep her dog would be a "reasonable accommodation" within the meaning of the regulation.

The second example given in section 100.204 involves a handicapped resident of a building in need of a specific parking space. Given the similarities between the example and the current case, the example is reproduced here in its entirety:

> Progress Gardens is a 300 unit apartment complex with 450 parking spaces which are available to tenants and guests of Progress Gardens on a first come first served basis. John applies for housing in Prospect Gardens. John is mobility impaired and is unable to walk more than a short distance and therefore requests that a parking space near his unit be reserved for him so he will not have to walk very far to get to his apartment. It is a violation of § 100.204 for the owner or manager to refuse to make this accommodation. Without a reserved space, John might be unable to live in Progress Gardens at all or, when he has to park in a space far from his unit, might have difficulty getting from his car to his apartment unit. The accommodation therefore is necessary to afford John an equal opportunity to use and enjoy a dwelling. The accommodation is reasonable because it is feasible and practical under the circumstances.

In their brief, defendants point out that the example in section 100.204 and [a] decision by the ALJ both deal with situations where there are sufficient parking spaces for all the residents of the building so that the only issue was how best to apportion the spaces. They argue that in this case, by way of contrast, there is a condition of scarcity with insufficient spaces for all residents.

Although there are clear differences between the example given in the CFR and the present fact situation, these are differences of degree rather than of kind. It is not correct to state that the current problem deals with the allocation of scarce goods, whereas the situation in the CFR does not. The CFR example also clearly deals with a scarce good, namely, the valued parking spaces nearest the apartments. Giving the best spaces to handicapped individuals will clearly inconvenience those nonhandicapped individuals who also prize them. However, for the nonhandicapped individuals the prime parking spaces are a convenience, whereas for the handicapped they are instrumental to living as close to normal lives as possible.

In the situation at bar the good whose distribution is at issue is the parking space itself, not the best parking spaces. Although defendants correctly point out that the good in question here is more prized by the nonhandicapped than the good in the CFR example (i.e., nonhandicapped individuals value a parking space over no parking space far more than they value a prime parking space over a bad one), this is, in terms of the existence of a duty to accommodate, irrelevant as the handicapped will have the same preferences as the nonhandicapped, only of a far more intense degree due to their acute need (and not simple desire) for the spots. In other words, the fact that the stakes are higher in this situation is beside the point, as they are higher for everyone. Everyone has, as a result of his or her membership in the cooperative, a connection with the building's parking space which interests each to a different degree.

Defendants' only legal support for their position is found in cases involving seniority rights established under collective bargaining agreements between management and labor. Those cases are distinguishable both factually and legally. Factually, defendants' first come/first served policy is not a creature of contract. Nor does it fulfill any national goal recognized by statute. In a Title VII case involving allegations of religious discrimination, the Court refused to disturb the seniority system and force some workers to work for others on religious holidays on the ground that "[c]ollective bargaining, aimed at effecting workable and enforceable agreements between management and labor, lies at the core of our national policy, and seniority provisions are universally included in these contracts." The Court further noted that Title VII itself provides that a bona fide seniority system will not be unlawful under its provisions.

In another representative case, an asthmatic employee of the post office sued under the Rehabilitation Act, claiming that the post office refused to accommodate his handicap by giving him "permanent light duty" jobs. The court noted that the language of the Rehabilitation Act only prohibits discrimination against the individual when he is "otherwise qualified." The court held that under the seniority system embodied in the collective bargaining agreement, plaintiff had not worked the number of years that would qualify him for the position and that he was, thus, not "otherwise qualified" for the position.

Accordingly, based on the statute, the legislative history, case law, and regulations promulgated by HUD and mindful of the fact that this chapter "is to be construed generously to ensure the prompt and effective elimination of all traces of discrimination within the housing field," I conclude that a "reasonable accommodation" of plaintiff's needs by reason of her handicap will in all probability require modification of defendants' first come/first served policy. In insisting that the policy of first come/first served remain inviolable whatever plaintiff's handicap and needs, defendants display the frame of mind which Congress sought to alter by requiring reasonable accommodations of the needs of the handicapped.

Although plaintiff has demonstrated a clear likelihood of success in establishing that defendants violated the FHAA, it would be inappropriate at this early point in the litigation to determine in any detail the manner in which defendants should accommodate those of its residents who are handicapped. Such a finding at this point would be an unnecessary judicial intrusion into the affairs of a private entity, despite the fact that defendants up to now appear to have given this aspect of its affairs little thought. As noted, defendants up to now have refused to make any accommodation. It is expected that this ruling will stimulate them to consider the available options by which they may fulfill their statutory duties.

Although this Court will not at this point determine what measures may ultimately prove necessary to accommodate plaintiff's handicap in a reasonable fashion, this is not an obstacle to ruling that plaintiff must in the interim be given the space she requires until such time as the trial of this matter is concluded or another reasonable accommodation is worked out. Defendants have not suggested that plaintiff, as one out of over 400 members of her cooperative, is making a demand out of line with the ratio of handicapped to nonhandicapped drivers in New York City. Nor have they suggested that she must compete with other handicapped drivers for the space or that she is not entitled to priority among them. Defendants have failed to propose other solutions, and plaintiff's irreparable harm outweighs any harm to defendants in meeting plaintiff's immediate needs.

Accordingly, plaintiff's motion for a preliminary injunction is granted, and defendants are hereby enjoined from refusing to provide plaintiff with a parking space on the lobby/ground floor of Cadman Towers' garage at 101 Clark Street in Brooklyn, New York, in reasonable proximity to the building lobby.

NOTES AND QUESTIONS

1. The facts in the previous case indicate that the Board was "suspicious of plaintiff's handicap." This highlights the challenge of "hidden" disabilities. A person who does not look like there is a disability may not seem to need accommodations. This can be true for mental illness, diabetes, epilepsy, fibromyalgia, and other conditions. What kinds of documentation should Phyllis Shapiro be required to present to verify that she has a disability entitling her to a reasonable accommodation? Is she more likely to be covered today than before the ADA Amendments Act of 2008?

2. The *Casey Martin* case in Chapter 4 also involves a case where documentation of his condition would probably be required because he is seeking a significant exception to the rule, as is the case with the *Shapiro* situation. To what extent might decision makers be denying accommodations or exceptions because they are concerned about opening the floodgates? In the case of golf tournaments, will the golfer with a mild heart condition now want a cart for a local tournament that does not allow them? If Cadman Towers gives Phyllis Shapiro a parking space (and one close to the entrance) are there concerns that many other residents will now ask for exceptions? In what situations might these concerns be legitimate? Does the potential for others to seek the same accommodation affect whether it would be unduly burdensome to grant an exception?

PROBLEMS

1. Should a city be required to allow residents to put paved parking spaces in front of their homes to facilitate access? *Trovato v. City of Manchester*, 992 F. Supp. 493 (D.N.H. 1997) (holding that failure to allow such an exemption violates the

FHA).

2. Must parking ever be provided free of charge? *Hubbard v. Samson Mgt. Corp.*, 994 F. Supp. 187 (S.D.N.Y. 1998) (FHA might required apartment complex that has free unreserved parking to provide some reserved spaces without charge); *United States v. California Mobile Home Park Management Co.*, 29 F.3d 1413 (9th Cir. 1994) (requiring waiver of daily parking fee for frequent home health care aide who provided daily services for a child with a respiratory disease).

[2]   Accommodating Mental Illness and Substance Abuse

The challenge for individuals with mental illness and housing are many. The cases that follow demonstrate some of the issues with respect to reasonable accommodations and discrimination. The challenge may be that where an individual does not have access to adequate mental health treatment (which may be due to unemployment because of mental illness), the behavior may become unacceptable. These individuals may be evicted from housing as a result. There is evidence that individuals with mental illness are disproportionately represented in the homeless population. For a discussion of the relationship of various laws, see Laura Rothstein, *Protections for Persons with Mental Disabilities: Americans with Disabilities Act and Related Federal and State Law*, Chapter 9 *in* Law, Mental Health, and Mental Disorder (Bruce D. Sales & Daniel W. Shuman eds., Brooks/Cole Publishing Co. 1996).

CITY WIDE ASSOCIATES v. PENFIELD
409 Mass. 140, 564 N.E. 2d 1003 (1991)

O'Connor, Justice:

[This case involved a 77-year-old tenant who suffered from a serious mental disability manifested by hearing voices from the walls of her apartment. The tenant hit the walls with a broom or stick, threw objects or water at the walls in response to these hallucinations. Some nicks and gouges and water damage has resulted in the amount of approximately $519. This is a federal housing project, so § 504 of the Rehabilitation Act was applied.]

"The Supreme Court [has] struck a balance between the statutory rights of the handicapped to be integrated into society and the legitimate interests of federal grantees in preserving the integrity of their programs: while a grantee need not be required to make 'fundamental' or 'substantial' modifications to accommodate the handicapped, it may be required to make 'reasonable' ones."

In this case, the judge was confronted with the question whether the landlord's obligation under § 504 reasonably to accommodate the tenant's mental illness and resulting damage to the apartment required the landlord to permit the tenant to continue to occupy the apartment despite the tenant's violation of the lease provision prohibiting defacement or damaging of the dwelling unit. [The tenant had struck the walls with a broom.] The judge reasoned that "[b]ecause the tenant pleads unlawful discrimination as an affirmative defense the burden is on her to prove her claim. As with any other discrimination claim, the burden is on the tenant to prove a prima facie case of discrimination. The burden of production (but not the ultimate burden of persuasion) then shifts to the respondent to prove that the challenged act was not discriminatory." Neither the landlord nor the tenant contests that allocation of the burdens of production of evidence and persuasion.

According to the judge's memorandum, the tenant met her burdens of production and persuasion by proposing a modification of her obligations under the tenancy agreement which the judge concluded would constitute a "reasonable accommodation" of the tenant's handicap and thus would entitle her to continued possession at least in the absence of further significant damage. The proposal was that the landlord would "forbear from further eviction steps (presumably, as long as the tenant's conduct does not change substantially) to give her an opportunity to pursue a program of outreach and counselling." This, the judge concluded, was "a reasonable step as long as more substantial damage is not caused. The [landlord] has not shown that it would be greatly prejudiced by holding off further and giving the tenant further opportunity to find the assistance needed to address the problem." In arriving at his conclusion that the tenant was "qualified" to remain in the unit "absent a substantial change in circumstances," the judge expressly took into account the cost of the damage caused by the tenant due to her mental illness, which he characterized as "small" (less than one month's rent), the fact that, under the contract between the landlord and HAP, the landlord was entitled to reimbursement of up to two months rent for tenant-caused damage, and the lack of evidence that other tenants were affected by the defendant tenant's conduct.

Whether a tenant's proposed accommodation of a disability is "reasonable" within the meaning of the relevant decisions is not susceptible of precise measurement, but we are persuaded that the judge exercised proper judgment in this case. Indeed, the landlord's only argument that meets the requirements of [state law] is that the tenant failed to show that she would cooperate with any program involving counselling or medication or otherwise take steps to correct the mental condition that prompted her destructive conduct. Even so, given the superficiality of the damage, the reimbursement available to the landlord, as found by the judge, and the absence of evidence of adverse impact on other tenants, we agree with the judge that, in the absence of further significant damage, the tenant is "otherwise qualified" under § 504, and that eviction on this record would be discriminatory and therefore unlawful.

PROBLEMS

1. Is it permissible for landlords to ask prospective tenants about prior drug use? What about prior criminal records that might relate to drugs? *Campbell v. Minneapolis Pub. Hous. Auth.*, 175 F.R.D. 531 (D. Minn. 1997) (housing applicant could not be asked about prior drug use).

2. Mr. A suffers from manic depression and applies to rent an apartment at Pleasant Acres Apartment Complex in Big City, USA. His application noted his mental condition, and he had excellent references and a medical report stating that he could live in a socially responsible manner. His application, however, was denied. The apartment manager had learned of several criminal acts by Mr. A that had occurred over the four years preceding his application, including deflating a

government official's car tires, spray-painting a police car, and making a bomb threat. Is the action by Pleasant Acres a violation of the FHA? Should the rental application be permitted to ask questions about mental history? If it were found that such questions were impermissible under the FHA, would Mr. A be likely to win an injunction against denying his apartment rental? *Quaker Hill Place v. Saville*, 523 A.2d 947 (Del. Super. 1987).

[3]   Accommodations for Assistance or Service Animals

Individuals with a range of disabilities often have an animal to assist or provide support in some other way. These situations can raise a variety of issues, including whether the individual has a disability (to be entitled to nondiscrimination or accommodation), whether the individual is otherwise qualified (including whether the animal presents a danger to safety or health or is disruptive in some way), and whether the modification of a policy is reasonable. The following case is one of the early decision addressing this issue.

CROSSROADS APARTMENTS ASS'N v. LEBOO
152 Misc. 2d 830, 578 N.Y.S.2d 1004 (City Ct. 1991)

JOHN R. SCHWARTZ, JUDGE:

Factual Background

The tenant, Kenneth LeBoo, is a forty-nine year old male with a long history of mental illness dating back to the late 1960's. His mental condition has been diagnosed as panic disorder with agoraphobia, mixed personality disorder, and chronic anxiety with a history of episodic alcohol abuse. The landlord, Crossroads, is an apartment complex located within the City of Rochester, New York, which consists of 518 residential apartment units. 496 of these apartment units are subject to a federally-funded Section 8 Housing Assistance Payment Contract. LeBoo has been a tenant since 1978, pursuant to a written lease and receives Section 8 assistance. No real problems existed between the parties until LeBoo obtained the subject cat in the spring of 1990. Mr. LeBoo alleges he acquired the cat to help alleviate his intense feeling of loneliness, anxiety and depression, which are daily manifestations of his mental illness.

Upon discovering the cat in LeBoo's apartment, Crossroads commenced the instant proceeding. After brief discovery, both sides now move for summary judgment.

I.

New York Courts have long recognized the validity of "no-pet clauses" in leases, and harboring a pet when a lease contains a "no-pet clause" constitutes a substantial breach of the lease agreement. Acceptance of the rent over a period of time after discovery of the pet still does not render the "no-pet clause" unenforceable. Landlords may also selectively enforce the "no-pet clause."

II.

LeBoo further urges this Court to determine as a matter of law that he has established that Crossroads has violated Section 504 of the Rehabilitation Act of 1973 and the Fair Housing Amendments Act of 1988. To support his claim, he submits three expert affidavits which state that LeBoo's cat is necessary for him to use and enjoy his apartment.

Crossroads, on the other hand, urges this Court to determine as a matter of law that LeBoo has not established even "prima facie" the necessity of his cat to assist him in coping with his mental illness. They also submit an affidavit of a psychiatrist.

To prove that Crossroads has violated both acts, LeBoo must demonstrate that: 1) he is handicapped; 2) he is otherwise qualified for the tenancy; 3) that because of his disability, it is necessary for him to keep the pet in order for him to use and enjoy the apartment; and 4) reasonable accommodations can be made to allow him to keep the pet.

First, LeBoo is a handicapped person. There is no dispute about that factual issue. Both parties' doctors diagnose him as having a mental illness that makes him disabled.

Second, he is an otherwise qualified person for tenancy except for the pet. "An otherwise qualified person is one who is able to meet all of the program's requirements in spite of his handicap." LeBoo had lived at Crossroads twelve years without incident before he obtained his pet. Clearly, he meets all other criteria for tenancy, if not for the pet.

Third, LeBoo must prove that the pet is necessary for him to use and enjoy his apartment. To prevail on this issue, LeBoo must demonstrate that he has an emotional and psychological dependence on the cat which requires him to keep the cat in the apartment. To support his claim, LeBoo has submitted the affidavits of his treating psychiatrist, his clinical social worker, and a certified pet-assisted therapist. They all describe his mental illness, his course of treatment, and conclude that LeBoo receives therapeutic benefits from keeping and caring for his cat. Also, they conclude that the keeping of the cat assists him in his use and enjoyment of his apartment by helping him cope with the daily manifestations of his mental illness.

In opposition, Crossroads submits the affidavit of its psychiatrist who has seen LeBoo twice, examined all his relevant medical records, and concludes that there is "no significant clinical evidence that the cat is necessary or required for LeBoo to be able to fully use and enjoy his apartment." He further concludes in his report that LeBoo was placed on the drug Prozac around the same time he acquired the cat and LeBoo's clinical course since taking Prozac has been slightly less tumultuous.

Based on these conflicting opinions, this is not an issue ripe for summary judgment. Genuine issues of fact exist as to whether this cat is necessary for LeBoo to use and enjoy his apartment. "If and when the Court reaches the conclusion that a genuine and substantial issue of fact is presented, such determination requires the denial of the application for summary judgment." Here, there is a genuine triable issue of fact, namely, whether this cat is necessary for LeBoo to use and enjoy his apartment.

Fourth, can reasonable accommodations be made by Crossroads which would permit LeBoo to keep his cat? This also constitutes a question of fact. LeBoo alleges that allowing him to keep his cat would not result in any undue financial or operational hardship to Crossroads. He claims reasonable accommodations could be made to allow him to keep his cat.

However, accommodations which place "undue financial and administration burdens" on Crossroads would not be reasonable. The property manager of Crossroads, in her affidavit, states that the cat would cause an undue administrative burden, and would create health problems for other tenants. This affidavit creates a question of fact concerning this issue.

[The court denied the landlord's motion for summary judgment and struck the demand for jury trial.]

PROBLEMS

1. In *LeBoo*, documentation was presented to support the request for the accommodation. What kinds of documentation should be required both to demonstrate a covered "disability" and to justify the requested accommodation? How will this be addressed with respect to the concerns about the types and numbers of animals in Hypothetical Problem 8.1?

2. Would the courts be likely to allow pet deposits for assistance or support animals in an apartment complex that ordinarily does not permit pets?

D STRUCTURAL BARRIERS

The Fair Housing Act incorporates two major requirements relating to structural modifications of premises. These relate to obligations with respect to existing facilities and those related to new construction. The requirements mandating that new construction meet certain specific design standards apply only to multifamily dwellings designed or constructed for first occupancy after March 13, 1991. 42 U.S.C. § 3604(f)(3)(C), (4)-(9); 24 C.F.R. § 100.205. The specific design standards refer to features including entrances, common areas, doorways, environmental controls, bathrooms, and kitchens. Multifamily dwellings are those with four or more units. The applicable requirements depend on whether the structure has an elevator or not.

Most judicial interpretation has arisen from the FHA requirements relating to structural modifications. Except for housing covered by some other federal or state statute, little is required by the FHA with respect to removing barriers in existing housing. The FHA, however, does require that individuals with disabilities be allowed to make their own structural modifications at their own expense in certain cases. The types of modifications usually are those relating to features such as ramps and railings for individuals with mobility impairments. As the following case illustrates, however, modifications for other types of conditions may be required.

LINCOLN REALTY MANAGEMENT CO. v. PENNSYLVANIA HUMAN RELATIONS COMMISSION
143 Pa. Commw. 54, 598 A.2d 594 (1991)

McGinley, Judge:

Lincoln Realty Management Company (Lincoln), the manager of Audubon Court Apartments (Audubon), appeals an order of the Pennsylvania Human Relations Commission (Commission) issued August 28, 1990, as a result of a complaint filed with the Commission by Sally Atkinson (Atkinson), a tenant at Audubon. The Commission determined that Lincoln ejected Atkinson from her apartment solely because of her physical disability, and rejected any reasonable accommodations she proposed in violation of the provisions of the Pennsylvania Human Relations Act (Act).

Atkinson, who is extremely sensitive to a variety of chemicals and chemical products, entered into a one-year lease agreement for a unit in Audubon's Building C beginning in February, 1986. By letter dated May 6, 1986 Lincoln informed Atkinson that her lease would not be renewed for the upcoming year as Lincoln was unable to provide her with the special treatment and precautions her condition demanded. Atkinson did not vacate her apartment at the expiration of the lease term in February of 1987, and filed a complaint with the Commission. Additionally, on June 22, 1987, Atkinson obtained an injunction in the Montgomery County Court of Common Pleas enjoining Lincoln from using "any pest control substance, device or methodology not approved by [Atkinson], anywhere in the north side of building Unit C, and to provide 48 hours notice of any spray or 'bomb' application to any other building or grounds within 100 feet of building Unit C, until [Atkinson] no longer occupies her unit or 45 days from this date, whichever occurs first." Lincoln has not repainted Building C and no pest control has been undertaken in the building since the commencement of Atkinson's tenancy.

A hearing was held before the Commission on June 14 and 15, 1990. At the hearing, Atkinson testified that she was diagnosed as suffering with multiple chemical sensitivity in June, 1984. Atkinson presented a letter from her physician which states that Atkinson is unable to tolerate the presence of various chemical compounds, including but not limited to certain pesticides and herbicides. Atkinson testified that conditions in Audubon were tolerable when she moved into her apartment.

The hearing examiner found that Atkinson is handicapped within the meaning of the Act, that she established a prima facie case of discrimination, and that Lincoln did not make reasonable accommodations for her, and that Lincoln did not demonstrate that making reasonable accommodations imposed an undue hardship. The hearing examiner set forth the following remedial measures:

> 1) Should Atkinson desire to do so, Lincoln shall permit Atkinson to install a kitchen ceiling fan in unit C-301 by a licensed electrician of her choice, subject to the approval of Lincoln, the cost to be borne by Atkinson, 2) Lincoln shall cause the dishwasher in unit C-301 to be removed and the pipes sealed to prevent odors from seeping into unit C-301, the cost to be

borne by Lincoln. 3) Should Atkinson desire to do so, Lincoln shall permit Atkinson to install a washer and dryer in unit C-301, cost to be borne by Atkinson, 4) Lincoln shall install an exhaust fan in the laundry room of building C . . . and install a control switch on the first floor level, the cost to be borne by Lincoln. 5) When deemed appropriate, Lincoln shall either paint or wallpaper the hallways of building C, and if painted, Lincoln shall use a less toxic paint product. Prior to painting, Lincoln shall discuss the choice of paint with Atkinson and allow Atkinson to submit the name of a recommended product for Lincoln's consideration. Any increased cost of a less toxic product or its application shall be borne by Lincoln. 6) Lincoln shall attempt pest control in and around building C by formatting a . . . strategy which first strives to address any pest problem with the least toxic pesticide application possible. Lincoln shall discuss their plan with Atkinson well in advance of any actual treatments and give due consideration to any recommended course of action Atkinson may submit. Should either less toxic products or their application cost additional money, Lincoln shall bear the added costs. 7) Lincoln shall permit Atkinson to either cover her floors with tolerable floor coverings or leave them bare. The cost of personal floor coverings, if any are installed by Atkinson, shall be borne by Atkinson. When Atkinson vacates the unit, no additional cost shall be assessed by Lincoln for Atkinson's prior removal of carpeting. 8) Within 100 feet of building C, Lincoln shall attempt to implement an organic lawn care program, the cost thereof to be borne by Lincoln. 9) Lincoln shall provide to Atkinson at least two weeks notice of all pest treatments and lawn maintenance at Audubon which use toxic materials of any sort. Such notice shall include an accurate description of the scope of treatments and products to be used. 10) Lincoln shall continue to give Atkinson advance notice of all painting to be done in building C.

We now turn to the question of whether Lincoln did fail to reasonably accommodate Atkinson in the manner contemplated by federal law, and if so, whether the Commission's remedial order was proper. We note that the Commission derives its authority to order that reasonable accommodations be made after a finding of discrimination from Section 9(f) of the Act:

If, upon all the evidence at the hearing, the Commission shall find that a respondent has engaged in or is engaging in any unlawful discriminatory practice as defined in this act, the Commission shall state its findings of fact, and shall issue and cause to be served on such respondent an order requiring such respondent to cease and desist from such unlawful discriminatory practice and to take such affirmative action, including, but not limited to . . . the making of reasonable accommodations . . . as, in the judgement of the Commission, will effectuate the purposes of this act, and including a requirement for the report of the manner of compliance. Further, when fashioning an award, the Commission has broad discretion and its actions are entitled to deference by a reviewing court. The Commission's order will not be disturbed unless it can be shown that the order is a patent attempt to achieve ends other than can be fairly said to effectuate the policies of the Act.

The evidence adduced at the hearing reveals that Atkinson requested the following accommodations:

> that she be allowed to have her carpets removed, that she be allowed to install a washer and dryer in her apartment at her own cost and with the agreement that she would restore the premises at the end of her tenancy, that she be allowed to install an exhaust fan in the laundry room at her own cost, the premises to be restored at the end of her tenancy, and that Lincoln paint with products that she could tolerate, with the understanding that she would make up the difference in the cost of the paint.

Atkinson also requested notification of painting and pesticide application and that Lincoln attempt use of the least toxic methodology of pest control. Atkinson presented a letter from Lincoln's attorney permitting Atkinson to remove the carpets provided Atkinson set up an escrow account in the amount equal to 50% of the replacement cost to facilitate restoring the apartment to its original condition. Atkinson also testified that Lincoln gave her permission to install an exhaust fan in her kitchen provided she used an electrician of Lincoln's choice, however, she decided not to have the fan installed after discovering that Lincoln's electrician charged more than the electricians she contacted. The testimony was contradictory on the point of whether Atkinson was notified of all painting and pesticide applications during her tenancy.

Lincoln asserts that it did not renew Atkinson's lease because Lincoln felt that it was unable to accommodate her. Norman Brodsky (Brodsky), President of Lincoln, testified that he considered Atkinson's letters requesting the use of least-toxic methods of pest control to be an attempt to "enter into the management realm of [the] complex." Brodsky testified that he believed Atkinson was having a home built, and he decided that he "wouldn't do anything" until she was gone. Atkinson testified that Lincoln stopped treating for outdoor pests in the complex after she was harassed by one of the exterminators, but that this was not done at her request. Despite Lincoln's assertion of sympathy, Lincoln's policy amounted to sitting back and doing nothing. This is not the equivalent of making a reasonable accommodation. Lincoln did not work with Atkinson in making the reasonable accommodations which she did propose, as contemplated by the federal regulations.

However, the Commission's order directs Lincoln to make accommodations beyond those requested by Atkinson, at Lincoln's cost. Although the Commission has broad discretion in fashioning an award, and has the authority to order reasonable accommodations as set forth in Section 9(f) of the Act, it is unreasonable to expect Lincoln to make accommodations which Atkinson did not formally and reasonably request. In this regard certain necessary findings are absent from the record and, as a result, portions of the Commission's order are unsupported.

Certainly the portions of the order which direct Lincoln to give Atkinson notice of pesticide application and painting, proposed accommodations (9) and (10), fall within the spirit of the federal guidelines. Similarly, it is clear that if the federal guidelines are to apply, they require Lincoln to permit Atkinson to make modifications to her apartment at her own expense. This would include the directives that Atkinson be permitted to install a kitchen ceiling fan and a washer and dryer in the apartment at her own expense, proposed accommodations (1) and (3), both of which modifications she previously requested.

Concerning proposed accommodations (2), dishwasher removal, (4), laundry room exhaust fan, (5), painting, (6), pest control, and (8), organic lawn care, we vacate these portions of the Commission's order and remand for specific findings on whether Atkinson provided a reasonable description of these proposed modifications to Lincoln with any necessary assurances that modifications are to be made in a workmanlike manner, and whether Atkinson is willing to pay any increased costs resulting from these modifications, and if she is willing to restore the premises, reasonable wear and tear excepted.

As we have stated, 24 C.F.R. 100.203(a) permits the landlord to condition permission for a modification on a renter agreeing to restore the premises to the condition that existed before the modification, reasonable wear and tear excepted. The portion of the order dealing with carpet removal, proposed accommodation (7), is vacated and remanded for a determination of whether Lincoln's request that Atkinson escrow 50% of the replacement cost was actually for the restoration of the premises, taking reasonable wear and tear into account.

Finally, Lincoln contends that "attempting to keep Atkinson in a safe environment" has caused and will continue to cause undue hardship in the form of hazards to the other tenants and promote tenant unrest. Lincoln cites a letter received from a six-year tenant who declined to renew her lease because of insect infestation in her apartment. The record also reveals that this tenant's apartment was located in building J, which is unaffected by the order of the Commission. Although tenants in Atkinson's building have expressed dissatisfaction with the presence of insects, and lack of painting, the hearing examiner properly found this dissatisfaction to be a result of Lincoln's refusal to utilize any painting, pest control or lawn care procedures in Atkinson's building, not as a result of the adoption of a policy of reasonable accommodation.

The order of the Commission is affirmed in part, vacated in part, and the matter remanded for disposition consistent with the foregoing opinion.

PROBLEMS

1. The *Lincoln Realty* case discussed the concerns about tenant unrest and undue hardships for other tenants. Is this an instance of impermissible "cotenant preference" or is it a legitimate concern about the effect on other tenants? What if the other tenants were not inconvenienced, but just found her complaints to be annoying?

2. The court did not focus on whether Atkinson's sensitivity to a variety of chemicals was a disability. The hearing examiner had made that determination. If a tenant's sensitivity was only to a small number of chemicals, would that tenant qualify for protection? How would a court be likely to handle whether TRAVEL's clients with post traumatic stress disorder are "disabled/handicapped" under the FHA?

3. Landlady lives in and owns a large house which is divided into four apartments. She also owns an apartment building of twenty-five units next door.

Mr. A, who is paraplegic and uses a wheelchair, wants to rent an apartment from Landlady and prefers to rent an apartment in the house. There is a vacancy in both the house and the apartment building. If Mr. A would live in either building, he would need ramps at the front entrance, lowered doorknobs and light switches, and added railings in the bathroom. What are Landlady's obligations in terms of renting space to Mr. A, making the needed changes, and payment for the needed changes under federal law?

The following case highlights challenges of older buildings. In reading the case, consider what would be required of a three story apartment building constructed after the FHA effective date that did not have an elevator at all. Would that violate the FHA?

CONGDON v. STRINE
854 F. Supp. 355 (E.D. Pa. 1994)

Dalzell, District Judge:

I. *Factual Background*

The Congdons reside in an apartment at 499 W. Jefferson Street, Media, Pennsylvania ("the building"), which Strine owns. The Congdons have lived in this apartment since 1983. Their apartment is on the fourth floor and may be reached by use of the stairway or the elevator. During the first year of occupancy, the Congdons had a one-year lease; since that time their tenancy has been on a month to month basis.

Mrs. Congdon suffers from various diseases, and since 1992 has been largely confined to a wheelchair. Some time before January of 1993, the building's elevator "began to experience recurring breakdowns." Because of these breakdowns, Mrs. Congdon "has used the stairs and had some physical problems that may be related to her increased activity."

In April of 1993, the Congdons filed a complaint with the Bureau of Consumer Protection, Office of the Attorney General, Commonwealth of Pennsylvania, describing the problems with the elevator and their alleged discriminatory effects. The Congdons also filed complaints with the Delaware County Consumer Affairs Department, and on May 17, 1993, they filed a complaint with the U.S. Department of Housing and Urban Development ("HUD"), alleging a violation of the Fair Housing Act. The next day, HUD referred its complaint to the Pennsylvania Human Relations Commission.

On May 26, 1993, Strine advised the Congdons that their lease was not being renewed and that they were to vacate the premises by August 31, 1993. The Congdons did not vacate the premises by August 31, 1993. Strine took no action against them, however, and has neither taken further action to evict plaintiffs nor filed any legal proceedings against them. Strine offered to rent to the Congdons a ground floor apartment in the same building or, alternatively, an apartment in another building he owned, but the Congdons rejected both offers as unsuitable.

Denial of Housing under 42 U.S.C. § 3604(f)(1)

This case differs from most Title VIII cases in that there was no actual denial of housing. It is undisputed that Strine continues to rent an apartment to the Congdons and that Linda Congdon has been living in the apartment since 1983. There is no evidence that Strine discriminated in renting to Mrs. Congdon or that she has been denied housing. The Congdons essentially claim that the threatened eviction and the refusal to provide reasonable accommodations violate § 3604(f)(1). Thus, we must determine whether Strine's actions fall within the ambit of the "otherwise make unavailable or deny" language of § 3604(f)(1).

While a threat of eviction should not be taken lightly, Strine and his agents made offers to rent other apartments to the Congdons, including an offer to rent her an apartment in the same building on the first floor. Strine took no further actions to enforce the eviction notice. Indeed, Strine never denied housing to the Congdons. To the contrary, Strine undisputedly offered the Congdons alternatives, albeit not to their taste.

Although the Congdons do not specify what reasonable accommodations they think Strine must provide, we infer that they want Strine to provide better repairs to the elevator, a new elevator, or another apartment that is acceptable to Mrs. Congdon's needs for accessibility and parking. Taking as true that defendant failed to provide a trouble-free elevator or another apartment to plaintiffs' liking, the Congdons still were not denied housing. There is no evidence that Mrs. Congdon was unable to return to her apartment and had to spend the night elsewhere. The Congdons only allege that Mrs. Congdon at times "miss[ed] appointments and other daily activities" because she was unable to leave the apartment, Although it appears that Mrs. Congdon was inconvenienced, we do not find that these actions fall within the meaning of "make unavailable" or "deny" in § 3604(f)(1) any more than the occasional failure of the elevators in this courthouse "deny" courtrooms to litigants. Thus, we cannot find that defendant's conduct implicates § 3604(f)(1) of Title VIII.

Discriminatory Provision of Services under 42 U.S.C. § 3604(f)(2)

We next consider whether the Congdons make out a claim for a violation of 42 U.S.C. § 3604(f)(2), which provides in relevant part that it is unlawful:

> [t]o discriminate against any person in the terms, conditions, or privileges of sale or rental of a dwelling, or in the provision of services or facilities in connection with such dwelling, because of a handicap of — (A) that person; or (B) a person residing in . . . that dwelling . . . ;

The Congdons do not allege that their terms, conditions or privileges of the rental differed from other tenants. In essence, the Congdons claim that Strine discriminated against them by providing poor elevator service. They allege that Strine's maintenance practices regarding the elevator were discriminatory because the breakdown of the elevator understandably created more hardships for Mrs.

Congdon than it did to non-handicapped tenants.

"To make out a prima facie case under Title VIII, a plaintiff can show either discriminatory treatment . . . or discriminatory effect alone, without proof of discriminatory intent . . . " We shall consider the Congdons' "discriminatory treatment" and "discriminatory effect" theories separately.

For the Congdons to succeed on a "discriminatory treatment" claim, they need to show that Strine adopted and carried out his maintenance policies regarding the elevator with the intent to discriminate against Mrs. Congdon because of her disability. The Congdons have not submitted any facts to show that Strine had such a discriminatory motive with regard to the elevator maintenance policies.

Plaintiffs only generally allege that Strine was motivated by a discriminatory intent. They proffer no evidence that Strine acted differently in providing elevator services to Mrs. Congdon. The elevator's imperfections doubtless vexed all the tenants, not solely Mrs. Congdon. Strine thus did not stop providing elevator service exclusively to Mrs. Congdon.

Although we find no evidence of discriminatory treatment, plaintiffs need only show that Strine's policy regarding the elevator's maintenance had a discriminatory effect. In considering the scope of the FHAA, we agree with the Seventh Circuit's refusal "to conclude that every action which produces discriminatory effects is illegal."

Our Court of Appeals has observed that the legislative history of Title VIII suggests that the statute should be read expansively in order to "eliminate the adverse discriminatory effects of past and present prejudice in housing." With this breadth in mind, we will apply the factors set forth in *Arlington Heights* to guide our analysis. [Author's note: These factors are discussed in *Baxter*, reproduced at the beginning of this Chapter.]

The first factor looks at how strong is the plaintiffs' showing of discriminatory effect. The Congdons submit evidence alleging that the elevator often suffered mechanical problems or broke down completely. Mrs. Congdon avers that when the elevator broke down she "has been forced to remain in her apartment and to miss appointments and other daily activities." Clearly, the elevator breakdowns affected Linda Congdon more severely than non-disabled tenants. There were times when she was unable to access her apartment without assistance or hardship, and was in general less able to enjoy her apartment. Therefore, we find that plaintiffs have made a showing of discriminatory effect in the provision of services to Linda Congdon. The first factor thus weighs in plaintiffs' favor.

With regard to the second factor, we must again look to see if there is evidence of discriminatory intent. The Congdons have proffered no facts supporting their allegation of discriminatory intent. In fact, Strine has offered Mrs. Congdon occupancy in other apartments and maintains a repair and servicing contract for the elevator. The Congdons have submitted no evidence that the defendant wilfully kept the elevator in a state of disrepair because of Mrs. Congdon's disability. Therefore, the second factor weighs in Strine's favor.

The third factor, which asks us to consider "defendant's interest in taking the action complained of," also weighs in Strine's favor. Defendant has no business interest in having a faulty elevator that drives out frustrated tenants. Strine has a maintenance contract with an elevator servicing company precisely to serve his business interest of making it possible for all tenants to have elevator service. This company frequently serviced the offending elevator. We therefore can perceive no interest Strine would have in perpetuating faulty elevator service.

The fourth Metropolitan factor directs us to examine the relief plaintiffs seek, i.e., whether the Congdons want us to compel Strine affirmatively to provide services or whether they seek to restrain Strine from deliberately reducing the level of services he provides to Mrs. Congdon. This examination is predicated on the economic realities of affirmative relief: To require a defendant to appropriate money, utilize his land for a particular purpose, or take other affirmative steps toward integrated housing is a massive judicial intrusion on private autonomy.

The Congdons alternatively seek that this Court compel Strine to repair the elevator so that it always works properly, to replace the existing elevator with a new one, or to provide her with occupancy in another apartment. If the Congdons remain in their present unit (which seems to be their desire in view of their refusal to accept the alternatives proffered them), it seems that Strine would have to achieve the impossible to please them. Even a perfect landlord cannot maintain a completely problem-free elevator. Elevators are subject to malfunctioning like all mechanical devices.

The Congdons have not presented any facts which suggest that Strine is providing a level of services inferior to the level of services he provides to the other tenants in the building. Especially in view of the alternatives Strine has offered the Congdons, we find no basis in § 3604(f)(2) that authorizes us to order Strine to install a new elevator or to assure that the present one is trouble-free.

"Reasonable Accommodations"

The Congdons claim that Strine did not make a "reasonable accommodation" of Mrs. Congdon's disability. Although it is not clear from the complaint, it appears that plaintiffs base their claim on their allegations that Strine did not keep the elevator in better working condition, did not replace the elevator, or offer the Congdons another apartment that would accommodate Mrs. Congdon's disabilities.

Strine argues that he did make reasonable accommodations for Mrs. Congdon's disability in that he had a regular elevator maintenance contract, and offered the Congdons a first floor apartment in the same building, as well as another apartment in a building with two elevators. Lastly, Strine argues that forcing him to install a new elevator in the building would impose an undue financial burden because a new elevator would cost sixty-five to seventy thousand dollars, and such an expenditure would not be a reasonable accommodation for a month-to-month tenant.

The Congdons have not submitted any evidence of requests for reasonable accommodations that they made and were refused other than for a new elevator and to make the existing elevator trouble-free.

We agree with Strine that forcing him to install a new elevator would constitute, in this context, "a massive judicial intrusion on private autonomy." Such an intrusion would offend any decent respect for proportionality given that the Congdons seek a $65,000 capital expenditure when they are free to walk away from Strine on payment of only one month's rent. The Congdons' extravagant demand for such an "accommodation" thus cannot be deemed to be "reasonable."

As we have previously mentioned, Strine has a contract with an elevator maintenance company, and he submits undisputed evidence that repairs were made regularly. Thus, it does not seem that Strine failed to make a reasonable accommodation in his elevator maintenance for Mrs. Congdon's disability.

We are further fortified in our conclusion because of Strine's good faith effort to accommodate Mrs. Congdon by offering her occupancy in other apartments. Thus, we do not find discrimination pursuant to § 3604(f)(3).

NOTES

1. The previous case illustrates the challenges with facilities built before the effective date for making new multi-unit housing accessible. Landlords are not required to make existing housing accessible. The FHA requires landlords to allow individuals to make structural modifications at their own expense, so long as the property can be restored to its original condition, less ordinary wear and tear. 42 U.S.C. § 3604(f)(3)(A). It even provides that an escrow account can be negotiated to ensure that the restoration will occur. How does that affect the situation for TRAVEL in the hypothetical problem? Does it make a difference that the lease is for three years?

2. Buildings constructed for occupancy after March 13, 1991, for multiunit dwellings must meet specific access requirements. 42 U.S.C. § 3604(f)(3)(C). If an apartment complex were built that did not meet the accessibility requirements, which parties would be liable — contractor, developer, architect, engineer? How would that be determined? What indemnification might be part of the arrangement? See, e.g., *United States of America v. Gambone Brothers Development Co.*, 37 Nat'l Disability L. Rep. ¶ 254 (E.D. Pa. 2008); *Equal Rights Center v. Archstone Smith Trust*, 28 Nat'l Disability L. Rep. 238 (D. Md. 2009); *United States v. Shanrie Co, Inc.*, 37 Nat'l Disability L. Rep. ¶ 255 (S.D. Ill. 2008).

Another issue that courts have grappled with where there are mixed results involves the standing of advocacy organizations to bring certain actions. See, e.g., *Metropolitan St. Louis Equal Housing Opportunity Council v. Lighthouse Lodge*, 39 Nat'l Disability L. Rep. ¶ 106 (W.D. Mo. 2009); *Equal Rights Center v. AvalonBay Communities, Inc.*, 38 Nat'l Disability L. Rep. ¶ 237 (D. Md. 2009); *Disability Advocates Inc. v. Paterson*, 598 F. Supp. 2d 289 (E.D.N.Y. 2009). Is TRAVEL an advocacy organization or is it more like the complainant in the *Baxter* case?

E LEAST RESTRICTIVE ENVIRONMENT AND INDEPENDENT LIVING

One of the major principles of the ADA and the Rehabilitation Act is the concept of least restrictive environment. This principle, of course, is intended to apply to where people with disabilities live. The courts focused substantial attention on this issue in relation to the movement to deinstitutionalize individuals with mental retardation and mental illness in the 1970s and 1980s. The Supreme Court twice addressed the issue in the case of *Pennhurst State School & Hospital v. Halderman*, 465 U.S. 89 (1984) and 451 U.S. 1 (1981). The case was a class action of institutionalized individuals in Pennsylvania state institutions. They brought claims seeking a right to treatment and a right to treatment in the least restrictive environment. The advocates in the case sought relief under a number of legal theories, including constitutional equal protection and due process grounds, Section 504 of the Rehabilitation Act, and state laws. The substantive issues remained unresolved for fifteen years, however, because the Court used a procedural basis to avoiding deciding these issues.

Deinstitutionalization began to take place as a social policy even without a definitive mandate from the Supreme Court. The goal was to place individuals who had previously been living in large institutions in community placements such as group homes, foster families, or independent living arrangements with supportive services. In addition, it became extremely unlikely that new placements in the large institutions would occur. A number of difficulties in implementing these policies, however, soon became apparent. These included inadequate resources (funding, placements, and trained staffing) in the communities, and zoning and other restrictions related to location of group homes and similar housing.

Economic challenges beginning in 2008 added to the difficulties of the deinstitutionalization movement. State and local governmental agencies that had been providers and funding sources for providing health care services to individuals with disabilities in their homes were facing funding shortfalls and seeking economies of scale. In some instances, they may have determined that it was only economically feasible to provide these services in a nursing home, although in many situations individuals receiving these services could live independently in the mainstream of society if only these services were provided. A number of cases have challenged this kind of delivery of service as violating the mainstreaming mandate of the FHA, the ADA, and Section 504. These decisions are just beginning to establish the standards for this issue.

Olmstead v. L.C., 119 S. Ct. 2176 (1999), provided the assurance that the least restrictive environment principle was to be applied in placing individuals with disabilities. The excerpt from that opinion follows and clarifies the basis for this determination. Other cases in this section highlight the judicial response to some of the challenges to full implementation of community based placement and treatment for individuals with disabilities.

OLMSTEAD v. L.C.
119 S. Ct. 2176 (1999)

JUSTICE GINSBURG announced the judgment of the Court and delivered the opinion of the Court with respect to Parts I, II, and III-A, and an opinion with respect to Part III-B, in which O'CONNOR, SOUTER, AND BREYER, JJ., joined.

This case concerns the proper construction of the anti-discrimination provision contained in the public services portion (Title II) of the Americans with Disabilities Act of 1990, 42 U.S.C. § 12132. Specifically, we confront the question whether the proscription of discrimination may require placement of persons with mental disabilities in community settings rather than in institutions. The answer, we hold, is a qualified yes. Such action is in order when the State's treatment professionals have determined that community placement is appropriate, the transfer from institutional care to a less restrictive setting is not opposed by the affected individual, and the placement can be reasonably accommodated, taking into account the resources available to the State and the needs of others with mental disabilities. In so ruling, we affirm the decision of the Eleventh Circuit in substantial part. We remand the case, however, for further consideration of the appropriate relief, given the range of facilities the State maintains for the care and treatment of persons with diverse mental disabilities, and its obligation to administer services with an even hand.

I

In the opening provisions of the ADA, Congress stated findings applicable to the statute in all its parts. Most relevant to this case, Congress determined that

> "(2) historically, society has tended to isolate and segregate individuals with disabilities, and, despite some improvements, such forms of discrimination against individuals with disabilities continue to be a serious and pervasive social problem;

> "(3) discrimination against individuals with disabilities persists in such critical areas as . . . institutionalization . . . :

> . . . .

> "(5) individuals with disabilities continually encounter various forms of discrimination, including outright intentional exclusion, . . . failure to make modifications to existing facilities and practices, . . . [and] segregation . . . ." 42 U.S.C. §§ 12101(a)(2), (3), (5).

Congress then set forth prohibitions against discrimination in employment, public services furnished by governmental entities, and public accommodations provided by private entities. The statute as a whole is intended "to provide a clear and comprehensive national mandate for the elimination of discrimination against individuals with disabilities."

This case concerns Title II, the public services portion of the ADA. The provision of Title II centrally at issue reads:

"Subject to the provisions of this subchapter, no qualified individual with a
disability shall, by reason of such disability, be excluded from participation
in or be denied the benefits of the services, programs, or activities of a
public entity, or be subjected to discrimination by any such entity."

Title II's definition section states that "public entity" includes "any State or local
government," and "any department, agency, [or] special purpose district."
§§ 12131(1)(A), (B). The same section defines "qualified individual with a disability"
as

"an individual with a disability who, with or without reasonable modifications to rules, policies, or practices, the removal of architectural, communication, or transportation barriers, or the provision of auxiliary aids and
services, meets the essential eligibility requirements for the receipt of
services or the participation in programs or activities provided by a public
entity."

On redress for violations of § 12132's discrimination prohibition, Congress
referred to remedies available under § 505 of the Rehabilitation Act of 1973

Congress instructed the Attorney General to issue regulations implementing
provisions of Title II, including § 12132's discrimination proscription. The Attorney
General's regulations, Congress further directed, "shall be consistent with this
chapter and with the coordination regulations . . . applicable to recipients of
Federal financial assistance under [§ 504 of the Rehabilitation Act]." 42 U.S.C.
§ 12134(b). One of the § 504 regulations requires recipients of federal funds to
"administer programs and activities in the most integrated setting appropriate to
the needs of qualified handicapped persons." 28 CFR § 41.51(d) (1998).

As Congress instructed, the Attorney General issued Title II regulations, see 28
CFR pt. 35 (1998), including one modeled on the § 504 regulation just quoted; called
the "integration regulation," it reads:

"A public entity shall administer services, programs, and activities in the
most integrated setting appropriate to the needs of qualified individuals
with disabilities." 28 CFR § 35.130(d) (1998).

The preamble to the Attorney General's Title II regulations defines "the most
integrated setting appropriate to the needs of qualified individuals with disabilities"
to mean "a setting that enables individuals with disabilities to interact with
non-disabled persons to the fullest extent possible." 28 CFR pt. 35, App. A, p. 450
(1998). Another regulation requires public entities to "make reasonable modifications" to avoid "discrimination on the basis of disability," unless those modifications
would entail a "fundamenta[l] alter[ation]"; called here the "reasonable-
modifications regulation," it provides:

"A public entity shall make reasonable modifications in policies, practices,
or procedures when the modifications are necessary to avoid discrimination
on the basis of disability, unless the public entity can demonstrate that
making the modifications would fundamentally alter the nature of the
service, program, or activity." 28 CFR § 35.130(b)(7) (1998).

II

With the key legislative provisions in full view, we summarize the facts underlying this dispute. Respondents L.C. and E.W. are mentally retarded women; L.C. has also been diagnosed with schizophrenia, and E.W., with a personality disorder. Both women have a history of treatment in institutional settings. In May 1992, L.C. was voluntarily admitted to Georgia Regional Hospital at Atlanta (GRH), where she was confined for treatment in a psychiatric unit. By May 1993, her psychiatric condition had stabilized, and L.C.'s treatment team at GRH agreed that her needs could be met appropriately in one of the community-based programs the State supported. Despite this evaluation, L.C. remained institutionalized until February 1996, when the State placed her in a community-based treatment program.

E.W. was voluntarily admitted to GRH in February 1995; like L.C., E.W. was confined for treatment in a psychiatric unit. In March 1995, GRH sought to discharge E.W. to a homeless shelter, but abandoned that plan after her attorney filed an administrative complaint. By 1996, E.W.'s treating psychiatrist concluded that she could be treated appropriately in a community-based setting. She nonetheless remained institutionalized until a few months after the District Court issued its judgment in this case in 1997.

In May 1995, when she was still institutionalized at GRH, L.C. filed suit in the United States District Court for the Northern District of Georgia, challenging her continued confinement in a segregated environment. Her complaint invoked 42 U.S.C. § 1983 and provisions of the ADA, §§ 12131-12134, and named as defendants, now petitioners, the Commissioner of the Georgia Department of Human Resources, the Superintendent of GRH, and the Executive Director of the Fulton County Regional Board (collectively, the State). L.C. alleged that the State's failure to place her in a community-based program, once her treating professionals determined that such placement was appropriate, violated, *inter alia*, Title II of the ADA. L.C.'s pleading requested, among other things, that the State place her in a community care residential program, and that she receive treatment with the ultimate goal of integrating her into the mainstream of society. E.W. intervened in the action, stating an identical claim.[4]

[Lower court proceedings omitted.]

III

Endeavoring to carry out Congress' instruction to issue regulations implementing Title II, the Attorney General, in the integration and reasonable- modifications regulations, made two key determinations. The first concerned the scope of the ADA's discrimination proscription, 42 U.S.C. § 12132; the second concerned the obligation of the States to counter discrimination. As to the first, the Attorney

---

[4] L.C. and E.W. are currently receiving treatment in community-based programs. Nevertheless, the case is not moot. As the District Court and Court of Appeals explained, in view of the multiple institutional placements L.C. and E.W. have experienced, the controversy they brought to court is "capable of repetition, yet evading review."

General concluded that unjustified placement or retention of persons in institutions, severely limiting their exposure to the outside community, constitutes a form of discrimination based on disability prohibited by Title II. Regarding the States' obligation to avoid unjustified isolation of individuals with disabilities, the Attorney General provided that States could resist modifications that "would fundamentally alter the nature of the service, program, or activity." 28 CFR § 35.130(b)(7) (1998).

The Court of Appeals essentially upheld the Attorney General's construction of the ADA. As just recounted, the appeals court ruled that the unjustified institutionalization of persons with mental disabilities violated Title II; the court then remanded with instructions to measure the cost of caring for L.C. and E.W. in a community- based facility against the State's mental health budget.

We affirm the Court of Appeals' decision in substantial part. Unjustified isolation, we hold, is properly regarded as discrimination based on disability. But we recognize, as well, the States' need to maintain a range of facilities for the care and treatment of persons with diverse mental disabilities, and the States' obligation to administer services with an even hand. In evaluating a State's fundamental-alteration defense, the District Court must consider, in view of the resources available to the State, not only the cost of providing community-based care to the litigants, but also the range of services the State provides others with mental disabilities, and the State's obligation to mete out those services equitably.

A

We examine first whether, as the Eleventh Circuit held, undue institutionalization qualifies as discrimination "by reason of . . . disability." The Department of Justice has consistently advocated that it does. Because the Department is the agency directed by Congress to issue regulations implementing Title II, its views warrant respect. . . .

The State argues that L.C. and E.W. encountered no discrimination "by reason of" their disabilities because they were not denied community placement on account of those disabilities. Nor were they subjected to "discrimination," the State contends, because " 'discrimination' necessarily requires uneven treatment of similarly situated individuals," and L.C. and E.W. had identified no comparison class, i.e., no similarly situated individuals given preferential treatment. We are satisfied that Congress had a more comprehensive view of the concept of discrimination advanced in the ADA.

The ADA stepped up earlier measures to secure opportunities for people with developmental disabilities to enjoy the benefits of community living. The Developmentally Disabled Assistance and Bill of Rights Act (DDABRA), a 1975 measure, stated in aspirational terms that "[t]he treatment, services, and habilitation for a person with developmental disabilities . . . *should be* provided in the setting that is least restrictive of the person's personal liberty." In a related legislative endeavor, the Rehabilitation Act of 1973, Congress used mandatory language to proscribe discrimination against persons with disabilities. Ultimately, in the ADA, enacted in 1990, Congress not only required all public entities to refrain from discrimination, see 42 U.S.C. § 12132; additionally, in findings applicable to the entire statute,

Congress explicitly identified unjustified "segregation" of persons with disabilities as a "for[m] of discrimination."

Recognition that unjustified institutional isolation of persons with disabilities is a form of discrimination reflects two evident judgments. First, institutional placement of persons who can handle and benefit from community settings perpetuates unwarranted assumptions that persons so isolated are incapable or unworthy of participating in community life. Second, confinement in an institution severely diminishes the everyday life activities of individuals, including family relations, social contacts, work options, economic independence, educational advancement, and cultural enrichment. Dissimilar treatment correspondingly exists in this key respect: In order to receive needed medical services, persons with mental disabilities must, because of those disabilities, relinquish participation in community life they could enjoy given reasonable accommodations, while persons without mental disabilities can receive the medical services they need without similar sacrifice.

The State urges that, whatever Congress may have stated as its findings in the ADA, the Medicaid statute "reflected a congressional policy preference for treatment in the institution over treatment in the community." The State correctly used the past tense. Since 1981, Medicaid has provided funding for state-run home and community-based care through a waiver program. Indeed, the United States points out that the Department of Health and Human Services (HHS) "has a policy of encouraging States to take advantage of the waiver program, and often approves more waiver slots than a State ultimately uses."

We emphasize that nothing in the ADA or its implementing regulations condones termination of institutional settings for persons unable to handle or benefit from community settings. Title II provides only that "qualified individual[s] with a disability" may not "be subjected to discrimination." 42 U.S.C. § 12132. "Qualified individuals," the ADA further explains, are persons with disabilities who, "with or without reasonable modifications to rules, policies, or practices, . . . mee[t] the essential eligibility requirements for the receipt of services or the participation in programs or activities provided by a public entity." § 12131(2).

Consistent with these provisions, the State generally may rely on the reasonable assessments of its own professionals in determining whether an individual "meets the essential eligibility requirements" for habilitation in a community-based program. Absent such qualification, it would be inappropriate to remove a patient from the more restrictive setting. Nor is there any federal requirement that community-based treatment be imposed on patients who do not desire it. See 28 CFR § 35.130(e)(1) (1998) ("Nothing in this part shall be construed to require an individual with a disability to accept an accommodation . . . which such individual chooses not to accept."); 28 CFR pt. 35, App. A, p. 450 (1998) ("[P]ersons with disabilities must be provided the option of declining to accept a particular accommodation."). In this case, however, there is no genuine dispute concerning the status of L.C. and E.W. as individuals "qualified" for noninstitutional care: The State's own professionals determined that community- based treatment would be appropriate for L.C. and E.W., and neither woman opposed such treatment.[5]

B

The State's responsibility, once it provides community-based treatment to qualified persons with disabilities, is not boundless. The reasonable- modifications regulation speaks of "reasonable modifications" to avoid discrimination, and allows States to resist modifications that entail a "fundamenta[l] alter[ation]" of the States' services and programs. 28 CFR § 35.130(b)(7) (1998). The Court of Appeals construed this regulation to permit a cost-based defense "only in the most limited of circumstances," and remanded to the District Court to consider, among other things, "whether the additional expenditures necessary to treat L.C. and E.W. in community-based care would be unreasonable given the demands of the State's mental health budget."

The Court of Appeals' construction of the reasonable-modifications regulation is unacceptable for it would leave the State virtually defenseless once it is shown that the plaintiff is qualified for the service or program she seeks. If the expense entailed in placing one or two people in a community- based treatment program is properly measured for reasonableness against the State's entire mental health budget, it is unlikely that a State, relying on the fundamental-alteration defense, could ever prevail. Sensibly construed, the fundamental-alteration component of the reasonable-modifications regulation would allow the State to show that, in the allocation of available resources, immediate relief for the plaintiffs would be inequitable, given the responsibility the State has undertaken for the care and treatment of a large and diverse population of persons with mental disabilities.

When it granted summary judgment for plaintiffs in this case, the District Court compared the cost of caring for the plaintiffs in a community-based setting with the cost of caring for them in an institution. That simple comparison showed that community placements cost less than institutional confinements. As the United States recognizes, however, a comparison so simple overlooks costs the State cannot avoid; most notably, a "State . . . may experience increased overall expenses by funding community placements without being able to take advantage of the savings associated with the closure of institutions."

As already observed, the ADA is not reasonably read to impel States to phase out institutions, placing patients in need of close care at risk. Nor is it the ADA's mission to drive States to move institutionalized patients into an inappropriate setting, such as a homeless shelter, a placement the State proposed, then retracted, for E.W. Some individuals, like L.C. and E.W. in prior years, may need institutional care from time to time "to stabilize acute psychiatric symptoms." For other individuals, no placement outside the institution may ever be appropriate.

To maintain a range of facilities and to administer services with an even hand, the State must have more leeway than the courts below understood the

---

[5] We do not in this opinion hold that the ADA imposes on the States a "standard of care" for whatever medical services they render, or that the ADA requires States to "provide a certain level of benefits to individuals with disabilities." (Thomas, J., dissenting). We do hold, however, that States must adhere to the ADA's nondiscrimination requirement with regard to the services they in fact provide.

fundamental-alteration defense to allow. If, for example, the State were to demonstrate that it had a comprehensive, effectively working plan for placing qualified persons with mental disabilities in less restrictive settings, and a waiting list that moved at a reasonable pace not controlled by the State's endeavors to keep its institutions fully populated, the reasonable- modifications standard would be met.

For the reasons stated, we conclude that, under Title II of the ADA, States are required to provide community-based treatment for persons with mental disabilities when the State's treatment professionals determine that such placement is appropriate, the affected persons do not oppose such treatment, and the placement can be reasonably accommodated, taking into account the resources available to the State and the needs of others with mental disabilities. The judgment of the Eleventh Circuit is therefore affirmed in part and vacated in part, and the case is remanded for further proceedings consistent with this opinion.

JUSTICE STEVENS, concurring in part and concurring in the judgment. [Omitted.]

JUSTICE KENNEDY, with whom JUSTICE BREYER joins as to Part I, concurring in the judgment.

I

Despite remarkable advances and achievements by medical science, and agreement among many professionals that even severe mental illness is often treatable, the extent of public resources to devote to this cause remains controversial. Knowledgeable professionals tell us that our society, and the governments which reflect its attitudes and preferences, have yet to grasp the potential for treating mental disorders, especially severe mental illness. As a result, necessary resources for the endeavor often are not forthcoming. During the course of a year, about 5.6 million Americans will suffer from severe mental illness. E. Torrey, Out of the Shadows 4 (1997). Some 2.2 million of these persons receive no treatment. Millions of other Americans suffer from mental disabilities of less serious degree, such as mild depression. These facts are part of the background against which this case arises. In addition, of course, persons with mental disabilities have been subject to historic mistreatment, indifference, and hostility.

Despite these obstacles, the States have acknowledged that the care of the mentally disabled is their special obligation. They operate and support facilities and programs, sometimes elaborate ones, to provide care. It is a continuing challenge, though, to provide the care in an effective and humane way, particularly because societal attitudes and the responses of public authorities have changed from time to time.

Beginning in the 1950's, many victims of severe mental illness were moved out of state-run hospitals, often with benign objectives. According to one estimate, when adjusted for population growth, "the actual decrease in the numbers of people with severe mental illnesses in public psychiatric hospitals between 1955 and 1995 was 92 percent." This was not without benefit or justification. The so-called "deinstitutionalization" has permitted a substantial number of mentally disabled persons to receive needed treatment with greater freedom and dignity. It may be, moreover, that those who remain institutionalized are indeed the most severe cases. With reference to this case, as the Court points out, it is undisputed that the State's own treating professionals determined that community-based care was medically appropriate for respondents. Nevertheless, the depopulation of state mental hospitals has its dark side. According to one expert:

> "For a substantial minority . . . deinstitutionalization has been a psychiatric *Titanic*. Their lives are virtually devoid of 'dignity' or 'integrity of body, mind, and spirit.' 'Self-determination' often means merely that the person has a choice of soup kitchens. The 'least restrictive setting' frequently turns out to be a cardboard box, a jail cell, or a terror-filled existence plagued by both real and imaginary enemies."

It must be remembered that for the person with severe mental illness who has no treatment the most dreaded of confinements can be the imprisonment inflicted by his own mind, which shuts reality out and subjects him to the torment of voices and images beyond our own powers to describe.

It would be unreasonable, it would be a tragic event, then, were the Americans with Disabilities Act of 1990 (ADA) to be interpreted so that States had some incentive, for fear of litigation, to drive those in need of medical care and treatment out of appropriate care and into settings with too little assistance and supervision. The opinion of a responsible treating physician in determining the appropriate conditions for treatment ought to be given the greatest of deference. It is a common phenomenon that a patient functions well with medication, yet, because of the mental illness itself, lacks the discipline or capacity to follow the regime the medication requires. This is illustrative of the factors a responsible physician will consider in recommending the appropriate setting or facility for treatment. Justice Ginsburg's opinion takes account of this background. It is careful, and quite correct, to say that it is not "the ADA's mission to drive States to move institutionalized patients into an inappropriate setting, such as a homeless shelter . . . . "

In light of these concerns, if the principle of liability announced by the Court is not applied with caution and circumspection, States may be pressured into attempting compliance on the cheap, placing marginal patients into integrated settings devoid of the services and attention necessary for their condition. This danger is in addition to the federalism costs inherent in referring state decisions regarding the administration of treatment programs and the allocation of resources to the reviewing authority of the federal courts. It is of central importance, then, that courts apply today's decision with great deference to the medical decisions of the responsible, treating physicians and, as the Court makes clear, with appropriate deference to the program funding decisions of state policymakers.

[Part II of the opinion, which relates to Justice Kennedy's opinion that the case should be remanded is omitted.]

[The dissent by Justice Thomas, joined by Chief Justice Rehnquist and Justice Scalia, is omitted.]

As noted previously, there are a number of challenges to the location of group homes in residential areas. These include zoning restrictions of many types. The Supreme Court had addressed this in the case of *City of Cleburne v. Cleburne Living Center*, 473 U.S. 432 (1985), in Chapter 1, *supra*. In that case, the Court focused on the Constitutional test to be applied in the denial of a special use permit for a group home for individuals with mental retardation. The plaintiffs used the Constitution because the Fair Housing Act had not yet been amended to cover individuals with disabilities, and the Americans with Disabilities Act had not yet been enacted. It is unusual today, for advocates to seek redress in the kinds of cases that follow, using constitutional theories, because the Fair Housing Act and/or the Americans with Disabilities Act is much more likely to provide the basis for relief.

The *City of Belleville* case, excerpted earlier in the Chapter, involved a denial of a special use permit apparently because of fears and stereotypes about individuals with HIV. The issue raised was direct threat. That case should be kept in mind when reviewing the following decisions, which address spacing requirements and occupancy levels.

The following case addresses the issue of dispersal of community based programs within zoning restrictions.

FAMILYSTYLE v. CITY OF ST. PAUL
923 F.2d 91 (8th Cir. 1991)

WOLLMAN, CIRCUIT JUDGE:

Familystyle provides rehabilitative services to mentally ill persons and operates residential group homes for them in St. Paul, Minnesota. Familystyle sought special use permits for the addition of three houses to its existing campus of group homes, intending to expand its capacity from 119 to 130 mentally ill persons. Twenty-one of Familystyle's houses, including the three proposed additions, are clustered in a one and one-half block area. On the condition that Familystyle would work to disperse its facilities, the St. Paul City Council issued temporary permits for the three additional houses. Familystyle failed to meet the conditions of the special use permits, and the permits expired. After St. Paul denied renewal of the permits, Familystyle exchanged its license for one excluding the three additional houses.

Relying upon the provisions of the Fair Housing Amendment Act of 1988, Familystyle challenges the city ordinance and state laws that bar the addition of these three houses to its campus.

Minnesota requires facilities that provide residential services for people with mental illness and retardation to be licensed. Minnesota seeks through the licensing of group homes to place the mentally ill in the least restrictive environment possible and to allow them "the benefits of normal residential surroundings."

An integral part of the licensing process guarantees that residential programs are geographically situated, to the extent possible, in locations where residential services are needed, where they would be a part of the community at large, and where access to other necessary services is available. This licensing requirement reflects the goal of deinstitutionalization — a philosophy of creating a full range of community-based services and reducing the population of state institutions.

Minnesota's deinstitutionalization policy is formally acknowledged by its Comprehensive Adult Mental Health Act Housing Mission Statement, which requires that "the housing services provided as part of a comprehensive mental health service system . . . allow all persons with mental illness to live in stable, affordable housing, in settings that maximize community integration and opportunities for acceptance." Federal law affirms the deinstitutionalization philosophy in the Developmental Disabilities Assistance Act, in which Congress found that it is in the national interest to offer persons with developmental disabilities the opportunity, to the maximum extent feasible, to make decisions for themselves and to live in typical homes and communities where they can exercise their full rights and responsibilities as citizens. 42 U.S.C. § 6000(a)(8).

Deinstitutionalization of the mentally ill is advanced in Minnesota by requiring a new group home to be located at least a quarter mile from an existing residential program unless the local zoning authority grants a conditional use or special use permit. The St. Paul zoning code similarly requires community residential facilities for the mentally impaired to be located at least a quarter of a mile apart.

Section 3615 of the Fair Housing Act invalidates "any law of a State, a political subdivision, or other such jurisdiction that purports to require or permit any action that would be a discriminatory housing practice under this subchapter."

Familystyle argues that the Minnesota and St. Paul dispersal requirements are invalid because they limit housing choices of the mentally handicapped and therefore conflict with the language and purpose of the 1988 Amendments to the Fair Housing Act. We disagree. We perceive the goals of non-discrimination and deinstitutionalization to be compatible. Congress did not intend to abrogate a state's power to determine how facilities for the mentally ill must meet licensing standards. Minnesota's dispersal requirements address the need of providing residential services in mainstream community settings. The quarter-mile spacing requirement guarantees that residential treatment facilities will, in fact, be "in the community," rather than in neighborhoods completely made up of group homes that re-create an institutional environment — a setting for which Familystyle argues. We cannot agree that Congress intended the Fair Housing Amendment Act of 1988 to contribute to the segregation of the mentally ill from the mainstream of our society. The challenged state laws and city ordinance do not affect or prohibit a retarded or mentally ill person from purchasing, renting, or occupying a private residence or dwelling.

The state plays a legitimate and necessary role in licensing services for the mentally impaired. We agree with the district court that the dispersal requirement as part of the licensure process is a legitimate means to achieve the state's goals in the process of deinstitutionalization of the mentally ill. Accordingly, we conclude that the Minnesota Human Services Licensing Act and the St. Paul zoning code do not violate the Fair Housing Amendments Act of 1988.

Familystyle argues that the state and city dispersal requirements result in a disparate impact on and discriminatory treatment of the mentally ill.

[I]n a Title VIII case brought against a public defendant, the plaintiff has the initial burden of presenting a prima facie case of the discriminatory effect of the challenged law. If the law is shown to have such an effect, the burden shifts to the governmental defendant to demonstrate that its conduct was necessary to promote a governmental interest commensurate with the level of scrutiny afforded the class of people affected by the law under the equal protection clause.

We conclude that the appropriate level of scrutiny is that announced in *City of Cleburne v. Cleburne Living Center*, 473 U.S. 432, 446, (1985), in which the Court held that persons suffering from mental retardation do not constitute a suspect class. The second question in the disparate impact analysis under Title VIII then becomes whether legislation which distinguishes between the mentally impaired and others is "rationally related to a legitimate governmental purpose."

The district court found that although local and state dispersal requirements for group homes on their face limit housing choices for the mentally ill, the government's interest in deinstitutionalization sufficiently rebutted any discriminatory effect of the laws. Familystyle argues that the district court misapplied the factors relevant in evaluating the government's interest in dispersal requirements. We disagree.

The district court examined the reasons for the state and local law under the strict scrutiny standard. Although we believe that it is not necessary to evaluate the purposes so closely, we agree with the district court that the government's interests are valid. The state aims to integrate the mentally ill into the mainstream of society. One method to achieve that goal is to license group homes which advance the process of deinstitutionalization. Familystyle is a treatment facility that houses more than one hundred mentally ill patients. Further growth of the Familystyle treatment facility may well be counterproductive to the desegregation of the mentally ill.

Had the state or city intended to discriminate against the mentally ill, one sure way would be to situate all group homes in the same neighborhood — a situation for which Familystyle argues. The state's group home dispersal requirements are designed to ensure that mentally handicapped persons needing residential treatment will not be forced into enclaves of treatment facilities that would replicate and thus perpetuate the isolation resulting from institutionalization.

We are not persuaded that any intent to discriminate against the handicapped lies beneath the surface of the state and local dispersal requirements and the purposes of deinstitutionalization. We have been given no reason to believe that Familystyle is incapable of dispersing its group homes and integrating its clients into the community. Accordingly, we conclude that the goal of deinstitutionalization remains a valid and legitimate end that the State of Minnesota and the City of St. Paul are pursuing through legally acceptable means.

The district court's judgment is affirmed.

NOTE

Balancing Fair Housing and Free Speech Rights: In August of 1994, the Department of Housing and Urban Development investigated a housing discrimination complaint alleging that a group of private citizens had violated the FHA by opposing plans to turn a motel into a low-income housing project for recovering alcoholics and drug abusers. Although HUD seemed to initially take the position that such opposition was an FHA violation, it backed off from that position when First Amendment supporters challenged the HUD position. In an opinion piece by Roberta Achtenberg, assistant secretary for fair housing and equal opportunity at HUD, the following was the explanation for the HUD position:

> Congress has said . . . that the First Amendment does not protect all forms of speech when it comes to housing discrimination. For example, the First Amendment does not protect a landlord or a neighbor who employs intimidation or verbal abuse to discourage someone from moving into housing because of his race, religion or disability. Fair housing rights were held paramount . . . when an administrative law judge imposed a $300,000 fine on a Texas woman who engaged in a "relentless campaign of intimidation" to force African-American neighbors out of public housing . . . .
>
> . . . .
>
> First, people have a right to petition local officials for action, even though their motives may appear discriminatory. Where the efforts of neighbors or others appear primarily directed toward achieving a governmental decision — such as denial of a zoning variance — their behavior will most likely be considered protected free speech, no matter what their motives may be. Second, people have the right to protection from private actions aimed at denying them access to housing because of race, color, sex, religion, national origin, family status or disability. Where neighbors or others attempt to intimidate property owners into refusing to sell to someone because of his or her race, for example, or where disabled people are harassed so that they will not move into a neighborhood, such actions will likely be considered discriminatory activities not protected by the First Amendment.

Roberta Achtenberg, *On Tightrope Between Fair Housing, Free Speech*, HOUSTON CHRONICLE, Aug. 26, 1994, at A33.

PROBLEM

The *Familystyle* decision is a case where the court recognized the importance of balancing the integration principles of deinstitutionalization with the nondiscrimination principles of the Fair Housing Act. What would happen in a city where spacing requirements effectively preclude the addition of new group homes because, in certain neighborhoods where the spacing requirements would not be violated, it is not feasible to purchase or rent affordable housing?

If the *Familystyle* reasoning were applied to the case involving the TRAVEL hypothetical problem to have two transitional houses next to each other, what would be the likely result? Are the TRAVEL residences different from group homes for individuals with mental retardation who would otherwise live in institutions? Does it matter that the TRAVEL residents are only going to live in the housing for a limited time and that they are in the process of transitioning into the mainstream of society?

———

The following case involves the issue of whether, under the Fair Housing Act, a city may impose greater restrictions on the number of *unrelated* people than related people who may live in housing zoned for single-family dwellings. The Supreme Court in this opinion only addresses the question of whether such zoning ordinances are exempt from the Fair Housing Act. After reading the case, consider whether the application of the Fair Housing Act should operate to require accommodation in this case or to strike down the differentiation entirely as having a disparate discriminatory impact on group homes for individuals with disabilities.

CITY OF EDMONDS v. OXFORD HOUSE, INC.
514 U.S. 725 (1995)

JUSTICE GINSBURG delivered the opinion of the Court:

The Fair Housing Act (FHA or Act) prohibits discrimination in housing against, inter alios, persons with handicaps. Section 3607(b)(1) of the Act entirely exempts from the FHA's compass "any reasonable local, State, or Federal restrictions regarding the maximum number of occupants permitted to occupy a dwelling." This case presents the question whether a provision in petitioner City of Edmonds' zoning code qualifies for § 3607(b)(1)'s complete exemption from FHA scrutiny. The provision, governing areas zoned for single-family dwelling units, defines "family" as "persons [without regard to number] related by genetics, adoption, or marriage, or a group of five or fewer [unrelated] persons." Edmonds Community Development Code (ECDC) § 21.30.010 (1991).

The defining provision at issue describes who may compose a family unit; it does not prescribe "the maximum number of occupants" a dwelling unit may house. We hold that § 3607(b)(1) does not exempt prescriptions of the family-defining kind, i.e., provisions designed to foster the family character of a neighborhood. Instead, § 3607(b)(1)'s absolute exemption removes from the FHA's scope only total occupancy limits, i.e., numerical ceilings that serve to prevent overcrowding in living quarters.

I.

In the summer of 1990, respondent Oxford House opened a group home in the City of Edmonds, Washington for 10 to 12 adults recovering from alcoholism and drug addiction. The group home, called Oxford House-Edmonds, is located in a neighborhood zoned for single-family residences. Upon learning that Oxford House had leased and was operating a home in Edmonds, the City issued criminal citations to the owner and a resident of the house. The citations charged violation of the zoning code rule that defines who may live in single-family dwelling units. The occupants of such units must compose a "family," and family, under the City's defining rule, "means an individual or two or more persons related by genetics, adoption, or marriage, or a group of five or fewer persons who are not related by genetics, adoption, or marriage." Edmonds Community Development Code (ECDC) § 21.30.010. Oxford House-Edmonds houses more than five unrelated persons, and therefore does not conform to the code.

Oxford House asserted reliance on the Fair Housing Act, which declares it unlawful "[t]o discriminate in the sale or rental, or to otherwise make unavailable or deny, a dwelling to any buyer or renter because of a handicap of . . . that buyer or a renter." The parties have stipulated, for purposes of this litigation, that the residents of Oxford House-Edmonds "are recovering alcoholics and drug addicts and are handicapped persons within the meaning" of the Act.

Discrimination covered by the FHA includes "a refusal to make reasonable accommodations in rules, policies, practices, or services, when such accommodations may be necessary to afford [handicapped] person[s] equal opportunity to use and enjoy a dwelling." § 3604(f)(3)(B). Oxford House asked Edmonds to make a "reasonable accommodation" by allowing it to remain in the single-family dwelling it had leased. Group homes for recovering substance abusers, Oxford urged, need 8 to 12 residents to be financially and therapeutically viable. Edmonds declined to permit Oxford House to stay in a single-family residential zone, but passed an ordinance listing group homes as permitted uses in multifamily and general commercial zones.

Edmonds sued Oxford House in the United States District Court for the Western District of Washington seeking a declaration that the FHA does not constrain the City's zoning code family definition rule. Oxford House counterclaimed under the FHA, charging the City with failure to make a "reasonable accommodation" permitting maintenance of the group home in a single-family zone. The United States filed a separate action on the same FHA-"reasonable accommodation" ground, and the two cases were consolidated. . . .

The Ninth Circuit's decision [holding the exemption inapplicable] conflicts with an Eleventh Circuit decision declaring exempt under § 3607(b)(1) a family definition provision similar to the Edmonds prescription.

II.

The sole question before the Court is whether Edmonds' family composition rule qualifies as a "restrictio[n] regarding the maximum number of occupants permitted to occupy a dwelling" within the meaning of the FHA's absolute exemption. 42 U.S.C. § 3607(b)(1).[1] In answering this question, we are mindful of the Act's stated policy "to provide, within constitutional limitations, for fair housing throughout the United States." § 3601. We also note precedent recognizing the

---

[1] Like the District Court and the Ninth Circuit, we do not decide whether Edmonds' zoning code provision defining "family," as the City would apply it against Oxford House, violates the FHA's prohibitions against discrimination set out in 42 U.S.C. § 3604(f)(1)(A) and (f)(3)(B).

FHA's "broad and inclusive" compass, and therefore according a "generous construction" to the Act's complaint-filing provision. Accordingly, we regard this case as an instance in which an exception to "a general statement of policy" is sensibly read "narrowly in order to preserve the primary operation of the [policy]."

A.

Congress enacted § 3607(b)(1) against the backdrop of an evident distinction between municipal land use restrictions and maximum occupancy restrictions.

Land use restrictions designate "districts in which only compatible uses are allowed and incompatible uses are excluded." D. Mandelker, Land Use Law § 4.16, pp. 113–114 (3d ed. 1993). These restrictions typically categorize uses as single-family residential, multiple-family residential, commercial, or industrial.

Land use restrictions aim to prevent problems caused by the "pig in the parlor instead of the barnyard." *Village of Euclid v. Ambler Realty Co.*, 272 U.S. 365, 388 (1926). In particular, reserving land for single-family residences preserves the character of neighborhoods, securing "zones where family values, youth values, and the blessings of quiet seclusion and clean air make the area a sanctuary for people." *Village of Belle Terre v. Boraas*, 416 U.S. 1, 9 (1974). To limit land use to single-family residences, a municipality must define the term "family"; thus family composition rules are an essential component of single-family residential use restrictions.

Maximum occupancy restrictions, in contradistinction, cap the number of occupants per dwelling, typically in relation to available floor space or the number and type of rooms. These restrictions ordinarily apply uniformly to all residents of all dwelling units. Their purpose is to protect health and safety by preventing dwelling overcrowding.

We recognized this distinction between maximum occupancy restrictions and land use restrictions in *Moore v. City of East Cleveland*, 431 U.S. 494 (1977). In *Moore*, the Court held unconstitutional the constricted definition of "family" contained in East Cleveland's housing ordinance. East Cleveland's ordinance "select[ed] certain categories of relatives who may live together and declare[d] that others may not"; in particular, East Cleveland's definition of "family" made "a crime of a grandmother's choice to live with her grandson." In response to East Cleveland's argument that its aim was to prevent overcrowded dwellings, streets, and schools, we observed that the municipality's restrictive definition of family served the asserted, and undeniably legitimate, goals "marginally, at best." Another East Cleveland ordinance, we noted, "specifically addressed . . . the problem of overcrowding"; that ordinance tied "the maximum permissible occupancy of a dwelling to the habitable floor area." Justice Stewart, in dissent, also distinguished restrictions designed to "preserv[e] the character of a residential area," from prescription of "a minimum habitable floor area per person," in the interest of community health and safety.

Section 3607(b)(1)'s language — "restrictions regarding the maximum number of occupants permitted to occupy a dwelling" — surely encompasses maximum occupancy restrictions.[2] But the formulation does not fit family composition rules typically tied to land use restrictions. In sum, rules that cap the total number of occupants in order to prevent overcrowding of a dwelling "plainly and unmistakably," fall within § 3607(b)(1)'s absolute exemption from the FHA's governance; rules designed to preserve the family character of a neighborhood, fastening on the composition of households rather than on the total number of occupants living quarters can contain, do not.

B.

Turning specifically to the City's Community Development Code, we note that the provisions Edmonds invoked against Oxford House, ECDC § 16.20.010 and 21.30.010, are classic examples of a use restriction and complementing family composition rule. These provisions do not cap the number of people who may live in a dwelling. In plain terms, they direct that dwellings be used only to house families. Captioned "USES," ECDC § 16.20.010 provides that the sole "Permitted Primary Us[e]" in a single-family residential zone is "[s]ingle-family dwelling units." Edmonds itself recognizes that this provision simply "defines those uses permitted in a single family residential zone."

A separate provision caps the number of occupants a dwelling may house, based on floor area: "Floor Area. Every dwelling unit shall have at least one room which shall have not less than 120 square feet of floor area. Other habitable rooms, except kitchens, shall have an area of not less than 70 square feet. Where more than two persons occupy a room used for sleeping purposes, the required floor area shall be increased at the rate of 50 square feet for each occupant in excess of two." ECDC § 19.10.000. This space and occupancy standard is a prototypical maximum occupancy restriction.

Edmonds nevertheless argues that its family composition rule, ECDC § 21.30.010, falls within § 3607(b)(1), the FHA exemption for maximum occupancy restrictions, because the rule caps at five the number of unrelated persons allowed to occupy a single-family dwelling. But Edmonds' family composition rule surely does not answer the question: "What is the maximum number of occupants permitted to occupy a house?" So long as they are related "by genetics, adoption, or marriage," any number of people can live in a house. Ten siblings, their parents and grandparents, for example, could dwell in a house in Edmonds' single-family residential zone without offending Edmonds' family composition rule.

Family living, not living space per occupant, is what ECDC § 21.30.010 describes. Defining family primarily by biological and legal relationships, the provision also accommodates another group association: five or fewer unrelated people are allowed to live together as though they were family. This

---

[2] The plain import of the statutory language is reinforced by the House Committee Report, which observes: "A number of jurisdictions limit the number of occupants per unit based on a minimum number of square feet in the unit or the sleeping areas of the unit. Reasonable limitations by governments would be allowed to continue, as long as they were applied to all occupants, and did not operate to discriminate on the basis of race, color, religion, sex, national origin, handicap or familial status." H.R. Rep. No. 100-711, p. 31 (1988).

accommodation is the peg on which Edmonds rests its plea for § 3607(b)(1) exemption. Had the City defined a family solely by biological and legal links, § 3607(b)(1) would not have been the ground on which Edmonds staked its case. It is curious reasoning indeed that converts a family values preserver into a maximum occupancy restriction once a town adds to a related persons prescription "and also two unrelated persons."

Edmonds additionally contends that subjecting single-family zoning to FHA scrutiny will "overturn Euclidian zoning" and "destroy the effectiveness and purpose of single-family zoning." This contention both ignores the limited scope of the issue before us and exaggerates the force of the FHA's antidiscrimination provisions. We address only whether Edmonds' family composition rule qualifies for § 3607(b)(1) exemption. Moreover, the FHA antidiscrimination provisions, when applicable, require only "reasonable" accommodations to afford persons with handicaps "equal opportunity to use and enjoy" housing. § 3604(f)(1)(A) and (f)(3)(B).

The parties have presented, and we have decided, only a threshold question: Edmonds' zoning code provision describing who may compose a "family" is not a maximum occupancy restriction exempt from the FHA under § 3607(b)(1). It remains for the lower courts to decide whether Edmonds' actions against Oxford House violate the FHA's prohibitions against discrimination set out in § 3604(f)(1)(A) and (f)(3)(B). For the reasons stated, the judgment of the United States Court of Appeals for the Ninth Circuit is Affirmed.

NOTE

In 1996, the Eighth Circuit addressed the issue of whether the limitation on eight unrelated persons in a single family dwelling violated the Fair Housing Act. The group home involved provided a residence for recovering alcoholics and drug addicts. The opinion follows.

OXFORD HOUSE-C v. CITY OF ST. LOUIS
77 F.3d 249 (8th Cir. 1996)

GAFF, CIRCUIT JUDGE.

Rather than discriminating against Oxford House residents, the City's zoning code favors them on its face. The zoning code allows only three unrelated, nonhandicapped people to reside together in a single family zone, but allows group homes to have up to eight handicapped residents. Oxford House's own expert witness testified Oxford Houses with eight residents can provide significant therapeutic benefits for their members. The district court nevertheless found the City's zoning ordinances are discriminatory because the eight-person limit would destroy the financial viability of many Oxford Houses, and recovering addicts need this kind of group home. Even if the eight-person rule causes some financial hardship for Oxford Houses, however, the rule does not violate the Fair Housing Act if the City had a rational basis for enacting the rule.

We conclude the eight-person rule is rational. Cities have a legitimate interest in decreasing congestion, traffic, and noise in residential areas, and ordinances restricting the number of unrelated people who may occupy a single family residence are reasonably related to these legitimate goals. The City does not need to assert a specific reason for choosing eight as the cut-off point, rather than ten or twelve. "[E]very line drawn by a legislature leaves some out that might well have been included. That exercise of discretion, however, is a legislative, not a judicial, function." We conclude the City's eight-person restriction has a rational basis and thus is valid under the Fair Housing Act.

NOTES

Application of Americans with Disabilities Act to Housing Discrimination: It was previously noted that Section 504 of the Rehabilitation Act will only apply to discrimination in housing that has been federally subsidized. When the Americans with Disabilities Act was passed in 1990, it was recognized that housing already had comprehensive coverage as a result of the 1988 amendments to the Fair Housing Act. Only public accommodations, such as inns, hotels, motels, and places of lodging, were subject to Title III of the ADA and its prohibitions relating to nondiscrimination on the basis of disability. 42 U.S.C. § 12181(7)(a). Residential hotels, which serve both transient and more permanent populations, however, by virtue of their hybrid status, might be covered by both the FHA and the ADA in certain aspects of the facility. *Independent Hous. Servs. v. Fillmore Ctr. Ass'n*, 840 F. Supp. 1328 (N.D. Cal. 1993).

Many individuals with severe impairments could remain in their own homes with family members or living independently if they had attendant care. Whether attendant care of a particular type is mandated under a state array of social services has been the subject of debate in litigation. In two of the most interesting and creative challenges to denial of attendant care, the Third Circuit Court of Appeals addressed this issue in two different but related contexts.

In *Easley v. Snider*, 36 F.3d 297 (3d Cir. 1994), two severely disabled women sought attendant care services from the Pennsylvania Department of Public Welfare. Tracey Easley was living at home, and Florence Howard was living in a nursing home. The state attendant care program provided services such as getting in and out of bed, assistance with routine bodily functions (bathing, dressing, feeding), ancillary services (shopping, cleaning, laundry), and companion services (transportation, reading mail). The program mandated eligibility based on the individual being mentally alert, the purpose being that the recipient would be able to make decisions about and direct the services. Because Ms. Easley and Ms. Howard were not mentally alert, they had been determined to be ineligible. This criteria was challenged as violating the ADA because a reasonable modification of allowing a surrogate to direct the services could be provided.

The court upheld the eligibility requirement, examining the actual services provided through the program, whose objective is to achieve greater personal control and independence for individuals with physical disabilities. The proposed alteration of allowing a surrogate to make decisions would substantially alter the vision of the program. The court recognized that a state program that provides services to a subgroup of individuals with disabilities is permissible.

In a case in the same Circuit Court of Appeals, *Helen L. v. Didario*, 46 F.3d 325 (3d Cir. 1995), decided only a year later, the court also addressed the state program of providing attendant care and nursing home services to individuals with disabilities in Pennsylvania. In this case, the plaintiffs were nursing home residents who were both mentally alert, and who both needed assistance in daily living. The evidence indicated that they could function in their own homes with attendant care services. The state budget, however, did not have sufficient funds in the attendant care program, but did have funding in the nursing home budget. Although the cost in the nursing home was substantially greater than the cost would be for attendant care, both were denied attendant care services because of the allocation of these budget lines.

The court applied the least restrictive environment principles under the ADA and the Rehabilitation Act in finding that the denial of services in this case violated the ADA. The court held that since Pennsylvania had chosen to provide services under the ADA, it must do so in manner appropriate to the requirements of the statute.

QUESTION

Do any of the FHA, ADA, or Section 504 requirements prohibit a provider of assisted living services from providing a "tiered" level of services that require that residents in such buildings qualify for each level? See, e.g., *Herriot v. Channing House*, 37 Nat'l Disability L. Rep.¶ 212 (N.D. Cal. 2008) (continuing care retirement community did not discriminate against individual who needed 24-hour care for mobility challenges and dementia; individual wanted to remain in independent living portion after developing needs that required skilled nursing and assisted living).

F   ENFORCEMENT

Enforcement of the Fair Housing Act is possible either through complaint to the Department of Housing and Urban Development (HUD) or through direct complaint in court. Exhaustion of administrative remedies is not required before bringing action in court. The administrative complaint mechanism contemplates referral to state or local agencies if they exist and have substantially similar rights and remedies. The Attorney General of the United States may also bring action in cases where there appears to be a pattern or practice of resistance to compliance with the FHA. The Attorney General may also intervene in a private action. 42 U.S.C. § 3610–3614. See also *Shapiro v. Cadman Towers, Inc.*, reproduced in Section [C][1], *supra*.

The remedies available to successful complainants include civil penalties up to $50,000 and other appropriate relief. 42 U.S.C. § 3612. Actual and punitive damages and appropriate equitable relief also are allowed. Attorneys' fees and costs may be awarded in the court's discretion. 42 U.S.C. § 3612–3613. An unsettled issue with respect to Title II claims seeking damages in cases involving deinstitutionalization and community living is whether state agencies are immune from damage actions in such cases.

Chapter 9

HEALTH CARE AND INSURANCE

A   INTRODUCTION

Access to health care services is important to all Americans. For individuals with disabilities, it can be even more critical. Yet these individuals often face greater challenges than other Americans in receiving health care services. One barrier is discrimination by health care providers. Individuals with HIV, for example, often face discrimination and refusal to treat, either directly or indirectly. Reasonable accommodations (such as interpreters for individuals who are deaf) and accessible facilities (such as ramps to enter buildings and equipment usable by individuals with mobility impairments) may be necessary to ensure access.

The cost of health care is the most significant barrier, however. Unless an individual has some type of health insurance coverage, health care costs can be prohibitive. Health insurance is most often available through an employment setting. Those without jobs may not be able to afford individual health insurance policies, and even if they can afford them, they may not be able to obtain health insurance or the insurance may not adequately cover the treatments needed by the individual.

This chapter highlights the key federal statutes that are designed to ensure nondiscrimination in health coverage and to some degree access to health insurance. These statutes include the Rehabilitation Act, the Americans with Disabilities Act, the Health Insurance Portability and Accountability Act, the Genetic Information Non-Discrimination Act, the Mental Health Parity and Addiction Equity Act, and various state laws prohibiting discrimination. It should be apparent that these protections are quite limited in ensuring adequate health care for individuals with disabilities.

In addition, the chapter highlights some of the unique employment aspects of health care providers who themselves have disabilities, and how nondiscrimination policies address those situations.

B   NONDISCRIMINATION IN HEALTH CARE SERVICES

Until the 1990 passage of the Americans with Disabilities Act (ADA), 42 U.S.C. § 12101 et seq., the only major protection from nondiscrimination by health care providers was under Section 504 of the Rehabilitation Act, 29 U.S.C. § 794. This section applies only to recipients of federal financial assistance, however, leaving most individuals with disabilities with little remedy against discrimination. Most courts hold that receipt of Medicare or Medicaid constitutes federal financial assistance. Therefore, physicians and hospitals accepting these payments are covered by Section 504.

The ADA of 1990 broadened the protection for persons with disabilities against discrimination in the provision of health care services. Title II prohibits state and local governments providing health care services from discriminating based on disability. Title III prohibits discrimination by twelve categories of public accommodation. Included in the list as public accommodations are offices of health care providers. There is a conflict in the courts over whether health insurance contracts themselves are public accommodations subject to the anti-discrimination mandates of the ADA. For more discussion on the issue of whether health insurance contracts are public accommodations, see Section [D], below. For more information and cases on coverage, see LAURA ROTHSTEIN & JULIA ROTHSTEIN, DISABILITIES AND THE LAW Sec. 10:1 (2009).

Two major Supreme Court cases have addressed significant issues related to health care and individuals with disabilities under the Rehabilitation Act.[1] The first is *Alexander v. Choate*, 469 U.S. 287 (1984), excerpted in Chapter 1, in which the Court addressed the question of whether the state of Tennessee's policy of reducing the number of annual days of inpatient hospital care covered by its state Medicaid program violates Section 504. This policy has a disparate impact on individuals with disabilities, but because the proposed fourteen-day limitation does not deny disabled individuals meaningful access to Medicaid services or exclude them from those services, the policy was held not to violate Section 504.

The second decision, *Bowen v. American Hosp. Ass'n*, below, followed several years of political activity beginning in 1982. The issues are quite complex, because they involve religious, moral, medical, ethical, and legal questions and policies. While this kind of issue is not frequently addressed by the courts today, the decision provides an interesting overview of how regulations are promulgated, the deference given to medical providers, and the challenges in addressing these issues in a particularly emotional situation.

---

[1] Two other Supreme Court decisions have addressed health care issues indirectly, but these decisions do not have the significant precedential application that is found in the three decisions discussed in this chapter. *Irving Indep. Sch. Dist. v. Tatro*, 468 U.S. 883 (1984), excerpted in Chapter 7[B][2], *supra*, was not a Rehabilitation Act case. It addressed the question of whether catheterization is a "related service" rather than a "medical service" to determine whether schools are obligated to provide this service within the mandates of the Individuals with Disabilities Education Act (formerly the Education for All Handicapped Children Act).

Traynor v. Turnage, 485 U.S. 535 (1988), discussed in Chapter 2[B][6], *supra*, involved a Veterans' Administration policy against providing educational benefits for primary alcoholics. The decision is not a health care access case, but since the same reasoning could apply to health care benefits, it should be mentioned at this point. The Court held that this policy does not violate Section 504. This decision was based on an assessment that congressional intent was clear when Congress indicated that these benefits should not be made available to veterans whose delay in requesting them was a result of their own willful misconduct. The regulations implementing this legislation distinguish between primary alcoholism (considered to be the result of the person's willful misconduct) and secondary alcoholism which relates to organic diseases and disabilities resulting from the chronic use of alcohol. 38 C.F.R. § 3.301(c)(2).

BOWEN v. AMERICAN HOSPITAL ASS'N
476 U.S. 610 (1986)

STEVENS, J., announced the judgment of the Court.

I.

The American Medical Association, the American Hospital Association, and several other respondents challenge the validity of Final Rules promulgated on January 12, 1984, by the Secretary of the Department of Health and Human Services. These Rules establish "Procedures relating to health care for handicapped infants," and in particular require the posting of informational notices, authorize expedited access to records and expedited compliance actions, and command state child protective services agencies to "prevent instances of unlawful medical neglect of handicapped infants."

Although the Final Rules comprise six parts, only the four mandatory components are challenged here.[2] Subsection (b) is entitled "Posting of informational notice" and requires every "recipient health care provider that

---

[2] In subsection (a) the Department "encourages each recipient health care provider that provides health care services to infants" to establish an "Infant Care Review Committee (ICRC)" to assist in the development of treatment standards for handicapped infants and to provide assistance in making individual treatment decisions. In subsection (f), the Department describes its version of a model ICRC. Subsection (f) also provides that "[t]he activities of the ICRC will be guided by . . . [t]he interpretative guidelines of the Department." These guidelines, which are "illustrative" and "do not independently establish rules of conduct," set forth the Department's interpretation of § 504. Although they do not contain any definition of "discrimination," they do state that § 504 is not applicable to parents and that the regulation applies to only two categories of activities of hospitals: (1) refusals to provide treatment or nourishment to handicapped infants whose parents have consented to, or requested, such treatment; and (2) the failure or refusal to take action to override a parental decision to withhold consent for medically beneficial treatment or nourishment. With respect to the second category, the guidelines state that the hospital may not "solely on the basis of the infant's present or anticipated future mental or physical impairments, fail to follow applicable procedures on reporting such incidents to the child protective services agency or to seek judicial review." With respect to the first category, the guidelines do not state that § 504 categorically prohibits a hospital from withholding requested treatment or nourishment "solely on the basis of present or anticipated physical or mental impairments of an infant." Rather, the substantive guidelines and two of the illustrative examples recognize that the etiology of and prognosis for particular handicapping conditions may justify "a refusal to treat solely on the basis of those handicapping conditions." (§ 504 does not require "futile treatment"); (§ 504 does not require treatment of anencephaly because it would "do no more than temporarily prolong the act of dying"); (same with severely premature and low birth weight infants). In general, the guidelines seem to make a hospital's liability under § 504 dependent on proof that (1) it refused to provide requested treatment or nourishment solely on the basis of an infant's handicapping condition, and (2) the treatment or nourishment would have been medically beneficial. The guidelines also describe how HHS will respond to "complaints of suspected life threatening noncompliance" with § 504 in this context, progressing from telephone inquiries to the hospital to obtain information about the condition of the infant, to requests for access to records, and finally to onsite investigations and litigation in appropriate cases. The guidelines do not draw any distinction between cases in which parental consent has been withheld and those in which it has been given. Nor do they draw any distinction between cases in which hospitals have made a report of parental refusal to consent to treatment and those in which no report to a state agency has been made. They do announce that the "Department will also seek to coordinate its investigation with any related investigations by the state child protective services agency so as to minimize potential

provides health care services to infants in programs or activities receiving Federal financial assistance" — a group to which we refer generically as "hospitals" — to post an informational notice in one of two approved forms. Both forms include a statement that § 504 prohibits discrimination on the basis of handicap, and indicate that because of this prohibition "nourishment and medically beneficial treatment (as determined with respect for reasonable medical judgments) should not be withheld from handicapped infants solely on the basis of their present or anticipated mental or physical impairments." The notice's statement of the legal requirement does not distinguish between medical care for which parental consent has been obtained and that for which it has not. The notice must identify the telephone number of the appropriate child protective services agency and, in addition, a toll-free number for the Department that is available 24 hours a day. Finally, the notice must state that the "identity of callers will be kept confidential" and that federal law prohibits retaliation "against any person who provides information about possible violations."

Subsection (c), which contains the second mandatory requirement, sets forth "Responsibilities of recipient state child protective services agencies." Subsection (c) does not mention § 504 (or any other federal statute) and does not even use the word "discriminate." It requires every designated agency to establish and maintain procedures to ensure that "the agency utilizes its full authority pursuant to state law to prevent instances of unlawful medical neglect of handicapped infants." Mandated procedures must include (1) "[a] requirement that health care providers report on a timely basis . . . known or suspected instances of unlawful medical neglect of handicapped infants," (2) a method by which the state agency can receive timely reports of such cases, (3) "immediate" review of those reports, including "on-site investigation," where appropriate, (4) protection of "medically neglected handicapped infants" including, where appropriate, legal action to secure "timely court order[s] to compel the provision of necessary nourishment and medical treatment," and (5) "[t]imely notification" to HHS of every report of "suspected unlawful medical neglect" of handicapped infants. The preamble to the Final Rules makes clear that this subsection applies "where a refusal to provide medically beneficial treatment is a result, not of decisions by a health care provider, but of decisions by parents."

The two remaining mandatory regulations authorize "[e]xpedited access to records" and "[e]xpedited action to effect compliance." Subsection (d) provides broadly for immediate access to patient records on a 24-hour basis, with or without parental consent, "when, in the judgment of the responsible Department official, immediate access is necessary to protect the life or health of a handicapped individual." Subsection (e) likewise dispenses with otherwise applicable requirements of notice to the hospital "when, in the judgment of the responsible Department official, immediate action to effect compliance is necessary to protect the life or health of a handicapped individual." The expedited compliance provision is intended to allow "the government [to] see[k] a temporary restraining order to sustain the life of a handicapped infant in imminent danger of death." Like the

disruption," indicating that the Department's investigations may continue even in cases that have previously been referred to a state agency.

provision affording expedited access to records, it applies without regard to whether parental consent to treatment has been withheld or whether the matter has already been referred to a state child protective services agency.

II.

The Final Rules represent the Secretary's ultimate response to an April 9, 1982, incident in which the parents of a Bloomington, Indiana, infant with Down's syndrome and other handicaps refused consent to surgery to remove an esophageal obstruction that prevented oral feeding. On April 10, the hospital initiated judicial proceedings to override the parents' decision, but an Indiana trial court, after holding a hearing the same evening, denied the requested relief. On April 12 the court asked the local Child Protection Committee to review its decision. After conducting its own hearing, the Committee found no reason to disagree with the court's ruling. The infant died six days after its birth.

Citing "heightened public concern" in the aftermath of the Bloomington Baby Doe incident, on May 18, 1982, the director of the Department's Office of Civil Rights, in response to a directive from the President, "remind[ed]" health care providers receiving federal financial assistance that newborn infants with handicaps such as Down's syndrome were protected by § 504.

This notice was followed, on March 7, 1983, by an "Interim Final Rule" contemplating a "vigorous federal role." The Interim Rule required health care providers receiving federal financial assistance to post "in a conspicuous place in each delivery ward, each maternity ward, each pediatric ward, and each nursery, including each intensive care nursery" a notice advising of the applicability of § 504 and the availability of a telephone "hotline" to report suspected violations of the law to HHS. Like the Final Rules, the Interim Rule also provided for expedited compliance actions and expedited access to records and facilities when, "in the judgment of the responsible Department official," immediate action or access was "necessary to protect the life or health of a handicapped individual." The Interim Rule took effect on March 22.

On April 6, 1983, respondents American Hospital Association et al. filed a complaint in the Federal District Court for the Southern District of New York seeking a declaration that the Interim Final Rule was invalid and an injunction against its enforcement. Little more than a week later, on April 14, in a similar challenge brought by the American Academy of Pediatrics and other medical institutions, the Federal District Court for the District of Columbia declared the Interim Final Rule "arbitrary and capricious and promulgated in violation of the Administrative Procedure Act." The District Judge in that case "conclude[d] that haste and inexperience ha[d] resulted in agency action based on inadequate consideration" of several relevant concerns and, in the alternative, found that the Secretary had improperly failed to solicit public comment before issuing the Rule.

On July 5, 1983, the Department issued new "Proposed Rules" on which it invited comment. Like the Interim Final Rule, the Proposed Rules required hospitals to post informational notices in conspicuous places and authorized expedited access to records to be followed, if necessary, by expedited compliance action. In a departure from the Interim Final Rule, however, the Proposed Rules required federally assisted state child protective services agencies to utilize their "full authority pursuant to State law to prevent instances of medical neglect of handicapped infants." Mandated procedures mirrored those contained in the Final Rules described above. The preamble and appendix to the Proposed Rules did not acknowledge that hospitals and physicians lack authority to perform treatment to which parents have not given their consent.

After the period for notice and comment had passed, HHS, on December 30, 1983, promulgated the Final Rules and announced that they would take effect on February 13, 1984. On March 12 of that year respondents American Hospital Association et al. amended their complaint and respondents American Medical Association et al. filed suit to declare the new regulations invalid and to enjoin their enforcement. The actions were consolidated. . . .

III.

On October 28, the New York Court of Appeals affirmed, but on the ground that the trial court should not have entertained a petition to initiate child neglect proceedings by a stranger who had not requested the aid of the responsible state agency.

IV.

The Solicitor General is correct that "handicapped individual" as used in § 504 includes an infant who is born with a congenital defect. If such an infant is "otherwise qualified" for benefits under a program or activity receiving federal financial assistance, § 504 protects him from discrimination "solely by reason of his handicap." It follows . . . that handicapped infants are entitled to "meaningful access" to medical services provided by hospitals, and that a hospital rule or state policy denying or limiting such access would be subject to challenge under § 504.

However, no such rule or policy is challenged, or indeed has been identified, in this case. Nor does this case, in contrast to the *University Hospital* litigation, involve a claim that any specific individual treatment decision violates § 504. This suit is not an enforcement action, and as a consequence it is not necessary to determine whether § 504 ever applies to individual medical treatment decisions involving handicapped infants. Respondents brought this litigation to challenge the four mandatory components of the Final Rules on their face, and the Court of Appeals' judgment which we review merely affirmed the judgment of the District Court which "declared invalid and enjoined enforcement of [the final] regulations, purportedly promulgated pursuant to section 504 of the Rehabilitation Act of 1973."

V.

It is an axiom of administrative law that an agency's explanation of the basis for its decision must include "a 'rational connection between the facts found and the choice made.'" Agency deference has not come so far that we will uphold regulations whenever it is possible to "conceive a basis" for administrative action.

Before examining the Secretary's reasons for issuing the Final Rules, it is essential to understand the pre-existing state-law framework governing the provision of medical care to handicapped infants. In broad outline, state law vests decisional responsibility in the parents, in the first instance, subject to review in exceptional cases by the State acting as parens patriae. Prior to the regulatory activity culminating in the Final Rules, the Federal Government was not a participant in the process of making treatment decisions for newborn infants. We presume that this general framework was familiar to Congress when it enacted § 504. It therefore provides an appropriate background for evaluating the Secretary's action in this case.

The Secretary has identified two possible categories of violations of § 504 as justifications for federal oversight of handicapped infant care. First, he contends that a hospital's refusal to furnish a handicapped infant with medically beneficial treatment "solely by reason of his handicap" constitutes unlawful discrimination. Second, he maintains that a hospital's failure to report cases of suspected medical neglect to a state child protective services agency may also violate the statute. We separately consider these two possible bases for the Final Rules.

VI.

In the immediate aftermath of the Bloomington Baby Doe incident, the Secretary apparently proceeded on the assumption that a hospital's statutory duty to provide treatment to handicapped infants was unaffected by the absence of parental consent. He has since abandoned that view. Thus, the preamble to the Final Rules correctly states that when "a non-treatment decision, no matter how discriminatory, is made by parents, rather than by the hospital, section 504 does not mandate that the hospital unilaterally overrule the parental decision and provide treatment notwithstanding the lack of consent." A hospital's withholding of treatment when no parental consent has been given cannot violate § 504, for without the consent of the parents or a surrogate decisionmaker the infant is neither "otherwise qualified" for treatment nor has he been denied care "solely by reason of his handicap."

Indeed, it would almost certainly be a tort as a matter of state law to operate on an infant without parental consent. This analysis makes clear that the Government's heavy reliance on the analogy to race-based refusals which violate § 601 of the Civil Rights Act is misplaced. If, pursuant to its normal practice, a hospital refused to operate on a black child whose parents had withheld their consent to treatment, the hospital's refusal would not be based on the race of the child even if it were assumed that the parents based *their decision* entirely on a mistaken assumption that the race of the child made the operation inappropriate.

Now that the Secretary has acknowledged that a hospital has no statutory treatment obligation in the absence of parental consent, it has become clear that the Final Rules are not needed to prevent hospitals from denying treatment to handicapped infants. The Solicitor General concedes that the administrative record contains no evidence that hospitals have ever refused treatment authorized either by the infant's parents or by a court order. Even the Secretary never seriously maintained that posted notices, "hotlines," and emergency on-site investigations were necessary to process complaints against hospitals that might refuse treatment requested by parents. The parental interest in calling such a refusal to the attention of the appropriate authorities adequately vindicates the interest in enforcement of § 504 in such cases, just as that interest obviates the need for a special regulation to deal with refusals to provide treatment on the basis of race which may violate § 601 of the Civil Rights Act.

The Secretary's belated recognition of the effect of parental nonconsent is important, because the supposed need for federal monitoring of hospitals' treatment decisions rests *entirely* on instances in which parents have refused their consent. Thus, in the Bloomington, Indiana, case that precipitated the Secretary's enforcement efforts in this area, as well as in the *University Hospital* case that provided the basis for the summary affirmance in the case now before us, the hospital's failure to perform the treatment at issue rested on the lack of parental consent. The Secretary's own summaries of these cases establish beyond doubt that the respective hospitals did not withhold medical care on the basis of handicap and therefore did not violate § 504; as a result, they provide no support for his claim that federal regulation is needed in order to forestall comparable cases in the future.

The Secretary's initial failure to recognize that withholding of consent by parents does not equate with discriminatory denial of treatment by hospitals likewise undermines the Secretary's findings in the preamble to his proposed rulemaking. In that statement, the Secretary cited four sources in support of the claim that "Section 504 [is] not being uniformly followed." None of the cited examples, however, suggests that recipients of federal financial assistance, as opposed to parents, had withheld medical care on the basis of handicap.

Notwithstanding the ostensible recognition in the preamble of the effect of parental nonconsent on a hospital's obligation to provide care, in promulgating the Final Rules the Secretary persisted in relying on instances in which parents had refused consent to support his claim that, regardless of its "magnitude," there is sufficient evidence of "illegality" to justify "establishing basic mechanisms to allow for effective enforcement of a clearly applicable statute." We have already discussed one source of this evidence -"the several specific cases cited in the preamble to the proposed rule." Contrary to the Secretary's belief, these cases do not "support the proposition that handicapped infants may be subjected to unlawful discrimination." In addition to the evidence relied on in prior notices, the Secretary included a summary of the 49 "Infant Doe cases" that the Department had processed before December 1, 1983. Curiously, however, by the Secretary's own admission none of the 49 cases had "resulted in a finding of discriminatory withholding of medical care." In fact, in the entire list of 49 cases there is no finding that a hospital failed or refused to provide treatment to a handicapped infant for which parental consent had been given.

Notwithstanding this concession, the Secretary "believes three of these cases demonstrate the utility of the procedural mechanisms called for in the final rules." ("[T]hese cases provide additional documentation of the need for governmental involvement and the appropriateness of the procedures established by the final rules"). However, these three cases, which supposedly provide the strongest support for federal intervention, fail to disclose any discrimination against handicapped newborns in violation of § 504. For example, in Robinson, Illinois, the Department conducted an on-site investigation when it learned that the "hospital (at *the parents' request*) failed to perform necessary surgery." After "[t]he parents refused consent for surgery," "the hospital referred the matter to state authorities, who accepted custody of the infant and arranged for surgery and adoption," all "in compliance with section 504." The Secretary concluded that "the involvement of the state child protective services agency," at the behest of the hospital, "was the most important element in bringing about corrective surgery for the infant. . . . Had there been no *governmental* involvement in the case, the outcome might have been much less favorable." 49 Fed. Reg. at 1649 (emphasis added).

The Secretary's second example illustrates with even greater force the effective and nondiscriminatory functioning of state mechanisms and the consequent lack of support for federal intervention. In Daytona Beach, Florida, the Department's hotline received a complaint of medical neglect of a handicapped infant; immediate contact with the hospital and state agency revealed that "the parents did not consent to surgery" for the infant. Notwithstanding this information, which was confirmed by both the hospital and the state agency, and despite the fact that the state agency had "obtained a court order to provide surgery" the day *before* HHS was notified, the Department conducted an on-site investigation. In the third case, in Colorado Springs, Colorado, the Department intervened so soon after birth that "the decisionmaking process was in progress at the time the OCR [Office of Civil Rights] inquiry began," and "it is impossible to say the surgery would not have been provided without this involvement." "However," the Secretary added, "the involvement of OCR and the OCR medical consultant was cooperatively received by the hospital and apparently constructive."

In sum, there is nothing in the administrative record to justify the Secretary's belief that "discriminatory withholding of medical care" in violation of 504 provides any support for federal regulation.

VII.

As a backstop to his manifestly incorrect perception that withholding of treatment in accordance with parental instructions necessitates federal regulation, the Secretary contends that a hospital's failure to report parents' refusals to consent to treatment violates § 504, and that past breaches of this kind justify federal oversight.

By itself, § 504 imposes no duty to report instances of medical neglect — that undertaking derives from state-law reporting obligations or a hospital's own voluntary practice. Although a hospital's selective refusal to report medical neglect of handicapped infants might violate § 504, the Secretary has failed to point to any specific evidence that this has occurred. The 49 actual investigations summarized in the preamble to the Final Rules do not reveal *any* case in which a hospital either failed, or was accused of failing, to make an appropriate report to a state agency. Nor can we accept the Solicitor General's invitation to infer discriminatory nonreporting from the studies cited in the Secretary's proposed rulemaking. Even assuming that cases in which parents have withheld consent to treatment for handicapped infants have gone unreported, that fact alone would not prove that the hospitals involved had discriminated on the basis of handicap rather than simply failed entirely to discharge their state-law reporting obligations, if any, a matter which lies wholly outside the nondiscrimination mandate of § 504.

The particular reporting mechanism chosen by the Secretary — indeed the entire regulatory framework imposed on state child protective services agencies — departs from the nondiscrimination mandate of § 504 in a more fundamental way. The mandatory provisions of the Final Rules omit any direct requirement that hospitals make reports when parents refuse consent to recommended procedures. Instead, the Final Rules command *state agencies* to require such reports, regardless of the state agencies' own reporting requirements (or lack thereof). Far from merely preventing state agencies from remaining calculatedly indifferent to handicapped infants while they tend to the needs of the similarly situated nonhandicapped, the Final Rules command state agencies to utilize their "full authority" to "prevent instances of unlawful medical neglect of handicapped infants." The Rules effectively make medical neglect of handicapped newborns a state investigative priority, possibly forcing state agencies to shift scarce resources away from other enforcement activities — perhaps even from programs designed to protect handicapped children outside hospitals. The Rules also order state agencies to "immedia- te[ly]" review reports from hospitals, to conduct "on-site investigation[s]," and to take legal action "to compel the provision of necessary nourishment and medical treatment" — all without any regard to the procedures followed by state agencies in handling complaints filed on behalf of nonhandicapped infants. These operating procedures were imposed over the objection of several state child protective services agencies that the requirement that they turn over reports to HHS "conflicts with the confidentiality requirements of state child abuse and neglect statutes" — thereby requiring under the guise of nondiscrimination a service which state law denies to the nonhandicapped.

The complaint-handling process the Secretary would impose on unwilling state agencies is totally foreign to the authority to prevent discrimination conferred on him by § 504. "Section 504 seeks to assure evenhanded treatment," "neither the language, purpose, nor history of § 504 reveals an intent to impose an affirmative-action obligation" on recipients of federal financial assistance. The Solicitor General also recognizes that § 504 is concerned with discrimination and with discrimination alone. In his attempt to distinguish the Secretary's 1976 determination that it "is beyond the authority of section 504" to promulgate regulations "concerning adequate and appropriate psychiatric care or safe and humane living conditions for persons institutionalized because of handicap or concerning payment of fair compensation to patients who perform work," the Solicitor General explains:

> "This conclusion of course was consistent with the fact that, as relevant here, Section 504 is essentially concerned only with discrimination in the relative treatment of handicapped and nonhandicapped persons and does not confer any absolute right to receive particular services or benefits under federally assisted programs."

The Final Rules, however, impose just the sort of absolute obligation on state agencies that the Secretary had previously disavowed. The services state agencies are required to make available to handicapped infants are in no way tied to the level of services provided to similarly situated nonhandicapped infants. Instead, they constitute an "*absolute* right to receive particular services or benefits" under a federally assisted program. Even if a state agency were scrupulously impartial as between the protection it offered handicapped and nonhandicapped infants, it could still be denied federal funding for failing to carry out the Secretary's mission with sufficient zeal.

It is no answer to state, as does the Secretary, that these regulations are a necessary " 'metho[d] . . . to give reasonable assurance' of compliance." For while the Secretary can require state agencies to document their *own* compliance with § 504, nothing in that provision authorizes him to commandeer state agencies to enforce compliance by *other* recipients of federal funds (in this instance, hospitals). State child protective services agencies are not field offices of the HHS bureaucracy, and they may not be conscripted against their will as the foot soldiers in a federal crusade.

VIII.

Section 504 authorizes any head of an Executive Branch agency — regardless of his agency's mission or expertise — to promulgate regulations prohibiting discrimination against the handicapped. As a result of this rulemaking authority, the Secretary of HHS has "substantial leeway to explore areas in which discrimination against the handicapped pos[es] particularly significant problems and to devise regulations to prohibit such discrimination."

Even according the greatest respect to the Secretary's action, however, deference cannot fill the lack of an evidentiary foundation on which the Final Rules must rest. The Secretary's basis for federal intervention is perceived discrimination against handicapped infants in violation of § 504, and yet the Secretary has pointed to no evidence that such discrimination occurs. Neither the fact that regulators generally may rely on generic information in a particular field or comparable experience gained in other fields, nor the fact that regulations may be imposed for preventative or prophylactic reasons, can substitute for evidence supporting the Secretary's own chosen rationale. For the principle of agency accountability recited earlier means that "an agency's action must be upheld, if at all, on the basis articulated by the agency itself."

The need for a proper evidentiary basis for agency action is especially acute in this case because Congress has failed to indicate, either in the statute or in the legislative history, that it envisioned federal superintendence of treatment decisions traditionally entrusted to state governance. "[W]e must assume that the implications and limitations of our federal system constitute a major premise of all congressional legislation, though not repeatedly recited therein." Congress therefore "will not be deemed to have significantly changed the federal-state balance" — or to have authorized its delegates to do so — "unless otherwise the purpose of the Act would be defeated." Although the nondiscrimination mandate of § 504 is cast in language sufficiently broad to suggest that the question is "not one of authority, but of its appropriate exercise[,] [t]he propriety of the exertion of the authority must be tested by its relation to the purpose of the [statutory] grant and with suitable regard to the principle that whenever the federal power is exerted within what would otherwise be the domain of state power, the justification of the exercise of the federal power must clearly appear." That is, "it must appear that there are findings, supported by evidence, of the essential facts . . . which would justify [the Secretary's] conclusion." The administrative record does not contain the reasoning and evidence that is necessary to sustain federal intervention into a historically state-administered decisional process that appears — for lack of any evidence to the contrary — to be functioning in full compliance with § 504.

This response, together with its previous remarks, makes irresistible the inference that the Department regards its mission as one principally concerned with the quality of medical care for handicapped infants rather than with the implementation of § 504. We could not quarrel with a decision by the Department to concentrate its finite compliance resources on instances of life-threatening discrimination rather than instances in which merely elective care has been withheld. But nothing in the statute authorizes the Secretary to dispense with the law's focus on discrimination and instead to employ federal resources to save the lives of handicapped newborns, without regard to whether they are victims of discrimination by recipients of federal funds or not. Section 504 does not authorize the Secretary to give unsolicited advice either to parents, to hospitals, or to state officials who are faced with difficult treatment decisions concerning handicapped children. We may assume that the "qualified professionals" employed by the Secretary may make valuable contributions in particular cases, but neither that assumption nor the sincere conviction that an immediate "on-site investigation" is "necessary to protect the life or health of a handicapped individual" can enlarge the statutory powers of the Secretary.

The administrative record demonstrates that the Secretary has asserted the authority to conduct on-site investigations, to inspect hospital records, and to participate in the decisional process in emergency cases in which there was no colorable basis for believing that a violation of § 504 had occurred or was about to occur. The District Court and the Court of Appeals correctly held that these investigative actions were not authorized by the statute and that the regulations which purport to authorize a continuation of them are invalid.

The judgment of the Court of Appeals is affirmed.

QUESTIONS

1.   Does this decision strike down the use of infant care review committees? See footnote 2 in the *Bowen* decision.

2.   The Section 504 regulations included a provision that the decision about whether to treat or not should not include consideration of the negative effect of the child's condition on others, including parents, siblings, and society. Is it possible not to do that? Should the impact on others be a valid consideration?

NOTES

1. *Institutional Ethics Committees:* The types of committees suggested in the regulations addressed in the *Bowen* case have been implemented in a number of hospitals. There are several practical issues relating to the implementation of such committees. These issues include how members of the committee are appointed, what their term of appointment is and how they are removed, what their decisionmaking authority is, what liability is involved, and other practical issues relating to when they meet, whether they vote or reach consensus, etc. For a discussion of these issues, see Alexander Morgan Capron, *Legal Perspectives on Institutional Ethics Committees*, 11 J. COLLEGE & UNIV. L. 417 (1985).

2. *Values as Factors in Decisionmaking:* Decisionmaking involving issues of seriously ill newborns obviously includes values that will be incorporated into standards to be applied. One's moral and/or religious perspective on life will affect whether any of the following standards are applied: biological life should be preserved at all costs; what the infant would want; can the infant relate to life adequately to have some meaning; the cost of the infant's life to others. For a discussion of these issues, see Rebecca Dresser, *Life, Death, and Incompetent Patients: Conceptual Infirmities and Hidden Values in the Law*, 28 ARIZ. L. REV. 373 (1986).

3. *Medicaid Prioritization and Health Care Rationing:* As a response to rising health care costs, many states base Medicaid funding prioritization on certain conditions. Medicaid is federally funded, but state administered. For that reason both Section 504 of the Rehabilitation Act and Title II of the Americans with Disabilities Act could be implicated in challenges that such plans discriminate on the basis of disability in violation of federal discrimination laws. What is the likelihood that plaintiffs would succeed in such an action? For a discussion of this issue, see Robert J. Moosy, Jr., *Health Care Prioritization and the ADA: The Oregon Plan 1991-1993*, 31 HOUS. L. REV. 265 (1994); David Orentlicher, *Rationing and the Americans with Disabilities Act*, 217 JAMA 308 (1994).

4. The ADA and Rehabilitation Act were amended by the ADA Amendments Act of 2008 (ADAAA), which took effect on January 1, 2009. As earlier chapters demonstrate, Congress passed the amendments to overturn a number of United States Supreme Court opinions interpreting the ADA and their application by the lower federal courts that had the effect of significantly narrowing the definition of individuals with disabilities. Some of these opinions concluded that persons with serious impairments such as mental retardation, deafness, diabetes and cancer were not individuals with disabilities and were therefore not protected by the Act from discrimination. The ADAAA will have the effect of including a broader group of persons within the definition of persons with disabilities. For more information on the ADAAA, see Chapters 1 and 2.

The *Bowen* decision provides a perspective on the application of Section 504 of the Rehabilitation Act to treatment of seriously ill newborns. The decision does not really address the discrimination issue, but rather focuses on the validity of the regulations on this issue promulgated pursuant to Section 504.

The following decision focuses more on the discrimination issue in the context of the ADA and withdrawal of treatment from a seriously ill newborn. The same analysis would be likely to apply in a Section 504 claim. On appeal, the Fourth Circuit did not address the ADA claim. *In re Baby K*, 16 F.3d 590 (4th Cir. 1994). The court instead found that the hospital had violated the Emergency Medical Treatment and Active Labor Act, 42 U.S.C. § 1395dd(b), (e)(3)(A), which mandates the provision of life-sustaining treatment in emergency situations. The appellate court did not comment on the ADA or Section 504.

IN RE BABY K
832 F. Supp. 1022 (E.D. Va. 1993)

HILTON, DISTRICT JUDGE:

Findings of Fact

1. Plaintiff Hospital is a general acute care hospital located in Virginia that is licensed to provide diagnosis, treatment, and medical and nursing services to the public as provided by Virginia law. Among other facilities, the Hospital has a Pediatric Intensive Care Department and an Emergency Department.

2. The Hospital is a recipient of federal and state funds including those from Medicare and Medicaid and is a "participating hospital" pursuant to 42 U.S.C. § 1395cc.

3. The Hospital and its staff (including emergency doctors, pediatricians, neonatologists and pediatric intensivists) treat sick children on a daily basis.

4. Defendant Ms. H, a citizen of the Commonwealth of Virginia, is the biological mother of Baby K, an infant girl born by Caesarean section at the Hospital on October 13, 1992. Baby K was born with anencephaly.

5. Anencephaly is a congenital defect in which the brain stem is present but the cerebral cortex is rudimentary or absent. There is no treatment that will cure, correct, or ameliorate anencephaly. Baby K is permanently unconscious and cannot hear or see. Lacking a cerebral function, Baby K does not feel pain. Baby K has brain stem functions primarily limited to reflexive actions such as feeding reflexes (rooting, sucking, swallowing), respiratory reflexes (breathing, coughing), and reflexive responses to sound or touch. Baby K has a normal heart rate, blood pressure, liver function, digestion, kidney function, and bladder function and has gained weight since her birth. Most anencephalic infants die within days of birth.

6. Baby K was diagnosed prenatally as being anencephalic. Despite the counselling of her obstetrician and neonatologist that she terminate her pregnancy, Ms. H refused to have her unborn child aborted.

7. A Virginia court of competent jurisdiction has found defendant Mr. K, a citizen of the Commonwealth of Virginia, to be Baby K's biological father.

8. Ms. H and Mr. K have never been married.

9.   Since Baby K's birth, Mr. K has, at most, been only distantly involved in matters relating to the infant. Neither the Hospital nor Ms. H ever sought Mr. K's opinion or consent in providing medical treatment to Baby K.

10.   Because Baby K had difficulty breathing immediately upon birth, Hospital physicians provided her with mechanical ventilator treatment to allow her to breathe.

11.   Within days of Baby K's birth, Hospital medical personnel urged Ms. H to permit a "Do Not Resuscitate Order" for Baby K that would discontinue ventilator treatment. Her physicians told her that no treatment existed for Baby K's anencephalic condition, no therapeutic or palliative purpose was served by the treatment, and that ventilator care was medically unnecessary and inappropriate. Despite this pressure, Ms. H continued to request ventilator treatment for her child.

12.   Because of Ms. H's continued insistence that Baby K receive ventilator treatment, her treating physicians requested the assistance of the Hospital's "Ethics Committee" in overriding the mother's wishes.

13.   A three person Ethics Committee subcommittee, composed of a family practitioner, a psychiatrist, and a minister, met with physicians providing care to Baby K. On October 22, 1992, the group concluded that Baby K's ventilator treatment should end because "such care is futile" and decided to "wait a reasonable time for the family to help the caregiver terminate aggressive therapy." If the family refused to follow this advice, the committee recommended that the Hospital should "attempt to resolve this through our legal system."

14.   Ms. H subsequently rejected the committee's recommendation. Before pursuing legal action to override Ms. H's position, the Hospital decided to transfer the infant to another health care facility.

15.   Baby K was transferred to a nursing home ("Nursing Home") in Virginia on November 30, 1992 during a period when she was not experiencing respiratory distress and thus did not need ventilator treatment. A condition of the transfer was that the Hospital agreed to take the infant back if Baby K again developed respiratory distress to receive ventilator treatment which was unavailable at the Nursing Home. Ms. H agreed to this transfer.

16.   Baby K returned to the Hospital on January 15, 1993 after experiencing respiratory distress to receive ventilator treatment. Hospital officials again attempted to persuade Ms. H to discontinue ventilator treatment for her child. Ms. H again refused. After Baby K could breathe on her own, she was transferred back to the Nursing Home on February 12, 1993.

17.   Baby K again experienced breathing difficulties on March 3, 1993 and returned to the Hospital to receive ventilator treatment.

18.   On March 15, 1993, Baby K received a tracheotomy, a procedure in which a breathing tube is surgically implanted in her windpipe, to facilitate ventilator treatment. Ms. H agreed to this operation.

19.   After no longer requiring ventilator treatment, Baby K was transferred back to the Nursing Home on April 13, 1993 where she continues to live.

20.   Baby K will almost certainly continue to have episodes of respiratory distress in the future. In the absence of ventilator treatment during these episodes, she would suffer serious impairment of her bodily functions and soon die.

21.   Ms. H visits Baby K daily. The mother opposes the discontinuation of ventilator treatment when Baby K experiences respiratory distress because she believes that all human life has value, including her anencephalic daughter's life. Ms. H has a firm Christian faith that all life should be protected. She believes that God will work a miracle if that is his will. Otherwise, Ms. H believes, God, and not other humans, should decide the moment of her daughter's death. As Baby K's mother and as the only parent who has participated in the infant's care, Ms. H believes that she has the right to decide what is in her child's best interests.

22.   On the Hospital's motion, a guardian ad litem to represent Baby K was appointed pursuant to Virginia Code § 8.01-9.

23.   Both the guardian ad litem and Mr. K share the Hospital's position that ventilator treatment should be withheld from Baby K when she experiences respiratory distress.

24.   The Hospital has stipulated that it is not proposing to deny ventilator treatment to Baby K because of any lack of adequate resources or any inability of Ms. H to pay for the treatment.

Conclusions of Law

Pursuant to the Declaratory Judgment Act, 28 U.S.C. § 2201, the Hospital has sought declaratory and injunctive relief under four federal statutes and one Virginia statute: the Emergency Medical Treatment and Active Labor Act, 42 U.S.C. § 1395dd; the Rehabilitation Act of 1973, 29 U.S.C. § 794; the Americans with Disabilities Act of 1990, 42 U.S.C. § 12101 et seq.; the Child Abuse Amendments of 1984, 42 U.S.C. § 5102 et seq.; and the Virginia Medical Malpractice Act, Va.Code § 8.01-581.1 et seq.

I. *Emergency Medical Treatment and Active Labor Act*

[Discussion of this issue omitted.]

II. *Rehabilitation Act*

Section 504 of the Rehabilitation Act prohibits discrimination against an "otherwise qualified" handicapped individual, solely by reason of his or her handicap, under any program or activity receiving federal financial assistance. Hospitals such as plaintiff that accept Medicare and Medicaid funding are subject to the Act. Baby K is a "handicapped" and "disabled" person within the meaning of the Rehabilitation Act of 1973. A "handicapped individual" under the Rehabilitation Act "includes an infant who is born with a congenital defect."

Section 504's plain text spells out the necessary scope of inquiry: Is Baby K otherwise qualified to receive ventilator treatment and is ventilator treatment being threatened with being denied because of an unjustified consideration of her anencephalic handicap? The Hospital has admitted that the sole reason it wishes to withhold ventilator treatment for Baby K over her mother's objections, is because of Baby K's anencephaly — her handicap and disability.

When the Rehabilitation Act was passed in 1973, Congress intended that discrimination on the basis of a handicap be treated in the same manner that Title VI of the Civil Rights Act treats racial discrimination. This analogy to race dispels any ambiguity about the extent to which Baby K has statutory rights not to be discriminated against on the basis of her handicap. It also shatters the Hospital's contention that ventilator treatment should be withheld because Baby K's recurring breathing troubles are intrinsically related to her handicap. No such distinction would be permissible within the context of racial discrimination. In addition, the Hospital was able to perform a tracheotomy on Baby K. This surgery was far more complicated than linking her to a ventilator to allow her to breathe. Just as an AIDS patient seeking ear surgery is "otherwise qualified" to receive treatment despite poor long term prospects of living, Baby K is "otherwise qualified" to receive ventilator treatment despite similarly dismal health prospects. Thus, the Hospital's desire to withhold ventilator treatment from Baby K over her mother's objections would violate the Rehabilitation Act.

III. *Americans with Disabilities Act*

Section 302 of the Americans with Disabilities Act ("ADA") prohibits discrimination against disabled individuals by "public accommodations." The Hospital is a public accommodation under the ADA.

Section 302(a) of the ADA states a general rule of nondiscrimination against the disabled:

> "General rule. No individual shall be discriminated against on the basis of disability in the full and equal enjoyment of the goods, services, facilities, privileges, advantages, or accommodation of any place of public accommodations by any person who owns, leases (or leases to), or operates a place of public accommodation." 42 U.S.C. § 12182(a).

In contrast to the Rehabilitation Act, the ADA does not require that a handicapped individual be "otherwise qualified" to receive the benefits of participation. Further, section 302(b)(1)(A) of the ADA states that "[i]t shall be discriminatory to subject an individual or class of individuals on the basis of a disability . . . to a denial of the opportunity of the individual or class to participate in or benefit from the goods, services, facilities, privileges, advantages, or accommodations of an entity." 42 U.S.C. § 12182(b)(1)(A)(i).

The Hospital asks this court for authorization to deny the benefits of ventilator services to Baby K by reason of her anencephaly. The Hospital's claim is that it is "futile" to keep alive an anencephalic baby, even though the mother has requested such treatment. But the plain language of the ADA does not permit the denial of ventilator services that would keep alive an anencephalic baby when those life-saving services would otherwise be provided to a baby without disabilities at the parent's request. The Hospital's reasoning would lead to the denial of medical services to anencephalic babies as a class of disabled individuals. Such discrimination against a vulnerable population class is exactly what the American with Disabilities Act was enacted to prohibit. The Hospital would therefore violate the ADA if it were to withhold ventilator treatment from Baby K.

IV. *Child Abuse Act*

[Discussion of application of Child Abuse Act, Virginia Medical Malpractice Act, and Constitutional and Common Law Issue omitted.]

For the foregoing reasons, the Hospital's request for a declaratory judgment that the withholding of ventilator treatment from Baby K would not violate the Emergency Medical Treatment and Active Labor Act, the Rehabilitation Act of 1973, the Americans with Disabilities Act, the Child Abuse Amendments of 1984, and the Virginia Medical Malpractice Act should be DENIED. Under the Emergency Medical Treatment and Active Labor Act, the Rehabilitation Act of 1973, and the Americans with Disabilities Act, the Hospital is legally obligated to provide ventilator treatment to Baby K. The court makes no ruling as to any rights or obligations under the Child Abuse Amendments of 1984 and under the Virginia Medical Malpractice Act.

An appropriate order shall issue.

QUESTIONS

The lower court in *Baby K* states that, unlike the Rehabilitation Act, the ADA does not require that an individual be otherwise qualified in order to state a claim. Does that statement make any sense? Isn't the requirement that an individual be otherwise qualified implicit in all disability discrimination statutes? Would a deaf patient with serious back problems who went to an ophthalmologist for treatment of the back problems, who subsequently refused to treat him, be able to claim discrimination on the basis of his disability (deafness)? Or would the ophthalmologist be able to claim that the patient is not otherwise qualified because the patient is not seeking the treatment for which the physician has expertise?

NOTES

1. *The ADA and Standards of Emergency Care.* Some commentators have questioned the role of courts in resolving "essentially medical matters." For a discussion of this, see George J. Annas, *Asking the Courts to Set the Standard of Emergency Care — The Case of Baby K,* 330 NEW ENG. J. MED. 1542 (1994). See also Schrode, *Life in Limbo: Revising Policies for Permanently Unconscious Patients,* 31 HOUS. L. REV. 1609 (1995).

2. *Right to Die and Assisted Suicide.* The *Bowen* and *Baby K* cases focus on termination of treatment for seriously ill newborns and infants. The issues are somewhat different with respect to adults and others who are not infants regarding termination of treatment. In 1990, the Supreme Court in *Cruzan v. Director, Missouri Dep't of Health*, 497 U.S. 261 (1990), recognized a right to die in certain instances. That case involved a woman who was comatose and whose condition was irreversible. Since that time, there has been a great deal of media attention to the issue of the right to die by alert and competent individuals who are suffering from painful, terminal diseases. Substantial attention also has been given to the right to assisted suicide.

States have begun to consider a variety of responses to these difficult and complex legal, medical, ethical, and religious issues. Both Oregon and Washington have passed laws that permit a terminally ill patient to request and receive medication to end his or her life. Both of these "Death with Dignity Acts" require that the patient be a state resident, be diagnosed by at least two physicians as terminal and within six months of death, be informed of medical options, be competent, and enter into the decision voluntarily. Both also require oral and written requests and two witnesses in addition to the physicians. Both specify that no person shall qualify solely because of age or disability. The Washington statute specifically states that the medication is to be self-administered, but although the intent behind the Oregon statute is for self-administration of medication, it is not explicit in the statute. See ORS § 127.800 (2007); Rev. Code Wash. § 70.245.010 (2009). Vermont, Michigan and California considered similar measures which did not pass. The Oregon statute took effect in 1997, while the Washington statute took effect in 2009. A study of ten years of experience with the Oregon statute revealed that only 341 persons ended their lives using the Act's protections of the 296,000 who died in Oregon during the same time period. See Dan Colburn, *Death with Dignity Act Applies to Very Few*, THE OREGONIAN (Aug. 5, 2009). There is a question about whether these laws violate Title II of the ADA. A patient who meets the other requirements, but whose condition physically prevents self-administration may argue that the law discriminates against him because of his disability. How would the courts be likely to treat such a challenge? What if an individual who is severely disabled and in extreme pain, but not terminally ill, wishes to have such a prescription? Would the Oregon and Washington statutes be discriminatory on that basis?

The Oregon Death with Dignity Act has received a substantial amount of media attention. Many of its critics are individuals who are severely disabled. These groups sometimes argue that such statutes will be the precursor of statutes permitting euthanasia of incompetent and severely disabled individuals. See *Judge Weighs Suicide Law*, WASHINGTON POST, Dec. 20, 1994, at A8.

The Supreme Court addressed the Oregon Death with Dignity Act, and held that the U.S. Attorney General may not bar dispensing controlled substances used for assisted suicide where there is a medical regime allowing that conduct. See *Gonzales v. Oregon*, 126 S. Ct. 904, 163 L. Ed. 2d 748 (2006).

For discussions of this issue, see Marc C. Siegel, *Lethal Pity: The Oregon Death with Dignity Act, Its Implications for the Disabled, and the Struggle for Equality in an Able-Bodied World*, 16 LAW & INEQ. J. 259 (1998); Stephen L. Mikochik, *Assisted Suicide and Disabled People*, 46 DEPAUL L. REV. 987 (1997).

3. *End of Life Issues.* A controversial issue with disability rights implications involves end of life and who can make decisions about that. The Terry Schiavo case in 2005 received substantial media attention and interest by the public. The case involved a dispute between the husband of Terry Schiavo, who wanted to withhold nutrition and hydration because of his acceptance of medical evidence that she no longer had viable brain activity. The parents of Terry Schiavo disagreed and challenged his decision. There were a number of judicial decisions addressing various legal theories in this case. One of those decisions was based on disability discrimination law. In *Schiavo v. Schiavo*, 403 F.3d 1289 (11th Cir. 2005), the court held that even if the hospice that cared for Terry Schiavo was a public accommodation, its compliance with the state judge's order to withhold nutrition and hydration was not discrimination on the basis of disability. The court held that neither the ADA nor the Rehabilitation Act was intended to apply to decisions involving the termination of life support or medical treatment.

4. *National Health Care Reform.* There is no question that the country needs health care reform. Nearly 47 million persons lack insurance, and, therefore, find it difficult to secure health care. President Obama has made health care reform one of the primary objectives of his presidency. At the time of the writing of this book, at least five bills are circulating the House of Representatives and the Senate, and opposition to the bills has become very vocal. People fear the high cost of the health care reform and potential governmental control over health care decisions. One of the greatest fears is that the government will intrude upon end of life decisions, requiring people who are old, sick and disabled to end their lives. They fear that "grandma" will face a "death panel" that will require her to end her life. While there is little support for this fear in the bills currently being discussed in Congress, rationing of health care is an important issue to discuss. In effect, rationing of health care already occurs. Those who do not have health insurance generally do not get the care they need. A system that covers everyone will necessarily ration care, some say, or otherwise become prohibitively expensive. See Peter Singer, *Why We Must Ration Health Care*, NY TIMES (July 19, 2009). Others argue that cost cutting measures that change how health care is delivered in less expensive and more effective ways are viable alternatives to rationing. See Atul Gawande, et al., *10 Steps to Better Health Care*, NY TIMES (Aug. 13, 2009).

Persons with disabilities have an important stake in the outcome of the health care reform debate because of their need for medical services. Disability advocates argue that health care reform is necessary, but they have urged federal legislators to amend Medicaid to remove its institutional biases. That is, many persons with disabilities can get benefits under Medicaid only if they are living in institutional settings. Advocates argue that community-based care would be superior and less expensive. Thus, advocates have urged Congress to pass the Community Living Assistance Services and Supports Act (CLASS) and the Community Choice Act, which would give support to families with persons with disabilities for national insurance without forcing them into poverty to collect Medicaid, and would remove the institutional bias of Medicaid. They encourage that these acts be incorporated into health care reform. See *Health Care Reform: Key Disability Issues*, http://www.thearc.org/NetCommunity/Document.Doc?id=1585.

HYPOTHETICAL PROBLEM 9.1

Consider the following hypothetical problem after reading the Supreme Court opinion in *Bragdon v. Abbott* and the lower court's opinion on remand. In determining whether Shanon is a person with a disability, use the definition of disability recently enacted in the ADAAA:

Shanon Burke is a college student who attends State University. She has a history of asthma, and uses medication and an inhaler for her asthma. She returned to college in August 2009 and within a few weeks, there was a rapid spread among the students of the H1N1 virus. The University Health Services establishes a protocol for isolating students with the H1N1 virus, which encourages sick students to stay in their room and to have their parents take them home as soon as possible. By mid-October, Shanon begins to feel ill with influenza symptoms of achiness, high fever, listlessness and vomiting. Because of her asthma, she experiences difficulty breathing. Shanon goes to the student health services, but when she arrives, the health services makes her enter through the backdoor into a "waiting room" for students with flu symptoms. Shanon goes into the waiting room, but the nurse tells her that the health services is overwhelmed and that she should call her parents (who live 6 hours away by car) to pick her up and take her home. The nurse also tells her she may go back to her dorm room for the next 8 hours, but that she should notify her roommate to evacuate the room. The nurse calls Shanon's roommate, Maria, and tells her to leave the room until the next day. The school will clean the room after Shanon leaves and then Maria will be permitted to return to the room.

Shanon is very sick and getting sicker by the moment. She calls her parents to find that they are both out of town, and will not be able to pick her up until the next day. Shanon can not fly home because the FAA has instigated a temporary rule stating that persons with flu symptoms may not fly. The Health Services refuses to allow Shanon to stay there because they consider Shanon a threat to the health of workers and other students at the Health Services. Shanon explains to the Health Services that her asthma is much worse and that she can not breathe. Health Services refuses to give Shanon a bed and sends her back to her empty dorm room. Shanon has a bad night, and her parents arrive early the next day. Shanon can barely breathe and her parents rush her to the closest hospital emergency room where they begin to treat Shanon. While Shanon survives, her lungs are seriously damaged and her asthma is much worse as a result of the University Health Services' refusal to treat her.

Does Shanon have an action against the University under Title II or Title III of the ADA or under Section 504 of the Rehabilitation Act? If so, what is the University's best defense? Analyze the arguments the University will make and the response that Shanon's attorney will make when Shanon brings a lawsuit against the University. What type of evidence should the University counsel attempt to find to support its case? What evidence should Shanon's attorney look for to support her case?

The previous cases and discussion addressed discrimination by terminating treatment. Discrimination can occur, of course, in the context of denial of treatment or providing treatment in a segregated setting or only where additional costs are paid. Litigation involving health care discrimination arises most frequently in the context of individuals seeking treatment who have HIV or AIDS. The following case addresses that issue through the Supreme Court's decision. While previous Supreme Court cases had addressed health care in the context of the Rehabilitation Act, this was the first health care access case decided under the Americans with Disabilities Act.

BRAGDON v. ABBOTT
118 S. Ct. 2196 (1998)

JUSTICE KENNEDY delivered the opinion of the Court.

We address in this case the application of the Americans with Disabilities Act of 1990 (ADA) to persons infected with the human immunodeficiency virus (HIV). We granted certiorari to review, first, whether HIV infection is a disability under the ADA when the infection has not yet progressed to the so-called symptomatic phase; and, second, whether the Court of Appeals, in affirming a grant of summary judgment, cited sufficient material in the record to determine, as a matter of law, that respondent's infection with HIV posed no direct threat to the health and safety of her treating dentist.

[Author's Note: This portion of the opinion only addresses whether HIV is a direct threat. The portion regarding whether Sidney Abbott is disabled under the ADA is excerpted in Chapter 2.]

I

Respondent Sidney Abbott has been infected with HIV since 1986. When the incidents we recite occurred, her infection had not manifested its most serious symptoms. On September 16, 1994, she went to the office of petitioner Randon Bragdon in Bangor, Maine, for a dental appointment. She disclosed her HIV infection on the patient registration form. Petitioner completed a dental examination, discovered a cavity, and informed respondent of his policy against filling cavities of HIV-infected patients. He offered to perform the work at a hospital with no added fee for his services, though respondent would be responsible for the cost of using the hospital's facilities. Respondent declined.

The petition for certiorari presented three other questions for review. The questions stated:

> 3. When deciding under title III of the ADA whether a private health care provider must perform invasive procedures on an infectious patient in his office, should courts defer to the health care provider's professional judgment, as long as it is reasonable in light of then-current medical knowledge?

4. What is the proper standard of judicial review under title III of the ADA of a private health care provider's judgment that the performance of certain invasive procedures in his office would pose a direct threat to the health or safety of others?

5. Did petitioner, Randon Bragdon, D. M. D., raise a genuine issue of fact for trial as to whether he was warranted in his judgment that the performance of certain invasive procedures on a patient in his office would have posed a direct threat to the health or safety of others?

Of these, we granted certiorari only on question three. The question is phrased in an awkward way, for it conflates two separate inquiries. In asking whether it is appropriate to defer to petitioner's judgment, it assumes that petitioner's assessment of the objective facts was reasonable. The central premise of the question and the assumption on which it is based merit separate consideration.

Again, we begin with the statute. Notwithstanding the protection given respondent by the ADA's definition of disability, petitioner could have refused to treat her if her infectious condition "pose[d] a direct threat to the health or safety of others." 42 U.S.C. § 12182(b)(3). The ADA defines a direct threat to be "a significant risk to the health or safety of others that cannot be eliminated by a modification of policies, practices, or procedures or by the provision of auxiliary aids or services." *Ibid.* Parallel provisions appear in the employment provisions of Title I. §§ 12111(3), 12113(b).

The ADA's direct threat provision stems from the recognition in *School Bd. of Nassau Cty. v. Arline*, 480 U.S. 273, 287 (1987), of the importance of prohibiting discrimination against individuals with disabilities while protecting others from significant health and safety risks, resulting, for instance, from a contagious disease. In *Arline*, the Court reconciled these objectives by construing the Rehabilitation Act not to require the hiring of a person who posed "a significant risk of communicating an infectious disease to others." Congress amended the Rehabilitation Act and the Fair Housing Act to incorporate the language. It later relied on the same language in enacting the ADA. Because few, if any, activities in life are risk free, *Arline* and the ADA do not ask whether a risk exists, but whether it is significant.

The existence, or nonexistence, of a significant risk must be determined from the standpoint of the person who refuses the treatment or accommodation, and the risk assessment must be based on medical or other objective evidence. As a health care professional, petitioner had the duty to assess the risk of infection based on the objective, scientific information available to him and others in his profession. His belief that a significant risk existed, even if maintained in good faith, would not relieve him from liability. To use the words of the question presented, petitioner receives no special deference simply because he is a health care professional. It is true that *Arline* reserved "the question whether courts should also defer to the reasonable medical judgments of private physicians on which an employer has relied." At most, this statement reserved the possibility that employers could consult with individual physicians as objective third-party experts. It did not suggest that an individual physician's state of mind could excuse discrimination without regard to the objective reasonableness of his actions.

Our conclusion that courts should assess the objective reasonableness of the views of health care professionals without deferring to their individual judgments does not answer the implicit assumption in the question presented, whether petitioner's actions were reasonable in light of the available medical evidence. In assessing the reasonableness of petitioner's actions, the views of public health authorities, such as the U.S. Public Health Service, CDC, and the National Institutes of Health, are of special weight and authority. The views of these organizations are not conclusive, however. A health care professional who disagrees with the prevailing medical consensus may refute it by citing a credible scientific basis for deviating from the accepted norm.

We have reviewed so much of the record as necessary to illustrate the application of the rule to the facts of this case. For the most part, the Court of Appeals followed the proper standard in evaluating the petitioner's position and conducted a thorough review of the evidence. Its rejection of the District Court's reliance on the Marianos affidavits was a correct application of the principle that petitioner's actions must be evaluated in light of the available, objective evidence. The record did not show that CDC had published the conclusion set out in the affidavits at the time petitioner refused to treat respondent.

A further illustration of a correct application of the objective standard is the Court of Appeals' refusal to give weight to the petitioner's offer to treat respondent in a hospital. Petitioner testified that he believed hospitals had safety measures, such as air filtration, ultraviolet lights, and respirators, which would reduce the risk of HIV transmission. Petitioner made no showing, however, that any area hospital had these safeguards or even that he had hospital privileges. His expert also admitted the lack of any scientific basis for the conclusion that these measures would lower the risk of transmission. Petitioner failed to present any objective, medical evidence showing that treating respondent in a hospital would be safer or more efficient in preventing HIV transmission than treatment in a well-equipped dental office.

We are concerned, however, that the Court of Appeals might have placed mistaken reliance upon two other sources. In ruling no triable issue of fact existed on this point, the Court of Appeals relied on the 1993 CDC Dentistry Guidelines and the 1991 American Dental Association Policy on HIV. This evidence is not definitive. As noted earlier, the CDC Guidelines recommended certain universal precautions which, in CDC's view, "should reduce the risk of disease transmission in the dental environment." U.S. Dept. of Health and Human Services, Public Health Service, CDC, Recommended Infection Control Practices for Dentistry. The Court of Appeals determined that, "[w]hile the guidelines do not state explicitly that no further risk-reduction measures are desirable or that routine dental care for HIV-positive individuals is safe, those two conclusions seem to be implicit in the guidelines' detailed delineation of procedures for office treatment of HIV-positive patients." In our view, the Guidelines do not necessarily contain implicit assumptions conclusive of the point to be decided. The Guidelines set out CDC's recommendation that the universal precautions are the best way to combat the risk of HIV transmission. They do not assess the level of risk.

Nor can we be certain, on this record, whether the 1991 American Dental Association Policy on HIV carries the weight the Court of Appeals attributed to it. The Policy does provide some evidence of the medical community's objective assessment of the risks posed by treating people infected with HIV in dental offices. It indicates:

> Current scientific and epidemiologic evidence indicates that there is little risk of transmission of infectious diseases through dental treatment if recommended infection control procedures are routinely followed. Patients with HIV infection may be safely treated in private dental offices when appropriate infection control procedures are employed. Such infection control procedures provide protection both for patients and dental personnel.

We note, however, that the Association is a professional organization, which, although a respected source of information on the dental profession, is not a public health authority. It is not clear the extent to which the Policy was based on the Association's assessment of dentists' ethical and professional duties in addition to its scientific assessment of the risk to which the ADA refers. Efforts to clarify dentists' ethical obligations and to encourage dentists to treat patients with HIV infection with compassion may be commendable, but the question under the statute is one of statistical likelihood, not professional responsibility. Without more information on the manner in which the American Dental Association formulated this Policy, we are unable to determine the Policy's value in evaluating whether petitioner's assessment of the risks was reasonable as a matter of law.

The court considered materials submitted by both parties on the cross motions for summary judgment. The petitioner was required to establish that there existed a genuine issue of material fact. Evidence which was merely colorable or not significantly probative would not have been sufficient.

We acknowledge the presence of other evidence in the record before the Court of Appeals which, subject to further arguments and examination, might support affirmance of the trial court's ruling. For instance, the record contains substantial testimony from numerous health experts indicating that it is safe to treat patients infected with HIV in dental offices. We are unable to determine the import of this evidence, however. The record does not disclose whether the expert testimony submitted by respondent turned on evidence available in September 1994.

There are reasons to doubt whether petitioner advanced evidence sufficient to raise a triable issue of fact on the significance of the risk. Petitioner relied on two principal points: [f]irst, he asserted that the use of high-speed drills and surface cooling with water created a risk of airborne HIV transmission. The study on which petitioner relied was inconclusive, however, determining only that "[f]urther work is required to determine whether such a risk exists." Petitioner's expert witness conceded, moreover, that no evidence suggested the spray could transmit HIV. His opinion on airborne risk was based on the absence of contrary evidence, not on positive data. Scientific evidence and expert testimony must have a traceable, analytical basis in objective fact before it may be considered on summary judgment.

Second, petitioner argues that, as of September 1994, CDC had identified seven dental workers with possible occupational transmission of HIV. These dental workers were exposed to HIV in the course of their employment, but CDC could not determine whether HIV infection had resulted. It is now known that CDC could not ascertain whether the seven dental workers contracted the disease because they did not present themselves for HIV testing at an appropriate time after their initial exposure. It is not clear on this record, however, whether this information was available to petitioner in September 1994. If not, the seven cases might have provided some, albeit not necessarily sufficient, support for petitioner's position. Standing alone, we doubt it would meet the objective, scientific basis for finding a significant risk to the petitioner.

Our evaluation of the evidence is constrained by the fact that on these and other points we have not had briefs and arguments directed to the entire record. In accepting the case for review, we declined to grant certiorari on question five, which asked whether petitioner raised a genuine issue of fact for trial. As a result, the briefs and arguments presented to us did not concentrate on the question of sufficiency in light [of] all of the submissions in the summary judgment proceeding. "When attention has been focused on other issues, or when the court from which a case comes has expressed no views on a controlling question, it may be appropriate to remand the case rather than deal with the merits of that question in this Court." This consideration carries particular force where, as here, full briefing directed at the issue would help place a complex factual record in proper perspective. Resolution of the issue will be of importance to health care workers not just for the result but also for the precision and comprehensiveness of the reasons given for the decision.

We conclude the proper course is to give the Court of Appeals the opportunity to determine whether our analysis of some of the studies cited by the parties would change its conclusion that petitioner presented neither objective evidence nor a triable issue of fact on the question of risk. In remanding the case, we do not foreclose the possibility that the Court of Appeals may reach the same conclusion it did earlier. A remand will permit a full exploration of the issue through the adversary process.

The determination of the Court of Appeals that respondent's HIV infection was a disability under the ADA is affirmed. The judgment is vacated, and the case is remanded for further proceedings consistent with this opinion.

NOTES AND QUESTIONS

1. On remand, the Court of Appeals in *Bragdon* once again held that there was inadequate evidence of a direct threat, and affirmed the grant of summary judgment to the plaintiff. The court stated:

> In compliance with the Court's directive, we have reexamined the evidence to determine whether summary judgment was warranted. In order to reverse our course, we would have to find, contrary to our original intuition, either that (i) Ms. Abbott did not merit judgment as a matter of law even in the absence of disputed facts, or (ii) that Dr. Bragdon had

submitted sufficient evidence to create a genuine issue of material fact as to his direct threat defense. In our reexamination, we apply conventional summary judgment jurisprudence, drawing all reasonable factual inferences in favor of Dr. Bragdon. Despite the leniency of this approach, we do not indulge "conclusory allegations, improbable inferences, and unsupported speculation."

A. *Ms. Abbott's Evidence.*

The Supreme Court raised questions regarding whether the Guidelines, which state that use of the universal precautions therein described "should reduce the risk of disease transmission in the dental environment," necessarily imply that the reduction of risk would be to a level below that required to show direct threat. We have reconsidered this point.

The CDC did not write the 1993 Guidelines in a vacuum, but, rather, updated earlier versions issued in 1986 and 1987, respectively. The 1986 text calls the universal precautions "effective for preventing hepatitis B, acquired immunodeficiency syndrome, and other infectious diseases caused by bloodborne viruses." The 1987 edition explains that use of the universal precautions eliminates the need for additional precautions that the CDC formerly had advocated for handling blood and other bodily fluids known or suspected to be infected with bloodborne pathogens. Neither the parties nor any of the amici have suggested that the 1993 rewrite was intended to retreat from these earlier risk assessments, and we find no support for such a position in the Guidelines' text. Thus, we have again determined that the Guidelines are competent evidence that public health authorities considered treatment of the kind that Ms. Abbott required to be safe, if undertaken using universal precautions.

Second, the Court questioned the appropriate weight to accord the Policy, expressing concern that the Policy might be based in whole or in part on the Association's view of dentists' ethical obligations, rather than on a pure scientific assessment. The supplemental briefing that we requested yielded a cornucopia of information regarding the process by which the Policy was assembled. We briefly recount the undisputed facts.

The Association formulates scientific and ethical policies by separate procedures, drawing on different member groups and different staff complements. The Association's Council on Scientific Affairs, comprised of 17 dentists (most of whom hold advanced dentistry degrees), together with a staff of over 20 professional experts and consultants, drafted the Policy at issue here. By contrast, ethical policies are drafted by the Council on Ethics, a wholly separate body. Although the Association's House of Delegates must approve policies drafted by either council, we think that the origins of the Policy satisfy any doubts regarding its scientific foundation.

For these reasons, we are confident that we appropriately relied on the Guidelines and the Policy. Moreover, as the Supreme Court acknowledged, these two pieces of evidence represent only a fraction of the proof advanced to support Ms. Abbott's motion. For example, she proffered the opinions of several prominent experts to the effect that, in 1994, the cavity-filling procedure could have been performed safely in a private dental office, as well as proof that no public health authority theretofore had issued warnings to health care providers disfavoring this type of treatment for asymptomatic HIV-positive patients. These materials, in and of themselves, likely suffice to prove Ms. Abbott's point. Thus, we again conclude, after due reevaluation, that Ms. Abbott served a properly documented motion for summary judgment.

B. *Dr. Bragdon's Evidence.*

We next reconsider whether Dr. Bragdon offered sufficient proof of direct threat to create a genuine issue of material fact and thus avoid the entry of summary judgment. In *Abbott II*, we canvassed eight items of evidence adduced by Dr. Bragdon in an effort to demonstrate a genuine issue of material fact. The Supreme Court suggested that one such piece of evidence — the seven cases that the CDC considered "possible" HIV patient-to-dental worker transmissions — should be reexamined.

The Court's concern revolved around how the word "possible" was understood in this context at the relevant time. To frame the issue, the Court noted that the CDC marks an HIV case as a "possible" occupational transmission if a stricken worker, who had no other demonstrated opportunity for infection, simply failed to present himself for testing after being exposed to the virus at work. The Court speculated that if this definition of "possible" was not available in September 1994, the existence of seven "possible" cases "might have provided some, albeit not necessarily sufficient, support for [Dr. Bragdon's] position." In other words, if a dentist knew of seven "possible" occupational transmissions to dental workers without understanding that "possible" meant no more than that the CDC could not determine whether workers were infected occupationally, he might reasonably regard the risk of treating an HIV-infected patient to be significant.

Upon reexamination of the record, we find that the CDC's definition of the word "possible," as used here, had been made public during the relevant period. The record contains two scientific articles published before Ms. Abbott entered Dr. Bragdon's office which explained this definition. Since an objective standard pertains here, the existence of the list of seven "possible" cases does not create a genuine issue of material fact as to direct threat.

In his supplemental briefing and oral argument, Dr. Bragdon has drawn our attention again to the CDC's report of 42 documented cases of occupational transmission of HIV to health-care workers (none of whom were dental workers). He repeats his argument that, because dental workers are subject to dangers similar to those faced by other health-care workers, these cases can be extrapolated to create an issue of fact as to the degree of risk to dental workers in September 1994. We previously held that this evidence was insufficient without a documented showing that the risks to dentists and other health-care workers are comparable, and the appellant offers us no cogent reason to change our view. The Supreme Court did not question our position on this front, and Dr. Bragdon points to no record support that we previously might have overlooked.

Our assessment of Dr. Bragdon's, and his amici's, other reprised arguments similarly remains unchanged. Each piece of evidence to which they direct us is still "too speculative or too tangential (or, in some instances, both) to create a genuine issue of material fact."

163 F.3d 87 (1st Cir. 1998).

2. Once the hospital is on notice that a physician to whom it extends practice privileges is discriminating against individuals with disabilities, is the hospital also in violation of the ADA if it continues to extend privileges to that physician? Even if the physician is not subject to Section 504, if discriminatory conduct by a physician with privileges is made known to the hospital, does it have an obligation to investigate and to take appropriate action? If it fails to do so, is it in violation of Section 504? See also *Doe v. Jamaica Hosp.*, 202 A.D.2d 386, 608 N.Y.S.2d 518 (1994) (physician who refused to treat a patient with AIDS would not be subject to § 504 because the physician did not receive federal financial assistance).

3. Would it matter whether both the ADA and Section 504 were being violated? Which avenue of redress should be used? Why?

4. *Medical Care for Patients with HIV.* In addition to *Bragdon*, there have been a number of other decisions where courts have found violations of the ADA or Section 504 by health care providers who refused to treat individuals with HIV. In *Miller v. Spicer*, 822 F. Supp. 158 (D. Del. 1993), the court held that there was a violation of Section 504 when an emergency room surgeon refused to treat an individual whom he thought to be HIV-positive. A complaint against Philadelphia emergency medical technicians and firefighters involved a refusal to assist people with AIDS. Part of the settlement included an agreement to undergo AIDS awareness training. *U.S. Department of Justice Complaint No. 204-62-24* (settled March 18, 1994). A refusal to treat an HIV-positive patient cost a dental care center $100,000 in damages and penalties. The settlement with the Department of Justice also included an agreement to establish a policy prohibiting bias on the basis of AIDS and staff training. *United States v. Castle Dental Soc'y*, No. CA-H933140 (S.D. Tex., settled Sept. 22, 1994). See also LAURA ROTHSTEIN & JULIA ROTHSTEIN, DISABILITIES AND THE LAW § 10.04 (2009).

In *Lesley v. Hee Man Chie*, 250 F.3d 47 (1st Cir. 2001), the court held that a pregnant woman who was transferred to a different hospital after testing HIV positive was not discriminated against because she was unable to show that the transfer was not linked to legitimate medical necessity. In *Green v. City of Welch*, 467 F. Supp. 2d 656 (S.D. W. Va. 2006), the court allowed a suit to go forward where the estate of a man with HIV claimed CPR assistance was denied to the decedent because of his HIV status. For other cases, see LAURA ROTHSTEIN & JULIA ROTHSTEIN, DISABILITIES AND THE LAW Sec. 10:2 (2009).

C ARCHITECTURAL BARRIERS AND REASONABLE ACCOMMODATION

The previous section highlights situations in which an individual with a disability might be refused or denied health care services because of prejudices of the provider. While this may often be the case of individuals with HIV or with individuals with mental retardation, the more common barrier to health care service access involves architectural barriers and the need for reasonable accommodations, including auxiliary aids and services or other accommodations.

It is probable that most major health care programs, such as hospitals and clinics, have accessible ramped entrances, because wheelchairs and gurneys are commonly used in these facilities. These facilities are also likely to be accessible with respect to restrooms and other similar facilities. The facilities that are less likely to be accessible are health care offices located in the residence of the provider or in commercial facilities other than hospitals and clinics.

Although most major hospitals are recipients of federal financial assistance, individual physicians and other health care providers, as a general rule, are not. For that reason, the Americans with Disabilities Act is substantially more comprehensive in its protection of individuals with disabilities. The physical facility access requirements are much stronger under the ADA, as Chapter 4 on Public Accommodations illustrates. A private health care provider generally would fall within the definition of a "public accommodation" under Title III of the ADA, and thus would be required to remove barriers to the extent it is readily achievable to do so, in addition to being required to make new construction accessible. The importance of access to health care providers is recognized in the regulations relating to new construction of buildings that are to be used for public accommodations. There is an exemption that allows certain of these facilities to be built without an elevator, where the facility is less than three stories or has less than 3,000 square feet per story. 28 C.F.R. § 36.401(d). This exemption does not apply, however, when the facility is intended to be used for professional offices of health care providers.

By contrast, Section 504 of the Rehabilitation Act only applies to recipients of federal financial assistance, such as hospitals. Before the passage of the ADA, these facilities were required to be accessible when viewed in their entirety. The ADA applies the same standard. If the facility is operated by a state or local governmental entity, Title II accessibility requirements would apply. If the facility is privately operated, Title III would apply in many instances.

Because of the exemption under 28 C.F.R. § 36.401(d), under the ADA and the Rehabilitation Act's application only to facilities receiving federal financial assistance, a wheelchair user who wants to visit a dentist office on the second floor of a building without an elevator may have no remedy under the ADA or the Rehabilitation Act. Under both statutes, however, the service providers may be expected to relocate a visit as an accommodation (such as a lawyer meeting in an alternative location). This will be unlikely to work, however, in the instance of health care providers whose unique equipment cannot be easily moved.

The ADA regulations also provide guidance on places of public accommodation in private residences. They require that the portions of the residence used exclusively for the residence need not meet access requirements. Those portions that are used as public accommodations, however, must meet access requirements in areas including the front sidewalk, the entrance, and portions of the residence (including restrooms) used by the public. 28 C.F.R. Section 36.207.

A related challenge for individuals with mobility and similar impairments can be that the health care office is accessible with respect to getting in and around the facility, but the equipment is not accessible. Special chairs for eye exams and dental treatment, for example, may be difficult to use for someone with a mobility impairment. Examination tables may be technically "accessible," but the providers may not be experienced at assisting individuals with spinal cord injuries in getting on and off a table for routine medical types of exams, such as annual gynecological exams.

With the advent of managed care, individuals with disabilities who have chronic health care needs face unique obstacles. In many managed care programs, the selection of physicians is limited, as is access to specialists without going through the primary care physician. An individual with mobility impairments may have particular difficulties if the offices of the listed providers are not accessible. Even if they are accessible, transportation difficulties may be a severe barrier. The bus system may not be completely accessible, and even if it is accessible, substantially more time might be required to use an accessible transportation system. In addition, although the entrance to the provider's office might be accessible, fixed equipment, such as a dental chair, might not be accessible for an individual with a mobility impairment. In *Anderson v. Department of Pub. Welfare*, 1 F. Supp. 2d 456 (E.D. Pa. 1998), the court held that health maintenance providers must ensure that the services viewed in their entirety are accessible, but this does not resolve many of the details about what that means.

There has been very little case law to provide guidance on physical access in health care provider facilities. There has, however, been some judicial guidance on the issue of reasonable accommodations in the health care provider context.

One area that has received substantial judicial attention involves the issue of providing interpreter service to individuals who are deaf at hospitals and in other health care settings. The issue can involve the feasibility of ensuring that appropriate communication services are available as well as the cost for providing such services.

HYPOTHETICAL PROBLEM 9.2

Read the following hypothetical Problem, and, after reading *Aikens* and *Mayberry*, prepare to discuss the problem.

Charlie Cortez is a two year old child who was born hearing-impaired. Charlie's parents, Anna and Mario Cortez, are not hearing-impaired. They suspect there is something wrong with Charlie's hearing because he does not react to loud noises and because his speech is delayed. They go to a group of doctors in Los Angeles who specialize in hearing difficulties to have Charlie diagnosed. The diagnosis is that Charlie is hearing-impaired, and that he would likely be helped by a device called the cochlear implant. The doctor they see, Jon Walter, recommends that

Anna and Mario take Charlie to Dr. Hugh Malloy, who he believes is one of the best ear surgeons in the City. Dr. Walter tells Anna and Mario that Dr. Malloy is hearing-impaired himself and that he has a hearing-impaired son. When Anna and Mario take Charlie to see Dr. Malloy, through an interpreter, he tells them that Charlie would likely be able to hear fairly well and would develop good speech habits if had a cochlear implant. Dr. Malloy, however, tells them that he will not do the surgery on Charlie. He believes that persons with deafness from birth should learn to sign and lip read and to become part of the deaf community. The device will keep Charlie from that experience, and it is Malloy's practice to refuse to give children cochlear implants because, although he had his own son get a cochlear implant, he believes it is more harmful than not having the cochlear implant because of the separation from the deaf community. Anna and Mario are very upset and want to force Dr. Malloy to perform the surgery because they know he is the best ear surgeon in town. When he refuses, they visit a lawyer to see if they have a cause of action of discrimination against Dr. Malloy based on the ADA. Consider the different arguments the plaintiffs' and defendant's lawyers would make in this case. Would it make a difference if Dr. Malloy was the only specialist in town who knew how to put in cochlear implants?

The following two cases raise the issue in different contexts. First, in *Aikins*, the court addressed the obligation in a hospital setting, including liability issues related to both the hospital and the treating physician. The *Mayberry* decision looks at the issue from the perspective of the individual health care provider.

AIKINS v. ST. HELENA HOSPITAL
843 F. Supp. 1329 (N.D. Cal. 1994)

FERN M. SMITH, DISTRICT JUDGE:

Background

The events giving rise to this lawsuit occurred between October 30 and November 4, 1992. Mrs. Aikins is a deaf woman whose husband, Harvey Aikins, suffered a massive cardiac arrest at approximately 8:00 p.m. on October 30, 1992. Following Mr. Aikins's attack, Mrs. Aikins went to the home of some neighbors and had them call 911. According to Mrs. Aikins, the paramedics arrived at her home approximately four minutes after the call to 911, which defendants assert was approximately fifteen minutes after Mr. Aikins suffered the attack. The paramedics then transported Mr. Aikins to St. Helena Hospital.

Dr. Lies was working in St. Helena's emergency room when Mr. Aikins was brought in. Dr. Lies is an independent contractor on staff at the hospital. He exercises no authority over hospital policy. When the paramedics informed Dr. Lies that they had arrived within four minutes of Mr. Aikins's attack, Dr. Lies decided to perform an emergency angioplasty. He attempted to consult Mrs. Aikins and to obtain her consent, but Mrs. Aikins could not understand him and requested that interpreters be provided. A hospital operator with some knowledge of fingerspelling was summoned and attempted to fingerspell Dr. Lies's comments for Mrs. Aikins. The woman became frustrated, however, and gave up her efforts within a minute. Shortly thereafter, Mrs. Aikins's neighbors arrived and attempted to mediate between Dr. Lies and Mrs. Aikins. Dr. Lies asserts that the neighbors "were quite able to communicate with [Mrs. Aikins]" and relayed to her his opinion that, with immediate medical intervention, Dr. Lies might be able to save Mr. Aikins's life. Mrs. Aikins submits that the neighbors only passed her a terse note stating that Mr. Aikins may have had a massive cardiac arrest and that he was "brain dead."

Subsequently, Mrs. Aikins went to the hospital's administrative office and made further attempts to secure interpreter services. At approximately 9:00 p.m., she was approached by a member of the hospital staff who sought to obtain her signature on forms consenting to the emergency procedure. Although the forms say that "[y]our signature on this form indicates . . . (2) that the operation procedure set forth above has been adequately explained to you by your physician, (3) that you have had a chance to ask questions, [and] (4) that you have received all of the information you desire concerning the operation or procedure . . . ," Mrs. Aikins claims that she was told only that "Dr. Lies needed [her] signature to permit him to perform surgery to save [her] husband's life." Dr. Lies claims that, although he believed that it was unnecessary under the circumstances to obtain Mrs. Aikins's consent to the surgery, "given [her] disability, [he] wanted her to be involved."

Later that evening, Dr. Lies contacted Mrs. Aikins's daughter, Francine Stern, to request that she fly up to Calistoga from Los Angeles to help her mother. Ms. Stern, who was Mr. Aikins's stepdaughter, is a fluent signer. Ms. Stern told Dr. Lies that she would be unable to come up until November 2nd.

Mrs. Aikins went to her husband's room at approximately 12:30 on the night of the operation. She claims that the nurse on duty told her that Mr. Aikins would not survive without life support and that Mrs. Aikins then requested that life support be discontinued. She then went to the administrative office, accompanied by a deaf friend, to request interpreter services again. Both the office and another nurse whom Mrs. Aikins and her friend later encountered in Mr. Aikins's room allegedly told Mrs. Aikins that the hospital had no means of procuring interpreter services.

The following day, October 31, 1992, Mr. Aikins showed no neurologic improvement, prompting Dr. Lies to question Mrs. Aikins about the length of time between the heart attack and the arrival of the paramedics. Dr. Lies submits that it was during this questioning, seemingly conducted through Mrs. Aikins's in-laws, that he first learned that fifteen minutes, not four, had elapsed between Mr. Aikins's heart attack and the commencement of CPR. Based on this new information, Dr. Lies ordered an EEG. The EEG was performed on November 1, 1992, at 9:00 a.m. and revealed that Mr. Aikins had no brain activity.

On November 2nd, Mrs. Aikins's daughter arrived and participated in a meeting with Dr. Lies and Mrs. Aikins. Mrs. Aikins claims that this meeting was the first opportunity that she had to communicate directly with Dr. Lies and to receive complete answers to her questions. As a result of the meeting, Mrs. Aikins requested that her husband's life support be discontinued. Mr. Aikins died two days later.

Discussion

I. *Plaintiffs' Standing to Seek Injunctive Relief*

Defendants have challenged CAD's [California Association of the Deaf] standing to participate in this lawsuit.

The Supreme Court has developed a three-part test for standing, a constitutional prerequisite growing out of Article III's "case or controversy" requirement. See U.S. Const. art. III, § 2, cl. 1. The first prong of the test is the "injury in fact" requirement: "[T]he plaintiff must have suffered an 'injury in fact' — an invasion of a legally-protected interest which is (a) concrete and particularized; and (b) 'actual or imminent, not "conjectural" or "hypothetical.'"" The second and third elements of the test are causation and redressability. As it is clear that defendants caused whatever violation of the relevant statutes may have occurred, and that a favorable decision of this Court would redress any injuries caused by violation of the statutes, only the first aspect of the inquiry is at issue here.

City of Los Angeles v. Lyons, 461 U.S. 95 (1983), established that a plaintiff seeking injunctive relief premised upon an alleged past wrong must demonstrate a "real and immediate threat" of repeated future harm to satisfy the injury in fact prong of the standing test.

Mrs. Aikins has not shown her standing to seek injunctive relief under *Lyons*. In her complaint, Mrs. Aikins alleges only that she is a deaf individual and within the protection of the ADA, the Rehabilitation Act, and various state statutes. Mrs. Aikins further states that she owns a mobile home seven miles from St. Helena Hospital and that she stays at the home for several days each year. These allegations do not establish the "real and immediate threat" of future harm that *Lyons* requires. Mrs. Aikins has shown neither that she is likely to use the hospital in the near future, nor that defendants are likely to discriminate against her when she does use the hospital. The Court cannot infer from Mrs. Aikins's limited experience with Dr. Lies and St. Helena Hospital that defendants routinely fail to comply with applicable anti-discrimination statutes.

Plaintiffs rely on *Greater Los Angeles Council on Deafness, Inc., et al., Plaintiffs-Appellants, v. Malcolm Baldrige*, 827 F.2d at 1353, to establish their standing for injunctive relief. In that case, plaintiffs were GLAD, a nonprofit organization dedicated to furthering the interests of deaf and hearing-impaired individuals, an attorney for GLAD who had filed an administrative complaint with the Department of Commerce, and two deaf individuals acting on their own behalf and as representatives of a class of similarly situated persons. Plaintiffs sought a writ of mandamus against the Department of Commerce, alleging that the department had failed to act on an administrative complaint that charged a public television station with violation of the Rehabilitation Act for failure to provide closed-captioned hearing. Plaintiffs alleged that the department's failure to act on the complaint was itself a violation of the Act. In holding that plaintiffs had standing to pursue their claim for injunctive relief, the Ninth Circuit noted that "[t]he actual or threatened injury required by Article III may exist solely by virtue of a statute that creates legal rights, the invasion of which creates standing." The court found that the Rehabilitation Act was such a statute.

Council on Deafness is distinguishable from this case. Implicitly at issue in that case was whether defendant's alleged violation of the Rehabilitation Act was an "injury in fact" sufficient to confer standing on plaintiffs. If the claimed violation constituted an injury, there was no question as to the imminence of the harm occasioned by the injury. Plaintiffs had filed an administrative complaint, on which defendant had failed to act; thus, the claimed injury was ongoing. Here, by contrast, imminence has not been shown. Although an alleged violation of the ADA and the Rehabilitation Act is an injury sufficient to give rise to an Article III case or controversy, Mrs. Aikins has not shown that defendants' alleged discrimination is ongoing and that she is likely to be served by defendants in the near future. Mrs. Aikins's claims for injunctive relief are accordingly dismissed with leave to amend to show that Mrs. Aikins faces a real and immediate threat of future injury at the hands of defendants.

CAD's standing to seek injunctive relief suffers from the same defects. An association seeking to bring suit on behalf of its members must show: (1) that its members would have standing to sue in their own right; (2) that the interests that it seeks to protect are germane to the organization's purpose; and (3) that neither the claim asserted nor the relief requested require the participation of individual members. CAD has alleged only that it is a nonprofit organization with at least eight hundred members, organized for the purpose of serving the needs of deaf individuals "through advocacy, education and referral," and that some members of CAD "have been or likely will be served by defendants. . . . " Although these allegations are sufficient to satisfy the second and third requirements for associational standing, they fail to show that CAD's members would have standing to sue in their own right. CAD's claims are accordingly dismissed with leave to amend to show standing to seek injunctive relief only.

Plaintiffs' Claims under the Americans with Disabilities Act

Plaintiffs claim that defendants violated the Americans with Disabilities Act ("ADA") by denying Mrs. Aikins access to information in connection with the treatment of her husband. The ADA provides, in pertinent part: "No individual shall be discriminated against on the basis of disability in the full and equal enjoyment of the goods, services, facilities, privileges, advantages, or accommodations of any place of public accommodation by any person who owns, leases (or leases to), or operates a place of public accommodation." 42 U.S.C. § 12182(a).

A. *The ADA Does Not Apply to Dr. Lies*

Dr. Lies contends that plaintiffs' claims against him under the ADA must fail because the Act does not apply to him in his capacity as an independent contractor with St. Helena. The regulations implementing the ADA alter the language of the statute slightly to read as follows: "No individual shall be discriminated against on the basis of disability . . . by any private entity who owns, leases (or leases to), or operates a place of public accommodation." 28 C.F.R. § 36.201(a) (1993). The preamble to the regulation notes that the change was designed to make clear that the regulation "places the ADA's nondiscrimination obligations on 'public accommodations' rather than on 'persons' or 'places of public accommodation.' " 36 C.F.R. App. B § 36.104 (1993).

The statute and the regulation both indicate that individuals may be liable under the ADA if they "own, lease (or lease to), or operate" a place of public accommodation. 42 U.S.C. § 12182(a); 28 C.F.R. § 35.201(a) (1993). The use of language relating to ownership or operation implies a requirement of control over the place providing services. Dr. Lies, however, is an independent contractor with St. Helena. He is not on the hospital's board of directors, and he has no authority to enact or amend hospital policy. Because he lacks the power to control hospital policy on the use of interpreters, this Court holds that Dr. Lies is not a proper defendant under the ADA.

Plaintiffs contend that this construction of the ADA undercuts the Act's purpose. Noting that the Act defines "public accommodation" to include the "professional office of a health care provider," 42 U.S.C. § 12181(7)(F), plaintiffs maintain that the Act would clearly cover Dr. Lies had he provided services to Mr. and Mrs. Aikins at his own office. They argue that he should not be able to escape liability under the ADA merely because in this case he provided services outside his office. "To hold otherwise," plaintiffs suggest, "would allow individuals to discriminate whenever they provide part of their services outside of their place of public accommodation while disallowing the very same type of discrimination for those services provided at the place of public accommodation."

Plaintiffs' policy argument does not warrant a departure from the statute's implicit requirement of ownership or control. The Court's construction of the Act is not at odds with the ADA's fundamental purpose of eliminating discrimination against individuals with disabilities, see 42 U.S.C. § 12101(b)(1), because it retains accountability for those in a position to ensure nondiscrimination.

B. *St. Helena Has Not Shown That It Complied with the Act as a Matter of Law*

St. Helena does not dispute that the ADA applies to it, see 42 U.S.C. § 12181(7)(F), but claims that it complied with the Act as a matter of law. Alternatively, St. Helena argues that compliance is excused, as it would impose an undue burden on the hospital. The regulations implementing the ADA provide that a "public accommodation shall furnish appropriate auxiliary aids and services where necessary to ensure effective communication with individuals with disabilities." 28 C.F.R. § 36.303(c) (1993). This requirement is tempered by the general qualification that a public accommodation may treat disabled individuals in need of auxiliary aids and services differently from other individuals if "the public accommodation can demonstrate that [ensuring equality of treatment] would . . . result in an undue burden, i.e., significant difficulty or expense." § 36.303(a) (1993).

St. Helena bases its contention that it complied with the ADA as a matter of law on the following evidence and allegations: that its human resources department had in place a policy of providing interpreters to those in need of them; that the hospital posted signs notifying the public that information about T.D.D. services could be obtained by going to the switchboard; that the switchboard operator and the office of human resources maintained lists of interpreters; that Mr. Aikins's medical records contain a statement that "there were interpreters present at all times during the discussion with the patient and the family"; and that "the complaint is replete with descriptions of instances where information was exchanged between plaintiff Aikins and members of the St. Helena hospital staff." Defendant argues alternatively that provision of an interpreter on a twenty-four hour a day basis would impose an undue burden on the hospital.

The record does not reveal that St. Helena complied with the ADA as a matter of law. St. Helena has not demonstrated that it communicated effectively with plaintiff Aikins during her husband's stay in the hospital. Indeed, the hospital's allegations that communication was effective are undercut not only by plaintiff's own account of the episode but also by the fact that, for between twenty-four to thirty-six hours, Dr. Lies was under the concededly mistaken impression that Mr. Aikins had been without CPR for only four minutes following his heart attack, a critical fact. Furthermore, although the regulations provide that the hospital "shall furnish" appropriate auxiliary aids and services for non-hearing individuals, § 36.303(c), it appears that St. Helena relied almost exclusively on Mrs. Aikins to provide her own interpreters. There exists a genuine dispute as to the issue of St. Helena's compliance with the ADA.

Finally, the Court cannot say as a matter of law that provision of interpreters would have imposed an undue burden on the hospital. The regulations set out criteria for determining whether a proposed accommodation imposes an undue burden within the meaning of section 36.303(a). Section 36.104 provides, in pertinent part:

> In determining whether an action would result in an undue burden, factors to be considered include — (1) The nature and cost of the action needed under this part; (2) The overall financial resources of the site or sites involved in the action; the number of persons employed at the site; the effect on expenses and resources; legitimate safety requirements that are necessary for safe operation . . . ; or the impact otherwise of the action upon the operation of the site; (3) The geographic separateness, and the administrative or fiscal relationship of the site or sites in question to any parent corporation or entity; (4) If applicable, the overall financial resources of any parent corporation or entity; the overall size of the parent corporation or entity with respect to the number of its employees; the number, type, and location of its facilities; and (5) If applicable, the type of operation or operations of any parent corporation or entity, including the composition, structure, and functions of the workforce of the parent corporation or entity.

§ 36.104 (1993). The question whether provision of interpreter services on some basis would pose an undue burden on St. Helena raises material issues of fact.

692   HEALTH CARE AND INSURANCE   CH. 9

Dobard v. San Francisco Bay Area Rapid Transit District, 1993 U.S. Dist. LEXIS 13677, 3 Am. Disabilities Cas. (BNA) 203 (N.D. Cal. Sept. 7, 1993), cited by defendant, does not warrant a different conclusion. In that case defendant transit authority provided plaintiff with both a sign language interpreter and a sound amplification device in connection with his attendance at a public board meeting. Plaintiff argued that defendant nonetheless violated the ADA by refusing to provide plaintiff with a computer aided transcription device, the auxiliary aid of his choice. The court in *Dobard* found that plaintiff had failed to state a claim for violation of the ADA, as defendant was not required to employ the most advanced technology but only to ensure that communication was effective. Plaintiffs herein are not arguing for an absolute right to a particular auxiliary aid. Rather, they claim a right to effective communication with the hospital. St. Helena, unlike the defendant in *Dobard*, allegedly made no effort to provide Mrs. Aikins with auxiliary aids, relying upon Mrs. Aikins to marshal her own communication resources.

III. *Plaintiffs' Claims under the Rehabilitation Act*

A. *Mrs. Aikins is an "Otherwise Qualified" Individual Within the Meaning of the Act*

[Dr. Lies apparently concedes that he is subject to Section 504 by receiving Medicare and Medicaid reimbursements.]

Defendant Lies argues that plaintiffs' claims under section 504 should be dismissed because plaintiff Aikins is not an "otherwise qualified" individual within the meaning of the Act.

[In another decision] the Second Circuit concluded that the Act applies to all services offered by a covered entity, not just those relating to the entity's central function. "The fact that a particular recipient institution is primarily engaged in the provision of one category of service does not exempt it from Regulation 104.3(k) in its provision of other services."

Although [that decision] is not binding upon this Court, its reasoning is sound. That Mrs. Aikins was not a patient at St. Helena should not preclude her from raising claims under the Rehabilitation Act based on the hospital's failure to communicate effectively with her in connection with its treatment of her husband. Mrs. Aikins was "otherwise qualified" to discuss her husband's condition with hospital officials, including Dr. Lies.

Defendant Lies next argues that California law precludes Mrs. Aikins from being "otherwise qualified" in the circumstances presented by this case. He submits that Mrs. Aikins's consent to the procedures performed on her husband was not necessary; as a consequence she was not required to be consulted or kept informed of her husband's condition. Defendant attempts to analogize from *Bowen v. American Hospital Association*, 476 U.S. 610 (1986), wherein a plurality of the Court stated that a "hospital's withholding of treatment when no parental consent has been given cannot violate § 504." The plurality reasoned that, in the absence of the required parental consent, the infant is neither "otherwise qualified" within the meaning of the Act, nor denied treatment "solely because of his handicap."

Defendant maintains that Mrs. Aikins is not "otherwise qualified" because her consent to her husband's treatment was not required.

Defendant's argument is unavailing. Dr. Lies's argument that emergency circumstances vitiated the requirement of informed consent is undercut by his own statement that, "[t]hough it was clear to me that Mr. Aikins presented an immediate medical emergency, thus making informed consent unnecessary, I had time to, and so did seek to, advise Mrs. Aikins and obtain her consent." Having undertaken to obtain Mrs. Aikins's consent, defendant was obligated to do so in a nondiscriminatory manner. More important, Mrs. Aikins's claims relating to inadequate communication span a period of almost seventy-two hours, from the time of her husband's admission to the hospital until the time that his life support was disconnected. Whatever emergency existed at the time of Mr. Aikins's admission to the hospital had subsided by the time the decision was made to discontinue his life support. Finally *Bowen* is distinguishable. That case essentially involved a failure of causation. It was the parents' refusal of consent, not the infant's disability, that would have resulted in the denial of treatment. By contrast, it was precisely Mrs. Aikins's disability that caused defendants to communicate with her in an allegedly inadequate manner.

B. *Defendants Have Not Shown That They Complied with the Act as a Matter of Law*

Defendants finally argue that they complied with the Rehabilitation Act as a matter of law. Defendant Lies argues that Mr. Aikins received precisely the same treatment that he would have received had Mrs. Aikins not been deaf. Defendant St. Helena maintains that it provided all that it was required to provide under the Act.

Both arguments are without merit. Even if Mr. Aikins received exactly the care that he would have received had Mrs. Aikins not been deaf, Dr. Lies misses the point. Mrs. Aikins's claims relate to her exclusion from meaningful participation in the decisions affecting her husband's treatment, not to the appropriateness of the treatment itself. As to the hospital's argument, the Court cannot infer from defendant's reference to its policies on interpreters and its own self-serving statements that it communicated effectively with plaintiff at all times that it complied with the Rehabilitation Act as a matter of law.

IV. *Availability of Damages under the Federal Statutes*

Defendants argue that Mrs. Aikins is not entitled to compensatory relief under either the ADA or the Rehabilitation Act. They are correct about the ADA. In cases involving claims under subchapter three of the ADA, the Act provides only for injunctive relief. Section 12188(a)(1) states that the remedies available to persons subjected to discrimination in violation of that subchapter are those set forth in 42 U.S.C. § 2000a-3(a). 42 U.S.C. § 12188(a)(1). § 2000a-3(a) provides:

> Whenever any person has engaged or there are reasonable grounds to believe that any person is about to engage in any act or practice prohibited

by section 2000a-2 of this title, a civil action for preventive relief . . . may be instituted by the person aggrieved . . . .

42 U.S.C. § 2000a-3(a). [T]he Supreme Court [has] held that a plaintiff suing under section 2000a-3(a) cannot recover damages. Plaintiffs appear to concede the unavailability of compensatory relief under the ADA in their opposition papers.

Because plaintiffs lack standing on the present record to assert claims for injunctive relief, the unavailability of damages under the ADA requires dismissal of all claims under the ADA. Such dismissal is without prejudice to plaintiffs' reinstating the ADA claims for injunctive relief upon a proper showing of standing.

As to Mrs. Aikins's claims under the Rehabilitation Act, the Ninth Circuit has held that damages are available for violations of the Act. Section 794a provides, in pertinent part: "The remedies, procedures, and rights set forth in title VI of the Civil Rights Act of 1964 [codified at 42 U.S.C. section 2000d et seq.] shall be available to any person aggrieved by any act or failure to act by any recipient of Federal assistance . . . under section 794 of this title." 29 U.S.C. § 794a(a)(2). The settled interpretation of section 794a in the Ninth Circuit is that money damages are available for violations of section 504 of the Rehabilitation Act.

V. *Plaintiffs' State Law Claims*

[Discussion of state law claims omitted.]

QUESTIONS

1. What would Mrs. Aikins' damages be? Suppose the hospital billed Mrs. Aikins for procedures that she would not have approved had there been adequate communication? Would she and/or her insurance provider be able to recover the costs of those procedures?

2. If this were a state or local governmental hospital, would Mrs. Aikins be entitled to damages under Title II of the ADA?

3. In Part IV of *Aikins*, the court dismissed the plaintiffs' claims for injunctive relief under the ADA for lack of standing, but made clear that dismissal was without prejudice of reinstating the ADA claim for injunctive relief "upon a proper showing of standing." Considering the entire *Aikins* opinion, what would constitute a proper showing of standing that would permit reinstatement of the ADA claim for injunctive relief?

MAYBERRY v. VON VALTIER
843 F. Supp. 1160 (E.D. Mich. 1994)

Woods, District Judge:

Defendant, Cheryl C. Von Valtier, is a physician licensed to practice medicine in the State of Michigan. Plaintiff, Shirley Mayberry, is a 67 year old deaf woman. Since 1987, Dr. Von Valtier has treated Ms. Mayberry as her family physician. Ms.

Mayberry testified that she was able to lipread until she completely lost her hearing in 1990, and that she is able to understand simple notes. Ms. Mayberry and Dr. Von Valtier communicated during physical examinations by passing notes back and forth, or by using a signor. The signor was often one of Ms. Mayberry's children, and on three occasions a professional interpreter had been used. Dr. Von Valtier testified that visits with Ms. Mayberry took twice as long with an interpreter than when they passed notes, but that she did not mind spending the extra time.

On March 15, 1991, Ms. Mayberry brought her daughter Claudia Langston to her appointment with Dr. Von Valtier. Ms. Langston told Dr. Von Valtier that her mother's hearing had gotten progressively worse. During that visit, Dr. Von Valtier discovered that the back pain Ms. Mayberry had earlier complained of was higher than she had originally understood. Dr. Von Valtier wrote the following note on her chart: "[Ms. Mayberry] [s]tates pain has not moved, but this is higher than I had understood her to say. Probably due to poor communication." Ms. Langston swears in her affidavit that Dr. Von Valtier told her that an interpreter made communication with Ms. Mayberry clearer and easier than writing notes. In addition, Dr. Von Valtier told her that she wanted Ms. Mayberry to have an interpreter when she was seen at her medical office.

On three occasions, Ms. Mayberry had an interpreter from Deaf, Hearing and Speech Services — Senior Citizens present during appointments with Dr. Von Valtier. On two of those occasions, once in 1989 and once in 1990, Dr. Von Valtier did not have to pay for the interpreter. On the third occasion, December 18, 1992, Ms. Mayberry was due to have a general examination, and she requested an interpreter because she felt she needed one. Dr. Von Valtier's office consented to pay for the interpreter's services pursuant to its duty under the Americans with Disabilities Act. Dr. Von Valtier wrote to Ms. Mayberry on January 7, 1993, summarizing the results of her examination.

Dr. Von Valtier was billed $28.00 by Monalee Ferrero for her interpreting services. Dr. Von Valtier paid the bill, and sent the following letter to Ms. Ferrero.

> Enclosed is payment for your services to Shirley Mayberry in this office 12/18/92. The Medicare payment for Mrs. Mayberry's office visit has been received, and I would now like to explain why I won't be able to utilize your services in the future, or indeed why I really can't afford to take care of Mrs. Mayberry at all. My regular fee for a 15 minute office visit is $40.00. I spent about 45 minutes with Mrs. Mayberry on December 12, 1992, for this I was paid $37.17 by Medicare and (hopefully) $9.29 by Mrs. Mayberry. My office overhead expense rate is a rather steady 70% of my gross receipts, which means that for that 45 minutes I was able to "pocket" $13.94, that is, until I paid your bill for $28.00. I certainly hope that the Federal Government does not further slash this outrageous profit margin. A copy of this letter was also sent to Ms. Mayberry.

After Ms. Mayberry received the letter addressed to Ms. Ferrero, she became angry and called Dr. Von Valtier's office to ask for her records. Ms. Mayberry admits that she did not ask Dr. Von Valtier what she intended by the letter. Ms. Mayberry interpreted the letter to mean that Dr. Von Valtier would not hire an interpreter for her again, and that she had been discharged as a patient. At her deposition, Dr. Von Valtier explained that the letter was poorly written and ambiguous, and it was not her intention to discharge Ms. Mayberry from her practice, nor did she intend to refuse to pay for an interpreter in the future. Dr. Von Valtier claims to have a specific protocol for discharging patients, and that protocol was not initiated in this case. Dr. Von Valtier sums up the purpose of her letter as a protest of the Americans with Disabilities Act, saying:

> I felt that although this ADA is the law of the land, and I have to obey it, I don't think it's fair. I wanted to protest it. I feel that I have a right to protest it even though I have to obey it. And this was one protest that I could make because of the fact that for six years, Shirley Mayberry and I successfully communicated with each other with pencil and paper.

Plaintiff's complaint alleges that she has been denied future treatment by defendant because she is deaf. Plaintiff alleges that defendant's actions in refusing to provide interpreter services in the future, and in terminating her medical care, amounts to discrimination in violation of the Americans with Disabilities Act of 1990 (ADA), Section 504 of the Federal Rehabilitation Act of 1973, and the Michigan Handicappers' Civil Rights Act.

A. *Americans with Disabilities Act (ADA)*

The ADA defines discrimination as including a failure to take necessary steps to ensure that no individual with a disability is denied services because of the absence of auxiliary aids and services. The Department of Justice has promulgated regulations to implement the ADA, and states in its commentary on the final regulations: The auxiliary aid requirement is a flexible one. A public accommodation can choose among various alternatives as long as the result is effective communication. The regulations include examples of auxiliary aids and services required to be furnished where necessary to ensure effective communication. The examples given for persons with hearing losses include qualified interpreters and notetakers. 28 CFR § 36.303(b)(1). The effective communication requirement of the ADA has been interpreted such that Congress expects places of public accommodation to consult with disabled persons when it comes to auxiliary aids for effective communication, but Congress does not mandate primary consideration of their expressed choices. 28 CFR 36.303, App. B.

The construction provision of the ADA states that the standards of title V of the Rehabilitation Act of 1973, and its regulations, are to apply, except where the ADA has explicitly adopted a different standard. 42 U.S.C. § 12201(a). In order to make out a prima facie case under title III of the ADA, the plaintiff must prove (1) that she has a disability; (2) that defendant's office is a place of public accommodation; and (3) that she was discriminated against by being refused full and equal enjoyment of medical treatment because of her disability. Defendant maintains that intent to discriminate is a fourth element of plaintiff's prima facie case, relying on traditional disparate-treatment/disparate-impact and burden-shifting analyses used in discrimination cases.

Federal courts have struggled with the issue of whether intent to discriminate is an element to stating a prima facie case under the Rehabilitation Act. This Court will look to the cases interpreting the Rehabilitation Act for guidance, as there are no reported cases analyzing the requirements for sustaining a claim under the effective communication by a public accommodation provisions of the ADA. The [Supreme] Court [has] refused to hold that all showings of disparate impact on the handicapped constitute prima facie cases under § 504, nor would it hold that proof of discriminatory intent was necessary in every case.

A disparate impact case is one in which a facially neutral practice impacts more harshly on one group of people than on others. For example, if defendant Von Valtier had announced a policy not to hire sign language interpreters for any patient, the impact would obviously be more profound on deaf patients. Such a policy, however, is not facially neutral in the same manner as the policy to reduce the number of annual inpatient hospital days that state Medicaid would pay for, which was the issue in *Alexander v. Choate*. The case presently before the Court does not involve a disparate impact, as plaintiff alleges that defendant specifically declined to provide her with an interpreter because she was disabled. Even though the Supreme Court addressed the issue of intent in a case where the discrimination complained of was in the form of a policy's impact rather than specific treatment, other courts have come to the same conclusion.

One of the stated purposes of the ADA is "to provide a clear and comprehensive national mandate for the elimination of discrimination against individuals with disabilities." 42 U.S.C. § 12101(b)(1). Congress specifically found that "individuals with disabilities continually encounter various forms of discrimination, including outright intentional exclusion [and] the discriminatory effects of . . . communication barriers. . . . " 42 U.S.C. § 12101(a)(5). Given that statement, Congress appears to have intended the ADA to address the discriminatory effects of benign actions or inaction, as well as intentional discrimination. Based on the cases analyzing alleged violations of § 504, the Court concludes that the Rehabilitation Act does not require a plaintiff to prove discriminatory intent in order to make out a prima facie case of handicap discrimination. The Court will apply the modified burden-shifting analysis developed in cases under the Rehabilitation Act to the ADA.

In order to set forth a prima facie case under title III of the ADA, plaintiff must prove that she has a disability, that defendant's office is a place of public accommodation, and that she was denied full and equal medical treatment because of her disability. Plaintiff must additionally show that she was denied treatment under circumstances which give rise to the inference that such denial was based solely on her handicap. If plaintiff succeeds in stating a prima facie case, the burden shifts to defendant to prove either that plaintiff was not denied medical treatment, or that such denial was not unlawful. The burden then shifts back to plaintiff to rebut defendant's reasons as pretext for unlawful discrimination.

In her attempt to make out a prima facie case under title III of the ADA, plaintiff has clearly proven that she has a disability and that defendant's office is a place of public accommodation. Plaintiff has also produced evidence giving rise to an inference that she was unlawfully discriminated against by being refused full and equal enjoyment of medical treatment because of her disability. As proof that defendant intended to refuse to hire an interpreter in the future, and to discharge plaintiff, plaintiff submits defendant's own words in the February 22, 1993 letter to Ms. Ferrero. In addition, plaintiff provides the affidavit of her daughter Ms. Langston which states that defendant wanted plaintiff to bring an interpreter to future appointments. Plaintiff also points to a note written by defendant on plaintiff's chart, that defendant misunderstood the exact location of plaintiff's pain due to poor communication. Finally, plaintiff submits a note written by defendant which instructs plaintiff to see an ophthalmologist, and suggests that she "take someone with her who signs so you can explain problem & answer their questions completely."

The burden of proof shifts to defendant to prove that she did not refuse to hire an interpreter for plaintiff, nor did she refuse to treat plaintiff in the future. Defendant may attempt to show that an interpreter was not necessary to ensure effective communication with plaintiff during her medical appointments. Furthermore, places of public accommodation are exempt from complying with the ADA if they can demonstrate that taking such steps would fundamentally alter the nature of the services being offered, or would result in an undue burden. 42 U.S.C. § 12182(b)(2)(A)(iii). Defendant, however, admitted at her deposition that she could afford to pay Ms. Ferrero's fee for interpreter services.

Defendant maintains that her letter to Ms. Ferrero was a protest of the ADA, and that she could adequately communicate with plaintiff by passing notes back and forth. The issue is how far defendant was willing to take her protest. It is true that plaintiff did not ask defendant what she intended by her letter, but it is not implausible for plaintiff to believe that defendant meant her words literally. Plaintiff has submitted evidence which would tend to show that passing notes did not result in effective communication with defendant. Commentary by the Department of Justice states that "[i]t is not difficult to imagine a wide range of communications involving areas such as health, legal matters, and finances that would be sufficiently lengthy or complex to require an interpreter for effective communication." 28 CFR § 36.303, App. B.

Plaintiff has come forth with enough evidence to survive summary judgment on her ADA claim. Plaintiff, however, is not entitled to money damages under the ADA, which limits the remedies available to private individuals to those set forth in the Civil Rights Act of 1964, 42 U.S.C. § 2000a-3(a). 42 U.S.C. § 12188(a)(1). Such remedies include permanent or temporary injunctions and restraining orders. Only when the Attorney General becomes involved in the matter may the Court award monetary damages to aggrieved persons. 42 U.S.C. § 12188(b)(2)(B). Plaintiff is permitted to seek injunctive relief under the ADA, as well as attorneys fees. 42 U.S.C. § 12188(b)(2), 12205.

[Rehabilitation Act and state law claims discussion is omitted.]

Defendant's motion for summary judgment is *Denied* in its entirety.

So Ordered.

QUESTIONS

1. Does the fact that Dr. Von Valtier could "afford to pay" for the interpreter mean that it is not an undue burden?

2. Would it make a difference in the analysis of undue burden if the accommodation needed were a ramp to permit access to individuals with a mobility impairment instead of an interpreter?

3. Would it matter if Dr. Von Valtier had a large number of patients with hearing impairments who needed interpreter service?

NOTES

1. The ADAAA states that auxiliary aids and services include "qualified interpreters or other effective methods of making aurally delivered materials available to individuals with hearing impairments." 42 U.S.C. § 12103 (1)(A).

2. *Mental Health Counseling Services for Deaf and Hearing-Impaired Individuals.* When the health care treatment in question involves psychological or psychiatric counseling where confidentiality is an important issue, are deaf recipients of the treatment or counseling entitled to have counselors who themselves sign and who understand the needs of the deaf community? The following excerpt from *Tugg v. Towey*, 864 F. Supp. 1201 (S.D. Fla. 1994), notes the court's response to several deaf and hearing-impaired individuals seeking counseling following Hurricane Andrew in Florida in 1993. The court granted a preliminary injunction, noting the following:

> Section 35.164 [of Title II, ADA regulations] also places a limit on the lengths a public entity must go to provide auxiliary aids. It states that a public entity is not required to take any action if "it can demonstrate [the action] would result in a fundamental alteration in the nature of a device, program or activity or [create] an undue financial and administration burden." . . . Under those circumstances the public entity has the burden of demonstrating that providing the auxiliary aid for the disabled individual would create such a hardship. This determination must be made by the head of the public entity, who must set forth in writing the reasons why the entity cannot comply with the wishes of the disabled individual, after considering all available resources.

> At the hearing, the Court invited the Defendants to address the issue of the harm they will suffer if the injunction is entered. Specifically, the Court asked for a cost benefit analysis the Defendants had conducted concluding that (1) providing the Plaintiffs with mental health counselors who possessed sign language ability and experience working with the deaf was too expensive to fit within the HRS budget and (2) that HRS's chosen alternative of providing qualified interpreters would cost the Defendants less money or create a lesser burden.

> The Defendants replied that no such cost benefit analysis had been conducted. The evidence produced at the hearing indicated that under

HRS's intended plan, it will cost an HRS contracting mental health provider a minimum of $35 per hour to provide a sign language interpreter in addition to the cost of the mental health counselor. Without the benefit of any accurate figures, logic would indicate that it would cost less to employ one individual to perform two tasks (signing and counseling) than two individuals to perform those same tasks. Counsel for the Defendants disputed this at the hearing, stating that because the pool of individuals meeting these qualifications is so small [estimating that the number in Dade and Monroe counties is four] the cost of securing their services would be higher. The Defendants, however, did not produce evidence to support this argument. The Defendants also did not demonstrate that they had complied with the requirements . . . which [mandate] that the public entity set forth its findings as to why it rejected the auxiliary aid sought by a disabled individual after considering all available resources.

What if the plaintiffs seeking such services were in a small rural area of North Dakota? Is it likely that defendants would be more likely to ultimately succeed in demonstrating both undue financial and undue administrative burden?

3. In *Aikins*, it was the wife of the patient, not the patient himself, seeking the accommodation. In another case involving accommodation of someone other than the patient, a visitor to a hospital patient requested that she be able to hook up her breathing apparatus to the hospital's oxygen port when visiting her husband's room. The court held that the hospital was not required to provide this accommodation. *Dryer v. Flower Hospital*, 383 F. Supp. 2d 934 (N.D. Ohio 2005).

D   HEALTH INSURANCE

The previous sections addressed the challenges of discrimination, environmental barriers, and the need for reasonable accommodations as barriers to health care for individuals with disabilities. While these barriers are significant, the major barrier is having health insurance to pay for health care services. Because most health insurance is tied to the workplace, individuals with disabilities face two problems.

First, they must be able to obtain and keep a job. Employers concerned about the high cost of health care for individuals with disabilities have a disincentive in many cases to hire such individuals even though it violates disability discrimination laws to do so. And as health insurance costs rise, employers may increasingly decide not to provide health insurance to any of their employees. These individuals may be able to receive health care services, however, through Medicare (if they are permanently and totally disabled) or Medicaid (if they are disabled and with very limited income).

Second, some individuals with disabilities, because of the limitations of their conditions, may not be able to work. Obtaining health care coverage through an individual health insurance policy is not a viable option for many individuals with disabilities. It is extremely expensive to purchase individual health insurance. The policy may not cover the types of treatments that the individual needs or there may be limited coverage for preexisting conditions. The Health Insurance Portability and Accountability Act (HIPAA), 42 U.S.C. § 300gg, passed in 1996, prohibits disability based discrimination in health insurance only with regard to employer-sponsored group health plans. HIPAA is important because it prohibits treating health conditions as a preexisting condition for purposes of limiting or excluding benefits. Thus, a person who changes employment becomes eligible for health insurance with the new employer.

The Health Insurance Reform proposed by President Obama may ameliorate the problem of persons with disabilities who can not afford health insurance.

With respect to insurance providers, there are a number of issues under the ADA, the Rehabilitation Act, and even some state laws. The first question is whether the ADA was intended to exempt health insurance programs from Title III application because traditionally health insurance has been regulated by the states. Most courts have not found there to be an exemption.

With respect to all insurance (health, life, and other insurance) there is an additional issue — whether Title III would apply only to accessing the service and not to distinctions related to the coverage itself. There is no question that insurance offices are public accommodations covered by Title III. There is, however, an unresolved question as to whether Title III regulates the *content* of the insurance policy. The majority and dissenting opinions in the next case illustrate the reasoning behind the two views.

JOHN DOE AND RICHARD SMITH v. MUTUAL OF OMAHA INSURANCE COMPANY
179 F.3d 557 (7th Cir. 1999)

OPINION BY: POSNER

Mutual of Omaha appeals from a judgment that the AIDS caps in two of its health insurance policies violate the public accommodations provision of the Americans with Disabilities Act. One policy limits lifetime benefits for AIDS or AIDS-related conditions (ARC) to $25,000, the other limits them to $100,000, while for other conditions the limit in both policies is $1 million. Mutual of Omaha has stipulated that it "has not shown and cannot show that its AIDS Caps are or ever have been consistent with sound actuarial principles, actual or reasonably anticipated experience, bona fide risk classification, or state law." It also concedes that AIDS is a disabling condition within the meaning of the Americans with Disabilities Act. Since the Supreme Court held in *Bragdon* that infection with the AIDS virus (HIV) is a disabling condition from the onset of the infection before any symptoms appear, it is apparent that both ARC and AIDS are disabilities. Mutual of Omaha does not question this, but argues only that the Americans with Disabilities Act does not regulate the content of insurance policies.

Title III of the Act, in section 302(a), provides that "no individual shall be discriminated against on the basis of disability in the full and equal enjoyment of the goods, services, facilities, privileges, advantages, or accommodations of any place of public accommodation" by the owner, lessee, or operator of such a place. The core meaning of this provision, plainly enough, is that the owner or operator of a store, hotel, restaurant, dentist's office, travel agency, theater, Web site, or other facility (whether in physical space or in electronic space) that is open to the public cannot exclude disabled persons from entering the facility and, once in, from using the facility in the same way that the nondisabled do. The owner or operator of, say, a camera store can neither bar the door to the disabled nor let them in but then refuse to sell its cameras to them on the same terms as to other customers.

Mutual of Omaha does not refuse to sell insurance policies to such persons — it was happy to sell health insurance policies to the two plaintiffs. But because of the AIDS caps, the policies have less value to persons with AIDS than they would have to persons with other, equally expensive diseases or disabilities. This does not make the offer to sell illusory, for people with AIDS have medical needs unrelated to AIDS, and the policies give such people as much coverage for those needs as the policies give people who don't have AIDS. If all the medical needs of people with AIDS were AIDS-related and thus excluded by the policies, this might support an inference that Mutual of Omaha was trying to exclude such people, and such exclusion, as we shall see, might violate the Act. But that is not argued.

Since most health-insurance policies contain caps, the position urged by the plaintiffs would discriminate among diseases. Diseases that happened to be classified as disabilities could not be capped, but equally or more serious diseases that are generally not disabling, such as heart disease, could be. Moreover, the plaintiffs acknowledge the right of an insurance company to exclude coverage for an applicant's pre-existing medical conditions. If the applicant is already HIV-positive when he applies for a health-insurance policy, the insurer can in effect cap his AIDS-related coverage at $0. This "discrimination" is not limited to AIDS or for that matter to disabilities, which is why the plaintiffs do not challenge it; but it suggests that the rule for which they contend is at once arbitrary and unlikely to do much for people with AIDS.

The insurance company asks us to compare this case to one in which a person with one leg complains of a shoestore's refusal to sell shoes other than by the pair, or in which a blind person complains of a bookstore's refusal to stock books printed in Braille. We do not understand the plaintiffs to be contending that such complaints are actionable under section 302(a), even though there is a sense in which the disabled individual would be denied the full and equal enjoyment of the services that the store offers. In fact, it is apparent that a store is not required to alter its inventory in order to stock goods such as Braille books that are especially designed for disabled people. But it is apparent as a matter of interpretation rather than compelled by a simple reading which would place the present case on the other side of the line; and so the case cannot be resolved by reference simply to the language of section 302(a).

The common sense of the statute is that the content of the goods or services offered by a place of public accommodation is not regulated. A camera store may not refuse to sell cameras to a disabled person, but it is not required to stock cameras specially designed for such persons. Had Congress purposed to impose so enormous a burden on the retail sector of the economy and so vast a supervisory responsibility on the federal courts, we think it would have made its intention clearer and would at least have imposed some standards. It is hardly a feasible judicial function to decide whether shoestores should sell single shoes to one-legged persons and if so at what price, or how many Braille books the Borders or Barnes and Noble bookstore chains should stock in each of their stores. There are defenses to a prima facie case of public-accommodation discrimination, but they would do little to alleviate the judicial burden of making standardless decisions about the composition of retail inventories. The only defense that might apply to the Braille case or the pair of shoes case is that the modification of a seller's existing practices that is necessary to provide equal access to the disabled "would fundamentally alter the nature of . . . [the seller's] services," and it probably would not apply to either case and certainly not to the Braille one.

The plaintiffs might be able to distinguish the shoestore hypothetical by pointing out that a nondisabled person might be in the market for one shoe simply because he had lost a shoe; in refusing to sell single shoes the store thus would not be refusing to adapt its service to a class of customers limited to disabled people. But the Braille case, and many others that we can imagine (such as a furniture store's decision not to stock wheelchairs, or a psychiatrist's refusal to treat schizophrenia, as distinct from his refusing to treat schizophrenics for the psychiatric disorders in which he specializes, or a movie theater's refusal to provide a running translation into sign language of the movie's soundtrack), cannot be so distinguished, although some of them might find shelter in the "fundamental alteration" defense. All are cases of refusing to configure a service to make it as valuable to a disabled as to a nondisabled customer.

It might seem that the AIDS caps could be distinguished from the "refusal to stock" cases because the caps include complications of AIDS. If being infected by HIV leads one to contract pneumonia, the cost of treating the pneumonia is subject to the AIDS cap; if a person not infected by HIV contracts pneumonia, the costs of treating his pneumonia are fully covered. It looks, therefore, like a difference in treatment referable solely to the fact that one person is disabled and the other not.

But this is not correct. The essential point to understand is that HIV doesn't cause illness directly. What it does is weaken and eventually destroy the body's immune system. As the immune system falters, the body becomes prey to diseases that the system protects us against. These "opportunistic" diseases that HIV allows, as it were, to ravage the body are exotic cancers and rare forms of pneumonia and other infectious diseases. To refer to them as "complications" of HIV or AIDS is not incorrect, but it is misleading, because they are the chief worry of anyone who has the misfortune to be afflicted with AIDS. An AIDS cap would be meaningless if it excluded the opportunistic diseases that are the most harmful consequences of being infected by the AIDS virus.

What the AIDS caps in the challenged insurance policies cover, therefore, is the cost of fighting the AIDS virus itself and trying to keep the immune system intact plus the cost of treating the opportunistic diseases to which the body becomes prey when the immune system has eroded to the point at which one is classified as having AIDS. The principal opportunistic diseases of AIDS, such as Kaposi's sarcoma, *Pneumocystis carinii pneumonia*, AIDS wasting, and esophageal candidiasis, are rarely encountered among people who are not infected by HIV — so rarely as to be described frequently as "AIDS-defining opportunistic infections." The frequency of *Pneumocystis carinii* pneumonia, for example, "among patients infected with human immunodeficiency virus (HIV) far exceeds that among other immuno-compromised hosts" and is "a leading cause of opportunistic infection and death among AIDS patients in industrialized countries." It is these *distinctive* diseases that are the target (along with the costs of directly treating infection by HIV) of the AIDS caps. This is not a case of refusing, for example, to provide the same coverage for a broken leg, or other afflictions not peculiar to people with AIDS, to such people, which would be a good example of discrimination by reason of disability.

It is true that as the immune system collapses because of infection by HIV, the patient becomes subject to opportunistic infection not only by the distinctive AIDS-defining diseases but also by a host of diseases to which people not infected with HIV are subject. Even when they are the same disease, however, they are far more lethal when they hit a person who does not have an immune system to fight back with. Which means they are not *really* the same disease. This is not a point that is peculiar to AIDS. The end stage of many diseases is an illness different from the one that brought the patient to that stage; nowadays when a person dies of pneumonia, it is usually because his body has been gravely weakened by some other ailment. If a health insurance policy that excluded coverage for cancer was interpreted not to cover the pneumonia that killed a patient terminally ill with cancer, this would not be "discrimination" against cancer.

To summarize the discussion to this point, we cannot find anything in the Americans with Disabilities Act or its background, or the nature of AIDS and AIDS caps, to justify so radically expansive an interpretation as would be required to bring these cases under section 302(a) without making an unprincipled distinction between AIDS caps and other product alterations — unless it is section 501(c)(1) of the Act. That section provides that Title I (employment discrimination against the disabled) and Title III (public accommodations, the title involved in this case) "shall not be construed to prohibit or restrict an insurer . . . from underwriting risks, classifying risks, or administering such risks that are based on or not inconsistent with State law," unless the prohibition or restriction is "a subterfuge to evade the purposes" of either title. § 12201(c). Even with the "subterfuge" qualification, section 501(c) is obviously intended for the benefit of insurance companies rather than plaintiffs and it may seem odd therefore to find the plaintiffs placing such heavy weight on what is in effect a defense to liability. But a defense can cast light on what is to be defended against, that is, what the prima facie case of a violation is. Suppose, for example, that a statute regulated the sale of "animals" but it was unclear whether the legislature had meant to include fish. Were there a statutory exclusion for goldfish, it would be pretty clear that "animals" included fish, since otherwise there would be no occasion for such an exclusion. And, with that clarified, the advocate of regulating the sale of a particular goldfish would have to show only that the exclusion was somehow inapplicable to him. That is the plaintiffs' strategy here. They use the insurance provision to show that section 302(a) regulates content, then argue that the excluding provision is narrow enough to allow them to challenge the coverage limits in Mutual of Omaha's policies. There is even some legislative history, which the plaintiffs hopefully call "definitive," to section 501(c) that suggests that an insurance company can limit coverage on the basis of a disability only if the limitation is based either on claims experience or on sound actuarial methods for classifying risks. And Mutual of Omaha conceded itself out of relying on section 501(c)'s safe harbor by stipulating that it cannot show that its AIDS caps are based on sound actuarial principles or claims experience or are consistent with state law.

The plaintiffs argue, consistent with our goldfish example, that the insurance exemption has no function if section 302(a) does not regulate the content of insurance policies, and so we should infer that the section does not regulate that content. But this reasoning is not correct. If it were, it would imply that section 302(a) regulates the content not only of insurance policies but also of all other products and services, since the section is not limited to insurance. The insurance industry may have worried that the section would be given just the expansive interpretation that the district court gave it in this case, and so the industry may have obtained the rule of construction in section 501(c) just to backstop its argument that section 302(a) regulates only access and not content. Or it may have worried about being sued under section 302(a) for refusing to sell an insurance policy to a disabled person. Remember that the right of full and equal enjoyment as we interpret it includes the right to buy on equal terms and not just the right to enter the store. For Mutual of Omaha to take the position that people with AIDS are so unhealthy that it won't sell them health insurance would be a prima facie violation of section 302(a). But the insurance company just might be able to steer into the safe harbor provided by section 501(c), provided it didn't run afoul of the "subterfuge" limitation, as it would do if, for example, it had adopted the AIDS caps to deter people who know they are HIV positive from buying the policies at all.

The legislative history is consistent with this interpretation. Both committee reports on which the plaintiffs rely give the example of refusing to sell an insurance policy to a blind person, as does the gloss placed on section 501(c) by the Department of Justice. A refusal to sell insurance to a blind person is not the same thing as a provision in the policy that if the insured becomes blind, the insurer will not pay the expense of his learning Braille. We find nothing in the language or history of the statute to suggest that the latter refusal would be unlawful. The Department's *Technical Assistance Manual, supra,* § III-3.11000, contains somewhat broader language than either the statute or the regulation or the committee reports, language about insurers' being forbidden to discriminate on the basis of disability in the sale, terms, or conditions of insurance contracts; but basically this just parrots the statute and the regulation and does not indicate a focused attention to coverage limits. There is, as we have pointed out, a difference between refusing to sell a health-insurance policy at all to a person with AIDS, or charging him a higher price for such a policy, or attaching a condition obviously designed to deter people with AIDS from buying the policy (such as refusing to cover such a person for a broken leg), on the one hand, and, on the other, offering insurance policies that contain caps for various diseases some of which may also be disabilities within the meaning of the Americans with Disabilities Act.

We conclude that section 302(a) does not require a seller to alter his product to make it equally valuable to the disabled and to the nondisabled, even if the product is insurance. This conclusion is consistent with all the appellate cases to consider this or cognate issues.

Evans, *Circuit Judge*, dissenting.

The Americans with Disabilities Act is a broad, sweeping, protective statute requiring the elimination of discrimination against individuals with disabilities. Because I believe the insurance policies challenged in this case discriminate against people with AIDS in violation of the ADA, I dissent.

The majority believes we are being asked to regulate the content of insurance policies — something we should not do under the ADA. But as I see it we are not being asked to regulate content; we are being asked to decide whether an insurer can discriminate against people with AIDS, refusing to pay for them the same expenses it would pay if they did not have AIDS. The ADA assigns to courts the task of passing judgment on such conduct. And to me, the Mutual of Omaha policies at issue violate the Act.

Chief Judge Posner's opinion likens the insurance company here to a camera store forced to stock cameras specially designed for disabled persons. While I agree that the ADA would not require a store owner to alter its inventory, I think the analogy misses the mark. The better analogy would be that of a store which lets disabled customers in the door, but then refuses to sell them anything but inferior cameras. To pick up on another analogy raised at oral argument, we are not being asked to force a restaurant to alter its menu to accommodate disabled diners; we are being asked to stop a restaurant that is offering to its nondisabled diners a menu containing a variety of entrees while offering a menu with only limited selections to its disabled patrons. Section 501(c)'s "safe harbor" would allow Mutual of Omaha to treat insureds with AIDS differently than those without AIDS if the discrimination were consistent with Illinois law or could be justified by actuarial principles or claims experience. But Mutual of Omaha conceded that its AIDS and ARC caps do not fall under the ADA's safe harbor protection.

The parties stipulated that the very same affliction (e.g., pneumonia) may be both AIDS-related and not AIDS-related and that, in such cases, coverage depends solely on whether the patient has AIDS. In my view that is more than enough to trigger an ADA violation. Chief Judge Posner reasons that, although the policies appear to discriminate solely based on an insured's HIVstatus, they really don't, when you consider the nature of AIDS. He suggests that the phrase "AIDS related conditions" embodies a unique set of symptoms and afflictions that would make it easy for the insurance company to determine with certainty whether an expense incurred for a particular illness is "AIDS-related" and therefore subject to the cap. His analysis — charitable to Mutual of Omaha to be sure — may very well be medically sound. But it doesn't come from the insurance policies. The policies don't even hint at what illnesses or afflictions might fall within the ARC exclusion. Nor has the medical community embraced an accepted definition for what "conditions" are "AIDS-related." The practical effect of all this, as Mutual of Omaha concedes, is that coverage for certain expenses would be approved or denied based solely on whether the insured had AIDS. Given that the ADA is supposed to signal a "clear and comprehensive national mandate for the elimination of discrimination against individuals with disabilities," I would use the statute to right the wrong committed by Mutual of Omaha.

NOTES AND QUESTIONS

1. Which arguments are more convincing? Those of Judge Posner in the majority opinion in *Mutual of Omaha* or those of Judge Evans' dissent? Why? For other cases deciding this issue, see *Chabner v. United of Omaha Life Insurance Co.*, 225 F.3d 1042 (9th Cir. 2000) (holding that Title III does not permit individuals to challenge the substantive provisions of insurance contracts), and *Carparts Distrib. Ctr., Inc. v. Automotive Wholesaler's Ass'n*, 37 F.3d 12 (1st Cir. 1994) (remanding for determination as to Title III application). This has not yet been resolved by the Supreme Court.

2. In a preliminary order in the case of *Carparts Distrib. Ctr., Inc. v. Automotive Wholesaler's Ass'n*, 37 F.3d 12 (1st Cir. 1994), the court overruled the lower court, and held that Title III (Public Accommodations) was not limited to actual physical structures with definite physical boundaries in which an individual would physically enter to use the facilities or obtain services. This decision means that a health benefit plan provided through an employer might be considered to be a Title III public accommodation. The case involves a health benefit plan offered to auto parts distributor members. The plan placed a cap on AIDS-related illnesses. The case also was brought under Title I. The First Circuit held that a health care plan that acts as an agent of an employer or is controlled by the employer may be subject to Title I of the ADA. For a more recent decision in this issue, review *Parker*, in Chapter 4[A], *supra*.

3. For an argument that *Doe* was wrongly decided, see Jeffrey W. Stempel, *An Inconsistently Sensitive Mind: Richard Posner's Cerebration of Insurance Law and Continuing Blind Spots of Econominalism*, 7 CONN. INS. L.J. 7, 65–68 (2000-2001) (arguing that Judge Posner should not have equated the situation present in *Doe* in which the plaintiff was already a policyholder with a decision to deny coverage to someone who has AIDS as a pre-existing condition).

4. There was a second reason upon which Judge Posner relied to find no violation of Title III. He concluded that if Title III regulates the content of an insurance policy, it would violate the McCarran-Ferguson Act, which prohibits courts from construing any federal act that does not directly regulate insurance to impair state insurance law. This is likely the strongest argument for finding that the ADA does not apply to the content of insurance policies, see Jeffrey W. Stempel, 7 CONN. INS. L.J. 7, 69 (2000-2001), but, at least according to Professor Stempel, is still insufficient for finding for the insurance company.

5. 42 U.S.C. § 12201(c) (Section 501(c)) creates an exception to Title III. It states:

> (c) Insurance. Subchapters I through III of this chapter [Titles I through III] and Title IV of this Act shall not be construed to prohibit or restrict —
>
>> 1. an insurer, hospital, or medical service company, health maintenance organization, or any agent or entity that administers benefit plans, or similar organizations from underwriting risks, classifying risks, or administering such risks that are based on or not inconsistent with State law; or

2. a person or organization covered by this chapter from establishing, sponsoring, observing or administering the terms of a bona fide benefit plan that are based on underwriting risks, classifying risks, or administering such risks that are based on or not inconsistent with State law; or

3. a person or organization covered by this chapter from establishing, sponsoring, observing, or administering the terms of a bona fide benefit plan that is not subject to State laws that regulate insurance.

Paragraphs (1), (2) and (3) shall not be used as a subterfuge to evade the purposes of subchapter I and III of this chapter. [titles I and III].

Why did the plaintiffs in *Mutual of Omaha* raise this section to support their claim? Why did Mutual of Omaha not use this section as a defense? Explain. For a discussion of Section 501(c) and its legislative history, see H. Miriam Farber, Note, *Subterfuge: Do Coverage Limitations and Exclusions in Employer-Provided Health Care Plans Violate the Americans with Disabilities Act?* 69 N.Y.U. L. Rev. 850 (1994).

———————

Assuming that health insurance programs are subject to the ADA, either as an employment benefit under Title I or as a public accommodation under Title III, there are a number of other issues that arise with respect to individuals with disabilities. One major issue is whether caps on benefits or denial of benefits for certain conditions is permissible. Related to that issue is whether insurers must provide parity for mental and physical conditions. The ADA expects that distinctions be based on legitimate actuarial data or reasonable experience.

Finally, employees may not be terminated to deprive them of employment benefits, including insurance. The Employee Retirement Income Security Act (ERISA), 29 U.S.C. §§ 1000–1461 prohibits that directly, and the ADA may also apply in some cases to prohibit such action.

For case citations and further discussion related these issues, see Laura Rothstein & Julia Rothstein, Disabilities and the Law § 10.02 (2009).

Access to health insurance is a complex matter for individuals with disabilities. The issues to be addressed in this area include whether health insurance is even covered under the ADA, whether differential treatment for different conditions is permissible, and whether discrimination in health insurance in other respects is permitted.

As a policy matter, individuals with disabilities face an even greater obstacle to coverage than all of the barriers listed above. Currently most individuals obtain health insurance through the workplace. Employers offer it as a benefit in the vast majority of employment settings. For individuals who are unemployed, it can be very difficult to obtain health insurance coverage. One concern was partially addressed in 1996. That concern was that because many health insurance policies did not cover pre-existing conditions, individuals who wanted to change jobs would not do so because of concerns about insurance coverage. The Health Insurance Portability and Accountability Act of 1996 (HIPAA), 42 U.S.C. § 300gg, provides that neither commercial health insurance nor employer-sponsored health insurance may treat health information as a preexisting condition for purposes of limiting or excluding benefits. Thus, a person who changes employment becomes eligible for health insurance with the new employer.

NOTES

1. *Caps on Fertility Treatment:* As was noted above, insurance plans that deny coverage for certain diseases may be found to violate the ADA. Would a cap on fertility treatment or a denial of benefits for fertility treatment violate the ADA? Is this issue affected by the decision in *Bragdon v. Abbott*, earlier in this Chapter. Would an insurance company's decision not to fund Viagra be affected by the ADA?

2. *Mental Health Parity.* One of the most contentious issues about discriminatory treatment involves the distinction between benefits for treating physical conditions and mental health conditions. Most courts dealing with this issue have held that the ADA does not prohibit an employer under Title I from offering a plan that grants differential benefits for physical and mental illnesses. See, e.g., *Fuller v. J.P. Morgan Chase & Co.*, 423 F.3d (2d Cir. 2005) (holding that it is not a violation of the ADA for an employer-provided long term disability plan to distinguish between physical and mental illness and even though the plaintiff's bipolar disease may have a biological cause, the disorder was still caused by a mental illness). This controversy ultimately resulted in the passage of mental health parity legislation in 2008.

The Paul Wellstone and Pete Domenici Mental Health Parity and Addiction Equity Act of 2008 (MHPAEA), 29 U.S.C. § 1185a and 42 U.S.C. § 300gg-5, took effect in January 2009. Its purpose is to assure parity in the insurance coverage of mental health and addiction related treatments with coverage of other non-mental health and addiction treatments. The MHPAEA applies to group health plans or health insurance coverage offered in connection with group plans that provide both medical and surgical benefits and new mental health or substance use disorder benefits. It states that:

1. financial requirements such as deductibles, copayments, co-insurance and out-of-pocket expenses that are applicable to the mental health or substance use disorder benefits may not be more restrictive than those applied to medical and surgical benefits;

2. there can be no separate cost sharing requirements that are applicable only with respect to mental health or substance use disorder benefits; and

3. limits on frequency of treatment, number of visits, days of coverage or other similar limits on the scope of duration of treatment applicable to mental health or substance use disorders may not be more restrictive than those for other medical and surgical benefits.

The MHPAEA does not apply to group health plans of small employers with fewer than 50 employees, and it has cost exemptions for plans whose costs rise as a result of compliance with the Act 2% or more in the first plan year and 1% in any subsequent year. The cost exemption allows the plan not to adhere to the MHPAEA for one plan year.

While the MHPAEA contains these exceptions and exemptions, it improves insurance parity for mental health and addiction disorder services over the previous Mental Health Parity Act of 1996. The Mental Health Parity Act of 1996 regulated only spending caps, and required that plans offering mental health coverage have the same caps for mental and physical health. Insurers were able to side-step these requirements by converting spending caps to inpatient-day and outpatient-visit limits. The new MHPAEA does not permit this behavior. Nonetheless, it applies only when the group plans offer mental health benefits or substance use benefits. It does not mandate coverage of mental illnesses or illnesses related to substance abuse. Besides the federal restrictions on insurance coverage, there are at least 46 states that provide some form of mental health parity legislation. For more information, see Jeffrey M. Barrett, Comment, *A State of Disorder: An Analysis of Mental-Health Parity in Wisconsin and a Suggestion for Future Legislation*, 2008 WIS. L. REV. 1159.

3. *Applicability of the ADA to Employer Provided Insurance.* Health benefits provided directly by the employer might be covered under Title I of the ADA. While the ADA is a broad non-discrimination mandate, it offers a safe harbor to insurance companies and employers whose risk assessment leads to more expensive insurance to persons with disabilities so long as the purpose of the assessment is not a subterfuge to evade the purposes of the Act.

4. *National Health Care Reform.* President Obama's national health care reform envisions that most of the uninsured Americans will have coverage through their employers, through Medicare or Medicaid, through a private insurer, through a publicly funded insurance program (the "public option"), or through non-profit co-operatives. Some versions of the bill mandate the employer to provide health benefits or to pay a tax into a fund to cover those employees who are not covered. Others do not include the employer mandate. How will national health care reform, if enacted, affect persons with disabilities who are employed? How will it affect those who are not employed?

5. *Genetic Information Non-Discrimination Act (GINA).* GINA applies both to employers who provide insurance and to health insurance providers. See Chapter 3 for a discussion of GINA and employers' responsibilities. For health insurers, the Act amends the Employee Retirement Income Security Act of 1974 (ERISA), the Public Health Service Act, the Internal Revenue Code of 1986, and the Social Security Act (medigap provisions). For group insurance plans, GINA prohibits the use of genetic information to increase group rates. It also prohibits the group health plan or a health insurer offering insurance in connection with a group plan from requiring genetic tests of individuals or family members, or from using the results of such genetic tests to set premiums. A "research exception" permits insurers to request, but not require, genetic testing under certain conditions, including that taking a genetic test must be voluntary, that non-compliance may not affect insurance premiums, and that the information gleaned from a genetic test may not be used for underwriting purposes. The Act also prohibits group health insurers from requesting, requiring or purchasing genetic information for underwriting purposes.

With reference to individual health insurance plans, the Act prohibits insurers from using genetic information for establishing rules for eligibility, and for setting premium rates. It also prohibits using the manifestation of a disease in a family member of the applicant for insurance for eligibility or premium rates, and prohibits use of genetic information as a "pre-existing condition" for the individual. It does not prohibit the use of the manifestation of disease of the individual for purposes of defining eligibility or rates, or of a family member if the family member is covered by the policy in question.

TABLE OF CASES

[References are to pages]

[References are to pages]

[References are to pages]

[References are to pages]

[References are to pages]

[References are to pages]

INDEX

* *

I-1

[References are to pages.]

[References are to pages.]

[References are to pages.]

[References are to pages.]

[References are to pages.]

[References are to pages.]